Prentice Hall
Psychology

TEACHER'S EDITION

Prentice Hall
Psychology

Katherine P. Minter
Westwood High School, Texas

William J. Elmhorst
Marshfield High School, Wisconsin

Prentice Hall

Boston   Columbus   Indianapolis   New York   San Francisco   Upper Saddle River
Amsterdam   Cape Town   Dubai   London   Madrid   Milan   Munich   Paris   Montreal   Toronto
Delhi   Mexico City   Sao Paulo   Sydney   Hong Kong   Seoul   Singapore   Taipei   Tokyo

We would like to thank all of the students who allowed us to use their photos in our book. Credits and acknowledgments from other sources and reproduced, with permission, in this text book appear on pages C-1–C-4.

The credits for images appearing in the Teaching Module are as follows:
T22 Yuri Arcurs/Shutterstock
T25 CandyBoxPhoto/Shutterstock
T27 Goodluz/Shutterstock
T29 Dean Mitchell/Shutterstock
T30 Dean Mitchell/Shutterstock
T32 lightpoet/Shutterstock
T35 Diego Cervo/Shutterstock

This work is protected by United States Copyright laws and is provided solely for the use of teachers and administrators in teaching courses and assessing student learning in their classes and schools. Dissemination or sale of any part of this work (including on the World Wide Web) will destroy the integrity of the work and is not permitted.

Copyright © 2012 by Pearson Education, Inc., Upper Saddle River, New Jersey 07458. Pearson Prentice Hall. All rights reserved. Printed in the United States of America. This publication is protected by copyright, and permission should be obtained from the publisher prior to any prohibited reproduction, storage in a retrieval system, or transmission in any form or by any means, electronic, mechanical, photocopying, recording, or likewise. For information regarding permission(s), write to: Rights and Permissions Department, One Lake Street, Upper Saddle River, New Jersey 07458.

Pearson, Prentice Hall, and Pearson Prentice Hall are trademarks in the U.S. and/or in other countries of Pearson Education, Inc. or its affiliates.

10 9 8 7 6 5 4 3 2 1

Prentice Hall
is an imprint of

www.pearsonschool.com

ISBN-13: 978-0-205-05548-7
ISBN-10:   0-205-05548-6

Scientific Inquiry Domain

CHAPTER 1: The Science of Psychology 2
Module 1: Psychology's Domains 4
Module 2: Research Methods and Ethics 16
Module 3: Statistics 26

Biopsychology Domain

CHAPTER 2: The Biological Perspective 40
Module 4: The Nervous System 42
Module 5: The Brain 54
Module 6: Heredity, Environment, and Adaptation 66

CHAPTER 3: Sensation and Perception 76
Module 7: Sensation 78
Module 8: Perception 94

CHAPTER 4: Consciousness: Sleep, Dreams, Hypnosis, and Drugs 108
Module 9: Sleep and Dreams 110
Module 10: Hypnosis and Drugs 123

Developmental and Learning Domain

CHAPTER 5: Development Across the Life Span 140
Module 11: Topics in Development 142
Module 12: Prenatal, Infant and Childhood Development 147
Module 13: Adolescence and Adulthood 162

CHAPTER 6: Learning and Language Development 176
Module 14: Classical Conditioning 178
Module 15: Operant Conditioning 184
Module 16: Cognitive Learning and Observational Learning 195
Module 17: Language 201

Social Context Domain

CHAPTER 7: Social Psychology 212
Module 18: Social Influence 214
Module 19: Social Cognition 224
Module 20: Social Interaction 232

CHAPTER 8: Culture and Gender ... 248
Module 21: Culture ... 250
Module 22: Gender ... 261

Cognition Domain

CHAPTER 9: Memory ... 272
Module 23: Encoding and Storage ... 274
Module 24: Retrieval and Retrieval Failure ... 285

CHAPTER 10: Cognition: Thinking and Intelligence ... 304
Module 25: Thinking ... 306
Module 26: Intelligence ... 321

Individual Variations Domain

CHAPTER 11: Motivation and Emotion ... 340
Module 27: Motivation ... 342
Module 28: Emotion ... 358

CHAPTER 12: Theories of Personality ... 374
Module 29: Perspectives on Personality ... 376
Module 30: Assessment and Issues in Personality ... 391

CHAPTER 13: Psychological Disorders ... 408
Module 31: Defining Abnormal Behavior ... 410
Module 32: Types of Psychological Disorders ... 418

Applications of Psychological Science Domain

CHAPTER 14: Psychological Therapies ... 444
Module 33: Psychotherapies ... 446
Module 34: Biomedical Therapies and Issues in Therapy ... 465

CHAPTER 15: Stress and Health ... 480
Module 35: Stress and Stressors ... 482
Module 36: Coping with Stress and Promoting Wellness ... 495

CHAPTER 16: Applied Psychology and Psychology Careers ... 512
Module 37: Careers in Psychology ... 514

Contents

PREFACE xxvii

TIMELINE OF IMPORTANT DATES IN PSYCHOLOGY xxx

Scientific Inquiry Domain

CHAPTER 1: The Science of Psychology 2

Module 1: Psychology's Domains 4
   Trace the Development of Psychology 4
      What is Psychology? What are its goals? 4
      What is the history of psychology as a scientific discipline? 5
   CLASSIC STUDIES IN PSYCHOLOGY: Psychologist Mary Cover Jones and "Little Peter" 9
      What are the major modern psychological perspectives? 10
      How is the field of psychology continuing to grow and change? 11
   Identify Psychology's Subfields 12
      Why do psychologists perform research? 12
      What are the major subfields of psychology? 12
      How does psychology benefit society? 14
   Practice Quiz 15

Module 2: Research Methods and Ethics 16
   Understand Psychological Research Methods 16
      What is the scientific method? 16
      What methods do researchers use to study behavior? 17
      How do researchers ensure their results are valid? 21
      Why do some researchers study animals instead of people? 22
   Consider Ethical Issues in Psychological Research 23
      What ethical guidelines do psychologists follow when they research humans? 23
      Are there different ethical guidelines for research with animals? 24
   APPLYING PSYCHOLOGY TO EVERYDAY LIFE: Stereotypes, Athletes, and Test Performance 24
   Practice Quiz 25

Module 3: Statistics 26
   Learn the Basic Concepts of Data Analysis 26
      What are descriptive statistics? 26
      What types of tables and graphs represents patterns in data? 28
      What are correlation coefficients? What do they tell researchers about relationships? 31
      What are inferential statistics? 33
      How do the concepts of validity and reliability relate to statistics? ... 33
   Practice Quiz 34

CHAPTER SUMMARY 35
ASSESSMENT 36
CONCEPT SUMMARY 38

Biopsychology Domain

CHAPTER 2: The Biological Perspective 40

Module 4: The Nervous System 42
- Understand the Structure and Function of the Nervous System 42
  - What are the major divisions of the human nervous system? 42
  - What are neurons, and how do they work? 42
  - What are the functions of the different parts of the central nervous system? 47
- Explain How the Neuroendocrine System Functions 50
  - How are the endocrine glands connected to the nervous system? 50
  - How do hormones affect our thoughts and behavior? 51
  - What effects do hormones have on the immune system? 51
- *Practice Quiz* 53

Module 5: The Brain 54
- Learn How Scientists Study the Nervous System 54
  - How do people study the brain? 54
  - What advances have made the brain easier to study? 55
  - What are some recent innovations in neuroscience? 56
- Understand the Structure and Function of the Brain 57
  - What are the different parts of the brain, and what does each part do? 57
  - How does the left side of the brain differ from the right side? 62
  - APPLYING PSYCHOLOGY TO EVERYDAY LIFE: Reflections on Mirror Neurons 64
- *Practice Quiz* 65

Module 6: Heredity, Environment, and Adaptation 66
- Discover How Biology and Experience Interact 66
  - How do genetic factors determine who we are? 66
  - How do heredity and environmental factors interact to affect our development? 67
  - How do evolved tendencies influence our behavior? 69
- *Practice Quiz* 70

CHAPTER SUMMARY 71
ASSESSMENT 72
CONCEPT SUMMARY 74

CHAPTER 3: Sensation and Perception 76

Module 7: Sensation 78
- Understand Sensation and Perception 78
  - What are the distinctions between sensation and perception? 78
  - What is a sensory threshold? What is sensory adaptation? 78
- Explore How the Senses Work 80
  - What forms of energy can humans sense? 80
  - How does the sense of vision work? 81
  - How does the sense of hearing work? 86

How do the senses of taste and smell work, and how are they alike? 88
What other sensory systems does the human body use? 91
Practice Quiz 93

Module 8: Perception 94
Learn How We Perceive the World 94
What is the nature of attention? 94
What are perceptual constancies, and why are they important? 94
What are the Gestalt principles of perception? 95
What are monocular and binocular depth cues? 96
CLASSIC STUDIES IN PSYCHOLOGY: The Visual Cliff 97
How do visual illusions work? 99
How do our experiences and expectations influence perception? 100
APPLYING PSYCHOLOGY TO EVERYDAY LIFE: Does Subliminal Advertising Really Work? 101
Practice Quiz 102
CHAPTER SUMMARY 103
ASSESSMENT 104
CONCEPT SUMMARY 106

CHAPTER 4: Consciousness: Sleep, Dreams, Hypnosis, and Drugs 108
Module 9: Sleep and Dreams 110
Understand the Relationship between Conscious and Unconscious Processes 110
What are the different levels of consciousness? 110
What is the difference between explicit and implicit processing? 111
Explain How and Why We Sleep and Dream 111
What is the circadian rhythm, and how does it relate to sleep? 112
What theories exist about the functions of sleep? 113
How does the sleep cycle work? 113
What are the different types of sleep disorders? 116
PSYCHOLOGY IN THE NEWS: Murder While Sleepwalking 117
Do dreams serve a function? 119
APPLYING PSYCHOLOGY TO EVERYDAY LIFE: Are You Sleep Deprived? 120
Practice Quiz 122
Module 10: Hypnosis and Drugs 123
Describe Meditation and Hypnosis 123
How does meditation affect consciousness? 123
How does hypnosis work, and why is it controversial? 124
Understand the Effects of Psychoactive Drugs 126
What are the major categories of psychoactive drugs? 126
How do drugs function at the synaptic level? 131
What are the effects of psychoactive drugs? 132
How do cultural pressures and expectations influence drug use? 133
Practice Quiz 134

CHAPTER SUMMARY **135**
ASSESSMENT **136**
CONCEPT SUMMARY **138**

Developmental and Learning Domain

CHAPTER 5: Development Across the Life Span **140**

Module 11: Topics in Development 142
    Describe Methods and Issues in Life Span Development 142
        How do biological and environmental factors influence development? ... 142
        What are some major research issues in developmental psychology? 143
        How do psychologists study development? 144
        What are critical periods and sensitive periods? 144
    Practice Quiz 146

Module 12: Prenatal, Infant and Childhood Development 147
    Learn about Prenatal and Newborn Development 147
        How do humans develop from conception through birth? 147
        What reflexes and abilities do newborns have? 150
    Describe Development During Infancy and Childhood 151
        What kinds of physical changes take place in infancy and childhood? ... 151
        How do infants and children develop cognitive skills? 152
        What are the stages of language development? 155
        How do babies begin to develop relationships with others? 156
    CLASSIC STUDIES IN PSYCHOLOGY: Harlow and Contact Comfort 158
    How do children develop socially and emotionally? 158
    Practice Quiz 161

Module 13: Adolescence and Adulthood 162
    Describe Development During Adolescence 162
        What physical changes happen during adolescence? 162
        How do reasoning and morality develop during adolescence? 163
        How do adolescents form their identities? 164
        What role do family members and peers play in adolescent development? ... 164
    Describe Development During Adulthood 165
        What social and cognitive changes occur during adulthood? 165
        What physical changes happen during adulthood? 166
        How do scientists explain why aging occurs? 167
        What are the stages of death and dying? 168
    APPLYING PSYCHOLOGY TO EVERYDAY LIFE: ADHD—Not Just for Children ... 169
    Practice Quiz 170

CHAPTER SUMMARY 171
ASSESSMENT 172
CONCEPT SUMMARY 174

CHAPTER 6: Learning and Language Development 176

Module 14: Classical Conditioning 178
   Explain the Process of Classical Conditioning 178
      What are the principles of classical conditioning? 178
      How can classical conditioning be specialized to affect emotions? ... 181
      How does classical conditioning function in our everyday lives? 182
   Practice Quiz 182

Module 15: Operant Conditioning 184
   Explain the Process of Operant Conditioning 184
      What is Thorndike's law of effect? 184
      What are the principles of operant conditioning? 185
      What are some specializations of operant conditioning? 187
   CLASSIC STUDIES IN PSYCHOLOGY: Biological Constraints on Operant Conditioning 190
      How does operant conditioning function in everyday life? 192
   APPLYING PSYCHOLOGY TO EVERYDAY LIFE: How to Make Punishment More Effective 193
   Practice Quiz 194

Module 16: Cognitive Learning and Observational Learning 195
   Identify the Aspects of Cognitive and Observational Learning 195
      What occurs in observational learning? 195
      How does observational learning function in everyday life? 196
      What is cognitive learning theory? 197
   Practice Quiz 199

Module 17: Language 201
   Identify the Structural Features of Language 201
      What is language, and how is it structured? 201
      How are language and thought related? 202
   Explain Theories and Stages of Language Acquisition 204
      How is language acquired? 204
      What are the theories of language acquisition? 204
   Identify Areas of the Brain Associated with Language 205
      Which parts of the brain are associated with language, and how does brain damage affect language? 205
   Practice Quiz 206

CHAPTER SUMMARY 207
ASSESSMENT 208
CONCEPT SUMMARY 210

Social Context Domain

CHAPTER 7: Social Psychology ... 212

Module 18: Social Influence ... 214
  Explore How Social Influence Affects Behavior ... 214
    Do people act differently in different situations? ... 214
    How does the presence of others affect an individual's behavior? ... 215
    How do group dynamics influence behavior? ... 219
    How can an individual change a group's behavior? ... 220
  APPLYING PSYCHOLOGY TO EVERYDAY LIFE: Anatomy of a Gang ... 221
  Practice Quiz ... 223

Module 19: Social Cognition ... 224
  Understand the Effects of Social Cognition ... 224
    What are attitudes, and how do they relate to behavior? ... 224
    How can attitudes be changed? ... 228
    How do people use attribution theory to explain the actions of others? ... 229
  Practice Quiz ... 231

Module 20: Social Interaction ... 232
  Describe Different Kinds of Social Relations ... 232
    How are prejudice and discrimination different? ... 232
  CLASSIC STUDIES IN PSYCHOLOGY: Brown Eyes, Blue Eyes ... 233
    What factors govern attraction and love? ... 235
    How does aggressive behavior develop? ... 238
    What is prosocial behavior? ... 240
  Practice Quiz ... 242

CHAPTER SUMMARY ... 243
ASSESSMENT ... 244
CONCEPT SUMMARY ... 246

CHAPTER 8: Culture and Gender ... 248

Module 21: Culture ... 250
  Understand Culture's Role in Psychology ... 250
    What is culture? ... 250
    How does culture vary across time and place? ... 251
    How does culture influence our conceptions of self and identity? ... 255
    What are some major areas of cross-cultural psychology research? ... 257
  Practice Quiz ... 260

Module 22: Gender ... 261
  Learn How Gender Identity Develops ... 261
    What is gender, and what is gender identity? ... 261
    What factors influence the development of gender identity? ... 262
    How do men and women differ in thinking, social behavior, and personality? ... 264

APPLYING PSYCHOLOGY TO EVERYDAY LIFE: Closing the Math and Science "Gender Gap" 265
Practice Quiz 266

CHAPTER SUMMARY **267**
ASSESSMENT **268**
CONCEPT SUMMARY **270**

Cognition Domain

CHAPTER 9: Memory 272

Module 23: Encoding and Storage 274
Learn How the Brain Encodes Memories 274
What are levels of processing? 275
How are memories encoded in the brain? 276
How can we make encoding more effective? 279
Understand How Memories Are Stored in the Brain 280
How is information stored in long-term memory? 280
How and where are memories stored in the brain? 282
Practice Quiz 284

Module 24: Retrieval and Retrieval Failure 285
Learn How Memories Are Retrieved From the Brain 285
What kinds of cues help people remember? 285
What factors influence how memories are retrieved? 286
How can we improve our ability to retrieve memories? 289
Can memories change? How reliable are they? 290
CLASSIC STUDIES IN PSYCHOLOGY: Elizabeth Loftus and Eyewitnesses 292
Why do we forget? 293
How does amnesia occur? 296
APPLYING PSYCHOLOGY TO EVERYDAY LIFE: Current Research in Alzheimer's Disease 297
Practice Quiz 298

CHAPTER SUMMARY **299**
ASSESSMENT **300**
CONCEPT SUMMARY **302**

CHAPTER 10: Cognition: Thinking and Intelligence 304

Module 25: Thinking 306
Understand the Basic Elements of Thought 306
How are mental images and concepts involved in the process of thinking? 306
What methods do people use to solve problems and make decisions? 311
Can a machine be made to think like a person? 313
PSYCHOLOGY IN THE NEWS: Artificial Intelligence (AI) 313

  Identify Obstacles to Thought 314
   What are some obstacles to problem solving? 314
   What are some obstacles to making good judgments? 316
   What are some obstacles to decision making? 318
  APPLYING PSYCHOLOGY TO EVERYDAY LIFE: Improving Your Cognitive Health 319
  Practice Quiz 320
Module 26: Intelligence 321
  Compare and Contrast Perspectives on Intelligence 321
   How do psychologists define intelligence? 321
   What are some established theories of intelligence? 321
   What are intellectual disability and giftedness? 323
  Learn How Intelligence Is Measured 327
   What is the history of intelligence testing? 327
   How is intelligence measured today? 328
   How can we determine whether intelligence tests are reliable and valid? 329
  Consider Key Issues in Intelligence Research 330
   How are intelligence tests used in the real world? 330
   How do heredity and environment influence intelligence? 331
  Practice Quiz 334
CHAPTER SUMMARY **335**
ASSESSMENT **336**
CONCEPT SUMMARY **338**

Individual Variations Domain

CHAPTER 11: Motivation and Emotion **340**
Module 27: Motivation 342
  Explain Major Theories of Motivation 342
   What are the major cognitive and biological theories of motivation? 342
   What is the humanist theory of motivation? 346
  Describe Motivated Behaviors 349
   What factors motivate eating? 349
   What factors motivate sexual behavior and orientation? 351
   What factors motivate achievement? 354
   Are there other ways in which humans and animals are motivated? 355
  Practice Quiz 357
Module 28: Emotion 358
  Understand Theories of Emotion and Emotional Expression 358
   What are the biological, behavioral, and cognitive components of emotion? 358
   What are the major theories of emotion? 360
   How do cultural and environmental factors influence emotional expression? 363

Analyze Emotional Behaviors in Depth 364
   What biological and environmental factors influence the expression and experience
      of fear? 364
CLASSIC STUDIES IN PSYCHOLOGY: The Angry/Happy Man. 365
   What biological and environmental factors influence the expression and experience
      of happiness?. 366
APPLYING PSYCHOLOGY TO EVERYDAY LIFE: A How-To of Happiness?. 367
Practice Quiz 368

CHAPTER SUMMARY 369
ASSESSMENT 370
CONCEPT SUMMARY 372

CHAPTER 12: Theories of Personality 374

Module 29: Perspectives on Personality 376
   Evaluate the Major Theories of Personality 376
      What is the psychodynamic theory of personality?. 376
      How do behaviorists and social cognitive theorists explain personality? 383
      How do humanistic psychologists explain personality? 385
      What are historical and current views of the trait perspective? 387
   Practice Quiz 390

Module 30: Assessment and Issues in Personality 391
   Learn How Personality Is Assessed. 391
      What techniques do researchers use to measure personality? Are these techniques reliable
         and valid? 391
   Consider Key Issues in Personality Research 396
      What part do biology and culture play in personality? 396
      Is personality stable, or can it change over time?. 397
      How can personality influence our health and our work?. 398
      What is self-esteem, and how does it affect us?. 399
      How do cultural perspectives relate to personality? 399
   APPLYING PSYCHOLOGY TO EVERYDAY LIFE: Personality Testing on the Internet 400
   Practice Quiz 402

CHAPTER SUMMARY 403
ASSESSMENT 404
CONCEPT SUMMARY 406

CHAPTER 13: Psychological Disorders 408

Module 31: Defining Abnormal Behavior 410
   Understand Historical, Cultural, and Current Views of Abnormality. 410
      How has mental illness been explained in the past and in other cultures?. 410
   CURRENT ISSUES IN PSYCHOLOGY: A Look at Abnormality in Various Cultures 411
      What is psychologically abnormal behavior? 412
      What are the major models of abnormality? 413

What is stigma, and how does it relate to mental illness? 415
How do psychological disorders impact individuals, their families, and society? 416
Practice Quiz 417

Module 32: Types of Psychological Disorders 418
Learn About Psychological Disorders, Their Symptoms, and Their Causes 418
What is the DSM classification system? 418
What are the challenges of diagnosing a mental illness? 421
What are the different types of anxiety disorders and their causes? 421
What are the different types of somatoform disorders and their causes? 424
What are the different types of dissociative disorders and their causes? 426
What are the different types of mood disorders and their causes? 427
What are the main symptoms, types, and causes of schizophrenia? 430
What are the different types of personality disorders and their causes? 433
How can family and social influences affect the experience of mental illness? 436
APPLYING PSYCHOLOGY TO EVERYDAY LIFE: Seasonal Affective Disorder 436
Practice Quiz 438

CHAPTER SUMMARY 439
ASSESSMENT 440
CONCEPT SUMMARY 442

Applications of Psychological Science Domain

CHAPTER 14: Psychological Therapies 444

Module 33: Psychotherapies 446
Understand Perspectives on Treating Psychological Disorders 446
What are the two modern ways in which psychological disorders can be treated,
and how have they been treated in the past? 446
Who can treat psychological disorders, and what training is required? 447
Identify Psychological Treatments and Evaluate Their Effectiveness 448
What are the different types of psychotherapy? 448
How effective is psychotherapy? 459
What other factors influence the effectiveness of therapy? 460
APPLYING PSYCHOLOGY TO EVERYDAY LIFE: What Is EMDR? 462
Practice Quiz 464

Module 34: Biomedical Therapies and Issues in Therapy 465
Identify Biomedical Therapies and Evaluate Their Effectiveness 465
What are biomedical forms of therapy, and how effective are they? 465
Should children and adolescents be treated with the same drugs used for adults? 469
Consider Legal, Ethical, and Professional Challenges in Therapy 470
What ethical challenges do therapists face when they deliver treatment? 470
What resources support people with psychological disorders and their families? 473
Practice Quiz 474

CHAPTER SUMMARY **475**
ASSESSMENT **476**
CONCEPT SUMMARY **478**

CHAPTER 15: Stress and Health 480

Module 35: Stress and Stressors 482
    Understand the Causes and Consequences of Stress 482
        How do psychologists define stress? 482
        What kinds of events and situations can cause stress? 483
        How can stress affect physiological and psychological health? 488
    APPLYING PSYCHOLOGY TO EVERYDAY LIFE: Suicide in America 492
    Practice Quiz 494

Module 36: Coping with Stress and Promoting Wellness 495
    Learn Strategies for Promoting Mental and Physical Health 495
        How do people think about stress? 495
        What are effective and ineffective ways to deal with stressors? ... 499
        What are some strategies for coping with stress? 500
        What is optimism, and how can people become more optimistic? .. 503
        What are some ways to promote wellness? 505
    Practice Quiz 506

CHAPTER SUMMARY **507**
ASSESSMENT **508**
CONCEPT SUMMARY **510**

CHAPTER 16: Applied Psychology and Psychology Careers 512

Module 37: Careers in Psychology 514
    Identify Educational Requirements for Careers in Psychology 514
        What are the degree requirements for psychological professionals? . 515
        What resources are available for people who want to study psychology in the future? 518
    Explore Career Options in Psychology 520
        What types of careers are available to someone with a bachelor's degree in psychology? ... 520
        How does psychology interact with other career fields? 522
    CURRENT ISSUES IN PSYCHOLOGY: Workplace Violence 525
    APPLYING PSYCHOLOGY TO EVERYDAY LIFE: Techniques Used by Sports Psychologists 527
    Practice Quiz 528

CHAPTER SUMMARY **529**
ASSESSMENT **530**
CONCEPT SUMMARY **532**

GLOSSARY/GLOSARIO **GL-1**
REFERENCES **R-1**
CREDITS **CR-1**
NAME INDEX **NI-1**
SUBJECT INDEX **SI-1**

Learner-Centered, Achievement-Driven Approach

Prentice Hall Psychology celebrates the fascinating field of psychology—its science, its history, its mysteries, its applications—by focusing on today's students. This learner-centered approach encourages dialogue and recognizes the importance of active engagement inside *and* outside the classroom. *Prentice Hall Psychology's* uniquely integrated textbook and media program awakens students' curiosity and energizes their desire to learn and succeed.

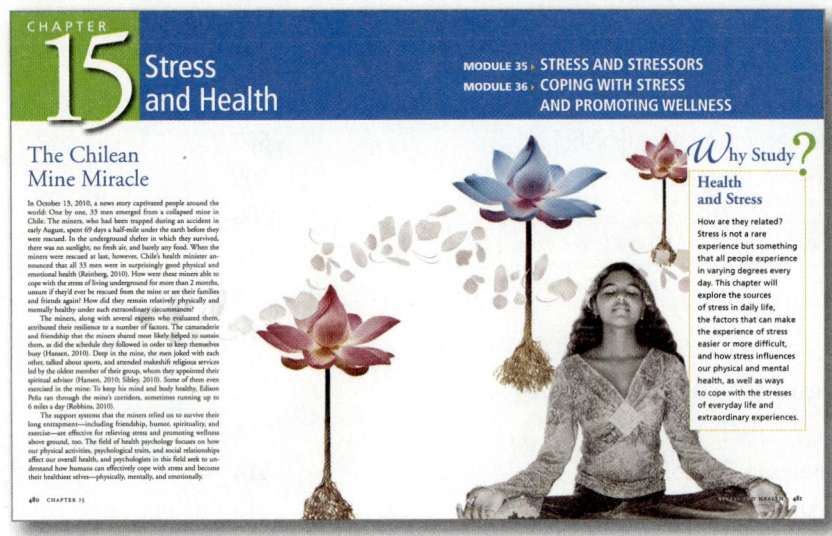

Chapter Opening Prologues are designed to capture student interest immediately. Taken from a case study or recent events in the news, these openers engage students in the material from the very start. The design truly captures students' imagination and adds to the appeal of the chapter content.

Each module is structured around detailed **Module Goals and Learning Objectives** based on APA recommendations. These goals and objectives, which correspond to the APA's newest National Standards for High School Psychology Curricula, provide students and teachers with an overview of the major concepts and questions they will encounter. The phrasing of the learning objectives encourages students to think critically about key concepts. Teachers can refer to the module goals and learning objectives to determine which sections of the text to emphasize in their courses.

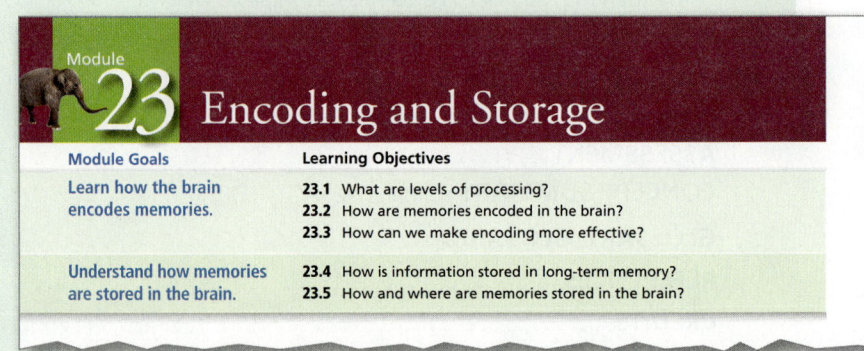

Student Voice Questions encourage students to stop, to clarify, and to think critically. Written by students for students, these questions create a dialogue between the text and the reader and encourage students to ask similar questions.

> My parents and I moved ▶ to this country when I was 6 years old. It's been a lot easier for me to adapt to our new culture than it has been for my parents. Is that normal?

identity with their new culture are (Mok et al., 2007).

My parents and I moved to thi easier for me to adapt to our new normal?

When it comes to transitionin a difference: When researchers stu States during the 1980s and 199 migrants saw themselves as mor themselves as more American th other words, the children had ac When families move from one "acculturation gap" between pare and nature of the gap depends on and the culture of origin. Child they can't clearly remember their difficulty adjusting to their new tries with cultures very similar t adjusting as well.

Children born into a culture

---

display rules learned ways of controlling displays of emotion in social settings.

participants tended to control their facial expressions, smiling or appearing calm and composed even when they felt afraid or angry. The American participants, on the other hand, continued to show their true emotions through facial expressions when the experimenter was present (Ekman, 1972; Friesen, 1972). Why does this happen? Each culture has its own **display rules**, or learned ways of controlling displays of emotion in social settings. LINK *to Chapter Eleven: Motivation and Emotion, pp. 363–364.* Psychologists now believe that there is a connection between a culture's individualism or collectivism and its display rules. In other words, your culture's individualist or collectivist tendencies will at least partially determine the degree to which you control your expressions of emotion in social situations (Matsumoto et al., 1998).

Intelligence Cultural factors affect psychologists' research not only in the study of emotion but also in the study of human intelligence. What does it mean to be intelligent? Does it mean that you have a high IQ, earn straight As and attend a prestigious university? Not necessarily. Not only is this a narrow definition of intelligence, but it also fails to take cultural considerations into account. LINK *to Chapter Ten: Thinking and Intelligence, p. 321.* IQ scores, letter grades, and college acceptances are sometimes considered to be signs of intelligence in the United States, but in other cultures, intelligence is measured differently.

The intelligence researcher Robert Sternberg and his colleagues studied children in Kenya to determine how well they could identify natural herbal medicines used frequently in their community. The researchers also gave the Kenyan children two intelligence tests. When they reviewed their results, the researchers discovered that there was actually a *negative* relationship between the children's ability to correctly identify the medicines and their scores on one of the intelligence tests. In other words, the better a child did on the

▶ Watch a video with Robert Sternberg discussing cultural influences on intelligence on **mypsychlab.com**

LINK feature It is often difficult for students to make connections from topics in one chapter to topics in other chapters. To help students identify interrelated concepts, throughout each chapter, whenever one topic has a relationship to another within the text, a LINK symbol is shown, followed by specific chapter and page number cross references. These links refer to content covered within the same chapter, in earlier chapters, or in subsequent chapters—giving students a real sense of the connections throughout the text material.

Vocabulary Terms and Running Glossary To help students recognize and understand the important terms introduced in each chapter, **Vocabulary Terms** are set in bold at first use and explained in the text. Additionally, the terms appear in a **Running Glossary** in the margin of the same page on which they are introduced; the term appears in bold along with its definition.

schizophrenia severe disorder in which the person suffers from disordered thinking, bizarre behavior, hallucinations, and inability to distinguish between fantasy and reality.

psychotic term applied to a person who is no longer able to perceive what is real and what is fantasy.

delusions false beliefs held by a person who refuses to accept evidence of their falseness.

Schizophrenia includes several different kinds of symptoms, the most common of which are **delusions**. Although delusions are not prominent in all forms of schizophrenia, they are the symptom that most people associate with this disorder. Delusions are false beliefs about the world that the person holds; these beliefs tend to remain fixed and unshakable even in the face of evidence that disproves them. Common schizophrenic delusions include *delusions of persecution* in which people believe that others are trying to hurt them in some way; *delusions of reference* in which people believe that other people, television characters, and even books are specifically talking to them; *delusions of influence* in which people believe that they are being controlled by external forces, such as the devil, aliens, or cosmic forces; and *delusions of grandeur* in which people are convinced that they can save the world or have a special mission (APA, 2000). Contrary to popular belief, schizophrenia is *not* characterized by the development of multiple separate personalities. Dissociative identity disorder, the controversial disorder associated with the phenomenon of multiple personalities, is not the same as schizophrenia.

Dr. John Nash is a famous mathematician who won the Nobel Prize for economics in 1994. Dr. Nash's fame, however, is mostly due to the fact that

430 CHAPTER 13

All vocabulary terms set in bold in the text also appear in a **Glossary** at the end of the book. To provide further support for students, including those whose first language is Spanish, the **Glossary/Glosario** at the end of the book lists key terms and definitions in English along with those same key terms and definitions in Spanish.

Glossary/Glosario

A

absolute threshold: the lowest level of stimulation that a person can consciously perceive 50 percent of the time the stimulation is present by 50 percent of the people tested. 79
umbral absoluto: nivel más bajo de estimulación que puede percibir la persona de manera consciente el 50 por ciento de las veces que la estimulación está presente por parte del 50 por ciento de las personas sometidas a prueba.

accommodation: the process of altering or adjusting old schemes to fit new information and experience, or, as a monocular clue, the brain's use of information about the changing thickness of the lens of the eye in response to looking at objects that are close or far away. 98, 153
adaptación: proceso de alterar o adecuar viejos procesos para ajustar información y experiencia nueva o, como pista monocular, uso de información por parte del cerebro concerniente al espesor cambiante del cristalino en respuesta a la visión de objetos cercanos o lejanos.

acute stress disorder (ASD): a disorder resulting fr[...] major stressor, with symptoms of anxiety, disse[...] nightmares, sleep disturbances, problems in c[...] ments in which people seem to "relive" the eve[...] flashbacks for as long as one month following [...]
trastorno de estrés agudo: trastorno que se p[...] tado de la exposición a un factor estresante ma[...] ansiedad, disociación, pesadillas recurrentes, po[...] sueño, problemas de concentración y moment[...] sona parece "revivir" el suceso en sueños y rev[...] períodos de hasta un mes después de ocurrid[...]

adaptation-level phenomenon: the tendency to ev[...] ences in terms of previous experiences and adj[...] cordingly. 366
fenómeno adaptación-nivel: tendencia a eval[...] nuevas en términos de experiencias anteriores[...] vas en consecuencia.

- View The Image on **mypsychlab.com**
- Watch on **mypsychlab.com**
- Listen on **mypsychlab.com**
- Explore on **mypsychlab.com**
- Simulate on **mypsychlab.com**
- Study and Review on **mypsychlab.com**
- Read on **mypsychlab.com**
- Map The Concepts on **mypsychlab.com**

MyPsychLab icons indicate that students can find related video, podcasts, simulations, practice quizzes, and more within MyPsychLab to expand their learning. There are many more resources available within MyPsychLab than those highlighted in the book, but the icons draw attention to some of the most high-interest materials available at **www.mypsychlab.com.**

For a complete overview of MyPsychLab, see pages xxviii–xxix.

Practice Quizzes are included at the end of each module. Each quiz features 10 multiple-choice questions designed to assess students' comprehension of module material. Practice quizzes encourage students to stop, review, and reinforce their learning before moving on to a new module.

Practice Quiz

Pick the best answer.

1. Which of the following statements about culture is true?
   a. It is possible to identify with more than one culture.
   b. It is not difficult to move from one culture to another.
   c. Cultural factors do not affect most aspects of people's daily lives.
   d. No country can contain more than one culture.

2. A culture may have certain rules, traditions, or beliefs that people are expected to follow.

7. Which of the following statements is the best illustration of an independent self-concept?
   a. "I am a friendly and considerate person."
   b. "I am a mother to three small boys."
   c. "I am a teacher in a public high school."
   d. "I am a member of the basketball team."

8. Which of the following is NOT a culture-bound action?
   a. smiling
   b. shaking hands
   c. giving a thumbs-up

▼ **Assessments** are also found at the end of each chapter. These end-of-chapter tests assess students' comprehension of key points and provide students a variety of opportunities to strengthen their analytical skills. Each test features a **vocabulary review** section; an extensive **multiple-choice assessment** aligned to the chapter learning objectives; two **short-essay questions** that encourage students to think critically about psychology topics; and a **project assignment** that allows students to participate in a hands-on project or experiment related to the chapter material.

▲ Each chapter contains a content **Summary** and a comprehensive list of **Vocabulary Terms** used in that chapter, allowing students to review key terms quickly and locate each term within the text.

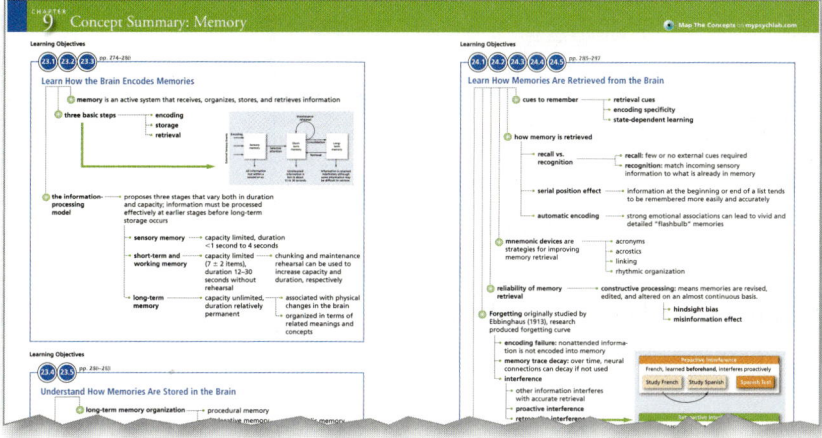

Concept Summaries, at the end of each chapter, provide students with a graphic summary of the chapter's content. By pulling the content together in this highly visual manner, students will better understand the connections and grasp how the chapter material fits together.

Other features of each chapter include special sections covering interesting topics related to the material, especially topics of diversity and cultural interest: *Classic Studies in Psychology, Psychology in the News,* and *Current Issues in Psychology.* These are not set off from the text in boxes, making it more likely that students will read the enriching material. Questions for Further Study allow students to think critically about the content they have just read.

LEARNER-CENTERED APPROACH   xxi

Teaching and Learning Package

The **Teacher's Edition** of *Prentice Hall Psychology* contains teaching tips, classroom activities, and other valuable materials designed to support teachers as they use this program in the classroom. Each page of the Student Edition is reproduced in this wraparound edition and annotated with additional information developed by high school teachers for high school teachers—including lesson-plan ideas, discussion questions, background information that expands on the material presented in the Student Edition, and strategies for adapting instruction to meet the needs of diverse learners. The supplementary information and creative teaching ideas in the Teacher's Edition help teachers save valuable time before, during, and after class.

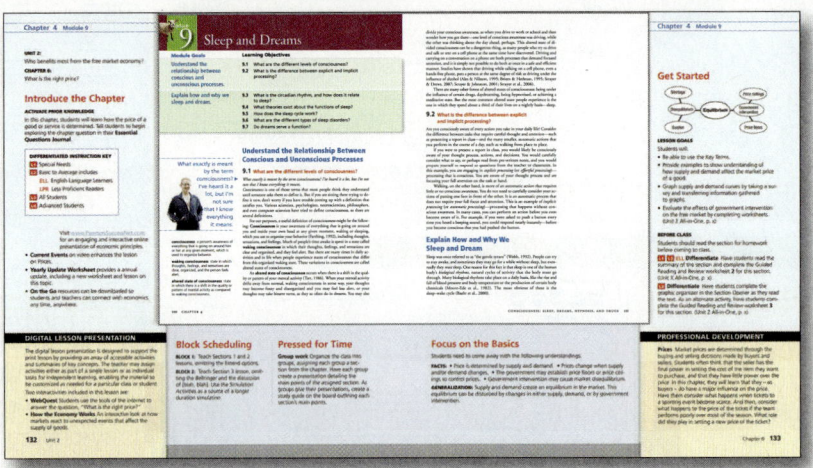

Teacher's Resource DVD The Teacher's Resource Manual, Test Bank, Exam*View*®, and PowerPoint Slides, are available on the Teacher Resource DVD, which provides a convenient way for teachers to access key supplementary materials at home or at school.

The **Teacher's Resource Manual** offers an in-depth collection of resources. For each module, you'll find activities, exercises, assignments, handouts, and demos for in-class use, as well as guidelines on integrating the many Pearson media resources into your classroom and syllabus. The electronic format features click-and-view hot links that allow teachers to quickly review or print any resource from a particular chapter. This resource saves prep work and helps maximize classroom time.

The **Test Bank** contains a primary test bank with more than 3,200 questions. Each chapter includes a two page Total Assessment Guide that lists all of the test items in an easy-to-reference grid. The Total Assessment Guide organizes all test items by learning objective and question type (factual, conceptual, and applied).

An additional feature of this test bank is the inclusion of rationales for the correct answer and the key distracter in the multiple-choice questions. The rationales help teachers further evaluate the questions they are choosing for their tests, giving them the option to use the rationales as an answer key for their students.

A second bank of over 2,000 questions is available. This additional bank has been class-tested and provides statistical item analysis for each question.

The *Prentice Hall Psychology* test bank comes with **ExamView®**, a powerful assessment-generation program that allows teachers to create and print quizzes and exams. This easy-to-use, customizable program enables teachers to view, edit, and add questions; transfer questions to test; print multiple tests for each chapter; and print multiple versions of tests.

Interactive PowerPoint Slides bring the text's powerful design right into the classroom, drawing students into the lesson and providing wonderful interactive activities, visuals, and videos. A video walk-through is available for teachers and provides clear guidelines on using and customizing the slides. The slides are built around the program learning objectives and offer multiple pathways or links between content areas.

How to Access Resources

Most of the teacher supplements and resources for this text are available electronically for download to qualified adopters from the Pearson Instructor Resource Center (IRC). Upon adoption or to preview, please go to PearsonSchool.com/Access_Request and select "Option 1." Teachers will be required to complete a brief one-time registration subject to verification of educator status. Upon verification, access information and instructions will be sent via email. Once logged into the IRC, enter your text ISBN in the "Search our Catalog" box to locate these resources.

TEACHING AND LEARNING PACKAGE

MyPsychLab
Engage, Assess, Succeed

What is **MyPsychLab**? **MyPsychLab** is a dynamic, easy-to-use learning and assessment tool that provides a wealth of resources for *Prentice Hall Psychology* geared to meet the diverse needs of today's students and teachers. **MyPsychLab** offers many accessible tools that encourage students to read their text and help them improve results. It combines original online materials with powerful online assessments to engage students, assess their learning, and help them succeed. **MyPsychLab** helps ensure students are always learning and always improving.

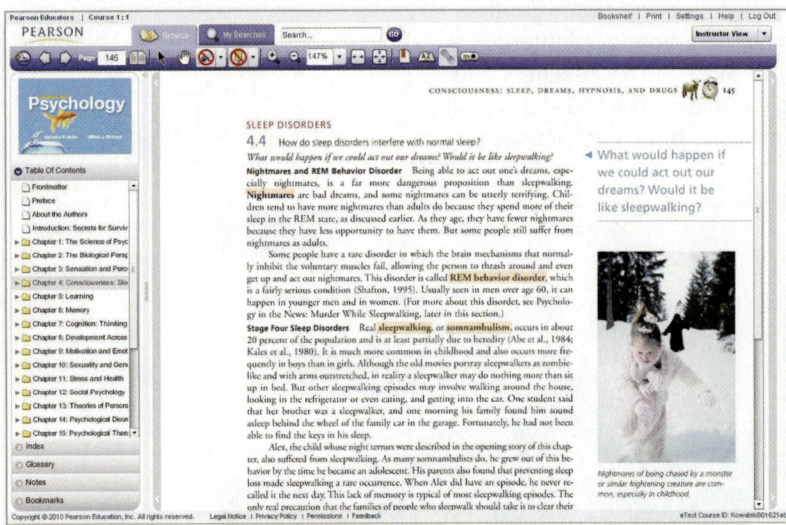

Pearson eText and Audio Textbook

- **Pearson eText** offers a complete interactive student text online. Students can navigate page-by-page, move directly to a chapter or section, or use the search feature to locate all references throughout the entire book. Pearson's interactive eText allows students to highlight, add study notes, bookmark pages, and access multimedia—videos, simulations, glossary—all at the point of use.
- **Audio Textbook** provides the complete *Prentice Hall Psychology* text in audio format. The audio text can be used stand-alone or in conjunction with the print textbook to help students read and understand each concept.

Interactive Study Tools and Assignments

MyPsychLab provides a wealth of interactive study tools to support a variety of student learning styles. Students will find video clips, simulations, animations, podcasts, flash cards, and more.

- **Downloadable Flash Cards** are another quick and easy way for students to quiz themselves on key content.
- **Psychology Library** offers numerous student tools and resources, including study skills and plagiarism tutorials, an APA documentation guide, and more.

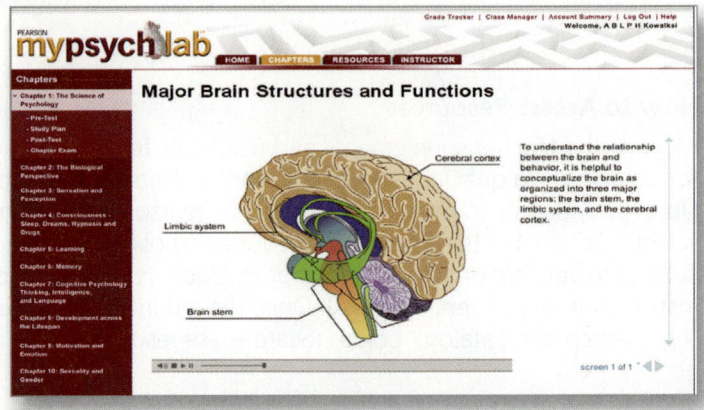

Assessments and Grade Tracker

For each chapter of the book, MyPsychLab offers a pre-test, post-test, and chapter exam. Based on the results of the pre-test, MyPsychLab creates a customized study plan for each student, identifying areas of strength and weakness and providing extra support where needed. With Grade Tracker, students can follow their own progress and teachers can monitor the work of the entire class. Automated grading of these tests and assignments helps both students and teachers save time and improve results.

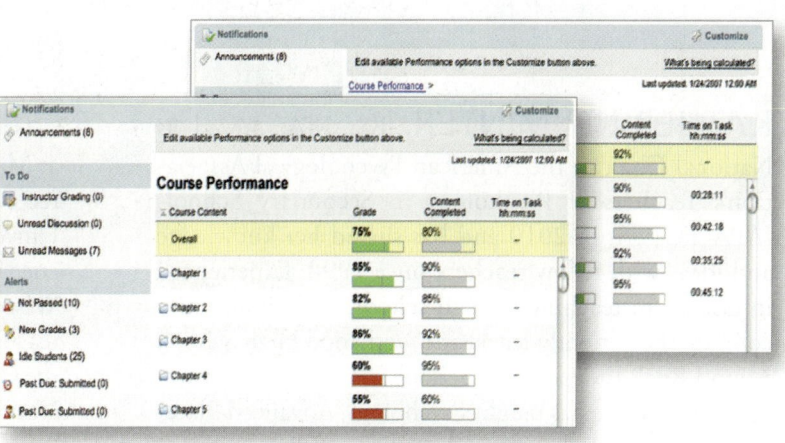

Class Prep for teachers. Now available in MyPsychLab

Finding, sorting, organizing, and presenting your teacher resources is faster and easier than ever before with **Class Prep**. This fully searchable database contains hundreds and hundreds of our best teacher resources, such as lecture launchers and discussion topics, in-class and out-of-class activities and assignments, handouts, as well as video clips, photos, illustrations, charts, graphs, and animations. Teachers can search or browse by topic, and it is easy to sort results by type, such as photo, document, or animation. Teachers can create personalized folders to organize and store materials or download the resources. Teachers can even present material in class directly from **Class Prep!**

How to Access MyPsychLab

Students and teachers are granted access to MyPsychLab with Pearson eText upon textbook purchase. High school teachers can obtain preview or adoption access for MyPsychLab in one of the following ways:

Preview Access

- Teachers can request preview access online by visiting **PearsonSchool.com/Access_Request,** using Option 2/3. Preview access information will be sent to the teacher via **email.**

Adoption Access

- With the purchase of this program, a Pearson Adoption Access Card, with codes and complete instructions, will be delivered with your textbook purchase. (ISBN: 0-13-034391-9)
- Ask your sales representative for an Adoption Access Code Card (ISBN: 0-13-034391-9)

Or

- Visit **PearsonSchool.com/Access_Request,** using Option 2/3. Adoption access information will be sent to the teacher via **email.**

Students, ask your teacher for access.

MyPsychLab xxv

About the Authors

KATHERINE MINTER, BS, MA, served as National Chair of the American Psychological Association's Teachers of Psychology in Secondary Schools (APA-TOPSS) in 2010 and has shared her knowledge and ideas with fellow teachers since 1992. Experienced in classroom teaching at high schools and community colleges, she currently teaches at Westwood High School, Round Rock Independent School District, near Austin, Texas. Katherine has taught Psychology, Advanced Placement (AP) Psychology, and International Baccalaureate (IB) Psychology at both the Standard Level and Higher Level. She has been a College Board Consultant since 1994, an AP Reader for 11 years, and an IB Trainer and IB Examiner. Katherine has been recipient of the College Board "Teaching Excellence Award" (1996), named "Westwood Teacher of the Year" (2001), and selected for the 2008 APA-TOPSS National Award for "Excellence in Teaching." She is also author of a teacher's manual for AP Psychology. In addition to teaching and writing, Katherine loves reading, traveling, gardening, and spending time with her family.

WILLIAM ELMHORST is a psychology teacher at Marshfield High School in Marshfield, Wisconsin. He received his Master of Arts in Education from Viterbo University in La Crosse, Wisconsin, and his Master of Science in Education Administration from the University of Wisconsin-Superior in Superior, Wisconsin. Will has been teaching Psychology for 14 years and is also a reader for the College Board's AP Psychology exam. He served as the National Chair of the APA affiliate board TOPSS in 2009, has published several articles on best practices in teaching psychology, and has authored Pearson Education's *AP* Test Prep Series: AP Psychology* workbook. Will also teaches an online Introduction to Psychology class for the University of Wisconsin Colleges. His research interests are diverse, and he is currently researching late 19th century science fiction, with a focus on psychology in the works of H. G. Wells. During time off from teaching, he enjoys travel with his family and spending time outdoors.

With content advisers:

SAUNDRA K. CICCARELLI is a professor of psychology at Gulf Coast Community College in Panama City, Florida. She received her PhD in Developmental Psychology from George Peabody College of Vanderbilt University in Nashville, Tennessee. Sandy has been teaching Introductory Psychology and Human Development at Gulf Coast Community College for more than 29 years. In addition to her textbooks—*Psychology, Psychology: An Exploration,* and *Psychology, AP* Edition*—Sandy has authored numerous ancillary materials for several introductory psychology and human development texts.

J. NOLAND WHITE is an associate professor of psychology at Georgia College & State University (GCSU) in Milledgeville, Georgia. He received both his BS and MS in Psychology from GCSU and joined the faculty there in 2001, after receiving his PhD in Counseling Psychology from the University of Tennessee in Knoxville. In April 2008, he was a recipient of the GCSU Excellence in Teaching Award.

Preface

From beginning to end, *Prentice Hall Psychology* was developed with high school students' and teachers' unique goals and concerns in mind. An engaging, clearly written textbook can motivate students to learn, so we wrote in a style that draws students to an ongoing dialogue and introduces them to psychology—its history, its breadth, its mysteries, and its applications. Examples and explanations are tailored to high school students' interests and needs to help them understand the fundamental concepts of psychology and show them that psychology is a current, relevant, and endlessly fascinating field. In *Prentice Hall Psychology,* students will find the academic support they need to succeed in class—and the current references, accessible language, and humor that will motivate them to explore how psychological principles play a role in their everyday lives.

Organization and Curriculum Standards

We understand, too, that high school teachers value a flexible curriculum that addresses key learning objectives and standards. *Prentice Hall Psychology* is organized around and correlated to the latest National Standards for High School Psychology Curricula, put forth by the American Psychological Association (APA). To ensure that *Prentice Hall Psychology* reflects the current concerns of high school educators and the larger psychology community, each Learning Objective in this text is linked to a specific national standard. In fact, the organization of our text mirrors the organization of the standards. Like the standards, this book is divided into seven domains, and each chapter of this book addresses one or two standards from the 20 Standards Areas, providing complete and comprehensive coverage. Teachers can feel comfortable knowing that when they use *Prentice Hall Psychology* in their classrooms, they are addressing key standards in a way that is both academically rigorous and student friendly.

The modular design of *Prentice Hall Psychology* provides teachers the flexibility they need to structure their courses around their unique classroom goals. Every effort has been made to ensure that each module stands alone and may be taught in any order. Students do not need to read earlier modules to fully understand later modules. Because these modules are much shorter than traditional textbook chapters, they help students focus on a few pages of text at a time without feeling overwhelmed with information. Learning Objectives at the beginning of each module give students and teachers at-a-glance information about the topics covered within, and practice quizzes at the end of each module encourage students to review frequently and retain the material they've learned.

These carefully crafted features, along with the others described, make *Prentice Hall Psychology* an innovative and invaluable resource for students and teachers alike. We are deeply indebted to the reviewers who have taken the time to give insightful feedback and suggestions for this program, especially the numerous high school psychology teachers who have helped us shape this book.

Acknowledgements

This program reflects the input and feedback of many educators and students who shared their thoughts with us. We are especially grateful to the many high school teachers who contributed to decisions about text organization, content coverage, and pedagogical innovation, helping us keep focused on what is most important to teachers and students in the classroom. We are indebted to the teachers who gave us their time, their energy, and their invaluable feedback as we developed this text and its supplementary materials. We are gratified with the results and hope that you find this text as inviting as we do!

Reviewers

Debra Adams, Osceola High School

Jordana Bales, Bronx High School of Science

John Billingslea, Franklin High School

Rich Biser, Blue Ridge Community and Technical College

Emily Box, Adlai E. Stevenson High School

Beth Burkhead, The Career Center

Bradley Cravens, Dr. Phillips High School

Angela Darrenkamp, Owen J. Roberts High School

Margaret Davidson, Rockwall-Heath High School

James Denson, Kempsville High School

Audrey Erickson, Moorhead High School

Tami Eshleman, North Platte High School

Joe Geiger, Carl Sandburg High School

Louis Farrar, Charter Oak High School

Jay Heilman, Prospect High School

Eileen Hermansen, Rancho Buena Vista High School

Steve Jones, City of Medicine Academy

Terri Lindenberg, Lake Park High School

Karen Lozzi, Whitman-Hanson Regional High School

Mara Marks, Desert Pines High School

Mark Minnick, Southside High School

Nate Naughton, Arlington Catholic High School

Robert Nelson, J. J. Pearce High School

Kimberly Patterson, Cypress Bay High School

Carolyn Rosenfeld, Ridgewood High School

Daria Schaffeld, Prospect High School

Stefanie Scher, Fort Lauderdale High School

Mark Schmidt, Springfield High School

Dr. Marie T. Smith, Thomas S. Wootton High School

Susan Spencer, Northern Highlands Regional High School

Mary Spilis, Northview High School

Larry R. Stombaugh, The Career Center

Sejal Vaughn, Glenbrook South High School

Desi Vuillaume, Carl Sandburg High School

Cyndi Wright, Aliso Niguel High School

In addition to the many reviewers who guided this book, we would like to extend our grateful acknowledgment to our extraordinary content advisors, Saundra Ciccarelli and Noland White, the authors of *Psychology*, a college-level introductory psychology course. Sandy and Noland's love of psychology, their dedication to students, and their humor inspired us and this book in countless ways.

Without the dedicated team at Pearson, this book would not have been possible. We would like to extend our thanks to Yolanda de Rooy, President; Craig Campanella, Editorial Director; and Jessica Mosher, Editor-in-Chief for their support of this project. Amber Mackey, Senior Sponsoring Editor, managed the project with the help of editorial assistants Paige Clunie and Jackie Moya. Elaine Shema, Product Management/Marketing for Humanities School, guided the project with expertise at every stage, and Gina Sluss, Director, Interdivisional Sales, provided invaluable direction and insight. Nancy Gilbert, Joan Mazzeo, Jennifer Ribnicky, Andrea Sheehan, and Joyce Kneuer all contributed greatly to making the book the best that it could be. Harriet Tellem, Senior Production Project Manager, expertly directed the project through the production process, along with Sherry Lewis, Senior Operations Specialist, and support from Maureen Richardson, Managing Editor. Anne Nieglos and Nancy Wells provided art direction for the book's wonderful design.

Katherine Minter: My heartfelt gratitude goes to my students, who have been my greatest teachers over many years. My coauthor, Will Elmhorst, my friend and colleague, was knowledgeable, supportive, and patient. He is not only a first-rate teacher but a first-rate human being as well. For giving a public school teacher an opportunity to contribute to the broader teaching of the science of psychology, my thanks go to the whole team at Pearson. My deep appreciation particularly goes to Amber Mackey, who encouraged me to take on this project and who, with expertise, flexibility, and good humor, skillfully guided this project to its conclusion. Caroline Carlson at Words & Numbers, worked with us all the way, making sure we were unified in style and tone. Finally, my love goes to my husband, Larry, and children, Sarah and Andrew, for always supporting my adventure.

Will Elmhorst: I would like to thank the team at Pearson for their guidance and support, especially Amber Mackey, who was always "just an email away," and Caroline Carlson at Words & Numbers, for her respect toward new ideas and creativity. I would also like to extend my thanks to my colleagues for sharing their insights. Especially deeply felt thanks go to Kay Minter for being such a strong coauthor and a good friend. Finally, and most importantly, I express my love and thanks to my wife, Jill, and my children, Noah, Taylor, and Collin, for their enduring love and support. We did it, guys!

Katherine Minter	**William Elmhorst**
Westwood High School	Marshfield High School
Austin, Texas	Marshfield, Wisconsin

Important Dates in Psychology

Use this timeline to get a better understanding of key dates in the history of psychology.

1929 Hans Berger introduces EEG method for studying the human brain.

1920 Francis Sumner becomes the first African American to receive a PhD in psychology at Clark University.

1906 Ivan Pavlov publishes his findings on classical conditioning.

1920 Watson and Rayner publish the "Little Albert" experiment.

1848 Phineas Gage suffers brain damage and provides a famous case study of the effects of brain damage.

1906 Ramon y Cajal discovers that the nervous system is composed of individual cells.

1921 The first neurotransmitter, acetylcholine, is discovered.

1884 James-Lange theory of emotion proposed.

360 Plato writes the *Theaetetus* examining theories of perception, knowledge, and truth.

1859 Charles Darwin publishes the theory of natural selection, which influences the field of evolutionary psychology.

1908 Yerkes-Dodson law proposed to explain relationship between performance and arousal.

1921 The Rorschach Inkblot Test is developed.

350 Aristotle writes *De Anima* about the relationship of the soul to the body.

1900 Freud publishes *The Interpretation of Dreams*.

1921 Allport proposes a trait theory of personality.

B.C.E. 400 C.E. 1650 1860 1900 1920

430 Hippocrates proposes that mental illnesses are caused by an imbalance of four major fluids in the human body.

1649 Descartes publishes *The Passion of the Soul*, outlining the pineal gland as the seat of the soul.

1860 Gustav Fechner is often credited with performing the first scientific experiments that would form the basis for experimentation in psychology.

1890 William James publishes his book, *Principles of Psychology*.

1904 Spearman proposes a general factor of intelligence.

1911 Thorndike proposes the Law of Effect.

1930 Tolman and Honzik demonstrate latent learning in rats.

1912 Gestalt psychology first developed by Max Wertheimer.

1930 Jean Piaget proposes four stages of cognitive development.

1861 Broca's Area and its role in speech production is discovered.

1892 American Psychological Association (APA) founded and G. Stanley Hall elected first president.

1912 The intelligence quotient is developed by William Stern.

1933 Sigmund Freud proposes the concepts of id, ego, and superego.

1874 Wernicke's Area and its role in language comprehension is discovered.

1894 Margaret Floy Washburn is the first woman to receive a PhD in psychology at Cornell University.

1905 Mary Whiton Calkins becomes the first female president of the APA.

1913 Carl Jung develops his theory of the collective conscious.

1934 Lev Vygotsky proposes concept of zone of proximal development.

1935 Henry Murray creates the Thematic Apperception Test.

1905 Freud proposes his psychosexual theory of personality development.

1935 Prefrontal lobotomy developed by Dr. Antonio Egas Moniz.

1905 The first widely used IQ test, the Binet-Simon, was created.

1915 Freud first proposes the concept of defense mechanisms.

1879 Wilhelm Wundt establishes the first laboratory of psychology in Leipzig, Germany.

1938 B.F. Skinner introduces the concept of operant conditioning.

1938 Electroconvulsive shock first used on a human patient.

1939 Clark and Clark classic study on prejudice conducted.

1942 Carl Rogers develops client-centered therapy.

1942 The Minnesota Multiphasic Personality Inventory is created.

1950 Erik Erikson proposes his psychosocial stages of personality development.

1951 Soloman Asch's classic study on conformity conducted.

1952 The first edition of the *Diagnostic and Statistical Manual of Mental Disorders (DSM)* is published.

1952 Chlorpromazine first drug treatment introduced for the treatment of schizophrenia.

1961 Carl Rogers creates the concepts of ideal self, real self, conditional positive regard, and unconditional positive regard.

1961 Muzafer Sherif conducts the "Robber's Cave" study.

1967 Seligman demonstrates learned helplessness in dogs.

1967 Holmes and Rahe create the Social Readjustment Rating Scale.

1967 Beck proposes a cognitive theory for explaining depression.

1968 Roger Sperry demonstrates hemispheric specialization with split-brain patients.

1977 The stress-vulnerability model of schizophrenia proposed by Zubin and Spring.

1977 Thomas and Chess conduct studies of different types of infant temperament.

1978 Elizabeth Loftus puts into question the validity of eyewitness testimony with discovery of misinformation effect.

1979 Mary Ainsworth uses the Strange Situation experiment to study infant attachment styles.

1979 Thomas Bouchard begins the Minnesota study of twins reared apart to identify the influence of genetics and the environment on personality traits.

1994 Herrnstein and Murray publish *The Bell Curve*.

1995 Goleman proposes idea of emotional intelligence.

2000 Genetic researchers finish mapping human genome.

2002 Steven Pinker publishes *The Blank Slate* arguing the concept of *tabula rasa*.

2002 New Mexico is the first state to allow licensed psychologists to prescribe drug treatments for psychological disorders.

1940   1960   1970   1990   2010

1948 Alfred Kinsey begins survey research on sexual behavior.

1953 The American Psychological Association publishes the first edition of *Ethical Standards in Psychology*.

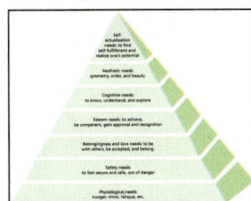

1954 Abraham Maslow proposes a hierarchy of needs to describe human motivation.

1955 Albert Ellis proposes rational emotive behavioral therapy.

1956 Hans Selye proposes the General Adaptation Syndrome to describe responses to stress.

1959 Festinger and Carlsmith publish their study on cognitive dissonance.

1959 Harlow and Zimmerman demonstrate the importance of contact comfort with their study on infant monkeys.

1962 Cognitive arousal theory of emotion proposed by Schacter and Singer.

1963 Albert Bandura's "Bobo doll" study is conducted.

1963 Stanley Milgram conducts his classic study on obedience.

1963 Lawrence Kohlberg creates his theory of moral development.

1966 Masters and Johnson introduce four stages of sexual response cycle.

1974 Friedman and Rosenman discover link between heart disease and Type-A personality.

1974 The PET scan is first introduced as a brain imaging technique.

1981 David Wechsler begins to devise IQ tests for specific age groups.

1983 Gardner first proposes his theory of multiple intelligences.

1985 Robert Sternberg proposes the triarchic theory of intelligence.

1989 Albert Bandura proposes the concept of reciprocal determinism.

1996 McCrae and Costa propose the Big Five Personality dimensions.

1997 Elisabeth Kubler-Ross publishes *On Grief and Grieving*, exploring the process of grieving through expansion of her theory of the five stages of death from *On Death and Dying* (1969).

2004 Alexander Storch presents possibility of obtaining stem cells from adults to repair damaged neural tissue.

2005 FDA mandates black box warnings of increased suicide risk on antidepressants.

2008 Law passed requiring insurance companies to provide equal coverage for mental health services.

2009 US President Barack Obama lifts federal funding limits on scientific research involving human stem cells.

2013 *DSM-V* scheduled for publication.

xxxi

TEACHING PSYCHOLOGY

Table of Contents

Raising the achievement level of all students is the number one challenge facing teachers today. To assist in meeting this challenge, we've enlisted a team of respected authors and consultants who specialize in psychology education, instructional design, and differentiated instruction. In the following pages, you'll find the key elements woven throughout this program to assure teaching and learning success.

TEACHING PSYCHOLOGY
- Why Teach Psychology? T1
- What Makes *Prentice Hall Psychology* Unique? T2
- How Can Technology Help? T4

PROGRAM ORGANIZATION
- Organization and Curriculum Standards T6

DIFFERENTIATED INSTRUCTION
- Table of Contents T17
- The Value of Differentiated Instruction T18
- Strategies for Specific Student Populations T20
- Strategies to Engage All Learners T24
- Developing Reading Skills T32
- Developing Student Writing Skills T33
- Supporting Media Literacy T34

ASSESSMENT
- The Need for Assessment T36
- Ongoing Assessment T36
- Encouraging Student Self-Assessment T37
- Using Rubrics T38

PLANNING YOUR INSTRUCTION
- Simplify Your Planning Using this Program T40
- Yearly and Semester Pacing Guides T42
- Block Scheduling Guide T45
- Chapter Lesson Planner T48

Why Teach Psychology?

Psychology touches every aspect of our lives. As we work, play, study, and simply interact every day, we are experiencing countless psychological phenomena. Our brains and bodies react to information and situations—sometimes in predictable (but often in unpredictable) ways. Such is the fascination of psychology—searching for the predictable, exploring the mysteries of the unpredictable.

The Science of Psychology

Though the ideas of psychology are seen in the writings of ancient civilizations, psychology as its own field of study is only a little over 130 years old. In that time, the science of psychology has expanded greatly. Scientists' understanding of the human mind and how it influences human behavior is constantly growing and evolving. In the past 130 years, our understanding of language and its acquisition, learning, emotions, human development, mental illness, and even our own basic, everyday behaviors has been enormously broadened because of the work of psychologists. Even so, the work has only just begun. The human brain still holds countless mysteries to be unlocked by science, and the psychologist's work may never truly be complete. The science of psychology is exciting, ever-moving, and deeply personal. It is the study of who we are—why we do what we do, why things sometimes go wrong in our development and behavior, and how to make things go right.

Developing Scientific and Critical Thinking Skills

Research is the cornerstone of psychology. The work of research psychologists informs real-world applications of psychological knowledge in countless areas of life. Honing these skills—familiarity with the scientific method, interpreting data, and simply reading people and understanding their actions and motivations—will serve students well in their academic and professional careers. Psychology teaches students to ask pertinent questions, observe situations critically, and move beyond their beliefs toward the facts of research. From Pavlov, for example, students may learn about conditioned behavior. But although it is the research that made Pavlov famous, perhaps the most important thing students can learn from him is his recognition that he was seeing a behavioral phenomenon even though he had set out to study digestion, and his willingness to switch from his original course in search of a fuller understanding of this behavior. In Pavlov's research, there is a lesson in the powers of observation and openness to experience that can benefit all students.

Applying Psychology

Taking a psychology class will undoubtedly inspire some students to become psychologists themselves. But all students can benefit from a basic understanding of psychology. Understanding psychology helps a teacher motivate students and instruct them to study more effectively. A basic understanding of psychology can help parents to effectively raise—and discipline—their children. Psychology can help a lawyer better read a witness, a doctor diagnose a patient, a pastor comfort the grieving, and a first-year college student deal with a new roommate. And as much as an understanding of psychology is useful in helping students and the adults they will become, navigating a world filled with other diverse people, psychology can also be helpful as students deal with their own difficulties in life. Studying psychology helps students understand that they are not alone, whether they face learning difficulties, body issues, depression, or loneliness. It gives students a window into why they may be experiencing these things, what to do when these issues become serious, and how they can either work their way through them or reach out for help. Students can see a whole body of science, information, theories, and modes of treatment to address their concerns about themselves and possibly those around them. Studying psychology helps students become more effective in their most important and basic role in the world—relating to others and understanding themselves.

TEACHING PSYCHOLOGY

What Makes *Prentice Hall Psychology* Unique?

Prentice Hall Psychology is a multidimensional program designed around the American Psychological Association's *National Standards for High School Psychology Curricula*. It helps students of all abilities gain an understanding of key principles of psychological science and see applications in the real world. The print Student Edition and Teacher Edition are supported online by a rich array of resources in MyPsychLab.

Learner-Centered

A learner-centered approach encourages dialogue and recognizes the importance of actively engaging students. This program offers a number of strategies designed to draw the student into an ongoing dialogue about psychology with the goal of awakening students' curiosity and energizing their desire to learn more.

1. Active Engagement Chapter Opening prologues are designed to capture student interest immediately. Taken from an exciting case study or recent events in the news, these openers are designed to engage student interest from the start. Throughout the chapters, student readers will find a friendly and inviting tone.

> My parents and I moved to this country when I was 6 years old. It's been a lot easier for me to adapt to our new culture than it has been for my parents. Is that normal?

2. Student Voice Questions appear in the margin. These questions encourage students to stop, clarify, and think critically. Written by students for students, these questions are designed to create a dialogue between the text and the reader. This Teacher's Edition provides additional support for using these questions as a starting point for class discussions.

3. Practice Quizzes are included at the end of each module. Practice quizzes encourage students to stop, review, and reinforce their learning before moving on to a new module.

4. Concept Summaries appear at the end of each chapter, providing students with a graphic

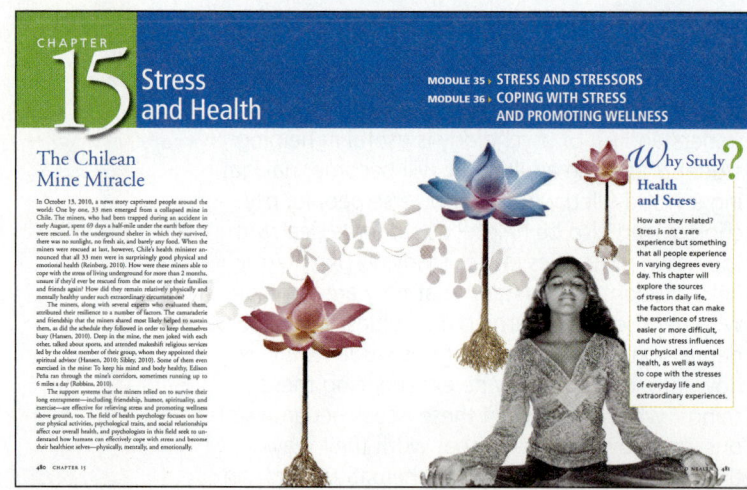

T2

summary of the chapter's content. By pulling the content together in this highly visual manner, students will better understand the connections and grasp how the chapter material fits together.

Achievement-Driven

Students are motivated to succeed when goals and expectations are clearly laid out and attainable. This program offers a number of strategies designed to encourage students to focus on key learning objectives aligned with the APA's *National Standards for High School Psychology Curricula* and to assist teachers in continually assessing students' progress in mastering these objectives.

1. Modular Design Each chapter is divided into two to four modules. These short modules help student focus on a few pages at a time without getting overwhelmed with information.

2. Learning Objectives Each module is organized around numbered Learning Objectives, which identify the most important concepts in the module. Teacher's resources, such as the Test Bank, Teacher's Manual, and PowerPoint slides, are all organized around the Learning Objectives, creating a fully integrated program of study.

3. Leveled Instruction This Teacher's Edition provides differentiated instruction options for reaching all students, using appropriate pedagogy and activities for students of all abilities and learning styles.

4. Technology to Assist Learning Rich digital assets such as audio, video, animations, and simulations in MyPsychLab provide multiple ways for learners to access the content. Extensive assessments, including Pretests, Posttests, and Chapter Exams, allow students and teachers to monitor progress.

Module 23: Encoding and Storage

Module Goals	Learning Objectives
Learn how the brain encodes memories.	23.1 What are levels of processing?
	23.2 How are memories encoded in the brain?
	23.3 How can we make encoding more effective?
Understand how memories are stored in the brain.	23.4 How is information stored in long-term memory?
	23.5 How and where are memories stored in the brain?

PROGRAM ORGANIZATION

DIFFERENTIATED INSTRUCTION

ASSESSMENT

PLANNING YOUR INSTRUCTION

DIFFERENTIATED INSTRUCTION KEY

Look for these symbols to help you adjust steps in each lesson to meet your students' needs.

- **L1** Special Needs
- **L2** Basic
  - **ELL** English Language Learners
  - **LPR** Less Proficient Readers
- **L3** All Students
- **L4** Advanced Students

How Can Technology Help?

Visit www.PearsonSchool.com/PHpsychology

MyPsychLab

Students can use a wide array of 21st-century learning tools to personalize learning. No matter where they are or what time of day it is, students have access to their work.

Pearson eText and Audio Textbook

- **Pearson eText** offers a complete interactive student text online. Students can navigate page-by-page, move directly to a chapter or section, or use the search feature to locate all references throughout the book. Pearson's interactive eText allows students to highlight, add study notes, bookmark pages, and access video clips, simulations, and the glossary—all at the point-of-use.

- **Audio Textbook** provides the complete *Prentice Hall Psychology* text in audio format. The audio text can be used stand alone or in conjunction with the print textbook to help students not only to read the text but also to understand each concept.

Interactivities help students gain deeper understanding of key concepts.

- Media assignments
- *Psychology In the News* audio podcasts
- Video clips
- Explorations and simulations

Electronic Flash Cards enable students to quiz themselves on key content, and they are downloadable to mobile devices.

Psychology Library offers numerous student tools and resources, including study skills and plagiarism tutorials, an APA documentation guide, and more.

Assessments and Grade Tracker For each chapter of the book, MyPsychLab offers a pretest, a posttest, and a chapter exam. Based on the results of the pretest, MyPsychLab creates a customized study plan for each student, identifying areas of strength and weakness and providing extra support where needed. With Grade Tracker, students can follow their own progress and teachers can monitor the work of the entire class. Automated grading of tests and assignments helps both students and teachers save time and improve results.

Class Prep for teachers in MyPsychLab: Finding, sorting, organizing, and presenting your teacher resources is fast and easy with Class Prep. This fully searchable database contains hundreds of teacher resources, such as lecture launchers and discussion topics, in-class and out-of-class activities and assignments, handouts, as well as video clips, photos, illustrations, charts, graphs, and animations.

Teachers can search or browse by topic, and it is easy to sort results by type, such as photograph, document, or animation. Teachers can create personalized folders to organize and store materials, or download the resources. Teachers can present material in class directly from Class Prep.

PROGRAM ORGANIZATION

ASSESSMENT

Organization and Curriculum Standards

What should students know and how should they show what they know at the end of their high school psychology class? *Prentice Hall Psychology* is organized around and correlated to the latest *National Standards for High School Psychology Curricula*, published by the American Psychological Association (APA). These Standards help teachers across the country design curricula for teaching scientific psychology that are consistent in content, level, and quality. The Standards also help teachers plan assessment of student learning based on specific learning objectives. Like the Standards, this book is divided into seven domains, and each chapter of this book addresses one or two standards from the 20 Standards Areas, providing complete and comprehensive coverage. *Prentice Hall Psychology* addresses all the Standard Areas in a way that is both academically rigorous and student-friendly.

Flexible Organization with Modules

Each chapter in *Prentice Hall Psychology* is divided into two to four shorter modules. The modular design provides teachers with flexibility to structure their courses around their unique classroom goals. Every effort has been made to ensure that each module stands alone, and they may be taught in any order. Students do not need to read earlier modules in order to fully understand later modules. Because these modules are much shorter than traditional textbook chapters, they help students focus on a few pages of text at a time without feeling overwhelmed with information. In addition, each module is structured around one or two module goals that help students identify what they should learn from the modules. Each module ends with a Practice Quiz to assess student comprehension of the module's content. The Practice Quizzes encourage students to stop, review, and reinforce their learning.

Learning Objectives

Based on APA recommendations, each module contains numbered Learning Objectives that provide an overview of the major concepts in the module. The Learning Objectives set clear expectations for what students should learn from the module, so they are not left struggling to identify the most important points of their reading. The phrasing of the Learning Objectives encourages students to think critically about the module's key concepts. Both the bulleted summary and the visual concept summary at the end of each chapter are organized around the Learning Objectives, further reinforcing students' understanding of the key concepts.

The Learning Objectives also provide a framework for teachers to assess performance and use assessment to promote improved student learning. The teacher resources, including the Test Bank, Teacher's Manual, and PowerPoint slides, are all organized around the Learning Objectives, providing teachers with a fully integrated system of teaching and assessment. For even more flexibility, this organization also allows teachers to choose which Learning Objectives they will include or leave out of their curriculum, and it is easy for teachers to select test items and other classroom resources that coordinate with the Learning Objectives they will cover. The Learning Objectives are closely aligned and correlated to the detailed Performance Standards detailed in the APA's *National Standards for High School Psychology Curricula*.

Correlation to APA's *National Standards for High School Psychology Curricula*

Prentice Hall Psychology provides complete and comprehensive coverage of the APA's *National Standards for High School Psychology Curricula*. The chart below lists the standards and shows which pages in *Prentice Hall Psychology* focus on each standard.

STANDARD	SE PAGE(S)
I. SCIENTIFIC INQUIRY DOMAIN	
IA. PERSPECTIVES IN PSYCHOLOGICAL SCIENCE	
IA-1. Development of psychology as an empirical science	
IA-1.1 Define psychology as a discipline and identify its goals as a science.	4–5
IA-1.2 Describe the emergence of psychology as a scientific discipline.	5–9
IA-1.3 Describe perspectives employed to understand behavior and mental processes.	10–11
IA-1.4 Recognize the evolving nature of psychology as a scientific discipline.	11–12
IA-2. Major subfields within psychology	
IA-2.1 Discuss the value of both basic and applied psychological research with human and nonhuman animals.	12
IA-2.2 Describe the major subfields of psychology.	12–14
IA-2.3 Identify the important role psychology plays in addressing the public interest.	14
IB. RESEARCH METHODS AND STATISTICS	
IB-1. Research methods used to study behavior and mental processes	
IB-1.1 Describe the scientific method and its role in psychology.	16–17
IB-1.2 Describe and compare descriptive, correlational, and experimental research.	17–21
IB-1.3 Define systematic procedures used to improve the validity of research findings.	21–22
IB-1.4 Discuss how and why psychologists use nonhuman animals in research.	22–23
IB-2. Ethical issues in research with human and nonhuman animals	
IB-2.1 Identify ethical standards psychologists must address regarding research with human participants.	23
IB-2.2 Identify ethical guidelines psychologists must address regarding research with nonhuman animals.	24
IB-3. Basic concepts of data analysis	
IB-3.1 Define descriptive statistics and explain how they are used by psychological scientists.	26–2
IB-3.2 Define correlation coefficients and explain their appropriate interpretation.	31–32
IB-3.3 Interpret graphical representations of data.	28–31
IB-3.4 Explain other inferential statistics, including statistical significance.	33
IB-3.5 Explain how validity and reliability of observations and measurements relate to data analysis.	33

(continued)

STANDARD	SE PAGE(S)
II. BIOPSYCHOLOGY DOMAIN	
IIA. BIOLOGICAL BASES OF BEHAVIOR	
IIA-1. Structure and function of the nervous system in human and nonhuman animals	
IIA-1.1 Identify the major divisions and subdivisions of the human nervous system.	42
IIA-1.2 Identify the parts of the neuron and describe the basic process of neural transmission.	42–47
IIA-1.3 Differentiate the structures and functions of the various parts of the central nervous system.	47–50
IIA-1.4 Describe the lateralization of brain functions.	57–63
IIA-1.5 Discuss the mechanisms of, and the importance of, plasticity of the nervous system.	56
IIA-2. Structure and function of the neuroendocrine system	
IIA-2.1 Describe how the endocrine glands are linked to the nervous system.	50
IIA-2.2 Describe the effects of hormones on behavior and mental processes.	51
IIA-2.3 Describe hormone effects on the immune system.	51–52
IIA-3. The interaction between biological factors and experience	
IIA-3.1 Describe concepts in genetic transmission.	66–67
IIA-3.2 Describe the interactive effects of heredity and environment.	67–69
IIA-3.3 Explain how evolved tendencies influence behavior.	69–70
IIA-4. Methods and issues related to biological advances	
IIA-4.1 Identify tools used to study the nervous system.	54
IIA-4.2 Describe advances made in neuroscience.	55–56
IIA-4.3 Discuss issues related to scientific advances in neuroscience and genetics.	56–57
IIB. SENSATION AND PERCEPTION	
IIB-1. The processes of sensation and perception	
IIB-1.1 Discuss the historical distinctions between sensation and perception.	78
IIB-1.2 Explain the concepts of threshold and adaptation.	79–80
IIB-2. The capabilities and limitations of sensory processes	
IIB-2.1 List forms of energy for which we do and do not have sensory receptors.	80–81
IIB-2.2 Describe the visual sensory system.	81–85
IIB-2.3 Describe the auditory sensory system.	86–88
IIB-2.4 Describe the olfactory and gustatory sensory systems.	88–90
IIB-2.5 Describe other important sensory systems.	91–92

(continued)

STANDARD	SE PAGE(S)
IIB-3. Interaction of the person and the environment in determining perception	
IIB-3.1 Explain Gestalt principles of perception.	95–96
IIB-3.2 Describe binocular and monocular depth cues.	96–99
IIB-3.3 Describe the importance of perceptual constancies.	94–95
IIB-3.4 Describe perceptual illusions.	99–100
IIB-3.5 Describe the nature of attention.	94
IIB-3.6 Explain how experiences and expectations influence perception.	100–101
IIC. CONSCIOUSNESS	
IIC-1. The relationship between conscious and unconscious processes	
IIC-1.1 Identify states of consciousness.	110–111
IIC-1.2 Distinguish between processing which is conscious (explicit) and other processing which happens without conscious awareness (implicit).	111
IIC-2. Characteristics of sleep and theories that explain why we sleep and dream	
IIC-2.1 Describe the circadian rhythm and its relation to sleep.	112
IIC-2.2 Describe the sleep cycle.	113–116
IIC-2.3 Describe and compare theories about the functions of sleep.	113
IIC-2.4 Describe types of sleep disorders.	116–119
IIC-2.5 Compare theories about the functions of dreams.	119–120
IIC-3. Categories of psychoactive drugs and their effects	
IIC-3.1 Characterize the major categories of psychoactive drugs and their effects.	126–131
IIC-3.2 Describe how psychoactive drugs act at the synaptic level.	131–132
IIC-3.3 Evaluate the biological and psychological effects of psychoactive drugs.	132–133
IIC-3.4 Explain how culture and expectations influence the use and experience of drugs.	133
IIC-4. Other states of consciousness	
IIC-4.1 Describe meditation and relaxation and their effects.	123–124
IIC-4.2 Describe hypnosis and controversies surrounding its nature and use.	124–126
III. DEVELOPMENT AND LEARNING DOMAIN	
IIIA. LIFE SPAN DEVELOPMENT	
IIIA-1. Methods and issues in life span development	
IIIA-1.1 Explain the interaction of environmental and biological factors in development, including the role of the brain in all aspects of development.	142–143

(continued)

PROGRAM ORGANIZATION

ASSESSMENT

STANDARD	SE PAGE(S)
IIIA. LIFE SPAN DEVELOPMENT	
IIIA-1.2 Explain issues of continuity/discontinuity and stability/change.	143
IIIA-1.3 Distinguish methods used to study development.	144
IIIA-1.4 Describe the role of sensitive and critical periods in development.	144–146
IIIA-1.5 Discuss issues related to the end of life as pertinent to any period in development.	
IIIA-2. Theories of life span development	
IIIA-2.1 Discuss theories of cognitive development.	152–155
IIIA-2.2 Discuss theories of moral development.	163–164
IIIA-2.3 Discuss theories of social development.	158–160
IIIA-3. Prenatal development and the newborn	
IIIA-3.1 Describe physical development from conception through birth and identify influences on prenatal development.	147–149
IIIA-3.2 Describe newborns' reflexes and abilities.	150–151
IIIA-4. Infancy (the first 2 years of life)	
IIIA-4.1 Describe physical and motor development.	151
IIIA-4.2 Describe how infant perceptual abilities and intelligence develop.	152–155
IIIA-4.3 Describe the development of attachment and the role of the caregiver.	156
IIIA-4.4 Describe the development of communication and language.	155–156
IIIA-5. Childhood	
IIIA-5.1 Describe physical and motor development.	151
IIIA-5.2 Describe how memory and thinking ability develops.	152–155
IIIA-5.3 Describe social and emotional development through childhood.	158–160
IIIA-6. Adolescence	
IIIA-6.1 Identify major physical changes.	162–163
IIIA-6.2 Describe the development of reasoning and morality.	163–164
IIIA-6.3 Describe identity formation.	164
IIIA-6.4 Discuss the role of family and peers in adolescent development.	164–165
IIIA-7. Adulthood and aging	
IIIA-7.1 Identify major physical changes associated with adulthood and aging.	166–167
IIIA-7.2 Describe cognitive and social development in adulthood.	165–166
IIIA-7.3 Discuss physical, cognitive, social, and emotional issues in aging.	167–169

(continued)

STANDARD	SE PAGE(S)
IIIB. LEARNING	
IIIB-1. Classical conditioning	
IIIB-1.1 Describe the principles of classical conditioning.	178–180
IIIB-1.2 Describe specializations of classical conditioning.	181–182
IIIB-1.3 Apply classical conditioning to everyday life.	182
IIIB-2. Operant conditioning	
IIIB-2.1 Describe the Law of Effect.	184–185
IIIB-2.2 Describe the principles of operant conditioning.	185–187
IIIB-2.3 Describe specializations of operant conditioning.	187–192
IIIB-2.4 Apply operant conditioning to everyday life.	192–193
IIIB-3. Observational learning	
IIIB-3.1 Describe the principles of observational learning.	195
IIIB-3.2 Apply observational learning to everyday life.	196
IIIC. LANGUAGE DEVELOPMENT	
IIIC-1. Structural features of language	
IIIC-1.1 Describe the structure and function of language.	201–202
IIIC-1.2 Discuss the relationship between language and thought.	202–204
IIIC-2. Theories and developmental stages of language acquisition	
IIIC-2.1 Explain the process of language acquisition.	204
IIIC-2.2 Evaluate the theories of language acquisition.	204–205
IIIC-3. Language and the brain	
IIIC-3.1 Identify the brain structures associated with language.	205–206
IIIC-3.2 Discuss how damage to the brain affects language.	205–206
IV. SOCIAL CONTEXT DOMAIN	
IVA. Social Interactions	
IVA-1. Social cognition	
IVA-1.1 Describe attributional explanations of behavior.	229–230
IVA-1.2 Describe the relationship between attitudes (implicit and explicit) and behavior.	224–228
IVA-1.3 Identify persuasive methods used to change attitudes.	228–229

(continued)

PROGRAM ORGANIZATION

STANDARD	SE PAGE(S)
IVA-2. Social influence	
IVA-2.1 Describe the power of the situation.	214
IVA-2.2 Describe effects of others' presence on individuals' behavior.	215–219
IVA-2.3 Describe how group dynamics influence behavior.	219–220
IVA-2.4 Discuss how an individual influences group behavior.	220–221
IVA-3. Social relations	
IVA-3.1 Discuss the nature and effects of prejudice and discrimination.	232–235
IVA-3.2 Describe determinants of prosocial behavior.	240–241
IVA-3.3 Discuss influences upon aggression and conflict.	238–240
IVA-3.4 Discuss factors influencing attraction and relationships.	235–238
IVB. Culture and Gender	
IVB-1. Culture	
IVB-1.1 Define culture.	250–251
IVB-1.2 Identify cultural variations across time and place.	251–254
IVB-1.3 Discuss the relationship between culture and conceptions of self and identity.	255–256
IVB-2. Gender	
IVB-2.1 Define gender and discuss the development of gender identity.	261–262
IVB-2.2 Identify gender similarities and differences.	264–265
IVB-2.3 Discuss the biological and environmental factors that relate to the development of gender identity.	262–263
V. COGNITION DOMAIN	
VA. Memory	
VA-1. Encoding of memory	
VA-1.1 Characterize the difference between shallow (surface) and deep (elaborate) processing.	275
VA-1.2 Identify factors that influence encoding.	276–279
VA-1.3 Discuss strategies for improving the encoding of memory.	279–280
VA-2. Storage of memory	
VA-2.1 Describe the differences between working memory and long-term memory.	280–282
VA-2.2 Identify and explain biological processes related to how memory is stored.	282–283
VA-2.3 Discuss types of memory and causes of amnesia.	296–297
VA-2.4 Discuss strategies for improving the storage of memories.	282–283

(continued)

STANDARD	SE PAGE(S)
VA-3. Retrieval of memory	
VA-3.1 Analyze the importance of retrieval cues in memory.	285–286
VA-3.2 Explain the role that interference plays in retrieval.	293–295
VA-3.3 Discuss the factors influencing how memories are retrieved.	286–289
VA-3.4 Explain how memories can be malleable.	290–292
VA-3.5 Discuss strategies for improving the retrieval of memories.	289–290
VB. Thinking	
VB-1. Processes and functions comprising thought	
VB-1.1 Define processes involved in the manipulation and understanding of information.	306–310
VB-1.2 Define processes involved in problem solving and decision making.	310–312
VB-1.3 Discuss nonhuman problem-solving abilities.	312–313
VB-2. Obstacles related to thought	
VB-2.1 Describe obstacles to problem solving.	314–316
VB-2.2 Describe obstacles to decision making.	318–319
VB-2.3 Describe obstacles to making good judgments.	316–318
VC. Intelligence	
VC-1. Perspectives on intelligence	
VC-1.1 Discuss intelligence as a general factor.	321
VC-1.2 Discuss alternative conceptualizations of intelligence.	321–322
VC-1.3 Describe the extremes of intelligence.	323–327
VC-2. Assessment of intelligence	
VC-2.1 Discuss the history of intelligence testing.	327–328
VC-2.2 Identify contemporary ways of assessing human abilities.	328–329
VC-2.3 Identify measures of and data on reliability and validity for intelligence test scores.	329–330
VC-3. Issues in intelligence	
VC-3.1 Discuss uses of intelligence testing.	330–331
VC-3.2 Discuss the influences of biological factors and environmental factors on intelligence.	331–333

(continued)

PROGRAM ORGANIZATION

STANDARD	SE PAGE(S)
VI. INDIVIDUAL VARIATIONS DOMAIN	
VIA. Motivation	
VIA-1. Perspectives on motivation	
VIA-1.1 Explain biologically based theories of motivation.	342–346
VIA-1.2 Explain cognitively based theories of motivation.	342–346
VIA-1.3 Explain humanistic theories of motivation.	346–348
VIA-2. Domains of motivated behavior in humans and nonhuman animals	
VIA-2.1 Discuss eating behavior.	349–351
VIA-2.2 Discuss sexual behavior and orientation.	351–354
VIA-2.3 Discuss achievement motivation.	354–355
VIA-2.4 Discuss other ways in which humans and nonhuman animals are motivated.	355–356
VIB. Emotion	
VIB-1. Perspectives on emotion	
VIB-1.1 Explain the biological and cognitive components of emotion.	358–360
VIB-1.2 Discuss the concept of basic human emotions and the evidence related to it.	358–360
VIB-1.3 Differentiate among theories of emotional experience.	360–363
VIB-2. Emotional expression	
VIB-2.1 Explain how biological factors influence emotional expression.	358–359
VIB-2.2 Explain how culture and gender influence emotional interpretation and expression.	363–364
VIB-2.3 Explain how other environmental factors influence emotional expression.	363–364
VIB-3. Domains of emotional behavior	
VIB-3.1 Identify biological and environmental influences on the expression and experience of fear.	364–365
VIB-3.2 Identify biological and environmental influences on the expression and experience of happiness.	366–367
VIC. Personality	
VIC-1. Perspectives on personality	
VIC-1.1 Evaluate psychodynamic theories.	376–383
VIC-1.2 Evaluate trait theories.	387–389
VIC-1.3 Evaluate humanistic theories.	385–387
VIC-1.4 Evaluate social cognitive theories.	383–385

(continued)

STANDARD	SE PAGE(S)
VIC-2. Assessment of personality	
VIC-2.1 Differentiate personality assessment techniques.	391–395
VIC-2.2 Discuss the reliability and validity of personality assessment techniques.	391–395
VIC-3. Issues in personality	
VIC-3.1 Discuss biological and situational influences.	396–397
VIC-3.2 Discuss stability and change.	397–398
VIC-3.3 Discuss connections to health and work.	398–399
VIC-3.4 Discuss self-esteem.	399
VIC-3.5 Analyze how individualistic and collectivistic cultural perspectives relate to personality.	399–400
VID. Psychological disorders	
VID-1. Perspectives on abnormal behavior	
VID-1.1 Define psychologically abnormal behavior.	412–413
VID-1.2 Describe historical and cross-cultural views of abnormality.	410–412
VID-1.3 Describe major models of abnormality.	413–415
VID-1.4 Discuss how stigma relates to abnormal behavior.	415–416
VID-1.5 Discuss the impact of psychological disorders on the individual, family, and society.	416
VID-2. Categories of psychological disorders	
VID-2.1 Identify the components of the DSM classification system.	418–420
VID-2.2 Discuss the challenges associated with diagnosis.	421
VID-2.3 Describe symptoms and causes of major categories of psychological disorders (including schizophrenic, mood, anxiety, and personality disorders).	421–436
VID-2.4 Evaluate how family and societal influences affect an individual's experience of psychological disorders.	436
VII. APPLICATIONS OF PSYCHOLOGICAL SCIENCE DOMAIN	
VIIA. Treatment of Psychological Disorders	
VIIA-1. Perspectives on treatment	
VIIA-1.1 Identify changes in treatment related to social and historical context.	446–447
VIIA-1.2 Match methods of treatment to psychological perspectives.	448–459
VIIA-1.3 Recognize that psychologists use a variety of treatment options.	448–459
VIIA-1.4 Identify treatment providers for psychological disorders and the training required for each.	447–448

(continued)

PROGRAM ORGANIZATION

STANDARD	SE PAGE(S)
VIIA-2. Categories of treatment and types of treatment providers	
VIIA-2.1 Identify biomedical treatments. 465–469	
VIIA-2.2 Identify psychological treatments. 448–459	
VIIA-2.3 Evaluate the efficacy of treatments for particular disorders.	459–460
VIIA-2.4 Describe appropriate treatments for different age groups.	469–470
VIIA-2.5 Identify other factors that improve the efficacy of treatment.	460–462
VIIA-3. Legal, ethical, and professional issues in the treatment of psychological disorders	
VIIA-3.1 Identify ethical challenges involved in delivery of treatment.	470–473
VIIA-3.2 Identify national and local resources available to support individuals with psychological disorders and their families (e.g., NAMI and support groups).	473
VIIB. Health	
VIIB-1. Stress and coping	
VIIB-1.1 Define stress as a psychophysiological reaction.	482–483
VIIB-1.2 Identify and explain potential sources of stress.	483–488
VIIB-1.3 Explain physiological and psychological consequences for health.	488–492
VIIB-1.4 Identify and explain physiological, cognitive, and behavioral strategies to deal with stress.	495–498, 500–503
VIIB-2. Behaviors and attitudes that promote health	
VIIB-2.1 Identify ways to promote mental health and physical fitness.	505
VIIB-2.2 Describe the characteristics and factors that promote resilience and optimism.	503–504
VIIB-2.3 Distinguish between effective and ineffective means of dealing with stressors and other health issues.	499
VIIC. Careers	
VIIC-1. Educational requirements	
VIIC-1.1 Identify degree requirements for psychologists and psychology-related careers.	515–518
VIIC-1.2 Identify resources to help select programs for further study.	518–520
VIIC-2. Career options	
VIIC-2.1 Identify careers in psychology.	520–522
VIIC-2.2 Identify careers related to psychology.	522–527

DIFFERENTIATED INSTRUCTION

Table of Contents

THE VALUE OF DIFFERENTIATED INSTRUCTION T18
- How is Instruction Differentiated? T18
- How Does This Improve Learning T18
- How Do We Implement Differentiated Instruction T18
- Leveled Assessments Give More Options T19

STRATEGIES FOR SPECIFIC STUDENT POPULATIONS T20
- Special Needs T20
- English Language Learners T21
- Less Proficient Readers T22
- Advanced Learners T23

STRATEGIES TO ENGAGE ALL LEARNERS T24
- Classroom Management T24
- Discussion Strategies T26
    - Idea Wave Discussion T26
    - Think-Write-Pair-Share T26
    - Numbered Heads T27
    - Click and Clunk T28
    - Peer Tutoring and Peer Feedback T28
    - Socratic Discussion T28
    - Debate T29
- Making Class Fun and Meaningful T29
    - Opinion Line T30
    - Jigsaw T30
    - Conversation Wall T31

DEVELOPING READING SKILLS T32

DEVELOPING STUDENT WRITING SKILLS T33

SUPPORTING MEDIA LITERACY T34

TEACHING PSYCHOLOGY

PROGRAM ORGANIZATION

DIFFERENTIATED INSTRUCTION

ASSESSMENT

PLANNING YOUR INSTRUCTION

DIFFERENTIATED INSTRUCTION

The Value of Differentiated Instruction

It's basic, but it's true—not all students learn in the same manner and not all students have the same academic background or abilities. The "one size fits all" approach has not been proved to be the most successful strategy. As educators, we need to respond to a variety of student learning styles, readiness levels, and interests by developing and using instructional strategies that address the needs of diverse learners. Under the *No Child Left Behind* mandate, educators are required to work to close the achievement gap. All students are expected to master state academic standards. Our goal as teachers is to enable 100 percent of students to achieve success on the high-stakes assessment tests. It is critical to properly match the difficulty level of tasks with the ability level of students. Giving students tasks that they perceive as too hard lowers their expectations of success. However, giving students assignments that they think are too easy undermines their feelings of competence. Therefore, it is important for a program to give teachers leveled activities that allow them to match tasks with the abilities of their individual students.

How Is Instruction Differentiated?

It is vital to determine the readiness, interests, and learning styles of all students. Diagnostic tests and assessments will help define the specific needs of students. Then once strengths and weaknesses are determined, you can differentiate curriculum through three facets.

Content

What students learn may be layered to fit their interests and talents. The level of concepts, generalizations, and skills that students can acquire will often depend on the complexity of thinking skills required. All students must master the same standards, but depth of learning should be adjusted to meet the needs of diverse learners.

Process

The process of instruction involves differentiating learning activities and strategies. Content can be accessed, or processed, through a combination of methods, such as direct instruction, inquiry-based learning, cooperative learning, and information-processing models. It can be done as a class, in groups or pairs, or individually. Differentiating instruction is also an essential tool for adapting technology into classroom activities. Technology, such as online activities, can provide an ideal opportunity for engaging students. It can be used also to provide additional opportunities to access content. A complete psychology program makes content available in a variety of formats, including text, audio, visuals, and interactivities.

Product

In the end, what students produce demonstrates skills and concepts they have learned. When evaluating student understanding, once again, we cannot assume that "one size fits all." The style, depth, and complexity of the product vary to match ability levels and learning styles. Various methods of assessment—activities, portfolios, performance-based assessment, rubrics, as well as standard tests—can measure students' progress in ways that are fair to multiple styles of learners.

How Does This Improve Learning?

Differentiated instruction provides multiple paths for students to access, use, and transfer understanding of concepts. It integrates instructional strategies to meet the needs of a diverse population of students, and thereby enables all students to achieve success. By using differentiated instruction, we allow students to take more responsibility for learning and create a community of learners who cooperate and respect each other.

How Do We Implement Differentiated Instruction?

The mission of *Prentice Hall Psychology* is to provide standards-based instruction in ways that allow all students to participate and to achieve.

Our program provides options so that diverse learners meet established goals, using different content, processes, and products to get there.

Our effective support helps you close the achievement gap.

Teaching Support Helps You Modify Instruction

The **Teacher's Edition** provides continuous professional development throughout the program, starting with strategies for specific populations at the beginning of this textbook. The **Teacher's Edition** was designed to make it easy for teachers to modify instruction for diverse learners. Specific activities help you adapt instruction for individual students in five categories: less proficient readers, English language learners, advanced students, special needs, and basic (all) population. Resources are identified as being appropriate for use by each of these categories. All resources are also assigned a level—special needs, basic, all students, and advanced—so you know exactly how to assign tasks of appropriate difficulty.

Varied Resources Address Different Populations

The program also delivers content through a wide variety of formats—including text, audio, video, slides, and interactive activities—appealing to all of your students.

- Pearson eText and the audio textbook in MyPsychLab provide students with multiple ways to access the book's content.
- Interactive PowerPoint slides provide a compelling visual presentation that benefits all learners.
- Video clips in MyPsychLab bring concepts to life.

Using technology as a tool to differentiate content enables students to access content in an engaging method. MyPsychLab includes:

- Interactive Flash Cards help students learn and review key terms. The Flash Cards can be downloaded to mobile devices.
- Simulations and Explorations in MyPsychLab provide an interactive way for students to learn.
- *Psychology in the News* podcasts engage students with audio content.

Leveled Assessments Give More Options

The program offers a variety of assessment methods. This allows you to choose the style and level of assessment to meet the needs of your students.

- **Test Bank and Exam*View*® Test Generator** software provide the tools to create leveled tests that adapt to individual needs. Each question in the Test Bank is linked to its corresponding Learning Objective and categorized by type (factual, conceptual, or applied) and by level (easy, moderate, or difficult). Each chapter of the Test Bank contains a Total Assessment Guide that organizes all test items by learning objective and question type in an easy-to-reference grid.
- **Assessments in MyPsychLab.** For each chapter of the book, MyPsychLab offers a pretest, posttest, and chapter exam. Based on the results of the pretest, MyPsychLab creates a customized study plan for each student, identifying areas of strength and weakness and providing extra support where needed.

DIFFERENTIATED INSTRUCTION KEY

Look for these symbols to help you adjust steps in each lesson to meet your students' needs.

- **L1** Special Needs
- **L2** Basic
  - **ELL** English Language Learners
  - **LPR** Less Proficient Readers
- **L3** All Students
- **L4** Advanced Students

DIFFERENTIATED INSTRUCTION

Strategies for Specific Student Populations

Differentiated instruction can be fostered through modifying instruction to address individual needs. To increase student achievement, teachers can use strategies for specific student populations to offer specialized support. Lesson plans in this **Teacher's Edition** provide differentiated instruction strategies and suggest ancillary support. The following pages provide general guidelines for modifying instruction for students with special needs, English language learners, less proficient students, and advanced learners.

Special Needs

Students with special education needs are a highly heterogeneous group of learners, presenting unique cognitive, behavioral, social, and physical needs. To help create a classroom culture that supports the participation and achievement of students with such needs, set clear expectations and provide reasonable choices for all students. Lessons should be planned with individual adaptations and modifications. Offer instructional activities that foster the development of relationships among students and between students and teachers.

Preteach

Preteaching helps prepare students for learning.

- Preteach critical terms and high-use academic words by reviewing the key terms in the side columns.
- Provide preferred seating in the front of the class for students who need interpreters, space for a guide dog, or face-to-face talk for reading lips.

Teach

Using a variety of approaches enhances lessons.

- Provide an overview of key ideas and concepts presented in the text using outlines, maps, or study guides.
- Present all ideas orally and visually, and when possible, incorporate tactile and kinesthetic experiences as well.
- Require students to demonstrate that they are listening and following along (e.g., taking notes, running a finger along the text).
- Incorporate active reading strategies (e.g., choral reading, paired reading) to assist in maintaining attention.
- Provide adaptive materials as appropriate (e.g., enlarged print, Braille edition, captions for the video program).
- Incorporate the same comprehension and learning strategies over time to allow for mastery.

Assess

Students need to know what is expected.

- Assess students' understanding by asking them to write questions about what they have learned, identify what they find unclear or confusing, or complete short quick-writes of the key points.
- When having students work in groups or pairs, set up procedures that maintain each student's accountability (e.g., students each having to write, draw, or state a response).

- Make sure that you have adequately scaffolded tasks for special needs students and equipped them with writing instruction and practice that builds the prerequisite skills.
- When appropriate, have students manage and chart their academic performance, homework and assignment completion, and behavior.
- Provide outlines of what is to be done, with suggested dates and timelines for project completion.

English Language Learners

Students who are learning English are the fastest growing segment of the school-age population. These students require frontloading, or reteaching in order to grasp challenging literacy tasks, such as those encountered in a psychology textbook. Since English Language Learners (ELL) may be approaching an assignment with limited background knowledge and weak English vocabulary, concentrate on activities that build strong conceptual and linguistic foundations, guide them through the text's organization, and model appropriate comprehension strategies. The following practices will support ELL students in making strides in their second-language literacy.

Preteach

English Language Learners require extra preparation.

- Introduce essential words in meaningful contexts, through simple sentences drawing on familiar issues, scenarios, and vocabulary. Ask students to write the definitions in their own words and then identify the words when they occur within the reading.
- Use realia and visuals (e.g., photographs, objects, color transparencies) to make the concepts less abstract.
- Lead a quick text prereading, or "text tour," focusing student attention on illustrations, titles and subtopics, and boldfaced words.
- Suggest students use the vocabulary flashcards in MyPsychLab, which are presented in both English and Spanish.

Teach

Many of these techniques will benefit all learners.

- Get students physically involved with the page, using sticky notes or small pieces of cardboard to focus and guide their reading.
- Have students engage in repeated readings of the same brief passage to build word recognition, fluency, and reading rate.
- Praise students' efforts to experiment with new language in class, both in writing and in speaking.

Assess

Students will demonstrate learning in different ways.

- Ask students to demonstrate their understanding by drawing upon different language skills: formal and informal writing assignments, posters, small group tasks, and oral presentations.
- Make sure students understand assessment criteria in advance. Distribute rubrics. Whenever possible, provide models of student work to emulate, along with an example of work that fails to meet the specified assessment criteria.

DIFFERENTIATED INSTRUCTION

Less Proficient Readers

Less proficient readers are individuals who begin the year 1 or more years below grade level yet do not qualify for special education services. They may or may not be ELLs. They may be underprepared for the academic challenges due to difficulties with attention and memory, learning strategies, or vocabulary and reading fluency. It is especially important to engage these students in challenging lessons while incorporating support or instructional scaffolding to increase their likelihood of success.

Preteach

Preteaching helps build students' confidence.

- *For Difficulties with Attention and Memory:* Gain attention by requesting a simple physical response (e.g., "Everyone, eyes on me, please."). Then keep the lesson pace brisk—a "perky not pokey" pace is helpful.

- *For Difficulties with Learning Strategies:* Clarify the rationale for learning a new strategy in terms students value. Directly teach any requisite skills needed to perform the strategy.

- *For Difficulties with Vocabulary and Fluency:* Directly teach meanings of critical vocabulary required for full understanding of the lesson.

Teach

Lessons have to address specific, different needs.

- *For Difficulties with Attention and Memory:* Emphasize connections between new and known information. Engage students in collaborative "read/reflect/discuss/note" cycle.

- *For Difficulties with Learning Strategies:* Explicitly model the use of the strategy, including a significant focus on thinking aloud during the execution of each step in the strategy. Discuss where else in or out of school students could use the strategy.

- *For Difficulties with Vocabulary and Fluency:* Intentionally revisit newly acquired vocabulary during discussion. Suggest that students use the vocabulary flashcards in MyPsychLab.

Assess

Assessment must accommodate special needs.

- *For Difficulties with Attention and Memory:* Ask students to reorganize, prioritize, and otherwise reflect on the key aspects of the lesson. Have them explain key content to a partner. Monitor and reteach as necessary.

- *For Difficulties with Learning Strategies:* Include explicit use of strategies taught as part of the quiz, report, project, and other formal assessments.

- *For Difficulties with Vocabulary and Fluency:* Randomly call on students to provide examples of the vocabulary word under examination.

Advanced Learners

Advanced Learners need modified instruction to achieve their highest potential. They tend to understand complex concepts quickly, learn more rapidly and in greater depth, and may have interests that are different from their peers. Teachers can modify pacing and offer enrichment to allow for exploring topics in-depth, manipulating ideas in novel ways, and making connections to other disciplines.

Preteach

These students may have extensive background.

- Before beginning a new unit, have students write, verbalize, or draw what they know about the topic and present this information to peers.
- Ask students to brainstorm what they'd like to learn, and then work with them to create a plan for advanced study based on their interests.

Teach

Activate students' ability to think creatively and see connections.

- Help students adjust the pace of their learning, speeding through concepts they master quickly or slowing down to study content in depth. The Teacher's Edition provides ideas for ways to extend content.
- Challenge students to tackle more complex topics and offer frequent opportunities to focus on abstract ideas.
- Provide opportunities for in-depth research on student-directed topics. Have students explore topics on the Internet under your direction.
- Encourage students to make connections between content they are learning and other disciplines such as language, arts, science, and math. For example, students might want to read about the multidisciplinary aspects of the concept they are studying.

Assess

Assessment can take many forms.

- Give students responsibility for part of the assessment of their learning. Allow them to plan, design, and monitor the project or assignment.
- Encourage students to apply standards-based understanding to new situations. Challenge them to take information and use it in novel ways.

DIFFERENTIATED INSTRUCTION

Strategies to Engage All Learners

All students may benefit from strategies that we often consider "differentiation." While these strategies are necessary for success with students with special needs, they also aid many on-level students who are kinesthetic or visual learners or those who struggle with organization. Here are some tips to keep in mind as you plan:

- **Clarify behavioral expectations** for the lesson. Use rubrics and work with students to create rubrics for class activities and projects. Modeling what students are to do or providing students with examples of finished products are necessary for student success. Explicit instructions do not water down the curriculum; they make it clear so that all students can access it.

- **Use visuals throughout the lesson.** Outlining key ideas, writing key phrases and vocabulary on the overhead projector or board, or putting notes on the overhead projector or board are critical supports for many students. You may want to provide some students with a copy of your overheads or notes ahead of time so that they can follow along. For other students, make a partial or blank copy of the graphic or outline you will be using and require students to write in key information as it is discussed. It is very helpful if you model this filling-in procedure for students. It also helps them to overcome problems with spelling or capturing complex ideas using only a few words.

- **Explicitly teach skills.** Model note taking as you present information to the classroom. Collect and review the students' notes and provide suggestions for improvement. Teach study skills, listening skills, and reading skills along with the content.

- **Incorporate active reading strategies.** Build vocabulary by teaching the meaning of prefixes and suffixes. Have students make study cards of unfamiliar words. Have students read and summarize the paragraph in their own words. Monitor their work to clarify any misunderstandings.

- **Use a variety of strategies to teach and assess understanding.** Present ideas orally and visually and, when possible, incorporate tactile and kinesthetic experiences. Think beyond the common modes of reading and writing. Students could present information orally, create a poster or visual representation of a work, make an audio recording of their ideas, or act out their understanding. These activities take into consideration multiple intelligences and can provide access for all learners in the classroom.

- **Assist in time management.** When requiring students to complete projects or long-term assignments, provide a calendar that breaks down the requirements by due dates. Go over the checklist with students and monitor their use of the checklist and task completion as the assignment proceeds. Many students will experience significant difficulties in self-managing the time needed to complete complex and long-term assignments.

- **Incorporate students' strengths and interests** to connect them to content and activities.

Classroom Management

Creating a positive learning environment enables all students to reach their full potential. In a supportive, respectful setting, students perform and behave better. Teachers who use effective motivational and management strategies that actively engage students and appeal to individual learning styles and needs create classrooms that enhance students' academic and personal lives.

The following are some tips for classroom management:

- **Make learning relevant.** Help students make connections between their own lives and the classroom content. Ask students to list questions about the topic that they would like to learn about. Allow students to extend the lesson by exploring subtopics of their choice. Use journal exercises to enable students to demonstrate understanding in their own words and through their own experiences.

> **BELLRINGER**
>
> Draw a two-column chart on the board for students to copy onto paper. The left column's heading should be "What I Already Know About Psychology." The right column's heading should be "What I Predict I Will Learn." Have students complete their charts with brief notations.

- **Be organized—and help students be organized.** Many students have difficulty organizing their time. Break down assignments into short tasks. Require students to submit a plan for completing a large project. Teach skills such as notebook organization. Hand out assignment sheets ahead of time, allowing students to organize their time for the upcoming week or unit. Keep a master notebook with class notes, handouts, and homework that students may consult if they miss a day of class.

- **Have students begin work in class.** Prior to class dismissal, check to ensure that each student has a good start and understands what is expected.

- **Provide time for students to collect their thoughts.** This gives more reflective learners time to consider the answer. Explain this procedure to the class before using it. Tell students the questions that you will be asking during tomorrow's class in order to give them time overnight to prepare their responses.

- **Use an instructional warmup activity.** Use the bellringers activities in the Teacher's Edition to grab students' attention and immediately engage them in a task.

- **Use group activities.** Collaborative work encourages students to be supportive of each other, creating positive interdependence. Explain the task clearly. Teach collaborative skills (such as problem solving, time management, accepting criticism).

- **Use peer tutoring.** This technique helps teachers accommodate academic diversity. All students can be actively involved in tasks they can perform successfully. Students work in pairs to assist each other in learning, which leads to improved self-esteem, personal interaction, and positive attitudes about school. Steps for using this strategy are on the next page.

TEACHING PSYCHOLOGY

PROGRAM ORGANIZATION

DIFFERENTIATED INSTRUCTION

ASSESSMENT

PLANNING YOUR INSTRUCTION

DIFFERENTIATED INSTRUCTION

DISCUSSION STRATEGIES

Simple structures for discussion can help students extract and process meaning from reading the text. These strategies guide students to a more productive and inclusive class discussion, while enabling students to "take ownership" of the information.

Strategy: Idea Wave Discussion

Purpose: To support all students in actively listening and responding academically to a critical question within a more elaborate unified-class discussion.

How to do it:

1. Pose an open-ended question or task (e.g., *What methods do researchers use to study behavior?*).

2. Provide a model response on the board (e.g., *Researchers use experiments to study behavior.*).

3. Give students time to consider what they know about the topic and record a number of responses.

   L2 Differentiate Provide two or three sentence starters and ask students to write one or two of their ideas using a sentence starter. These starters should include key academic vocabulary and sentence structures that students wouldn't ordinarily use in casual conversation (e.g., *In studying behavior, researchers may choose an experiment over descriptive methods because...*).

4. As students jot down ideas, pick volunteers to jumpstart the subsequent class discussion.

   L2 Differentiate Get a few answers from students who wouldn't ordinarily respond voluntarily and bolster their confidence by affirming their idea prior to the actual discussion.

   L2 Differentiate Read aloud your model response and have students read along with you a second time to build reading fluency.

5. Have students share their responses with a partner to build confidence and accountability to respond, even if all students do not participate in the class discussion.

6. Move around the class in a fast-paced, but structured manner (e.g., down rows, around tables).

   L4 Differentiate After this structured debriefing, call on a few volunteers who have additional answers.

7. Provide an active listening and note-taking task during the discussion. Ask students to jot down two ideas, such as two perspectives with which you agree, two additional examples, and so forth.

8. If there tends to be repetition in responses, ask students to point out similarities rather than stating that their idea has already been mentioned. Require that students use language for acknowledging other ideas (e.g., *My idea builds upon _____'s idea. I also believe that...*).

Strategy: Think-Write-Pair-Share

Purpose: To engage students in responding to instruction.

How to do it:

1. **Think** Students listen while the teacher poses a question or task related to the reading or classroom discussion. The level of questions should vary from lower level literal to higher order inferential or analytical.

   L1 L2 ELL Differentiate Write questions on the board or provide them on a piece of paper.

2. **Write** Provide quiet thinking or writing time for students to deal with the question and go back to the text or review notes. Have students record their ideas in their notebooks.

   L1 L2 Differentiate Consider providing academic sentence starters for students to complete as a means of encouraging more thoughtful and formal responses.

T26

3. **Pair/Share** Cue students to find a partner and share their written response, noting similarities and differences. Teach students to encourage one another to clarify and justify their responses. To add more accountability for active listening, ask students to share their partner's idea during the structured debriefing and require that they begin their response with a citation expression (e.g., *My partner pointed out / emphasized / predicted that ...*).

4. Randomly call on students to share during a class discussion after they have rehearsed answers with their partners.

5. Invite volunteers to contribute additional ideas and points of view to the discussion after calling on a reasonable number of students.

6. Direct students to go back to their notes and add any important information garnered during the partner and class discussions.

Strategy: Numbered Heads

Purpose: To engage all students in responding to questions in order to assess reading comprehension and content understanding.

How to do it:

1. Seat students in groups of four and number off 1 through 4.

2. After asking a question or assigning a task, give students a specified amount of time to discuss a response. This time should generally be no longer than 90 seconds to prevent students from wandering off task.

3. Remind students to pay attention to each member of the group because only one member will be chosen to represent the group's ideas.

4. Call a number, 1 through 4, and ask students with that number to raise their hands to respond in a whole-class discussion.

5. Add comments, extend key ideas, ask follow-up questions, and make connections between students' comments. If you have a classroom with native English speakers and ELLs, you may ask an English speaker to take notes on the board as the discussion progresses, using key words and ideas.

6. Finish up by asking students to write a two- to four-sentence summary of the discussion and have a few students read their summaries out loud.

TEACHING PSYCHOLOGY

PROGRAM ORGANIZATION

DIFFERENTIATED INSTRUCTION

ASSESSMENT

PLANNING YOUR INSTRUCTION

DIFFERENTIATED INSTRUCTION

Strategy: Click and Clunk

Purpose: To gauge student understanding of a reading selection or course content.

How to do it:

1. After students have read a selection or finished covering a topic in class, ask students to write down one or two pieces of information or ideas that "clicked," meaning that students feel that they understand well.
2. Then have them write down one or two pieces of information or ideas that "clunked," meaning they did not understand them.
3. Rotate around the room, asking students to list their "clicks" and "clunks." Use the information to guide your follow-up lessons, skipping information that students already understand and spending more time with the information they do not understand. Alternatively, you may collect their lists to read after class.

Strategy: Peer Tutoring and Peer Feedback

Purpose: To pair students of the same or different abilities to help learn or practice educational tasks.

How to do it:

1. Give students directions and model appropriate methods of how to assist each other. List the do's and don'ts of helping someone with the work.
2. Pair students. Match students based on need and personality, or on ability. Students may alternate roles as tutor/tutee or the more advanced student may be assigned the tutor role to a struggling student. As the curriculum progresses, you may want to change the pairing.
3. Clearly define the objectives of peer tutoring. Give a specific assignment or task to work on. These tasks supplement classroom instruction; they do not teach new material or skills.
4. The tutor should give immediate corrective feedback. Students should be reminded that the feedback should be constructive and positive.
5. Monitor the tutoring process to be sure students stay on task and assess student learning. Walk around the room and engage students frequently.
6. Ask students for feedback about the process. Checklists or self-reporting forms can give students opportunities to discuss the experience. Formal assessments can also provide evaluation of achievement.

Strategy: Socratic Discussion

Purpose: To encourage students to come to a consensus about ideas through structured discussion.

How to do it:

1. Pose a question to the class. Emphasize that the class will try to reach a consensus (agreement) about the answer. If they cannot come to agreement, they will still try to come to a deeper understanding together. Some questions to start a discussion may be:
   - What assumptions does the author make?
   - How does this connect to other things that we have learned?
   - What is the significance of the article?
2. Establish rules for the discussion.
   - Students must focus on ideas.
   - Information from readings and class materials must be used to substantiate claims. Every opinion needs proof.
   - Students may not disagree with one another. Instead, they must find something to build on or ask for clarification on a point.
   - Students should take notes, so when it is their turn to speak, they can comment accurately on the statements from which they would like to build.
3. Discuss. As much as possible, allow the discussion to be student directed. Do not act as a participant. You may also consider a system for ensuring that all students participate. For example, you may give each student three paperclips to throw in a bucket when they contribute. A rule may be that everyone must contribute once before anyone may contribute three times.
4. Debrief. Following a Socratic discussion, it is important to have an open discussion afterward in which students may discuss what they found difficult about the exercise and how it made them think differently.

Note: When possible, it is beneficial to use a defined text, such as a primary source, as the basis for a discussion. They must, however, be given ample time to read and make notes about the text. When a text is the basis for a discussion, it is also important that students only discuss what is in that text, rather than bring in information they have learned in other settings.

Modifications: When a class is too large for a single discussion, break the class into two groups, with an inner and outer circle. Partners may then take turns participating in the discussion. The one in the outside circle should take notes about the comments the partner made. For example, "One interesting point was ____ because . . ." or "I'd like to know more about . . ." Alternatively, have two discussions, one following the other.

Strategy: Debate

Purpose: To help students learn to make arguments with strong points and counterpoints.

How to do it:

1. Present a question to students that can be logically answered several different ways.

Whenever possible, debates should be based on readings rather than students' opinions alone.

2. Begin by assigning students to one of four groups: A1, A2, B1, or B2. Give each side its argument. Groups A1 and A2 will argue against groups B1 and B2. However, the groups will prepare differently.

3. Assign groups A1 and B1 to brainstorm and research the arguments FOR their positions and summarize them in a three-to-four sentence opening statement.

4. Assign groups A2 and B2 to brainstorm and research the arguments AGAINST their positions and come up with counter arguments to support their points.

5. Provide time for students to review sources and make notes on their own, then let each team (A and B) review their case as a group.

Making Class Fun and Meaningful

Too often, students become bored and listless in the classroom. The chief culprits for this are lessons that are filled with routine, lecture, and/or content that matters little to them. Students who experience classes that are provocative and animated are more engaged with learning and are more motivated.

DIFFERENTIATED INSTRUCTION

Here are some tips to manipulate the pace and rhythm of the class.

Strategy: Opinion Line

Purpose: To engage all students by making them active participants and able to defend their position on a given topic.

How to do it:

1. Ask students to write or think about their opinion on a topic that has answers at two extremes *(e.g., schools move start/end times to later hours to accommodate students' sleep needs.)*. Meanwhile, post the two extremes *(e.g., "Strongly agree" and "Strongly disagree")* at either end of the wall. If it makes sense, post "I don't know" or "neutral" in the middle.
2. After students write their answers, ask them to stand against the wall, at the point where they think they stand in the opinion continuum.
3. Ask several students to explain their positions, either by choosing or asking for volunteers. Tell them that they may move if they are swayed by a classmate's argument.
4. Give students 2 minutes to revise their original opinion, allowing them to discuss their positions with each other and then repositioning themselves if necessary.
5. You may want to follow up by asking a question that invites students to explain their position or consider arguments made in the course of the activity.

Strategy: Jigsaw

Purpose: To allow students to cover one topic in-depth, becoming the instructors for the rest of the class, while allowing the class to cover large amounts of information.

How to do it:

1. When you have many topics to cover in a short period of time, divide the class into numbered groups *(e.g., 1, 2, 3, 4)* and assign each group a different topic. These may be referred to as "expert groups," as the members will become "experts" in their topics.
2. Give each group a task *(e.g., make a study guide, prepare a presentation)* that demands that they summarize the key points and significance of the topic. For classes with lower-level students, you may consider giving students a worksheet on which they record important information.

3. Divide the class into new, lettered groups (e.g., A, B, C, D...) that include a member from each of the numbered groups (e.g., group A has one member from group 1, one from group 2, and so on).
4. Assign the new groups a new task that requires them to teach each other the information they learned in their numbered group (e.g., give a presentation) or requires collaboration (e.g., make a plan).

Strategy: Conversation Wall

Purpose: To give students an opportunity to share ideas and reflect on the work of their classmates.

How to do it:

1. Post stimuli and "conversation boards" around the classroom. The stimuli may be student work (produced individually or in groups) or materials that are new to students, such as images or quotations written on poster board. The conversation boards are blank posters or sheets of paper. Alternatively, students may be given a few sticky notes for comments.
2. Give students a set amount of time to look at the stimuli posted around the room. Each activity should have a defined objective, such as, "comment on the poster that you think is most informative and explain why" or "comment on a quotation that makes you think about the content in a different way."
3. Remind students that they may react to another comment as well as a stimulus.
4. Assign several students or groups of students to look at the comments from each stimulus and summarize the "conversation."
5. Use the summaries to launch a class discussion about the content.

DIFFERENTIATED INSTRUCTION

Developing Reading Skills

Due to the increased emphasis on reading required by the *No Child Left Behind* (NCLB) legislation, psychology teachers may be called on to help improve their students' reading skills. These skills are critical to prepare students for academic success. A teacher using a graph about intelligence test scores can teach math skills and psychology concepts at the same time. The connection between reading and psychology is especially important. Many state and local assessments require students to read and interpret informational texts. Therefore, psychology teachers may assist in raising scores by integrating reading instruction into their teaching of psychology content.

How does *Prentice Hall Psychology* Enhance Reading Skills?

Too often the text is too hard for some students, and far too easy for others. So educators "teach to the middle of the class," trying to keep everyone on board, but always worrying about all the students who are falling off both edges. By providing practice quizzes and differentiated instruction, *Prentice Hall Psychology* helps all students access the material.

Differentiated Instruction helps meet the needs of students with reading difficulties or disabilities. By using strategies provided in the teacher lesson (such as scaffolding questions and allowing less proficient readers to answer first), students of all levels can access the material and fully participate in class discussions.

eFlashcards in MyPsychLab provide students with an alternate method to access a key term. Using an interactive format, students explore the definitions of key terms and concepts.

Concept Summaries at the end of each chapter help struggling readers find the key points in the text and make visual connections between the concepts in the chapter.

Bellringers are warmup activities that help students recall prior knowledge or preview the content they will be learning about. The more a reader knows about the topic, context, or issue, the better his or her comprehension will be.

Developing Student Writing Skills

Teachers often assume that if they teach content effectively, their students will be able to communicate what they have learned in writing on state assessments. However, many students falter when asked to write because they don't know how to construct a response that shows what they have learned.

Teachers can help students improve their performance by embedding expository writing tasks in class activities, homework assignments, and tests throughout the year. Take time with students to work through the process of analyzing the task and framing their response. To be successful, students will need to learn how to analyze the prompt, budget their time and answer space, plan and write their response, and then edit their first drafts.

Good writing prompts are key to successful responses. A good prompt will:

- test what students have been taught, whether defined by state standards or your own course outline;
- communicate what is expected of students in terms of format, length, and level of detail, such as the number of examples or reasons; and
- be doable in the time and space allocated for the task.

A good prompt provides multiple access points to help students with different learning styles, backgrounds, and abilities engage with the task.

This may be done by breaking the task into parts that build from lower- to higher-order thinking skills. This sequencing provides a point of entry for weaker students who may not be capable of completing the entire task and enables them to respond in a limited way.

Assessing the Product

The goal of a writing program should be to empower students to assess and improve their own work. For this to happen, students need to have a clear vision of what good writing looks like and how to bring their own work up to that standard.

An effective way to communicate your expectations is through the consistent use of generic rubrics and/or scoring guides. Generic rubrics describe levels of performance on various aspects of a written task, such as writing mechanics or development of a clear thesis statement. Scoring guides, in contrast, describe levels of performance for each specific task. Teachers can use both of these tools to communicate efficiently with students about their written work.

How Does *Prentice Hall Psychology* Address Writing Skills?

Research shows that writing about what you read actually helps you learn new information. *Prentice Hall Psychology* provides continuous opportunities for students to prepare and practice writing skills.

End-of-chapter writing prompts Two writing prompts appear at the end of each chapter, giving students regular writing practice.

Lesson Activities often require students to use writing skills as they work on projects such as reporting on research or responding to critical thinking questions.

"We are drowning in information but starved for knowledge." —John Naisbitt,

Megatrends: Ten New Directions Transforming Our Lives

TEACHING PSYCHOLOGY

PROGRAM ORGANIZATION

DIFFERENTIATED INSTRUCTION

ASSESSMENT

PLANNING YOUR INSTRUCTION

DIFFERENTIATED INSTRUCTION

Supporting Media Literacy

Defining Media Literacy

People define *media literacy* in many ways. Some educators understand it to mean teaching students how to use technology. Others see it as meaning teaching them how to evaluate the media. In fact, we need to teach students both the technical and the critical thinking aspects of media literacy in order to equip them with the 21st-century skills they need to navigate today's electronic and media-rich era.

Teenagers are spending more time using a wider array of technologies than ever before. What are the challenges for teachers?

- How do we channel this familiarity and time spent with technology toward technology that teaches and informs as well as entertains?
- How do we ensure that we and our students are taking full advantage of the opportunities for learning that technology in the classroom can provide?
- How do we make sure that our students are critical consumers of the media that they are surrounded by on a daily basis?

Teaching with and About Technology

Studies indicate that students in "technology-rich environments" experience increased achievement in all major subject areas (Sivin-Kachela, 1998). By integrating technology into the classroom, teachers not only help students learn the critical tools they need to thrive in a digital age, they also enhance social studies content.

Technology provides easily accessible ways to both present core content and engage students. Audio and video bring dynamic moments to life. Primary sources provide the personal experience. The Internet unlocks a vast array of materials. Together, these materials make psychology come alive in the classroom.

Teaching Critical Thinking About Media

Media can be a powerful tool not just to teach through technology but also to teach critical thinking skills. Studies show that media literacy training increases students' ability to access, analyze, and evaluate media messages (Yates, 2001). Students need to learn to analyze what they see and hear as well as what they read. In a psychology course, sources include research articles, quotations, charts, and graphs used to display facts and information and news reports on television, the Internet, and newspapers. These are ideal instruments for fostering 21st-century skills for critical thinking, including

- comparing viewpoints
- identifying bias
- evaluating evidence
- interpreting cause and effect
- decision making

By embedding these media skills into your course, you not only enhance key concepts but also teach students key analysis skills, many of which are tested on high-stakes exams and in written assessments. In addition, media-literate students will become more effective consumers, decision-makers, and citizens, able to succeed in the classroom and beyond.

Media literacy is essential for students in today's classroom as well as in the world at large. *Prentice Hall Psychology* supports media literacy in an exciting variety of ways, helping students at all levels become more active and engaged learners. Assets in MyPsychLab provide opportunities to integrate media literacy.

Access Content

Differentiated instruction is designed to help all students access content—no matter their level of ability or learning style. Technology is one method of information delivery that appeals to a variety of students through a variety of learning styles: visual/spatial, auditory/verbal, kinesthetic/body, and logical/mathematical. MyPsychLab features multimedia assets for busy learners and teachers.

- eText
- Audio text
- Interactive Flash Cards in English and Spanish
- Interactive simulations and explorations

Enrich and Reinforce Learning

Authentic learning means students will be able to transfer knowledge to new situations. When students use and apply their understandings or further explore concepts, learning becomes more real. Using technology to extend the lesson reinforces learning and improves the retention level of students. These activities make psychology more relevant and meaningful.

- *Psychology in the News* audio podcasts
- Video clips
- Simulations and Explorations

Assessment

Monitoring comprehension can take form in multiple ways. For some, using the online format is more engaging and therefore gives more motivation to succeed. MyPsychLab provides automatically graded quizzes and tests with immediate feedback that shows students, which questions they answered correctly, which answers they answered incorrectly, and what the correct answer is.

"Media literacy is...absolutely critical. It's going to make the difference between whether the kids are a tool of the mass media or whether the mass media is a tool for kids to use." —Linda Ellerbee, producer/host, *Nick News*

TEACHING PSYCHOLOGY

PROGRAM ORGANIZATION

DIFFERENTIATED INSTRUCTION

ASSESSMENT

PLANNING YOUR INSTRUCTION

ASSESSMENT

The Need for Assessment

Why Do We Need To Assess Student Learning?

Assessment should be viewed as a process, not an activity that quickly evaluates instruction or student learning. As such, the goal of assessment is to focus, guide, and support instruction and subsequently learning. When making an assessment, the teacher isn't just "testing" but rather is making thoughtful observations about the student's strengths and weaknesses. It is not a value judgment (good/bad) but an analysis of student performance against specific goals and criteria. As a process, the goal of assessment is to assemble information from a variety of sources.

Assessment happens constantly, although you probably don't give a quiz every day. It takes a variety of formats. Traditional assessments focus on written work, such as essays. Performance assessments are geared toward students who prefer to show what they've learned in a less verbal or written format. Alternative assessments range from metacognitive activities, such as journals, to student-generated assessments, such as portfolios.

Formative Assessment

Formative assessment is self-assessment. It provides feedback to modify teaching and learning activities. Formative assessments are conducted throughout the instructional process to monitor students' progress and provide feedback on strengths and weaknesses. The key is feedback.

Feedback allows students to correct conceptual errors and encourages instructors to modify their methods. It provides students with an understanding of what they are doing well, links to classroom learning, and gives specific input to adjust the learning process.

Summative Assessment

Summative assessments are used to judge progress. They are meant to gauge student learning at particular points in time. Common summative assessments occur at the end of chapters or units or school terms to determine what students know and do not know. Like formative assessments, they reveal areas that need review before moving on to new topics.

Balancing Assessments

Proper utilization of assessment tools in the classroom will lead to greater learning. Incorporating a variety of assessments (in both format and product), observations, and communications with and between students allows for a more fully developed picture of your students' learning process. The more information you have about your students, the better you can determine teaching effectiveness and the quality of student learning.

Assessment Informs Instruction

Assessment is a never-ending cycle. With the spotlight now on improving student performance and providing differentiated instruction, it is essential to use assessment to target goals, identify strategies to achieve results, monitor progress, and assess results to inform lesson planning.

Ongoing Assessment

Assessments may fall in either the formative or the summative category. However, depending on their use, these evaluations may provide information for both categories.

Formative Assessments

Practice Quizzes at the end of each module measure students' comprehension of the module material. What have students learned and what do you need to revisit?

ExamView Test Bank questions assess understanding and foster remediation by providing text page numbers for quick references to content.

MyPsychLab Assessments For each chapter in the book, MyPsychLab contains a pretest, posttest, and chapter exam, all of which are automatically graded and provide instant feedback to students on their results. Students take the pretest after reading the chapter to measure their understanding. The pretest generates a customized study plan for each student that directs remediation in areas of weakness and

T36

identifies areas of strength. After remediation, students take the posttest to evaluate their progress.

Grade Tracker Reports in MyPsychLab help you understand where your students are in the learning process and determine an effective strategy for moving them to the next stage.

Teacher's Edition includes remediation suggestions for chapter assessments to re-teach key concepts to struggling students.

Summative Assessment

ExamView Test Bank allows teachers to easily create tests from banks of thousands of questions, which can be sorted by difficulty levels to provide leveled quizzes and tests.

MyPsychLab Assessments After taking the pretest and posttest in MyPsychLab, students take the chapter exam to assess their progress and identify any outstanding areas of weakness.

End-of-Chapter Assessments test students' comprehension and provide opportunities for students to strengthen and apply their analytical skills.

Rubrics can also be used as a summative evaluation of understanding.

Encouraging Student Self-Assessment

As mentioned earlier, formative assessment is self-assessment. Successful people take time to reflect on what they have accomplished and what needs to be adjusted as they work toward their goals.

Students need to evaluate their own progress and accept responsibility to manage and adjust their own learning. As part of the educational process, teachers must help students understand the importance of and methods used to achieve such reflection and self-evaluation.

To Develop Self-Assessment General Strategies

- Set aside a few minutes at the middle and end of the lesson to ask: What have we learned? What questions do you have about this?
- Require that a self-assessment be attached to every formal product or performance.
- Include a 1-minute essay at the end of a class, in which students summarize the two or three main points and the questions that they still have.
- Have students write their questions on an index card as homework. Then, in small groups, have them find the common issues and use these questions to begin class.

Checking Understanding

Students also should use the following checks of their understanding of skills and concepts offered by *Prentice Hall Psychology* before moving on to the next topic.

Practice Quizzes at the end of each module allow students to stop and check their understanding; they can review and reinforce their learning before moving on to a new module.

Chapter Summaries review the module goals and learning objectives. The learning objectives are phrased as questions, so students can reinforce and confirm their understanding.

Chapter Assessments enable students to check their understanding and prepare for test-taking success.

TEACHING PSYCHOLOGY

PROGRAM ORGANIZATION

DIFFERENTIATED INSTRUCTION

ASSESSMENT

PLANNING YOUR INSTRUCTION

T37

ASSESSMENT

Using Rubrics

Assessing a student's understanding and abilities can't be a matter of right vs. wrong or simple checklists. You have to assess for how sophisticated or effective the work is; you have to consider to what extent a learning task was done well. So you need assessment guides—rubrics.

Scoring rubrics can be **holistic** (to provide a single overall impression of performance) or **analytic** (to permit separate descriptions and subscores for varied traits of performance). In either case, rubrics are most effective when they are accompanied by anchors or exemplars Ð examples or models of responses for each score point.

Rubrics provide teachers with a tool for increasing the validity and consistency of their assessment, and they provide students with clear performance targets, expectations about what is most important, and criteria for evaluating *and* improving their own work.

Perhaps the greatest advantage of rubrics lies in their capacity to clearly communicate "what quality looks like" to students and to help them see where they stand along the continuum of quality. Then, learners better understand what they are aiming for and learn to self-assess and self-adjust accordingly. Good rubrics and clear samples completely demystify the goals, tasks, and scoring of work.

What Makes a Rubric Good?
The best rubrics:

1. Discriminate among performances validly, not arbitrarily—by the *central* features of performance, not by that which is easiest to see, count up, or score.
2. Do not combine completely independent criteria in the same descriptors. To combine "very clear" and "very organized" in the same descriptor, for example, often creates a problem since a paper might be clear but not organized and vice versa; why give them the same score when the performance is so different?
3. Are based on analysis of many specific work samples, of the widest possible range. In other words, all potential student performances should fit somewhere in the rubric.
4. Rely on descriptive language—what quality or its absence looks like—as opposed to relying heavily on mere comparatives or value language (e.g., "not as thorough as" or "excellent product") to make the discrimination.
5. Avoid making the lowest score points just sound bad. The lowest score should rather describe what novice performance looks like.
6. Highlight the judging of the impact of performance—the effect or bottom-line success of the work, given the purpose—as opposed to overrewarding just the processes, the content used, or a good-faith effort made. Ultimately, performance is about results—Was the paper *persuasive*? The problem *solved*? The speech *informative*? And so on. Make sure students understand the purpose of the task as reflected in appropriate criteria.
7. Intelligently weight the various criteria relative to one another. Giving 25% equally to four criteria is easy but rarely valid. Surely "mechanics" is less important than "persuasiveness" in an essay. Give percentages that reflect the relative importance of each criterion to the others.

Misconception Alerts

1. Perhaps the most common misunderstanding about rubrics is that they can be developed only *after* a specific task has been designed. But the rubric is meant as a bridge between any of a variety of unique performance tasks and a more general target. For example, a rubric for judging the effectiveness of an essay should be applicable to *any* essay, and thus can and should be written *before* a particular writing prompt is developed. In other words, the qualities of an effective essay guide the rubric's development. You may add specific indicators to a rubric to make it unique and more helpful to the student, but you should know the general criteria of performance before you go to design a unique task.
2. A common mistake in rubric design is to turn qualitative differences in work quality into arbitrary quantities or quotas. For example, many

rubrics give a higher score if you have more footnotes or reasons. This is clearly invalid: An essay with one compelling, well-supported argument and a single footnote may be far more persuasive than an essay with three weakly developed and supported reasons and five footnotes. Though more time-consuming, it pays to describe the differences in quality at each level, by studying samples of work of varying quality.

Sample Rubric: Assessing an Oral Presentation

Grading Criteria	Excellent	Acceptable	Minimal	Unacceptable
Preparation 20%	Gathers information from many reputable sources; prepares thorough and helpful notes (or speaks clearly from memory); creates attractive visual aids to support the presentation.	Gathers information from varied and appropriate sources; prepares notes or visual aids to use during presentation.	Gathers minimal information from one or two sources; the sources may or may not be appropriate or sufficient; does not prepare many notes or visual aids.	Gathers limited information from one easy-to-find source; may not be able to complete task because of lack of preparation.
Content 20%	Abundance of material clearly relates to topic; points are interesting and clear; presentation has coherent thesis.	Has adequate information about the topic; makes good points; has a thesis.	Not enough adequate or total content provided; some information may not be relevant; thesis is simple or unclear.	Information included has little connection to the topic. No explicit or acceptable thesis is provided.
Organization 30%	Information is well organized and logically ordered; argument is easy to follow; conclusion is clear.	Most information is presented in logical order; argument is generally clear and easy to follow.	Ideas loosely connect; organization and flow are choppy and somewhat difficult to follow.	Seemingly random or unconnected information is presented. There is no sense of an organization having been thought through.
Speaking Skills 30%	Is engaging, poised, and confident during the presentation; speaks clearly, naturally, and fluently.	Is mostly engaging during the presentation; speaks clearly and fluently during most of presentation.	Is not very engaging; speech is wooden, enunciation is not always clear; lots of "er" or "um," no eye contact, and so forth.	Appears uninterested, afraid or unfocused during presentation; is difficult to understand.

(Teacher also posts 4 video clips to anchor the score points of the rubric and thus "teach" what the expectations are and what the descriptors mean.)

Checklist

When practicing your presentation, ask yourself if you've met these criteria for a top grade:

__ Did I use information from varied and appropriate sources?
__ Are all my sources reliable?
__ Do I have notes about my presentation?
__ Do I use helpful visual aids?
__ Do I have a thesis?
__ Is all the information in my presentation clearly related to my topic?
__ Do my evidence and arguments support my thesis?
__ Is there a logical order to my presentation that is easy to follow?
__ Do I have an introduction, clear position, and conclusion?
__ Do I speak clearly?
__ Is my voice natural and pleasant sounding?
__ Is my voice loud enough?
__ Do I make eye contact or otherwise engage my listeners?

PLANNING YOUR INSTRUCTION

Simplify Your Planning Using This Program

Where Do I Start?

Right here! These pages will guide you through the program's unique organization and describe the many resources that will enrich our teaching.

How Do I Teach the Chapter?

Begin each chapter with the Chapter Opener, previewing the content to come with the students. At the end of the chapter, use the Chapter Summary and Assessments to help students explore their understanding of the content and strengthen their analytical skills.

What Should I Use to Plan and Prepare?

Start your planning with the **Pacing Guides** to give you a time frame for the year's curriculum. Then use the **Lesson Planner** before each section to give you a summary of the lesson plan in the Teacher's Edition, with suggestions for incorporating resources into your instruction.

How Do I Differentiate Instruction?

Prentice Hall Psychology provides opportunities for differentiated instruction:

- **Teacher's Edition** provides a core lesson for the entire class, but within that lesson you will find strategies and modified instruction geared toward different levels of student ability and learning styles.
- **Concept Summaries** at the end of each chapter provide a visual overview of the chapter to give struggling readers and visual learners additional support.
- **MyPsychLab** provides students with another format to access the material.

What Are These Features?

- **Little Red Boxes** Within the core lesson plan, you will notice red boxes labeled **L1, L2, L3,** or **L4.** These denote differentiation suggestions for different levels of students. In planning your lesson, you should review the lesson plan and resources to determine which differentiation suggestions are appropriate for your class. "ELL" or "LPR" following the label denotes an activity tailored specifically for English Language Learners or Less Proficient Readers. Many teachers, however, find these strategies helpful for other students, too.
- **"Bellringer"** You have a lot to do at the beginning of the class: attendance, returning papers, and other housekeeping. These Bellringers are short activities that engage students upon their arrival, allowing you to get organized. They are best used consistently, providing a routine for students to begin working without explicit instructions to do so.
- **Teacher Prep** On the chapter level, we summarize the most important points to help you focus on the essential facts, concepts, and generalizations that students must grasp. This feature is designed to be a helpful reminder in the 3 minutes between periods or when you choose to create your own lesson plan to cover the content.

How Does the Program Help Me Develop as a Teacher?

The Teacher's Edition provides these built-in professional development features:

- **Lesson plans** Margin notes provide pedagogy, strategies, and activities to teach and extend the content.
- **Differentiated Instruction** Lessons provide leveled instruction, giving support for struggling students, modifications of lessons to address cultural differences, and enrichment for advanced students.
- **Teaching Tips** These tips prepare you for common misconceptions, pitfalls, and other ways to present a concept.

How Can I Use Technology in My Classroom?

Prentice Hall Psychology with MyPsychLab allows you to integrate a wealth of online learning tools into your class. MyPsychLab is a dynamic and easy-to-use learning and assessment tool geared toward meeting the diverse needs of today's students with engaging content that helps students succeed. MyPsychLab contains the Pearson eText, a complete and interactive text online that teachers and students can refer to anytime. You will also find media assets such as video clips, simulations, animations, and podcasts that engage students and support a variety of learning styles.

Teachers have access to Class Prep in MyPsychLab. This searchable database contains hundreds of our best teaching resources such as lecture launchers and discussion topics, in-class and out-of-class demonstrations and assignments, handouts, as well as video clips, photographs, illustrations, charts, graphs, and animations. You can search or browse by topic and you can create personalized folders to organize and store material.

TEACHING PSYCHOLOGY

PROGRAM ORGANIZATION

DIFFERENTIATED INSTRUCTION

ASSESSMENT

PLANNING YOUR INSTRUCTION

T41

PLANNING YOUR INSTRUCTION

YEAR AND SEMESTER PACING GUIDE

The following pacing guides show how the chapters of *Prentice Hall Psychology* can be adapted to fit your specific course focus and time constraints. The year guide is representative of a course based on 36 weeks or 180 days. The semester guide is representative of a course that lasts for 18 weeks or 90 days.

1 PERIOD = 50 MIN. 1 BLOCK = 90 MIN.	SEMESTER COURSE PERIODS	SEMESTER COURSE BLOCKS	FULL-YEAR COURSE PERIODS	FULL-YEAR COURSE BLOCKS
SCIENTIFIC INQUIRY DOMAIN				
Chapter 1: The Science of Psychology				
Module 1: Psychology's Domains	2	1	4	2
Module 2: Research Methods and Ethics	2	1	4	2
Module 3: Statistics	2	1	4	2
Total Days for Chapter/Domain	**6**	**3**	**12**	**6**
BIOPSYCHOLOGY DOMAIN				
Chapter 2: The Biological Perspective				
Module 4: The Nervous System	2.5	1.25	5	2.5
Module 5: The Brain	2.5	1.25	5	2.5
Module 6: Heredity, Environment, and Adaptation	1	.5	2	1
Total Days for Chapter	**6**	**3**	**12**	**6**
Chapter 3: Sensation and Perception				
Module 7: Sensation	2.5	1.25	5	2.5
Module 8: Perception	2.5	1.25	5	2.5
Total Days for Chapter	**5**	**2.5**	**10**	**5**
Chapter 4: Consciousness: Sleep, Dreams, Hypnosis, and Drugs				
Module 9: Sleep and Dreams	2.5	1.25	5	2.5
Module 10: Hypnosis and Drugs	2.5	1.25	5	2.5
Total Days for Chapter	**5**	**2.5**	**10**	**5**
Total Days for Domain	**16**	**8**	**32**	**16**

DEVELOPMENTAL AND LEARNING DOMAIN				
Chapter 5: Development Across the Life Span				
Module 11: Topics in Development	2.5	1.25	5	2.5
Module 12: Prenatal, Infant and Childhood Development	2.5	1.25	5	2.5
Module 13: Adolescence and Adulthood	1	.5	2	1
Total Days for Chapter	**6**	**3**	**12**	**6**
Chapter 6: Learning and Language Development				
Module 14: Classical Conditioning	1	.5	2	1
Module 15: Operant Conditioning	1.5	.75	3	1.5
Module 16: Cognitive Learning and Observational Learning	1	.5	2	1
Module 17: Language	1.5	.75	3	1.5
Total Days for Chapter	**5**	**2.5**	**10**	**5**
Total Days for Domain	**11**	**5.5**	**22**	**11**
SOCIAL CONTEXT DOMAIN				
Chapter 7: Social Psychology				
Module 18: Social Influence	2.5	1.25	5	2.5
Module 19: Social Cognition	2.5	1.25	5	2.5
Module 20: Social Interaction	1	.5	2	1
Total Days for Chapter	**6**	**3**	**12**	**6**
Chapter 8: Culture and Gender				
Module 21: Culture	2.5	1.25	5	2.5
Module 22: Gender	2.5	1.25	5	2.5
Total Days for Chapter	**5**	**2.5**	**10**	**5**
Total Days for Domain	**11**	**5.5**	**22**	**11**
COGNITION DOMAIN				
Chapter 9: Memory				
Module 23: Encoding and Storage	2.5	1.25	5	2.5
Module 24: Retrieval and Retrieval Failure	2.5	1.25	5	2.5
Total Days for Chapter	**5**	**2.5**	**10**	**5**
Chapter 10: Cognition: Thinking and Intelligence				
Module 25: Thinking	2.5	1.25	5	2.5
Module 26: Intelligence	2.5	1.25	5	2.5
Total Days for Chapter	**5**	**2.5**	**10**	**5**
Total Days for Domain	**10**	**5**	**20**	**10**

TEACHING PSYCHOLOGY

PROGRAM ORGANIZATION

DIFFERENTIATED INSTRUCTION

ASSESSMENT

PLANNING YOUR INSTRUCTION

PLANNING YOUR INSTRUCTION

INDIVIDUAL VARIATIONS DOMAIN				
Chapter 11: Motivation and Emotion				
Module 27: Motivation	2.5	1.25	5	2.5
Module 28: Emotion	2.5	1.25	5	2.5
Total Days for Chapter	**5**	**2.5**	**10**	**5**
Chapter 12: Theories of Personality				
Module 29: Perspectives on Personality	2.5	1.25	5	2.5
Module 30: Assessment and Issues in Personality	2.5	1.25	5	2.5
Total Days for Chapter	**5**	**2.5**	**10**	**5**
Chapter 13: Psychological Disorders				
Module 31: Defining Abnormal Behavior	2.5	1.25	5	2.5
Module 32: Types of Psychological Disorders	2.5	1.25	5	2.5
Total Days for Chapter	**5**	**2.5**	**10**	**5**
Total Days for Domain	**15**	**7.5**	**30**	**15**
APPLICATIONS OF PSYCHOLOGICAL SCIENCE DOMAIN				
Chapter 14: Psychological Therapies				
Module 33: Psychotherapies	2.5	1.25	5	2.5
Module 34: Biomedical Therapies and Issues in Therapy	2.5	1.25	5	2.5
Total Days for Chapter	**5**	**2.5**	**10**	**5**
Chapter 15: Stress and Health				
Module 35: Stress and Stressors	3	1.5	6	3
Module 36: Coping with Stress and Promoting Wellness	3	1.5	6	3
Total Days for Chapter	**6**	**3**	**12**	**6**
Chapter 16: Applied Psychology and Psychology Careers				
Module 37: Careers in Psychology	2	1	4	2
Total Days for Chapter	**2**	**1**	**4**	**2**
Total Days for Domain	**13**	**6.5**	**26**	**13**

Block Scheduling Guide

This pacing chart is for a nine-week teaching block. Each class day is 90 minutes long. Two days of the 45-day block are set aside for review and for final exams.

Chapter 1	The Science of Psychology	# of Days
Day 1	Module 1: Psychology's Domains	1
Day 2	Module 2: Research Methods and Ethics	1
Day 3	Module 3: Statistics	1
	Total days for Chapter 1	**3**
Chapter 2	**The Biological Perspective**	**# of Days**
Day 4	Module 4: The Nervous System	1
Day 5	Module 5: The Brain	1
Day 6	Module 6: Heredity, Environment, and Adaptation	1
	Total days for Chapter 2	**3**
Chapter 3	**Sensation and Perception**	**# of Days**
Days 7–8	Module 7: Sensation	1.5
Days 8–9	Module 8: Perception	1.5
	Total days for Chapter 3	**3**
Chapter 4	**Consciousness: Sleep, Dreams, Hypnosis, and Drugs**	**# of Days**
Days 10–11	Module 9: Sleep and Dreams	1.5
Days 11–12	Module 10: Hypnosis and Drugs	1.5
	Total days for Chapter 4	**3**
Chapter 5	**Development Across the Life Span**	**# of Days**
Day 13	Module 11: Topics in Development	1
Day 14	Module 12: Prenatal, Infant and Childhood Development	1
Day 15	Module 13: Adolescence and Adulthood	1
	Total days for Chapter 5	**3**
Chapter 6	**Learning and Language Development**	**# of Days**
Day 16	Module 14: Classical Conditioning	1
Day 17	Module 15: Operant Conditioning	1
Day 18	Module 16: Cognitive Learning and Observational Learning	1
Day 19	Module 17: Language	1
	Total days for Chapter 6	**4**

TEACHING PSYCHOLOGY

PROGRAM ORGANIZATION

DIFFERENTIATED INSTRUCTION

ASSESSMENT

PLANNING YOUR INSTRUCTION

PLANNING YOUR INSTRUCTION

Chapter 7	Social Psychology	# of Days
Day 20	Module 18: Social Influence	1
Day 21	Module 19: Social Cognition	1
Day 22	Module 20: Social Interaction	1
	Total days for Chapter 7	**3**
Chapter 8	Culture and Gender	# of Days
Day 23	Module 21: Culture	1
Day 24	Module 22: Gender	1
	Total days for Chapter 8	**2**
Chapter 9	Memory	# of Days
Days 25–26	Module 23: Encoding and Storage	1.5
Days 26–27	Module 24: Retrieval and Retrieval Failure	1.5
	Total days for Chapter 9	**3**
Chapter 10	Cognition: Thinking and Intelligence	# of Days
Days 28–29	Module 25: Thinking	1.5
Days 29–30	Module 26: Intelligence	1.5
	Total days for Chapter 10	**3**
Chapter 11	Motivation and Emotion	# of Days
Day 31	Module 27: Motivation	1
Day 32	Module 28: Emotion	1
	Total days for Chapter 11	**2**
Chapter 12	Theories of Personality	# of Days
Day 33	Module 29: Perspectives on Personality	1
Day 34	Module 30: Assessment and Issues in Personality	1
	Total days for Chapter 12	**2**
Chapter 13	Psychological Disorders	# of Days
Day 35	Module 31: Defining Abnormal Behavior	1
Day 36	Module 32: Types of Psychological Disorders	1
	Total days for Chapter 13	**2**
Chapter 14	Psychological Therapies	# of Days
Day 37	Module 33: Psychotherapies	1
Day 38	Module 34: Biomedical Therapies and Issues in Therapy	1
	Total days for Chapter 14	**2**

Chapter 15	Stress and Health	# of Days
Days 39–40	Module 35: Stress and Stressors	1.5
Days 40–41	Module 36: Coping with Stress and Promoting Wellness	1.5
	Total days for Chapter 15	**3**
Chapter 16	Applied Psychology and Psychology Careers	# of Days
Days 42–43	Module 37: Careers in Psychology	2
	Total days for Chapter 16	**2**
Day 44	Review	1
Day 45	Final Exam	1

TEACHING PSYCHOLOGY

PROGRAM ORGANIZATION

DIFFERENTIATED INSTRUCTION

ASSESSMENT

PLANNING YOUR INSTRUCTION

PLANNING YOUR INSTRUCTION

Chapter 1 The Science of Psychology

CHAPTER RESOURCES

Introduce the Chapter	Assessment	Additional Support	Module
• Module Goals and Learning Objectives • MyPsychLab interactivities • Bellringer activities	• ExamView Test Bank • MyPsychLab Assessments • End-of-Chapter Assessments	• Differentiation suggestions throughout each lesson • Teacher's Manual resources • Interactive PowerPoint slides and Standard PowerPoint slides	Module 1 Psychology's Domains Module 2 Research Methods and Ethics Module 3 Statistics

MODULE 1

Psychology's Domains

Module Goals
- Trace the development of psychology.
- Identify psychology's subfields.

Summary of Teaching Strategies

Students will explore the definition of psychology and learn about its goals. They will trace the history of psychology by reading about famous psychologists and the major modern psychological perspectives. They will discuss why psychologists perform research and will identify the major subfields of psychology.

Learning Objectives

1.1 What is psychology? What are its goals?
1.2 What is the history of psychology as a scientific discipline?
1.3 What are the major modern psychological perspectives?
1.4 How is the field of psychology continuing to grow and change?
1.5 Why do psychologists perform research?
1.6 What are the major subfields of psychology?
1.7 How does psychology benefit society?

Key Module Resources

- Explore: Using Information from the Internet; History of Psychology Websites; Psychology in Different Cultures; Careers in Psychology; Find a Psychologist on the Internet
- Class Demonstrations: Toasting the Contributions of Early Psychologists; Which Famous Psychologist Am I?; Psychological Perspectives; Psychologists Are Scientists

MODULE 2

Research Methods and Ethics

Module Goals
- Understand psychological research methods.
- Consider ethical issues in psychological research.

Summary of Teaching Strategies

Students will explore different psychological research methods researchers use to study behavior, including nonexperimental methods, the correlation method, and experimental methods. Students will learn how researchers ensure their findings are valid and will consider ethical issues in psychological research involving humans and animals.

Learning Objectives

2.1 What is the scientific method?

2.2 What methods do researchers use to study behavior?

2.3 How do researchers ensure their findings are valid?

2.4 Why do some researchers study animals instead of people?

2.5 What ethical guidelines do psychologists follow when they research humans?

2.6 Are there different ethical guidelines for research with animals?

Key Module Resources
- Explore: Observational Research; Understanding Correlational and Experimental Research; Debate the Use of Animals in Research
- Class Demonstrations: Quiz on Correlation; Critical Thinking; Discussing Controversies in Research
- Critical Thinking: Writing About Psychology
- Cultural Connections: Minorities and Mental Health

MODULE 3

Statistics

Module Goal
- Learn the basic concepts of data analysis.

Summary of Teaching Strategies

Students will learn the basic concepts of data analysis by exploring descriptive statistics, tables and graphs, correlation coefficients, and inferential statistics. Students will also analyze how the concepts of validity and reliability relate to statistics.

Learning Objectives

3.1 What are descriptive statistics?

3.2 What types of tables and graphs represent patterns in data?

3.3 What are correlation coefficients? What do they tell researchers about relationships?

3.4 What are inferential statistics?

3.5 How do the concepts of validity and reliability relate to statistics?

Key Module Resources
- Explore: Evaluating Internet Websites; Using Word Webs; Using the Internet to Find Research Results
- Class Demonstrations: Understanding Statistics; Writing About Graphs; Collaborative Learning
- Critical Thinking: Making a Verbal Presentation

TEACHING PSYCHOLOGY

PROGRAM ORGANIZATION

DIFFERENTIATED INSTRUCTION

ASSESSMENT

PLANNING YOUR INSTRUCTION

PLANNING YOUR INSTRUCTION

Chapter 2 The Biological Perspective

CHAPTER RESOURCES

Introduce the Chapter	Assessment	Additional Support	Module
• Module Goals and Learning Objectives • MyPsychLab interactivities • Bellringer activities	• ExamView Test Bank • MyPsychLab Assessments • End-of-Chapter Assessments	• Differentiation suggestions throughout each lesson • Teacher's Manual resources • Interactive PowerPoint slides and Standard PowerPoint slides	Module 4 The Nervous System Module 5 The Brain Module 6 Heredity, Environment, and Adaptation

MODULE 4

The Nervous System

Module Goals
- Understand the structure and function of the nervous system.
- Explain how the neuroendocrine system functions.

Summary of Teaching Strategies

Students will explore the structure and functions of the nervous system and study how the neuroendocrine system functions.

Learning Objectives

4.1 What are the major divisions of the human nervous system?
4.2 What are neurons, and how do they work?
4.3 What are the functions of the different parts of the central nervous system?
4.4 How are the endocrine glands connected to the nervous system?
4.5 How do hormones affect our thoughts and behavior?
4.6 What effects do hormones have on the immune system?

Key Module Resources

- Explore: Using Information from the Internet; Studying Squid; Effects of Drugs on the Body and the Brain; Too Much or Too Little: Writing About Hormone Imbalances
- Class Demonstrations: Using Reaction Time to Show the Speed of Neurons; Learning About Neurotransmitters; Discussing Neurotransmitters; Handling Stress; Learning About the Endocrine Glands; Debate on a Healthy Lifestyle

MODULE 5

The Brain

Module Goals
- Learn how scientists study the nervous system.
- Understand the structure and function of the brain.

Summary of Teaching Strategies

Students will learn how scientists study the brain, including the use of computed tomography scans, magnetic resonance imaging, positron emission tomography, and electroencephalographs. They will study the different parts of the brain and what the parts do. They will assess how the left side of the brain differs from the right side.

Learning Objectives

5.1 How do people study the brain?
5.2 What advances have made the brain easier to study?
5.3 What are some recent innovations in neuroscience?
5.4 What are the different parts of the brain, and what does each part do?
5.5 How does the left side of the brain differ from the right side?

Key Module Resources

- Explore: The Brain Diagram
- Class Demonstrations: Review of Brain-Imaging Techniques; Critical Thinking; Discussing Controversies in Neuroscience; The Importance of a Wrinkled Cortex; Parts of the Brain; Split Brain; Left-Brained vs. Right Brained
- Cultural Connections: Your Brain on Culture
- Critical Thinking: Discussing Workplace Problems for the Left-Handed

MODULE 6

Heredity, Environment, and Adaptation

Module Goal

- Discover how biology and experience interact.

Summary of Teaching Strategies

Students will learn how genetic factors determine who we are and how heredity and environmental factors interact to affect our development. They also will discuss how evolved tendencies influence our behavior.

Learning Objectives

6.1 How do genetic factors determine who we are?

6.2 How do heredity and environmental factors interact to affect our development?

6.3 How do evolved tendencies influence our behavior?

Key Module Resources

- Explore: Writing About Heredity
- Class Demonstrations: Research with Twins; Take a Stand

TEACHING PSYCHOLOGY

PROGRAM ORGANIZATION

DIFFERENTIATED INSTRUCTION

ASSESSMENT

PLANNING YOUR INSTRUCTION

PLANNING YOUR INSTRUCTION

Chapter 3 The Biological Perspective

CHAPTER RESOURCES

Introduce the Chapter	Assessment	Additional Support	Module
• Module Goals and Learning Objectives • MyPsychLab interactivities • Bellringer activities	• ExamView Test Bank • MyPsychLab Assessments • End-of-Chapter Assessments	• Differentiation suggestions throughout each lesson • Teacher's Manual resources • Interactive PowerPoint slides and Standard PowerPoint slides	Module 7 Sensation Module 8 Perception

MODULE 7

Sensation

Module Goals
- Understand sensation and perception.
- Explore how senses work.

Summary of Teaching Strategies

Students will explain the distinctions between sensation and perception. They will define sensory threshold and sensory adaptation. They will examine how the senses of vision, hearing, taste, smell, and touch work.

Learning Objectives

7.1 What are the distinctions between sensation and perception?

7.2 What is a sensory threshold? What is sensory adaptation?

7.3 What forms of energy can humans sense?

7.4 How does the sense of vision work?

7.5 How does the sense of hearing work?

7.6 How do the senses of taste and smell work, and how are they alike?

7.7 What other sensory systems does the human body use?

Key Module Resources

- Explore: Understanding Selective Attention; Mapping the Blind Spot; Learning About Sound Waves; Teaching Classmates; Preventing Hearing Impairment
- Class Demonstrations: Exploring Just Notable Difference; Sensory Adaptation; Understanding the Retina; Rods and Cones; Color Blindness in Daily Life; Exploring Taste; Understanding Flavor; The Body's Sensitivity to Touch
- Critical Thinking: The Senses

MODULE 8

Perception

Module Goal
- Learn how we perceive the world.

Summary of Teaching Strategies

Students will consider the nature of attention and perceptual constancies, and why they are important. They will explore Gestalt principles such as figure-ground relationships, proximity, similarity, closure, and continuity. Students will investigate the Visual Cliff experiment and will assess how visual illusions work. Finally, they will student how perception is influenced by expectations and experiences.

Learning Objectives

8.1 What is the nature of attention?

8.2 What are perceptual constancies?

8.3 What are the Gestalt principles of perception?

8.4 What are monocular and binocular depth cues?

8.5 How do visual illusions work?

8.6 How do our experiences and expectations influence perception?

Key Module Resources

- Explore: In Search of Perceptual Illusions; The Visual Cliff
- Class Demonstrations: Perceptual Constancies; Depth Perception in Art; Optical Illusions; Expectancy and Perception
- Critical Thinking: Controversies in Perception

TEACHING PSYCHOLOGY

PROGRAM ORGANIZATION

DIFFERENTIATED INSTRUCTION

ASSESSMENT

PLANNING YOUR INSTRUCTION

PLANNING YOUR INSTRUCTION

Chapter 4 Consciousness: Sleep, Dreams, Hypnosis, and Drugs

CHAPTER RESOURCES

Introduce the Chapter	Assessment	Additional Support	Module
• Module Goals and Learning Objectives • MyPsychLab interactivities • Bellringer activities	• ExamView Test Bank • MyPsychLab Assessments • End-of-Chapter Assessments	• Differentiation suggestions throughout each lesson • Teacher's Manual resources • Interactive PowerPoint slides and Standard PowerPoint slides	Module 9 Sleep and Dreams Module 10 Hypnosis and Drugs

MODULE 9

Sleep and Dreams

Module Goals
- Understand the relationship between conscious and unconscious processes.
- Explain how and why we sleep and dream.

Summary of Teaching Strategies
Students will study the different levels of consciousness and explain the difference between explicit and implicit processing. They will investigate how and why people sleep and dream and will assess the different kinds of sleep disorders. Finally, they will explore how daytime experiences affect dreaming.

Learning Objectives

9.1 What are the different levels of consciousness?

9.2 What is the difference between explicit and implicit processing?

9.3 What is the circadian rhythm, and how does it relate to sleep?

9.4 What theories exist about the functions of sleep?

9.5 How does the sleep cycle work?

9.6 What are the different types of sleep disorders?

9.7 Do dreams serve a function?

Key Module Resources
- Explore: Sleep Studies Online; Brain Waves: Their Unique Qualities and Benefits; Investigating Sleep Disorders
- Class Demonstrations: Debate: Consciousness; Circadian Rhythms; Think Fast; The Sleepwalking Defense; Dream Analysis "á la Freud"; Debate: High School Start/End Times
- Critical Thinking: Make a Connection; Writing About Dreaming

MODULE 10

Hypnosis And Drugs

Module Goals
- Describe meditation and hypnosis.
- Understand the effects of psychoactive drugs.

Summary of Teaching Strategies

Students will explore how meditation and hypnosis can reduce stress. They will study the different kinds of psychoactive drugs, how they function, what effects they produce, and how drug use is affected by depression, anxiety, anger, and peer pressure.

Learning Objectives

10.1 How does meditation affect consciousness?

10.2 How does hypnosis work, and why is it controversial?

10.3 What are the major categories of psychoactive drugs?

10.4 How do drugs function at the synaptic level?

10.5 What are the effects of psychoactive drugs?

10.6 How do cultural pressures and expectations influence drug use?

Key Module Resources

- Explore: Investigating Hypnosis; Exploring Teen Alcohol Abuse; Ecstasy Rising Video
- Class Demonstrations: Hypnosis: Dissociation or Social Role-Playing?; Examine Statistics on Teen Drug Use; Stimulant Awareness PSA Campaign; Prescriptions for Disaster?; Debate: Should Laws Against Illegal Drugs Be Strengthened?; What Drug Am I?; Subtle Pressure in Advertisements for Legal Drug Use

---

TEACHING PSYCHOLOGY

PROGRAM ORGANIZATION

DIFFERENTIATED INSTRUCTION

ASSESSMENT

PLANNING YOUR INSTRUCTION

PLANNING YOUR INSTRUCTION

Chapter 5 Development Across the Life Span

CHAPTER RESOURCES

Introduce the Chapter	Assessment	Additional Support	Module
• Module Goals and Learning Objectives • MyPsychLab interactivities • Bellringer activities	• ExamView Test Bank • MyPsychLab Assessments • End-of-Chapter Assessments	• Differentiation suggestions throughout each lesson • Teacher's Manual resources • Interactive PowerPoint slides and Standard PowerPoint slides	Module 11 Topics in Development Module 12 Prenatal, Infant and Childhood Development Module 13 Adolescence and Adulthood

MODULE 11

Topics in Development

Module Goal

- Describe methods and issues in life span development.

Summary of Teaching Strategies

Students will investigate how biological and environmental factors influence human development. They also will describe how researchers study development and assess major issues in developmental psychology. Last, they will explain how particular experiences affect critical periods and sensitive periods.

Learning Objectives

11.1 How do biological and environmental factors influence development?

11.2 What are some major research issues in developmental psychology?

11.3 How do psychologists study development?

11.4 What are critical periods and sensitive periods?

Key Module Resources

- Explore: Using Information from the Internet; Developmental Psychology Websites
- Class Discussion: Questions in Development

MODULE 12

Prenatal, Infant and Childhood Development

Module Goals

- Learn about prenatal and newborn development.
- Describe development during infancy and childhood.

Summary of Teaching Strategies

Students will learn about prenatal and newborn development and then will describe development during infancy and childhood. They will assess the physical changes that take place, the development of cognitive skills and language, and how children develop emotionally and socially.

Learning Objectives

12.1 How do humans develop from conception through birth?

12.2 What reflexes and abilities do newborns have?

12.3 What kinds of physical changes take place in infancy and childhood?

12.4 How do infants and children develop cognitive skills?

12.5 What are the stages of language development?

12.6 How do babies begin to develop relationships with others?

12.7 How do children develop socially and emotionally?

Key Module Resources

- Explore: The Visible Embryo; Measuring Intelligence in Infants; Facts and Myths About Autism; Childhood Development Websites; Jean Piaget Websites; Using Videos to Teach Developmental Concepts; Is Television Bad for Children?
- Class Demonstrations: Educating People About Teratogens; Piaget's Stages; Piaget's Stages of Cognitive Development; Talk Baby Talk; Designing a Day Care; Erikson's Stages

MODULE 13

Adolescence and Adulthood

Module Goals
- Describe development during adolescence.
- Describe development during adulthood.

Summary of Teaching Strategies

Students will describe development during adolescence, including physical changes, levels of morality, the formation of identity, and the influence of parents and peer pressure.

Learning Objectives

13.1 What physical changes occur during adolescence?

13.2 How do reasoning and morality develop during adolescence?

13.3 How do adolescents form their identities?

13.4 What role do family members and peers play in adolescent development?

13.5 What social and cognitive changes occur during adulthood?

13.6 What physical changes happen during adulthood?

13.7 How do scientists explain why aging occurs?

13.8 What are the stages of death and dying?

Key Module Resources
- Explore: Being a Leader and a Follower
- Class Demonstrations: Moral Development; Stereotypes of Aging;
- Critical Thinking: Writing About Personal Fables
- Class Discussion: A Nation of Wimps?
- Cultural Connection: Exploring Attitudes About Aging

TEACHING PSYCHOLOGY

PROGRAM ORGANIZATION

DIFFERENTIATED INSTRUCTION

ASSESSMENT

PLANNING YOUR INSTRUCTION

PLANNING YOUR INSTRUCTION

Chapter 6 Learning and Language Development

CHAPTER RESOURCES

Introduce the Chapter	Assessment	Additional Support	Module
• Module Goals and Learning Objectives • MyPsychLab interactivities • Bellringer activities	• ExamView Test Bank • MyPsychLab Assessments • End-of-Chapter Assessments	• Differentiation suggestions throughout each lesson • Teacher's Manual resources • Interactive PowerPoint slides and Standard PowerPoint slides	Module 14 Classical Conditioning Module 15 Operant Conditioning Module 16 Cognitive Learning and Observational Learning Module 17 Language

MODULE 14

Classical Conditioning

Module Goal

- Explain the process of classical conditioning.

Summary of Teaching Strategies

Students will investigate aspects of classical conditioning, including its principles and how it works in people's everyday lives. In addition, they will study how phobias can be learned when something unpleasant is paired with a neutral stimulus.

Learning Objectives

14.1 What are the principles of classical conditioning?

14.2 How can classical conditioning be specialized to affect emotions?

14.3 How does classical conditioning function in our everyday lives?

Key Module Resources

- Explore: Classical Conditioning and Television Advertisements; Writing About Phobias
- Class Demonstrations: Finding Examples of Classical Conditioning; Classical Conditioning in Humans

MODULE 15

Operant Conditioning

Module Goal

- Explain the process of operant conditioning.

Summary of Teaching Strategies

Students will explain the theory behind Thorndike's law of effect and will study the principles of operant conditioning, including the effects of reinforcement and punishment. In addition, they will assess the role of shaping and schedules of fixed and variable intervals and ratios.

Learning Objectives

15.1 What is Thorndike's law of effect?

15.2 What are the principles of operant conditioning?

15.3 What are some specializations of operant conditioning?

15.4 How does operant conditioning function in everyday life?

Key Module Resources

- Explore: Investigating Clicker Training; Animal Training at Sea World; Learning About Token Economies; Learning Theory in Everyday Life
- Class Demonstrations: Operant Conditioning in Human Behavior; Exploring Shaping
- Critical Thinking: Primary and Secondary Reinforcers
- Class Discussions: Controversies in Learning; Superstition and Operant Conditioning

T58

MODULE 16

Cognitive Learning and Observational Learning

Module Goal
- Identify the aspects of cognitive and observational learning.

Summary of Teaching Strategies

Students will understand how people learn behavior by watching others perform that behavior. They will explore how observational learning requires attention, memory, capability, and the desire to perform a behavior. Finally, they will describe how cognitive learning theory focuses on the role of thought processes in learning.

Learning Objectives

16.1 What occurs in observational learning?

16.2 How does observational learning function in everyday life?

16.3 What is cognitive learning theory?

Key Module Resources
- Explore: Techniques and Methods of Learning; Understanding Depression
- Class Demonstrations: Tie Your Shoes; Human Cognitive Maps

MODULE 17

Language

Module Goals
- Identify the structural features of language.
- Explain theories and stages of language acquisition.
- Identify areas of the brain associated with language.

Summary of Teaching Strategies

Students will be able to define language and explain how it is structured. They will understand the relationship between language and thought, the acquisition of language, and how language is affected by problems in the brain.

Learning Objectives

17.1 What is language, and how is it structured?

17.2 How are language and thought related?

17.3 How is language acquired?

17.4 What are the theories of language acquisition?

17.5 Which parts of the brain are associated with language, and how does brain damage affect language?

Key Module Resources
- Explore: Do Animals Have Language? A Survey
- Class Demonstrations: Toasting the Contributions of Early Psychologists; Which Famous Psychologist Am I?; Psychological Perspectives; Psychologists Are Scientists
- Critical Thinking: Writing About Bilingualism
- Cultural Connection: Language and Culture
- Class Discussion: "Nonhandicapping" Language

TEACHING PSYCHOLOGY

PROGRAM ORGANIZATION

DIFFERENTIATED INSTRUCTION

ASSESSMENT

PLANNING YOUR INSTRUCTION

PLANNING YOUR INSTRUCTION

Chapter 7 Social Psychology

CHAPTER RESOURCES

Introduce the Chapter	Assessment	Additional Support	Module
• Module Goals and Learning Objectives • MyPsychLab interactivities • Bellringer activities	• ExamView Test Bank • MyPsychLab Assessments • End-of-Chapter Assessments	• Differentiation suggestions throughout each lesson • Teacher's Manual resources • Interactive PowerPoint slides and Standard PowerPoint slides	Module 18 Social Influence Module 19 Social Cognition Module 20 Social Interaction

MODULE 18

Social Influence

Module Goal

- Explore how social influence affects behavior.

Summary of Teaching Strategies

Students will explain how the presence of others influences our behavior, feelings, and thoughts. They will describe the meaning of conformity, compliance, and obedience. Students will investigate groupthink and the influence of group interactions. Finally, they will understand how leaders develop and how they affect the groups they lead.

Learning Objectives

18.1 Do people act differently in different situations?

18.2 How does the presence of others affect an individual's behavior?

18.3 How do group dynamics influence behavior?

18.4 How can an individual change a group's behavior?

Key Module Resources

- Explore: The Influence of Obedience on Historical Events; Leadership Styles
- Class Demonstrations: Conforming Behavior; Compliance Techniques; Classroom Version of Milgram's Study of Obedience; Group Polarization
- Critical Thinking: Reading and Writing About Groupthink and Bullying; Cultivate the Student Voice

MODULE 19

Social Cognition

Module Goal

- Understand the effects of social cognition.

Summary of Teaching Strategies

Students will define attitudes and will explain how they are formed, how they affect interactions, and how they can be changed. They will investigate attribution theory and will understand that the fundamental attribution error is the tendency to overestimate the influence of internal factors on the behavior of other people while underestimating the influence of the situation.

Learning Objectives

19.1 What are attitudes, and how do they relate to behavior?

19.2 How can attitudes be changed?

19.3 How do people use attribution theory to explain the actions of others?

Key Module Resources

- Explore: Applying Knowledge of Persuasion Techniques
- Class Demonstrations: Applying Models of Attitude Formation; Inducing Cognitive Dissonance; Take Attribution Theory for a Spin; Exploring the Fundamental Attribution Error
- Critical Thinking: Applying the Attitude Formation Model

MODULE 20

Social Interaction

Module Goal

- Describe different kinds of social relations.

Summary of Teaching Strategies

Students will explain the difference between prejudice and discrimination and between attraction and love. They will describe antisocial and prosocial behavior and their effects on social relations.

Learning Objectives

20.1 How are prejudice and discrimination different?

20.2 What factors govern attraction and love?

20.3 How does aggressive behavior develop?

20.4 What is prosocial behavior?

Key Module Resources

- Explore: Surf the Stanford Prison Experiment's Website
- Class Demonstrations: Headbands and Stereotypes; Theories About Prejudice; Defining Aggression; Analyzing Cartoons; Creating an Experiment to Test the Bystander Effect
- Critical Thinking: Overcoming Prejudice; Decoding the Love Triangle
- Class Discussion: Looking for Love

TEACHING PSYCHOLOGY

PROGRAM ORGANIZATION

DIFFERENTIATED INSTRUCTION

ASSESSMENT

PLANNING YOUR INSTRUCTION

Chapter 8 Culture and Gender

CHAPTER RESOURCES

Introduce the Chapter
- Module Goals and Learning Objectives
- MyPsychLab interactivities
- Bellringer activities

Assessment
- ExamView Test Bank
- MyPsychLab Assessments
- End-of-Chapter Assessments

Additional Support
- Differentiation suggestions throughout each lesson
- Teacher's Manual resources
- Interactive PowerPoint slides and Standard PowerPoint slides

Module
Module 21 Culture
Module 22 Gender

MODULE 21

Culture

Module Goal
- Understand culture's role in psychology.

Summary of Teaching Strategies

Students will define culture and explain how cultures are shaped at different times and in different places. They will describe the differences between collectivist and individualist cultures. They will investigate cross-cultural psychological research into areas such as emotion and intelligence. Finally, they will understand that what is considered "abnormal behavior" varies across cultures.

Learning Objectives

21.1 What is culture?

21.2 How does culture vary across time and place?

21.3 How does culture influence our conceptions of self and identity?

21.4 What are some of the major areas of cross-cultural psychology research?

Key Module Resources
- Explore: Depicting Norms; Celebrations and Rituals in Other Cultures; Expressing Emotions; What Is Normal?
- Class Demonstrations: Cultural Differences and Similarities; Debating Acculturation; Discussing Independence and Interdependence; Creating a Culture-Fair Intelligence Test
- Critical Thinking: Discussing Individualism and Collectivism

MODULE 22

Gender

Module Goal
- Learn how gender identity develops.

Summary of Teaching Strategies
Students will define gender and gender identity and will understand how biological and environmental factors affect gender identity. They will explain how differences between women and men seem to be disappearing as society treats the genders more equally. Students will also describe how males and females are socialized differently, which influences personality.

Learning Objectives
- 22.1 What is gender, and what is gender identity?
- 22.2 What factors influence the development of gender identity?
- 22.3 How do men and women differ in thinking, social behavior, and personality?

Key Module Resources
- Explore: Career Stereotypes
- Class Demonstrations: Analyzing Children's Toys; Exploring Gender Roles
- Critical Thinking: Controversies in Gender

TEACHING PSYCHOLOGY

PROGRAM ORGANIZATION

DIFFERENTIATED INSTRUCTION

ASSESSMENT

PLANNING YOUR INSTRUCTION

PLANNING YOUR INSTRUCTION

Chapter 9 Memory

CHAPTER RESOURCES

Introduce the Chapter
- Module Goals and Learning Objectives
- MyPsychLab interactivities
- Bellringer activities

Assessment
- ExamView Test Bank
- MyPsychLab Assessments
- End-of-Chapter Assessments

Additional Support
- Differentiation suggestions throughout each lesson
- Teacher's Manual resources
- Interactive PowerPoint slides and Standard PowerPoint slides

Module
Module 23 Encoding and Storage
Module 24 Retrieval and Retrieval Failure

MODULE 23

Encoding And Storage

Module Goals
- Learn how the brain encodes memories.
- Understand how memories are stored in the brain.

Summary of Teaching Strategies
Students will explain the information processing model, which suggests that there are levels of depth within memory. They will understand that the stages of memory are sensory memory, short-term memory, and long-term memory and that information enters the nervous system through the senses. They will describe how chunking can increase the amount of information that can be held in short-term memory and that information can be transferred into long-term memory through elaborative rehearsal.

Learning Objectives
23.1 What are levels of processing?
23.2 How are memories encoded in the brain?
23.3 How can we make encoding more effective?
23.4 How is information stored in long-term memory?
23.5 How and where are memories stored in the brain?

Key Module Resources
- Explore: Using Information from the Internet; Amnesia and Implicit Memory
- Class Demonstrations: Cultural Reminders; The Cocktail Party Effect; Do We Make Accurate Copies of Events in Our Memories?; The Value of Chunking; Time-Gap Experience; Memory Networks
- Critical Thinking: Memory Storage

MODULE 24

Retrieval And Retrieval Failure

Module Goal
- Learn how memories are retrieved from the brain.

Summary of Teaching Strategies
Students will understand that almost anything in one's surroundings is capable of becoming a cue for memory retrieval. They will describe how information at the beginning or end of a list tends to be remembered more easily and accurately and that mnemonic devices such as acrostics, acronyms, linking, and rhythmic organization can help people recall information stored in long-term memory. They will explore how memories are revised, edited, and altered and how false memories can be created through the suggestion of others. Finally, they will investigate why people forget and how amnesia occurs.

Learning Objectives
24.1 What kinds of cues help people remember?
24.2 What factors influence how memories are retrieved?
24.3 How can we improve our ability to retrieve memories?
24.4 Can memories change? How reliable are they?
24.5 Why do we forget?
24.6 How does amnesia occur?

Key Module Resources
- Explore: Serial Position Effect; Retrieval of Memories; How False Memories Are Formed; How Reliable Are Memories?; Causes of Amnesia
- Class Demonstrations: Context and Its Effect on Memory; Controversies in Memory; Patriot Games; Memory Distortion; Forgetting; Decay and Interference in Short-Term Memory
- Critical Thinking: Aging, Culture, and Memory

TEACHING PSYCHOLOGY

PROGRAM ORGANIZATION

DIFFERENTIATED INSTRUCTION

ASSESSMENT

PLANNING YOUR INSTRUCTION

PLANNING YOUR INSTRUCTION

Chapter 10 Cognition: Thinking and Intelligence

CHAPTER RESOURCES

Introduce the Chapter	Assessment	Additional Support	Module
• Module Goals and Learning Objectives • MyPsychLab interactivities • Bellringer activities	• ExamView Test Bank • MyPsychLab Assessments • End-of-Chapter Assessments	• Differentiation suggestions throughout each lesson • Teacher's Manual resources • Interactive PowerPoint slides and Standard PowerPoint slides	Module 25 Thinking Module 26 Intelligence

MODULE 25

Thinking

Module Goals
- Understand the basic elements of thought.
- Identify obstacles to thought.

Summary of Teaching Strategies

Students will understand the difference between mental images and concepts. They will explore mechanical solutions and heuristics to solve problems and make decisions, and they will assess artificial intelligence. Last, they will discuss obstacles to problem solving and making good judgments and decisions.

Learning Objectives

25.1 How are mental images and concepts involved in the process of thinking?

25.2 What methods do people use to solve problems and make decisions?

25.3 Can a machine be made to think like a person?

25.4 What are some obstacles to problem solving?

25.5 What are some obstacles to making good judgments?

25.6 What are some obstacles to decision making?

Key Module Resources

- Explore: Types of Concepts; The Availability Heuristic; Improving Cognitive Health
- Class Demonstrations: Mental Imagery; Learning a Concept; Prototypes; Problem Solving; Functional Fixedness; Creative Thinking; Creativity Quiz
- Critical Thinking: Writing About Insight
- Class Debate: Artificial Intelligence
- Class Discussion: "Gut" Feelings

MODULE 26

Intelligence

Module Goals

- Compare and contrast perspectives on intelligence.
- Learn how intelligence is measured.
- Consider key issues in intelligence research.

Summary of Teaching Strategies

Students will define intelligence and identify theories of intelligence. They will understand intellectual disability and giftedness. They will explore how intelligence testing developed and how it is conducted today, along with standards of testing validity and reliability. Finally, students will assess how heredity and environment influence intelligence.

Learning Objectives

26.1 How do psychologists define intelligence?

26.2 What are some established theories of intelligence?

26.3 What are intellectual disability and giftedness?

26.4 What is the history of intelligence testing?

26.5 How is intelligence measured today?

26.6 How can we determine whether intelligence tests are reliable and valid?

26.7 How are intelligence tests used in the real world?

26.8 How do heredity and environment influence intelligence?

Key Module Resources

- Explore: Intellectual Disability; Intelligence and Mental Capacity in Film; Online IQ Tests; Can You "Become Smarter"?
- Class Demonstrations: Defining Intelligence; Late Bloomers; Creating a Culturally Fair Intelligence Test
- Class Discussion: Gardner's Multiple Intelligences; The Bell Curve
- Class Debate: Using Standardized Tests
- Critical Thinking: Cultural Bias in Intelligence Tests; Controversies in Intelligence

TEACHING PSYCHOLOGY

PROGRAM ORGANIZATION

DIFFERENTIATED INSTRUCTION

ASSESSMENT

PLANNING YOUR INSTRUCTION

PLANNING YOUR INSTRUCTION

Chapter 11 Motivation and Emotion

CHAPTER RESOURCES

Introduce the Chapter
- Module Goals and Learning Objectives
- MyPsychLab interactivities
- Bellringer activities

Assessment
- ExamView Test Bank
- MyPsychLab Assessments
- End-of-Chapter Assessments

Additional Support
- Differentiation suggestions throughout each lesson
- Teacher's Manual resources
- Interactive PowerPoint slides and Standard PowerPoint slides

Module
Module 27 Motivation
Module 28 Emotion

MODULE 27

Motivation

Module Goals
- Explain the major theories of motivation.
- Describe motivated behaviors.

Summary of Teaching Strategies

Students will explore major cognitive and biological theories of motivation, including early instinct approaches, drive-reduction approaches, arousal theory, the incentive approach, McClelland's psychological needs, expectancy-value theories, and humanist theory. Students also will investigate factors that motivate eating, sexual behavior/orientation, and achievement.

Learning Objectives

27.1 What are the major cognitive and biological theories of motivation?

27.2 What is the humanist theory of motivation?

27.3 What factors motivate eating?

27.4 What factors motivate sexual behavior and orientation?

27.5 What factors motivate achievement?

27.6 Are there other ways in which humans and animals are motivated?

Key Module Resources

- Explore: Personality Assessment; Abraham Maslow; Your Brain on Food; Privileges Based on Sexual Orientation
- Class Demonstrations: Types of Motivation; Achievement and Motivation; Identifying Human Motives; Incentives; Treatment of Obesity; Evaluating Diet Plans; Physique Preferences; Controversies in Motivation; Comparison of Theories of Motivation; Hierarchy of Belongingness

MODULE 28

Emotion

Module Goals

- Understand theories of emotion and emotional expression.
- Analyze emotional behaviors in depth.

Summary of Teaching Strategies

Students will investigate biological, behavioral, and cognitive components of emotion, the major theories of emotion, and the influence of cultural and environmental factors on emotional expression. Finally, they will analyze fear and happiness in depth.

Learning Objectives

28.1 What are the biological, behavioral, and cognitive components of emotion?

28.2 What are the major theories of emotion?

28.3 How do cultural and environmental factors influence emotional expression?

28.4 What biological and environmental factors influence the expression and experience of fear?

28.5 What biological and environmental factors influence the expression and experience of happiness?

Key Module Resources

- Explore: Kismet the Sociable Robot; How Cognitions Influence Emotions; Positive Psychology
- Class Demonstrations: Vocal Cues and Emotion; Physiological Experiences of Emotion; Smile When You Say That; Cultural Meanings of Nonverbal Gestures; Scent and Emotion; The Pursuit of Happiness

---

TEACHING PSYCHOLOGY

PROGRAM ORGANIZATION

DIFFERENTIATED INSTRUCTION

ASSESSMENT

PLANNING YOUR INSTRUCTION

PLANNING YOUR INSTRUCTION

Chapter 12 Theories of Personality

CHAPTER RESOURCES

Introduce the Chapter
- Module Goals and Learning Objectives
- MyPsychLab interactivities
- Bellringer activities

Assessment
- ExamView Test Bank
- MyPsychLab Assessments
- End-of-Chapter Assessments

Additional Support
- Differentiation suggestions throughout each lesson
- Teacher's Manual resources
- Interactive PowerPoint slides and Standard PowerPoint slides

Module
- Module 29 Perspectives on Personality
- Module 30 Assessment and Issues in Personality

MODULE 29

Perspectives on Personality

Module Goal
- Evaluate the major theories of personality.

Summary of Teaching Strategies
Students will learn that the three parts of the personality are the id, ego, and superego. They will understand that behaviorists define personality as a set of learned responses and that the social cognitive view of personality includes the concept of reciprocal determinism in which the environment, characteristics of the person, and the behavior itself all interact. They will explore humanistic psychologists' belief that self-actualization depends on proper development of the self-concept, which includes the real self and the ideal self. Finally, students will explore the five trait dimensions that have support across cultures, called the Big Five: openness, conscientiousness, extraversion, agreeableness, and neuroticism.

Learning Objectives

29.1 What is the psychodynamic theory of personality?

29.2 How do behaviorists and social cognitive theorists explain personality?

29.3 How do humanistic psychologists explain personality?

29.4 What are the history and current views of the trait perspective?

Key Module Resources

- Explore: First Look at the Four Theories of Personality; Learning More About the Neo-Freudians; Birth Order; Photographs at the Freud Museum in London
- Class Demonstrations: Role Playing the Id, Ego, and Superego; Exploring Defense Mechanisms; Are You In or Out? "Musical Chairs"; Harmony or Anxiety?; Exploring Cattell's Self-Report Inventory; What's My Career Personality?; Celebrity Analysis
- Class Discussion: Fixations and Personality Type
- Critical Thinking: Creating a Character with Personality

MODULE 30

Assessment and Issues In Personality

Module Goals
- Learn how personality is assessed.
- Consider key issues in personality research.

Summary of Teaching Strategies

Students will investigate whether personality measurement techniques are reliable and valid. They will consider the parts played by culture and biology in personality, whether personality can change, and how personality influences people's health and work. They will explore the role of self-esteem and the four basic dimensions of personality along which cultures may vary.

Learning Objectives

30.1 What techniques do researchers use to measure personality? Are these techniques reliable and valid?

30.2 What part do biology and culture play in personality?

30.3 Is personality stable, or can it change over time?

30.4 How can personality influence our health and our work?

30.5 What is self-esteem, and how does it affect us?

30.6 How do cultural perspectives relate to personality?

Key Module Resources

- Explore: Personality Assessments; Genetics and Personality; Learning More About How Personality Can Affect Health and Work; Personality Tests on the Internet
- Class Demonstrations: Projective Test Assessment; Assessing the "Personality" of Personality Assessments
- Critical Thinking: Debating Employers' Use of Personality Tests; Interview with an Elder
- Cultural Connection: Collectivistic vs. Individualistic Cultures
- Class Debate: The Value of Personality Testing

TEACHING PSYCHOLOGY

PROGRAM ORGANIZATION

DIFFERENTIATED INSTRUCTION

ASSESSMENT

PLANNING YOUR INSTRUCTION

PLANNING YOUR INSTRUCTION

Chapter 13 Psychological Disorders

CHAPTER RESOURCES

Introduce the Chapter
- Module Goals and Learning Objectives
- MyPsychLab interactivities
- Bellringer activities

Assessment
- ExamView Test Bank
- MyPsychLab Assessments
- End-of-Chapter Assessments

Additional Support
- Differentiation suggestions throughout each lesson
- Teacher's Manual resources
- Interactive PowerPoint slides and Standard PowerPoint slides

Module
Module 31 Defining Abnormal Behavior
Module 32 Types of Psychological Disorders

MODULE 31

Defining Abnormal Behavior

Module Goal
- Understand historical, cultural, and current views of abnormality.

Summary of Teaching Strategies
Students will explore explanations of mental illness in other times and cultures, and will describe abnormal behavior from a psychological perspective. Students will understand that biological models propose that psychological disorders have a biological cause; psychological models explain disordered behavior as the result of thought-related malfunctioning; and the biopsychosocial model proposes that biological, psychological, and sociological factors interact to cause abnormal behavior. Students will define stigma and how it affects the mentally ill. Finally, students will discuss the effects of psychological disorders on people and society.

Learning Objectives

31.1 How has mental illness been explained in the past and in other cultures?

31.2 What is psychologically abnormal behavior?

31.3 What are the major models of abnormality?

31.4 What is stigma, and how does it relate to mental illness?

31.5 How do psychological disorders impact individuals, their families, and society?

Key Module Resources
- Explore: The Biological Model; The Stigma of Mental Illness
- Class Demonstrations: Making Connections; Explaining Psychopathology
- Class Discussion: What Is "Abnormal" in Our Culture?
- Critical Thinking: Writing About Psychology

MODULE 32

Types Of Psychological Disorders

Module Goal
- Learn about psychological disorders, their symptoms, and their causes.

Summary of Teaching Strategies

Students will understand the DSM classification system and will discuss problems in diagnosing mental disorders. They will study types and causes of anxiety disorders, somatoform disorders, dissociative disorders, mood disorders, schizophrenia, and personality disorders. Last, they will explore the effects of family and social influences on mental illness.

Learning Objectives

32.1 What is the DSM classification system?

32.2 What are the challenges of diagnosing a mental illness?

32.3 What are the different types of anxiety disorders and their causes?

32.4 What are the different types of somatoform disorders and their causes?

32.5 What are the different types of dissociative disorders and their causes?

32.6 What are the different types of mood disorders and their causes?

32.7 What are the main symptoms, types, and causes of schizophrenia?

32.8 What are the different types of personality disorders and their causes?

32.9 How can family and social influences affect the experience of mental illness?

Key Module Resources

- Explore: The Axes of the *DSM-IV-TR*; Most Common Mental Disorders in the United States; Misdiagnosis of Mental Disorders; Dissociative Disorders in the News; Bipolar Disorder; Contributing to the Mental Health of Loved Ones

- Class Demonstrations: Exploring Phobias; Anxiety Disorder "Catchphrase"; How Do the Four Main Psychological Models Explain Anxiety?; Somatoform Scenarios; Getting the Word Out About Depression; A Monologue Demonstrating Schizophrenia; Reviewing the Symptoms of Schizophrenia; Profiling Personality Disorders; Writing About Psychological Disorders

- Critical Thinking: Writing About Psychology; Dispelling Myths About Schizophrenia; Teen Moodiness or Borderline Personality Disorder?

- Class Discussion: Psychology in Film

TEACHING PSYCHOLOGY

PROGRAM ORGANIZATION

DIFFERENTIATED INSTRUCTION

ASSESSMENT

PLANNING YOUR INSTRUCTION

PLANNING YOUR INSTRUCTION

Chapter 14 Psychological Therapies

CHAPTER RESOURCES

Introduce the Chapter
- Module Goals and Learning Objectives
- MyPsychLab interactivities
- Bellringer activities

Assessment
- ExamView Test Bank
- MyPsychLab Assessments
- End-of-Chapter Assessments

Additional Support
- Differentiation suggestions throughout each lesson
- Teacher's Manual resources
- Interactive PowerPoint slides and Standard PowerPoint slides

Module
Module 33 Psychotherapies
Module 34 Biomedical Therapies and Issues in Therapy

MODULE 33

Psychotherapies

Module Goals
- Understand perspectives on treating psychological disorders.
- Identify psychological treatments and evaluate their effectiveness.

Summary of Teaching Strategies
Students will learn that the two modern forms of therapy are psychotherapy and biomedical therapy and that psychiatrists, psychoanalysts, psychiatric social workers, and psychologists all treat psychological disorders. Students will analyze different types of therapies, such as person-centered therapy, behavior therapies, cognitive therapy, rational-emotive behavior therapy, and group therapy. Finally, students will explore the effectiveness of psychotherapy.

Learning Objectives

33.1 What are the two modern ways in which psychological disorders can be treated, and how have they been treated in the past?

33.2 Who can treat psychological disorders, and what training is required?

33.3 What are the different types of psychotherapy?

33.4 How effective is psychotherapy?

33.5 What other factors influence the effectiveness of therapy?

Key Module Resources
- Explore: Using Information from the Internet; Psychoanalysis; Carl Rogers; You Are What You Think; Group Therapy; Mental Health Resources in the Community
- Class Demonstrations: Systematic Desensitization; Modify Your Behavior; Rational-Emotive Therapy; Group Therapy
- Class Discussion: On Being Sane in Insane Places; How Can I Find a Good Therapist?
- Critical Thinking: Phobias; Controversies in the Treatment of Mental Illness
- Cultural Connections: Cultural Beliefs About Therapy; Navajo Medicine
- Class Debate: EMDR

MODULE 34

Biomedical Therapies and Issues in Therapy

Module Goals

- Identify biomedical therapies and evaluate their effectiveness.
- Consider legal, ethical, and professional challenges in therapy.

Summary of Teaching Strategies

Students will explore biomedical therapies, including drug therapy, electroconvulsive therapy (ECT), and psychosurgery. They will investigate the use of adult drugs for children and adolescents and will learn about legal, ethical, and professional issues in therapy. Finally, they will study resources available for the mentally ill.

Learning Objectives

34.1 What are biomedical forms of therapy, and how effective are they?

34.2 Should children and adolescents be treated with the same drugs used for adults?

34.3 What ethical challenges do therapists face when they deliver treatment?

34.4 What resources support people with psychological disorders and their families?

Key Module Resources

- Explore: Antidepressants and Adolescents; Ethical Issues; Treatment Options
- Class Demonstration: Interviewing Mental-Health Professionals
- Class Discussion: Should Psychologists Prescribe Medications?; The Ethics of Electroconvulsive Therapy; Prefrontal Lobotomies; Therapists' Visit to the Classroom

TEACHING PSYCHOLOGY

PROGRAM ORGANIZATION

DIFFERENTIATED INSTRUCTION

ASSESSMENT

PLANNING YOUR INSTRUCTION

PLANNING YOUR INSTRUCTION

Chapter 15 Stress and Health

CHAPTER RESOURCES

Introduce the Chapter
- Module Goals and Learning Objectives
- MyPsychLab interactivities
- Bellringer activities

Assessment
- ExamView Test Bank
- MyPsychLab Assessments
- End-of-Chapter Assessments

Additional Support
- Differentiation suggestions throughout each lesson
- Teacher's Manual resources
- Interactive PowerPoint slides and Standard PowerPoint slides

Module
- Module 35 Stress and Stressors
- Module 36 Coping with Stress and Promoting Wellness

MODULE 35

Stress and Stressors

Module Goal
- Understand the causes and consequences of stress.

Summary of Teaching Strategies

Students will define stress and explain its environmental, social, and psychological causes. They will also explore its effects on the immune system, heart health, and the body's ability to fight cancer. They will investigate anxiety disorders such as acute stress disorder (ASD) and post-traumatic stress disorder (PTSD).

Learning Objectives

35.1 How do psychologists define stress?

35.2 What kinds of events and situations can cause stress?

35.3 How can stress affect physiological and psychological health?

Key Module Resources
- Explore: Catastrophes and Stress; Stress and Health; Post-Traumatic Stress Disorder
- Class Demonstrations: Students' Daily Hassles; Stress at Work; Thinking Critically About Stress; Health Beliefs and Coping; Controversies About Stress; The Many Faces of Stress
- Class Discussion: What Is the Purpose of Stress?
- Cultural Connections: Adapting to a New Culture

MODULE 36

Coping with Stress and Promoting Wellness

Module Goal
- Learn strategies for promoting mental and physical health.

Summary of Teaching Strategies

Students will understand that how one cognitively assesses a stressor has a lot to do with one's personality. They will discuss ways to deal with stress, learn how to be more optimistic, and investigate behaviors and lifestyle choices that promote physical and mental health.

Learning Objectives

36.1 How do people think about stress?

36.2 What are effective and ineffective ways to deal with stressors?

36.3 What are some strategies for coping with stress?

36.4 What is optimism, and how can people become more optimistic?

36.5 What are some ways to promote wellness?

Key Module Resources
- Explore: Laughing out Loud to Good Health
- Class Demonstrations: Perception and Stress; Personality and Stress; Type A Behavior Patterns; Coping with Final Exam Stress; Defense Mechanisms; Lifestyle Awareness Triangle; The Control Process; Relax Before the Big Game
- Cultural Connections: Breakdown or Smash-Up?

Chapter 16 Applied Psychology and Psychology Careers

CHAPTER RESOURCES

Introduce the Chapter
- Module Goals and Learning Objectives
- MyPsychLab interactivities
- Bellringer activities

Assessment
- ExamView Test Bank
- MyPsychLab Assessments
- End-of-Chapter Assessments

Additional Support
- Differentiation suggestions throughout each lesson
- Teacher's Manual resources
- Interactive PowerPoint slides and Standard PowerPoint slides

Module
- Module 37 Careers in Psychology

MODULE 37

Careers In Psychology

Module Goals
- Identify educational requirements for careers in psychology.
- Explore career options in psychology.

Summary of Teaching Strategies

Students will investigate the degree requirements for various psychological professionals and the resources available to people who want to study psychology. Finally, they will learn what career options are open to persons with bachelor's degrees in psychology and will understand how psychology is used in other career fields.

Learning Objectives

37.1 What are the degree requirements for psychological professionals?

37.2 What resources are available for people who want to study psychology in the future?

37.3 What types of careers are available to someone with a bachelor's degree in psychology?

37.4 How does psychology interact with other career fields?

Key Module Resources
- Explore: "Passport to Psychology" Portfolio Project; Let the Experts Do the Talking; Interview an Expert
- Research: "Passport to Psychology" Portfolio Project
- Critical Thinking: "Passport to Psychology" Portfolio Project; How Can a Degree in Psychology Transfer to Other Careers?; Preventing Violence in the Workplace
- Class Discussion: Think Like a Forensic Psychologist
- Application: Think Like an Environmental Psychologist
- Final Project: Psychology Career Fair

TEACHING PSYCHOLOGY

PROGRAM ORGANIZATION

DIFFERENTIATED INSTRUCTION

ASSESSMENT

PLANNING YOUR INSTRUCTION

T77

CHAPTER 1 • Module 1

Launch the Chapter

CHAPTER GOALS AND LEARNING OBJECTIVES

Module 1 Psychology's Domains

Trace the development of psychology.

1.1 What is psychology? What are its goals?
1.2 What is the history of psychology as a scientific discipline?
1.3 What are the major psychological perspectives?
1.4 How is the field of psychology continuing to grow and change?

Identify psychology's subfields.

1.5 Why do psychologists perform research?
1.6 What are the major subfields of psychology?
1.7 How does psychology benefit society?

Module 2 Research Methods and Ethics

Understand psychological research methods.

2.1 What is the scientific method?
2.2 What methods do researchers use to study behavior?
2.3 How do researchers ensure their findings are valid?
2.4 Why do some researchers study animals instead of people?

Consider ethical issues in psychological research.

2.5 What ethical guidelines do psychologists follow when they research humans?
2.6 Are there different ethical guidelines for research with animals?

Module 3 Statistics

Learn the basic concepts of data analysis.

3.1 What are descriptive statistics?
3.2 What types of tables and graphs represent patterns in data?
3.3 What are correlation coefficients? What do they tell researchers about relationships?
3.4 What are inferential statistics?
3.5 How do the concepts of validity and reliability relate to statistics?

DIFFERENTIATED INSTRUCTION KEY

Look for these symbols to help you adjust steps in each lesson to meet your students' needs.

- **L1** Special Needs
- **L2** Basic
  - **ELL** English Language Learners
  - **LPR** Less Proficient Readers
- **L3** All Students
- **L4** Advanced Students

CHAPTER 1

The Science of Psychology

What Can Psychology Do for Me?

Have you ever wondered . . .

. . . why using common sense doesn't always work?
. . . how you could develop a better memory?
. . . if psychics really communicate with the dead?
. . . why it's so easy for little children to learn another language when it's so hard for adults?
. . . what happens when you faint?
. . . if ESP really exists?
. . . why you find some people attractive but not others?
. . . why you get nervous?
. . . what scores on an IQ test really mean?
. . . how the salesperson managed to talk you into buying more than you wanted to buy?
. . . how different men and women really are?
. . . why you sleep and why you dream?
. . . if hypnosis is real?
. . . why people tend to get sick right before final exams?
. . . why identical twins aren't so identical when it comes to their personalities?

If you've ever been curious about any of these questions, this book is for you. Psychologists study all of these things and more. If you've puzzled about it, thought about doing it, or actually done it, chances are psychology has an explanation for it.

CORRELATION TO APA STANDARDS FOR CHAPTER 1

IA. PERSPECTIVES IN PSYCHOLOGICAL SCIENCE

IA-1. Development of psychology as an .... pp. 4–12
empirical science
IA-2. Major subfields within psychology .... pp. 12–14

IB. RESEARCH METHODS AND STATISTICS

IB-1. Research methods used to study behavior .... pp. 16–23
and mental processes
IB-2. Ethical issues in research with human and .... pp. 23–24
nonhuman animals
IB-3. Basic concepts of data analysis .... pp. 26–33

MODULE 1 ▶ **PSYCHOLOGY'S DOMAINS**
MODULE 2 ▶ **RESEARCH METHODS AND ETHICS**
MODULE 3 ▶ **STATISTICS**

Why Study? Psychology

Psychology not only helps you understand why other people do the things they do, but it also helps you better understand yourself and your reactions to other people. Psychology can help you understand how your brain and body are connected, how to improve your learning abilities and memory, and how to deal with the stresses of life. By learning about psychology and its research methods, you will learn how to think critically about the world around you.

SCHEDULING

	1 Period = 50 min. 1 Block = 90 min.	Semester Course (18 weeks/90 days) Periods/Blocks		Full-Year Course (36 weeks/180 days) Period/Blocks	
Module 1		2	1	4	2
Module 2		2	1	4	2
Module 3		2	1	4	2
Total Days for Chapter		6	3	12	6

CHAPTER 1 • Module 1

Teacher Prep

Psychology is defined as the scientific study of behavior and mental processes. The goals of psychology are to describe, explain, predict, and control the behaviors and mental processes of both humans and animals. The goals of psychology can be thought of in terms of what, why, when, and how behaviors and mental processes occur.

The field of psychology is relatively new (around 125 years old) but has its origins in the much older fields of physiology and philosophy.

Today there are six major perspectives within the field of psychology: (1) psychodynamic, (2) behaviorism, (3) humanistic, (4) cognitive, (5) sociocultural, and (6) biopsychological.

Psychologists use the scientific method to reduce bias and error in their observations. The steps of the scientific method include asking a question, turning the question into a hypothesis (a statement about what someone believes is the actual answer), testing the hypothesis, drawing a conclusion, and reporting the findings. The findings can then be further strengthened if other researchers conduct a study and draw the same conclusions as you did—in other words, if other researchers replicate your findings. The method used to test the hypothesis depends on which of the four goals of psychology you are attempting to achieve.

Understanding the scientific method can help you in your daily life as you apply the four principles of critical thinking to problems you face day to day. The four criteria are that (1) most truths need to be tested, (2) all evidence is not equal, (3) authorities are not always right, and (4) an open mind is still important.

CHAPTER 1 • Module 1

Focus

RESOURCES
For this module, consult the appropriate sections of the Teacher's Manual, Test Bank, and PowerPoint slides, all found on the Teacher's Resource DVD, and the interactive study tools for students on MyPsychLab.

BEFORE CLASS
Students should read the section for homework before coming to class.

BELLRINGER
Draw a two-column chart on the board for students to copy onto paper. The left column's heading should be "What I Already Know About Psychology." The right column's heading should be "What I Predict I Will Learn." Have students complete their charts with brief notations.

Teach

BRAINSTORM
Have students share their ideas from the Bellringer in a brainstorm session. Encourage students to revisit their charts during the course to see if their predictions are correct.

COVER THE MODULE
1.1 What is psychology? What are its goals?
- *Psychology* is the scientific study of behavior and mental processes.
- Behavior includes all of our outward actions and reactions.
- Mental processes refer to all the internal, covert activity of our minds, such as thinking, feeling, and remembering.
- **Four Goals of Psychology**
  - Description: *What is happening?*
  - Explanation: *Why is it happening?*
  - Prediction: *When will it happen again?*
  - Control: *How can it be changed?*

4 Chapter 1 The Science of Psychology

Module 1 Psychology's Domains

Module Goals	Learning Objectives
Trace the development of psychology.	1.1 What is psychology? What are its goals?
	1.2 What is the history of psychology as a scientific discipline?
	1.3 What are the major modern psychological perspectives?
	1.4 How is the field of psychology continuing to grow and change?
Identify psychology's subfields.	1.5 Why do psychologists perform research?
	1.6 What are the major subfields of psychology?
	1.7 How does psychology benefit society?

Trace the Development of Psychology

1.1 What is psychology? What are its goals?

Psychology is the scientific study of behavior and mental processes. *Behavior* includes anything we do that can be measured, including all of our outward actions and reactions, such as talking, facial expressions, and movement. The term *mental processes* refers to all the internal activity of our minds, such as thinking, feeling, and remembering. Why "scientific"? To study behavior and mental processes in both animals and humans, researchers have to observe them objectively. Psychologists don't want to let their personal judgments cause them to make incorrect observations. They want to measure as carefully as they can, so they use the scientific method—a way to ask and answer questions based on observations.

Psychology's Goals In psychology, there are four goals that aim at uncovering the mysteries of human and animal behavior: description, explanation, prediction, and control.

Description begins with an observation—something that has been seen, heard, or felt. Description involves observing a behavior and noting everything about it: what is happening, where it happens, to whom it happens, and under what circumstances it seems to happen. For example, a teacher might notice that her second-grade students seem more hyperactive after lunch on Thursdays. The hyperactive behavior is disruptive to her class. That is *what* she is observing in students' outward behavior. The description of what the students are doing gives a starting place for the next question: *Why* are they doing it?

To find out why the students' behavior has changed, the teacher considers what is different about Thursdays compared to other days of the week. In other words, she is trying to find an *explanation* for the students' behavior. Finding explanations for behavior is a very important step in the process of forming theories of behavior. A *theory* is a set of ideas, combined in a logical way, that explains and connects known facts and predicts events. The

psychology the scientific study of behavior and mental processes.

4 CHAPTER 1

Terms

- psychology • structuralism • functionalism • psychoanalysis • behaviorism
- psychodynamic perspective • cognitive perspective • cognitive neuroscience
- sociocultural perspective • biopsychological perspective • evolutionary psychology
- positive psychology • clinical psychology • counseling psychology • developmental psychology • experimental psychology • social psychology • personality psychology
- physiological psychology • comparative psychology • industrial/organizational (I/O) psychology

teacher observes that students are allowed to drink caffeinated beverages with lunch on Thursdays. She forms the theory that caffeinated drinks lead to hyperactive behavior in children. The goal of description provides the observations, and the goal of explanation helps build the theory.

Theories, especially when strengthened by scientific evidence, help us explain the world around us. Researchers may have many different theories about behavior, and all of their theories may be based on careful observation and facts, but until scientific tests are performed, there is no way to tell if any of the theories are correct.

If all tests indicate that caffeinated drinks lead to hyperactive behavior in children, then the next step would be trying to determine what is likely to happen if the situation stays the same. Determining what will happen in the future is a *prediction*. In the example, the teacher might predict that students will exhibit hyperactive, disruptive behavior each time they drink caffeinated beverages. Clearly, something needs to be done to change this prediction, which is the point of the last of the four goals of psychology: changing or modifying behavior.

The focus of *control*, or the modification of some behavior, is to change a behavior from an undesirable one (such as disruptive behavior) to a desirable one (such as focused behavior). In the example of the second-grade classroom, the teacher and the school would work together to find a strategy that works best for the students and teachers.

▲ *The researcher in the foreground is watching the children through a one-way mirror to get a description of their behavior. Observations such as these are just one of many ways that psychologists have of investigating behavior. Why is it important for the researcher to be behind a one-way mirror?*

1.2 What is the history of psychology as a scientific discipline?

In the Beginning: Wundt, Introspection, and the Laboratory

How long has psychology been around?
Psychology, a relatively new field in the realm of the sciences, is only about 130 years old. (See Figure 1.1 on page 6.) It's not that no one thought about what makes people tick before then; on the contrary, there were philosophers, medical doctors, and other scientists who thought about little else. But it all started to come together in a laboratory in Leipzig, Germany, in 1879. It was here that Wilhelm Wundt (VILL-helm Voont, 1832–1920), a physiologist and physicist, attempted to apply scientific principles to the study of the human mind. Wundt was trained in philosophy and physiology, and many of his experiments also related to psychophysics, which was an attempt to apply the laws of natural world to the mind. Wundt believed that the mind was made up of thoughts, experiences, emotions, and other basic elements. To inspect these nonphysical elements, Wundt's students had to learn to think objectively about their own thoughts—after all, they could hardly read someone else's mind.

This was really the first attempt by anyone to bring objectivity and measurement to the concept of psychology and the mind. This attention to objectivity (the state of being impartial or unbiased), together with the establishment of the first true experimental laboratory in psychology, is why Wundt is known as the "father of psychology."

◀ How long has psychology been around?

THE SCIENCE OF PSYCHOLOGY 5

CHAPTER 1 • Module 1

COVER THE MODULE

1.2 What is the history of psychology as a scientific discipline?

- **In the Beginning: Wundt, Introspection, and the Laboratory**
  - Psychology began as a science of its own in Germany in 1879 with the establishment of Wilhelm Wundt's psychology laboratory.
    - He developed the technique of objective introspection, which involves the process of objectively examining and measuring one's own thoughts and mental activities.

DISCUSS THE STUDENT VOICE QUESTION

Ask: **Are you surprised that psychology is a relatively new field of study. Why might it have taken many centuries for psychology to develop as a science?** *(Possible answer: The idea that the mind should be measured and studied objectively probably could not have been thought of until science itself was measured and studied objectively.)*

UNDERSTANDING VISUALS

Direct students' attention to the question in the photo caption. It is important that the researcher not be seen by the subjects, who should be observed acting naturally.

Explore

USING INFORMATION FROM THE INTERNET

Send students to a History of Psychology Timeline at
http://psychology.okstate.edu/museum/history/

This website features a History of Psychology Timeline from early civilization to the 20th century. Recommend this to your students as a way of organizing their studying, by placing the right people and the right ideas at the right time.

Module 1 Psychology's Domain   **5**

CHAPTER 1 • Module 1

COVER THE MODULE (continued)

- Edward Titchener, a student of Wundt, brought psychology in the form of structuralism to America.
  - *Structuralism* was focused on studying the structure of the mind.
  - Structuralism died out in the early 20th century.
  - In 1894, Margaret F. Washburn, a student of Titchener, was the first woman to receive a Ph.D. in psychology, and she published *The Animal Mind*.
- William James and functionalism
  - William James proposed a countering point of view called functionalism, which stresses the way in which the mind allows us to adapt.
  - *Functionalism* **influenced** the modern fields of educational psychology, evolutionary psychology, and industrial/organizational psychology.

L1 DIFFERENTIATED INSTRUCTION

Special Needs Teach critical psychology terms by reviewing the key terms in the side columns.

▲ German physiologist Wilhelm Wundt participates in an experiment in his laboratory as students look on.

Titchener and Structuralism in America One of Wundt's students was Edward Titchener (1867–1927). Titchener expanded on Wundt's original ideas, calling his new viewpoint **structuralism** because the focus of study was the structure of the mind. He believed that every experience could be broken down into its individual emotions and sensations (Brennan, 2002). Although Titchener agreed with Wundt that consciousness, the state of being aware of external events, could be broken down into its basic elements, Titchener also believed that objective introspection, or the awareness of events that take place in the mind, could be used on thoughts as well as on physical sensations. For example, Titchener might have asked his students to introspect ("look inward") about things that are blue rather than actually giving them a blue object and asking for reactions to it. Such an exercise might have led to something like the following: "What is blue? There are blue things, like the sky or a bird's feathers. Blue is cool and restful, blue is calm . . . " and so on, trying to thoroughly understand all the parts that go into the experience of *blue*.

One of Wundt's students was an American named G. Stanley Hall, who went on to found the first psychology laboratory in the United States. Hall received the first Ph.D. in psychology in the United States, founded the American Psychological Association (APA), and became its first president.

Structuralism was a dominant force in the early days of psychology. However, a competing view arose not long after Wundt established his German laboratory.

structuralism early perspective in psychology associated with Wilhelm Wundt and Edward Titchener, in which the focus of study is the structure or basic elements of the mind.

William James and Functionalism Unlike Wundt and Titchener, an American scholar at Harvard University named William James (1842–1910) was more interested in studying the importance of consciousness to everyday life than he was in actually analyzing consciousness. He believed that the scientific study of consciousness itself was not yet possible because conscious ideas are constantly flowing like an ever-changing stream, and once you start thinking about what you were just thinking about, what you were thinking about is no longer what you *were* thinking about, it's what you *are* thinking about, and . . . excuse me, I'm a little dizzy. I think you get the picture, anyway.

FIGURE 1.1 Psychology's Early Days: A Timeline

1879 Wilhelm Wundt's psychology laboratory opens in Leipzig, Germany.

1890 William James publishes *Principles of Psychology*.

1900 Sigmund Freud publishes *The Interpretation of Dreams*.

1882 G. Stanley Hall opens the first psychology laboratory in the United States at Johns Hopkins University.

1892 Edward Titchener develops structuralism.

6 CHAPTER 1

Class Demonstration (Kinesthetic)

TOASTING THE CONTRIBUTIONS OF EARLY PSYCHOLOGISTS

Purpose: Students discuss the contributions of early psychologists.

Time: 15 minutes

Description: After reading about the contributions of historical figures in psychology, assign each team of students to a different figure. Students begin by individually preparing "toasts" to their assigned figure. Toasts should honor the accomplishments of contributors, as opposed to "roasting," and should be creative. Teams should then stand up and share their toasts out loud with the class, which should select the one they like best. One of the benefits of this exercise is that it provides exposure to contributors who are often overlooked in historical discussions.

Instead, James focused on how the mind helps people *function* in the real world—how people work, play, and adapt to their surroundings—a viewpoint he called **functionalism** (how people "function" better as a result of their experience).

James was heavily influenced by naturalist Charles Darwin's ideas about *natural selection*, in which physical traits that help an animal adapt to its environment and survive are passed on to its offspring, becoming part of the animal's traits. If physical traits could aid in survival, James thought, why couldn't behavioral traits do the same? For example, a behavior such as avoiding the eyes of others in an elevator can be seen as a way of protecting one's personal space—a kind of territorial protection that may have its roots in the primitive need to protect one's home and source of food and water from intruders (Manusov & Patterson, 2006), or as a way of avoiding what might seem like a challenge to another person.

One of James's early students at Harvard University was Mary Whiton Calkins, who completed every course and requirement for earning a Ph.D. but was denied that degree by Harvard because she was a woman. Calkins eventually established a psychological laboratory at Wellesley College. Her work was some of the earliest research in the area of human memory and the psychology of the self. In 1905, she became the first female president of the APA (Furumoto, 1979).

Women were not the only minority to make contributions in the early days of psychology. In 1920, for example, Francis Cecil Sumner became the first African American to earn a Ph.D. in psychology at Clark University. He eventually became the chair of the psychology department at Howard University and is assumed by many to be the father of African American psychology (Guthrie, 2004). **Explore** on **mypsychlab.com**

Beginning in the mid-1930s, George I. Sánchez, a Hispanic psychologist, helped identify bias in testing and in the education of Mexican American and Navajo students. Sánchez's research and activism led to many reforms in education that continued throughout the 20th century. In the 1950s, John Garcia, another Hispanic psychologist, made an important contribution to the field of psychology with his research on a biological foundation for taste aversion (the tendency to associate food or taste with a negative reaction, such as illness).

Today, representation of minority groups in psychology continues to grow. For example, Asian American psychologist David Matsumoto is a renowned

▲ Mary Whiton Calkins, despite being denied a Ph.D. degree by Harvard because she was a woman, became the first female president of the APA and had a successful career as a professor and researcher.
Source: Archives of the History of American Psychology, the University of Akron.

Explore a timeline of important dates in psychology on **mypsychlab.com**

functionalism early perspective in psychology associated with William James, in which the focus of study is how the mind allows people to adapt, live, work, and play.

1905
Mary Whiton Calkins becomes the first female president of the American Psychological Association.

1920
Francis Cecil Sumner becomes the first African American to earn a Ph.D. in psychology.

| 1905 | 1910 | 1915 | 1920 | 1925 |

1913
John B. Watson develops behaviorism.

1924
Mary Cover Jones publishes her study of "Little Peter."

THE SCIENCE OF PSYCHOLOGY 7

Explore

HISTORY OF PSYCHOLOGY WEBSITES

- **Archives of the History of American Psychology: www.uakron.edu/ahap**

  "Psychology's attic," maintained at the University of Akron Center for the History of Psychology.

- **Classics in the History of Psychology: http://psychclassics.yorku.ca/**

  This document repository, complete with a search engine, allows students to read excerpts from classic papers in psychology.

- **History of Psychology: http://psych.athabascau.ca/html/aupr/history.shtml**

  The Centre for Psychology Resources' History of Psychology page has many websites to choose from, including broad topics and those specific to the history of psychology. Students can learn more about psychology's past or investigate the history of a particular topic that interests them.

CHAPTER 1 • Module 1

EXTEND THE LESSON

Multicultural Focus Tell students that Mary Whiton Calkins (1863–1930) attended Harvard University and worked with William James, but because Harvard did not officially admit women into graduate programs, Calkins never received a Ph.D. from Harvard.

Like women, African Americans faced many obstacles to their education and participation in psychology. Most white institutions would not accept African-American students, and when they were able to enroll, they often experienced discrimination. In addition, few undergraduate African-American colleges offered a major in psychology until after the 1940s. Not only was earning the Ph.D. difficult, but employment opportunities were scarce for African-American psychologists since neither white universities nor organizations in the private sector would hire them. Most taught at African-American colleges, where opportunities to engage in research were limited, thus restricting opportunities for professional recognition.

Ask: Why is it important to have representation of minority groups in psychology? (*Possible answer: Because there are many minority groups within the general population, psychologists can help people better if those minorities are represented in the field.*)

MULTIMEDIA CONTENT AVAILABLE AT www.mypsychlab.com

Explore a timeline of important dates in psychology on **mypsychlab.com**

Module 1 Psychology's Domain **7**

CHAPTER 1 • Module 1

COVER THE MODULE (continued)

- Sigmund Freud's theory of *psychoanalysis*
  - Freud's theory was influenced by the sexually repressed Victorian Age in which he lived.
  - Freud proposed in his theory of psychoanalysis that the unconscious mind controls much of our conscious behavior.

  LINK to *Chapter Twelve: Theories of Personality*, pp. 376–383

- Pavlov, Watson, and the dawn of behaviorism

  LINK to *Chapter Six: Learning and Language Development*, p. 178

  - John Watson proposed a science of behavior called *behaviorism*, which focused on the study of observable stimuli and responses.
  - Much of his work was based on Ivan Pavlov's discovery of classic conditioning.
  - Watson demonstrated that a phobia could be learned by conditioning a baby ("Little Albert") to be afraid of a white rat. Due to the ethical concerns about this study, it would never be replicated.
  - Mary Cover Jones later demonstrated that a learned phobia could be counterconditioned.

DISCUSS THE STUDENT VOICE QUESTION

Because Freud may be the only psychologist with which students are familiar, point out that his theories are no longer as influential as they once were. Remind students that this is just one example of how the field of psychology continues to evolve over time.

---

expert in the field of cultural psychology. His research on blind judo athletes has shown that some facial expressions and other forms of nonverbal behavior are not learned by sight, but are common among humans and impossible to conceal. His findings have been used in lie detection and emotion recognition in corporate, criminal, and personal settings.

Since those early days, psychology has seen an increase in all minorities, although the percentages of the minority groups are still far too small when compared to the percentage of the overall population that the minority group represents.

Sigmund Freud's Theory of Psychoanalysis

What about Freud? Everybody talks about him when they talk about psychology. Are his ideas still in use?

Sigmund Freud was a noted Austrian medical doctor—a neurologist, someone who specializes in disorders of the nervous system. Freud's patients suffered from nervous disorders for which he and other doctors could find no physical cause. Therefore, they thought the cause must be in the mind, and that is where Freud began to explore. He proposed that there is an *unconscious* (unaware) mind into which we push, or *repress*, all of our threatening urges and desires. He believed that these repressed urges, in trying to surface, created the nervous disorders in his patients (Freud et al., 1990). LINK to *Chapter Twelve: Theories of Personality, pp. 376–383*.

Freud's ideas are still influential today, although in a somewhat modified form. He had a number of followers, many of whom became famous by altering his theory to fit their own viewpoints, but his basic ideas are still discussed and debated.

Freudian **psychoanalysis**, the theory and therapy based on Freud's ideas, has been the basis of much modern *psychotherapy* (a process in which a trained psychological professional helps a person gain insights into and change his or her behavior), but another major and competing viewpoint has been more influential in the field of psychology as a whole.

Pavlov, Watson, and the Dawn of Behaviorism Ivan Pavlov, like Freud, was not a psychologist. He was a Russian physiologist who, working with dogs, had shown that a reflex (an involuntary reaction) such as salivation, which is normally produced by actually having food in one's mouth, could be caused to occur in response to a totally new and formerly unrelated stimulus (an event that provokes a response), such as the sound of a ticking metronome. He would turn on the metronome, give the dogs food, and they would salivate. After several repetitions, the dogs would salivate to the sound of the metronome *before* the food was presented—a learned (or "conditioned") reflexive response (Klein & Mowrer, 1989). This process was called *conditioning*. LINK to *Chapter Six: Learning and Language Development, p. 178*.

In the early 1900s, psychologist John B. Watson challenged the functionalist viewpoint, as well as psychoanalysis, with his own "science of behavior," or **behaviorism** (Watson, 1924). Watson wanted to bring psychology back to a focus on scientific inquiry, and he felt that the only way to do that was to ignore the whole "consciousness" issue (and "unconsciousness" issue, which he believed never could be scientifically measured) and to focus only on *observable behavior*—something that could be directly seen and measured. He had read of Pavlov's work and thought that conditioning could be applied to humans and could form the basis of his new perspective of behaviorism.

▶ What about Freud? Everybody talks about him when they talk about psychology. Are his ideas still in use?

▲ Psychologist Sigmund Freud walks with his daughter, Anna, also a psychoanalyst.

psychoanalysis the theory and therapy based on the work of Sigmund Freud, emphasizing the revealing of unconscious conflicts.

behaviorism the science of behavior that focuses on observable behavior only.

8 CHAPTER 1

Class Demonstration

WHICH FAMOUS PSYCHOLOGIST AM I?

Purpose: Students review the major historical figures in psychology.

Time: Approximately 15 minutes

Description: The purpose of this activity is to familiarize students with the names and contributions of notable psychologists. Prepare a sign for volunteer students to wear on their back; make sure that students do not see the name assigned to them. After discussing the history of psychology, have the volunteers stand in front of the class and instruct them to try to guess the name of the psychologist on their back by asking only yes/no questions of classmates. After hearing the answers, volunteers must guess their psychologist's name.

While Freud believed that all behavior stems from unconscious motivation, Watson believed that all behavior is learned. Freud had stated that a *phobia*, an irrational fear, is really a symptom of an underlying, repressed conflict and cannot be "cured" without years of psychoanalysis to uncover and understand the repressed material. Watson, however, believed that phobias are learned through the process of conditioning. Watson wanted to prove that all behavior was a result of a stimulus–response relationship such as that described by Pavlov.

In what has come to be known as the "Little Albert" experiment, Watson exposed a 9-month-old boy, "Little Albert," to a variety of stimuli, such as a white rat, a rabbit, a monkey, masks, and burning newspapers. Initially, the child showed no fear of any of the stimuli. Watson again exposed the child to the objects, striking a metal pipe with a hammer when the rat was shown. The loud noise startled Albert, causing him to cry. After repeated pairings of the loud noise with the sight of the white rat, Albert became conditioned to fear the sight of the rat, crying even when there was no loud noise. This experiment was significant in that it seemed to prove that humans could be conditioned to have phobias as a result of a stimulus–response relationship. Watch on **mypsychlab.com**

Watch classic video footage of John Watson and Little Albert on **mypsychlab.com**

Classic Studies In Psychology

Psychologist Mary Cover Jones and "Little Peter"

Mary Cover Jones was one of John Watson's students. During the 1920s, she wanted to explore the concept of learned phobias, so, based on the "Little Albert" experiment, she used a white rabbit to create a phobic reaction in a child named "Little Peter" (Jones, 1924). Once the child was conditioned to fear the rabbit, Jones began a process called *counterconditioning*, in which the old conditioning (fear of the rabbit) would be replaced, or countered, by new conditioning. Peter was brought into one corner of a room, while the rabbit was placed in the opposite corner. Peter was then given some food (something he liked quite a bit). Although Peter may have been nervous, he began to eat and experienced the pleasurable sensations associated with eating. This pattern was repeated over several sessions, with the rabbit being brought a little closer each time. Eventually, Peter was no longer showing any fear of the rabbit at all. He had come to associate the pleasurable feeling of eating with the experience of being near the rabbit.

Questions for Further Discussion

1. In the early 1900s, women did not have many opportunities to pursue careers as researchers, especially compared to men. What might the field of psychology look like today if Mary Cover Jones had not overcome the obstacles she faced from society? In what ways did Mary Cover Jones's research help redefine the field of psychology?
2. What concerns, if any, might a parent have with the "Little Albert" experiment? Would the same concerns apply to the "Little Peter" experiment? Why or why not?

▲ Mary Cover Jones, one of the early pioneers of behavior therapy, earned her master's degree under the supervision of John B. Watson. She had a long and distinguished career, including the publication in 1952 of the first educational television course in child development.

THE SCIENCE OF PSYCHOLOGY 9

CHAPTER 1 • Module 1

DEBATE

Briefly review the "Little Albert" experiment with the class. Then divide students into two teams and have them debate whether they think the experiment was ethical. Ask them to consider whether they would have been willing to conduct this experiment. Would they have allowed their own child to participate? Did the outcome of the experiment negate any negative aspects of the procedure?

MULTIMEDIA CONTENT AVAILABLE AT
www.mypsychlab.com

Watch Classic video footage of John Watson and Little Albert on **mypsychlab.com**

CLASSIC STUDIES IN PSYCHOLOGY

1. By overcoming obstacles against women in psychology, Jones was able to make valuable contributions to psychology. Her experiments in counterconditioning showed that "old" conditioning could be replaced by "new" conditioning. This indicated that people could be helped to learn new ways of reacting.
2. In the "Little Albert" experiment, a child was traumatized, a situation against which any parent would protest. In the "Little Peter" experiment, the child was counterconditioned, so that the traumatic reaction was replaced by a positive one.

Critical Thinking

WRITING ABOUT PSYCHOLOGY

Purpose: Students complete a brief 1-minute writing assignment that involves critical thinking, personalizing, or deeper processing of information.

Time: 1–5 minutes

Description: Students are given several minutes to answer, in writing, a question posed by the teacher. This assignment can be used to verify attendance, to start discussion, to assess student knowledge, and to provide opportunities for critical thinking. Ask students if they have ever read a self-help book or listened to a radio show or watched a talk show with a guest psychologist. What did they think of the psychologist's advice?

Module 1 Psychology's Domain 9

CHAPTER 1 • Module 1

COVER THE MODULE

1.3 What are the major modern psychological perspectives?

- *Psychodynamic Perspective*
  - Freud's theory is still in use today but reflects less emphasis on repressed desires.
  - Even those who use his techniques modify them for modern use.
- *Behavioral Perspective*
  - B.F. Skinner's operant conditioning of voluntary behavior became a major force in the 20th century. He introduced the concept of reinforcement to behaviorism.

  LINK to *Chapter Six: Learning and Language Development, pp. 185–186*

- *Humanistic Perspective*
  - Humanism, which focuses on free will and the human potential for growth, was developed by Abraham Maslow and Carl Rogers, among others, and emphasized achieving one's ideal self.
- *Cognitive Perspective*
  - Cognitive psychology is the study of learning, memory, language, and problem solving.

  LINK to *Chapter Ten: Cognitive Thinking and Intelligence, pp. 321–327*

  - The field of *cognitive neuroscience* includes the study of the brain and nervous system when engaged in cognitive processes.

  LINK to *Chapter Two: The Biological Perspective, p. 55*

10 Chapter 1 The Science of Psychology

▲ These brain scans show the increasing malfunction of the brains of people with a mental disorder called schizophrenia, highlighting one focus of the biological perspective.

psychodynamic perspective a modern version of psychoanalysis that is more focused on the development of a sense of self and the discovery of other motivations behind a person's behavior than repressed desires.

cognitive perspective modern perspective that focuses on memory, intelligence, perception, problem solving, and learning.

cognitive neuroscience study of the physical changes in the brain and nervous system during thinking.

1.3 What are the major modern psychological perspectives?

Even today, there isn't one single perspective that is used to explain all human behavior and mental processes. There are actually six major modern perspectives, with two of those being holdovers from the early days of the field. Today's psychologists recognize that each perspective helps us understand a different aspect of human behavior and mental processing, and no single perspective answers all the questions. These differing, occasionally overlapping perspectives guide research and help move psychology forward.

Psychodynamic Perspective Freud's theory is still in use today by many professionals in therapy situations. It is far less common today than it was a few decades ago, however, and even those who use his techniques modify them for modern use. In the more modern **psychodynamic perspective**, the focus is still on the unconscious mind and its influence over conscious behavior and on early childhood experiences, but with less of an emphasis on repressed desires and more emphasis on the development of a sense of self and the discovery of other motivations behind a person's behavior.

Behavioral Perspective Like psychoanalysis, behaviorism is still also very influential. When its primary supporter, John B. Watson, moved on to a career in advertising, B. F. Skinner became the new leader of the field. Skinner not only continued research in classical conditioning but also developed a theory of how voluntary behavior is learned called *operant conditioning* (Skinner, 1938). In this theory, behavioral responses (or "operants") that are followed by pleasurable consequences are strengthened, or *reinforced*. For example, a preschooler who cries and is rewarded by getting his mother's attention will cry again in the future. **LINK** to *Chapter Six: Learning and Language Development, pp. 185–186.*

Humanistic Perspective The humanistic perspective, often known as the "third force" in psychology, owes far more to the early roots of psychology in the field of philosophy than it does to the more scientific fields of medicine and physiology. Two of the earliest and most famous founders of humanistic psychology were Abraham Maslow (1908–1970) and Carl Rogers (1902–1987). Both Maslow and Rogers emphasized the human potential, the ability of each person to become the best person he or she could be (Maslow, 1968; Rogers, 1961). They believed that studying animals in laboratories (as the behaviorists did) or people with nervous disorders (as the psychoanalysts did) could not lead to a better understanding of this human potential for *self-actualization*, as Maslow termed it—achieving one's full potential or ideal self.

Cognitive Perspective Cognitive psychology, the study of how the mind processes information, focuses on how people think: how they remember, store, and use information. It became a major force in the field in the 1960s. Its focus on memory, intelligence, perception, thought processes, problem solving, language, and learning has become a major force in psychology. **LINK** to *Chapter Ten: Cognition: Thinking and Intelligence, pp. 321–327.*

Within the **cognitive perspective**, the relatively new field of **cognitive neuroscience** includes the study of the physical workings of the brain and nervous system when engaged in memory, thinking, and other cognitive

10 CHAPTER I

Class Demonstration

PSYCHOLOGICAL PERSPECTIVES

<u>Purpose</u>: Students apply what they have learned about psychological perspectives.

<u>Time</u>: Approximately 15 minutes

<u>Description</u>: Students will practice analyzing the behavior of a fictional character, using the major psychological perspectives. Read the following description to the class:

"Joe is a high school student. He has been absent from school a lot lately. There is some concern that he may drop out." Each team of four students is assigned to a different psychological perspective; use a folded piece of paper handed to each team. Give teams a few minutes to think about "Joe" and generate an explanation for his behavior, given their assigned perspective. Each team then shares its explanation with the rest of the class, which then tries to guess which psychological perspective was used.

processes. Cognitive neuroscientists use tools for imaging the structure and activity of the living brain, and the emerging field of brain imaging is important to the study of cognitive processes. LINK to Chapter Two: The Biological Perspective, p. 55.

Sociocultural Perspective The **sociocultural perspective** actually combines two areas of study: *social psychology*, which is the scientific study of how a person's thoughts, feelings, and behavior are influenced by the real, imagined, or implied presence of others; and *cultural psychology*, which is the study of cultural behaviors, values, and expectations. These two areas are both about the effect that people have on one another, either individually or in a larger group, such as a culture (Peplau & Taylor, 1997).

The sociocultural perspective reminds people that how they and others behave (or even think) is influenced not only by whether they are alone, with friends, in a crowd, or part of a group, but also by the social norms, fads, class differences, and ethnic-identity concerns of the particular culture in which they live.

Biopsychological Perspective *Biopsychology*, or the study of the biological bases of behavior and mental processes, is not really as new a perspective as one might think. In the **biopsychological perspective**, human and animal behavior is seen as a direct result of events in the body. Hormones, heredity, brain chemicals (called neurotransmitters), tumors, and diseases are some of the biological causes of behavior and mental events. LINK to Chapter Two: The Biological Perspective, pp. 40–64.

1.4 How is the field of psychology continuing to grow and change?

As you can probably tell, psychology has changed over time, and it will continue to change in the future as new technologies are developed, new theories are adopted, and new discoveries are made. Lately, psychologists have performed significant research in several new or developing areas of psychology, including evolutionary psychology and positive psychology.

Evolutionary psychology examines potential links between human behavior and Charles Darwin's theory of evolution. The evolutionary perspective focuses on the biological bases for universal mental characteristics that all humans share. It seeks to explain general mental strategies and traits, such as why we lie, how attractiveness influences mate selection, why fear of snakes is so universal, and why people like music and dancing, among many others. In this perspective, the mind is seen as a set of information-processing machines, designed by the same process of natural selection that Darwin (1859) first theorized. For example, evolutionary psychologists would view the human behavior of not eating substances that have a bitter taste (such as poisonous plants) as an adaptive behavior that evolved as early humans came into contact with such bitter plants. Those who ate the bitter plants would die, while those who spit them out survived to pass their "I don't like this taste" genes on to their offspring. Therefore, detecting bitter tastes became an "adaptive trait" that promoted survival.

Psychologist Martin Seligman is widely recognized as one of the founders of **positive psychology**, a perspective that recommends shifting the focus of

▲ *Psychologists with an evolutionary perspective would be interested in how this couple selected each other as partners.*

sociocultural perspective perspective that focuses on the relationship between social behavior and culture.

biopsychological perspective perspective that attributes human and animal behavior to biological events occurring in the body, such as genetic influences, hormones, and the activity of the nervous system.

evolutionary psychology perspective that focuses on the biological bases of universal mental characteristics that all humans share.

positive psychology a viewpoint that recommends shifting the focus of psychology away from the negative aspects to a more positive focus on strengths, well-being, and the pursuit of happiness.

THE SCIENCE OF PSYCHOLOGY 11

CHAPTER 1 • Module 1

COVER THE MODULE *(continued)*

- *Sociocultural Perspective*
  - The sociocultural perspective combines social psychology and cultural psychology.
- *Biopsychological Perspective*
  - Biopsychology emerged as the study of the biological bases of behavior. Hormones, brain chemistry, brain structure, and diseases are the focus of this perspective.

EXTEND THE LESSON

Discuss how difficult it is to analyze behavior from only one perspective. Point out that there is no "right" perspective. Each perspective explains behavior in a different way. Discuss how the most complete explanation of a behavior involves gathering information from each perspective.

COVER THE MODULE

1.4 How is the field of psychology continuing to grow and change?

- Psychology will continue to change as new technologies are developed, new theories are adopted, and new discoveries are made.
- *Evolutionary psychology* examines potential links between human behavior and Charles Darwin's theory of evolution.
- *Positive psychology* recommends shifting the focus of psychology from the negative to strengths, well-being, and happiness.

Explore

PSYCHOLOGY IN DIFFERENT CULTURES

It is important to remember that all cultures have implicit or explicit psychological theories of how the mind works that have been developing for thousands of years. Psychology as a scientific discipline is common in industrial and "modernizing" countries, while in poorer nations, psychology has still to be licensed and regulated. Ask students to select different countries and to conduct library or Internet research on what the field of psychology is like in their chosen country. Have them report their findings back to the class. Some questions for students to focus on include the following: (1) Are psychologists licensed in the country? Is psychology considered a scientific discipline in that country? (2) Are there any particular issues in psychology relative to that country's culture?

Module 1 Psychology's Domain 11

CHAPTER 1 • Module 1

COVER THE MODULE

1.5 Why do psychologists perform research?

- Research allows psychologists to collect data from the real world to test their theories.
- Research results can be applied to everyday problems.

COVER THE MODULE

1.6 What are the major subfields of psychology?

- *Clinical psychologists* diagnose and treat psychological disorders in people.
- *Counseling psychologists* work with people who have less severe problems, such as work or family problems.

LINK to Chapter Sixteen: Careers in Psychology, pp. 517–518

DISCUSS THE STUDENT VOICE QUESTION

After you have covered the information on the major subfields of psychology, ask students if they think any of these areas might be interesting as a career field. If so, how do they think they could be helpful to others by studying that subfield?

---

clinical psychology area of psychology in which the psychologists diagnose and treat people with psychological disorders that may range from mild to severe.

counseling psychology area of psychology in which the psychologists help people with problems of adjustment.

psychology away from the negative (abuse, anxiety, depression, all the things that can go wrong) to a more positive focus on strengths, well-being, and the pursuit of happiness (Myers, 1993). According to social psychologist David G. Myers, a leader in the field of happiness research, happiness is the key to many things: the perception of the world as a safer place, healthier living, and even the ability to make decisions more easily. Happy people are also more likely to help others (Pizarro & Salovey, 2002; Salovey et al., 2000). Positive psychologists' research findings may help more people learn how to live happy and satisfying lives.

Identify Psychology's Subfields

1.5 Why do psychologists perform research?

Many practicing psychologists spend their time conducting research on both human and animal subjects. But why is research so important to psychology?

We have already discussed how psychologists come up with theories to explain human behaviors. Theories are strongest when they are supported with scientific evidence—with facts and data from the real world. That's where research comes in: Research allows psychologists to collect facts and data that (hopefully) support their theories. When a psychologist wants to determine whether her theory is accurate, she will put it to the test by performing an experiment or another type of research study. Sometimes, research results may even lead to new theories. And research results can be applied to everyday problems, too. For example, research into the causes of psychological disorders like depression and anxiety can lead to the development of new therapies that help people with those disorders live healthier lives.

1.6 What are the major subfields of psychology?

> *What types of career opportunities are available for someone who wants to work in the field of psychology?*

Although many psychologists work as counselors, delivering therapy to people who need help, a nearly equal number of psychologists do other tasks: researching, teaching, designing equipment and workplaces, and developing educational methods, for example. (See Figure 1.2a.) Most psychologists work in several different areas of interest, as shown in Figure 1.2b.

Not all psychologists do counseling or therapy. Specialists who work in **clinical psychology** diagnose and treat psychological disorders in people. The clinical psychologist cannot prescribe drugs or medical therapies but instead listens to the client's problems, administers psychological tests, and provides possible explanations and advice. There is a difference between psychologists and psychiatrists: Psychiatrists are medical doctors and can prescribe medication, while most psychologists do not have the medical training or authority to prescribe medication. LINK *to Chapter Sixteen: Careers in Psychology, pp. 517–518.*

Counseling psychology is similar to clinical psychology in that this type of psychologist diagnoses and treats problems. The difference is that a

---

Class Demonstration

PSYCHOLOGISTS ARE SCIENTISTS

Make the point that all psychologists, regardless of their area of expertise, are indeed scientists. First, write the word "psychologist" on the board and ask students to describe some traits of the typical psychologist. Students may answer: caring, patient, warm, soothing, good listener, giving advice, and so forth. After erasing these responses, write the word "scientist" on the board and ask students to do the same for the typical scientist. Their responses likely will indicate that traits of "scientists" (such as analytical, brilliant, and conducting research) are very different from their perceptions of "psychologists." Some students may catch on and ask, "But aren't psychologists scientists?" Lead the class into a discussion of why their perceptions are so divergent.

FIGURE 1.2 Work Settings and Subfields of Psychology
(a) There are many different work settings for psychologists. Although not obvious from the chart, many psychologists work in more than one setting. For example, a clinical psychologist may work in a hospital setting as well as teach at a university or college (J. Tsapogas et al., 2006). (b) This pie chart shows the specialty areas of psychologists who recently received their doctorates (T. B. Hoffer et al., 2007). Note: Due to rounding, percentages may not total to 100 percent.

counseling psychologist usually works with people who have less severe problems, such as adjustment to stress, marriage, family life, work problems, and so on.

Developmental psychology focuses on the study of change, or development. Developmental psychologists are interested in changes in the way people think, in how people relate to others, and in the ways people feel over the entire span of life. These psychologists may do research in various areas of development. LINK *to Chapter Five: Development Across the Life Span, p. 143.*

Experimental psychology encompasses areas such as learning, memory, thinking, perception, motivation, and language. The focus of these psychologists is on doing research and conducting studies and experiments with both people and animals in these various areas.

Social psychology focuses on how human behavior is affected by the presence of other people. Social psychologists perform research in areas such as prejudice, attitude change, aggressive behavior, and interpersonal attraction. LINK *to Chapter Seven: Social Psychology, pp. 212–241.*

Personality psychology focuses on the differences in personality among people. These psychologists study the ways in which people are both alike and different. They look at the development of personality and do personality assessment. They may form new theories of how personality works or develops. LINK *to Chapter Twelve: Theories of Personality, pp. 383–387.*

Physiological psychology focuses on the study of the biological bases of behavior. Physiological psychologists study the brain, the nervous system, and the influence of the body's chemicals on human behavior. They study

developmental psychology area of psychology in which the psychologists study the changes in the way people think, relate to others, and feel as they age.

experimental psychology area of psychology in which the psychologists primarily do research and experiments in the areas of learning, memory, thinking, perception, motivation, and language.

social psychology area of psychology in which the psychologists focus on how human behavior is affected by the presence of other people.

personality psychology area of psychology in which the psychologists study the differences in personality among people.

physiological psychology area of psychology in which the psychologists study the biological bases of behavior.

THE SCIENCE OF PSYCHOLOGY

Explore

CAREERS IN PSYCHOLOGY

Have someone from a career counseling center give a talk on opportunities for psychology majors (he or she may also have data on the current employment status of recent psychology graduates). Better yet, invite to class (1) a psychologist from an applied setting (e.g., a clinician in private practice, an industrial/organizational psychologist, a sports or forensic psychologist) or (2) a psychologist who works in an academic setting to talk about career opportunities and experiences. Consider having students supply a list of questions or topics (prescreened by you) for the visitor.

CHAPTER 1 • Module 1

COVER THE MODULE (continued)

- *Developmental psychologists* focus on the study of change.
- *Experimental psychologists* conduct research with people and animals in the areas of learning, memory, thinking, perception, motivation, and language.
- *Social psychologists* study how human behavior is affected by the presence of other people.
- *Personality psychologists* study the ways in which people are both alike and different.
- *Physiological psychologists* study the brain, the nervous system, and the influence of the body's chemicals on human behavior.

LINK *to Chapter Five: Development Across the Life Span, p. 143; Chapter Seven: Social Psychology, pp. 212–241; Chapter Twelve: Theories of Personality, pp. 383–387; Chapter Two: The Biological Perspective, p. 51*

L2 ELL DIFFERENTIATED INSTRUCTION

English Language Learners Use visuals, such as Figure 1.2, to make concepts less abstract. Ask one or more volunteers to read aloud the information in these charts to the rest of the class.

FAST FACT

According to the U.S. Bureau of Labor Statistics, demand for clinical psychologists is expected to increase because of the rising healthcare costs associated with unhealthy lifestyles such as smoking, alcoholism, and obesity, which have made prevention and treatment more important.

TEACHING TIP

Outlining key ideas and writing key phrases and vocabulary on the board, an overhead projector, or in PowerPoint slides are critical supports for many students.

Module 1 Psychology's Domain

CHAPTER 1 • Module 1

COVER THE MODULE (continued)
- *Comparative psychologists* focus on the study of animals and animal behavior.
- *Industrial/organizational (I/O) psychologists* study relationships between people and their work environments.

MULTIMEDIA CONTENT AVAILABLE AT
www.mypsychlab.com

👁 Watch a video on the subfields of psychology on **mypsychlab.com**

COVER THE MODULE
1.7 How does psychology benefit society?
- All psychologists' mission is to help people.
- Researchers conduct experiments on nonhumans, which can improve the lives of humans.

EXTEND THE LESSON
Have students investigate the role of psychology in addressing social problems. Divide the class into teams of four. Assign each team to a category of social problems, such as workplace changes; new genetic knowledge; and deteriorating social or economic conditions.

Give each team a newspaper, or have them access a newspaper via the Internet. Have students look for specific articles or examples of their subtopic and then report back to their group. How many articles did they find? Students may be surprised at how many articles would be of interest to psychologists. Do any of the articles present experimental information? This can show how psychology can be used to address personal and societal problems. How do students think that current events influence what psychologists choose to study?

---

comparative psychology area of psychology in which the psychologists study animals and their behavior for the purpose of comparing and contrasting it to human behavior.

industrial/organizational (I/O) psychology area of psychology concerned with the relationships between people and their work environment.

👁 Watch a video on the subfields of psychology on **mypsychlab.com**

the effects of drug use and the genetic influences that may exist on some kinds of abnormal and normal human behavior. LINK to Chapter Two: *The Biological Perspective, p. 51.*

Comparative psychology focuses exclusively on animals and animal behavior. By comparing and contrasting animal behavior with what is already known about human behavior, comparative psychologists contribute to the understanding of human behavior.

Industrial/organizational (I/O) psychology is concerned with the relationships between people and their work environments. I/O psychologists perform such tasks as helping workers improve their efficiency, designing work areas that spark productivity, and creating materials that assess how well employees are performing in the workplace. 👁 Watch on **mypsychlab.com**

1.7 How does psychology benefit society?

Psychologists can work in a number of different subfields and have dozens of different specialties, but all psychologists have one important mission in common: to help others. Through research, counseling, treatment, and teaching, psychologists aim to understand how the human mind works and use that understanding to improve people's lives. Research into tough social issues such as racial prejudice and violence can lead to strategies for minimizing these issues in real communities. Research in the field of human factors psychology, which focuses on interactions between humans and machines, can lead to engineering improvements such as designing airline cockpits that help pilots perform their jobs more accurately and efficiently. Psychologists' increasing understanding of developmental issues during childhood can strengthen school curriculums and guide parents' approaches to raising their children. And well-trained counselors and therapists can help people work through difficult personal issues and overcome the challenges of psychological disorders. These are only a few of the many ways in which psychology can improve the daily lives of people around the world.

Researchers conduct experiments to observe humans and nonhuman subjects. Findings on nonhuman subjects can be applied to human study in some cases. Findings are also beneficial to animal study. For example, research can lead to the development of medications and other treatments that can prolong animals' lives. Furthermore, research on nonhuman subjects can also help improve our lives because of the topics that can be studied with animals that would not be ethical to study with human participants.

Explore

FIND A PSYCHOLOGIST ON THE INTERNET

<u>Purpose</u>: Students learn about the profession of psychology.

<u>Time</u>: 20 minutes

<u>Description</u>: Have students search the Internet for the homepage of a psychologist. College and university psychology departments, clinics, hospitals, and research institutes are possibilities. Then have them answer the following questions: (1) Who did you find? (2) What kind of job does this psychologist have (e.g., teacher, researcher, therapist)? (3) In what type of setting does this psychologist work? (4) What additional information do you have about this person? Can you tell what theoretical perspective he or she might have? Training? Area of expertise? Research interests? Have students share their information using a bulletin board, PowerPoint slides, or a printed booklet.

Practice Quiz

Pick the best answer.

1. In the definition of psychology, *behavior* means
   a. mental processes
   b. internal physical functions
   c. outward actions and reactions
   d. abilities that make humans unique from other animals

2. Experimental psychologists, who design experiments to determine the causes of behavior, would be most interested in the goal of
   a. description
   b. explanation
   c. prediction
   d. control

3. Which of the following early psychologists would have been most likely to agree with the statement "The study of the mind should focus on how it allows us to adapt to our surroundings"?
   a. Wilhelm Wundt
   b. William James
   c. John B. Watson
   d. Sigmund Freud

4. In the experiment with "Little Peter," what did Mary Cover Jones use as a stimulus to decrease Little Peter's fear of the rabbit?
   a. a white rat
   b. food
   c. a loud noise
   d. relaxation

5. Which of the following pairs represents the two psychology perspectives that were also part of the historical beginnings of psychology?
   a. humanism and behaviorism
   b. humanism and cognitive psychology
   c. psychodynamics and behaviorism
   d. psychodynamics and cognitive psychology

6. Which perspective studies the storage and retrieval of information in the human brain?
   a. psychoanalysis
   b. behaviorism
   c. cognitive psychology
   d. evolutionary psychology

7. Which researcher studied biases in the testing of Mexican American and Navajo students?
   a. Francis Cecil Sumner
   b. David Matsumoto
   c. John Garcia
   d. George I. Sánchez

8. Specialists who diagnose and treat psychological disorders most likely work in the subfield of
   a. clinical psychology
   b. experimental psychology
   c. social psychology
   d. physiological psychology

9. Which subfield of psychology focuses exclusively on animals and animal behavior?
   a. comparative psychology
   b. counseling psychology
   c. experimental psychology
   d. developmental psychology

10. Which of the following is a relatively new, developing area of study in psychology?
    a. functionalism
    b. psychoanalysis
    c. positive psychology
    d. behaviorism

THE SCIENCE OF PSYCHOLOGY 15

CHAPTER 1 • Module 1

Assess

Assign the Module 1 Practice Quiz.
Use the Practice Quiz to identify gaps in student understanding.

REMEDIATE

Have students, individually or in groups, review the module goals, learning objectives, and key terms.
Refer students to the Concept Summary on p. 38 for review.

Close

As a class, discuss how students think that psychology can benefit modern society. How do psychologists render an important service to people?

Practice Quiz Answers

1. c
2. b
3. b
4. b
5. a
6. c
7. d
8. a
9. a
10. c

Module 1 Psychology's Domain 15

CHAPTER 1 • Module 2

Focus

RESOURCES

For this module, consult the appropriate sections of the Teacher's Manual, Test Bank, and PowerPoint slides, all found on the Teacher's Resource DVD, and the interactive study tools for students on MyPsychLab.

BEFORE CLASS

Students should read the section for homework before coming to class.

BELLRINGER

Ask students if they have ever tried to guess a person's occupation based solely on the person's appearance. For example: People wearing suits are executives. Men with long hair are musicians. Point out that such guesses are often incorrect. In contrast, psychology is about trying to determine facts and reduce uncertainty.

Teach

COVER THE MODULE

2.1 What is the scientific method?

- The *scientific method* is a way to determine facts and control the possibilities of error and bias when observing behavior.
- The five steps in the scientific method are formulating the question, developing a hypothesis, testing the hypothesis, drawing conclusions, and reporting the results.

FAST FACT

Ask students if they can provide a synonym for *hypothesis*. (A synonym for hypothesis *is* proposition. The word hypothesis *is from the Greek* hypo *["under"]* + thesis *["placing"].)*

Module 2: Research Methods and Ethics

Module Goals	Learning Objectives
Understand psychological research methods.	2.1 What is the scientific method?
	2.2 What methods do researchers use to study behavior?
	2.3 How do researchers ensure their findings are valid?
	2.4 Why do some researchers study animals instead of people?
Consider ethical issues in psychological research.	2.5 What ethical guidelines do psychologists follow when they research humans?
	2.6 Are there different ethical guidelines for research with animals?

Understand Psychological Research Methods

2.1 What is the scientific method?

While there are many fields and approaches to psychology, they all use the same basic tools of science: the scientific method. In psychology, researchers want to see only what is really there, not what their personal opinions, or biases, might want them to see. So they use the **scientific method**, a system for reducing bias and maintaining objectivity in the measurement of data.

The first step in any investigation is to have a question to investigate, right? So the first step in the scientific method is this:

1. **Formulating the Question:** You notice something interesting happening in your surroundings for which you would like an explanation. For example, a teacher may observe that students are more hyperactive on Thursdays, the day the cafeteria offers caffeinated drinks at lunchtime. You wonder if the caffeine in the drinks could be creating the hyperactive behavior in the students.

2. **Developing a Hypothesis:** Based on your initial observations about what is going on in the classroom, you form an educated guess about the explanation for your observations, putting it into the form of a statement that can be tested in some way. This statement is called a **hypothesis**. For example, you might say, "Students who drink caffeinated beverages will become more hyperactive."

3. **Testing the Hypothesis:** The method you use to test your hypothesis will depend on what kind of answer you think you might get. You might make more detailed observations or do a survey in which you ask questions of a large number of people, or you might design an experiment in which you deliberately change one thing to see if that one adjustment causes changes in the behavior you are observing. In the example, the best method would probably be an experiment because only

scientific method system of gathering data so that bias and error in measurement are reduced.

hypothesis tentative explanation of a phenomenon based on observations.

Terms

- scientific method • hypothesis • naturalistic observation • observer effect • observer bias • laboratory method • case study • survey method • representative sample • population • correlation • correlation coefficient • experiment • operational definition • informed consent • independent variable • dependent variable • confounding variable • experimental group • control group • random assignment • placebo effect • experimenter effect • double-blind experiment the experimental method determines cause and effect; no other research method can control variables so well to be able to do this. You could design an experiment in which you randomly select a group of students, and then randomly assign them to two groups. Give the experimental group 20 milligrams of caffeine (about the equivalent of a cup of weak tea) in a noncaffeinated, sugar-free beverage, and give the control group the beverage without caffeine in it. Then measure the hyperactivity observed in both groups over the same period of time.

4. **Drawing Conclusions:** After your measurements are made, you must organize the raw data, describe it through statistical methods, and draw conclusions from your results. Using descriptive and inferential statistical techniques, you will analyze the data you have collected and determine whether you've discovered a cause-and-effect relationship. (Module 3 of this textbook explains these statistical methods in more detail.) Once you have measured results from both groups, you will find that either your hypothesis was supported—which means that your little experiment worked, or your measurements supported your initial observations—or it was not supported, which means that you need to go back to the beginning and think of another possible explanation for what you have observed. (Could it be that something else in the drinks—perhaps sugar—made students more hyperactive? Could it be a change in the classroom environment on Thursdays after lunch?)

5. **Report Your Results:** The final step is to write up exactly what you did, why you did it, how you did it, and what you found, so that others can learn from what you have already accomplished—or failed to accomplish. Even if your research gave you the answer you expected, your investigation might have been done incorrectly, or the results might have been a fluke or due to chance alone. If others can perform the same study over again and get the same results you got (a process called replication), it gives much more support to your findings.

2.2 What methods do researchers use to study behavior?

Nonexperimental Methods Sometimes, researchers want to describe what is happening to a group of animals or people. The best way to look at the behavior of animals or people is to watch them behave in their normal environment. To study people, researchers might want to observe them in their workplaces, their homes, or on playgrounds. This strategy is called **naturalistic observation**.

Naturalistic observation allows researchers to get a realistic picture of how behavior occurs because they are actually watching that behavior. For example, if a researcher wanted to know how adolescents behave with members of the opposite sex in a social setting, she might go to the mall on a weekend night.

Of course, researchers must take precautions. In many cases, animals or people who know they are being watched will not behave normally, in a process called the **observer effect**, so often the observer needs to remain hidden from view, or *unobtrusive*.

One of the disadvantages of naturalistic observation is the possibility of **observer bias**. That happens when the person doing the observing has a particular opinion or expectation about what he or she is going to see. If that

naturalistic observation the study of people or animals in their natural environment.

observer effect tendency of people or animals to behave differently from normal when they know they are being observed.

observer bias tendency of observers to see what they expect to see.

▲ *Researcher Jane Goodall watches chimpanzees behave in their natural environment. How might her presence have affected the behavior of the chimpanzees?*

THE SCIENCE OF PSYCHOLOGY 17

CHAPTER 1 • Module 2

CHECK FOR UNDERSTANDING

This is a good place to make a distinction between questions that can be scientifically studied and those that cannot. Ask: **Can the question "What is the meaning of life?" be studied using the scientific method? Why or why not?** (Answer: No; the meaning of life is a question of belief for each person. It cannot be studied by objectively gathering evidence.) **Can the question "Does life exist on Mars?" be studied using the scientific method? Why or why not?** (Answer: Yes; scientists can try to answer this question through measurements, experimentation, and other methods.)

COVER THE MODULE

2.2 What methods do researchers use to study behavior?

- **Nonexperimental Methods**
  - *Naturalistic observations* involve watching animals or people in their natural environments but have the disadvantage of lack of control.
    - One of the control problems is related to the *observer effect*, which refers to the fact that people may behave differently when they know they are being watched.
    - The *observer bias* is related to the reality that observers often "see what they expect to see."
    - Each naturalistic setting is unique, so observations may not hold true for other times or places.

UNDERSTANDING VISUALS

Direct students' attention to the question in the photo caption. It is possible that Jane Goodall's presence could have created fear or tension in the chimpanzees, causing them to behave in a way that was not "natural" for them.

Cultural Connections

MINORITIES AND MENTAL HEALTH

Are minorities in America less likely than whites to receive good mental health care? Divide students into small groups and have them use library or Internet resources to research one of these groups: African Americans, American Indians and Alaskan Natives, Asian Americans and Pacific Islanders, or Hispanic Americans. The resources page on the www.mypsychlab.com website can be used. Students should learn about problems in receiving mental health care for their minority group and prepare a short presentation using software or audiovisual resources, a bulletin board display, or a written report.

Module 2 Research Methods and Ethics

CHAPTER 1 • Module 2

COVER THE MODULE (continued)
- **Nonexperimental Methods** (continued)
  - *Laboratory observations* involve watching animals or people in an artificial but controlled situation, such as a laboratory. A disadvantage of this method is that subjects may not behave the same way as they would in a natural environment.
  - *Case studies* are detailed investigations of one individual or one group over a period of time. One concern is that researchers cannot apply the results to other similar people. Also, the person conducting the study may be biased.
  - *Surveys* involve asking standardized questions of large groups of people who represent a sample of the population of interest. Concerns include response bias and accuracy of responses.

EXTEND THE DISCUSSION
Ask students if they have ever completed a survey. Where and how was the survey conducted? What are some advantages and disadvantages of the survey method?

L4 DIFFERENTIATED INSTRUCTION
Advanced Learners Challenge students to tackle more complex topics, and offer frequent opportunities to focus on abstract ideas.

TEACHING TIP
When evaluating student understanding, do not assume that "one size fits all." The style, depth, and complexity of what students produce vary to match student ability levels and learning styles.

---

is the case, sometimes that person sees only those actions that support that expectation and ignores actions that do not fit.

Another disadvantage is that each naturalistic setting is unique and unlike any other. Observations that are made at one time in one setting may not hold true for another time, even if the setting is similar, because the conditions are not going to be exactly the same time after time—researchers don't have that kind of control over the natural world. For example, think about the researcher who decides to observe teenagers at the mall. If she made her observations on the day before winter vacation, she would probably see very different behaviors than she would if she made her observations on the day before midterm exams.

Sometimes, observing behavior in animals or people is just not practical in a natural setting. In this case, perhaps the **laboratory method** would be best. In a laboratory, variables in the environment, such as light level or presence of others, can be kept under control, so sometimes it makes more sense to observe subjects in a laboratory setting, even though that setting does not represent the "real world." Of course, a disadvantage to the laboratory method is that subjects may not behave the same as they would in a natural environment.

Another descriptive technique is called the **case study**, in which one individual, or one individual group, such as a family, is studied in great detail, usually over a long period of time. In a case study, researchers try to learn everything they can about that individual. The advantage of the case study is the tremendous amount of detail it provides. It may also be the only way to get certain kinds of information. For example, one famous case study is the story of Phineas Gage, who had a large metal rod driven through his head during a mining accident and suffered a major personality change as a result (Damasio et al., 1994). Psychologists learned a lot about the nature of the brain, and the effects of brain damage, by studying Gage's case. Researchers couldn't study that with naturalistic observation, and an experiment was out of the question. Imagine anyone responding to an ad in the newspaper that read:

> Wanted: 50 people to suffer nonfatal brain damage for scientific study of the brain. Will pay all medical expenses.

The disadvantage of the case study is that researchers cannot apply the results to other similar people. What researchers find in one case will not necessarily apply or generalize to others. Another weakness of this method is that case studies are a form of detailed observation and are vulnerable to bias on the part of the person conducting the case study, just as observer bias can occur in naturalistic or laboratory observation.

Sometimes what psychologists want to know about is pretty personal and potentially embarrassing to research subjects. The only way to find out about very private behavior is to ask questions. In the **survey method**, researchers ask a series of questions about the topic they are studying. Surveys can be conducted in person, on the telephone, on the Internet, or with a questionnaire. In this way, researchers can ask a lot of questions and survey literally hundreds of people.

Of course, there are disadvantages to surveys. People do not always tell the truth on surveys, for example. And researchers have to be very careful about the group of people they survey. If they want to find out what high school students think about politics, they can't really ask every single high school

▲ On the left in this photograph is a model of Phineas Gage's head; on the right is Gage's actual skull. Damage at the top of the skull indicates the location at which a steel rod was driven through the skull.

laboratory method method of conducting research in a controlled environment.

case study study of one individual in great detail.

survey method method of conducting research in the form of interviews.

18 CHAPTER 1

Explore

OBSERVATIONAL RESEARCH
Introduce students to research methods by helping them become more aware of their everyday surroundings. The local mall or other public spot can be a "laboratory" to observe human behavior. Ask students to observe others in a particular setting and to record their observations. In class, have students share their findings and generate discussion about potential hypotheses that may provide a better understanding of the behaviors they observed.

18 Chapter 1 The Science of Psychology

student in the United States. But they can select a **representative sample** from that group. They could randomly select a certain number of students from several different high schools across the United States, for example. One method of gathering a random sample could be to make a list of the names of all of the students in a high school, and then draw names, like a lottery. Why randomly select? Because the sample has to be *representative* of the **population**, which is the entire group in which the researcher is interested. If researchers survey a lot of high schools and select their *participants* (people who are part of the study) randomly, they will be more certain of getting answers that a broad selection of students would typically give.

Correlation Method There are only two methods that allow researchers to know more than just a description of what has happened: correlations and experiments. Correlation is actually a statistical technique, a particular way of organizing numerical information so that it is easier to look for patterns and relationships in the information.

A **correlation** is a measure of the relationship between two or more variables. A *variable* is anything that can change or vary: scores on a test, temperature in a room, gender, and so on. For example, researchers might be curious to know whether or not cigarette smoking is connected to life expectancy—the number of years a person can be expected to live. Obviously, the scientists can't hang around people who smoke and wait to see when those people die. The only way to find out if smoking and life expectancy are related to each other is to use the medical records of people who have already died. Researchers would look for two facts from each record: the number of cigarettes the person smoked per day and the age of the person at death.

Now the researcher has two sets of numbers for each person in the study that go into a mathematical formula to produce a number called the **correlation coefficient**. The correlation coefficient is one number that represents two things: the direction of the relationship and its strength.

Direction? How can a mathematical relationship have a direction?

Whenever researchers talk about two variables being related to each other, what they really mean is that knowing the value of one variable allows them to *predict* the value of the other variable. For example, if researchers found that smoking and life expectancy are indeed related, they should be able to predict how long someone might live if they know how many cigarettes a person smokes in a day. But which way does that prediction work? If a person smokes a lot of cigarettes, does that mean that he or she will live a longer life or a shorter one? Does life expectancy go up or down as smoking increases? That's what is meant by the *direction* of the relationship.

So if we found that the correlation between cigarette smoking and life expectancy was high, does that mean that smoking causes your life expectancy to be shortened?

Not exactly. The biggest error that people make concerning correlation is to assume that it means one variable is the cause of the other. It is important to know that *correlation does not prove causation*. Just because two variables are related to each other, researchers cannot assume that one of them causes the other one to occur. They could both be related to some other variable that is the cause of both. For example, cigarette smoking and life expectancy could be linked only because people who smoke may be less likely to take care of their health by eating right and exercising, whereas people who do not smoke may tend to eat healthier foods and exercise more than smokers do.

Explore on **mypsychlab.com**

---

representative sample randomly selected sample of subjects from a larger population of subjects.

population the entire group of people or animals in which the researcher is interested.

correlation a measure of the relationship between two variables.

correlation coefficient a number derived from the formula for measuring a correlation and indicating the strength and direction of a correlation.

◀ *Direction? How can a mathematical relationship have a direction?*

◀ *So if we found that the correlation between cigarette smoking and life expectancy was high, does that mean that smoking causes your life expectancy to be shortened?*

Explore how correlations do not prove causation on **mypsychlab.com**

THE SCIENCE OF PSYCHOLOGY 19

CHAPTER 1 • Module 2

COVER THE MODULE *(continued)*

- **Correlation Method**
  - *Correlation* is a statistical technique that allows researchers to discover and predict relationships between variables of interest.
    - The *correlation coefficient* is the number indicating the strength and the direction of the relationship between two variables.
    - Positive correlations exist when increases in one variable are matched by increases in the other variable.
    - Negative correlations exist when increases in one variable are matched by decreases in the other variable.
    - Correlations cannot be used to prove cause-and-effect relationships.

DISCUSS THE STUDENT VOICE QUESTION

Use this question to check students' understanding of correlation. Make sure they realize that correlation does not prove causation. The two variables could both be related to some other variable that is the cause of both.

MULTIMEDIA CONTENT AVAILABLE AT www.mypsychlab.com

Explore how correlations do not prove causation on **mypsychlab.com**

Class Demonstration

QUIZ ON CORRELATION

Purpose: Students identify positive and negative correlation. The teacher assesses how well students understand the difference between positive and negative correlations.

Time: 5-10 minutes

Description: Ask students to write the term *positive correlation* on one side of a piece of paper and *negative correlation* on the other side. Then read a list of prepared examples of correlations, such as the following: (1) The more I eat, the more I weigh. (2) The more time I spend at the mall, the less money I have. (3) The less I study, the poorer my grades are.

After you read an item, students should indicate by holding up their paper whether the example is an illustration of positive or negative correlation. Ask volunteers to verify the correct answer.

Module 2 Research Methods and Ethics

CHAPTER 1 • Module 2

UNDERSTANDING VISUALS

Direct students' attention to the cartoon on this page. Ask a volunteer to provide the definition of a correlation. *(Answer: A measure of the relationship between two variables.)* Ask another volunteer to explain what is happening in the cartoon. *(Answer: A bird "executive" is studying two charts. One chart is titled "Hour of Rising." It indicates an increase in the hour of rising. The other chart is titled "Worm Acquisition." It indicates a decrease in the number of worms acquired.)* Ask: **What is the direction of the relationship between the two charts?** *(Answer: As the hour of rising goes up, worm acquisition goes down.)*

COVER THE MODULE *(continued)*

- **Experimental Method**
  - The *experiment* is the only research method that allows researchers to determine the cause of a behavior.
  - *Operational definitions* require researchers to clearly define the variables to be measured.
  - *Informed consent* is permission from a person to participate in an experiment, after the risks and purposes have been explained.
  - The *independent variable* in an experiment is the variable that is deliberately manipulated by the experimenter to see if related changes occur in the behavior or responses of the participants and is given to the experimental group.
  - The *dependent variable* in an experiment is the measured behavior or responses of the participants.

To sum up, a correlation will tell researchers if there is a relationship between the variables (see the word "relation" inside the word "correlation"?), how strong the relationship is, and in what direction the relationship goes. If researchers know the value of one variable, they can predict the value of the other. To learn more about relationships such as these, see the expanded discussion on correlations in the next module.

Experimental Method The only research method that will allow researchers to determine the cause of a behavior is the **experiment**. In an experiment, researchers deliberately change, or manipulate, the variable they think is causing some behavior while holding all the other variables that might interfere with the experiment's results constant and unchanging. That way, if they see changes in behavior, they know that those changes must be due to the single manipulated variable. For example, in our discussion of the steps in the scientific method, we talked about how to study the effects of drinking caffeinated beverages on students' hyperactive behavior. The most logical way to study that particular relationship is through an experiment.

First, researchers would need to define exactly what they mean by "students" (second-grade boys and girls) and "hyperactive behavior," so that the behavior can be measured. These are called **operational definitions**, because they specifically name the operations (steps or procedures) that the experimenter must use to control or measure the variables in the experiment. An operational definition of hyperactive behavior might be a checklist of very specific actions such as fidgeting, interrupting, and so on that an observer could mark off as students do the items on the list. If the observers were just instructed to look for "hyperactive behavior," they might have multiple interpretations of what that behavior looks like.

Researchers might start by selecting the students from the target population they want to use in the experiment. The best method to do that is through random selection of a sample of students from a population determined by the researchers, just as a sample would be selected for a survey. Ideally, researchers would decide on the age of student they wanted to study—say, children who are 7 to 8 years old. Then researchers would go to various schools and randomly select a certain number of students of that age. Parents of students who will participate in the experiment must be informed of the intentions of the experiment so that they may give their **informed consent** for their children to participate in the study.

Another important step is to decide on the variable the researchers want to manipulate and the variable they want to measure to see if there are any changes. In the example of hyperactivity and caffeinated drinks, the variable that researchers think causes hyperactive behavior is the caffeine in the beverages. Researchers would want to manipulate that in some way. To do that, they would have to serve caffeinated drinks to the participants and try to measure the participants' hyperactive behavior afterward.

The name for the variable that is manipulated in any experiment is the **independent variable** because it is *independent* of anything the participants do. The participants in the study do not get to choose or vary the independent variable, and their behavior does not affect this variable at all. In our example, the independent variable would be the presence or absence of caffeine.

Source: © The New Yorker Collection 1994 Leo Cullum from cartoonbank.com. All Rights Reserved.

experiment a deliberate manipulation of a variable to see if corresponding changes in behavior result, allowing the determination of cause-and-effect relationships.

operational definition definition of a variable of interest that allows it to be measured.

informed consent permission from a person (or a parent or guardian, in the case of minors) to participate in an experiment after the risks and purpose of the experiment have been explained.

independent variable variable in an experiment that is manipulated by the experimenter.

Class Demonstration

CRITICAL THINKING

<u>Purpose</u>: Students think critically about research claims in the tabloids.

<u>Time</u>: 20 minutes

<u>Description</u>: Instruct students to bring in a research claim from a tabloid magazine or newspaper. Tabloids often have wild headlines like "Dogs and Cats Have Exciting Dreams." Teams should work together to design a hypothetical experiment to test these research claims. If scientists wanted to test the claim, how could they do it? Teams should write a description of their experiment and identify all the major components (hypothesis, independent variable, dependent variable). Ask students to present their work to the class.

The response of the participants to the manipulation of the independent variable *is* a dependent relationship, so the response of the participants that is measured is known as the **dependent variable**. Their behavior, if the hypothesis is correct, should *depend* on whether or not they were exposed to the independent variable, and in the example, the dependent variable would be the measure of hyperactive behavior in the children.

Explore on **mypsychlab.com**

2.3 How do researchers ensure their findings are valid?

If researchers do all of this and find that the students' behavior is hyperactive, can they say that the hyperactive behavior was caused by the caffeine in the drinks?

No, what has been described so far is not enough. The researchers may find that the students who drank the caffeinated beverages are hyperactive, but how would they know if their hyperactive behavior was caused by the caffeinated drinks or was just the natural behavior of those particular students?

The best way to control for these **confounding variables** is to have two groups of participants: those who drink a caffeinated beverage, and those who drink a nearly identical but noncaffeinated beverage. Then the researchers would measure the hyperactive behavior in both groups. If the hyperactive behavior is significantly greater in the group that drank the caffeinated beverage, then researchers can say that, in this experiment, drinking caffeinated beverages *caused* more hyperactive behavior.

The group that is exposed to the independent variable (caffeine in the example) is called the **experimental group**. The other group that gets either no treatment or some kind of treatment that should have no effect (like the group that drinks the noncaffeinated drink in the example) is called the **control group**.

As we discussed, random selection is the best way to choose the participants for any study. Participants must then be assigned to either the experimental group or the control group. **Random assignment** of participants to one of the groups is the best way to ensure control over other interfering variables. Drawing names from a hat or flipping a coin are both means of random assignment.

Experimental Hazards: The Placebo Effect and the Experimenter Effect There are a few other problems that might arise in any experiment, even with the use of control groups and random assignment. These problems are especially likely when studying people, because people are often influenced by their own thoughts or biases about what is happening in an experiment. For example, say there is a new drug that is supposed to improve memory in people who are in the very early stages of *Alzheimer's disease* (a form of mental deterioration that occurs in some people as they grow old). Researchers would want to test the drug to see if it really is effective in helping to improve memory, so they would get a sample of people who are in the early stages of the disease, divide them into two groups, give one group the drug, and then test for improvement.

But there's a problem with this experiment. What if the researchers do find that the drug group had greater memory improvement than the group that received nothing? Can they really say that the drug itself caused the improvement? Or is it possible that the participants who received the drug *knew* that they were supposed to improve in memory and, therefore, made a major

If researchers do all of this and find that the students' behavior is hyperactive, can they say that the hyperactive behavior was caused by the caffeine in the drinks?

Explore how to distinguish independent and dependent variables on **mypsychlab.com**

dependent variable variable in an experiment that represents the measurable response or behavior of the subjects in the experiment.

confounding variable variable in an experiment that may unintentionally affect the dependent variable

experimental group subjects in an experiment who are subjected to the independent variable.

control group subjects in an experiment who are not subjected to the independent variable and who may receive a placebo treatment.

random assignment process of assigning subjects to the experimental or control groups randomly so that each subject has an equal chance of being in either group.

THE SCIENCE OF PSYCHOLOGY 21

CHAPTER 1 • Module 2

MULTIMEDIA CONTENT AVAILABLE AT
www.mypsychlab.com

Explore how to distinguish independent and dependent variables on **mypsychlab.com**

COVER THE MODULE

2.3 How do researchers ensure their findings are valid?

DISCUSS THE STUDENT VOICE QUESTION

Use this question to introduce the idea that researchers must control for variables by using two groups of participants.

- *Confounding variables* may unintentionally affect the dependent variable.
- The *experimental group* includes participants who are subjected to the independent variable, while the *control group* consists of participants who are not subjected to the independent variable.
- One of the best ways to ensure control over interfering variables is through random assignment, the process of assigning subjects randomly to the experimental or control groups. *Random assignment* of participants helps to control for individual differences both within and between the groups that might otherwise interfere with the experiment's outcome.
- **Experimental Hazards**
  - Even with the use of control groups and random assignment, problems can arise in experiments.
  - People are often influenced by their own thoughts or biases about what is happening in an experiment.

Explore

UNDERSTANDING CORRELATIONAL AND EXPERIMENTAL RESEARCH

Many students have difficulty understanding the difference between correlational research and experimental research. It might be useful to walk the class through an example where both kinds of research are illustrated with the same variables. One example that could be used this way is the relationship between the viewing of violent television and aggression. In this example, either variable could plausibly be caused by the other (or by some third factor); so the step up from correlational to experimental research, where causality can be determined, can be seen as useful.

Module 2 Research Methods and Ethics 21

CHAPTER 1 • Module 2

COVER THE MODULE (continued)
- **Experimental Hazards** (continued)
  - The expectations and biases of participants in a study can influence their behavior. For example, in the *placebo effect*, participants' beliefs may be more significant in creating an improvement than is a drug or a procedure.
  - The *experimenter effect* is the tendency of an experimenter's expectations to unintentionally affect a study's results.
  - Experiments in which neither the experimenters nor the subjects know who is in the control group and who is in the experimental group are called *double-blind studies*. These procedures are designed to minimize both experimenter and placebo effects.

COVER THE MODULE
2.4 Why do some researchers study animals instead of people?
- Some advantages in using animals in research include animals' shorter life spans; the ease with which animals and their environments can be controlled; the simplicity of their behavior; and the fact that animals can be used in ways that humans cannot.
- However, researchers who experiment with animals must act ethically.

DISCUSS THE STUDENT VOICE QUESTION
Use this question to check students' understanding of the topic. After covering the text material, ask a volunteer to answer the question. Ask another student to determine if the answer is correct.

---

placebo effect phenomenon in which the expectations of the participants in a study can influence their behavior.

experimenter effect tendency of the experimenter's expectations for a study to unintentionally influence the results of the study.

double-blind experiment study in which neither the experimenter nor the subjects know if the subjects are in the experimental or control group.

▲ This elderly woman has Alzheimer's disease, which causes a severe loss of recent memory. If she were given a drug to improve her memory, the researcher could not be certain that any improvement shown was caused by the drug rather than by the elderly woman's belief that the drug would work. The expectations of any person in an experimental study can affect the outcome of the study, a phenomenon known as the placebo effect.

► But why not just study people in the first place?

effort to do so? The improvement may have had more to do with participants' *belief* in the drug than the drug itself, a phenomenon known as the **placebo effect**: The expectations and biases of the participants in a study can influence their behavior.

Another way that expectations about the outcome of the experiment can influence the results is called the **experimenter effect**. It has to do with the expectations of the experimenter, not the participants. Sometimes observers are biased—they see what they expect to see. When a researcher is measuring the dependent variable, which is usually some form of behavior, it is possible that he or she could give the participants accidental clues about how they are supposed to respond—with body language, tone of voice, or even eye contact.

Fortunately, there are ways to control for these effects. The classic way to control for the placebo effect is to give the control group an actual *placebo*—some kind of treatment that does not affect behavior at all. The participants in both the experimental and the control groups would not know whether or not they got the real drug or the placebo. If their expectations have any effect at all on the outcome of the experiment, the experimenter will be able to tell by looking at the results for the control group and comparing them to the experimental group.

Researchers can control for the experimenter effect by designing studies in which neither the participants nor the experimenters know who is in the control group and who is in the experimental group. This type of study is called a **double-blind experiment**. Everything in a double-blind experiment gets coded in some way or tracked by an assistant to the experimenter known as a *confederate*, but only after all the measurements have been taken can the experimenter determine who was in the experimental group and who was in the control group.

2.4 Why do some researchers study animals instead of people?

In many research situations, psychologists study animals to find out about behavior, often drawing comparisons between what the animals do and what people might do under similar conditions.

But why not just study people in the first place?

Some research questions are extremely important but difficult or impossible to answer by using human participants. Animals live shorter lives, so looking at long-term effects becomes much easier. Animals are also easier to control—the scientist can control diet, living arrangements, and even genetic relatedness. And animals engage in much simpler behavior than humans do, making it easier to see the effects of manipulations. But the biggest reason that researchers use animals in some research is that animals can be used in ways that researchers could never use people. For example, it took a long time for scientists to prove that the tars and other harmful substances in tobacco cause cancer because they had to do correlational studies with people and experiments only with animals. When you think that without animal research there would be no vaccines for deadly diseases, no insulin treatments for diabetics, no transplants, and so on, the value of the research and its benefits to humankind far outweigh the hazards to which the research

---

Explore

DEBATE THE USE OF ANIMALS IN RESEARCH
Divide the class into two teams. Be sure to include students of differing learning styles and abilities on each team. Direct the teams to conduct library or Internet research on the topic of using animals in psychological experiments. Consider designating a student on each team as a captain to direct the work of classmates. Then have the two teams meet in a class debate with one team taking the position that experimentation on animals is justified and the other team arguing that it is not justified. At the end of the debate, take a class vote to determine which position the majority of students support.

animals are exposed. Whenever researchers perform experiments on animals, however, it is important for them to act responsibly and ethically.

Consider Ethical Issues in Psychological Research

These days, when psychologists perform research on humans or animals, they know it is especially important to ensure that all research participants are treated ethically. Ethical treatment means that people who volunteer for a study can expect that no physical or psychological harm will come to them.

2.5 What ethical guidelines do psychologists follow when they research humans?

"He says he wants a lawyer."

Source: © The New Yorker Collection 1999 Tom Chalkley from cartoonbank.com. All Rights Reserved.

There are quite a few ethical concerns when dealing with human subjects in an experiment or other type of study. To help make sure ethical standards are maintained, institutional review boards (IRBs) are used to scrutinize research proposals. Here are the most common ethical guidelines:

1. **Humanitarian:** Rights and well-being of participants must be weighed against the study's value to science. In other words, people come first, research second.
2. **Informed Consent:** Participants must be allowed to make an informed decision about participation. This means that researchers have to explain the study to the people they want to include before they do anything to them or with them, and the explanation has to be in terms that the participants can understand. When conducting research with minors, like students in a school, consent forms need to be signed by parents or guardians before any research and data gathering can be conducted. Otherwise, the school and researcher are in violation of government regulations.
3. **Justification:** Deception must be justified. In some cases, it is necessary to deceive the participants because the study would not work any other way. The participants have to be told after the study exactly why the deception was important. This is called *debriefing*.
4. **Right to Withdraw:** Participants may withdraw from the study at any time. The participants must be allowed to drop out for any reason.
5. **Risks and Benefits:** Participants must be protected from risks or told explicitly of risks. For example, if researchers are using electrical equipment, they must ensure that no participant will experience a physical shock from faulty equipment.
6. **Debriefing:** Investigators must debrief participants, telling the true nature of the study and expectations of results. This is important in all types of studies but particularly in those involving deception.
7. **Confidentiality:** Data must remain confidential. Psychologists today tend to report only group results rather than results for a single individual, so no single person can possibly be recognized from the results (APA, 2002).

THE SCIENCE OF PSYCHOLOGY 23

CHAPTER 1 • Module 2

COVER THE MODULE

2.5 What ethical guidelines do psychologists follow when they conduct research with humans?

- Protection of rights and well-being of participants
- Informed consent
- Justification when deception is used
- Right of participants to withdraw at any time
- Protection of participants from physical or psychological harm
- Debriefing of participants at the end of the study
- Confidentiality

UNDERSTANDING VISUALS

Direct students' attention to the cartoon on this page. Ask a volunteer to explain what is happening in the cartoon. *(Answer: A chimp is using sign language to communicate with researchers that he wants a lawyer, probably to protect the chimp's rights.)*

FAST FACT

Ask students if they think it would be ethical to clone humans. *(Many scientists and physicians believe that it would be unethical to attempt to clone humans. Physicians from the American Medical Association and scientists with the American Association for the Advancement of Science have issued formal public statements advising against human reproductive cloning. The U.S. Congress has considered the passage of legislation that could ban human cloning.)*

L2 LPR DIFFERENTIATED INSTRUCTION

Less Proficient Readers For students who have difficulties with vocabulary and fluency, directly teach meanings of critical vocabulary required for full understanding of the lesson.

Critical Thinking

WRITING ABOUT PSYCHOLOGY

Divide students into pairs that are as equally balanced as possible in terms of ability levels. Then refer the duos back to the discussion of the "Little Peter" experiment on page 9. Have students use the list of seven ethical guidelines on this page to write a description of how they might conduct this experiment today. What would they do—or not do—in order to maintain ethical standards? Ask volunteer duos to read their work to the class.

Module 2 Research Methods and Ethics 23

CHAPTER 1 • Module 2

COVER THE MODULE

2.6 Are there different ethical guidelines for research with animals?

- Animals in psychological research should not be exposed to *unnecessary* pain and suffering.

EXTEND THE DISCUSSION

Tell students that a positive result of the debate over animal research has been the close examination of the American Psychological Association ethical code for the humane treatment of animals and the passage of stricter federal welfare regulations governing the care of research animals. Most psychological organizations, however, oppose proposals to ban or greatly reduce animal research. They feel that protective legislation for animals is desirable but must not risk research that increases scientific understanding and improves human welfare.

APPLYING PSYCHOLOGY TO EVERYDAY LIFE

1. Experimental group: athletes who answered the questionnaire before taking the intellectual test; control group: athletes who answered the questionnaire after taking the test; independent variable: when students answer the questionnaire (before or after the test); dependent variable: how well students perform on the intellectual test

2. Possible answer: Educators could stress to athletes that they are graded on the basis of classroom performance, not athletic ability.

UNDERSTANDING VISUALS

Direct students' attention to the question in the photo caption. Academic performance could indeed be influenced by a negative stereotype.

2.6 Are there different ethical guidelines for research with animals?

Just as there are with humans, there are ethical considerations when dealing with animals in research. With animals, though, the focus is on avoiding exposing them to any *unnecessary* pain or suffering. So if surgery is part of the study, it is done under anesthesia. If the research animal must die for the effects of some drug or other treatment to be examined in an autopsy, the death must be accomplished humanely. Animals are used in only about 7 percent of all psychological studies (Committee on Animal Research and Ethics, 2004).

Applying Psychology to Everyday Life

Stereotypes, Athletes, and Test Performance

Many people have a negative stereotype of student athletes—that they are graded and promoted on the basis of their ability on the athletic field and not on the basis of classroom performance. If you are an athlete, can that negative stereotype have a negative impact on your test performance? Wesleyan University researchers Matthew Jameson, Robert Diehl, and Henry Danso have some evidence that such stereotypes can have just that kind of negative impact (Jameson et al., 2007).

In their experiment, 72 male college athletes took an intellectual test. Half of the athletes answered a brief questionnaire before taking the test, while the other half received the same questionnaire after taking the test. The questionnaire asked three questions, with the third question being, "Rate your likelihood of being accepted to the university without the aid of athletic recruiting." This "high threat" item was designed to bring the negative stereotype of athletes to the forefront of students' minds.

The results? Those students who answered the "high threat" question *before* the intellectual test scored significantly lower on that test than those who answered the question *after* the test. The researchers also found a correlation between the students' exposure to the "high threat" stereotype condition and accuracy on the intellectual test: The more students believed that they got into college primarily because of their athletic ability, the worse they performed on the subsequent test. Jameson and colleagues concluded that obvious negative stereotypes in higher education may be an important cause of the tendency of college athletes to underperform in academics.

▲ *Could knowing that other people might think your success in school is due to your athletic ability and not to your intelligence make you perform poorly on an academic test?*

Questions for Further Discussion

1. In this experiment, which group was the experimental group and which was the control? What was the independent variable? The dependent variable?
2. What might educators do to try to prevent the effect of the "dumb jock" negative stereotype on student athletes?

Class Demonstration

DISCUSSING CONTROVERSIES IN RESEARCH

<u>Purpose</u>: Students have a chance to think about and discuss controversial topics in research methods.

<u>Time</u>: 15 minutes

<u>Description</u>: Pose one or more of the following controversial questions to the class. Students should share their answers and contribute to further class discussion: (1) Should researchers be allowed to deceive participants if the knowledge gained could benefit humanity? (2) Should infants be used in psychological research, even with parental consent? (3) Should observational studies conducted in public places require informed consent?

Practice Quiz

Pick the best answer.

1. In the scientific method, the first step is
   a. reporting your results
   b. perceiving a question
   c. drawing conclusions
   d. testing your hypothesis

2. In a naturalistic observation, the phenomenon in which the behavior of the subjects being observed changes because they are being watched is called
   a. observer bias
   b. participant observation
   c. observer effect
   d. representative sampling

3. Which of the following is the main disadvantage of a case study?
   a. Its results cannot be truly unbiased.
   b. Its results cannot be generalized to other similar conditions.
   c. It is not easily done due to the large number of subjects.
   d. It is not detailed enough to address most research questions.

4. When researchers select study participants from several different parts of the population, they are selecting a
   a. representative sample
   b. control group
   c. random assignment
   d. experimental group

5. Which of the following is NOT a piece of information that researchers can determine from a correlation?
   a. whether there is a relationship between two variables
   b. the direction of a relationship between two variables
   c. the strength of a relationship between two variables
   d. the cause of a relationship between two variables

6. The group that receives no treatment or an ineffective treatment in an experiment is known as the
   a. control group
   b. experimental group
   c. placebo group
   d. random group

7. The variable that an experimenter purposefully manipulates in order to create a change is called the
   a. dependent variable
   b. independent variable
   c. confounding variable
   d. hypothetical variable

8. What is the name for a study in which neither the experimenter nor the participants know who is in the control group and who is in the experimental group?
   a. placebo study
   b. case study
   c. double-blind study
   d. bias-free study

9. Which of the following is NOT a common ethical rule in psychological research?
   a. Participants have to give informed consent.
   b. Data about individual participants must remain confidential.
   c. The rights and well-being of the participants must come first.
   d. Deception cannot be used in any studies with human beings.

10. Why do psychologists use animals in research?
    a. Animals have more complicated brains than people do.
    b. Animals are more psychologically interesting than people are.
    c. We can do things to animals that we cannot do to people.
    d. We understand more about people than we do about animals.

THE SCIENCE OF PSYCHOLOGY 25

Practice Quiz Answers

1. b
2. c
3. b
4. a
5. d
6. a
7. b
8. c
9. d
10. c

CHAPTER 1 • Module 2

Assess

Assign the Module 2 Practice Quiz.
Use the Practice Quiz to identify gaps in student understanding.

REMEDIATE

Have students, individually or in groups, review the module goals, learning objectives, and key terms.
Refer students to the Concept Summary on p. 38 for review.

Close

As a class, discuss whether students think that fewer controls or stricter controls are needed over psychological research methods. What might be the consequences of loosening controls? Of strengthening controls?

CHAPTER 1 • Module 3

Focus

RESOURCES
For this module, consult the appropriate sections of the Teacher's Manual, Test Bank, and PowerPoint slides, all found on the Teacher's Resource DVD, and the interactive study tools for students on MyPsychLab.

BEFORE CLASS
Students should read the section for homework before coming to class.

BELLRINGER
Write on the board: **Why does the study of psychology require a knowledge of statistics? Write an answer of one or two sentences.** Once class is ready to begin, ask several volunteers to read their answers aloud.

Teach

INTRODUCE THE TOPIC
Explain to students that psychologists use research data to (1) summarize information and (2) make judgments about that data. *Statistics* are used for both these activities.

COVER THE MODULE
3.1 What are descriptive statistics?
- *Descriptive statistics* are a way of organizing numbers and summarizing them so they can be understood.
  - Measures of central tendency are used to summarize data and provide a score that seems typical of the sample.
  - Measures of variability indicate the range of data.

TEACHING TIP
Because students may be intimidated by the mathematical concepts in this module, consider using peer tutoring and feedback to help them learn the content. Match students based on need and personality or on ability. A more advanced student can be assigned the tutor role to a struggling peer.

26 Chapter 1 The Science of Psychology

Module 3 Statistics

Module Goal
Learn the basic concepts of data analysis.

Learning Objectives
- 3.1 What are descriptive statistics?
- 3.2 What types of tables and graphs represent patterns in data?
- 3.3 What are correlation coefficients? What do they tell researchers about relationships?
- 3.4 What are inferential statistics?
- 3.5 How do the concepts of validity and reliability relate to statistics?

Learn the Basic Concepts of Data Analysis

Many students wonder why the science of psychology requires knowledge of mathematical concepts like statistics. The answer is simple: Psychologists base their conclusions on research findings. Data are collected (using the various research methods discussed in the previous module), and they have to be analyzed. Statistics is the field that gives us the tools to do that. An understanding of basic statistics can help you think critically about psychological research. It can also help you understand the statistical claims you read or hear about every day from sources like advertisements, political polls, and salespeople.

Psychologists have to be able to do two things with the data they collect. The first is to summarize the information from a study or experiment. This is the role of **descriptive statistics**. The second is to make judgments and decisions about the data. We are interested in whether groups differ from each other. We are also interested in how one group of variables is related to another. This second emphasis is known as **inferential statistics**.

Statistical analysis is a way of trying to account for the error that exists in almost any body of data, and **statistics** is the branch of mathematics that is concerned with the collection and interpretation of data from samples (Agresti & Finlay, 1997; Aron et al., 2005). Psychology is only one of many fields that use descriptive and inferential statistics.

3.1 What are descriptive statistics?

Descriptive statistics are a way of organizing numbers and summarizing them so that they can be understood. There are two main types of descriptive statistics:
- *Measures of Central Tendency.* Measures of central tendency are used to summarize the data and give you one score that seems typical of your sample.
- *Measures of Variability.* Measures of variability are used to indicate the range of data. Are most data close to the average, or are they spread out more widely?

descriptive statistics a way of organizing numbers and summarizing them so that patterns can be determined.

inferential statistics statistical analysis of two or more sets of numerical data to reduce the possibility of error in measurement and to determine if the differences between the data sets are greater than chance variation would predict.

statistics branch of mathematics concerned with the collection and interpretation of numerical data.

26 CHAPTER 1

Terms

- descriptive statistics • inferential statistics • statistics • measures of central tendency
- mean • median • mode • measures of variability • range • standard deviation
- frequency distribution • histogram • polygon • normal curve • bell curve
- statistically significant • reliability • validity

Measures of Central Tendency One way to sum up numerical data is to find out what a "typical" score might be, or some central number around which all the others seem to fall. This kind of summation is called a **measure of central tendency**. There are three different measures of central tendency: the mean, the median, and the mode.

The most commonly used measure of central tendency is the **mean**. To find the mean, you add up all the numbers in a particular set and then divide them by how many numbers there are. This is usually the way teachers get the grade point average for a particular student, for example. If Rochelle's grades on the tests she has taken so far are 86, 92, 87, and 90, then the teacher would add $86 + 92 + 87 + 90 = 355$, and then divide 355 by 4 (the number of scores) to get the mean, or grade point average, of 88.75.

I remember that sometimes my teacher would "curve" the grades for a test, and it was always bad when just one person did really well and everyone else did lousy.

Yes, the mean does not work as well when there are extreme scores, as you would have if only two students out of an entire class had a perfect score of 100 and everyone else scored in the 70s or lower. If you want a truer measure of central tendency in such a case, you need one that isn't affected by extreme scores. The **median** is just such a measure. A median is the score that falls in the middle of an *ordered* distribution of scores. Half of the scores will fall above the median, and half of the scores will fall below it. If the distribution contains an odd number of scores, it's just the middle number, but if the number of scores is even, it's the average of the two middle scores. Look at Table 3.1 for an example of the median.

◀ I remember that sometimes my teacher would "curve" the grades for a test, and it was always bad when just one person did really well and everyone else did lousy.

Table 3.1	Intelligence Test Scores for 10 People		
NAME	IQ	NAME	IQ
Allison	240	Fethia	100
Ben	105	George	100
Carol	103	Hal	100
Denise	103	Inga	98
Evan	102	Jay	95

The mean IQ of this group would be 114.6, but the median would be 101 (the average between Evan with 102 and Fethia with 100, the average of the two middle numbers).

The **mode** is another measure of central tendency in which the most frequent score is taken as the central measure. In the numbers given in Table 3.1, the mode would be 100 because that number appears more times than any other. Three people have that score. This is the simplest measure of central tendency.

Measures of Variability Descriptive statistics can also determine how much the scores in a distribution differ, or vary, from the central tendency of the data. These **measures of variability** are used to discover how "spread out" the scores are from each other. The more the scores cluster around the central scores, the smaller the measure of variability will be, and the more widely the scores differ from the central scores, the larger this measurement will be.

measures of central tendency numbers that best represent the most typical score of a frequency distribution.

mean the average score within a group of scores, calculated by adding all of the scores and then dividing by the number of scores.

median the middle score in an ordered distribution of scores, or the mean of the two middle numbers; the 50th percentile.

mode the most frequent score in a distribution of scores.

measures of variability measurement of the degree of differences within a distribution or how the scores are spread out.

THE SCIENCE OF PSYCHOLOGY 27

CHAPTER 1 • Module 3

COVER THE MODULE (continued)

Measures of Central Tendency

- There are three different measures of central tendency.
  - The *mean* is the most commonly used measure of central tendency. It is found by adding all the numbers in a set and then dividing them by how many numbers there are. The mean does not work well when there are extreme scores.
  - The *median* is the score that falls in the middle of an ordered distribution of scores.
  - The *mode* is the most frequent score in a group of scores. It is the simplest measure of central tendency.

CHECK FOR UNDERSTANDING

To reinforce students' understanding of measures of central tendency, direct their attention to Table 3.1 in the text. Write the scores from the table on the board, in ascending numerical order. Ask volunteers to show how the mean *(114.6)*, the median *(101)*, and the mode *(100)* are obtained.

Class Demonstration (Kinesthetic)

UNDERSTANDING STATISTICS

The following approach can be used to give students a kinesthetic and visual sense of descriptive statistics. Ask students a question with an answer that can be ordered numerically. For example, you could use age or height. Students should line themselves up according to their answers. You can then use the data to calculate the mean (average number), and students can number off themselves in order to locate the median (middle number). Students can also determine the mode (the most frequent number).

Module 3 Statistics 27

CHAPTER 1 • Module 3

COVER THE MODULE (continued)

- **Measures of Variability**
  - *Measures of variability* are used to determine how "spread out" scores are from each other. There are two ways that variability is measured.
    - The *range* is the difference between the highest score and the lowest score in the set of numbers. It is the simpler method.
    - The *standard deviation* is a number that represents how far away the scores in a data set are from the mean. This figure can be determined using computers or calculators.

COVER THE MODULE

3.2 What types of tables and graphs represent patterns in data?

- Graphs or charts help researchers look for patterns. They represent research findings in a visual form. The type of graph or chart chosen by a researcher is the one that most accurately represents the data found.

Frequency Distributions

- A *frequency distribution* is a table or graph that shows how often different numbers appear in a particular set of scores.

TEACHING TIP

Encourage students to use the following steps to analyze graphic data:

1. **Identify the type of information presented.** Note the title, all labels, and any key.
2. **Read the data.** Look at specific elements on the graph, and determine what the numbers represent. Then determine the relationship between the numbers.
3. **Interpret the graph and draw conclusions.** Look for patterns or trends, such as changes over time or comparisons of different groups.

There are two ways that variability is measured. The simpler method is by calculating the **range** of the set of scores, or the difference between the highest score and the lowest score in the set of scores. The range is somewhat limited as a measure of variability when there are extreme scores in the distribution. For example, if you look at Table 3.1, the range of those IQ scores would be 240–95, or 145. But if you just look at the numbers, you can see that there really isn't that much variation except for that one high score of 240.

The other measure of variability that is commonly used is called the **standard deviation**. The standard deviation is a number that represents how far away the scores in a data set are from the mean. The mathematical formula for finding the standard deviation looks complicated, but the steps in Table 3.2 explain how to find the standard deviation for a set of data.

Table 3.2	How to Find the Standard Deviation
1.	Calculate the data set's mean.
2.	Subtract the mean from each individual score to find out how much each score differs from the mean.
3.	Square each deviation score.
4.	Add up all of the squares you calculated in Step 3.
5.	Divide the total you calculated in Step 4 by the number of scores in the data set.
6.	Find the square root of the number you calculated in Step 5. This square root is the standard deviation.

This procedure may look complicated to you, but be assured that computers and inexpensive calculators can figure out the standard deviation simply by entering the numbers and pressing a button. No one finds a standard deviation by hand anymore.

3.2 What types of tables and graphs represent patterns in data?

How do psychologists analyze the data they collect during research? Just looking at a long list of numbers isn't usually very helpful, so researchers make a graph or chart and search for patterns. While statistical calculations represent research findings in the form of numbers, graphs and charts represent these same findings in a visual form. What type of graph or chart is best? It depends on the data: Researchers try to choose the graph or chart that most accurately represents the data they have found.

Frequency Distributions A **frequency distribution** is a table or graph that shows how often different numbers, or scores, appear in a particular set of scores. For example, let's say that you have a sample of 30 people, the size of a psychology class. You ask them how many glasses of water they drink each day. You could represent the answers as shown in Table 3.3. Just by looking at

range the difference between the highest and lowest scores in a distribution.

standard deviation a statistical measure of the average variation from the mean score.

frequency distribution table or graph that shows how often different numbers or scores appear in a particular set of scores.

Class Demonstration

WRITING ABOUT GRAPHS

Have students bring to class graphs from newspapers, magazines, or the Internet. Give each student a graph and ask them to write three statements about the graph they received. Tell students to exchange their graphs and statements with a classmate, who should review the writings against the graphs to determine if the statements are correct.

Table 3.3 A Frequency Distribution

NUMBER OF GLASSES PER DAY	NUMBER OF PEOPLE OUT OF 59 (FREQUENCY)
1	0
2	1
3	2
4	4
5	5
6	6
7	5
8	4
9	2
10	1

this table, it is clear that typical people drink between four and eight glasses of water a day.

Tables can be useful, especially when dealing with small sets of data. Sometimes a more visual presentation gives a better "picture" of the patterns in a data set, and that is when researchers use graphs to plot the data from a frequency distribution. One common graph is a **histogram**. Figure 3.1 shows how the same data from Table 3.3 would look in a histogram.

FIGURE 3.1 A Histogram
Histograms provide a visual way to look at data from frequency distributions. In this graph, for example, the height of the bars indicates that most people drink four to eight glasses of water (represented by the five highest bars in the middle of the graph).

histogram graph showing a frequency distribution.

THE SCIENCE OF PSYCHOLOGY 29

CHAPTER 1 • Module 3

COVER THE MODULE *(continued)*

Frequency Distributions *(continued)*

- Tables are useful when dealing with small amounts of data.
- A *histogram* is a graph showing a frequency distribution.
- Another type of graph used in frequency distribution is the polygon, which is a line graph.

UNDERSTANDING VISUALS

Direct students to Figure 3.1 on this page and Figure 3.2 at the top of the next page. Stress that although Figure 3.1 shows a histogram and Figure 3.2 shows a polygon, both graphs show the same data.

FAST FACT

Ask students why psychologists should have to deal with statistics. *(Statistics is crucial to the field of psychology. Remind students that people with good research and statistical skills are much more employable and make more money than those who do not try to master research skills. Job seekers need all the skills they can get in today's world.)*

Class Demonstration

COLLABORATIVE LEARNING

Ask the class to work as one group to create a frequency distribution. Tell them to use the entire class as a sample and ask a question to which answers can be quantified, such as how many tunes they have on their iPods or how many times they text message in one day. Next, tell them to represent their answers in a table showing a frequency distribution. Then have half the class create a histogram from the table and the other half create a polygon from the table. If appropriate, students can use software to create their graphs. Finally, ask students to display their graphs for class viewing.

Module 3 Statistics 29

CHAPTER 1 • Module 3

COVER THE MODULE (continued)

- **The Normal Curve**
  - The normal curve (also called the *bell curve*) is a special frequency *polygon* in which the scores are symmetrically distributed around the mean. The mean, median, and mode are located on the same point on the curve.
  - The *normal curve* is used as a model for the measurement of such things as intelligence, height, or weight.

L4 DIFFERENTIATED INSTRUCTION

Advanced Learners The Rice Virtual Lab in Statistics, located at http://onlinestatbook.com/rvls.html, includes links to an online statistics textbook, simulations and demonstrations, case studies, and basic statistical analysis tools. Advanced students can check out this website for more information about the topics in this module.

FAST FACT

Quantitative psychologists study methods and techniques for the measurement of human attributes, the statistical and mathematical modeling of psychological processes, the design of research studies, and the analysis of psychological data. The American Psychological Association states that quantitative psychology is vital to all aspects of psychology: science, education, public interest, and practice.

EXTEND THE LESSON

Tell students that the Internet is a valuable tool that provides links to many sources of information, such as government agencies, schools and universities, businesses, and individuals. However, not all of these sources are reliable. Therefore, students must learn to determine which websites are trustworthy. Refer them to the Explore activity below to practice this skill.

FIGURE 3.2 A Polygon
A polygon is a line graph that can represent the data in a frequency distribution in much the same way as a bar graph but allows the shape of the data to be easily viewed.

Another type of graph used in frequency distributions is the **polygon**, a line graph. Figure 3.2 shows the same data in a polygon graph.

The Normal Curve Frequency polygons allow researchers to see the shape of a set of data easily. For example, the number of people drinking glasses of water in Figure 3.2 is easily seen to be centered about six glasses (central tendency) but drops off below four glasses and above eight glasses a day (variability). Our frequency polygon has a high point, and the frequency decreases on both sides.

A common frequency distribution of this type is called the **normal curve**. It has a very specific shape and is sometimes called the **bell curve**. Look at Figure 3.3. This curve is almost a perfect normal curve, and many things in life are not that perfect. The normal curve is used as a model for many things that are measured, such as intelligence, height, or weight, but even those measures only

polygon line graph showing a frequency distribution.

normal curve special frequency polygon in which the scores are symmetrically distributed around the mean, and the mean, median, and mode are all located on the same point on the curve with scores decreasing as the curve extends from the mean.

bell curve alternate name for the normal curve, which is said to be shaped like a bell.

Standard Deviations	-4	-3	-2	-1	0	1	2	3	4
Wechsler IQ	40	55	70	85	100	115	130	145	160
Stanford-Binet 4 IQ	36	52	68	84	100	116	132	148	164
Cumulative %	0.003	0.135	2.275	15.856	50.00	84.134	97.725	99.865	99.997

FIGURE 3.3 A Normal Curve
The normal curve, also known as the bell curve because of its unique shape, is often the way in which certain characteristics such as intelligence or weight are represented in the population. The highest point on the curve typically represents the average score in any distribution. Scores on intelligence tests are typically represented by the normal curve.

30   CHAPTER 1

Explore

EVALUATING INTERNET WEBSITES

Digital literacy is an essential 21st-century skill. Ask students to locate a psychology-related website on the Internet and evaluate it by following these steps: (1) Identify the sources of the information on the website. Is the author credible? (2) Determine when the information was written. Is it current? (3) Verify information by looking at other sources. Compare the information with that provided on government sites or those sponsored by respected organizations. Discuss students' responses as a class.

FIGURE 3.4 A Frequency Polygon
Skewed distributions are those in which the most frequent scores occur at one end or the other of the distribution, as represented by this frequency polygon in which most people are seen to drink seven to eight glasses of water each day.

come close to a perfect distribution (provided large numbers of people are measured). One of the reasons that the normal curve is so useful is that it has very specific relationships to measures of central tendency and to the standard deviation.

Distributions aren't always normal in shape. Some distributions are described as *skewed*. This occurs when the distribution is not equal on both sides of a central score with the highest frequency (like in our example). Instead, the scores are concentrated toward one side of the distribution. For example, what if a study of people's water-drinking habits in a different class revealed that most people drank around seven to eight glasses of water daily, with no one drinking more than eight? The frequency polygon shown in Figure 3.4 reflects this very different distribution.

Skewed distributions are called positively or negatively skewed, depending on where the scores are concentrated. A concentration in the high end of the distribution would be called *negatively skewed*, while a concentration in the low end would be called *positively skewed*. In Figure 3.4, most of the scores are concentrated in the high end of the distribution, so this distribution is negatively skewed.

3.3 What are correlation coefficients? What do they tell researchers about relationships?

A *correlation* is a measure of the relationship between two or more variables. For example, if you wanted to know if scores on the SAT are related to grade point average, you could get SAT scores and GPAs from a group of people and enter those numbers into a mathematical formula, which will produce a number called the correlation coefficient. The correlation coefficient represents the strength and direction of the relationship between variables.

The correlation coefficient that researchers get from the formula will either be a positive number or a negative number. If positive, the two variables increase

THE SCIENCE OF PSYCHOLOGY 31

CHAPTER 1 • Module 3

COVER THE MODULE *(continued)*
- **The Normal Curve** *(continued)*
  - Distributions are not always normal in shape. Skewed distributions occur when the distribution is not equal on both sides of a central score with the highest frequency. Rather, the scores are concentrated toward one side of the distribution.
    - Skewed distributions are considered positively skewed (that is, a concentration in the low end of the distribution) or negatively skewed (that is, a concentration in the high end of the distribution).

CHECK FOR UNDERSTANDING
Direct students' attention to Figure 3.4. Ask a volunteer to say whether the distribution shown there is positively or negatively skewed. *(Answer: negatively skewed.)* Why? *(Answer: Most of the scores are concentrated in the high end of the distribution.)*

COVER THE MODULE
3.3 What are correlation coefficients? What do they tell researchers about relationships?
- A correlation measures the relationship between two or more variables. The correlation coefficient represents the strength and direction of the relationship between variables.
- A correlation coefficient is either a positive number or a negative number. If it is positive, the two variables increase in the same direction. If it is negative, the two variables have an opposite relationship—as one increases, the other decreases.

Explore

USING WORD WEBS

A word web consists of a word or topic in a circle in the center of a piece of paper. Subtopics are then placed in circles around the main circle, with lines attaching the subtopic circles to the main circle. This visual can help students understand how the subtopics relate to the main topic. Have students work in groups to choose a topic for psychological research. Once they have selected a general topic, have them create a word web of possible subtopics and then list sources of information for researching the subtopics. Circulate to provide guidance with topic selection and brainstorming subtopics and information sources. Ask groups to present their word webs to classmates for explanation and discussion.

Module 3 Statistics **31**

CHAPTER 1 • Module 3

COVER THE MODULE (continued)

- The correlation coefficient is the number, ranging from −1.00 to +1.00, indicating the strength of the relationship between the two variables. The closer the number is to ±1.00, the stronger is the relationship.
- The closer the number is to zero, the weaker is the relationship.
- A correlation coefficient of 0.00 represents no correlation at all. A correlation coefficient of +1.00 is a perfect positive correlation. This rarely occurs in the real world.
- Positive correlations exist when increases in one variable are matched by increases in the other variable.
- Negative correlations exist when increases in one variable are matched by decreases in the other variable.

L2 DIFFERENTIATED INSTRUCTION

Students Who Struggle with Organization Model note taking as you present information in the classroom. Teach study skills, listening skills, and reading skills along with content.

---

32 Chapter 1 The Science of Psychology

---

in the same direction—as one goes up, the other goes up; as one decreases, the other also decreases. If negative, the two variables have an inverse (or opposite) relationship. As one increases, the other decreases. If researchers find that the more cigarettes a person smoked, the younger that person was when he or she died, that would mean that the correlation between the two variables is negative. (As smoking goes up, life expectancy goes down—an inverse relationship.)

The strength of the relationship between the variables will be determined by the actual number itself. That number will always range between +1.00 and −1.00. If the relationship is a strong one, the number will be closer to +1.00 or to −1.00. A correlation of +.89 would be a very strong positive correlation. That might represent the relationship between scores on the SAT and an IQ test, for example. A correlation of −.89 would be equally strong but negative. That would be more like the correlation researchers would probably find between smoking cigarettes and the age at which a person dies.

Notice that the closer the number is to zero, the weaker the relationship becomes. Researchers would probably find that the correlation coefficient for the relationship between people's weight and the number of freckles they have is pretty close to zero, for example. A correlation coefficient of 0.00 represents no correlation whatsoever. A correlation coefficient of +1.00 is a perfect positive correlation and probably indicates an error in calculation. (See Figure 3.5 for graphical examples of correlations.)

What are some other examples of strong and weak correlations in the real world? Consider the strong correlation between a person's level of education and the size of his or her income: People who have completed higher levels of schooling often make more money than those who have less education. Of course, you know by now that although these variables do seem to be related, there is no guarantee that, in all cases, a person with a higher level of education will earn more money than a person with a lower level of education.

On the other hand, variables such as the color of a person's hair and the number of books that a person reads per month have a weak correlation. That is, there is little or no consistent relationship between the two.

FIGURE 3.5 Examples of Correlations
Five scatter plots showing direction and strength of correlation. It should be noted that perfect correlations, whether positive or negative, rarely occur in the real world.

32 CHAPTER 1

Critical Thinking

MAKING A VERBAL PRESENTATION

Review with students the five scatter plots in Figure 3.5, showing types of correlation. Next, assign one type of correlation to each student in the class. Tell students to think of an example of the type of correlation to which they were assigned. Then have each student present his or her example to classmates, explaining how the example meets the criteria of the correlation.

3.4 What are inferential statistics?

In any analysis that compares two or more sets of data, there is always the possibility of error in the data, and it is always possible that luck, or chance, has played a role in the experiment. When researchers want to know if the differences they find in data are large enough to be caused by the experimental manipulation and *not* just by chance, they have to use a kind of statistical technique that can take those chance variations into account. These kinds of statistical analysis use inferential statistics.

All inferential statistics have one thing in common: They look for differences in group measurements that are **statistically significant**. Statistical significance is a way to test differences to see how likely those differences are to be real and not just caused by the random variations in behavior that exist in everything animals and people do.

Tests of significance give researchers the probability that the results of their experiment were caused by chance and not by their experimental manipulation. There are many different types of tests that researchers use to calculate statistical significance. In general, researchers are satisfied when these tests indicate that there is a 95 percent likelihood that their experimental results did not occur by chance. In reading scientific journals, you may see an equation that represents this significance as $p < .05$. In words, this states that the probability that these results have occurred by chance is less than 5 out of 100, thus the results are statistically significant.

3.5 How do the concepts of validity and reliability relate to statistics?

In psychology, as in other scientific fields, it's important that research results be both reliable and valid. The term **reliability** describes how consistent a result is. For example, if you perform an experiment five times and get similar results each time, you can say that your experiment is reliable. **Validity**, on the other hand, describes whether an experiment measures the thing that it is supposed to measure. Imagine that you decide to test young children's knowledge of U.S. geography by having them solve arithmetic problems. This test would not be valid because scores on a math test do not measure geographical knowledge. Validity can also describe the extent to which a test predicts future actions correctly. A standardized test for high school students has *predictive validity* if most students who score high on the test also perform well in college (and most students who do not score as well do not perform as well in college).

Statistical concepts can help researchers determine whether their tests are reliable and valid. If a data set's mean, median, and mode are all close to each other, and if most of the data are closely grouped (meaning that they have a small range, or a low standard deviation), the data set most likely represents a reliable study, because the results are consistent. Strong positive or negative correlations can suggest that research results are valid, and weak correlations can suggest the opposite: For example, if there is no correlation between students' scores on a standardized test and their performance in college, then that standardized test does not have predictive validity.

You may not need to perform statistical calculations yourself during your time in high school, but if you are interested in exploring psychology further in college or as a career, you will likely use all of these statistical concepts to analyze your own research and the research of others. For now, just remember that statistical analysis is one of a psychologist's most important and helpful tools.

statistically significant referring to differences in data sets that are larger than chance variation would predict.

reliability the tendency of a test to produce the same scores again and again each time it is given to the same people.

validity the degree to which a test actually measures what it is supposed to measure.

THE SCIENCE OF PSYCHOLOGY 33

CHAPTER 1 • Module 3

COVER THE MODULE

3.4 What are inferential statistics?

- Inferential statistics are techniques that look for differences in group measurements that are *statistically significant*, meaning how likely those differences are to be real and not just caused by random variations.

- In general, researchers are satisfied when tests indicate that there is a 95 percent likelihood that their experimental results did not occur by chance.

EXTEND THE LESSON

Explain to students that inferential statistics allow researchers to draw conclusions, or make *inferences*, about whether the results of research are true only for the specific group involved or whether the results can be applied to, or *generalized* to, the larger population from which the study participants were selected.

COVER THE MODULE

3.5 How do the concepts of validity and reliability relate to statistics?

- *Reliability* describes how consistent is a result. If a data set's mean, median, and mode values are close to each other, and if the data have a low standard deviation, the data most likely are reliable.

- *Validity* describes whether an experiment measures the thing that it is supposed to measure. Strong positive or negative correlations can suggest that research results are valid.

CHECK FOR UNDERSTANDING

Some students may have difficulty understanding that reliability and validity do not mean the same thing. Point out that reliability means that a test will produce the same results every time it is performed on the same group. Validity is concerned with whether a test actually measures what it is supposed to measure.

Explore

USING THE INTERNET TO FIND RESEARCH RESULTS

Have student groups look at the Research in Action section of the APA website at **www.apa.org**. With your approval, each group should select a topic and read about the research findings on that topic, their significance, and their practical applications. Groups should present a summary of what they have discovered, using software or audiovisual resources.

CHAPTER 1 • Module 3

Assess

Assign the Module 3 Practice Quiz.

Use the Practice Quiz to identify gaps in student understanding.

REMEDIATE

Have students, individually or in groups, review the module goals, learning objectives, and key terms.

Refer students to the Concept Summary on p. 38 for review.

Close

As a class, discuss how psychologists use statistics to summarize research results and then make judgments about the data. If researchers did not use statistics in this way, could we have confidence in study results?

Practice Quiz

Pick the best answer.

1. Another name for a bar graph is a
   a. polygon
   b. histogram
   c. normal curve
   d. line graph

2. A table that shows how often different scores appear in a set of scores is called a
   a. frequency distribution
   b. bell curve
   c. bar graph
   d. central tendency

3. In the set of numbers 2, 2, 2, 3, 5, 5, 6, 8, 15, what is the median?
   a. 2
   b. 3
   c. 5
   d. 15

4. In the set of numbers 2, 2, 2, 3, 5, 5, 6, 8, 15, what is the mode?
   a. 2
   b. 3
   c. 5
   d. 15

5. In a skewed distribution, the scores
   a. have two high points instead of one
   b. fall to one side of the distribution
   c. are evenly distributed around the mean
   d. are all identical to each other

6. The normal curve is a special kind of
   a. inferential statistic
   b. frequency distribution
   c. measure of central tendency
   d. correlational coefficient

7. Which of the following lets researchers know how spread out their data are?
   a. measures of central tendency
   b. measures of variability
   c. inferential statistics
   d. significant statistics

8. When a researcher wants to know if her results are likely to be caused by something other than chance, she wants to determine the results'
   a. correlation coefficient
   b. statistical significance
   c. measure of variability
   d. median score

9. When you add up all the numbers in a set of scores and divide the total by how many numbers there are, you are finding the
   a. mean
   b. median
   c. mode
   d. range

10. Which of the following correlation coefficients represents a strong negative correlation?
    a. +0.85
    b. 0.00
    c. −0.10
    d. −0.79

Practice Quiz Answers

1. b
2. a
3. c
4. a
5. b
6. b
7. b
8. b
9. a
10. d

CHAPTER 1 Summary

🔊 **Listen** on mypsychlab.com

Module 1: Psychology's Domains

Trace the development of psychology.

1.1 What is psychology? What are its goals?
- Psychology is the scientific study of behavior and mental processes.
- Its goals are description, explanation, prediction, and control.

1.2 What is the history of psychology as a scientific discipline?
- In 1879 psychology began as a science of its own with the establishment of Wilhelm Wundt's psychology laboratory in Germany.
- Early viewpoints included structuralism and functionalism.

1.3 What are the major modern psychological perspectives?
- The major perspectives are psychodynamic, behavioral, humanistic, cognitive, sociocultural, and biopsychological.

1.4 How is the field of psychology continuing to grow and change?
- Evolutionary psychology and positive psychology are two relatively new and intriguing areas of research.

Identify psychology's subfields.

1.5 Why do psychologists perform research?
- Research allows psychologists to collect data to support theories.

1.6 What are the major subfields of psychology?
- Major subfields include clinical, counseling, developmental, experimental, social, personality, physiological, comparative, and industrial/organizational psychology.

1.7 How does psychology benefit society?
- Through research, counseling, treatment, and teaching, psychologists aim to understand the mind and improve lives.

Module 2: Research Methods and Ethics

Understand psychological research methods.

2.1 What is the scientific method?
- The steps are formulating a question, developing a hypothesis, testing the hypothesis, drawing conclusions, and reporting results.

2.2 What methods do researchers use to study behavior?
- Researchers use descriptive methods, correlational methods, and experiments to study behavior.

🔊 **Listen** to an audio file of your chapter on mypsychlab.com

2.3 How do researchers ensure their findings are valid?
- Random assignment of participants to experiment groups helps control for differences within and between groups.

2.4 Why do some researchers study animals instead of people?
- Animals live shorter lives, are easier to control, and can be used in ways that would be unethical if applied to humans.

Consider ethical issues in psychological research.

2.5 What ethical guidelines do psychologists follow when they research humans?
- Guidelines include the protections of participants' rights and well-being, informed consent, justification when deception is used, the right of participants to withdraw at any time, protection of participants from harm, confidentiality, and debriefing.

2.6 Are there ethical guidelines for research with animals?
- Animals must not be exposed to any unnecessary pain or suffering, and all treatment must be humane.

Module 3: Statistics

Learn the basic concepts of data analysis.

3.1 What are descriptive statistics?
- Descriptive statistics include measures of central tendency and measures of variability.

3.2 What tables and graphs represent patterns in data?
- Frequency distribution tables, histograms (bar graphs), and polygons (line graphs) can all be used to represent data.

3.3 What are correlation coefficients?
- The correlation coefficient measures the direction and strength of a relationship between two variables.

3.4 What are inferential statistics?
- Inferential statistics help determine whether effects are caused by experimental manipulation and not just by chance.

3.5 How do validity and reliability relate to statistics?
- Reliability describes how consistent a result is, and validity describes whether an experiment measures what it is supposed to measure.

Vocabulary Terms

psychology p. 4
structuralism p. 6
functionalism p. 7
psychoanalysis p. 8
behaviorism p. 8
psychodynamic perspective p. 10
cognitive perspective p. 10
cognitive neuroscience p. 10
sociocultural perspective p. 11
biopsychological perspective p. 11
evolutionary psychology p. 11
positive psychology p. 12
clinical psychology p. 12
counseling psychology p. 13
developmental psychology p. 13
experimental psychology p. 13

social psychology p. 13
personality psychology p. 13
physiological psychology p. 14
comparative psychology p. 14
industrial/organizational (I/O) psychology p. 14
scientific method p. 16
hypothesis p. 16
naturalistic observation p. 17
observer effect p. 17
observer bias p. 17
laboratory method p. 18
case study p. 18
survey method p. 18
representative sample p. 19
population p. 19

correlation p. 19
correlation coefficient p. 19
experiment p. 20
operational definition p. 20
informed consent p. 20
independent variable p. 20
dependent variable p. 21
confounding variable p. 21
experimental group p. 21
control group p. 21
random assignment p. 21
placebo effect p. 22
experimenter effect p. 22
double-blind experiment p. 22
descriptive statistics p. 26
inferential statistics p. 26

statistics p. 26
measure of central tendency p. 27
mean p. 27
median p. 27
mode p. 27
measures of variability p. 27
range p. 28
standard deviation p. 28
frequency distribution p. 28
histogram p. 29
polygon p. 30
normal curve p. 30
bell curve p. 30
statistically significant p. 33
reliability p. 33
validity p. 33

THE SCIENCE OF PSYCHOLOGY 35

CHAPTER 1 • Chapter Summary and Vocabulary

Chapter Summary

Encourage students to carefully review and study the summary. Explain that it provides an overview of key concepts presented in the text.

Have students identify what they find unclear or confusing. Call on volunteers to provide answers, examples, or definitions.

Vocabulary Terms

Remind students that terms are defined within the chapter at point of use. If they are not sure of a term's definition, they should look up the definition on the page.

Encourage students to create study cards of unfamiliar words or to go to **www.mypsychlab.com** for flash cards. Have them test themselves or a classmate. Advanced students can explain the terms in their own words.

Critical Thinking

MAKING CONNECTIONS

Have students complete the following activity to connect the ideas in this chapter. Send them to the Multimedia Library for Chapter 1 at **www.mypsychlab.com** to view the video titled "Carlos," which shows how easily people were fooled by a fake "psychic channeler." Then lead a class discussion based on the following questions: (1) Why was it so easy for the fake channeler to get people to believe him? (2) How might research into the fake channeler have established the truth? (3) What kinds of research methods might a person use in order to discover the truth in this situation?

CHAPTER 1 Assessment

Study and Review on mypsychlab.com

Vocabulary Review
Match each vocabulary term to its definition.

1. functionalism
2. statistics
3. behaviorism
4. evolutionary psychology
5. psychoanalysis
6. hypothesis
7. case study
8. experiment
9. reliability
10. validity

a. The tendency of a test to produce the same scores again and again each time it is given to the same people.
b. The branch of mathematics concerned with the collection and interpretation of numerical data.
c. The theory and therapy based on the work of Sigmund Freud.
d. The early perspective in psychology associated with William James, in which the focus of study is how the mind allows people to adapt, live, work, and play.
e. A study of one individual in great detail.
f. The degree to which a test actually measures what it is supposed to measure.
g. A tentative explanation of a phenomenon based on observations.
h. A perspective that focuses on the biological bases of universal mental characteristics that all humans share.
i. A deliberate manipulation of a variable to see if corresponding changes in behavior result, allowing the determination of cause-and-effect relationships.
j. The science of behavior that focuses on observable behavior only.

Writing about Psychology
Respond to each question in complete sentences.

1. Which of the six modern psychological perspectives is most interesting to you? Choose one perspective and give a brief description of that perspective. Then, explain why it interests you. Finally, give at least two examples of real-life problems that the perspective could help psychologists solve.
2. Imagine that you are a psychologist who wants to determine how different amounts of sleep affect students' test scores. Your hypothesis is that students who get 8 hours of sleep during the night will perform better on a test the next day than students who get less sleep. Describe an experiment that you could design to test this hypothesis. Be sure to identify the independent variable and the dependent variable. Also identify potential sources of bias or error, and explain the steps you would take to account for these biases.

Psychology Project
Although women and members of minority groups were not always fully represented in the early days of psychology, they have always made important contributions to the field. This project will give you a chance to study one psychologist's contributions in depth.

Materials:
- access to print or electronic reference resources
- a pencil and paper, or other note-taking materials
- poster board, markers, and craft supplies (optional)

Instructions:
1. Choose an influential psychologist to research. The psychologist may be historical or current, but he or she must be a woman or a member of a minority group. You may want to choose one of the psychologists discussed in this textbook, or you may ask your teacher or librarian for help finding a list of possible psychologists to research.
2. Once you have chosen your psychologist, use print or electronic resources to learn as much as you can about the person you have chosen. Ask yourself, "How did this person begin a psychology career? What are his or her areas of interest? Why is his or her research important? What is one challenge to his or her most important research? What is one strength of his or her most important research? Did this person have to overcome any special challenges?" Take notes as you gather information.
3. Share what you have learned with your classmates by delivering a short oral presentation about your psychologist or creating a poster filled with the information you've collected.

CHAPTER 1 • Assessment

VOCABULARY REVIEW

1. d
2. b
3. j
4. h
5. c
6. g
7. e
8. i
9. a
10. f

WRITING ABOUT PSYCHOLOGY

1. Students' answers should show evidence of careful thought in describing the psychological perspective of particular interest to them, along with the selection of two problems that could be solved by using that perspective.
2. Students should display a clear understanding of what the terms *hypothesis, independent variable*, and *dependent variable* mean. They should also realize that there is a potential for bias or error in their experiments. For example, what if some students eat breakfast before the test and others do not?

PSYCHOLOGY PROJECT

Consider checking students' choices of psychologists before they begin their study. Have students who create posters mount them on classroom walls or the bulletin board. Set aside some class time for students who make oral presentations on their selections. Afterwards, conduct a class discussion about what challenges the female and minority psychologists had to overcome in order to be successful in their field.

Internet Resources

AmoebaWeb: http://psychology.vanguard.edu/amoebaweb/
From Vanguard University Department of Psychology, contains nicely organized tables of links to web pages related to various topics in psychology.

Psych Web: www.psychwww.com
Many psychology-related links maintained by Russ Dewey, assistant professor emeritus of psychology at Georgia Southern University.

APA PsycNET: http://psycnet.apa.org/
Allows you to search for psychology journal articles, books, and web content.

Psychology Central: www.psych-central.com/
Web links and online resources for psychology students and faculty.

Test Yourself

Pick the best answer.

1. Which early theorist developed his perspective on psychology by basing it on Charles Darwin's ideas about natural selection?
   a. Wilhelm Wundt
   b. William James
   c. John B. Watson
   d. Sigmund Freud

2. Which of the following theorists brought structuralism to America?
   a. Wilhelm Wundt
   b. Edward Titchener
   c. William James
   d. Sigmund Freud

3. Which of the following terms describes a number around which all numbers in a data set seem to fall?
   a. measure of variability
   b. measure of central tendency
   c. measure of frequency
   d. measure of significance

4. Which perspective focuses on topics such as perception, learning, and memory?
   a. cognitive psychology
   b. evolutionary psychology
   c. sociocultural psychology
   d. positive psychology

5. Which perspective assumes that human behavior may have developed in certain directions because it served a useful function in preserving the species?
   a. psychoanalysis
   b. humanism
   c. cognitive psychology
   d. evolutionary psychology

6. Which subfield of psychology studies how people change during their lifetimes?
   a. developmental psychology
   b. clinical psychology
   c. physiological psychology
   d. social psychology

7. In an experiment, which participants are subjected to the independent variable?
   a. participants in the control group
   b. participants in the experimental group
   c. all of the participants
   d. none of the participants

8. The process through which researchers explain the true nature of a psychological study to participants is known as
   a. closure
   b. debriefing
   c. ethics
   d. deception

9. Potential participants in a psychological research study must be allowed to
   a. make an informed decision about participating in the study
   b. have access to all the data collected during research
   c. know the independent variable and the dependent variable ahead of time
   d. read and approve any publication that describes the results of the study

10. Which of the following terms is a measure of the relationship between two or more variables?
    a. central tendency
    b. statistical significance
    c. correlation coefficient
    d. standard deviation

11. A psychologist is interested in finding out why identical twins have different personalities. This psychologist is most interested in the goal of
    a. description
    b. explanation
    c. prediction
    d. control

12. Jenna suffers from a nervous tic of washing her hands repeatedly and being unable to resist washing them again and again. How would the psychodynamic perspective most likely explain Jenna's hand-washing behavior?
    a. as a disorder with a biological basis
    b. as a conditioned response to dirt
    c. as an evolutionary adaptation
    d. as a result of repressed conflicts

13. Which group of three psychologists shared similar ideas about human behavior?
    a. Watson, Pavlov, and Skinner
    b. Titchener, Freud, and Pavlov
    c. Rogers, Watson, and Freud
    d. Wundt, Skinner, and Maslow

14. A person who has suffered a major stroke and is now experiencing severe personality problems because of the damage would be best advised to see a
    a. psychiatrist
    b. counseling psychologist
    c. psychology professor
    d. industrial/organizational psychologist

15. The main advantage of laboratory observation is
    a. the degree of control it allows the observer
    b. the amount of participation it allows the observer
    c. the elimination of the observer effect
    d. the strengthening of observer biases

16. Which of the following is a similarity between biopsychology and evolutionary psychology?
    a. Both perspectives believe that behaviors have biological bases.
    b. Both perspectives believe in the importance of conditioned behavior.
    c. Both perspectives are based on Charles Darwin's theory of natural selection.
    d. Both perspectives are based on the study of hormones and brain chemicals.

17. A researcher designs an experiment to test the effects of playing video games on memory. What would be the dependent variable?
    a. scores on a memory test
    b. playing video games
    c. the number of participants
    d. the researcher's biases

18. An experimenter decides to test the effectiveness of a new drug by giving the drug to 100 randomly selected people after explaining the drug's desired effects. All 100 people have positive, statistically significant reactions to the drug. Based on this information, which of the following criticisms of this study is most valid?
    a. The experiment did not have an independent variable and a dependent variable.
    b. The experiment did not test a large enough group of participants.
    c. The results did not illustrate a cause-and-effect relationship.
    d. The results could have been affected by the placebo effect.

19. In the set of numbers 2, 3, 5, 7, what is the range?
    a. 2
    b. 3
    c. 5
    d. 7

CHAPTER 1 • Assessment

TEST YOURSELF

1. b
2. b
3. b
4. a
5. d
6. a
7. b
8. b
9. a
10. c
11. b
12. d
13. a
14. a
15. a
16. a
17. a
18. d
19. c

Ready for Testing

STUDENTS KNOW THEY ARE READY FOR TESTING IF THEY ARE ABLE TO . . .

- Define *psychology* and describe the goals that psychologists hope to achieve.
- Describe the history of psychology.
- Discuss the current state of psychology, including the most common perspectives and major professions in the field.
- Describe the scientific method and discuss its strengths and weaknesses.
- Explain the basic guidelines and ethical concerns of psychological research.
- Explain the basic concepts of data analysis.

CHAPTER 1 • Concept Summary

MULTIMEDIA CONTENT AVAILABLE AT
www.mypsychlab.com

Map the Concepts on **mypsychlab.com**

Study and Review Flashcards on **mypsychlab.com**

STUDY TIPS

Choosing a Place to Study Explain to students that *where* they study can be as important as *how* they study. A good study spot has several important features. It should be a quiet place, with a minimum of distractions. Distractions can come in many forms, including noise, conversation, visitors, and telephone calls. Studying in a place where temptations to play video or computer games exist can make it harder to concentrate. Instead, students should choose a spot in which there is little else to do besides study. In addition, the study area should have good lighting and not be too comfortable. Studying in bed can prompt even those with the best intentions to drop off to sleep! Have students make a list of five possible study spots and ask them to try each one. Have them rate each spot on a scale from 1 to 10.

CHAPTER 1 Concept Summary: The Science of Psychology

Learning Objectives

1.1 1.2 1.3 1.4 pp. 4–12

Trace the Development of Psychology

- **psychology** is the scientific study of behavior and mental processes
- **the history of psychology**
  - structuralism
  - functionalism
  - psychoanalysis
  - behaviorism
- **major modern perspectives**
  - psychodynamic
  - behavioral
  - humanistic
  - cognitive
  - sociocultural
  - biopsychological

1.5 1.6 1.7 pp. 12–14

Identify Psychology's Subfields

- **major subfields of psychology**
  - clinical psychology
  - counseling psychology
  - developmental psychology
  - experimental psychology
  - social psychology
  - personality psychology
  - physiological psychology
  - comparative psychology
  - industrial/organizational (I/O) psychology

Learning Objectives

2.1 2.2 2.3 2.4 pp. 16–23

Understand Psychological Research Methods

- **scientific method**
  - formulating the question
  - developing a hypothesis
  - testing the hypothesis
  - drawing conclusions
  - reporting your results
- **research methods**
  - **nonexperimental methods**
    - naturalistic observation
    - laboratory observation
    - case studies
    - surveys
  - **correlation**
    - is a measure of relationship between two or more variables
    - does not prove causation
  - **experiments**
    - manipulating the **independent variable** to affect the **dependent variable**
    - using **random assignment** to create the **experimental group** and the **control group**
    - experimental hazards: **placebo effect** and **experimenter effect**

What Every Student Should Know About...

PROCRASTINATION

The individual who frequently engages in procrastination postpones important projects. Many different types of projects begin to develop, and deadlines seem to appear all at once. Things soon begin to become overwhelming, and many students simply do not have any idea where to begin first, and then they feel helpless and out of control. Prioritizing your schedule can prevent this state of things from ever occurring in the first place. Ask yourself: What is most important to you? What needs doing right now? What is the best manner to go about doing it? Try writing down your responsibilities. This method is very advantageous for two reasons: When you write down everything that needs to be done, you have a very clear idea of what each project involves; and by doing that, you are able to identify what needs to be done first.

Learning Objectives

2.5 **2.6** pp. 23–24

Consider Ethical Issues in Psychological Research

- guidelines for research with humans
  - institutional review board (IRB)
  - humanitarian
  - informed consent
  - justification
  - right to withdraw
  - risks and benefits
  - debriefing
  - confidentiality
- guidelines for research with animals
  - psychologists avoid exposing animals to any unnecessary pain or suffering

"He says he wants a lawyer."

Learning Objectives

3.1 **3.2** **3.3** **3.4** **3.5** pp. 26–33

Learn the Basic Concepts of Data Analysis

- **descriptive statistics**
  organize and summarize data
  - measures of central tendency
    - mean
    - median
    - mode
  - measures of variability
    - range
    - standard deviation
- **frequency distributions**
  can be represented graphically; one special type of distribution is the normal curve
- **correlation coefficients**
  represent the direction and strength of the relationship between two variables
- **inferential statistics**
  determine if results are caused by something more than chance
- **reliability and validity**
  measures of central tendency, measures of variability, and correlations can help determine whether a test is reliable and valid

THE SCIENCE OF PSYCHOLOGY 39

Comprehension Check

INEFFECTIVE THERAPIES

To check their understanding, students can visit the Multimedia Library section of the www.mypsychlab.com site and explore the Ineffective Therapies activity. Advanced students can work alone, while on-level and struggling students can work in pairs or small groups. Students will receive immediate feedback on their answers.

CHAPTER 1 • Concept Summary

STUDY TIPS

Learning Styles Explain that figuring out their particular way of absorbing information can go a long way toward helping students study more effectively. The simplest and most useful grouping of learning styles divides people into visual, auditory, and kinesthetic/tactile learners. Have students consider the following questions to help them recognize their preferred learning style: Do they remember information best when they read it, hear it, or take notes about it? When learning new vocabulary, do they tend to visualize the word, sound out the word, or write the word down? Are they likely to forget names but remember faces? Remember names but forget faces? Remember what they were doing or where they were when meeting someone new? These examples illustrate visual, auditory, and kinesthetic learners, in that order. Visual learners need quiet study time and learn well using outlines. Auditory learners do well with group discussions and audiotapes or podcasts. Kinesthetic learners benefit from short study sessions and role playing.

Chapter 1 Concept Summary 39

CHAPTER 2 • Module 4

Launch the Chapter

CHAPTER GOALS AND LEARNING OBJECTIVES

Module 4 The Nervous System

Understand the structure and function of the nervous system.

4.1 What are the major divisions of the human nervous system?

4.2 What are neurons, and how do they work?

4.3 What are the functions of the different parts of the central nervous system?

Explain how the neuroendocrine system functions.

4.4 How are the endocrine glands connected to the nervous system?

4.5 How do hormones affect our thoughts and behavior?

4.6 What effects do hormones have on the immune system?

Module 5 The Brain

Learn how scientists study the nervous system.

5.1 How do people study the brain?

5.2 What advances have made the brain easier to study?

5.3 What are some recent innovations in neuroscience?

Understand the structure and function of the brain.

5.4 What are the different parts of the brain, and what does each part do?

5.5 How does the left side of the brain differ from the right side?

Module 6 Heredity, Environment, and Adaptation

Discover how biology and experience interact.

6.1 How do genetic factors determine who we are?

6.2 How do heredity and environmental factors interact to affect our development?

6.3 How do evolved tendencies influence our behavior?

DIFFERENTIATED INSTRUCTION KEY

Look for these symbols to help you adjust steps in each lesson to meet your students' needs.

- **L1** Special Needs
- **L2** Basic
  - **ELL** English Language Learners
  - **LPR** Less Proficient Readers
- **L3** All Students
- **L4** Advanced Students

CHAPTER 2
The Biological Perspective

Half a Mind?

Michelle M. is a 29-year-old woman who holds a part-time job and loves to read, watch movies, and spend time with her family. She has the amazing ability to tell you exactly what day of the week on which any particular calendar date fell, and she's a whiz at solitaire. If you were to look at her, you would see that in addition to wearing glasses (like so many other people), Michelle's right wrist is a bit bent and slightly twisted. She can use this hand just fine, although she is actually left-handed. She wears a brace to support her right leg.

You might think that Michelle is very lucky to still have so many normal functions, since the weakness on her right side might indicate that she had suffered a moderate stroke at some time in her past, but you'd be wrong. Michelle is more than lucky—she's astonishing. The weakness in her right side comes from the fact that Michelle was born with basically half a brain—the right half—and nothing but a fluid-filled cavity in the left side of her skull.

Michelle's case has fascinated doctors who study the brain. Her condition has existed since the womb, when some unknown accident caused the left side of her brain to fail to develop, while the right side grew normally. The left side of the brain, as you will see later in this chapter, normally controls skills such as speech, reading, analytical thinking, and understanding abstract concepts. Michelle, with no left brain, can do all those things well, with the exception of abstraction—she's a pretty detail-oriented, concrete person (Doidge, 2007).

How can Michelle function so normally when she's missing half of her brain? That's just one mystery that we will explore in the pages to come.

CORRELATION TO APA STANDARDS FOR CHAPTER 2

IIA. BIOLOGICAL BASES OF BEHAVIOR

IIA-1. Structure and function of the nervous system in human and nonhuman animals .... pp. 42–50, 56, 57–63

IIA-2. Structure and function of the neuroendocrine system .... pp. 50–52

IIA-3. The interaction between biological factors and experience .... pp. 66–70

IIA-4. Methods and issues related to biological advances .... pp. 54–57

MODULE 4 ▸ **THE NERVOUS SYSTEM**
MODULE 5 ▸ **THE BRAIN**
MODULE 6 ▸ **HEREDITY, ENVIRONMENT, AND ADAPTATION**

Why Study?

The Nervous System and the Glands

How could we possibly understand any of our behavior, thoughts, or actions without knowing something about the incredible organs that allow us to perceive the world, think, and respond to it? If we can understand how the brain, the nerves, and the glands interact to control feelings, thoughts, and behavior, we can begin to truly understand the complex organism called a human being.

THE BIOLOGICAL PERSPECTIVE   41

SCHEDULING

1 Period = 50 min. 1 Block = 90 min.	Semester Course (18 weeks/90 days) Periods/Blocks		Full-Year Course (36 weeks/180 days) Period/Blocks	
Module 4	2.5	1.25	5	2.5
Module 5	2.5	1.25	5	2.5
Module 6	1	0.5	2	1
Total Days for Chapter	6	3	12	6

CHAPTER 2 • Module 4

Teacher Prep

The nervous system is divided into the central nervous system and the peripheral nervous system. The autonomic nervous system is divided into the parasympathetic and sympathetic divisions. Neurons have dendrites, which receive input; a soma, or cell body; and axons, which carry the neural message to other cells.

The spinal cord transmits messages to and from the brain. The brain and the spinal cord communicate with the rest of the body through the peripheral nervous system.

The nervous system triggers endocrine glands to release hormones into the bloodstream, affecting thoughts and behavior. Some hormones can help the immune system function properly; others can weaken the system.

Modern scientists perform tests on people with existing brain damage.

Brain-imaging techniques include CT scans, MRI and fMRI scans, PET scans, and EEGs.

Researchers have explored the possibility of using stem cells to repair damaged or diseased brain tissue. Researchers have also discovered the existence of mirror neurons.

The structures of the hindbrain control life-sustaining functions, sleep, arousal, and movement. The structures of the limbic system are involved in emotions, motivation, and learning. The cortex processes sensory information, controls voluntary muscles, and performs higher mental functions. The left side controls language, writing, and logical thought. The right side controls spatial perception, facial recognition, patterns, melodies, and emotions.

DNA molecules form genes, which interact to determine many of our physical traits and predispositions.

Our thoughts and behaviors are affected not only by biological predispositions, but also by the influence of our parents, our peers, and the cultures in which we participate.

Chapter 2 The Biological Perspective   **41**

CHAPTER 2 • Module 4

Focus

RESOURCES
For this module, consult the appropriate sections of the Teacher's Manual, Test Bank, and PowerPoint slides, all found on the Teacher's Resource DVD, and the interactive study tools for students on MyPsychLab.

BEFORE CLASS
Students should read the section for homework before coming to class.

BELLRINGER
Students may find the presence of a chapter on "biology" puzzling in a psychology textbook. Point out our tendency to take for granted the normal functioning of the nervous system. Only when there is damage through stroke, disease, or brain trauma do we realize its importance. Ask volunteers to share any stories they have about such experiences.

Teach

COVER THE MODULE

4.1 What are the major divisions of the human nervous system?
- The nervous system is a complex network of cells that carry information to and from all parts of the body.

4.2 What are neurons, and how do they work?
- **Structure of the Neuron: the Nervous System's Building Block**
  - *Neurons* are specialized cells in the nervous system that receive and send messages.
  - Neurons have *dendrites*, which receive input; a *soma*, or cell body; and *axons*, which carry the neural message to other cells.

42 Chapter 2 The Biological Perspective

Module 4: The Nervous System

Module Goals

Understand the structure and function of the nervous system.

Explain how the neuroendocrine system functions.

Learning Objectives

4.1 What are the major divisions of the human nervous system?
4.2 What are neurons, and how do they work?
4.3 What are the functions of the different parts of the central nervous system?
4.4 How are the endocrine glands connected to the nervous system?
4.5 How do hormones affect our thoughts and behavior?
4.6 What effects do hormones have on the immune system?

Understand the Structure and Function of the Nervous System

4.1 What are the major divisions of the human nervous system?

This chapter will discuss a complex system of cells, organs, and chemicals that work together to produce behavior, thoughts, and actions. The first part of this complex arrangement is the *nervous system*, a network of cells that carries information to and from all parts of the body. Before beginning the discussion on the cells that make up the nervous system, take a look at Figure 4.1. This figure shows the organization of the various parts of the nervous system and will help in understanding how all the different parts work together in controlling the way people and animals think, act, and feel.

4.2 What are neurons, and how do they work?

Neurons are specialized cells in the nervous system that receive and send messages within that system. Whether they are located in the brain or in other parts of the body, all neurons have a special structure that helps them communicate with each other.

Structure of the Neuron—the Nervous System's Building Block
The parts of the neuron that receive messages from other cells are called **dendrites**. The name *dendrite* comes from the Greek word for "tree," and this structure does indeed look like the branches of a tree. The dendrites are attached to the cell body, or **soma**, which is the part of the cell that contains the nucleus and keeps the entire cell alive and functioning. The **axon** is a fiber attached to the soma, and its job is to carry messages out to other cells. (See Figure 4.2 on page 44.)

neuron the basic cell that makes up the nervous system and that receives and sends messages within that system.

dendrites branchlike structures that receive messages from other neurons.

soma the cell body of the neuron responsible for maintaining the life of the cell.

axon tubelike structure that carries the neural message to other cells.

42 CHAPTER 2

Terms

- neuron • dendrites • soma • axon • myelin • action potential • axon terminals
- synaptic vesicles • neurotransmitter • receptor sites • central nervous system (CNS)
- sensory neuron • motor neuron • interneuron • peripheral nervous system (PNS)
- autonomic nervous system (ANS) • sympathetic division (fight-or-flight system)
- parasympathetic division • endocrine glands • hormones • pituitary gland
- pineal gland • thyroid gland • pancreas • adrenal glands • gonads

FIGURE 4.1 An Overview of the Nervous System

- Nervous system
  - Central nervous system: The brain and spinal cord
    - Brain: Interprets and stores information and sends orders to muscles, glands, and organs
    - Spinal Cord: Pathway connecting the brain and the peripheral nervous system
  - Peripheral nervous system: Transmits information to and from the central nervous system
    - Autonomic nervous system: Automatically regulates glands, internal organs and blood vessels, pupil dilation, digestion, and blood pressure
      - Parasympathetic division: Maintains body functions under ordinary conditions; saves energy
      - Sympathetic division: Prepares the body to react and expend energy in times of stress
    - Somatic nervous system: Carries sensory information and controls movement of the skeletal muscles

A layer of fatty substances called **myelin** wraps around the shaft of the axons, forming a protective sheath. It is very similar to the concept of a laptop power cable. Within the cable are lots of copper wires coated in plastic. The plastic serves the same insulating purpose for the wires as the myelin sheath does for the axons. Bundled all together, they form a cable that is much stronger and less vulnerable to breakage than any wire alone would be. It works the same way in the nervous system. Bundles of myelin-coated axons travel together in "cables" called *nerves*.

Myelin not only insulates the neuron but also offers a little protection from damage and speeds up the electrical message traveling down the axon. As shown in Figure 4.2, sections of myelin bump up next to each other on the axon, similar to the way sausages are linked together. The places where the myelin seems to bump are actually small spaces on the axon called the nodes of Ranvier, which are not covered in myelin. When the electrical impulse travels down an axon surrounded with myelin, it "jumps" between the myelin sheath sections to the places where the axon is accessible at the nodes. That makes the message go much faster down the coated axon than it would down an uncoated axon of a neuron.

myelin fatty substances that coat the axons of neurons to insulate, protect, and speed up the neural impulse.

The Electrochemical Message of the Neuron

Exactly how does this "electrical message" work inside the cell?
A neuron that's at rest—not currently firing a neural impulse or message—is actually electrically charged. The inside of the cell is really a semiliquid (jelly-like) solution in which there are charged particles, or *ions*. There is also a

◄ Exactly how does this "electrical message" work inside the cell?

THE BIOLOGICAL PERSPECTIVE 43

Explore

USING INFORMATION FROM THE INTERNET

Send students to the website Neuroscience for Kids at
http://faculty.washington.edu/chudler/neurok.html
Tell them not to be put off by the name! This site can be enjoyed by people of all ages who want to learn about the brain. It is a fun, superbly organized site providing information and links to other neuroscience sites. It includes informative pages covering brain basics, higher functions, spinal cord, peripheral nervous system, the neuron, sensory systems, methods and techniques, drug effects, and neurological and mental disorders. Ask students to select a topic that interests them and present a brief oral or written review of what they learned.

CHAPTER 2 • Module 4

COVER THE MODULE *(continued)*

- *Myelin* insulates and protects the axons of neurons that travel in the body.
- These axons are bundled together in "cables" called nerves.
- Myelin also speeds up the neural message.
- When the electrical impulse travels down an axon surrounded with myelin, this coating makes the message go faster down the coated axon than it would down an uncoated axon.

UNDERSTANDING VISUALS

Explain that Figure 4.1 provides an important overview of the nervous system, with which students must familiarize themselves. Refer back to this figure as you cover Module 4, and encourage students to review it to help understand the lesson's content.

DISCUSS THE STUDENT VOICE QUESTION

Some students may have trouble grasping the idea of an "electrical message." Take time to explain the presence of positive and negative ions inside and outside the neurons. Use the visual imagery of the tiny opening, or "gates," in the membrane, allowing substances to enter or leave the cells.

CHAPTER 2 • Module 4

COVER THE MODULE (continued)

- **The Electrochemical Message of the Neuron**
  - A neuron at rest—not currently firing a neural impulse or message—is electrically charged.
  - The inside of the cell contains charged particles called ions. The semiliquid solution surrounding the outside of the cell also contains ions. The ions inside the cell are mainly negatively charged, while the ions outside the cell are mostly positively charged.
  - When the cell is in resting potential, sodium ions outside the cell cannot enter. But when the cell receives a strong enough stimulation from another cell, gates open and allow sodium ions to rush in.

UNDERSTANDING VISUALS

Because the scientific aspect of how neurons work may intimidate some students, consider making slides of Figures 4.2 and 4.3 and displaying them for class viewing. Point out—or have students point out—the different elements of the illustrations as you discuss the figures' content.

FIGURE 4.2 The Structure of the Neuron

semiliquid solution surrounding the outside of the cell that contains ions. While there are both positive and negative ions inside and outside of the cell, the ions inside the cell are mostly negatively charged, and the ions outside the cell are mostly positively charged.

The cell membrane itself is *semipermeable*. This means some substances that are outside the cell can enter through tiny openings, or *gates*, in the membrane, while other substances in the cell can go outside. The negatively charged ions inside the cell, however, are so big that they can't get out, which leaves the inside of the cell primarily negative when at rest. Outside the cell are lots of positively charged sodium ions, but they are unable to enter the cell membrane when the cell is at rest—the ion gates that would allow them in are closed. But because the outside sodium ions are positive and the inside ions are negative, and because opposite electrical charges attract each other, the sodium ions will cluster around the membrane. This difference in charges is an electrical potential.

When the cell is in a state called the *resting potential*, the sodium ions are outside the cell. The sodium ions cannot enter when the cell is at rest, because even though the cell membrane has all these gates, the *particular* gates for the big sodium ions aren't open yet. In this state, the cell membrane is *impermeable* (nothing can pass through it). But when the cell receives a strong stimulation from another cell (meaning that the dendrites are activated), the cell membrane opens up those *particular* gates, one after the other, in domino fashion, all down its surface, allowing the

Explore

STUDYING SQUID

Direct students to **www.mypsychlab.com** to watch the Chapter 2 video entitled "Studying Squid." Then have them answer these questions: (1) Why do scientists study this squid? (2) What is it about the squid that is so valuable to scientists? (3) Considering what you learned in Chapter 1 about the ethics of research using animals, do you think it is ethical for scientists to use squids for research? Students can answer the questions in writing or in a class discussion.

FIGURE 4.3 The Neural Impulse Action Potential

The Neuron at Rest
During the resting potential, the neuron is negatively charged inside and positively charged outside.

The Neural Impulse
The action potential occurs when positive sodium ions enter into the cell, causing a reversal of the electrical charge from negative to positive.

The Neural Impulse Continues
As the action potential moves down the axon toward the axon terminals, the cell areas behind the action potential return to their resting state of a negative charge as the positive sodium ions are pumped to the outside of the cell, and the positive potassium ions rapidly leave.

---

sodium ions to rush into the cell. That causes the inside of the cell to become mostly positive and the outside of the cell to become mostly negative, because many of the positive sodium ions are now inside the cell—at the point where the first gate opened. This electrical-charge reversal, called *depolarization*, will start at the part of the axon closest to the soma (the first gate) and then proceed down the axon in a kind of chain reaction, like dominos falling one after the other. (Picture a long hallway with many doors in which the first door opens, then the second, and so on, all the way down the hall.) This electrical-charge reversal is known as the **action potential** because the electrical impulse is now in action rather than at rest. Each action potential sequence takes about one-thousandth of a second, so the neural message travels very fast—from 2 miles per hour in the slowest, shortest neurons to 270 miles per hour in other neurons. (See Figure 4.3.) As the action potential travels down the axon, the parts of the cell that the action potential has already left behind return to the resting state.

If the stimulus that originally causes the neuron to fire is very strong, will the neuron fire more strongly than it would if the stimulus were weak?

Neurons actually have a threshold for firing, and all it takes is a stimulus that is just strong enough to get past that threshold to make the neuron fire. When a neuron does fire, it fires in an *all-or-none* fashion. Neurons are either firing at full strength or not firing at all; there's no such thing as "partial" firing of a neuron. It would be like turning on a light switch—it's either on or off.

> If the stimulus that originally causes the neuron to fire is very strong, will the neuron fire more strongly than it would if the stimulus were weak?

action potential the release of the neural impulse consisting of a reversal of the electrical charge within the axon.

THE BIOLOGICAL PERSPECTIVE 45

CHAPTER 2 • Module 4

COVER THE MODULE *(continued)*

- When a cell is stimulated, the inside becomes mostly positive while the outside becomes mostly negative.
- This electrical-charge reversal, called depolarization, proceeds down the axon in a chain reaction. This is known as the action potential because the electrical impulse is now in action, rather than at rest.

EXTEND THE DISCUSSION

Use "The Wave," an activity at sports arenas, as an analogy for the action potential. Like "The Wave," the action potential travels the length of the neuron; the neuron does not experience the action potential all at once. To extend the analogy, mention that right after people stand up in "The Wave," they are somewhat tired and must recover (i.e., refractory period) to be prepared for the next go-round (i.e., action potential).

DISCUSS THE STUDENT VOICE QUESTION

Emphasize that neurons have a threshold for firing, and the stimulus needs to be just strong enough to make the neuron fire. This firing is an all-or-nothing situation. The example of turning a light switch on and off may be helpful for students to remember.

Class Demonstration (Kinesthetic)

USING REACTION TIME TO SHOW THE SPEED OF NEURONS

Have students form a line by holding hands. Instruct them to close their eyes and squeeze the hand of the person next to them when they feel the person on the opposite side squeeze their hand. The last person in line should signal you that his or her hand has been squeezed by raising a free hand. Use a stopwatch to record the elapsed time. Repeat the process until the reaction times seem stable. Take the final reaction time and divide by the number of students to get the average reaction time. Next, have the students squeeze the next person's shoulder. The average reaction time should now decrease since the sensory information has a shorter distance to travel. The difference in average reaction times represent—roughly—the average conduction time for sensory information between the hand and shoulder.

Module 4 The Nervous System

CHAPTER 2 • Module 4

COVER THE MODULE (continued)

- **Sending the Message to Other Cells—the Synapse**
  - *Synaptic vesicles* in the end of the *axon terminal* release *neurotransmitter* chemicals into the synapse, or gap, between one cell and the next.
  - The neurotransmitter molecules fit into *receptor sites* on the next cell, stimulating or inhibiting that cell's firing.

DISCUSS THE STUDENT VOICE QUESTION

Direct students' attention to Figure 4.4. Tell students to point out the different elements of the illustration as you read aloud the first two paragraphs on the page.

TEACHING TIP

Creating a positive learning environment enables all students to reach their full potential. In a supportive, respectful setting, students perform and behave better. Teachers who use effective motivational and management strategies that actively engage students and appeal to individual learning styles and needs create classrooms that enhance students' academic and personal lives.

Sending the Message to Other Cells—the Synapse

▶ What happens when the action potential reaches the end of the axon?

What happens when the action potential reaches the end of the axon? Look once again at Figure 4.2. The end of the axon actually fans out into several shorter fibers called **axon terminals**. The tip of each axon terminal has a little knob on it. Figure 4.4 shows this knob blown up to giant size. Notice that the knob (called the *synaptic knob* or sometimes the *terminal button, knob,* or *bulb*) is not empty. It has a number of little saclike structures in it called **synaptic vesicles**. The word *vesicle* is Latin and means a "little blister" or "fluid-filled sac."

Inside the synaptic vesicles are chemicals suspended in fluid, which are *molecules* of substances called **neurotransmitters**. The name is simple enough—they are inside a neuron and they are going to transmit a message. Next to the synaptic knob is the dendrite of another neuron (see Figure 4.4). Between them is a fluid-filled space called the *synapse* (also known as the *synaptic cleft* or *synaptic gap*). Instead of an electrical charge, the vesicles at the end of the axon contain the molecules of neurotransmitters, whereas the surface of the dendrite right next to the axon contains special little locks called **receptor sites**. These locks only accept a particular molecule of neurotransmitter, just as a keyhole will only accept a particular key.

How do the neurotransmitters get across the gap? Recall the action potential making its way down the axon after the neuron has been stimulated. When that action potential, or electrical charge, reaches the synaptic vesicles, the

axon terminals branches at the end of the axon.

synaptic vesicles saclike structures found inside the synaptic knob containing chemicals.

neurotransmitter chemical found in the synaptic vesicles that, when released, has an effect on the next cell.

receptor sites holes in the surface of the dendrites or certain cells of the muscles and glands, which are shaped to fit only certain neurotransmitters.

FIGURE 4.4 The Synapse
The neuron's electrical impulse reaches the synaptic knobs, triggering the release of the neuron's chemical messengers, called neurotransmitters, from the synaptic vesicles and into the cleft.

46 CHAPTER 2

Class Demonstration

LEARNING ABOUT NEUROTRANSMITTERS

<u>Purpose</u>: Students learn about the major neurotransmitters and their effects.

<u>Time</u>: 15 minutes

<u>Description</u>: Each student team member is assigned to a different neurotransmitter. Students may be asked to complete their research outside class, or you may give students 5 minutes in class to look up the information in the textbook. Students meet in expert groups to make sure they have the correct information on their assigned neurotransmitter. Students return to their teams and present information on their neurotransmitter.

46 Chapter 2 The Biological Perspective

synaptic vesicles release their neurotransmitters into the synaptic cleft. The molecules then float across the synapse, and many of them fit themselves into the receptor sites, activating the next cell and stimulating that cell's action potential.

So far, we've been talking about the synapse as if neurotransmitters always cause the next cell to fire its action potential (or, in the case of a muscle or gland, to contract or start secreting its chemicals). But the neurons must have a way to be turned *off* as well as on. Otherwise, when a person burns a finger, the pain signals from those neurons would not stop until the burn was completely healed. Muscles are told to contract or relax, and glands are told to secrete or stop secreting their chemicals. The neurotransmitters found at various synapses around the nervous system (and there are at least 50 to 100 identified neurotransmitters and theoretically several times that number exist) can either turn cells on (called an *excitatory* effect) or turn cells off (called an *inhibitory* effect), depending on exactly what synapse is being affected. (See Table 4.1 for a list of some neurotransmitters and their functions.) **Explore** on mypsychlab.com

Explore neurons and neurotransmitters on mypsychlab.com

Table 4.1	Some Neurotransmitters and Their Functions
NEUROTRANSMITTERS	**FUNCTIONS**
Acetylcholine	• Excitatory or inhibitory • Involved in arousal, attention, and memory • Controls muscle contractions
Serotonin	• Excitatory or inhibitory • Involved in mood, sleep, and appetite
Dopamine	• Excitatory or inhibitory • Involved in control of movement and sensations of pleasure
Endorphins	• Inhibitory neural regulators • Involved in pain relief

4.3 What are the functions of the different parts of the central nervous system?

The nervous system is divided into two main parts: the central nervous system, which consists of the spinal cord and brain and is in the "central" part of the body, and the peripheral nervous system, which extends to the periphery (outlying edges) of the body. The **central nervous system (CNS)** is composed of the brain and the spinal cord. Both the brain and spinal cord are composed of neurons and other cells that control the life-sustaining functions of the body as well as all thought, emotion, and behavior.

The brain is the core of the nervous system, the part that makes sense of the information received from the senses, makes decisions, and sends commands out to the muscles and the rest of the body. Without the spinal cord, however, the brain would be useless.

The *spinal cord* is a long bundle of neurons that serves two vital functions for the nervous system. Look at the cross-sectional view of the spinal cord in Figure 4.5. Notice that it seems to be divided into two areas, one around the outside and one inside the cord. If it were a real spinal cord, the outer section would appear white and the inner section would seem gray. That's because the outer section is composed mainly of myelinated axons ("white matter"), whereas the inner

central nervous system (CNS) part of the nervous system consisting of the brain and spinal cord.

THE BIOLOGICAL PERSPECTIVE

Class Demonstration

DISCUSSING NEUROTRANSMITTERS

Psychoactive drugs affect consciousness because of their effects on synaptic transmission. For example, cocaine and amphetamines prolong the action of certain neurotransmitters, and opiates imitate the action of natural neuromodulators called the endorphins. The neurotransmitters dopamine, norepinephrine, and serotonin are associated with some severe forms of mental illness. There are probably only a few ounces of these substances in the body, but they may have a profound effect on mood, memory, perception, and behavior. Ask: **Why is it important to know how neurotransmitters work in the body?**

CHAPTER 2 • Module 4

COVER THE MODULE (continued)

- The neurotransmitters found at various synapses around the nervous system can turn cells on (excitatory effect) or turn cells off (inhibitory effect).
- The neurotransmitter acetylcholine controls muscle contractions. Serotonin is involved in mood, sleep, and appetite. Dopamine is involved in the control of movement and sensations of pleasure. Endorphins are involved in pain relief.

MULTIMEDIA CONTENT AVAILABLE AT
www.mypsychlab.com

Explore neurons and neurotransmitters on **mypsychlab.com**

COVER THE MODULE

4.3 What are the functions of the different parts of the central nervous system?

- The *nervous system* is divided into the central nervous system, consisting of the spinal cord and brain, and the peripheral nervous system, extending to the outlying edges of the body.
- Both the brain and the spinal cord are composed of neurons and other cells that control body functions, thought, emotion, and behavior.
- The brain is the nervous system's core. It makes decisions and sends messages to the rest of the body.

CHAPTER 2 • Module 4

COVER THE MODULE (continued)

- The spinal cord serves two functions:
  - The outer part of the cord transmits messages to and from the brain, while the inner part controls life-saving reflexes such as the pain response.
- Spinal cord reflexes involve sensory neurons, interneurons, and motor neurons, forming a simple reflex arc.

DISCUSS THE STUDENT VOICE QUESTION

Tell students that the word *peripheral* comes from the Greek word *peripheria*, meaning "carrying around." Therefore, the *peripheral* nervous system involves the nerves and neurons that are not in the *central* nervous system.

L3 DIFFERENTIATED INSTRUCTION

It is critical to properly match the difficulty level of tasks with the ability level of students. Giving students tasks that they perceive as too hard lowers their expectations of success. However, giving students assignments that they think are too easy undermines their feeling of competence.

FIGURE 4.5 The Spinal Cord Reflex
The pain from the burning heat of the candle flame stimulates the sensory nerve fibers, which carry the message up to the interneurons in the middle of the spinal cord. The interneurons then send a message out by means of the motor nerve fibers, causing the hand to jerk away from the flame.

1 Flame stimulates pain receptors (sensory neurons).
2 Sensory neurons excite interneurons in the dorsal gray portion of the spinal cord.
3 Interneurons excite motor neurons in the ventral gray portion of the spinal cord.
4 Motor nerves exit the spinal cord, excite the muscle, and initiate a movement.

section is mainly composed of somas (cell bodies) of neurons ("gray matter"). The purpose of the outer section is to carry messages from the body up to the brain and from the brain down to the body. It is simply a message pipeline.

The inside section, which is made up of cell bodies, is actually a primitive sort of "brain." This part of the spinal cord is responsible for certain reflexes—very fast lifesaving reflexes. To understand how the spinal cord reflexes work, it is important to know there are three basic types of neurons: **sensory neurons** that carry messages from the senses to the spinal cord and then up to the brain; **motor neurons** that carry messages from the brain down the spinal cord and into the periphery of the body; and **interneurons** that receive sensory messages, but provide a "reflex arc" that bypasses the brain and sends motor messages back into the periphery of the body for even faster response than the brain could make. (See Figure 4.5.) Touch a flame or a hot stove with your finger, for example, and a sensory neuron will send the pain message up to the spinal column, where it enters into the central area of the spinal cord. The interneuron in that central area will then receive the message and send out a response along a motor neuron, causing your finger to pull back. This all happens very quickly. If the pain message had to go all the way up to the brain before a response could be made, the response time would be greatly increased and more damage would be done to your finger. Of course, the pain message does eventually get to the brain, where other motor responses may be triggered, like saying "Ouch!" and putting the finger in your mouth.

▶ *OK, but how does the CNS communicate with the rest of the body?*

The term *peripheral* refers to things that are not in the center or that are on the edges of the center. The **peripheral nervous system**, or **PNS** (see Figure 4.6), is made up of all the nerves and neurons that are not contained in the CNS. This system allows the brain and spinal cord to communicate with the sensory systems of the eyes, ears, skin, and mouth and allows the brain and spinal cord to control the muscles and glands of the body. The PNS can be divided into two major systems, the *somatic nervous system* and the **autonomic nervous system (ANS)**.

The Somatic Nervous System and the Autonomic Nervous System The somatic nervous system controls the senses and the skeletal muscles—the muscles that allow us to move our bodies. Often, we use these muscles voluntarily. When people are walking, raising their hands in class,

sensory neuron a neuron that carries information from the senses to the CNS.

motor neuron a neuron that carries messages from the CNS to the muscles of the body.

48 CHAPTER 2

Explore

EFFECTS OF DRUGS ON THE BODY AND THE BRAIN

The website for the PBS series "Moyers on Addiction: Close to Home" features interesting animations of how various drugs of abuse work in the body and the brain. Send students to **www.thirteen.org/closetohome** to view these animations. Drugs covered include alcohol, marijuana, cocaine, nicotine, opiates, and stimulants. Ask volunteers to report to the class on what they learned. What effects do these drugs have on humans? Are there certain ways of using these drugs that cause reactions in the body more quickly or more slowly?

picking a flower to smell, or directing their gaze toward a pretty picture, they are using the somatic nervous system.

The ANS, on the other hand, controls muscles that we cannot voluntarily control, like the muscles of the internal organs. It is in charge of many of the body's automatic functions, including breathing, digestion, heart rate, and the release of hormones into the bloodstream.

The ANS is further divided into two systems, the **sympathetic division** and the **parasympathetic division** (also known as the sympathetic branch and the parasympathetic branch). The sympathetic division is usually called the *fight-or-flight system* because it allows people and animals to deal with all kinds of stressful events. LINK *to Chapter Fifteen: Stress and Health,*

interneuron a neuron found in the center of the spinal cord that receives information from the sensory neurons and sends commands to the muscles through the motor neurons. Interneurons also make up the bulk of the neurons in the brain.

peripheral nervous system (PNS) all nerves and neurons that are not contained in the brain and spinal cord but that run through the body itself.

autonomic nervous system (ANS) division of the PNS consisting of nerves that control all of the involuntary muscles, organs, and glands.

sympathetic division (fight-or-flight system) part of the ANS that is responsible for reacting to stressful events and bodily arousal.

parasympathetic division part of the ANS that restores the body to normal functioning after arousal and is responsible for the day-to-day functioning of the organs and glands.

FIGURE 4.6 The Peripheral Nervous System

THE BIOLOGICAL PERSPECTIVE 49

CHAPTER 2 • Module 4

COVER THE MODULE *(continued)*

- **The Somatic Nervous System and the Autonomic Nervous System**
  - The somatic nervous system contains the sensory pathway, or neurons carrying messages to the central nervous system, and the motor pathway, or neurons carrying messages from the central nervous system to the voluntary muscles.
  - The *autonomic nervous system* consists of the parasympathetic division and the sympathetic division.
    - The *sympathetic division* is our fight-or-flight system reacting to stress.
    - The *parasympathetic division* restores and maintains normal day-to-day functioning of the organs.

  LINK *to Chapter Fifteen: Stress and Health, p. 488*

EXTEND THE DISCUSSION

Ask students to think of a time when they were very frightened. What sorts of bodily symptoms did they experience? Then have them think of a time when they were very calm and relaxed. What sorts of bodily symptoms did they experience? List students' comments on the board.

FAST FACT

Ask students if they can explain the difference between *distress* and *eustress*. *(Distress, the most familiar type of stress, has negative implications, while the term* eustress *is used to describe a positive form of stress, usually related to desirable events such as winning at athletics, getting married, or celebrating a holiday.)*

Class Demonstration

HANDLING STRESS

Divide the class into pairs or small teams. Ask students to think about ways they have for managing both mental and physical stress. Do they think their coping mechanisms are helpful (e.g., getting more sleep) or potentially harmful (e.g., overeating)? Have them create posters or PowerPoint slides listing and illustrating their stress management methods. Then tell them to research healthy ways to cope, and add these techniques to their audiovisual presentations. Finally, have students post their materials in the classroom or make presentations to their classmates.

Module 4 The Nervous System **49**

CHAPTER 2 • Module 4

COVER THE MODULE (continued)
- The sympathetic division helps the body deal with stress by expending energy reserves.
- The parasympathetic division mends energy reserves and is responsible for most of the daily functions of the body.

MULTIMEDIA CONTENT AVAILABLE AT
www.mypsychlab.com

◉→ Simulate the autonomic nervous system on **mypsychlab.com**

COVER THE MODULE

4.4 How are the endocrine glands connected to the nervous system?

- Glands are body organs that secrete chemicals. *Endocrine glands* secrete their chemicals directly into the bloodstream for fast distribution.
- The chemicals secreted by endocrine glands are *hormones*. When they are triggered by the nervous system, hormones flow into the bloodstream and are carried to target organs.

---

p. 488. Emotions during these events might be anger (hence, the term *fight*) or fear (that's the *flight* part, obviously) or even extreme joy or excitement. Yes, even joy can be stressful. Anything that gets your heart pumping and your palms sweaty is considered *autonomic arousal*—from the sight of a pretty girl or handsome guy to the sight of a salivating lion looking directly at you. The sympathetic division's job is to get the body ready to deal with the stress by making the heart pump faster, increasing the lungs' breathing rate, and shutting down functions like digestion that aren't important in stressful situations. The sympathetic division "expends energy reserves."

If the sympathetic division can be called the fight-or-flight system, the parasympathetic division might be called the eat-drink-and-rest system. The parasympathetic division "mends energy reserves" and is active in those processes that restore the body's reserves of energy. The parasympathetic division is responsible for most of the ordinary, day-to-day functions of the body, and it also restores the body to normal functioning after a stressful situation ends. It slows the heart and breathing, constricts the pupils, and reactivates digestion. In a sense, the parasympathetic division allows the body to put back all the energy it burned, which is why people are often very hungry *after* the stress is all over.

Following a stressful event, the activity of the sympathetic division will be replaced by the activation of the parasympathetic division. If the stress goes on too long or is too intense, the person might actually collapse (as a deer might do when being chased by another animal). This collapse occurs because the parasympathetic division overresponds in its inhibition of the sympathetic activity. The heart slows, blood vessels open up, blood pressure in the brain drops, and fainting can be the result. ◉→ Simulate on **mypsychlab.com**

Explain How the Neuroendocrine System Functions

4.4 How are the endocrine glands connected to the nervous system?

Glands are organs in the body that secrete chemicals. Some glands, such as salivary glands and sweat glands, affect the functioning of the body but do not affect behavior. Other glands, called **endocrine glands**, are a system of ductless glands that secrete their chemicals directly into the bloodstream for faster distribution around the body. The chemicals secreted by this type of gland are called **hormones** (from a Greek word meaning "to excite"). When they are triggered by the nervous system, these hormones flow into the bloodstream, which carries them to their target organs. These hormone chemicals then fit into receptor sites on target organs and excite them to function.

For example, during a stressful situation, the sympathetic division of the ANS is activated. The nervous system stimulates glands in the endocrine system known as the *adrenal glands*, and the adrenal glands release stress-related hormones into the bloodstream. These stress hormones will travel to all parts of the body and fit into receptor sites at various target organs—notably, the heart, muscles, and lungs. The hormones stimulate these organs to work harder.

◉→ Simulate the autonomic nervous system on **mypsychlab.com**

endocrine glands glands that secrete chemicals called hormones directly into the bloodstream.

hormones chemicals released into the bloodstream by endocrine glands.

50 CHAPTER 2

Explore

TOO MUCH OR TOO LITTLE: WRITING ABOUT HORMONE IMBALANCES

Students can use Internet or library resources to learn about disorders caused by problems within the endocrine system. Have students write a short report on one of these disorders: (1) *Hypopituitary dwarfism*. If the pituitary secretes too little growth hormone during childhood, the person will be very small, although normally proportioned. (2) *Hyperthyroidism*. The thyroid secretes too much thyroxin, resulting in an overly active metabolism, making a person thin, nervous, and excitable. (3) *Acromegaly*. Oversecretion of the growth hormone after the major growth period is ended results in the bones in the face, hands, and feet increasing in size, producing abnormally large hands, feet, and facial bone structure.

50 Chapter 2 The Biological Perspective

4.5 How do hormones affect our thoughts and behavior?

Hormones affect behavior and emotions by controlling many of the muscles and organs in our bodies. For example, when we get scared, the hormone adrenaline is released, which speeds up the heart rate. Some hormones produced by the endocrine glands can even affect the brain.

What hormones does each of the glands produce? How do those hormones affect our bodies?

The **pituitary gland** is located in the brain itself. It's sometimes called the *master gland* because it controls or influences all of the other endocrine glands. One part of the pituitary controls the levels of salt and water in the body. Another part of the pituitary secretes several hormones that influence the activity of the other glands. Most notable of these hormones is a *growth hormone* (called GH) that controls and regulates the increase in size as children grow from infancy to adulthood. The pituitary also controls things associated with pregnancy, such as production of milk for nursing infants and the onset of labor.

The **pineal gland** is also located in the brain, near the back. It secretes a hormone called *melatonin*, primarily at night, which reacts to the changing hours of daylight over the year and influences the sleep–wake cycle in humans and some animals. When melatonin is present, we become sleepy. When melatonin recedes, we become awake. LINK to *Chapter Four: Consciousness: Sleep, Dreams, Hypnosis, and Drugs, p. 123.*

The **thyroid gland** is located inside the neck and secretes a hormone called *thyroxin* that regulates metabolism (the conversion of food into energy that can be used by the body).

The **pancreas** controls the level of blood sugar in the body by secreting *insulin* and *glucagons*. Glucagons are hormones secreted by the pancreas, which oppose the action of insulin by stimulating an increase in blood sugar levels. Insulin allows our bodies to metabolize sugar into usable forms. If the pancreas secretes too little insulin, it results in *diabetes*. If it secretes too much insulin, it results in *hypoglycemia*, or low blood sugar, which causes a person to feel hungry all the time and often become overweight as a result.

Everyone has two **adrenal glands**, one on top of each kidney, that release epinephrine to stimulate the sympathetic system when people are under stress. Among other things, the adrenal glands produce more than 30 different hormones called *corticoids* (also called steroids). One of the most important of these adrenal hormones is *cortisol*, which is released when the body experiences stress, both physical stress (such as illness, surgery, or extreme heat or cold) and psychological stress (such as an emotional upset).

The **gonads** are the sex glands, including the *ovaries* in the female and the *testes* in the male. They secrete hormones that regulate sexual behavior and reproduction. They do not control all sexual behavior, though. In a very real sense, the brain itself is the master of the sexual system.

Explore on **mypsychlab.com**

4.6 What effects do hormones have on the immune system?

The endocrine system is linked not only to the nervous system but also to the *immune system*, the system of cells, organs, and chemicals in the body that responds to attacks on the body from diseases and injuries. While many

What hormones does each of the glands produce? How do those hormones affect our bodies?

Explore the endocrine glands on **mypsychlab.com**

pituitary gland gland located in the brain that secretes human growth hormone and influences all other hormone-secreting glands (also known as the master gland).

pineal gland endocrine gland located near the base of the cerebrum; secretes melatonin.

thyroid gland endocrine gland found in the neck; regulates metabolism.

pancreas endocrine gland; controls the levels of sugar in the blood.

adrenal glands endocrine glands located on top of each kidney that secrete over 30 different hormones to deal with stress, regulate salt intake, and provide a secondary source of sex hormones affecting the sexual changes that occur during adolescence.

gonads sex glands; secrete hormones that regulate sexual development and behavior as well as reproduction.

THE BIOLOGICAL PERSPECTIVE 51

CHAPTER 2 • Module 4

COVER THE MODULE

4.5 How do hormones affect our thoughts and behavior?

- The *pituitary gland* is found in the brain. It controls or influences all other endocrine glands.
- The *pineal gland* is also located in the brain. It secretes melatonin, a hormone that regulates our sleep-wake cycle in response to changes in light.

LINK to *Chapter Four: Consciousness: Sleep, Dreams, Hypnosis, and Drugs, p. 123*

- The *thyroid gland* is located inside the neck. It controls metabolism (the burning of energy) by secreting thyroxin.
- The *pancreas* controls the level of sugar in the blood by secreting insulin and glucagons. Too much insulin produces hypoglycemia, while too little causes diabetes.
- The *adrenal glands*, one on top of each kidney, control our stress reactions. The adrenal cortex secretes over 30 different corticoids (steroids).
- The *gonads* are the ovaries in women and testes in men. They secrete hormones to regulate sexual behavior and reproduction.

MULTIMEDIA CONTENT AVAILABLE AT
www.mypsychlab.com

Explore the endocrine glands on **mypsychlab.com**

COVER THE MODULE

4.6 What effects do hormones have on the immune system?

Class Demonstration

LEARNING ABOUT THE ENDOCRINE GLANDS

Purpose: Students review and discuss the endocrine glands.

Time: 15 minutes

Description: Students should choose a partner and create flash cards of the endocrine glands on scraps of paper. One student could create cards with the name of the gland on one side and the name of the hormone it produces on the other. The other student could create cards with the hormone on one side and the function of the hormone on the other. To save class time, you may want to require students to complete the flash cards at home and bring them to class. Using the cards, students can alternate playing the role of teacher and learner.

CHAPTER 2 • Module 4

COVER THE MODULE (continued)

- Some hormones can help the immune system function properly, while others can weaken it.
  - Hormones produced by the thymus gland help develop cells that attack infections and diseases. The hormone cortisol can negatively affect the immune system's ability to function.

LINK to *Chapter Fifteen: Stress and Health*, p. 490

EXTEND THE DISCUSSION

Tell students that scientists have found that exercise works the body's communication system in order to deal with stress. It forces the body's central and sympathetic nervous systems to get the muscular, cardiovascular, and renal systems to communicate much more closely than usual to handle stress.

---

hormones do not affect the body's ability to fight illness and injury, some hormones can help the immune system function properly, and other hormones can actually weaken the immune system.

Hormones produced by the *thymus gland* (located near the top of the sternum), for example, seem to play an important role in the successful development of cells that attack infections and diseases. Without these hormones, the cells that help our immune system work properly wouldn't be able to develop, and we couldn't fight off infections. On the other hand, the hormone cortisol can negatively affect the immune system's ability to function. While low levels of cortisol can be helpful and healthy, higher levels of cortisol, or cortisol in the system for sustained periods of time, can inhibit the cells that attack infections and diseases, making people with high cortisol levels more prone to sickness and infection. Have you ever noticed that when you feel stressed out for a long period of time, you are more likely to come down with a cold? Stress triggers the release of cortisol, so it's no surprise that long periods of stress can make your immune system weaker. LINK to *Chapter Fifteen: Stress and Health, p. 490.*

Class Demonstration

DEBATE ON A HEALTHY LIFESTYLE

Many students see their lives stretching before them and assume that there is no point in trying to live a "healthy" life at such a young age. Yet teenagers have more control over their health than they might think. For example, research shows that a large percentage of cancer-related deaths are directly linked to lifestyle choices such as smoking, drinking, a lack of exercise, and an unhealthy diet. Avoiding cigarettes and alcohol, exercising regularly, and eating healthy foods are a great start to a healthier lifestyle. Conduct a class debate on whether teens should make good lifestyle choices now, in order to improve their health. Is there value in following these methods as a young person? Or, is this something that teens should be concerned about only when they are older?

Practice Quiz

Pick the best answer.

1. Which part of the neuron receives messages from other cells?
   a. axon
   b. dendrite
   c. soma
   d. myelin

2. When the action potential reaches the end of the axon terminal, it causes the release of
   a. an electrical spark that sets off the next cell
   b. positively charged ions that excite the next cell
   c. negatively charged ions that inhibit the next cell
   d. neurotransmitters that excite or inhibit the next cell

3. If you burn your finger, your immediate reaction will probably involve all BUT which of the following?
   a. the brain
   b. the spinal cord
   c. sensory neurons
   d. motor neurons

4. If you are typing on the computer keyboard, the motions of your fingers on the keys are probably being controlled by the
   a. autonomic nervous system
   b. somatic nervous system
   c. sympathetic division
   d. parasympathetic division

5. Which of the following parts of the nervous system connects the brain to the peripheral nervous system?
   a. the spinal cord
   b. the autonomic nervous system
   c. the somatic nervous system
   d. the sympathetic division

6. The protective sheath that wraps around a neuron's axon is made of
   a. dendrites
   b. myelin
   c. synapses
   d. hormones

7. The hormone cortisol is produced by the
   a. pituitary gland
   b. thyroid gland
   c. pineal gland
   d. adrenal glands

8. The gap between two neurons is known as the
   a. neurotransmitter
   b. receptor site
   c. axon terminal
   d. synapse

9. What job do interneurons perform?
   a. They carry messages from the senses to the spinal cord.
   b. They carry messages from the spinal cord to the muscles and glands.
   c. They connect the sensory neurons to the motor neurons.
   d. They connect the sympathetic division to the parasympathetic division.

10. How do hormones produced by the thymus gland affect the immune system?
    a. They strengthen the immune system.
    b. They weaken the immune system.
    c. They first strengthen and later weaken the immune system.
    d. They have no effect on the immune system.

THE BIOLOGICAL PERSPECTIVE

CHAPTER 2 • Module 4

Assess

Assign the Module 4 Practice Quiz.
Use the Practice Quiz to identify gaps in student understanding.

REMEDIATE

Have students, individually or in groups, review the module goals, learning objectives, and key terms.
Refer students to the Concept Summary on p. 74 for review.

Close

As a class, discuss why students think it would be important to understand how hormones affect the human immune system.

TEACHING TIP

Make learning relevant. Help students make connections between their own lives and the classroom content. Ask students to list questions about the topic about which they would like to learn. Allow students to extend the lesson by exploring subtopics of their choice.

Practice Quiz Answers

1. b
2. b
3. a
4. b
5. a
6. b
7. d
8. d
9. c
10. a

Module 4 The Nervous System

CHAPTER 2 • Module 5

Focus

RESOURCES
For this module, consult the appropriate sections of the Teacher's Manual, Test Bank, and PowerPoint slides, all found on the Teacher's Resource DVD, and the interactive study tools for students on MyPsychLab.

BEFORE CLASS
Students should read the section for homework before coming to class.

BELLRINGER
Chances are good that in any given class, you will have several students who will report having had a concussion in the past, usually as a result of participation in sports activities or as a result of an automobile accident. You can ask the students to discuss their experiences with the class, explaining what kind of physiological and cognitive effects occurred.

Teach

COVER THE MODULE

5.1 How do people study the brain?
- Researchers cannot destroy areas of human brains, but they can test people who already have brain damage or they can study animals' brains.
- Scientists can study the brain by using *deep lesioning* to destroy certain areas of the brain in laboratory animals or by electrically stimulating those areas.

Module 5: The Brain

Module Goals
Learn how scientists study the nervous system.

Understand the structure and function of the brain.

Learning Objectives
- 5.1 How do people study the brain?
- 5.2 What advances have made the brain easier to study?
- 5.3 What are some recent innovations in neuroscience?
- 5.4 What are the different parts of the brain, and what does each part do?
- 5.5 How does the left side of the brain differ from the right side?

Learn How Scientists Study the Nervous System

5.1 How do people study the brain?

The brain has never been easy to study. Many early "scientists" dissected the brains of those who had died—both animals and people—to try to see how the brain worked. The problem, of course, is that it is impossible to tell what a structure in the brain is supposed to do if it's dead. This method did, however, achieve some success. In 1861, French surgeon Paul Broca performed autopsies and located the speech center of the brain. Without having access to a functioning brain, several researchers also studied the image of the brain: In 1508, Leonardo da Vinci drew sketches of the brain, and in the late 19th century/early 20th century, Santiago Ramón y Cajal used sketches and advanced staining methods to study the brain and how neurons communicate.

These days, how do researchers study human brain function? It should be obvious that researchers can't destroy areas of the brains of human beings. But they can test people who already have brain damage and assess what they can or cannot do. It isn't an ideal way to study the brain, however, as no two case studies of human brain damage are likely to be in exactly the same area of the brain and involve exactly the same amount of damage.

One way to get some idea of what the various areas of the brain control is to study animals or people with damage to those areas. In animals, that may mean researchers purposefully damage a part of an animal's brain to study that area scientifically. Then researchers test the animal to see what has happened to its abilities. Or they may electrically stimulate some particular area of the animal's brain and watch the result. Both the destruction and stimulation of brain tissue are accomplished by the same basic process. After the animal is *anesthetized* (given a treatment that prevents the animal from feeling any pain), a thin wire insulated everywhere but the very tip is surgically inserted into the brain of the test animal. If brain tissue is to be destroyed, an electrical current strong enough to kill off the neurons at the tip of the wire is sent through it. This is called **deep lesioning**.

deep lesioning insertion of a thin, insulated wire into the brain through which an electrical current is sent that destroys the brain cells at the tip of the wire.

54 CHAPTER 2

Terms

- deep lesioning • computed tomography (CT) • magnetic resonance imaging (MRI) • positron emission tomography (PET) • functional MRI (fMRI) • electroencephalograph (EEG) • neuroplasticity • stem cells • medulla • pons • reticular formation (RF) • cerebellum • limbic system • thalamus • hypothalamus • homeostasis • hippocampus • amygdala • cortex • cerebral hemisphere • corpus callosum • occipital lobe • parietal lobes • somatosensory cortex • temporal lobes • frontal lobes • motor cortex • association areas

54 Chapter 2 The Biological Perspective

5.2 What advances have made the brain easier to study?

Looking at Structure Scientists now have several ways to look inside the human brain without harm to the person. One way is to take a series of X-rays of the brain, aided by a computer. This is called a **CT scan** (CT stands for computed tomography, or mapping "slices" of the brain by computer). CT scans can show stroke damage, tumors, injuries, and abnormal brain structure. (See Figure 5.1b.)

As good as a CT scan can be, it still doesn't show very small details within the brain. A newer technique called **magnetic resonance imaging**, or **MRI**, provides much more detail, even allowing doctors to see the effects of very small strokes. (See Figure 5.1c.) The person getting an MRI scan will be placed inside a machine that generates a powerful magnetic field. The magnetic field allows the computer to create a three-dimensional image of the brain and display "slices" of that image on a screen. Watch on mypsychlab.com

Looking at Function While CT and MRI scans can show the structure of the brain, researchers who want to see the brain in action may use a **PET scan** (positron emission tomography). (See Figure 5.1d.) In this method, the person is injected with a radioactive glucose (a kind of sugar; harmless to the patient). The computer detects the activity of the brain cells by looking at which cells are using up the radioactive glucose and projecting the image of that activity onto a monitor. The computer uses colors to indicate different levels of activity. Areas that are very active usually show up as white or very light, whereas areas that are inactive are dark blue. With this method, researchers can have the person perform different tasks while the computer shows what his or her brain is doing during the task. In most brain surgeries, the patient is awake and in no pain, since there are no pain receptors in the brain (only in the skin

computed tomography (CT)
brain-imaging method using computer-controlled X-rays of the brain.

magnetic resonance imaging (MRI)
brain-imaging method using radio waves and magnetic fields of the body to produce detailed images of the brain.

positron emission tomography (PET)
brain-imaging method in which a radioactive sugar is injected into the subject and a computer compiles a color-coded image of the activity of the brain, with lighter colors indicating more activity.

Watch a video on brain scans on **mypsychlab.com**

FIGURE 5.1 Studying the Brain
(a) An example of an EEG readout. (b) A CT scan showing the detail of a center cross section of the brain. (c) An MRI showing enhanced detail of the same view of the brain as in the CT scan. (d) A PET scan showing activity of the brain, using colors to indicate different levels of activity. (e) An fMRI scan, showing the brain from three different angles.

THE BIOLOGICAL PERSPECTIVE

Cultural Connections

YOUR BRAIN ON CULTURE

Cultural neuroscience is an exciting, growing field that uses brain-imaging technology to expand our understanding of how environment and beliefs can shape mental function. Almost unknown just a few years ago, the field has become an important area of research. While cultural neuroscience has shown mainly how culture shapes biology, researchers are also beginning to examine how biology shapes culture. In the end, cultural neuroscience could usher in an era of greater understanding between people from different cultures. Ask students to use library or Internet resources to learn more about this field and report back to the class on their findings.

CHAPTER 2 • Module 5

COVER THE MODULE

5.2 What advances have made the brain easier to study?

- There are several ways in which scientists can look into a human brain without damaging the person.
  - *CT* scans are computer-aided X-rays of the brain and show a great deal of brain structure.
  - *MRI* scans use a magnetic field and a computer to give researchers an even more detailed look at the structure of the brain.
  - *PET* scans use a radioactive sugar injected into the bloodstream to track the activity of brain cells, which is enhanced and color-coded by a computer. They allow researchers to see the brain in action.

MULTIMEDIA CONTENT AVAILABLE AT
www.mypsychlab.com

Watch a video on brain scans on **mypsychlab.com**

Module 5 The Brain

CHAPTER 2 • Module 5

COVER THE MODULE (continued)

- An *fMRI* allows researchers to look at the activity of the brain during various mental tasks.
- The *EEG* machine allows researchers to look at the activity of the surface of the brain through the use of microelectrodes placed on the scalp and connected to an amplifier and a computer for data recording and analysis.

COVER THE MODULE

5.3 What are some recent innovations in neuroscience?

- The brain has the ability to constantly change both the structure and the function of many of its cells in response to experience and even trauma.
- Scientists are studying the possibility of using stem cells to repair damaged or diseased brain tissue.

MULTIMEDIA CONTENT AVAILABLE AT
www.mypsychlab.com

((•—Listen to the Psychology in the News podcast and learn more about stem cells on
mypsychlab.com

CHECK FOR UNDERSTANDING

To ensure that students understand the ways in which the brain can be studied, ask: **What means do scientists use to study brain structure?** *(Answer: CT scan and MRI.)* **How do scientists study brain function?** *(Answer: PET scan, fMRI, and EEG.)*

---

of the scalp, for which a local anesthetic is used). Therefore, during surgery, the patient can help the surgeon by responding to questions.

Although traditional MRI scans only show structure, there is a technique called **functional MRI (fMRI)** in which the computer tracks changes in the oxygen levels of the blood. (See Figure 5.1e.) By placing this picture of where the oxygen goes in the brain on top of the picture of the brain's structure, researchers can tell what areas of the brain are active. By combining such images taken over a period of time, a sort of "video" of the brain's functioning can be made (Lin et al., 2007). fMRIs can give more detail, tend to be clearer than PET scans, and are fast becoming an incredibly useful tool for research into the workings of the brain.

Another harmless, painless way to study the activity of the living brain is to record the electrical activity of the cortex just below the skull. This has been done for years by using a device called an **electroencephalograph (EEG)**. Small metal disk electrodes are placed directly on the scalp, using a jellylike substance to help conduct the electrical messages from the cortex just below. These electrodes are connected to an amplifier and then to a computer to view the information. The resulting electrical output forms waves (see Figure 5.1a) that indicate many things, such as stages of sleep, seizures, and even the presence of tumors. The EEG can also be used to determine which areas of the brain are active during various mental tasks that involve memory and attention. However, the EEG only allows researchers to look at the activity of the surface of the brain.

5.3 What are some recent innovations in neuroscience?

Neuroplasticity Damage to the brain, and to the central nervous system as a whole, was once thought to be permanent. Neurons in the brain and spinal cord were not seen as capable of repairing themselves. When people recovered from a stroke, for example, it was assumed that healthy brain cells took over the function of the damaged ones. Scientists have known for a while now that some forms of central nervous system damage can be repaired by the body's systems; and in recent years, great strides have been made in repairing spinal cord damage. The brain actually exhibits a great deal of **neuroplasticity**, the ability to constantly change both the structure and function of many cells in the brain in response to experience and even trauma (Neville & Bavelier, 2000; Rossini et al., 2007; Sanders, Weber-Fox, & Neville, 2008). Scientists have been able to implant nerve fibers from outside the spinal cord onto a damaged area and then "coax" the damaged spinal nerves to grow through these "tunnels" of implanted fibers (Cheng et al., 1996). The first human trials have already begun (Blits & Bunge, 2006; Bunge & Pearse, 2003). It is also now known that the brain can change itself quite a bit by adapting neurons to serve new functions when old neurons die or are damaged. Dendrites grow and new connections are formed in at least some areas of the brain, as people learn new things throughout life (Abraham & Williams, 2003).

Stem Cell Research Researchers are constantly looking for new ways to repair the brain. In the past few years, some researchers have developed a new and promising treatment for people with damage from strokes and diseases such as Parkinson's and Alzheimer's: They have been researching the possibility of transplanting **stem cells** to repair damaged or diseased brain tissue.

Stem cells are like "generic cells" and can become other types of cells, such as blood cells, nerve cells, and brain cells (National Institutes of Health, 2007). Stem cells are found in many of the organs of the body, bone marrow, and human placentas, which are readily available after each birth. An ongoing con-

functional MRI (fMRI) a specialized MRI scan that tracks changes in oxygen levels of the blood to show which areas of the brain are active.

electroencephalograph (EEG) equipment designed to record the brain wave patterns produced by electrical activity of the surface of the brain.

neuroplasticity the ability within the brain to constantly change both the structure and function of many cells in response to experience or trauma.

stem cells special cells found in all the tissues of the body that are capable of becoming other cell types when those cells need to be replaced due to damage or wear and tear.

56 CHAPTER 2

Class Demonstration

REVIEW OF BRAIN-IMAGING TECHNIQUES

Ask students to tell which brain-imaging technique could answer each of the following questions: (1) How do the brains of children and adults differ with regard to energy consumption? *(PET)* (2) In what ways do brain waves change as a person falls asleep? *(EEG)* (3) In which part of the brain has a stroke patient experienced a disruption of blood flow? *(CT, MRI)* (4) What is the precise location of a suspected brain tumor? *(CT, MRI)* (5) How can brain structures be examined without exposing a patient to radiation? *(MRI)*

56 Chapter 2 The Biological Perspective

troversy concerns the source of stem cells, which can be obtained from human embryos, from either terminated pregnancies or fertilization clinics. A study conducted by neurologist Alexander Storch of the University of Ulm in Germany and his colleagues may hold hope for the future of stem cell treatments without the controversial need to use human embryonic tissue (Hermann et al., 2006). In this study, the researchers were able to convert bone marrow stem cells from mice into cells resembling neural stem cells. The authors go on to describe the possibility of such conversion taking place in adult bone marrow stem cells.

Listen on mypsychlab.com

medulla the first large swelling at the top of the spinal cord, forming the lowest part of the brain, which is responsible for life-sustaining functions such as breathing, swallowing, and heart rate.

Listen to the Psychology in the News podcast and learn more about stem cells in mypsychlab.com

Understand the Structure and Function of the Brain

5.4 What are the different parts of the brain, and what does each part do?

Now it's time to look at the various structures of the brain, starting from the bottom and working up to the top. (A word of caution: This text won't be discussing every single part of the brain, only the parts interesting to psychologists as explorers of human behavior. Many parts of the brain also overlap in their functions, but a full understanding of the brain is not truly possible within one module of an introductory psychology text.)

The Hindbrain and Beyond The **medulla** (which, oddly enough, means "marrow" or "inner substance") is located at the top of the spinal column. In Figure 5.2, it is the first "swelling" at the top of the spinal cord, just at the very

Corpus callosum Connects left and right hemispheres of the brain.

Cerebral cortex Controls complex thought processes.

Thalamus Part of the forebrain that relays information from sensory organs to the cerebral cortex.

Hypothalamus Part of the forebrain that regulates the amount of fear, thirst, sexual drive, and aggression we feel.

Cerebellum Part of the hindbrain that controls balance and maintains muscle coordination.

Pituitary gland Regulates other endocrine glands.

Pons Part of the hindbrain that relays messages between the cerebellum and the cortex.

Hippocampus Plays a role in our learning, memory, and ability to compare sensory information to expectations.

Reticular formation A system of nerves running from the hindbrain and through the midbrain to the cerebral cortex, controlling arousal and attention.

Medulla Part of the hindbrain where nerves cross from one side of the body to the opposite side of the brain.

FIGURE 5.2 The Major Structures of the Human Brain

THE BIOLOGICAL PERSPECTIVE 57

CHAPTER 2 • Module 5

COVER THE MODULE

5.4 What are the different parts of the brain, and what does each part do?

- **The Hindbrain**
  - The *medulla* is at the very bottom of the brain and the top of the spinal column. It controls life-sustaining functions such as breathing and swallowing. The nerves from each side of the body also cross over in this structure to opposite sides.

FAST FACT

Ask: **Do you think people are awake or asleep during brain surgery?** *(Students may be surprised, and horrified, to find out that people are often awake during brain surgery. It is fairly routine for the surgeon to stimulate an awake patient's brain during surgery, to verify the function of the areas the surgeon is working near. During surgery, the scalp, bone, and membranes covering the brain must be anesthetized, so that the patient does not feel pain. The brain itself does not have pain receptors, so working on the brain is not physically painful for the patient.)*

Explore

THE BRAIN DIAGRAM

Try asking students to draw their own colorful rendition of the human brain, an active learning strategy that ensures that they encode and think about the parts of the brain rather than passively glossing over them in the text. Prior to the class period in which you will be discussing the brain, ask students to read Module 5 and to hand-draw a diagram of the brain (in a cross-section) on a sheet of white unlined paper. For each of the following sections of the brain, students should color and label the appropriate structure, and also list one or two of its major functions: (a) the cerebral cortex, including the four lobes, (b) the thalamus, (c) the hypothalamus, (d) the hippocampus, (e) the amygdala, (f) the cerebellum, (g) the pons, and (h) the medulla.

Module 5 The Brain 57

CHAPTER 2 • Module 5

COVER THE MODULE (continued)

- The *pons* is above the medulla and acts as a bridge between the lower part of the brain and the upper part. It influences sleep, dreaming, arousal, and coordination of movement on the left and right sides of the body.
- The *reticular formation* runs through the medulla and the pons and controls our selective attention and arousal.
- The *cerebellum* is found at the base and back of the brain and coordinates fine, rapid motor movement, learned reflexes, posture, and muscle tone.

MULTIMEDIA CONTENT AVAILABLE AT
www.mypsychlab.com

Simulate the cerebrum on mypsychlab.com

- **Structures Under the Cortex**
  - The cortex, the outer wrinkled covering of the brain, is about one quarter of an inch thick.
  - The *limbic system* consists of the thalamus, hypothalamus, hippocampus, and amygdala. This system is involved in emotions, motivation, and learning.

---

bottom of the brain. This is the part of the brain that a person would least want to have damaged, as it controls life-sustaining functions such as heartbeat, breathing, and swallowing. In the medulla, the sensory nerves coming from the left and right sides of the body cross over, so that sensory information from the left side of the body goes to the right side of the brain and vice versa.

The **pons** is the larger "swelling" just above the medulla. This term means "bridge," and the pons is indeed the bridge between the lower parts of the brain and the upper sections. As in the medulla, there is a crossover of nerves, but in this case, it is the motor nerves carrying messages from the brain to the body. This allows the pons to coordinate the movements of the left and right sides of the body. The pons also influences sleep, dreaming, and arousal.

The **reticular formation (RF)**, also known as the *reticular activating system* (or RAS), is an area of neurons running through the middle of the medulla and the pons and slightly beyond. These neurons are responsible for people's ability to attend to certain kinds of information in their surroundings. Basically, the RF allows people to ignore constant, unchanging information (such as the noise of an air conditioner) and become alert to changes in information (for example, if the air conditioner stopped, most people would notice immediately).

At the base of the skull, behind the pons and below the *cerebrum* (or main part of the brain that's divided into hemispheres), is a structure that looks like a small brain. (See Figure 5.2.) This is the **cerebellum** (meaning "little brain"). The cerebellum is the part of the lower brain that controls all involuntary, rapid, fine motor movement, such as balance and posture. People can sit upright because the cerebellum controls all the little muscles needed to keep them from falling out of their chairs. It also coordinates voluntary movements that have to happen in rapid succession, such as walking, diving, skating, gymnastics, dancing, playing a musical instrument, and even the movements of speech. Learned reflexes, skills, and habits are also stored here, which allows them to become more or less automatic. For example, riding a bicycle is an example of a learned reflex that is stored in the cerebellum. Once you learn how to ride a bike, you never really forget.

The first brain tissue affected by alcohol is the cerebellum. When a police officer stops a driver suspected of driving under the influence of alcohol, the police officer might give a sobriety test asking a person to put a pointer finger at the tip of the nose or walk heel to toe in a straight line; it is cerebellar functioning that's being tested here.

Structures Under the Cortex The cortex is the outer wrinkled covering of the brain. In a human brain, it is about one-quarter of an inch thick. The cortex is the outer layer of the cerebrum, the large mass divided into left and right hemispheres. But there are a number of important structures located just under the cortex, in the forebrain, and above the brain stem. Each of these structures plays a part in our behavior. (See Figure 5.3.) Simulate on mypsychlab.com

The **limbic system** includes the thalamus, hypothalamus, hippocampus, and amygdala. In general, the limbic system is involved in emotions, motivation, and learning.

Have you ever had to go to the emergency room of a hospital? You may find yourself getting past the receptionist, but most of the time, you have to wait to see a nurse before you ever get to see the doctor. These nurses ask people questions about their complaints. They may be able to partially treat minor complaints before the person sees a doctor. Then they will send the person to a treatment room with the equipment that might be needed for the ailment, and eventually, the person will see a doctor. In other words, the nurse evaluates the information you give, and then sends you to the right person to solve your problem.

Simulate the cerebrum on mypsychlab.com

pons the larger swelling above the medulla that connects the top of the brain to the bottom and that plays a part in sleep, dreaming, left–right body coordination, and arousal.

reticular formation (RF) an area of neurons running through the middle of the medulla and the pons and slightly beyond that play a role in general arousal, alertness, and sleep.

cerebellum part of the lower brain located behind the pons that controls and coordinates involuntary, rapid, fine motor movement.

limbic system a group of several brain structures located under the cortex and involved in learning, emotion, memory, and motivation.

58   CHAPTER 2

Class Demonstration

CRITICAL THINKING

Purpose: Students complete a brief 1-minute assignment that involves critical thinking, personalizing, or deeper processing of information.

Time: 1–5 minutes

Description: Allow students a few minutes to answer these questions. This assignment can be used in a variety of ways—to verify attendance, to start discussion, to assess student knowledge, and to provide opportunities for critical thinking. Give students the following topic: "**Brain function**: If you could enhance the function of one structure in your brain, what would it be? Suppose a television network wanted to create a superhero with your enhanced brain capabilities. What would you name the superhero?"

Thalamus Part of the forebrain that relays information from sensory organs to the cerebral cortex.

Mamillary body Neurons that act as a relay station, transmitting information between fornix and thalamus.

Fornix Pathway of nerve fibers that transmits information from hippocampus to the mamillary bodies.

Hypothalamus Part of the forebrain that regulates the amount of fear, thirst, sexual drive, and aggression we feel.

Amygdala Influences our motivation, emotional control, fear response, and interpretations of nonverbal emotional expressions.

Hippocampus Plays a role in our learning, memory, and ability to compare sensory information to expectations.

FIGURE 5.3 The Limbic System

The **thalamus** ("inner chamber") is in some ways similar to an emergency room nurse. This somewhat football-shaped tissue in the center of the brain acts as a relay station for incoming sensory information. In fact, the thalamus is like Grand Central Station, handling the amount of incoming and outgoing traffic of sensory messages. Additionally, like a nurse, the thalamus might perform some processing of that sensory information before sending it on to the part of the cortex that deals with that kind of sensation—hearing, sight, touch, or taste. Damage to the thalamus might result in the loss or partial loss of any or all of those sensations. **LINK** to Chapter Three: Sensation and Perception, pp. 80–92.

The size of a pea but an extremely powerful, important part of the forebrain is located just below and in front of the thalamus. (See Figure 5.3.) The **hypothalamus** ("below the inner chamber") monitors homeostasis, which regulates body temperature, thirst, hunger, sleeping and waking, sexual activity, and emotions. It sits right above the pituitary gland and actually controls the pituitary, so the ultimate regulation of hormones lies with the hypothalamus. **Homeostasis** ("standing still") refers to the body's tendency to maintain balance.

The **hippocampus** is the Greek word for "seahorse," and this name was given to this structure of the brain because the first scientists who dissected the brain thought it looked like the curled tail of a seahorse. Today, we might recognize the hippocampus as looking like the thick, curled horn of a mountain ram, which begins in the front of the ram's head, goes toward the back, and then curls around toward the front on both sides of the head. Research has shown that the hippocampus is instrumental in processing memories and then sending them for storage around the cortex. The hippocampus wraps around the area of the thalamus, so there is half in each hemisphere at the temporal lobe, and electrical stimulation of the temporal lobe may produce memory- or dream-like experiences. **Simulate** on **mypsychlab.com**

Simulate the limbic system on **mypsychlab.com**

thalamus part of the limbic system located in the center of the brain, this structure relays sensory information from the lower part of the brain to the proper areas of the cortex and processes some sensory information before sending it to its proper area.

hypothalamus small structure in the brain located below the thalamus and directly above the pituitary gland, responsible for motivational behavior such as sleep, hunger, thirst, and sex.

homeostasis the tendency of the body to maintain a steady state.

hippocampus curved structure located within each temporal lobe, responsible for the formation of long-term memories and the storage of memory for location of objects.

THE BIOLOGICAL PERSPECTIVE 59

CHAPTER 2 • Module 5

COVER THE MODULE (continued)

- The *thalamus* is the switching station that sends sensory information to the proper areas of the cortex.
- **LINK** to *Chapter Three: Sensation and Perception, pp. 80–92*
- The *hypothalamus* controls hunger, thirst, sleep, sexual behavior, sleeping and waking, and emotions. It also controls the pituitary gland.
- *Homeostasis* refers to the body's tendency to maintain balance.
- The *hippocampus* is the part of the brain responsible for storing memories and remembering locations of objects.

MULTIMEDIA CONTENT AVAILABLE AT
www.mypsychlab.com

Simulate the limbic system on **mypsychlab.com**

EXTEND THE DISCUSSION

Tell students that the idea of the body being "in balance" is important. Physical problems that can be caused from a homeostatic imbalance include dehydration, diabetes, hypoglycemia (lower than normal glucose), hyperglycemia (high blood sugar), and any disease caused by a toxin in the bloodstream. These difficulties result from the presence of an increased amount of a particular substance in the body, putting it "out of balance."

Class Demonstration

DISCUSSING CONTROVERSIES IN NEUROSCIENCE

Purpose: Students have a chance to think about and discuss controversial topics in the field of neuroscience.

Time: 15 minutes

Description: Pose one or more of the following controversial questions to the class. Students should share their answers and contribute to further class discussion. Consider using one of the topics for a class debate. (1) Is neural transplant surgery (using fetal brain tissue) to treat brain damage ethical? (2) Should sports that can cause brain damage, such as football, boxing, and mixed martial arts, be banned?

CHAPTER 2 • Module 5

COVER THE MODULE *(continued)*
- The *amygdala* controls our fear responses and memory of fearful stimuli.
- **The Cortex**

DISCUSS THE STUDENT VOICE QUESTION
No doubt students will be interested to learn that the brain has a smooth outer covering before birth and then gets wrinkled as the brain increases in size and complexity.

- The *cortex* is divided into two *cerebral hemispheres* connected by a thick band of neurons called the *corpus callosum*.
- The *occipital lobes* at the back and base of each hemisphere process vision and contain the primary visual cortex.
- The *parietal lobes* at the top and back of the cortex contain the *somatosensory area*, which processes our sense of touch, temperature, and body position. Taste is also processed in this lobe.
- The *temporal lobes* contain the primary auditory area and are also involved in understanding language.

60 Chapter 2 The Biological Perspective

The **amygdala** ("almond") is an area of the brain located at the tip of the hippocampus on each side. These two structures seem to be responsible for fear responses and memory of fear. Information from the senses goes to the amygdala before the upper part of the brain (the cortex) is even involved, so that people can respond to danger very quickly, sometimes before they are consciously aware of what is happening. In 1939 researchers found that monkeys with large amounts of their temporal lobes removed—including the amygdala—were completely unafraid of snakes and humans, both normally fear-provoking stimuli (Klüver & Bucy, 1939). Case studies of humans with damage to the amygdala also show a link to decreased fear response (Adolphs et al., 2005).

The Cortex The **cortex** is the outermost part of the brain, which is the part of the brain most people picture when they think of what the brain looks like. It is made up of tightly packed neurons and actually is only about one-tenth of an inch to one-quarter of an inch thick on average (Fischl et al., 2001; MacDonald et al., 2000; Zilles, 1990). The tissue appears grayish pink because the tightly packed neural bodies (somas) are gray and the small blood vessels appear pink. The cortex is very recognizable surface anatomy because it is full of wrinkles.

Why is the cortex so wrinkled?

The wrinkling of the cortex allows a much larger area of cortical cells to exist in the small space inside the skull. If the cortex were to be taken out, ironed flat, and measured, it would be about 2 to 3 square feet. As the brain develops before birth, it forms a smooth outer covering on all the other brain structures. This will be the cortex, which will get more and more wrinkled as the brain increases in size and complexity.

The cortex is divided into two sections called the **cerebral hemispheres**, which are connected by a thick, tough band of neural fibers (axons) called the **corpus callosum**, which means "colossal body." (See Figure 5.2.) The corpus callosum allows the left and right hemispheres to communicate with each other. In general, the left hemisphere controls the right side of the body, and the right hemisphere controls the left side of the body. Consequently, a person who had a stroke leaving the left arm paralyzed would probably have damage in the right hemisphere.

The cortex is divided into parts called "lobes." (See Figure 5.4.) At the base of the cortex, toward the back of the brain, is an area in each hemisphere called the **occipital lobe**. (The term *occipital* refers to the rear of the head.) This area processes visual information from the eyes in the *primary visual cortex*. The *visual association cortex*, also in this lobe, is the part of the brain that helps identify and make sense of the visual information from the eyes.

The **parietal lobes** (*parietal* means "wall") are at the top and back of the brain, just under the parietal bone in the skull. This area contains the **somatosensory cortex**, an area of neurons (see Figure 5.5 on page 62) running down the front of the parietal lobes on either side of the brain. This area processes information from the skin and internal body receptors for touch, temperature, and body position. The somatosensory cortex is laid out in a rather interesting way: The cells at the top of the brain receive information from the bottom of the body, and as one moves down the area, the signals come from higher and higher in the body. It's almost as if a little upside-down person were laid out along this area of cells.

The beginning of the **temporal lobes** (*temporal* means "of or near the temples") is found just behind the temples of the head. These lobes contain the *primary auditory cortex* and the *auditory association area*. If a person receives a

> Why is the cortex so wrinkled? ▶

amygdala brain structure located near the hippocampus, responsible for fear responses and memory of fear.

cortex outermost covering of the brain consisting of densely packed neurons, responsible for higher thought processes and interpretation of sensory input.

cerebral hemispheres the two sections of the cortex on the left and right sides of the brain.

corpus callosum thick band of neurons that connects the right and left cerebral hemispheres.

occipital lobe section of the brain located at the rear and bottom of each cerebral hemisphere containing the visual centers of the brain.

parietal lobes sections of the brain located at the top and back of each cerebral hemisphere containing the centers for touch, taste, and temperature sensations.

somatosensory cortex area of neurons running down the front of the parietal lobes responsible for processing information from the skin and internal body receptors for touch, temperature, body position, and possibly taste.

temporal lobes areas of the cortex located just behind the temples containing the neurons responsible for the sense of hearing and meaningful speech.

Class Demonstration

THE IMPORTANCE OF A WRINKLED CORTEX

Ask students to explain why the cerebral cortex is wrinkled. There are usually a few students who correctly answer that the wrinkled appearance of the cerebral cortex allows it to have a greater surface area while fitting in a relatively small space (i.e., the head). To demonstrate this point, hold a plain white sheet of paper in your hand and then crumple it into a small, wrinkled ball. Note that the paper retains the same surface area, yet it is now much smaller and is able to fit into a much smaller space, such as your hand. You can then mention that the brain's actual surface area, if flattened out, would be roughly the size of a newspaper page. Laughs usually erupt when the class imagines what our heads would look like if we had to accommodate an unwrinkled, newspaper-sized cerebral cortex!

FIGURE 5.4 The Lobes of the Brain: Occipital, Parietal, Temporal, and Frontal

frontal lobes areas of the cortex located in the front and top of the brain, responsible for higher mental processes and decision making, as well as the production of fluent speech.

motor cortex section of the frontal lobe located at the back, responsible for sending motor commands to the muscles of the somatic nervous system.

association areas areas within each lobe of the cortex responsible for the coordination and interpretation of information, as well as higher mental processing.

blow to the side of the head, that person will probably "hear" a ringing sound. Oddly enough, the sense of taste also seems to be processed in the temporal lobe, deep inside a fold of the cortex, rather than anywhere in the parietal lobe (Fresquet et al., 2004).

The lobes at the front of the brain are named, naturally, **frontal lobes**. Here are found all the higher mental functions of the brain: planning, personality, memory storage, complex decision making, and areas devoted to the speaking of language. The frontal lobe also helps control emotions by means of its connection to the limbic system.

The frontal lobes also contain the **motor cortex**, a band of neurons located at the back of each lobe. (See Figure 5.5 on page 62.) These cells control the movements of the body's voluntary muscles by sending commands out to the somatic division of the peripheral nervous system. The motor cortex is laid out just like the somatosensory cortex, which is right next door in the parietal lobes.

You've mentioned association cortex a few times. Do the other lobes of the brain contain association cortex as well?

Association areas are made up of neurons in the cortex that are devoted to making connections between the sensory information coming into the brain and stored memories, images, and knowledge. In other words, association areas help people make sense of incoming sensory input. Although the association areas in the occipital and temporal lobes have already been mentioned, much of the brain's association cortex is in the frontal lobes. The left frontal lobe is home to *Broca's area*, which is devoted to the production of speech. Another important association area, *Wernicke's area* (pronounced "vair ni keys"), is

◀ You've mentioned association cortex a few times. Do the other lobes of the brain contain association cortex as well?

THE BIOLOGICAL PERSPECTIVE 61

CHAPTER 2 • Module 5

COVER THE MODULE (continued)

- The *frontal lobes* contain the *motor cortex*, which controls the voluntary muscles, and are also where all the higher mental functions occur, such as planning and complex decision making.
- An area called Broca's area in the left frontal lobe is responsible for producing fluent, understandable speech.
- An area called Wernicke's area in the left temporal lobe is responsible for the understanding of language.

🅛🅘🅝🅚 *to Chapter Six: Learning and Language Development, p. 205*

CHECK FOR UNDERSTANDING (KINESTHETIC)

Ask volunteers to come to the front of the room and act out a behavior (e.g., problem solving, balancing an object, smelling an object). The behaviors can be either student-generated or teacher-generated. The other students must try to guess which lobe of the brain is responsible for that behavior: frontal, occipital, temporal, or parietal.

DISCUSS THE STUDENT VOICE QUESTION

Tell students that they can remember the meaning of *association areas* by recalling that a synonym for *association* is *connection*. Association areas help people make *connections* between incoming sensory information and the memories, images, and knowledge already stored in the brain.

Class Demonstration

PARTS OF THE BRAIN

Prepare a list of questions dealing with the structures of the brain, such as: "This structure plays an important role in our balance" [cerebellum]. "This part of the hindbrain relays messages between the cerebellum and the cortex" [pons]. "This part of the forebrain relays information from sensory organs to the cerebral cortex" [thalamus].

Read a question and call on the first raised hand. If students provide the correct answer, they (or their team, or their side of the room) get a playing card. If they provide an incorrect answer, they must return a playing card to the teacher. Play continues for a specified period of time, or until all the questions have been answered. The person, or team, or side of the room tries to make the best five-card poker hand they can, using the cards they earned. The winner can be rewarded with extra credit points.

Module 5 The Brain 61

CHAPTER 2 • Module 5

UNDERSTANDING VISUALS

Direct students' attention to Figure 5.5. Stress that the motor cortex controls the movements of the body's voluntary muscles, while the somatosensory cortex processes information from the skin and internal body receptors for touch, temperature, and body position. However, both cortexes are organized in a similar manner.

COVER THE MODULE

5.5 How does the left side of the brain differ from the right side?

DISCUSS THE STUDENT VOICE QUESTION

Use this question to introduce the idea of hemisphere specialization. Split-brain patients undergo a treatment called *corpus callosotomy* (often because of severe epilepsy). The procedure involves severing a part of the corpus callosum, which connects the two hemispheres of the brain and allows them to communicate. In split-brain patients, the two halves of the brain have less ability to communicate with each other.

- Studies with split-brain patients, in which the corpus callosum has been severed, reveal that the left side of the brain seems to control language, writing, logical thought, analysis, and mathematical abilities. The left side also processes information sequentially.

62 Chapter 2 The Biological Perspective

FIGURE 5.5 The Motor and Somatosensory Cortex
Cells at the top of the motor cortex control muscles at the bottom of the body, whereas cells at the bottom of the motor cortex control muscles at the top of the body. Body parts are drawn larger or smaller according to the number of cortical cells devoted to that body part. The somatosensory cortex is organized in much the same manner.

located in the left temporal lobe and helps us understand the meaning of words. **LINK** *to Chapter Six, Learning and Language Development, p. 205.*

5.5 How does the left side of the brain differ from the right side?

> I've heard that some people are right-brained and some are left-brained. Are the two sides of the brain really that different?

I've heard that some people are right-brained and some are left-brained. Are the two sides of the brain really that different?

Most people tend to think of the two cerebral hemispheres as identical twins. Both sides have the same four lobes and are arranged in much the same way. But language seems to be confined to only the left hemisphere in about 90 percent of the population (Toga & Thompson, 2003). What other special tasks do the two hemispheres engage in, and how do researchers know about such functions?

Roger Sperry was a pioneer in the field of hemisphere specialization. He won a Nobel Prize for his work in demonstrating that the left and right hemispheres of the brain specialize in different activities and functions (Sperry, 1968). In looking for a way to cure epilepsy (muscle spasms or seizures), Sperry cut through the corpus callosum, the thick band of neural fibers that joins the two hemispheres. In early research with animals, this technique worked to lessen the seizures and seemed to have no side effects. The first people to have this procedure done also experienced relief from their severe epileptic symptoms, but testing found that (in a sense) they now had two brains in one body because the communication between the two hemispheres had been severed.

Class Demonstration (Kinesthetic)

SPLIT BRAIN

Purpose: Students experience what it would feel like to have a split brain.

Time: 15 minutes

Description: This activity allows students to feel some of the difficulty and frustration following split-brain surgery, where the person's hemispheres can no longer communicate directly. Students should sit next to a partner. Each student plays the role of one hemisphere. Their outside arms should go behind their backs or remain still during the exercise. Arms closest to the partner should cross each other so that each "hemisphere" is controlling the opposite hand. The teacher can provide a series of tasks such as tying a shoe, opening a can with an opener, sealing an envelope, and tearing open a bag of chips. The exercises will be quite difficult because each student is controlling only one hand, and the hands must work together to complete the task.

The special testing involves sending messages to only one side of the brain, which is now possible because the connecting tissue, the corpus callosum, has been cut. In a split-brain patient, if a picture of a ball is flashed to the right side of the screen, the image of the ball will be sent to the left occipital lobe. The person will be able to say that he or she sees a ball. If a picture of a hammer is flashed to the left side of the screen, the person will not be able to *verbally* identify the object or be able to state with any certainty that something was seen. But if the left *hand* (controlled by the right hemisphere) is used, the person can point to the hammer he or she "didn't see." The right occipital lobe clearly saw the hammer, but the person could not *verbalize* that fact (Sperry, 1968). By doing studies such as these, researchers have found that the two hemispheres of the brain have decidedly different specialties (see Figure 5.6). ⊙→ Simulate on mypsychlab.com

⊙→ Simulate split-brain experiments on mypsychlab.com

Left Hemisphere
- Spoken language
- Written language
- Mathematical calculations
- Logical thought processes
- Analysis of detail
- Reading

Right Hemisphere
- Visual-spatial perception
- Music and artistic processing
- Emotional thought and recognition
- Pattern recognition
- Facial recognition

FIGURE 5.6 Specialization of the Two Hemispheres

THE BIOLOGICAL PERSPECTIVE 63

CHAPTER 2 • Module 5

COVER THE MODULE (continued)
- The right side of the brain processes globally and controls emotional expression, spatial perception, recognition of faces, patterns, and melodies, and emotions.
- The left hemisphere controls spoken language in most individuals.

MULTIMEDIA CONTENT AVAILABLE AT
www.mypsychlab.com

⊙→ Simulate split-brain experiments on **mypsychlab.com**

UNDERSTANDING VISUALS

Direct students' attention to Figure 5.6, and ask: **What generalizations can you make about how the two hemispheres are specialized?** *(Possible answer: The left hemisphere appears to specialize in logic and detail, while the right hemisphere is concerned with emotion and sensation.)*

L1 DIFFERENTIATED INSTRUCTION

Special Needs Students with special educational needs are a highly heterogeneous group of learners, presenting unique cognitive, behavioral, social, and physical needs. To help create a classroom culture that supports the participation and achievement of students with such needs, set clear expectations and provide reasonable choices for all students.

Class Demonstration (Kinesthetic)

LEFT-BRAINED VS. RIGHT-BRAINED

Ask students to move their right hand and right foot simultaneously in a clockwise direction for a few seconds. Next, ask that the right hand and left foot be moved in a clockwise direction. Then, have students make circular movements in opposite directions with the right hand and the left foot. Finally, have students attempt to move the right hand and right foot in opposite directions. This generally produces laughter, as students discover that this procedure is most difficult to do even though they are sure—before they try it—that it would be no problem to perform. A simple alternative activity is to ask students to pat their head and to rub their stomach clockwise and then switch to a counterclockwise motion. The pat will show slight signs of rotation as well.

Module 5 The Brain

CHAPTER 2 • Module 5

COVER THE MODULE (continued)

- **Reflections on Mirror Neurons**
  - Mirror neurons are special brain cells that fire not only when we perform a motor action, but also when we see someone else perform the same action.
  - Their discovery has changed the way researchers think about social interactions and perception.
  - Instead of trying to understand someone only through thinking, it is very possible that mirror neurons are the neurological foundation that allows us to simulate intentions and the emotions behind those actions.
  - The roles of mirror neurons are currently being investigated in disorders that involve deficits in social interaction.

APPLYING PSYCHOLOGY TO EVERYDAY LIFE

1. Possible answer: yawning when seeing someone else yawning
2. Possible answer: If children watch an adult forming words and making sounds, mirror neurons could help the children do the same.

Applying Psychology to Everyday Life

Reflections on Mirror Neurons

While using implanted electrodes to examine neural activity in macaque monkeys, psychologist Giacomo Rizzolatti and his colleagues at the University of Parma, in Italy, made an interesting discovery (Rizzolatti et al., 1996). The researchers wanted to determine which neurons were specifically involved in controlling the movement of the hands. They discovered that the same neurons that fired when the monkeys clutched a piece of food would also fire when the monkeys merely *watched the researchers* handle food. These premotor cortex neurons, which fire not only when an animal performs an action but also when an animal observes that same action being performed by another, are called *mirror neurons*. Brain-imaging techniques in human studies indicate that we, too, have mirror neurons (Buccino et al., 2001, 2004; Iacoboni et al., 1999).

Psychologists are very excited about what the existence of mirror neurons means for social interaction and its influence on the brain and perception. Have you ever winced and ducked when watching someone in a soccer game get hit? Blame those mirror neurons. Do you see someone looking happy and feel you just have to smile, too? Mirror neurons again. We are naturally social creatures, reacting to the mere sight of what we see others doing.

Does the knowledge researchers are gathering about mirror neurons have any practical applications? Some studies find that when a stroke patient needs to relearn a motor skill, watching another person perform that skill can be effective in regaining it (Binkofski & Buccino, 2006; Ertelt et al., 2007). Additionally, treatment of phantom-limb pain in amputees uses a mirror technique to help ease the discomfort that patients are experiencing. The implications for therapy with psychological disorders have not yet been fully explored. In a sense, we "learn" without having to actually "participate" in the activity. Could having depressed patients watch others enjoying themselves and laughing lift the depression? If a child with an intense fear of dogs watched someone calmly pet and play with a dog, would that help the child become less afraid? The future is ours to see—through the looking glass of social interactions.

▲ As this boy imitates the motions his father goes through while shaving, certain areas of his brain are more active than others. But even if the boy were only watching his father, those same neurons would mirror his father's actions.

Questions for Further Discussion

1. What other examples can you think of that might involve mirror neurons?
2. In what ways might mirror neurons be involved in how children learn to speak and form words?

Critical Thinking

DISCUSSING WORKPLACE PROBLEMS FOR THE LEFT-HANDED

There are millions of people who are left-handed, which presents a severe problem in the workplace. Left-handed individuals are more likely to have accidents at work than are right-handed individuals. Accommodations such as being able to rearrange the work area and having tools available that are either left- or right-hand adapted would make the workplace a safer place. Have students suggest ways that the workplace could be made safer or even what could be done in the classroom that would make it easier for students who are left-handed to take notes or tests. What about the computer mouse? The mouse is actually made for people who are right-handed. How adaptable must a left-handed person become in order not to be frustrated by using a right-handed mouse?

Practice Quiz

Pick the best answer.

1. Which of the following techniques uses a radioactive sugar to look at the functioning of the brain?
   a. EEG
   b. CT
   c. MRI
   d. PET

2. Which brain structure is most responsible for our balance, posture, and muscle tone?
   a. medulla
   b. cerebellum
   c. reticular formation
   d. pons

3. If you have problems storing away new memories, which area of your brain is most likely damaged?
   a. hippocampus
   b. hypothalamus
   c. cerebellum
   d. amygdala

4. In which of the following lobes of the cortex would you find the primary auditory area?
   a. frontal
   b. temporal
   c. occipital
   d. parietal

5. Which lobe controls higher mental functions such as thinking and problem solving?
   a. frontal
   b. parietal
   c. temporal
   d. corpus

6. Which of the following is true of split-brain patients?
   a. They can easily name objects in their left visual field.
   b. They cannot see objects in their left visual field.
   c. They can easily name objects in their right visual field.
   d. They cannot see objects in their right visual field.

7. Which of the following areas of the brain seems to be responsible for fear responses?
   a. thalamus
   b. amygdala
   c. corpus callosum
   d. somatosensory cortex

8. Parts of the brain that are responsible for coordinating sensory information with stored memories, images, and knowledge are called
   a. association areas
   b. peripheral locations
   c. subcortical structures
   d. cerebral hemispheres

9. Special cells that can manufacture other cell types when those cells need to be replaced are known as
   a. blood cells
   b. motor cells
   c. stem cells
   d. sensory cells

10. The brain's ability to adapt to serve new functions after it has been damaged is an example of
    a. deep lesioning
    b. action potential
    c. neuroplasticity
    d. mirroring

THE BIOLOGICAL PERSPECTIVE 65

Practice Quiz Answers

1. d
2. b
3. a
4. b
5. a
6. b
7. b
8. a
9. c
10. c

CHAPTER 2 • Module 5

Assess

Assign the Module 5 Practice Quiz.
Use the Practice Quiz to identify gaps in student understanding.

REMEDIATE

Have students, individually or in groups, review the module goals, learning objectives, and key terms.
Refer students to the Concept Summary on p. 75 for review.

Close

As a class, discuss what students found to be the most interesting or surprising thing they learned about the brain in this module. Ask: **Why is it important for psychologists to understand how the brain works?** *(Possible answer: It is important to understand how the brain works in order to understand how it interacts to control feelings, thoughts and behavior)*

L2 LPR DIFFERENTIATED INSTRUCTION

Less Proficient Readers For students with difficulties with attention and memory, gain attention by requesting a simple physical response (e.g., "Everyone, eyes on me, please"). Then keep the lesson pace brisk.

CHAPTER 2 • Module 6

Focus

RESOURCES
For this module, consult the appropriate sections of the Teacher's Manual, Test Bank, and PowerPoint slides, all found on the Teacher's Resource DVD, and the interactive study tools for students on MyPsychLab.

BEFORE CLASS
Students should read the section for homework before coming to class.

BELLRINGER
Write on the board: **Which is more important to human development: nature or nurture? Write an answer of one or two sentences.** Once class is ready to begin, ask several volunteers to read their answers aloud.

Teach

INTRODUCE THE TOPIC
- Nature versus nurture
  - The issue of nature (heredity) versus nurture (environmental) influences has been debated for years.
  - *Nature* is the influence of heredity on personality, physical growth, intellectual growth, and social interactions.
  - *Nurture* is the influence of environment on all of those things and includes parenting styles, socioeconomic factors, physical surroundings, and anything else that may influence how one develops.

COVER THE MODULE
6.1 How do genetic factors determine who we are?
- Genetics is the science of heredity.
- *DNA* contains genetic material. Molecules of DNA link and form long strands.
- A *gene* is a section of DNA having the same arrangement of chemical elements.
- A fertilized egg contains 23 chromosomes from the mother and 23 from the father.

66 Chapter 2 The Biological Perspective

Module 6: Heredity, Environment, and Adaptation

Module Goal
Discover how biology and experience interact.

Learning Objectives
6.1 How do genetic factors determine who we are?
6.2 How do heredity and environmental factors interact to affect our development?
6.3 How do evolved tendencies influence our behavior?

Discover How Biology and Experience Interact

There's no denying it: Our biology plays an important role in determining our behavior. The nervous system in general and the brain in particular help us act and react to the world around us. But are all of our actions and reactions determined by biology?

This is a question that psychologists have explored and debated for years. Psychologists are curious about whether our personalities, behaviors, and abilities are determined by our **nature** (our genetic traits and inherited characteristics) or by our **nurture** (the environmental factors that surround us throughout our lives and influence our development). These days, most psychologists believe that both nature *and* nurture play important roles in human development. Our inherited genetic traits go a long way toward determining whom we grow up to be, but biology isn't the only force that shapes us. We are also constantly shaped by our family, friends, culture, and day-to-day experiences. In the next few pages, we'll take a look at a variety of factors that influence human development and behavior.

FIGURE 6.1 DNA Molecule

nature the influence of our DNA that dictates the inherited characteristics that influence our personality, physical growth, intellectual growth, and social interactions.

nurture the influence of the environment on personality, physical growth, intellectual growth, and social interactions.

DNA (deoxyribonucleic acid) special molecule that contains the genetic material of the organism.

gene section of DNA having the same arrangement of chemical elements.

chromosome tightly wound strand of genetic material or DNA.

dominant referring to a gene that actively controls the expression of a trait.

6.1 How do genetic factors determine who we are?

Genetics is the science of heredity. Understanding how genes transmit human characteristics and traits involves defining a few basic terms.

DNA (deoxyribonucleic acid) is a very special kind of molecule. See Figure 6.1 for a representation of DNA. Because of DNA's unique spiral, double-helix shape, each molecule of DNA is linked end to end with the others, forming a very long strand. Each section of DNA containing a certain sequence (ordering) of these amines is called a **gene**. These genes are located on rod-shaped structures called **chromosomes**, which are found in the nucleus of a cell.

A mother's egg (ovum) has 23 chromosomes, and a father's sperm has 23 chromosomes. A fertilized egg (a zygote) has 46 chromosomes. As the zygote begins cell division, every cell in its body will have 46 chromosomes: 23 from the mother and 23 from the father. The 46 chromosomes can be arranged in pairs, with one member of each pair coming from the mother and the other member from the father.

Dominant and Recessive Genes Some genes that are more active in influencing a trait are called **dominant**. A dominant gene will always be

66 CHAPTER 2

Terms

- nature • nurture • DNA (deoxyribonucleic acid) • gene • chromosome • dominant
- recessive • predisposition • evolution • natural selection

expressed in the observable trait. A person with a dominant brown hair color gene will have brown hair, no matter what the other gene is, because brown is the most dominant of all the hair colors. Some genes tend to recede, or fade, into the background when paired with a more dominant gene, so they are called **recessive**. Blond hair color is the most recessive color and will only show up in a person's hair color if that person has a blond hair color gene from each parent.

What about red hair? And how come some people have mixed hair color, like a strawberry blond?

Sometimes certain kinds of genes tend to group themselves with certain other genes, like the genes for blond hair and blue eyes. Other genes are so equally dominant or equally recessive that they combine their traits in the organism. For example, genes for blond hair and red hair are recessive. When a child inherits one of each from his or her parents, instead of one or the other controlling the child's hair color, they may blend together to form a strawberry-blond mix.

Genes play a role in determining what we look like and how we act, but it's important to remember that, in many cases, DNA only creates genetic **predispositions** (genetic tendencies or possibilities). If a person is predisposed to develop a certain type of cancer, it does not mean that he is guaranteed to have that type of cancer—it simply means that, for him, getting that type of cancer is more of a possibility than it is for someone without that predisposition. Genes determine predispositions, but not all predispositions become realities.

◀ What about red hair? And how come some people have mixed hair color, like a strawberry blond?

6.2 How do heredity and environmental factors interact to affect our development?

Is a person like Hitler born that way, or did something happen to make him the person he was?

How much of a person's personality and behavior are determined by nature and how much are determined by nurture? This is a key question, and the answer is quite complicated. It is also quite important: Was someone like Hitler the result of bad genes? Or was it bad parenting or life-altering experiences in childhood? Or was it a unique combination of both hereditary and environmental influences? After many years of scientific research, most developmental psychologists now agree that the last possibility is the most likely explanation for most of human development: All that people are and all that people become is the product of an interaction between nature and nurture (Ridley, 1999). Our DNA may determine the outlines of our lives, but external forces—including parents, peers, and cultural expectations—have a tremendous amount of power over who we become.

The Effect of Parents and Peers When you hear the word "nurture," you might automatically think of parents. Parents and other close family members and friends are generally responsible for taking care of children, and the family environment can affect a person's behaviors and skills, particularly during childhood. For example, while most abused children do not grow up to become abusive adults, most abusive adults were abused or neglected as children (Kempe & Kempe, 1978).

You can see the influences of family in smaller ways, too. Think about your own close family members: How have your tastes in movies and books, your political or religious beliefs, and your academic and athletic interests been

◀ Is a person like Hitler born that way, or did something happen to make him the person he was?

recessive referring to a gene that only influences the expression of a trait when paired with an identical gene.

predisposition tendency or possibility

THE BIOLOGICAL PERSPECTIVE **67**

CHAPTER 2 • Module 6

COVER THE MODULE *(continued)*
- **Dominant and Recessive Genes**
  - *Dominant* genes control the expression of a trait.
  - *Recessive* gene traits are only expressed when paired with another recessive gene for the same trait.
  - In many cases, DNA creates only genetic *predispositions*, which are tendencies or possibilities. Not all predispositions become realities.

DISCUSS THE STUDENT VOICE QUESTION
Make sure students understand that certain kinds of genes can group themselves with certain other genes. Some genes are so equally dominant or equally recessive that they combine their traits in the organism. For example, when a child inherits certain genes from both parents, instead of one or the other controlling, something like hair color, the genes may blend together.

COVER THE MODULE
6.2 How do heredity and environmental factors interact to affect our development?

DISCUSS THE STUDENT VOICE QUESTION
Point out that this type of question is at the heart of the nature-versus-nurture controversy. Most human development is likely a function of nature *and* nurture.

- **The Effect of Parents and Peers**
  - The family environment can affect a person's behaviors, particularly in childhood.
  - Experiences with one's peers can also shape one's personality.

Explore

WRITING ABOUT HEREDITY
Ask students to use library or Internet resources to research the topic of dominant and recessive genes and their role in heredity. Then have them write a short report on whether there are any physical characteristics in their own family tree that appear to be dominant, such as eye color, height, hair color, dimples, and so forth. Tell them to list such dominant traits. Have volunteers report their findings during class.

Module 6 Heredity, Environment, and Adaptation **67**

CHAPTER 2 • Module 6

DISCUSS THE STUDENT VOICE QUESTION
This question should help students understand that one's environment does not consist solely of one's family.

COVER THE MODULE (continued)
- **The Effect of Culture**
  - The culture in which one lives can have a great impact on beliefs and behaviors.
- **Twin Studies**
  - Researchers study twins in order to determine how much of their identical genetic makeup influences their behavior and personality.
- **Adoption Studies**
  - The Minnesota/Texas Adoption Project studied the similarities between adopted children and their biological parents, finding that adopted children shared more similarities with their biological parents than with their adoptive parents.

UNDERSTANDING VISUALS
Direct students' attention to the question in the photo caption. A possible answer could include the idea that these girls belong to a culture that promotes the idea of girls as athletes. In addition, their parents and/or peers might have encouraged them to participate in sports.

▶ My sister and I were raised by the same parents, but we're totally different people. If we grew up in the same environment, why are we so different?

▲ What environmental forces might encourage these girls to train as soccer players? What roles might parents and peers play in shaping the girls' behavior?

68 CHAPTER 2

---

shaped by the people who raised you? Your family's values have most likely shaped your personality in a number of ways.

My sister and I were raised by the same parents, but we're totally different people. If we grew up in the same environment, why are we so different?

Two siblings raised by the same parents may have very different interests and talents—and that's perfectly normal. Parenting is an important environmental factor to consider in our discussion of the nature–nurture issue, but it certainly isn't the only factor.

People do not spend all their time with their parents; the older they get, the more likely they are to be influenced by their friends, classmates, teachers, neighbors, bosses, and coworkers. Our experiences with our peers can shape our personalities and interests in the same way that our experiences with our parents can. Your parents might influence your love for Thai food, while your friends might influence your fashion choices. And if all of your friends have a certain accent, you might find yourself developing that accent, too.

The Effect of Culture Family members and peers are two small parts of a larger *culture*—a society that shares a set of beliefs and behaviors. The culture in which we live can have an enormous effect on our thoughts and actions. A culture's understood rules, or *norms*, tell us what behavior is acceptable or unacceptable. Cultural norms can influence a wide variety of beliefs and behaviors, from what we eat to how we worship. In many cases, cultural norms help us decide what behaviors are "normal" or "abnormal." There is no biological basis for saying "please" and "thank you" at the dinner table, but in many cultures, using polite language is an important example of "normal" behavior.

Twin Studies Researchers find it valuable to study the behavior of twins in order to get a better understanding of the question of nature vs. nurture. Identical twins share 100 percent of the same genes. They are often raised in the same household. However, they are not the same people. How much of their identical genetic makeup influences their behavior and personality?

Psychologist Thomas Bouchard conducted a famous experiment in twin studies, known as the Minnesota Twin Family Study. In this experiment, Bouchard studied twins who were raised apart. He found that these twins displayed some remarkable similarities in behavior and personality traits. For example, the "Jim twins," James Lewis and James Springer, were separated as infants and raised with no knowledge of one another. When they were reunited, at the age of 39, they found that they shared many of the same interests and habits, both married women named Linda, divorced, and remarried women named Betty. Both had a dog named Toy. One named his son James Alan, and the other named his son James Allan.

Not all of the twins studied shared such remarkable characteristics. The Minnesota Twin Family Study has been criticized because some of the twins raised apart had contact with each other, and some were raised in the homes of relatives, which could arguably share similar cultural qualities. However, Bouchard's findings seem to suggest that there may be some genetic influence on almost all areas of human behavior.

Adoption Studies Another famous study, the Minnesota/Texas Adoption Project, examines the similarities between adopted children and their biological parents, whom they have never met. Researchers have followed participants in the study for more than 20 years and found that adopted children

---

Class Demonstration

RESEARCH WITH TWINS
Some studies of twins who have been reared apart have shown that they have striking similarities in interests and attitudes. However, critics argue that if you ask enough questions, you can find a long list of commonalities between total strangers. Divide four-member teams into *A*'s and *B*'s. Have the *A*'s ask the *B*'s 20 or so questions and record anything they have in common. They might ask questions about music preferences, food likes, and personality traits. Then the *B*'s should interview the *A*'s. Ask the pairs to reunite and share their responses with the team. Were students able to find commonalities with their partner?

68 Chapter 2 The Biological Perspective

share more similiarities with their biological parents than with their adoptive parents. Though this seems to suggest that genetics (nature) plays a strong role in behavioral tendencies, the nature vs. nurture question has yet to be satisfactorily answered by any one study.

6.3 How do evolved tendencies influence our behavior?

Many psychologists believe that human behavior is shaped not only by biology and environment but also by evolutionary forces: tendencies that have developed gradually over many generations to help humans survive. Psychologists who are interested in these tendencies study how human behavior relates to the basic evolutionary principles proposed more than 100 years ago by famous British scientist Charles Darwin.

Charles Darwin and Natural Selection Like many other 19th century scientists, Darwin accepted the theory of **evolution**, which states that species of plants and animals change gradually over the course of many generations. But why did these changes occur? Darwin noticed that many of the changes seemed to give organisms some sort of advantage in their natural environments. For example, if dark-colored moths can hide from predators more easily than light-colored moths can, it's likely that in a few generations, there will be many more dark-colored moths than light-colored moths. Why? The moths' dark color gives them an advantage when it comes to survival. This means that, in general, dark-colored moths will live long enough to have baby dark-colored moths, while light-colored moths will be eaten by predators before they can reproduce.

This scenario is one simple example of Darwin's groundbreaking theory of **natural selection**. Darwin argued that traits and behaviors that provide a survival advantage are more likely than other characteristics to be passed on to future generations. The concepts of evolution and natural selection were controversial during Darwin's time, and they remain somewhat controversial today, but most scientists accept Darwin's theories because they accurately illustrate the changes that take place in plant and animal populations over time. In particular, the concepts of evolution and natural selection have been adopted by evolutionary psychologists in order to explain human behavior.

Hold on a minute—are my behaviors affected by evolution?

What would you do if a poisonous snake slithered toward you, or if a big, hairy spider crawled across your bedroom floor? If you're like most people, you'd probably scream and try to get away from the snake or the spider as quickly as possible. But what's the cause of your behavior?

Evolutionary psychologists would argue that our fear when we see a dangerous animal is an evolved behavior that helps us survive. Many generations ago, humans who reacted with fear to dangerous animals were more likely to survive than humans who weren't afraid of those animals, so the fear response has been passed down to modern-day humans—even those of us who only encounter poisonous animals at the zoo and in movies. We are "hard-wired" to fear snakes because that fear has helped our species survive. Plenty of other human behaviors can be explained in a similar way. We tend to like the taste of fatty foods, for example, because in ancient hunting and gathering societies, fat was an important source of calories and an important substance for survival. Humans who enjoyed the taste of fatty foods were more likely to get enough calories in their diet and, as a result, they were more likely to survive than humans who didn't like the taste of fat.

▲ In 1859, naturalist Charles Darwin published *The Origin of Species*, which introduced the theory of natural selection.

◀ Hold on a minute—are my behaviors affected by evolution?

evolution a process of gradual change over time.

natural selection principle stating that inherited characteristics that give a survival advantage are more likely to be passed on to future generations.

THE BIOLOGICAL PERSPECTIVE 69

Class Demonstration (Kinesthetic)

TAKE A STAND

Designate one side of the room as the "Heredity" side and the other as the "Experience" side. Acknowledge that everyone probably agrees that both nature and nurture contribute to development. Students should then choose which they believe to be the most important set of influences. Those who think genetics exert greater influence than experience should go to the Heredity side. Students who think that experience is more important should go to the Experience side. Tell them that everyone has to take a side; give students a few minutes to decide. Next, each student is allowed 30 seconds to explain his or her position. Alternate between the two sides. When all students have finished, allow students to switch sides. Students who switch sides should then explain what changed their mind.

CHAPTER 2 • Module 6

COVER THE MODULE

6.3 How do evolved tendencies influence our behavior?

- **Charles Darwin and Natural Selection**
  - The theory of *evolution* states that species of plants and animals change gradually over the course of many generations.
  - Darwin's theory of *natural selection* argues that traits and behaviors that provide a survival advantage are more likely than other characteristics to be passed on to future generations.

DISCUSS THE STUDENT VOICE QUESTION

Explain to students that many human behaviors can be explained as evolved behaviors that have helped humans survive.

L2 ELL DIFFERENTIATED INSTRUCTION

English Language Learners Students who are learning English require front-loading, or preteaching, in order to grasp challenging literacy tasks. Since ELL students may be approaching an assignment with limited background knowledge and weak English vocabulary, concentrate on activities that build strong conceptual and linguistic foundations, guide them through the text's organization, and model appropriate comprehension strategies.

Module 6 Heredity, Environment, and Adaptation **69**

CHAPTER 2 • Module 6

Assess

Assign the Module 6 Practice Quiz.

Use the Practice Quiz to identify gaps in student understanding.

REMEDIATE

Have students, individually or in groups, review the module goals, learning objectives, and key terms.

Refer students to the Concept Summary on p. 75 for review.

Close

As a class, briefly discuss the various influences that student believe have affected their development, such as parents, peers, and culture. Do students believe that one of these influences has been more important in their lives than others?

Some evolutionary psychologists believe that mating preferences between human men and women can also be explained in evolutionary terms. They argue, for instance, that men have evolved to look for female partners who are young, healthy, and able to have many children. Women, on the other hand, look for men who are mature and stable, and who will help to take care of a family. In evolutionary psychology's view, many of our romantic decisions and behaviors can be explained by our desire to ensure the survival of our species. Many people are critical of this perspective because it is nearly impossible to prove, and it tends to reinforce harmful or unfair gender stereotypes. Still, the field of evolutionary psychology asserts that many of our everyday behaviors are shaped by influences that have evolved over thousands of years.

▲ How would you react to this black widow spider? Humans' fear of spiders can be explained as an evolved behavior.

Practice Quiz

Pick the best answer.

1. How many chromosomes do humans have in each cell of their bodies?
   a. 10
   b. 22
   c. 23
   d. 46

2. Which of the following is the most dominant hair color?
   a. brown
   b. blond
   c. red
   d. gray

3. Genes that tend to "fade into the background" when paired with more influential genes are called
   a. dominant
   b. recessive
   c. chromosomes
   d. autosomes

4. If a person is predisposed to burning in the sun, which of the following is true?
   a. The person will definitely experience sunburns.
   b. The person will definitely not experience sunburns.
   c. The person is unlikely to experience sunburns.
   d. The person may experience sunburns, depending on environmental factors.

5. A person who believes that our environments and experiences are entirely responsible for our personalities, skills, and behaviors believes in the power of
   a. nature over nurture
   b. nurture over nature
   c. both nature and nurture
   d. neither nature nor nurture

6. Which of the following is an example of a hereditary influence?
   a. a genetic disease
   b. parental discipline
   c. cultural values
   d. peer pressure

7. Twins who grow up with the same parents in the same environment will most likely be
   a. identical in every way
   b. similar in some ways and different in others
   c. completely different in every way
   d. identical in terms of genetics but opposite in terms of behavior

8. A culture's understood rules of behavior are
   a. beliefs
   b. guidelines
   c. norms
   d. values

9. Charles Darwin was the first to propose the theory of
   a. evolution
   b. natural selection
   c. genetics
   d. environmental influences

10. Which of the following human behaviors is most likely an evolved tendency?
    a. shopping at a mall
    b. attending school
    c. driving cars and trucks
    d. spitting out poisonous foods

70 CHAPTER 2

Practice Quiz Answers

1. d
2. a
3. b
4. d
5. a
6. a
7. a
8. c
9. b
10. d

70 Chapter 2 The Biological Perspective

CHAPTER 2 Summary

🔊 **Listen** on **mypsychlab.com**

Module 4: The Nervous System
Understand the structure and function of the nervous system.

4.1 What are the divisions of the human nervous system?
- The nervous system is divided into the central nervous system and the peripheral nervous system. The ANS is divided into the parasympathetic and sympathetic division.

4.2 What are neurons, and how do they work?
- Neurons have dendrites, which receive input, a soma or cell body, and axons that carry the neural message to other cells.

4.3 What are the functions of the different parts of the central nervous system?
- The spinal cord transmits messages to and from the brain. The brain and the spinal cord communicate with the rest of the body through the peripheral nervous system.

Explain how the neuroendocrine system functions.

4.4 How are the endocrine glands connected to the nervous system?
- The nervous system triggers endocrine glands to release hormones into the bloodstream. These hormones can affect thoughts and behavior.

4.5 How do hormones affect our behavior?
- Hormones regulate growth, sleep, metabolism, blood sugar levels, stress reactions, and other physical functions.

4.6 What effects do hormones have on the immune system?
- Some hormones can help the immune system function properly, and others can weaken the immune system.

Module 5: The Brain
Learn how scientists study the nervous system.

5.1 How do people study the brain?
- Early scientists examined brains of people who had died. Modern scientists perform tests on people with existing brain damage.

Listen to an audio file of your chapter on **mypsychlab.com**

5.2 What advances have made the brain easier to study?
- Brain-imaging techniques include CT scans, MRI and fMRI scans, PET scans, and EEGs.

5.3 What are some recent innovations in neuroscience?
- Researchers have explored the possibility of using stem cells to repair damaged or diseased brain tissue. Researchers have also discovered the existence of mirror neurons.

Understand the structure and function of the brain.

5.4 What are the different parts of the brain?
- The structures of the hindbrain control life-sustaining functions, sleep, arousal, and movement. The structures of the limbic system are involved in emotions, motivation, and learning. The cortex processes sensory information, controls voluntary muscles, and performs higher mental functions.

5.5 How does the left side of the brain differ from the right side?
- The left side controls language, writing, and logical thought. The right side controls spatial perception, facial recognition, patterns, melodies, and emotions.

Module 6: Heredity, Environment, and Adaptation
Discover how biology and experience interact.

6.1 How do genetic factors determine who we are?
- DNA molecules form genes, which interact to determine many of our physical traits and predispositions.

6.2 How do heredity and environmental factors interact to affect our development?
- Our thoughts and behaviors are affected not only by biological predispositions but also by the influence of our parents, our peers, and the cultures in which we participate.

6.3 How do evolved tendencies influence our behavior?
- Charles Darwin's theory of natural selection can explain human behaviors like avoiding dangerous animals and enjoying fatty foods.

Vocabulary Terms

neuron p. 42
dendrites p. 42
soma p. 42
axon p. 42
myelin p. 43
action potential p. 45
axon terminals p. 46
synaptic vesicles p. 46
neurotransmitter p. 46
receptor sites p. 46
central nervous system p. 47
sensory neuron p. 48
motor neuron p. 48
interneuron p. 49
peripheral nervous system p. 49
autonomic nervous system p. 49

sympathetic division p. 49
parasympathetic division p. 49
endocrine glands p. 50
hormones p. 50
pituitary gland p. 51
pineal gland p. 51
thyroid gland p. 51
pancreas p. 51
adrenal glands p. 51
gonads p. 51
deep lesioning p. 54
computed tomography p. 55
magnetic resonance imaging p. 55
positron emission tomography p. 55
functional MRI p. 56
electroencephalograph p. 56

neuroplasticity p. 56
stem cells p. 56
medulla p. 57
pons p. 58
reticular formation (RF) p. 58
cerebellum p. 58
limbic system p. 58
thalamus p. 59
hypothalamus p. 59
homeostasis p. 59
hippocampus p. 59
amygdala p. 60
cortex p. 60
cerebral hemispheres p. 60
corpus callosum p. 60
occipital lobe p. 60
parietal lobes p. 60
somatosensory cortex p. 60

temporal lobes p. 60
frontal lobes p. 61
motor cortex p. 61
association areas p. 61
nature p. 66
nurture p. 66
DNA p. 66
gene p. 66
chromosome p. 66
dominant p. 66
recessive p. 67
predisposition p. 67
evolution p. 69
natural selection p. 69

THE BIOLOGICAL PERSPECTIVE 71

CHAPTER 2 • Chapter Summary and Vocabulary

Chapter Summary

Encourage students to carefully review and study the summary. Explain that it provides an overview of key concepts presented in the text.

Have students identify what they find unclear or confusing. Call on volunteers to provide answers, examples, or definitions.

Vocabulary Terms

Remind students that terms are defined within the chapter at point of use. If they are not sure of a term's definition, they should look up the definition on the page.

Encourage students to create study cards of unfamiliar words or to go to **www.mypsychlab.com** for flash cards. Have them test themselves or a classmate. Advanced students can explain the terms in their own words.

Critical Thinking

MAKING CONNECTIONS

Have students complete the following activity to connect the ideas in this chapter. Send them to the Multimedia Library for Chapter 2 at **www.mypsychlab.com** to view the video titled "MKM and Brain Scans," which discusses an advanced procedure for brain surgery. Then lead a class discussion based on the following questions: (1) Why is the MKM system considered such an important advance in neurosurgery? (2) Why is it important for brain surgery to be so precise? (3) What is the benefit to the patient of using this process?

CHAPTER 2 • Assessment

VOCABULARY REVIEW

1. j	6. g
2. a	7. e
3. h	8. i
4. f	9. d
5. c	10. b

WRITING ABOUT PSYCHOLOGY

1. Students' answers should show evidence of careful thought and accuracy in describing ways in which both biological and environmental forces have affected them.
2. Students should display a clear understanding of how different parts of the brain help them perform an activity.

PSYCHOLOGY PROJECT

Be sensitive to students' descriptions of emotional experiences, which they may think of as personal and private. Consider asking volunteers to share any responses they feel comfortable discussing in the classroom.

72 Chapter 2 The Biological Perspective

CHAPTER 2 Assessment

✓ Study and Review on mypsychlab.com

Vocabulary Review

Match each vocabulary term to its definition.

1. soma
2. neuron
3. hypothalamus
4. hormones
5. medulla
6. neurotransmitters
7. cerebellum
8. dendrites
9. temporal lobe
10. gene

a. The basic cell that makes up the nervous system and that receives and sends messages within that system.
b. Section of DNA having the same arrangement of chemical elements.
c. The first large swelling at the top of the spinal cord, forming the lowest part of the brain, which is responsible for life-sustaining functions such as breathing, swallowing, and heart rate.
d. The area of the cortex located just behind the temples containing the neurons responsible for the sense of hearing and meaningful speech.
e. Part of the lower brain located behind the pons that controls and coordinates involuntary, rapid, fine motor movement.
f. Chemicals released into the bloodstream by endocrine glands.
g. Chemicals found in the synaptic vesicles that, when released, have an effect on the next cell.
h. The small structure in the brain located below the thalamus and directly above the pituitary gland, responsible for motivational behavior.
i. The branchlike structures that receive messages from other neurons.
j. The cell body of the neuron responsible for maintaining the life of the cell.

Writing about Psychology

Respond to each question in complete sentences.

1. How have you been shaped by nature and by nurture? Describe at least three ways in which biological forces have affected your personality, skills, behavior, or appearance. Then describe at least three ways in which environmental forces have affected you. Be sure to explain why each force is either biological or environmental.
2. Choose an activity that you enjoy, such as playing a sport, creating art, or talking with friends. Then explain how at least three different parts of the brain help you perform that activity.

Psychology Project

What does it really feel like when the sympathetic division controls the body? Keep a journal and record your nervous system's responses to emotional situations.

Materials:
- small notebook
- pencil or pen

Instructions:

1. Over the course of 1 week, pay close attention to your behavior in stressful and nonstressful situations. At the end of each day, use a notebook to write down any emotional experiences you had that day, whether those experiences involved fear, anger, joy, or excitement.
2. For each experience you record, write a few notes about how your body responded to the experience. Did your heart beat faster before the math test? Did your stomach lurch as you waited in line for the roller coaster? Write down as many physical details as you can remember.
3. At the end of the week, analyze your findings. What physical sensations did you experience in response to each event? Did you respond differently to a scary situation than you did to an exciting situation? How did your physical responses to emotional experiences differ from your normal, everyday behaviors and feelings? Based on what you know about the sympathetic and parasympathetic divisions of the autonomic nervous system, why do you think you felt the way you did? Record your responses to these questions in your notebook.

72 CHAPTER 2

Internet Resources

Neuroguide.com – Neurosciences on the Internet: www.neuroguide.com/

A resource for all things related to neuroscience: databases, diseases, research centers, software, biology, psychology, journals, tutorials, and much more.

Neuropsychology Central: www.neuropsychologycentral.com/

Contains links to resources related to neuropsychology, including brain images, and extensive, well-organized links to other sites.

Brain and Behavior: http://serendip.brynmawr.edu/bb/

This mega-site contains many links to information about the brain, behavior, and the bond between the two. Students can complete several interactive exercises to learn more about brain functions.

Brain Connection: The Brain and Learning: www.brainconnection.com/

A newspaper-style web page that contains interesting articles, news reports, activities, and commentary on brain-related issues.

Test Yourself

Pick the best answer.

1. Which part of the neuron sends information to other cells?
   a. axon
   b. dendrite
   c. soma
   d. myelin

2. When a neuron is in the resting potential state, where are the sodium ions?
   a. only inside the cell
   b. only outside the cell
   c. both inside and outside the cell
   d. usually inside the cell, but sometimes outside the cell

3. Which part of the nervous system controls the voluntary muscles?
   a. somatic nervous system
   b. autonomic nervous system
   c. sympathetic division
   d. parasympathetic division

4. Your heart races. You begin to breathe faster. Your pupils enlarge and your appetite is gone. Which of the following has just been activated?
   a. the central nervous system
   b. the somatic nervous system
   c. the sympathetic division
   d. the parasympathetic division

5. Which technique of studying the brain actually damages neurons?
   a. EEG
   b. CT
   c. fMRI
   d. deep lesioning

6. Which part of the brain stem must be developed in order to allow a young child to sit upright?
   a. medulla
   b. pons
   c. reticular formation
   d. cerebellum

7. George has a small stroke that results in a partial paralysis of his left side. The damaged area is most likely in which lobe of his brain?
   a. right frontal
   b. left frontal
   c. right parietal
   d. left temporal

8. Which of the following is a specialty of the left hemisphere of the brain?
   a. controlling the left hand
   b. nonverbal communication
   c. emotional thought
   d. mathematical calculations

9. Which of the following statements is TRUE about hormones?
   a. Hormones attack the immune system and cause sickness and infection.
   b. Hormones support the immune system and attack infections and disease.
   c. Hormones can either help or lower the functioning of the immune system.
   d. Hormones have no connection to the functioning of the immune system.

10. Britta has naturally blond hair. What do we know about Britta's parents?
    a. Both of Britta's parents must have blond hair.
    b. Neither of Britta's parents must have blond hair.
    c. At least one of Britta's parents must have blond hair.
    d. Both of Britta's parents must have at least one gene for blond hair.

11. The rod-shaped structures found in the nuclei of cells are called
    a. DNA
    b. amines
    c. genes
    d. chromosomes

12. Scientists have been able to repair some forms of spinal cord damage by implanting nerve fibers from outside of the spinal cord onto a damaged area and then "coaxing" the damaged spinal nerves to grow through these "tunnels" of implanted fibers. This ability of the brain to change both the structure and function of many cells is known as
    a. homeostasis
    b. neuroplasticity
    c. resting potential
    d. acting potential

13. Which of the following is likely to be mostly influenced by cultural forces?
    a. your eye color
    b. your height
    c. your food allergies
    d. your taste in music

14. Which of the following statements about environmental influences is most accurate?
    a. Children's behavior is influenced mostly by their parents.
    b. Children's behavior is influenced mostly by their peers.
    c. Parents and peers both influence children's behavior.
    d. Neither parents nor peers can influence children's behavior.

15. In general, evolutionary psychologists believe that we are attracted to mates who
    a. have a good sense of humor
    b. share most of our interests
    c. will make good parents
    d. live nearby

16. Which of the following people is famous for his research into evolution and natural selection?
    a. Charles Darwin
    b. Roger Sperry
    c. Paul Broca
    d. Leonardo da Vinci

17. Which of the following is NOT a cultural norm?
    a. saying "thank you" after receiving a gift
    b. treating men and women equally
    c. being afraid of poisonous animals
    d. celebrating birthdays with a party

18. Which hormone is secreted by the pituitary gland?
    a. human growth hormone
    b. insulin
    c. thyroxin
    d. cortisol

CHAPTER 2 • Assessment

TEST YOURSELF

1. a		10. d	
2. b		11. d	
3. a		12. b	
4. c		13. d	
5. d		14. c	
6. d		15. c	
7. a		16. a	
8. d		17. c	
9. c		18. a	

Ready for Testing

STUDENTS KNOW THEY ARE READY FOR TESTING IF THEY ARE ABLE TO . . .

- Explain what neurons are and how they work to transfer and process information.
- Introduce the peripheral nervous system and describe its role in the body.
- Discuss the role of the endocrine system.
- Describe the methods used to observe the structure and activity of the brain.
- Identify the basic structures of the brain and explain their functions.
- Explain how biology and experience interact.

CHAPTER 2 • Concept Summary

MULTIMEDIA CONTENT AVAILABLE AT
www.mypsychlab.com

Map the Concepts on **mypsychlab.com**

Study and Review Flashcards on **mypsychlab.com**

STUDY TIPS

Organization Point out to students that organizing their personal spaces and items, such as desks, backpacks, lockers, and study spaces, will save time and help avoid the frustration caused by searching fruitlessly for missing assignments or notebooks. Organizing information will help make studying easier and more productive. Suggest that students use three-ring binders, pouches, and boxes to organize their personal space. They should take time each week to sort through old papers, deciding which to keep and which to discard. Those that are kept should be filed in an appropriate location for easy reference later.

74 Chapter 2 The Biological Perspective

CHAPTER 2
Concept Summary: The Biological Perspective

Learning Objectives

4.1 4.2 4.3   pp. 42–50

Understand the Structure and Function of the Nervous System

- **neurons** are specialized cells in the nervous system
  - have specialized components
  - have a resting potential and action potential
  - are separated by a gap called the synapse
  - are affected by neurotransmitters

- **central nervous system**
  - **brain** — takes information from senses, processes it, makes decisions, sends commands to rest of body
  - **spinal cord** — carries information to and away from the brain

- **peripheral nervous system**
  - **somatic nervous system** — controls voluntary muscles of the body
  - **autonomic nervous system** — controls automatic functions of the body
    - parasympathetic division
    - sympathetic division

Learning Objectives

4.4 4.5 4.6   pp. 50–52

Explain How the Neuroendocrine System Functions

- **endocrine glands** are triggered by the nervous system to secrete hormones into the bloodstream
  - pituitary gland
  - pineal gland
  - thyroid gland
  - pancreas
  - adrenal glands

- **hormones**
  - can affect thought and behavior
  - can strengthen or weaken the immune system

74 CHAPTER 2

What Every Student Should Know About . . .

DOING ONLINE RESEARCH

Wikis such as Wikipedia represent a new direction in online community development. Anyone who has a web browser can add to and edit existing information on a wiki. However, because wikis change constantly, they may or may not provide the most reliable or respected information on a source. Explain to students that when doing research on a topic in psychology, they can browse the Wikipedia entry on the topic, but then they should turn to a more academically approved resource, such as an encyclopedia of psychology, for further information. In other words, they should use such Internet resources as wikis for introductory information but not as official research sources they cite in their work.

Learning Objectives

5.1 5.2 5.3   pp. 54–57

Learn How Scientists Study the Nervous System

- techniques for studying brain function
  - dissection of dead brains
  - deep lesioning in animals
  - case studies of brain-damaged individuals
  - imaging techniques
- structure
  - CT
  - MRI
- function
  - fMRI
  - EEG
  - PET

Learning Objectives

5.4 5.5   pp. 57–64

Understand the Structure and Function of the Brain

- structures of the brain
  - the hindbrain
    - medulla
    - pons
    - reticular formation
    - cerebellum
  - the limbic system
    - thalamus
    - hypothalamus
    - hippocampus
    - amygdala
  - the cortex
    - frontal lobes
    - temporal lobes
    - parietal lobes
    - occipital lobes
- the cerebral hemispheres govern brain functions, and some brain functions are governed by one hemisphere more than the other

Learning Objectives

6.1 6.2 6.3   pp. 66–70

Discover How Biology and Experience Interact

- **nature** involves the influence of inherited characteristics
  - genetics
    - dominant and recessive genes
    - genetic predispositions
- **nurture** involves the influence of the environment
  - parent and peer influences
  - cultural influences
- **evolved tendencies** can also influence our behavior

THE BIOLOGICAL PERSPECTIVE   75

Comprehension Check

PHYSIOLOGICAL BASES OF BEHAVIORAL PROBLEMS

To check their understanding, students can visit the Multimedia Library section of the www.mypsychlab.com site and explore the simulation titled "Physiological Bases of Behavioral Problems." Advanced students can work alone, while on-level and struggling students can work in pairs or small groups. Students will receive immediate feedback on their answers.

CHAPTER 2 • Concept Summary

STUDY TIPS

Making Outlines Point out that preparing a good outline before starting to write ensures that writing progresses more quickly and is more focused. An outline also will help students identify whether they have too much or not enough information and how their ideas connect. Have students first identify the topic of their essay and then list the main points they want to make. Under each main point, students should list the details that support that point. Generally speaking, each detail in their outline will translate into at least one paragraph in their final essay. After students have completed these steps, have them review the items and place them in the most logical order. Explain that once they begin writing, they may decide to make changes in the outline, but the outline will serve as the general plan for their essays.

Chapter 2 Concept Summary   75

CHAPTER 3 • Module 7

Launch the Chapter

CHAPTER GOALS AND LEARNING OBJECTIVES

Module 7 Sensation

Understand sensation and perception.

7.1 What are the distinctions between sensation and perception?

7.2 What is a sensory threshold? What is sensory adaptation?

Explore how senses work.

7.3 What forms of energy can humans sense?

7.4 How does the sense of vision work?

7.5 How does the sense of hearing work?

7.6 How do the senses of taste and smell work, and how are they alike?

7.7 What other sensory systems does the human body use?

Module 8 Perception

Learn how we perceive the world.

8.1 What is the nature of attention?

8.2 What are perceptual constancies?

8.3 What are the Gestalt principles of perception?

8.4 What are monocular and binocular depth cues?

8.5 How do visual illusions work?

8.6 How do our experiences and expectations influence perception?

DIFFERENTIATED INSTRUCTION KEY

Look for these symbols to help you adjust steps in each lesson to meet your students' needs.

L1 Special Needs

L2 Basic

　ELL English Language Learners

　LPR Less Proficient Readers

L3 All Students

L4 Advanced Students

CHAPTER 3

Sensation and Perception

Seeing Sounds and Hearing Colors: Synesthesia

"There was a piece of music by a group called Uman. The first note was grey and it was like a band of grey with a slight curve to it, and it was a gradient—light grey going to dark grey—it had gold specks on it. The background was black but it was being broken up by other colours, moving shapes of fuchsia and there was a small sound like a click, almost like a drumbeat, something being struck, and as it was struck, a black shape appeared, and the shapes appeared from left to right, going horizontally across the bottom of this—like a movie screen that I was watching. And the shapes were so exquisite, so simple, so pure and so beautiful, I wanted somehow to be able to capture them, but they were moving too quickly and I couldn't remember them all."

—Carol Steen (1996), New York artist and synesthete, quoted from ABC Radio National Transcripts, Health Report with Robin Hughes

Ms. Steen is a most unusual artist because she is able to perceive a world where sounds have colors and shapes, an ability she often turns into unusual and beautiful sculptures. A *synesthete* is a person with synesthesia, which literally means "joined sensation". People with this condition are rare—about one in 25,000. In the synesthete, the signals that come from the sensory organs, such as the eyes or the ears, go to places in the brain where they weren't originally meant to be, causing those signals to be interpreted as more than one sensation. A fusion of sound and sight is most common, but touch, taste, and even smell can enter into the mix (Cytowic, 1989).

Although research on the physical causes of synesthesia is ongoing, some studies suggest that areas of the left side of the brain deep inside the temporal lobe and nearby in the parietal lobe may be responsible (Ramachandran et al., 2002; Rouw & Scholte, 2007). **LINK** to Chapter Two: The Biological Perspective, pp. 60–61.

CORRELATION TO APA STANDARDS FOR CHAPTER 3

IIB. SENSATION AND PERCEPTION

IIB-1 The processes of sensation and perception . . . . pp. 78–80

IIB-2 The capabilities and limitations of sensory processes . . pp. 80–92

IIB-3 Interaction of the person and the environment in determining perception. . . . . pp. 94–101

MODULE 7 ▸ SENSATION

MODULE 8 ▸ PERCEPTION

Why Study?

Sensation and Perception

Without sensations to tell us what is outside our own body and mental world, we would live entirely in our own minds, separate from one another and unable to find food or any other basics that sustain life. Sensations are the mind's window to the world that exists around us. Without perception, we would be unable to understand what all those sensations mean—perception is the process of interpreting the sensations we experience so that we can act upon them.

SCHEDULING

1 Period = 50 min. 1 Block = 90 min.	Semester Course (18 weeks/90 days) Periods/Blocks		Full-Year Course (36 weeks/180 days) Periods/Blocks	
Module 7	2.5	1.25	5	2.5
Module 8	2.5	1.25	5	2.5
Total Days for Chapter	5	2.5	10	5

Teacher Prep

Sensation occurs when the sensory receptors are stimulated by information from the outside world and send that information to the brain. Perception occurs when the brain interprets and organizes sensations. Absolute thresholds are the smallest amount of energy needed for conscious detection of a stimulus at least half the time it is present. Sensory adaptation occurs when the sensory receptors stop responding to a constant stimulus.

Light enters the eye and is focused through the cornea, passes through the aqueous humor, and then goes through the pupil. The lens focuses light on the retina, where it passes through ganglia and bipolar cells to stimulate the rods and cones. Sound enters the ear through the visible outer structure and travels to the eardrum, the small bones of the middle ear, and the inner ear. Auditory receptors in the inner ear send signals to the brain. Taste buds in the tongue receive molecules of substances, which fit into receptor sites. The olfactory receptors in the upper part of the nasal passages receive molecules of substances and create neural signals that are sent to the brain.

The somesthetic senses include the skin senses and the vestibular senses (touch, pain, motion, and balance). Size constancy is the tendency to perceive objects as remaining the same size. Shape constancy is the tendency to perceive objects as remaining the same shape. Brightness constancy is the tendency to perceive objects at a certain brightness.

The Gestalt principles of perception are figure–ground relationships, closure, similarity, continuity, contiguity, and common region.

Illusions are perceptions that do not correspond to reality or are distortions of visual stimuli. Culture is one of many factors that can influence perception.

CHAPTER 3 • Module 7

Focus

RESOURCES

For this module, consult the appropriate sections of the Teacher's Manual, Test Bank, and PowerPoint slides, all found on the Teacher's Resource DVD, and the interactive study tools for students on MyPsychLab.

BEFORE CLASS

Students should read the section for homework before coming to class.

BELLRINGER

Ask students to write down short definitions of *sensation* and *perception*.

Teach

INTRODUCE THE TOPIC

Stress to students that it is important to understand the difference between the two terms they defined in the Bellringer activity: *Sensation* is the physical experience of seeing or hearing or sensing in some other way; *perception* is the psychological process of giving meaning to what has been sensed.

COVER THE MODULE

7.1 What are the distinctions between sensation and perception?

- *Sensation* is the activation of receptors located in the eyes, ears, skin, nasal cavities, and tongue.
- *Perception* is the process by which sensations are interpreted and organized in a meaningful fashion.

7.2 What is a sensory threshold? What is sensory adaptation?

- **Sensory Thresholds**
  - A *just noticeable difference* (jnd) is the smallest difference between two stimuli that is detectable 50% of the time.
  - Weber's law of just noticeable differences states that the jnd between two stimuli is always a constant.

Module 7: Sensation

Module Goals	Learning Objectives
Understand sensation and perception.	7.1 What are the distinctions between sensation and perception?
	7.2 What is a sensory threshold? What is sensory adaptation?
Explore how the senses work.	7.3 What forms of energy can humans sense?
	7.4 How does the sense of vision work?
	7.5 How does the sense of hearing work?
	7.6 How do the senses of taste and smell work, and how are they alike?
	7.7 What other sensory systems does the human body use?

Understand Sensation and Perception

7.1 What are the distinctions between sensation and perception?

There is so much information in the world outside of the body and brain. That information has to have a way to get into the brain, where it can be used to determine actions and responses. The way into the brain is through the sensory organs and the process of **sensation**. When you use your sense of sight to look around your neighborhood, or when you use your sense of hearing to listen to your favorite song at a concert, you are using sensory processes to take in information about the world around you. But that information comes in as raw data, meaningless pieces of information about the external word, captured by our senses.

The process of bringing meaning to the raw data is called **perception**. Through perception, your brain collects the data, organizes it, and interprets it to give those sensations meaning. At a concert, your ears receive sound waves, but your brain perceives those sounds as music—specifically, the opening notes of your favorite song. Sensation and perception are distinct processes, but they work together to help us make sense of ourselves and our surroundings.

7.2 What is a sensory threshold? What is sensory adaptation?

Sensory Thresholds The various sense organs—eyes, ears, nose, skin, and taste buds—are actually quite sensitive to stimulation. People have been investigating sensory abilities for a long time. Ernst Weber (1795–1878) did studies to determine the smallest detectable difference between two weights. His research led to the formulation known as Weber's law of **just noticeable differences** (**jnd**, or the **difference threshold**). A jnd is the

sensation the process that occurs when special receptors in the sense organs are activated, allowing various forms of outside stimuli to become neural signals in the brain.

perception the method by which the sensations experienced at any given moment are interpreted and organized in some meaningful fashion.

just noticeable difference (jnd, or the difference threshold) the smallest difference between two stimuli that is detectable 50 percent of the time by 50 percent of the people tested.

78 CHAPTER 3

Terms

- sensation • perception • just noticeable difference (jnd, or the difference threshold)
- absolute threshold • habituation • sensory adaptation • visual accommodation • rods
- cones • transduction • blind spot • dark adaptation • light adaptation • trichromatic theory • afterimages • opponent-process theory • hertz (Hz) • pinna • auditory canal
- cochlea • auditory nerve • pitch • place theory • frequency theory • volley principle
- gestation • somesthetic senses • skin senses • kinesthetic sense • vestibular senses

78 Chapter 3 Sensation and Perception

smallest difference between two stimuli that is detectable by 50 percent of people. For example, suppose you're eating pasta and you need to put five teaspoons of Parmesan cheese on top before you can taste the cheese. How much more cheese would you need to add to make your pasta taste even cheesier? Let's say that in order to make a noticeable difference to the pasta's taste half of the time, you'd have to add one teaspoon of cheese. Since the total amount of cheese already on the pasta is five teaspoons, the percentage of change needed to detect a just noticeable difference is one fifth, or 20 percent. Weber's law states that this percentage of change will remain constant, no matter how much cheese is already on the pasta. If you had 10 teaspoons of cheese on your pasta, you would have to add another 20 percent, or two teaspoons, to be able to taste the difference half of the time.

Gustav Fechner (1801–1887) expanded on Weber's work by studying something he called the **absolute threshold** (Fechner, 1860). An absolute threshold is the lowest level of stimulation that a person can consciously detect 50 percent of the time the stimulation is present. (Remember, the jnd is detecting a difference *between two* stimuli.) For example, how much salt must be added to a glass of pure water before the change in taste can be detected in at least half of the taste tests? For some examples of absolute thresholds for various senses, see Table 7.1.

Table 7.1	Examples of Absolute Thresholds
SENSE	**THRESHOLD**
Sight	A candle flame at 30 miles on a clear, dark night
Hearing	The tick of a watch 20 feet away in a quiet room
Smell	One drop of perfume diffused throughout a three-room apartment
Taste	1 teaspoon of sugar in 2 gallons of water
Touch	A bee's wing falling on the cheek from 1 centimeter above

Habituation and Sensory Adaptation It is interesting to know that the lower centers of the brain sort through sensory stimulation and "ignore" or screen out conscious attention to stimuli that do not change. The brain is only interested in changes in information. That's why people don't really "hear" the noise of the air conditioner unless it suddenly cuts off or the noise made in some classrooms unless it gets very quiet. Although they actually are *hearing* it, they aren't paying attention to it. This is called **habituation**, and it is the way the brain deals with unchanging information from the environment. L I N K *to Chapter Two: The Biological Perspective, p. 47.*

Sometimes I can smell the odor of the garbage can in the kitchen when I first come home, but after a while the smell seems to go away—is this also habituation?

Another process by which constant, unchanging information from the sensory receptors is "ignored" is a different process from habituation. The difference is that in habituation the sensory receptors are still responding to stimulation, but the lower centers of the brain are not sending the signals from those receptors to the cortex. In **sensory adaptation**, the receptor cells *themselves* become less responsive to an unchanging stimulus—the

absolute threshold the lowest level of stimulation that a person can consciously perceive 50 percent of the time the stimulation is present by 50 percent of the people tested.

habituation tendency of the brain to stop attending to constant, unchanging information.

sensory adaptation tendency of sensory receptor cells to become less responsive to a stimulus that is unchanging.

◀ Sometimes I can smell the odor of the garbage can in the kitchen when I first come home, but after a while the smell seems to go away— is this also habituation?

SENSATION AND PERCEPTION 79

CHAPTER 3 • Module 7

COVER THE MODULE (continued)

- *Absolute thresholds* are the smallest amount of energy needed for conscious detection of a stimulus at least half the time it is present.

- **Habituation and Sensory Adaptation**
  - *Habituation* occurs when the brain ignores a constant stimulus.

  L I N K to Chapter Two: The Biological Perspective, p. 47

DISCUSS THE STUDENT VOICE QUESTION

Help students understand the difference between habituation (when the brain stops attending to constant information) and sensory adaptation (when sensory receptor cells become less responsive to an unchanging stimulus).

- *Sensory adaptation* occurs when the sensory receptors stop responding to a constant stimulus.

EXTEND THE DISCUSSION

Explain to students that our senses automatically adjust to the level of stimulation they are receiving, so they can be as sensitive as possible without getting overloaded. As a result, our senses become less sensitive when the overall level of stimulation is high but more sensitive when the overall level of stimulation is low. This explains, for example, why the tick of a watch is more annoying in a quiet room than on a busy street.

Class Demonstration

EXPLORING JUST NOTABLE DIFFERENCE

Purpose: Students complete a demonstration on the difference threshold.

Time: 20 minutes

Description: Provide teams of students with two paper cups and a bag of marbles, or something similar that can be incrementally weighted and measured. Tell the class how many marbles should be used in each cup (e.g., 10). Students should take turns being the research participant. They close their eyes, and the cups with 10 marbles each are placed in their hands. Then teammates take the cups and add a marble to one cup to see whether the research participant can feel any difference. Marbles are added one at a time until the participant feels certain that one cup is now heavier. Each student takes a turn and comes up with an average jnd. Groups can compare their findings, and the teacher can record data for the class on the board.

Module 7 Sensation 79

CHAPTER 3 • Module 7

COVER THE MODULE

7.3 What forms of energy can humans sense?

- Sensory receptor cells are stimulated by different kinds of energy, such as visible light, vibrations, pressure, temperature, or chemical substances. Other forms of energy, such as x-rays, radio waves, gravitational energy, and nuclear energy, cannot be directly sensed by humans because of the lack of receptor neurons sensitive to those energy forms.

L4 DIFFERENTIATED INSTRUCTION

Advanced Learners These students need modified instruction to achieve their highest potential. They tend to understand complex concepts quickly, learn more rapidly and in greater depth, and have interests that are different from their peers. Modify pacing and offer enrichment to allow for exploring topics in depth, manipulating ideas in novel ways, and making connections to other disciplines.

---

receptors are no longer sending signals to the brain. Without sensory adaptation, clothes would probably drive people crazy, because they would be constantly aware of every piece of clothing or jewelry they had on. They would feel the seat of the chair they are sitting on constantly, instead of only when they moved. And bad odors like the garbage can smell would never go away.

Explore How the Senses Work

7.3 What forms of energy can humans sense?

Sensation occurs when special receptor sites on neurons in the sense organs are activated, allowing various forms of outside stimuli to become neural signals in the brain. The *sensory receptors* are specialized forms of neurons, the cells that make up the nervous system. Instead of receiving neurotransmitters from other cells, these receptor cells are stimulated by different kinds of energy—for example, the receptor neurons in the eyes are triggered by electromagnetic energy in the form of visible light, whereas vibrations trigger the receptors in the ears. Touch receptors are triggered by pressure or temperature, and the receptors in taste and smell are activated by chemical substances. (See Figure 7.1.)

FIGURE 7.1 Some Forms of Energy We Can Sense

80 CHAPTER 3

Class Demonstration

SENSORY ADAPTATION

Involve the class in this simple exercise for demonstrating sensory adaptation with touch. Bring to class a number of samples of very coarse sandpaper and distribute them to students. After rubbing their index fingers gently over the paper a few times, students should rate its coarseness on a scale from 1 (very soft) to 7 (very coarse). After a minute or two, have them rub the same finger over the paper and again rate its coarseness. Ask students to explain their findings. *(Their senses should have adapted to the coarseness, and thus the ratings for the second time should be lower.)*

80 Chapter 3 Sensation and Perception

There are many other forms of energy—such as X-rays, radio waves, gravitational energy, and nuclear energy—that humans can't sense directly because we don't have receptor neurons sensitive to these types of energy. For example, although we can see and hear the effects of low-frequency electromagnetic waves when we turn on the TV, the radio, or the microwave oven, we can't sense the waves themselves.

7.4 How does the sense of vision work?

The Nature of Light

I've heard that light is waves, but I've also heard that light is made of particles—which is it?

Light is a complicated phenomenon: It is electromagnetic energy with the properties of both waves and particles. Albert Einstein first proposed that light is actually tiny "packets" of waves. These "wave packets" are called photons and have specific wavelengths associated with them (Lehnert, 2007; van der Merwe & Garuccio, 1994).

◀ I've heard that light is waves, but I've also heard that light is made of particles—which is it?

There are three aspects to the perception of light: *brightness*, *color*, and *saturation*. *Brightness* is determined by the amplitude of the wave—how high or how low the wave actually is. The higher the wave, the brighter the light appears to be. Low waves are dimmer. *Color*, or hue, is determined by the length of the wave. Long wavelengths are found at the red end of the *visible spectrum* (the portion of the whole spectrum of light that is visible to the human eye; see Figure 7.2), whereas shorter wavelengths are found at the blue end.

Saturation refers to the purity of the color people perceive: A highly saturated red, for example, would contain only red wavelengths, whereas a less-saturated red might contain a mixture of wavelengths. For example, when a child is using only the red paint from a set of poster paints, the paint on the paper will look like a pure red, but if the child mixes in some white paint, the paint will look pink. The hue is still red but it will be less of a saturated red because of the presence of white wavelengths. Mixing in black or gray would also lessen the saturation.

FIGURE 7.2 The Visible Spectrum The wavelengths that people can see are only a small part of the whole electromagnetic spectrum.

The Structure of the Eye The best way to talk about how the eye processes light is to talk about what happens to an image being viewed, as the photons of light from that image travel through the eye. Refer to Figure 7.3 on page 82 to follow the path of the image.

The surface of the eye is covered in a clear membrane called the *cornea*. The cornea not only protects the eye but also focuses most of the light coming into the eye (vision-improving techniques such as LASIK surgery actually use this fact by making small incisions in the cornea to change the focus in the eye).

The next visual layer is a clear, watery fluid called the *aqueous humor*. This fluid is continually replenished and supplies nourishment to the eye. The light from the visual image then enters the interior of the eye through a hole, called

SENSATION AND PERCEPTION 81

CHAPTER 3 • Module 7

COVER THE MODULE

7.4 How does the sense of vision work?

- **The Nature of Light**

DISCUSS THE STUDENT VOICE QUESTION

Emphasize that light is energy with the properties of both waves and particles. It may be helpful for students to think of light as packets of waves.

- Brightness corresponds to the amplitude of light waves, while color corresponds to the length of the light waves.
- Saturation is the psychological interpretation of wavelengths that are all the same (highly saturated) or varying (less saturated).

- **The Structure of the Eye**

  - Light enters the eye and is focused through the cornea, passes through the aqueous humor, and then passes through the hole in the iris muscle called the pupil.
  - The iris can change the size of the pupil to let more or less light into the eye.

L3 DIFFERENTIATED INSTRUCTION

Auditory/Verbal Learners When these students learn something new, they should state the information in their own words out loud or to a study partner.

Explore

UNDERSTANDING SELECTIVE ATTENTION

Send students to the Chapter 3 simulation titled "Selective Attention" at www.mypsychlab.com. Have them complete the simulation and then report back as to how they fared in the demonstration. Conduct a brief class discussion of what students learned. What would happen if humans could not "select out" certain stimuli in their environment? What is the value of being able to select certain stimuli?

Module 7 Sensation 81

CHAPTER 3 • Module 7

COVER THE MODULE (continued)

- The lens can change shape from thick to thin in the process called *visual accommodation*, which allows the eye to focus on objects that are near or far away.
- The retina is a light-sensitive area at the back of the eye containing special neuron cells: ganglion cells, bipolar cells, and *rods* and *cones*. The latter turn light into electrochemical messages for the brain.
- The *blind spot* is the "hole" in the retina where all the axons of the ganglion cells leave the retina to become the optic nerve. This area is insensitive to light.

MULTIMEDIA CONTENT AVAILABLE AT
www.mypsychlab.com

⊙→ Simulate the structures of the eye on mypsychlab.com

TEACHING TIP

Use group activities. Collaborative work encourages students to be supportive of each other, creating positive interdependence. Explain the task clearly. Teach collaborative skills, such as problem solving, time management, and accepting constructive criticism.

FIGURE 7.3 Structure of the Eye
Light enters the eye through the cornea and pupil. The iris controls the size of the pupil. From the pupil, light passes through the lens to the retina, where it is transformed into nerve impulses. The nerve impulses travel to the brain along the optic nerve.

3. **Pupil** Iris opening that changes size depending on the amount of light in the environment
4. **Lens** Changes shape to bring objects into focus
2. **Iris** Its muscles control the size of the pupil
5. **Retina** Contains photoreceptor cells
6. **Fovea** Central area of retina; greatest density of photoreceptors
1. **Cornea** Bends light waves so the image can be focused on the retina
7. **Optic nerve** Sends visual information to the brain
8. **Blind spot (optic disc)** Where the optic nerve leaves the eye. There are no photoreceptor cells here
Blood vessels

the *pupil*, in a round muscle called the *iris* (the colored part of the eye). The iris can change the size of the pupil, letting more or less light into the eye. That also helps focus the image; people try to do the same thing by squinting.

Behind the iris, suspended by muscles, is another clear structure called the *lens*. The flexible lens finishes the focusing process begun by the cornea and can change its shape from thick to thin in a process called **visual accommodation**, which allows the eye to focus on objects that are close or far away.

Once through the lens, light passes through a large, open space filled with a clear, jelly-like fluid called the *vitreous humor*. This fluid, like the aqueous humor, also nourishes the eye and gives it shape.

⊙→ Simulate the structures of the eye on **mypsychlab.com**

⊙→ Simulate on **mypsychlab.com**

The final stop for light within the eye is the *retina*, a light-sensitive area at the back of the eye containing three layers of specialized neuron cells: ganglion cells, bipolar cells, and the special neurons sensitive to light waves (*photoreceptors* called **rods** and **cones**). (See Figure 7.4a and b.) The rods and the cones are the business end of the retina—the parts that actually receive the photons of light and turn them into electrochemical messages for the brain. These messages are sent through the bipolar cells (called bipolar or "two-ended" because they connect the rods and cones to the ganglion cells in the optic nerve) to the ganglion neuron axons. The axons bundle that energy into the optic nerve, which takes the message to the brain. (See Figure 7.5 on page 84.) This transformation of one form of energy to another form is called **transduction**.

The eyes don't adapt to constant stimuli under normal circumstances because of their frequent quick movements. But if people stare with one eye at one spot long enough, as an image moves down the retina tissue, the image will briefly disappear. This is due to a "hole" in the retina—the place where all the axons of those ganglion cells leave the retina to become the optic nerve—which has no rod and cone neurons to sense images. This area is referred to as the **blind spot**. You can demonstrate the blind spot for yourself by following the directions in Figure 7.4c.

visual accommodation the change in the thickness of the lens as the eye focuses on objects that are far away or close.

rods visual sensory receptors found at the back of the retina, responsible for noncolor sensitivity to low levels of light.

cones visual sensory receptors found at the back of the retina, responsible for color vision and sharpness of vision.

transduction the transformation of energy from one form to another.

blind spot the area in the retina where the axons of the three layers of retinal cells exit the eye to form the optic nerve, insensitive to light.

82 CHAPTER 3

Explore

MAPPING THE BLIND SPOT

There are no visual receptors where the optic nerve leaves the eye and enters the brain. This area is called the optic disc or blind spot. We do not notice this blind area because most of us have two working eyes, and when an object falls into this area in one eye, the other eye can visually process the information. A good website on mapping the blind spot can be found at: http://serendip.brynmawr.edu/bb/blindspot/

Ask students to visit the site and prepare a brief report on what they find. The report can be in the form of a written document, a poster, or an audiovisual presentation.

82 Chapter 3 Sensation and Perception

FIGURE 7.4 The Parts of the Retina

(a) Light passes through ganglion and bipolar cells until it reaches and stimulates the rods and cones. Nerve impulses from the rods and cones travel along a nerve pathway to the brain. (b) On the right of the figure is a photomicrograph of the long, thin rods and the shorter, thicker cones; the rods outnumber the cones by a ratio of about 20 to 1. (c) The blind spot demonstration. Hold the book in front of you. Close your right eye and stare at the picture of the dog with your left eye. Slowly bring the book closer to your face. The picture of the cat will disappear at some point because the light from the picture of the cat is falling on your blind spot.

How the Eye Works Rods and cones are each responsible for different aspects of vision. The rods (about 120 million of them in each eye) are found all over the retina except in the very center, which contains only cones. Rods are sensitive to changes in brightness, but not to changes in wavelength, so they see only in black and white and shades of gray. In addition, their visual acuity, or sharpness, is low. That's why things seen in low levels of light, such as during twilight or in a dimly lit room, are fuzzy and grayish. Because rods are located predominantly in the periphery of the retina, they are responsible for peripheral vision.

Because rods work well in low levels of light, they are also the cells that allow the eyes to adapt to low light. **Dark adaptation** occurs as the eye recovers its ability to see when going from a brightly lit state to a dark state. (The light-sensitive pigments that allow us to see are able to regenerate or "recharge" in the dark.) The brighter the original light was, the longer it takes the rods to adapt to the new lower levels of light (Bartlett, 1965). This is why the bright headlights of an oncoming car can leave a person less able to see for a while after the oncoming car has passed. Fortunately, this is usually a temporary condition because the bright light was on so briefly and the rods readapt to the dark night relatively quickly. Full dark adaptation, which occurs when going from more constant light to darkness (for example, when turning out one's bedroom lights), takes about 30 minutes. As people get older, this process takes longer, causing many older persons to be less able to see at night and in darkened rooms (Klaver et al., 1998). This age-related change can cause *night blindness*, in which a person has difficulty seeing well enough to drive at night or get around in a darkened room or house. Some research indicates that taking supplements such as vitamin A can reverse or relieve this symptom in some cases (Jacobson et al., 1995).

dark adaptation the recovery of the eye's sensitivity to visual stimuli in darkness after exposure to bright lights.

SENSATION AND PERCEPTION 83

CHAPTER 3 • Module 7

COVER THE MODULE *(continued)*

- **How the Eye Works**
  - Rods detect changes in brightness but do not see color and function best in low levels of light. They do not respond to different colors and are found everywhere in the retina except the center.
  - *Dark adaptation* occurs as the eye recovers its ability to see when going from bright light to the dark.

UNDERSTANDING VISUALS

If students want assistance in understanding Figure 7.4, refer them to the Chapter 3 Explore Multimedia feature on the www.mypsychlab.com website titled "Light and the Optic Nerve."

EXTEND THE LESSON

Have each student blindfold one eye at the beginning of class. Conduct class in your usual fashion, and after about 30 minutes, darken the room. Ask the students to remove their blindfolds. The differential sensitivity of the two eyes is immediately apparent.

Class Demonstration (Kinesthetic)

UNDERSTANDING THE RETINA

Ask students to bring a flashlight from home. Students should stand and face a light-colored wall (not the chalkboard or any dark surface). Darken the room and tell students the retina is essentially a "web" of blood vessels and neurons. We actually look through blood vessels and neurons all the time. We cannot see the neurons, but we can see the blood vessels if we look hard enough. Tell students to look at the wall and tilt their heads downward slightly and look up with their eyes at about a 45-degree angle onto the wall. Students should hold the flashlight (turned on) next to one of their eyes and flicker the light. They should be able to see a web of blood vessels out of the corner of their eye, and if they focus closely enough on this web, they will see that the blood vessels all converge at one point, where the optic nerve begins—the blindspot.

Module 7 Sensation 83

CHAPTER 3 • Module 7

COVER THE MODULE *(continued)*
- Cones are sensitive to colors and work best in bright light. They are responsible for the sharpness of visual information and are found in the eye's center.
- *Light adaptation* is the recovery of the eye's sensitivity to visual stimuli in light after exposure to darkness.
- **Perception of Color**

DISCUSS THE STUDENT VOICE QUESTION

Explain to students that there is an ongoing discussion about the role the cones play in the sensation of color.
- The *trichromatic theory* of color perception assumes three types of cones: red, green, and blue. All colors would be perceived as combinations of these three.

L3 DIFFERENTIATED INSTRUCTION

Visual/Verbal Learners Have students write out key information in whole sentences or phrases in their own words. When they look at diagrams, they should write out a description.

FIGURE 7.5 Crossing of the Optic Nerve

Light rays enter the eyes to fall on the retina. Light falling on the left side of each eye's retina (from the right visual field, shown in yellow) will stimulate a neural message that will travel along the optic nerve to the left visual cortex in the occipital lobe of the left hemisphere. Notice that the message from the left eye goes directly to the left occipital lobe, while the message from the right eye crosses over to the left hemisphere (the optic chiasm is the point of crossover). The optic nerve tissue from both eyes joins together to form the left optic tract before going on to the left occipital lobe. For the left visual field (shown in blue), the messages from both right sides of the retinas will travel along the right optic track to the right visual cortex in the same manner.

▲ *In trichromatic theory, the three types of cones combine to form different colors much as these three colored lights combine.*

> You said the cones are used in color vision. There are so many colors in the world—are there cones that detect each color? Or do all cones detect all colors? ▶

light adaptation the recovery of the eye's sensitivity to visual stimuli in light after exposure to darkness.

trichromatic theory theory of color vision that proposes three types of cones: red, blue, and green.

When going from a darkened room to one that is brightly lit, the opposite process occurs. The cones have to adapt to the increased level of light, and they accomplish this **light adaptation** much more quickly than the rods adapt to darkness—it takes a few seconds at most (Hood, 1998). There are 6 million cones in each eye; of these, 50,000 have a private line to the optic nerve (one bipolar cell for each cone). This means that the cones, found toward the center of the retina, and even more concentrated in an area called the *fovea*, are the receptors for visual acuity. It also means that the cones need a lot more light to function than the rods do, so cones work best in bright light, which is also when people see things most clearly. Cones are also sensitive to different wavelengths of light, so they are responsible for color vision.

Perception of Color

You said the cones are used in color vision. There are so many colors in the world—are there cones that detect each color? Or do all cones detect all colors?

Although experts in the visual system have been studying color and its nature for many years, at this point in time, there is an ongoing theoretical discussion about the role the cones play in the sensation of color.

Two theories about how people see colors were originally proposed in the 1800s. The first is called the **trichromatic** ("three colors") **theory**. First proposed by Thomas Young in 1802 and later modified by Hermann von Helmholtz in 1852, this theory proposed three types of cones: red cones, blue cones, and green cones, one for each of the three primary colors of light.

Most people probably think that the primary colors are red, yellow, and blue, but these are the primary colors when talking about *painting*—not when talking about *light*. Paints *reflect* light, and the way reflected light mixes is different from the way direct light mixes. For example, if an artist were to blend red, yellow, and blue paints together, the resulting paint mixture would be

84 CHAPTER 3

Class Demonstration

RODS AND CONES

Cones are sensitive to color but not as sensitive to light. By contrast, rods are sensitive to light but do not register color information. Thus, in dim light, when the rods are doing most of the work, it is difficult to see colors. To demonstrate this phenomenon, bring in several pieces of construction paper of different colors. Ten minutes before you want to demonstrate the concept, dim the lights until you can just barely see. Then hold up the pieces of paper and ask the students to write down what color they think the paper is. After you turn on the lights, review the correct colors with your students. How accurate were they?

black. But if the artist were to blend red, green, and blue lights together by focusing lights of those colors on one common spot, the result would be white, not black.

In the trichromatic theory, different shades of color correspond to different amounts of light received by each of these three types of cones. These cones then fire their message to the brain's vision centers. It is the combination of cones and the rate at which they are firing that determine the color that will be seen. For example, if the red and green cones are firing in response to a stimulus at fast enough rates, the color the person sees is yellow. If the red and blue cones are firing fast enough, the result is magenta. If the blue and green cones are firing fast enough, a kind of cyan color (blue-green) appears. Look again at Figure 7.2, the visible spectrum. Adding the long red wavelengths to the much shorter green ones will produce something in the middle—yellow.

The trichromatic theory would, at first glance, seem to be more than adequate to explain how people perceive color. But there's an interesting phenomenon that this theory cannot explain. If a person stares at a picture of the American flag for a little while—say, a minute—and then looks away to a blank white wall or sheet of paper, that person will see an afterimage of the flag. **Afterimages** occur when a visual sensation persists for a brief time even after the original stimulus is removed. The person would also notice rather quickly that the colors of the "flag" in the afterimage are all wrong—green for red, black for white, and yellow for blue. If you follow the directions for Figure 7.6, in which the "flag" is yellow, green, and black, you should see a flag with the usual red, white, and blue.

Hey, now the afterimage of the flag has normal colors! Why does this happen?

The phenomenon of the color afterimage is explained by the second theory of color perception, called the **opponent-process theory** (De Valois & Jacobs, 1968; Hurvich, 1969). In this theory, there are four primary colors: red, green, blue, and yellow. The cones are arranged in pairs, red with green and blue with yellow. If one member of a pair is stimulated, the other member cannot be working—so there are no reddish-greens or bluish-yellows.

How does this cause the color afterimage? If a person tires out one of the members of the pairs (by looking at a red image for about a minute, for example), it weakens that member's ability to inhibit the other cell. When the person then looks away from the red image, there will be a green afterimage as the other member of the pair fires away.

So, which theory of color vision is the "right" one? Actually, both theories may be correct. We have good reason to believe that both trichromatic theory and opponent-process theory play a part in color vision.

What happens when there are problems with the cones in the eye's retina? This condition can cause color blindness. People who are color-blind cannot differentiate between certain colors: For example, people whose red or green cones are not working will have trouble telling the difference between red and green. Because color blindness is an inherited genetic condition linked to the chromosomes that determine an individual's sex, males are more likely to be color-blind than females are. Read on **mypsychlab.com**

FIGURE 7.6 Color Afterimage
Stare at the white dot in the center of this oddly colored flag for about 30 seconds. Now look at a white piece of paper or a white wall. Notice that the colors are now the normal, expected colors of the American flag. They are also the primary colors that are opposites of the colors in the picture and provide evidence for the opponent-process theory of color vision.

Hey, now the afterimage of the flag has normal colors! Why does this happen?

Read and learn more about color blindness on **mypsychlab.com**

afterimages images that occur when a visual sensation persists for a brief time even after the original stimulus is removed.

opponent-process theory theory of color vision that proposes four primary colors with cones arranged in pairs: red and green, blue and yellow.

SENSATION AND PERCEPTION 85

CHAPTER 3 • Module 7

COVER THE MODULE *(continued)*

- *Afterimages* occur when a visual sensation persists for a brief period, even after the original stimulus is removed.
- The *opponent-process theory* of color perception assumes four primary colors: red, green, blue, and yellow. Cones are arranged in pairs, and when one member of a pair is activated, the other is not.
- Both theories may be correct.
- Colorblindness is either a total lack of color perception or color perception that is limited to yellows and blues or to reds and greens only.

CHECK FOR UNDERSTANDING

Ask: What is the difference between the trichromatic theory and the opponent-process theory? *(The trichromatic theory proposes three types of cones: red, blue, and green. The opponent-process theory proposes four primary colors with cones arranged in pairs: red and green, and blue and yellow.)*

MULTIMEDIA CONTENT AVAILABLE AT
www.mypsychlab.com

Read and learn more about color blindness on **mypsychlab.com**

Class Demonstration

COLOR BLINDNESS IN DAILY LIFE

<u>Purpose</u>: Students discuss how color blindness influences daily living.

<u>Time</u>: 15 minutes

<u>Description</u>: Ask for volunteers to be the "experts" on color blindness. The volunteer could be someone who suffers from color blindness or knows someone in their family who does. Color blindness is relatively common, especially in males, so there may be a few people in a class who can volunteer. Students can surround the "experts" and ask questions. Experts should be encouraged to share information on how people with color blindness adapt to daily living and under what circumstances color blindness poses problems. For example, people who have trouble with red and green may have to memorize the position of the lights at an intersection, since they cannot rely on information about color.

Module 7 Sensation 85

CHAPTER 3 • Module 7

COVER THE MODULE

7.5 How does the sense of hearing work?

- **Perception of Sound: Good Vibrations**
  - Sound has three aspects: pitch (frequency), loudness, and timbre (purity).
  - People are limited in the range of frequencies they can hear. Frequency is measured in cycles (waves) per second, or *hertz (Hz)*.

UNDERSTANDING VISUALS

Direct students' attention to Figure 7.7. Ask volunteers to read aloud the chart showing decibels of various stimuli. Then ask students if they are surprised by this information. What, if any, concerns do they have about the stimuli above the thresholds for potential ear damage and physical pain?

TEACHING TIP

After students have covered a topic in class, ask them to write down one or two pieces of information or ideas that they believe they understand well. Then have them write down one or two ideas that they did not understand well. Rotate around the room, asking students to list their "clicks" and "clunks." Use the information to guide your follow-up lessons, skipping information that students already understand and spending more time on ideas they do not understand.

---

hertz (Hz) cycles or waves per second, a measurement of frequency.

7.5 How does the sense of hearing work?

Perception of Sound: Good Vibrations The properties of sound are similar to those of light, as both senses rely on waves. But the similarity ends there, as the physical properties of sound are different from those of light. Sound waves do not come in little packets the way light comes in photons. Sound waves are simply the vibrations of the molecules of air that surround us. Sound waves do have the same properties of light waves, though—wavelength, amplitude, and purity. Wavelengths are interpreted by the brain as the frequency or *pitch* (high, medium, or low). Amplitude is interpreted as *volume*, how soft or loud a sound is. (See Figure 7.7.) Finally, what would correspond to saturation or purity in light is called *timbre* in sound, or the level of richness in the tone of the sound. And just as people rarely see pure colors in the world around us, they also seldom hear pure sounds. The everyday noises that surround people do not allow them to hear many pure tones.

Just as a person's vision is limited by the visible spectrum of light, a person is also limited in the range of frequencies he or she can hear. Frequency is measured in cycles (waves) per second, or **hertz (Hz)**. Human limits are between 20 and 20,000 Hz, with the most sensitivity from about 2,000 to 4,000 Hz, the range most important for conversational speech (Goldstein, 2006).

FIGURE 7.7 Sound Waves and Decibels
(a) A typical sound wave. The higher the wave, the louder the sound; the lower the wave, the softer the sound. If the waves are close together in time (high frequency), the pitch will be perceived as high. Waves that are farther apart (low frequency) will be perceived as having a lower pitch.
(b) Decibels of various stimuli. A *decibel* is a unit of measure for loudness. Psychologists study the effects that noise has on stress, learning, performance, aggression, and psychological and physical well-being. Research on the hazards of loud noises led the National Basketball Association to put an 85-decibel limit on the sound system played at basketball arenas (Heisler, 1995).

Pain threshold
- 135: Headphones turned to highest volume
- 125: Jackhammer, 3 feet away
- 120: Sound causes pain
- 110: Live rock music

Potential ear damage
- 100: Chain saw or subway train going by, 20 feet away
- 85–90: Prolonged exposure to any sound above this level causes hearing loss
- 70: Vacuum cleaner
- 60: Normal conversation between persons 3 feet apart
- 40: Quiet office
- 30: Library
- 15: Normal breathing

86 CHAPTER 3

Explore

LEARNING ABOUT SOUND WAVES

Send students to the **www.mypsychlab.com** website for Chapter 3 to review the Explore feature titled "Frequency and Amplitude of Sound Waves." Then have them use library or Internet resources to research the upper and lower limits of frequencies that humans and various animals can hear. Finally, ask students to create a chart or table, using software if possible, showing the results of their research.

---

86 Chapter 3 Sensation and Perception

FIGURE 7.8 The Structure of the Ear

(a) This figure shows the entire ear, beginning with the outer ear. The vestibular organ includes the semicircular canals and the otolith organs (inside the round structures just above the cochlea). (b) The middle ear. Sound waves entering through the ear canal cause the eardrum to vibrate, which causes each of the three bones of the middle ear to vibrate, amplifying the sound. The stirrup rests on the oval window, which transmits its vibration to the fluid in the inner ear. (c) The inner ear. Large spaces are filled with fluid that vibrates as the oval window vibrates. The basilar membrane contains the organ of Corti, which sends signals to the auditory cortex of the brain by way of the auditory nerve. (d) A close-up view of the basilar membrane with the hair cells of the organ of Corti. Notice the axons leaving the hair cells to form the auditory nerve.

(In comparison, dogs can hear between 50 and 60,000 Hz, whereas dolphins can hear up to 200,000 Hz.) To hear the higher and lower frequencies of music on an mp3 player, for example, a person would need to increase the amplitude or volume—which explains why some people like to "crank it up."

The Structure of the Ear: Follow the Vibes The ear is a series of structures, each of which plays a part in the sense of hearing, as shown in Figure 7.8.

The **pinna** is the visible, external part of the ear that serves as a kind of concentrator, funneling the sound waves from the outside into the structure of the ear. The pinna is also the entrance to the **auditory canal** (or ear canal), the short tunnel that runs down to the *tympanic membrane*, or eardrum. When sound waves hit the eardrum, they cause three tiny bones in the middle ear to vibrate.

The three tiny bones in the middle ear are known as the hammer, anvil, and stirrup (malleus, incus, and stapes). The names come from the shape of each of the bones. The vibration of these three bones amplifies the vibrations from the eardrum. The stirrup, the last bone in the chain, causes a membrane (the oval window) covering the opening of the inner ear to vibrate.

Explore on **mypsychlab.com**

The oval window's vibrations set off another chain reaction within the inner ear. The inner ear is a snail-shaped structure called the **cochlea**, which is filled with fluid. When the oval window vibrates, it causes the fluid in the cochlea to vibrate. This fluid surrounds a membrane running through the middle of the cochlea called the *basilar membrane*. The basilar membrane is the resting place of the *organ of Corti*, which contains the receptor neurons for the sense of hearing. When the basilar membrane vibrates, it sends bursts of energy that vibrate through the organ of Corti. On the organ of Corti are special cells called *hair cells*, which are the receptors for sound. When the bursts of energy from the basilar membrane are strong enough to move these hairs, the hair cells send electrochemical messages through the **auditory nerve** and into the brain, where the temporal lobe's auditory cortex will interpret the sounds.

Explore the structures of the ear on **mypsychlab.com**

pinna the visible part of the ear.

auditory canal short tunnel that runs from the pinna to the eardrum.

cochlea snail-shaped structure of the inner ear that is filled with fluid.

auditory nerve bundle of axons from the hair cells in the inner ear.

SENSATION AND PERCEPTION 87

CHAPTER 3 • Module 7

COVER THE MODULE *(continued)*

- **The Structure of the Ear: Follow the Vibes**
  - Sound enters the ear through the visible outer structure, or *pinna*; travels to the eardrum; and then travels to the small bones of the middle ear.
  - The *auditory canal* is a short tunnel running down to the eardrum.
  - A bone called the stirrup rests on the oval window, causing the *cochlea* and basilar membrane to vibrate with sound.
  - The organ of Corti on the basilar membrane contains the auditory receptors, which send signals through the *auditory nerve* to the brain, as they vibrate, about sound qualities.
  - The louder the sound in the outside world, the stronger are the vibrations that stimulate the cells, which the brain interprets as loudness.

MULTIMEDIA CONTENT AVAILABLE AT
www.mypsychlab.com

Explore the structures of the ear on **mypsychlab.com**

L3 DIFFERENTIATED INSTRUCTION

The level of concepts, enduring understandings, and skills students can acquire will often depend on the complexity of thinking skills required. All students must master the same standards, but depth of learning should be adjusted to meet the needs of diverse learners.

Explore

TEACHING CLASSMATES

Ask for class volunteers to go to the **www.mypsychlab.com** website for Chapter 3 and watch the video titled "Listening to Blues Test," which details a new method for determining which drugs to use in treating depressed patients. After viewing the video, the volunteers should meet with small groups of classmates in order to report on what they saw. This gives the volunteers a chance to act as teachers to their colleagues. Consider making this an extra-credit project for students.

Module 7 Sensation **87**

CHAPTER 3 • Module 7

COVER THE MODULE (continued)

- **Theories of Pitch**
  - *Place theory* states that the location of the hair cells on the organ of Corti correspond to different pitches of sound. This explains moderate to high pitches.
  - *Frequency theory* states that the speed with which the basilar membrane vibrates corresponds to different pitches of sound. This explains low pitches.
  - *Volley principle* states that neurons take turns firing for sounds above 400 Hz and below 4000 Hz.

FAST FACT

Ask: **What is "perfect pitch"?** *(Perfect pitch is the ability to identify the pitch of a musical tone without the need to hear another tone for reference. It occurs in about 0.1% of the population, and those who have it tend to have been raised in a musical family.)*

DISCUSS THE STUDENT VOICE QUESTION

After you cover the theory of pitch, use the student voice question to check students' understanding of the topic.

- **Types of Hearing Impairments**
  - Conductive impairment means that sound vibrations cannot be passed from the eardrum to the cochlea.
  - Sensorineural impairment involves problems either in the inner ear or in the auditory pathways and cortical areas of the brain.
  - Tinnitus is a continuous ringing in one's ears.

MULTIMEDIA CONTENT AVAILABLE AT
www.mypsychlab.com

Listen to the Psychology in the News podcast on cochlear implants on **mypsychlab.com**

---

88 Chapter 3 Sensation and Perception

> I think I have it straight—but all of that just explains how soft and loud sounds get to the brain from the outside. How do we hear different kinds of sounds, like high pitches and low pitches?

Listen to the Psychology in the News podcast on cochlear implants on **mypsychlab.com**

pitch psychological experience of sound that corresponds to the frequency of the sound waves; higher frequencies are perceived as higher pitches.

place theory theory of pitch that states that different pitches are experienced by the stimulation of hair cells in different locations on the organ of Corti.

frequency theory theory of pitch that states that pitch is related to the speed of vibrations in the basilar membrane.

volley principle theory of pitch that states that frequencies from about 400 Hz to 4000 Hz cause the hair cells (auditory neurons) to fire in a volley pattern, or take turns in firing.

gustation the sensation of a taste.

88 CHAPTER 3

Thus, the sound waves go in through the pinna and vibrate the eardrum, which then vibrates the hammer, anvil, and stirrup, which in turn vibrate the oval window. This causes the fluid in the cochlea to vibrate, which vibrates the basilar membrane, which then causes the organ of Corti to move up and bend its hair cells, which send signals about hearing to the brain. The louder the sound in the outside world, the stronger the vibrations that stimulate more of those hair cells, which the brain interprets as loudness.

I think I have it straight—but all of that just explains how soft and loud sounds get to the brain from the outside. How do we hear different kinds of sounds, like high pitches and low pitches?

Theories of Pitch Pitch refers to how high or low a sound is. For example, the bass tones in the music pounding through the wall of your apartment from the neighbors next door are low in pitch, whereas the scream of a 2-year-old child is a very high pitch. There are two theories about how the brain receives information about pitch: According to **place theory**, the pitch a person hears depends on where the hair cells that are stimulated are located on the organ of Corti. For example, if the person is hearing a high-pitched sound, all of the hair cells near the oval window will be stimulated, but if the sound is low-pitched, all of the hair cells that are stimulated will be located farther away on the organ of Corti. However, **frequency theory** states that pitch is related to how fast the basilar membrane vibrates. The faster this membrane vibrates, the higher the pitch; the slower it vibrates, the lower the pitch.

It turns out that both theories are correct, at least up to a certain point. The frequency theory works for low pitches, and place theory works for moderate to high pitches. Is there another explanation? Yes, and it is the **volley principle**, which accounts for pitches from about 400 Hz up to about 4000 Hz (Breedlove et al., 2007; Klein & Thorne, 2007). (Most human conversation falls within this range of pitches.) In this explanation, groups of auditory neurons take turns firing in a process called volleying. If a person hears a tone of about 3000 Hz, it means that three groups of neurons have taken turns sending the message to the brain—the first group for the first 1000 Hz, the second group for the next 1000 Hz, and so on.

Types of Hearing Impairments *Hearing impairment* is the term used to refer to difficulties in hearing. There are a few different types of hearing impairments. *Conductive impairment* means that sound vibrations cannot be passed from the eardrum to the cochlea. The cause might be a damaged eardrum or damage to the bones of the middle ear (usually from an infection). In *sensorineural impairment*, the problem lies either in the inner ear or in the auditory pathways and cortical areas of the brain. Normal aging causes loss of hair cells in the cochlea, and exposure to loud noises can damage hair cells. *Tinnitus* is a fancy word for a continuous ringing in one's ears that remains after a sound has ceased, and it can also be caused by infections or loud noises—including loud music in headphones, so you might want to turn down that music player! **Listen** on **mypsychlab.com**

7.6 How do the senses of taste and smell work, and how are they alike?

Gustation: How We Taste the World The sense of taste (**gustation**) and the sense of smell—both chemical senses—are very closely related. Have you ever noticed that when your nose is all stopped up, your sense of taste is

---

Explore

PREVENTING HEARING IMPAIRMENT

Explain to students that it is important to realize that hearing loss caused by loud noise can be prevented. There are steps they can take to reduce their risk of this type of hearing loss. Ask pairs or small groups of students to conduct library or Internet research into how they can reduce the risk of permanent hearing damage. Then have them use their findings to create posters or audiovisual presentations about the topic. Mount their posters in the classroom and have students make their presentations to their classmates.

affected, too? That's because the sense of taste is really a combination of taste and smell. Without the input from the nose, there are actually only five kinds of taste sensors in the mouth.

Taste buds are the common name for the taste neurons. There are about 10,000 taste buds on the tongue, and each bud has hundreds of taste neurons within it. Most taste buds are located on the tongue, but there are a few on the roof of the mouth, the cheeks, and under the tongue as well. How sensitive people are to various tastes depends on how many taste buds they have; some people have can have up to 25,000 taste buds! Those people are called "supertasters" and need far less seasoning in their food than those with fewer taste buds (Bartoshuk, 1993).

So taste buds are those little bumps I can see when I look closely at my tongue?

No, those "bumps" are called *papillae*, and the taste buds line the walls of these papillae. (See Figure 7.9.) Each taste bud has about 20 neuron cells for taste. These receptors receive molecules of various substances that fit into the neuron's receptor sites, like a key into a lock. When the molecules (dissolved in saliva) fit into the receptors, a signal is fired to the brain, which then interprets the taste sensation.

In 1916 a German psychologist named Hans Henning proposed that there are four primary tastes: sweet, sour, salty, and bitter. Most of us are familiar with these four tastes, but in 1909, a Japanese chemist named Kikunae Ikeda discovered a fifth: a pleasant "brothy" taste associated with foods like chicken soup, tuna, kelp, cheese, and soy products, among others. Ikeda named this taste *umami*. In 1996, Bernd Lindemann supported the idea that there is a fifth kind of taste receptor that detects *umami*.

The five taste sensations work together, along with the sense of smell and the texture, temperature, and "heat" of foods, to produce thousands of taste sensations. Although researchers used to believe that certain tastes were located on certain places on the tongue, it is now known that all of the taste sensations are processed all over the tongue (Bartoshuk, 1993).

◀ So taste buds are those little bumps I can see when I look closely at my tongue?

FIGURE 7.9 The Tongue and Taste Buds—A Crosscut View of the Tongue
(a) The right side of this drawing shows the nerves in the tongue's deep tissue. (b) The taste bud is located inside the papillae and is composed of small cells that send signals to the brain when stimulated by molecules of food. (c) Microphotograph of the surface of the tongue, showing two different sizes of papillae. The taste buds are located under the surface of the larger red papillae, whereas the smaller and more numerous papillae form a touch-sensitive rough surface that helps in chewing and moving food around the mouth.

SENSATION AND PERCEPTION

Class Demonstration

EXPLORING TASTE

Students may be surprised to learn that food must be dissolved in water in order to be tasted. That is, some kind of liquid must be available to bind solid food to the appropriate taste receptor (e.g., sweet, sour, bitter, or salty). Try this simple exercise that demonstrates the crucial role of saliva in taste. First, have students wipe their tongue dry (the drier, the better) with the back of their hand. Then, walk around the room with a bowl of sugar and have students take a small pinch and place it on the tip of their tongue. They should not be able to taste anything until their mouth gradually moistens—with renewed saliva, the sweet taste should come flooding back.

CHAPTER 3 • Module 7

COVER THE MODULE

7.6 How do the senses of taste and smell work, and how are they alike?

- **Gustation: How We Taste the World**
  - *Gustation* is the sense of taste. Taste buds in the tongue receive molecules of substances, which fit into receptor sites.
  - The five basic types of taste are sweet, sour, salty, bitter, and umami (brothy).
  - The five tastes work with the sense of smell and the texture, temperature, and heat of foods to produce thousands of taste sensations.
  - All of the taste sensations are processed all over the tongue.

DISCUSS

Discuss with students the fact that many smokers experience a diminished ability to taste certain flavors. Smoking affects receptors on the tongue and in the nasal passages, thereby affecting the ability to taste. Cigarettes contain chemicals that blunt the ability of the taste buds to register the senses. Because a significant amount of smoke is exhaled through the nose, these same chemicals affect the olfactory nerve endings, too.

L1 DIFFERENTIATED INSTRUCTION

Special Needs When appropriate, have students manage and chart their academic performance, homework and assignment completion, and behavior.

CHAPTER 3 • Module 7

COVER THE MODULE (continued)
- **The Sense of Scents: Olfaction**
  - *Olfaction* is the sense of smell. The olfactory receptors in the upper part of the sinus cavity receive molecules of substances and create neural signals, which then go to the olfactory bulbs under the frontal lobes.

FAST FACT
Smell remains the least studied and least understood of the senses. Although it is relatively primitive (compared to the sophisticated intricacies of vision), scientists still do not have a complete understanding of the rules governing how smell works.

DISCUSS THE STUDENT VOICE QUESTION
Remind students that sensory adaptation is the reason why people do not continue to smell odors after a time.

CHECK FOR UNDERSTANDING
Ask students to explain this statement: "The sense of taste is really a combination of taste and smell." (**Possible answer:** *The mouth contains only five kinds of taste sensors. However, the nose contains over 1,000 different types of olfactory neuron receptors. Input from the nose is necessary to the sense of taste.*)

---

olfaction (olfactory sense) the sensation of smell.

Wait a minute—you mean that when I can smell something like a skunk, ▶ there are little particles of skunk odor IN my nose?

The Sense of Scents: Olfaction The ability to smell odors is called **olfaction**, or the **olfactory sense**. Our noses collect odors, but the part of the olfactory system that actually turns odors into signals the brain can understand is located at the top of the nasal passages, known as the epithelium tissue. This area is only about an inch square in each cavity, yet it contains about 10 million olfactory neuron receptors. (See Figure 7.10.) There are only five different types of taste neuron receptors, but there are over 1,000 different types of olfactory neuron receptors.

These neuron receptors each have about a half dozen to a dozen little "hairs" that project into the cavity. These "hairs" are called *cilia*. Like taste buds, there are receptor sites on these hair cells that send signals to the brain when stimulated by the molecules of substances that are in the air moving past them.

Wait a minute—you mean that when I can smell something like a skunk, there are little particles of skunk odor IN my nose?

Yes. When a person is sniffing something, the sniffing serves to move molecules of whatever the person is trying to smell into the nose and into the nasal cavities. That's okay when it's the smell of baking bread, apple pie, flowers, and the like, but when it's skunk, rotten eggs, limburger cheese—well, try not to think about it too much.

Remember when sensory adaptation was covered earlier in the module? The text stated that certain sensory receptors become less sensitive to a constant stimulus as time goes by, so that eventually a person no longer perceives the stimulus. This adaptation is why people don't continue to smell the odor of the kitchen garbage can after being home for a while—thank goodness!

FIGURE 7.10 The Olfactory Receptors
(a) A cross section of the nose and mouth. This drawing shows the nerve fibers inside the nasal cavity that carry information about smell directly to the olfactory bulb just under the frontal lobe of the brain (shown in green). (b) A diagram of the cells in the nose that process smell. The olfactory bulb is on top. Notice the cilia, tiny hairlike cells that project into the nasal cavity. These are the receptors for the sense of smell.

90 CHAPTER 3

Class Demonstration

UNDERSTANDING FLAVOR
Students usually are not aware of the fact that the sense of taste determines only roughly half of what we consider to be flavor. Flavor is, in fact, a combination of taste and smell. Give each of your students a jellybean. Ask the students to pinch their nose closed when they first place the jelly bean in their mouth. After they have chewed the jellybean with their nose plugged, ask them to unplug their nose and notice the difference. They will then be able to perceive much more of the flavor of the jellybean and be much more likely to be able to identify the flavor.

7.7 What other sensory systems does the human body use?

So far, we have discussed vision, hearing, taste, and smell. That leaves touch. What we think of as the sense of touch is really several sensations, originating in several different places in—and on—the body. It's really more accurate to refer to these as the body senses, or **somesthetic senses**. The first part of that word, *soma*, means "body," and the second part, *esthetic*, means "feeling." There are three somesthetic sense systems: the **skin senses** (having to do with touch, pressure, temperature, and pain), the **kinesthetic sense** (having to do with the location of body parts in relation to the ground and to each other), and the **vestibular senses** (having to do with movement, balance, and body position).

Perception of Touch, Pressure, and Temperature Here's a good trivia question: What organ of the body is about 20 square feet in size? The answer is the skin. Skin is an organ that receives and transmits information from the outside world to the central nervous system. Information about light touch, deeper pressure, hot, cold, and even pain is collected by special neurons in the skin's layers.

How exactly does pain work? Why is it that sometimes I feel pain deep inside? Are there pain receptors there, too?

Yes, there are pain neuron receptor sites in the internal organs as well as receptors for pressure. How else would people have a stomachache or intestinal pain? Or get that feeling of pressure when they've eaten too much or their bladder is full?

There are actually different types of pain. There are receptors that detect pain (and pressure) in the organs, a type of pain called *visceral pain*. (The "viscera" are the internal organs of the body.) But pain sensations in the skin, muscles, tendons, and joints are carried on large nerve fibers and are called *somatic pain*. Somatic pain is the body's warning system that something is being, or is about to be, damaged and tends to be sharp and fast. Another type of somatic pain is carried on small nerve fibers and is slower and more of a general ache. This somatic pain acts as a kind of reminder system, keeping people from further injury by reminding them that the body has already been damaged. For example, if you hit your thumb with a hammer, the immediate pain sensation is of the first kind—sharp, fast, and bright. But later the bruised tissue simply aches, letting you know to take it easy on that thumb.

Pain: Gate-Control Theory The best current explanation for how the sensation of pain works is called *gate-control theory*, first proposed by Melzack and Wall (1965) and later refined and expanded (Melzack & Wall, 1996). In this theory, the pain signals must pass through a "gate" located in the spinal cord. The activity of the gate can be closed by nonpain signals coming into the spinal cord from the body and by signals coming from the brain. The gate is not a physical structure but instead represents the relative balance in neural activity of cells in the spinal cord that receive information from the body and then send information to the brain.

Pain stimulates the pain receptor neurons to release a chemical called *substance P* (for pain, naturally). Substance P released into the spinal cord activates other neurons that send their messages through spinal gates (opened

somesthetic senses the body senses consisting of the skin senses, the kinesthetic sense, and the vestibular senses.

skin senses the sensations of touch, pressure, temperature, and pain.

kinesthetic sense sense of the location of body parts in relation to the ground and each other.

vestibular senses the sensations of movement, balance, and body position.

How exactly does pain work? Why is it that sometimes I feel pain deep inside? ◀ Are there pain receptors there, too?

▲ Her sense of touch is allowing this blind girl to "read" a Braille book with her fingers. The fingertips are extremely sensitive to fine differences in texture, allowing her to distinguish between small dots representing the different letters of the alphabet.

SENSATION AND PERCEPTION 91

CHAPTER 3 • Module 7

COVER THE MODULE

7.7 What other sensory systems does the human body use?

- The sense of touch is really several sensations, called somesthetic senses.
  - The three *somesthetic sense* systems are the *skin senses*, the *kinesthetic sense*, and the *vestibular senses*.
- **Perception of Touch, Pressure, and Temperature**
  - Special neurons in the skin collect information about light touch, deeper pressure, hot, cold, and pain.
  - The different types of pain include visceral pain (in the body's internal organs) and somatic pain (in the skin, muscles, tendons, and joints).

DISCUSS THE STUDENT VOICE QUESTION

Use the question to check students' comprehension of the topic.

- **Pain: Gate Control Theory**
  - The gate-control theory of pain states that when receptors sensitive to pain are stimulated, a neurotransmitter called *substance P* is released into the spinal cord, activating other pain receptors by opening "gates" in the spinal column and sending the message to the brain.

Class Demonstration

THE BODY'S SENSITIVITY TO TOUCH

Various parts of the body differ greatly in their sensitivity to pressure. Distribute a single hairpin to student pairs. One student should pry the hairpin apart (so its prongs are roughly 1-inch apart) and press the hairpin against the back of the partner's forearm. The person being touched will report feeling only a single point of pressure. Next, the student should bend the prongs inward, so that they are only about 1/16 inch apart and place it on the partner's index fingertip. This time (despite the smaller difference between the prongs), the partner will have no trouble differentiating the two points, as the fingertip is much more sensitive than the forearm.

Module 7 Sensation 91

CHAPTER 3 • Module 7

COVER THE MODULE (continued)

- **The Kinesthetic Sense**
  - The kinesthetic sense allows the brain to know its position in space through the activity of special neuron receptors that are located in the skin, joints, muscles, and tendons.
- **The Vestibular Sense**
  - The vestibular sense also contributes to the body's sense of spatial orientation through the activity of the otolith organs (up and down movement) and the semicircular canals (movement through arcs).
  - Motion sickness is explained by the fact that information from the eyes conflicts with information from the vestibular sense, causing nausea.

EXTEND THE LESSON

Tell students that, for millions of people, pain is a part of daily life. However, a psychological approach called cognitive-behavioral therapy is often very effective in managing chronic pain. Patients are taught which factors affect pain, along with techniques to reduce pain, such as relaxation. Even limited control over the pain can reduce anxiety and tension, which, in turn, reduces the pain. Although the pain is not eliminated, many patients are better able to cope and to lead relatively normal lives.

---

by the pain signal). From the spinal cord, the message goes to the brain. The brain then interprets the pain information and sends signals that either open the spinal gates farther, causing a greater experience of pain, or close them, dampening the pain. Of course, this decision by the brain is influenced by the psychological aspects of the pain-causing stimulus. Anxiety, fear, and helplessness intensify pain, whereas laughter, distraction, and a sense of control can diminish it. (This is why people might bruise themselves and not know it if they were concentrating on something else.) Pain can also be affected by competing signals from other skin senses, which is why rubbing a sore spot can reduce the feeling of pain.

The Kinesthetic Sense The neuron receptors located in the skin, joints, muscles, and tendons, mentioned in the discussion of pain, are part of the body's sense of position in space—the location of the arms, legs, and so forth in relation to one another and in relation to the ground. This sense is called *kinesthesia*, from the Greek words *kinein* ("to move") and *aesthesis* ("sensation"). When you close your eyes and raise your hand above your head, you know where your hand is because the neuron receptors tell you about the changes in pressure within the muscles.

If you have ever gotten sick from traveling in a moving vehicle, you might be tempted to blame these neuron receptors. Actually, it's not the neuron receptors in the body that make people get sick. The culprits are special structures in the ear that make up the *vestibular sense*—the sense of balance.

The Vestibular Sense The name of this particular sense comes from a Latin word that means "entrance" or "chamber." The latter definition is probably the one that fits better here, as the structures for this sense are located in the innermost chamber of the ear. There are two kinds of vestibular organs, the otolith organs and the semicircular canals.

The *otolith organs* are tiny sacs found just above the cochlea. These sacs contain a gelatin-like fluid within which tiny crystals are suspended (much like pieces of fruit in a bowl of Jello). The head moves and the crystals cause the fluid to vibrate, setting off some tiny hairlike receptors on the inner surface of the sac, telling the person that he or she is moving forward, backward, sideways, or up and down.

The *semicircular canals* are three somewhat circular tubes that are also filled with fluid and will stimulate hairlike receptors when rotated. There are three tubes so that there is one in each of the three planes of motion. Remember learning in geometry class about the *x*-, *y*-, and *z*-axes? Those are the three planes through which the body can rotate, and when it does, it sets off the receptors in these canals. Ever spin around and around like a top when you were a kid? When you stopped, the fluid in the horizontal canal was still rotating and making you feel dizzy because your body was telling you that you were still moving, but your eyes were telling you that you had stopped.

▲ This tightrope-walking violinist is performing an amazing feat of coordination and muscular control. He must not only use his vestibular organs to help maintain his balance, but also his kinesthetic sense to be aware of exactly where each foot is in relation to the rope.

92 CHAPTER 3

Critical Thinking

THE SENSES

<u>Purpose</u>: Students complete a brief 1-minute assignment that involves critical thinking, personalizing, or deeper processing of information.

<u>Time</u>: 1–5 minutes

<u>Description</u>: Give students a few minutes to answer the following question, posed by the teacher. This assignment can be used in a variety of ways—to verify attendance, to start discussion, to assess student knowledge, and to provide opportunities for critical thinking. "**The Senses:** If you had to give up one of your senses, which one would you choose? Explain your answer."

---

92 Chapter 3 Sensation and Perception

Practice Quiz

Pick the best answer.

1. You have a piece of candy that you are holding in your mouth. After a while, the candy doesn't taste as strong as it did when you first tasted it. What has happened?
   a. habituation
   b. saturation
   c. sensory adaptation
   d. visual accommodation

2. Which of the following words best describes the brain's process of organizing and interpreting information from the outside world?
   a. sensation
   b. perception
   c. adaptation
   d. gustation

3. Which of the following represents the correct path of light through the eye?
   a. iris, cornea, lens, retina
   b. cornea, vitreous humor, iris, lens, aqueous humor, retina
   c. cornea, pupil, lens, vitreous humor, retina
   d. cornea, lens, pupil, iris, retina

4. Which theory of color vision accounts better for the afterimage?
   a. trichromatic theory
   b. opponent-process theory
   c. both trichromatic theory and opponent-process theory
   d. neither trichromatic theory nor opponent-process theory

5. The snail-shaped structure of the inner ear is known as the
   a. cochlea
   b. pinna
   c. stirrup
   d. eardrum

6. Which of the following sounds is most likely to have the highest pitch?
   a. a bass guitar
   b. a rumble of thunder
   c. a man's speaking voice
   d. a screaming young child

7. Which of the following is not one of the five basic tastes?
   a. sweet
   b. bitter
   c. spicy
   d. umami

8. After some time has passed, you can no longer smell the odor of wet paint that you noticed when you first walked into your classroom. Which is the most likely reason for this?
   a. The smell has gone away.
   b. Your olfactory bulb is missing.
   c. Your receptor cells are not working properly.
   d. You've adapted to the smell, even though it's still there.

9. Which of the following senses is most responsible for motion sickness?
   a. the kinesthetic sense
   b. the vestibular sense
   c. the olfactory sense
   d. the skin sense

10. Pain sensations in the skin, muscles, tendons, and joints that are carried on large nerve fibers are called
    a. visceral pain
    b. somatic pain
    c. referred pain
    d. indigenous pain

CHAPTER 3 • Module 7

Assess

Assign the Module 7 Practice Quiz.

Use the Practice Quiz to identify gaps in student understanding.

REMEDIATE

Have students, individually or in groups, review the module goals, learning objectives, and key terms.

Refer students to the Concept Summary on pp. 106–107 for review.

Close

As a class, discuss which sense students think is the most important. Make sure students provide a reasonable explanation for their viewpoints.

L3 DIFFERENTIATED INSTRUCTION

Tactile/Kinesthetic Learners These students need a "hands-on" opportunity to learn. Lab classes are very good ways for this type of learner to absorb material. Teachers who conduct lots of demonstrations and use field experience outside the classroom are helpful for this style of learner. Some kinesthetic learners benefit from writing notes during a lecture or from writing a summary of their notes afterward.

Practice Quiz Answers

1. c
2. b
3. c
4. b
5. a
6. d
7. c
8. d
9. b
10. b

CHAPTER 3 • Module 8

Focus

RESOURCES

For this module, consult the appropriate sections of the Teacher's Manual, Test Bank, and PowerPoint slides, all found on the Teacher's Resource DVD, and the interactive study tools for students on MyPsychLab.

BEFORE CLASS

Students should read the section for homework before coming to class.

BELLRINGER

Before class, gather three metal or plastic containers—for example, three that hold 8 ounces, 16 ounces, and 32 ounces. Put dirt or pebbles into each container so that all three are exactly the same weight (use a kitchen scale). Cover them with foil so the contents cannot be seen. Ask students to judge the lightest or heaviest. Most will be certain that the smallest container weighs the most and the largest weighs the least.

Teach

INTRODUCE THE TOPIC

Tell students that the Bellringer activity is an example of size–weight illusion. This effect is explained by our expectations. When we see the large container, we prepare our muscles to lift something heavy. When it is filled to only a portion of its capacity, it is picked up easily.

COVER THE MODULE

8.1 What is the nature of attention?

Humans are able to use their powers of attention to focus on certain stimuli in their environment and ignore the rest.

8.2 What are perceptual constancies, and why are they important?

- Perception is the interpretation and organization of sensations.
- *Size constancy* is the tendency to perceive objects as always being the same size, no matter how close or far away they are.

94 Chapter 3 Sensation and Perception

Module 8 Perception

Module Goal
Learn how we perceive the world.

Learning Objectives
- 8.1 What is the nature of attention?
- 8.2 What are perceptual constancies, and why are they important?
- 8.3 What are the Gestalt principles of perception?
- 8.4 What are monocular and binocular depth cues?
- 8.5 How do visual illusions work?
- 8.6 How do our experiences and expectations influence perception?

FIGURE 8.1 Shape Constancy
Three examples of shape constancy are shown here. The opening door is actually many different shapes, yet we still see it as basically a rectangular door. We do the same thing with a triangle and a circle—although when we look at them from different angles they cast differently shaped images on our retina, we experience them as a triangle and a circle because of shape constancy.

size constancy the tendency to interpret an object as always being the same actual size, regardless of its distance.

94 CHAPTER 3

Learn How We Perceive the World

Perception is the method by which the brain takes all the raw data sensations people experience at any given moment and allows them to be interpreted in some meaningful fashion in the brain. Perception has some individuality to it—no two people will perceive the world in exactly the same way. As individual as perception might be, however, there are some similarities in how people perceive the world around themselves.

8.1 What is the nature of attention?

What would the world be like if you could pay constant attention to every noise, sight, feeling, and smell around you? Think about what it would be like to read this book while paying attention to all the sensations in your environment: On the page in front of you, you see words, but you also see the white spaces between the lines and in the margins. The book's cover feels smooth against your fingertips. You can hear the pages crinkling, the traffic outside, your parents talking in the next room, your own heartbeat. You are aware of each breath you take. In a world like this, you'd be so distracted that it would be hard to get any reading done!

Luckily for all of us, we are able to use our powers of attention to focus on certain stimuli in our environment and ignore the rest. Whether we focus our attention on an object or sensation willingly or unwillingly, the simple act of paying attention is the first step in the process of perception.

8.2 What are perceptual constancies, and why are they important?

There's an old cartoon that shows a very large man speaking to a very small man. He's saying, "Excuse me for shouting—I thought you were much farther away." This cartoon makes use of the concept of a perceptual constancy for size. **Size constancy** is the tendency to interpret an object as always being the same size, regardless of its distance from the viewer (or the size of the image it casts on the retina). So if an object that is normally perceived to be about 6 feet tall appears very small on the retina, it will be interpreted as being very far away.

Terms

- size constancy • shape constancy • brightness constancy • Gestalt psychology
- figure-ground • reversible figures • proximity • similarity • closure • continuity
- contiguity • depth perception • monocular cues (pictorial depth cues) • binocular cues • linear perspective • relative size • overlap (interposition) • aerial perspective
- texture gradient • motion parallax • accommodation • convergence • binocular disparity • Müller-Lyer illusion • perceptual set (perceptual expectancy) • top-down processing • bottom-up processing

Another perceptual constancy is the tendency to interpret the shape of an object as constant, even when it changes on the retina. This **shape constancy** is why a person still perceives a coin as a circle even if it is held at an angle that makes it appear to be an oval on the retina. Dinner plates on a table are also seen as round, even though from the angle of viewing they are oval. (See Figure 8.1.)

The third form of perceptual constancy is called **brightness constancy**, the tendency to perceive the apparent brightness of an object as the same even when the light conditions change. If a person is wearing black pants and a white shirt, for example, in broad daylight the shirt will appear to be much brighter than the pants. But if the sun is covered by thick clouds, even though the pants and shirt have less light to reflect than previously, the shirt will still appear to be just as much brighter than the pants as before—because the difference between the amounts of light reflected from each piece of clothing is still the same as before (Zeki, 2001).

The perceptual constancies are important to all of us because they help us interact with our environment. Think about what the world would look like without perceptual constancies—can you imagine living in a confusing place full of constantly changing shapes and objects? Size, shape, and brightness constancies keep our perceptions stable and orderly.

8.3 What are the Gestalt principles of perception?

Nineteenth-century German psychologist Max Wertheimer (VERT-hi-mer) felt that psychological events such as perceiving and sensing could not be broken down into any smaller elements and still be properly understood. As a melody is made up of individual notes that can only be understood if the notes are in the correct relationship to one another, so perception can only be understood as a whole, entire event. Hence the familiar slogan, "The whole is greater than the sum of its parts."

Wertheimer and others devoted their efforts to studying sensation and perception in this new perspective, **Gestalt psychology**. *Gestalt* (Gesh-TALT) is a German word meaning "an organized whole" or "configuration," which fit well with the focus on studying whole patterns rather than small pieces of them. The Gestalt psychologists believed that people naturally seek out patterns ("wholes") in the sensory information available to them.

Figure–ground relationships refer to the tendency to perceive objects or figures as existing on a background. Figure 8.2 is an example of a **reversible figure**, in which the figure and the ground seem to switch back and forth.

Another very simple rule of perception is the tendency to perceive objects that are close to one another as part of the same grouping, a principle called **proximity**, or nearness. (See Figure 8.3.)

Similarity refers to the tendency to perceive things that look similar as being part of the same group. When members of a sports team wear uniforms that are all the same color, people viewing the game are able to perceive the team as one group even when they are scattered around the field or court.

Closure is the tendency to complete figures that are incomplete. In class, one teacher usually draws a series of curved lines, spaced an inch or so apart, in a circular pattern on the board. When students are asked what they see, they invariably say "a circle." But it isn't a circle at all—just curved lines laid out in a circular formation. The brain fills in the spaces between the arcs to perceive a circle, which has more meaning than a series of line segments.

The principle of **continuity** is easier to see than it is to explain in words. It refers to the tendency to perceive things as simply as possible with a continuous

FIGURE 8.2 Figure-Ground Illusion
What do you see when you look at this picture? Is it a goblet? Or two faces looking at each other? This is an example in which the figure and the ground seem to "switch" each time you look at the picture.

shape constancy the tendency to interpret the shape of an object as being constant, even when its shape changes on the retina.

brightness constancy the tendency to perceive the apparent brightness of an object as the same even when the light conditions change.

Gestalt psychology early perspective in psychology focusing on perception and sensation, particularly the perception of patterns and whole figures.

figure–ground the tendency to perceive objects, or figures, as existing on a background.

reversible figures visual illusions in which the figure and ground can be reversed.

proximity the tendency to perceive objects that are close to each other as part of the same grouping.

similarity the tendency to perceive things that look similar to each other as being part of the same group.

closure the tendency to complete figures that are incomplete.

continuity the tendency to perceive things as simply as possible with a continuous pattern rather than with a complex, broken-up pattern.

SENSATION AND PERCEPTION 95

CHAPTER 3 • Module 8

COVER THE MODULE (continued)

- *Shape constancy* is the tendency to perceive objects as remaining the same shape even when the shape of the object changes on the retina of the eye.
- *Brightness constancy* is the tendency to perceive objects as a certain level of brightness, even when the light is different.

COVER THE MODULE

8.3 What are the Gestalt principles of perception?

- *Gestalt* means "an organized whole." The *Gestalt psychologists* believe that people naturally seek out patterns in sensory information. These scientists developed several principles of perception that involve interpreting patterns in visual stimuli.
- The principles are figure-ground relationships, similarity, closure, continuity, contiguity, and common region.
  - *Figure-ground* relationships refer to the tendency to perceive objects or figures as existing on a background.
  - *Similarity* is the tendency to perceive things that look similar as being part of the same group.
  - *Closure* is the tendency to complete incomplete figures.
  - *Continuity* is the tendency to perceive things as simply as possible with a continuous pattern.

Class Demonstration

PERCEPTUAL CONSTANCIES

Purpose: Students teach each other about the perceptual constancies.

Time: 15 minutes

Description: This exercise should be completed in teams of three students. Each student is assigned to one of the perceptual constancies—size, shape, or brightness. Students have 5 minutes to read the section of the textbook on their assigned constancy and come up with several everyday examples that illustrate the constancy in action. Students then teach or present their constancy to the group. The teacher can randomly call on students to explain the constancy and give an example.

CHAPTER 3 • Module 8

COVER THE MODULE (continued)
- *Contiguity* is the tendency to perceive two things that happen close together in time as being related.
- *Common region* refers to the tendency to perceive objects that are in a common area as being in a group.

MULTIMEDIA CONTENT AVAILABLE AT
www.mypsychlab.com

Listen to a podcast on Gestalt principles of perception on **mypsychlab.com**

EXTEND THE LESSON
The Gestalt psychologists described perception as something in which "the whole is more than the sum of its parts." Be prepared to elaborate on this statement, because some students might find it troublesome. For example, point out that on very close examination, a newspaper photograph is just a bunch of dots, yet we perceive much more.

CHECK FOR UNDERSTANDING
To ensure that students understand the Gestalt principles, direct their attention to Figure 8.3. Ask volunteers to explain each of the examples shown in the illustration. If students need remediation, refer them to the **www.mypsychlab.com** website for the Chapter 3 simulation on Gestalt Laws of Perception.

COVER THE MODULE
8.4 What are monocular and binocular depth cues?
- *Depth perception* is the ability to see in three dimensions, which is necessary to judge how far away objects are located.

FIGURE 8.3 Gestalt Principles of Grouping
The Gestalt principles of grouping are shown here. These are the human tendency to organize isolated stimuli into groups on the basis of five characteristics: proximity, similarity, closure, continuity, and common region.

pattern rather than with a complex, broken-up pattern. Look at Figure 8.3 for an example of continuity. Isn't it much easier to see the figure on the left as two wavy lines crossing each other than as the little sections in the diagram to the right?

Contiguity isn't shown in Figure 8.3 because it involves not only nearness in space but also nearness in time. Basically, contiguity is the tendency to perceive two things that happen close together in time as being related. Usually the first occurring event is seen as causing the second event.

There is one other principle of perceptual grouping that was not one of the original principles. It was added to the list (and can be seen at the bottom of Figure 8.3) by Stephen Palmer (Palmer, 1992). In *common region*, the tendency is to perceive objects that are in a common area or region as being in a group. In Figure 8.3, people could perceive the stars as one group and the circles as another on the basis of similarity. But the colored backgrounds so visibly define common regions that people instead perceive three groups—one of which has both stars and circles in it. **Listen** on **mypsychlab.com**

8.4 What are monocular and binocular depth cues?

The ability to see the world in three dimensions is called **depth perception**. It's a handy ability because without it, you would have a hard time judging how far away objects are. The Classic Studies in Psychology section presents one of the most famous studies in the field of depth perception.

Listen to a podcast on Gestalt principles of perception on **mypsychlab.com**

contiguity the tendency to perceive two things that happen close together in time as being related.

depth perception the ability to perceive the world in three dimensions.

96 CHAPTER 3

Explore

IN SEARCH OF PERCEPTUAL ILLUSIONS
Students often can gain a better understanding of perceptual illusions by actively finding their own examples. Possible ways to document examples include taking photographs, cutting clippings out of magazines or newspapers, or describing the illusion in detail if it is not possible to obtain a sample (e.g., if it was seen in a movie). Real world examples abound, and students will likely enjoy their quest for the ultimate illusion. An added benefit is that students can share their examples with the rest of the class, who can try to identify the illusion portrayed. In this way, all students will have had access to numerous examples outside the text.

96 Chapter 3 Sensation and Perception

Classic Studies In Psychology

The Visual Cliff

In the late 1950s, psychologist Eleanor Gibson and her fellow researcher, Richard Walk, wondered if infants could perceive the world in three dimensions and thought up a way to test babies for depth perception (Gibson & Walk, 1960). They built a special table (see Figure 8.4) that had a big drop on one side. The surface of the table on both the top and the drop to the floor was covered in a patterned tablecloth, so that the different size of the patterns would be a cue for depth (remember, in size constancy, if something looks smaller, people assume it is farther away from them). The whole table was then covered by a clear glass top, so that a baby could safely be placed on or crawl across the "deep" side.

The infants tested in this study ranged from 6 months to 14 months old. They were placed on the middle of the table and then encouraged (usually by their mothers) to crawl over either the shallow side or the deep side. Most babies—81 percent—refused to crawl over the deep side, even though they could touch it with their hands and feel that it was solid. Because they were upset and seemed fearful when encouraged to crawl across the deep side, Gibson and Walk interpreted this as a very early sign of depth perception.

Questions for Further Discussion

1. Does the fact that 19 percent of the infants did crawl over the deep side of the visual cliff necessarily mean that those infants could not perceive the depth?
2. What other factors might explain the willingness of the 19 percent to crawl over the deep side?
3. Are there any ethical concerns in this experiment?
4. Ducks aren't bothered by the visual cliff at all—why would that be?

monocular cues (pictorial depth cues) cues for perceiving depth based on one eye only.

binocular cues cues for perceiving depth based on both eyes.

FIGURE 8.4 The Visual Cliff Experiment

In the visual cliff experiment, the table has both a shallow and a "deep" side, with glass covering the entire table. When an infant looks down at the deep-appearing side, the squares in the design on the floor look smaller than the ones on the shallow side, forming a visual cue for depth. Notice that this little girl seems to be very reluctant to cross over the deep-appearing side of the table, gesturing to be picked up instead.

There are various cues for perceiving depth in the world. Some require the use of only one eye (**monocular cues**) and some are a result of the slightly different visual patterns that exist when both eyes are used (**binocular cues**).

CHAPTER 3 • Module 8

CLASSIC STUDIES IN PSYCHOLOGY

1. No, the fact that some infants did crawl over the deep side of the visual cliff could have been attributed to reasons other than not perceiving the depth.
2. It is possible that the babies who were willing to crawl over the deep side did so because of their mother's encouragement or because their need to reach the mother was more critical than any fear they might have had.
3. The fact that some babies were upset and fearful could indicate that they were very distressed, raising an ethical issue in the experiment.
4. Possible answer: Ducks' sense of depth perception is different from that of humans'.

FAST FACT

Research has shown that infants as young as 3 months are able to perceive the visual cliff. When they are placed over the apparent "edge," they experience an increased breathing rate, widened eyes, and a quickened heart rate. However, these children do not yet understand that the result of going over the visual cliff is possibly falling. This insight comes once the child begins to crawl and experiences toppling over.

Explore

THE VISUAL CLIFF

Have students visit the www.mypsychlab.com website for Chapter 3 in order to try the visual cliff experiment for themselves. Tell them to write a short report describing their experience and relating it to the theory and research presented in the text. Do they understand why the babies might have refused to crawl over the deep side?

CHAPTER 3 • Module 8

COVER THE MODULE (continued)

- Monocular cues for depth perception include *linear perspective, relative size, overlap, aerial perspective, texture gradient, motion parallax,* and *accommodation.*
- Binocular cues for depth perception include *convergence* and *binocular disparity.*

EXTEND THE LESSON

For additional opportunities to understand pictorial depth cues, send students to the **www.myspychlab.com** website for the Chapter 3 simulation on the ABCs of perception.

L2 ELL DIFFERENTIATED INSTRUCTION

English Language Learners Make sure students understand assessment criteria in advance. Whenever possible, provide models of student work to emulate, along with an example of work that fails to meet the specific assessment criteria.

L3 DIFFERENTIATED INSTRUCTION

Engaging All Learners Incorporate students' strengths and interests. Use the students' abilities to connect them to content and activities.

---

linear perspective the tendency for parallel lines to appear to converge on each other.

relative size perception that occurs when objects that a person expects to be of a certain size appear to be small and are, therefore, assumed to be much farther away.

overlap (interposition) the assumption that an object that appears to be blocking part of another object is in front of the second object and closer to the viewer.

aerial perspective the haziness that surrounds objects that are farther away from the viewer, causing the distance to be perceived as greater.

texture gradient the tendency for textured surfaces to appear to become smaller and finer as distance from the viewer increases.

motion parallax the perception of motion of objects in which close objects appear to move more quickly than objects that are farther away.

accommodation as a monocular clue, the brain's use of information about the changing thickness of the lens of the eye in response to looking at objects that are close or far away.

convergence the rotation of the two eyes in their sockets to focus on a single object, resulting in greater convergence for closer objects and lesser convergence if objects are distant.

binocular disparity the difference in images between the two eyes, which is greater for objects that are close and smaller for distant objects.

Monocular cues are often referred to as **pictorial depth cues** because artists can use these cues to give the illusion of depth to paintings and drawings. Examples of these cues are discussed next.

1. **Linear perspective:** When looking down a long interstate highway, the two sides of the highway appear to merge together in the distance. This tendency for lines that are actually parallel to *seem* to come closer together is called **linear perspective**. It works in pictures because people assume that in the picture, as in real life, the converging lines indicate that the "ends" of the lines are a great distance away from where the people are as they view them.
2. **Relative size:** The principle of size constancy is at work in **relative size**, when objects that people expect to be of a certain size appear to be small and are, therefore, assumed to be much farther away. Movie makers use this principle to make their small models seem gigantic but off in the distance.
3. **Overlap:** If one object seems to be blocking another object, people assume that the blocked object is behind the first one and, therefore, farther away. This cue is also known as **interposition**.
4. **Aerial (atmospheric) perspective:** The farther away an object is, the hazier the object will appear to be, a perceptual cue called **aerial (atmospheric) perspective**. This is why distant mountains often look fuzzy, and buildings far in the distance are blurrier than those that are close.
5. **Texture gradient**: If there are any large expanses of pebbles, rocks, or patterned roads (such as a cobblestone street) nearby, go take a look at them one day. The pebbles or bricks that are close to you are very distinctly textured, but as you look farther off into the distance, their texture becomes smaller and finer. **Texture gradient** is another trick artists use to give the illusion of depth in a painting.
6. **Motion parallax:** The next time you're in a car, notice how the objects outside the car window seem to zip by very fast when they are close to the car, and objects in the distance, such as mountains, seem to move more slowly. This discrepancy in motion of near and far objects is called **motion parallax**.
7. **Accommodation:** A monocular cue that is not one of the pictorial cues, **accommodation** makes use of something that happens inside the eye. The lens of the human eye is flexible and held in place by a series of muscles. The discussion of the eye earlier in this chapter mentioned the process of visual accommodation as the tendency of the lens to change its shape, or thickness, in response to objects near or far away. The brain can use this information about accommodation as a cue for distance. Accommodation is also called a muscular cue.

As their name suggests, binocular cues require the use of two eyes:

1. **Convergence:** Another muscular cue, **convergence**, refers to the rotation of the two eyes in their sockets to focus on a single object. If the object is close, the convergence is pretty great (almost as great as crossing the eyes). If the object is far, the convergence is much less.
2. **Binocular disparity:** Binocular disparity is a scientific way of saying that because the eyes are a few inches apart, they don't see exactly the same image. The brain interprets the images on the retina to determine distance from the eyes. If the two images are very different,

---

Class Demonstration

DEPTH PERCEPTION IN ART

Purpose: Students create the illusion of depth on a flat surface.

Time: 15 minutes

Description: Artists face the task of creating the illusion of depth on a flat surface, and they use many of the monocular cues to do this. Give students 5 minutes to create a drawing that gives the illusion of depth. Using one or more of the monocular cues for depth listed in the textbook, students should have no trouble creating the illusion of depth on their paper. On the back of their paper, they should list the cue(s) used. Students should then hold up their drawing, while classmates point out the monocular cue(s). There are many variations to this activity. You could assign individual students or teams to a particular cue, and then each team shares their drawing with the class. Or, you could have teams work together and try to create a drawing that uses four or more cues.

the object must be pretty close. If they are almost identical, the object is far enough away to make the retinal disparity very small.

8.5 How do visual illusions work?

You've mentioned the word illusion *several times. Exactly what are illusions, and why is it so easy to be fooled by them?*

An *illusion* is a perception that does not correspond to reality. People *think* they see something when the reality is quite different. One can also think of illusions as visual stimuli that "fool" the eye. (Illusions are different from hallucinations in that a hallucination's origin is in the brain itself—a person is seeing or hearing something that is actually not there at all. An illusion is a distorted perception of something that *is* there.)

One of the most famous visual illusions, the **Müller-Lyer illusion**, is shown in Figure 8.5. The distortion happens when the viewer tries to determine if the two lines are exactly the same length. They are identical, but one line looks longer than the other. (It's always the line with the angles on the end facing outward.) Why is this illusion so powerful? The explanation is that most people in industrialized Western societies live in a world with lots of buildings. Buildings have corners. When a person is outside of a building, the corner of the building is close to that person, while the walls seem to be moving away. When the person is inside a building, the corner of the room seems to move away from the viewer, while the walls are coming closer. In the illusion, the line with the angles facing inward is like the outside of the building, and the one with the angles facing outward is like the inside of the room. In their minds, people "pull" the inward-facing angles toward them like the outside corners of a building, and they make the outward-facing angles "stretch" away from them like the inside corners of the room (Enns & Coren, 1995; Gregory, 1990).

Segall and colleagues (Segall et al., 1966) found that people in Western cultures, having carpentered buildings with lots of straight lines and corners (Segall and colleagues refer to this as a "carpentered world"), are far more susceptible to this illusion than people from non-Western cultures (having round huts with few corners—an "uncarpentered world"). Gregory (1990) found that Zulus, for example, rarely are fooled by this illusion. They live in round huts arranged in circles, use curved tools and toys, and experience few straight lines and corners in their world.

Another common illusion is the *moon illusion*, in which the moon on the horizon appears to be much larger than the moon in the sky (Plug & Ross, 1994). One explanation for this is that the moon high in the sky is all alone, with no cues for depth surrounding it. But on the horizon, the moon appears behind

Müller-Lyer illusion illusion of line length that is distorted by inward-turning or outward-turning corners on the ends of the lines, causing lines of equal length to appear to be different.

◀ You've mentioned the word *illusion* several times. Exactly what are illusions, and why is it so easy to be fooled by them?

FIGURE 8.5 The Müller-Lyer Illusion
(a) Which line is longer? In industrialized Western countries, people generally see the lines in part (a) in situations similar to those in part (b). According to one theory, people have become accustomed to seeing right angles in their environment and assume that the short, slanted lines are forming a right angle to the vertical line. They make that assumption because they are accustomed to seeing corners, such as the ones shown in figure (b) on the right. Consequently, in figure (b) on the left, they tend to perceive the line on the right as slightly longer than the line on the left.

SENSATION AND PERCEPTION 99

CHAPTER 3 • Module 8

COVER THE MODULE

8.5 How do visual illusions work?

DISCUSS THE STUDENT VOICE QUESTION

Use the question to check students' comprehension of the topic.

- Illusions are perceptions that do not correspond to reality, distortions of visual stimuli.
- The *Müller-Lyer illusion* involves the misperception of two lines of equal length as being different in length because of angles placed on each end of each line.
- The moon illusion occurs when the moon appears to be larger on the horizon than in the upper sky. It is explained by the apparent distance hypothesis, which involves a misinterpretation of size constancy.

EXTEND THE DISCUSSION

Flashing lights that create the perception of continuous motion illustrate the phi phenomenon. You can easily demonstrate this in class. Darken the room and flash two stationary lights on and off. Students will perceive the apparent movement of the light from one place to another, although the light sources never actually move.

Class Demonstration

OPTICAL ILLUSIONS

Purpose: Students discuss the science behind optical illusions.

Time: 15 minutes

Description: Each student should bring an optical illusion to class. Illusions are plentiful on the Internet, or students may photocopy one from the textbook. Students should take time to learn about the science behind the illusion and how the brain is fooled. In class, students can join a group with others who have similar illusions (e.g., afterimages, relative size, perceptual set). Have these groups meet in different "corners." After some discussion and consensus about each group of illusions, a spokesperson for the group can share with the class.

CHAPTER 3 • Module 8

COVER THE MODULE

8.6 How do our experiences and expectations influence perception?

- *Perceptual set* or expectancy refers to the tendency to perceive objects and situations a particular way because of prior experiences.
- *Top-down processing* involves the use of preexisting knowledge to organize individual features into a unified whole.

MULTIMEDIA CONTENT AVAILABLE AT
www.mypsychlab.com

⊙→ Simulate the concept of perceptual expectancy with an activity on ambiguous figures on **mypsychlab.com**

EXTEND THE LESSON

Send students to the online exhibits of San Francisco's Exploratorium at **www.exploratorium.edu/exhibits/f_exhibits.html**. Tell them to select a visual illusion and then write a short report, detailing how this illusion proves the idea that people have a tendency to perceive things a certain way because their previous experiences or expectations influence them.

L3 DIFFERENTIATED INSTRUCTION

Visual/Nonverbal Learners Have these students make flash cards with pictures or diagrams to aid in recall of key concepts.

▲ The moon illusion. When this moon is high in the night sky, it will still be the same size to the eye as it is now. Nevertheless, it is perceived to be much larger when on the horizon. In the sky, there are no objects for comparison, but on the horizon, objects such as this tree are seen as being in front of a very large moon.

⊙→ Simulate the concept of perceptual expectancy with an activity on ambiguous figures on **mypsychlab.com**

perceptual set (perceptual expectancy) the tendency to perceive things a certain way because previous experiences or expectations influence those perceptions.

top-down processing the use of preexisting knowledge to organize individual features into a unified whole.

FIGURE 8.6 Perceptual Set
Look at the drawing in the middle. What do you see? Now look at the drawings on each end. Would you have interpreted the middle drawing differently if you had looked at the drawing of the man or the sitting woman first?

100 CHAPTER 3

---

trees and houses, cues for depth that make the horizon seem very far away. The moon is seen as being behind these objects and, therefore, farther away from the viewer. Because people know that objects that are farther away from them and still seem large are very large indeed, they "magnify" the moon in their minds—a misapplication of the principle of size constancy. This explanation of the moon illusion is called the *apparent distance hypothesis*. This explanation goes back to the second century A.D. It was first written about by the Greek-Egyptian astronomer Ptolemy and later further developed by an eleventh-century Arab astronomer, Al-Hazan (Ross & Ross, 1976).

Sometimes people perceive an object as moving when it is really still. One example of this is the *autokinetic effect*. ("Autokinetic" means "self-moving.") In this effect, a small, stationary light in a darkened room will appear to move or drift because there are no surrounding cues to indicate that the light is *not* moving. Another is the *stroboscopic motion* seen in motion pictures and flip books, in which a rapid series of still pictures will seem to be in motion.

Another movement illusion related to stroboscopic motion is the *phi phenomenon*, in which lights turned on in sequence appear to move. For example, if a light is turned on in a darkened room and then turned off, and then another light a short distance away is flashed on and off, it will appear to be one light moving across that distance. This principle is used to suggest motion in many theater marquee signs, flashing arrows indicating direction that have a series of lights going on and off in a sequence, and even in strings of decorative lighting, such as the "chasing" lights seen on houses at holiday times.

8.6 How do our experiences and expectations influence perception?

People often misunderstand what is said to them because they were expecting to hear something else. People's tendency to perceive things a certain way because their previous experiences or expectations influence them is called **perceptual set** or **perceptual expectancy**. ⊙→ Simulate on **mypsychlab.com**

Although expectancies can be useful in interpreting certain stimuli, they can also lead people down the wrong path. For example, look at Figure 8.6. The drawing in the middle is a little hard to identify. People who start looking at these five drawings by looking at the drawing on the far left (which is clearly a man's face) tend to see the middle drawing as a man's face. But people who start looking from the far right (where the drawing is a kneeling woman with one arm over her chest and one touching her knee) see the middle picture as a woman. What you see depends on what you expect to see.

The way in which people interpret what they perceive can also influence their perception. For example, people can try to understand what they perceive by using information they already have (as is the case of perceptual expectancy). But if there is no existing information that relates to the new information, they can look at each feature of what they perceive and try to put it all together into one whole.

Anyone who has ever worked on a jigsaw puzzle knows that it's a lot easier to put it together if there is a picture of the finished puzzle to act as a guide. It also helps to have completed the puzzle before; people who have done that already know what it's going to look like when it's finished. In the field of perception, this is known as **top-down processing**—the use of preexisting knowledge to organize individual features into a unified whole. This is also a form of perceptual expectancy.

Class Demonstration

EXPECTANCY AND PERCEPTION

Conduct a "spelling bee in reverse." Ask students to pronounce a word out loud after you write it on the board. First write: MAC DONALD. Then write: MAC HENRY. Then: MAC MAHON. Finally, write: MAC HINERY. The latter will likely generate a chorus of Scottish-sounding surnames (e.g., "MacHinery") rather than the real pronunciation of *machinery*.

---

100 Chapter 3 Sensation and Perception

If the puzzle is one the person has never worked on before or if that person has lost the top of the box with the picture on it, he or she would have to start with a small section, put it together, and keep building up the sections until the recognizable picture appears. This analysis of smaller features and building up to a complete perception is called **bottom-up processing** (Cave & Kim, 1999). In this case, there is no expectancy to help organize the perception, making bottom-up processing more difficult in some respects. Fortunately, the two types of processing are often used together in perceiving the surrounding world.

Do people of different cultures perceive objects differently because of different expectancies? Some research suggests that this is true. For example, take a look at Figure 8.7. This figure is often called the "devil's trident." Europeans and North Americans insist on making this figure three dimensional, so they have trouble looking at it—the figure is impossible if it is perceived in three dimensions. But people in less technologically oriented cultures have little difficulty seeing or even reproducing this figure, because they see it as a two-dimensional drawing, quite literally a collection of lines and circles rather than a solid object (Deregowski, 1969). Explore on mypsychlab.com

bottom-up processing the analysis of the smaller features to build up to a complete perception.

FIGURE 8.7 The Devil's Trident
At first glance, this seems to be an ordinary three-pronged figure. But a closer look reveals that the three prongs cannot be real as drawn. Follow the lines of the top prong to see what goes wrong.

Explore top-down processing on mypsychlab.com

Applying Psychology to Everyday Life

Does Subliminal Advertising Really Work?

You may have heard about "subliminal advertising"—hidden messages in movies and on television that influence our purchasing behaviors even though we can't consciously perceive the messages. Are these messages real, and do they really work?

It is true that some stimuli are just strong enough to activate the sensory receptors but not strong enough for people to be consciously aware of them. Many people believe that these stimuli act upon the unconscious mind, influencing behavior in a process called *subliminal perception*. But can subliminal perception be used effectively in advertising?

Although the following story is now widely recognized as false, it has taken on the status of an urban legend—a story that is so often repeated that people have come to believe that it is true. The story highlights the fears that many people had concerning subliminal perception when psychologists first introduced the concept. The story goes like this: In 1957 a market researcher named James Vicary claimed that over a six-week period, 45,699 patrons at a movie theater in Fort Lee, New Jersey, were shown two advertising messages, *Eat Popcorn* and *Drink Coca-Cola*, while they watched the film *Picnic*. According to Vicary, these messages were flashed for 0.003 seconds once every 5 seconds. Vicary claimed that over the six-week period the sales of popcorn rose 57.7 percent and the sales of Coca-Cola rose 18.1 percent.

For years, Vicary's claims were often accepted as established facts; however, Vicary never described his study in print. Real researchers were unable to duplicate his findings. Finally, in a 1962 interview with *Advertising Age*, Vicary admitted what many researchers had long suspected: The original study was a complete deception—he never did it (Merikle, 2000; Pratkanis, 1992). Since then, researchers have gathered scientific evidence that subliminal perception has no scientific merit and does not work in advertising (Bargh et al., 1996; Moore, 1988; Pratkanis & Greenwald, 1988; Trappey, 1996; Vokey & Read, 1985).

SENSATION AND PERCEPTION 101

CHAPTER 3 • Module 8

COVER THE MODULE *(continued)*
- *Bottom-up processing* involves the analysis of smaller features, building up to a complete perception.

MULTICULTURAL FOCUS
Tell students that researchers have studied differences between the ways in which Westerners and East Asians view the world. These scientists have found evidence that East Asians, whose culture promotes group harmony, think in a more integrated, comprehensive way. They pay attention to all the elements of a scene, to context, and to the relationships between items. On the other hand, Western culture stresses personal independence and formal logic, so Westerners are more analytic and pay attention to particular objects and categories.

APPLYING PSYCHOLOGY TO EVERYDAY LIFE
Ask students if they are aware that various companies have been able to exploit people's belief in subliminal perception by marketing subliminal self-help audio and video tapes. The companies claim that regular use of the tapes can cure a variety of problems such as smoking, weight gain, and stress. Apparently, the tapes contain embedded subliminal messages that can be neither consciously seen nor heard. There have been several controlled studies designed to test the effectiveness of these tapes. None of these studies has found any evidence to prove the claims of the companies that market these tapes. There is no evidence that regular listening to subliminal audio self-help tapes or regular viewing of subliminal video self-help tapes is an effective method for overcoming problems. Ask students why they think the general public is so captivated with the idea of subliminal perception.

Explore top-down processing on mypsychlab.com

Critical Thinking

CONTROVERSIES IN PERCEPTION

<u>Purpose</u>: Students have a chance to think about, debate, and discuss controversial topics in sensation and perception.

<u>Time</u>: 15 minutes

<u>Description</u>: Pose the following issue to the class: "Subliminal perception should be allowed in advertising." Give students 15 minutes to write down whether they agree or disagree, and why. Then ask students to share their answers and contribute to further class discussion. Or, conduct a class debate on this topic.

Module 8 Perception 101

CHAPTER 3 • Module 8

Assess

Assign the Module 8 Practice Quiz.

Use the Practice Quiz to identify gaps in student understanding.

REMEDIATE

Have students, individually or in groups, review the module goals, learning objectives, and key terms.

Refer students to the Concept Summary on p. 107 for review.

Close

As a class, discuss why paying attention is the first step in perception. What are some of the factors that influence perception?

Practice Quiz

Pick the best answer.

1. The tendency to perceive a quarter as being round even when it is viewed at an angle is called
   a. size constancy
   b. shape constancy
   c. brightness constancy
   d. vision constancy

2. A reversible figure makes use of which principle of perception?
   a. shape constancy
   b. expectancy
   c. figure-ground relationships
   d. depth perception

3. Which of the following is NOT a monocular cue for depth?
   a. convergence
   b. linear perspective
   c. overlap
   d. texture gradient

4. The first time Joe had to put together a bicycle, it took a long time. Now that he has built several bicycles, he can put together a bicycle quickly and easily. Joe's improved speed and skill can be attributed to
   a. binocular disparity
   b. monocular depth cues
   c. top-down processing
   d. bottom-up processing

5. Tasha is waiting for her friend at the mall. She listens for the sound of her friend calling her name. She hears a word that sounds like her name and turns around, but she soon realizes that she's made a mistake: A stranger behind her was calling to his small child. Which of the following influenced Tasha's conviction that she heard her own name?
   a. depth perception
   b. bottom-up processing
   c. perceptual expectancy
   d. atmospheric perspective

6. The tendency to perceive objects close to each other as part of the same group is called
   a. similarity
   b. proximity
   c. contiguity
   d. continuity

7. Which of the following is an example of motion parallax?
   a. One object appears to overlap another object.
   b. An object looks very small when it is far away.
   c. An object looks fuzzy and blurry when it is far away.
   d. Nearby objects appear to move faster than distant objects.

8. Eleanor Gibson's research using the visual cliff suggests that
   a. infants are able to perceive depth
   b. infants are born with a fear of heights
   c. infants use monocular cues but not binocular cues
   d. infants understand Gestalt principles of perception

9. A visual stimulus that fools the eye into seeing something that's not real is called a(n)
   a. illusion
   b. hallucination
   c. perception
   d. false sensation

10. A person's cultural background will most likely affect his or her
    a. binocular disparities
    b. perceptual expectancies
    c. ability to perceive depth
    d. muscular cues for distance

Practice Quiz Answers

1. b
2. c
3. a
4. d
5. c
6. b
7. d
8. a
9. a
10. b

CHAPTER 3 Summary

Listen on mypsychlab.com

Module 7: Sensation
Understand sensation and perception.

7.1 What are the distinctions between sensation and perception?
- Sensation occurs when the sensory receptors are stimulated by information from the outside world. Sensory receptors send that information to the brain.
- Perception occurs when the brain interprets and organizes sensations in a meaningful fashion.

7.2 What is a sensory threshold? What is sensory adaptation?
- Absolute thresholds are the smallest amount of energy needed for conscious detection of a stimulus at least half the time it is present.
- Sensory adaptation occurs when the sensory receptors stop responding to a constant stimulus.

Explore how the senses work.

7.3 What forms of energy can humans sense?
- Humans' sensory receptors are stimulated by visible light waves, sound waves, thermal energy (heat), pressure, and chemical substances.

7.4 How does the sense of vision work?
- Light enters the eye and is focused through the cornea, passes through the aqueous humor, and then through the pupil. The lens focuses light on the retina, where it passes through ganglion and bipolar cells to stimulate the rods and cones.
- Rods detect changes in brightness but do not see color and function best in low levels of light. Cones are sensitive to colors and work best in bright light.

7.5 How does the sense of hearing work?
- Sound enters the ear through the visible outer structure and travels to the eardrum, the small bones of the middle ear, and the inner ear. Auditory receptors in the inner ear send signals to the brain.

7.6 How do the senses of taste and smell work, and how are they alike?
- Taste buds in the tongue receive molecules of substances, which fit into receptor sites. The five basic types of taste are sweet, sour, salty, bitter, and umami.
- The olfactory receptors in the upper part of the nasal passages receive molecules of substances and create neural signals that are sent to the brain.

Listen to an audio file of your chapter on mypsychlab.com

7.7 What other sensory systems does the human body use?
- The somesthetic senses include the skin senses and the vestibular senses (touch, pain, motion, and balance).

Module 8: Perception
Learn how we perceive the world.

8.1 What is the nature of attention?
- We are able to use our powers of attention to focus on certain stimuli in our environment and ignore the rest. Paying attention is the first step in perception.

8.2 What are perceptual constancies, and why are they important?
- Size constancy is the tendency to perceive objects as remaining the same size. Shape constancy is the tendency to perceive objects as remaining the same shape. Brightness constancy is the tendency to perceive objects at a certain brightness.

8.3 What are the Gestalt principles of perception?
- The Gestalt principles of perception are figure–ground relationships, closure, similarity, continuity, contiguity, and common region.

8.4 What are monocular and binocular depth cues?
- Monocular cues for depth perception include linear perspective, relative size, overlap, aerial perspective, texture gradient, motion parallax, and accommodation. Binocular cues for depth perception include convergence and binocular overlap.

8.5 How do visual illusions work?
- Illusions are perceptions that do not correspond to reality or are distortions of visual stimuli. Examples include the Müller-Lyer illusion and the moon illusion.

8.6 How do our experiences and expectations influence perception?
- We tend to use our preexisting knowledge and prior experiences to perceive objects and situations in particular ways, which may or may not be correct. Culture is one of many factors that can influence perception.

Vocabulary Terms

sensation p. 78
perception p. 78
just noticeable difference (jnd, or the difference threshold) p. 78
absolute threshold p. 79
habituation p. 79
sensory adaptation p. 79
visual accommodation p. 82
rods p. 82
cones p. 82
transduction p. 82
blind spot p. 82
dark adaptation p. 83
light adaptation p. 84
trichromatic theory p. 84

afterimages p. 85
opponent-process theory p. 85
hertz (Hz) p. 86
pinna p. 87
auditory canal p. 87
cochlea p. 87
auditory nerve p. 87
pitch p. 88
place theory p. 88
frequency theory p. 88
volley principle p. 88
gustation p. 88
olfaction (olfactory sense) p. 90
somesthetic senses p. 91
skin senses p. 91
kinesthetic sense p. 91

vestibular senses p. 91
size constancy p. 94
shape constancy p. 95
brightness constancy p. 95
Gestalt psychology p. 95
figure–ground p. 95
reversible figures p. 95
proximity p. 95
similarity p. 95
closure p. 95
continuity p. 95
contiguity p. 96
depth perception p. 96
monocular cues (pictorial depth cues) p. 97
binocular cues p. 97

linear perspective p. 98
relative size p. 98
overlap (interposition) p. 98
aerial perspective p. 98
texture gradient p. 98
motion parallax p. 98
accommodation p. 98
convergence p. 98
binocular disparity p. 98
Müller-Lyer illusion p. 99
perceptual set (perceptual expectancy) p. 100
top-down processing p. 100
bottom-up processing p. 101

SENSATION AND PERCEPTION 103

CHAPTER 3 • Chapter Summary and Vocabulary

Chapter Summary

Encourage students to carefully review and study the summary. Explain that it provides an overview of key concepts presented in the text.

Have students identify what they find unclear or confusing. Call on volunteers to provide answers, examples, or definitions.

Vocabulary Terms

Remind students that terms are defined within the chapter at point of use. If they are not sure of a term's definition, they should look up the definition on the page.

Encourage students to create study cards of unfamiliar words or to go to **www.mypsychlab.com** for flash cards. Have them test themselves or a classmate. Advanced students can explain the terms in their own words.

Critical Thinking

MAKING CONNECTIONS

Have students connect the information they have learned in this chapter. Divide students into pairs or small groups. Tell them that they have been given the job of creating a sixth sense for an alien in an upcoming movie. What would this sense entail? What would they call it? Have them create an audiovisual presentation of this sixth sense.

CHAPTER 3 Assessment

✓ Study and Review on mypsychlab.com

Vocabulary Review

Match each vocabulary term to its definition.

1. sensation
2. perception
3. cones
4. pinna
5. olfaction
6. pitch
7. accommodation
8. bottom-up processing
9. contiguity
10. linear perspective

a. The method by which the sensations experienced at any given moment are interpreted and organized in some meaningful fashion.
b. As a monocular clue, the brain's use of information about the changing thickness of the lens of the eye in response to looking at objects that are close or far away.
c. The tendency for parallel lines to appear to converge on each other.
d. Visual sensory receptors found at the back of the retina, responsible for color vision and sharpness of vision.
e. The visible part of the ear.
f. The analysis of the smaller features to build up to a complete perception.
g. The sensation of smell.
h. The process that occurs when special receptors in the sense organs are activated, allowing various forms of outside stimuli to become neural signals in the brain.
i. Psychological experience of sound that corresponds to the frequency of the sound waves.
j. The tendency to perceive two things that happen close together in time as being related.

Writing about Psychology

Respond to each question in complete sentences.

1. What is the difference between habituation and sensory adaptation? Describe each process, and give at least two examples of how each occurs in your everyday life.
2. Imagine that you are an artist who wants to create the illusion of a realistic, three-dimensional landscape in your painting. Describe at least four techniques you could use to create a perception of depth in a two-dimensional painting.

Psychology Project

How important are binocular depth cues? Perform this experiment to see what happens to your sense of depth perception when you close one eye.

Materials:
- a partner
- a beanbag or a small, soft ball
- a pencil and paper

Instructions:
1. Determine which partner will be the pitcher and which partner will be the catcher.
2. Stand several feet away from your partner in a clear area.
3. Have the pitcher throw the beanbag gently to the catcher ten times in a row. The catcher should keep both of his or her eyes open. Count how many throws are caught, and record that number on the paper.
4. Have the catcher close one eye. The pitcher should throw the beanbag gently to the catcher ten more times while the catcher's eye remains closed. Count how many throws are caught, and record that number on the paper.
5. Switch roles and repeat the experiment. Compare your results to your partner's.
6. Discuss the results. Was it easier to catch the beanbag with two eyes open or with one eye open? What monocular and binocular depth cues did you use during the activity? Which cues were not available to you when you closed one of your eyes?

CHAPTER 3 • Assessment

VOCABULARY REVIEW

1. h
2. a
3. d
4. e
5. g
6. i
7. b
8. f
9. j
10. c

WRITING ABOUT PSYCHOLOGY

1. In habituation, the sensory receptors are still responding to stimulation, but the lower centers of the brain are not sending the signals from the receptors to the cortex. In sensory adaptation, the receptor cells themselves become less responsive to an unchanging stimulus.
2. A perception of depth could be created through the use of linear perception, relative size, overlap, aerial (atmospheric) perspective, and texture gradient.

PSYCHOLOGY PROJECT

Monocular cues used during the activity include relative size, aerial perspective, motion parallax, and accommodation. Binocular cues used during the activity were convergence and binocular disparity. The binocular cues were lost when one eye was closed.

Internet Resources

Seeing, Hearing, and Smelling the World — Howard Hughes Medical Institute:
www.hhmi.org/senses/
This site provides excellent information about sensation, perception, and the brain.

How We See: www.accessexcellence.org/AE/AEC/CC/vision_background.html
This is a detailed website complemented by helpful diagrams that explain the nature of human vision.

Visual Illusions Gallery: http://dragon.uml.edu/psych/illusion.html
Includes links to various visual illusions, including negative afterimages.

Touch: http://sun.science.wayne.edu/~wpoff/cor/sen/touch.html
A review of major topics related to touch, including descriptions of anatomy, tactile stimuli, heat, pressure, pain, and damage to the tactile system.

Test Yourself

Pick the best answer.

1. Which of the following qualities is determined by the amplitude of a light wave?
   a. pitch
   b. color
   c. saturation
   d. brightness

2. Which of the following is responsible for controlling how much light enters the eye?
   a. cornea
   b. lens
   c. retina
   d. iris

3. Which type of retinal cell is responsible for peripheral vision?
   a. rods
   b. cones
   c. ganglion cells
   d. bipolar cells

4. Which set of colors are the primary colors when mixing light?
   a. red, yellow, and blue
   b. red, blue, and green
   c. blue, green, and yellow
   d. red, green, and yellow

5. The thin membrane stretched over the opening to the inner ear is the
   a. pinna
   b. cochlea
   c. oval window
   d. tympanic membrane

6. Which of the following explains how we hear sounds between 400 and 4000 Hz?
   a. place theory
   b. frequency theory
   c. the volley principle
   d. the Gestalt principle

7. Which type of hearing impairment is likely to develop when the bones of the middle ear are damaged?
   a. nerve hearing impairment
   b. stimulation hearing impairment
   c. brain pathway hearing impairment
   d. conduction hearing impairment

8. The sense of taste is most closely related to the sense of
   a. sight
   b. hearing
   c. smell
   d. touch

9. The "bumps" on the tongue that are visible to the eye are called
   a. taste buds
   b. papillae
   c. taste receptors
   d. olfactory receptors

10. The olfactory receptor cells are located
    a. at the tip of the nose
    b. on the roof of the mouth
    c. on the surface of the tongue
    d. at the tops of the nasal passages

11. We know when we are moving up and down in an elevator because of the movement of tiny crystals in the
    a. tendons
    b. outer ear
    c. otolith organs
    d. semicircular canals

12. Which of the following is a form of energy for which humans do NOT have sensory receptors?
    a. visible light
    b. radio waves
    c. sound waves
    d. thermal energy

13. Which of the following is NOT a perceptual constancy?
    a. size constancy
    b. color constancy
    c. shape constancy
    d. brightness constancy

14. Which of the following occurs when one object appears to block another object?
    a. overlap
    b. convergence
    c. texture gradient
    d. linear perspective

15. The Müller-Lyer illusion exists in cultures in which there are
    a. more men than women
    b. more women than men
    c. buildings with lots of curves
    d. buildings with lots of corners

16. Which of the following statements about perception is true?
    a. Perception must occur before sensation can occur.
    b. Most people perceive the world in exactly the same way.
    c. The first step in the process of perception is paying attention.
    d. The process of perception is not linked to cultural influences.

17. You find that you have to add 1 teaspoon of sugar to a cup of tea that already has 5 teaspoons of sugar in it to notice the difference in sweetness. If you have a cup of tea with 10 teaspoons of sugar in it, how many teaspoons would you have to add to notice the difference in sweetness at least half the time?
    a. 1
    b. 2
    c. 4
    d. 5

18. Allison opened her new jigsaw puzzle but soon realized that the puzzle pieces inside had nothing to do with the picture on the box. With no picture to follow, she realized she would have to use
    a. bottom-up processing
    b. top-down processing
    c. perceptual expectancy
    d. perceptual set

19. Which of the following describes a perception?
    a. tasting salt on your tongue
    b. seeing the color red in a painting
    c. feeling a sharp pain on your right arm
    d. recognizing your mother's voice on the phone
    e. brightness constancy

20. Which Gestalt principle is at work when a ventriloquist moves the dummy's mouth while doing the talking, making it seem like the dummy is talking?
    a. closure
    b. similarity
    c. continuity
    d. contiguity

CHAPTER 3 • Assessment

TEST YOURSELF

1. d
2. d
3. a
4. b
5. c
6. c
7. d
8. c
9. b
10. d
11. c
12. b
13. b
14. a
15. d
16. c
17. b
18. a
19. d
20. d

Ready for Testing

STUDENTS KNOW THEY ARE READY FOR TESTING IF THEY ARE ABLE TO . . .

- Define sensation and introduce some of the key concepts developed by researchers in the study of sensation.
- Explain in detail how our sense of sight and our sense of hearing work, and discuss some causes for impairments in these senses.
- Discuss the chemical senses of taste and smell and the lesser-known somesthetic senses of touch, body position, and balance.
- Describe our experience of perception, especially in relation to visual stimuli.

CHAPTER 3 • Concept Summary

MULTIMEDIA CONTENT AVAILABLE AT
www.mypsychlab.com

Map the Concepts on **mypsychlab.com**

Study and Review Flashcards on **mypsychlab.com**

STUDY TIPS

Making and Keeping a Schedule Schedules are indispensable tools for staying focused, getting things done, and not letting obligations or important tasks slip through the cracks. Suggest to students that they use a large monthly calendar for long-term items, such as test dates and project due dates. A separate weekly or even daily schedule should list every hour in the day. On this schedule, students should first block out time for those commitments that are inflexible, such as class time, work schedules, or practices. The time left each day is their free time, which must be used for meals, studying, errands, relaxation, and everything else. Explain that the more detailed and realistic a schedule is, the more useful it will be.

106 Chapter 3 Sensation and Perception

CHAPTER 3
Concept Summary: Sensation and Perception

Learning Objectives 7.1 7.2 pp. 78–80

Understand Sensation and Perception

- **sensation** process by which information from the outside world enters the brain
- **perception** process by which sensations are organized and interpreted in a meaningful fashion
- **sensory thresholds** describe the extent of our sensory abilities
- **habituation** the brain "ignores" unchanging information from the environment
- **sensory adaptation** sensory receptors become less responsive to unchanging stimuli

Learning Objective 7.3 pp. 80–81

Explore How the Senses Work

- forms of energy we can sense
  - light waves
  - sound waves
  - thermal energy
  - chemical substances

Learning Objective 7.4 pp. 81–85

Vision

- **light**
  - has psychological properties
    - brightness
    - color/hue
    - saturation
  - is a physical stimulus processed by the eye
- **seeing**
  - begins with the retinal receptor cells
    - rods
    - cones

Eye diagram labels: 1. Cornea, 2. Iris, 3. Pupil, 4. Lens, 5. Retina, 6. Fovea, 7. Optic nerve, 8. Blind spot (optic disc), Blood vessels, Light

Learning Objective 7.5 pp. 86–88

Hearing

- **sound**
  - has psychological properties
    - volume
    - frequency or pitch
    - timbre
  - is a physical stimulus processed by the ear

Ear diagrams:
- **entire ear** (a.): Pinna, Ear canal, Vestibular organ (semicircular canals), Auditory nerve, Eardrum, Cochlea
- **middle ear** (b.): Hammer, Anvil, Oval window, Stirrup, Eardrum, Middle ear
- **inner ear** (c.): Organ of Corti, Basilar membrane, Fluid in cochlea

106 CHAPTER 3

What Every Student Should Know About . . .

PREPARING EFFECTIVE ORAL PRESENTATIONS

Making a speech can be stressful. Here are some tips for overcoming nervousness: (1) *Breathe properly*. During the presentation, be sure to inhale completely and do not rush your breathing. (2) *Stay physically relaxed*. Most muscle tension occurs in the shoulders, neck, and arms. Before making the speech, practice recognizing what your muscles feel like when you are fully relaxed, so you can recognize muscle tension and make necessary adjustments. (3) *Eat carefully before the speech*. Avoid foods that are spicy, caffeinated, or carbonated. Water is the best liquid to drink before speaking. (4) *Maintain a positive attitude*. Your speech will be more effective if you can project enjoyment. (5) *Prepare thoroughly*. The more you can practice, the more comfortable you will be.

Learning Objective 7.6 pp. 88–90

- **taste/gustation**
  - made possible largely through the role of taste buds (taste receptor cells)
  - five basic tastes (receptor types)

Taste and Smell

- **smell/olfaction**
  - nose serves as a collection device
  - olfactory receptor cells are stimulated by molecules of chemical substances in the air

Taste pore, Taste hair, Receptor cell, Supporting cell, Outer layer of tongue, Nerve fiber

Olfactory bulb, Cilia of olfactory receptor cell, Olfactory epithelium

Learning Objective 7.7 pp. 91–92

Somesthetic Senses

- **skin senses** — having to do with touch, pressure, temperature, and pain
- **kinesthetic sense** — having to do with the location of body parts; processed by receptors in skin, joints, muscles, and tendons
- **vestibular sense** — having to do with movement and body position; processed by vestibular organs in the ear

Learning Objectives 8.1 8.2 8.3 8.4 8.5 8.6 pp. 94–101

Learn How We Perceive the World

- **perception** process by which information from the outside world enters the brain
  - **attention** allows us to focus on certain stimuli and ignore the rest
  - **perceptual constancies** help us interpret changes in size, shape and brightness
  - **Gestalt principles of perception** illustrate people's tendency to group objects together and perceive whole shapes
  - **depth cues** enable depth perception
  - **visual illusions** are stimuli that "fool" the eye into seeing something that does not correspond to reality
  - **perceptual set (perceptual expectancy)** our previous experiences and expectations influence our perceptions

SENSATION AND PERCEPTION 107

CHAPTER 3 • Concept Summary

STUDY TIPS

Study Groups Explain that study groups can be an excellent way to review information and study for tests. When deciding whom to include in their groups, students should consider which of their peers (1) have similar goals; (2) have comparable study habits, including the time of day they prefer to study (or are available) and their learning style; and (3) have a personality that will complement their own. Suggest that students avoid including friends in their study groups. This choice can lead to more socializing than studying. Students should also consider partners who will balance their own skills and knowledge, who are able to stay on track, and who are self-motivated and can motivate others to learn.

Comprehension Check

USING SENSES IN CAREERS

Ask students to think about the careers they hope to have one day. Which senses will be most important in these careers? For example, a chef, a plumber, and a dancer all make very different use of sensory information in their daily jobs. Have students discuss their possible careers and which senses they will use. Or, have them prepare short presentations using audiovisual resources.

CHAPTER 4 • Module 9

Launch the Chapter

CHAPTER GOALS AND LEARNING OBJECTIVES

Module 9 Sleep and Dreams

Understand the relationship between conscious and unconscious processes.

9.1 What are the different levels of consciousness?

9.2 What is the difference between explicit and implicit processing?

Explain how and why we sleep and dream.

9.3 What is the circadian rhythm, and how does it relate to sleep?

9.4 What theories exist about the functions of sleep?

9.5 How does the sleep cycle work?

9.6 What are the different types of sleep disorders?

9.7 Do dreams serve a function?

Module 10 Hypnosis and Drugs

Describe meditation and hypnosis.

10.1 How does meditation affect consciousness?

10.2 How does hypnosis work, and why is it controversial?

Understand the effects of psychoactive drugs.

10.3 What are the major categories of psychoactive drugs?

10.4 How do drugs function at the synaptic level?

10.5 What are the effects of psychoactive drugs?

10.6 How do cultural pressures and expectations influence drug use?

DIFFERENTIATED INSTRUCTION KEY

Look for these symbols to help you adjust steps in each lesson to meet your students' needs.

- **L1** Special Needs
- **L2** Basic
  - **ELL** English Language Learners
  - **LPR** Less Proficient Readers
- **L3** All Students
- **L4** Advanced Students

CHAPTER 4

Consciousness:
Sleep, Dreams, Hypnosis, and Drugs

A Scream in the Night

Imagine: It's a quiet night. Your 2-year-old son has been asleep for a few hours, and you and your spouse have just gone to bed. As you begin to drift off, you hear a bloodcurdling scream from the child's room. Both of you leap up and run to the nursery, where you find your son, bolt upright in bed, screaming at the top of his not-so-little lungs. You try to calm him down but soon realize that he is not even awake—he is terrified, yet asleep.

That is the experience Jenny and Jim had about once a month for the first few years of their son's life. Their son, Alex, suffered from *night terrors*, a relatively rare sleep disorder that occurs more often in children than adults and more often in boys than girls. It took Jenny and Jim several months and some research to find out that they could prevent most of these episodes by making sure that Alex always got a good night's sleep. One of the primary triggers of a night terror is a night or two of sleep loss just before the night of the episode.

CORRELATION TO APA STANDARDS FOR CHAPTER 4

IIC. CONSCIOUSNESS

IIC-1. The relationship between conscious . . . . pp. 110–111
and unconscious processes

IIC-2. Characteristics of sleep and theories . . . . pp. 112–120
that explain why we sleep and dream

MODULE 9 ▶ **SLEEP AND DREAMS**

MODULE 10 ▶ **HYPNOSIS AND DRUGS**

Why Study?

Consciousness

Consciousness, as humans experience it, is the key difference between humans and the lower animals. Waking, sleeping, dreaming, daydreaming, and other forms of conscious awareness make up the better part of the human experience. Drug use is on the rise, not only as recreation but also for many health and psychological conditions, including the treatment of children. It seems obvious that we need to understand how drugs affect our thinking and behavior in everyday life. In a very real sense, to understand consciousness is to understand what it means to be who we are.

CONSCIOUSNESS 109

CHAPTER 4 • Module 9

Teacher Prep

Consciousness is defined as a person's awareness of the world around him or her. Most waking hours are spent in waking consciousness, a state of awareness where thoughts and feelings are clear and organized. Altered states of consciousness are shifts in the quality or patterns of mental activity. The most common state of altered consciousness is sleep, but other examples include being under the influence of drugs or alcohol, daydreaming, or being hypnotized.

The sleep–wake cycle is a circadian rhythm, meaning one cycle takes 24 hours to complete, and is controlled by the hypothalamus. There are two theories about the functions of sleep: (1) the adaptive theory and (2) the restorative theory. When people go through the sleep cycle, they typically go through these stages: STAGE ONE (light sleep), STAGE TWO (sleep spindles), STAGES THREE and FOUR (deep sleep), and rapid eye movement (REM) sleep. As we sleep, we dream. Freud's method of dream analysis still plays a role in psychodynamic theory, but a more recent theory known as the activation-information-mode model has been developed to explain the function of dreams.

Meditation affects consciousness by refocusing attention to achieve a trance-like state to aid in relaxation. Hypnosis is a state of consciousness in which a person is susceptible to suggestion.

Psychoactive drugs affect consciousness by altering thinking, perception, and memory. There are four categories of psychoactive drugs: (1) stimulants, (2) depressants, (3) narcotics, and (4) hallucinogens. At the synaptic level, drugs either block or enhance the effects of neurotransmitters, and they may cause physical addiction and psychological dependence. Drug use is influenced by cultural pressures and expectations.

SCHEDULING

1 Period = 50 min. 1 Block = 90 min.	Semester Course (18 weeks/90 days) Periods/Blocks		Full-Year Course (36 weeks/180 days) Period/Blocks	
Module 9	2.5	1.25	5	2.5
Module 10	2.5	1.25	5	2.5
Total Days for Chapter	5	2.5	10	5

Chapter 4 Consciousness **109**

CHAPTER 4 • Module 9

Focus

RESOURCES

For this module, consult the appropriate sections of the Teacher's Manual, Test Bank, and PowerPoint slides, all found on the Teacher's Resource DVD, and the interactive study tools for students on MyPsychLab.

BEFORE CLASS

Students should read the section for homework before coming to class.

BELLRINGER

On the board, write the definition of consciousness. Below, create two columns. In the first column, write "waking consciousness" and write the definition, leaving space to add examples later. Do the same for "altered state." Ask students to think of an example for each state and write them down, with a brief description. Ask students to share their examples with the class. As they participate, ask the class to categorize the examples as "waking" or "altered state" and note the examples briefly on the board in the appropriate column.

Teach

COVER THE MODULE

9.1 What are the different levels of consciousness?

- *Consciousness*: awareness of everything going on around you and inside your own head, used to organize behavior
- *Waking consciousness*: feelings and sensations are clear and organized; the person feels alert
- *Altered state of consciousness*: a shift in the quality or pattern of mental activity as compared to waking consciousness

110 Chapter 4 Consciousness

Module 9
Sleep and Dreams

Module Goals

Understand the relationship between conscious and unconscious processes.

Explain how and why we sleep and dream.

Learning Objectives

9.1 What are the different levels of consciousness?
9.2 What is the difference between explicit and implicit processing?
9.3 What is the circadian rhythm, and how does it relate to sleep?
9.4 What theories exist about the functions of sleep?
9.5 How does the sleep cycle work?
9.6 What are the different types of sleep disorders?
9.7 Do dreams serve a function?

What exactly is meant by the term *consciousness*? ▶ I've heard it a lot, but I'm not sure that I know everything it means.

consciousness a person's awareness of everything that is going on around him or her at any given moment, which is used to organize behavior.

waking consciousness state in which thoughts, feelings, and sensations are clear, organized, and the person feels alert.

altered state of consciousness state in which there is a shift in the quality or pattern of mental activity as compared to waking consciousness.

Understand the Relationship Between Conscious and Unconscious Processes

9.1 What are the different levels of consciousness?

What exactly is meant by the term consciousness? *I've heard it a lot, but I'm not sure that I know everything it means.*

Consciousness is one of those terms that most people think they understand until someone asks them to define it. But if you are sitting there trying to define it now, don't worry if you have trouble coming up with a definition that satisfies you. Various scientists, psychologists, neuroscientists, philosophers, and even computer scientists have tried to define consciousness, so there are several definitions.

For our purposes, a useful definition of consciousness might be the following: **Consciousness** is your awareness of everything that is going on around you and inside your own head at any given moment, waking or sleeping, which you use to organize your behavior (Farthing, 1992), including thoughts, sensations, and feelings. Much of people's time awake is spent in a state called **waking consciousness** in which their thoughts, feelings, and sensations are clear and organized, and they feel alert. But there are many times in daily activities and in life when people experience states of consciousness that differ from this organized waking state. These variations in consciousness are called altered states of consciousness.

An **altered state of consciousness** occurs when there is a shift in the quality or pattern of your mental activity (Tart, 1986). When your mental activity drifts away from normal, waking consciousness in some way, your thoughts may become fuzzy and disorganized and you may feel less alert, or your thoughts may take bizarre turns, as they so often do in dreams. You may also

110 CHAPTER 4

Terms

• consciousness • waking consciousness • altered state of consciousness • circadian rhythm • microsleeps • sleep deprivation • adaptive theory • restorative theory • rapid eye movement (REM) • non-REM sleep (NREM) • alpha waves • theta waves • delta waves • REM paralysis • REM rebound • sleepwalking • nightmares • REM behavior disorder • night terrors • insomnia • sleep apnea • narcolepsy • activation-synthesis hypothesis • activation-information-mode model (AIM) divide your conscious awareness, as when you drive to work or school and then wonder how you got there—one level of conscious awareness was driving, while the other was thinking about the day ahead, perhaps. This altered state of divided consciousness can be a dangerous thing, as many people who try to drive and talk or text on a cell phone at the same time have discovered. Driving and carrying on a conversation on a phone are both processes that demand focused attention, and it is simply not possible to do both at once in a safe and efficient manner. Studies have shown that driving while talking on a cell phone, even a hands-free phone, puts a person at the same degree of risk as driving under the influence of alcohol (Alm & Nilsson, 1995; Briem & Hedman, 1995; Strayer & Drews, 2007; Strayer & Johnston, 2001; Strayer et al., 2006).

There are many other forms of altered states of consciousness: being under the influence of certain drugs, daydreaming, being hypnotized, or achieving a meditative state. But the most common altered state people experience is the one in which they spend about a third of their lives on a nightly basis—sleep.

9.2 What is the difference between explicit and implicit processing?

Are you consciously aware of every action you take in your daily life? Consider the difference between tasks that require careful thought and attention—such as presenting a report in class—and the many smaller, automatic actions that you perform in the course of a day, such as walking from place to place.

If you were to present a report in class, you would likely be consciously aware of your thought process, actions, and decisions. You would carefully consider what to say, or perhaps read from pre-written notes, and you would prepare yourself to respond to questions from the teacher or classmates. In this example, you are engaging in *explicit processing* (or *effortful processing*)—processing that is conscious. You are aware of your thought process and are focusing your full attention on the task at hand.

Walking, on the other hand, is more of an automatic action that requires little or no conscious awareness. You do not need to carefully consider your actions of putting one foot in front of the other. It is an automatic process that does not require your full focus and attention. This is an example of *implicit processing* (or *automatic processing*)—processing that happens without conscious awareness. In many cases, you can perform an action before you even become aware of it. For example, if you were asked to push a button every time you heard a beeping sound, you could respond nearly instantly—before you became conscious that you had pushed the button.

Explain How and Why We Sleep and Dream

Sleep was once referred to as "the gentle tyrant" (Webb, 1992). People can try to stay awake, and sometimes they may go for a while without sleep, but eventually they *must* sleep. One reason for this fact is that sleep is one of the human body's *biological rhythms*, natural cycles of activity that the body must go through. Many biological rhythms take place on a daily basis, like the rise and fall of blood pressure and body temperature or the production of certain body chemicals (Moore-Ede et al., 1982). The most obvious of these is the sleep–wake cycle (Baehr et al., 2000).

CHAPTER 4 • Module 9

COVER THE MODULE

9.2 What is the difference between explicit and implicit processing?

- Explicit processing: processing that is conscious in which a person is aware of his or her thought process and is focusing full attention on the task.
- Implicit processing: the process of performing an action automatically, requiring little or no conscious awareness.

INTRODUCTION TO SLEEP AND DREAMS

Write the following three questions on the board: "(1) Do people HAVE to sleep, and why or why not? (2) Why do people dream? (3) What happens if people don't sleep?"

Divide students into groups by counting by 3s. All the group 1 students will answer question 1, and so on. For 1 minute, have students silently write answers to their questions. Then break them into their respective groups to share their answers. Have them work to come up with a group-consensus answer to their question and then share it with the class.

Class Demonstration (Kinesthetic)

DEBATE: CONSCIOUSNESS

Purpose: Students debate the nature and purpose of consciousness.

Time: 20 minutes

Description: Write the following on the board: "Consciousness is like a steamwhistle, deriving from the locomotive's engine and revealing something about its processes but ultimately contributing nothing to the moving train."—Thomas Huxley

Explain that Thomas Huxley was a famous 19th-century scientist. Clarify the meaning of the quote with the class, making sure they understand the analogy between the train and the human brain. Then divide the class in half. One team will *agree*, and the other will *disagree*. Have students sit in their groups and brainstorm reasons, discussions, and support for their respective sides. Next, ask students to line up in their two teams, facing each other. Give the first student in one of the teams a soft ball. Explain the rules for the debate: When holding the ball, the student speaks by saying "I agree/disagree with this quote because. . . ." Then the student throws the ball to the student facing him or her on the other side. That student then counters. Keep score to determine the side that wins each "argument," according to the quality of the statements.

CHAPTER 4 • Module 9

COVER THE MODULE

9.3 What is the circadian rhythm, and how does it relate to sleep?

- A *circadian rhythm* is the sleep–wake cycle over a 24-hour period.
- The sleep–wake cycle is controlled by the hypothalamus.

LINK *to Chapter Two: The Biological Perspective, pp. 57–59.*

- People can live without sleep for a while but cannot do without it altogether.
- When unable to sleep, people slip into *microsleep* in which they fall asleep for only a few seconds.
- *Sleep deprivation* is a significant loss of sleep; many people do not realize they have it, but it can become a serious problem.

LINK *to Chapter Thirteen: Psychological Disorders, pp. 428–429.*

L1 DIFFERENTIATED INSTRUCTION

Special Needs Present all ideas orally and visually, and when possible, incorporate tactile and kinesthetic experiences as well.

UNDERSTANDING VISUALS

Ask: **Looking at Figure 9.1, how many more hours of REM sleep do you need, compared to your parents?** *(A typical high school student is 16 years old and needs 10 hours of REM sleep, compared to a 50-year-old parent, who needs about 6 hours.)*

112 Chapter 4 Consciousness

---

circadian rhythm a cycle of bodily rhythm that occurs over a 24-hour period.

microsleeps brief sidesteps into sleep lasting only a few seconds.

sleep deprivation any significant loss of sleep, resulting in problems in concentration and irritability.

9.3 What is the circadian rhythm, and how does it relate to sleep?

The sleep–wake cycle is a **circadian rhythm**. The term actually comes from two Latin words, *circa* ("about") and *diem* ("day"). So a circadian rhythm is a cycle that takes "about a day" to complete.

For most people, this means that they will experience several hours of sleep at least once during every 24-hour period. The sleep–wake cycle is ultimately controlled by the brain, specifically by an area within the *hypothalamus*, the tiny section of the brain that influences the glandular system. **LINK** *to Chapter Two: The Biological Perspective, pp. 57–59.*

Although people can do without sleep for a while, they cannot do without it altogether. In one experiment, rats were placed on moving treadmills over water. They couldn't sleep normally because they would then fall into the water and be awakened, but they did drift repeatedly into **microsleeps**, or brief sidesteps into sleep lasting only seconds (Goleman, 1982; Konowal et al., 1999). People can have microsleeps, too, and if this happens while they are driving a car or a truck, it's obviously bad news (Dinges, 1995; Lyznicki et al., 1998; Thomas et al., 1998). Microsleep periods are no doubt responsible for a lot of car accidents that occur when drivers have had very little sleep.

What will missing out on one night's sleep do to a person? For most people, a missed night of sleep will result in concentration problems and the inability to do simple tasks that normally would take no thought at all, such as loading a DVD into a player. More complex tasks, such as math problems, suffer less than these simple tasks (Chee & Choo, 2004; Lim et al., 2007).

Even so, **sleep deprivation**, or loss of sleep, is a serious problem, which many people have without realizing it. People stay up too late at night during the week, get up to go to work or school before they've really rested, and then try to pay off the "sleep debt" on the weekend. All of that disrupts the normal sleep–wake cycle and isn't good for anyone's health. Students, for example, may stay up all night to study for an important test the next day. In doing so, they will lose more information than they gain, as a good night's sleep is important for memory consolidation (Stickgold et al., 2000–2001) and the ability to think well (Fenn et al., 2003). Some typical symptoms of sleep deprivation include trembling hands, inattention, staring off into space, droopy eyelids, and general discomfort (Naitoh et al., 1989), as well as emotional symptoms such as irritability and even depression. **LINK** *to Chapter Thirteen: Psychological Disorders, pp. 428–429.*

FIGURE 9.1 Sleep Patterns of Infants and Adults

Infants need far more sleep than older children and adults. Both REM sleep and NREM sleep decrease dramatically in the first 10 years of life, with the greatest decrease in REM sleep. Nearly 50 percent of an infant's sleep is REM, compared to only about 20 percent for a normal, healthy adult. (Roffwarg, 1966)

112 CHAPTER 4

Class Demonstration

CIRCADIAN RHYTHMS

Purpose: Students examine their own circadian rhythms.

Time: 15 minutes

Description: On the board, write the following questions: "(1) If you have a difficult 1-hour workout to complete, at what time would you choose to do it? (2) If you have a paper to write, would you rather get up early or stay up late to write it? (3) Ideally, what time would you like to get up in the morning? Go to bed at night? (4) How alert are you when you first get up?" Divide the class into two teams, *A* and *B*. Pair *A*'s with *B*'s to interview each other. Through the interview, students determine if they are "morning-dominant" versus "night-dominant" people. Next, have them rejoin their teams, share what they learned, and discuss how their circadian rhythms affect their lives, education, and employment.

9.4 What theories exist about the functions of sleep?

Okay, so we obviously need to sleep. But what does it do for us? Why do we have to sleep at all?

According to the **adaptive theory** of why organisms sleep, sleep is a product of evolution (Webb, 1992). Animals and humans evolved different sleep patterns to avoid predators during the predators' normal hunting times, which are generally at night. If a prey animal (one the predator will eat) is out and about at night, it is likely to be eaten. If instead it is in a safe place sleeping and conserving energy, it remains safe.

The other major theory of why organisms sleep is called **restorative theory**, which states that sleep is necessary to the physical health of the body. During sleep, chemicals that were used up during the day's activities are replenished and cellular damage is repaired (Adam, 1980; Moldofsky, 1995). There is evidence that most bodily growth and repair occur during the deepest stages of sleep.

Which of these theories is correct? The answer is that both are probably needed to understand why sleep occurs the way it does. Adaptive theory explains why people sleep *when* they do, and restorative theory explains why people *need* to sleep.

How much sleep is enough sleep? The answer varies from person to person because of each person's age and possibly inherited sleep needs (Feroah et al., 2004), but most adults need about 7 to 9 hours of sleep each 24-hour period in order to function well. (See Figure 9.1.) Some people are short sleepers, needing only 4 or 5 hours, whereas others are long sleepers and need more than 9 hours of sleep (McCann & Stewin, 1988).

9.5 How does the sleep cycle work?

So, are there different kinds of sleep? Do you go from being awake to being asleep and dreaming—is it instant?

There are actually two kinds of sleep: **REM (rapid eye movement)** and **non-REM (NREM) sleep**. REM sleep is a relatively active type of sleep when most of a person's dreaming takes place, whereas non-REM sleep is a much deeper, more restful kind of sleep. In REM sleep, the voluntary muscles are inhibited, meaning that the person in REM sleep moves very little, whereas in non-REM sleep the person's body is free to move around. There are also several different stages of sleep that people go through each night in which REM sleep and non-REM sleep occur. A machine called an electroencephalograph (EEG) allows scientists to record brain wave activity as a person passes through the various stages of sleep and to determine what type of sleep the person has entered (Aserinsky & Kleitman, 1953). Figure 9.2 on page 114 illustrates brain waves of different stages of consciousness.

A person who is wide awake and mentally active will show a brain wave pattern on the EEG called *beta waves*. Beta waves are very small and very fast. As the person relaxes and gets drowsy, slightly larger and slower **alpha waves** appear. The alpha waves are eventually replaced by even slower and larger **theta waves**, which indicate Stage One sleep. **Delta waves**, the slowest and largest waves, replace theta waves during the deepest cycle of sleep.

Non-REM Stage One: Light Sleep As theta wave activity increases and alpha wave activity fades away, people are said to be entering Stage One sleep, or light sleep. If people are awakened at this point, they will probably not believe that they were actually asleep. In this state between sleep and wake-

◄ *Okay, so we obviously need to sleep. But what does it do for us? Why do we have to sleep at all?*

◄ *So, are there different kinds of sleep? Do you go from being awake to being asleep and dreaming— is it instant?*

adaptive theory theory of sleep proposing that animals and humans evolved sleep patterns to avoid predators by sleeping when predators are most active.

restorative theory theory of sleep proposing that sleep is necessary to the physical health of the body and serves to replenish chemicals and repair cellular damage.

rapid eye movement (REM) stage of sleep in which the eyes move rapidly under the eyelids and the person is typically experiencing a dream.

non-REM (NREM) sleep any of the stages of sleep that do not include REM.

alpha waves brain waves that indicate a state of relaxation or light sleep.

theta waves brain waves indicating the early stages of sleep.

delta waves long, slow waves that indicate the deepest stage of sleep.

CONSCIOUSNESS: SLEEP, DREAMS, HYPNOSIS, AND DRUGS 113

Explore

SLEEP STUDIES ONLINE

The following website provides a video for students to watch, showing a patient's experience with a sleep study: **www.sleepmed.md/page/2245**

CHAPTER 4 • Module 9

COVER THE MODULE

9.4 What theories exist about the function of sleep?

- The *adaptive theory*: Humans and animals evolved sleep patterns to avoid predators at normal hunting times.
- The *restorative theory*: Sleep is necessary to the physical health of the body.
- The average person needs about 7 to 9 hours of sleep, but each person's age and inherited sleep needs can vary this number.

DISCUSS THE STUDENT VOICE QUESTION

The adaptive theory gives an explanation for why we sleep at night. The restorative theory proposes that we sleep so our body can restore chemicals used during the day and so cellular damage can be repaired. During the deepest stages of sleep, evidence has shown that most bodily repair and growth occur.

COVER THE MODULE

9.5 How does the sleep cycle work?

- Two kinds of sleep:
  - *REM (rapid eye movement)*: The eyes move rapidly, the person is experiencing a dream, and voluntary muscles are inhibited.
  - *Non-REM (NREM)*: a deeper, more restful sleep in which muscles are not inhibited
- *Beta waves*: brain waves shown when a person is alert and awake
- *Alpha waves*: occur with drowsiness, larger and slower than beta waves
- *Theta waves*: larger and slower than alpha; indicate Stage One sleep
- *Delta waves*: slowest and largest waves; indicate the deepest level of sleep

DISCUSS THE STUDENT VOICE QUESTION

There are four stages of NREM sleep and one stage of REM. People move through these stages gradually, from Stages One through Four, then back to Stage One again. At that point, REM sleep occurs, and then the cycle starts over. REM sleep occurs about every 90 minutes through the night. People dream throughout all stages, but dreams during REM are often longer and more detailed.

CHAPTER 4 • Module 9

COVER THE MODULE (continued)
- NREM Sleep Stage One: light sleep
  - Occurs as theta waves increase
  - Many people experience *hypnagogic images*, which are bits of what may become dreams but are usually flashes of light.
- NREM Sleep Stage Two: sleep spindles
  - Body temperatures drop as people drift to sleep and heart rate slows.
  - EEG shows *sleep spindles*, brief bursts of activity lasting a second or two.

FAST FACT
An EEG works by recording the electrical activity along the scalp that is produced by the firing of neurons on the brain. The activity is recorded through electrodes placed on the scalp that record the activity as graphs (wavy lines) on a computer or on paper.

UNDERSTANDING VISUALS
Ask: **What happens to the waves' appearance at the various sleep stages? How does this correspond to what you know about how the body and brain respond during a person's sleep cycle?** *(The waves' appearance becomes flatter and wider with every increasing sleep stage. This coincides with the slowing heart rate, lower body temperature, and slower breathing.)*

L2 ELL DIFFERENTIATED INSTRUCTION
English Language Learners Ask students to demonstrate their understanding by drawing upon different language skills: formal and informal writing assignments, posters, small group tasks, and oral presentations.

114 Chapter 4 Consciousness

FIGURE 9.2 Brain Waves of Different State of Conciousness
Our brains show different wave patterns depending on our state of conciousness. Notice how the brain waves are slower and longer when we are in a deeper state of sleep.

fulness, they may also experience vivid visual events called *hypnagogic images* (Mavromatis, 1987; Mavromatis & Richardson, 1984). These images are bits and pieces of what may eventually become dreams but are most often seen as flashes of light. Some people have very vivid images that seem realistic. Many researchers now believe that people's visions of ghostly visits, alien abductions, and near-death experiences may be most easily explained by these images (Moody & Perry, 1993).

Non-REM Stage Two: Sleep Spindles As people drift further into sleep, their body temperature continues to drop. Heart rate slows, breathing becomes more shallow and irregular, and the EEG will show the first signs of

114 CHAPTER 4

Explore

BRAIN WAVES: THEIR UNIQUE QUALITIES AND BENEFITS
Send students to www.brainwavesblog.com/beta-brain-waves-information/. This website has links to interesting articles on the five basic brain waves. Divide the class into five groups and assign each group one brain wave to read about. Have the groups write down five "fun facts" about their assigned brain wave to share with the class. When they return with their facts, create groups of five students, one from each "brain wave" group, to share the facts. Have each group vote on its favorite fact to share with the whole class.

sleep spindles, brief bursts of activity lasting only a second or two. Theta waves still predominate in this stage, but if people are awakened during this stage, they will be aware of having been asleep.

Non-REM Stage Three and Stage Four: Delta Waves Roll In
In the third stage of sleep, the delta waves—the slowest and largest waves—make their appearance. In Stage Three, delta waves make up only about 20 to 50 percent of the brain wave pattern.

Once delta waves account for more than 50 percent of total brain activity, the person is said to have entered Stage Four sleep, the deepest stage of sleep. It is during this stage that the body is at its lowest level of functioning. Eventually, the delta waves become the dominant brain activity for this stage of sleep. See Figure 9.3 to show movement through the sleep stages throughout one night.

People in deep sleep are very hard to awaken. If something does wake them, they may be very confused and disoriented at first. It is not unusual for people to wake up in this kind of disoriented state only to hear the crack of thunder and realize that a storm has come up. Children, who need deep sleep so that their bodies will grow, are even harder to wake up when in this state than are adults.

What Happens in REM Sleep?
After spending some time in Stage Four, the sleeping person will go back up through Stage Three, Stage Two, and then into a stage in which body temperature increases to near-waking levels, the eyes move rapidly under the eyelids, the heart beats much faster, and brain waves resemble beta waves—the kind of brain activity that usually signals wakefulness. The person is still asleep but in the stage known as REM sleep.

When a person in REM sleep is awakened, he or she almost always reports being in a dream state (Shafton, 1995). REM sleep is, therefore, associated with dreaming, and 90 percent of dreams actually take place in REM sleep. People do have dreams in the other non-REM (or NREM) stages, but REM dreams tend to be more vivid, more detailed, longer, and more bizarre than the dreams of NREM sleep. NREM dreams tend to be more like thoughts about daily occurrences and far shorter than REM dreams (Foulkes & Schmidt, 1983; Takeuchi et al., 2003). Fortunately, the body is unable to act upon these dreams under normal conditions because the voluntary muscles are paralyzed during REM sleep, a condition known as **REM paralysis**.

REM paralysis the inability of the voluntary muscles to move during REM sleep.

FIGURE 9.3 A Typical Night's Sleep
The graph shows the typical progression through the night of Stages 1–4 and REM sleep. Stages 1–4 are indicated on the *y*-axis, and REM stages are represented by the green curves on the graph. The REM periods occur about every 90 minutes through the night (Dement, 1974).

CONSCIOUSNESS: SLEEP, DREAMS, HYPNOSIS, AND DRUGS   115

CHAPTER 4 • Module 9

COVER THE MODULE *(continued)*

- NREM Sleep Stages Three and Four: delta waves roll in
  - In Stage Three, delta waves make up 20 to 50 percent of the brain wave pattern.
  - Once brain waves make up more than 50 percent of brain waves, the person has entered into Stage Four sleep.
  - During Stage Four, the body is at its lowest level of functioning.
- REM Sleep:
  - After completing Stage Four, a person will cycle backward through Stages Three, Two, and One, then into REM.
  - Body temperatures rise to near-waking levels, eyes move rapidly under eyelids, heart beats faster.
  - Voluntary muscles are paralyzed, known as *REM paralysis*.
  - Brain waves almost resemble beta waves.
  - Ninety percent of dreams occur during REM sleep.

FAST FACT
Ask: **When do you think the body performs most of its physical repairs?** *(The body performs most of its physical repairs during Stages Three and Four, or "deep sleep." During REM sleep, the body restores the mind. REM sleep consolidates information taken in during the day, forms neural connections to strengthen memory, and replenishes the chemicals serotonin and dopamine, which contribute to happy moods.)*

Class Demonstration (Kinesthetic)

THINK FAST
Print images of brain waves from the various sleep stages from images online: (1) one image of awake, alert beta; (2) one image of awake, relaxed alpha; (3) two images of Sleep Stage One: theta; (4) two images of Sleep Stage Two: sleep spindles; (5) two images of Sleep Stage Three: deep NREM delta and theta; (6) two images of Sleep Stage Four: deep NREM: delta; and (7) one image of REM. Copy two sets of these images and cut them up into individual images if necessary. Place sets in envelopes labeled 1 and 2.

Divide the class into teams of 10 students. Hand the students on each team an image from the envelopes for their teams. Do not let them see the images until you say "Go." When you say "Go," the students must look at their images and line themselves up in the correct order of how the brain waves would appear during a normal sleep cycle. The team that lines up correctly first wins.

Module 9 Sleep and Dreams   115

CHAPTER 4 • Module 9

COVER THE MODULE *(continued)*

- Need for NREM vs. REM sleep
  - NREM helps the body recover from physical activity.
  - REM sleep helps recovery from emotional stress.
  - *REM rebound*: if a person is deprived of REM sleep the night before, the following night he or she will experience greater amounts of REM sleep.

MULTIMEDIA CONTENT AVAILABLE AT
www.mypsychlab.com

Simulate the stages of sleep on mypsychlab.com

COVER THE MODULE

9.6 What are the different types of sleep disorders?

- *Sleepwalking,* or *somnambulism*
  - Is partially due to heredity
  - Occurs in 20 percent of the population, more common in boys, and more frequently in childhood
  - Occurs during Stages Three and Four
- *Nightmares*: bad dreams
  - Occur more frequently in children due to their extra time in REM sleep
  - More dangerous than sleepwalking because of *REM behavior disorder* in which nightmares can be acted out
- *Night terrors*: a state of panic during Stage Four sleep
  - More common in children and disappears as child ages

116 Chapter 4 Consciousness

REM rebound increased amounts of REM sleep after being deprived of REM sleep on earlier nights.

Simulate the stages of sleep on mypsychlab.com

▶ Why do some people sleepwalk?

▲ Nightmares of being chased by a monster or similar frightening creature are common, especially in childhood.

116 CHAPTER 4

The Need for REM Sleep Why two kinds of sleep? And why would REM sleep ever be considered restful when the body is almost awake and the brain is so active? REM sleep seems to serve a different purpose than does NREM, or deep sleep. After a very physically demanding day, people tend to spend more time in NREM deep sleep than is usual. But an emotionally stressful day leads to increased time in REM sleep (Horne & Staff, 1983). Perhaps the dreams people have in REM sleep are a way of dealing with the stresses and tensions of the day, whereas physical activity would demand more time for recovery of the body in NREM sleep. Also, if deprived of REM sleep (as would occur with the use of sleeping pills or other depressant drugs), a person will experience greatly increased amounts of REM sleep the next night, a phenomenon called **REM rebound** (Vogel, 1975, 1993).

Simulate on mypsychlab.com

9.6 What are the different types of sleep disorders?

Why do some people sleepwalk?
Real **sleepwalking**, or **somnambulism**, typically occurs during Stages Three and Four sleep. It occurs in about 20 percent of the population and is at least partially due to heredity (Abe et al., 1984; Kales et al., 1980). It is much more common in childhood and also occurs more frequently in boys than in girls. Although the old movies portray sleepwalkers as zombie-like with arms outstretched, in reality, a sleepwalker may do nothing more than sit up in bed. But other sleepwalking episodes may involve walking around the house, looking in the refrigerator or even eating, or getting into the car. Sleepwalking actions are usually routine, but some sleepwalkers do things (like rearranging furniture) that they wouldn't normally do if they were awake.

Alex, the child whose night terrors were described in the opening story of this chapter, also suffered from sleepwalking. As many somnambulists do, he grew out of this behavior by the time he became an adolescent. His parents also found that preventing sleep loss made sleepwalking a rare occurrence. When Alex did have an episode, he never recalled it the next day. This lack of memory is typical of most sleepwalking episodes. The only real precaution that the families of people who sleepwalk should take is to clear their floors of obstacles and to put hard-to-reach locks on the doors.

Being able to act out one's dreams, especially nightmares, is a far more dangerous proposition than sleepwalking. **Nightmares** are bad dreams, and some nightmares can be utterly terrifying. Children tend to have more nightmares than adults do because they spend more of their sleep in the REM state, as discussed earlier. As they age, they have fewer nightmares because they have less opportunity to have them. But some people still suffer from nightmares as adults.

Some people have a rare disorder in which they are able to thrash around and even get up and act out nightmares. This disorder is called **REM behavior disorder**, and it is a fairly serious condition (Shafton, 1995). Usually seen in men over age 60, it can also happen in younger men and in women.

Night terrors are a rare disorder, although one that is more likely in children and also likely to disappear as the child grows older (Garland & Smith, 1991). A night terror is essentially a state of panic experienced while sound asleep, usually during Stage Four sleep. People may sit up, scream, run around the room, or flail at some unseen attacker. It is not uncommon for people experiencing night terrors to sweat profusely and feel unable to breathe.

Explore

INVESTIGATING SLEEP DISORDERS

Send students to www.webmd.com/sleep-disorders/default.htm. WebMd.com has a comprehensive site for sleep disorders. There are many activities and resources available for enrichment on this topic, including videos, quizzes for self-assessment, and articles about how to improve sleep. Have students select an element of the site to investigate and then write a short report about what they have found.

Psychology in the News

Murder While Sleepwalking

According to a compilation of information by Dr. Lawrence Martin, associate professor at Case Western Reserve University and specialist in sleep medicine, at least 20 cases of "murder while sleepwalking" have been recorded. The term *sleepwalking* as used in these cases most likely refers to the very real condition called REM behavior disorder rather than ordinary sleepwalking. Use of this disorder as a defense in a murder trial has sometimes been successful. Here are short descriptions of three cases and their outcomes.

Case One: In 1987, Kenneth Parks, a 23-year-old man from Toronto, Canada, got up early in the morning, got in his car, and drove 23 kilometers (about 14 miles) to the home of his wife's parents. He killed his mother-in-law, attacked his father-in-law, and then drove to the police. Once there, he told them that he thought he had killed some people. Parks had no motive and had been suffering from severe insomnia. He did have a history of sleepwalking; and his defense team, which included sleep experts and psychiatrists, concluded that he was indeed unaware of his actions at the time of the crime. He was acquitted (Denno, 2002; Martin, 2004).

Case Two: Scott Falater, 43 years old, was accused of murdering his wife in 1997. Falater had performed a series of very deliberate and time-consuming actions in cleaning up after the murder. But Falater claimed to have been sleepwalking during all of these actions. Although sleep experts for the defense stated that Falater's story was possible, the prosecution pointed to marital troubles as motive. Most damaging to his case was the witness who stated that 3 weeks before the murder, Falater had been discussing the case of Kenneth Parks and Parks's acquittal for murder based on a sleepwalking defense. The jury found Falater guilty of murder in the first degree and he was given a life sentence (Martin, 2004; Tresniowski, 1999).

Case Three: In 2003, Jules Lowe of Manchester, England, attacked and killed his 82-year-old father while sleepwalking. Lowe had a history of sleepwalking, was under great stress, and had no motive to kill his father. Sleep expert Dr. Irshaad Ebrahim testified that tests showed Lowe to have been sleepwalking at the time of the attack. In 2005, Lowe was acquitted (Smith-Spark, 2005).

▲ Scott Falater testifies at his trial for the murder of his wife, which he claims he committed while he was sleepwalking.

Questions for Further Discussion

1. Should sleepwalking be a valid defense for a crime as serious as murder? What about other kinds of crimes?
2. What kind of evidence should be required to convince a jury that a crime was committed while sleepwalking?

Considering that people suffering a night terror episode are in a deep stage of sleep and breathing shallowly, one can understand why breathing would seem difficult when they are suddenly active. Most people do not remember what happened during a night terror episode, although a few people can remember vividly the images and terror they experienced.

sleepwalking (somnambulism) an episode, occurring during Stages Three and Four sleep, of moving around or walking around in one's sleep.

nightmares bad dreams occurring during REM sleep.

REM behavior disorder a rare disorder in which the mechanism that blocks the movement of the voluntary muscles fails, allowing the person to thrash around and even get up and act out nightmares.

night terrors relatively rare disorder in which the person experiences extreme fear and screams or runs around during deep sleep without waking fully.

CONSCIOUSNESS: SLEEP, DREAMS, HYPNOSIS, AND DRUGS 117

CHAPTER 4 • Module 9

PSYCHOLOGY IN THE NEWS

1. Possible points to discuss:
   - *Automism* is the word used for the sleepwalking defense, which states that the person made only physical movements and did not intend to commit the crime.
   - If a person is asleep, can he or she be held responsible for actions taken while in an altered state of consciousness?
   - How does motive factor in? Even if a person were to briefly think about harming someone but not act on the thought, but then do so while asleep, does this make him or her any more or less guilty?
   - If this is a valid defense, how are those who commit these crimes different from other murderers? Should they be treated differently?

2. For most cases where acquittal was the verdict, the defense:
   - Used the insanity defense, claiming defendant was "not in his right mind" at the time of the crime.
   - Established a history of sleepwalking while presenting proof that the defendant had no prior "disease of the mind."
   - Provided evidence that the defendant had no memory of the crime and/or no prior motive.

EXTEND THE DISCUSSION

Ask students if they believe a person in this situation should go free, go to a mental hospital, or go to jail. Students should provide an explanation for their decision.

Class Demonstration

THE SLEEPWALKING DEFENSE

Have students go online to explore other cases where the sleepwalking defense was used. Ask them to present their cases to the class in the form of a "case brief." Then have them relate the cases to their discussions from above by explaining (1) what defense was used; (2) whether the defendant was acquitted; and (3) whether they agree or disagree with the jury's verdict.

A helpful website for research is: http://health.usnews.com/health-news/family-health/sleep/articles/2009/05/08/7-criminal-cases-that-invoked-the-sleepwalking-defense

Module 9 Sleep and Dreams 117

CHAPTER 4 • Module 9

COVER THE MODULE (continued)

- Difference between nightmares and night terrors: nightmares occur during REM sleep, and night terrors occur during NREM, so people can move while experiencing them
- *Insomnia*: the inability to get to sleep, stay asleep, or get good-quality sleep
  - Causes are psychological (e.g., worrying or anxiety) and physiological (e.g., pain or too much caffeine).
- *Sleep apnea*: occurs during snoring; a person stops breathing for nearly 30 seconds or more
  - Causes excessive sleepiness during the day and heart problems
- *Narcolepsy*: a person falls immediately into REM sleep during the day without warning, especially when the person experiences strong emotions.

DISCUSS THE STUDENT VOICE QUESTION

There are two main differences between a nightmare and a night terror. First, nightmares are remembered immediately upon waking, but a person experiencing a night terror does not remember anything. Second, since a night terror occurs during NREM sleep, people can move around, making this a more dangerous experience. Nightmares usually occur during REM sleep, when people typically cannot move.

> But that sounds like the description of a nightmare—what's the difference?

But that sounds like the description of a nightmare—what's the difference?

There are some very real differences between night terrors and nightmares. Nightmares are usually vividly remembered immediately upon waking. A person who has had a nightmare, unlike a person experiencing a night terror, will actually be able to come awake and immediately talk about the bad dream. Perhaps the most telling difference is that nightmares occur during REM sleep rather than deep non-REM sleep, which means that people don't move around in a nightmare as they do in a night terror experience.

Most people think that **insomnia** is the inability to sleep. Although that is the literal meaning of the term, in reality, insomnia is defined as the inability to get to sleep, stay asleep, or get a good quality of sleep (Kryger, Lavie, & Rosen, 1999). There are many causes of insomnia, both psychological and physiological. Some of the psychological causes are worrying, trying too hard to sleep, or having anxiety. Some of the physiological causes are too much caffeine, indigestion, or aches and pains.

There are several steps people can take to help with sleep. Obvious ones are taking no caffeinated drinks or foods that cause indigestion before bedtime, taking medication for pain, and dealing with anxieties in the daytime rather than facing them at night. That last bit of advice is easy to say but not always easy to do. Here are some other helpful hints (Kupfer & Reynolds, 1997):

1. Go to bed only when you are sleepy.
2. Use your bed only for sleep, not studying nor watching television.
3. Don't try too hard to get to sleep, and especially do not look at the clock and calculate how much sleep you aren't getting.
4. Keep to a regular schedule. Go to bed at the same time and get up at the same time.

Snoring is fairly common, occurring when the breathing passages (nose and throat) get blocked. Most people snore only when they have a cold or some other occasional problem, but some people snore every night, sometimes quite loudly. It is this type of snoring that is often associated with a condition called **sleep apnea**, in which the person stops breathing for nearly half a minute or more. When breathing stops, there will be a sudden silence, followed shortly by a gasping sound as the person struggles to get air into the lungs. Many people do not wake up while this is happening, but they do not get a good, restful night's sleep because of the apnea.

Apnea is a serious problem. Not only does it disturb nightly sleep, making the person excessively sleepy in the daytime, but it also can cause heart problems (Flemons, 2002). If a person suspects the presence of apnea, a visit to a physician is the first step in identifying the disorder and deciding on a treatment. With mild apnea, treatment may be a device worn on the nose at night to open the nostrils and prevent blockage. Other treatments include losing excess weight and using sprays designed to shrink the tissues lining the throat.

Some very young infants also experience a kind of apnea due to immaturity of the brain stem. These infants are typically placed on monitors that sound an alarm when breathing stops, allowing caregivers to help the infant begin breathing again.

A disorder affecting one in every 2,000 persons, **narcolepsy** is a kind of "sleep seizure." In narcolepsy, the person may slip suddenly into REM sleep during the day (especially when the person experiences strong emotions). Another symptom is excessive daytime sleepiness that results in the person falling asleep throughout the day at inappropriate times and in inappropriate places

insomnia the inability to get to sleep, stay asleep, or get a good quality of sleep.

sleep apnea disorder in which the person stops breathing for nearly half a minute or more.

narcolepsy sleep disorder in which a person falls immediately into REM sleep during the day without warning.

Critical Thinking

MAKE A CONNECTION

Purpose: Help students personally connect to the topic and find examples.

Time: 10 minutes

Description: Ask students to spend a few minutes writing answers to the following questions: "(1) Have you or someone you know experienced any of the sleep disorders discussed? (2) Describe the experience. (3) How, if at all, did these disorders affect his or her everyday life? (4) Were these disorders treated? (5) What was the outcome?" If students say they have no experiences to write about, ask that they imagine and describe what a person suffering from one of these disorders may experience. Volunteers can share their responses with the class.

(Overeem et al., 2001). These sleep attacks may occur many times and without warning, making the operation of a car or other machinery very dangerous for the *narcoleptic* (person who suffers from narcolepsy). Treatments of narcolepsy include medications like stimulants and behavioral changes like avoiding substances that interfere with sleep when it is needed. Table 9.1 has a more detailed list of known sleep disorders. **Listen** on **mypsychlab.com**

Listen to the Psychology in the News podcast about sleep deprivation and obesity on **mypsychlab.com**

Table 9.1 Sleep Disorders

NAME OF DISORDER	PRIMARY SYMPTOMS
Somnambulism	Sitting, walking, or performing complex behavior while asleep
Night terrors	Extreme fear, agitation, screaming while asleep
Hypersomnia	Excessive daytime sleepiness
Nocturnal leg cramps	Painful cramps in calf or foot muscles
Restless leg syndrome	Uncomfortable feeling in legs causing movement and loss of sleep
Enuresis	Urinating while asleep in bed
Narcolepsy	Slipping into REM sleep during the day
Sleep apnea	Breathing momentarily stops during sleep

9.7 Do dreams serve a function?

Because we spend a large part of our lives asleep, most of us are very familiar with one of sleep's most notable features: dreaming. Dreams have long been a source of curiosity. People of ancient times tried to find meaning in dreams. Some saw dreams as prophecy, some as messages from the spirits. But the real inquiry into the process of dreaming began with the publication of Freud's *The Interpretation of Dreams* (1900).

Freud's Interpretation: Dreams as Wish Fulfillment Sigmund Freud (1856–1939) believed that the problems of his patients stemmed from conflicts and events that had been buried in their unconscious minds since childhood. One of the methods Freud devised to get at these early memories was to examine the dreams of his patients, believing that conflicts, events, and desires of the past would be represented in the dreams.

The *manifest content* of a dream is the actual dream itself, as we remember it when we wake up. For example, if Chad has a dream in which he is trying to climb out of a bathtub, the manifest content of the dream is exactly that—he's trying to climb out of a bathtub.

But, of course, Freud would no doubt find more meaning in Chad's dream than is at first evident. He believed dreams contain hidden truths, or *latent content*, expressed through symbols. In the dream, the water in the tub might symbolize the waters of birth, and the tub itself might be Chad's mother's womb. Chad may have been dreaming about being born in Freudian terms. Today, many professionals are no longer as fond of Freud's dream analysis as they once were, although dream analysis still plays a part in psychodynamic therapy. **LINK** to Chapter Fourteen: *Psychological Therapies, p. 449.*

▲ *Dreams are often filled with unrealistic and imaginative events and images. A common dream is that of flying. What do you think flying might represent in a dream?*

CONSCIOUSNESS: SLEEP, DREAMS, HYPNOSIS, AND DRUGS

CHAPTER 4 • Module 9

MULTIMEDIA CONTENT AVAILABLE AT www.mypsychlab.com

Listen to the Psychology in the News podcast about sleep deprivation and obesity on **mypsychlab.com**

COVER THE MODULE

9.7 Do dreams serve a function?

- The first inquiry into dreaming began with Freud's *The Interpretation of Dreams*.
- Freud believed that dream content was manifesting from conflicts of the unconscious mind.
  - *Manifest content*: the actual dream itself
  - *Latent content*: the symbolic meaning of the dream
- Freud's dream analysis is no longer used except in portions of psychodynamic therapy.

LINK to Chapter Fourteen: *Psychological Therapies, p. 449.*

UNDERSTANDING VISUALS

Direct students' attention to the question in the photo caption. Flying can possibly represent freedom, liberation, joy, the resolution of a conflict, rising above a conflict, or breaking away from physical pain.

Class Demonstration

DREAM ANALYSIS "á la FREUD"

Purpose: Students make a personal connection to Freud's dream interpretation theory.

Time: 15 minutes (Ask students to keep a dream journal for about a week before you plan to do this activity in your class. Have them record any dreams they remember every morning as soon as they wake up.)

Description: Have students choose a dream from their journals and write down as much *manifest content* as they can remember, being as detailed as possible. Ask students to work in pairs and exchange their manifest contents. Either for homework or in class, have students research the dream's hidden meaning on the Internet or provide materials for them to use in their analysis. Useful websites include:

- Basic information about how Freud approached dream interpretation: http://en.wikipedia.org/wiki/The_Interpretation_of_Dreams
- Dream Symbols Dictionary: www.dreaminterpretation-dictionary.com/dreams-dictionary.html

CHAPTER 4 • Module 9

COVER THE MODULE (continued)

- *Activation-synthesis hypothesis*: A dream is a different way of thinking, due to random neural firing that triggers memories and past experiences.
- *Activation-information-mode model (AIM)*: When composing a dream, the brain pulls from pieces of a person's experience from the previous day(s).
- When people dream, they reflect events of everyday life.
  - Gender differences between men and women

DISCUSS THE STUDENT VOICE QUESTION

Freud believed that dreams had underlying meaning, while Hobson and McCarley hypothesized that dreams were nothing more than the brain pulling information from daily activities and experiences. Hobson and McCarley's hypothesis seems incomplete because it leaves out an explanation for why, at times, people experience truly insightful dreams. From a purely psychological standpoint, the theory also explains dreams during REM sleep, but it does not explain dreams experienced during NREM.

L3 DIFFERENTIATED INSTRUCTION

Auditory/Verbal Learners These students take information best by listening. Group discussions and a lecture format in which the teacher talks about the subject are of the most benefit to this style of learning.

My dreams can be really weird, but sometimes they seem pretty ordinary or even seem to mean something. ▶ Can dreams be more meaningful?

activation-synthesis hypothesis explanation that states that dreams are created by the higher centers of the cortex to explain the activation by the brain stem of cortical cells during REM sleep periods.

activation-information-mode model (AIM) revised version of the activation-synthesis explanation of dreams in which information that is accessed during waking hours can have an influence on the synthesis of dreams.

120   CHAPTER 4

The Activation-Synthesis Hypothesis In a theory called the **activation-synthesis hypothesis** (Hobson, 1988; Hobson & McCarley, 1977; Hobson et al., 2000), a dream is merely another kind of thinking that occurs when people sleep. It is less realistic because it comes not from the outside world of reality, but from within the brain due to random neural firing that triggers people's memories and experiences of the past. The frontal lobes, which people normally use in daytime thinking, are more or less shut down during dreaming, which may also account for the unrealistic and often bizarre nature of dreams (Macquet & Franck, 1996).

My dreams can be really weird, but sometimes they seem pretty ordinary or even seem to mean something. Can dreams be more meaningful?

Hobson and colleagues have reworked the activation-synthesis hypothesis to reflect concerns about dream meaning, calling it the **activation-information-mode model**, or **AIM** (Hobson et al., 2000). In this newer version, information that is accessed during waking hours can have an influence on dreams. In other words, when the brain is "making up" a dream, it uses meaningful bits and pieces of the person's experiences from the previous day or the last few days rather than just random items from memory.

What do People Dream About? Calvin Hall collected over 10,000 dreams and concluded that most dreams reflect the events that occur in everyday life (Hall, 1966). Although most people dream in color, people who grew up in the era of black and white television sometimes have dreams in black and white. There are gender differences, although whether those differences are caused by hormonal/genetic influences, sociocultural influences, or a combination of influences remains to be seen. In his book *Finding Meaning in Dreams*, Dr. William Domhoff (1996) concluded that across many cultures, men more often dream of other males whereas women tend to dream about males and females equally. Men across various cultures also tend to have more physical aggression in their dreams than do women, with women more often being the victims of such aggression in their dreams.

Girls and women tend to dream about people they know, personal appearance concerns, and family and home. Boys and men tend to have more male characters in their dreams, which are also typically in outdoor or unfamiliar settings and may involve weapons, tools, cars, and roads.

In some dreams, people run, jump, talk, and do all of the actions that they do in normal daily life. Then there are dreams of flying, falling, and trying to do something and failing, all of which are very common dreams across many cultures (Domhoff, 1996).

Applying Psychology to Everyday Life

Applying Psychology to Everyday Life: Are You Sleep Deprived?

Sleep deprivation has long been considered a fact of life for many people. Sleep deprivation was one of the factors indicated in such disasters as the explosion of the *Challenger*, the Exxon *Valdez* oil spill, and the Chernobyl disaster.

Here are some other sleep deprivation facts (data taken from Williamson & Feyer, 2000):

- 30 to 40 percent of all heavy truck accidents can be attributed to driver fatigue.

Critical Thinking

WRITING ABOUT DREAMING

Purpose: Students discuss their opinions on the meaning of dreams while justifying their statements with examples from personal experience.

Time: 15 minutes

Description: Have students write their answers to the following questions: "Whose theory do you personally believe to be the best description for why we dream? Is it Freud's dream analysis or McCarley and Hobson's activation-information-mode theory?" Have students choose a dream from their dream journals (if they kept one) to back up their opinions. If they did not keep a dream journal, ask that they try to use a dream that they can recall. Alternatively, ask students how recurring dreams factor into these theories. Ask if they have had recurring dreams. If so, have them summarize those dreams and hypothesize about why they may be experiencing them.

- Drivers who have been awake for 17 to 19 hours are more dangerous than drivers with a blood alcohol level of .05.
- Sleep deprivation is linked to higher levels of stress, anxiety, depression, and unnecessary risk taking.

Clearly, sleep deprivation is a serious and all-too-common problem. Many of the sleep disorders that were discussed in this chapter are themselves causes of sleep deprivation. Sleep apnea, narcolepsy, sleepwalking, night terrors, and a condition called "restless leg syndrome," in which a person constantly moves his or her legs because they feel tingly, are all causes. Yet these problems are not the sole, or most common, cause of sleep deprivation.

The most obvious cause is the refusal of many people to go to sleep at a reasonable time, so that they can get the 8 hours of sleep that most adults need in order to function well (Bonnet & Arand, 1995). People want to watch that last bit of news, spend time on social networking Web sites, or get a little more homework done. Another reason for sleep loss is stress and worry. Finally, some medications that people take, both prescription and over-the-counter, interfere with the sleep–wake cycle. For example, decongestants that some people take to relieve sinus congestion may cause a racing heartbeat, preventing them from relaxing enough to sleep.

According to Fahey (1993), you may be sleep deprived if you:
- actually need your alarm clock to wake up.
- find getting out of bed in the morning is a struggle.
- feel tired, irritable, or stressed out for much of the day.
- have trouble concentrating or remembering.
- fall asleep watching TV, in lectures, or warm rooms.
- fall asleep after heavy meals.
- fall asleep within 5 minutes of getting into bed. (A well-rested person actually takes 15 to 20 minutes to fall asleep.)

▲ The student in the background is unable to stay awake during his class, indicating that he is seriously sleep deprived. Has this happened to you?

CONSCIOUSNESS: SLEEP, DREAMS, HYPNOSIS, AND DRUGS   121

CHAPTER 4 • Module 9

APPLYING PSYCHOLOGY TO EVERYDAY LIFE

- Open this discussion by asking students to take 1 minute to write about the following question: "What is the longest amount of time you have ever gone without sleep? Describe how you felt and any changes in functioning that you experienced."
- Allow students to share their experiences.
- Have students take a quiz to assess their current levels of sleep. A good one is available online at: **www.sleepandhealth.com/are-you-sleep-deprived-short-quiz**.

EXTEND THE LESSON

The text states that drivers who have been awake for 17 to 19 hours are more dangerous than drivers with a blood alcohol level of .05. Lead a discussion:

- Have students ever driven while drowsy? What did they do to prevent themselves from falling into microsleep?
- Discuss how most of their methods (e.g., opening a car window) would not be effective and describe effective alternatives.
- Do students feel there should be laws against knowingly driving while drowsy? If so, what should the laws state? What should the punishment be?

Class Demonstration

DEBATE: HIGH SCHOOL START/END TIMES

Purpose: Students examine the circadian rhythms of their own age group and how their levels of sleep deprivation are affected by traditional high school start/end times.

Time: From 5 minutes through the whole class period (depending on how in-depth the debate becomes)

Description: Studies have shown that adolescents have greater sleep needs than adults because of changes in their circadian rhythms. The following website provides information in great detail about the sleep needs of teenagers: **www.pbs.org/wgbh/pages/frontline/shows/teenbrain/from/**

Have students sit in a circle. Allow students to pass a softball to one another to indicate who should be speaking. Debate the following questions: (1) Should schools move start/end times to later hours to accommodate students' sleep needs? (2) How will this affect students' jobs and afterschool activities?

Module 9 Sleep and Dreams   121

CHAPTER 4 • Module 9

Assess

Assign the Module 9 Practice Quiz.

Use the Practice Quiz to identify gaps in student understanding.

REMEDIATE

Have students, individually or in groups, review the module goals, learning objectives, and key terms.

Refer students to the Concept Summary on p. 138 for review.

Close

Divide students into three groups: (1) sleep cycle, (2) sleep disorders, and (3) dreaming. Have students work together in their groups to prepare a mini-presentation for the class, answering the following questions:

- How would you summarize the key information in these topics?
- What was the most surprising/interesting thing you learned from this section?
- What is one way you can apply something you learned to your everyday life?

TEACHING TIP

Have students begin individual work in class. Prior to class dismissal, check to ensure that each student has a good start and understands what is expected.

Practice Quiz

Pick the best answer.

1. When our mental activity undergoes a shift in quality or pattern, this is called a(n)
   a. hallucination
   b. circadian rhythm
   c. waking consciousness
   d. altered state of consciousness

2. The sleep/wake cycle is a(n) _____ rhythm, normally occurring every 24 hours.
   a. annual
   b. monthly
   c. circadian
   d. adaptive

3. Which theory of sleep offers an explanation of why humans sleep during the nighttime?
   a. reactive theory
   b. microsleep theory
   c. REM theory
   d. adaptive theory

4. Which of the following is not a characteristic of REM sleep?
   a. paralysis of voluntary muscles
   b. increased heart rate
   c. slower, deeper breathing
   d. vivid, detailed dreaming

5. In which disorder does breathing stop for nearly half a minute or more?
   a. sleep apnea
   b. night terrors
   c. narcolepsy
   d. REM behavior disorder

6. Which of the following is bad advice for someone suffering from insomnia?
   a. Keep a regular schedule.
   b. Do not study or watch TV in bed.
   c. Lie in bed until you fall asleep, even if it takes several hours.
   d. Avoid drugs that slow down the nervous system.

7. If you are in REM sleep but are able to move around and act out your dreams, you may have a rare condition called
   a. REM behavior disorder
   b. nightmare disorder
   c. narcolepsy
   d. insomnia

8. If you suddenly and without warning slip into REM sleep during the day, you may have the condition called
   a. sleep apnea
   b. insomnia
   c. narcolepsy
   d. somnambulism

9. In Freud's theory, the symbolic content of dreams is called
   a. manifest content
   b. latent content
   c. activation-synthesis content
   d. AIM content

10. Compared to women, men across all cultures are more likely to dream about all of the following except
    a. personal appearance
    b. male characters
    c. the outdoors
    d. physical aggression

Practice Quiz Answers

1. d
2. c
3. d
4. c
5. a

6. c
7. a
8. c
9. b
10. a

Module 10: Hypnosis and Drugs

Module Goals
Describe meditation and hypnosis.

Understand the effects of psychoactive drugs.

Learning Objectives
- **10.1** How does meditation affect consciousness?
- **10.2** How does hypnosis work, and why is it controversial?
- **10.3** What are the major categories of psychoactive drugs?
- **10.4** How do drugs function at the synaptic level?
- **10.5** What are the effects of psychoactive drugs?
- **10.6** How do cultural pressures and expectations influence drug use?

Describe Meditation and Hypnosis

Sleep is the most common altered state of consciousness, but meditation and hypnosis are two additional ways in which an altered state of consciousness can be achieved.

10.1 How does meditation affect consciousness?

Meditation is a mental series of exercises meant to refocus attention and achieve a trancelike state of consciousness. Meditation can produce a state of relaxation that can aid in coping with the physiological reactions to a stressful situation.

Have you ever found yourself staring out into space, or at some little spot on the wall or table, only to realize that your mind has seemed completely blank for the last several minutes?

The state just described is really nothing more than **concentrative meditation**, the form of meditation best known to the general public. In concentrative meditation, the goal is to focus the mind on some repetitive or unchanging stimulus (such as a spot or the sound of one's own heart beating) so that the mind can forget daily hassles and problems and the body can relax. In fact, Herbert Benson (Benson, 1975; Benson et al., 1974a, 1974b) found that meditation produces a state of relaxation in which blood pressure is lowered, alpha waves (brain waves associated with relaxation) are increased, and the amount of melatonin secreted at night (the hormone that helps induce sleep) is increased.

Research shows that concentrative meditation is a helpful way to relax and lower blood pressure (Barnes et al., 1997; Rainforth et al., 2007; Schneider et al., 1995; Wenneberg et al., 1997). The advantage of meditation is that people can do it almost anywhere, even in the classroom just before a big test.

Other research has suggested that concentrative meditation can reduce the levels of chronic pain (Kabat-Zinn et al., 1986), and reduce the symptoms of anxiety, depression, and hostility (Kabat-Zinn et al., 1985).

Another kind of meditation is less well known and not as easily achieved. It is called **receptive meditation** and involves trying to expand consciousness outward. The best description of what this is like is to think about a time when

▲ This man is practicing Zen yoga meditation. Meditation increases relaxation and helps to lower blood pressure and muscle tension.

meditation mental series of exercises meant to refocus attention and achieve a trancelike state of consciousness.

concentrative meditation form of meditation in which a person focuses the mind on some repetitive or unchanging stimulus so that the mind can be cleared of disturbing thoughts and the body can experience relaxation.

receptive meditation form of meditation in which a person attempts to become aware of everything in immediate conscious experience, or an expansion of consciousness.

CONSCIOUSNESS: SLEEP, DREAMS, HYPNOSIS, AND DRUGS 123

Terms
- meditation • concentrative meditation • receptive meditation • hypnosis
- social-cognitive theory of hypnosis • psychoactive drugs • stimulants • depressants
- narcotics • hallucinogenics • amphetamines • cocaine • nicotine • caffeine
- barbiturates • benzodiazepines • alcohol • opium • morphine • heroin • hallucinogens • LSD (lysergic acid diethylamide) • PCP • MDMA (ecstasy or X) • stimulatory hallucinogenics • mescaline • psilocybin • marijuana • physical dependence
- withdrawal • psychological dependence

CHAPTER 4 • Module 10

Focus

RESOURCES
For this module, consult the appropriate sections of the Teacher's Manual, Test Bank, and PowerPoint slides, all found on the Teacher's Resource DVD, and the interactive study tools for students on MyPsychLab.

BEFORE CLASS
Students should read the section for homework before coming to class.

BELLRINGER
Have the classroom lights dimmed and soft music playing as students enter the room. Guide them through a concentrative meditation experience. Turn off the music; instruct students to find a comfortable sitting position and not to speak. Have them close their eyes and breathe normally for 30 seconds, then clear their minds and think of nothing but the expansion and contraction of their abdomens as they breathe. Continue for 5 to 10 minutes. Last, have them focus on any sensations or sounds they experience. After 1 minute, students can open their eyes and discuss the following: (1) How did they feel physically and emotionally before the exercise, and then after? (2) Does meditation lead to heightened states of consciousness, alertness, or creativity?

Teach

COVER THE MODULE
10.1 How does meditation affect consciousness?

- *Meditation* is a series of mental exercises meant to refocus attention and achieve a trancelike state of consciousness.
- *Concentrative meditation*: focusing the mind on a repetitive stimulus
  - Blood pressure lowers, alpha waves increase, more melatonin secreted at night; reduces levels of chronic pain, anxiety, depression, and hostility
- *Receptive meditation*: expand consciousness outward, becoming aware of everything in immediate conscious experience

Module 10 Hypnosis and Drugs 123

CHAPTER 4 • Module 10

MULTICULTURAL FOCUS

Ask students to research how meditation relates to culture in areas such as India and Southeast Asia. Ask students to prepare a 2-minute presentation with visual aid to share their findings with the class.

FAST FACT

The word "hypnosis" comes from the Greek god *Hypnos*, the god controlling sleep. He lived in the land of eternal darkness, *Erebos*, located beyond the gates of the rising sun. His mother was *Nyx* ("night"), and his twin brother was *Thanatos* ("peaceful death"). His sons were the *Oneiroi* ("dreams").

COVER THE MODULE

10.2 How does hypnosis work, and why is it controversial?

- *Hypnosis* is a state of consciousness in which a person is susceptible to suggestion.
- Four steps to hypnotize a person, in which a person is instructed to (1) focus on what is said, (2) relax and feel tired, (3) "let go" and accept suggestions, and (4) use a vivid imagination.
- People cannot be hypnotized against their will; the person who is hypnotized is in complete control. The hypnotist guides a person into a more relaxed state, but the person hypnotizes himself or herself.

MULTIMEDIA CONTENT AVAILABLE AT
www.mypsychlab.com

👁 Watch a video about hypnosis on **mypsychlab.com**

---

hypnosis state of consciousness in which a person is especially susceptible to suggestion.

you were awed by nature. Perhaps you were standing at the ocean's edge on a starry night and suddenly became aware of how vast the universe really is. Or perhaps you were walking in the woods and listening to all the little sounds of the birds and animals surrounding you. Your attention was focused outward rather than inward, and this is similar to the state that this type of meditation tries to achieve.

Regardless of which form of meditation people choose to try, the effects are similar (Murphy & Donavan, 1997). Meditation for only 20 minutes can produce lowered blood pressure in people with hypertension (high blood pressure). It can calm anxiety, help people get to sleep, and help people deal with stress.

10.2 How does hypnosis work, and why is it controversial?

Hypnosis (from the Greek word *hypnos*, meaning "sleep") is a state of consciousness in which a person is especially susceptible to suggestion. There are several key steps in inducing hypnosis. According to Druckman and Bjork (1994), although every hypnotist may have a different style or use different words, these four steps are always present:

1. The hypnotist tells the person to focus on what is being said.
2. The person is told to relax and feel tired.
3. The hypnotist tells the person to "let go" and accept suggestions easily.
4. The person is told to use vivid imagination.

The real key to hypnosis seems to be a heightened state of suggestibility. People can be hypnotized when active and alert, but only if they are willing to be hypnotized. Only 80 percent of all people can be hypnotized, and only 40 percent are good hypnotic subjects. People who fantasize a lot, who daydream and have vivid imaginations, as well as people who get "really into" whatever task they are doing, are more susceptible to hypnosis than others (Silva & Kirsch, 1992).

Fact or Myth: What Can Hypnosis Really Do?

Is it true that people can be hypnotized into doing things that they would never do under normal conditions?

Books, movies, and television programs have often misrepresented the effects of hypnosis. Although the popular view is that the hypnotized person is acting involuntarily, the fact is that the hypnotized person is really the one in control. In fact, the hypnotist may only be a guide into a more relaxed state, while the subject actually hypnotizes himself or herself (Kirsch & Lynn, 1995). People cannot be hypnotized against their will.

For a concise look at what hypnosis can and cannot do, see Table 10.1.

In general, hypnosis is a way to help people relax and control pain. These subjective experiences are very much under people's mental influence. Actual physical behavior is harder to change, and that is why hypnosis is not as effective at changing eating habits or helping people to stop smoking (Druckman & Bjork, 1994). Hypnosis is sometimes used in psychological therapy to help people cope with anxiety or deal with cravings for food or drugs.

There are two views of why hypnosis works. One emphasizes the role of *dissociation*, or a splitting of conscious awareness, whereas the other involves a kind of social role-playing. 👁 Watch on **mypsychlab.com**

▶ Is it true that people can be hypnotized into doing things that they would never do under normal conditions?

👁 Watch a video about hypnosis on **mypsychlab.com**

124 CHAPTER 4

Explore

INVESTIGATING HYPNOSIS

Students can learn more about hypnosis at the following websites.

- Students can take a test to see how susceptible they are to hypnosis: **www.behyp.com/hypnosis_quiz.html**
  - *Note: Students do not have to enter e-mail addresses to see results.*
- Students can experience a simulation of hypnosis on **www.mypsychlab.com**

- Students can learn more about how hypnosis aids in:
- Cessation of smoking: **www.worldwidehealth.com/health-article-Does-Hypnosis-Work-to-Help-You-Quit-Smoking.html**
- Pain management: **www.psychwww.com/asc/hyp/painhypn.html**
- A history of hypnosis can be found at: **www.wayneperkins.net/hypnosis/history.html**

124 Chapter 4 Consciousness

Table 10.1 Facts about Hypnosis

HYPNOSIS CAN:	HYPNOSIS CANNOT:
Create amnesia of whatever happens during the hypnotic session, at least for a brief time (Bowers & Woody, 1996).	Give people superhuman strength. (People may use their full strength under hypnosis, but it is no more than they had before hypnosis.)
Relieve pain by allowing a person to remove conscious attention from the pain (Holroyd, 1996).	Reliably enhance memory. (There's an increased risk of false memory retrieval because of the suggestible state hypnosis creates.)
Alter sensory perceptions. (Smell, hearing, vision, time sense, and the ability to see visual illusions can all be affected by hypnosis.)	Regress people back to childhood. (Although people may act like children, they do and say things children would not.)
Help people relax in situations that normally would cause them stress, such as flying on an airplane (Muhlberger et al., 2001).	Regress people to some "past life." There is no scientific evidence for past life regression (Lilienfeld et al., 2004).

Hypnosis as Dissociation: The Hidden Observer Ernest Hilgard (1991; Hilgard & Hilgard, 1994) believed that hypnosis worked only on the immediate conscious mind of a person, while a part of that person's mind (a "hidden observer") remained aware of all that was going on. It's the same kind of dissociation that takes place when people drive somewhere familiar and then wonder how they got there. One part of the mind, the conscious part, is thinking about dinner or a date or something else, while the other part is doing the actual driving. When people arrive at their destination, they don't really remember the actual trip. In the same way, Hilgard believes that there is a hidden part of the mind that is very much aware of the hypnotic subject's activities and sensations, even though the "hypnotized" part of the mind is blissfully unaware of these same things.

In one study (Miller & Bowers, 1993), subjects were hypnotized, instructed to feel no pain, and told to put their arms in ice water. There had to be pain—many people can't even get an ice cube out of the freezer without *some* pain—but some subjects reported no pain at all. The subjects who were successful at denying the pain also reported that they imagined being at the beach or in some other place that allowed them to dissociate from the pain. Even outside the research lab, many people struggling with chronic pain or illness find that hypnosis can help them manage their pain effectively.

Hypnosis as Social Role-Playing: The Social-Cognitive Explanation
The other theory of how hypnosis works began with an experiment in which people who were *not* hypnotized were instructed to behave as if they were (Sarbin & Coe, 1972). These people had no trouble copying many actions previously thought to require a hypnotic state, such as being rigidly suspended between two chairs. Researchers (Sarbin & Coe, 1972) also found that people who were not familiar with hypnosis, and had no idea what the "role" of a hypnotic subject was supposed to be, could not be hypnotized.

CHAPTER 4 • Module 10

COVER THE MODULE *(continued)*

- Hypnosis as dissociation: Ernest Hilgard believed hypnosis works on the immediate conscious mind, while another part of the mind (hidden observer) is aware of what is going on.
- Hypnosis as social role playing, *the social-cognitive explanation*: The person being hypnotized inadvertently plays a "role" in which he or she carries out his or her own expectations for how a hypnotized person would behave.

UNDERSTANDING VISUALS

Discuss Table 10.1 with the class. First, ask students to describe their prior knowledge of the scope and ability of hypnosis. Then ask that they look at the chart; ask if any of the items on the chart about what hypnosis can and cannot do surprises them.

L4 DIFFERENTIATED INSTRUCTION

Advanced Learners Encourage students to make connections between content they are learning and other disciplines such as language arts, science, and math. For example, students might want to read about the impact of technology on the psychology concept they are studying.

Class Demonstration

HYPNOSIS: DISSOCIATION OR SOCIAL ROLE-PLAYING?

Lead the class in an exercise in suggestion. Tell the class that they are going to experience hypnosis. Begin with a brief description of the four steps of hypnosis. Then perform either activity below:

1. Bring out a small, sealed jar of odorless liquid colored with food coloring. Open the jar and tell the class that it is an exotic, aromatic liquid; add details such as wrinkling your nose to indicate an odor. Ask students to raise their hand as soon as they smell the liquid.

2. Behave as if you have an itch. Slowly begin scratching and describe in detail the pleasurable sensation of scratching an itch such as a tickle on the back or nose. Suggest that students may be developing an itch that is getting progressively stronger, and they cannot help but scratch.

After the exercise is over, ask students (1) to take a moment to write about their experience being "hypnotized" and then (2) to admit whether they believed they were actually in a dissociative state or whether they were playing a "role" so as not to be left out of the experience.

CHAPTER 4 • Module 10

COVER THE MODULE (continued)

- *Psychoactive drugs* alter thinking, perception, and memory.
  - Drugs were developed for useful purposes but become dangerous when a dependence is formed, causing a person to take increasing quantities and a possible overdose.

COVER THE MODULE

10.3 What are the major categories of psychotic drugs?

- *Stimulants*: increase function of nervous system by causing neurons to fire more rapidly, causing heart to beat and brain to work faster

LINK *to Chapter Two: The Biological Perspective, pp. 42–47.*

- *Depressants*: decrease function of nervous system
- *Narcotics*: opium-related drugs that suppress pain
- *Hallucinogenics*: produce hallucinations or increased feelings of relaxation and intoxication

LINK *to Chapter Two: The Biological Perspective, p. 50.*

MULTIMEDIA CONTENT AVAILABLE AT
www.mypsychlab.com

Simulate psychoactive drugs on mypsychlab.com

FAST FACT

Ask: **Do you think illegal drug use among teens is increasing or decreasing?** *(According to the website teendrugabuse.us, illegal drug use among teens is declining, but abuse of prescription drugs is increasing because many teens believe these drugs to be "safe.")*

126 Chapter 4 Consciousness

---

social-cognitive theory of hypnosis theory that assumes that people who are hypnotized are not in an altered state but are merely playing the role expected of them in the situation.

psychoactive drugs drugs that alter thinking, perception, and memory.

stimulants drugs that increase the functioning of the nervous system.

depressants drugs that decrease the functioning of the nervous system.

narcotics a class of opium-related drugs that suppress the sensation of pain by binding to and stimulating the nervous system's natural receptor sites for endorphins.

hallucinogenics drugs including synthesized hallucinogens and marijuana that produce hallucinations or increased feelings of relaxation and intoxication.

amphetamines stimulants that are synthesized (made) in laboratories rather than being found in nature.

Simulate psychoactive drugs on mypsychlab.com

Add to those findings the later findings of Kirsch (2000) that expectancies of the hypnotized person play a big part in how the person responds and what the person does under hypnosis. The **social-cognitive theory of hypnosis** assumes that people who are hypnotized are not in an altered state but are merely playing the role expected of them in the situation. They might believe that they are hypnotized, but in fact it is all a very good performance, so good that even the "subjects" are unaware that they are role-playing. **LINK** *to Chapter Seven: Social Psychology, pp. 218–219.*

Understand the Effects of Psychoactive Drugs

Whereas some people seek altered states of consciousness in sleep, daydreaming, meditation, or hypnosis, others try to access a different type of altered state. They use substances called **psychoactive drugs** that alter thinking, perception, memory, or some combination of those abilities. Many of the drugs discussed in the following sections are very useful and were originally developed to help people. Some allow sedation so that operations that would otherwise be impossible can be performed, whereas others help people deal with the pain of injuries or disease. Still, others may be used in helping to control various conditions, such as sleep disorders or attention deficits in children and adults.

The usefulness of these drugs must not blind us to the dangers of misusing or abusing them. When taken for pleasure, to get "high" or to dull psychological pain, or when taken without the supervision of a qualified medical professional, these drugs can pose serious risks to one's health and may even cause death. One danger of such drugs is their potential to create either a physical or psychological dependence, both of which can lead to a lifelong pattern of abuse as well as the risk of taking increasingly larger doses, leading to one of the clearest dangers of dependence: a drug overdose.

Simulate on mypsychlab.com

10.3 What are the major categories of psychoactive drugs?

This module will describe several of the major drug categories: **stimulants** (drugs that excite, or increase, the functioning of neurons and the nervous system), **depressants** (drugs that inhibit, or decrease, the functioning of neurons and the nervous system), **narcotics** (painkilling depressant drugs derived from the opium poppy), and **hallucinogenics** (drugs that alter perceptions and may cause hallucinations).

Stimulants In simple terms, stimulants "speed up" the nervous system by causing neurons to fire more rapidly. **LINK** *to Chapter Two: The Biological Perspective, pp. 42–47.* As a result, the heart may beat faster or the brain may work faster. Many of these drugs are called "uppers" for this reason.

Amphetamines are stimulants that are synthesized (made) in laboratories rather than being found in nature. Truck drivers, shift workers, and students report use of amphetamines to stay awake for long hours, and many doctors used to prescribe these drugs as diet pills for overweight people, but only on a short-term basis and under strict medical supervision.

Like other stimulants, amphetamines cause the neurons of the sympathetic nervous system to go into overdrive. **LINK** *to Chapter Two: The Biological*

126 CHAPTER 4

Class Demonstration

EXAMINE STATISTICS ON TEEN DRUG USE

Have students research statistics on teen drug use, such as those found on SADD's website: www.sadd.org/stats.htm. As a class, create graphs on the board or on a PowerPoint slide comparing use by teens of various types of drugs. Then ask the class to discuss the following questions: (1) Which category of drugs is the most widely used? (2) Which specific drug is the most widely used? (3) Are students surprised by the statistics? Why or why not?

Perspective, p. 50. Stimulants cause people to burn up whatever energy reserves they have. When the energy reserves are exhausted, or the drug wears off, a "crash" is inevitable.

This is why people who take amphetamines quickly develop a *drug tolerance*, meaning that they have adapted to the drug and no longer experience an effect from taking a small amount of it. When the "crash" or depression comes, the tendency is to take more pills to get back "up." The person taking these pills finds that it takes more and more pills to get the same stimulant effect. Doses can easily become toxic and deadly. Nausea, vomiting, high blood pressure, and strokes are possible, and addicts can become delusional (losing contact with what is real) and paranoid (thinking people are out to "get" them). Violence is a likely outcome, both against the self and others (Kratofil et al., 1996).

Unlike amphetamines, **cocaine** is a natural drug found in coca plant leaves. It produces feelings of euphoria (a feeling of exaggerated happiness), energy, power, and pleasure. It also deadens pain and suppresses the appetite. Many years ago, cocaine was thought to be a "wonder drug," and people like Sigmund Freud used it as a painkiller. Once Freud became aware of the drug's addictive qualities, however, he stopped using it immediately and began to write about the harmful properties of cocaine.

Cocaine is a highly dangerous drug, not just because of its addictive properties. Some people have convulsions and may even die when using cocaine for the first time (Lacayo, 1995). Cocaine has devastating effects on the children born to mothers who use it, causing learning disabilities, hyperactivity, delayed language development, and tremors, among other symptoms (Blatt et al., 2000; Frank et al., 2001).

Although cocaine users do not go through the same kind of physical withdrawal symptoms that users of heroin, alcohol, and other physically addictive drugs go through, users will experience a severe mood swing into depression (the "crash"), followed by extreme tiredness, nervousness, an inability to feel pleasure, and paranoia.

As addictive as cocaine is, there is one other stimulant that comes in at a very close second: **nicotine**. The Surgeon General's Report (Centers for Disease Control and Prevention [CDC], 1992) reports that nicotine produces addiction in 99 percent of the people who use it.

Nicotine is a relatively mild but nevertheless toxic stimulant, producing a slight "rush" or sense of arousal as it raises blood pressure and accelerates the heart, as well as providing a rush of sugar into the bloodstream (Rezvani & Levin, 2001). As is the case with many stimulants, it also has a relaxing effect on most people and seems to reduce stress (Pormerleau & Pormerleau, 1994).

Although the amount of nicotine in a cigarette is low, first-time smokers often experience nausea as a result of the toxic effects after just a few puffs. Nicotine use, combined with other harmful additives found in cigarettes, can lead to health problems in many parts of the body, including the lungs, heart, and brain. Every year, nearly 438,000 people in the United States die from illnesses related to smoking.

Quitting is a good idea but hard to accomplish for many people. The majority of people who quit will start smoking again, even after having quitted for years. Why is it so difficult to quit? In terms of its addictive power, nicotine is more powerful than heroin or alcohol (Henningfield et al., 1990). The physical withdrawal symptoms can be as bad as those resulting from alcohol, cocaine, or heroin abuse (Epping-Jordan et al., 1998).

cocaine a natural drug derived from the leaves of the coca plant.

nicotine the active ingredient in tobacco.

CHAPTER 4 • Module 10

COVER THE MODULE *(continued)*

- People taking stimulants burn up energy; when the drugs wear off, a "crash" occurs. People tend to take more stimulants to combat the crash, and a vicious cycle begins.
- People taking stimulants experience a *drug tolerance*.
- *Cocaine* is found in the coca plant leaves, produces euphoria, energy, power, and pleasure.
- *Nicotine* is the second-most addictive stimulant, producing addiction in 99 percent of users, causing a "rush" by raising blood pressure, accelerating the heart, and sending sugar into the bloodstream.

CHECK YOUR UNDERSTANDING

Divide the class into teams. Quickly read the definitions of the terms/concepts discussed so far about drugs, and as you read them, ask a representative from each team to stand up when he or she knows the answer. Allow the first student to give the answer; if it is correct, award the team a point, and if it is incorrect, allow the other teams a chance to answer. Rotate team representatives for each question.

TEACHING TIP

For class discussions, consider a system for ensuring that all students participate. For example, you may give each student three paperclips to throw in a bucket when he or she contributes. A rule may be that everyone must contribute once before anyone may contribute three times.

Class Demonstration

STIMULANT AWARENESS PSA CAMPAIGN

Purpose: Students perform further research into the stimulants described in the text and create a public service announcement (PSA) to share with the class about their findings.

Time: One class period

Description: Divide students into groups of three or four. Assign each group a stimulant from the text. Send the groups to the following website to research their topics:

http://teens.drugabuse.gov/facts/facts_stim1.php

Have each group create a PSA "commercial" to present to the class, including the definition of the stimulant, how it affects the body, how it is harmful, and how addiction is treated (if at all).

CHAPTER 4 • Module 10

COVER THE MODULE *(continued)*

- *Caffeine* is a natural stimulant found in coffee, tea, soda, energy drinks, chocolate, and over-the-counter medication.
- *Depressants* slow or inhibit neuron functioning in the central nervous system.
- *Barbiturates* (major tranquilizers) are sedatives ranging from mild sedation to unconsciousness and coma.
- *Benzodiazepines* (minor tranquilizers) are used to lower anxiety and reduce stress.
- *Alcohol* is the most commonly used and abused depressant.

LINK *to Chapter 5: Development Across the Life Span, p. 148.*

L3 DIFFERENTIATED INSTRUCTION

Engaging All Learners A major mistake made by many students is to come to class without having read the material first. Explain to students that if they come to class totally unprepared, they will have no idea what is important enough to write down. Reading the material first will give them a good idea of exactly what is important about the topic.

MULTIMEDIA CONTENT AVAILABLE AT
www.mypsychlab.com

Watch videos on alcohol and the brain as well as alcoholism on **mypsychlab.com**

▲ Sleep deprivation causes this man to struggle to wake up. Caffeine can help with alertness but may worsen his sleep deprivation when he tries to get a decent night's sleep tonight.

Watch videos on alcohol and the brain as well as alcoholism on **mypsychlab.com**

caffeine a mild stimulant found in coffee, tea, and several other plant-based substances.

barbiturates depressant drugs that have a sedative effect.

benzodiazepines drugs that lower anxiety and reduce stress.

alcohol the chemical resulting from fermentation or distillation of various kinds of vegetable matter.

Medications can help smokers deal with the cravings for nicotine while they try to quit, as well as nicotine-containing gums and patches that deliver the drug in a much lower dose, allowing the smoker to control the cravings until quitting completely (Benowitz, 1996; Henningfield, 1995; Stitzer & De Wit, 1998).

One stimulant that many people use every day is **caffeine**, the stimulant found in coffee, tea, most sodas, energy drinks, chocolate, and even many over-the-counter drugs.

Caffeine is another natural substance, like cocaine and nicotine, and is found in coffee beans, tea leaves, cocoa nuts, and at least 60 other types of plants (Braun, 1996). It is a mild stimulant, helps maintain alertness, and can increase the effectiveness of some pain relievers such as aspirin. Caffeine is often added to pain relievers for that reason and is the key ingredient in medications meant to keep people awake. Negative effects of caffeine include insomnia and even anxiety when taken in large doses.

Depressants Another class of psychoactive drugs is *depressants*, drugs that slow or inhibit neuron functioning in the central nervous system.

Commonly known as the *major tranquilizers* (drugs that have a strong depressant effect) or sleeping pills, **barbiturates** are drugs that have a sedative (sleep-inducing) effect. The effects, depending on dosage levels, range from mild sedation or sleepiness to unconsciousness or coma. Overdoses can lead to death as breathing and heart action are stopped. Barbiturates are highly addictive and users can quickly develop a tolerance.

The *minor tranquilizers* (drugs having a relatively mild depressant effect) are called **benzodiazepines**. These drugs are used to lower anxiety and reduce stress. They are considered safer than barbiturates and are now the drugs of choice to treat sleep problems, nervousness, and anxiety. However, even these minor tranquilizers can be addictive, and large doses can be dangerous.

The most commonly used and abused depressant is **alcohol**, the chemical resulting from fermentation or distillation of various kinds of vegetable matter. Anywhere from 10 to 20 million people in the United States alone suffer from alcoholism. Aside from the obvious health risks to the liver, brain, and heart, alcohol is associated with loss of work time, loss of a job, loss of economic stability, and loss of strong family relationships.

Watch on **mypsychlab.com**

According to the National Center for Health Statistics (National Center for Health Statistics [NCHS], 2007), the number of alcohol-induced deaths in 2003 was 20,687. Of these deaths, 12,360 were attributed to liver disease caused by alcoholism. Alcohol was involved in nearly 22.5 percent of the fatal traffic crashes for drivers under 21, and 24.8 percent of the fatal crashes for those over 21 (NIAAA, 2007).

Pregnant women should not drink at all, as alcohol can damage the growing embryo, causing mental retardation and physical deformity. **LINK** *to Chapter Five: Development Across the Life Span, p. 148.* Heart disease has also been linked to alcoholism (Abbott et al., 1994).

Figure 10.1 shows the effects of various numbers of drinks on the average person's behavior. Alcohol has the effect of depressing inhibitions, which are the social rules people have learned that allow them to function in society. This means that when people drink alcohol, they are more likely to do

128 CHAPTER 4

Explore

EXPLORING TEEN ALCOHOL ABUSE

Send students to the following website: **www.medicinenet.com/alcohol_and_teens/article.htm**. Assign each student a topic from the page to read. Ask each student to create a small poster outlining the key ideas from the article. The poster should be titled "What every teen should know about (insert article topic)." Students then use their posters as the basis for a 2-minute class presentation. At the conclusion of all presentations, ask volunteers to describe the fact they learned about teen alcohol abuse that most surprised them. Will this fact change students' attitudes or actions concerning alcohol use?

Key: 1 drink equals 1 can of beer, 1 glass of wine, or 1 shot of most liquors.

Source: Adapted from the *Moderate Drinking Skills Study Guide*. (2004). Eau-Claire, WI: University of Wisconsin.

FIGURE 10.1 How Drinks Affect Behavior

things they'd never do when not under the influence of alcohol. In addition, motor skills, reaction time, and speech are all negatively affected by alcohol consumption. Aside from its health risks and physical dangers, alcohol can have serious and devastating financial and legal consequences for those who use it illegally or irresponsibly.

Narcotics *Narcotics* (from the Greek word *nark* meaning "numbness") are a class of drugs that suppress the sensation of pain (Olin, 1993). They also slow down the action of neurons in the nervous system. All narcotics are a derivative of a particular plant-based substance—opium.

Opium, made from the opium poppy, has pain-relieving and euphoria-inducing properties that have been known for at least 2,000 years. In 1803, opium was developed for use as a medication by a German physician. The new form—**morphine**—was thought, like cocaine, to be a "wonder drug," although its addictive qualities soon became a major concern to physicians and their patients. Morphine is still used today but in carefully controlled doses and for short periods of time.

opium substance derived from the opium poppy from which all narcotic drugs are derived.

morphine narcotic drug derived from opium, used to treat severe pain.

CONSCIOUSNESS: SLEEP, DREAMS, HYPNOSIS, AND DRUGS 129

CHAPTER 4 • Module 10

COVER THE MODULE (continued)

- Narcotics suppress the sensation of pain and are all derived from a plant-based substance called opium.
- Opium comes from the poppy and has pain-relieving and euphoric properties.
- Morphine, a new form of opium, is still used today in small, controlled doses.

UNDERSTANDING VISUALS

Binge drinking is defined as having five or more drinks on one occasion. A nationwide survey showed that 13 percent of eighth-graders, 25 percent of tenth-graders, and 30 percent of twelfth-graders said they had participated in binge drinking within 2 weeks prior to the survey. Looking at Figure 10.1, ask students for their reactions to these findings. What dangers does binge drinking pose for teens?

TEACHING TIP

During class discussions about drugs and alcohol, be sensitive to these topics to ensure that student interactions do not become too personal or that certain students are not targeted by classmates.

Class Demonstration (Kinesthetic)

PRESCRIPTIONS FOR DISASTER?

In this activity, students will examine teen abuse of painkillers in greater depth. In each corner of the classroom, hang the following signs: *strongly agree, somewhat agree, strongly disagree,* and *somewhat disagree*. Have students read the *New York Times* article, "When Teenagers Abuse Prescription Drugs, the Fault May Be the Doctor's" found at: www.nytimes.com/learning/teachers/featured_articles/20051227tuesday.html

Read aloud the first statement below and have students move to the area of the room that best describes their opinion. As a group, students should then discuss their thoughts and elect one spokesperson to explain the group viewpoint to the class. Proceed in turn with the remaining statements: (1) Teens should not be allowed to take a prescription painkiller that is addictive. (2) If a teen becomes addicted to a prescription drug, it is the parents' or doctor's fault. (3) Pharmaceutical companies should be held responsible if teens become addicted to their drugs. (4) Teens should tell an adult if they or someone they know is addicted to painkillers.

CHAPTER 4 • Module 10

COVER THE MODULE (continued)

- *Heroin* is a derivative of morphine that is more addictive than opium or morphine.
- Opium and its derivatives mimic action of endorphins so well that the nervous system stops production of neurotransmitters. When a person stops taking the drug, there is no protection against pain, causing severe withdrawal.
- *Hallucinogens* cause the brain to alter interpretation of sensations, causing false sensory perceptions called *hallucinations*.
- Three synthetically created hallucinogens: LSD, PCP, and MDMA
- Three naturally occurring hallucinogens: *mescaline*, psilocybin, and marijuana

FAST FACT

A link has been found that suggests that ergot poisoning (LSD is synthesized from ergot) may have been to blame for the bizarre behaviors that prompted the Salem Witch Trials. Ergot was a naturally occurring grain fungus available at the time of the trials, and behaviors cited at the trials such as muscle spasms, vomiting, hallucinations, delusions, and crawling sensations are all consistent with ergot poisoning.

---

heroin narcotic drug derived from opium that is extremely addictive.

hallucinogens drugs that cause false sensory messages, altering the perception of reality.

LSD (lysergic acid diethylamide) powerful synthetic hallucinogen.

PCP synthesized drug now used as an animal tranquilizer that can cause stimulant, depressant, narcotic, or hallucinogenic effects.

MDMA (Ecstasy or X) designer drug that can have both stimulant and hallucinatory effects.

stimulatory hallucinogenics drugs that produce a mixture of psychomotor stimulant and hallucinogenic effects.

mescaline natural hallucinogen derived from the peyote cactus buttons.

Heroin was also hailed as a new wonder drug—a derivative of morphine that did not have many of morphine's disagreeable side effects. The theory was that heroin was a purer form of the drug. It did not take long, however, for doctors and others to realize that heroin was even more powerfully addictive than morphine or opium. Opium and its derivatives, morphine and heroin, duplicate the action of endorphins so well that the nervous system slows or stops its production of the neurotransmitters. When the drug wears off, there is no protection against any kind of pain, causing severe symptoms of withdrawal. The addict who tries to quit using the drug feels such pain that the urge to use again becomes unbearable.

Hallucinogenics **Hallucinogens** cause the brain to alter its interpretation of sensations (Olin, 1993), so that sensations cross over each other—colors have sound, sounds have smells, and so on. False sensory perceptions, called *hallucinations*, are often experienced, especially with the more powerful hallucinogens.

Several hallucinogens were developed in the laboratory instead of being found in nature. Perhaps because these drugs are manufactured, they are often more potent than drugs found in the natural world.

LSD, or **lysergic acid diethylamide**, is synthesized from a grain fungus called *ergot*. LSD is one of the most potent, or powerful, hallucinogens (Lee & Shlain, 1986). It takes only a very tiny drop of LSD to achieve a "high."

Some people feel that LSD helps them to expand their consciousness or awareness of the world around them. Colors seem more intense, sounds more beautiful, and so on. But the fact is that LSD takes people out of the real world and dumps them into a world of the brain's creation. This is not always a pleasant experience: "Bad trips" are common, and there is no way to control what kind of "trip" the brain is going to take.

One danger of LSD is its effect on a person's ability to perceive reality. Real dangers and hazards in the world may go unnoticed by a person "lost" in an LSD fantasy, and people under the influence of this drug may make poor decisions, such as trying to drive while high.

Another extremely dangerous synthesized drug is **PCP** (which stands for *p*henyl *c*yclohexyl *p*iperidine). PCP users can experience hallucinations and distorted sensations, and PCP can also lead to acts of violence or suicide (Brecher, 1988; Cami et al., 2000). Users may physically injure themselves unintentionally because PCP causes them to feel no warning signal of pain.

The synthetic drug MDMA is capable of producing hallucinations as well. In fact, both **MDMA** (also known as **Ecstasy** or simply **X**) and PCP are now classified as **stimulatory hallucinogenics**, drugs that produce a mixture of psychomotor stimulant and hallucinogenic effects (Shuglin, 1986). Although many users of MDMA believe that it is relatively harmless, it can be deadly. Deaths from MDMA use are often the result of dehydration or a heat stroke that occurs from a rise in temperature when the body cannot cool itself.

A number of substances found in nature can produce hallucinogenic effects. These drugs are potentially dangerous, especially when used in conjunction with driving a vehicle or performing some other task that requires focused attention.

Mescaline comes from the peyote cactus and has long been a part of many Native American religious and spiritual rituals. Native Americans have used mescaline to produce sensations of being out of one's own body or talking with spirits (Lyvers, 2003).

Explore

ECSTASY RISING VIDEO

Students can learn more about the drug ecstasy by viewing the following video, available online through Google Videos at
http://video.google.com

Title: Ecstasy Rising

Source: ABC News – Primetime Special with Peter Jennings (4/1/2004)

Run Time: 18:44

Description: Introduces the effects and government-professed hazards of the drug ecstasy.

Uses: The presentation of altered states of consciousness, discussion about why drugs are used, and the real and professed dangers of chemically altering consciousness. Also good for following topics: methods of psychology (research flaws, experimenter bias, and replication), consciousness, motivation, social influences, health, and well-being.

Follow up with a discussion of students' thoughts on the use of ecstasy in the United States and whether it is as dangerous as it seems.

▲ Cannabis is reported to relieve pain in cases of multiple sclerosis and chronic pain from nerve damage. Such use is controversial as cannabis is classified as an illegal drug in some countries.

psilocybin natural hallucinogen found in certain mushrooms.

marijuana mild hallucinogen (also known as *pot* or *weed*) derived from the leaves and flowers of a particular type of hemp plant.

Psilocybin (sigh-luh-SIGH-bun) is another naturally occurring hallucinogen, contained in a certain kind of mushroom, often referred to as "magic mushrooms." Like mescaline, it has also been used in similar rituals by several native cultures (Aghajanian & Marek, 1999).

One of the best known and most commonly abused of the hallucinogenic drugs, **marijuana** (also called *pot* or *weed*) comes from the leaves and flowers of the hemp plant called *cannabis sativa*. Marijuana can produce a feeling of well-being, mild intoxication, and mild sensory distortions or hallucinations (Olin, 1993; Tart, 1970).

The effects of marijuana are relatively mild compared to the other hallucinogens. This does not mean, however, that marijuana is "safe." On the contrary, using marijuana can lead to numerous health problems (not to mention legal problems). Higher doses of marijuana can cause hallucinations, delusions, and the all-too-common paranoia. Newer studies suggest that long-term marijuana use can produce signs of withdrawal such as irritability, memory difficulties, sleep difficulties, and increased aggression (Block & Ghoneim, 1993; Budney et al., 2001; Kouri et al., 1999; Pope et al., 2001).

Even at mild doses, it is not safe to operate heavy machinery or drive a car while under the influence of marijuana. The drug's effect on a person's reaction time and perception of surroundings is too damaging to the ability to make the split-second decisions that are required in driving.

10.4 How do drugs function at the synaptic level?

What do psychoactive drugs actually do to a person's brain?
Your entire nervous system—brain, spinal cord, and nerves—is filled with cells called neurons. Neurons receive and process information within your body, allowing you to move, think, and experience emotions. Essentially, neurons control every thought, behavior, and emotion you have. Neurons receive messages from chemical molecules called neurotransmitters, which

◀ What do psychoactive drugs actually do to a person's brain?

CONSCIOUSNESS: SLEEP, DREAMS, HYPNOSIS, AND DRUGS

CHAPTER 4 • Module 10

COVER THE MODULE *(continued)*

- Marijuana is a mild hallucinogen, producing mild euphoria and relaxation in users. Larger doses can lead to hallucinations and paranoia.
- Many people believe that marijuana is "safe" because it is mild. However, studies show that long-term use cause irritability, memory difficulties, sleep difficulties, and increased aggression.

COVER THE MODULE

10. 4 How do drugs function at the synaptic level?
- Neurons are cells that make up the nervous system and control every thought, behavior, and emotion.
- Neurons receive messages from neurotransmitters.

DISCUSS THE STUDENT VOICE QUESTION

The text describes what happens in the brain in order for the drugs to take effect. The following website has pictures of the brain after prolonged use of various types of drugs: **www.amenclinics.com/brain-science/spect-image-gallery/spect-atlas/images-of-alcohol-and-drug-abuse/**. Show the photos to the class for a strong visual pertaining to how drugs affect the brain.

L2 LPR DIFFERENTIATED INSTRUCTION

Less Proficient Readers For students with difficulties with vocabulary and fluency, randomly call on these students to provide examples of the vocabulary word under examination.

Class Demonstration

DEBATE: SHOULD LAWS AGAINST ILLEGAL DRUGS BE STRENGTHENED?

Pose the above question to the class. Divide the class into two teams. Team *A* is assigned the favorable position, and Team *B* is assigned the opposing view. Allow students a few minutes to work together to plan their arguments. Team *A* forms an inner circle, and Team *B* forms an outer circle. Students from each team face each other in pairs. Students have 30 seconds to present arguments to one another. Then have students take one step to the right. Repeat the process until all arguments have been presented. Bring the class back together. Have students debrief and share their personal opinions on the topic.

Module 10 Hypnosis and Drugs **131**

CHAPTER 4 • Module 10

COVER THE MODULE (continued)

LINK to Chapter Two: The Biological Perspective, pp. 42–47.

- Psychoactive drugs interfere with neurons and transmitters.
  - Some drugs are *antagonists*, blocking effects of neurotransmitters.
  - Others are *agonists*, enhancing neurotransmitters' effects.
- Alcohol interferes with neurotransmitters controlling muscles and movement, releasing GABA, a neurotransmitter that is a depressant.
- Cocaine enhances neurotransmitters that control mood, causing euphoria.

COVER THE MODULE

10.5 What are the effects of psychoactive drugs?

- *Physical dependence* occurs when the body cannot function normally without a certain drug.
- Signs of physical dependence include drug tolerance and *withdrawal*.
- *Psychological dependence* occurs when a person believes a drug is necessary to his or her emotional well-being.

DISCUSS THE STUDENT VOICE QUESTION

Review: Which drugs cause physical dependence and which ones do not? Ask students to list some reasons why a person can be psychologically dependent. How does the drug "help" a person in this situation? What other methods might people use to cope with whatever is causing them to use the drug?

---

physical dependence condition occurring when a person's body becomes unable to function normally without a particular drug.

withdrawal physical symptoms that can include nausea, pain, tremors, crankiness, and high blood pressure, resulting from a lack of an addictive drug in the body systems.

psychological dependence the feeling that a drug is needed to continue a feeling of emotional or psychological well-being.

> But not all drugs produce physical dependence, right? For example, some people say that you can't get physically dependent on marijuana. If that's true, why is it so hard for some people to quit smoking pot?

---

pass information from one neuron to the next and tell neurons how to act in certain situations. **LINK** to Chapter Two: The Biological Perspective, pp. 42–47.

Psychoactive drugs, however, interfere with the physiology of neurons and the use of their neurotransmitters. Some drugs serve as antagonists, blocking the effects of neurotransmitters, while other drugs serve as agonists, increasing neurotransmitters' effects. When this happens, the neurons in a person's body are not getting the correct information, which causes a person's physical functioning, emotions, movements, or thoughts to dramatically change.

Alcohol, for instance, interferes with the neurotransmitters that control muscles and movement. Alcohol indirectly stimulates the release of a neurotransmitter called GABA, the brain's major depressant (Brick, 2003). GABA slows down or stops neural activity. As more GABA is released, the brain's functioning becomes more and more inhibited, depressed, or slowed down. That's why a person who is heavily under the influence of alcohol has trouble moving and speaking normally.

Cocaine, on the other hand, enhances the effects of the neurotransmitters that control mood. So the neurons receive far more information than they should—they are receiving messages from both the neurotransmitters and the chemicals in cocaine. This sends the neurons into overdrive, which causes a euphoric rush. Different drugs have varying effects on neurotransmitters, which can alter everything from memory and muscle movement to hunger and sleep.

10.5 What are the effects of psychoactive drugs?

Drugs that people can become physically dependent on cause the user's body to crave the drug (Abadinsky, 1989; Fleming & Barry, 1992; Pratt, 1991). After using the drug for some period of time, the body becomes unable to function normally without the drug and the person is said to be dependent or addicted, a condition commonly called **physical dependence**.

One sign of physical dependence is the development of a drug tolerance (Pratt, 1991). As the person continues to use the drug, larger and larger doses of the drug are needed to achieve the same initial effects.

Another sign of physical dependence is that the user experiences symptoms of **withdrawal** when deprived of the drug. Depending on the drug, these symptoms can range from headaches, nausea, and irritability to severe pain, cramping, shaking, and dangerously elevated blood pressure. These physical sensations occur because the body is trying to adjust to the absence of the drug. Many users will take more of the drug to alleviate the symptoms of withdrawal, which makes the entire situation worse.

But not all drugs produce physical dependence, right? For example, some people say that you can't get physically dependent on marijuana. If that's true, why is it so hard for some people to quit smoking pot?

Not all drugs cause physical dependence; some cause **psychological dependence**, or the belief that the drug is needed to continue a feeling of emotional or psychological well-being, which is a very powerful factor in continued drug use. The body may not need or crave the drug, and people may not experience the symptoms of physical withdrawal or tolerance, but

132 CHAPTER 4

Class Demonstration (Kinesthetic)

WHAT DRUG AM I?

Purpose: Students review what they have learned about psychoactive drugs.

Time: 15 minutes

Description: Tape a piece of paper on the back of each student with the name of a drug. Students circulate in the classroom, asking each other questions such as "Am I a stimulant?" and "How do I affect the user?" to gather information to deduce what drug is written on their back. Once they have guessed correctly, they can remove the paper and help other students. Alternatively, divide the class in half. Give each student in one group a folded piece of paper with the name of a drug on it. Students describe how a person would behave while taking the drug. Students in the other half pretend to be "ER doctors" and ask questions of each other to "diagnose" the drug each student is describing. Switch roles.

they will continue to use the drug because they *think* they need it. In this case, it is the rewarding properties of using the drug that cause a dependency to develop.

Although not all drugs produce physical dependence, *any* drug can become a focus of psychological dependence. Psychological dependencies can last forever. Some people who gave up smoking pot decades ago still say that the craving returns every now and then (Roffman et al., 1988).

10.6 How do cultural pressures and expectations influence drug use?

Drug use, unfortunately, remains an all-too-common problem in today's society. In many cases, people use drugs partly to deal with pressures from the outside world.

Some of these pressures are psychological. People who feel depressed often turn to drugs because they feel that their lives are meaningless, hopeless, and directionless. This can occur especially among school dropouts and the unemployed (Newcomb & Harlow, 1986). Others who are at risk for drug use include people who have recently left home (Bachman et al., 1997), or who suffer from anger, anxiety, or insomnia.

External forces can play a role in drug use as well. Among teenagers in particular, peer pressure can lead to experimentation with drugs. If a teen's friends are using drugs, that teen will be more likely to end up using them, too. They may use drugs because they think it will make them more popular with their peers. Alcohol and other drugs are often found at parties and other social gatherings, which increases the pressure on teenagers to "fit in with the crowd."

By the same token, if a teen's friends stop using drugs, that teen will be more likely to stop using them, too. Alcohol and drug use also decreases when people marry and have children. They no longer want to take part in such risky behavior now that they have a responsibility to their family.

Culture also plays a role in substance use and abuse. For example, in some areas of the United States, the use of medical marijuana is permitted, although recreational use is not. In Scotland, drinking whiskey is considered socially acceptable and a national pastime, while drinking is forbidden in Islamic cultures such as Pakistan, Qatar, and Sudan. Some cultures may incorporate the use of drugs into religious rituals and ceremonies, while other strictly forbid the use of any such substance.

As you have learned in this section, psychoactive drugs can have a very harmful impact on people's health and well-being. Although peer influence may sometimes seem intimidating, it is important to make an extra effort to resist these social pressures. The negative consequences of drug use can be devastating—and even deadly.

CHAPTER 4 • Module 10

COVER THE MODULE

10.6 How do cultural pressures and expectations influence drug use?

- Psychological pressures: people suffering from depression, anxiety, anger, or insomnia turn to drugs because of feelings of hopelessness
- External forces such as peer pressure, especially with teenagers
- Cultural pressures advocating drug use as a "national pastime" or incorporating it into religious rituals and ceremonies, or forbidding the use of any such substance

L3 DIFFERENTIATED INSTRUCTION

Tactile/Kinesthetic Learners When these students study, they should read information out loud while walking back and forth.

Class Demonstration

SUBTLE PRESSURE IN ADVERTISEMENTS FOR LEGAL DRUG USE

<u>Purpose</u>: Students recognize "cultural pressure" in the form of advertisements for legal drugs.

<u>Time</u>: 25 to 30 minutes

<u>Description</u>: Have students bring in an advertisement from a magazine, newspaper, website, and so forth (or search through sources you provide to find one) that markets a legal drug, such as alcohol, cigarettes, diet pills, beer, chewing tobacco, sleeping aids, and/or energy drinks. Group students according to type of product. Have students draw conclusions about the commonalities in the ads for how the drug is marketed. Have a spokesperson for the group share findings with the class. As an extension, have students make up a product for their product category and create an advertisement. Discuss with students how products are aimed at a target audience, and how drugs are marketed in such a way that consumers may not perceive them as drugs at all.

CHAPTER 4 • Module 10

Assess

Assign the Module 10 Practice Quiz.

Use the Practice Quiz to identify gaps in student understanding.

REMEDIATE

Have students, individually or in groups, review the module goals, learning objectives, and key terms.

Refer students to the Concept Summary on p. 139 for review.

Close

Ask each student to take a turn answering the following question: "How do meditation, hypnosis, and drugs affect consciousness? Give an example and discuss the health benefits and/or drawbacks of the example."

Practice Quiz

Pick the best answer.

1. Kareem is relaxing in a chair with his eyes closed. As he sits quietly, he is focusing on the sound of his own breathing and clearing his mind of other thoughts. Kareem is practicing
   a. sensory deprivation
   b. receptive meditation
   c. coping-based meditation
   d. concentrative meditation

2. Which of the following is not one of the steps in inducing hypnosis?
   a. putting the person to sleep
   b. telling the person to relax
   c. telling the person to use vivid imagination
   d. telling the person to focus on what is being said

3. Hypnosis has been successfully used to
   a. reduce sensations of pain
   b. regress a person back to infancy
   c. give a person superhuman strength
   d. reliably enhance memory

4. In the _____ theory of hypnosis, hypnotized people are not in an altered state but are merely playing the role expected of them.
   a. social-cognitive
   b. dissociative
   c. expectancy
   d. alternative

5. All narcotics are derived from
   a. cannabis
   b. opium
   c. mescaline
   d. morphine

6. Which of the following hallucinogens is not a synthetically created drug?
   a. psilocybin
   b. LSD
   c. PCP
   d. MDMA

7. Which of the following is not a depressant?
   a. alcohol
   b. benzodiazepine
   c. nicotine
   d. barbiturate

8. Which of the following was originally thought to be a more pure form of morphine, with fewer side effects?
   a. heroin
   b. caffeine
   c. marijuana
   d. cocaine

9. What are two signs of physical dependence?
   a. drug tolerance and psychological cravings
   b. drug tolerance and withdrawal
   c. psychological cravings and nausea
   d. withdrawal and nausea

10. Alcohol and drug use is less frequent among
    a. school dropouts and the unemployed
    b. people who suffer from anger, anxiety, or insomnia
    c. teens whose friends use drugs
    d. people with a spouse and children

Practice Quiz Answers

1. d
2. a
3. a
4. a
5. b
6. a
7. c
8. a
9. b
10. d

CHAPTER 4 Summary

🎧 Listen on **mypsychlab.com**

Module 9: Sleep and Dreams
Understand the relationship between conscious and unconscious processes.

9.1 What are the different levels of consciousness?
- Consciousness is a person's awareness of everything that is going on at any given moment. Most waking hours are spent in waking consciousness. Altered states of consciousness are shifts in the quality or pattern of mental activity.

9.2 What is the difference between explicit and implicit processing?
- Explicit processing is processing that is conscious, in which you are aware of your thought process. Implicit processing happens without conscious awareness.

Explain how and why we sleep and dream.

9.3 What is the circadian rhythm, and how does it relate to sleep?
- Sleep is a circadian rhythm, lasting 24 hours, and is a product of the activity of the hypothalamus.

9.4 What theories exist about the function of sleep?
- Adaptive theory states that sleep evolved as a way to conserve energy and keep animals safe from predators that hunt at night.
- Restorative theory states that sleep provides the body with an opportunity to restore chemicals that have been depleted during the day.

9.5 How does the sleep cycle work?
- The stages of the sleep cycle are Stage One (light sleep), Stage Two (sleep spindles), Stages Three and Four (deep sleep), and REM sleep. People cycle through these stages throughout a typical night's sleep.

9.6 What are the different types of sleep disorders?
- Sleep disorders include REM behavior disorder, night terrors, sleep apnea, insomnia, and narcolepsy.

Listen to an audio file of your chapter on **mypsychlab.com**

9.7 Do dreams serve a function?
- The activation-information-mode model states that information experienced during waking hours can influence dream synthesis.

Module 10: Hypnosis and Drugs
Describe meditation and hypnosis.

10.1 How does meditation affect consciousness?
- Meditation can produce a state of relaxation and reduce the physical reactions common to stressful situations.

10.2 How does hypnosis work, and why is it controversial?
- Hypnosis is a state of consciousness in which a person is especially susceptible to suggestion. Hypnosis can produce amnesia, reduce pain, and alter sensory impressions.

Understand the effects of psychoactive drugs.

10.3 What are the major categories of psychoactive drugs?
- Stimulants increase the activity of the nervous system. Depressants decrease the activity of the nervous system. Narcotics are pain-relieving drugs derived from the opium poppy. Hallucinogens alter perceptions and may cause hallucinations.

10.4 How do drugs function at the synaptic level?
- The chemicals in drugs can either block or enhance the effects of neurotransmitters.

10.5 What are the effects of psychoactive drugs?
- Drugs may produce physical addiction and psychological dependence.

10.6 How do cultural pressures and expectations influence drug use?
- Depression, anger, anxiety, and peer pressure can all influence drug use.

Vocabulary Terms

consciousness p. 110
waking consciousness p. 110
altered state of consciousness p. 110
circadian rhythm p. 112
microsleeps p. 112
sleep deprivation p. 112
adaptive theory p. 113
restorative theory p. 113
rapid eye movement p. 113
non-REM sleep p. 113
alpha waves p. 113
theta waves p. 113
delta waves p. 113
REM paralysis p. 115

REM rebound p. 116
sleepwalking p. 117
nightmares p. 117
REM behavior disorder p. 117
night terrors p. 117
insomnia p. 118
sleep apnea p. 118
narcolepsy p. 118
activation-synthesis hypothesis p. 120
activation-information-mode model (AIM) p. 120
meditation p. 123
concentrative meditation p. 123
receptive meditation p. 123

hypnosis p. 124
social-cognitive theory of hypnosis p. 126
psychoactive drugs p. 126
stimulants p. 126
depressants p. 126
narcotics p. 126
hallucinogenics p. 126
amphetamines p. 126
cocaine p. 127
nicotine p. 127
caffeine p. 128
barbiturates p. 128
benzodiazepines p. 128
alcohol p. 128

opium p. 129
morphine p. 129
heroin p. 130
hallucinogens p. 130
LSD p. 130
PCP p. 130
MDMA (Ecstasy or X) p. 130
stimulatory hallucinogenics p. 130
mescaline p. 130
psilocybin p. 131
marijuana p. 131
physical dependence p. 132
withdrawal p. 132
psychological dependence p. 132

CONSCIOUSNESS: SLEEP, DREAMS, HYPNOSIS, AND DRUGS

Critical Thinking

MAKING CONNECTIONS

Have students create a poster "mind map" of the chapter and the personal connections he or she made. Have students put a symbolic or photographic image of themselves in the center. For every section in bold in the summary, ask that they choose a photo/magazine cutout or a print from a website to represent one connection he or she made to the material in that section. Each image must be accompanied by a one- or two-sentence description of the image, the connection, and what the student learned. Students can present posters to the class as review.

CHAPTER 4 • Module 10

Chapter Summary

Encourage students to carefully review and study the summary. Explain that it provides an overview of key concepts presented in the text.

Have students identify what they find unclear or confusing. Call on volunteers to provide answers, examples, or definitions.

Vocabulary Terms

Remind students that terms are defined within the chapter at point of use. If they are not sure of a term's definition, they should look up the definition on the page.

Encourage students to create study cards of unfamiliar words or go to **www.mypsychlab.com** for flashcards. Have them test themselves or a classmate. Advanced students can explain the terms in their own words.

CHAPTER 4 • Module 10

VOCABULARY REVIEW

1. g
2. c
3. a
4. e
5. f
6. j
7. b
8. h
9. i
10. d

WRITING ABOUT PSYCHOLOGY

1. The student's answers should provide three examples of each implicit and explicit processing as well as at least two reasons per example explaining how implicit/explicit processing apply.

2. Answers should clearly state whether the student agrees or disagrees. The student should provide three strong explanations for why he or she took this position, including (1) discussions of whether the actions performed while in hypnosis were feasible for what hypnosis can and cannot accomplish, (2) discussion of dissociation, and (3) social role-playing.

PSYCHOLOGY PROJECT

Have students keep a brief journal recording the experiment. Students should:

- Record the time of day and conditions under which the experiment began.
- Record the starting heart rate for the activity.
- Describe briefly where the meditation took place, the environment, and the activities undertaken while meditating.
- Record the new calculated heart rate.
- Discuss how the heart rate changed.
- Include at least one paragraph describing how activities such as meditation affect the body.

CHAPTER 4 Assessment

Study and Review on mypsychlab.com

Vocabulary Review
Match each vocabulary term to its definition.

1. altered state of consciousness
2. rapid eye movement (REM)
3. meditation
4. hypnosis
5. stimulants
6. depressants
7. narcotics
8. hallucinogenics
9. physical dependence
10. psychological dependence

a. Mental series of exercises meant to refocus attention and achieve a trancelike state of consciousness.
b. A class of opium-related drugs that suppress the sensation of pain by binding to and stimulating the nervous system's natural receptor sites for endorphins.
c. Stage of sleep in which the eyes move rapidly under the eyelids and the person is typically experiencing a dream.
d. The feeling that a drug is needed to continue a feeling of emotional or psychological well-being.
e. State of consciousness in which the person is especially susceptible to suggestion.
f. Drugs that increase the functioning of the nervous system.
g. State in which there is a shift in the quality or pattern of mental activity as compared to waking consciousness.
h. Drugs including marijuana that produce hallucinations or increased feelings of relaxation and intoxication.
i. Condition occurring when a person's body becomes unable to function normally without a particular drug.
j. Drugs that decrease the functioning of the nervous system.

Writing about Psychology
Respond to each question in complete sentences.

1. Think about everything you have done since you woke up this morning. Which actions required implicit processing? Which used explicit processing? Give at least three examples of each and explain why they involved implicit or explicit processing.

2. A friend mentions to you that she does not believe in hypnosis. She thinks that people cannot really be hypnotized and that people who claim to be hypnotists are lying. Do you agree or disagree? Use your knowledge of hypnosis to explain your position.

Psychology Project
Meditation or resting peacefully can calm your mind, but can these practices also calm your body? Find out how sitting peacefully affects your heart rate.

Materials:
- a stopwatch or clock
- a quiet, comfortable place to sit
- meditation audio instructions or calming music (optional)

Instructions:

1. Plan a time to perform your experiment. Choose a time just after you have been engaging in normal activities like going to school or taking a walk. Do not perform the experiment immediately after sleeping or exercising.

2. Find your pulse on your neck or wrist (you may need someone to help you) and count how many heartbeats you feel in a 10-second period. Multiply this number by 6 to find your heart rate in beats per minute. This is your starting heart rate.

3. Sit in a quiet, comfortable place and meditate or rest peacefully for at least 20 minutes. You may wish to listen to calming music or follow instructions for guided meditation. Avoid thinking about anything that makes you feel stressed or excited.

4. After at least 20 minutes have passed, calculate your heart rate again, following the instructions in step 2. Has your heart rate changed? How do you think activities like meditation or resting peacefully affect the body?

Internet Resources

Association for the Scientific Study of Consciousness: http://assc.caltech.edu/

National Institute on Alcohol Abuse and Alcoholism-NIH: www.niaaa.nih.gov/

Neuroscience for Kids: The Effects of Drugs on the Nervous System: http://faculty.washington.edu/chudler/introb.html#drug

Test Yourself

Pick the best answer.

1. Which of the following situations is not an altered state of consciousness?
   a. You are daydreaming.
   b. You have been hypnotized.
   c. You are concentrating on a math test.
   d. You are asleep.

2. Which is the best example of implicit processing?
   a. talking with friends
   b. walking to class
   c. taking notes in class
   d. asking the teacher a question

3. Which of the following statements about REM sleep is FALSE?
   a. The eyes move rapidly back and forth under the eyelids.
   b. Most people report that they were dreaming if awakened.
   c. Brain waves resemble waking beta waves.
   d. Lack of REM sleep produces psychological disorders.

4. The symptoms of sleep deprivation include all but which of the following?
   a. trembling hands
   b. inability to concentrate
   c. feeling of general discomfort
   d. REM paralysis.

5. The restorative theory of sleep best explains
   a. when we sleep
   b. why we need to sleep
   c. where we sleep
   d. how we sleep

6. In which stage of sleep do night terrors occur?
   a. Stage One
   b. Stage Two
   c. Stage Three
   d. Stage Four

7. Which of the following is true about night terrors?
   a. They are the same thing as nightmares.
   b. They are always vividly remembered afterward.
   c. They are more common in children.
   d. They take place in one of the lighter stages of sleep.

8. A sleep disorder that may require the use of a device to open the nostrils is called
   a. sleep apnea
   b. insomnia
   c. narcolepsy
   d. somnambulism

9. What theory holds that information that is accessed during waking hours can have an influence on dreams?
   a. latent content theory
   b. manifest content theory
   c. activation-synthesis hypothesis
   d. activation-information-mode model

10. Which is the best example of receptive meditation?
    a. Focusing on the sound of your heartbeat
    b. Staring at one particular spot for several minutes
    c. Closing your eyes and clearing your head
    d. Listening to the sounds of wildlife

11. Hypnotism has been shown to do all of the following except
    a. create amnesia of whatever happens during the hypnotic session
    b. provide pain relief
    c. alter sensory perceptions
    d. regress people back to their early childhood experiences

12. Jackie once used marijuana, but quit when she got married. Although she had no problem quitting, she still finds that every now and then she gets a strong craving to use marijuana again. Her craving is most likely the result of
    a. psychological dependence
    b. physical dependency
    c. withdrawal
    d. none of the above

13. Nicole does not drink at home or when she goes to parties. However, when she goes on vacation overseas, her host family offers her a glass of wine with dinner each night, which she accepts. Which BEST explains Nicole's behavior?
    a. Nicole was given more opportunities to drink overseas than at home.
    b. Nicole was peer-pressured into drinking by her host family when she went overseas.
    c. Nicole comes from a country where drinking and drug use are not permitted.
    d. Nicole visited a country where drinking a glass of wine with dinner is socially accepted.

14. In the hospital, an elderly cancer patient is given a drug derived from the opium poppy. This drug relieves her pain and inhibits the functioning of her nervous system. This drug is most likely classified as a
    a. depressant
    b. hallucinogen
    c. stimulant
    d. narcotic

15. Cocaine _____ the neurotransmitters that control mood.
    a. eliminates
    b. inhibits
    c. excites
    d. has no effect on

16. You hear about an accident that took place at 3 A.M., when a driver drifted into oncoming traffic. Given the early morning time, you suspect that the driver may have experienced a
    a. lapse in judgment
    b. microsleep episode
    c. hypnogogic episode
    d. hallucination

CONSCIOUSNESS: SLEEP, DREAMS, HYPNOSIS, AND DRUGS 137

CHAPTER 4 • Module 10

TEST YOURSELF

1. c	9. d
2. b	10. d
3. d	11. d
4. d	12. a
5. b	13. d
6. d	14. d
7. c	15. c
8. a	16. b

Ready for Testing

STUDENTS KNOW THEY ARE READY FOR TESTING IF THEY ARE ABLE TO . . .

- Define consciousness and discuss the different levels of consciousness.
- Explain the factors that control sleep, theories on the purpose of sleep, the stages of sleep, and disorders of sleep.
- Discuss dreams and three theories that attempt to explain the purpose of dreams.
- Talk about the effects of sleep deprivation.
- Introduce the phenomenon of hypnosis and two theories suggesting the underlying mechanism.
- Describe properties and potential dangers of psychoactive drugs, including stimulants, depressants, narcotics, and hallucinogens.

Chapter 4 Assessment 137

CHAPTER 4 • Module 10

MULTIMEDIA CONTENT AVAILABLE AT
www.mypsychlab.com

Map the Concepts on **mypsychlab.com**

Study and Review Flashcards on **mypsychlab.com**

STUDY TIPS

Essay Tests When faced with an essay test, students should scan the test and note the number of questions and the point value of each. They should then budget their time accordingly. Before beginning to write, encourage students to read the question carefully and be sure to do what it asks. Key words to look for include *analyze, explain, identify, demonstrate, compare, contract,* and *define*. Jotting down an outline can help students organize their thoughts and may get them some points if they run out of time. Stress that if the test is handwritten, neatness counts. They may find it preferable to draw a line through mistakes rather than erasing. This tends to be quicker and easier to read. If students are having trouble understanding the question, suggest they try to put it in their own words. When they have finished writing, have students proofread their work if at all possible, and make sure they have answered all the parts of each question.

CHAPTER 4 — Concept Summary: Consciousness

Learning Objectives 9.1 9.2 pp. 110–111

Understand the Relationship between Conscious and Unconscious Processes

- **consciousness** is a person's awareness of everything that is going on around him or her at any given moment
  - waking consciousness
  - altered states of consciousness can be caused by
    - sleep and dreams
    - hypnosis
    - meditation
    - drugs
- **levels of processing**
  - **explicit processing** is conscious
  - **implicit processing** happens without conscious awareness

Learning Objectives 9.3 9.4 9.5 9.6 9.7 pp. 112–121

Explain How and Why We Sleep and Dream

- **sleep** is one of the body's **circadian** (daily) **biological rhythms**
  - **theories of sleep**
    - **adaptive theory** explains when we sleep
    - **restorative theory** explains why we sleep
  - **sleep stages**
    - **non-REM Stage One** (light sleep)
    - **non-REM Stage Two** (sleep spindles)
    - **non-REM Stages Three & Four** (delta waves)
    - **REM sleep** (dreams)
- **sleep disorders**
  - insomia
  - sleep apnea
  - narcolepsy
- **dreams**
  - **Freud's interpretation**: wish fulfillment—conflicts, events, and desires represented in symbolic forms in dreams
  - **activation-synthesis hypothesis**

138 CHAPTER 4

What Every Student Should Know About . . .

CREATING A PORTFOLIO

Explain the purpose of portfolios to students. Tell them that their teachers will likely be the main audience for portfolios that they create as students. As an instructional tool, the portfolio serves as both a record of their progress in a particular course and as a means of assessment (which might be provided as a grade, or might be presented as a written evaluation from the teacher). As they advance in their coursework, their portfolios will become of more interest to their field or discipline. Their portfolio of work can serve as a networking tool, helping them to connect their work to the work of others. Similarly, the portfolios they create to assist them when they are applying to college or looking for a job can help others see both the quality of the work they have done and the processes they employ to accomplish that work.

138   Chapter 4 Consciousness

Sleep, Dreams, Hypnosis, and Drugs

Map The Concepts on mypsychlab.com

CHAPTER 4 • Module 10

Learning Objectives

10.1 10.2 pp. 123–126

Describe Meditation and Hypnosis

- **meditation** is a mental series of exercises meant to achieve a trancelike state of consciousness
  - concentrative meditation
  - receptive meditation
- **hypnosis** is a state of consciousness during which a person is more susceptible to suggestion

Learning Objectives

10.3 10.4 10.5 10.6 pp. 126–133

Understand the Effects of Psychoactive Drugs

- **major categories of drugs**
  - **stimulants** increase functioning of nervous system
  - **depressants** have sedative effect
  - **narcotics** are euphoria-producing and pain-relieving drugs derived from opium
  - **hallucinogens** alter brain's interpretation of sensations
- **drugs interfere with neurotransmitters**
  - alcohol blocks neurotransmitters that control muscles and movement
  - cocaine enhances effects of neurotransmitters that control mood
- **effects of psychoactive drugs**
  - physical dependence
  - psychological dependence

Number of Drinks / Behavior
- Release of inhibitions
- Judgment impaired
- Coordination and level of alertness lowered
- Reaction time significantly slowed
- Muscle control and speech impaired
- Loss of self-control
- Sensory and motor capabilities depressed
- Double vision and legal blindness
- Unfit to drive for up to 10 hours
- Lethal dosage for about 50% of people
- Alcohol poisoning/overdose

Key: 1 drink equals 1 can of beer, 1 glass of wine, or 1 shot of most liquors.

CONSCIOUSNESS: SLEEP, DREAMS, HYPNOSIS, AND DRUGS

STUDY TIPS

Test-Taking Skills A few simple strategies should help most students improve their performance on tests. A positive attitude toward the test and their own abilities is a top priority. Beyond that, students should scan the entire test before beginning to work. Using this approach, they should answer the easiest questions first and then focus on the more difficult ones. This strategy boosts confidence, and the simpler questions may contain information that helps with more difficult ones. When answering questions, students should be sure to read the entire question before responding and to read any instructions thoroughly. If they find a question confusing, they should ask the teacher for clarification. Focusing on one question at a time can help with concentration. Finally, if students find themselves getting anxious, they should stop working and take a few deep breaths to help them relax.

Comprehension Check

ADVICE FOR A YOUNGER STUDENT

To gauge students' grasp of the contents of this chapter, ask them to write down what they would say to a younger student who asked about taking drugs. What are some of the physical and mental effects of using drugs? How can students deal with cultural pressures to take drugs?

CHAPTER 5

Development Across the Life Span

Launch the Chapter

CHAPTER GOALS AND LEARNING OBJECTIVES

Module 11 Topics in Development

Describe methods and issues in life span development.

- 11.1 How do biological and environmental factors influence development?
- 11.2 What are some major research issues in developmental psychology?
- 11.3 How do psychologists study development?
- 11.4 What are critical periods and sensitive periods?

Module 12 Prenatal, Infant and Childhood Development

Learn about prenatal and newborn development.

- 12.1 How do humans develop from conception through birth?
- 12.2 What reflexes and abilities do newborns have?

Describe development during infancy and childhood.

- 12.3 What kinds of physical changes take place in infancy and childhood?
- 12.4 How do infants and children develop cognitive skills?
- 12.5 What are the stages of language development?
- 12.6 How do babies begin to develop relationships with others?
- 12.7 How do children develop socially and emotionally?

Module 13 Adolescence and Adulthood

Describe development during adolescence.

- 13.1 What physical changes occur during adolescence?
- 13.2 How do reasoning and morality develop during adolescence?
- 13.3 How do adolescents form their identities?
- 13.4 What role do family members and peers play in adolescent development?

Describe development during adulthood.

- 13.5 What social and cognitive changes occur during adulthood?
- 13.6 What physical changes happen during adulthood?
- 13.7 How do scientists explain why aging occurs?
- 13.8 What are the stages of death and dying?

Home Alone at Two: A Lesson in Survival Instincts

Don was separated from his wife, Lisa. She had custody of their 2-year-old daughter, and he had been trying to reach her to check on the little girl. Finally, he contacted the police and found out that his wife had been in jail for nearly 3 weeks, arrested on an aggravated battery charge. Lisa told him that their daughter was with neighbors, but after knocking on door after door without success, Don finally got the apartment manager to let him into his wife's apartment. There was his precious little child, covered in dirt and dried ketchup. She grabbed him and didn't let go.

The 2-year-old child had survived alone in the apartment for 19 days by drinking water from the bathroom sink and eating mustard, ketchup, dried spaghetti, and a few other items she was able to find in the bottom sections of the refrigerator and cupboards of the kitchen. Although malnourished, she had managed to find enough to eat to survive until rescued by her father, who was amazed at her relatively good condition.

The day after arriving at the hospital to be treated for malnutrition and dehydration, the plucky little girl was sitting up in her hospital bed, laughing and playing with the nurses.

This true story, which occurred in September 2003, shows not only the power of the drive to survive in human beings but also the adaptive nature of children, even young children, to explore their environment and find ways to cope with adversity.

CORRELATION TO APA STANDARDS FOR CHAPTER 5

IIIA. LIFE SPAN DEVELOPMENT

IIIA-1.	Methods and issues in life span development	pp. 142–146
IIIA-2.	Theories of life span development	pp. 152–155, 158–160, 163–164
IIIA-3.	Prenatal development and the newborn	pp. 147–151
IIIA-4.	Infancy (the first 2 years of life)	pp. 151–156
IIIA-5.	Childhood	pp. 151–155, 158–160
IIIA-6.	Adolescence	pp. 162–165
IIIA-7.	Adulthood and aging	pp. 166–169

MODULE 11 ▸ TOPICS IN DEVELOPMENT

MODULE 12 ▸ PRENATAL, INFANT AND CHILDHOOD DEVELOPMENT

MODULE 13 ▸ ADOLESCENCE AND ADULTHOOD

Why Study?

Human Development

Understanding how we come to be the people we are is a critical step in understanding ourselves as we are today, as well as whom we may become as we grow older. From the moment of conception, we are each headed down a pathway of change, influenced by our biology, environment, and social interactions, to a destination that is the same for all of us. The twists and turns of the pathway are what make each of us unique individuals. In this chapter, we'll look at the influences that help determine our developmental pathway through life.

DEVELOPMENT ACROSS THE LIFE SPAN 141

SCHEDULING

	Semester Course (18 weeks/90 days) Periods/Blocks		Full-Year Course (36 weeks/180 days) Period/Blocks	
1 Period = 50 min. 1 Block = 90 min.				
Module 11	2.5	1.25	5	2.5
Module 12	2.5	1.25	5	2.5
Module 13	1	0.5	2	1
Total Days for Chapter	6	3	12	6

CHAPTER 5 • Module 11

Teacher Prep

Human development is the scientific study of the changes that occur in people as they age from conception to death. Developmental psychologists investigate the effects of aging on psychological processes using longitudinal, cross-sectional, and cross-sequential studies. One of the biggest debates among developmental psychologists is the question of *nature* versus *nurture*. Nature refers to the influence of everything you inherited genetically from your biological parents, and nurture refers to the influence your environment has had on your development.

Many people believe that conception represents the beginning of life. Over the course of three phases, the fertilized egg becomes a baby. The process includes cell specialization and organ formation.

Most infants are able to perform five innate reflexes. Touch is the most well-developed sense, followed by smell, sound, and taste. Vision is the least functional.

The brain triples in weight during the first 2 years of life. Piaget believed that children pass through four cognitive stages: sensorimotor, preoperational, concrete operations, and formal operations. Children go through five stages of speech development and form attachment with their primary caregivers.

Adolescence is the period from around age 14 to the early 20s and is most clearly identified by the physical changes that occur in puberty. Mentally, many adolescents are moving into Piaget's formal operational stage of development.

Adulthood can be roughly identified as the period from the early 20s until death. Most adults experience diminished perception and health problems. Hormonal changes cause menopause and andropause. The stages of death and dying are denial, anger, bargaining, depression, and acceptance.

DIFFERENTIATED INSTRUCTION KEY

Look for these symbols to help you adjust steps in each lesson to meet your students' needs.

L1 Special Needs
L2 Basic
  ELL English Language Learners
  LPR Less Proficient Readers
L3 All Students
L4 Advanced Students

Chapter 5 Development Across the Life Span **141**

CHAPTER 5 • Module 11

Focus

RESOURCES

For this module, consult the appropriate sections of the Teacher's Manual, Test Bank, and PowerPoint slides, all found on the Teacher's Resource DVD, and the interactive study tools for students on MyPsychLab.

BEFORE CLASS

Students should read the section for homework before coming to class.

BELLRINGER

Write the following developmental stages on the board: **infants, children, adolescents, adults, the elderly**. For each stage, have students briefly write an explanation of the development of the body, development of thinking skills, and development of social and emotional lives.

Teach

INTRODUCE THE TOPIC

Ask volunteers to share their answers from the Bellringer exercise.

COVER THE MODULE

11.1 How do biological and environmental factors influence development?

- *Nature* is the influence of heredity on personality, physical growth, intellectual growth, and social interactions.
- *Nurture* is the influence of environment on all of those things, including parenting styles, socioeconomic factors, physical surroundings, and anything else that may influence how one develops.
- **Genetic Influences**
  - *Dominant* genes control the expression of a trait.
  - *Recessive* gene traits are only expressed when paired with another recessive gene for the same trait.
  - Almost all traits are the result of combinations of genes working together.

142 Chapter 5 Development Across the Life Span

Module 11: Topics in Development

Module Goal
Describe methods and issues in life span development.

Learning Objectives
- 11.1 How do biological and environmental factors influence development?
- 11.2 What are some major research issues in developmental psychology?
- 11.3 How do psychologists study development?
- 11.4 What are critical periods and sensitive periods?

Describe Methods and Issues in Life Span Development

What is development? In the context of life, **human development** is the scientific study of the changes that occur in people as they age, from conception until death. This chapter will touch on a wide range of topics in psychology, such as personality, cognition (how we think and process information), biological processes, and social interactions. But in this chapter, all of those topics will be studied in the context of the process of human development.

11.1 How do biological and environmental factors influence development?

For years, psychologists have tried to understand what influences our behavior more—biological or environmental factors. The expression "nature vs. nurture" summarizes this debate. **Nature** refers to the influence of genetic characteristics we inherit and are born with, while **nurture** refers to the influence of environmental factors, including our families, peers, and culture.

Most psychologists now agree that both nature and nurture influence development and behavior. The characteristics we are born with help to determine who we become, but so does our environment. For instance, a girl's genes may determine that she will grow up to be tall and have swift reflexes. However, genetics alone will not make her into a star basketball player. **LINK** to Chapter Two: The Biological Perspective, pp. 66–67.

Genetic Influences Each of our cells contains 23 pairs of **chromosomes**—rod-shaped structures made up of **DNA**. (See Figure 11.1.) DNA consists of strands of chemical elements called *amines* that are arranged in sequences. Pieces of these DNA strands, consisting of particular patterns of amines, are known as **genes**. **LINK** to Chapter Two: The Biological Perspective, p. 66.

One-half of each pair of chromosomes is inherited from the mother, and the other half is inherited from the father. The particular combination of genes a person inherits influences his or her development.

Genes may be dominant or recessive. A **dominant** gene will always be expressed, determining what trait will physically appear in the person possessing

human development the scientific study of the changes that occur in people as they age, from conception until death.

nature the influence of our inherited characteristics on our personality, physical growth, intellectual growth, and social interactions.

nurture the influence of the environment on personality, physical growth, intellectual growth, and social interactions.

chromosome tightly wound strand of genetic material or DNA.

DNA (deoxyribonucleic acid) special molecule that contains the genetic material of the organism.

gene section of DNA having the same arrangement of chemical elements.

dominant referring to a gene that actively controls the expression of a trait.

recessive referring to a gene that only influences the expression of a trait when paired with an identical gene.

physical development development of the body.

cognitive development development of thinking and reasoning skills such as problem solving and memory.

142 CHAPTER 5

Terms

- human development • nature • nurture • chromosome • DNA (deoxyribonucleic acid) • gene • dominant • recessive • physical development • cognitive development • psychosocial development • temperament • attachment • longitudinal design • cross-sectional design • cross-sequential design • critical period • sensitive period that gene. However, a **recessive** gene will not be expressed if paired with a different, dominant gene. Genes are sometimes directly responsible for a person's having a particular trait. However, often genes do not determine a specific trait, but rather a tendency or a *predisposition*.

Environmental Influences The environmental influences that surround us before birth and during our lives significantly affect our development. These influences include our immediate environment, such as family and friends, as well as the larger culture in which we participate.

Parents or other caretakers influence children's behavior, knowledge and skills, and values. In early childhood, caretakers model the most basic human behaviors, such as talking and eating. Later, children encounter a wider circle of influences. They may participate in a sport or develop academic interests because of a friend or teacher. Finally, the culture at large influences personality and behavior. For instance, in many parts of the United States, most people learn to drive in their mid- to late teens. A teenager from a culture that places less importance on driving might not learn this skill until much later, if ever.

11.2 What are some major research issues in developmental psychology?

"Human development" seems like such a huge topic. What are some of the major issues developmental psychologists look at? What kinds of development do they study? As a field of research, developmental psychology is particularly concerned with two big questions:
- **Continuity or discontinuity:** Does development happen in a smooth, continuous progression, or in a series of clear-cut stages?
- **Stability or change:** What remains stable over the course of human development, and what changes?

Neither question has a simple answer; it depends largely on which aspect of development is under discussion. The characteristics psychologists examine fall into three broad areas: physical, cognitive, and psychosocial development.

Physical development, or development of the body, is fairly discontinuous, occurring in clearly defined stages. Our physical characteristics and skills also change over time. You may have observed these developmental patterns in babies or adolescents who undergo dramatic physical changes in a short time.

Cognitive development, or development of thinking and reasoning skills, is fairly continuous, and it changes over time. Some psychologists have proposed clear stages of cognitive development in childhood and adolescence. However, there is some debate about these stages, and in any case, a person's transition between stages is gradual. Furthermore, cognitive development is continuous in that certain skills tend to develop steadily throughout life.

Psychosocial development encompasses our emotional and social lives. Aspects that are studied include **temperament**, a child's innate personality and emotional characteristics; **attachment**, the first emotional bond a child forms with its primary caretaker; and finally, the psychological characteristics and social relationships a person has throughout childhood, adolescence, and adulthood. Research suggests that temperament is somewhat influenced by the environment but remains fairly stable over time. The process of forming an emotional attachment with the primary caregiver is continuous. While attachment style remains stable through infancy and may influence later relationships, our overall psychosocial development undergoes many changes.

psychosocial development development affecting our emotional and social lives.

temperament a child's innate personality and emotional characteristics, observable in infancy; the enduring characteristics with which each person is born.

attachment the first emotional bond a child forms with its primary caretaker.

◀ *"Human development" seems like such a huge topic. What are some of the major issues developmental psychologists look at? What kinds of development do they study?*

FIGURE 11.1 DNA Molecule
The rungs of this twisted ladderlike structure are the amines that carry the genetic codes for building the proteins that make up life.

DEVELOPMENT ACROSS THE LIFE SPAN **143**

CHAPTER 5 • Module 11

COVER THE MODULE (continued)

- **Environmental Influences**
  - These influences include our immediate environment, such as family and friends, as well as the larger culture in which we participate.

COVER THE MODULE

11.2 What are some major research issues in developmental psychology?

- One question in determining development is that of whether development occurs as gradual increases in the quantity of knowledge and skills or in discrete stages of qualitative change.
- The other question explores stability versus change—what remains stable over the course of human development, and what changes?
- These questions are answered using three broad areas of development: physical, cognitive (thinking and reasoning skills), and psychosocial (emotional and social).

DISCUSS THE STUDENT VOICE QUESTION

Ask students to think about their development to this point. What do they think has changed about them in the course of their lives? What has remained stable? Can they pinpoint any changes that happened suddenly versus changes that happened gradually?

L3 DIFFERENTIATED INSTRUCTION

Various methods of assessment—activities, portfolios, performance-based assessment, rubrics, as well as standard tests—can measure students' progress in ways that are fair to many styles of learners.

Explore

USING INFORMATION FROM THE INTERNET

Send students to the developmental psychology page of the Centre for Psychology Resources at http://psych.athabascau.ca/html/aupr/developmental.shtml.

This website contains numerous links to sites related to developmental psychology. Ask students to pick a timeframe in life span development (i.e., adolescence, old age, infancy) and explore two or three relevant links from this site. Have them write a brief report on what they found.

Module 11 Topics in Development **143**

CHAPTER 5 • Module 11

COVER THE MODULE

11.3 How do psychologists study development?
- The three special research methods used in developmental research are the longitudinal design, the cross-sectional design, and the cross-sequential design.
  - *Longitudinal design*: one group of people is followed and assessed at different times as the group ages.
  - *Cross-sectional design*: several different age groups are studied at one time.
  - *Cross-sequential design*: a combination of longitudinal and cross-sectional designs.

11.4 What are critical periods and sensitive periods?
- *Critical periods*: relatively short times when a child is most susceptible to the presence or absence of particular environmental stimuli.
  - Occur during gestation, infancy, and early childhood.
- *Sensitive periods*: those times when a child is especially receptive to learning from certain experiences.
  - May span months or even years.

11.3 How do psychologists study development?

Psychologists who study human development face unique challenges in conducting research—specifically, the problem of age. In any experiment, the participants who are exposed to the independent variable—that is, the variable the experimenter deliberately manipulates—should be randomly assigned to the different experimental conditions. The problem in developmental research is that the age of the study participants should always be an independent variable, but people cannot be randomly assigned to different age groups.

There are some special designs that are used in researching age-related changes. In a study with a **longitudinal design**, one group of people is followed and assessed *at different times* as the group ages. One famous longitudinal study started in 1964 when the British television documentary now known as *The Up Series* began. The documentary films are based on the lives of 14 individuals from different socioeconomic classes and has followed them from age 7 into adulthood, updating their television audience every 7 years. In a study with a **cross-sectional design**, several different age groups are studied *at one time*. Testing a group of fifth graders and then testing a group of ninth graders to see which group has faster reflexes is one example of a cross-sectional study. Finally, some studies have a **cross-sequential design**, which is a combination of the longitudinal and cross-sectional designs. For example, the Seattle Longitudinal Study was started in 1956 by K. Warner Schaie to study the effects of aging. The study started with 500 people ranging from 20 to 60 years old. Every 7 years, the study is updated and new participants are added. After more than 50 years, over 6,000 people have joined the remaining 26 from the original group. You can see how such a research design can become complicated and expensive.

Differences between age groups are often a problem in developmental research. For example, in comparing the IQ scores of 30-year-olds to 80-year-olds to see how aging affects intelligence, questions arise concerning whether differing educational experiences and opportunities might affect IQ scores, in addition to any effects of aging. Table 11.1 compares different research designs.

11.4 What are critical periods and sensitive periods?

Developmental psychologists also consider critical periods and sensitive periods. These periods are especially important for acquiring traits or skills that are vital to long-term development. During these periods, exposure to harmful stimuli, or failure to expose a child to the right stimuli, can permanently impair development.

The **critical periods** that occur during gestation, infancy, and early childhood are relatively short times when a child is most susceptible to the presence or absence of particular environmental stimuli. They are associated with major developmental milestones—for instance, development of an embryo's brain or an infant's vision. Problems during critical periods can lead to serious developmental challenges for the rest of a person's life. An embryo that doesn't receive proper nutrition early in development may experience permanent neurological deficits, and a baby who does not see light during the first few months of life will suffer degeneration of the optical neurons and loss of vision.

The concept of a critical period is especially important in understanding the development of language. Most psychologists agree that childhood is a critical period for language development. Adults can encourage language learning by talking or reading to the child and providing multiple opportunities to hear spoken language. In contrast, a child who is not exposed to language will find it extremely difficult to learn later on.

longitudinal design research design in which one group of people is followed and assessed at different times as the group ages.

cross-sectional design research design in which several different age groups are studied at one time.

cross-sequential design a combination of the longitudinal and cross-sectional designs in which different participants of various ages are compared at several points in time.

critical period a time when a child is developmentally most susceptible to the presence or absence of particular stimuli in the environment and must progress to the next stage of development if development is to continue normally.

Class Discussion

QUESTIONS IN DEVELOPMENT

Purpose: Students have a chance to think about and discuss questions about development and the current scientific consensus—or debates—on these topics.

Time: 15 minutes

Description: Select one of the following controversies from development and pose it to the class. Have students explore psychological research that addresses these questions and present some findings to the class for discussion. At the end of the discussion, ask whether anyone's opinion has changed by hearing what others have said.

- Are there any developmental differences between children who are cared for primarily in the home versus children who go to day care? What are the immediate- and long-term differences, if any?
- Should preschool children have academic instruction? What is appropriate academic instruction at age 2? Age 3? Age 4? Age 5?
- Does television violence influences children's behavior more than adults' behavior? If so, what is the influence on children at age 5 versus age 10? Versus age 15?
- Are older people happier than younger people?

Table 11.1 — A Comparison of Three Developmental Research Designs

CROSS-SECTIONAL DESIGN

Different participants of various ages are compared at one point in time to determine age-related *differences*.

- Group One: 20-year-old participants
- Group Two: 40-year-old participants
- Group Three: 60-year-old participants

Research done in 2010

Advantages: quick, relatively inexpensive, and easier to accomplish than the longitudinal design

Disadvantages: cannot be used to compare an individual to that same individual as he or she ages

LONGITUDINAL DESIGN

The **same** participants are studied at various ages to determine age-related *changes*.

- Study One: 20-year-old participants — Research done in 1970
- Study Two: Same participants were 40 years old — Research done in 1990
- Study Three: Same participants are now 60 years old — Research done in 2010

Advantages: examines real age-related changes as those changes occur in the same individuals

Disadvantages:
- requires time, money, and effort involved to follow participants over the years
- may result in loss of participants when they move away, lose interest, or die

CROSS-SEQUENTIAL DESIGN

Different participants of various ages are compared at several points in time, to determine both age-related *differences* and age-related *changes*.

- Study One: Group One: 20-year-old participants; Group Two: 40-year-old participants — Research done in 2005
- Study Two: Group One: participants are now 25 years old; Group Two: participants are now 45 years old — Research done in 2010

One famous case study often used as evidence for a critical period of language development is the case of Genie, a child who was severely abused and neglected by her family until she was rescued at the age of 13. After spending most of her childhood in virtual isolation, Genie was not able to say more than a handful of words. While she did eventually learn about 200 words after her rescue, she was not able to understand the rules of grammar that govern the construction of English sentences (Curtiss et al., 1974). It's important to keep in mind that we don't know what Genie's language ability was before she was isolated, and the abuse she suffered may have permanently affected her ability to learn, but Genie's experience does illustrate how difficult it can be to learn certain information after the relevant developmental period has passed.

Sensitive periods, during which a child is especially receptive to learning from certain experiences, are also important. These periods may span months or even years. For instance, attachment to a primary caregiver forms during infancy. The period from birth until about 18 months is a sensitive period when babies are especially responsive to caretaking and interactions with adult

sensitive period a time when a child is susceptible to stimuli and receptive to learning from particular types of experiences.

CHAPTER 5 • Module 11

EXTEND THE LESSON

Day Care and Social Development Discuss with students Frank Mott's longitudinal study of 2,387 children investigating whether various forms of infant care were related to the child's performance on tests of physical, cognitive, and social development several years later. Controlling for a wide range of factors, Mott found no statistically significant association between day care in infancy and the child's later motor or social development. As for cognitive development, the children who had been in day care as infants scored *higher* than those who had been at home. Mott found that healthy baby girls benefitted most from day care; healthy baby boys neither gained nor lost by being in day care; and unhealthy baby boys gained more from being in their mothers' care. Mott concluded that "no type of infant care arrangement can be generalized as being uniformly preferable or detrimental."

Most psychologists today, instead of assuming that day care is universally helpful *or* harmful, are asking different questions.

Ask: What are some better questions to ask when assessing the effects of day care on children's development? *(Possible answers: What is the quality of this particular day care? Which children do well and which do poorly in different environments? How do parents contribute to the day care experience?)*

Explore

DEVELOPMENTAL PSYCHOLOGY WEBSITES

- **Developmental Psychology – The Psychology of Development:**
  http://psychology.about.com/od/developmentalpsychology/Developmental_Psychology.htm
  Learn more about developmental psychology throughout the life span.

- **PediaView – Developmental Psychology:**
  http://pediaview.com/openpedia/Developmental_psychology
  Find information on research methods, research areas, theories of development, stages of development, and more at this site.

- **Helping Psychology – Developmental Psychology Research Methods:**
  http://helpingpsychology.com/developmentalpsychology
  This page from Helping Psychology discusses research methods used in the field of developmental psychology. It also contains links to information on developmental psychology itself, as well as the different methods of research and examples of each.

CHAPTER 5 • Module 11

Assess

Assign the Module 11 Practice Quiz.

Use the Practice Quiz to identify gaps in student understanding.

REMEDIATE

Have students, individually or in groups, review the module goals, learning objectives, and key terms.

Refer students to the Concept Summary on p. 174 for review.

Close

As a class, discuss why human development is important to psychologists. How does a better understanding of the way people move through the life span advance the field of psychology?

---

caretakers. Early childhood also includes sensitive periods for the development of gross and fine motor skills and social skills. Sensitive periods differ from critical periods in that, if a child does not develop specific traits or skills during a sensitive period, there is more likelihood of "catching up" later on.

Topics such as the influence of genetics and the environment, stability versus change, and critical and sensitive periods are relevant to all stages of human development. Modules 12 and 13 explain in more detail how fundamental issues like these influence our whole lives, from birth to old age.

Practice Quiz

Pick the best answer.

1. In what type of research design are several different age groups of participants studied at one time?
   a. case study
   b. longitudinal
   c. cross-sectional
   d. cross-sequential

2. Which of these is generally true of recessive genes?
   a. They are not located on the chromosome.
   b. They are not expressed unless paired with a similar gene.
   c. They are the cause of genetic defects.
   d. They do not determine specific traits.

3. Which of the following affects the human brain's development?
   a. genetic influences
   b. environmental influences
   c. both genetic and environmental influences
   d. neither genetic nor environmental influences

4. Which aspect of development is the least continuous?
   a. physical development
   b. cognitive development
   c. emotional development
   d. social development

5. Which of these is an example of nature affecting development?
   a. a class taken in school
   b. an inherited mental illness
   c. peer pressure from other children
   d. imitation of a parent's actions

6. If a woman's diet in the first weeks of pregnancy does not include enough folic acid, it may permanently harm the baby's brain development. This period could be described as
   a. temperamental
   b. sensitive
   c. critical
   d. continuous

7. Which of the following is the most stable over time?
   a. one's body
   b. one's temperament
   c. one's moral reasoning
   d. one's social relationships

8. The case study of Genie has been used to support the theory of
   a. critical periods in language development
   b. continuity's superiority over discontinuity
   c. the interaction between genetics and the environment
   d. the instability of childhood development

9. Tasha designs a research project in which she studies the same participants when they are 2-years old, 4-years old, and 6-years old. Tasha is using a
   a. case study research design
   b. longitudinal research design
   c. cross-sectional research design
   d. cross-sequential research design

10. Which of the following areas includes emotional development?
    a. physical development
    b. cognitive development
    c. psychosocial development
    d. sensitive development

146 CHAPTER 5

Practice Quiz Answers

1. c
2. b
3. c
4. a
5. b

6. c
7. b
8. a
9. b
10. c

146 Chapter 5 Development Across the Life Span

Module 12: Prenatal, Infant and Childhood Development

Module Goals

Learn about prenatal and newborn development.

Describe development during infancy and childhood.

Learning Objectives

- 12.1 How do humans develop from conception through birth?
- 12.2 What reflexes and abilities do newborns have?
- 12.3 What kinds of physical changes take place in infancy and childhood?
- 12.4 How do infants and children develop cognitive skills?
- 12.5 What are the stages of language development?
- 12.6 How do babies begin to develop relationships with others?
- 12.7 How do children develop socially and emotionally?

Learn About Prenatal and Newborn Development

12.1 How do humans develop from conception through birth?

Conception is the moment at which a sperm and an egg unite to form a single cell. The period from conception to birth lasts approximately 9 months. During this time, as the single cell develops into a complete infant, many things can positively or negative influence its development.

When an egg (or **ovum**) and a sperm unite in the process of **fertilization**, the resulting single cell, called a **zygote**, will have a total of 46 chromosomes. Normally, the zygote will divide, first into two cells, then four, and so on, in a process called *mitosis*. Each new cell also has 46 chromosomes, because the DNA molecules duplicate themselves before each division. Eventually, the mass of cells becomes a baby. Sometimes, in the earliest stages of cell division after conception, the cell division process doesn't work exactly this way, and twins or multiples result, as shown in Figure 12.1.

conception the moment at which a sperm and egg unite to form a single cell.

ovum the female sex cell, or egg.

fertilization the union of the ovum and sperm in the fallopian tube.

zygote a single cell that contains all the information needed to form a complete human being, resulting from the union of ovum and sperm.

Identical twins
1. Accounting for about 1 in 250 births, these are created when a single egg is fertilized by one sperm.
2. The egg splits into halves. Each develops into a fetus with the same genetic composition.

Fraternal twins
1. Twice as common as identicals, fraternals arise when two eggs are released at once.
2. If both are fertilized by separate sperm, two fetuses form. Genetically, they are just ordinary siblings.

FIGURE 12.1 Identical and Fraternal Twins

Identical twins are the same sex and look exactly alike because they come from a single fertilized egg that splits. They are also called monozygotic twins ("mono" means "one"). Fraternal twins may be of different sexes and do not look as much alike because they come from different eggs. They are also called dizygotic twins ("di" means "two").

DEVELOPMENT ACROSS THE LIFE SPAN 147

Terms

- conception • ovum • fertilization • zygote • germinal period • embryonic period
- fetal period • teratogen • uterus • placenta • umbilical cord • embryo • fetus
- assimilation • accommodation • sensorimotor stage • object permanence
- preoperational stage • egocentrism • centration • conservation • concrete operations stage • formal operations stage • expressive language delay

---

CHAPTER 5 • Module 12

Focus

RESOURCES

For this module, consult the appropriate sections of the Teacher's Manual, Test Bank, and PowerPoint slides, all found on the Teacher's Resource DVD, and the interactive study tools for students on MyPsychLab.

BEFORE CLASS

Students should read the section for homework before coming to class.

BELLRINGER

Ask students if they see any dangers in a heavy reliance on set stages in observing children's development. How might dividing development into stage be helpful for psychologists? How might it be disadvantageous for psychologists and parents alike?

Teach

COVER THE MODULE

12.1 How do humans develop from conception through birth?

- The fertilized egg is called a zygote and divides into many cells, eventually forming the baby.
  - Monozygotic twins are formed when the zygote splits into two separate masses of cells, each of which will develop into a baby identical to the other.
  - Dizygotic twins are formed when the mother's body releases multiple eggs and at least two are fertilized, or when another ovulation occurs, even though the mother has already become pregnant.

Module 12 Development 147

CHAPTER 5 • Module 12

COVER THE MODULE (continued)

The Germinal, Embryonic, and Fetal Periods

- The *germinal period* is the first 2 weeks of pregnancy in which the dividing mass of cells moves down the fallopian tube and into the uterus.
- The *embryonic period* begins at 2 weeks after conception and ends at 8 weeks.
  - The vital organs and structures of the baby form during this period, making it a critical one for teratogens to affect the development of those organs and structures.
- The *fetal period* is from the beginning of the ninth week until the birth of the baby. Tremendous growth occurs, length and weight increase, and organs continue to become fully functional.

DISCUSS THE STUDENT VOICE QUESTION

Ask students to offer ideas about why it might be important for psychologists to understand the development of humans in the womb, the effects of teratogens on a fetus, even the biological processes that result in twins. How might these processes shed light on human behavior?

> How does a mass of cells become a baby, with eyes, nose, hands, feet, and so on? How do all those different things come from the same original cell?

The Germinal, Embryonic, and Fetal Periods

How does a mass of cells become a baby, with eyes, nose, hands, feet, and so on? How do all those different things come from the same original cell?

In discussing pregnancy, many people refer to trimesters—the three 3-month segments that make up the 9-month gestation period. For the purposes of understanding development, however, pregnancy can be divided into three periods of differing length: the **germinal period**, lasting about 2 weeks; the **embryonic period**, lasting from the second through the eighth week of pregnancy; and the **fetal period**, lasting from the eighth week of pregnancy until the baby is born. Figure 12.2 summarizes what happens during each of these periods.

Critical Periods in Prenatal Development The embryonic period includes definite critical periods. The structural development of the arms and legs, for example, is only affected during the time that they are developing (3.5 to 8 weeks), whereas the heart's structure is most affected very early in this period (2.5 to 6.5 weeks). Other physical and structural problems can occur with the central nervous system (2 to 5 weeks), eyes (3.5 to 8.5 weeks), and the teeth and roof of the mouth (about 7 to 12 weeks).

Prenatal Hazards Any factor such as a drug, chemical, virus, or other factor that can cause a birth defect is called a **teratogen**. Table 12.1 shows some common teratogens and their possible negative effects.

---

germinal period first 2 weeks after fertilization, during which the zygote moves down to the uterus and begins to implant in the lining.

embryonic period the period from 2 to 8 weeks after fertilization, during which the major organs and structures of the organism develop.

fetal period the time from about 8 weeks after conception to the birth of the child.

teratogen any factor that can cause a birth defect.

uterus the muscular organ that will contain and protect the developing infant.

placenta a specialized organ that develops out of fetal tissue, providing nourishment and filtering away waste products.

umbilical cord cord that connects the baby to the placenta and implants itself in the uterine wall.

embryo name for the developing organism from 2 weeks to 8 weeks after fertilization.

fetus name for the developing organism from 8 weeks after fertilization to the birth of the baby.

Table 12.1	Common Teratogens
TERATOGENIC AGENT	**EFFECT ON DEVELOPMENT**
Rubella	Blindness, deafness, heart defects, brain damage
Marijuana	Irritability, nervousness, tremors; infant is easily disturbed, startled
Cocaine	Decreased height, low birth weight, respiratory problems, seizures, learning difficulties; infant is difficult to soothe
Alcohol	Fetal alcohol syndrome (mental retardation, delayed growth, facial malformation), learning difficulties, smaller than normal head size
Nicotine	Miscarriage, low birth weight, stillbirth, short stature, mental retardation, learning disabilities
Mercury	Mental retardation, blindness
Syphilis	Mental retardation, deafness, meningitis
Caffeine	Miscarriage, low birth weight
Radiation	Higher incidence of cancers, physical deformities
High Water Temperatures	Increased chance of neural tube defects

Source: Shepard, T. H. (2001).

Class Demonstration

EDUCATING PEOPLE ABOUT TERATOGENS

Divide the class into small groups. Tell students that each group is a business that creates public service announcements (PSAs). The business has been hired to design a PSA to educate pregnant women about the dangers of teratogens. Each group should prepare a PSA that it believes will help these women understand what teratogens are and how they can be harmful to the unborn child. The PSA could be a radio announcement, television commercial, or a newspaper/magazine advertisement. Students can create a poster or an audiovisual presentation for their PSA. When students have completed their work, have them present it to their classmates.

Germinal Period: Weeks 1–2

Major Developmental Events

1. Fertilization takes place in the fallopian tube, where the single cell zygote is formed.
2. Mass of cells divides, moves to the uterus.
3. The zygote attaches to the wall of the **uterus**.
4. **Placenta** and **umbilical cord** form.
5. Cells begin to differentiate, or develop into the specialized cells that make up different parts of the human body.

Embryonic Period: Weeks 3–8

Major Developmental Events

1. The **embryo** begins to receive nourishment through the placenta. It becomes vulnerable to hazards that pass to it from the mother.
2. Cells continue to specialize.
3. Embryo grows to be 1 inch long and develops primitive eyes, nose, lips, teeth, arms, legs, and a beating heart.

Fetal Period: Weeks 9–38 (approximately)

Major Developmental Events

1. The **fetus** continues to grow and develop fat. Its length increases by about 20 times and its weight increases from about 1 ounce to a little over 7 pounds.
2. Muscles begin to contract in month three. In months four and five, the mother feels the baby's fluttering and kicking movements.
3. Organs continue to develop and become functional.
4. Miscarriages are most common in the first 3 months and usually caused by unpreventable genetic defects.

FIGURE 12.2 Stages of Prenatal Development

DEVELOPMENT ACROSS THE LIFE SPAN 149

CHAPTER 5 • Module 12

EXTEND THE LESSON

Bring pictures of sonograms to class and see if students can identify the various anatomical parts of the fetus. (You may want to make an overhead out of a sonogram.) Try contacting a local hospital or clinic for access to sample sonograms. Or check websites, such as WebMD at **www.webmd.com**, under the topic "fetal ultrasound."

FAST FACT

Ask: **When do you think an embryo has the features and internal organs of a full-grown adult?** *(An embryo in its seventh week has the features and all the internal organs of a full-grown adult, even though it is only 1 inch long.)*

L1 DIFFERENTIATED INSTRUCTION

Special Needs Assess students' understanding by asking them to write questions about what they have learned, identify what they find unclear or confusing, or complete short quick-writes of the key points.

Explore

THE VISIBLE EMBRYO

Ask students to visit The Visible Embryo website at **www.visembryo.com**. Encourage them to explore the various stages of development by providing a list of questions for them to answer, such as the following:

- When are the lungs capable of breathing air? *(weeks 26 to 27)*
- When do fingerprints form? *(weeks 16 to 17)*
- When can it be distinguished whether the fetus is male or female? *(Carnegie Stage 20)*
- When and why does the fetal brain appear wrinkled? *(weeks 28 to 29; to provide more surface area and maximize brain cells)*

Module 12 Development

CHAPTER 5 • Module 12

COVER THE MODULE

12.2 What reflexes and abilities do newborns have?

- Four critical areas of adjustment for the newborn are respiration, digestion, circulation, and temperature regulation.

- Infants are born with reflexes that help them survive until more complex learning is possible. These reflexes include:
  - sucking
  - rooting
  - Moro (startle)
  - grasping
  - stepping

MULTIMEDIA CONTENT AVAILABLE AT
www.mypsychlab.com

Watch video footage on newborn reflexes on mypsychlab.com

DISCUSS THE STUDENT VOICE QUESTION

Discuss each of the five newborn reflexes with the class. Have any of the students observed these reflexes in an infant? Do they know how to trigger these reflexes? Ask students how each reflex might be necessary to an infant's survival.

150 Chapter 5 Development Across the Life Span

What can babies do? Aren't they pretty much unaware of what's going on around them at first? ▶

Watch video footage on newborn reflexes on **mypsychlab.com**

12.2 What reflexes and abilities do newborns have?

Immediately after birth, several changes occur. The respiratory system fills the lungs with air, bringing oxygen into the blood. Blood now circulates only within the infant's system because the umbilical cord has been cut. Body temperature is now regulated by the infant's own activity and insulating body fat rather than by amniotic fluid. The digestive system probably takes the longest to adjust to life outside the womb. In the meantime, the infant's extra body fat provides fuel until the infant can take in enough nourishment.

Reflexes

What can babies do? Aren't they pretty much unaware of what's going on around them at first?

Babies come into this world able to interact with it. Newborns have a set of *innate* (existing from birth), automatic behavior patterns called *reflexes*. Until a baby learns more complex means of interaction, reflexes help it to survive. Figure 12.3 shows five newborn reflexes. Pediatricians use these and other reflexes to determine whether the nervous system is working properly. **Watch** on **mypsychlab.com**

Baby, Can You See Me? Baby, Can You Hear Me? Sensory Development Although most senses are fairly well developed at birth, some take more time to reach "full power." The sense of touch is the best developed, which makes perfect sense when one realizes how much skin-to-womb

FIGURE 12.3 Five Newborn Reflexes
Shown here are five reflexes used to make sure the newborn's nervous system is healthy. These include (a) the grasping reflex, (b) the startle or Moro reflex, (c) the rooting reflex, in which a baby whose cheek is touched will turn toward the hand, open its mouth, and begin searching for the nipple, (d) the stepping reflex, and (e) the sucking reflex.

150 CHAPTER 5

Explore

MEASURING INTELLIGENCE IN INFANTS

Discuss with students that there are several instruments that are designed to assess intellectual functioning in infants and very young children. These measures may be examining different aspects of intelligence, such as physical, psychomotor, and social and emotional development, rather than the verbally based measures typically used by intelligence tests. Although these measures may not accurately predict later intelligence, they can be useful in identifying potential developmental problems.

Divide the class into groups and assign each group a specific test: the Bayley Scales of Infant Development, the Denver Developmental Screening Test–Revised, the Gesell Developmental Schedules, or the Brazelton Neonatal Assessment Scale. Have each group research their test—what it is named for, what it measures, how it is administered, and so forth—and report their findings to the class.

contact the baby experienced in the last months of pregnancy. The sense of smell is also highly developed. Breast-fed babies soon learn to smell the difference between their own mother's milk and another woman's milk.

Taste is also nearly fully developed. At birth, babies show a preference for sweets. By 4 months, they have developed a preference for salty tastes. Sour and bitter, two other taste sensations, result in the baby's spitting up (Ganchrow et al., 1983).

Hearing is functional before birth but may take a little while to reach its full potential after birth. From birth, newborns seem most responsive to high and low pitches, as heard in human voices.

The least functional sense at birth is vision. As stated in Chapter Three, the eye is quite a complex organ. **LINK** *to Chapter Three: Sensation and Perception, pp. 81–85.* The rods, which detect only changes in brightness and have little visual acuity, are fairly well developed at birth, but the cones, which detect color and provide sharpness of vision, take another 6 months to fully develop. So the newborn has relatively poor color perception for about 2 months and can more easily see contrasting lights and darks (Adams, 1987).

The newborn also has fairly "fuzzy" vision. Until the muscles that hold the lenses of the eye in place mature, the newborn cannot shift its focus from close to far. Thus, newborns have a fixed distance for clear vision of about 7 to 10 inches (Slater, 2000). **Explore** on **mypsychlab.com**

Explore infants' perceptual and cognitive milestones on **mypsychlab.com**

Describe Development During Infancy and Childhood

12.3 What kinds of physical changes take place in infancy and childhood?

From Crawling to a Blur of Motion: Motor Development Infants make tremendous progress in motor skills from birth to about age 2. Nutrition, care, and health affect development. One important way to protect an infant's health is to make sure that immunizations against various illnesses are given at the appropriate times.

Figure 12.4 on the next page shows some of the major physical milestones of infancy. (The age ranges listed are averages based on large samples. A normally developing infant may reach these milestones earlier or later than average.)

As the baby becomes a child, physical development is less dramatic, but still significant. Height and weight continue to increase rapidly until about age 5, after which the rate of growth becomes slower and steadier until about age 10 or 12. Muscle strength and coordination improve. Gross motor development, involving large muscle groups such as the legs and arms, improves first. Children develop the ability to perform more complex activities that require them to coordinate different parts of their bodies—for instance, running or throwing a ball. Fine motor skills, involving the smaller muscles such as the muscles of the fingers, gradually improve through the preschool years. If given a pencil, a typical toddler could only scribble with it, whereas a child of 5 or 6 can begin to perform the complex motions of writing the alphabet.

DEVELOPMENT ACROSS THE LIFE SPAN 151

CHAPTER 5 • Module 12

COVER THE MODULE *(continued)*

- Touch, smell, and taste are the most developed senses at birth.
- Hearing is functional before birth but may take a little while to reach its full potential after birth.
- The sense of vision is the least well-developed sense at the time of birth. Vision is blurry and lacking in full color perception until about 6 months of age.

LINK *to Chapter Three: Sensation and Perception, pp. 81–85*

MULTIMEDIA CONTENT AVAILABLE AT
www.mypsychlab.com

Explore infants' perceptual and cognitive milestones on **mypsychlab.com**

COVER THE MODULE

12.3 What kinds of physical changes take place in infancy and childhood?

- Gross and fine motor skills develop at a fast pace during infancy and early childhood.
- Infants learn to raise their heads, roll over, sit up, and walk.

Explore

FACTS AND MYTHS ABOUT AUTISM

The developmental disorder known as autism has become a very controversial topic. Autism is defined as a complex neurological disorder that typically appears during the first 3 years of life. First identified by Dr. Leo Kanner in 1943, autism has become the target of both professionals and parents. The professionals are researching ways to improve the behavior and outlook for autistic children, while the parents are trying to understand a very misunderstood disorder. Myths about autism abound.

Have students research autism myths on the Internet (e.g., visit http://abcnews.go.com/Health/ColdandFluNews/story?id=6089162&page=1, or search using the term "autism myths"). Ask students which myths they found that surprised them.

Module 12 Development 151

CHAPTER 5 • Module 12

COVER THE MODULE

12.4 How do infants and children develop cognitive skills?

- In infancy and early childhood, the brain develops rapidly, and connections between brain neurons are established.

LINK to *Chapter Two: The Biological Perspective,* pp. 42–47

EXTEND THE LESSON

People have asked psychologists whether it is possible to speed up a child's cognitive development. Most researchers agree that such pressure is detrimental if a child is not developmentally prepared to learn.

Ask students to identify a benefit of encouraging children to speed their intellectual development and a possible disadvantage. *(Possible answers: Advantage: The child may learn early in life to value intellectual skills such as reading and problem-solving. Disadvantage: The child may feel stressed and pressured by the parents to be perfect and, as a result, learn to dislike intellectual activities.)*

L2 ELL DIFFERENTIATED INSTRUCTION

English Language Learners During class discussions, consider providing academic sentence starters for students to complete as a means of encouraging more thoughtful and formal responses.

FIGURE 12.4 Six Motor Milestones
Typical milestones in motor development are shown here: (a) raising head and chest—2 to 4 months, (b) rolling over—2 to 5 months, (c) sitting up with support—4 to 6 months, (d) sitting up without support—6 to 7 months, (e) crawling—7 to 8 months, and (f) walking—8 to 18 months.

12.4 How do infants and children develop cognitive skills?

By age 1, the average infant has tripled its birth weight and added another foot to its height. The brain triples its weight in the first 2 years, reaching about 75 percent of its adult weight. By age 5, the brain is at 90 percent of its adult weight. This increase makes it possible for the child to make tremendous advances in cognitive development, including thinking, problem solving, and memory.

In infancy and early childhood, the brain develops rapidly and connections between brain neurons are established. During the early stages of brain development, synaptic connections are formed at an explosive rate. Each new experience in a child's life helps establish new connections between different groups of cells, and the number of connections in the brain increases dramatically. By the time a child is about 18 months old, neurons develop their myelin sheaths, which insulate the cells and increase their efficiency. As a result, the developing brain becomes more able to respond to complex new experiences. You might think of it as a self-perpetuating cycle: The more a young child learns, the more capable he or she becomes of learning more.

Brain cells increase their connections until puberty, when those connections that are not used frequently are eliminated in a process called *synaptic pruning*. When it comes to connections between neurons, "use it or lose it" is an appropriate mantra—nerve cells that are used often become even stronger, while nerve cells that are neglected are pruned. **LINK** to *Chapter Two: The Biological Perspective,* pp. 42–47.

Explore

CHILDHOOD DEVELOPMENT WEBSITES

- **The Child Psychologist: www.childpsychology.com/**
  This megasite provides a wealth of links to other information about developmental psychology.

- **ChildStats: http://childstats.gov/**
  This government site provides statistics about a range of behaviors and trends during childhood.

- **Early Childhood Development: www.ecdgroup.com**
  International resources in support of young children and their families are the focus here.

- **ISIS: www.isisweb.org/**
  International Society on Infant Studies offers information about infant development and abilities.

Piaget's Theory: Four Stages of Cognitive Development One way of examining cognitive development is found in the work of Jean Piaget. Piaget developed his theory from detailed observations of infants and children. He contributed significantly to our understanding of how children think about the world. Children do not think like "little adults." Rather, their thinking is quite different from that of adults.

Piaget believed that children form mental schemes as they experience new situations and events. For example, if a mother points to a picture of an apple and tells her child, "That's an apple," the child forms a scheme for "apple" that resembles the picture. Piaget also believed that children first try to understand new things in terms of schemes they already possess, a process called **assimilation**. The child might see an orange and say "apple" because both objects are round. When corrected, the child might alter the scheme for apple to include "round" and "red." The process of altering or adjusting old schemes to fit new information and experiences is **accommodation** (Piaget, 1952, 1962, 1983).

Piaget also proposed that there are four distinct stages of cognitive development that occur from infancy to adolescence, as shown in Table 12.2 (Piaget, 1952, 1962, 1983). During the **sensorimotor stage**, infants use their senses and motor abilities to learn about the world. At first, they have only their inborn

Table 12.2	Piaget's Stages of Cognitive Development	
STAGE		**COGNITIVE DEVELOPMENT**
Sensorimotor	Birth to 2 years old	Children explore the world using their senses and ability to move. They develop object permanence, or the knowledge that objects exist even when they can't be seen, as well as the understanding that concepts and mental images represent objects, people, and events.
Preoperational	2 to 7 years old	Young children can mentally represent and refer to objects and events with words or pictures and they can pretend. However, they can't logically reason or simultaneously consider many characteristics of an object.
Concrete Operations	7 to 12 years old	Children at this stage are able to conserve, reverse their thinking, and classify objects in terms of their many characteristics. They can also think logically and understand analogies but only about concrete events.
Formal Operations	12 years old to adulthood	People at this stage can use abstract reasoning about hypothetical events or situations, think about logical possibilities, use abstract analogies, and systematically examine and test hypotheses. Not everyone can eventually reason in all these ways.

assimilation in this case, the process of trying to understand new things in terms of schemes one already possesses.

accommodation in this case, the process of altering or adjusting old schemes to fit new information and experiences.

sensorimotor stage Piaget's first stage of cognitive development, in which the infant uses its senses and motor abilities to interact with objects in the environment.

DEVELOPMENT ACROSS THE LIFE SPAN 153

CHAPTER 5 • Module 12

COVER THE MODULE *(continued)*

- **Piaget's Theory: Four Stages of Cognitive Development**
  - Jean Piaget proposed that children go through four distinct stages of cognitive development:
    - Sensorimotor: sensory and physical interaction with the world.
    - Preoperational: language becomes a tool of exploration.
    - Concrete operations: logical thought becomes possible.
    - Formal operations: abstract concepts are understood and hypothetical thinking develops.

EXTEND THE LESSON

Discuss Piaget's concepts of assimilation and accommodation with students. Ask students to give examples of how young children may use assimilation to describe new things. (For example, a child who has a dog might identify all furry, four-legged animals as "dog" or might call a semi-truck a "car.") How might a child then use accommodation to change his or her definitions? (For example, the child may expand the definition of "dog" to include furry, four-legged animals that bark or the definition of "car" to include vehicles with only four wheels.)

L3 DIFFERENTIATED INSTRUCTION

Tactile/Kinesthetic Learners These students should sit near the front of the classroom and take notes by jotting down key terms and making pictures or charts to help them remember what they are hearing.

Class Demonstration (Kinesthetic)

PIAGET'S STAGES

<u>Purpose</u>: Students role-play Piaget's stages.

<u>Time</u>: 10 minutes or longer

<u>Description</u>: Students generate a role play in which a child is interacting with an adult. Assign pairs of students to one of Piaget's stages along with a scenario. Possible scenarios are: Santa asks a little boy what he would like for Christmas; a little girl eats at a restaurant with her parents.

The student playing the role of the child speaks in a way that is consistent with the Piagetian stage he or she has been assigned. For example, if a little girl is ordering at a restaurant, she may ask for a scoop of ice cream in a cone because it is bigger than the same scoop in a cup, to illustrate the preoperational child stage. Pairs may practice their role plays a few times and then perform them for the class. The audience then tries to guess which Piagetian stage is being illustrated.

Module 12 Development

CHAPTER 5 • Module 12

COVER THE MODULE (continued)

- During the sensorimotor stage (birth to 2 years old), children develop *object permanence* (the knowledge that an object exists even when it's not in sight).
- During the *preoperational stage* (2 to 7 years), children are limited by:
  - *egocentrism*
  - *centration*

MULTIMEDIA CONTENT AVAILABLE AT
www.mypsychlab.com

Watch classic footage on sensorimotor development with Jean Piaget on **mypsychlab.com**

DISCUSS THE STUDENT VOICE QUESTION

Ask students if they remember how old they were when they stopped believing in childhood icons like Santa Claus and the Tooth Fairy. Did they figure it out on their own? If someone, such as a sibling, told them when they were very young that such things do not exist, did they believe them at first? Do the ages during which students believed or ceased believing generally follow Piaget's stages?

Why is it so easy for children to believe in Santa Claus and the Tooth Fairy when they're little? ▶

Watch classic footage on sensorimotor development with Jean Piaget on **mypsychlab.com**

object permanence the knowledge that an object exists even when it is not in sight.

preoperational stage Piaget's second stage of cognitive development in which the preschool child learns to use language as a means of exploring the world.

egocentrism the inability to see the world through anyone else's eyes.

centration in Piaget's theory, the tendency of a young child to focus only on one feature of an object while ignoring other relevant features.

conservation in Piaget's theory, the ability to understand that simply changing the appearance of an object does not change the object's nature.

concrete operations stage third stage of cognitive development in which the school-age child becomes capable of logical thought processes but is not yet capable of abstract thinking.

154 CHAPTER 5

---

involuntary reflexes to interact with objects and people. As sensory and motor development progresses, they begin to interact deliberately with objects by grasping, pushing, tasting, and so on. Infants move from simple repetitive actions, such as grabbing their toes, to complex patterns, such as trying to put a shape into a sorting box. These experiences promote new dendrite growth and connections around the brain. **Watch** on **mypsychlab.com**

By the end of this stage, infants have fully developed a sense of **object permanence**, the knowledge that an object exists even when it is not in sight. For example, playing "peek-a-boo" helps teach infants that Mommy's face is always going to be behind her hands. This is a critical step in developing language (and eventually abstract thought), as words themselves are symbols of things that may not be present. Symbolic thought, which is the ability to represent objects in one's thoughts with symbols such as words, becomes possible by the end of this stage.

Why is it so easy for children to believe in Santa Claus and the Tooth Fairy when they're little?

During the **preoperational stage** (ages 2–7), children develop language and more complex concepts. Now able to move about freely, they no longer rely solely on their senses and motor skills. They can ask questions and explore their surroundings more fully. Pretending and make-believe play become possible. Children at this stage can understand, through symbolic thinking, that a line of wooden blocks can "stand in" for a train.

However, very young children are limited in several ways. They can use simple mental concepts but are not yet capable of logical thought. They believe that anything that moves is alive. They tend to believe that what they see is literally true. Thus, when children of this age see a person dressed as Santa Claus, Santa becomes real to them. It doesn't occur to them to think about why it would be physically impossible for Santa to visit every child's house in one night.

Another limitation is **egocentrism**, the inability to see the world through anyone else's eyes except one's own. The preoperational child believes everyone else has the same understandings and priorities as he or she does. For example, a child may cover her eyes when she knows she is breaking a rule—the reasoning being that if she can't see her parents, they can't see *her*. Egocentrism is not the same as being egotistical or selfish. It would also be egocentric, but completely unselfish, if 4-year-old Kenny wants to give his grandmother an action figure for her birthday because that's what *he* would want.

Children in this stage are also easily misled by appearances. A child who complains that his piece of pie is smaller than his brother's may be quite happy once his original piece is cut into two pieces, because now he thinks he has "more." He has focused only on the number of pieces, not the actual amount of the pie. Focusing only on one feature of some object is called **centration**.

In the bottom example in Figure 12.5, children will not see that both rows have the same number of coins, because they focus, or center, on the top row's longer *appearance*. Centration is one reason that children fail to understand that changing the way something looks does not change its amount, its volume, or its mass. The understanding that even when an object's appearance changes, its essential nature is "conserved" or kept intact is called **conservation**.

In the **concrete operations stage** (ages 7–12), children become capable of conservation and reversible thinking. They learn to consider all the relevant features of any given object. They begin to think more logically about beliefs such as Santa Claus and ask questions. Eventually, aided by what they learn in school, they come to more rational conclusions.

Class Demonstration

PIAGET'S STAGES OF COGNITIVE DEVELOPMENT

Pose the following scenarios to students.

- A 4-year-old insists small people must live in the television because they are right there behind the glass. Identify the stage and the phenomenon being displayed by the child.
- A child adept at roller skating goes ice skating for the first time. She keeps trying to stand and move just as on roller skates but falls again and again. According to Piaget, what is necessary for mastery of this new skill?
- An 8-year-old boy threatens to tell his parents when he is given only one of the three candy bars he and his 10-year-old brother are told to share. The older child then breaks his brother's bar in half and gives him two pieces. This satisfies both children because they each have two pieces. Identify the cognitive stages of these children and the disadvantage that allows the younger child to be cheated.

Type of conservation	Initial presentation	Transformation	Question	Preoperational child's answer
Liquids	Two equal glasses of liquid	Pour one into a taller, narrower glass.	Which glass contains more?	The taller one.
Number	Two equal lines of pennies	Increase spacing of pennies in one line.	Which line has more pennies?	The longer one.

FIGURE 12.5 Measuring Conservation Skills
Experimenters often measure children's conservation skills by pouring equal amounts of water into two glasses of the same size and shape. When the water from one glass is poured into a taller, narrower glass, children incorrectly assume that the second glass has more water than the first one. In the second example, pennies are laid out in two equal lines. When the pennies in the top line are then spaced out, the child who cannot yet conserve will assume that there are actually more pennies in that line.

The major limitation of this stage is children's inability to deal effectively with *abstract concepts* that do not have some physical, *concrete*, touchable reality. For example, "freedom" is an abstract concept. People can define it but cannot see or touch it. The *concrete concepts* that children of this age understand relate to objects, written rules, and real things that they can see, touch, or at least see in their minds.

In the last of Piaget's stages, **formal operations** (age 12 to adulthood), abstract thinking becomes possible. Teenagers not only understand concepts that have no physical reality, but also they get deeply involved in hypothetical thinking, or thinking about possibilities and even impossibilities, asking questions such as "What if everyone just got along?" or "If women were in charge of more countries, would there be fewer wars?" Piaget did not believe that everyone would necessarily reach formal operations. Studies show that only about half of all adults in the United States have reached the formal operations stage (Sutherland, 1992).

Piaget's research has been very influential, especially in education. However, some researchers question his idea of distinct stages of cognitive development (Courage & Howe, 2002; Feldman, 2003; Schwitzgebel, 1999; Siegler, 1996). Others point out that preschoolers are not as egocentric as Piaget seemed to believe (Flavell, 1999) and that object permanence exists much earlier than Piaget thought (Aguiar & Baillargeon, 2003; Baillargeon, 1986).

12.5 What are the stages of language development?

The development of language is a very important milestone in cognitive development because language allows children to think in words rather than images, to ask questions, to communicate their needs and wants, and to

formal operations stage Piaget's last stage of cognitive development in which the adolescent becomes capable of abstract thinking.

CHAPTER 5 • Module 12

COVER THE MODULE (continued)

- During the concrete operations stage (7 to 12 years), children are unable to deal with abstract concepts.
- Not everyone necessarily reaches the formal operations stage (12 years to adulthood).

EXTEND THE DISCUSSION

Piaget used experiments involving conservation to demonstrate centration—the narrowly focused thought that characterizes preoperational youngsters. In his conservation experiments, Piaget wanted to determine when children realize that important characteristics of objects stay the same despite changes in their physical experience. In the conservation of liquid problem, children are shown identical glasses filled with the same amount of juice. After children agree that the two glasses have the same amount of juice in them, juice is poured from one glass into a taller, thinner glass. The children are then asked if the amount of juice present in the taller, thinner glass is now more, less, or the same as in the shorter, wider glass.

Ask students if any of them could conduct conservation experiments with younger siblings, cousins, or friends. Have them videotape their experiments to share with the class or simply report their findings.

FAST FACT

Jean Piaget's scientific career began with his work with mollusks when he was an adolescent.

Explore

JEAN PIAGET WEBSITES

- **Jean Piaget Archives: www.unige.ch/piaget/PiagetGB.html**
  Maintained by the University of Geneva, this archive offers students a glimpse into the workings of Piaget's mind. Available in three languages, to boot!
- **Jean Piaget Society: www.piaget.org/**
  A society named in honor of Piaget, focused on the overall processes of cognitive development.
- **Learning and Teaching:**
  www.learningandteaching.info/learning/piaget.htm
  An overview of Piaget's key ideas, plus some key criticisms of his theories.

CHAPTER 5 • Module 12

COVER THE MODULE

12.5 What are the stages of language development?
- The five stages of language development are:
  - Cooing (vowel-like sounds)
  - Babbling (adding consonant sounds)
  - One-word speech ("Cookie!" for "I want a cookie!")
  - Telegraphic speech ("unnecessary" words omitted, as in a telegram)
  - Whole sentences (by around age 6)
- While some language is learned through imitation and reinforcement, infants may possess a language acquisition device that governs the learning of language during infancy and early childhood.

COVER THE MODULE

12.6 How do babies begin to develop relationships with others?
- Babies form an attachment with a primary caregiver.
- Mary Ainsworth identified four different types of attachment.

▲ This infant has already learned some of the basics of language, including the use of gestures to indicate meaning and enhance communication.

form concepts (L. Bloom, 1974; P. Bloom, 2000). Current theories of language development focus on environmental influences such as child-directed speech—the way adults and older children talk to infants and very young children, with higher pitched, repetitious, sing-song speech patterns—as well as infants' use of gestures and signs. Infants and toddlers attend more closely to child-directed speech, which creates a learning opportunity (Dominey & Dodane, 2004; Fernald, 1984, 1992; Küntay & Slobin, 2002). Infants also seem to understand far more language than they can produce, a phenomenon known as **expressive language delay** (Stevenson et al., 1988). They may be able to only produce one or two words while understanding longer sentences. **LINK** *to Chapter Six: Learning and Language Development, p. 205.*

There are several stages of language development that all children experience, regardless of their home culture or native language (Brown, 1973):

1. **Cooing:** At around 2 months of age, babies begin to make vowel-like sounds.
2. **Babbling:** At about 6 months, infants add consonant sounds to the vowels to make a babbling sound. Deaf children decrease their babbling after 6 months while increasing their use of primitive hand signs and gestures (Petitto & Marentette, 1991; Petitto et al., 2001).
3. **One-word speech:** Around age 1, most children begin to say actual words, typically nouns that may seem to represent an entire phrase of meaning. They are called *holophrases* (whole phrases in one word) for that reason. For example, a child might say "Milk!" and mean "I want some milk!"
4. **Telegraphic speech:** At around 18 months, toddlers begin to string words together to form short, simple sentences such as "Baby eat" or "Doggie go bye-bye." Only the words that carry the meaning of the sentence are used.
5. **Whole sentences:** As children move through the preschool years, they learn to use grammatical terms and construct longer sentences. By age 6 or so, they are nearly as fluent as adults, although their vocabulary is relatively limited.

12.6 How do babies begin to develop relationships with others?

The emotional bond that forms between an infant and a primary caregiver is called attachment. Attachment is a very important development in the infant's social and emotional life, usually forming within the first 6 months and showing up in a number of ways during the second 6 months, such as wariness of strangers and fear of being separated from the caregiver. Usually, the primary attachment is to the mother, but infants can attach to fathers and to other caregivers as well. Despite cultural differences in parenting styles, children in all cultures attach to caregivers and demonstrate similar attachment styles. Attachment is an important first step in forming relationships with others, which may set the stage for later relationships (Hu & Meng, 1996; Juffer & Rosenboom, 1997; Keromoian & Leiderman, 1986).

Mary Ainsworth (Ainsworth, 1985; Ainsworth et al., 1978) measured infants' attachment to their mothers by exposing them to a series of leave-takings

expressive language delay the apparent ability of infants to understand far more language than they can produce.

Class Demonstration

TALK BABY TALK

Ask students to do their best imitations of "baby talk," that high-pitched, drawn-out pattern that babies seem to love. Tell other students to pay attention to the way the baby talk sounds. Explain that Patricia Kuhl, a neuroscientist at the University of Washington, studied mothers in Sweden, Russia, and Seattle as they talked to their infants. Swedish, Russian, and English have substantially different vowel systems, yet the vowel sounds that are common to each language—"ee," "ah," and "oo"—were the same sounds that were unintentionally accentuated in the mothers' speech. These parents did not accentuate all sounds or raise the pitch of all words, as might someone pretending to speak "baby talk." Rather, acoustic profiles of some 2,363 words across all three groups revealed that just these important vowels were exaggerated and, according to Kuhl, for good reason. By providing an infant with unambiguous examples of what vowel sounds belong together, the task of language acquisition is presumably made that much easier.

and returns of their mothers and a stranger. Her team identified four attachment styles:

1. **Secure** babies were willing to leave their mothers' laps upon entering the room. They explored happily, looking back at their mothers and returning to them periodically (sort of like "touching base"). When the stranger came in, these infants were wary but calm as long as their mothers were nearby. When the mothers left, the infants got upset. When the mothers returned, the infants approached them, were easily soothed, and were glad.
2. **Avoidant** babies, although somewhat willing to explore, did not "touch base." They did not look at the stranger or their mothers and reacted very little to their mothers' absence or their return, seeming to have no interest or concern.
3. **Ambivalent** babies had mixed feelings. They were clinging, unwilling to explore, and very upset by the stranger regardless of the mothers' presence. They protested mightily when their mothers left and were hard to soothe. When the mothers returned, the infants would demand to be picked up, but at the same time push the mothers away or kick them.
4. **Disorganized-disoriented** babies, identified in later studies by other researchers (Main & Hesse, 1990; Main & Solomon, 1990), seemed unable to decide how to react to their mothers' return. They would approach their mothers with their eyes turned away, as if afraid to make eye contact. They seemed fearful and had a dazed and depressed expression.

It should come as no surprise that the mothers of each of the four types of infants also behaved differently. Mothers of secure infants were loving, warm, sensitive to their infant's needs, and responsive to attempts at communication. Mothers of avoidant babies were unresponsive, insensitive, and coldly rejecting. Mothers of ambivalent babies tried to be responsive but were inconsistent and insensitive to the baby's actions, often talking to the infant about something totally unrelated to its actions. Mothers of disorganized-disoriented babies were found to be abusive or neglectful.

Attachment is not necessarily the result of the mother's behavior alone. The infant's temperament may also influence the mother's reactions (Goldsmith & Campos, 1982; Skolnick, 1986). For example, an infant with a difficult temperament is hard to soothe, so its mother might come to avoid unnecessary contact.

Critics of Ainsworth's research wonder if infants and mothers would behave differently in more familiar surroundings. However, other attachment research using home-based assessments has supported Ainsworth's findings (Blanchard & Main, 1979). Other studies also support the concept of attachment styles and stability of attachment over the first 6 years of life (Lutkenhaus et al., 1985; Main & Cassidy, 1988; Owen et al., 1984; Wartner et al., 1994).

As day care has become more common, many parents have been concerned about its effect on attachment. Studies find that, while high-quality day care is important, especially for cognitive development, positive development—including attachment—is more clearly related to the quality of parenting at home (Belsky, 2005; Belsky & Johnson, 2005; Belsky et al., 2007).

CHAPTER 5 • Module 12

COVER THE MODULE (continued)

- There are three basic infant temperaments: easy (regular, adaptable, and happy), difficult (irregular, nonadaptable, and irritable), and slow-to-warm-up (need to adjust gradually to change).
- The four types of attachment identified by Ainsworth are:
  - Secure
  - Avoidant (unattached)
  - Ambivalent (insecurely attached)
  - Disorganized (insecurely attached and sometimes abused or neglected)

EXTEND THE DISCUSSION

Spanking has had a controversial history as an element of effective child-rearing. Some Scandinavian cultures have found the practice so abhorrent that it has been outlawed as a form of parental discipline. On the other hand, some private schools and many parents believe it is an effective, socially acceptable, parental-choice practice for shaping a child's behavior. Ask your students to debate the merits of spanking and the potential consequences it holds for developing a child's future behavior. Should this simply be a parental decision, or should there be legislation governing this activity? In particular, does spanking lead children to become more violent? Ask your students to read more about both sides of this issue before discussing it in class. Here are some suggested sources for students to consult: (1) American Academy of Pediatrics' view on corporal punishment and spanking—note specifically their definition of what spanking is and is not; and (2) Diana Baumrind, developmental psychologist who conducted research on parenting styles.

Explore

USING VIDEOS TO TEACH DEVELOPMENTAL CONCEPTS

It is often difficult to illustrate developmental processes that occur in infancy and childhood in the classroom. One technique that is often suggested is to bring infants or children to the classroom for in-class demonstrations, but this method has several problems. Although there are many good commercially produced videos of topics related to infant and child development, several teachers have advocated the use of homemade videos. A major advantage of homemade videos is the ability to develop brief teaching modules that address specific concepts that you are interested in covering in your class. Rather than edited videos illustrating specific developmental issues, consider using unedited videos and having students analyze the video for illustrations of concepts that have been discussed in class.

CHAPTER 5 • Module 12

CLASSIC STUDIES IN PSYCHOLOGY

- Harlow's classic research with infant rhesus monkeys demonstrated the importance of contact comfort in the attachment process, contradicting the earlier view that attachment was merely a function of associating the mother with the delivery of food

LINK to Chapter Six, Learning and Language Development, p. 186

1. Possible answer: I think that the monkeys raised with the surrogates might be confused when associating with other monkeys. I believe these monkeys would be able to tell the difference between the surrogates and the actual monkeys.

COVER THE MODULE

12.7 How do children develop socially and emotionally?

- Erikson developed eight stages of social development, the first four occurring in infancy and childhood.

UNDERSTANDING VISUALS

Direct students to the photograph of one of Harlow's baby rhesus monkeys on this page. Ask students if they find the outcome of the experiment surprising? Why or why not?

L2 LPR DIFFERENTIATED INSTRUCTION

Less Proficient Readers For students with difficulties with vocabulary and fluency, intentionally revisit newly acquired vocabulary during discussions.

Classic Studies in Psychology

Harlow and Contact Comfort

When psychologists first began to study attachment, they assumed that the infant bonded with the mother because the infant learned to associate her with satisfaction of primary drives such as hunger and thirst. **LINK** to Chapter Six: Learning and Language Development, p. 186.

However, psychologist Harry Harlow felt that attachment had to be influenced by more than that. Noticing that the rhesus monkeys in his lab clung to the soft cloth pad lining their cages, Harlow designed a study to examine *contact comfort,* the seeming attachment of the monkeys to something soft (Harlow, 1958).

Harlow isolated eight baby rhesus monkeys shortly after their birth, placing each in a cage with two surrogate (substitute) "mothers." One surrogate was a block of wood covered in soft padding and terry cloth. The other was a wire form. Both were heated from within. Half of the monkeys fed from a bottle held by their wire "mother," while the other half fed from a bottle held by their soft "mother." Harlow then recorded the time each monkey spent with each "mother." If this time is taken to indicate attachment, then learning theory would predict that the monkeys would spend more time with whichever surrogate was used to feed them.

The results? Regardless of which surrogate fed them, the monkeys all spent significantly more time with the soft, cloth-covered surrogate and very little time with the wire surrogate. Harlow and his colleagues concluded that "contact comfort was an important basic affectional or love variable" (Harlow, 1958, p. 574). Harlow's work represents one of the earliest investigations into the importance of touch in the attachment process and remains an important study in human development.

▲ *Baby rhesus monkeys preferred the soft cloth "mother" even when it was the wire "mother" that provided food.*

Question for Further Discussion

1. Even though the cloth surrogate was warm and soft and seemed to provide contact comfort, do you think that the monkeys raised in this way would behave normally when placed into contact with other monkeys? How might they react?

12.7 How do children develop socially and emotionally?

Erikson's Theory Psychologist Erik Erikson explored how our first social interactions and those we have later on affect development throughout our lives. Ultimately, Erikson concluded that social development occurred in eight stages, the first four of which take place in infancy and childhood (Erikson, 1950; Erikson & Erikson, 1997). Each stage presents an emotional *crisis,* or a kind of turning point, in personality. The crisis must be successfully navigated for normal, healthy psychological development. Table 12.3 summarizes the conflict in each stage and its implications for future development (Erikson, 1950; Erikson & Erikson, 1997).

158 CHAPTER 5

Class Demonstration (Kinesthetic)

DESIGNING A DAY CARE CENTER

Purpose: Students think about the important elements of a good day care center.

Time: 45 minutes

Description: Students work in teams and create an advertising flyer for a new day care center for preschool-aged children. You may want to provide poster board or paper. The flyer should include information on the kinds of programs and activities the day care center will offer. Students should base their programs on the information presented in the textbook about the developmental needs of this age group. Students then display their flyers and walk around the room viewing other students' work. You may want students to vote on which day care center they find most appealing. Have the class engage in a larger discussion about the important components of day care or the kinds of information that parents use in making day care choices for their children.

158 Chapter 5 Development Across the Life Span

Table 12.3 Erikson's Psychosocial Stages of Development

STAGE	DEVELOPMENTAL CRISIS	SUCCESSFUL OUTCOME	UNSUCCESSFUL OUTCOME
1. Infant Birth to 1 year old	**Trust Versus Mistrust** Babies learn to trust or mistrust others based on whether their basic needs are met.	The baby learns to trust people and expect life to be pleasant.	The baby learns not to trust.
2. Toddler 1 to 3 years old	**Autonomy Versus Shame and Doubt** Toddlers realize that they can direct their own behavior.	Toddlers who successfully direct their own behavior learn to be independent.	Toddlers whose attempts at independence are blocked learn self-doubt and shame.
3. Preschool Age 3 to 5 years old	**Initiative Versus Guilt** Preschoolers are challenged to control their own behavior.	Preschoolers who succeed in taking responsibility feel capable and develop initiative.	Preschoolers who fail in taking responsibility feel irresponsible, anxious, and guilty.
4. Elementary School Age 5 to 12 years old	**Industry Versus Inferiority** School-aged children learn new social and academic skills and compare themselves with others.	When children succeed in working to learn new skills, they develop feelings of industry, competence, and self-esteem.	If children fail to develop new abilities, they feel incompetent, inadequate, and inferior.
5. Adolescence 13 to early 20s	**Identity Versus Role Confusion** Adolescents must decide who they want to be in terms of occupation, beliefs, attitudes, and behavior.	Adolescents who succeed in defining who they are develop a strong sense of identity.	Adolescents who fail to define their identity become confused and withdrawn or want to inconspicuously blend in with the crowd.

Continued

DEVELOPMENT ACROSS THE LIFE SPAN 159

CHAPTER 5 • Module 12

COVER THE MODULE *(continued)*

- Erikson's first four stages of psychosocial development occur in childhood.
  - In trust versus mistrust, the infant must gain a sense of predictability and trust in its caretakers or risk developing a mistrustful nature.
  - In autonomy versus shame and doubt, the toddler needs to become physically independent.
  - In initiative versus guilt, the preschool child is developing emotional and psychological independence.
  - In industry versus inferiority, school-age children are gaining competence and developing self-esteem.
- Erikson's fifth stage, identity versus role confusion, occurs in adolescence.

EXTEND THE DISCUSSION

Give students some time to read over Table 12.3. Based on their own experience, do they agree with the crises presented? What criticisms do they have of the crises and/or their outcomes? For example, do they believe that one is either successful or unsuccessful in working through the crises? Do they think that Erikson meant the crises to be so cut and dried, or did he possibly mean for them to exist on a continuum?

Explore

IS TELEVISION BAD FOR CHILDREN?

Television plays a powerful and influential role in children's daily lives. At the heart of this issue lies the controversy over whether excessive television viewing by children is harmful to their intellectual development and/or promotes aggressive behavior. There is no easy answer, as proponents on both sides of the issue cite a variety of studies to support their cause. Thus, while some argue that viewing violent television is correlated with aggressive behavior, others contend that there is no relationship or even that viewing pro-social programs can lead to an increase in helpful behavior. Similarly, although research shows no correlation between the amount of television viewed and IQ, others suggest that television prevents children from engaging in other intellectually challenging activities. Students will likely have strong opinions on this issue and will enjoy the chance to explore the controversy in greater depth. Assign students to research and defend both sides of this issue. Have them present their findings and opinions to the class.

Module 12 Development 159

CHAPTER 5 • Module 12

COVER THE MODULE (*continued*)

- Erikson's last three stages—intimacy versus isolation, generativity versus stagnation, and ego integrity versus despair—occur in adulthood.

FAST FACT

Ask students if they can guess what phrase was famously coined by Erikson. The answer: "identity crisis." They may be even more interested to know the context: "Identity crisis is the failure to achieve ego identity during adolescence."

EXTEND THE DISCUSSION

Bring a variety of children's books to class and use them to illustrate developmental principles. Children's books apply a tremendous range of principles in developmental psychology. Implicit in most books are important lessons that attempt to strengthen children's development in some way. Popular topics include moral development (lying, stealing); coping with adversity and stress (death, divorce); techniques to advance cognitive and intellectual skills; issues of identity development and self-esteem; physical development and change (toilet training); social and relationship issues (how to share); coping with fears (e.g., of the dark); tolerance of diversity (racial and religious differences); gender role development; and so on. Divide students into small groups, distribute two or three books to each group, and have them identify the relevant developmental concepts applicable to each book. Allow groups to take turns making short presentations and soliciting comments and questions.

Table 12.3 Erikson's Psychosocial Stages of Development (Continued)

STAGE	DEVELOPMENTAL CRISIS	SUCCESSFUL OUTCOME	UNSUCCESSFUL OUTCOME
6. Early Adulthood 20s and 30s	Intimacy Versus Isolation Young adults must learn to share who they are with another person in a close, committed relationship.	People who succeed in this task will have satisfying intimate relationships.	Adults who fail at this task will be isolated from other people and may be lonely.
7. Middle Adulthood 40s and 50s	Generativity Versus Stagnation The challenge is to be creative, productive, and nurture the next generation.	Successful adults are creative, productive, and nurturant, thereby benefiting themselves, their family, community, country, and future generations.	Adults are passive and self-centered and feel that they have done nothing for the world or the next generation.
8. Late Adulthood 60s and beyond	Ego Integrity Versus Despair The issue is whether a person will reach wisdom, spiritual tranquility, a sense of wholeness, and acceptance of his or her life.	Elderly people who succeed in addressing this issue will enjoy life and not fear death.	Elderly people who fail will feel that their life is empty and will fear death.

Class Demonstration (Kinesthetic)

ERIKSON'S STAGES

Purpose: Students discuss Erickson's stages of development.

Time: 15 minutes

Description: Give each student a piece of paper with a developmental question. The questions represent Erickson's eight stages of psychosocial development: (1) Can I trust the world? (2) Can I control my own behaviors? (3) Can I become independent of my parents by exploring my limits? (4) Can I master the skills I need to adapt? (5) Who am I? What do I believe and feel? What are my attitudes? (6) Can I fully give myself to another? (7) What can I offer the generations to follow? (8) Have I found contentment and satisfaction through my life's work and play? Once all questions have been assigned, ask students to line up or order themselves according to Erickson's eight stages. Alternatively, place a timeline on the floor with ages of the life span and have students stand on an age at which they would be most likely to ask their assigned question.

Practice Quiz

Pick the best answer.

1. The first 2 weeks of pregnancy are called the
   a. gestational period
   b. germinal period
   c. embryonic period
   d. fetal period

2. Which of the following does not happen during the germinal period?
   a. A dividing mass of cells travels to the uterus.
   b. Cells begin to differentiate into specialized human cells.
   c. The zygote attaches itself to the uterus.
   d. Toxins passing through the placenta can affect developing organs.

3. Which sense is least functional at birth?
   a. touch
   b. taste
   c. hearing
   d. vision

4. Which motor milestone occurs first in infants?
   a. standing
   b. raising the head and chest
   c. rolling over
   d. sitting with support

5. A child who has just developed object permanence is in which of Piaget's stages?
   a. sensorimotor
   b. preoperational
   c. concrete operational
   d. formal operational

6. The fertilized egg is called a(n)
   a. zygote
   b. ovum
   c. sperm
   d. gene

7. "I play cars" is an example of which stage of language development?
   a. babbling
   b. holophrases
   c. telegraphic speech
   d. whole sentences

8. According to Ainsworth, which kind of attachment is shown by a baby who demands to be picked up when the mother returns, but then pushes her away?
   a. secure
   b. avoidant
   c. ambivalent
   d. disorganized-disoriented

9. According to Harlow's research, which of the following surrogate mothers would infant monkeys most likely prefer?
   a. a cold wire surrogate with a milk bottle
   b. a warm wire surrogate with a milk bottle
   c. a warm wire surrogate without a milk bottle
   d. a warm cloth surrogate without a milk bottle

10. In which of Erikson's stages does a child learn self-control and begin to feel more capable?
    a. autonomy versus shame and doubt
    b. initiative versus guilt
    c. industry versus inferiority
    d. identity versus role confusion

DEVELOPMENT ACROSS THE LIFE SPAN 161

Practice Quiz Answers

1. b
2. d
3. d
4. b
5. a
6. a
7. c
8. c
9. d
10. b

CHAPTER 5 • Module 12

Assess

Assign the Module 12 Practice Quiz.

Use the Practice Quiz to identify gaps in student understanding.

REMEDIATE

Have students, individually or in groups, review the module goals, learning objectives, and key terms.

Refer students to the Concept Summary on pp. 174–175 for review.

Close

Discuss with students the many theories of childhood development. Ask students, without looking back through the book, to name the different types of theories discussed in this module. Remind them of any they may miss. Why are so many theories necessary? How do they help psychologists understand human behavior?

CHAPTER 5 • Module 13

Focus

RESOURCES

For this module, consult the appropriate sections of the Teacher's Manual, Test Bank, and PowerPoint slides, all found on the Teacher's Resource DVD, and the interactive study tools for students on MyPsychLab.

BEFORE CLASS

Students should read the section for homework before coming to class.

BELLRINGER

Ask students if they think the changes that occur during adolescence and adulthood are as important as the many changes children experience. Why or why not? If they all agree that they are as important, play the devil's advocate.

Teach

COVER THE MODULE

- Adolescence is the period of life from about age 13 to the early 20s during which physical development reaches completion.
- 13.1 What physical changes happen during adolescence?
- Puberty is a period of about 4 years during which the sexual organs and systems fully mature.
- Secondary sex characteristics such as body hair, breasts, deepening voices, and growth spurt occur.

LINK *to Chapter Eight, Culture and Gender, pp. 250–256*

TEACHING TIP

Be prepared for some students to react with embarrassment during the discussion of physical changes in adolescence. Others may laugh or make jokes. Remind students that psychology is a science and that such topics should be treated "professionally."

162 Chapter 5 Development Across the Life Span

Module 13 Adolescence and Adulthood

Module Goals	Learning Objectives
Describe development during adolescence.	**13.1** What physical changes happen during adolescence?
	13.2 How do reasoning and morality develop during adolescence?
	13.3 How do adolescents form their identities?
	13.4 What role do family members and peers play in adolescent development?
Describe development during adulthood.	**13.5** What social and cognitive changes occur during adulthood?
	13.6 What physical changes happen during adulthood?
	13.7 How do scientists explain why aging occurs?
	13.8 What are the stages of death and dying?

Describe Development During Adolescence

Adolescence lasts from the beginning of **puberty** to the early 20s, when a young person is no longer physically a child but is not yet an independent, self-supporting adult. Adolescence isn't necessarily determined by chronological age. It also concerns how a person deals with life issues such as work, family, and relationships. Although most people enter adolescence at approximately the same time, they may leave it earlier or later than others.

Conceptions of adolescence also differ across cultures. In some cultures, individuals go through special ceremonies or rites of passage that symbolize the transition from childhood to adulthood. For example, many girls from Latin American cultures have *Quinceañera* celebrations on their 15th birthdays, during which they change from flat-heeled shoes to high heels and move from dancing with their fathers to dancing with male friends. The Jewish tradition of accepting responsibility for one's religious faith and becoming a *Bar* or *Bat Mitzvah* on one's 13th birthday is another example of a cultural representation of adolescence. A variety of cultural and social factors determine, in part, when a child becomes an adolescent and when an adolescent becomes an adult. LINK *to Chapter Eight: Culture and Gender, pp. 250–256.*

13.1 What physical changes happen during adolescence?

The clearest physical sign of the beginning of adolescence is the onset of puberty. Puberty refers to the physical changes in both *primary sex characteristics* (growth of the actual sex organs such as the penis or the uterus) and *secondary*

puberty the physical changes in both primary and secondary sex characteristics that occur as part of sexual development.

162   CHAPTER 5

Terms

- puberty • personal fable • imaginary audience • preconventional morality
- conventional morality • postconventional morality • generativity • ego integrity
- menopause • andropause • activity theory

sex characteristics (such as breasts in females, deeper voices in males, and body hair for both males and females) that occur as part of sexual development.

Puberty is caused by a complex series of glandular activities, stimulated by the pituitary gland (also called the "master gland"). Puberty often begins about 2 years after the beginning of the growth spurt—the rapid period of growth that takes place at around age 10 for girls and around age 12 for boys—and lasts for about 4 years. While scientists have identified ages at which puberty often begins, there is a fairly wide range of time during which a person may enter puberty. Some people enter puberty earlier than their peers; some people enter puberty later. A young person experiencing the early or late onset of puberty can find this time emotionally stressful, but it's important to know that while people do not all develop at the same rate, the physical differences that seem so dramatic during adolescence tend to decrease over time and even out in adulthood.

13.2 How do reasoning and morality develop during adolescence?

◀ *If I'm remembering correctly, teenagers should be in Piaget's formal operational stage. So why don't many teenagers think just like adults?*

Adolescents' cognitive development is less visible than physical development, but they still undergo major cognitive changes. Many adolescents move into Piaget's final stage in which abstract thinking becomes possible thanks to the final development of the brain's frontal lobes, responsible for organizing, understanding, and decision making (Giedd et al., 1999; Sowell et al., 1999). They begin to think about hypothetical or ideal situations. However, not all adolescents (or adults) use formal operational processes equally well. Recent research has suggested that the development of the brain's frontal lobe, which is responsible for organizing, understanding, and decision making, is not complete until the early to mid-20s (Knox, 2010). The teen brain is different from the adult brain, and these differences may be partially responsible for lapses in judgment and decision making during adolescence.

During adolescence, egocentrism shows up in individuals' excessive concern with their own thoughts. They do a lot of introspection (turning inward) and may believe their thoughts are as important to others as to themselves. This adolescent egocentrism may emerge in the form of the personal fable or the imaginary audience (Elkind, 1985; Lapsley et al., 1986; Vartanian, 2000).

The **personal fable** is the tendency of many adolescents to believe they are special and unique, and that no one else could ever have or understand the thoughts and feelings they have. Because they feel unique, teenagers may feel somehow protected from the dangers of the world. "It can't happen to me, I'm special" is the underlying belief.

The **imaginary audience** shows up as extreme self-consciousness, especially about others' opinions of their looks or behavior. Adolescents may mistakenly believe everyone is as focused on them as they are on themselves.

Moral Development Another important cognitive advance concerns the teenager's understanding of "right" and "wrong." Influenced by Piaget and others, developmental psychologist Lawrence Kohlberg (1973) proposed three levels of moral development, which are summarized in Table 13.1 on the next page. Although these stages are associated with certain age groups, adolescents and adults can be found at all three levels.

personal fable type of thought common to adolescents in which young people believe themselves to be unique and protected from harm.

imaginary audience type of thought common to adolescents in which young people believe that other people are just as concerned about the adolescent's thoughts and characteristics as they themselves are.

DEVELOPMENT ACROSS THE LIFE SPAN 163

CHAPTER 5 • Module 13

COVER THE MODULE

13.2 How do reasoning and morality develop during adolescence?

- Adolescents engage in two kinds of egocentric thinking, called the imaginary audience and the personal fable.
  - *Imaginary audience* shows up as extreme self-consciousness.
  - *Personal fable* is demonstrated by adolescents when they feel that they are so special that nothing bad could ever happen to them.

DISCUSS THE STUDENT VOICE QUESTION

Aside from the cognitive changes outlined here, ask students if they can think of other reasons why adolescents do not think like adults.

EXTEND THE LESSON

Many of the negative stereotypes about adolescents involve their "laziness" and inability to pay attention and complete tasks. Most students probably can recall situations in which their parents seemed frustrated by their behaviors and decisions. There is a general sense that teenagers are "flaky" and seem to "lose their minds" during puberty. It may make students relieved to find out that many of the attention and concentration problems of adolescence are related to a lack of brain maturation. Recent studies have demonstrated that the brain areas related to multitasking, which are located in the frontal cortex, continue to develop throughout adolescence. Another source of conflict between parents and teens is associated with teen sleeping patterns. Contrary to earlier beliefs that teens are just lazy, research has shown that teenagers need to sleep longer and later than adults in order to function optimally.

Critical Thinking

WRITING ABOUT PERSONAL FABLES

Purpose: Students complete a brief assignment that involves critical thinking about personal fables.

Time: 15 minutes

Description: Review with students the definition of the term "personal fable." Ask them to write a brief paragraph that describes a personal fable they themselves have held or one they have heard other adolescents express. Have volunteers read their paragraphs and ask the remaining students for comments. Could any of these personal fables be harmful or even dangerous?

CHAPTER 5 • Module 13

COVER THE MODULE (continued)

- **Moral Development**
  - Lawrence Kohlberg proposed three levels of moral development:
    - *Preconventional morality*: consequences determine morality.
    - *Conventional morality*: conformity is right.
    - *Postconventional morality*: moral principles are determined by the individual.

13.3 How do adolescents form their identities?

- In Erikson's identity versus role confusion crisis, the job of the adolescent is to achieve some consistent sense of self from among all the roles, values, and futures open to him or her.

DISCUSS THE STUDENT VOICE QUESTION

This question should spark some lively discussion among students who are experiencing this very issue. Do students feel caught in Erikson's conflict? How do they think their families, peers, and the world around them are shaping who they are (or, maybe, preventing them from finding their real identities)?

COVER THE MODULE

13.4 What role do family members and peers play in adolescent development?

- Conflict with parents may encourage adolescent independence.

---

preconventional morality first level of Kohlberg's stages of moral development in which the child's behavior is governed by the consequences of the behavior.

conventional morality second level of Kohlberg's stages of moral development in which the child's behavior is governed by conforming to the society's norms of behavior.

postconventional morality third level of Kohlberg's stages of moral development in which the person's behavior is governed by moral principles that have been decided on by the individual and that may be in disagreement with accepted social norms.

Kohlberg's theory has been criticized as being male-oriented, especially since he used only males in his studies (Gilligan, 1982). Carol Gilligan (1982) proposed that men and women have different perspectives when determining which actions are moral: Men value fairness and justice more, while women have an "ethic of care" that leads them to focus on doing the least harm to people. Researchers, however, have not found consistent support for these gender differences (Walker, 1991). Another common criticism is that Kohlberg's assessment focuses on hypothetical rather than real situations.

Table 13.1 Kohlberg's Three Levels of Morality

LEVEL OF MORALITY	HOW RULES ARE UNDERSTOOD	EXAMPLE
Preconventional morality (typically very young children)	The consequences determine morality; behavior that is rewarded is right; that which is punished is wrong.	A child who steals a toy from another child and does not get caught does not see that action as wrong.
Conventional morality (older children, adolescents, and most adults)	Conformity to social norms is right; nonconformity is wrong.	A child criticizes his or her parent for speeding because speeding is against the posted laws.
Postconventional morality (about 20 percent of the adult population)	Moral principles determined by the person are used to determine right and wrong and may disagree with societal norms. The person understands and accepts the societal consequences of his or her actions.	A reporter who wrote a controversial story goes to jail rather than reveal the source's identity.

13.3 How do adolescents form their identities?

▶ How do teenagers figure out who they are?

How do teenagers figure out who they are?
Personal and social development in adolescence primarily concerns the search for a consistent sense of self or personal identity. According to Erikson, the adolescent must face the psychosocial crisis of identity versus role confusion. (See Table 12.3.) The teenager must choose among many options for values and beliefs concerning things like political issues, career paths, and marriage (Feldman, 2003) in order to form a consistent sense of self. Erikson believed that teens who have successfully resolved the conflicts of earlier stages are much better "equipped" to find their own identities.

13.4 What role do family members and peers play in adolescent development?

Parent/Teen Conflict Even for the majority of adolescents who develop a consistent sense of self, there will be conflicts with parents. Many researchers believe that a certain amount of "rebellion" and conflict is a necessary step in

---

Class Demonstration

MORAL DEVELOPMENT

<u>Purpose</u>: Students create moral dilemmas using Kohlberg's three levels of morality.

<u>Time</u>: 15 minutes

<u>Description</u>: Divide students into small groups and have each group write one example or scenario for each of Kohlberg's three levels of morality. Then have a volunteer from each group read one of the group's examples to the class. Students from other groups should guess the level of morality to which the example relates.

gradually becoming independent. As intense as they may seem, parent–child conflicts generally focus on trivial issues—hair, clothing, music, and so on. On major moral issues, most parents and teens would be quite surprised to realize that they are in agreement.

Peer Pressure Erik Erikson believed that teenagers who had successfully resolved earlier developmental crises would find it easier to resist peer pressure to engage in unhealthy or illegal activities. Unfortunately, less successful teens enter adolescence with a lack of trust in others, feelings of guilt and shame, low self-esteem, and dependency on others. Peer pressure is quite effective on teenagers who desperately want to "fit in" and have an identity of some sort and who feel they must conform to be accepted. Teens may join sports teams, clubs, or even gangs and allow their fellow group members to influence their choices and behaviors. Many teenagers play the part of the model child for the parents, the good student for the teachers, and the "cool" juvenile delinquent to their friends. They are confused about which of the many roles they play factor into their own identities. Watch on **mypsychlab.com**

Actresses Lindsay Lohan, Amanda Seyfried, Lacey Chabert, and Rachel McAdams on the set of Mark S. Waters's comedy movie Mean Girls. *This movie portrays the ins and outs of peer pressure and the desire to fit in that many adolescents face.*

Watch a video on peer pressure on **mypsychlab.com**

Describe Development during Adulthood

Adulthood can also be divided into three periods: young adulthood, middle age, and late adulthood. While the concepts of middle age and late adulthood are firmly established in many Western cultures, these age categories are not universal constructs. For example, women from the Oriya culture in India do not consider middle age to be a distinct period of their lives. Women begin their lives as daughters and, when they marry, become wives and daughters-in-law. This shift in social status marks a significant change in women's responsibilities within the Oriya culture, and there is no differentiation between young adulthood and middle age (Shweder, 1998, 2003). The concept of old age is similarly subjective across cultures. For example, the degree to which elders are respected, honored, and looked after by younger adults differs from one society to the next.

13.5 What social and cognitive changes occur during adulthood?

Social Changes: Erikson's Theories of Adulthood Erikson saw the primary task of young adulthood to be finding a mate and developing true intimacy—an emotional and psychological closeness based on one's previously developed ability to trust, share, and care, while still maintaining one's sense of self. (See Table 12.3.) LINK *to Chapter Seven: Social Psychology, p. 237.* Young adults who are distrustful or unsure of their own identities may find *isolation* instead—loneliness, shallow relationships, and even a fear of real intimacy. For example, many marriages soon end in divorce, with one partner leaving the relationship to explore personal concerns and unfinished issues of identity.

In midlife, people who have found intimacy can now focus outward. Erikson saw this as parenting the next generation and helping them through their crises, a process he called **generativity**. Educators, supervisors, health care

generativity providing guidance to one's children or the next generation, or contributing to the well-being of the next generation through career or volunteer work.

DEVELOPMENT ACROSS THE LIFE SPAN **165**

CHAPTER 5 • Module 13

COVER THE MODULE *(continued)*

- Adolescents without a strong sense of self are vulnerable to peer pressure.

MULTIMEDIA CONTENT AVAILABLE AT www.mypsychlab.com

Watch a video on peer pressure on **mypsychlab.com**

EXTEND THE LESSON

Ask students to call out the first thoughts that come to mind when they hear the word "adolescent." Write their responses on the board, allowing ample time for students to share their thoughts. Discuss the patterns that emerge from this list. Is adolescence seen primarily as a carefree time? A time of stress? What themes come up repeatedly in your students' perceptions? Use this discussion to link their experiences to the topics covered in the textbook.

COVER THE MODULE

13.5 What social and cognitive changes occur during adulthood?

- Adulthood begins in the early twenties and ends with death in old age. It can be divided into young adulthood, middle adulthood, and late adulthood.
- Erikson's crisis of young adulthood is intimacy versus isolation in which the young person must establish an intimate relationship, usually with a mate.

LINK *to Chapter Seven: Social Psychology, p. 237*

- The crisis of middle adulthood is generativity versus stagnation in which the task of the middle adult is to help the next generation through its crises, either by parenting, mentoring, or a career that leaves some legacy to the next generation.

Explore

BEING A LEADER AND A FOLLOWER

Resentment of authority is so common among American adolescents that it is tempting to think of it as normal. Differentiating between legitimate authority and arbitrary authority is a task of identity establishment. Identity formation includes being able to take the role of leader or follower in the appropriate circumstances. Ask students to think about their roles as leaders and followers and to write down how they personally serve as both. Beside each item, ask them to assess whether their role is positive or negative (reminding them that it is possible for follower to be a positive role). How can they make the negative situations positive?

Module 13 Adolescence and Adulthood **165**

CHAPTER 5 • Module 13

COVER THE MODULE *(continued)*

- Erikson's final crisis is integrity versus despair in which an old adult must come to terms with mortality.
- Reaction times slow down, but intelligence and memory remain relatively stable.

COVER THE MODULE

13.6 What physical changes happen during adulthood?

- While the 20s are the peak of physical health, in the 30s the signs of aging become more visible, and in the 40s, visual problems may occur, weight may increase, strength may decrease, and height begins to decrease.
- Women experience a physical decline in the reproductive system called the climacteric, ending at about age 50 with *menopause*, when a woman's estrogen levels are at zero and her reproductive capabilities are at an end.

TEACHING TIP

Take time with students to work through the process of analyzing writing tasks and framing their response. To be successful, students need to learn how to analyze a prompt, budget their time and answer space, plan and write their response, and then edit their first draft.

---

professionals, doctors, and community volunteers are generative positions. Other possibilities include engaging in a career or major life work that becomes one's legacy. Those who cannot focus outward and are still dealing with unresolved conflicts—including parents who focus on their own needs rather than their children's—are *stagnated*.

In late adulthood, people may feel a sense of urgency as the realities of physical aging and the approaching end of life become harder to ignore. Erikson (1980) believed that at this time, people engage in a *life review* in which they look back on their lives. They must deal with mistakes, regrets, and unfinished business. If they ultimately conclude that their lives were relatively full and come to terms with regrets and losses, they experience a feeling of **ego integrity** or wholeness. Integrity is the final completion of the identity, or ego. If people have many regrets and a lot of unfinished business, they feel *despair*—deep regret over unaccomplished goals and dreams.

Cognitive Changes during Adulthood Adults' intellectual abilities do not decline overall, although speed of processing (or reaction time) does slow down. A middle-aged person may take a little longer than a younger adult to solve a problem, but will also bring more life experience and knowledge to bear on the problem, which counters the lack of speed. In one study (Nunes & Kramer, 2009), researchers tested older and younger air traffic controllers' performance on a variety of cognitive and job-related tasks. Although the older participants' age negatively affected their performance, their greater experience made up for the effects of age, suggesting that experienced older adults can solve real-world problems just as quickly and effectively as less experienced younger people.

Many middle-aged people notice changes in memory as they find themselves struggling to remember a word or name. This difficulty in retrieval is probably not evidence of a physical decline or the beginning of Alzheimer's disease. More likely, it is caused by the stresses a middle-aged person experiences and the sheer amount of information he or she must keep straight (Craik, 1994; Launer et al., 1995; Sands & Meredith, 1992). Our fast-paced, technology-driven twenty-first century lifestyle increasingly demands that we multitask in ways that humans haven't yet fully adapted to.

13.6 What physical changes happen during adulthood?

Physical changes in young adulthood are relatively minimal. The 20s are a time of peak physical health, sharp senses, fewer insecurities, and mature cognitive abilities. However, even then, the signs of aging, such as wrinkles, are beginning. By one's 30s, vision and hearing begin to decline. Hearing loss may begin in one's 40s and 50s but often does not become noticeable until later.

Most adults in their 40s experience greater security without the concerns of adolescence and the career-focused worries of young adulthood. However, physical aging continues: Skin gets more wrinkles, hair turns gray (or falls out), vision and hearing decline further, and physical strength may decline (Frontera et al., 1991). Some adults gain weight as metabolism slows. Many lose height—about half an inch for every decade after 40, and up to 8 inches or more for people with the bone loss disease, osteoporosis (Cummings & Melton, 2002). Although sexual functioning usually does not decline, opportunities for sexual activity may decrease (Hodson & Skeen, 1994; Williams, 1995).

Women undergo major physical changes in their 40s in preparation for the end of reproduction. The reproductive organs begin functioning

ego integrity sense of wholeness that comes from having lived a full life and the ability to let go of regrets; the final completion of the ego.

166 CHAPTER 5

Class Discussion

A NATION OF WIMPS?

Students may enjoy discussing an article from *Psychology Today* that suggests the reason many people are finding parenting to be less enjoyable, and children are experiencing increasingly higher rates of disorders/problems, is overprotective parenting styles. It is suggested that the parental tendency to "protect" children from any type of discomfort and failure is preventing children from developing the coping strategies they will need later in life. The argument is made that this desire to make a child's life completely successful and painless is creating fragile children who grow into adults who are sorely lacking in resilience and independence skills. The article also suggests that the constant pressure parents are feeling to make their children's lives perfect is emotionally exhausting to the parents and detracts from the positive aspects of being a parent. Find the article at http://cms.psychologytoday.com/articles/pto-20041112-000010.html

inconsistently, as levels of the female hormone estrogen decline. The uterus slowly begins to shrink, menstrual cycles become irregular, and some women experience "hot flashes," sudden sensations of heat and sweating. The period of 5 to 10 years over which these changes occur is called perimenopause. Most women cease ovulation and menstruation altogether in their early 50s. This change is called **menopause** (Mishell, 2001).

Do men go through anything like menopause?
Men also go through sexual changes, but they are much more gradual. **Andropause** (Carruthers, 2001) usually begins in males in their 40s with a decline in several hormones, primarily testosterone. Physical symptoms are also less dramatic but no less troubling: fatigue, irritability, possible problems in sexual functioning, and reduced sperm count. Males, however, rarely lose all reproductive ability.

Effects of Aging on Health Many health problems first occur in middle age. Their causes include hereditary and lifestyle factors, which sometimes include bodily wear and tear caused by poor self-care in young adulthood. Common health problems include high blood pressure, skin cancer, heart problems, arthritis, and obesity. Sleep problems may also take their toll. The most common causes of death in middle age are heart disease, cancer, and stroke—in that order (McGinnis & Foege, 1993). Watch on mypsychlab.com

Do men go through anything like menopause?

Watch a video about physical development after age 40 mypsychlab.com

13.7 How do scientists explain why aging occurs?

There are a number of theories of why people physically age. Some theories point to biological changes in cellular structure, whereas others focus on how external stresses influence body tissues and functioning.

Cellular Clock Theory One biologically based theory is the *cellular clock theory* (Hayflick, 1977). According this theory, known as the "Hayflick Limit" (named after the research credited with its discovery), cells are limited in the number of times they can reproduce to repair damage. Evidence for this theory is the existence of *telomeres*, structures on the ends of chromosomes that shorten each time a cell reproduces (Martin & Buckwalter, 2001). When telomeres are too short, cells cannot reproduce and damage accumulates, resulting in the effects of aging.

Wear-and-Tear Theory The *wear-and-tear theory of aging* points to outside influences such as stress, physical exertion, and bodily damage. Damaged tissues accumulate and produce the effects of aging as organs and cell tissues simply wear out with repeated use and abuse. For example, *collagen*, the natural elastic tissue that allows the skin to be flexible, "wears out," becoming less and less "stretchy," causing skin to sag and wrinkle (Cua et al., 1990; Kligman & Balin, 1989).

Free Radical Theory The *free radical theory*, proposed by doctor Denham Harman in the 1950s, gives a biological explanation for the cellular damage described by the wear-and-tear theory. *Free radicals* are oxygen molecules that have an unstable electron (negative particle). They bounce around cells, stealing electrons from other molecules and increasing the damage to cellular structures. As people age, more and more free radicals do more and more damage, producing the effects of aging (Hauck & Bartke, 2001; Knight, 1998).

menopause the cessation of ovulation and menstrual cycles and the end of a woman's reproductive capability.

andropause gradual changes in the sexual hormones and reproductive system of middle-aged males.

DEVELOPMENT ACROSS THE LIFE SPAN 167

CHAPTER 5 • Module 13

COVER THE MODULE *(continued)*

- Men go through *andropause*, a less dramatic change in testosterone and other male hormones, beginning in the mid-20s.
- Many health problems such as high blood pressure, skin cancers, and arthritis begin in middle age, with the most common causes of death in middle age being heart disease, cancer, and strokes.

DISCUSS THE STUDENT VOICE QUESTION

Ask students if they were surprised to read that men experience changes similar to those women experience in menopause. Did any of their preconceived ideas about women and men in their 40s change after reading this module?

MULTIMEDIA CONTENT AVAILABLE AT www.mypsychlab.com

Watch a video about physical development after age 40 on mypsychlab.com

COVER THE MODULE

13.7 How do scientists explain why aging occurs?

- The cellular clock theory is based on the idea that cells only have so many times that they can reproduce, and once that limit is reached, damaged cells begin to accumulate.
- The wear-and-tear theory of physical aging states that as time goes by, repeated use and abuse of the body's tissues cause it to be unable to repair all the damage.
- The free radical theory states that oxygen molecules with an unstable electron move around the cell, damaging cell structures as they go.

Class Demonstration

STEREOTYPES OF AGING

<u>Purpose</u>: Students compare stereotypes of older adults.

<u>Time</u>: 15 minutes

<u>Description</u>: Divide students into small teams for this brainstorming activity. Have them use the roundtable method to generate stereotypes of older adults. The groups compile their responses into one list and then present them to the class. Ask students to compare the number of positive and negative stereotypes. This activity can be an effective transition to a discussion on negative stereotypes of the elderly.

Module 13 Adolescence and Adulthood

CHAPTER 5 • Module 13

COVER THE MODULE (continued)

- **Activity Theory**
  - Research strongly indicates that remaining active and involved results in the most positive adjustment to aging.

DISCUSS THE STUDENT VOICE QUESTION

Discuss the idea of "use it or lose it" with students. Ask students if they have seen this principle at work in their own lives, among their families and friends. What are some barriers older people might face in trying to remain active?

COVER THE MODULE

13.8 What are the stages of death and dying?

- Denial: the person refuses to believe that the diagnosis of death is real.
- Anger: the person experiences feelings of helplessness to change things.
- Bargaining: the dying person tries to make a deal.
- Depression: the person feels sadness from losses already experienced.
- Acceptance: the person has accepted the inevitable and quietly awaits death.

FAST FACT

Researchers have suggested that the brain could continue to function efficiently for 150 or 200 years if it were supported by other bodily systems. Scientists believe that although the brain does change as we age, cognitive loss is largely preventable through exercise (of both body and mind), rest, and effective management of stress.

168 Chapter 5 Development Across the Life Span

> I've heard that most older people just want to be left alone and have some peace and quiet. Is that true?

This older woman volunteers as a teacher's aide in an elementary school, an activity that helps her use her mind, feel productive, and stay involved in her community.

activity theory theory of adjustment to aging that assumes older people are happier if they remain active in some way, such as volunteering or developing a hobby.

168 CHAPTER 5

Activity Theory

I've heard that most older people just want to be left alone and have some peace and quiet. Is that true?

Activity theory (Havighurst et al., 1968) proposes that older people adjust better to aging when they remaining active and involved in life, even if their careers must end. Older people who volunteer at hospitals or schools, participate in hobbies, and maintain a social life are happier and live longer than those who withdraw from activity. Some people believe that the elderly voluntarily withdraw, but often it is not their choice. Others simply stop inviting them to social activities and including them in their lives.

People who exercise their mental abilities are far less likely to develop memory problems and even senile dementias such as Alzheimer's disease (Ball et al., 2002; Colcombe et al., 2003; Fiatarone, 1996). "Use it or lose it" is the phrase to remember. For example, working challenging crossword puzzles can help someone maintain healthy cognitive functioning. Reading, having an active social life, going to plays, taking classes, and staying physically active can all have a positive impact on the brain's continued well-being (Bosworth & Schaie, 1997; Cabeza et al., 2002; Singh-Manoux et al., 2003).

13.8 What are the stages of death and dying?

There are several ways of looking at the process of dying. One of the more well-known theories is that of Elisabeth Kübler-Ross (Kübler-Ross, 1997), who conducted extensive interviews with dying people and their caregivers.

Kübler-Ross believed people go through five stages of reaction when faced with death (Backer et al., 1994; Kübler-Ross, 1997). These stages are as follows: *denial*, in which people are unable to believe that the diagnosis of death is real; *anger*, which is really anger at death itself and the feelings of helplessness to change things; *bargaining*, in which the dying person tries to make a deal with doctors or even with God; *depression*, which is sadness from losses already experienced and those yet to come; and *acceptance*, when the person has accepted reality and quietly awaits death. (Of course, some people do not have time to go through all of these stages or go through them in a different order.) (Schneidman, 1983, 1994)

Some theorists do not agree with the stage idea, seeing the process of dying as a series of emotional ups and downs (Schneidman, 1983, 1994; Weisman, 1972). Still others question the idea of common reactions among dying people, stating that the person's medical condition and treatment, personality before diagnosis, and other life history factors make the process of dying unique and unpredictable (Kastenbaum & Costa, 1977). The danger in holding too strictly to a stage theory is that people may mistakenly feel there is a "right" way to face death and a "wrong" way.

Death and Dying Across the Life Span While many of us associate death with old age, people can die at any point during the life span. Infants can face life-threatening complications during and after birth, including *sudden infant death syndrome*, or *SIDS*, which causes infants to suddenly stop breathing. SIDS has no known cause, but it can cause parents to feel extraordinary grief and guilt. Children and young adults most frequently die from accidents, but by middle adulthood, disease has surpassed accidents as the leading cause of death.

Cultural Connection

EXPLORING ATTITUDES ABOUT AGING

Ask students to use library or Internet resources to explore what their culture thinks about aging. If appropriate, they can also discuss with older relatives. (If all or most of the students are from similar cultures or ethnic groups, ask them to select other cultures to explore for this exercise.) Divide the class into small groups and have them discuss what they have learned about this topic. Give groups 10 to 15 minutes for discussion; then reconvene the class and have each group present their findings. Are there any common themes? Do all the cultures explored consider aging to be negative? Have such stereotypes had any impact on students' own attitudes about growing older?

People tend to view death differently depending on their age and their level of development. Young children, for example, tend to think of death as a temporary state (Kastenbaum, 1985), and many children may consider death to be similar to sleep. Older children, however, eventually come to understand the finality of death. Some people believe that children who are terminally ill generally do not understand that they are dying, but anthropologist Myra Bluebond-Langner says that is not the case: She has interviewed many seriously ill children, all of whom have understood that they are dying. Some state this knowledge outright, while others talk more generally about not going back to school or not being able to attend an upcoming party, but children are certainly capable of understanding—and even accepting—their own deaths (Peterson, 2009).

While adolescents understand the universal nature of death, they do not always believe that the bad things that happen to other people could happen to them. Because adolescents' personal fables tell them that they are special and even invulnerable, they are more likely to engage in risky behavior that can lead to death. As people age, they begin to think about death more realistically, but death is not easy to face at any stage of life.

Applying Psychology to Everyday Life

ADHD—Not Just for Children

Attention-deficit hyperactivity disorder, or *ADHD*, has long been recognized and treated in children. In the last few decades, professionals have come to understand that ADHD may persist into adulthood (Barkley et al., 2001; Goldstein, 1997; Murphy & LeVert, 1995; Nadeau, 1995). Its causes are not clear, but some research points to a biological basis that includes hereditary factors (Barkley, 1998; Faraone et al., 1993, 2000). Other contributing factors may include prenatal influences, prematurity, high levels of lead in the body, and even prefrontal brain damage. Between 30 percent and 50 percent of children diagnosed with ADHD will continue to have attentional and behavioral problems as adults that may negatively affect their professional and personal lives (Barkley et al., 2001; Searight et al., 2000), and that could be relieved with treatment.

Although hyperactivity tends to decrease, the symptoms of adult ADHD are essentially the same as the ones children experience. These symptoms often include inability to pay attention to details, feeling restless, and being impatient and disorganized (Barkley et al., 2001; Wender et al., 2001).

Adult ADHD may be treated with medications, but there are other ways for adults with ADHD to cope. Joining a support group, for example, is an excellent idea. Other possible treatment activities include marital counseling, vocational counseling, other forms of psychotherapy, and perhaps changing occupations to ones that more appropriately fit the ADHD adult's personality and energy level (Goldstein, 1997; Murphy & LeVert, 1995; Nadeau, 1995; Silver, 2000).

Question for Further Discussion
1. What might be appropriate careers for someone with ADHD? What might be careers for which the ADHD adult would not be well suited?

DEVELOPMENT ACROSS THE LIFE SPAN 169

CHAPTER 5 • Module 13

APPLYING PSYCHOLOGY TO EVERYDAY LIFE

- Many children with ADHD grow up to be adults with ADHD, which may affect their work and relationships.
- Treatment—with medication or some form of counseling—can be very beneficial.

1. Possible answer: People with ADHD might do better in a career that allows them to be outdoors a lot or to work on their own. Careers that probably would not work well for people with ADHD would include those that involve office work or close detail, such as being an accountant or a bank teller.

MULTICULTURAL FOCUS

Point out to students that, despite its universality (or perhaps because of it), death is treated very differently by different cultures. Native Americans, for example, believe that when they die, they rejoin with nature and become part of the spirit world. Buddhists, on the other hand, believe that although their body may die, their spirit remains and will attach to a new body and a new life. Among Asians, stoic attitudes among the grieving are common, while Hispanics are encouraged to express their grief. Some Jewish mourners may observe a period where visitors are not received, while the Irish may hold a wake, or a gathering in celebration of the deceased. Point out to students that these cultural approaches to death, the dead, and grieving in a large way shape our own attitudes toward death itself. Ask volunteers if they would like to share some of their families' observances of death.

Class Demonstration

CRITICAL THINKING

Purpose: Students complete a brief assignment that involves critical thinking, personalizing, or deeper processing of information.

Time: 5 minutes

Description: Give students several minutes to answer a question that you pose. These assignments can be used in a variety of ways—to verify attendance, to start discussion, to assess student knowledge, and to provide opportunities for critical thinking. Here are some examples: (1) Write your own obituary. If you were to die today, how would people describe your life? (2) Would you want to know right now the age at which you're going to die? Why or why not? Would you live your life differently if you knew you had limited time left? Explain. (3) What do you think it means to have a midlife crisis? Do you think everyone goes through this? What do you think causes a midlife crisis?

CHAPTER 5 • Module 13

Assess

Assign the Module 13 Practice Quiz.

Use the Practice Quiz to identify gaps in student understanding.

REMEDIATE

Have students, individually or in groups, review the module goals, learning objectives, and key terms.

Refer students to the Concept Summary on p. 175 for review.

Close

Discuss with students the ways in which—although childhood is a time of enormous physical and developmental change—adolescents and adults face many changes as well. Ask students if they learned anything about adolescents that they did not already know. If so, do these new insights help them deal better with or at least find more common ground with their peers? In the same vein, do students find that they have a better understanding of their parents and grandparents and the struggles they may face? Has it changed their attitudes toward, or maybe even their relationships with, their families?

L4 DIFFERENTIATED INSTRUCTION

Advanced Learners Provide opportunities for in-depth research on student-directed topics. Have students explore topics on the Internet under your direction.

Practice Quiz

Pick the best answer.

1. Which of the following refers to the feeling of being unique and protected from harm?
   a. personal fable
   b. moral dilemma
   c. imaginary audience
   d. adolescent rebellion

2. According to Kohlberg, most adolescents are at which level of morality?
   a. overly conventional
   b. preconventional
   c. conventional
   d. postconventional

3. According to Erikson, the adolescent's primary challenge is to
   a. learn to feel successful at new tasks
   b. develop a consistent sense of self
   c. form relationships based on true intimacy
   d. resist peer pressure successfully

4. Conflicts between adolescents and their parents or caregivers usually focus on
   a. issues of morality
   b. issues of little real importance
   c. issues of personal responsibility
   d. issues of academic success

5. A sense of completeness of one's ego, or identity, is called
   a. life review
   b. intelligence
   c. integrity
   d. generativity

6. How did Carol Gilligan question Kohlberg's theory of morality?
   a. She proposed that people's basic morality is more similar than Kohlberg believed.
   b. She proposed that most adults have a postconventional moral perspective.
   c. She proposed that Kohlberg's subjects would act differently in real-life situations.
   d. She proposed that men and women have different perspectives when determining which actions are moral.

7. The period of 5 or 10 years during which a woman's reproductive system begins to decline is called
   a. ovulation
   b. andropause
   c. perimenopause
   d. menopause

8. Adam, a middle-aged man, might outperform a younger person on a cognitive task because
   a. his reaction time has improved over the years
   b. his stressful life makes his mind sharper
   c. he has more life experience to draw upon.
   d. his sense of generativity makes him more confident

9. Which of these is most likely to help Joanne, a 65-year-old woman, adjust positively to aging?
   a. staying active in her community
   b. withdrawing from social demands
   c. giving up her career
   d. accepting that her life will end soon

10. According to this theory of aging, shortened telomeres cause cells to age.
    a. cellular clock theory
    b. wear-and-tear theory
    c. free radical theory
    d. activity theory

Practice Quiz Answers

1. a
2. c
3. b
4. b
5. c
6. d
7. c
8. c
9. a
10. a

CHAPTER 5 Summary

Listen on mypsychlab.com

Module 11: Topics in Development
Describe methods and issues in life span development.

11.1 How do biological and environmental factors influence development?
- Biological factors include genetic traits and predispositions. Environmental factors include experiences, social environment, and culture.

11.2 What are some major research issues in developmental psychology?
- Research explores continuity vs. discontinuity, stability vs. change, and physical, cognitive, and psychosocial development.

11.3 How do psychologists study development?
- Researchers perform longitudinal, cross-sectional, and cross-sequential studies.

11.4 What are critical periods and sensitive periods?
- Critical and sensitive periods occur when a child is susceptible to stimuli and receptive to learning from particular experiences.

Module 12: Prenatal, Infant, and Childhood Development
Learn about prenatal and newborn development.

12.1 How do humans develop from conception through birth?
- Over the course of three phases, the fertilized egg becomes a baby. This process includes cell specialization and organ formation.

12.2 What reflexes and abilities do newborns have?
- Infants are born with reflexes including rooting and sucking. Touch, smell, and taste are the most developed senses at birth.

Describe development during infancy and childhood.

12.3 What kinds of physical changes take place in infancy and childhood?
- Infants learn to raise their heads, roll over, sit up, crawl, and walk. Children's gross and fine motor skills improve.

12.4 How do infants and children develop cognitive skills?
- Piaget believed children pass through four cognitive stages: sensorimotor, preoperational, concrete operations, and formal operations.

12.5 What are the stages of language development?
- The stages are cooing, babbling, one-word speech, telegraphic speech, and speaking in whole sentences.

Listen to an audio file of your chapter on mypsychlab.com

12.6 How do babies begin to develop relationships with others?
- Babies form an attachment with a primary caregiver. Attachment styles are secure, avoidant, ambivalent, and disorganized-disoriented.

12.7 How do children develop socially and emotionally?
- Children must resolve four conflicts: trust vs. mistrust, autonomy vs. shame and doubt, initiative vs. guilt, and industry vs. inferiority.

Module 13: Adolescence and Adulthood
Describe development during adolescence.

13.1 What physical changes happen during adolescence?
- Before puberty, children experience a growth spurt. At puberty, children begin to develop adult sexual characteristics.

13.2 How do reasoning and morality develop during adolescence?
- Egocentrism appears in the personal fable and imaginary audience. Many adolescents function at the conventional or even postconventional level of morality.

13.3 How do adolescents form their identities?
- Adolescents face the conflict of identity vs. role confusion and must begin to determine their personal values and their path in life.

13.4 What role do others play in adolescent development?
- Conflict with parents may encourage independence. Adolescents without a strong sense of self are vulnerable to peer pressure.

Describe development during adulthood.

13.5 What social and cognitive changes happen in adulthood?
- Adults must resolve three major conflicts: intimacy vs. isolation, generativity vs. stagnation, and integrity vs. despair. Perception and reaction time slows.

13.6 What physical changes happen in adulthood?
- Most adults experience diminished perception and health problems. Hormonal changes cause menopause and andropause.

13.7 How do scientists explain why aging occurs?
- There are four major theories of aging: cellular clock theory, wear-and-tear theory, free-radical theory, and activity theory.

13.8 What are the stages of death and dying?
- The stages are denial, anger, bargaining, depression, and acceptance.

Vocabulary Terms

human development p. 142
nature p. 142
nurture p. 142
chromosome p. 142
DNA (deoxyribonucleic acid) p. 142
gene p. 142
dominant p. 142
recessive p. 142
physical development p. 142
cognitive development p. 142
psychosocial development p. 143
temperament p. 143
attachment p. 143
longitudinal design p. 144
cross-sectional design p. 144
cross-sequential design p. 144
critical period p. 144
sensitive period p. 145
conception p. 147
ovum p. 147
fertilization p. 147
zygote p. 147
germinal period p. 148
embryonic period p. 148
fetal period p. 148
teratogen p. 148
uterus p. 148
placenta p. 148
umbilical cord p. 148
embryo p. 148
fetus p. 148
assimilation p. 153
accommodation p. 153
sensorimotor stage p. 153
object permanence p. 154
preoperational stage p. 154
egocentrism p. 154
centration p. 154
conservation p. 154
concrete operations stage p. 154
formal operations stage p. 155
expressive language delay p. 156
puberty p. 162
personal fable p. 163
imaginary audience p. 163
preconventional morality p. 164
conventional morality p. 164
postconventional morality p. 164
generativity p. 165
ego integrity p. 166
menopause p. 167
andropause p. 167
activity theory p. 168

DEVELOPMENT ACROSS THE LIFE SPAN 171

Critical Thinking

MAKING CONNECTIONS

Have students complete the following activity to connect the ideas in this chapter. Send them to the Multimedia Library for Chapter 5 at **www.mypsychlab.com** to listen to "Ages and Stages of Cognitive and Moral Development," interviews with people who are in different stages of development according to Erikson. Then lead a class discussion based on the following questions: (1) How do the children and adults interviewed fit into the categories as defined by Erikson? (2) Do the people interviewed appear to be facing their crises in a healthy way, according to Erikson? How so? How not? (3) From which interview did students learn the most? Which did they find the most interesting?

CHAPTER 5 • Chapter Summary and Vocabulary

Chapter Summary

Encourage students to carefully review and study the summary. Explain that it provides an overview of key concepts presented in the text.

Have students identify what they find unclear or confusing. Call on volunteers to provide answers, examples, or definitions.

Vocabulary Terms

Remind students that terms are defined within the chapter at point of use. If they are not sure of a term's definition, they should look up the definition on the page.

Encourage students to create study cards of unfamiliar words or to go to **www.mypsychlab.com** for flash cards. Have them test themselves or a classmate. Advanced students can explain the terms in their own words.

CHAPTER 5 • Module 13

VOCABULARY REVIEW

1. e	6. d
2. i	7. c
3. g	8. h
4. b	9. a
5. j	10. f

WRITING ABOUT PSYCHOLOGY

1. Examples of student responses may be that nature could affect development in the form of a chromosomal disorder such as Down syndrome or a birth defect such as fetal alcohol syndrome. Nurture could affect development in situations of child abuse. Students may use the example of attachment to illustrate how these two work together. A baby's temperament (nature) plus parenting style (nurture) equal attachment style.

2. Students should display not only an understanding of the general list of characteristics of their chosen age range but also the various stages in which someone of this age may fit, according to Piaget, Erikson, and Kohlberg. If it is a young child, his or her language stage, for example, may also be a relevant factor.

PSYCHOLOGY PROJECT

Ask students to submit to you the name and age of the person they chose to study and that person's relationship to the student. Ensure that students who chose to observe children receive proper permission from the child's parent or guardian. When the project is completed, consider dividing students into groups according to the age range studied, and ask them to compare where their findings were consistent and inconsistent with Erikson's.

CHAPTER 5 Assessment

Study and Review on mypsychlab.com

Vocabulary Review

Match each vocabulary term to its definition.

1. sensitive period
2. longitudinal design
3. conservation
4. activity theory
5. generativity
6. attachment
7. personal fable
8. teratogen
9. critical period
10. expressive language delay

a. A time when a child is developmentally most susceptible to the presence or absence of particular stimuli in the environment and must progress to the next stage of development if development is to continue normally.
b. Theory of adjustment to aging that assumes older people are happier if they remain active in some way, such as volunteering or developing a hobby.
c. Type of thought common to adolescents in which young people believe themselves to be unique and protected from harm.
d. The first emotional bond a child forms with its primary caretaker.
e. A time when a child is susceptible to stimuli and receptive to learning from particular types of experiences.
f. The apparent ability of infants to understand far more language than they can produce.
g. In Piaget's theory, the ability to understand that simply changing the appearance of an object does not change the object's nature.
h. Any factor that can cause a birth defect.
i. Research design in which one group of people is followed and assessed at different times as the group ages.
j. Providing guidance to one's children or the next generation, or contributing to the well-being of the next generation through career or volunteer work.

Writing about Psychology

Respond to each question in complete sentences.

1. Throughout our lives, development is influenced by both nature (genetic and biological factors) and nurture (environmental factors). Describe two ways nature influences development and two ways nurture influences development. Then describe an example of how nature and nurture can interact, or affect each other, during development.

2. Choose one specific age range (for example, ages 13–15) and summarize the major developmental changes a person of that age would typically experience. Include specific details about physical, cognitive, and psychosocial changes. Summarize examples of stability that you might see as a person goes through this period.

Psychology Project

What does psychosocial development look like in real life? Conduct observations or interviews to help you understand Erikson's theories.

Materials:
- a notebook
- an audio recorder
- a pencil and paper

Instructions:

1. Choose a person of a different age group to study. You may choose to *observe* a child you know who is between the ages of 2 and 10 or to *interview* an adult who is at least 30. For this project, it is best to work with people you know quite well, such as family members or close friends.
2. Review Erikson's eight developmental stages. Based on the age of the person you are observing or interviewing, determine which stage is most appropriate to focus on.
3. Plan your interview/observation session in advance. Review the appropriate developmental stage and think about what day-to-day concerns are most relevant.
4. Identify related questions you might ask your interviewee, or related behaviors you might expect to see in the child you are observing. Write down your questions or predictions. (If you are observing a child, especially if the child is very young, you might want to prepare a few questions to ask the child's family.)
5. Conduct and record your observation or interview. Take careful notes, even if you are recording the session. Don't hesitate to ask follow-up questions if necessary.
6. Write a one-page report summing up what you learned from the observation or interview. Are your findings consistent with Erikson's theory? If so, how? If not, what was different?

Internet Resources

Intute: www.intute.ac.uk/psychology/
A point of departure for your search for information about human development.

Suite 101: www.suite101.com/welcome.cfm/developmental_psychology
A collection of information on all aspects of human development.

Child Development Institute: www.childdevelopmentinfo.com/
Aimed toward answering parents' questions, this site nonetheless offers a great deal of information for anyone interested in childhood developmental stages.

Test Yourself

Pick the best answer.

1. The period of pregnancy that contains the clearest examples of critical periods is the
   a. fetal period
   b. germinal period
   c. embryonic period
   d. fertilization period

2. Which of the following best describes the relationship between age and task performance?
   a. The older you are, the faster you will complete a task.
   b. The younger you are, the better you will complete a task.
   c. Old age negatively impacts performance but experience positively impacts performance.
   d. Old age positively impacts performance but experience negatively impacts performance.

3. Which reflex describes a baby moving her head when someone touches her cheek?
   a. sucking
   b. startle
   c. rooting
   d. grasping

4. Which of the newborn's senses is the most fully developed at birth?
   a. hearing
   b. smell
   c. taste
   d. touch

5. In which of Piaget's stages does the child become capable of understanding conservation?
   a. sensorimotor
   b. preoperational
   c. concrete operations
   d. formal operations

6. A toddler who is punished for hitting someone and, as a result, concludes that hitting is wrong is using which type of moral reasoning?
   a. unconventional
   b. preconventional
   c. conventional
   d. post conventional

7. Erikson's conflict of intimacy versus isolation primarily concerns people in which age group?
   a. adolescents
   b. young adults
   c. middle-aged adults
   d. older adults

8. Which of the following physical changes usually occurs before puberty, rather than during puberty?
   a. in girls, the onset of menstruation
   b. in boys, the development of facial hair
   c. in both sexes, a dramatic growth spurt
   d. in both sexes, the development of pubic hair

9. According to Erikson, adults who are not dealing successfully with the developmental crises of middle adulthood will
   a. be unable to nurture others because they are too self-centered.
   b. form shallow relationships that do not involve true intimacy.
   c. play many different roles and be unsure of who they are.
   d. be intensely afraid of death and full of regrets.

10. Ego integrity can be defined as
    a. being confident that your mind is still sharp, despite aging.
    b. feeling that you have led a full and rewarding life.
    c. feeling a sense of greater security in your forties.
    d. being in a close relationship where you can still be true to yourself.

11. With which type of attachment are abusive and/or neglectful mothers associated?
    a. secure
    b. avoidant
    c. ambivalent
    d. disorganized-disoriented

12. Which of the following is NOT part of dealing with the conflict of identity versus role confusion?
    a. forming political opinions
    b. developing personal values
    c. beginning to think about possible careers
    d. deciding whether to have children

13. Kashif, a toddler, holds his empty cup up to his mothers and says "Milk!" His use of the word is correctly labeled
    a. cooing
    b. babbling
    c. a holophrase
    d. telegraphic speech

14. Samantha, a teenager, refuses to go to school because she is convinced that everyone will laugh at her new haircut. Samantha's thinking is an example of
    a. the personal fable
    b. role confusion
    c. the imaginary audience
    d. formal operations

15. The way collagen tissue becomes less elastic as we get older is a good example of which theory of aging?
    a. cellular clock
    b. wear-and-tear
    c. free radical
    d. activity

16. A child who believes the Tooth Fairy is a real person is in which of Piaget's cognitive stages?
    a. sensorimotor
    b. preoperational
    c. concrete operational
    d. formal operational

17. Emily is a psychology researcher studying Kohlberg's stages of moral development in children and teenagers. She wants to study subjects when they are 6, 12, and 18 years old. Emily's research is funded by a grant that only provides money for 3 years of research, so Emily must complete her research in 3 years. Which research design best meets Emily's needs?
    a. cross-sectional
    b. longitudinal
    c. cross-sequential
    d. case study

18. At age 9, Pedro is in Piaget's concrete operations stage. Which of the following is most likely true?
    a. Pedro is completely unable to see the world through anyone's eye but his own.
    b. Pedro will automatically assume that the tallest glass contains the most juice.
    c. Pedro has trouble understanding abstract concepts, such as the true meaning of "friendship."
    d. Pedro spends a lot of time thinking about hypothetical situations and the future.

19. Paul is an elderly cancer patient whose doctor tells him he has only a few months to live. He promises the doctor he will make whatever lifestyle changes are necessary, if only he can have more time. In which stage of reacting to death is Paul?
    a. denial
    b. anger
    c. bargaining
    d. depression

CHAPTER 5 • Assessment

TEST YOURSELF

1. c	11. d
2. c	12. d
3. c	13. c
4. d	14. c
5. c	15. b
6. b	16. b
7. b	17. a
8. c	18. c
9. a	19. c
10. b	

Ready for Testing

STUDENTS KNOW THEY ARE READY FOR TESTING IF THEY ARE ABLE TO . . .

- Introduce the research methods and major issues in developmental psychology, including the nature-versus-nurture controversy.
- Describe the stages of prenatal development and potential hazards.
- Discuss the theories of Piaget with regard to cognitive development.
- Describe physical and cognitive development in infancy and childhood including language development.
- Explain the concept of personality, including the idea of temperament, attachment theory, and Erikson's psychosocial model.
- Identify the major stages of development in adolescence and adulthood.
- Discuss theories of aging and Kübler-Ross's stages of dying.
- Understand how ADHD affects adults.

CHAPTER 5 • Concept Summary

MULTIMEDIA CONTENT AVAILABLE AT
www.mypsychlab.com

- Map the Concepts on mypsychlab.com
- Study and Review Flashcards on mypsychlab.com

STUDY TIPS

Setting Priorities Many students get derailed in their studying by an inability to set priorities. Explain to students that doing so can help them focus on the right tasks at the right time, and for the right amount of time. The first step in setting priorities is to write down all assignments and tasks that must be completed, along with the date by which each must be accomplished. Stress that students should write down (or input into a software program) their assignments, not rely on memory. Have students look at their assignment lists. Which items must be done first? Which can wait? Point out that all tasks do not have equal urgency, nor should easy tasks be given first priority merely because they are less difficult to perform. Next, ask students to rewrite their list in order of importance. They can then use this list to schedule their time each day. Suggest they check off each task as it is accomplished.

CHAPTER 5 Concept Summary: Development Across

Learning Objectives

11.1 11.2 11.3 11.4   pp. 142–146

Describe Methods and Issues in Life Span Development

- **nature and nurture**
  - **nature** is the influence of genetic and biological factors on development
  - **nurture** is influence of environmental factors on development

- **major research issues**
  - physical
  - cognitive
  - psychosocial
  - is development **continuous** or **discontinuous?**
  - which aspects of development are **stable,** and which **change** over time?

- **research designs**
  - longitudinal
  - cross-sectional
  - cross-sequential

- **critical and sensitive periods**

Learning Objectives

12.1 12.2   pp. 147–151

Learn about Prenatal and Newborn Development

- **prenatal development is the period from conception to birth**
  - germinal period: weeks 1–2
  - embryonic period: weeks 3–8
  - fetal period: weeks 9–38 (approximately)

- **Newborn development immediately after birth**
  - **Sensory development**
    - Touch, taste, and smell are well developed
    - Hearing is functional but not well developed
    - Vision is least developed
  - **Physical development**
    - Body systems start to function
    - Babies are born with innate reflexes, such as grasping, startle, rooting, stepping, and sucking

174 CHAPTER 5

What Every Student Should Know About...

PLAGIARISM

Tell students that plagiarism means using someone else's work—published or unpublished words, ideas, or illustrations—without giving the creator of that work the appropriate credit. Presenting another's work as one's own is equivalent to lying, a form of dishonesty. Handing in a paper as one's own amounts to intentional plagiarism. In the same way, buying a paper from an Internet source and handing it in, even with minor changes to wording, is plagiarism. Also, paying someone to write a paper that a student then hands in as his or hers is plagiarism. Finally, handing in a paper of one's own that someone else has heavily revised is plagiarism. The penalties for plagiarism can be severe. Students risk a failing grade or even disciplinary action such as suspension or expulsion.

the Life Span

Map The Concepts on mypsychlab.com

Learning Objectives 12.3 12.4 12.5 12.6 12.7 pp. 151–160

Describe Development during Infancy and Childhood

- **physical development**
  - Birth to 2 years is a period of rapid development
  - Motor milestones within the first 2 years include: lifting head and chest, rolling over, sitting with and without support, crawling, walking

- **cognitive development**
  - Piaget's stages
    - **Sensorimotor stage**
    - **Preoperational stage**
    - **Concrete operational stage**
    - **Formal operational stage**
  - Stages of language development: cooing, babbling, holophrases, telegraphic speech, whole sentences

- **Psychosocial development**
  - Attachment styles: secure, avoidant, ambivalent, disorganized-disoriented
  - Erikson's theory suggests that children face a series of crises that must be navigated
    - Trust vs. mistrust
    - Autonomy vs. shame and doubt
    - Intiative vs. guilt
    - Industry vs. inferiority

Learning Objectives 13.1 13.2 13.3 13.4 pp. 162–165

Describe Development during Adolescence

- **physical changes** → **puberty** is the development of adult primary and secondary sexual characteristics

- **Kohlberg's levels of morality:**
  - preconventional
  - conventional
  - postconventional

- **family and peers** may motivate adolescents' independence

Learning Objectives 13.5 13.6 13.7 13.8 pp. 165–169

- **social and cognitive changes:** Erikson's developmental crises of adulthood
  - intimacy vs. isolation
  - generativity vs. stagnation
  - ego integrity vs. despair

- **physical changes** → **menopause** in women and **andropause** in men

Describe Development during Adulthood

- **why aging occurs:** cellular clock, wear-and-tear, free radical, and activity theories

- **stages of death and dying:** denial, anger, bargaining, depression, acceptance

DEVELOPMENT ACROSS THE LIFE SPAN 175

CHAPTER 5 • Assessment

STUDY TIPS

Summarizing To help students prepare for college, have them practice summarizing. Give them several minutes to summarize one section of the chapter in one to three sentences. In groups of three, they should share their summaries and work together to agree on the most succinct summary possible. Share these summaries with the class and see if it is possible to write a better one. A good summary should identify the main idea(s) and conclusions of the section without including too many details or examples.

Comprehension Check

AGES AND STAGES OF COGNITIVE AND MORAL DEVELOPMENT

To check their understanding of developmental stages, students can visit the Multimedia Library section of the www.mypsychlab.com site and explore the Ages and Stages of Cognitive and Moral Development activity. Advanced students can work alone, while on-level and struggling students can work in pairs or small groups. Students will receive immediate feedback on their answers.

Chapter 5 Assessment

CHAPTER 6 • Module 14

Launch the Chapter

CHAPTER GOALS AND LEARNING OBJECTIVES

Module 14 Classical Conditioning

Explain the process of classical conditioning.

14.1 What are the principles of classical conditioning?

14.2 How can classical conditioning be specialized to affect emotions?

14.3 How does classical conditioning function in our everyday lives?

Module 15 Operant Conditioning

Explain the process of operant conditioning.

15.1 What is Thorndike's law of effect?

15.2 What are the principles of operant conditioning?

15.3 What are some specializations of operant conditioning?

15.4 How does operant conditioning function in everyday life?

Module 16 Cognitive Learning and Observational Learning

Identify the aspects of cognitive and observational learning.

16.1 What occurs in observational learning?

16.2 How does observational learning function in everyday life?

16.3 What is cognitive learning theory?

Module 17 Language

Identify the structural features of language.

17.1 What is language, and how is it structured?

17.2 How are language and thought related?

Explain theories and stages of language acquisition.

17.3 How is language acquired?

17.4 What are the theories of language acquisition?

Identify areas of the brain associated with language.

17.5 Which parts of the brain are associated with language, and how does brain damage affect language?

DIFFERENTIATED INSTRUCTION KEY

Look for these symbols to help you adjust steps in each lesson to meet your students' needs.

- **L1** Special Needs
- **L2** Basic
- **ELL** English Language Learners
- **LPR** Less Proficient Readers
- **L3** All Students
- **L4** Advanced Students

CHAPTER 6
Learning and Language Development

Why White Coats Made the Baby Scream

When Stephanie was an infant, she was constantly getting sick and spent a lot of her infancy in the doctor's office. Antibiotics were delivered by injection. The shots were obviously painful and caused Stephanie to scream and cry.

Of course, the doctor in his white coat and the nurse in her white uniform were always present, as well as the white paper covering the examining table. It didn't take too many visits before Stephanie would scream when she saw the "white coat" people coming toward her—especially the nurse, who was usually the one who delivered the hated shot.

When she was 1 year old, her mother took her to a photography studio to have her portrait made. In those days, the photographer wore a white jacket to look more professional and took the pictures on a carpeted platform with a white sheet draped across it. Stephanie threw a fit, crying and screaming. The photographer had to take his jacket off and remove the white drape. After about an hour, she was finally calm enough to pose for the picture on a bare platform. Why did Stephanie have this reaction?

Stephanie's reaction to the photo session was a result of a special type of learning called *classical conditioning*. In this type of learning, objects or situations (such as white coats and being up on a table) can become associated or paired with other kinds of situations (such as the pain of injections). Once the association is made, similar objects or situations can cause the same response (e.g., screaming in fear) that the earlier situation caused.

CORRELATION TO APA STANDARDS FOR CHAPTER 6

IIIB. LEARNING

IIIB-1.	IIIB-1. Classical conditioning	pp. 178–182
IIIB-2.	Operant conditioning	pp. 184–193
IIIB-3.	Observational learning	pp. 195–196

IIIC. LANGUAGE DEVELOPMENT

IIIC-1.	Structural features of language	pp. 201–204
IIIC-2.	Theories and developmental stages of language acquisition	pp. 204–205
IIIC-C.	Basic concepts of data analysis	pp. 205–206

MODULE 14 ▸ CLASSICAL CONDITIONING

MODULE 15 ▸ OPERANT CONDITIONING

MODULE 16 ▸ COGNITIVE LEARNING AND OBSERVATIONAL LEARNING

MODULE 17 ▸ LANGUAGE

Why Study? Learning

If we had not been able to learn, we would have died out as a species long ago. Learning is the process that allows us to adapt to the changing conditions of the world around us. We can alter our actions until we find the behavior that leads us to survival and rewards, and we can eliminate actions that have been unsuccessful in the past. Without learning, there would be no buildings, no agriculture, no lifesaving medicines, and no human civilization.

LEARNING AND LANGUAGE DEVELOPMENT 177

SCHEDULING

1 Period = 50 min. 1 Block = 90 min.	Semester Course (18 weeks/90 days) Periods/Blocks		Full-Year Course (36 weeks/180 days) Period/Blocks	
Module 14	1	0.5	2	1
Module 15	1.5	0.75	3	1.5
Module 16	1	0.5	2	1
Module 17	1.5	0.75	3	1.5
Total Days for Chapter	5	2.5	10	5

CHAPTER 6 • Module 14

Teacher Prep

An unconditioned stimulus can be paired with a neutral stimulus to create a conditioned stimulus. Phobias can be learned when something unpleasant is paired with a neutral stimulus.

Thorndike's law holds that if a behavior is followed by a pleasurable consequence, the behavior will be repeated. Operant conditioning is the learning of voluntary behavior through the effects of pleasant and unpleasant consequences to responses. Reinforcement encourages learning voluntary behavior. Punishment discourages learning voluntary behavior. Shaping involves a stepped process of learning by getting a person or animal to perform a behavior. Reinforcement can be applied through partial reinforcement, continuous reinforcement, and schedules of fixed and variable intervals and ratios. Applied behavior analysis uses the shaping process to mold a desired response. Biofeedback and neurofeedback measure learning progress.

People learn behavior by watching others perform that behavior. Observational learning requires attention, memory, capability, and the desire to perform a behavior. Cognitive learning theory focuses on the role of thought processes on learning.

Language is a system of symbols used to communicate. Piaget believed that people learn concepts first and later acquire the words that describe that concept. Vygotsky believed that language helps develop concepts. Language is acquired through a series of stages. Chomsky believed that humans are born with an ability to understand and learn how to speak language. Environmental factors, such as an adult's tone toward a child, also influence language acquisition. Broca's area is associated with language production; Wernicke's area is associated with language comprehension.

Module 14 Learning and Language Development

CHAPTER 6 • Module 14

Focus

RESOURCES

For this module, consult the appropriate sections of the Teacher's Manual, Test Bank, and PowerPoint slides, all found on the Teacher's Resource DVD, and the interactive study tools for students on MyPsychLab.

BEFORE CLASS

Students should read the section for homework before coming to class.

BELLRINGER

Ask students to write down short answers to these questions: Name a skill that you learned easily and quickly. How did you learn this skill? Why was it easy to learn? Now think of a skill that was difficult to learn. Why was it difficult to learn?

Teach

INTRODUCE THE TOPIC

Explain to students that learning is any relatively permanent change in behavior brought about by experience or practice. It is different from maturation, which is controlled by the genes.

LINK to Chapter Nine, Memory, p. 279

COVER THE MODULE

14.1 What are the principles of classical conditioning?

- Important concepts/terminology: *reflex* (involuntary response) and *stimulus* (any object, event, or experience that causes a *response,* or reaction, of an organism).
- Ivan Pavlov accidentally discovered the phenomenon in which one stimulus can, through pairing with another stimulus, produce a similar response. He called this *classical conditioning*.

LINK to Chapter One, The Science of Psychology, pp. 5–9

Module 14 Classical Conditioning

Module Goal

Explain the process of classical conditioning.

Learning Objectives

14.1 What are the principles of classical conditioning?
14.2 How can classical conditioning be specialized to affect emotions?
14.3 How does classical conditioning function in our everyday lives?

Explain the Process of Classical Conditioning

The term *learning* is one of those concepts whose meaning is crystal clear until one has to put it in actual words. **Learning** is any relatively permanent change in behavior brought about by experience or practice.

The "relatively permanent" part of the definition refers to the fact that when people learn anything, some part of their brain is physically changed to record what they've learned. Research strongly suggests that once people learn something, it is always present somewhere in memory (Barsalou, 1992). They may be unable to retrieve it, but it's there. LINK *to Chapter Nine: Memory, p. 279.*

Not all change is accomplished through learning. Any kind of change in the way an organism *behaves* is learning. Changes like an increase in height or the size of the brain are another kind of change controlled by a genetic blueprint. This kind of change is called *maturation*, which is not the same as learning. For example, children learn to walk when they do because their nervous systems, muscle strength, and sense of balance have reached the point where walking is possible for them—all factors controlled by maturation, not by how much practice those children have had in trying to walk.

14.1 What are the principles of classical conditioning?

In the early 1900s, research scientists were unhappy with psychology's primary focus on mental activity. LINK *to Chapter One: The Science of Psychology, pp. 5–9.* Many were looking for a way to bring some kind of objectivity and scientific research to the field. It was a Russian *physiologist* (a person who studies the workings of the body) named Ivan Pavlov (1849–1936) who accidentally stumbled across the basic principles of a particular kind of learning (Pavlov, 1906, 1926). His famous experiments are now known as "Pavlov's dogs."

Pavlov had built a device that would accurately measure the amount of saliva produced by dogs when they were fed a measured amount of food. Normally, when food is placed in the mouth of any animal, the salivary glands automatically start releasing saliva to help with chewing and digestion. This is a normal *reflex* (involuntary response) in both animals and humans. A *stimulus* can be defined as any object, event, or experience that causes a *response*, the reaction of an organism. In the case of Pavlov's dogs, the food is the stimulus and salivation is the response.

Pavlov noticed that his dogs began salivating when they weren't expected to, such as when they saw the food bowl. Pavlov spent the rest of his career studying what he termed **classical conditioning**, learning to make a reflex re-

learning any relatively permanent change in behavior brought about by experience or practice

classical conditioning learning in which one learns an involuntary response when a stimulus that normally causes a particular response is paired with a new, neutral stimulus. After enough pairings, the new stimulus will also cause the response to occur.

Terms

• learning • classical conditioning • unconditioned stimulus (UCS) • unconditioned response (UCR) • neutral stimulus (NS) • conditioned stimulus (CS) • conditioned response (CR) • stimulus generalization • stimulus discrimination • extinction • spontaneous recovery • conditioned emotional response (CER) • vicarious conditioning • conditioned taste aversion • biological preparedness

Before Conditioning
Neutral Stimulus (NS) Bell → No Salivation

During Conditioning
Neutral Stimulus (NS) Bell + Unconditioned Stimulus (UCS) Food → Unconditioned Response (UCR) Salivation

After Conditioning
Conditioned Stimulus (CS) Bell → Conditioned Response (CR) Salivation

FIGURE 14.1 Classical Conditioning
Before conditioning takes place, the sound of the bell does not cause salivation and is a neutral stimulus, or NS. During conditioning, the sound of the bell occurs just before the presentation of the food, the UCS. The food causes salivation, the UCR. When conditioning has occurred after several pairings of the bell with the food, the bell will begin to elicit a salivation response from the dog without any food. This is learning, and the sound of the bell is now a CS and the salivation to the bell is the CR.

sponse to a stimulus other than the original, natural stimulus that normally produces it. (The term *conditioning* is a synonym for "learning.")
⊙▸─ Simulate on **mypsychlab.com**

Elements of Classical Conditioning Pavlov did a classic experiment in which he paired the ringing of a bell with the presentation of food to see if the dogs would eventually salivate to the sound of the bell. Pavlov knew that dogs naturally salivate in response to food. In this situation, the food is called the **unconditioned stimulus (UCS).** The term *unconditioned* means "unlearned" or "naturally occurring." This stimulus ordinarily leads to an involuntary reflex response called the **unconditioned response (UCR).** In the example of Pavlov's dogs, salivation is the unconditioned response to food. It occurs because of genetic "wiring" in the nervous system.

Before conditioning began, Pavlov's dogs did not have any reaction to the sound of a ringing bell. However, Pavlov determined that almost any kind of stimulus could become associated with the unconditioned stimulus if it is paired with that unconditioned stimulus often enough. So, he began to pair the presentation of food with the ringing of a bell: Just before the dogs were given food, they heard the bell ring. At this point, the bell was called a **neutral stimulus (NS)** because it had no effect on salivation. After being paired with the food many times, however, the bell came to produce the same salivation response as the food itself. In a sense, the bell predicted the arrival of food. Because the bell was no longer neutral, it became a **conditioned stimulus (CS).** The response to the CS of salivation is called the **conditioned response (CR).** Figure 14.1 illustrates the elements of Pavlov's experiment.

⊙▸─ Simulate Pavlov's classical conditioning experiment on **mypsychlab.com**

unconditioned stimulus (UCS) a naturally occurring stimulus that leads to an involuntary (reflex) response.

unconditioned response (UCR) an involuntary (reflex) response to a naturally occurring or unconditioned stimulus.

neutral stimulus (NS) stimulus that has no effect on the desired response.

conditioned stimulus (CS) stimulus that becomes able to produce a learned reflex response by being paired with the original unconditioned stimulus.

conditioned response (CR) learned reflex response to a conditioned stimulus.

LEARNING AND LANGUAGE DEVELOPMENT 179

CHAPTER 6 • Module 14

MULTIMEDIA CONTENT AVAILABLE AT
www.mypsychlab.com

⊙▸─ Simulate Pavlov's classical conditioning experiment on **mypsychlab.com**

COVER THE MODULE (continued)

- **Elements of Classical Conditioning**
  - The *unconditioned stimulus (UCS)* is the stimulus that is naturally occurring and produces the reflex, or involuntary *unconditioned response (UCR)*. Both are called "unconditioned" because they are not learned.
  - The *conditioned stimulus (CS)* begins as a *neutral stimulus (NS)*, but when paired with the UCS, it eventually begins to elicit the reflex on its own. The reflex response to the CS is called the *conditioned response (CR)*, and both stimulus and response are learned.
  - Pavlov paired a sound with the presentation of food to dogs and discovered several principles of classical conditioning: the NS and the UCS must be paired several times, and the CS must precede the UCS by only a few seconds.

UNDERSTANDING VISUALS

During your discussion of the elements of classical conditioning, direct students' attention to Figure 14.1 for a review of Pavlov's experiment. Ask a volunteer to explain what the figure illustrates.

Class Demonstration

FINDING EXAMPLES OF CLASSICAL CONDITIONING

This activity works well if you begin with your own example before asking students to do so. Play a clip of music from the movie *Jaws*. Students will usually begin to laugh and, when asked, will say that they are thinking of the shark from *Jaws*. Point out that the movie has conditioned us to be afraid when we hear that music by consistently pairing it with bloody shark attacks. Now ask students to generate their own examples of classical conditioning in the movies. These examples may include famous lines that we associate with certain movies, particular characters, songs, or symbols. Call on students to "present" (i.e., say, sing, act, etc.) the conditioned stimulus (CS) in their example for the rest of the class. Call on volunteers to guess what the stimulus refers to.

Module 14 Classical Conditioning

CHAPTER 6 • Module 14

DISCUSS THE STUDENT VOICE QUESTION
Use this question to lead into an explanation of the difference between stimulus generalization and stimulus discrimination. It is logical to assume that the dogs salivated to the doorbell, but emphasize that they learned to tell the difference between the bell sounds because only the real CS was followed with food.

COVER THE MODULE *(continued)*
- *Stimulus generalization* occurs when stimuli similar to the UCS evoke the CR but to a lesser degree.
- *Stimulus discrimination* occurs when presentation of a stimulus similar to the CS without the UCS leads to this stimulus not producing generalization.
- **Extinction and Spontaneous Recovery**
  - *Extinction* is the disappearance of or weakening of the CR following the removal of the UCS.
  - *Spontaneous recovery* is the reappearance of the CR after a pause in extinction trials.

CHECK FOR UNDERSTANDING
Ask volunteers to explain the concepts of (1) stimulus generalization and stimulus discrimination and (2) extinction and spontaneous recovery. Students who need remediation can visit the www.mypsychlab.com website for Chapter 6 to review these processes.

▶ That seems simple enough. But I wonder—did Pavlov's dogs salivate to the doorbell, too?

stimulus generalization the tendency to respond to a stimulus that is only similar to the original conditioned stimulus with the conditioned response.

stimulus discrimination the tendency to stop making a generalized response to a stimulus that is similar to the original conditioned stimulus because the similar stimulus is never paired with the unconditioned stimulus.

extinction the disappearance or weakening of a learned response following the removal or absence of the unconditioned stimulus (in classical conditioning) or the removal of a reinforcer (in operant conditioning).

spontaneous recovery the reappearance of a learned response after extinction has occurred.

180 CHAPTER 6

Notice that the responses, CR (conditioned response) and UCR (unconditioned response), are essentially the same—salivation. They simply differ in strength and what they are the response *to*. An *unconditioned* stimulus (UCS) is always followed by an *unconditioned* response (UCR), and a *conditioned* stimulus (CS) is always followed by a *conditioned* response (CR).

Is this rocket science? No, not really. Classical conditioning is actually one of the simplest forms of learning. Does your dog come running when she hears the pantry door opening? This is an example of classical conditioning: The dog has come to associate the sound of the pantry door (CS) with the pleasure and excitement (UCR) of eating supper (UCS), and so the sound produces a feeling of pleasure and excitement (CR).

That seems simple enough. But I wonder—did Pavlov's dogs salivate to the doorbell, too?

Pavlov found that similar-sounding bells would produce the same conditioned response from his dogs. This tendency to respond to a stimulus that is only similar to the original conditioned stimulus is called **stimulus generalization**. However, because only the real CS was followed with food, the dogs learned to tell the difference, or *discriminate*, between the "fake" bells and the real one, a process called **stimulus discrimination**. Stimulus discrimination occurs when an organism learns to respond to different stimuli in different ways.

Extinction and Spontaneous Recovery What would have happened if Pavlov had stopped giving the dogs food after the real CS? Pavlov did just that, and the dogs gradually stopped salivating to the sound of the bell. When the bell (CS or conditioned stimulus) was repeatedly presented in the absence of the UCS (unconditioned stimulus or food, in this case), the salivation (CR or conditioned response) "died out" in a process called **extinction**.

Why does the removal of an unconditioned stimulus lead to extinction of the conditioned response? One theory is that the presentation of the CS alone leads to new learning. During extinction, the UCS–CS association that was learned is weakened, as the CS no longer predicts the UCS. In the case of Pavlov's dogs, through extinction, they learned not to salivate to the bell as it no longer predicted that food was on its way.

However, once you learn something, it's almost impossible to "unlearn" it. Pavlov waited a few weeks, putting the bell away. There were no more training sessions and the dogs were not exposed to the bell's ringing in that time at all. But when Pavlov took the bell back out and rang it, the dogs all began to salivate, although it was a fairly weak response and didn't last very long. This brief recovery of the conditioned response, called **spontaneous recovery**, proves that the CR isn't dead and gone; it's just suppressed or inhibited. As time passes, this inhibition weakens, especially if the original conditioned stimulus has not been present for a while. (See Figure 14.2 for an illustration of extinction and spontaneous recovery.)

People experience classical conditioning in many ways. A person who has been hit from behind in a car accident, for example, will spend the next few weeks cringing every time another vehicle gets too close to the rear of the car. That cringing reaction is a conditioned response. The crash itself was the UCS (unconditioned stimulus) and the closeness of the other cars becomes a CS (conditioned stimulus). The cringing reaction will eventually become extinct if the person comes close to many other cars without experiencing another crash, but spontaneous recovery (reacting briefly and with less strength to an approaching car) is still possible even after extinction.

Class Demonstration

CLASSICAL CONDITIONING IN HUMANS
A well-known demonstration involves puffing air (UCS) through a drinking straw directed at a subject's eye, which causes an eye blink (UCR). Precede the puff with a finger snap or another appropriate neutral stimulus. Set up pairs of students in which one student is the experimenter and the other is the subject. In the first set of trials, the experimenter should expose the subject to several pairings of the neutral and unconditioned stimuli. In the second set of trials, the experimenter should vary presentations of the neutral stimulus such that it sometimes precedes the UCS and sometimes does not. The second set of trials should demonstrate that the subject blinks in response to the neutral stimulus even when it is not followed by the UCS. Thus, the neutral stimulus will have become a CS and the eye blink will have become a CR.

180 Chapter 6 Learning and Language Development

FIGURE 14.2 Extinction and Spontaneous Recovery
This graph shows the acquisition, extinction, spontaneous recovery, and reacquisition of a conditioned salivary response. Typically, the measure of conditioning is the number of drops of saliva elicited by the CS on each trial. Note that on the day following extinction, the first presentation of the CS elicits quite a large response.

14.2 How can classical conditioning be specialized to affect emotions?

Later scientists took Pavlov's concepts and expanded them to explain not only animal behavior but also human behavior. One of the earliest of these studies showed that even an emotional response could be conditioned.

Little Albert and the White Rat John B. Watson, the founder of *behaviorism* (the study of observable behavior), firmly believed that all behavior could be explained in terms of learning, including even the *phobias* (irrational fear responses) that the Freudian camp thought were deeply rooted in the unconscious mind. His classic experiment with an 18-month-old boy, called "Little Albert," and a white rat was a demonstration of learning a phobia (Watson & Rayner, 1920). **LINK** to *Chapter One: The Science of Psychology, p. 9*.

Watson, collaborating with graduate student Rosalie Rayner, paired the presentation of the white rat to the baby with a loud, scary noise that was produced by striking an iron bar with a hammer behind Albert's head. Although the baby was not afraid of the rat, he was naturally afraid of the loud noise and started to cry. Soon, every time the baby saw the rat, he started to cry. In conditioning terms, the loud noise was the UCS, the fear of the noise the was UCR, the white rat became the CS, and the fear of the rat (the phobia) was the CR.

This experiment demonstrates the power of conditioning, but it also raises ethical concerns. Watson and Rayner's experiment took place nearly a century ago, and causing a baby to develop a phobia in this way would not be considered ethical today. Albert's family did not give informed consent, and Albert was harmed without being given follow-up treatment for his phobia of white furry things. **Watch** on **mypsychlab.com**

The learning of phobias is a very good example of a certain type of classical conditioning, the **conditioned emotional response (CER).** CERs are some of the easiest forms of classical conditioning to accomplish, and our lives are full of them. The next time you watch television, watch the commercials closely. Advertisers often use certain objects or certain types of people in their ads to generate a specific emotional response in viewers, hoping that the emotional response will become paired with their product. Glamorous models and baby animals are some of the examples of stimuli the advertising world uses to catch our attention.

Watch classic footage of Little Albert on **mypsychlab.com**

conditioned emotional response (CER) emotional response that has become classically conditioned to occur to learned stimuli, such as fear of dogs or the emotional reaction that occurs when seeing an attractive person.

LEARNING AND LANGUAGE DEVELOPMENT 181

CHAPTER 6 • Module 14

COVER THE MODULE

14.2 How can classical conditioning be specialized to affect emotions?

- **Little Albert and the White Rat**
  - John Watson was able to demonstrate that an emotional disorder called a *phobia* could be learned through classical conditioning by exposing a baby to a white rat and a loud noise, producing conditioned fear of the rat in the baby.

LINK to Chapter One, The Science of Psychology, p. 9

MULTIMEDIA CONTENT AVAILABLE AT
www.mypsychlab.com

Watch classic footage of Little Albert on **mypsychlab.com**

- *Conditional emotional response (CER)* is an emotional response that has become classically conditioned to occur to learned stimuli.

FAST FACT

Ask: How many people in the United States do you think suffer from some sort of phobia? *(According to the National Institute of Mental Health, more than 10 million adults in the U.S. suffer from some sort of phobia.)*

L2 LPR DIFFERENTIATED INSTRUCTION

Less Proficient Readers For students with difficulties with learning strategies, clarify the rationale for learning a new strategy in terms the students value. Directly teach any requisite skills needed to perform the strategy.

Explore

CLASSICAL CONDITIONING AND TELEVISION ADVERTISEMENTS

Ask students to watch television at home and pay special attention to the advertisements they see. Tell them to select one or two ads and take notes, analyzing the pairing of emotion-provoking stimuli (possible classical conditioning) with products. For example, a commercial that advertises tires might portray a mother and her baby driving on a dark, rainy night (fearful stimulus), with the implication being that fear can be avoided by choosing the proper brand of tire. Another ad might show an attractive person approaching someone who is drinking a particular brand of beverage, suggesting that an individual can attract a desirable person (pleasant stimulus) by drinking the right kind of soda. Have students report their findings in class and discuss.

Module 14 Classical Conditioning **181**

CHAPTER 6 • Module 14

COVER THE MODULE (continued)

- *Vicarious conditioning* is the classical conditioning of a reflex response or emotion by watching the reaction of another person.

COVER THE MODULE

14.3 How does classical conditioning function in our everyday lives?

- *Conditioned taste aversions* occur when an organism becomes nauseated some time after eating a certain food, which then becomes aversive to the organism.
- **Biological Preparedness**
  - Some kinds of conditioned responses are more easily learned because of *biological preparedness*, which may cause humans to associate certain stimuli with danger to survival.

EXTEND THE LESSON

Explain to students that impulse buying is a joy to many retailers but a scourge to many consumers. It is also a behavior of great interest to consumer psychologists, who want to know why people give in to their impulses. Researchers in this field are in demand by advertisers, manufacturers, and retailers who want advice on how to capture the attention of potential customers and get people to open their wallets.

CHECK FOR UNDERSTANDING

Ask: **Why does classical conditioning have limitations as a learning technique?** *(There is no way to teach entirely new behaviors within the framework of classical conditioning.)*

---

vicarious conditioning classical conditioning of a reflex response or emotion by watching the reaction of another person.

conditioned taste aversion development of a nauseated or aversive response to a particular taste because that taste was followed by a nausea reaction, occurring after only one association.

biological preparedness referring to the tendency of animals to learn certain associations, such as taste and nausea, with only one or few pairings due to the survival value of the learning.

It is even possible to become classically conditioned by simply watching someone else respond to a stimulus in a process called **vicarious conditioning** (Bandura & Rosenthal, 1966). Many years ago, children received vaccination shots in school. The nurse lined the children up, and one by one, they had to go forward to get a needle in the arm. When some children received their shots, they cried quite a bit. By the time the nurse got near the end of the line of children, they were all crying—many of them before she ever touched needle to skin. They had learned their fear response from watching the reactions of the other children.

14.3 How does classical conditioning function in our everyday lives?

Are there any foods that you just can't eat anymore because of a bad experience with them? Believe it or not, your reaction to that food is a kind of classical conditioning.

Many experiments have shown that laboratory rats will develop a **conditioned taste aversion** for any liquid or food they swallow up to 6 hours before becoming nauseated. Researchers like John Garcia (1989) found that rats that were given a sweetened liquid and then given something that caused nausea would not touch the sweetened liquid again (Berteretche et al., 2004).

Biological Preparedness Conditioned taste aversions, along with phobic reactions, are an example of something called **biological preparedness**. Most mammals find their food by smell and taste and will learn to avoid any food that smells or tastes like something they ate just before becoming ill. The mammalian body, which has adapted over time to promote survival, seems to be prepared to associate smells and tastes with getting sick (Garcia & Koelling, 1966; Seligman, 1970). Although most conditioning requires repeated pairings of CS with UCS, for nausea, one pairing may be all that is necessary.

Classical conditioning can be an effective learning technique, but it does have its limitations. For example, while new stimuli can be paired with old responses, there is no way to teach an entirely new behavior within the framework of classical conditioning.

Practice Quiz

Pick the best answer.

1. Which of the following illustrates the classical conditioning concept of acquisition?
   a. A neutral stimulus is repeatedly paired with a neutral response.
   b. A conditioned stimulus is repeatedly paired with an unconditioned stimulus.
   c. A neutral stimulus is repeatedly paired with an unconditioned stimulus.
   d. A conditioned stimulus is repeatedly paired with a conditioned response.

2. Ed noticed that whenever he used his electric can opener, his cat would come into the kitchen and act hungry—mewing pitiably. He reasoned that because he used the can opener to open the cat's food, the sound of the can opener had become a(n)
   a. unconditioned stimulus
   b. conditioned stimulus
   c. conditioned response
   d. neutral stimulus

Explore

WRITING ABOUT PHOBIAS

Ask students to use library or Internet resources to research phobias. Have them prepare a short written report on a phobia of interest to them. Reports should include an explanation of what the phobia is and how it is manifested. How has classical conditioning played a role in the phobia? Can students think of a way to use classical conditioning to reverse the phobia?

3. Stephanie, a young child, developed a fear of white coats as a result of painful shots given to her by doctors and nurses dressed in white coats. The fact that she was afraid not only of white coats worn by doctors and nurses but also those worn by photographers is an example of
   a. extinction
   b. reinforcement
   c. spontaneous recovery
   d. stimulus generalization

4. Which of the following illustrates the phenomenon of spontaneous recovery?
   a. A dog, which has been conditioned to salivate at the sound of a bell, begins to salivate at the sound of all bells.
   b. A dog, which has been conditioned to salivate at the sound of a bell, ceases to salivate at the bell and salivates only when food is present.
   c. A dog, whose conditioned response to a bell has been extinguished, briefly displays the conditioned response to the bell.
   d. A dog, whose conditioned response to a bell has been extinguished, briefly displays a new and different response to the bell.

5. Which of the following statements about the ethics of Watson's "Little Albert" experiment is most accurate?
   a. This experiment would be performed in exactly the same way today because it produced valuable results that broadened human knowledge.
   b. This experiment would be performed in exactly the same way today because it did not result in lasting damage to Little Albert.
   c. This experiment would be performed differently today; researchers would ask a young child for his consent to participate in the study.
   d. This experiment would be performed differently today; researchers would not create a phobia in a young child and leave that phobia untreated.

6. What did Watson's classic experiment with "Little Albert" demonstrate?
   a. the learning of a phobia
   b. the biological basis of fear
   c. the existence of vicarious conditioning
   d. the extinction of a conditioned response

7. Often, people with certain types of cancer must take chemotherapy treatments. The drugs used in these treatments are powerful and usually cause strong nausea reactions. If Cindy had scrambled eggs for breakfast and then took a chemotherapy treatment later that same morning, which of the following responses is most likely to occur?
   a. Cindy will develop a strong liking for scrambled eggs.
   b. Cindy will be able to eat scrambled eggs with no nausea at all.
   c. Cindy will get nauseated the next time she tries to eat scrambled eggs.
   d. Cindy will get nauseated the next time she tries to eat any sort of food.

8. In order for conditioning to take place, the neutral stimulus must
   a. replace the unconditioned stimulus
   b. occur at the same time as the unconditioned stimulus
   c. be removed before the unconditioned stimulus is presented
   d. have a physical resemblance to the unconditioned stimulus

9. What must be removed in order for extinction to occur?
   a. unconditioned stimulus
   b. conditioned stimulus
   c. generalized stimulus
   d. neutral stimulus

10. Companies who use popular actors and actresses in their ad campaigns are trying to create a _____ in people who look at their advertisements.
    a. neutral response
    b. higher order response
    c. vicarious response
    d. conditioned emotional response

LEARNING AND LANGUAGE DEVELOPMENT 183

Practice Quiz Answers
1. c
2. b
3. d
4. c
5. d
6. a
7. c
8. b
9. a
10. d

CHAPTER 6 • Module 14

Assess

Assign the Module 14 Practice Quiz.

Use the Practice Quiz to identify gaps in student understanding.

REMEDIATE

Have students, individually or in groups, review the module goals, learning objectives, and key terms.

Refer students to the Concept Summary on p. 210 for review.

Close

Point out that before covering this module, students may have thought of the definition of *learning* as simply "studying." As a class, discuss the psychological definition of *learning* ("any relatively permanent change in behavior brought about by experience or practice").

Module 14 Classical Conditioning 183

CHAPTER 6 • Module 15

Focus

RESOURCES
For this module, consult the appropriate sections of the Teacher's Manual, Test Bank, and PowerPoint slides, all found on the Teacher's Resource DVD, and the interactive study tools for students on MyPsychLab.

BEFORE CLASS
Students should read the section for homework before coming to class.

BELLRINGER
Ask students to write down a behavior they would like to modify, either an undesirable behavior that they would like to eliminate or a desirable behavior that they would like to strengthen. Tell them to think about this behavior as you discuss operant conditioning.

Teach

INTRODUCE THE TOPIC
Make sure students understand the difference between involuntary (reflexive) and voluntary behaviors. Classical conditioning occurs with involuntary behavior, while operant conditioning is the kind of behavior that applies to voluntary behavior.

COVER THE MODULE
15.1 What is Thorndike's law of effect?
- Edward Thorndike conducted experiments with cats in "puzzle boxes" in order to explore the laws of learning voluntary responses.
- Thorndike developed the law of effect: a response followed by a pleasurable consequence will be repeated, but a response followed by an unpleasant consequence will not be repeated.

184 Chapter 6 Learning and Language Development

Module 15 Operant Conditioning

Module Goal
Explain the process of operant conditioning.

Learning Objectives
- 15.1 What is Thorndike's law of effect?
- 15.2 What are the principles of operant conditioning?
- 15.3 What are some specializations of operant conditioning?
- 15.4 How does operant conditioning function in everyday life?

Explain the Process of Operant Conditioning

There are two kinds of behavior that all organisms are capable of exhibiting: involuntary (reflexive) and voluntary. If Inez blinks her eyes because a gnat flies close to them, that's a reflex and totally involuntary. But if she then swats at the gnat to shoo it away, that's a voluntary choice. She *had* to blink, but she *chose* to swat.

Classical conditioning is the kind of learning that occurs with reflexive, involuntary behavior. The kind of learning that applies to *voluntary* behavior is called **operant conditioning**, which is both different from and similar to classical conditioning.

15.1 What is Thorndike's law of effect?

Edward L. Thorndike (1874–1949) was one of the first researchers to explore and attempt to outline the laws of learning voluntary responses, although the field was not yet called operant conditioning. Thorndike placed a hungry cat inside a "puzzle box" from which the only escape was to press a lever located on the floor of the box. Cats definitely do *not* like being confined, as anyone who has ever tried to stuff one into a travel box will know (and probably have the scars to prove it). There was also a dish of food *outside* the box, so the cat was highly motivated to get out. Thorndike observed that the cat would move around the box, pushing and rubbing up against the walls in an effort to escape. Eventually, the cat would accidentally push the lever, opening the door. Upon escaping, the cat was fed from a dish placed just outside the box. The lever is the stimulus, the pushing of the lever is the response, and the consequence is both escape (good) and food (even better).

The cat did not learn to push the lever and escape right away. It did not immediately realize that the lever would help it escape, but after a number of trials (and many errors) in a box like this one, the cat took less and less time to push the lever that would open the door. It's important not to assume that the cat had "figured out" the connection between the lever and freedom—Thorndike kept moving the lever to a different position, and the cat had to learn the whole process over again. The cat would simply continue to rub and push in the same general area that led to food and freedom the last time, each time getting out and getting fed a little more quickly.

operant conditioning the learning of voluntary behavior through the effects of pleasant and unpleasant consequences to responses.

184 CHAPTER 6

Terms

- operant conditioning • law of effect • operant • reinforcer • primary reinforcer
- secondary reinforcer • positive reinforcement • negative reinforcement
- punishment • punishment by application • punishment by removal • shaping
- successive approximations • discriminative stimulus • partial reinforcement effect
- continuous reinforcement • fixed interval schedule of reinforcement • variable interval schedule of reinforcement • fixed ratio schedule of reinforcement • variable ratio schedule of reinforcement • instinctive drift • behavior modification • token economy • applied behavior analysis (ABA) • biofeedback • neurofeedback

Based on this research, Thorndike developed the **law of effect**: If an action is followed by a pleasurable consequence, it will tend to be repeated. If an action is followed by an unpleasant consequence, it will tend not to be repeated (Thorndike, 1911). This is the basic principle behind learning voluntary behavior. In the case of the cat in the box, pushing the lever was followed by a pleasurable consequence (getting out and getting fed), so pushing the lever became a repeated response.

Thorndike's work began the study of voluntary learning, but the person who had the greatest influence on the field and who gave it the name *operant conditioning* was B. F. Skinner. He is also known as behaviorism's biggest supporter.

15.2 What are the principles of operant conditioning?

B. F. Skinner (1904–1990), an American behaviorist working at Harvard, assumed leadership of the field of behaviorism after John Watson. Like Watson, he believed that psychologists should study only measurable, observable behavior. In addition to his knowledge of Pavlovian classical conditioning, Skinner used Thorndike's work to explain all behavior as the product of learning. He even gave the learning of voluntary behavior a special name: *operant conditioning* (Skinner, 1938). Voluntary behavior is what people and animals do to *operate* in the world. Voluntary behavior, for Skinner, is **operant** behavior, and the learning of such behavior is operant conditioning.

The heart of operant conditioning is the effect of consequences on behavior. In classical conditioning, learning a reflex depends on what comes *before* the response—the unconditioned stimulus and what will become the conditioned stimulus. These two stimuli are the *antecedent* stimuli (antecedent means something that comes before another thing). But in operant conditioning, learning depends on what happens *after* the response—the consequence. Operant conditioning could be summed up as this: "If I do this, what's in it for me?"

"What's in it for me?" represents the concept of **reinforcement**. Skinner defined reinforcement as anything that, when following a response, causes that response to be more likely to happen again. Typically, this means that reinforcement is a consequence that is in some way pleasurable to the organism or meets the organism's needs, which relates back to Thorndike's law of effect. The "pleasurable consequence" is what's in it for the organism. (This could be getting food when you are hungry, but it might also mean *avoiding* something, such as taking out the garbage.)

Skinner had his own research device called a "Skinner box" or "operant conditioning chamber." His early research often involved placing a rat into one of these chambers and training it to push down on a bar to get food.

⊙→ Simulate on **mypsychlab.com**

Primary and Secondary Reinforcers The events or items that can be used to reinforce behavior are not all alike. Let's say that a friend of yours asks you to help her repaint her bedroom. In return for your help, she offers you $25 or a sandwich. You'll most likely choose the money, right? With $25, you could buy more than one sandwich.

Now, pretend that your friend offers the same deal to her 3-year-old cousin who likes to play around with paint: $25 or a sandwich. Most children at that age have no real idea of the value of money, so the child will probably choose the sandwich. The money and the sandwich represent two basic kinds

⊙→ Simulate operant conditioning on **mypsychlab.com**

law of effect law stating that if an action is followed by a pleasurable consequence, it will tend to be repeated, and if followed by an unpleasant consequence, it will tend not to be repeated.

operant any behavior that is voluntary.

reinforcer any event or object that, when following a response, increases the likelihood of that response occurring again.

LEARNING AND LANGUAGE DEVELOPMENT 185

CHAPTER 6 • Module 15

COVER THE MODULE

15.2 What are the principles of operant conditioning?

- B. F. Skinner named the learning of voluntary responses *operant conditioning*, because voluntary responses are what we use to operate on the world around us.
- *Operant* conditioning focuses on the effects of consequences on behavior.
- Skinner developed the concept of *reinforcement*, the process of strengthening a response by following it with a pleasurable, rewarding consequence.

MULTIMEDIA CONTENT AVAILABLE AT www.mypsychlab.com

⊙→ Simulate operant conditioning on **mypsychlab.com**

CHECK FOR UNDERSTANDING

If students have problems understanding Skinner's work, send them to the **www.mypsychlab.com** website for Chapter 6 to watch the video of a pigeon in a "Skinner box."

EXTEND THE LESSON

Point out to students that handing over a credit card to a salesperson is immediately rewarded by the delivery of a desired item into your hands; the payment is not due until much later. Thus, through a process of operant conditioning, credit card use becomes more likely. Even the mere presence of a credit card increases the likelihood and magnitude of spending. When a card is repeatedly paired with the responses involved in spending, it becomes a stimulus for "spending behavior."

Class Demonstration

OPERANT CONDITIONING IN HUMAN BEHAVIOR

Because much of the operant conditioning research presented in textbooks is conducted with animals, students sometimes have difficulty seeing its relevance to human behavior. Try this simple demonstration, which can be used to generate a discussion of human operant conditioning. While discussing operant conditioning, interrupt your lecture with a question that you know will elicit a mostly positive response (e.g., "How many of you live within five miles of school?"). Most students will raise their hands in response to your question. Tell them to hold that position, and ask if anyone told them to raise their hands or even mentioned raising hands. Then ask students to explain their behavior in terms of operant conditioning, and use this activity as a springboard for generating other examples of operant conditioning in humans.

Module 15 Operant Conditioning **185**

CHAPTER 6 • Module 15

COVER THE MODULE (continued)

- **Primary and Secondary Reinforcers**
  - A *primary reinforcer* is something like food or water that satisfies a basic, natural drive.
  - A *secondary reinforcer* is something that becomes reinforcing only after being paired with a primary reinforcer.
- **Positive and Negative Reinforcement**
  - In *positive reinforcement*, a response is followed by the presentation of a pleasurable stimulus.
  - In *negative reinforcement*, a response is followed by the removal or avoidance of an unpleasant stimulus.
- **Two Kinds of Punishment**
  - *Punishment* is any event or stimulus that, when following a response, makes that response less likely to happen again.
    - In *punishment by application*, a response is followed by the application or experiencing of an unpleasant stimulus, such as a spanking.
    - In *punishment by removal*, a response is followed by the removal of some pleasurable stimulus, such as taking away a child's toy for misbehavior.

MULTIMEDIA CONTENT AVAILABLE AT
www.mypsychlab.com

Listen podcast on positive reinforcement on mypsychlab.com

---

primary reinforcer any reinforcer that is naturally reinforcing by meeting a basic biological need, such as hunger, thirst, or touch.

secondary reinforcer any reinforcer, such as praise, tokens, or gold stars, that becomes reinforcing after being paired with a primary reinforcer.

positive reinforcement the reinforcement of a response by the addition or experiencing of a pleasurable stimulus (a reward following a response).

negative reinforcement the reinforcement of a response that removes or allows escape from something unpleasant.

punishment any event or object that, when following a response, makes that response less likely to happen again.

punishment by application the punishment of a response by the addition or experiencing of an unpleasant stimulus.

punishment by removal the punishment of a response by the removal of a pleasurable stimulus.

▶ *I'm confused—I thought negative reinforcement, or taking something away, was a kind of punishment?*

---

of *reinforcers*, defined as items or events that when following a response will strengthen it. The reinforcing properties of money must be learned, but food gives immediate reward in the form of taste and satisfying hunger.

A reinforcer, such as a sandwich, that satisfies a basic need like hunger is called a **primary reinforcer**. Examples would be any kind of food (hunger drive), liquid (thirst drive), or touch (pleasure drive). The behavior of infants, toddlers, preschool-age children, and animals can be easily reinforced by using primary reinforcers.

A **secondary reinforcer**, such as money, however, gets its reinforcing properties from being associated with primary reinforcers in the past. A child who is given money soon realizes that the ugly green paper can be traded for toys and treats—primary reinforcers.

Secondary reinforcers get their reinforcing power from the process of classical conditioning. After all, the pleasure people feel when they eat, drink, or get a back rub is an involuntary response, and any involuntary response can be classically conditioned to occur to a new stimulus. In the case of money (a neutral stimulus that has no meaning to young children), the toys and treats are a UCS for pleasure (the UCR) and the money is presented just before the treats are obtained. The money eventually becomes a CS paired with pleasure.

Positive and Negative Reinforcement Reinforcers can also differ in the way they are used. Any response that results in a removal or escape from something unpleasant will likely occur again. If a person's behavior gets pain to stop, the person is much more likely to do that same thing again—which is part of the reason people can get addicted to painkilling medication.

In operant conditioning, the term *reinforcement* always means that a behavior is being strengthened. Sometimes, behaviors are strengthened because they are rewarded. The reinforcement of a response by the *addition* of a pleasurable consequence, such as a reward or a pat on the back, is called **positive reinforcement**. Other times, however, behaviors are strengthened because they eliminate something negative. The reinforcement of a response by the *removal* of, or the escape from, an unpleasant stimulus is called **negative reinforcement**. (See Figure 15.1.)

Two Kinds of Punishment

I'm confused—I thought negative reinforcement, or taking something away, was a kind of punishment?

People get confused because "negative" sounds like it ought to be something bad, like a kind of punishment. **Punishment** is actually the opposite of reinforcement. It is any event or stimulus that, when following a response, causes that response to be less likely to happen again. Punishment *weakens* responses, whereas reinforcement (no matter whether it is positive or negative) *strengthens* responses.

Punishment by application occurs when something unpleasant (such as a spanking or scolding) is added to the situation or *applied*. This is the kind of punishment that many child development specialists strongly recommend parents avoid using with their children because it can easily escalate into abuse (Dubowitz & Bennett, 2007; Saunders & Goddard, 1998; Straus, 2000; Straus & Stewart, 1999; Straus & Yodanis, 1994; Trocmé et al., 2001).

Punishment by removal is the kind of punishment most often confused with negative reinforcement. In this type of punishment, behavior is punished

---

Critical Thinking

PRIMARY AND SECONDARY REINFORCERS

<u>Purpose</u>: Students complete a brief one-minute assignment that involves critical thinking, personalizing, or deeper processing of information.

<u>Time</u>: 1–5 minutes

<u>Description</u>: Give students a few minutes to answer the following question. This assignment can be used in a variety of ways—to verify attendance, to start discussion, to assess student knowledge, and to provide opportunities for critical thinking.

"**Reinforcers:** Identify some of the primary and secondary reinforcers in your life. What rewards motivate you most?"

FIGURE 15.1 Two Forms of Reinforcement
In the example of positive reinforcement, a child earns a good grade and receives a pleasurable consequence: a hug from a parent. In the example of negative reinforcement, the noise outside a child's window is preventing the child from sleeping. The child removes the unpleasant stimulus (the loud noise) by wearing headphones.

by the removal of something pleasurable or desired after the behavior occurs, such as placing a child in time-out (removing the attention of the others in the room). This type of punishment is far more acceptable to child development specialists because it involves no physical aggression and avoids many of the problems caused by more aggressive punishments.

The confusion over the difference between negative reinforcement and punishment by removal makes it worth examining the difference just a bit more. The difference between them lies in *what* is taken away: In the case of negative reinforcement, it is an *unpleasant* thing; in the case of punishment by removal, it is a *pleasant* or desirable thing. For a comparison of negative reinforcement and punishment by removal, see Table 15.1 on the next page.

Listen on **mypsychlab.com**

Listen to the podcast on positive reinforcement on **mypsychlab.com**

15.3 What are some specializations of operant conditioning?

Operant conditioning is more than just the reinforcement of simple responses. For example, have you ever tried to teach a pet to do a trick? If you have, you probably know that training animals involves more than simple reinforcement.

LEARNING AND LANGUAGE DEVELOPMENT 187

CHAPTER 6 • Module 15

COVER THE MODULE (continued)

- A person who uses aggressive punishment, such as spanking, can act as a model for aggressive behavior. This will increase aggressive behavior in the one being punished, an undesirable response.
- Punishment of both kinds normally has only a temporary effect on behavior.
- Punishment can be made more effective by making it immediate, consistent, and by pairing punishment of the undesirable behavior with reinforcement of the desirable one.

UNDERSTANDING VISUALS

Students often have difficulty distinguishing between negative reinforcement and punishment by removal. Direct their attention to Table 15.1 on p. 188. Reiterate that in the case of negative reinforcement, an unpleasant thing is taken away. In the case of punishment by removal, a pleasant or desirable thing is taken away.

L4 DIFFERENTIATED INSTRUCTION

Advanced Learners Help students adjust the pace of their learning, speeding through concepts they master quickly or slowing down to study content in depth. This Teacher's Edition provides ideas for ways to extend content in the Extend sections of the lesson plan.

Class Discussion

CONTROVERSIES IN LEARNING

Purpose: Students have a chance to think about, debate, and discuss controversial topics in learning.

Time: 15 minutes

Description: Divide the class in half. Pose the following controversial topic for debate, with one half of the students arguing for the topic and the other half against. Tell students to think about what they have learned in this chapter as they formulate their arguments. "**Topic**: Corporal punishment is an effective tool for teaching children."

Module 15 Operant Conditioning

CHAPTER 6 • Module 15

COVER THE MODULE

15.3 What are some specializations of operant conditioning?

- **Shaping**
  - *Shaping* is the reinforcement of *successive approximations* (small steps) to some final goal, allowing behavior to be molded from simple behavior already present in the organism.

- **Extinction, Generalization, and Spontaneous Recovery in Operant Conditioning**
  - Extinction is the removal of reinforcement to decrease/stop behavior.
  - Generalization involves responding to similar stimuli with the expectation of reward.
  - A *discriminative stimulus* is a specific stimulus that provides a cue for making a response.
  - Spontaneous recovery is the recurrence of a conditioned response after extinction.

CHECK FOR UNDERSTANDING

For additional opportunities to understand extinction and spontaneous recovery, send students to the www.mypsychlab.com website for the Chapter 6 exploration of these processes.

Table 15.1	Negative Reinforcement vs. Punishment by Removal
EXAMPLE OF NEGATIVE REINFORCEMENT	**EXAMPLE OF PUNISHMENT BY REMOVAL**
Taking the car to the mechanic's shop to eliminate the unpleasant noise coming from the engine.	Losing the privilege of driving because you got into too many accidents.
Doing homework to stop a parent's constant reminders.	Losing grade points on an assignment because it was turned in late.

Shaping Teaching an animal complex tricks is an example of a process in operant conditioning called **shaping**, in which small steps toward some ultimate goal are reinforced until the goal itself is reached.

For example, if Jody wanted to train his dog to jump through a hoop, he would have to start with the hoop on the ground and then call the dog through the hoop, using the treat as bait. After Rover steps through the hoop (as the shortest way to the treat), Jody should give Rover the treat (positive reinforcement). Then he could raise the hoop just a little, reward Rover for walking through it again, raise the hoop, reward him . . . until Rover is jumping through the hoop to get the treat. The goal is achieved by reinforcing each **successive approximation** (small steps one after the other that get closer and closer to the goal; Skinner, 1974).

Extinction, Generalization, and Spontaneous Recovery in Operant Conditioning *Extinction* in classical conditioning involves the removal of the UCS, the unconditioned stimulus that associated with the CS during acquisition. Extinction in operant conditioning involves the removal of all forms of reinforcement. Have you ever seen a child throw a temper tantrum in the checkout line because he or she wants a treat? Many exasperated parents will cave in and give the child the treat, positively reinforcing the tantrum. The parent is also being negatively reinforced for giving in, because the obnoxious behavior stops. The only way to get the tantrum behavior to stop permanently is to remove the reinforcement, which means no treat, and if possible, no attention or eye contact from the parent.

In operant conditioning, *generalization* occurs when operantly conditioned responses are generalized to stimuli that are similar to the original stimulus. For example, a baby may refer to every man she sees as "Dada." The name "Dada" begins as a baby's response to the presence of her own father and is reinforced by his delight and attention to her. At first, she will generalize her "Dada" response to any man. As other men fail to reinforce her for this response, she'll learn to discriminate between them and her father and only call her father "Dada." In this way, the man who is actually her father becomes a **discriminative stimulus**, which is any stimulus that provides the organism with a cue for making a certain response in order to obtain reinforcement.

Spontaneous recovery (the recurrence of a conditioned response after extinction) will also happen with operant responses. Anyone who has ever trained animals to do several different tricks will say that when first learning a new trick, most animals will try to get reinforcers by performing their *old*

shaping technique in which a person is rewarded for gradually coming closer to demonstrating a desirable behavior by reinforcing steps toward the desired behavior and extinguishing behaviors that move away from the desired behavior.

successive approximations small steps in behavior, one after the other, that lead to a particular goal behavior.

discriminative stimulus any stimulus, such as a stop sign or a doorknob, that provides the organism with a cue for making a certain response in order to obtain reinforcement.

188 CHAPTER 6

Class Demonstration (Kinesthetic)

EXPLORING SHAPING

Divide students into four-person teams, with one member as the "lab rat" and the other three team members as the "scientists." The goal is for the "scientists" to shape the "rats'" behavior. Ask the "rats" to briefly leave the room. With the rest of the class, select a particular behavior that the "rats" must exhibit. For example, the class may decide that the "rats" must go to their desks and pick up their textbooks. Once a behavior has been selected, call the "rats" back in and seat them with their teams. Each team must get their "rat" to complete the behavior by rewarding successive steps. Each "rat" must listen to the teammates for rewards and punishments. When you say "go," the "rats" should begin to move about the room. When the "rat" moves toward the desired behavior, the team rewards the "rat" by saying "good." If the "rat" moves away from the desired behavior, the team punishes the "rat" by saying "bad." After the "rats" have all been successful at completing their desired behavior, you can discuss shaping in more detail.

188 Chapter 6 LEARNING AND LANGUAGE DEVELOPMENT

tricks. Rover might very well have tried to roll over, speak, and shake paws to get that treat before finally walking through the hoop.

The Schedules of Reinforcement The timing of reinforcement can make a tremendous difference in the speed at which learning occurs and the strength of the learned response. Skinner (1956) found that reinforcing each and every response was not necessarily the best schedule of reinforcement for long-lasting learning.

Alicia's mother gives her a quarter every night she remembers to put her dirty clothes in the clothes hamper. Bianca's mother gives her a dollar at the end of the week, but only if she has put her clothes in the hamper every night. Alicia learns more quickly than does Bianca because responses that are reinforced each time they occur are more easily and quickly learned.

As soon as continuous reinforcement stops, the behavior extinguishes. When the quarters stop coming, Alicia stops immediately. Bianca, however, has expected to get a reinforcer only after *seven correct responses*. When the reinforcers stop, Bianca might continue to put the clothes in the hamper for several more days or even another whole week, hoping that the reinforcer will eventually come anyway.

Bianca's behavior illustrates the **partial reinforcement effect** (Skinner, 1956): Any response that is reinforced after some, but not all, correct responses will be more resistant to extinction than a response that receives **continuous reinforcement** (a reinforcer for each and every correct response). Although it may be easier to teach a new behavior using continuous reinforcement, partially reinforced behavior is harder to extinguish. In the real world, people tend to receive partial reinforcement (such as a paycheck or grades) rather than continuous reinforcement for their work.

Partial reinforcement can be accomplished according to different patterns or schedules. When the *timing* of the response is more important, it is called an *interval schedule*. When it is the *number* of responses that is important, the schedule is called a *ratio schedule*, because a certain number of responses is required for each reinforcer (e.g., 50 raffle tickets for each prize). The other way in which schedules of reinforcement can differ is in whether the number of responses or interval of time is *fixed* (the same in each case) or *variable* (a different number or interval is required in each case). So, it is possible to have a fixed interval schedule, a variable interval schedule, a fixed ratio schedule, and a variable ratio schedule (Skinner, 1961).

The kind of reinforcement schedule most people are more familiar with is called a **fixed interval schedule of reinforcement**, in which a reinforcer is received after a certain, fixed interval of time has passed. If a researcher were teaching a rat to press a lever to get food pellets, he might require it to push the lever every 2 minutes to get a pellet. It wouldn't matter how many times the rat pushed the lever, it would only get the pellet after 2 minutes had passed.

People are reinforced on this kind of schedule, too. When do you study the hardest? Isn't it right before a test? If you know when the test is to be given, that's like having a fixed interval of time that is predictable, and you can save your greatest studying efforts until closer to the exam. (Some students save *all* of their studying for the night before the exam, which is not exactly the best strategy.)

So, if a scheduled test is a fixed interval, what sorts of things happen on a variable interval schedule?

In a **variable interval schedule of reinforcement**, the interval of time after which the organism must respond in order to receive a reinforcer changes

partial reinforcement effect the tendency for a response that is reinforced after some, but not all, correct responses to be very resistant to extinction.

continuous reinforcement the reinforcement of each and every correct response.

fixed interval schedule of reinforcement schedule of reinforcement in which the interval of time that must pass before reinforcement becomes possible is always the same.

variable interval schedule of reinforcement schedule of reinforcement in which the interval of time that must pass before reinforcement becomes possible is different for each trial or event.

◀ So, if a scheduled test is a fixed interval, what sorts of things happen on a variable interval schedule?

LEARNING AND LANGUAGE DEVELOPMENT 189

Explore

INVESTIGATING CLICKER TRAINING
Tell students that clicker training is a form of animal training using operant conditioning principles. Send students to www.clickertrain.com/whatis.html for a concise informational article on the topic. Ask students to prepare a short written report or an audiovisual presentation about what they have learned. They should be sure to explain how this type of training reflects operant conditioning principles.

CHAPTER 6 • Module 15

COVER THE MODULE *(continued)*
- **The Schedules of Reinforcement**
  - *Partial reinforcement*, in which only some correct responses are followed by reinforcement, is much more resistant to extinction. This is called the partial reinforcement effect.
  - *Continuous reinforcement* occurs when each and every correct response is followed by a reinforcer.
  - In a *fixed interval schedule of reinforcement*, at least one correct response must be made within a set interval of time to obtain reinforcement.
  - In a *variable interval schedule of reinforcement*, reinforcement follows a varying interval of time.

DISCUSS THE STUDENT VOICE QUESTION
Use the question to check students' comprehension of the topic.

TEACHING TIP
A good writing prompt provides multiple access points to help students with different learning styles, backgrounds, and abilities engage with the task. This may be done by breaking the task into parts that build from lower- to higher-order thinking skills. This sequencing provides a point of entry for weaker students who may not be capable of completing the entire task and enables them to respond in a limited way.

Module 15 Operant Conditioning **189**

CHAPTER 6 • Module 15

COVER THE MODULE (continued)

- In a fixed ratio schedule of reinforcement, a certain number of responses are required before reinforcement is given.
- In a variable ratio schedule of reinforcement, a varying number of responses is required to obtain reinforcement.

MULTIMEDIA CONTENT AVAILABLE AT www.mypsychlab.com

⊙→ Simulate the schedules of reinforcement on mypsychlab.com

CHECK FOR UNDERSTANDING

Ask: **When should a reinforcer be given?** *(as soon as possible after the desired behavior)* **Why should only the desired behavior be reinforced?** *(Otherwise, it undermines learning the behavior.)*

---

fixed ratio schedule of reinforcement schedule of reinforcement in which the number of responses required for reinforcement is always the same.

variable ratio schedule of reinforcement schedule of reinforcement in which the number of responses required for reinforcement is different for each trial or event.

⊙→ Simulate the schedules of reinforcement on mypsychlab.com

---

from one time to the next. For example, a rat might receive a food pellet every 5 minutes on average. Sometimes it might be 2, sometimes 10, but the rat must push the lever at least once after that interval to get the pellet. Because the rat can't predict how long the interval is going to be, it pushes the bar more or less continuously. Once again, speed is not important, so the rate of responding is slow but steady.

If you use social networking Web sites like Facebook, you are probably used to a variable interval schedule of reinforcement: You have to log in to accept friend requests and respond to your friends' messages. You never know when you are going to get reinforcement—a friend request or a message—but you might begin to log in frequently and steadily to see if anything's changed.

In ratio schedules, it is the *number* of responses that counts. In a **fixed ratio schedule of reinforcement**, the number of responses required to receive each reinforcer will always be the same number.

Anyone who does piecework, in which a certain number of items have to be completed before payment is given, is reinforced on a fixed ratio schedule. Some sandwich shops give out punch cards that get punched one time for each sandwich purchased. When the card has 10 punches, for example, the person might get a free sandwich.

A **variable ratio schedule of reinforcement** is one in which the number of responses changes from one trial to the next. In the rat example, the rat might be expected to push the lever an *average* of 20 times to get reinforcement. That means that sometimes the rat would push the lever only 10 times before a reinforcer comes, but at other times it might take 30 lever pushes or more.

The variable ratio schedule of reinforcement provokes just as rapid a response rate as the fixed ratio schedule because the *number* of responses still matters. For example, people who play slot machines are being reinforced on a variable ratio schedule of reinforcement (they hope). They put their coins in (response), but they don't know how many times they will have to do this before reinforcement (the jackpot) comes. People who do this tend to sit there until they either win or run out of money. They don't dare stop because the "next one" might hit that jackpot.

Regardless of the schedule of reinforcement one uses, there are some things that can be done to make reinforcement of a behavior as effective as possible. For example, timing is important: A reinforcer should be given as immediately as possible after the desired behavior. Delaying reinforcement tends not to work well, especially when dealing with animals and small children. Care should also be taken to reinforce *only* the desired behavior—for example, many parents make the mistake of giving a child who has not done some chore the promised treat anyway, which completely undermines the child's learning of that chore or task. ⊙→ Simulate on mypsychlab.com

Classic Studies in Psychology

Biological Constraints on Operant Conditioning

Raccoons are fairly intelligent animals and are sometimes used in learning experiments. In a typical experiment designed to study how organisms learn, a behaviorist would use shaping and reinforcement to teach a raccoon a trick. The goal might be to get the raccoon to pick up several coins and drop them into a metal container, for which the

190 CHAPTER 6

Class Discussion

SUPERSTITION AND OPERANT CONDITIONING

Tell students that superstition develops when a behavior coincidentally happens to be followed by a reinforcer and, as a result, the behavior is repeated. For example, athletes may go through rituals, such as adjusting their caps or tapping their spikes with a bat. An explanation for these behaviors is that at one time, the behavior happened to be followed by hitting a home run. These behaviors often do not easily extinguish because circumstances provide intermittent reinforcement for them. If a batter goes through a ritual every time he or she steps to the plate, he or she will, from time to time, again be reinforced for these actually unrelated behaviors. Ask students to name other superstitions they are familiar with. Are these superstitious responses resistant to extinction? *(Possible answer: Yes, because if the individual believes the superstition is valid, omitting the "necessary" act might produce other changes in his or her behavior that would directly affect the event in question.)*

190 Chapter 6 Learning and Language Development

raccoon would be rewarded with food. The behaviorist starts by reinforcing the raccoon for picking up a single coin. Then the metal container is introduced and the raccoon is now required to drop the coin into the slot on the container in order to get reinforcement.

It is at this point that operant conditioning seems to fail. Instead of dropping the coin in the slot, the raccoon puts the coin in and out of the slot and rubs it against the inside of the container, then holds it firmly for a few seconds before finally letting it go. When the requirement is upped to two coins, the raccoon spends several minutes rubbing them against each other and dipping them into the container, without actually dropping them in. In spite of the fact that this dipping and rubbing behavior is not reinforced, it gets worse and worse until conditioning becomes impossible. How can this be? Why has operant conditioning failed?

Researchers Keller and Marian Breland concluded that the raccoon was reverting to instinctual behavior (Breland & Breland, 1961). Instinctual behavior is genetically determined and not under the influence of learning—it has developed over long periods of time because it has promoted survival. Apparently, even though the animals were at first able to learn the tricks, as the coins became more and more associated with food, the animals began to drift back into the instinctual patterns of behavior that they used with real food. Raccoons rub their food between their paws and dip it in and out of water. The Brelands called this tendency to revert to genetically controlled patterns **instinctive drift**.

In their 1961 paper describing these and other examples of instinctive drift, the Brelands (both trained by Skinner himself) determined that three assumptions that most Skinnerian behaviorists believed were not actually true. The three false assumptions:

1. The animal comes to the laboratory a "tabula rasa," or "blank slate," and can therefore be taught anything with the right conditioning.
2. Differences between species of animals are insignificant.
3. All responses are equally able to be conditioned to any stimulus.

As became quickly obvious in their studies with these animals, each animal comes into the world (and the laboratory) with certain genetically determined instinctive patterns of behavior already in place. These instincts, called *species-specific behaviors*, differ from species to species, with the result that there are some responses that simply cannot be trained into an animal regardless of conditioning. To quote Breland and Breland (1961):

"It is our reluctant conclusion that the behavior of any species cannot be adequately understood, predicted, or controlled without knowledge of its instinctive patterns, evolutionary history, and ecological niche." (p. 684)

Questions for Further Discussion

1. How can these research findings about animal behavior be generalized to human behavior?
2. What kinds of behavior might people do that would be resistant to conditioning?

▲ *Raccoons commonly dunk their food in and out of water before eating. This "washing" behavior is controlled by instinct and difficult to change even using operant techniques.*

instinctive drift tendency for an animal's behavior to revert to genetically controlled patterns.

LEARNING AND LANGUAGE DEVELOPMENT 191

CHAPTER 6 • Module 15

CLASSIC STUDIES IN PSYCHOLOGY

- Instinctive behavior in animals is resistant to conditioning or modification.
- Although an animal may change its behavior at first through conditioning, the behavior will revert to the instinctual pattern in a process called *instinctive drift*.
- Species-specific behaviors are genetically determined instinctive patterns of behavior already in place. They differ from species to species, with the result that some responses simply cannot be trained into an animal, regardless of conditioning.

1. Just like animals, humans come into the world with certain genetically determined instinctive behavior patterns. And, as with animals, it may be impossible to train certain responses into humans.
2. Possible answers: the need to eat when hungry; the need to sleep when tired.

L3 DIFFERENTIATED INSTRUCTION

Visual/Verbal Learners These students learn best when looking at material, particularly things that are written down. Reading the textbook, using classroom notes, and having a teacher who uses overhead projections, writes on the board, or uses visual multimedia presentations are very helpful. Visual/verbal learners, because they focus on reading and taking notes, tend to learn best when studying alone rather than in a group.

Explore

ANIMAL TRAINING AT SEA WORLD

Have students visit www.seaworld.org/infobooks/Training/home.html. This is a great site for students to explore "fun" applications of operant conditioning principles. Ask students to prepare a short written report or audiovisual presentation on how Sea World trains its animals. Students should be sure to explain how operant conditioning comes into play in Sea World's methods.

Module 15 Operant Conditioning

CHAPTER 6 • Module 15

COVER THE MODULE

15.4 How does operant conditioning function in everyday life?

- *Operant conditioning* can be used in many settings on both animals and people to change, or modify, behavior. This use is termed *behavior modification* and includes the use of reinforcement and shaping to alter behavior.
- *Token economies* are a type of behavior modification in which secondary reinforcers, or tokens, are used.
- *Applied behavior analysis (ABA)* is the modern version of behavior modification and makes use of shaping by breaking desired behavior down into discrete steps.
- *Biofeedback* is the use of feedback about biological conditions to bring involuntary responses under control.
- *Neurofeedback* is a modified version of biofeedback in which the person is connected to an electroencephalograph, which records the brain's electrical activity.

EXTEND THE LESSON

Send students to the www.mypsychlab.com website for Chapter 6 to listen to the podcast titled "Psychology in the News: Biofeedback." Then discuss some ways in which students think biofeedback can be used to help patients.

FAST FACT

Behavior therapy has grown in popularity over the past several decades. In many cases (e.g., the treatment of phobias and obsessive-compulsive disorder), it is the treatment of choice.

15.4 How does operant conditioning function in everyday life?

Operant conditioning principles such as reinforcement and the process of shaping have been used for many years to change undesirable behavior and create desirable responses in animals and humans—particularly in schoolchildren. The term **behavior modification** refers to the application of operant conditioning (and sometimes classical conditioning) to bring about such changes.

Sometimes, *tokens* (secondary reinforcers that can be traded in for other kinds of reinforcers) are used to modify behavior. A teacher who gives her well-behaved students gold stars is using tokens to promote good behavior. The use of tokens to modify behavior is called a **token economy**. The system of money is very much a token economy. People work and are rewarded with money, which they then trade for food, shelter, and so on.

Another tool that behaviorists can use to modify behavior is the process of *time-out*. Time-out is a form of mild punishment by removal in which a misbehaving animal, child, or adult is placed in a special area away from the attention of others. When used with children, time-out should be limited to 1 minute for each year of age with a maximum time-out of 10 minutes (longer than that and the child can forget why the time-out occurred).

Applied behavior analysis (ABA) is the modern term for a form of behavior modification that uses the shaping process to mold a desired behavior or response. It can be said to have begun with the work of Lovaas (1964) and his associates, although the basic techniques are those first outlined by Skinner. Lovaas used small pieces of candy as reinforcers to teach social skills and language to children with *autism*. (Autism is a disorder in which the person has great difficulty in communicating with others).

In ABA, skills are broken down to their simplest steps and then taught to the child through a system of reinforcement. Prompts are given as needed when the child is learning a skill or refuses to cooperate. As the child begins to master a skill and receives reinforcement in the form of treats or praise, the prompts are gradually withdrawn until the child can do the skill independently. Typical uses for ABA are dealing with children with disorders, training animals, and developing effective teaching methods for children and adults of all levels of mental abilities (Baer et al., 1968).

Other techniques for modifying behavior have been developed so that even behavior that is normally considered involuntary, such as blood pressure, muscle tension, and hyperactivity, can be brought under conscious control. For nearly 60 years, scientists have known how to use feedback of a person's biological information (such as heart rate) to create a state of relaxation (Margolin & Kubic, 1944). **Biofeedback** is the traditional term used to describe this kind of biological feedback of information, and through its use, many problems (such as pain and anxiety) can be relieved or controlled.

A relatively newer technique called **neurofeedback** has been used to treat children's attention problems in the classroom. Although this technique uses the latest in technology, the basic principles behind it are much older. Neurofeedback involves trying to change brain wave activity. In neurofeedback, the person is connected to an *electroencephalograph*, a machine that records the brain's electrical activity. Neurofeedback devices can be integrated into video game–style programs (Radford, 2004). Playing a video game to help solve anxiety and attention problems? To many people, it probably sounds like a perfect solution.

behavior modification the use of operant conditioning techniques to bring about desired changes in behavior.

token economy the use of objects called tokens to reinforce behavior; tokens can be accumulated and exchanged for desired items or privileges.

applied behavior analysis (ABA) modern term for a form of behavior modification that uses shaping techniques to mold a desired behavior or response.

biofeedback using feedback about biological conditions to bring involuntary responses, such as blood pressure and relaxation, under voluntary control.

neurofeedback form of biofeedback using brain-scanning devices to provide feedback about brain activity in an effort to modify behavior.

Explore

LEARNING ABOUT TOKEN ECONOMIES

Divide students into pairs or small groups. Have them research the topic of token economies, using library or Internet resources. Ask them to consider the following questions: What is a token economy? How are token economies used in education? What are some of the steps in implementing a token economy in the classroom? What are advantages and disadvantages of using a token economy? Do you think using a token economy in your classroom would be helpful? Why or why not? Ask students to report back via a short written report or an audiovisual presentation.

Applying Psychology to Everyday Life

How to Make Punishment More Effective

If you babysit, volunteer with children, or have younger siblings, you may find yourself in the role of disciplinarian. How can you maintain order in a way that's both effective and ethical? Try to remember a few simple rules:

1. **Punishment should immediately follow the behavior it is meant to punish.** If the punishment comes long after the behavior, it will not be associated with that behavior. (This is also true of reinforcement.)

2. **Punishment should be consistent.** If you say that a certain punishment will follow a certain behavior, then you must make sure to follow through and do what you promised to do. Punishment for a particular behavior should stay at the same intensity or increase slightly but never decrease. For example, if a child is scolded for jumping on the bed the first time, the second time this behavior happens, the child should also be punished by scolding or by a stronger penalty, such as removal of a favorite toy.

3. **Punishment of the wrong behavior should be paired, whenever possible, with reinforcement of the right behavior.** Instead of yelling at a 2-year-old for eating with her fingers, you should pull her hand gently out of her plate while saying something such as, "No, we eat with our fork," and then placing the fork in the child's hand and praising her for using it. "See, you are doing such a good job with your fork. I'm so proud of you." Pairing punishment with reinforcement allows caretakers to use a much milder punishment and still be effective. It also teaches the desired behavior rather than just suppressing the undesired one.

Question for Further Discussion

1. What types of penalties are most commonly used to discipline children? Do you think these penalties are effective within the framework of operant conditioning? If not, how would you change these penalties to be more effective?

CHAPTER 6 • Module 15

APPLYING PSYCHOLOGY TO EVERYDAY LIFE

- Punishment should immediately follow the behavior it is meant to punish.
- Punishment should be consistent.
- Punishment of the wrong behavior should be paired, whenever possible, with reinforcement of the right behavior.

1. Possible answer: I think that physical punishment, such as spanking, is used much too often in disciplining children, even though it doesn't seem to achieve the desired effect. It only teaches children to be violent. A better method would be to pair punishment with reinforcement, which teaches the desired behavior.

CLASS DISCUSSION

Tell students: "Think of cases in your own life when punishment worked effectively and other cases when it did not. What were the differences between the two situations? Why did it work in some cases but not in others? How do your own experiences compare to the discussion in the text on the circumstances under which aversive control is likely to be most effective? Can you add new conditions to those listed in the text?"

Explore

LEARNING THEORY IN EVERYDAY LIFE

The principles of operant and classical conditioning have been used extensively to help people. Assign each member of a four-student team to a different application listed below. Students should use library or Internet resources to explore in detail the learning principles operating in these situations. Then, in class, allow students to share and teach others what they have learned. **Applications:** alcohol aversion therapy; the use of guide dogs to help the disabled; weight-loss clinics; parenting techniques to raise children.

CHAPTER 6 • Module 15

Assess

Assign the Module 15 Practice Quiz.

Use the Practice Quiz to identify gaps in student understanding.

REMEDIATE

Have students, individually or in groups, review the module goals, learning objectives, and key terms.

Refer students to the Concept Summary on p. 210 for review.

Close

As a class, revisit the behaviors students noted in the Bellringer activity. How could students use operant conditioning to modify the behaviors?

Practice Quiz

Pick the best answer.

1. Bennie is afraid of birds. When he sees a bird in his back yard, he screams and causes the bird to fly away. Bennie's screaming behavior is an example of
   a. positive reinforcement
   b. punishment by application
   c. punishment by removal
   d. negative reinforcement

2. Jessica's mother was upset to find that Jessica had used her crayons to draw flowers on her bedroom wall. Her mother took the crayons away from her and made Jessica wash the drawings off the wall. Which of the following best describes Jessica's punishment?
   a. punishment by application
   b. punishment by negative reinforcement
   c. punishment by both application and removal
   d. punishment by both positive and negative reinforcement

3. Elizabeth's parents want her to put her clothes in the hamper. At first, they praise her for putting the clothes together in one pile. Then they praise her for getting the clothes on the same side of the room as the hamper. When she gets the clothes on top of the hamper, she gets praise. Finally, her parents praise her when she puts her clothes in the hamper. This process is an example of
   a. shaping
   b. punishment
   c. negative reinforcement
   d. a discriminative stimulus

4. Ella is teaching her parrot a new word. Every time the parrot says a sound that is close to the new word, she gives it a treat. But the parrot keeps repeating other words it has learned in the past, trying to get a treat that way. The parrot is exhibiting
   a. extinction
   b. discrimination
   c. generalization
   d. spontaneous recovery

5. Mr. Elliot told his students that if his door was open, it meant that he was available to them and would gladly answer any questions they might have. But if his door was pushed shut, it meant that he was busy and would prefer not to answer questions at that time. Which of the following best describes Mr. Elliot's open door in terms of operant conditioning?
   a. The open door provides punishment by application.
   b. The open door provides negative reinforcement.
   c. The open door facilitates a fixed interval schedule of reinforcement.
   d. The open door is a discriminative stimulus for asking questions.

6. Which of the following illustrates an instance of instinctive drift?
   a. A dog salivates in response to a ringing bell.
   b. A circus elephant is unable to learn a difficult trick from its trainer.
   c. A mouse learns to navigate a maze and receives a reward for exiting the maze.
   d. A bird associates a certain toy with food and begins to treat that toy as it would treat food.

7. An elementary school teacher gives students a sticker each time the students raise their hands before speaking in class. When a student has earned 10 stickers, he or she is given an extra 5 minutes of recess. What process is the teacher using?
   a. behavior modification and/or a token economy
   b. neurofeedback
   c. partial reinforcement
   d. applied behavior analysis

8. Alex works at a local bookstore. He receives his paycheck every 2 weeks. What schedule of reinforcement is illustrated in this scenario?
   a. fixed interval
   b. variable interval
   c. fixed ratio
   d. variable ratio

194 CHAPTER 6

Practice Quiz Answers

1. d	**5.** d
2. c	**6.** b
3. a	**7.** a
4. d	**8.** a

194 Chapter 6 Learning and Language Development

Module 16: Cognitive Learning and Observational Learning

Module Goal
Identify the aspects of cognitive and observational learning.

Learning Objectives
- 16.1 What occurs in observational learning?
- 16.2 How does observational learning function in everyday life?
- 16.3 What is cognitive learning theory?

Identify the Aspects of Cognitive and Observational Learning

16.1 What occurs in observational learning?

One learning theory that departs from the traditional theories of Pavlov and Skinner and also depends on cognition is that of **observational learning**, the learning of new behavior through the observation of a model (watching someone else who is performing that behavior).

Bandura and the Bobo Doll Bandura's classic study in observational learning involved having a preschool child in a room in which the experimenter and a model interacted with toys in the room in front of the child (Bandura et al., 1961). In one condition, the model interacted with the toys in a nonaggressive manner, ignoring the presence of an inflatable clown doll called a "Bobo doll." In another condition, the model became very aggressive with the Bobo doll, kicking it and yelling at it. Watch on mypsychlab.com

When each child was left alone in the room and had the opportunity to play with the toys, a camera filming through a one-way mirror caught the children who were exposed to the aggressive model beating up on the Bobo doll in exact imitation of the model. The children who saw the model ignore the doll did not act aggressively toward the doll. Obviously, the aggressive children had learned their aggressive actions from merely watching the model—with no reinforcement necessary.

But would that child have imitated the model if the model had been punished? Wouldn't the consequences of the model's behavior make a difference?

In later studies, Bandura showed a film of a model beating up the Bobo doll. In one group, the children saw the model rewarded afterward. In another, the model was punished. When placed in the room with toys, the children in the first group beat up the doll, but the children in the second group did not.

However, when Bandura told the children in the second group that he would give them a reward if they could show him what the model in the film did, each child duplicated the model's actions (Bandura, 1965). Apparently, consequences do matter in motivating a person to imitate a particular model. In fact, Bandura began this research to investigate possible links between children's exposure to violence on television and aggressive behavior toward others.

Watch footage from Bandura's Bobo doll experiment on **mypsychlab.com**

◀ But would that child have imitated the model if the model had been punished? Wouldn't the consequences of the model's behavior make a difference?

observational learning learning new behavior by watching a model perform that behavior.

LEARNING AND LANGUAGE DEVELOPMENT 195

CHAPTER 6 • Module 16

Focus

RESOURCES
For this module, consult the appropriate sections of the Teacher's Manual, Test Bank, and PowerPoint slides, all found on the Teacher's Resource DVD, and the interactive study tools for students on MyPsychLab.

BEFORE CLASS
Students should read the section for homework before coming to class.

BELLRINGER
Ask students to write down an instance when they learned to do something by watching someone else perform the behavior.

Teach

INTRODUCE THE TOPIC
Explain to students that *observational learning* is learning through watching others perform, or model, certain actions.

COVER THE MODULE
16.1 What occurs in observational learning?
- **Bandura and the Bobo Doll**
  - Bandura's famous Bobo doll experiment demonstrated that young children will imitate the aggressive actions of a model even when there is no reinforcement for doing so.

MULTIMEDIA CONTENT AVAILABLE AT
www.mypsychlab.com

Watch footage from Bandura's Bobo doll experiment on **mypsychlab.com**

Terms

- cobservational learning • latent learning • insight • learned helplessness

Module 16 Cognitive and Observational Learning 195

CHAPTER 6 • Module 16

COVER THE MODULE

16.2 How does observational learning function in everyday life?

- Bandura determined that four elements needed to be present for observational learning to occur.
  - Attention: The learner must first pay attention to the model.
  - Memory: The learner must also be able to retain the memory of what was done.
  - Imitation: The learner must be capable of imitating the actions of the model.
  - Motivation: The learner must have the desire to perform the action.

MULTIMEDIA CONTENT AVAILABLE AT www.mypsychlab.com

Simulate Bandura's study on observational learning on **mypsychlab.com**

CLASS DISCUSSION

Remind students that researchers have studied for years the effects of violent television on children in order to determine if it makes children more aggressive. This topic has taken on increased interest currently with the proliferation of violent video games and Internet activities. Ask students if they think there is a connection between children and teens watching violence and then acting aggressively. Students should provide evidence to support their viewpoints.

▲ *Albert Bandura's famous Bobo doll experiment. This doll was used to demonstrate the impact of observing an adult model performing aggressive behavior on the later aggressive behavior of children. The children in these photos are imitating the adult model's behavior even though they believe they are alone and are not being watched.*

While there is a body of evidence stretching over nearly two decades that suggests a relationship between viewing violent television and an increased level of aggression in children (Bushman & Huesmann, 2001; Huesmann & Eron, 1986), this evidence is based on correlational data. Correlations do not prove that viewing violence on TV is the *cause* of the increased violence. What if naturally aggressive children just like to watch more violent shows?

16.2 How does observational learning function in everyday life?

Bandura (1986) concluded, from these studies and others, that observational learning required the presence of four elements: attention, memory, imitation, and motivation.

To learn anything through observation, the learner must first pay *attention* to the model. For example, the first time you go to a concert with friends, you might want to watch your friends to learn how they act at concerts: whether they dance, clap, or sing along with the band. Certain characteristics of models can make attention more likely. People pay more attention to others whom they perceive as similar to themselves and to people whom they respect or perceive as attractive.

The learner must also be able to retain the *memory* of what was done. If your friend shows you how to install and run a new computer program, you have to remember those steps in order to put the program on your own computer later on.

The learner must be capable of reproducing, or *imitating*, the actions of the model. A 2-year-old might be able to watch someone tie shoelaces and might even remember most of the steps, but the 2-year-old's chubby little fingers will not have the dexterity necessary for actually tying the laces.

Finally, the learner must have the desire or *motivation* to perform the action. At that concert, for example, you might not care whether your friends will think you're weird if you sit in the audience instead of dancing up by the stage. Also, if a person expects a reward, that person will be much more likely to imitate the observed behavior. Successful models are powerful figures for imitation, but rarely would we motivated to imitate someone who fails or is punished. Simulate on **mypsychlab.com**

Simulate Bandura's study on observational learning on **mypsychlab.com**

196 CHAPTER 6

Class Demonstration

TIE YOUR SHOES

The purpose of this activity is to educate students on the prevalence of behaviors that are acquired by observational learning. The activity involves students teaching other students to tie shoes. Have students pair up; one member of the pair should be wearing shoes with laces. Ask students with laces to untie their shoes. The partner, referred to as the "Teacher," provides instructions on how to tie shoes. Assuming nothing, the student should follow the instructions without inference of any kind (e.g., which lace to grab with which hand; how to make "bunny" ears). The "Teacher" cannot point to the laces nor do any type of prompting. After several minutes of probable frustration, ask the "Teacher" to use vicarious or participant modeling.

196 Chapter 6 Learning and Language Development

16.3 What is cognitive learning theory?

In the early days of behaviorism, the original focus of Watson, Skinner, and many of their followers was on observable, measurable behavior. Anything that might be occurring inside a person or animal's head during learning was considered to be of no interest to the behaviorist because it could not be seen or directly measured. Other psychologists, however, were still interested in the mind's influence over behavior. Gestalt psychologists, for instance, were studying the way that the human mind tried to force a pattern on stimuli in the world around the person. LINK *to Chapter One: The Science of Psychology, pp. 5–12.*

This continued interest in the mind was followed, in the 1950s and 1960s, by the comparison of the human mind to the workings of those fascinating "thinking machines," computers. Soon afterward, interest in *cognition*, the way in which the brain processes information, began to dominate experimental psychology. Many behavioral psychologists could no longer ignore the thoughts, feelings, and expectations that clearly existed in the mind and that seemed to influence observable behavior. Some eventually began to develop a cognitive learning theory to supplement the more traditional theories of learning (Kendler, 1985). Three important figures often cited as key theorists in the development of cognitive learning theory are the early psychologists Edward Tolman and Wolfgang Köhler and the modern psychologist Martin Seligman.

Tolman's Maze-Running Rats: Latent Learning One of Edward Tolman's best-known experiments in learning involved teaching three groups of rats the same maze, one at a time (Tolman & Honzik, 1930). In the first group, each rat was placed in the maze and reinforced with food for making its way out the other side. The rat was then placed back in the maze, reinforced, and so on until the rat could successfully solve the maze with no errors the typical maze-learning experiment.

The second group of rats never received any reinforcement upon exiting the maze. They were simply put back in again and again, until the 10th day of the experiment, when they received reinforcement for the first time. The third group of rats, serving as a control group, was also not reinforced and was not given reinforcement for the entire duration of the experiment.

A strict Skinnerian behaviorist would predict that only the first group of rats would learn the maze successfully because learning depends on reinforcing consequences. During the first 9 days, the first group of rats did indeed solve the maze after a certain number of trials, whereas the second and third groups seemed to wander aimlessly around the maze.

On the 10th day, the second group of rats received reinforcement for the first time. It *should* have taken them as long as the first group to solve the maze. Instead, they began to solve the maze almost immediately. Tolman concluded that the rats in the second group had learned where all the paths were and stored this knowledge away as a kind of "mental map," or *cognitive map* of the maze's layout. The rats in the second group had learned and stored that learning away mentally but had not *demonstrated* this learning. Tolman called this **latent learning** (*latent* means "hidden"). Figure 16.1 graphs the results of Tolman's study.

Köhler's Smart Chimp: Insight Learning Another exploration of the cognitive elements of learning came about almost by accident. Wolfgang Köhler (1887–1967) studied animal learning in a primate research lab in the Canary Islands off the coast of North Africa. In one of his more

latent learning learning that remains hidden until its application becomes useful.

LEARNING AND LANGUAGE DEVELOPMENT 197

CHAPTER 6 • Module 16

COVER THE MODULE

16.3 What is cognitive learning theory?

- Cognitive learning theory states that learning requires cognition, or the influence of an organism's thought processes.

LINK *to Chapter One, The Science of Psychology, pp. 5–12*

- **Tolman's Maze-Running Rats: Latent Learning**
  - Tolman found that rats that were allowed to wander in a maze but were not reinforced still showed evidence of having learned the maze once reinforcement became possible. He termed this hidden learning *latent learning*, a form of cognitive learning.

UNDERSTANDING VISUALS

In order to help students understand the information presented in Figure 16.1 on p. 198, encourage them to visit the www.mypsychlab.com website for Chapter 6 and review the simulation titled "Cognitive Learning."

REINFORCE THE LESSON

Students can visit the www.mypsychlab.com website for Chapter 6 and work through the simulation titled "How Good Is Your Cognitive Map?" in order to see for themselves how cognitive maps work.

Class Demonstration

HUMAN COGNITIVE MAPS

Humans use a variety of cognitive maps to represent important environments. Have students generate a cognitive map for a relevant environment, such as your school campus. Ask students to sketch a map of the campus. Compare and contrast the features included in (and excluded from) students' maps by having a few students with detailed maps sketch theirs on the board. Discuss how and why students' maps differ. What landmarks were central to most maps? Were any features commonly left out? These and other questions should spark an interesting discussion on the role of experience in developing cognitive maps.

Module 16 Cognitive and Observational Learning

CHAPTER 6 • Module 16

COVER THE MODULE (continued)

- **Köhler's Smart Chimp: Insight Learning**
  - Köhler found evidence of insight, the sudden perception of the relationships among elements of a problem, in chimpanzees.
  - More research has found support for the concept of animal insight, but controversy remains over how to interpret these studies.

FAST FACT

Ask: **Which animal has the largest brain of all land mammals?** *(The answer is the Asian elephant. According to recent research, Asian elephants fail to understand the underlying purpose of tasks and instead follow training in a rote manner. This challenges previous research that suggested elephants are capable of insight.)*

COVER THE MODULE (continued)

- **Seligman's Depressed Dogs: Learned Helplessness**
  - Seligman found that dogs who had been placed in an inescapable situation failed to try to escape when it became possible to do so, remaining in the painful situation as if helpless to leave. Seligman called this phenomenon *learned helplessness* and found parallels between learned helplessness and depression.
  - L**I**N**K** to Chapter One, The Science of Psychology, pp. 11–12

---

famous studies (Köhler, 1925), he set up a problem for Sultan, one of the chimpanzees. Sultan wanted a banana that was placed just out of his reach outside his cage, so he used a stick from the cage to rake the banana into the cage.

Then the banana was placed just out of reach of Sultan's extended arm with the stick in his hand. At this point, there were two sticks lying around in the cage, which could be fitted together to make a single pole that would be long enough to reach the banana. Sultan first tried one stick, then the other. Then, Sultan pushed one stick out of the cage as far as it would go toward the banana and then pushed the other stick behind the first one. Of course, when he tried to draw the sticks back, only the one in his hand came. When Köhler returned the second stick, Sultan examined both sticks carefully. He then fitted them together and retrieved his banana. Köhler called Sultan's rapid "perception of relationships" **insight** and determined that insight could not be gained through trial-and-error learning alone (Köhler, 1925).

FIGURE 16.1 Learning Curves for Three Groups of Rats
In the results of the classic study of latent learning, Group 1 was rewarded on each day, while Group 2 was rewarded for the first time on Day 11. Group 3 was never rewarded. Note the immediate change in the behavior of Group 2 on Day 12 (Tolman & Honzik, 1930).

Although Thorndike believed animals could not demonstrate insight, Köhler's work demonstrates that insight, requiring a sudden "coming together" of all the elements of a problem in a kind of "aha" moment not predicted by traditional studies, was not limited to humans. More recent research has also found support for the concept of animal insight (Heinrich, 2000; Heyes, 1998; Zentall, 2000), but there is still controversy over how to interpret the results of those studies (Wynne, 1999).

Seligman's Depressed Dogs: Learned Helplessness American cognitive psychologist Martin Seligman is now most famous for founding the field of *positive psychology*, a new way of looking at the entire concept of mental health and therapy. L**I**N**K** *to Chapter One: The Science of Psychology, pp. 11–12.* But in the mid- to late 1960s, Seligman and his colleagues accidentally discovered an unexpected phenomenon while doing experiments on dogs using classical conditioning (Seligman, 1975). Their original intention was to study escape and avoidance learning. Seligman and colleagues presented a tone followed by a harmless but painful electric shock to one group of dogs (Overmier & Seligman, 1967; Seligman & Maier, 1967). The dogs in this group were harnessed so that they could not escape the shock. The researchers assumed that the dogs would learn to fear the sound of the tone and later try to escape from the tone before being shocked.

These dogs, along with another group of dogs that had not been conditioned to fear the tone, were placed into a special box consisting of a low fence that divided the box into two compartments. The dogs could easily see over

insight the seemingly sudden perception of relationships among various parts of a problem, allowing the solution to the problem to come quickly.

198 CHAPTER 6

Explore

TECHNIQUES AND METHODS OF LEARNING

There are many websites that are dedicated to improving learning and memory. Students can learn a variety of aids to improving learning and memory, including "accelerated learning," "lateral thinking," and "creative enhancement." Have each student on a team spend approximately 30 minutes surfing the Internet for the best techniques for improving learning. Then, when students return to class, have them share what they learned with their team and ask the team to come up with a list of the five best techniques for improving learning. Discuss whether they reflect the principles of classical conditioning, operant conditioning, or cognitive learning. The teams can then present their information to the rest of the class in written or oral form.

198 Chapter 6 Learning and Language Development

the fence and jump over if they wished—which is precisely what the second group of dogs did as soon as the shock occurred. However, when the tone the first group of dogs had been conditioned to fear sounded, the conditioned dogs just sat there. In fact, those dogs showed distress but didn't try to jump over the fence *even when the shock itself began*.

Why would the conditioned dogs refuse to move when shocked? The dogs had apparently learned in the original tone/shock situation that there was nothing they could do to escape the shock. So when placed in a situation in which escape was possible, the dogs still did nothing because they had learned to be "helpless." They believed they could not escape, so they did not try.

I know some people who seem to act just like those dogs—they live in a horrible situation but won't leave. Is this the same thing?

Seligman extended this theory of **learned helplessness**, the tendency to fail to act to escape from a situation because of a history of repeated failures in the past, to explain *depression*. Depressed people often stay in unpleasant work environments or bad marriages or relationships rather than trying to escape or better their situation. Seligman proposed that this depressive behavior is a form of learned helplessness. Depressed people may have learned in the past that they seem to have no control over what happens to them (Alloy & Clements, 1998). A sense of powerlessness and hopelessness is common to depressed people, and certainly, this would seem to apply to Seligman's dogs as well.

Think about how this might apply to other situations. There are many students who feel that they are bad at math because they have had problems with it in the past. Is it possible that this belief could make them not try as hard or study as much as they should? Isn't this kind of thinking also an example of learned helplessness?

learned helplessness the tendency to fail to act to escape from a situation because of a history of repeated failures in the past.

◀ I know some people who seem to act just like those dogs—they live in a horrible situation but won't leave. Is this the same thing?

Practice Quiz

Pick the best answer.

1. Attention, memory, imitation, and motivation are the four elements required for the process of
   a. insight
   b. latent learning
   c. observational learning
   d. spontaneous recovery

2. In Edward Tolman's maze study, the fact that the group of rats receiving reinforcement only after the 10th day of the study solved the maze far more quickly than did the rats who had been reinforced from the first day can be interpreted to mean that these particular rats
   a. were much smarter than the other rats
   b. had already learned the maze in the first 9 days
   c. had the opportunity to cheat by watching the other rats
   d. were able to learn only because they had not received much reinforcement

continued

LEARNING AND LANGUAGE DEVELOPMENT

CHAPTER 6 • Module 16

DISCUSS THE STUDENT VOICE QUESTION

This question could lead to an interesting discussion with students about why a person in a "bad" situation might not try to escape it. For example, women with abusive partners may not be able to escape their situation for a variety of reasons. Discuss what some of these factors might be.

TEACHING TIP

When discussing depression and learned helplessness, be sensitive to the fact that for some students, the topic may be difficult or disturbing.

EXTEND THE DISCUSSION

Point out that learned helplessness can affect both physical and mental health. Sufferers may experience health problems if they neglect diet, exercise, and medical treatment, erroneously thinking that they don't have the power to change. The more that persons perceive events as uncontrollable, the more stress they experience and the less hope they feel about making changes in their lives.

L3 DIFFERENTIATED INSTRUCTION

Engaging All Learners Clarify behavioral expectations for each lesson. Use rubrics and work with students to create rubrics for class activities and project. Modeling what students are to do or providing students with examples of finished products is necessary for student success. Explicit instructions do not water down the curriculum; they make it clear so that all students can access it.

Explore

UNDERSTANDING DEPRESSION

Depression is a real illness, and sufferers pay a high price in terms of relationship problems, family difficulties, and lost work productivity. Depressed persons tend to feel helpless and hopeless and to blame themselves for having these feelings. People who are depressed may become overwhelmed and exhausted and may stop participating in their routine activities. They may withdraw from family and friends. Yet, depression is a treatable illness. Ask students to use library or Internet resources to research depression and how it can be treated, including the use of cognitive therapy. Ask volunteers to report their findings back to the class. How do students think cognitive therapy might be helpful for treating depression?

CHAPTER 6 • Module 16

Assess

Assign the Module 16 Practice Quiz.

Use the Practice Quiz to identify gaps in student understanding.

REMEDIATE

Have students, individually or in groups, review the module goals, learning objectives, and key terms.

Refer students to the Concept Summary on p. 210 for review.

Close

As a class, discuss examples from students' experience of latent learning, insight learning, and learned helplessness.

---

continued

3. Martin Seligman found many similarities between his "helpless" dogs and people suffering from
   a. depression
   b. agoraphobia
   c. schizophrenia
   d. aggressive behavior syndrome

4. Wolfgang Köhler determined that his chimpanzee's two-stick solution to the banana problem was an example of insight because it was
   a. sudden and rapid
   b. the result of trial-and-error learning
   c. arrived at after a long period of time
   d. based on natural biological behaviors

5. In Albert Bandura's study with the Bobo doll, the children in the group that saw the model punished did not imitate the model at first. They would only imitate the model if given a reward for doing so. The fact that these children had obviously learned the behavior without actually performing it is an example of
   a. observational learning
   b. insight learning
   c. operant conditioning
   d. classical conditioning

6. In _____, a person will learn something but will not display this learned behavior because there is no incentive to show what they have learned.
   a. depression
   b. latent learning
   c. vicarious learning
   d. learned helplessness

7. A teacher tells her students that they will have recess as soon as they put their art supplies away. This is an example of
   a. attention
   b. motivation
   c. imitation
   d. memory

8. People who study what goes on a person's mind as he or she learns are interested in
   a. latent learning theory
   b. cognitive learning theory
   c. observational learning theory
   d. motivational learning theory

9. Fatimah decides to run in a 5k race. However, she does not join a race immediately. She trains for 3 months before signing up. Which of the following elements best describes why she waits to run?
   a. attention: she wants to see someone else run a race before she tries herself
   b. memory: she has to be able to remember how to pace herself throughout the race
   c. imitation: she has to be physically able to run a 5k race before she can succeed
   d. motivation: she has to find a race that best fits her interests and her busy schedule

10. A jar with a small purse of seeds and a long piece of wire is placed in a room with a crow. The crow attempts to use the wire to push the seed purse out of the jar. When this fails, the crow examines the jar, then takes out the piece of wire. The crow bends the wire into a hook, and uses this hook to pull the purse out of the jar. Which of the following did this crow display?
    a. insight
    b. attention
    c. memory
    d. aggression

200   CHAPTER 6

Practice Quiz Answers

1. c
2. b
3. a
4. a
5. a
6. b
7. b
8. b
9. c
10. a

Module 17: Language

Module Goals

- Identify the structural features of language.
- Explain theories and stages of language acquisition.
- Identify areas of the brain associated with language.

Learning Objectives

- **17.1** What is language, and how is it structured?
- **17.2** How are language and thought related?
- **17.3** How is language acquired?
- **17.4** What are the theories of language acquisition?
- **17.5** Which parts of the brain are associated with language, and how does brain damage affect language?

Identify the Structural Features of Language

17.1 What is language, and how is it structured?

We may all learn different things from our life experiences, and we may study different subjects in school, but one thing that almost everyone in the world learns is language. **Language** is a system for combining symbols (such as letters and words) so that an infinite number of meaningful statements can be made for the purpose of communicating with others through writing, speech, or both. Language allows people not only to communicate with one another but also to represent their own internal mental activity. In other words, language is a very important part of how people think.

The Levels of Language Analysis The structures of languages all over the world share common characteristics. Languages involve words, word order, word meanings, the rules for making words into other words, the sounds that exist within a language, the rules for practical communication with others, and the meanings of sentences and phrases. If a language is designed to be written, it also involves letters or characters used to write words and sentences.

Grammar Grammar is the system of rules governing the structure and use of a language. According to Noam Chomsky, an American linguist at MIT, humans have an innate ability to understand and produce language through a device he calls the *language acquisition device*, or *LAD* (Chomsky, 2006; Chomsky et al., 2002). While humans may learn the *specific* language (English, Spanish, Mandarin, etc.) through the processes of imitation, reinforcement, and shaping, the ability to acquire the complexities of the grammar of a language are, according to Chomsky, to some degree "wired in" to the developing brain. Grammar includes rules for syntax (the order of words), morphology (the study of the formation of words), phonemes (the basic sounds of language), and pragmatics (the practical social expectations and uses of language).

language a system for combining symbols (such as words) so that an unlimited number of meaningful statements can be made for the purpose of communicating with others.

grammar the system of rules governing the structure and use of a language.

LEARNING AND LANGUAGE DEVELOPMENT 201

Terms

- language • grammar • syntax • morphemes • semantics • phonemes • pragmatics
- cognitive universalism • Broca's aphasia • Wernicke's aphasia

---

CHAPTER 6 • Module 17

Focus

RESOURCES

For this module, consult the appropriate sections of the Teacher's Manual, Test Bank, and PowerPoint slides, all found on the Teacher's Resource DVD, and the interactive study tools for students on MyPsychLab.

BEFORE CLASS

Students should read the section for homework before coming to class.

BELLRINGER

Ask students to think about what their world would be like if there were no such thing as language. Have them jot down a few sentences about their thoughts.

Teach

COVER THE MODULE

17.1 What is language and how is it structured?

- Language is a system for combining symbols so that an infinite number of meaningful statements can be created and communicated to others.
- **The Levels of Language Analysis**
  - Languages involve words, word order, word meanings, rules for making words into other words, the sounds within a language, rules for practical communication, and the meanings of sentences and phrases. Written languages also involve letters or characters used to write words and sentences.
- **Grammar**: The system of rules governing the structure and use of a language.

Module 17 Language **201**

CHAPTER 6 • Module 17

COVER THE MODULE *(continued)*

- **Syntax:** A system of rules for combining words and phrases to form grammatically correct sentences.
- **Morphemes:** The smallest units of meaning within a language.
- **Semantics:** Rules for determining the meaning of words and sentences.
- **Phonemes:** The basic units of sound in a language.
- **Pragmatics:** This deals with the practical aspects of communicating with others. It involves knowing just what rhythm and emphasis to use when communicating with others (intonation).

17.2 How are language and thought related?

- Jean Piaget theorized that concepts preceded and aided the development of language. Concepts became the "pegs" upon which words are "hung."
- Lev Vygotsky believed that language helped develop concepts and could help a child learn to control behavior.
- Evidence seems to bear out Vygotsky's view: Children tend to use more private speech when learning how to socialize with other children or when working on a difficult task.

▲ Pragmatics involve the practical aspects of communicating. This young mother is talking and then pausing for the infant's response. In this way, the infant is learning about taking turns, an important aspect of language development. What kinds of games do adults play with infants that also aid the development of language?

syntax the system of rules for combining words and phrases to form grammatically correct sentences.

morphemes the smallest units of meaning within a language.

semantics the rules for determining the meaning of words and sentences.

phonemes the basic units of sound in language.

pragmatics aspects of language involving the practical ways of communicating with others, or the social "niceties" of language.

202 CHAPTER 6

Syntax **Syntax** is a system of rules for combining words and phrases to form grammatically correct sentences. Syntax is quite important, as just a simple mix-up can cause sentences to be completely misunderstood. For example, "John kidnapped the boy" has a different meaning from "John, the kidnapped boy," although all four words are the same (Lasnik, 1990).

Morphemes **Morphemes** are the smallest units of meaning within a language. For example, the word *playing* consists of two morphemes, *play* and *ing*. Morphemes themselves are governed by **semantics**, rules for determining the meaning of words and sentences. Sentences can have the same semantic meaning while having different syntax: "Johnny hit the ball" and "the ball was hit by Johnny."

Phonemes **Phonemes** are the basic units of sound in a language. The *a* in the word *car* is a very different phoneme from the *a* in the word *day*, even though it is the same letter of the alphabet. One of the biggest problems for people who are trying to learn another language is the inability to both hear and pronounce the phonemes of that other language. Although infants are born with the ability to recognize all phonemes (Werker & Lalonde, 1988), after about 9 months, that ability has deteriorated and the infant recognizes only the phonemes of the language to which the infant is exposed (Boysen-Bardies et al., 1989).

Pragmatics The **pragmatics** of language deal with the practical aspects of communicating with others. Pragmatics involve knowing things like how to take turns in a conversation, the use of gestures to emphasize a point or indicate a need for more information, and the different ways in which one speaks to different people (Yule, 1996). For example, adults use simpler words when they speak to small children than they do when speaking to other adults. Both adults and children use higher-pitched voices and many repeated phrases when talking to infants. Part of the pragmatics of language includes knowing just what rhythm and emphasis to use when communicating with others, called *intonation*. When speaking to infants, adults and children are changing the intonation when they use a higher pitch and stress certain words differently than others.

17.2 How are language and thought related?

Two very influential developmental psychologists, Jean Piaget and Lev Vygotsky, often debated the relationship of language and thought (Duncan, 1995). Piaget (1926, 1962) theorized that concepts preceded and aided the development of language. In a sense, concepts become the "pegs" upon which words are "hung." Piaget also noticed that preschool children seemed to spend a great deal of time talking to themselves—even when playing with other children. Each child would be talking about something totally unrelated to the speech of the other, in a process Piaget called *collective monologue*. Piaget believed that this kind of nonsocial speech was very egocentric and that as the child became more socially involved and less egocentric, these non-social-speech patterns would reduce.

Vygotsky, however, believed almost the opposite. He theorized that language helped develop concepts and could help the child learn to control behavior (Vygotsky, 1962, 1978, 1987). For Vygotsky, the word helped form the concept: Once a child had learned the word "mama," the various elements of "mama-ness"—*warm, soft, food, safety,* and so on—could come together around that word. Vygotsky also believed that the "egocentric" speech of the preschool child was actually a way for the child to form thoughts and control

---

Critical Thinking

WRITING ABOUT BILINGUALISM

Although many educators believe that bilingual and multilingual children should be taught in English and in their native language (both to preserve their culture and because it has cognitive benefits), other educators and members of Congress are pushing to assimilate non-native speakers into U.S. culture by placing them in classes where only English is taught. Ask your students to write a short paper that explains their perspective on this issue. Which side of the argument do they believe is correct? If there are enough contrasting opinions, consider holding a class debate on the topic.

actions. Socializing with other children would demand much more self-control and behavioral regulation on the part of the preschool child; therefore, Vygotsky believed that private speech would actually *increase* as children became more socially active. The evidence seems to bear out Vygotsky's view: Children tend to use more private speech when learning how to socialize with other children or when working on a difficult task (Berk, 1992; Berk & Spuhl, 1995; Bivens & Berk, 1990).

Cognitive Universalism Does language influence the way we think? The belief that language shapes thoughts was once an accepted hypothesis, but more recent studies have suggested that thought concepts are universal and not actually shaped by language. For example, in one study, researchers assumed that a language's color names would influence the ability of the people who grew up with that language to distinguish among and perceive colors. The study found that basic color terms did directly influence color recognition memory (Lucy & Shweder, 1979). But an earlier series of studies of the perception of colors (Rosch-Heider, 1972; Rosch-Heider & Olivier, 1972) had already found just the opposite effect: Members of the Dani tribe, whose language has only two names for colors, were no different in their ability to perceive all of the colors than were the English speakers in the study. More recent studies (Davies et al., 1998a, 1998b; Laws et al., 1995; Pinker & Bloom, 1990) support Rosch-Heider's findings and the idea of a **cognitive universalism** (concepts are universal and influence the development of language).

Animal Studies in Language

I've heard that chimpanzees can be taught to use sign language. Is this for real, or are the chimps just performing tricks like the animals in the circus or the zoo?

Language is defined as the use of symbols, and symbols are things that stand for something else. In human language, symbols are used quite deliberately and voluntarily, and abstract symbols have no meaning until people assign meaning to them. Can animals be taught to use abstract symbols that represent language?

cognitive universalism theory that concepts are universal and influence the development of language.

> I've heard that chimpanzees can be taught to use sign language. Is this for real, or are the chimps just performing tricks like the animals in the circus or the zoo?

▲ *Kanzi looks at the keyboard used in teaching language to chimpanzees. Kanzi's language abilities were learned through watching researchers train his mother rather than directly—much as a human infant learns through listening to the speech of adults.*

LEARNING AND LANGUAGE DEVELOPMENT 203

Explore

DO ANIMALS HAVE LANGUAGE? A SURVEY

A fairly large number of people believe that animals have language abilities. Most scientific data on the point, however, indicate that animals *communicate* but do not use a complicated system of symbols and syntax to convey ideas. The following three questions can be used by students as an informal survey of people (such as family members or friends) regarding the issue of animal language: (1) Do you believe that animals have language? If so, what specific species? (2) Why or why not? (3) Why do you think humans have such well-developed language abilities?

Students can potentially learn a great deal by teaching those whom they survey (presumably, there will be many people who may not grasp the vast difference between animal communication and human language).

CHAPTER 6 • Module 17

COVER THE MODULE *(continued)*

- *Cognitive universalism* is the theory that concepts are universal and influence the development of language.

- **Animal Studies in Language**
  - Researchers have tried to teach animals how to use sign language. Kanzi, a bonobo chimpanzee, learned to press abstract symbols on a computer keyboard by observing his mother. His language is considered to be "real," but the language of such animals cannot compare to the level of language development of a human child. There is no evidence that these animals have mastered syntax.

MULTIMEDIA CONTENT AVAILABLE AT
www.mypsychlab.com

Read and learn more about animal studies and language on **mypsychlab.com**

L1 DIFFERENTIATED INSTRUCTION

Special Needs Provide preferred seating in the front of the class, face-to-face talk for students who read lips, interpreters, or space for a guide dog as necessary.

Module 17 Language 203

CHAPTER 6 • Module 17

COVER THE MODULE

17.3 How is language acquired?
- Language is acquired through a stepped learning process.
- Cooing involves producing vowel sounds (at 2 months of age).
- Babbling is creating consonant sounds (about 6 months old).
- Children speak actual word at about 1 year. They speak in holophrases, single words meant to represent entire phrases of meaning.
- At around 18 months, children begin to group words together in short sentences.
- At age 6, children are as fluent in language as an adult; they simply have a limited vocabulary.

LINK to Chapter Five, Development Across the Life Span, pp. 115–156

COVER THE MODULE

17.4 What are the theories of language acquisition?
- The earliest theories of language development were based on Skinnerian principles of reinforcement.
- Chomsky argued that language was an innate part of human nature. Real-world evidence supports this theory. The stages of language acquisition are universal across cultures.
- New theories concentrate on environmental factors that go into language acquisition.

Read and learn more about animal studies and language on **mypsychlab.com**

It's true that there have been attempts to teach animals how to use sign language. The most successful of these experiments has been with Kanzi, a bonobo chimpanzee trained to press abstract symbols on a computer keyboard (Savage-Rumbaugh & Lewin, 1994). Kanzi watched his mother use the keyboard and appeared to learn how to use the symbols through that observation. At last count, Kanzi could understand about 150 spoken English words. He has managed to follow correctly complex instructions up to the level of a two-and-a-half-year-old child (Savage-Rumbaugh et al., 1998). Kanzi also makes sounds that seem to have consistent meaning across different situations (Taglialatela et al., 2003). Researchers were able to identify four sounds that seemed to represent banana, grapes, juice, and the word *yes*.

Is it real language? The answer seems to be "yes." However, none of the animals can compare to the level of language development of a 3-year-old human child (Pinker, 1995). And, as yet, there is no evidence that any of the animals trained in language have been able to master syntax (Demers, 1988; Johnson, 1995; Pinker, 1995). **Read** on **mypsychlab.com**

Explain Theories and Stages of Language Acquisition

17.3 How is language acquired?

We acquire language through a stepped learning process. Initially, 2-month-old infants are only capable of producing vowel sounds, a stage known as *cooing*. They begin *babbling*, or creating consonant sounds, at about 6 months old, but do not begin speaking actual words until about 1 year. At this age, most children speak in *holophrases*, single words meant to represent entire phrases of meaning. Children begin to group words together in short sentences at around 18 months of age, gaining more complexity and more understanding of grammar and syntax as they mature. By the time they are 6 years old, children are as fluent in the language as an adult; they simply have a limited vocabulary. **LINK** to Chapter Five: Development Across the Life Span, pp. 115–156.

17.4 What are the theories of language acquisition?

The earliest theories of language development were based on Skinnerian principles of reinforcement. However, Chomsky argued that language was an innate part of human nature. He claimed that all humans are born with a LAD (language acquisition device) schema that allows them to learn and use language. The LAD "listens" to the language input of the infant's world and then begins to produce language sounds and eventually words and sentences in a pattern found across cultures. According to Chomsky, children use this innate language "program" to analyze and comprehend the language they hear. They use this schema to reproduce the language sounds and eventually speak the language. Real-world evidence supports Chomsky's theory: Infants are capable of learning any language, babies in the babbling stage of language acquisition can recreate the sounds of every language in the world, and the stages

Cultural Connection

LANGUAGE AND CULTURE

Languages are a part of the larger culture of the communities that speak them. Humans use language as a way of signaling their relationship with one cultural group and their dissimilarity from others. Divide the class into several teams. Give the teams some time to make a list of specific words and phrases that are part of the "language" of their own cultures, whether these are particular ethnic groups, races, genders, or age groups. Then ask a volunteer from each group to reproduce the group's list on the board, create a PowerPoint slide, or use any other appropriate method. After all the lists are visible, review them with the class. Are there any words or phrases shown that are unfamiliar to any students? Are there similarities or differences between the lists? How are the lists representative of the cultures from which they come?

of language acquisition are universal across cultures. Also, universal are the brain regions dedicated to forming and comprehending speech. Children who are raised from a very young age to speak more than one language will learn those languages easily and will often be able to speak them throughout their lives. (In contrast, it is much more difficult to learn and retain another language as a teenager or an adult.)

New theories in language concentrate on the environmental factors that go into language acquisition. The way adults speak to babies is one factor; adults use a higher pitched, repetitive sing-song voice, to which infants and toddlers are very responsive (Dominey & Dodane, 2004; Fernald, 1984, 1992; Küntay & Slobin, 2002). Studies have also shown a phenomenon called *expressive language delay* in infants, where children understand much more than they can reproduce (Stevenson et al., 1988). Until they learn how to utilize the language they hear, infants use gestures and signs to communicate. **LINK** *to Chapter Five: Development Across the Life Span, p. 156.*

Identify Areas of the Brain Associated with Language

17.5 Which parts of the brain are associated with language, and how does brain damage affect language?

Broca's Area In the left frontal lobe of most people's brains is an area devoted to the production and articulation of speech. **LINK** *to Chapter Two: The Biological Perspective, p. 61.* More specifically, this area allows a person to speak smoothly and fluently. It is called *Broca's area* after 19th-century neurologist Paul Broca, who first studied people with damage to this area (Leonard, 1997). Damage to Broca's area causes an inability to get words out in a smooth, connected fashion. People with this condition may know exactly what they want to say and understand what they hear others say, but they cannot control the actual production of their own words. Speech is halting and words are often mispronounced, such as saying "cot" instead of "clock" or "non" instead of "nine." Some words may be left out entirely, such as "the" or "for." This is called **Broca's aphasia**. *Aphasia* refers to an inability to use or understand either written or spoken language (Goodglass et al., 2001).

Wernicke's Area In the left temporal lobe (again, in most people) is an area called *Wernicke's area*, named after the physiologist and Broca's contemporary, Carl Wernicke, who first studied problems arising from damage in this location. This area of the brain appears to be involved in comprehending the meaning of words (Goodglass et al., 2001). **LINK** *to Chapter Two: The Biological Perspective, p. 61–62.* A person with **Wernicke's aphasia** is able to speak fluently and pronounce words correctly, but uses the entirely wrong words. For example, Elsie suffered a stroke, damaging her temporal lobe. When a nurse tried to take her blood pressure, Elsie said, "Oh, that's so Saturday hard." Elsie *thought* she was making sense. She also had trouble understanding what the people around her were saying to her.

Broca's aphasia condition resulting from damage to Broca's area, causing the affected person to be unable to speak fluently, to mispronounce words, and to speak haltingly.

Wernicke's aphasia condition resulting from damage to Wernicke's area, causing the affected person to be unable to understand or produce meaningful language.

LEARNING AND LANGUAGE DEVELOPMENT 205

CHAPTER 6 • Module 17

COVER THE MODULE

17.5 Which parts of the brain are associated with language, and how does brain damage affect language?

- **Broca's Area**
  - This area is in the left frontal lobe of the brain and is devoted to the production and articulation of speech. Damage to the area causes an inability to get words out in a smooth, connected fashion. The resulting condition is called *Broca's aphasia*.
  - **LINK** *to Chapter Two, The Biological Perspective, p. 61*

- **Wernicke's Area**
  - This area is in the left temporal lobe of the brain and is involved in comprehending the meaning of words. Damage to the area causes a person to speak fluently and pronounce words correctly but to use the entirely wrong words. The resulting condition is called *Wernicke's aphasia*.
  - **LINK** *to Chapter Two, The Biological Perspective, pp. 61–62*

Class Discussion

"NONHANDICAPPING" LANGUAGE

According to the American Psychological Association, the use of certain words or phrases can express gender, ethnic, or racial bias either intentionally or unintentionally. The same is true of language referring to persons with disabilities, which in many instances can express negative and disparaging attitudes. The guiding principle for "nonhandicapping" language is to maintain the integrity of individuals as whole human beings by avoiding language that (1) implies that a person as a whole is disabled (e.g., *disabled person*); (2) equates a person with his or her condition (e.g., *epileptic*); (3) has superfluous, negative overtones (e.g., *stroke victim*); and (4) is regarded as a slur (e.g., *cripple*). Conduct a class discussion about this topic. What do students think about the use of "nonhandicapping" language?

Module 17 Language **205**

CHAPTER 6 • Module 17

Assess

Assign the Module 17 Practice Quiz.

Use the Practice Quiz to identify gaps in student understanding.

REMEDIATE

Have students, individually or in groups, review the module goals, learning objectives, and key terms.

Refer students to the Concept Summary on p. 211 for review.

Close

Ask students if they know of anyone who has experienced trouble with language due to brain damage. How was the person able to cope?

TEACHING TIP

Many students falter when asked to write because they don't know how to construct a response that shows what they have learned. Teachers can help students improve their performance by embedding expository writing tasks in class activities, homework assignments, and tests throughout the semester.

Practice Quiz

Pick the best answer.

1. The system of rules for combining words and phrases to make meaningful sentences is called
   a. syntax
   b. phonics
   c. pragmatics
   d. grammar

2. Grammar includes all but which of the following aspects of language?
   a. tone of spoken words
   b. order of words
   c. formation of words
   d. structure of language

3. Which of the following is an English phoneme?
   a. the word *ball*
   b. the word *play*
   c. the suffix *ing*
   d. the sound *sh*

4. The Dani have only two words for color, yet can distinguish between many different colors. This finding specifically supports the language theory of
   a. Chomsky
   b. Rosch-Heider
   c. Broca and Wernicke
   d. Lucy and Shweder

5. According to Chomsky, grammar is
   a. impossible for older children and adults to learn
   b. innately understood by the developing human brain
   c. identical in content across all languages and cultures
   d. not a requirement for any relatively simple language

6. The first language sounds infants begin to make are
   a. vowels
   b. consonants
   c. animal sounds
   d. partial words

7. Which of the following best describes Chomsky's LAD theory?
   a. A child will talk to itself as a way to determine actions and organize thoughts.
   b. A child is as fluent as an adult in a language by the age of 5.
   c. A child is able to understand what is said to it, even if it is unable to respond.
   d. A child is born with the ability to recognize any language, although it loses that ability as it matures.

8. Henry's speech is halting, and many of his words are mispronounced. Henry most likely has
   a. Broca's aphasia
   b. Wernicke's aphasia
   c. Rosch-Heider disorder
   d. Seligman's disorder

9. Knowing how to take turns in a conversation is an example of
   a. syntax
   b. pragmatics
   c. accelerated aphasia
   d. cognitive universalism

10. For most people, which portion of the brain is associated with comprehending the meanings of words?
    a. right parietal lobe
    b. cerebellum
    c. left temporal lobe
    d. left frontal lobe

Practice Quiz Answers

1. a
2. a
3. d
4. b
5. b
6. a
7. c
8. a
9. b
10. c

CHAPTER 6 Summary

Listen on mypsychlab.com

Module 14: Classical Conditioning
Explain the process of classical conditioning.

14.1 What are the principles of classical conditioning?
- An unconditioned stimulus can be paired with a neutral stimulus to create a conditioned stimulus.

14.2 How can classical conditioning be specialized to affect emotions?
- Phobias can be learned when something unpleasant is paired with a neutral stimulus.

14.3 How does classical conditioning function in our everyday lives?
- Mammals learn to avoid food that makes them sick through a process called biological preparedness.

Module 15: Operant Conditioning
Explain the process of operant conditioning.

15.1 What is Thorndike's law of effect?
- If a behavior is followed by a pleasurable consequence, the behavior will be repeated.

15.2 What are the principles of operant conditioning?
- Operant conditioning is the learning of voluntary behavior through the effects of pleasant and unpleasant consequences to responses. Reinforcement encourages learning voluntary behavior. Punishment discourages learning voluntary behavior.

15.3 What are some specializations of operant conditioning?
- Shaping involves a stepped process of learning by getting a person or animal to perform a behavior.
- Reinforcement can be applied through partial reinforcement, continuous reinforcement, and schedules of fixed and variable intervals and ratios.

15.4 How does operant conditioning function in everyday life?
- Applied behavior analysis uses the shaping process to mold a desired behavior or response. Biofeedback and neurofeedback can be used to measure learning progress.

Listen to an audio file of your chapter on **mypsychlab.com**

Module 16: Cognitive Learning and Observational Learning
Identify the aspects of cognitive and observational learning.

16.1 What occurs in observational learning?
- People learn behavior by watching others perform that behavior.

16.2 How does observational learning function in everyday life?
- Observational learning requires attention, memory, capability, and the desire to perform a behavior.

16.3 What is cognitive learning theory?
- It focuses on the role of thought processes on learning.

Module 17: Language
Identify the structural features of language.

17.1 What is language, and how is it structured?
- Language is a system of symbols used to communicate, consisting of grammar, syntax, morphemes, phonemes, semantics, and pragmatics.

Explain theories of language acquisition.

17.2 How are language and thought related?
- Piaget believed that people learn concepts first, and later acquire the words that describe that concept. Vygotsky believed that language helped develop concepts.

17.3 How is language acquired?
- Language is acquired through a series of stages: cooing, babbling, one-word speech, telegraphic speech, and whole sentences.

17.4 What are the theories of language acquisition?
- Chomsky believed that humans are born with an ability to understand and learn how to speak language. Environmental factors, such as an adult's tone toward a child, also influence language acquisition.

Identify areas of the brain associated with language.

17.5 Which parts of the brain are associated with language, and how does brain damage affect language?
- Broca's area is associated with language production; Wernicke's area is associated with language comprehension. Brain damage can result in Broca's aphasia (which affects language production) or Wernicke's aphasia (which affects language comprehension).

Vocabulary Terms

learning p. 178
classical conditioning p. 178
unconditioned stimulus (UCS) p. 179
unconditioned response (UCR) p. 179
neutral stimulus (NS) p. 179
conditioned stimulus (CS) p. 179
conditioned response (CR) p. 179
stimulus generalization p. 180
stimulus discrimination p. 180
extinction p. 180
spontaneous recovery p. 180
conditioned emotional response (CER) p. 181
vicarious conditioning p. 182

conditioned taste aversion p. 182
biological preparedness p. 182
operant conditioning p. 184
law of effect p. 185
operant p. 185
reinforcement p. 185
primary reinforcer p. 186
secondary reinforcer p. 186
positive reinforcement. p. 186
negative reinforcement. p. 186
punishment p. 186
punishment by application p. 186
punishment by removal p. 186
shaping p. 188
successive approximation p. 188
discriminative stimulus p. 188

partial reinforcement effect p. 189
continuous reinforcement p. 189
fixed interval schedule of reinforcement p. 189
variable interval schedule of reinforcement p. 189
fixed ratio schedule of reinforcement p. 190
variable ratio schedule of reinforcement p. 190
instinctive drift p. 191
behavior modification p. 192
token economy p. 192
applied behavior analysis (ABA) p. 192
biofeedback p. 192

neurofeedback p. 192
observational learning p. 195
latent learning p. 197
insight p. 198
learned helplessness p. 199
language p. 201
grammar p. 201
syntax p. 202
morphemes p. 202
semantics p. 202
phonemes p. 202
pragmatics p. 202
cognitive universalism p. 203
Broca's aphasia p. 205
Wernicke's aphasia p. 205

LEARNING AND LANGUAGE DEVELOPMENT 207

CHAPTER 6 • Chapter Summary and Vocabulary

Chapter Summary

Encourage students to carefully review and study the summary. Explain that it provides an overview of key concepts presented in the text.

Have students identify what they find unclear or confusing. Call on volunteers to provide answers, examples, or definitions.

Vocabulary Terms

Remind students that terms are defined within the chapter at point of use. If they are not sure of a term's definition, they should look up the definition on the page.

Encourage students to create study cards of unfamiliar words or to go to **www.mypsychlab.com** for flash cards. Have them test themselves or a classmate. Advanced students can explain the terms in their own words.

Critical Thinking

EXPLORING THE DIFFERENT FORMS OF LEARNING

Have students connect the information they have learned in this chapter. Divide students into pairs or small groups. Ask them to generate as many of the implicit norms or rules for "classroom behavior" as they can. These include things like sitting in chairs at desks, staying quiet when the teacher is talking, raising your hand when you want to speak, exiting when the bell rings, and so forth. How did students learn these classroom norms? Responses to this question can be used to illustrate the different forms of learning. Many of these norms are learned through direct observation. Some may have been reinforced through rewards and punishments from other students, while others are learned because they are reinforced by the teacher's attention or peer approval. After students have had a few minutes to generate their responses, have them share their answers with the class.

CHAPTER 6 • Assessment

VOCABULARY REVIEW

1. c	6. a
2. g	7. h
3. i	8. b
4. j	9. e
5. d	10. f

WRITING ABOUT PSYCHOLOGY

1. Students' answers should describe Pavlov's experiment correctly and use the key terms UCS, UCR, NS, CS, and CR. In addition, the students' examples from everyday life should also use these key terms correctly.

2. Students should correctly define reinforcement as an event or object that, when following a response, increases the likelihood of that response occurring again. In contrast, punishment is any event or object that, when following a response, makes that response less likely to occur.

PSYCHOLOGY PROJECT

Students should recognize that a conditioned emotional response (CER) is an emotional response that has become classically conditioned to occur to learned stimuli. Advertisers often use certain objects or types of people to generate a specific emotional response in viewers, hoping that the emotional response will become paired with their product.

CHAPTER 6 Assessment

Study and Review on mypsychlab.com

Vocabulary Review

Match each vocabulary term to its definition.

1. pragmatics
2. conditioned stimulus
3. negative reinforcement
4. latent learning
5. operant conditioning
6. classical conditioning
7. punishment by removal
8. discriminative stimulus
9. extinction
10. unconditioned stimulus

a. learning in which one learns an involuntary response when a stimulus that normally causes a particular response is paired with a new, neutral stimulus. After enough pairings, the new stimulus will also cause the response to occur.
b. any stimulus, such as a stop sign or a doorknob, that provides the organism with a cue for making a certain response in order to obtain reinforcement.
c. aspects of language involving the practical ways of communicating with others, or the social "niceties" of language.
d. the learning of voluntary behavior through the effects of pleasant and unpleasant consequences to responses.
e. the disappearance or weakening of a learned response following the removal or absence of the unconditioned stimulus (in classical conditioning) or the removal of a reinforcer (in operant conditioning).
f. a naturally occurring stimulus that leads to an involuntary (reflex) response.
g. stimulus that becomes able to produce a learned reflex response by being paired with the original unconditioned stimulus.
h. the punishment of a response by the removal of a pleasurable stimulus.
i. the reinforcement of a response by the removal or escape from an unpleasant stimulus.
j. learning that remains hidden until its application becomes useful.

Writing About Psychology

Respond to each question in complete sentences.

1. Explain Pavlov's process of conditioning his dogs. Be sure to use the key terms unconditioned stimulus (UCS), unconditioned response (UCR), neutral stimulus (NS), conditioned stimulus (CS), and conditioned response (CR). Then, describe an example of classical conditioning in everyday life. Be sure to identify the UCS, UCR, NS, CS, and CR in your example.
2. Describe the difference between reinforcement and punishment. Use examples to illustrate your descriptions.

Psychology Project

Explore techniques that advertisers use to evoke conditioned emotional responses in their audience.

Materials:
- a print advertisement OR a screen capture of a commercial with brief description OR a transcript of a radio advertisement

Instructions:

1. Select an advertisement or commercial that you think is designed to evoke an emotional response.
2. Write a brief visual analysis of this advertisement. Use the following questions as a guide as you write:
   - What conditioned emotional response is the advertisement designed to evoke in the viewer?
   - What visual or audio features are used to bring about this emotion?
   - Is the advertisement successful? Why or why not?
3. Share your advertisement and analysis with a classmate.

Internet Resources

Association for Applied Behavior Analysis:
www.abainternational.org/
An international organization "dedicated to promoting the experimental, theoretical, and applied analysis of behavior."

Operant and Classical Conditioning:
www.brembs.net/learning/drosophila/general_introduction.html
Compares and contrasts operant and classical conditioning. Provides helpful diagrams that students can use while learning about learning.

Can Chimps Talk?
www.geocities.com/RainForest/Vines/4451/nova_CanChimpsTalk1.html
Transcript of a NOVA program.

Center for the Study of Language and Information:
www-csli.stanford.edu/
This independent research center founded by researchers from Stanford University provides information about their current and past publications.

Test Yourself

Pick the best answer.

1. Who added the concept of reinforcement to learning theory?
   a. Watson
   b. Skinner
   c. Thorndike
   d. Pavlov

2. A child has been classically conditioned to fear a white rat. If the child also shows fear when shown a white rabbit, this is called
   a. stimulus generalization
   b. discriminative stimulation
   c. successive approximation
   d. secondary reinforcement

3. The area of the brain devoted to producing speech is known as _____ and is located in the _____.
   a. Broca's area; left frontal lobe
   b. Broca's area; left temporal lobe
   c. Wernicke's area; left frontal lobe
   d. Wernicke's area; left temporal lobe

4. Jared learns how to prepare his father's famous chili recipe by watching his father in the kitchen for many years. This kind of learning is known as
   a. insight learning
   b. operant learning
   c. conditioned learning
   d. observational learning

5. Which of the following is an example of punishment by application?
   a. putting a child in time-out
   b. taking away a toy or treat
   c. ignoring a tantrum
   d. giving a spanking or a scolding

6. The raccoon in the Brelands' shaping experiment began displaying _____ when it learned to associate the coins with food.
   a. biofeedback
   b. instinctive drift
   c. vicarious conditioning
   d. biological preparedness

7. Pavlov conditioned his dogs to salivate at the ring of a bell. If Pavlov began snapping his fingers at the same time he rang the bell, his finger snap could become a(n)
   a. unconditioned stimulus
   b. neutral stimulus
   c. second conditioned stimulus
   d. discriminative stimulus

8. Which of the following is NOT a required element of effective observational learning?
   a. memory
   b. imitation
   c. punishment
   d. motivation

9. Chomsky believed that humans were born with an innate "program" that allowed them to listen to and learn a language. He called this
   a. Egocentric Speech
   b. Language Acquisition Development
   c. Learned Language Adaptation
   d. Linguistic Relativity Hypothesis

10. The basic units of sound in a language are known as
    a. phonemes
    b. morphemes
    c. semantics
    d. pragmatics

11. Which of the following is the best example of Thorndike's law of effect in action?
    a. A man sits on a chair and is stung by a bee. A week later, the man sits on the same chair again and is not stung.
    b. A child goes to piano lessons for 3 weeks before she becomes sick and misses a lesson. She returns to her lessons after 1 week's absence.
    c. A student studies hard for a test and receives an excellent grade as a result. The student studies hard for the next test, too.
    d. A woman answers the door when the doorbell rings, but no one is there. The next time the doorbell rings, the woman answers the door again.

12. Kashif speaks in one-word holophrases, saying "Toy!" to mean, "I want my toy!" Assuming that Kashif's speech has developed at an average pace, approximately how old is Kashif?
    a. 3 months old
    b. 6 months old
    c. 1 year old
    d. 2 years old

13. Sherry wants her dog to "heel" on command. At first, she gives the dog a treat for coming to her when she speaks the command, "Heel!" Then she rewards the dog only when it stands at her side when she gives the command. Finally, she rewards the dog only when it is at her side and facing front. Sherry is using
    a. shaping
    b. instinctive drift
    c. higher-order conditioning
    d. a fixed ratio schedule of reinforcement

14. Dumont's grandmother recently had a stroke. Now, she uses incorrect words when she speaks, which makes it difficult to understand what she is trying to say. She also has trouble understanding him when he talks. She most likely has
    a. spatial neglect
    b. Wernicke's aphasia
    c. split-brain
    d. Broca's aphasia

15. To ensure that his students are studying, Mr. Wagner will give them occasional pop quizzes. Through what type of schedule are his students being reinforced?
    a. A fixed interval schedule
    b. A fixed ratio schedule
    c. A variable interval schedule
    d. A variable ratio schedule

16. Rosch-Heider, who studied cognitive universalism, would most likely agree with the language development theories of
    a. Vygotsky
    b. Piaget
    c. both Vygotsky and Piaget
    d. neither Vygotsky nor Piaget

LEARNING AND LANGUAGE DEVELOPMENT

CHAPTER 6 • Assessment

TEST YOURSELF

1. b	9. b
2. a	10. a
3. a	11. c
4. d	12. c
5. d	13. a
6. b	14. b
7. c	15. c
8. c	16. b

Ready for Testing

STUDENTS KNOW THEY ARE READY FOR TESTING IF THEY ARE ABLE TO . . .

- Define learning.
- Explain what classical conditioning is, how it works, and how it was discovered.
- Describe the mechanisms of operant conditioning, its application in the real world, and the researchers who contributed to our understanding of the process.
- Introduce cognitive learning theory.
- Define observational learning and describe Bandura's classic experiments in the area of observational learning.
- Explain the basis of language and the relationship between language and thought processes.

CHAPTER 6 • Concept Summary

MULTIMEDIA CONTENT AVAILABLE AT
www.mypsychlab.com

Map the Concepts on **mypsychlab.com**

Study and Review Flashcards on **mypsychlab.com**

STUDY TIPS

Rewriting and Color-Coding Notes While rewriting notes is time-consuming, it is also an excellent way to review. By rewriting their notes, students can make them neater and better organized. As they rewrite, they may see relationships among ideas that they missed in class, and they can refer to their reading assignments to help fill in gaps in their notes or clarify a troublesome point. Suggest that students rewrite their notes as soon as possible after class, while the lecture is still fresh in their minds. Color-coding can make rewriting more fun and can also help to organize material. Students might consider using different colors for different types of information (i.e., terms or dates), to highlight important information or to show relationships among ideas.

CHAPTER 6
Concept Summary: Learning and

Learning Objectives
14.1 **14.2** **14.3** pp. 178–182

Explain the process of classical conditioning

- **key elements**
  - unconditioned stimulus (UCS)
  - unconditioned response (UCR)
  - conditioned stimulus (CS)
  - conditioned response (CR)
- **key features**
  - stimulus generalization
  - stimulus discrimination
  - extinction
  - spontaneous recovery

Learning Objectives
15.1 **15.2** **15.3** **15.4** pp. 184–192

Explain the process of operant conditioning

- **reinforcement** is any event or stimulus that, when following a response, increases the probability that the response will occur again
- **punishment** is any event or stimulus that, when following a response, decreases the probability that the response will occur again

Positive Reinforcement

Learning Objectives
16.1 **16.2** **16.3** pp. 195–199

Identify the aspects of cognitive and observational learning

- **observational learning** is the learning of a new behavior through the observation of a model
  - Bandura and "Bobo doll" study
- **key elements for learner**
  - pay attention to the model
  - able to remember what was done
  - capable of reproducing, or imitating, the actions of the model
  - have the desire or motivation to perform the action
- **cognitive learning theory** focuses on role of thought processes on learning

210 CHAPTER 6

What Every Student Should Know About . . .

PRIORITIZING

Life for many students is a balancing act. Attending classes takes up only part of the day. Family obligations, work, friends, exercise sessions, recreation . . . the list goes on. It is clear that today's students need to be good at "multitasking" and setting priorities. Priorities are defined as what is most important to a person. Everyone's priorities are different. Although family and church might be a priority for one person, sports and socializing might be a priority for another. Identifying one's priorities assists the person in accomplishing goals and in achieving success.

210 Chapter 6 Learning and Language Development

Language Development

Map The Concepts on mypsychlab.com

Learning Objectives

17.1 pp. 201–202

Identify the structural features of language

- **language** is a system of combining symbols to communicate
  - grammar
  - syntax
  - morphemes
  - phonemes
  - semantics
  - pragmatics

- **the relationship between language and thought**
  - does language influence thought or does thinking influence language?
  - animal studies in language

Learning Objectives

17.2 **17.3** **17.4** pp. 202–205

Explain theories and stages of language acquisition

- **Piaget** — people learn concepts first, and later acquire words to describe that concept.
- **Vygotsky** — language helps develop concepts.
- **Language learning process** — cooing, babbling, one-word speech, telegraphic speech, whole sentences.
- **Chomsky** — proposed the **Language Acquisition Device (LAD)**

Learning Objective

17.5 pp. 205–206

Identify areas of the brain associated with language.

- **Broca's area** in the left frontal lobe affects language production
- **Wernicke's area** in the left temporal lobe affects language comprehension

LEARNING AND LANGUAGE DEVELOPMENT

CHAPTER 6 • Concept Summary

STUDY TIPS

Consistent Notebook Organization An organized notebook is an important study tool. Suggest that students consider using one large notebook with dividers. The advantage of this approach is less time spent searching for the right notebook or discovering that students have left the notebook they need at home, at school, or in their locker. Many find that a three-ring binder works best, because pages can easily be added or removed and homework papers and tests can be punched for inclusion. Make sure students use the tab dividers in the notebook so they can easily find the subject they need; organizing the sections in order of their schedule is one option. Recommend that students include a separate section for listing homework assignments, so they do not have to page through each subject to find their assignments. A front pocket is handy for keeping homework assignments. Encourage students to go through their notebooks weekly to discard old papers and make sure the pages are in the right sections.

Comprehension Check

ROLE MODELS: WHO AND WHY

Much attention in the popular media is given to the notion of role models. Social learning theory supports the idea that many of our behaviors are learned through observation and imitation. Ask students to identify the characteristics of individuals likely to serve as role models. Why are particular individuals more likely to become role models? What characterizes the relationship between the learner and the role model? Next, consider the imitative behavior that is often observed between "best friends" who share expressions, gestures, and other behaviors. Can peers be role models for one another? Using principles of learning discussed in the chapter, how can students explain such behaviors?

CHAPTER 7 • Module 18

Launch the Chapter

CHAPTER GOALS AND LEARNING OBJECTIVES

Module 18 Social Influence

Explore how social influence affects behavior.

18.1 Do people act differently in different situations?

18.2 How does the presence of others affect an individual's behavior?

18.3 How do group dynamics influence behavior?

18.4 How can an individual change a group's behavior?

Module 19 Social Cognition

Understand the effects of social cognition.

19.1 What are attitudes, and how do they relate to behavior?

19.2 How can attitudes be changed?

19.3 How do people use attribution theory to explain the actions of others?

Module 20 Social Interaction

Describe different kinds of social relations.

20.1 How are prejudice and discrimination different?

20.2 What factors govern attraction and love?

20.3 How does aggressive behavior develop?

20.4 What is prosocial behavior?

DIFFERENTIATED INSTRUCTION KEY

Look for these symbols to help you adjust steps in each lesson to meet your students' needs.

- **L1** Special Needs
- **L2** Basic
- **ELL** English Language Learners
- **LPR** Less Proficient Readers
- **L3** All Students
- **L4** Advanced Students

CHAPTER 7

Social Psychology

The Unresponsive Bystander: Why Did No One Help?

On March 13, 1964, at about 3:15 in the morning, a man who didn't even know Catherine "Kitty" Genovese caught her in the parking lot of her apartment complex, stabbed her, left, and then came back nearly half an hour later to assault and kill her in the entryway of the complex. A police investigation determined that while several neighbors heard Kitty's screams or saw some part of the assault, most of the witnesses to the attack did not help her—they may have been uncertain about what was happening, they may have thought Kitty was out of danger after the first assault, or they may have thought that other people would take responsibility and help. Of the few witnesses who did try to help (by shouting at the attacker, for example), no one could do enough to prevent the murder (Delfiner, 2001; Gado, 2004; Rosenthal, 1964).

Forty-three years later on June 23, 2007, 27-year-old LaShanda Calloway was killed during an argument in a convenience store. It took 2 minutes for someone to call 911. Surveillance video captured the attack, including the five shoppers who stepped over her bleeding form and continued shopping. One customer did stop—to take a picture of Ms. Calloway as she lay dying on the floor (Hegeman, 2007).

Events such as these have prompted innovations like the development of the 911 emergency call system, and they have inspired psychologists to ask questions about why witnesses behave the way they do in violent or dangerous situations. How could people coldly and callously step over a bleeding, dying woman and then continue to shop? Were they simply afraid to get involved? Or did all those people simply assume that the situation was someone else's responsibility? Could LaShanda Calloway have been saved if someone had tried to stop the bleeding or render some kind of first aid?

CORRELATION TO APA STANDARDS FOR CHAPTER 7

IVA. SOCIAL INTERACTIONS

IVA-1. Social cognition	pp. 224–230
IVA-2. Social influence	pp. 214–221
IVA-3. Social relations	pp. 232–241

MODULE 18 ▸ **SOCIAL INFLUENCE**
MODULE 19 ▸ **SOCIAL COGNITION**
MODULE 20 ▸ **SOCIAL INTERACTION**

Why Study?

Social Psychology

Human beings are social creatures—we have adapted over time to meet our survival needs by living with others, working with others, and playing with others. The people who surround us impact our beliefs and values, decisions and assumptions, and how we think about other people in general. Why are some people prejudiced toward certain others? Why do we obey some people but not others? What causes us to like, to love, or to hate others? These answers and more are found in the study of social psychology.

SOCIAL PSYCHOLOGY 213

CHAPTER 7 • Module 18

Teacher Prep

Social psychology is the scientific study of how a person's behavior, thoughts, and feelings are influenced by the real, imagined, or implied presence of others. Social psychology is divided into three areas of study: (1) social influence, (2) social cognition, and (3) social interaction.

(1) Social influence is the process in which the presence of other people influences the behavior, thoughts, and feelings of an individual. Within this area of study, the following topics are discussed: *Conformity* is changing one's behavior to more closely match the actions of others, and behaviors, including compliance and obedience. *Groupthink* is a type of conformity in which people place more importance on maintaining the cohesiveness of the group rather than assessing the reality of the situation with which the group is concerned.

(2) Social cognition studies the ways people think about other people and includes attitudes and attributions. *Attitude* is the tendency to respond positively or negatively toward a certain person, object, idea, or situation. Attitudes are made up of three components: affect, behavior, and cognition. *Attribution* is the process of explaining human behavior. Attribution theory explains how people make attributions and includes situational and dispositional cause.

(3) Social interaction is the relationships and interactions between people. Social interactions include prejudice and discrimination, liking and loving, and aggression and prosocial behavior.

SCHEDULING

1 Period = 50 min. 1 Block = 90 min.	Semester Course (18 weeks/90 days) Periods/Blocks		Full-Year Course (36 weeks/180 days) Period/Blocks	
Module 18	2.5	1.25	5	2.5
Module 19	2.5	1.25	5	2.5
Module 20	1	0.5	2	1
Total Days for Chapter	6	3	12	6

Chapter 7 Social Psychology 213

CHAPTER 7 • Module 18

Focus

RESOURCES

For this module, consult the appropriate sections of the Teacher's Manual, Test Bank, and PowerPoint slides, all found on the Teacher's Resource DVD, and the interactive study tools for students on MyPsychLab.

BEFORE CLASS

Students should read the section for homework before coming to class.

BELLRINGER

Before study begins on this module, it may be interesting to conduct your own classroom version of the Solomon Asch experiment. Prior to the lesson, place students in groups. Inside envelopes that students will open when the activity begins include "scripts" for the confederates in each group and one set of actual directions for the "participant" in each group. Make copies or transparencies of the lines from Asch's experiment for students to view once the activity begins. Allow students to discuss in groups and then share their answers with the class. Once your experiment has been revealed to the "participants," lead a discussion about how close the class results came to those of Asch.

Teach

COVER THE MODULE

- *Social psychology* is the scientific study of how behavior, thoughts, and feelings are influenced by the real, imagined, or implied presence of others.

18.1 Do people act differently in different situations?

- *Social influence* is the process through which the presence of others influences thoughts, feelings, and behavior of an individual.

214 Chapter 7 Social Psychology

Module 18 Social Influence

Module Goal
Explore how social influence affects behavior.

Learning Objectives
- 18.1 Do people act differently in different situations?
- 18.2 How does the presence of others affect an individual's behavior?
- 18.3 How do group dynamics influence behavior?
- 18.4 How can an individual change a group's behavior?

Explore How Social Influence Affects Behavior

How does society affect our thoughts and behavior? Like other areas of psychology, the field of social psychology looks at behavior and mental processes, but it also considers the social world in which we exist. **Social psychology** is the scientific study of how behavior, thoughts, and feelings are influenced by the real, imagined, or implied presence of others.

18.1 Do people act differently in different situations?

Social psychologists like to talk about "the power of the situation," but what does this phrase really mean? Think about how the actions you perform every day are affected by the people around you. Do you behave the same way when you're hanging out with your friends and when you're attending a challenging class at school? When you go to see a movie with other people, do you find yourself laughing when others laugh, even if you probably wouldn't think the movie was very funny if you watched it by yourself? Maybe you are funny and outspoken when you're around your friends and family members, but you're more shy and reserved when you meet strangers or authority figures. These examples all illustrate the power that social situations have over our thoughts and our behavior. Our ideas and actions don't remain consistent from day to day and from place to place—they are constantly influenced by the different situations in which we find ourselves and by the different people who make up our social world.

People share this world with other people. From our infancy, others have an impact on our actions, personality, and growth. We continue to interact with others, and their presence influences our behavior, feelings, and thoughts. For example, a pioneer in social psychology named Kurt Lewin conducted research on leadership styles and found that the productivity and attitudes of a group could change dramatically when the leader's leadership style changed (Lewin et al., 1939). This finding is one example of a process called **social influence**. People can influence others to obey, or disobey, authority figures. The mere presence of others can even influence how people perform tasks.

social psychology the scientific study of how a person's thoughts, feelings, and behavior are influenced by the real, imagined, or implied presence of others.

social influence the process through which the real or implied presence of others can directly or indirectly influence the thoughts, feelings, and behavior of an individual.

214 CHAPTER 7

Terms

- social psychology • social influence • conformity • consumer psychology
- compliance • foot-in-the-door technique • door-in-the-face technique
- norm of reciprocity • lowball technique • that's-not-all technique • obedience
- social facilitation • social impairment • social loafing • groupthink

18.2 How does the presence of others affect an individual's behavior?

Conformity Have you ever seen someone looking up at something? Did the urge to look up to see what that person was looking at become so strong that you actually found yourself looking up? This common practical joke clearly demonstrates the power of **conformity**: changing one's own behavior to more closely match the actions of others.

In 1936, social psychologist Muzafer Sherif conducted a study in which small groups of two or three participants at a time were exposed to a single point of light in a dark room. Involuntary movements of the eye will cause the light to appear to move, but the participants were not told of that effect. **LINK** to Chapter Three: Sensation and Perception, pp. 81–84. They reported the distance that they perceived the light moving. But when a confederate (a person chosen by the experimenter to deliberately manipulate the situation) also gave estimates, the real participants changed their answers to be similar to the confederate's estimates (Sherif, 1936). Although we know that the perception of light's motion is not objectively measurable, this study raised the question: Do people conform so easily under measurable conditions?

Solomon Asch (1951) conducted the first of his classic studies on conformity by inviting seven participants to participate in an experiment on visual judgment. They were shown three black lines of varying lengths, followed by a single line. The task was to match most closely the length of the single line to one of the three. (See Figure 18.1.) Notice that in Sherif's experiment, there was no "right" answer to the question of how far the stimulus moved, because the stimulus (the point of light) was not actually moving at all. In Asch's experiment, however, the stimuli (the three lines) were clearly of different lengths, so subjects were able to give correct or incorrect answers.

Watch on **mypsychlab.com**

conformity changing one's own behavior to match that of other people.

Watch a video conformity on **mypsychlab.com**

FIGURE 18.1 Matching Lines in Asch's Study

Participants in Asch's famous study on conformity were first shown the three lines on the left. They were then shown the line on the right and asked to determine which of the three lines on the left it was most similar to. Which line would you pick? What if you were one of several people, and everyone who answered ahead of you chose line 3? How would that affect your answer? *Source:* Adapted from Asch (1956).

SOCIAL PSYCHOLOGY 215

CHAPTER 7 • Module 18

COVER THE MODULE

18.2 How does the presence of others affect an individual's behavior?

- *Conformity* is changing one's own behavior to more closely match the actions of others.
- Muzafer Sherif conducted a study in 1936 to learn about conformity behaviors by asking participants to estimate the distance covered by a light appearing to move. Participants changed their answers to more closely align with the answers of a "confederate."

LINK to Chapter Three: Sensation and Perception, pp. 81–84

- Solomon Asch conducted a study in 1951 asking participants to compare lines of varying lengths.
  - Asch found that participants conformed to incorrect answers one-third of the time.
  - Also, conformity decreased if at least one person who agreed with participants was present.

MULTIMEDIA CONTENT AVAILABLE AT
www.mypsychlab.com

Watch a video on conformity on **mypsychlab.com**

Class Demonstration

CONFORMING BEHAVIOR

Give the class the following instructions and allow students a few minutes to write their answers: "For **one** of the following situations, describe what you would wear and how you would behave: (1) at a movie with your friends vs. with your friends' parents and family members, (2) at a sports event in which you are participating vs. one in which you are the audience, (3) babysitting or in a position of authority around smaller children vs. hanging out with friends."

Once students are finished writing, place them in groups according to the situation each student wrote about. Ask the group members to share their answers with each other, and then, with the class reassembled, ask the following questions: "(1) How is our behavior affected by the presence of others? (2) Why do people conform? (3) Is it good or bad to conform? Why?" Have students share their answers with the class.

CHAPTER 7 • Module 18

COVER THE MODULE (continued)

- **Compliance**
  - *Compliance* occurs when people change their behavior due to others' requests or directions.
  - *Consumer psychology* studies why people buy things or are persuaded to make purchases
    - *Foot-in-the-door technique:* asking for a small commitment, and once compliance is gained, asking for a larger commitment
    - *Door-in-the-face technique:* asking for a large commitment and after being refused, asking for a smaller, more reasonable commitment
    - *Norm of reciprocity:* assumption that if someone does something for a person, that person should do something for the other in return
    - *Lowball technique:* getting a commitment from a person and then raising the cost of the commitment
    - *That's-not-all technique:* the persuader makes an offer and adds something extra to make the offer look better and to activate the norm of reciprocity

DISCUSS THE STUDENT VOICE QUESTION

Ask students if they or anyone they know has fallen for any of the compliance techniques and have them share the stories with the class.

L3 DIFFERENTIATED INSTRUCTION

During class discussions, have students share their responses with a partner to build confidence and accountability to respond, even if all students do not participate in the discussion.

I have a friend who watches infomercials and buys stuff that isn't worth the money or that doesn't work like it's supposed to work. Why do people fall for pitches like that? ▶

consumer psychology branch of psychology that studies the habits of consumers in the marketplace.

compliance changing one's behavior as a result of other people directing or asking for the change.

foot-in-the-door technique asking for a small commitment and, after gaining compliance, asking for a bigger commitment.

door-in-the-face technique asking for a large commitment and being refused, and then asking for a smaller commitment.

norm of reciprocity assumption that if someone does something for a person, that person should do something for the other in return.

lowball technique getting a commitment from a person and then raising the cost of that commitment.

The experiment was not about visual judgment; in fact, there was only one true participant in each group of seven. The others had been instructed to pick the same *incorrect* answer. Would the real participant, always placed next to last, change what he knew was correct to conform to the group's opinion? Surprisingly, the participants conformed to the group answer over one-third of the time. Asch also found that conformity increased with each confederate's additional incorrect answer until four incorrect answers had been given (Asch, 1951). In a later experiment, Asch (1956) found that conformity decreased if at least one other person who agreed was present.

Are women more likely to conform than men? In private, conformity is no greater for women than for men, but if a public response is required, women tend to show a bit more conformity than men (Eagly, 1987; Eagly et al., 2000). This effect may be due to the socialization that women receive in being agreeable and supportive.

Compliance

I have a friend who watches infomercials and buys stuff that isn't worth the money or that doesn't work like it's supposed to work. Why do people fall for pitches like that?

Marketing products is very much a psychological process. In fact, the whole area of **consumer psychology** studies why people buy things and how people are persuaded to make purchases. But infomercials are not the only way people try to get others to do what they want them to do. **Compliance** occurs when people change their behavior due to others' requests or directions. The person or group asking for the change typically doesn't have any real authority or power; when that authority does exist and behavior is changed as a result, it is called *obedience*. A number of techniques to arouse compliance in others have been used in the world of marketing—for example, door-to-door salespeople commonly use these techniques.

Let's say that a neighbor asks you to water his plants while he is on vacation. You agree, thinking that it's a rather small request. Later, the neighbor asks if you would also walk and feed his dogs every day while he is away. This seems more involved and requires more time and energy. If you are like most people, you will probably comply with this second, larger request because you have already agreed to the smaller one and want to behave consistently with your previous response (Cialdini et al., 1995; Dillard, 1990, 1991; Freedman & Fraser, 1966). This is called the **foot-in-the-door technique** because the first small request acts as an opener. (Salespeople once literally stuck a foot in a potential customer's door to prevent the occupant from shutting it so they could continue their sales pitch.)

Another method of gaining compliance is the **door-in-the-face technique** (Cialdini et al., 1975). In this method, the larger request comes first, and it is usually refused. This is followed by a second smaller and more reasonable request that often gains compliance. What if that neighbor first asked you to take care of his dog and cat in your home? If you refused to do so, the neighbor might ask if you would at least water his plants, which you would probably do.

This technique relies on the **norm of reciprocity**: If someone does something for you, you feel obligated to return the favor (Gouldner, 1960). This is also the principle behind free samples and gifts, such as stickers that accompany sales pitches or requests for donations.

A third compliance technique is called the **lowball technique** (Burger & Petty, 1981). In this technique, once a commitment is made, the cost of that

216 CHAPTER 7

Class Demonstration (Kinesthetic)

COMPLIANCE TECHNIQUES

As a homework assignment, ask students to gather as many examples of the compliance techniques from their own life experiences as they can. When students return to class with their examples, group students according to the types of compliance examples they found. Have each group select its favorite example and act out a skit for the class that demonstrates the example. Here are some examples of each technique students may find:

- Foot-in-the-door: A sibling asks Mom for a small toy or treat at the store, and then when asked to choose one, chooses a larger one than originally allowed.

- Door-in-the-face: A student asks Mom to have a friend stay overnight and when she refuses, the student then asks if the friend can come for dinner or for a few hours after school.

- Norm of reciprocity: Mom carpools one way to an activity, and then another mother carpools on the way back.

- Lowball: A sibling asks for one cookie from the plate and then takes more cookies from the plate without asking.

216 Chapter 7 Social Psychology

commitment is increased. If you've ever made a big purchase—like a car or a computer—you probably know that the commitment to buy the item at a low price is quickly followed by the addition of other costs: extended warranties, additional options, taxes and fees, and so on, causing you to spend more money than you'd anticipated. This technique can backfire when a consumer becomes angry about the "hidden" costs and walks out without making a purchase.

Finally, there is the now familiar technique of the infomercial salesperson: the **that's-not-all technique**. See if this sounds familiar: "But wait—that's not all! If you call now, we'll send you this 15-piece set of genuine faux carving knives as a bonus!"

In this compliance tactic, while the consumer considers the offer, but before the decision is made, the pitcher adds something to activate the norm of reciprocity (Burger, 1986). The consumer feels as though the seller is being generous, and the consumer should comply as a return favor.

People of different cultures are not equally susceptible to these techniques. Research has shown that people in individualist cultures (such as the United States) are more likely to comply with the second request of the foot-in-the-door technique than are people in collectivist cultures (such as in Japan). This suggests that people in collectivist cultures are less concerned with being consistent with previous behavior because they are less focused on their inner motivation than are people in individualist cultures (Cialdini et al., 1999; Petrova et al., 2003). **LINK** to Chapter Eight: Culture and Gender, pp. 255–256.

Obedience There is a difference between compliance and **obedience**, defined as changing one's behavior at the direct order of an authority figure. A salesperson has no real power, but an authority figure is a person with social power—such as a police officer, a teacher, or a work supervisor—and the right to demand certain behavior from people. How far will people go in obeying the commands of an authority figure?

Social psychologist Stanley Milgram was aware of Asch's studies of conformity and wondered how much impact social influence could have on behavior. He designed what has become one of the most famous experiments in the history of psychology, known as "Milgram's Study of Obedience to Authority."

In a carefully designed experiment, participants signed up to research the effects of punishment on learning behavior (Milgram, 1964a, 1974). The participants believed that they had randomly been assigned to either a "teacher" role or a "learner" role. In fact, the "learner" was always an actor who would pretend to react to what the "teacher" did. The task for the "learner" was a simple memory test. **Watch** on mypsychlab.com

The "teacher" (who was actually the sole participant in the experiment) was told to punish the "learner" for incorrect answers by administering electrical shocks through a machine. For each mistake the "learner" made, the "teacher" was instructed to increase the level of shock by 15 volts. The "learner" (who was not actually shocked) was out of sight of the teacher—but the teacher could hear his reactions to the shocks. According to a script, the "learner" reacted to the increasing shocks by showing discomfort, begging, screaming, and eventually falling silent as if unconscious—or dead. (See Table 18.1 on the next page for samples of the scripted responses.) As the "teachers" hesitated to continue administering the shocks, the experimenter in his authoritative white lab coat said, for example, "You must continue," and insisted he would take responsibility for the safety of the "learner."

Watch classic video footage on Milgram's obedience study on mypsychlab.com

that's-not-all technique a sales technique in which the persuader makes an offer and then adds something extra to make the offer look better before the target person can make a decision.

obedience changing one's behavior at the command of an authority figure.

SOCIAL PSYCHOLOGY **217**

CHAPTER 7 • Module 18

COVER THE MODULE *(continued)*

- **Obedience**
  - *Obedience* involves changing one's behavior at the command of an authority figure.
  - Stanley Milgram designed a famous experiment in which "teachers" supposedly shocked "learners" at the insistence of the experimenter.

MULTIMEDIA CONTENT AVAILABLE AT
www.mypsychlab.com

Watch classic video footage on Milgram's obedience study on **mypsychlab.com**

FAST FACT

The original Simulated Shock Generator and Event Recorder, or *shock box*, through which "punishment" was administered in Milgram's experiment, is now located in the Archives of the History of American Psychology at the University of Akron.

Class Demonstration (Kinesthetic)

CLASSROOM VERSION OF MILGRAM'S STUDY OF OBEDIENCE

Conduct the following demonstration as an introduction to your lecture on Milgram:

1. Announce that the following activity is for a "participation grade" worth a large percentage of students' final grade and that participation is mandatory.

2. Go through a series of increasingly bizarre requests with the class. For example:
   - Ask students to switch seats with one another.
   - Ask students to exchange their watches/accessories with another student.
   - Ask students to empty their pockets/purses/backpacks in the middle of the floor.
   - Ask students to stand up individually and do something silly in front of the class.

3. End the session with a big round of applause. Once students return to their seat, lead the class in a discussion of their thoughts during the activity, why they participated, at what point they may have wanted to stop participating, and whether we should always obey authority.

Module 18 Social Influence **217**

CHAPTER 7 • Module 18

EXTEND THE LESSON

As noted in the text, Milgram's study raised the ethical issue: *How far should researchers be willing to go to answer a question?*

LINK to Chapter One: The Science of Psychology, pp. 23–24

Place signs in each corner of the room that read: (1) Strongly Agree, (2) Somewhat Agree, (3) Strongly Disagree, and (4) Somewhat Disagree. Present the following statements and have students move to the corner of the room that best describes their opinion. Have students discuss their thoughts as a group and then share with the class.

- Milgram's study was ethical.
- There should be no limits placed on psychological studies in order to make discoveries that would help to avoid life-threatening situations.
- Milgram's study would be allowed to happen today.

TEACHING TIP

Be a role model for respecting others. Teenagers can be sensitive to criticism and correction, particularly from a teacher. Your actions will set the tone for how classmates treat one another.

Table 18.1	Sample Script Items from Milgram's Classic Experiment
VOLTAGE	**LEARNER'S SCRIPT**
150	"Ugh! Experimenter! That's all. Get me out of here. I told you I had heart trouble. My heart's starting to bother me now. Get me out of here, please. My heart's starting to bother me. I refuse to go on. Let me out."
210	"Ugh! Experimenter! Get me out of here. I've had enough. I *won't* be in this experiment any more."
300	(*Agonized scream*) "I absolutely refuse to answer any more. Get me out of here. You can't hold me here. Get me out. Get me out of here."
330	(*Intense and prolonged agonized scream*) "Let me out of here. Let me out of here. My heart's bothering me. Let me out, I tell you. (*Hysterically*) Let me out of here. Let me out of here. You have no right to hold me here. Let me out! Let me out! Let me out of here! Let me out! Let me out!"

Source: Milgram (1964a, 1974).

Milgram surveyed a wide range of people prior to the experiments to predict how far the participants would go in giving shocks. Many believed that the most participants would refuse to go on as soon as the "learner" protested when the "teacher" reached 150 volts. No one thought that any participant would go up to the highest voltage.

So were they right? Far from it—in the first set of experiments, 65 percent of the "teachers" administered the experiment's final 450-volt shock level, although many were obviously uncomfortable and begged to be allowed to stop. Of those who finally did stop, not one "teacher" stopped before reaching 300 volts!

No one was more stunned than Milgram by how obedient people could be. These experiments have been repeated at various times in the United States and in other countries, and the percentage of participants who went all the way has remained between 61 and 66 percent (Blass, 1999).

That's incredible—I just don't believe that I could do something like that to someone else.

Researchers have not identified any one trait or group of traits that consistently predicts who will obey in experiments similar to Milgram's original studies (Blass, 1991). The people who "went all the way" were simply average people, caught in a situation of "obey or disobey" the authority.

Milgram's research also raised a serious ethical question: How far should researchers be willing to go to answer a question of interest? Milgram's experiment involved excessive deception and caused participants severe psychological distress; under the current ethical rules that exist for such research, this study would most likely not be allowed to happen today. **LINK** to Chapter One: *The Science of Psychology*, pp. 23–24.

Task Performance: Social Facilitation and Social Loafing Social influence can also affect an individual's task performance. The ease of a task can have an impact: If a task is perceived as easy, the presence of other people seems

> *That's incredible—I just don't believe that I could do something like that to someone else.*

218 CHAPTER 7

Explore

THE INFLUENCE OF OBEDIENCE ON HISTORICAL EVENTS

Assign students **one** of the following three topics to research: (1) the Nazi regime and the Holocaust; (2) civil disobedience during the Civil Rights Movement; or (3) the My Lai massacre during the Vietnam War. Have students write down answers to the following questions while researching:

- Who were the leaders or authority figures?
- What laws or orders were participants expected to obey?
- What actions were taken by participants in obedience/disobedience?
- What were the consequences of these actions?
- What motivated participants to obey/disobey? Did they believe they had a choice? Why or why not?
- Based upon your findings, is it acceptable to disobey authority figures? When? Why?

To extend the exploration, have students meet in groups to share their findings and finally present their group findings to the class.

218 Chapter 7 Social Psychology

to improve performance, but if the task is perceived as difficult, the presence of others has a negative effect on performance. The positive effect is called **social facilitation**, and the negative influence is sometimes called **social impairment** (Aiello & Douthitt, 2001; Michaels et al., 1982; Zajonc, 1965).

In both social facilitation and social impairment, the presence of other people increases arousal (Zajonc, 1965, 1968; Zajonc et al., 1970). In social facilitation, the presence of others increases arousal just enough to improve performance. But when the task is difficult, arousal is too high, resulting in impaired performance. For example, the presence of others might help you perform well in a play if you've memorized your lines, but it might hurt your ability to give an improvised speech for which you're unprepared.

The rules of social influence affect different individuals differently. For example, people who are lazy may work well alone, but tend to do worse working in groups. This phenomenon is called **social loafing** (Karau & Williams, 1993, 1997; Latané et al., 1979). It is easier for a lazy person (a "loafer") to hide laziness when doing group work because someone in the group will most likely ensure that the task is completed successfully. But when the social loafer works alone, there is no one else to whom the work can be shifted. Interestingly, it appears that Chinese people, who hold a more interdependent cultural viewpoint, tend to assume that each individual within the group is still nearly as responsible for the group's outcome as the group at large (Menon et al., 1999). Chinese people are, therefore, less likely to exhibit social loafing than are Americans.

18.3 How do group dynamics influence behavior?

Groupthink occurs when people within a group feel it is more important to maintain the group's cohesiveness, or unity and togetherness, than it is to consider facts realistically (Hogg & Hains, 1998; Janis, 1972, 1982; Schafer & Crichlow, 1996). One example of the dangerous consequences of groupthink is the *Challenger* disaster of 1986: The launch of the space shuttle *Challenger*, which had been delayed for several days, was finally about to take place when engineers raised concerns that the seals holding the shuttle together would not function properly in the cold weather. The management team decided not to act on the engineers' concerns, and the *Challenger* broke into pieces 2 minutes after its launch, killing everyone on board. Why did the managers say nothing? If they experienced groupthink, they may have felt invulnerable right before the high-profile launch, they may have explained away the engineers' warnings, and they may have felt under pressure to keep silent and let the long-delayed launch proceed as scheduled. The characteristics of groupthink are outlined in Table 18.2 on the next page.

Several things can be done to minimize the possibility of groupthink (Hart, 1998; McCauley, 1998; Moorhead et al., 1998). Choosing impartial leaders and seeking alternate opinions beyond the group both help. Voting should be done in secret, and all group members should be held responsible for decisions made by the group.

Group interaction can also cause *deindividuation*, a person's loss of his or her sense of self caused by the stimulating feeling of being in a group combined with the lack of responsibility that comes from being in a crowd. A self-aware, restrained individual, in the excitement of a group, might forget his or her own moral guidelines and restraints. Large protests that turn into riots are examples of deindividuation in action: In such instances, self-awareness and

social facilitation the tendency for the presence of other people to have a positive impact on the performance of an easy task.

social impairment the tendency for the presence of other people to have a negative impact on the performance of a difficult task.

social loafing the tendency for people to put less effort into a simple task when working with others on that task.

groupthink kind of thinking that occurs when people place more importance on maintaining group cohesiveness than on assessing the facts of the problem with which the group is concerned.

SOCIAL PSYCHOLOGY 219

CHAPTER 7 • Module 18

COVER THE MODULE *(continued)*

- **Task Performance: Social Facilitation and Social Loafing**
  - Task performance is affected by social influence.
  - *Social facilitation* is the tendency for the presence of others to have a positive impact on an easy task due to increased arousal.
  - *Social impairment* is the tendency for the presence of others to have a negative impact on the performance of a difficult task due to arousal that is too high.
  - *Social loafing* is the tendency for people to put less effort into a simple task when working with others than when working alone.

COVER THE MODULE

18.3 How do group dynamics influence behavior?

- *Groupthink* occurs when people place more importance on the cohesiveness of the group than on assessing the facts of the situation.
  - Deindividualism is a person's loss of self caused by stimulation of the group and feelings of lack of individual responsibility due to the crowd.
  - Group polarization is the strengthening of shared beliefs through discussion.

CLASS DISCUSSION

Ask students to think of a time when they did something they would not ordinarily have done because they were in a group situation. Ask for volunteers to share. Then ask why they believe they changed their standards of behavior, what their motivations were, and what the consequences were. Do they think they should be held responsible for their actions?

Critical Thinking

VIEW A FILM AND WRITE ABOUT BULLYING

Remind students that people in groups develop a number of dynamic processes that separate them from a random collection of individuals. These processes include roles, relations, the need to belong, social influence, and effects on behavior. Then have students watch the short animated film entitled "Bully Dance," from the National Film Board of Canada. The film can be found at:

http://rippleeffect.edublogs.org/2011/02/23/our-social-dilemma/

Point out that group dynamics can be both a positive and a negative force in social situations. Ask students to react to the film in a class discussion, answering the following questions: "Who should be held responsible and/or punished for acts of bullying by a group? Just the 'leader' or the entire group?" Then ask students to think of a time when they were involved with or witnessed an act of bullying involving group dynamics. Have them privately write themselves a letter describing their thoughts about the incident and about how to change their behavior to make the situation better.

Module 18 Social Influence 219

CHAPTER 7 • Module 18

COVER THE MODULE

18.4 How can an individual change a group's behavior?

- Influential leaders are individuals who affect the behavior of an entire group.
- The great person theory of leadership states that leaders are extraordinary people who lead because they are born to do it.

UNDERSTANDING VISUALS

After having students review Table 18.2, ask them how each characteristic makes groupthink more powerful and dangerous. Then, as a class, brainstorm ways for a person in a groupthink situation to combat each characteristic and prevent it from continuing.

TEACHING TIP

In discussing topics such as groupthink, bullying, and gangs, be sensitive to students' comfort level with what they are willing to volunteer in class.

L1 DIFFERENTIATED INSTRUCTION

Special Needs Provide an overview of key ideas and concepts presented in the text using outlines, graphic organizers, or study guides.

Table 18.2 Characteristics of Groupthink

CHARACTERISTIC	DESCRIPTION
Invulnerability	Members feel they cannot fail.
Rationalization	Members explain away warning signs and help each other rationalize their decision.
Lack of introspection	Members do not examine the ethical implications of their decision because they believe that they cannot make immoral choices.
Stereotyping	Members stereotype their enemies as weak, stupid, or unreasonable.
Pressure	Members pressure each other not to question the prevailing opinion.
Lack of disagreement	Members do not express opinions that differ from the group consensus.
Self-deception	Members share in the illusion that they all agree with the decision.
Insularity	Members prevent the group from hearing disruptive but potentially useful information from people who are outside the group.

Source: Janis (1972, 1982).

self-control are often abandoned in favor of a "mob mentality" characterized by irresponsible, uninhibited group behavior.

Deindividuation and groupthink aren't the only potential consequences of extensive group interaction. If you talk with people who share your political opinions, the whole group will most likely hold those opinions more and more strongly; these are the effects of *group polarization*, the strengthening of shared beliefs through discussion (Moscovici & Zavalloni, 1969). For example, if you feel fairly optimistic that you will do well on your upcoming psychology test, and you discuss the test with a group of classmates who are also optimistic, you will most likely feel even more optimistic about the test than you did before interacting with the group. Group polarization is often harmless and occasionally beneficial, but it can be dangerous when people who promote acts of violence, hatred, or terrorism get together to discuss radical beliefs.

18.4 How can an individual change a group's behavior?

Just as groups of people can affect an individual's behavior, it's possible for an individual to change the behavior of an entire group. Think about influential leaders from Queen Elizabeth I to Dr. Martin Luther King, Jr. and beyond. Where do leaders come from, and how do they develop their influence over others?

The *great person theory* of leadership, often attributed to 19th century Scottish historian Thomas Carlyle, states that leaders are extraordinary people who lead because they are born to do it. Supporters of this leadership theory might point to Napoleon or George Washington as examples of people born

---

Class Demonstration

GROUP POLARIZATION

Before class, obtain a copy of a Likert scale. (These are easily available on the Internet.) Then choose a "controversial" idea that students will have some sort of opinion about, such as "the next test in class should be taken in a group for a group grade" or "students who have an A in the class are exempt from the exam." Ask students to use the Likert scale to rate their opinion on the topic. Divide students into like-minded groups and have them share their ideas on the topic. Again ask students to rate their opinion on the topic on the Likert scale. Results should be typical of group polarization, with students feeling more strongly than they did before about the issue. Follow the activity with a discussion about why students felt more strongly after having spoken with a group.

to greatness. However, this view ignores external conditions, such as poverty, lack of access to education, the need to put aside one's own goals to care for family members, and other factors that could prevent a "born leader" from leading. Greatness alone is not enough to guarantee successful leadership.

The *transactional view* of leadership proposes that many factors combine to form the right conditions for the right kind of leader. A leader who succeeds under certain conditions may not flourish if the conditions change. For example, Carly Fiorina was a businesswoman and a well-liked leader who worked her way up at AT&T and, as an executive vice president, directed the spinoff of Lucent Technologies. Fiorina used an aggressive and innovative management style to transform Lucent into one of the largest and most profitable technology companies in the 1990s (Burrows, 1999). In 2005, she became CEO of Hewlett-Packard, but her aggressive style, which resulted in a controversial merger of HP and Compaq, did not fit that organization's needs, and Fiorina was forced to resign (Magid, 2005).

A third view of leadership, the *transformational view*, proposes that transformational leaders have certain personality traits that inspire change in individuals and in organizations. A study of 90 effective leaders (Bennis & Nanus, 1985) found that these leaders create positive change among their followers by paying attention to their followers' needs, encouraging creativity and independent thinking, motivating their followers to pursue a vision, and earning their followers' respect and trust.

There are two major leadership styles, both of which affect the group. Leaders can be *task-oriented*, or skilled at getting the goals of the group accomplished efficiently and well. This type of leader often motivates the group, models a personal energy, and challenges the group to do their best, sometimes by encouraging competition. Leaders can also be *relationship-oriented*, or skillful at getting people in the group to work together in harmony. This type of leader is friendly, motivating, and caring, and challenges members of the group to share responsibility and work together (Fiedler, 1967).

Applying Psychology to Everyday Life

Anatomy of a Gang

Why do people join gangs? In the United States today, the term *gang* is generally used to describe a group of people involved in violent or criminal activities, but if gang activities are so often dangerous and illegal, why would anyone want to be a member?

For individuals who feel like outcasts, or who feel like they don't have a place in mainstream society, gangs can offer an alternative social structure. Most humans have a strong desire to be part of a group, and the tight-knit nature of gangs can be appealing to people who feel isolated or alone in the world. Many young people who join gangs come from homes in which there is domestic tension or a lack of parental supervision (Vigil, 1988); for these individuals, who may feel rejected by their biological families, a gang can provide a sense of protection, family, and belonging.

In order to earn respect, acceptance, and status in the gang, a new member may feel pressured to conform to the group's expectations by acting in ways that feel unnatural to him. For example, a new gang

---

CHAPTER 7 • Module 18

COVER THE MODULE *(continued)*

- The transactional view of leadership holds that many factors combine to form the right conditions for the right kind of leader.
  - Certain leadership styles may flourish in one environment but fail in another.
- The transformational view of leadership says that transformational leaders have certain personality traits that inspire change in individuals and organizations.
- There are two major leadership styles:
  - Task-oriented leaders are skilled at getting the goals of the group accomplished efficiently and well.
  - Relationship-oriented leaders are skilled at getting people in the group to work together in harmony.

APPLYING PSYCHOLOGY TO EVERYDAY LIFE

- People join gangs for the following reasons:
  - They feel like outcasts or that they do not have a place in society.
  - Humans have a strong desire to be a part of a group, and gangs offer social structure to those who feel isolated.
  - Young people who come from troubled or broken homes find a sense of protection, family, and belonging in gangs.
- To gain acceptance in a gang, a new member feels pressure to conform to the group's expectations, acting in ways that feel unnatural (e.g., the new member may act aggressive or uncaring, even if he is not comfortable with being that way).

Explore (Kinesthetic)

LEADERSHIP STYLES

Students can read biographies of famous leaders at the following website:

www.thefamouspeople.com/political-leaders.php

Host a "Leadership Conference" in your classroom:

1. Allow students to choose a leader of interest to explore, subject to your approval.
2. Students should come dressed as the person they studied and assume the personality of the leader. Students should prepare a short "speech" that includes the leader's lifetime accomplishments and the students' analysis of (1) the leadership view they subscribe to for how their leader was created and (2) the leadership style the leader used to affect the group.
3. Allow students to walk around and "meet" each other, sharing their information.

To add an element of fun, allow the students to vote on the "lifetime achievement award" for their favorite leader of the day.

CHAPTER 7 • Module 18

APPLYING PSYCHOLOGY TO EVERYDAY LIFE *(continued)*

- Gang members experience deindividuation, losing their sense of individuality and melding into the group.
  - These members are more likely to commit violent or illegal acts because the gang's moral code has replaced their own.
- Gang members on the fringe of the gang have an easier time leaving than do those who hold a central role or have been in the gang for a long time.

FAST FACT

As you read out the following statistics to the class, ask for that percentage of students in the room to stand up, so that students can visually conceptualize how prevalent gangs have become.

- Current surveys indicate that approximately 7 percent of teenagers are involved in gangs.
- 20 percent of teens personally know someone who has been killed or injured by gang members.

EXTEND THE LESSON

Divide students into three groups (obedience, groupthink, and leadership style), and have them work together to formulate a list of all the ways their topic affects gang social structure and behavior. Possible answers:

- Obedience can contribute to gang behavior as members push their own moral limits to follow the direction of their leader.
- Groupthink is critical in gang mentality. In order to preserve the group's cohesiveness, every characteristic of groupthink is applicable and exploited.
- A task-oriented leader motivates gang members by expecting the "best" of gang members and fostering competition. A relationship-oriented leader cultivates a cohesive, close-knit group working together in harmony and uses this relationship to motivate members.

---

member may try to "prove" himself by acting aggressive, violent, or uncaring, even if he is not entirely comfortable with his own actions—the desire to be part of a group motivates him to conform to the group's rules and behaviors (Vigil, 1988).

Over time, gang members may experience deindividuation, losing some or all of their sense of self. They may think of themselves not as independent individuals but as part of a group. Gang members who feel deindividualized are typically more likely to commit violent or illegal acts because they feel less responsible for their actions than they otherwise might, and because the gang's moral code has replaced their individual morals and ethics (Skarin et al., 2009).

Because gangs have such powerful social influence over their members, it can be difficult for people to leave gangs for good. According to the U.S. Department of Justice's National Gang Center, while members who have remained on the fringes of a gang can leave the gang relatively easily, long-term gang members or members who have taken on central roles in the gang may struggle to leave—in part because they have come to depend on the gang for protection, social status, and a sense of identity.

Question for Further Discussion

1. What are other ways in which various forms of social influence—such as obedience, groupthink, and leadership—might contribute to gang formation and behavior?

Critical Thinking

CULTIVATE THE STUDENT VOICE

Divide students into groups and have them research ways either to help gang members escape gangs or to prevent teens from joining gangs. Have them create public service announcement (PSA) skits to report their information. Have the class vote on the best PSA and give them the option of filming the group's skit to play on the school's media system to spread the word about what they've learned.

Practice Quiz

Pick the best answer.

1. Solomon Asch's 1951 study with a standard line and comparison lines showed the influence of
   a. compliance
   b. obedience
   c. persuasion
   d. conformity

2. Which of the following is not a characteristic of groupthink?
   a. pressure
   b. objectivity
   c. invulnerability
   d. rationalization

3. Francisco wants to buy a new computer. He sees a computer being sold for what he thinks is a reasonable price, so he commits to buying it. After he makes this commitment, however, he is forced to spend even more money on a warranty, an anti-theft plan, and required software for the computer. Which technique has Francisco been manipulated by?
   a. lowball technique
   b. that's-not-all technique
   c. foot-in-the-door technique
   d. door-in-the-face technique

4. Which of the following techniques relies on the norm of reciprocity?
   a. lowball technique
   b. social loafing technique
   c. foot-in-the-door technique
   d. door-in-the-face technique

5. Milgram's classic 1964 experiment found that
   a. the foot-in-the-door technique is rarely effective
   b. most people are surprisingly obedient to authority
   c. the presence of others improves the performance of easy tasks
   d. women and men are equally likely to conform in group situations

6. Jenna always did well in during group projects because she allowed the rest of the group to do most of the work, but she shared in the good grade. Her new teacher requires each student to complete a different section of a project to prevent students like Jenna from
   a. social loafing
   b. deindividuation
   c. rationalization
   d. invulnerability

7. Gang members who feel deindividualized are typically more likely to
   a. commit violent acts
   b. leave the gang early on
   c. become powerful gang leaders
   d. report gang activity to law enforcement officials

8. The great person theory of leadership states that extraordinary people
   a. will emerge as leaders in any situation
   b. will be in the right place at the right time
   c. will demonstrate the skills needed by the group
   d. will not necessarily be extraordinary if the situation changes

9. Emily refuses to eat her dinner. Her father tells her she cannot go play until she eats all the food on her plate. She folds her arms and refuses. Her father then tells her to eat half her Brussels sprouts and take three bites of salad. Emily happily gobbles up the limited amount of food and rushes outside to play. Which technique did Emily's father use?
   a. lowball
   b. that's not all
   c. door-in-the-face
   d. foot-in-the-door

10. The branch of psychology devoted to figuring out why people buy things is
    a. social psychology
    b. marketing psychology
    c. compliance psychology
    d. consumer psychology

CHAPTER 7 • Module 18

Assess

Assign the Module 18 Practice Quiz.

Use the Practice Quiz to identify gaps in student understanding.

REMEDIATE

Have students, individually or in groups, review the module goals, learning objectives, and key terms.

Refer students to the Concept Summary on p. 246 for review.

Close

Pose the following questions: "What is the *most* important thing teens should know from what you learned in this section? Why?"

As a class, discuss the top five issues and then narrow them down to the number one choice.

Practice Quiz Answers

1. d
2. b
3. a
4. d
5. b
6. a
7. a
8. a
9. c
10. d

CHAPTER 7 • Module 19

Focus

RESOURCES

For this module, consult the appropriate sections of the Teacher's Manual, Test Bank, and PowerPoint slides, all found on the Teacher's Resource DVD, and the interactive study tools for students on MyPsychLab.

BEFORE CLASS

Students should read the section for homework before coming to class.

BELLRINGER

Have students create a list of topics about which they have likely formed attitudes. Examples include choice of music, foods, or sports teams and teen issues such as underage drinking, parental authority, exercise, and so forth. Allow students to share. Then ask how they believe they formed these attitudes.

Teach

COVER THE MODULE

- Social cognition focuses on the ways people think about others and how our thoughts influence our behavior.
- 19.1 What are attitudes, and how do they relate to behavior?
- An *attitude* is a tendency to respond positively or negatively toward an idea, person, object, or situation.
- Attitudes are learned through experiences and contact with others and are taught by parents, teachers, and others of importance.
- **The ABC Model of Attitudes**
  - A = Affective Component: the emotional component describing the way a person feels toward an object, a person, or a situation

224 Chapter 7 Social Psychology

Module 19 Social Cognition

Module Goal
Understand the effects of social cognition.

Learning Objectives
19.1 What are attitudes, and how do they relate to behavior?
19.2 How can attitudes be changed?
19.3 How do people use attribution theory to explain the actions of others?

Understand the Effects of Social Cognition

Social cognition focuses on the ways in which people think about other people and how those thoughts influence behavior. One area of social cognition concerns the formation and influence of attitudes on the behavior and perceptions of others.

19.1 What are attitudes, and how do they relate to behavior?

An **attitude** can be defined as a tendency to respond positively or negatively toward a certain idea, person, object, or situation (Triandis, 1971). This tendency, developed through peoples' experiences, can affect the way they behave toward those ideas, people, objects, and situations and can include opinions, beliefs, and biases. In fact, attitudes influence the way people view things *before* they've actually been exposed to them (Petty et al., 2003).

How can an attitude have an effect on something that hasn't happened yet?
People are not born with attitudes (although you may know a toddler who makes you question that statement). Attitudes are learned through experiences and contact with others as well as direct instruction from parents, teachers, and other important people. Because attitudes involve positive or negative evaluations, it is possible to go into a new situation, meet a new person, or be exposed to a new idea with one's "mind already made up" (Eagly & Chaiken, 1993; Petty et al., 2003). For example, many children are known for being picky eaters. A child may have tried a food with a certain characteristic, such as a green color, and disliked it. Now the child may have a negative attitude toward all green foods.

The ABC Model of Attitudes Attitudes are actually made up of three different parts, or components, as shown in Figure 19.1 (Eagly & Chaiken, 1993, 1998).

The *affective component* of an attitude is the way a person feels toward an object, person, or situation. *Affect* is used in psychology to mean "emotions" or "feelings," so the affective component might also be called the emotional component. For example, some people might feel that country music is fun and uplifting.

How can an attitude have an effect on something that hasn't happened yet?

attitude a tendency to respond positively or negatively toward a certain person, object, idea, or situation.

224 CHAPTER 7

Terms

- attitude • cognitive dissonance • persuasion • elaboration likelihood model
- central-route processing • peripheral-route processing • attribution • attribution theory • situational cause • dispositional cause • fundamental attribution error

FIGURE 19.1 The ABC Model of Attitudes

The *behavior component* of an attitude is the action that a person takes in regard to the person, object, or situation. For example, a person who feels that country music is fun is likely to turn to a country music station on the car radio, buy country music CDs, or go to a country music concert.

Finally, the *cognitive component* of an attitude is the way a person thinks about the person, object, or situation. These thoughts, or cognitions, include beliefs and ideas about the focus of the attitude. For example, the country music lover might believe that country music is superior to other forms of music.

A person may hold a *general attitude* about something without reflecting that attitude in his or her behavior and see no contradiction. For example, doctors generally hold the attitude that people should protect their health and promote wellness, yet plenty of doctors pay little attention to their own well-being. A very *specific attitude*, such as "exercise is important to my immediate health" makes it more likely to be reflected in behavior (Ajzen, 2001; Ajzen & Fishbein, 2000).

Attitudes do not always predict actual behavior, and strong attitudes are more likely to predict behavior than weak ones. A person who quits smoking because of failing health may have a stronger attitude toward secondhand smoke than someone who quits for financial reasons, for example. Importance of the attitude also plays a role—the more important the attitude appears, the more likely it is that the behavior will match it. Someone who is anti-smoking might be more likely to confront a smoker breaking the rules in a hospital, for example, than a smoker outside the building (Eagly & Chaiken, 1998).

Attitude Formation Attitudes are formed through different types of learning: direct contact, direct instruction, interaction with others, and vicarious or

SOCIAL PSYCHOLOGY 225

CHAPTER 7 • Module 19

COVER THE MODULE (continued)
- B = Behavior Component: the action a person takes in regard to the person, object, or situation
- C = Cognitive Component: the way a person thinks about the person, object, or situation
- General attitude: a person holds an attitude without reflecting it in his or her behavior and without seeing the contradiction
- Specific attitude: an attitude that is more likely to be reflected in behavior

L2 LPR DIFFERENTIATED INSTRUCTION

Less Proficient Readers Less proficient readers are individuals who begin the year 1 or more years below grade level yet do not qualify for special education services. They may or may not be English Language Learners. They may be underprepared for the academic challenges due to difficulties with attention and memory, learning strategies, or vocabulary and reading fluency. It is especially important to engage these students in challenging lessons while incorporating support or instructional scaffolding to increase their likelihood of success.

L3 DIFFERENTIATED INSTRUCTION

Visual/Verbal Learners Ask these students to visualize charts, diagrams, and figures. They can also redraw things from memory.

Critical Thinking

APPLYING THE ATTITUDE FORMATION MODEL

Ask students to choose one attitude from the Bellringer exercise (or one they can think of on their own about which they feel particularly strongly) to elaborate upon. Ask them to analyze their attitude formation according to the ABC model of attitudes. Have them create a chart similar to the one in Figure 19.1 to "map" their selected attitude. Finally, ask students if they believe they hold a general or specific attitude and to explain why.

Module 19 Social Cognition **225**

CHAPTER 7 • Module 19

COVER THE MODULE (continued)

- **Attitude Formation**
  - Attitudes are influenced by: (1) direct contact, (2) direct instruction, (3) interaction with others, and (4) vicarious learning.
- **Cognitive Dissonance: When Attitudes and Behavior Clash**
  - *Cognitive dissonance* occurs when people do or say things that do not match their idea of themselves and thus they experience emotional discomfort.

DISCUSS THE STUDENT VOICE QUESTION

Ask students to think of examples of situations like this in their own experiences. Why do they think a person would get upset? Possible answers include embarrassment, shame, or the sudden revelation causing cognitive dissonance that the person has not thought through yet.

L3 DIFFERENTIATED INSTRUCTION

Auditory/Verbal Learners These students can read their notes or text material into a recorder or get study materials in audio form to play back later.

L3 DIFFERENTIATED INSTRUCTION

Engaging All Learners For some students, make a partial or blank copy of graphics or outlines you will be using in a lesson and require students to write in key information as it is discussed. It is very helpful if you model this filling-in procedure for students. It also helps them to overcome problems with spelling or with capturing complex ideas using only a few words.

FIGURE 19.2 Models of Attitude Formation
Attitudes are formed by direct contact with the person, idea, situation, or object that is the focus of the attitude. Attitudes can also be learned through direct instruction and interaction with others. Vicarious or observational learning is observation of other people's actions and reactions to various objects, people, or situations. An attitude can be learned by observing the emotional reactions of others, and behavior can be observed and imitated.

> Sometimes what people say and what they do are very different. I once pointed this out to a friend of mine who was behaving this way, and he got really upset over it. Why did he get so upset?

observational learning. Figure 19.2 illustrates how each element influences attitude formation.

Attitudes are not only influenced by other people in an individual's immediate world but also by the larger world of the educational system (many attitudes may be learned in school or through reading books) and the mass media of magazines, television, and the movies—a fact of which advertisers and marketing experts are well aware (Gresham & Shimp, 1985; MacKenzie et al., 1986).

Cognitive Dissonance: When Attitudes and Behavior Clash

Sometimes what people say and what they do are very different. I once pointed this out to a friend of mine who was behaving this way, and he got really upset over it. Why did he get so upset?

When people find themselves doing things or saying things that don't match their idea of themselves, they experience an emotional discomfort (and physiological arousal) known as **cognitive dissonance** (Aronson, 1997; Festinger, 1957; Kelly et al., 1997). When people are confronted with the knowledge that something they have done or said was dumb, immoral, or illogical, they suffer an inconsistency in cognitions. For example, they may

226 CHAPTER 7

Class Demonstration

APPLYING MODELS OF ATTITUDE FORMATION

Have students create a mind map, similar to that in Figure 19.2, of an attitude they have formed. In the center of a large piece of paper or poster board, have students complete the following sentence: "I love this _____" or "I hate this _____." Then, ask that they draw or cut and paste pictures in each of the four corners of the paper for direct contact, direct instruction, interaction with others, and vicarious learning that display how they came to hold their attitude about the topic they chose.

have a cognition that says "I'm pretty smart" but also the cognition "That was a dumb thing to do," which causes *dissonance,* or a lack of agreement.

When people experience cognitive dissonance, the resulting tension and arousal are unpleasant, and their motivation is to change something to reduce the unpleasant feelings and tension. There are three things that people do to reduce cognitive dissonance:

1. Change their conflicting behavior to make it match their attitude.
2. Change their current conflicting attitude to justify their behavior.
3. Form new cognitions to justify their behavior.

Take Angelo, for example. He has been raised in a vegetarian family with strong beliefs about caring for animals. Needing money, Angelo gets a job as a bus boy at an all-you-can-eat steak house. Angelo knows that he will financially strain his family if he doesn't keep the job, but he feels terrible that he is earning money by compromising his principles. Angelo is experiencing cognitive dissonance. How can he reduce his discomfort? He could change his behavior by quitting and finding a job at a natural foods restaurant. Or he could change his beliefs; many of his friends are meat eaters anyway. Finally, he could form a new attitude and think of himself as a researcher or educator about vegetarianism. Explore on mypsychlab.com

In a classic experiment conducted at Stanford University by psychologist Leon Festinger and colleague James Carlsmith (1959), each male student volunteer was given a dull task of sorting wooden spools and turning wooden pegs. After the hour, the participants were told to tell the female volunteer in the waiting room that the task was fun. While half of the participants were paid only $1 to try to convince her, the other participants were paid $20 (a considerable sum in the late 1950s). The participants were then given a private survey to determine their enjoyment of the task.

At the time, many researchers would have predicted participants would like the task more if they were paid more because they were getting more reinforcement. But the participants paid only $1 were actually much more likely to report that the boring task had been interesting and fun. The reason is cognitive dissonance: They experienced discomfort at thinking that they would agree to lie to someone for only a dollar, so they talked themselves into believing that the spools really were interesting, after all, and fun, too! They had to change their attitude toward the task so that they could maintain their self-image of honesty. Those who were paid more experienced no dissonance, because they knew exactly why they were lying—for lots of money. (See Figure 19.3.)

Cognitive dissonance theory has often been challenged by other possible explanations. New research on dissonance is emerging, much of it using brain imaging technologies. These studies have found that the brain's left frontal cortex (the language and decision-making part) is particularly active when people are able to reduce dissonance (Harmon-Jones, 2000, 2004, 2006; Harmon-Jones et al., 2008). Since reducing cognitive dissonance is mainly a function of people "talking" themselves into or out of something, this finding is not surprising. But researchers at Yale University have found surprising evidence for cognitive dissonance in both 4-year-old humans and capuchin monkeys—two groups that are not normally thought to have developed the higher level mental abilities (Egan et al., 2007). Are monkeys and preschoolers more complex thinkers than we had assumed? Or are the cognitive processes used to resolve dissonance a lot simpler than previously indicated?

cognitive dissonance sense of discomfort or distress that occurs when a person's behavior does not correspond to that person's attitudes.

Explore cognitive dissonance and attitude change on mypsychlab.com

Inducement	Attitude
$1	+1.35
$20	−0.5
Control	−.45

*Based on a −5 to +5 scale, where −5 means "extremely boring" and +5 means "extremely interesting"

FIGURE 19.3 Cognitive Dissonance: Attitude Toward a Task
After completing a boring task, some participants were paid $1 and some $20 to convince others waiting to do the same task that the task was interesting and fun. Surprisingly, the participants who were paid only $1 seemed to change their own attitude toward the task, rating it as interesting, whereas those who were paid $20 rated the task no differently than a control group did. **Source:** Adapted from Festinger and Carlsmith (1959).

SOCIAL PSYCHOLOGY 227

CHAPTER 7 • Module 19

COVER THE MODULE (continued)

- People can do three things to reduce cognitive dissonance:
  - Change behavior to match attitude.
  - Change attitude to match behavior.
  - Form new cognitions to justify their behavior.

MULTIMEDIA CONTENT AVAILABLE AT
www.mypsychlab.com

Explore cognitive dissonance and attitude change on mypsychlab.com

EXTEND THE DISCUSSION

Ask students why the participants in Festinger and Carlsmith's study would have changed their attitude for only $1. What would their motivation be? Would the students behave in the same way the participants in the study did? Why or why not?

Alternatively, ask students if they can think of a time when, like Angelo, they went against their beliefs for a "good cause." What conflicts did they experience? How did they resolve them?

Class Demonstration

INDUCING COGNITIVE DISSONANCE

Draw a 5-point Likert scale on the board ranging from *strongly agree* to *strongly disagree* and number the options 1 through 5. (Likert scales are easily found on the Internet.) Ask students to privately rate their opinions about the following statements on a blank paper as you read them aloud: (1) Poverty and hunger are serious problems that need attention. (2) Bullying is one of the most important and difficult issues teens face in schools, and something must be done about it.

Next, have students flip their papers over and answer the following questions with a "yes" or "no" to indicate that they perform (or do not perform) the behavior on a regular basis: (1) Do you volunteer in homeless shelters, donate items or money to these causes, or take action to lessen the issues of poverty and hunger locally? (2) Have you personally taken action to stop bullying if you see it occurring?

Lead the class in a discussion comparing their answers to their attitudes on the issues and their behaviors. Did they experience any cognitive dissonance?

Module 19 Social Cognition 227

CHAPTER 7 • Module 19

COVER THE MODULE

19.2 How can attitudes be changed?

- *Persuasion* is the process by which one person tries to change the belief, opinion, position, or course of action of another through argument, pleading, or explanation.

UNDERSTANDING VISUALS

Review each of the concepts in Table 19.1 with students by using sample ads that you or they have collected ahead of class time. Create transparencies of the ads and discuss the source, message, and target audience of each.

MAKING CONNECTIONS

Table 19.1 states that "people in their late teens to mid-20s seem to be more susceptible to persuasion than older people." The advertising industry has identified children and teens as a goldmine of opportunity and has funded dozens of studies to learn how to best market to this age group. One industry newsletter, *Selling to Kids*, describes how many research firms hire psychologists and other experts to learn how best to market to teens to exploit their insecurities and vulnerabilities. Why? Because it is estimated that 78 percent of children influence what their parents buy, teens are being given more independence when it comes to choosing products on which to spend their money, and more and more teens have money to spend.

Ask students if they can think of ads they have seen recently that market directly to them and which techniques are used to do so.

---

persuasion the process by which one person tries to change the belief, opinion, position, or course of action of another person through argument, pleading, or explanation.

elaboration likelihood model model of persuasion stating that people will either elaborate on the persuasive message or fail to elaborate on it and that the future actions of those who do elaborate are more predictable than those who do not.

Obviously, there are still questions to be answered with new research in cognitive dissonance.

19.2 How can attitudes be changed?

Because attitudes are learned, they can change with new learning. The most effective way to change someone else's attitude is to use **persuasion**, the process by which one person tries to change the belief, opinion, position, or course of action of another person through argument, pleading, or explanation.

Persuasion is not a simple matter. There are several factors that become important in predicting how successful any persuasive effort at attitude change might be shown in Table 19.1.

How easily influenced a person is also relates to the way people tend to process information. In the **elaboration likelihood model** of persuasion

Table 19.1   Factors that Influence Persuasion

PERSUASIVE FACTOR	EXPLANATION	EFFECTIVE CHARACTERISTIC(S)
Source	The communicator who delivers the message	• Those who have the most influence are "experts," as well as those who seem trustworthy, attractive, and similar to the person receiving the message (Eagly & Chaiken, 1975; Petty & Cacioppo, 1986, 1996; Priester & Petty, 1995).
Message	The medium through which the source attempts to persuade the target	• The message should be clear and well organized (Booth-Butterfield, 1996). • The message is usually more effective when both sides of an argument are presented to an uncommitted audience (Crowley & Hoyer, 1994; Petty & Cacioppo, 1996; Petty et al., 2003). • Messages that produce fear are more effective if they produce only a moderate amount of fear and also instruct how to avoid the fear-provoking consequences (Kleinot & Rogers, 1982; Meyrick, 2001; Petty, 1995; Rogers & Mewborn, 1976).
Target Audience	The person or group receiving the message	• Audience characteristics are important in determining the effectiveness of the message. Age can be a factor, for example. People in their late teens to mid-20s seem to be more susceptible to persuasion than older people (Visser & Krosnick, 1998).

228   CHAPTER 7

Explore

APPLYING KNOWLEDGE OF PERSUASION TECHNIQUES

Ask students to bring in an advertisement that appeals to them from print sources of their choosing, or to bring in a detailed summary of an advertisement they saw on television. Ask students to analyze the ad's source, message, and target audience. Finally, place students in groups to share their findings. Students should discuss how effective the ads were in appealing to their age group.

This website has a detailed list and explanation of advertising techniques well-suited to the teenage audience:

www.media-awareness.ca/english/resources/educational/handouts/advertising_marketing/mtt_advertising_strategies.cfm

(Petty & Cacioppo, 1986), it is assumed that people either elaborate (add details and information) based on what they hear (the facts of the message) or they do not elaborate at all, preferring to pay attention to the surface characteristics of the message (length, who delivers it, how attractive the message deliverer is, etc.). Two types of processing are hypothesized in this model: **central-route processing**, in which people attend to the content of the message, and **peripheral-route processing**, in which people base their decisions on peripheral cues (factors outside of the message content itself) such as the expertise of the message source, length of the message, and other factors unrelated to message content (Petty & Cacioppo, 1986; Stiff & Mongeau, 2002). An example is if a jury member finds a defendant guilty based on his "shifty eyes" and not on evidence presented.

19.3 How do people use attribution theory to explain the actions of others?

Have you ever watched someone who was doing something you didn't understand? Chances are you were going through a number of possible explanations in your head. The need to explain the behavior of other people seems to be human nature. If no obvious answer is available, people tend to come up with their own reasons. People also need to explain their own behavior. If an explanation isn't obvious, it causes cognitive dissonance. The process of explaining human behavior is called **attribution**. When we make attributions, we ask, "What is causing this behavior? Where is the behavior coming from?"

Attribution theory was originally developed by social psychologist Fritz Heider (1958) as a way of not only explaining why things happen but also why people choose the particular explanations of behavior that they do. There are basically two kinds of explanations—those that involve an external cause and those that assume that causes are internal.

When the cause of behavior is assumed to be from external sources, it is said to be a **situational cause**. The observed behavior seems to be caused by the situation. For example, if John is late to class, his lateness might be explained by heavy traffic or bad weather. On the other hand, if the cause of behavior is assumed to come from within the individual, it is called a **dispositional cause**. In this case, it is the person's internal personality characteristics that are seen as the cause of the observed behavior. Someone might assume that John was late because he is careless, a dispositional cause.

Interestingly, researchers have found that when people are happy in a marriage, they tend to attribute a spouse's positive behavior to an internal cause ("He likes making me happy"), and they attribute a spouse's negative behavior to an external cause ("She must have had a difficult day"). But if the marriage is an unhappy one, the opposite attributions occur (Fincham et al., 2000; Karney & Bradbury, 2000).

The Fundamental Attribution Error The most well-known attributional bias is the **fundamental attribution error**, which is the tendency for people to overestimate the influence of another person's internal characteristics on behavior and underestimate the influence of the situation. In other words, people tend to explain the actions of others based on what "kind" of person they are rather than looking for outside causes such as social influences

central-route processing type of information processing that involves attending to the content of the message itself.

peripheral-route processing type of information processing that involves attending to factors not involved in the message, such as the appearance of the source of the message, the length of the message, and other noncontent factors.

attribution the process of explaining one's own behavior and the behavior of others.

attribution theory the theory of how people make attributions.

situational cause cause of behavior attributed to external factors, such as delays, the action of others, or some other aspect of the situation.

dispositional cause cause of behavior attributed to internal factors such as personality or character.

fundamental attribution error the tendency to overestimate the influence of internal factors in determining the behavior of others while underestimating situational factors.

CHAPTER 7 • Module 19

COVER THE MODULE (continued)

- How easily influenced people are relates to how they process information.
- In the elaboration likelihood model of persuasion, people will either elaborate on the persuasive message or fail to elaborate on it, and the future actions of those who do elaborate are more predictable than the actions of those who do not.
  - In *central-route processing*, people pay attention to the content of the persuasive message.
  - In *peripheral-route processing*, people pay attention to factors not involved in the content of the message, such as appearance or length.

COVER THE MODULE

19.3 How do people use attribution theory to explain the actions of others?

- People have an inherent need to explain their own behavior and that of others. If no explanation is available, it creates cognitive dissonance.
- *Attribution* is the process of explaining human behavior.
- *Attribution theory* explains how people make attributions.
  - *Situational cause* explains that the behavior is caused by the situation the individual was in, or factors outside the individual.
  - *Dispositional cause* explains that the behavior is due to personality or character, or other factors from within the individual.
- *Fundamental attribution* error is the tendency to overestimate the influence of internal factors and underestimate the external factors in determining the behavior of others.

Class Demonstration

TAKE ATTRIBUTION THEORY FOR A SPIN

As students enter the room for class, or at the very beginning of the class period, perform a behavior without explanation that will induce students to form an attribution. For example, walk into class 5 minutes late, ignore students when they arrive, and continue to work at your desk after class begins, or talk on your telephone during class.

Immediately ask students to write down what they thought about your behavior or how they would explain it. Create two columns on the board: (1) Situational Cause and (2) Dispositional Cause. Define the terms and then ask students to read their explanations aloud. As they do, put a check mark in the corresponding column. Lead the class in a discussion of how attribution theory was just demonstrated and analyze the class results for fundamental attribution error.

CHAPTER 7 • Module 19

COVER THE MODULE *(continued)*

- People assume internal causes for behavior more often than external causes because of the following:
  - They are aware of the situational causes of their own behavior, but an observer of a behavior does not have that perspective, so an assumption is made.
  - Actor-observer bias
- To reduce fundamental attribution error and actor-observer bias:
  - Notice how many people are displaying the same behavior.
  - Think about what you would do in the same situation.
- Fundamental attribution error appears to be cultural.
  - In a collectivistic culture, a person may behave to please others rather than to express his or her own attitudes.

MULTIMEDIA CONTENT AVAILABLE AT
www.mypsychlab.com

Explore internal and external attribution on **mypsychlab.com**

L3 DIFFERENTIATED INSTRUCTION

Tactile/Kinesthetic Learners These students can try using musical rhythms as memory aids, putting information to a rhyme or tune.

---

or situations (Blanchard-Fields et al., 2007; Harman, 1999; Jones & Harris, 1967; Leclerc & Hess, 2007; Weiner, 1985).

But why do we do that? Why not assume an external cause for everyone?

When people observe themselves, they are aware of the situational influences on their own behavior. For example, Tardy John knows that heavy traffic and an unexpected rainstorm made him late to work—he was *there*, after all. But someone else looking at John's behavior doesn't have the opportunity to see all of the possible situational influences and has only John himself in focus. This observer might assume that John's tardiness is caused by some internal personality flaw.

Other research has shown that when students are given an opportunity to make attributions about cheating, they demonstrate the fundamental attribution error and actor-observer bias: If others are cheating, it's because they are not honest people, but if the students themselves are cheating, it is because of the situation (Bogle, 2000).

Can the tendency to make these errors be reduced? There are several strategies for making errors in attribution less likely. One is to notice how many other people are doing the same thing. As teachers, we often have students who arrive late to class. When it is only one student and it happens frequently, the assumption is that the student is not very careful about time (dispositional cause). But when a large number of students come straggling in late, the assumption becomes "there must be a wreck on the bridge," which is a situational attribution. In other words, if a lot of people are doing something, it is probably caused by an outside factor.

Another way of reducing attribution error is to think about what you would do in the same situation. If you think that you might behave in the same way, the cause of behavior is probably situational. People should also make the effort of looking for causes that might not be obvious. If John were to look particularly "stressed out," for example, the assumption might be that something stressed him out, and that "something" might have been heavy traffic.

Although the fundamental attribution error has been found in American culture (Jones & Harris, 1967), it is not necessarily universal. Masuda and Kitayama (2004) had American and Japanese participants listen to a prewritten attitudinal statement read by a target and give their opinion on the target's real attitude. American participants made the classic error. The Japanese participants, however, assumed that the person might have been under social obligation to make the statement. In a collectivistic culture, a person might expect to write a paper to please a teacher or employer rather than to express his or her own attitudes. A summary of the research in cross-cultural differences in attribution provides further support for this idea (Peng et al., 2000).

Age is also a factor in how likely someone is to fall prey to the fundamental attribution error. Several studies (Blanchard-Fields & Horhota, 2005; Follett & Hess, 2002; Leclerc & Hess, 2007) have found that older adults show a stronger bias toward attributing the actions of another to internal causes than do younger people. **Explore** on **mypsychlab.com**

But why do we do that? Why not assume an external cause for everyone?

Explore internal and external attribution on **mypsychlab.com**

230 CHAPTER 7

Class Demonstration (Kinesthetic)

EXPLORING THE FUNDAMENTAL ATTRIBUTION ERROR

Remind students that the fundamental attribution error is the tendency for people to overestimate the influence of another person's internal characteristics on behavior and underestimate the influence of the situation. Then divide the class into student pairs. Ask each pair to write a short script or scenario in which a person exhibits a particular behavior. The pair should indicate (1) how the person's internal characteristics might be influencing the behavior and (2) how the specific situation might be influencing the behavior. Ask volunteers to act out their scenario for the rest of the class.

CHAPTER 7 • Module 20

Focus

RESOURCES
For this module, consult the appropriate sections of the Teacher's Manual, Test Bank, and PowerPoint slides, all found on the Teacher's Resource DVD, and the interactive study tools for students on MyPsychLab.

BEFORE CLASS
Students should read the section for homework before coming to class.

BELLRINGER
Ask students to take a few moments to create a list of as many words to describe human interactions or relationships they can think of. Put four columns on the board: (1) Prejudice/Discrimination, (2) Attraction/Love, (3) Aggression, and (4) Prosocial. Ask students to volunteer some items from their list and discuss with the class the column in which each item belongs. Track students' answers on the board.

Teach

INTRODUCE THE TOPIC
Explain to students that this module will discuss social interaction, which is the study of the relationships between people, both casual and intimate. The four categories from the Bellringer will frame the module.

COVER THE MODULE
20.1 How are prejudice and discrimination different?
- *Prejudice* is an attitude held by a person about the members of a particular social group.
- *Discrimination* is treating people differently because of prejudice.
- An *in-group* is a social group with whom an individual identifies ("us").
- An *out-group* is a social group with whom an individual does not identify ("them").
- A *stereotype* is a set of characteristics that people believe is shared by all members of a particular social category.

232 Chapter 7 Social Psychology

Module 20 Social Interaction

Module Goal
Describe different kinds of social relations.

Learning Objectives
20.1 How are prejudice and discrimination different?
20.2 What factors govern attraction and love?
20.3 How does aggressive behavior develop?
20.4 What is prosocial behavior?

Describe Different Kinds of Social Relations

Social influence and social cognition are two of the three main areas included in the field of social psychology. The third major area has to do with social interactions with others, or the relationships between people, both casual and intimate. Social interactions include prejudice and discrimination, liking and loving, and aggression and prosocial behavior.

20.1 How are prejudice and discrimination different?

When a person holds an unsupported and often negative stereotyped attitude about the members of a particular social group, it is called **prejudice**. When prejudicial attitudes cause members of a particular social group to be treated differently in situations that call for equal treatment, it is called **discrimination**. Prejudice is the attitude, and discrimination is the behavior that can result from that attitude. Therefore discrimination can be controlled and in some cases eliminated, but it is hard to control prejudicial attitudes. (While prejudicial attitudes themselves are not illegal in the United States, there are many laws that protect against discrimination, or prejudicial behavior.)

There are many kinds of prejudice and discrimination based on age, sex, race or ethnicity, weight, religion, economic status, and other physical and social characteristics. Prejudice can also be based on targeted groups that do not necessarily have a distinct characteristic in common. In any society, there will always be **in-groups** and **out-groups**, or "us" versus "them." The in-group is all the people with whom a particular person identifies and the out-groups are everyone else (Brewer, 2001; Hewstone et al., 2002; Tajfel & Turner, 1986). The formation of in-groups and out-groups begins in childhood (Ruble et al., 2004) and continues as children become adults.

Once an in-group is established, prejudice toward and discriminatory treatment of the out-group or groups soon follow (Brewer, 2001). Out-group members usually become stereotyped according to superficial characteristics, such as hair color. A **stereotype** is a set of characteristics that people believe is shared by all members of a particular social category (Fiske, 1998). Stereotypes (although not always negative) are very limiting, causing people to misjudge what others are like and often to treat them differently as a result. Once

prejudice negative attitude held by a person about the members of a particular social group.

discrimination treating people differently because of prejudice toward the social group to which they belong.

in-groups social groups with whom a person identifies; "us."

out-groups social groups with whom a person does not identify; "them."

stereotype a set of characteristics that people believe is shared by all members of a particular social category.

232 CHAPTER 7

Terms

- prejudice • discrimination • in-groups • out-groups • stereotype • realistic conflict theory • social cognitive theory • social identity theory • social identity • social comparison • stereotype vulnerability • self-fulfilling prophecy • equal status contact • interpersonal attraction • proximity • reciprocity of liking • romantic love • companionate love • aggression • social role • prosocial behavior • altruism • bystander effect • diffusion of responsibility

Practice Quiz

Pick the best answer.

1. On Paul's birthday, his girlfriend Beth doesn't treat him specially. Paul assumes that Beth simply doesn't care about him because she didn't recognize his special day. When he complains, she seems shocked and explains that her family never celebrated birthdays, and asks him if he'd like to go out to celebrate. Paul has possibly made the
   a. assumption error
   b. false consensus error
   c. social categorization error
   d. fundamental attribution error

2. In Asian cultures, people tend to explain the behavior of others as a result of
   a. genetics
   b. personality traits
   c. external, situational factors
   d. internal, dispositional factors

3. Elizabeth's room is almost always a mess. Her parents attribute this to Elizabeth's laziness, which is an example of a
   a. situational cause   c. fundamental cause
   b. superficial cause   d. dispositional cause

4. According to research, which of the following people is MOST likely to commit the fundamental attribution error?
   a. a young person from Japan
   b. an elderly person from Japan
   c. a young person from the United States
   d. an elderly person from the United States

5. Which of the following represents the cognitive component of an attitude?
   a. "I just love Italian food!"
   b. "I'm going to bake lasagna tonight."
   c. "Italian food is the best of the European cuisines."
   d. "Tonight we're going to a new Italian restaurant."

6. Lilly's mother always listens to the classic rock radio station, so Lilly has grown up hearing classic rock and noticing how much her mother enjoys it. Now Lilly says that classic rock is her favorite. Lilly's attitude toward classic rock was most likely acquired through
   a. indirect contact
   b. direct instruction
   c. vicarious learning
   d. interaction with others

7. Physical attractiveness is most involved in which of the following aspects of persuasion?
   a. the target   c. the source
   b. the message   d. the audience

8. Pamela hates when people use their cell phones during class. One day Pamela gets an urgent call during class, and she slips out to take the call. She tells herself that answering a phone during class isn't so bad after all. Pamela is reducing her sense of
   a. attitude formation
   b. cognitive dissonance
   c. social impairment
   d. justified conformity

9. Many times, food companies will market their products to young children by putting images of popular cartoon characters on cereal boxes, egg cartons, snack packs, and yogurt lids. These companies hope that which of the following will influence their target audience?
   a. central-route processing
   b. fundamental attribution error
   c. peripheral-route processing
   d. the elaboration likelihood model

10. In the famous Festinger experiment, participants were paid either $1 or $20 to lie to a woman in the waiting room about how interesting the task really was. The participants who convinced themselves that the task really was fun were the ones who were
    a. paid immediately   c. paid only $1
    b. paid after one day   d. paid $20

SOCIAL PSYCHOLOGY   231

CHAPTER 7 • Module 19

Assess

Assign the Module 19 Practice Quiz.

Use the Practice Quiz to identify gaps in student understanding.

REMEDIATE

Have students, individually or in groups, review the module goals, learning objectives, and key terms.

Refer students to the Concept Summary on p. 246 for review.

Close

Ask students to think of times when they have experienced cognitive dissonance because of (1) attitude and (2) attribution. How did they resolve this dissonance? Are there any examples of dissonance they are currently experiencing? How can they use what they have learned to resolve it?

Practice Quiz Answers

1. d   6. d
2. c   7. c
3. d   8. b
4. c   9. c
5. c   10. c

Module 19 Social Cognition   23

they are formed, stereotypes are difficult to shed (Cameron et al., 2001; Hamilton & Gifford, 1976).

The **realistic conflict theory** of prejudice states that increases in prejudice and discrimination are closely tied to increases in conflict between groups that seek a common resource, such as land or available jobs (Horowitz, 1985; Taylor & Moghaddam, 1994). History is filled with examples of this, including the conflict between early Crusaders and Muslims; conflicts between the Jewish people and the Germans; the conflict between Irish Catholics and Irish Protestants; and the conflict between the native population of you-name-the-country and the colonists who want that land. The section that follows is a classic study that illustrates how easily in-groups and out-groups can be formed and how quickly prejudice and discrimination follow. ⊙⃞Watch on mypsychlab.com

realistic conflict theory theory stating that prejudice and discrimination will be increased between groups that are in conflict over a limited resource.

⊙⃞Watch a video about prejudice on mypsychlab.com

Classic Studies in Psychology

Brown Eyes, Blue Eyes

In a small town in Iowa in 1968, a few days after the assassination of Dr. Martin Luther King, Jr., a second grade teacher named Jane Elliot tried to teach her students a lesson in prejudice and discrimination. She divided her students into two groups, those with blue eyes and those with brown eyes.

On the first day of the lesson, the blue-eyed children were given special privileges, such as extra time at recess and getting to leave first for lunch. She also told the blue-eyed children that they were superior to the brown-eyed children, telling the brown-eyed children not to bother taking seconds at lunch because it would be wasted. She kept the blue-eyed children and the brown-eyed children apart (Peters, 1971).

The blue-eyed children soon started to criticize, belittle, and become quite vicious in their attacks on the brown-eyed children. By the end of the first day, the blue-eyed children felt and acted superior, and the brown-eyed children were miserable, and even scored lower on tests. Two days later, the brown-eyed children became the favored group and the effects from the first 2 days appeared again but in reverse: The blue-eyed children began to feel inferior and their test scores dropped.

The fact that test scores reflected the treatment received by the out-group is a stunning one, raising questions about the effects of prejudice and discrimination on the education of children who are members of stereotyped out-groups. That the children were so willing to discriminate against their own classmates, some of whom were their close friends before the experiment, is also telling. In his book about this classroom experiment, *A Class Divided*, Peters (1971) reported that the students who were part of the original experiment, when reunited 15 years later to talk about the experience, said that they believed that this early experience with prejudice and discrimination helped them to become less prejudiced as young adults.

Questions for Further Discussion

1. How do you think adults might react in a similar experiment?
2. What are the ethical concerns regarding how Elliot treated the children in her classroom?

▲ On September 6, 1957, this high school in Little Rock, Arkansas, became integrated, allowing African American students to attend school with White students. The practice of segregating Black and White school children was discrimination, and the desegregation laws were aimed at stopping that discrimination. But the attitudes of prejudice persisted even after the legal discrimination was stopped and to some degree still exist today. The courts can make laws against discrimination, but changing prejudicial attitudes is much more difficult.

SOCIAL PSYCHOLOGY 233

CHAPTER 7 • Module 20

COVER THE MODULE (continued)

- *Realistic conflict theory* states that prejudice and discrimination will be increased between groups that are in conflict over a limited resource.

MULTIMEDIA CONTENT AVAILABLE AT www.mypsychlab.com

⊙⃞Watch a video about prejudice on mypsychlab.com

CLASSIC STUDIES IN PSYCHOLOGY

1. Because there have been so many efforts to educate people about discrimination and prejudice, one would hope that adults would react much more favorably. However, if the experiment were to be taken out of an educational atmosphere and placed into the social realm or that of the workforce, it is possible that adults would behave similarly to the children in the study. Can students think of examples of adults behaving in this manner? (Examples include the neighborhood in which adults live, wealth, attire, professional hierarchy of authority, etc.)

2. Today, it is doubtful that Elliot would have conducted this lesson because of ethical concerns and legal ramifications. The psychological and emotional harm that can result from the activity has been cited, as well as the effect on grades from the drop in test scores. Elliot did not tell the students beforehand of the exercise's purpose, and, in some later experiments, participants' frustration caused more anger, which enflamed the notions of prejudice rather than fostering more sensitivity.

Class Demonstration (Kinesthetic)

HEADBANDS AND STEREOTYPES

Create strips of paper large enough to wrap around students' heads as headbands. On each headband, write a stereotype. Ideas for stereotypes can be generated by students from classroom discussion, such as "quiet," "silly," "hot-tempered," "jock," and "geek." (Make sure that the stereotypes are not offensive.) Randomly distribute the headbands to students, who should put them on without knowing what the headbands say. Ask students to wear the headbands and move around the classroom "socializing." During conversation, students should treat each other according to the stereotype on the headband. Students then can try to guess what stereotype they are wearing by how they are being treated.

Module 20 Social Interaction 233

CHAPTER 7 • Module 20

COVER THE MODULE (continued)

- Conflicts between groups are usually greater when there are other stresses such as war, economic difficulties, or other misfortunes.
- A scapegoat is a person or group, typically members of an out-group, serving as the target for the negative emotions of the in-group.
- **How People Learn Prejudice**
  - In the *social cognitive theory*, prejudice is seen as an attitude that is formed in the same way other attitudes are formed through direct instruction, modeling, and other social influences on learning.
  - In the *social identity theory*, three processes form a person's identity within a group and the adoption of attitudes, concepts, and behaviors of the group:
    - Social categorization
    - Social identity
    - Social comparison
  - *Social identity* theory explains why people feel the need to stereotype others.
  - Prejudice may arise from the need to increase one's own self-esteem by looking down on others.
  - *Stereotype vulnerability* is the effect that a person's knowledge of another's stereotyped opinions can have on that person's behavior.

Conflicts between groups are usually greater when there are other pressures or stresses going on, such as war, economic difficulties, or other misfortunes. A *scapegoat* is a person or a group, typically a member or members of an out-group, who serves as the target for the frustrations and negative emotions of members of the in-group. (The term comes from the ancient Jewish tradition of sending a goat into the wilderness with the symbolic sins of the people on its head.)

Scapegoats are the group with the least power, and the newest immigrants to an area are typically those with the least power at that time. Many social psychologists believe that the rioting that took place in Los Angeles, California, in the spring of 1992 occurred in the areas it did for this reason. This was just after the infamous Rodney King beating. Rodney King was an African American man who suffered a violent beating by four police officers caught on videotape by a bystander. At the trial, the officers were found not guilty of assault with a deadly weapon. When news of the decision got out, Los Angeles streets erupted in a series of violent riots (Knight, 1996).

What puzzled many was that most of the rioting and violence took place beyond the neighborhoods of the mostly White police officers and beyond the African American neighborhoods, but tended to occur where Asian Americans and Asians, the most recent immigrants to the area, lived. When a group is new to an area, as the Asians were, that group has the least social power and influence. The rioters took out their frustrations *not* on the people seen as responsible for those frustrations but on the group with the least power to resist.

How People Learn Prejudice As was clearly demonstrated in the brown eyes–blue eyes experiment, even children are, under the right circumstances, prone to developing prejudiced attitudes. Several theories have been proposed to explain the origins and the persistence of prejudice. In **social cognitive theory,** prejudice is seen as an attitude that forms just as other attitudes form, through direct instruction, modeling, and other social influences on learning.

In **social identity theory**, three processes are responsible for the formation of a person's identity within a particular social group and the adoption of the attitudes, concepts, and behavior that go along with identification with that group (Tajfel & Turner, 1986). The first process is *social categorization*. Just as people assign categories to others (such as Black, White, student, teacher, and so on) to help organize information about those others, people also assign themselves to social categories to help determine how they should behave. The second element of social identity theory is *identification*, or the formation of one's **social identity**. A social identity is the part of one's self-concept that includes the view of oneself as a member of a particular social group—typically, the in-group. The third aspect of social identity theory is **social comparison**, Festinger's (1954) concept in which people compare themselves favorably to others to improve their own self-esteem: "Well, at least I'm better off than that person." (Members of the out-group make handy comparisons.)

Social identity theory helps to explain why people feel the need to categorize or stereotype others, producing the sense of "us versus them." Prejudice may result, at least in part, from the need to increase one's own self-esteem by looking down on others.

Not only do stereotypes affect the way people perceive others, but stereotypes can affect the way people see themselves and their own performance (Snyder et al., 1977). **Stereotype vulnerability** refers to the effect that a person's knowledge of another's stereotyped opinions can have on that person's behavior (Steele, 1992, 1997). Research has shown that when people are aware

social cognitive theory referring to the use of cognitive processes in relation to understanding the social world.

social identity theory theory in which the formation of a person's identity within a particular social group is explained by social categorization, social identification, and social comparison.

social identity the part of the self-concept including one's view of self as a member of a particular social category.

social comparison the comparison of oneself to others in ways that raise one's self-esteem.

stereotype vulnerability the effect that people's awareness of the stereotypes associated with their social group has on their behavior.

Class Demonstration

THEORIES ABOUT PREJUDICE

Read the story "The Sneetches" by Dr. Seuss to the class. Before you read, have the students count off in 4s. Ask the 1s to listen, while you read, for examples of social cognitive theory in the story; the 2s to listen for the three elements of social identity theory; the 3s to listen for stereotype vulnerability; and the 4s to listen for self-fulfilling prophecy. When you finish reading, have students to meet with their like-number group to share their findings. Tell each group to choose a spokesperson to share the group's compilations with the class. To conclude the discussion, ask students to share their ideas about who the "star-bellied" and "plain-bellied" sneetches are in today's world or in their school's social system. How do their stories relate to that of the sneetches? How do they think the conflict will be resolved?

of stereotypes that are normally applied to their own group by others, they feel anxious about behaving in ways that might support that stereotype. This fear results in anxiety and self-consciousness that have negative effects on their performance in a kind of **self-fulfilling prophecy** (the effect that expectations can have on outcomes).

Stereotype vulnerability is highly related to *stereotype threat* in which members of a stereotyped group are made anxious and wary of any situation in which their behavior might confirm a stereotype (Hyde & Kling, 2001; Steele, 1999). In one study, researchers administered a difficult verbal test to Caucasian and African American participants (Steele & Aronson, 1995). Half of the African American participants were asked to record their race on a question before the test, making them very aware of their minority status. Those participants showed a significant decrease in scores on the test when compared to the other participants, African American and Caucasian, who did not answer the question. They had more incorrect answers, had slower response times, answered fewer questions, and demonstrated more anxiety when compared to the other participants (Steele & Aronson, 1995).

Overcoming Prejudice The best weapon against prejudice is education: learning about people who are different from you in many ways. *Intergroup contact* is very common in college settings where students and faculty from many different backgrounds live, work, and study together. Because they go through many of the same experiences (midterms, finals, and so on), people from these diverse, varied backgrounds find common ground to build friendships and respect for one another's cultural, ethnic, or religious differences.

Contact between social groups can backfire under certain circumstances, however, as seen in a famous study (Sherif et al., 1961) called the "Robber's Cave." At a summer camp called Robber's Cave, 22 White, well-adjusted pre-teen boys were divided into two groups. The groups each lived separately and were kept apart for daily activities. During the second week, after in-group relationships had formed, the researchers scheduled highly competitive events pitting one group against the other. Intergroup conflict quickly occurred, with name-calling, fights, and hostility emerging between the two groups.

The third week involved making the two groups come together for pleasant, noncompetitive activities, in the hopes that cooperation would be the result. Instead, the groups used the activities of the third week as opportunities for more hostility. However, after several weeks of being forced to work together to resolve a series of crises created deliberately by the experimenters (such as a water shortage and a broken down truck), the boys lost their hostility toward each other and formed friendships between the groups. When dealing with the crises, the boys were forced into a situation of **equal status contact** in which they were all in the same situation with neither group holding power over the other. Equal status contact has been shown to reduce prejudice and discrimination. It appears that personal involvement with people from another group must be cooperative and occur when all groups have equal power or status to effectively reduce prejudice (Pettigrew & Tropp, 2000; Robinson & Preston, 1976).

20.2 What factors govern attraction and love?

Interpersonal attraction is one of the fundamental areas of social psychology. When we think about what attracts us to other people, one of the topics that usually arises is physical attractiveness. Some research suggests that physical

self-fulfilling prophecy the tendency of one's expectations to affect one's behavior in such a way as to make the expectations more likely to occur.

equal status contact contact between groups in which the groups have equal status, with neither group having power over the other.

interpersonal attraction liking or having the desire for a relationship with another person.

CHAPTER 7 • Module 20

COVER THE MODULE *(continued)*
- Self-fulfilling prophecy is the tendency of one's expectations to affect one's behavior in such a way that makes those expectations more likely to occur.
- **Overcoming Prejudice**
  - The best way is through education and intergroup contact.
  - Equal status contact is contact between groups in which the groups have equal status, with neither group having power over the other.

EXTEND THE LESSON
Ask students to first privately write down a list of the groups with which they identify or belong (e.g., Catholic, Hispanic, male, teenager, skater). Then have students think about the prejudices they hold concerning other groups, or of those prejudices for which they have been on the receiving end. How did they learn their prejudices? Did they experience a self-fulfilling prophecy as a result of these stereotypes?

L4 DIFFERENTIATED INSTRUCTION
Advanced Learners Encourage students to apply standards-based understanding to new situations. Challenge them to take information and use it in novel ways.

Critical Thinking

OVERCOMING PREJUDICE

Purpose: Students examine a famous historical example of a high school overcoming segregation and prejudicial attitudes.

Description: Arrange for students to view the movie *Remember the Titans*. Ask students to note the key ideas discussed so far in this chapter concerning prejudice, discrimination, stereotyping, how prejudice is learned, and stereotype vulnerability. Also, students should note how the concepts of intergroup contact and equal status contact were used by Herman Boone to bring together the students and the T. C. Williams High School community. Lead a discussion of the students' views of what was portrayed in the movie. What lessons could be applied to their own high school community?

CHAPTER 7 • Module 20

COVER THE MODULE

20.2 What factors govern attraction and love?

- *Interpersonal attraction* is liking or having the desire for a relationship with another person.
- Physical beauty is one of the main factors that influence people's choices.
- *Proximity* means that people are more likely to choose friends and lovers from the people available to them.
  - Mere exposure effect is people's tendency to prefer the things with which they are familiar (such as in repeated encounters with someone, due to proximity).
- People tend to be more attracted to others who are similar to them.
- Opposites do not attract, according to research. Complementary traits are commonly mistaken for opposite traits.
- *Reciprocity of liking* is the tendency of people to like other people who like them in return.

DISCUSS THE STUDENT VOICE QUESTION

Ask students to think about whether they could be attracted to someone with very different traits from theirs. Have volunteers explain what different traits would be acceptable and which ones might not be.

MULTIMEDIA CONTENT AVAILABLE AT
www.mypsychlab.com

Watch a video about attraction on **mypsychlab.com**

L2 ELL DIFFERENTIATED INSTRUCTION

English Language Learners Have students engage in repeated readings of the same brief passage to build word recognition, fluency, and reading rate.

---

proximity physical or geographical nearness.

reciprocity of liking tendency of people to like other people who like them in return.

Isn't there a saying about "opposites attract"? Aren't people sometimes attracted to people who are different instead of similar?

Watch a video about attraction on **mypsychlab.com**

We use the word love to describe many things. I love my family and I love my friends, but in different ways. Those aren't all the same kind of relationships.

236 CHAPTER 7

---

beauty is one of the main factors that influence people's choices for selecting people they want to know better, although other factors may become more important in later stages of relationships (Eagly et al., 1991; Feingold, 1992; White, 1980).

The closer together people are physically, such as in their working or living conditions, the more likely they are to form a relationship. **Proximity** refers to being physically near someone else. People choose friends and lovers from the people available to them, and availability depends heavily on proximity (Udry, 1971).

One theory about proximity involves the idea of repeated exposure to new stimuli. The more people experience something, the more they tend to like it. When people are in proximity to each other, repeated exposure may increase their attraction. People's tendency to prefer the things they are familiar with is known as the *mere exposure effect*.

People tend to like and be more attracted to people who are *similar* to them or have something in common—such as attitudes, beliefs, and interests (Hartfield & Rapson, 1992; Moreland & Zajonc, 1982; Neimeyer & Mitchell, 1998). When other people hold similar attitudes and beliefs and exhibit similar behaviors, it makes a person's own attitudes, beliefs, and behaviors seem more valid.

Isn't there a saying about "opposites attract"? Aren't people sometimes attracted to people who are different instead of similar?

Some people have very rewarding relationships with people who have *complementary* qualities (characteristics in one person that fill a need in the other) (Carson, 1969; Schmitt, 2002). Research does not support the view that opposites attract, however. It is similarity, not complementarity, which attracts people and helps them stay together (Berscheid & Reis, 1998; McPherson et al., 2001).

Finally, people have a very strong tendency to like people who like them, a simple but powerful concept referred to as **reciprocity of liking**. In one experiment, researchers paired college students with other students (Curtis & Miller, 1986). Neither student in each pair knew the other member. One member of each pair was randomly chosen to receive some information about whether the *other* student liked them or disliked him or her.

When the pairs of students were allowed to communicate again, the students who had been told that the other student liked them were friendlier, disclosed more information about themselves, agreed with the other person more, and behaved in a warmer manner. The other students came to like these students better as well, so liking produced more liking. Watch on **mypsychlab.com**

The only time that liking someone does not seem to make that person like the other in return is if a person suffers from feelings of low self-worth. A person with low self-worth may question the motives of the liker. Driven by mistrust, the liked may be mean to the liker, which, in most cases, turns off the liker in a kind of self-fulfilling prophecy (Murray et al., 1998).

Love is a Triangle—Robert Sternberg's Triangular Theory of Love

We use the word love to describe many things. I love my family and I love my friends, but in different ways. Those aren't all the same kind of relationships.

Dictionary definitions of love refer to a strong affection for another person due to kinship, personal ties, physical attraction, admiration, or common interests.

Psychologists generally agree that there are different kinds of love. One psychologist, Robert Sternberg, outlined a theory of three main components of love and the different types of love that combinations of them can produce

---

Class Discussion

LOOKING FOR LOVE

Ask students if they have seen television commercials for online matchmaking services, such as match.com or eHarmony.com. Lead a discussion based on the following questions: (1) How do people in the commercials describe the methods of attraction for finding a new relationship? (2) What characteristics or traits do they describe as being very important to them for a successful relationship? As an extension, have students reflect upon what most often governs their attraction to others. Ask volunteers to describe to the class which traits or aspects are more important to them and which are not as important.

236 Chapter 7 Social Psychology

(Sternberg, 1986, 1988, 1997). According to Sternberg, love consists of three basic components: intimacy, passion, and commitment. *Intimacy*, in Sternberg's view, refers to the feelings of closeness that one has for another person or the sense of having close emotional ties to another. Intimacy in this sense is not physical but psychological. Friends have an intimate relationship because they share secrets, feel strong emotional ties, and enjoy the presence of the other person.

Passion is the physical aspect of love. Passion refers to the emotional and physical arousal a person feels toward the other person. Holding hands, loving looks, and hugs can all be forms of passion.

Commitment involves the decisions one makes about a relationship. A short-term decision might be, "I think I'm in love." An example of a more long-term commitment is, "I want to be with this person for the rest of my life."

A love relationship between two people can involve one, two, or all three of these components in various combinations. The combinations can produce seven different forms of love, as can be seen in Figure 20.1. Once all three components of love are present, the couple has achieved *consummate love*.

Two well-researched forms of love from Sternberg's theory are romantic love and companionate love. When intimacy and passion are combined, the result is **romantic love**, which is sometimes called passionate love (Bartels & Zeki, 2000; Diamond, 2003; Hartfield, 1987). Romantic love is often the basis for a lasting relationship. In many Western cultures, the ideal relationship begins with liking, then becomes romantic love as passion is added, and finally becomes enduring as a commitment is made. ⊙ Watch on mypsychlab.com

When intimacy and commitment are the main components of a relationship, it is called **companionate love**. People in companionate love make a commitment to live together, usually in marriage. Consummate love often turns into companionate love during the middle years of a relationship's commitment, and companionate love often holds a marriage together through the

romantic love type of love consisting of intimacy and passion.

companionate love type of love consisting of intimacy and commitment.

⊙ Watch a video on Sternberg's triangular theory of love on mypsychlab.com

FIGURE 20.1 Sternberg's Triangular Theory of Love
This diagram represents the seven different kinds of love that can result from combining the three components of love: intimacy, passion, and commitment. Notice that some of these types of love sound less desirable or positive than others. What is the one key element missing from the less positive types of love? Source: Adapted from Sternberg (1986b).

SOCIAL PSYCHOLOGY 237

CHAPTER 7 • Module 20

COVER THE MODULE (continued)

- **Love Is a Triangle—Robert Sternberg's Triangular Theory of Love**
  - Three main components combine to produce seven different types of love:
    - Intimacy is the feelings of emotional closeness or emotional ties one person has for another.
    - Passion is the emotional and physical arousal a person feels toward another.
    - Commitment is the decisions one makes about a relationship.
  - *Romantic love* is the combination of intimacy and passion.
  - *Companionate love* is the combination of intimacy and commitment.

MULTIMEDIA CONTENT AVAILABLE AT
www.mypsychlab.com

⊙ Watch a video on Sternberg's triangular theory of love on **mypsychlab.com**

UNDERSTANDING VISUALS

Direct students' attention to the question in the figure caption. Intimacy is the missing element in the less positive forms of love.

EXTEND THE DISCUSSION

As a class, have students brainstorm famous couples, whether celebrity or fictional, to analyze according to Sternberg's triangular theory. Allow students to work in pairs, labeling the type of love they observe in the couples. Then have the students share their results with the class, as well as explain why they assigned that label.

Critical Thinking

DECODING THE LOVE TRIANGLE

Purpose: Students analyze relationships they have personally witnessed or experienced according to Sternberg's triangular theory of love. Then students create their own "perfect match."

Time: 20 minutes

Description: First, students should work individually to analyze, in writing, two relationships they know about. Next, have students imagine their "perfect match," using Sternberg's components. What would the person look like? What qualities of attraction would he or she have? What aspects of the relationship would help create Sternberg's components?

CHAPTER 7 • Module 20

COVER THE MODULE

20.3 How does aggressive behavior develop?

- *Aggression* occurs when one person physically or verbally hurts another.
- The frustration–aggression hypothesis holds that when a person is prevented from reaching a goal, frustration can cause aggressive behavior.
- Aggression has been explained as both a biological phenomenon and a learned behavior.
- **Aggression and Biology**
  - Studies of twins have shown that if one twin has a violent temper, the other is likely to have one as well.
  - The amygdala and areas of the limbic system have been shown to trigger aggression when stimulated.

L(i)N(k) to *Chapter Two: The Biological Perspective, pp. 57–59*

  - Alcohol releases inhibitions, making people less likely to control aggression.

DISCUSS THE STUDENT VOICE QUESTION

Ask students whether they believe alcohol calms people or makes them aggressive. Why do they think that alcohol is typically portrayed in advertising as helping people relax and have a good time?

L3 DIFFERENTIATED INSTRUCTION

Provide time for students to collect their thoughts. This gives more reflective learners time to consider the answer. Explain this procedure to the class before using it. Tell students the questions that you will be asking during tomorrow's class in order to give them time overnight to prepare their responses.

---

years of parenting, paying bills, and lessening physical passion (Gottman & Krokoff, 1989; Steinberg & Silverberg, 1987). In many non-Western cultures, companionate love is seen as more sensible. Parents or matchmakers, rather than the couple themselves, may choose a mate for young people on the basis of compatibility (Duben & Behar, 1991; Hortacsu, 1999; Jones, 1997; Thornton & Hui-Sheng, 1994).

20.3 How does aggressive behavior develop?

Unfortunately, violence toward others is another form of social interaction. When one person physically or verbally hurts another, psychologists call it **aggression**. Frustration, which occurs when a person is prevented from reaching a goal, can cause aggressive behavior, known as the *frustration–aggression hypothesis* (Berkowitz, 1993; Miller et al., 1941). Many sources of frustration can lead to aggressive behavior. Pain, for example, produces negative sensations that are intense and uncontrollable, leading to frustration and often aggressive acts (Berkowitz, 1993). Crowding, loud noises, excessive heat, and even bad smells can lead to aggressive behavior (Anderson, 1987; Rotton & Frey, 1985; Rotton et al., 1979; Zillmann et al., 1981).

Many early researchers, including Sigmund Freud (1930), believed that aggression was a basic human instinct. But if aggression is an instinct in all humans, the pattern of aggression should be similar across cultures. Modern approaches explain aggression as both a biological phenomenon and a learned behavior.

Aggression and Biology Studies of twins have shown a possible genetic basis to aggression: If one identical twin has a violent temper, the identical sibling will be more likely to have one, too. This happens more often with identical twins than with fraternal twins (Miles & Carey, 1997; Rowe et al., 1999). Biological explanations of aggression are also supported by studies that show that certain areas of the brain, including the amygdala and other structures of the limbic system, trigger aggressive responses when stimulated in animals and humans (Adams, 1968; Albert & Richmond, 1977; LaBar et al., 1995; Scott et al., 1997). L(i)N(k) to *Chapter Two: The Biological Perspective, pp. 57–59*.

Researchers previously believed that the sex hormone testosterone was linked to higher levels of aggression (Archer, 1991). However, a recent study (Eisenegger et al., 2010) found that women who were given testosterone and then asked to participate in a bargaining exercise actually bargained more fairly than those women who did not receive the hormone. The results of this study suggest that testosterone may actually enhance people's desire to defend their social status—and although people may defend their social status through aggression, they may also defend it through nonconfrontational methods such as bargaining.

Can alcohol make people more aggressive?
Alcohol does impact aggressive behavior. Psychologically, alcohol acts to release inhibitions, making people less likely to control their behavior. In one study, volunteers were asked to administer electric shocks before and after consuming alcohol in a study similar to Milgram's shock experiment. The volunteers believed that the test was about reaction time and learning, and that the responses were coming from real people (they were actually computer-simulated) (Bushman, 1997). Participants were much more aggressive in administering stronger shocks after drinking.

Can alcohol make people more aggressive? ▶

aggression actions meant to harm or destroy.

238 CHAPTER 7

Class Demonstration

DEFINING AGGRESSION

Provide a list of actions to students. Suggestions include the following: a woman spreads negative gossip about a colleague at work; a girl does not invite a friend to a party but invites all other mutual friends; a frustrated child punches a stuffed animal; a woman accidentally runs over her cat; a hockey player fist-fights another player during a game; a hungry child steals food from another child; a man fantasizes about murdering an enemy but does not commit the act; a soldier kills another in a war; a police officer must use extreme force to subdue a man under arrest. Have students work in groups of three to five. On a piece of poster board or paper in the center of the table, have students discuss and graph each action on a scale of 1–10 for level of aggression. Have the groups share their results with the class, explaining their justifications for each number.

▲ *This photograph shows a "guard" searching a "prisoner" in Zimbardo's famous Stanford prison experiment.*

The Power of Social Roles Although frustration, genetics, body chemicals, and even the effects of drugs can be blamed for aggressive behavior to some degree, much human aggression is influenced by learning. The social learning theory explanation for aggression states that aggressive behavior is learned by watching aggressive models get reinforced for their aggressive behavior (Bandura, 1980; Bandura et al., 1961). **LINK** *to Chapter Six: Learning and Language Development, pp. 195–196.* Aggressive models can be parents, siblings, friends, or people on television.

There is some evidence to suggest that taking on a particular *social role*, such as that of a soldier, can lead to an increase in aggressive behavior. A **social role** is the pattern of behavior that is expected in a particular social position. A deeply disturbing experiment, now among the most famous and controversial experiments in psychology, was conducted by famed social psychologist Philip Zimbardo at Stanford University in 1971. In the study, now known as the Stanford Prison Experiment, about 70 young men volunteered to participate for 2 weeks, embodying the social role of either a "guard" or a "prisoner." The "guards" were given uniforms and instructions not to use violence but to maintain control of the "prison." The "prisoners" were booked at a real jail, blindfolded, and transported to the campus "prison," actually the basement of one of the campus buildings. On day 2, the prisoners staged a revolt (not planned as part of the experiment), which was quickly crushed by the guards. The guards became increasingly more aggressive, using humiliation to control and punish the prisoners. For example, prisoners were forced to clean toilet bowls with their bare hands. Five prisoners became physically ill and were released. The entire experiment was canceled on day 6, after a prisoner reported that what the experimenters were doing to the men was terrible

social role the pattern of behavior that is expected of a person who is in a particular social position.

SOCIAL PSYCHOLOGY **239**

Explore

SURF THE STANFORD PRISON EXPERIMENT'S WEBSITE

The following website has a slideshow telling the story of this famous experiment, provides questions for further discussion on the topic, and lists links to Zimbardo's official webpage: **www.prisonexp.org/**. Send interested students to the site for additional information about the experiment. Ask volunteers to report back to the class on what they learned.

CHAPTER 7 • Module 20

COVER THE MODULE *(continued)*

- **The Power of Social Roles**
  - Human aggression is influenced by learning.
    - Social learning theory states that aggressive behavior is learned by watching aggressive models get reinforced for their aggressive behavior.

  LINK *to Chapter Six: Learning and Language Development, pp. 195–196*

  - A social role is the pattern of behavior that is expected of a person who is in a particular social position.
  - Philip Zimbardo's Stanford Prison Experiment highlighted the influence that social roles can have on ordinary people.

FAST FACT

Students may be interested to learn that in 2002, Philip Zimbardo appeared in the British reality television show *The Human Zoo*. Participants were observed inside a controlled setting while Zimbardo and a British psychologist analyzed their behavior.

TEACHING TIP

For students who need it, provide a structured environment with clear rules and schedules.

L3 DIFFERENTIATED INSTRUCTION

Auditory/Verbal Learners Encourage students to record class lectures (with your permission). They should take notes on the lecture sparingly, using the recording later to fill in parts they might have missed.

Module 20 Social Interaction **239**

CHAPTER 7 • Module 20

COVER THE MODULE (continued)

- **Violence in the Media and Aggression**
  - Various studies have consistently found that exposure to violent media significantly increases the likelihood that children will engage in physical and verbal aggression.
  - Factors that contribute to these findings include the normal aggressive behavior of the child as well as the age at which exposure begins.

MULTIMEDIA CONTENT AVAILABLE AT www.mypsychlab.com

Watch classic footage of Zimbardo's Stanford prison experiment on **mypsychlab.com**

Listen to the Psychology in the News podcast about violent video games and their effect on the brain on **mypsychlab.com**

EXTEND THE LESSON

Place the following signs in the four corners of the room: (1) Strongly Agree, (2) Somewhat Agree, (3) Somewhat Disagree, and (4) Strongly Disagree. Read the following statements and have students move to the area of the room that best describes their opinions. Once they have discussed the statements as a group, share each group's findings with the class.

- Children who play violent video games will grow up to be aggressive adults.
- Violent media should be blamed for violent acts by teens, such as the shootings at Columbine High School.

COVER THE MODULE

20.4 What is prosocial behavior?

- **Prosocial Behavior**
  - This is defined as socially desirable behavior that benefits others.
  - Altruism is prosocial behavior that is done with no expectation of reward and may involve the risk of harm to oneself.

(Zimbardo, 1971). The experiment raised some serious ethical concerns by causing distress to the participants and allowing the "guards" to humiliate the "prisoners," but the extreme and disturbing nature of the participants' behavior certainly highlighted the influence that social roles can have on perfectly ordinary people. **Watch** on **mypsychlab.com**

During the war in Iraq, between October and December 2003, investigators found numerous cases of cruel, humiliating, and other startling abuses of the Iraqi prisoners by the army military police stationed at the prison of Abu Ghraib (Hersh, 2004). The "guards" in Zimbardo's prison study were civilians, but the effect of putting on the uniform and taking on the social role of guard changed their behavior radically. Is it possible that a similar factor was at work at Abu Ghraib? Further research will be needed to determine to what degree social roles are at work in these kinds of real-life situations.

Violence in the Media and Aggression

I've heard that violent television programs can cause children to become more aggressive. How true is that?

Since the 1960s, researchers have examined the impact of television and other media violence on the aggressive behavior of children of various ages. The conclusions have all been similar: Children exposed to high levels of violent media are more aggressive than children who are not (Baron & Reiss, 1985; Bushman & Huesmann, 2000; Centerwall, 1989; Geen & Thomas, 1986; Huesmann & Miller, 1994; Huesmann et al., 1997; Huesmann et al., 2003; Villani, 2001). Several factors contribute to the level of aggression, including the normal aggressive tendencies of the child (more aggressive children prefer more aggressive media), as well as the age at which exposure begins (the younger the child, the greater the impact). The tolerance of aggression and physical punishment in the home also shows an increase in the aggressive impact of television.

Violent video games have also been blamed for violent behavior in children, especially young adolescents. In one study, second grade boys were allowed to play either an aggressive or a nonaggressive video game. After playing, the boys were allowed a free period. Boys who had played the aggressive video game demonstrated more verbal and physical aggression to both objects and people than boys who had played the nonaggressive game (Irwin & Gross, 1995).

There is clear and consistent evidence that even short-term exposure to violent media significantly increases the likelihood that children will engage in both physical and verbal aggression as well as have aggressive thoughts and emotions (Anderson et al., 2003). (Keep in mind, though, that the studies mentioned here do not prove that playing violent video games *causes* increased aggression.) **Listen** on **mypsychlab.com**

20.4 What is prosocial behavior?

Prosocial Behavior A far more pleasant form of human social interaction is **prosocial behavior**, or socially desirable behavior that benefits others rather than brings them harm. **Altruism** is one type of prosocial behavior: Helping someone in trouble with no expectation of reward and often without fear for one's own safety. Scientists who study the evolutionary and genetic bases of social organizations see altruistic behavior as a way of preserving one's genetic

prosocial behavior socially desirable behavior that benefits others.

altruism prosocial behavior that is done with no expectation of reward and may involve the risk of harm to oneself.

Class Demonstration

ANALYZING CARTOONS

Write the following scale on the board: 1 = mildly violent, 2 = moderately violent, 3 = extremely violent. As a class, define and give examples of each of these indicators (e.g., mild violence includes accidental harm, moderate violence includes purposeful punches, extreme violence includes murder and death). Show a children's action cartoon to the class. On a blank sheet of paper, ask students to write the number 1, 2, or 3 for every violent act they see during the show. Stop the video during regular increments (every 2–5 minutes) to allow students to tally the amount of violence that occurs during that time interval. Ask students to describe their thoughts on their findings.

material, even at the cost of one's own life. This is why the males of certain species of spiders, for example, seem to willingly become "dinner" for the females they have just fertilized, ensuring the continuation of their genes through the offspring (Koh, 1996). It also explains the parent who risks life and limb to save a child. Altruism is typified by the heroes we revere who give but ask nothing in return.

Why do people sometimes refuse to help when their own lives are not at risk, as in the cases of Kitty Genovese and LaShanda Calloway presented in the opening story? Social psychologists might explain that the lack of response was not due to indifference or a lack of sympathy but instead due to the bystander effect and diffusion of responsibility.

The **bystander effect** refers to the finding that the likelihood of a bystander (someone close in proximity) to help someone in trouble decreases as the number of bystanders increases. One person is far more likely to help than two people, and the addition of each new bystander decreases the possibility of helping behavior even more (Darley & Latané, 1968; Eagly & Crowley, 1986; Latané & Darley, 1969). Five shoppers stepped over the bleeding body of LaShanda Calloway, and none helped.

Diffusion of responsibility is a form of attribution in which a person fails to take responsibility because of the presence of other people who are seen to share the responsibility (Leary & Forsyth, 1987). "I was just following orders," "Other people were doing it," and "I thought someone would do something" are all examples of diffusion of responsibility. Kitty Genovese received almost no help because there were too many potential "helpers"—most of the witnesses thought surely someone else would step in.

What kind of decision-making process might people go through before deciding to help? Darley and Latané (1968) identified several decision points that a bystander faces before helping someone in trouble: A bystander must notice the situation, define the situation as an emergency, take personal responsibility to act, plan a course of action, and—finally—take action to help the person in trouble.

Other factors also influence the decision to help. For example, the more ambiguity there is in a situation, the less likely it becomes that the situation will be considered an emergency. If other people are nearby, especially if the situation is ambiguous, bystanders may rely on the actions of the others to help determine if their help is necessary. Since all the bystanders look to one another, it is likely that the situation will be seen as a nonemergency if no one acts with authority.

Another factor is the mood of the bystanders. People in a good mood are generally more likely to help than people in a bad mood, but oddly enough, people in a good mood are less likely to help if helping would destroy the good mood. Gender of the victim is also a factor, with women more likely to receive help than men if the bystander is male, but not if the bystander is female. Appearance matters, too: Physically attractive people are more likely to be helped, while victims who look like "they deserve what is happening" are also less likely to be helped. For example, a man who appears to be drunk and is dressed in shabby clothing will be passed by, but if he is dressed in a business suit, people are more likely to stop and help. Racial and ethnic differences between victim and bystander also decrease the probability of helping (Richards & Lowe, 2003; Tukuitonga & Bindman, 2002).

bystander effect referring to the effect that the presence of other people has on the decision to help or not help, with help becoming less likely as the number of bystanders increases.

diffusion of responsibility occurring when a person fails to take responsibility for actions or for inaction because of the presence of other people who are seen to share the responsibility.

CHAPTER 7 • Module 20

COVER THE MODULE (continued)

- Bystander effect is the effect that the presence of other people has on the decision of whether to help; the choice to help becomes less likely as the number of bystanders increases.
- Diffusion of responsibility is a form of attribution occurring when a person fails to take responsibility for actions or inaction because of the presence of others, who are believed to share the responsibility.
- Factors that influence the decision to help:
  - Ambiguity of the situation
  - Mood of the bystanders
  - Gender of the victim and bystander
  - Physical appearance of the victim
  - Racial and ethnic differences between the victim and bystander

L3 DIFFERENTIATED INSTRUCTION

By using strategies such as scaffolding questions and allowing less proficient readers to answer first, you can help students at all levels to access the material and fully participate in class discussions.

Class Demonstration (Kinesthetic)

CREATING AN EXPERIMENT TO TEST THE BYSTANDER EFFECT

Divide students into groups of four. Have each group choose a situation that could elicit help from other students (e.g., dropping books down a stairwell, spilling a purse or backpack in the cafeteria line, losing a contact lens). Each group should write a skit that shows how the students would conduct an experiment to measure how likely bystanders would be to assist a person involved in the situation the group chose. Ask the groups to act out their skit for their classmates, who should determine if the experiment has been correctly designed.

CHAPTER 7 • Module 20

Assess

Assign the Module 20 Practice Quiz.

Use the Practice Quiz to identify gaps in student understanding.

REMEDIATE

Have students, individually or in groups, review the module goals, learning objectives, and key terms.

Refer students to the Concept Summary on p. 247 for review.

Close

Ask students to discuss how the discoveries and experiments in social interaction psychology have affected our lives today. Where would we be without the discoveries and knowledge we have gained from them? How would society be different if we had not made these discoveries?

Practice Quiz

Pick the best answer.

1. Mental patterns that represent what a person believes about certain types of people are called
   a. schemas
   b. attitudes
   c. attributions
   d. stereotypes

2. Which of the following is best classified as an altruistic act?
   a. saving a loved one from danger
   b. making a living teaching children
   c. protecting a stranger from an attack
   d. using aggression only in self-defense

3. In Zimbardo's classic Stanford prison experiment, participants succumbed to the power of
   a. altruism
   b. social roles
   c. compliance
   d. self-fulfilling prophecy

4. Once a situation has been defined as an emergency, the next step in the decision-making process is
   a. noticing
   b. taking action
   c. requesting assistance
   d. taking responsibility

5. Research based on the bystander effect suggests that a victim is MOST likely to get help from a bystander if
   a. no one else is around
   b. the person is overweight
   c. the person seems unconscious
   d. several other people are passing by

6. The area of the brain that is most involved in aggression is the
   a. cortex
   b. amygdala
   c. cerebellum
   d. medulla oblongata

7. Which of the following is not a major cause of interpersonal attraction?
   a. similarity
   b. reciprocity of liking
   c. physical attractiveness
   d. complementary qualities

8. A person who has very low self-worth is less likely to be affected by the
   a. primacy effect
   b. proximity effect
   c. reciprocity of liking effect
   d. opposites attract effect

9. According to Sternberg, which of the following describes the feelings of emotional closeness between two people?
   a. passion
   b. intimacy
   c. infatuation
   d. commitment

10. Greta and Huan are no longer passionate in their long marriage, but they feel emotionally close, they nurture their relationship, and they have no intention of leaving each other. Greta and Huan's relationship can best be described as
    a. romantic love
    b. consummate love
    c. companionate love
    d. unconditional love

Practice Quiz Answers

1. d
2. c
3. b
4. d
5. a

6. b
7. d
8. c
9. b
10. c

CHAPTER 7 Summary

Listen on mypsychlab.com

Module 18: Social Influence
Explore how social influence affects behavior.

18.1 Do people act differently in different situations?
- The presence of others influences our behavior, feelings, and thoughts.

18.2 How does the presence of others affect an individual's behavior?
- Conformity occurs when we change our own behavior to match others'. Compliance occurs when we change our behavior as a result of another person's request. Obedience occurs when we change our behavior at the direct order of an authority figure.

18.3 How do group dynamics influence behavior?
- Groupthink occurs when a group feels it is more important to maintain group unanimity than to consider the facts realistically. Group interactions can also cause deindividuation and group polarization.

18.4 How can an individual change a group's behavior?
- Many factors influence the emergence of a great leader, including the leader's strengths and the organization's needs.

Module 19: Social Cognition
Understand the effects of social cognition.

19.1 What are attitudes, and how do they relate to behavior?
- Attitudes are tendencies to respond positively or negatively toward persons, objects, or situations. Attitudes have affective, behavioral, and cognitive components. Attitudes can be formed through direct instruction, interaction with others, and observation.

19.2 How can attitudes be changed?
- Persuasion is the process by which one person tries to change the belief, opinion, position, or course of action of another person through argument, pleading, or explanation. The key elements in persuasion are the source of the message, the message itself, and the target audience.

Listen to an audio file of your chapter on mypsychlab.com

19.3 How do people use attribution theory to explain the actions of others?
- Attribution is the process of explaining behavior. People make attributions based on situational and dispositional causes. The fundamental attribution error is the tendency to overestimate the influence of internal factors on the behavior of other people while underestimating the influence of the situation.

Module 20: Social Interaction
Describe different kinds of social relations.

20.1 How are prejudice and discrimination different?
- Prejudice is a negative attitude that a person holds about the members of a particular social group. Discrimination occurs when members of a social group are treated differently because of prejudice toward that group.

20.2 What factors govern attraction and love?
- Interpersonal attraction refers to liking or having the desire for a relationship with another person. Factors affecting liking include physical attractiveness, proximity, similarity, possession of complementary qualities, and reciprocity of liking.
- Love is a strong affection for another person due to kinship, personal ties, physical attraction, admiration, or common interests. Sternberg states that the three components of love are intimacy, passion, and commitment.

20.3 How does aggressive behavior develop?
- Aggression is behavior intended to hurt or destroy another person, which may be physical or verbal. Aggression may have a genetic or biological basis, but social roles are also powerful influences on the expression of aggression.

20.4 What is prosocial behavior?
- Prosocial behavior is behavior that is socially desirable and benefits others. Altruism is prosocial behavior in which a person helps someone else without expectation of reward or recognition, often without fear for his or her own safety.

Vocabulary Terms

social psychology p. 214
social influence p. 214
conformity p. 215
consumer psychology p. 216
compliance p. 216
foot-in-the-door technique p. 216
door-in-the-face technique p. 216
norm of reciprocity p. 216
lowball technique p. 216
that's-not-all technique p. 217
obedience p. 217
social facilitation p. 219
social impairment p. 219

social loafing p. 219
groupthink p. 219
attitude p. 224
cognitive dissonance p. 227
persuasion p. 228
elaboration likelihood model p. 228
central-route processing p. 229
peripheral-route processing p. 229
attribution p. 229
attribution theory p. 229
situational cause p. 229
dispositional cause p. 229

fundamental attribution error p. 229
prejudice p. 232
discrimination p. 232
in-groups p. 232
out-groups p. 232
stereotype p. 232
realistic conflict theory p. 233
social cognitive theory p. 234
social identity theory p. 234
social identity p. 234
social comparison p. 234
stereotype vulnerability p. 234

self-fulfilling prophecy p. 235
equal status contact p. 235
interpersonal attraction p. 235
proximity p. 236
reciprocity of liking p. 236
romantic love p. 237
companionate love p. 237
aggression p. 238
social role p. 239
prosocial behavior p. 240
altruism p. 240
bystander effect p. 241
diffusion of responsibility p. 241

SOCIAL PSYCHOLOGY 243

CHAPTER 7 • Chapter Summary and Vocabulary

Chapter Summary

Encourage students to carefully review and study the summary. Explain that it provides an overview of key concepts presented in the text.

Have students identify what they find unclear or confusing. Call on volunteers to provide answers, examples, and definitions.

Vocabulary Terms

Remind students that terms are defined within the chapter at point of use. If they are not sure of a term's definition, they should look up the definition on the page.

Encourage students to create study cards of unfamiliar words or go to **www.mypsychlab.com** for flash cards. Have them test themselves or a classmate. Advanced students can explain the terms in their own words.

Critical Thinking

MAKING CONNECTIONS

Have students complete the following activity to connect the ideas in this chapter. Send them to the Multimedia Library for Chapter 7 at **www.mypsychlab.com** to view the simulation titled "Social Influence 2," which has a more in-depth discussion of conformity. Lead the class discussion based on the following questions: (1) What are some motivations to conform? (2) How does our choice to conform affect our behavior, our attitude, our relationships, and our interactions with one another? (3) How does conformity affect our perceived social roles?

CHAPTER 7 • Assessment

VOCABULARY REVIEW

1. e
2. j
3. g
4. f
5. a
6. i
7. b
8. d
9. c
10. h

WRITING ABOUT PSYCHOLOGY

1. Students' answers should include a detailed description of the situation in which they chose to act differently than they would have normally, as well as answering whether they were affected by the desire to conform, comply, or obey. Excellent answers will also include a detailed explanation of why they chose to conform, comply, or obey.

2. Students' letters should include a specific statement of opinion on this topic, as well as three clear reasons why they oppose or support this plan, citing evidence from the text to support their views. Excellent answers will include specific citations of the concepts in the text as well as in-depth explanations of how these concepts are relevant to their argument.

PSYCHOLOGY PROJECT

Depending on the abilities of your students and the resources available to them at home, it may help to provide them with ads that you have selected that make use of the techniques for them to study. It may be interesting to open your classroom up to parents on the day students present and to allow students to set up displays for parents to browse during a "Marketing Convention" that you host.

CHAPTER 7 Assessment

Study and Review on mypsychlab.com

Vocabulary Review
Match each vocabulary term to its definition.

1. dispositional cause
2. attitude
3. stereotype vulnerability
4. bystander effect
5. cognitive dissonance
6. companionate love
7. conformity
8. central-route processing
9. obedience
10. prejudice

a. The sense of discomfort or distress that occurs when a person's behavior does not correspond to that person's attitudes.
b. Changing one's own behavior to be similar to that of other people.
c. Changing one's behavior at the command of an authority figure.
d. Involves attending to the content of the message instead of noncontent behaviors.
e. A cause of behavior attributed to internal factors such as personality or character.
f. The impact that the presence of other people has on the decision to help or not help, with help becoming less likely as the number of bystanders increases.
g. The effect that people's awareness of the stereotypes associated with their social group has on their behavior.
h. Negative attitude held by a person about the members of a particular social group.
i. Consists of intimacy and commitment.
j. A tendency to respond positively or negatively toward a certain person, object, idea, or situation.

Writing about Psychology
Respond to each question in complete sentences.

1. Do you ever behave differently in a group than you do when you are alone? Write about a time when you were influenced by a group to act differently than you would have acted otherwise. Was your behavior affected by the desire to conform, to comply, or to be obedient? Explain your response.

2. Imagine that a politician in your city or state plans to decrease violence in your community by banning the sale of violent video games. Do you think the politician's plan makes sense? Write a letter to the politician in which you explain why you support or oppose the plan. Use specific evidence from the chapter to support the points you make in your letter.

Psychology Project

How do people use compliance techniques in everyday life? Try to identify the use of compliance techniques in real-life advertisements.

Materials:
- magazines or newspapers with advertisements
- a television (optional)

Instructions:

1. Review the compliance techniques discussed in this chapter: the door-in the face technique, the foot-in-the-door technique, the that's-not-all technique, and the lowball technique.

2. Find several advertisements in magazines or newspapers, or watch several commercials on television. Identify one advertisement or commercial that uses one of the compliance techniques you've studied.

3. Give a short presentation to your class in which you describe the advertisement, identify the compliance technique it used, and explain how the technique was used. Finally, explain whether or not you think the advertisement's use of the technique was effective.

Internet Resources

Center for the Study and Prevention of Violence: www.colorado.edu/cspv/
A clearinghouse of information about this topic.

Advertising Age Magazine: www.adage.com/
The leading publication for the advertising industry.

VolunteerMatch: www.volunteermatch.org/
Ideas for making a difference through volunteering and giving of one's time, energy, or resources.

Anti-Defamation League Online: www.adl.org/
Homepage of this organization dedicated to eliminating prejudice and discrimination.

Test Yourself

Pick the best answer.

1. Research has found that higher levels of the hormone testosterone lead to an increase in
   a. aggressive behavior
   b. calm and rational behavior
   c. social-status-defending behavior
   d. psychologically disordered behavior

2. According to Sternberg, committed couples who also have intimacy and passion are in the form of love called
   a. romantic love
   b. consummate love
   c. companionate love
   d. unconditional love

3. Which explanation of prejudice assumes that the same processes that help form other attitudes form prejudiced attitudes?
   a. scapegoating
   b. authoritarian
   c. social cognitive
   d. social discrimination

4. Cognitive dissonance arises when
   a. stereotypes do not match reality
   b. attitudes do not match behaviors
   c. passion does not match commitment
   d. one partner's beliefs do not match the other's beliefs

5. Which of the following best explains why the "teachers" in Milgram's experiment did not stop when the "learners'" screamed?
   a. sadism
   b. obedience
   c. conformity
   d. groupthink

6. Which of the following is LEAST likely to prevent groupthink?
   a. seeking opinions from outside the group
   b. ensuring that the group leader is impartial
   c. discouraging questions and alternate solutions
   d. voting by secret ballot rather than by a show of hands

7. The behavioral component of prejudice is
   a. attitude
   b. aggression
   c. stereotyping
   d. discrimination

8. The part of one's self-concept that includes the view of oneself as a member of a group is known as
   a. social identity
   b. social influence
   c. social comparison
   d. social categorization

9. To which two processes do most social psychologists attribute the failure of Kitty Genovese's neighbors to help her?
   a. bystander effect and altruism
   b. aggression and diffusion of responsibility
   c. altruism and aggression
   d. bystander effect and diffusion of responsibility

10. Which theory of leadership proposes that effective leaders are born rather than made?
    a. great person theory
    b. transactional theory
    c. transformational theory
    d. task-oriented theory

11. Which of the following is the LEAST effective persuasive element?
    a. an expert source
    b. an attractive source
    c. an older target audience
    d. a clear, balanced message

12. Which of the following would make a potential relationship LEAST likely?
    a. proximity
    b. physical attraction
    c. similar characteristics
    d. complementary characteristics

13. Which of the following is the most accurate term for helping someone without the expectation of reward?
    a. altruism
    b. idealism
    c. prosocial behavior
    d. diffusion of responsibility

14. Which has the greatest effect on conformity?
    a. one's gender
    b. testosterone levels
    c. the number of bystanders
    d. whether one's culture is collectivist

15. Alexei does not show up for soccer practice one day. Which of the following explanations for Alexei's absence is dispositional?
    a. Alexei is irresponsible.
    b. Alexei is not feeling well.
    c. Alexei has a prior commitment.
    d. Alexei has decided to quit the soccer team.

16. Sandy plays tennis very well. Lately she seems to play even better when other people watch her. The difference in Sandy's playing is most likely due to
    a. social loafing
    b. social identity
    c. social facilitation
    d. social comparison

17. Tami asks her mother for permission to go to an all-night party at a friend's house. Her mother refuses. Tami accepts this decision, but then asks if she can at least go to a smaller party at another friend's house. Her mother allows her to go. Which compliance technique has Tami used?
    a. lowball
    b. that's-not-all
    c. foot-in-the-door
    d. door-in-the-face

18. Alec is a 16-year-old Caucasian male, Bella is a 16-year-old Caucasian female, and Charles is a 16-year-old African American male. All three students are taking a standardized math test. On the first page of the test, they must indicate their age, gender, and race. Which student is least likely to be affected by stereotype threat?
    a. Alec
    b. Bella
    c. Charles
    d. All of the students will be affected by stereotype threat.

19. Which situation would be MOST likely to result in an increase in prejudice?
    a. completing a common task together
    b. working in competitive teams to complete a race
    c. directing each person to interact with as many others as possible
    d. forcing people to cooperate in order to get credit for an assignment

SOCIAL PSYCHOLOGY

CHAPTER 7 • Assessment

TEST YOURSELF

1. c		11. c	
2. b		12. d	
3. c		13. a	
4. b		14. d	
5. b		15. a	
6. c		16. c	
7. d		17. d	
8. a		18. a	
9. d		19. b	
10. a			

Ready for Testing

STUDENTS KNOW THEY ARE READY FOR TESTING IF THEY ARE ABLE TO . . .

- Describe the role social influence plays on conformity, compliance, and obedience.
- Discuss the issues of social cognition, including the formation and development of attitudes, impressions, and attributions.
- Introduce concepts of social interaction, including prejudice, discrimination, interpersonal attraction, aggression, and altruism.

CHAPTER 7 • Concept Summary

MULTIMEDIA CONTENT AVAILABLE AT
www.mypsychlab.com

Map the Concepts on mypsychlab.com

Study and Review Flashcards on mypsychlab.com

STUDY TIPS

Taking Multiple Choice Tests When taking multiple choice tests, students should scan the entire document before they begin, noting the number of questions and their point values. They can then use this information to pace themselves. For each question, caution students to read all the choices before selecting an answer, eliminating those choices they know to be wrong. Suggest the following strategy: Cover up the answers and try to anticipate the correct answer. If your answer is among the choices, circle it but then read the others to make sure none is better. When "all of the above" is a choice, it is probably the correct answer if at least two choices are correct. Recommend that students not skip questions they are unsure about, however—this increases the chances of forgetting to go back and answer some questions. Instead, have them answer as best they can and then mark the question to return to if time permits.

CHAPTER 7 Concept Summary: Social Psychology

Learning Objectives 18.1, 18.2, 18.3, 18.4 — pp. 214–223

- **the power of the situation** can affect our thoughts, actions, and feelings
- **conformity** changing one's behavior to more closely match the actions of others
- **compliance** changing one's behavior due to another person's request or demand
  - foot-in-the-door technique
  - door-in-the-face technique
  - lowball technique
  - that's-not-all technique
- **obedience** changing one's behavior at the direct order of an authority figure
  - a classic study by Milgram demonstrated that people are much more obedient to authority than thought, even when their own moral boundaries are tested

Social Influence
- **task performance** can be affected by social influence
  - social facilitation = positive influence
  - social impairment = negative influence
  - social loafing
- **leadership**
  - great person theory
  - transactional view
  - transformational view

Learning Objectives 19.1, 19.2, 19.3 — pp. 224–231

- **attitudes**
  - comprise affective, behavioral, and cognitive components
  - are not great predictors of behavior
  - can be formed through several processes
  - can change through persuasion

Attitude toward country music

- Affect (feelings): I like country music; it's fun and uplifting.
- Behavior (actions): I buy country music CDs every chance I get. I only listen to a country music station on the radio; I'm going to a country music concert soon.
- Cognition (thoughts): I think country music is better than any other kind of music I hear on the radio.

Social Cognition
- **cognitive dissonance** emotional discomfort caused by behavior that does not match the attitude
- **attribution** how we explain people's behavior
  - situational causes
  - dispositional causes
  - fundamental attribution error

246 CHAPTER 7

What Every Student Should Know About . . .

STUDY SKILLS

Concentration is the ability to focus without distraction. These concentration techniques can help improve students' study skills: (1) Study at the same time and place every day, if possible. (2) Study when you are most alert. (3) Create good study habits from the beginning of the year or semester. Because it is easier to make a habit than break one, it is better to start out with positive behaviors. (4) Use relaxation techniques. When you are relaxed, your concentration is better. (5) Create a study area and use it for studying *only*. This is important because you are creating a positive habitual behavior. Every time you sit down to study, your mind knows that it is time to concentrate and learn. (6) Turn off the telephone, television, and other distracters.

Learning Objectives 20.1 20.2 20.3 20.4 pp. 232–242

- **interpersonal attraction** liking or having the desire for a relationship with someone else.
  - physical attractiveness
  - proximity
  - similarity
  - complementary qualities
  - reciprocity of liking

Sternberg's Triangular Theory of Love

- Liking — Intimacy only
- Romantic Love — Intimacy + Passion
- Companionate Love — Intimacy + Commitment
- Consummate Love — Intimacy + Passion + Commitment
- Infatuation — Passion only
- Fatuous Love — Passion + Commitment
- Empty Love — Commitment only

- **love** is strong affection for another person due to kinship, personal ties, sexual attraction, admiration, or common interests
- **Sternberg's triangular theory** suggests different components of love

Social Interaction

- **prejudice and discrimination**
  - rely on negative **stereotypes**
  - cause members of a social group to be treated differently
  - vary based on in-groups and out-groups

- **prosocial** or socially desirable behavior benefits others
  - altruism
  - can be influenced by helper's mood and victim's gender, attractiveness, or "just rewards"; racial and ethnic differences can decrease probability of helping
  - can be negatively affected by presence of others

- **aggression** occurs when one person verbally or physically hurts or tries to destroy another person; often the result of frustration
  - may be partly attributed to genetics
  - can be triggered by variations in brain function and by internal or external chemical influences
  - is influenced by learning

SOCIAL PSYCHOLOGY 247

CHAPTER 7 • Concept Summary

STUDY TIPS

SQ3R SQ3R stands for "Survey, Question, Read, Recite, Review." Explain to students that SQ3R is a reading method that will help them organize and remember information. When they sit down to read a section of their textbook using this method, students will first **survey** the section. This means skimming the headings, subheadings, and captions in the section, as well as introductory and concluding paragraphs. Students should then skim the section again, this time asking themselves **questions** such as "What is this section about?" and turning the headings and subheadings into questions. After considering these questions briefly, students should **read** the section, looking for the answers. While reading, students should also note key terms and review graphic organizers. When reading is complete, students **recite** information from the section. To do this, they can ask themselves questions aloud or summarize aloud what they have read or jot down key points in their own words. The **review** part of the method is ongoing over several days. To review what they have read, students can write questions about the content, skim the material, or create graphic organizers to summarize the material in the section. Students might also create flash cards of key points in the section that they can use while studying.

Comprehension Check

CHAPTER 7 POSTTEST

To check their understanding, students should revisit the story on page 212 about "The Unresponsive Bystander: Why Did No One Help?" Ask them to review the information and then write a personal statement on how they would have reacted if they had been a bystander at either of the events described. Would they have become involved? Why or why not?

Chapter 7 Concept Summary **247**

CHAPTER 8 • Module 21

Launch the Chapter

CHAPTER GOALS AND LEARNING OBJECTIVES

Module 21 Culture

Understand culture's role in psychology.

21.1 What is culture?

21.2 How does culture vary across time and place?

21.3 How does culture influence our conceptions of self and identity?

21.4 What are some of the major areas of cross-cultural psychology research?

Module 22 Gender

Learn how gender identity develops.

22.1 What is gender, and what is gender identity?

22.2 What factors influence the development of gender identity?

22.3 How do men and women differ in thinking, social behavior, and personality?

DIFFERENTIATED INSTRUCTION KEY

Look for these symbols to help you adjust steps in each lesson to meet your students' needs.

- **L1** Special Needs
- **L2** Basic
- **ELL** English Language Learners
- **LPR** Less Proficient Readers
- **L3** All Students
- **L4** Advanced Students

CHAPTER 8
Culture and Gender

Surviving Sorrow: Providing Culture-Based Support for Haiti

On February 12, 2010, a 7.0 earthquake hit Haiti, sending 33 aftershocks through the country and leaving massive destruction in its wake. An estimated 250,000 people lost their lives, and thousands of others were injured. 1.5 million people were left homeless and without access to food or water. There was an immediate worldwide effort to gather supplies and enlist volunteer medical staff to assist the survivors of the disaster.

The need for medical assistance was not limited to physical wounds and diseases; many of the people who survived the earthquake suffered from post-traumatic stress disorder (PTSD) and depression. An emergency department technician who worked in one of the field hospitals described in a letter how one woman came in physically intact, but felt listless, tired, and constantly had a headache. When he asked for her symptoms, she began instead to tell him of the daughter and parents she had lost the day of the earthquake, the trapped son whom she had been able to hear for days afterward but had been unable to rescue, and the husband who had died from his wounds a few days before. The technician believed that the woman suffered from PTSD and depression, so he sent her to the field hospital's psychologist. After experiencing a powerful therapy session with the psychologist through an interpreter, the woman left the hospital able to smile again.

Part of the healing process for those left behind will be learning how to cope with their losses and find a way to start again. To help people suffering from depression and PTSD, psychologists looked at Haitian culture to determine how to begin. Religion is a large part of Haitian culture, and prayer has often been used to help them through difficult situations. Community and family are also a very important part of the culture, so doctors sought ways to help local communities, schools, and villages and thus help the individuals as well. By understanding the Haitian culture and traditional practices, volunteers can help the survivors begin the healing process.

248 CHAPTER 8

CORRELATION TO APA STANDARDS FOR CHAPTER 8

IVB. CULTURE AND GENDER

IVB-1. Culture .... pp. 250–256
IVB-2. Gender .... pp. 261–265

Why Study? Culture and Gender

We are all affected by the social influences that shape our lives and determine our identities. Culture and gender are two of these influences that particularly affect how we perceive ourselves and how we perceive the world around us. By studying psychology from cross-cultural and gender-based perspectives, we can gain a broader, more diverse, and more thorough understanding of human thought and behavior.

SCHEDULING				
1 Period = 50 min. 1 Block = 90 min.	Semester Course (18 weeks/90 days) Periods/Blocks		Full-Year Course (36 weeks/180 days) Period/Blocks	
Module 21	2.5	1.25	5	2.5
Module 22	2.5	1.25	5	2.5
Total Days for Chapter	5	2.5	10	5

CHAPTER 8 • Module 21

Teacher Prep

Culture is a shared set of beliefs, behaviors, values, and attitudes held by a group of people or a society. It is learned, it is shared, and it changes over time. Cultures are shaped by geographic factors like climate and by human factors like population density.

Cultures may be individualist or collectivist. People living in individualist cultures tend to have an independent self-concept, while people who live in collectivist cultures tend to have an interdependent self-concept.

Psychologists run studies on individuals from different cultural groups and compare the results to determine whether patterns of thought and behavior are universal (found across all cultures) or culture-bound (found only in particular cultures). People in different cultures may share many of the same emotions, but the degree of individualism or collectivism in our culture can affect how we label and express those emotions. Intelligence does not have a universal definition, and there is no universal way of measuring it.

Gender is the psychological aspect of being masculine or feminine. The expectations of one's culture, the development of one's personality, and one's sense of identity are all affected by the concept of gender. Both biological and environmental factors influence gender identity.

Females score higher on tests of verbal abilities than do males, but males score higher on tests of mathematical skills and spatial skills. Differences seem to be disappearing as society has begun to view the two genders as more equal in ability. This is taken as a sign that more equal treatment in society has reduced the gender difference. Males and females are socialized differently, which influences personality. However, males tend to "report" when in conversation, while females tend to "relate" when conversing.

CHAPTER 8 • Module 21

Focus

RESOURCES
Consult the appropriate sections of the Instructor's Manual, Videos, PowerPoint slides, and Tests for this module.

BEFORE CLASS
Students should read the section for homework before coming to class.

BELLRINGER
Ask students to write down a short definition of the word *culture*.

Teach

INTRODUCE THE TOPIC
Students may think of the word *culture* as meaning its more popular definition: "the quality in a person or society that arises from a concern for what is regarded as excellent in arts, letters, manners, scholarly pursuits, and so forth." Stress that in psychology, *culture* refers to "a shared set of beliefs, behaviors, values, and attitudes held by a group of people."

COVER THE MODULE
21.1 What is culture?
- *Culture* refers to a shared set of beliefs, behaviors, values, and attitudes held by a group of people or a society.
- *Norms* are a culture's understood rules for expected behavior, values, beliefs, and attitudes.
- **Common Characteristics of Culture**
  - Culture is learned.
  - Culture is shared.
  - Culture changes over time.

250 Chapter 8 Culture and Gender

Module 21 Culture

Module Goal
Understand culture's role in psychology.

Learning Objectives
- 21.1 What is culture?
- 21.2 How does culture vary across time and place?
- 21.3 How does culture influence our conceptions of self and identity?
- 21.4 What are some major areas of cross-cultural psychology research?

Understand Culture's Role in Psychology

Psychology is devoted to the examination of human thought and behavior—but does everyone around the world think and act in the same way? As a matter of fact, they don't. No matter how independent we may think we are, our thoughts and behaviors are partially influenced by the beliefs and values of our culture. Every day, these cultural forces affect the decisions we make, the values we hold, and even the way in which we see ourselves.

21.1 What is culture?

In the field of psychology, the term **culture** refers to a shared set of beliefs, behaviors, values, and attitudes held by a group of people or a society. The culture in which we live can have an enormous effect on our thoughts and actions. A culture's understood rules, or **norms**, tell us what behavior is acceptable or unacceptable. Cultural norms can influence a wide variety of beliefs and behaviors, from what we eat to how we worship. In many cases, cultural norms help us decide what behaviors are "normal" or "abnormal." For example, despite what your mother may have told you when you were younger, there is no biological basis for saying "please" and "thank you" at the dinner table. However, in many cultures, using polite language is an important example of "normal" behavior.

Common Characteristics of Culture While no two cultures are exactly alike, all cultures do share a few common characteristics. Here are a few of the most important qualities that all cultures share:

Culture is learned. It is not a biological or genetic phenomenon; children learn cultural norms and values from their parents or guardians, or from the society in which they grow up.

Culture is shared. Culture is a social phenomenon that connects humans and helps them work together. According to psychologist David Matsumoto, a prominent researcher in the field of cross-cultural psychology, the rules established by a culture actually help to ensure that culture's survival (1999).

Culture changes over time. For example, in the not-so-distant past, American fathers rarely stayed home to take care of their children. Instead, they

culture a shared set of beliefs, behaviors, values, and attitudes held by a group of people or a society.

norms a culture's understood rules for expected behavior, values, beliefs, and attitudes.

250 CHAPTER 8

Terms

• culture • norms • acculturation • individualism • collectivism • independent self-concept • interdependent self-concept • cross-cultural psychology • universal • culture-bound • display rules

▲ People come from a variety of ethnic and cultural backgrounds, which influence how they think and behave. How might learning more about a person's cultural background help you understand his or her thoughts and behaviors?

were expected to provide financial support. Over the past several years, however, more and more American men have taken on childcare duties, and the idea of being a stay-at-home dad is far less unusual than it once was (Shaver, 2007). Cultural norms create an environment that shapes our behavior, but norms—like other environmental influences in our lives—can change drastically over time.

I think I get the big picture, but how are the things I do every day affected by my culture?

Have you ever shaken someone's hand or given a high five? What do those gestures mean to you? In many cultures within the United States, a handshake is a common form of greeting and a high five means "Good job!" If you tried to give a person from another culture a handshake or a high five, however, he or she might not understand what you were doing, because those gestures do not have the same meanings in different cultures. In Japan, for example, people traditionally greet each other by bowing rather than by shaking hands.

The language you speak, the spiritual beliefs you hold, and the moral values to which you adhere are also important parts of your culture that most likely impact you every day. When you chat with your friends, attend a religious service, or volunteer for a cause you believe in, you are acting under the influence of culture.

◀ I think I get the big picture, but how are the things I do every day affected by my culture?

21.2 How does culture vary across time and place?

Although all cultures have certain general characteristics in common, there is a huge amount of variation from one culture to the next. Around the world, cultures are shaped by geographic factors like climate and the availability of natural resources, as well as by human factors like population density and technological development (Matsumoto, 1993).

CULTURE AND GENDER 251

CHAPTER 8 • Module 21

UNDERSTANDING VISUALS

Direct students' attention to the photograph on this page and discuss the caption question. Students should recognize that understanding and respecting other people's perspectives are easier if you know the characteristics of their cultures.

DISCUSS THE STUDENT VOICE QUESTION

Ask students to provide a few examples of how their daily interactions with other people are affected by their culture.

EXTEND THE DISCUSSION

Explain to students that ethnocentrism involves judging other cultures against the standards of one's own culture. Ethnocentric people think their own way of doing things is "normal," while other people's ways of doing things are "abnormal." In other words, they forget that what may be considered normal or abnormal in their culture is not necessarily considered the same in another culture.

TEACHING TIP

When a class is too large for a single discussion, break the class into two groups, with inner and outer circles. Partners may then take turns participating in the discussion. Students should take notes about the comments their partner made.

Explore

DEPICTING NORMS

Remind students that norms are a culture's understood rules for expected behavior, values, beliefs, and attitudes. Then tell the class to assume that a student from a foreign culture has just enrolled in their school. Ask them to think about the norms particular to an American high school. What would they tell the new student about those cultural norms? Have students prepare a short written report, draw a poster, or create an audiovisual presentation on this topic.

Module 21 Culture 251

CHAPTER 8 • Module 21

COVER THE MODULE

21.2 How does culture vary across time and place?

- Although cultures have certain characteristics in common, there are many variations among cultures, which are shaped by geographic factors like climate and the availability of natural resources, as well as by human factors like population density and technological development.

- **Cultural Differences and Similarities: China and the United States**
  - American and Chinese cultural traditions may seem strange or surprising to other cultures, but they are common to the people who live with them daily.
  - Cultural differences do not imply that one culture is better or worse than another.
  - When we study how cultures vary, we gain a better understanding of other lifestyles and perspectives.

L3 DIFFERENTIATED INSTRUCTION

Engaging All Learners Assist in time management. When requiring students to complete projects or long-term assignments, provide a calendar that breaks down the requirements by due dates. Review the checklist with students and monitor their use of the checklist and task completion as the assignment proceeds. Many students will experience significant difficulties in self-managing the time needed to complete complex and long-term assignments.

252 Chapter 8 Culture and Gender

All of these factors, for example, affect life in the Lahaul Valley, a region nestled in the Himalayas in northern India. Currently, the valley can only be reached by traveling through one of the highest mountain passes in the world, the Rohtang Pass. This road is covered with snow for 6 months of the year, and many people have lost their lives trying to travel along the Rohtang Pass during the winter. As a result, the people of the Lahaul Valley generally cannot leave their homes for months at a time. During the cold winter months, there is no light, no mail delivery, and no fresh vegetables (Polgreen, 2010). Life in the Lahaul Valley is obviously very different from life in a major metropolitan area like Beijing or London, where the climate is milder, natural resources are more accessible, the population is larger and denser, and advanced technologies are easier to come by. In June 2010, however, work began on a tunnel that will bypass the Rohtang Pass and connect the Lahaul Valley to the rest of India year-round. This technological development will almost certainly lead to cultural changes as the people who live in the valley gain greater access to resources and become more able to interact with people outside their geographic area.

If you have traveled to another country—or even to another part of your own country—you have probably already seen the effects of cultural diversity in the real world. Even within the United States, there is a wealth of cultural variety: Ford and Toyota drivers in Lancaster County, Pennsylvania share the road with horses and buggies driven by their Amish neighbors. Some road signs in Texas give instructions in both Spanish and English, while some road signs in northern Maine feature both French and English phrases. If we tried to list all the differences and similarities among all the world's cultures, our list would take up the rest of this book (and it still wouldn't be complete!). Instead, we will take a look at differences and similarities between the cultures in two countries—China and the United States.

Cultural Differences and Similarities: China and the United States Many Chinese cultural traditions might seem unusual or surprising to an American audience, but keep in mind that many American cultural traditions would seem equally strange to a Chinese audience. Differences between cultures do not imply that one culture is better or worse than another. When we study how cultures vary, we gain a greater understanding of other lifestyles and other points of view, and we begin to appreciate the diversity that makes our world so interesting. We are also likely to find ways in which other cultures are not so different from our own.

In both China and the United States, celebrations and rituals that mark family events such as births, marriages, and deaths are important, but these events are celebrated differently in each culture. In the United States, for example, a baby shower is usually held a few weeks before the baby's birth, but in China, the baby shower is held after the baby arrives. In Western culture, it is traditional to wear black clothing to a funeral, but at traditional Chinese funerals, the dress code is slightly different: The immediate family of the deceased person wears black, but the grandchildren of the deceased wear blue, and the great-grandchildren wear light blue.

Brides in the United States often wear white gowns, but in China, the color white is associated with mourning and is generally avoided at traditional weddings. Red, on the other hand, symbolizes happiness in Chinese culture, and many Chinese brides wear red dresses. In China, it is traditional to give a newly married couple a check or cash in a red envelope as a wedding

252 CHAPTER 8

Class Activity

CULTURAL DIFFERENCES AND SIMILARITIES

Ask one or more teens or adults from other cultures to come to your class to discuss how life in their culture is similar to and different from that of the majority of your students. Consider having the class prepare questions ahead of time for your visitors, which you can review and pass on to the speakers.

Sometimes, a couple will choose to incorporate traditions from both cultures into their wedding. This couple has decided to have western attire for the bride and groom, although the rest of the bridal party is wearing traditional Chinese clothes.

gift, while in the United States, couples often create "wedding registries" on which they list the silverware, kitchen appliances, and other gifts they hope to receive from their guests. At many weddings in the United States, the bride and groom hug and shake hands with their guests after the ceremony, while at the end of a Chinese wedding reception, the bride and groom are joined by their parents and other relatives. The entire family thanks the guests for attending, a tradition which highlights the importance of the family in Chinese culture.

Despite the differences between traditional Chinese and traditional American weddings, it should be clear by now that in both cultures, weddings are important celebrations of family and friendship, involving quite a lot of planning, budgeting, feasting, and gift-giving. In addition, many modern wedding ceremonies in both China and America are marked by cross-cultural influences. For example, although many Chinese brides still wear red gowns, white wedding gowns have become more popular in China in recent years, likely due to Western influences. And a popular American wedding planning Web site offers brides- and grooms-to-be "Five ways to feng shui your wedding," suggesting tips for incorporating ancient Chinese traditions into Western-style celebrations. This type of cross-cultural communication and inspiration is currently thriving as people around the world become familiar with cultures outside their own.

Explore

CELEBRATIONS AND RITUALS IN OTHER CULTURES

Have students explore how another culture conducts its celebrations or rituals. Tell students to interview someone from a different culture, such as a relative, friend, or neighbor, and learn how a holiday or other significant event is celebrated in that culture. How is it different from the way in which that event is celebrated in the student's culture? Are there any similarities? Then have students report back to the class via a short written account of what they learned.

CHAPTER 8 • Module 21

COVER THE MODULE (continued)
- In both China and the United States, celebrations and rituals that mark family events are important.
- Many of these modern events are marked by cross-cultural influences that are incorporated into ceremonies, such as weddings.

EXTEND THE LESSON
Ask students who have traveled to other parts of the country or the world to discuss some of the cultural differences they have witnessed. Then ask, "Did those differences make the other cultures better or worse than your own culture—or just different from yours?"

L3 DIFFERENTIATED INSTRUCTION
Help students be organized. Many students have difficulty organizing their time. Break down assignments into short tasks. Require students to submit a plan for completing a large project. Teach skills such as notebook organization. Hand out assignment sheets ahead of time, allowing students to organize their time for the upcoming week or unit. Keep a master notebook with class notes, handouts, and homework that students may consult if they miss a day of class.

CHAPTER 8 • Module 21

COVER THE MODULE (continued)
- **Immigration and Acculturation**
  - *Acculturation* is the process of adapting to a new culture by adopting the new culture's beliefs and behaviors.
  - Some immigrants integrate their new identities into their existing identities, seeing themselves as members of both cultures simultaneously. Other immigrants, however, maintain their earlier cultural connections and resist identifying with their new culture.
  - Research suggests that immigrants who identify with both their birth culture and their new culture are likely to have large, interconnected social networks of friends from the new culture, while immigrants who do not identify with their new culture are less likely to have these types of friendships.
  - Age makes a difference when it comes to transitioning to a new culture. Children tend to acculturate more quickly than do adults.
  - Children born into a culture that is not their parents' native culture may also experience this cultural gap in their household.

DISCUSS THE STUDENT VOICE QUESTIONS
Use the student voice questions on this page as a starting point for a class discussion about acculturation. If any students are immigrants from other cultures, ask volunteers to share how the acculturation process has worked for them and their family.

Immigration and Acculturation

▶ *If there are so many differences between cultures, isn't it hard for people who move to a new culture to adjust?*

If there are so many differences between cultures, isn't it hard for people who move to a new culture to adjust?

For a variety of reasons, many people move from one culture to another at some point during their lives, and this transition can present psychological challenges. When individuals who are born and raised in one culture join a new culture, they may experience **acculturation**, the process of adapting to a new culture by adopting the new culture's beliefs and behaviors.

But adapting to a new culture is hardly a simple process, and not all immigrants come to identify with their new culture over time. For example, researchers have noted that some Chinese people who move to the United States integrate their new American identities into their existing Chinese identities, seeing themselves as members of both cultures simultaneously. Other Chinese immigrants to the United States, however, maintain their Chinese cultural connections and resist identifying with their new American culture. Research findings suggest that immigrants who identify with both their birth culture and their new culture are likely to have large, interconnected social networks of friends from the new culture, while immigrants who do not identify with their new culture are less likely to have these types of friendships (Mok et al., 2007).

▶ *My parents and I moved to this country when I was 6 years old. It's been a lot easier for me to adapt to our new culture than it has been for my parents. Is that normal?*

My parents and I moved to this country when I was 6 years old. It's been a lot easier for me to adapt to our new culture than it has been for my parents. Is that normal?

When it comes to transitioning to a new culture, age does appear to make a difference: When researchers studied Russians who had moved to the United States during the 1980s and 1990s, they discovered that while the adult immigrants saw themselves as more Russian than American, the children saw themselves as more American than Russian (Birman & Trickett, 2001). In other words, the children had acculturated more quickly than the adults had. When families move from one culture to another, there tends to be an "acculturation gap" between parents and their children, although the degree and nature of the gap depends on several factors, including the age of the child and the culture of origin. Children who move when they are so young that they can't clearly remember their culture of origin will probably not have much difficulty adjusting to their new culture, and people who immigrate to countries with cultures very similar to their own will likely have an easier time adjusting as well.

Children born into a culture which is not their parents' native culture may also experience this cultural gap in their households: Sometimes, when parents and children are born into different cultures, the parents' cultural expectations don't quite matchup with their children's cultural expectations (O'Brien, 2009). For example, an Indian American girl born in the United States may feel uncomfortable when her Indian-born parents suggest an arranged marriage for her, because while arranged marriages are fairly common in parts of India, they are not very common in the United States.

Regardless of whether immigrants to a new culture embrace that new culture, maintain their connections to their home culture, or try to incorporate both cultures into their lives, the process of immigration and acculturation can be challenging and stressful. But it also gives people from different backgrounds the opportunity to share their traditions with each other and celebrate the richness and diversity of cultures around the world.

acculturation the process of adapting to a new culture by adopting the new culture's beliefs and behaviors.

Class Activity

DEBATING ACCULTURATION
Explain to students that immigrants' responses to moving from one culture to another can vary considerably. Some immigrants integrate their new identities into their existing identities, considering themselves as members of both cultures. Other immigrants resist identifying with their new culture. Divide the class into two groups and conduct a debate on this topic: "It is better for immigrants to adapt to their new cultures as thoroughly as possible, rather than to hold on to their birth cultures." Tell students to provide support for their viewpoints.

21.3 How does culture influence our conceptions of self and identity?

Which is more important to you, your independence or your role as a member of your family? Do you think of yourself as an individual? Or do you see yourself as one member in a larger, interconnected community? Is it more important for you to meet your own personal goals or to help your friends and family meet their goals?

Whatever your answers to these questions are, it is likely that your answers have been shaped by cultural influences. Some cultures value **individualism**, meaning that they prioritize individuality, independence, and personal needs. Other cultures, however, value **collectivism**. These cultures emphasize the interdependence of all people in a group, and they tend to value group goals and needs more highly than individual goals and needs. Can you see how a person from an individualist culture and a person from a collectivist culture would answer the above questions differently?

Which cultures are individualist, and which are collectivist?

Most cultures are not 100 percent individualist or 100 percent collectivist. It makes sense to think about a scale with pure individualism on one end, pure collectivism on the other end, and most cultures falling somewhere in the middle. We can say in general, though, that cultures in the United States, Great Britain, France, and Australia tend to be more individualist, while cultures in places like Japan, China, Egypt, and Mexico tend to be more collectivist.

Individualism, Collectivism, and Self-Concept Psychologists have found that the degree to which a culture is individualist or collectivist can influence how people in that culture think of themselves. Two prominent researchers in cross-cultural psychology, Hazel Markus and Shinobu Kitayama, have spent years comparing how people think and act in individualist countries like the United States and in collectivist countries like Japan. Their research (1991) strongly supports the idea that people in the United States have an **independent self-concept**, meaning that Americans view themselves as entirely independent from their friends, family members, classmates, and coworkers, as shown in Figure 21.1 on the next page. They are more likely to describe themselves through references to their individual goals or desires; for example, an American might say, "I am a scientist" or "I am creative." In contrast, people in Japan have an **interdependent self-concept**, meaning that Japanese people view themselves in terms of their social roles and relationships. They see themselves as fundamentally connected to their friends, family members, classmates, and coworkers, and they are more likely to describe themselves through references to their social roles. While an American might say, "I am a scientist," a Japanese person might say, "I am a daughter and a sister." Table 21.1 on the next page shows more examples of independent and interdependent tasks.

Being brought up in an individualist or collectivist culture can also influence how people think of others. In the United States, we tend to attribute other people's behavior to their personalities and other internal characteristics rather than to their social positions and other external situations. LINK to *Chapter Seven: Social Psychology, p. 229–230.* But people raised in more collectivist cultures are more likely to attribute others' behavior to situational factors (Miller, 1984). For example, imagine that a man is walking quickly down

◀ Which cultures are individualist, and which are collectivist?

individualism a cultural style that emphasizes the importance of individuality, independence, and personal needs.

collectivism a cultural style that emphasizes the importance of interdependence, group goals, and group needs.

independent self-concept an individual's perception of self as entirely independent from others.

interdependent self-concept an individual's perception of self as fundamentally connected to others.

CULTURE AND GENDER 255

CHAPTER 8 • Module 21

COVER THE MODULE

21.3 How does culture influence our conceptions of self and identity?

- *Individualism* is a cultural style that emphasizes the importance of individuality, independence, and personal needs. Cultures in the United States, Great Britain, France, and Australia tend to be more individualist.

- *Collectivism* is a cultural style that emphasizes the importance of interdependence, group goals, and group needs. Cultures in Japan, China, Egypt, and Mexico tend to be more collectivist.

- **Individualism, Collectivism, and Self-Concept**
  - The degree to which a culture is individualist or collectivist can influence how people in that culture think of themselves.
  - People in the United States have an *independent self-concept*, meaning that they view themselves as entirely independent from others.
  - People in Japan have an *interdependent self-concept*, meaning that they view themselves in terms of their social needs and relationships.

LINK to *Chapter Seven: Social Psychology,* pp. 229–230.

FAST FACT

Ask volunteers the age at which they had their earliest childhood memory. Then explain that researchers have found that the average age of first memories varies up to 2 years among cultures. The way in which parents discuss—or do not discuss—the events in children's lives influences how the children will later remember those events. People who grow up in societies that focus on individual personal history, like the United States, will have different—and often earlier—childhood memories than will people who grow up in cultures that, like many Asian cultures, value interdependence.

Critical Thinking (Kinesthetic)

DISCUSSING INDIVIDUALISM AND COLLECTIVISM

Have the class sit in two circles, one circle inside the other, with each student facing a classmate "partner." Ask students to have a brief discussion with each other about whether they would prefer to live in an individualist culture or a collectivist culture. Tell students to give reasons for their opinions. After a few minutes, rotate the outer circle so that students have a new "partner." Continue rotating until the outer circle has moved completely around the inner circle.

CHAPTER 8 • Module 21

UNDERSTANDING VISUALS

Direct students' attention to Figure 21.1 and Table 21.1. Check for understanding by asking a volunteer to explain what Figure 21.1 shows and by having students come up with additional examples of independent and interdependent tasks for Table 21.1.

EXTEND THE LESSON

Tell students that *cultural relativism* is the belief that a culture should be evaluated according to its own standards, not those of any other culture. This means that there really are no good or bad cultures. Persons are better able to understand the standards of other cultures when they do not assume that their own is somehow better.

L1 DIFFERENTIATED INSTRUCTION

Special Needs Make sure that you have adequately scaffolded tasks for special-needs students and equipped them with writing instruction and practice that build the prerequisite skills.

Independent Self-Concept

Interdependent Self-Concept

FIGURE 21.1 Independent and Interdependent Self-Concepts
Source: Adapted from Markus & Kitayama, 1991.

the sidewalk, pushing aside people who stand in his way and not pausing to excuse himself or apologize. How would you explain this behavior? People from individualist cultures might say that the man is a rude, thoughtless person, while people from collectivist cultures would be more likely to consider external reasons for the man's behavior: They may think that he is late for an important meeting, or he is about to miss his train, or his wife is giving birth and he is trying to get to the hospital before the baby arrives.

Table 21.1	Independence vs. Interdependence
INDEPENDENT TASKS	**INTERDEPENDENT TASKS**
Be unique	Belong; try to fit in
Express yourself	Occupy your proper place
Meet your own goals	Help others meet their goals
Say what's on your mind	Be indirect; try to know what others are thinking

Source: Adapted from Markus & Kitayama, 1991.

Class Activity

DISCUSSING INDEPENDENCE AND INTERDEPENDENCE

Point out to the class that teenagers are at a time in their life span when they may struggle with wanting to be independent and yet needing to have connections with (and the approval of) their peers. Conduct a class discussion about which of these viewpoints students find most significant in their own life. Is it more important to be independent from others or to be part of a group? Why?

21.4 What are some major areas of cross-cultural psychology research?

Cross-cultural psychology, the study of human thought and behavior across cultures, is an important area of study in its own right, but it would be wrong to suggest that cross-cultural psychology is entirely separate from the other psychological perspectives discussed in this textbook. Cultural influences affect a huge range of research areas, from human development, cognition, and intelligence to emotion, motivation, personality, and abnormal behavior.

Because it took place largely in Europe and the United States, most early psychology research was strongly influenced by Western cultural forces such as democracy, Judeo-Christianity, secularism, and individualism. Psychologists and the people they studied were often all members of the same culture, and no one thought to question whether people raised in other cultures would think and behave differently in certain situations. These days, however, psychologists in all areas of the field are taking cultural influences into consideration in their research. Cross-cultural psychologists run studies on individuals from different cultural groups and compare the results to determine whether patterns of thought and behavior are **universal** (found across all cultures) or **culture-bound** (found only in particular cultures). Many aspects of human psychology appear to be universal. For example, evidence suggests that there are seven basic emotions shared across cultures: anger, fear, sadness, happiness, surprise, disgust, and contempt (Ekman, 1973; Ekman & Friesen, 1969, 1971). In many cases, however, psychologists are discovering that the behaviors they previously believed were universal may actually be strongly affected by culture.

What exactly are cross-cultural psychologists discovering? To answer that question, let's take a closer look at a few of the many areas of cross-cultural psychology research.

Emotion People in different cultures may share many of the same emotions, but the degree of individualism or collectivism in our culture can affect how we label and express those emotions. According to researcher Phoebe Ellsworth, we interpret experiences differently based on our cultural backgrounds, and those different interpretations of experiences lead to different emotional reactions. To illustrate her point, Ellsworth used fish—computer-animated fish, to be exact. She showed Chinese and American subjects animations of fish interacting with each other and then asked the subjects to label the fish's emotions. For example, one animation showed a blue fish being approached from both sides by a lot of other different-colored fish. When they saw this animation, most of the Chinese participants said that the blue fish was feeling happy, but most of the American participants said that the blue fish was feeling afraid. Ellsworth believes that this difference in responses is due in part to China's more collectivist culture and the United States' more individualist culture: It makes sense that the approach of a large group would seem like a happy event to collectivists and a potentially frightening event to individualists (Swanbrow, 1998).

People from different cultures not only label emotions differently, but also express emotions differently—at least when they are around others. In the 1970s, experimenters conducted research to determine how American and Japanese participants expressed their emotional reactions to a stressful film. They found that when the American and Japanese participants watched the film alone in a darkened theater, the participants made similar facial expressions (indicating anger and fear, for example) regardless of their cultural background. When they watched the film in the company of an experimenter, however, the Japanese

cross-cultural psychology the study of human thought and behavior across cultures.

universal found across all cultures.

culture-bound found only in particular cultures.

CHAPTER 8 • Module 21

COVER THE MODULE

21.4 What are some major areas of cross-cultural psychology research?

- *Cross-cultural psychology* is the study of human thought and behavior across cultures.
- Most early psychology research was strongly influenced by Western cultural forces. However, modern psychologists are taking cultural influences into consideration in their research.
- These psychologists want to determine whether patterns of thought and behavior are universal (found across all cultures) or *culture-bound* (found only in particular cultures).
- Many aspects of human psychology appear to be *universal*. Seven basic emotions are shared across cultures: anger, fear, sadness, happiness, surprise, disgust, and contempt.
- **Emotion**
  - The degree of individualism or collectivism in a culture can affect how people label and express emotions.
  - People interpret experiences differently, based on their cultural backgrounds, and those different interpretations of experiences lead to different emotional reactions.
  - People from different cultures also express emotions differently. Each culture has its own display rules, or learned ways of controlling displays of emotion in social settings.

L(I)(N)(K) to *Chapter Eleven: Motivation and Emotion, pp. 363–364*.

Explore (Kinesthetic)

EXPRESSING EMOTIONS

Send students to library or Internet resources to research ways in which emotions are expressed, or not expressed, in different cultures. Then have them select one of the examples they found and write a brief "scenario" in which a person from that culture experiences a situation that would lead him or her to feel an emotion such as anger, fear, sadness, happiness, surprise, disgust, or contempt. Students should include appropriate thoughts or dialogue that shows how the person might react to that emotion. Ask volunteers to present their scenarios to the class. If appropriate, consider having these students "act out" their scenarios for their classmates.

CHAPTER 8 • Module 21

COVER THE MODULE (continued)

- **Intelligence**
  - Intelligence is measured differently in various cultures.

  LINK to *Chapter Ten: Thinking and Intelligence,* p. 321.

  - Traditional IQ tests are not free from cultural bias. These tests reflect the language, norms, and valued skills of the cultures in which they are created.
  - The word *intelligence* does not have a universal definition, and there is no universal way of measuring it.

MULTIMEDIA CONTENT AVAILABLE AT
www.mypsychlab.com

Watch a video with Robert Sternberg discussing cultural influences on intelligence on **mypsychlab.com**

UNDERSTANDING VISUALS

Direct students' attention to the photograph on this page. Ask a volunteer to explain how the concept of intelligence is shaped by cultural forces. *(Possible answer: What makes a person "intelligent" in one culture may not be appropriate in another culture.)*

L2 ELL DIFFERENTIATED INSTRUCTION

English Language Learners Use realia and visuals (e.g., photographs, objects, color transparencies) to make the concepts less abstract.

258 Chapter 8 Culture and Gender

---

display rules learned ways of controlling displays of emotion in social settings.

participants tended to control their facial expressions, smiling or appearing calm and composed even when they felt afraid or angry. The American participants, on the other hand, continued to show their true emotions through facial expressions when the experimenter was present (Ekman, 1972; Friesen, 1972). Why does this happen? Each culture has its own **display rules**, or learned ways of controlling displays of emotion in social settings. **LINK** *to Chapter Eleven: Motivation and Emotion, pp. 363–364.* Psychologists now believe that there is a connection between a culture's individualism or collectivism and its display rules. In other words, your culture's individualist or collectivist tendencies will at least partially determine the degree to which you control your expressions of emotion in social situations (Matsumoto et al., 1998).

Intelligence Cultural factors affect psychologists' research not only in the study of emotion but also in the study of human intelligence. What does it mean to be intelligent? Does it mean that you have a high IQ, earn straight As and attend a prestigious university? Not necessarily. Not only is this a narrow definition of intelligence, but it also fails to take cultural considerations into account. **LINK** *to Chapter Ten: Thinking and Intelligence, p. 321.* IQ scores, letter grades, and college acceptances are sometimes considered to be signs of intelligence in the United States, but in other cultures, intelligence is measured differently.

The intelligence researcher Robert Sternberg and his colleagues studied children in Kenya to determine how well they could identify natural herbal medicines used frequently in their community. The researchers also gave the Kenyan children two intelligence tests. When they reviewed their results, the researchers discovered that there was actually a *negative* relationship between the children's ability to correctly identify the medicines and their scores on one of the intelligence tests. In other words, the better a child did on the medicine-identification task, the worse he or she did on the intelligence test. Within the cultural context of a small Kenyan village, this result makes sense: Most children have no use for Western schooling in their village, where their lives revolve around farming and other occupations that are valuable to their culture, so there is no reason for children to learn the information that would help them perform well on a standard Western intelligence test. Having a good working knowledge of herbal medicines, however, is very valuable to the community, and it is this type of intelligence that matters most within the culture (Sternberg, 2002). **Watch** on **mypsychlab.com**

Intelligence researchers are well aware that traditional IQ tests are not free from cultural bias: These tests reflect the language, the norms, and the valued skills of the cultures in which they are created. For example, if a question refers to the process of voting for elected officials, people who come from democratic cultures and are very familiar with the concept of voting will be able to answer the question more easily than people who come from cultures in which free elections and voting are unfamiliar concepts. Many intelligence test designers now believe that it may be impossible to create a test that is completely free of cultural bias (Carpenter et al., 1990). When we talk about what intelligence means and how it can be measured, it is important for us to remember that "intelligence" does not have a universal definition, and there is no universal way of measuring it. It takes different forms in different cultures.

Development Across the Life Span In the United States in the 21st century, most children attend school until they are at least 17 or 18 years old, and many teenagers and young adults attend college. We generally start our careers in our 20s; we generally find romantic partners and start families in our 20s and 30s. This path from childhood to adulthood may seem familiar and

Watch a video with Robert Sternberg discussing cultural influences on intelligence on **mypsychlab.com**

▲ A child from Kenya might not perform well on an IQ test that reflects American cultural expectations and values, but that same child might perform very well on an IQ test that reflects her own cultural background. How is the concept of "intelligence" shaped by cultural forces?

258 CHAPTER 8

Class Activity

CREATING A CULTURE-FAIR INTELLIGENCE TEST

Divide students into small groups. Instruct each group to come to a consensus about the kinds of questions that should be on a culture-fair intelligence test. After the groups have finished, ask each to report on its conclusions. Engage the entire class in discussions of each proposal, carefully examining how culture or specific experiences (e.g., education) might influence the results.

normal, but if you think about it for a few minutes, you'll realize that this "normal" developmental path is heavily influenced by cultural values and expectations. In some cultures, many people work, marry, and begin to raise families when they are still teenagers. According to a 2005 report by the United Nations Population Fund, for example, teenage marriage is not uncommon in parts of Africa and Southern Asia. In other cultures, particularly European and North American cultures, marriage rates have declined over time and the average age of people getting married for the first time has risen (Talbot, 2010).

Even within the United States, age-related roles and responsibilities can vary by culture: While a 14-year-old boy who lives in an apartment in New York City might spend his days going to school, doing homework, and playing basketball, a 14-year-old boy living on a farm in the Midwest might spend most of his days working on the farm and doing his school work with family members at home. He might learn to drive a tractor several years before other children his age learn to drive a car. When an individual takes on adult responsibilities at an earlier age, he or she may advance through the psychological stages of development (like those proposed by Freud, Erikson, & Kohlberg) more rapidly than his or her peers who grow up with different responsibilities and cultural expectations. Research has found, in fact, that while Kohlberg's stages of moral development do appear to be universal, the age at which people reach each of Kohlberg's stages differs across cultures (Chen & Farruggia, 2002).

Abnormal Behavior What behaviors are considered "abnormal?" The answer to this question differs from culture to culture, and there is no single, universal definition of abnormal behavior or mental illness. What appears strange, disturbing, or unhealthy to members of one culture may appear relatively normal to members of another culture, and even when an abnormal behavior seems to exist across cultures, it may be expressed in different ways. According to researchers David Lackland Sam and Virginia Moreira, "To deal with mental health is to deal with culture" (2002).

For example, Sam and Moreira point out that psychologists used to assume that depression was a universal mental illness. However, while people from Western cultures who are diagnosed with depression commonly report feeling unhappy, anxious, and not good enough, people from non-Western cultures who are diagnosed with depression commonly report physical symptoms like dizziness, headaches, and trouble sleeping. Does depression take different forms in different cultures? Can it even truly be called the same disorder in a Western culture and in a non-Western culture? Cross-cultural psychologists who investigate mental illness are still searching for answers to these questions.

Psychologists do know that some disorders are culture-bound—that is, they are only found in particular cultures. These syndromes are recognized as illnesses in the cultures in which they occur. Anorexia nervosa, for example, is an eating disorder that causes people to starve themselves in order to become thin. While anorexia is a relatively common disorder in the United States and other Western cultures, it is not usually found in non-Western cultures (Bemporad, 1997; Garner & Garfinkel, 1980). Similarly, the disorder *taijin kyofusho*, which is characterized by fear of embarrassing or offending others with one's appearance or actions, is found primarily in Japan and Korea (Jilek, 2001). LINK to *Chapter Thirteen: Psychological Disorders, pp. 411–412.*

The study of human thought and behavior across cultures fascinates many modern-day psychologists, and rightly so: Cross-cultural psychology can open our eyes to the differences that make our world fascinating and rich, and it can help us recognize the similarities that unite us all as human beings.

CHAPTER 8 • Module 21

COVER THE MODULE *(continued)*

- **Development Across the Life Span**
  - A "normal" developmental path is heavily influenced by cultural values and expectations.
  - Even within one country, age-related roles and responsibilities can vary by culture.
  - When individuals take on adult responsibilities at an earlier age, they may advance through the psychological stages of development more rapidly than their peers who grow up with different responsibilities and cultural expectations.

- **Abnormal Behavior**
  - There is no single, universal definition of *abnormal behavior* or *mental illness*.
  - Some disorders are culture-bound, being found only in particular cultures. These syndromes are recognized as illnesses in the cultures in which they occur.

LINK to *Chapter Thirteen: Psychological Disorders, pp. 411–412.*

L2 LPR DIFFERENTIATED INSTRUCTION

Less Proficient Readers For students with difficulties with vocabulary and fluency, intentionally revisit newly acquired vocabulary during discussions.

Explore

WHAT IS NORMAL?

Remind students that abnormal behavior varies across societies and countries. Each culture has its own ideas of what is considered normal and abnormal. Therefore, what is seen as a mental disorder in one society is not necessarily seen in the same way in another. In addition, cultures change over time in terms of what is acceptable behavior. What may seem normal today may have been seen as unacceptable in the past or may be frowned upon in the future. For example, women in Western cultures have not always worn masculine attire, such as pants. Have students select a specific behavior and then research the topic to learn how, when, and where the behavior has been considered normal and abnormal. Tell them to create a chart that lists the facts of what they have learned and then present it to the class.

CHAPTER 8 • Module 21

Assess

Assign the Module 21 Practice Quiz.

Use the Practice Quiz to identify gaps in student understanding.

REMEDIATE

Have students, individually or in groups, review the module goals, learning objectives, and key terms.

Refer students to the Concept Summary on p. 270 for review.

Close

As a class, discuss what students have learned about other cultures that interested or surprised them.

Practice Quiz

Pick the best answer.

1. Which of the following statements about culture is true?
   a. It is possible to identify with more than one culture.
   b. It is not difficult to move from one culture to another.
   c. Cultural factors do not affect most aspects of people's daily lives.
   d. No country can contain more than one culture.

2. A culture may have certain rules, traditions, or beliefs that people are expected to follow. These rules are known as
   a. norms
   b. roles
   c. display rules
   d. self-concepts

3. _____ thoughts and behaviors are those which are the same in many different cultures all over the world.
   a. Normal
   b. Universal
   c. Collective
   d. Culture-bound

4. Which of the following people is likely to make the fastest transition from an old culture to a new culture?
   a. a 10-year-old girl
   b. a 30-year-old man
   c. a 50-year-old woman
   d. an 80-year-old man

5. A man who thinks of himself in terms of his relationship to his family and coworkers is most likely from a(n) _____ culture.
   a. individualist
   b. collectivist
   c. developing
   d. industrialized

6. IQ tests are not a preferred measure of intelligence in cross-cultural psychology because
   a. The tests are outdated and do not analyze modern skills.
   b. IQ changes too quickly to be measured accurately.
   c. Intelligence takes different forms in different cultures.
   d. Psychologists cannot write tests in languages other than English.

7. Which of the following statements is the best illustration of an independent self-concept?
   a. "I am a friendly and considerate person."
   b. "I am a mother to three small boys."
   c. "I am a teacher in a public high school."
   d. "I am a member of the basketball team."

8. Which of the following is NOT a culture-bound action?
   a. smiling
   b. shaking hands
   c. giving a thumbs-up
   d. making a victory "V" sign with two fingers

9. In which of the following scenarios does display rules play a part?
   a. A girl moves to a new country with her family. She makes friends with people from her new culture but still feels like she is part of her old culture.
   b. A girl brings food and decorations from her home culture to school to share her cultural background with her friends.
   c. A girl watches a sad movie with friends. She wants to cry, but because she is with other people, she keeps her emotions to herself.
   d. A girl takes an IQ test designed in a culture different from her own, and she is not familiar with many of the terms and concepts used in the test.

10. Which of the following research questions would a cross-cultural psychologist most likely ask?
    a. Is there a biological basis for depression?
    b. Can moving to a new country cause depression?
    c. Are symptoms of depression different now than they were in the past?
    d. Do people in different countries experience depression in the same way?

260 CHAPTER 8

Practice Quiz Answers

1. a
2. a
3. b
4. a
5. b
6. c
7. c
8. a
9. c
10. d

260   Chapter 8 Culture and Gender

Module 22: Gender

Module Goal
Learn how gender identity develops.

Learning Objectives
22.1 What is gender, and what is gender identity?
22.2 What factors influence the development of gender identity?
22.3 How do men and women differ in thinking, social behavior, and personality?

Learn How Gender Identity Develops

22.1 What is gender, and what is gender identity?

Whereas sex can be defined as the *physical* characteristics of being male or female, **gender** is defined as the *psychological* aspects of being masculine or feminine. The expectations of one's culture, the development of one's personality, and one's sense of identity are all affected by the concept of gender.

Gender roles refer to a culture's expectations for the behavior of a person who is perceived as male or female, including attitudes, actions, and personality traits associated with a particular gender within that culture (Tobach, 2001; Unger, 1979). **Gender typing** is the process by which people learn their culture's preferences and expectations for proper "masculine" and "feminine" behavior. The process by which one develops a **gender identity** (a sense of being male or female) is influenced by both biological and environmental factors (in the form of parenting and other child-rearing behaviors), although which type of factor has greater influence is still controversial.

Most researchers today would agree that biology has an important role in gender identity, at least in certain aspects of gender identity and behavior (Diamond & Sigmundson, 1997; Money, 1994; Reiner, 1999, 2000). Those people born with genitalia that are not entirely male and not entirely female, and that may include characteristics of both male and female anatomy, are described as *intersex*. In one study, 25 intersex children were surgically altered and raised as females. Now, as older children and teenagers, they prefer male play activities. Fourteen of these children have openly declared themselves to be boys (Reiner, 2000). ◉ Watch on **mypsychlab.com**

Gender identity, like physical sex, is not always as straightforward as males who are masculine and females who are feminine. In some cases, people's sense of gender identity does not match their external appearance or even the sex chromosomes that determine whether they are male or female (Califia, 1997; Crawford & Unger, 2004; White, 2000). Such people are typically termed *transgendered*. Biology and environment both have an influence on the concept of a person's gender identity. In a syndrome called *gender identity disorder*, a person feels that he or she is occupying the body of the wrong sex; a man may feel that he was meant to be a woman or a woman may feel that she was meant to be a man (American Psychiatric Association, [APA] 2000). Some people with this disorder feel so strongly that they are in the wrong body that they

◉ Watch a video on gender on **mypsychlab.com**

gender the psychological aspects of being male or female.

gender roles a culture's expectations for masculine or feminine behavior, including attitudes, actions, and personality traits associated with being male or female in that culture.

gender typing the process of acquiring gender role characteristics.

gender identity the individual's sense of being male or female.

CULTURE AND GENDER 261

Terms
- gender • gender roles • gender typing • gender identity

CHAPTER 8 • Module 22

Focus

RESOURCES
For this module, consult the appropriate sections of the Teacher's Manual, Test Bank, and PowerPoint slides, all found on the Teacher's Resource DVD, and the interactive study tools for students on MyPsychLab.

BEFORE CLASS
Students should read the section for homework before coming to class.

BELLRINGER
Provide the following question to students, and ask them to jot down an answer: Which factor do you think is most influential in determining a person's gender identity—biology or environment? Why?

Teach

INTRODUCE THE TOPIC
Tell students that the Bellringer question is a controversial issue that is still relevant today, even after years of psychological research into the topic of gender.

COVER THE MODULE
22.1 What is gender, and what is gender identity?
- *Gender* is the psychological aspects of being male or female.
- *Gender roles* are the culture's expectation for male and female behavior and personality.
- *Gender typing* is the process by which people in a culture learn the appropriate gender role behavior.
- *Gender identity* is a person's sense of being male or female.

MULTIMEDIA CONTENT AVAILABLE AT
www.mypsychlab.com

◉ Watch a video on gender on **mypsychlab.com**

Module 22 Gender 261

CHAPTER 8 • Module 22

COVER THE MODULE

22.2 What factors influence the development of gender identity?

- **Biological Influences**
  - The external sexual characteristics of the genitals are biological influences.
  - There are also hormonal differences between men and women. The quantities of estrogen and testosterone differ between the sexes and affect development.
  - Infant girls exposed to male hormones before birth were found to be tomboys during early childhood. However, when they grew up, these girls became typically "female."

DISCUSS THE STUDENT VOICE QUESTION

Use this question and the one in the photograph caption on this page to discuss the nature vs. nurture controversy about gender. Point out how powerfully other people's expectations can affect the way in which children grow up.

L4 DIFFERENTIATED INSTRUCTION

Advanced Learners Before beginning a new unit, have students write, verbalize, or draw what they know about the topic and present this information to peers.

---

have surgery to become the sex they feel they were always meant to be. These people are generally termed *transsexuals* because they actually undergo sexual reassignment surgery. Although the causes of gender identity disorder are not fully understood, there is some evidence for both prenatal influences and early childhood experiences as causes (Stein, 1984; Ward, 1992; Zhou et al., 1995).

Many societies are not particularly accepting or tolerant of individuals with gender identity disorder, but several Native American tribes have long recognized the role of the male *winkte* (the Lakota word for "wants to be like a woman") in their societies. Traditionally, these tribes not only tolerated such individuals but also had important places for them in the social structure as caretakers of children, cooks, and menders and creators of clothing, and even involved them in certain rituals for bestowing luck upon a hunt (Medicine, 2002). Although some *winkte* (now often referred to as people with "two spirits") were homosexuals, many were not and would now be recognized as having an alternate gender identity. Unfortunately, as tribes have modernized and become more integrated into the larger European-dominated culture of the United States, the tolerant attitudes of other Native Americans toward the *winkte* have begun to be replaced with homophobic attitudes and aggressive behavior (Medicine, 2002). Perhaps some of this intolerance develops as a result of unfamiliarity with the biological, social, and cultural factors that can influence a person's gender identity.

▲ *In studies in which infant girls were exposed to androgens (male hormones) while in their mother's womb, the girls became "tomboys" as children, preferring to play with typically masculine toys and participate in male-dominated play activities. Yet when these same girls grew into puberty and adulthood, they became more feminine in their behavior. What do these findings mean for the nature/nurture controversy?*

22.2 What factors influence the development of gender identity?

Biological Influences What are the biological influences on gender? Aside from the obvious external sexual characteristics of the genitals, there are also hormonal differences between men and women. All humans have both estrogen and testosterone, but the quantities of each hormone differ between the sexes and affect development at all stages. Some researchers believe that exposure to these hormones during fetal development not only causes the formation of the sexual organs but also predisposes the infant to behavior that is typically associated with one gender or the other. There have been several studies of infant girls who were exposed to androgens, or male hormones, before birth (for example, in the form of miscarriage-preventing drugs). In these studies, the girls were found to be tomboys during early childhood—preferring to play with typically "boy" toys, wrestling and playing rough, and playing with boys rather than with other girls (Berenbaum & Snyder, 1995; Money & Mathews, 1982; Money & Norman, 1987). However, when these girls grew up, they became more typically "female" in their desire for marriage and motherhood, which many of these same researchers took as evidence that upbringing won out over the hormonal influences.

Was their early tomboy nature due to the influence of the male hormones?
This is difficult to determine, as the parents of these girls were told about their infants' exposure to male hormones during pregnancy and may have formed assumptions about the effects of such masculinizing hormones on their children. It is entirely possible that these girls were simply allowed, or even encouraged, to be more "masculine" as small children because the parents were expecting them to be masculine. As these same girls grew older, they were exposed to the gender-role expectations of teachers, friends, and the media, which may have influenced them to become more like the feminine gender stereotype in contrast to their earlier "masculine" style of behavior.

▶ *Was their early tomboy nature due to the influence of the male hormones?*

262 CHAPTER 8

Class Activity

ANALYZING CHILDREN'S TOYS

<u>Purpose</u>: Students examine how "male" and "female" toys promote and encourage gender differences.

<u>Time</u>: 15 minutes

<u>Description</u>: Give students 5 minutes to write down three of their favorite childhood toys. They should describe each toy and whether it was a stereotypical "male" or "female" toy or was gender neutral. They should also think about the kinds of skills and abilities that are encouraged by playing with that toy. For example, does the toy encourage spatial skills (e.g., erector set) or does it encourage the development of interpersonal skills (e.g., dolls)? Students should then partner with a classmate to share and discuss. Ask: **Could encouraging boys and girls to play with different toys lead to gender differences in skills and abilities? Explain.**

262 Chapter 8 Culture and Gender

Environmental Influences Even if the girls who were exposed to androgens prenatally were initially influenced by these hormones, it seems fairly clear that their later "reversion" to more feminine ways was at least somewhat influenced by the pressures of society. In most cultures, there are certain roles that males and females are expected to play (gender roles, in other words), and the pressure that can be brought to bear on a person who does not conform to these expectations can be tremendous. In most Western cultures, the pressure to be masculine can be as great or greater for males than the pressure to be feminine is for girls. The term *tomboy* is not generally viewed as an insult, but there are no positive terms for a boy who acts in a feminine manner—*sissy*, for example, is not a nice term at all. And although studies of parents' influence on their children's gender typing show that both parents have an impact, they also show that the fathers are almost always more concerned about their sons showing male gender behavior than their daughters showing female gender behavior (Lytton & Romney, 1991).

Culture and Gender A person's culture is also an environmental influence on gender identity. One study found that attitudes toward gender roles in cultures that are more individualist and have fairly high standards of living tend to be less traditional than those in collectivist cultures that have less wealth, although in both types of cultures, women were found to hold less traditional views than men (Gibbons et al., 1991). Other studies have found that the most nontraditional ideas about gender roles and gender behavior are found in countries such as the Netherlands, Germany, Italy, and England, whereas the most traditional ideas predominate in African and Asian countries, such as Nigeria, Pakistan, and Japan (Best & Williams, 2001). The United States, often seen as very nontraditional by researchers, actually was somewhere in the middle in these studies, perhaps due to the large variation in subcultures that exists within this multicultural country. Environment, even in the form of culture, seems to be at least a partial and perhaps a dominant influence on gender roles.

Several studies over the years have found differences in male and female brain activity: When completing language tasks, women use an area of the right hemisphere that is not as active in men, leading some to speculate that this is why women seem to recover faster than men from left hemisphere strokes that affect language (Jaeger et al., 1998; Skrandies et al., 1999). Whereas men use the right side of the brain for emotional expression and the left side for visual/spatial perception, women seem to use both sides (Argyle, 1986; Fischer, 1993; Jaeger et al., 1998; Kimura, 2002; Pittam et al., 1995; Skrandies et al., 1999). There are physical differences in male and female brains from birth with the male hypothalamus being somewhat larger than that of females in rats and humans (Kimura, 2002). Even in these biological differences, the influence of the environment in the form of parenting and cultural expectations cannot be ruled out. For example, in Western cultures, girls are encouraged to express and use their emotions while boys are encouraged to hide emotions and be calm, which might contribute to the different emphasis placed on each hemisphere for the two sexes (Argyle, 1986; Fischer, 1993; Pittam et al., 1995). Psychologist Eleanor Maccoby, a pioneering figure in gender studies, believes that the biological differences between males and females help to create different contexts in which boys and girls are raised; the aggressive nature of boys, for example, causes them to engage in more rough-and-tumble play and competitive games than girls (Maccoby, 1998).

Explore on mypsychlab.com

▲ Although Asian cultures are often more traditional concerning the roles that men and women play within society even in these cultures, gender roles are becoming more flexible, as this male preschool teacher in a Chinese classroom demonstrates. Why might gender roles in these countries be changing?

Explore gender stereotypes on mypsychlab.com

CULTURE AND GENDER 263

CHAPTER 8 • Module 22

COVER THE MODULE *(continued)*

- **Environmental Influences**
  - These include parenting, surroundings, and societal pressures on the formation of gender identity.

- **Culture and Gender**
  - Attitudes toward gender roles in cultures that are more individualistic and have fairly high standards of living tend to be less traditional than those in collectivist cultures that have less wealth.
  - Environment, even in the form of culture, seems to be at least a partial and perhaps a dominant influence on gender roles.
  - Studies have found differences in male and female brain activity. But even with such biological differences, environmental influences in the form of parenting and cultural expectations cannot be ruled out.
  - Psychologist Eleanor Maccoby believes that the biological differences between females and males help to create different contexts in which girls and boys are raised.

UNDERSTANDING VISUALS

Ask volunteers for answers to the question in the photograph caption. *(Possible answer: The effect of global communication—such as movies, television, and the Internet—may be influencing traditional cultures where gender roles are concerned.)*

Explore gender stereotypes on mypsychlab.com

Class Activity

EXPLORING GENDER ROLES

Purpose: Students generate examples of societal expectations for men and women.

Time: 10 minutes

Description: Divide students into teams. Ask the teams to generate examples of societal expectations for males and females. For example, the first student might say, "Boys don't cry." Team members should then continue to contribute responses for a fixed amount of time or until team members can no longer generate any more responses. To increase accountability, groups may be asked to record their responses. Lists can then be shared with the larger class for comparison and discussion.

CHAPTER 8 • Module 22

COVER THE MODULE

22.3 How do men and women differ in thinking, social behavior, and personality?

- **Cognitive Differences**
  - Cognitive differences between men and women include a male advantage in mathematical and spatial skills and a female superiority in verbal skills. These differences are now less than they were in former times.

- **Social and Personality Differences**
  - Males and females are socially taught to interact differently and express emotions differently. Men tend to talk with each other in a "report" style, while women tend to talk to each other in a "relate" style.
  - Gender differences play a significant role in our societies and in our personal lives. However, our genders may influence us, but they do not have to define and separate us.

FAST FACT

According to the National Institute of Mental Health, about 6 million American men suffer from depression each year. Rather than display traditional signs of depression (sadness, worthlessness, excessive guilt), these men may instead express their depression in terms of increases in fatigue, irritability and anger, loss of interest in work or hobbies, and sleep disturbances. Some researchers believe that the traditional male role, which limits emotional expression and emphasizes success, power, and competition, is associated with negative consequences such as depression, anxiety, and relationship difficulties.

One thing is clear: The issue of differences between men and women is one that will be discussed, debated, and researched for some time to come.

22.3 How do men and women differ in thinking, social behavior, and personality?

Although there are clear biological differences in males and females, including those that affect the size of certain structures in the brain (Allen & Gorski, 1991; Allen et al., 1989; Zhou et al., 1995), what differences exist in the behavior of males and females? Are those differences due to biology, socialization, or a combination of the two influences?

Cognitive Differences Researchers have long held that females score higher on tests of verbal abilities than do males, but males score higher on tests of mathematical and spatial skills (Diamond, 1991; Voyer et al., 1995). Another study, using MRI technology, found that men listen with the left hemisphere only, whereas women listen with both hemispheres, suggesting that women pay attention to the tone and emotion of statements as well as the content (Lurito et al., 2000). Early explanations of these differences in cognitive functioning involved physical differences in the way each sex used the two hemispheres of the brain as well as hormonal differences (Witelson, 1991). Other research, however, strongly suggests that psychological and social issues may be more responsible for these differences, as these differences have become less and less obvious in recent studies (Hyde & Plant, 1995; Kimura, 1999; Voyer et al., 1995; Watt, 2000). That the differences seem to be disappearing as society has begun to view the two genders as more equal in ability is taken as a sign that more equal treatment in society has reduced the gender difference.

More evidence that the gender differences between males and females in certain cognitive areas are disappearing comes from a follow-up to a 1992 study showing that girls actually begin their school experience with math and science skills that are equal to those of the boys of their age group, but that by the time they finish high school, the girls have become less skilled in those two areas than boys (American Association of University Women, 1992; Sadker & Sadker, 1994). The follow-up study, done 6 years later, showed that these differences had all but disappeared as the girls improved their skills (American Association of University Women, 1998).

▲ As children develop the concept of gender, they begin to imitate the behavior of those they see as similar to themselves. This young girl is learning that women wear cosmetics while she plays at helping her mother put on her makeup. As she grows, she will incorporate more of her mother's behavior and ideas about what it is to be female into her own personality.

Social and Personality Differences The differences normally cited between men and women in the ways they interact with others and in their personality traits are often the result of stereotyped thinking about the sexes. It is difficult to demonstrate differences that are not caused by the way boys and girls are socialized as they grow up. Generally, in the United States, boys are taught to hold in their emotions, not to cry, to be "strong" and "manly." Girls are encouraged to form emotional attachments, be emotional, and be open about their feelings with others.

In communication, research suggests that when men talk to each other, they tend to talk about current events, sports, and other events. This has been called a "report" style of communication and seems to involve switching topics frequently with attempts to dominate the conversation by certain members of the group. In contrast, women tend to use a "relate" style of communication with each other, revealing a lot about their private lives and showing

---

Critical Thinking

CONTROVERSIES IN GENDER

<u>Purpose</u>: Students have a chance to think about, debate, and discuss controversial topics in gender.

<u>Time</u>: 15 minutes

<u>Description</u>: Pose the topic below to the class. After students have a chance to think about the issue, ask them to share their answers and contribute to further class discussion. Topic: **If men and women were treated the same, gender differences would disappear.**

concern and sympathy. They tend to interrupt each other less and let everyone participate in the conversation (Argamon et al., 2003; Coates, 1986; Pilkington, 1998; Swann, 1998).

Whether they are biological or environmental in nature, gender differences play a significant and very real role in our societies and our personal lives. It's important to keep in mind, however, that the similarities between our genders greatly outweigh the differences. Our genders may influence us, but they do not have to define us or separate us.

Applying Psychology to Everyday Life

Closing the Math and Science "Gender Gap"

Male and female students enroll in math and science classes at equal rates in high school, and they perform equally well in their classes. But something happens when these students enter college: Fewer women than men pursue college majors in math, science, technology, and engineering (Schaffhauser, 2010). When they head into the workplace, the number of women involved in these fields shrinks even more. Only 11 percent of engineers, for example, are women (ScienceDaily, 2008). What's causing this gender gap?

There's no biological evidence to suggest that men are naturally better at math and science than women are. According to recent research, environment, not biology, seems to be the largest factor influencing the gender gap: The belief that women aren't good at math is a strong (although inaccurate) cultural stereotype, and it can discourage women from pursuing math-related careers (Schaffhauser, 2010). Female high school students don't sign up for electives like computer science at the same rates as male students do; it can be socially challenging to be the only girl in a class full of boys, and social pressures from both male and female classmates can make girls less inclined to sign up for these courses voluntarily (Strauss, 2005). When women land jobs in math and science, they are more likely to feel unsupported by their coworkers and frustrated by inflexible, overly demanding work schedules. As a result, men still make up the majority of workers in the high-paying fields of math, science, engineering, and technology (Schaffhauser, 2010).

What can be done to get more girls and women involved in these areas? The U.S. Department of Education (2007) makes several recommendations, including the following:

- Teach students that their math and science skills can be expanded and improved through effort and learning.
- Give students feedback that helps them improve their skills and feel good about their abilities in math and science.
- Teach students about women who have had successful careers in math and science.

Question for Further Discussion

1. Careers such as nursing and teaching at the elementary school level tend to be dominated by women. Why do you think more women than men pursue these careers, and what can be done to encourage men to explore these fields?

CHAPTER 8 • Module 22

APPLYING PSYCHOLOGY TO EVERYDAY LIFE

- There is no biological evidence suggesting that men are naturally better at math and science than women are. Environment, not biology, seems to be the main factor influencing the math and science gender gap.
- Cultural stereotypes can discourage women from pursuing such careers.
- To get more girls and women interested in these areas, suggestions include teaching students to feel good about their math and science abilities and publicizing women with successful careers in these fields.

1. Possible answer: Cultural stereotypes hold that nursing and teaching are "caring" fields that are appropriate for the "motherly" instincts of women. Therefore, more women than men pursue such careers. If such fields were promoted as scientific or technical-type areas, more men might be willing to explore them.

L3 DIFFERENTIATED INSTRUCTION

Visual/Nonverbal Learners These students learn best through the use of diagrams, pictures, charts, videos, and other image-oriented material rather than printed text. This type of learner, like the visual/verbal learner, also prefers to study alone.

Explore

CAREER STEREOTYPES

Extend the Applying Psychology to Everyday Life activity on this page. Divide the class into pairs or small groups. Ask students to select one career that is typically thought of as "female" (e.g., librarian) and one that is typically thought of as "male" (e.g., engineer). Tell them to do library or Internet research to find out what these jobs involve and what job skills are necessary to do them. Then have the pairs/groups discuss why they think these jobs have been stereotyped as "male" or "female." What might be done to get more persons of the opposite sex into those careers? Have students present their thoughts and information to the rest of the class for discussion.

CHAPTER 8 • Module 22

Assess

Assign the Module 22 Practice Quiz.

Use the Practice Quiz to identify gaps in student understanding.

REMEDIATE

Have students, individually or in groups, review the module goals, learning objectives, and key terms.

Refer students to the Concept Summary on p. 271 for review.

Close

As a class, discuss the careers in which students are interested. Are any of these careers stereotypically "male" or "female"? Have environmental or cultural influences played any role in students' choices?

Practice Quiz

Pick the best answer.

1. The term for the psychological aspect of being male or female is
   a. sex
   b. sexual orientation
   c. gender
   d. gender role

2. What is gender typing?
   a. a biological predisposition for behavior
   b. an environmental factor that affects one sex
   c. a physical differentiation between male and female
   d. a cultural perception of what is masculine and feminine

3. In many Western cultures, boys are expected to play with trucks while girls are expected to play with dolls. This is an example of
   a. gender roles
   b. gender identity
   c. gender typing
   d. gender discrimination

4. Which of the following statements about gender is true?
   a. A person's gender has absolutely nothing to do with his or her biological sex.
   b. A person's gender is entirely determined by his or her biological sex.
   c. A person's gender is influenced by biological characteristics but is not always determined by those characteristics.
   d. A person's gender is generally determined by cultural influences rather than by biological characteristics.

5. The Native American role of the *winkte*, in which a male assumes some of the typically female responsibilities of the tribe is an example of a(n)
   a. cultural gender stereotype
   b. alternative gender identity
   c. transcultural gender role
   d. environmental gender influence

6. Which of the following statements is true?
   a. Cultural and social factors have little influence over brain activities.
   b. Women use both brain hemispheres, while men use one hemisphere at a time.
   c. Men are always more analytical, while women are always more emotional.
   d. Gender-based differences in brain activity disappear with equal educational exposure.

7. Which of the following factors are MOST influential in the development of gender identity?
   a. economic and social factors
   b. physical and hormonal factors
   c. ethical and moral factors
   d. biological and environmental factors

8. Some girls exposed to male hormones in the womb engaged in more masculine play activities. However, as they aged, they began to engage in more feminine play activities. The girls' changing interests illustrate the effect of
   a. gender roles
   b. gender typing
   c. gender bias
   d. gender discrimination

9. In which of the following types of cultures are nontraditional gender roles most likely to thrive?
   a. conservative cultures
   b. historic cultures
   c. collectivist cultures
   d. individualist cultures

10. In the United States and in many other cultures, boys are generally taught to
    a. keep their feelings to themselves
    b. relate to others through conversation
    c. seek help from friends in tough times
    d. express their emotions freely

266 CHAPTER 8

Practice Quiz Answers

1. c
2. d
3. a
4. c
5. b

6. d
7. d
8. b
9. d
10. a

CHAPTER 8 Summary

Listen on mypsychlab.com

Module 21: Culture
Understand culture's role in psychology.

21.1 What is culture?
- Culture is a shared set of beliefs, behaviors, values, and attitudes held by a group of people or a society.
- Culture is learned, it is shared, and it changes over time.

21.2 How does culture vary across time and place?
- Cultures are shaped by geographic factors like climate and the availability of natural resources as well as by human factors like population density and technological development.

21.3 How does culture influence our conceptions of self and identity?
- Cultures may be individualist or collectivist. People living in individualist cultures tend to have an independent self-concept, identifying themselves as independent from others, while people who live in collectivist cultures tend to have an interdependent self-concept, identifying themselves in relation to others.

21.4 What are some major areas of cross-cultural psychology research?
- Psychologists run studies on individuals from different cultural groups and compare the results to determine whether patterns of thought and behavior are universal (found across all cultures) or culture-bound (found only in particular cultures).
- Emotion: People in different cultures may share many of the same emotions, but the degree of individualism or collectivism in our culture can affect how we label and express those emotions.
- Intelligence: It does not have a universal definition, and there is no universal way of measuring it. Intelligence takes different forms in different cultures.

Listen to an audio file of your chapter on **mypsychlab.com**
- Development across the life span: How and when people fulfill certain cultural and developmental stages in life, and what those stages are.
- Abnormal behavior: What is considered "normal" and accepted within a culture?

Module 22: Gender
Learn how gender identity develops.

22.1 What is gender, and what is gender identity?
- Gender is the psychological aspects of being masculine or feminine. The expectations of one's culture, the development of one's personality, and one's sense of identity are all affected by the concept of gender.

22.2 What factors influence the development of gender identity?
- Both biological (hormones, sex, and physical condition) and environmental factors (in the form of parenting, other child-rearing behaviors, and cultural influences) influence gender identity.

22.3 How do men and women differ in thinking, social behavior, and personality?
- Females score higher on tests of verbal abilities than do males, but that males score higher on tests of mathematical skills and spatial skills.
- Differences seem to be disappearing as society has begun to view the two genders as more equal in ability. This is taken as a sign that more equal treatment in society has reduced the gender difference.
- Males and females are socialized differently, which influences personality. However, males tend to "report" when in conversation, while females tend to "relate" when conversing.

Vocabulary Terms

culture p. 250
norms p. 250
acculturation p. 254
individualism p. 255
collectivism p. 255
independent self-concept p. 255
interdependent self-concept p. 255
cross-cultural psychology p. 257
universal p. 257
culture-bound p. 257
display rules p. 258
gender p. 261
gender roles p. 261
gender typing p. 261
gender identity p. 261

CULTURE AND GENDER 267

Critical Thinking

MAKING CONNECTIONS

Have students connect the information they have learned in this chapter. Divide students into pairs or small groups. Ask them to come up with a list of at least five ways in which their culture has affected or influenced their gender identity—positively or negatively. Then ask volunteers to read their lists to the class.

CHAPTER 8 • Summary and Vocabulary

Chapter Summary

Encourage students to carefully review and study the summary. Explain that it provides an overview of key concepts presented in the text.

Have students identify what they find unclear or confusing. Call on volunteers to provide answers, examples, or definitions.

Vocabulary Terms

Remind students that terms are defined within the chapter at point of use. If they are not sure of a term's definition, they should look up the definition on the page.

Encourage students to create study cards of unfamiliar words or to go to **www.mypsychlab.com** for flash cards. Have them test themselves or a classmate. Advanced students can explain the terms in their own words.

CHAPTER 8 • Assessment

VOCABULARY REVIEW

1. d
2. b
3. j
4. i
5. a
6. c
7. f
8. e
9. g
10. h

WRITING ABOUT PSYCHOLOGY

1. Students' responses should show an understanding of the definitions of individualist and collectivist cultures and how one of those cultures has affected their lives.
2. Students' answers should indicate that the writers understand the meaning of gender roles and stereotypes. Examples should be provided to support the answers.

PSYCHOLOGY PROJECT

The object of this activity is for students to realize that similarities and differences between cultures are normal and do not indicate superiority or inferiority. Remind students to be respectful and considerate during their interviews with classmates.

268 Chapter 8 Culture and Gender

CHAPTER 8 Assessment

Study and Review on mypsychlab.com

Vocabulary Review

Match each vocabulary term to its definition.

1. culture
2. norms
3. individualism
4. collectivism
5. acculturation
6. gender
7. culture-bound
8. universal
9. display rules
10. gender roles

a. The process of adapting to a new culture by adopting the new culture's beliefs and behaviors.
b. A culture's understood rules for expected behavior, values, beliefs, and attitudes.
c. The psychological aspects of being male or female.
d. A shared set of beliefs, behaviors, values, and attitudes held by a group of people or a society.
e. Found across all cultures.
f. Found only in particular cultures.
g. Learned ways of controlling displays of emotion in social settings.
h. A culture's expectations for masculine or feminine behavior, including attitudes, actions, and personality traits associated with being male or female in that culture.
i. A cultural style that emphasizes the importance of interdependence, group goals, and group needs.
j. A cultural style that emphasizes the importance of individuality, independence, and personal needs.

Writing About Psychology

Respond to each question in complete sentences.

1. Describe the culture you were raised in and identify whether it is more individualist or more collectivist. Then, give at least three examples of ways in which your cultural background has shaped your thoughts, beliefs, actions, values, or goals.
2. In the United States today, there is more equality between men and women than there has been in the past. Do you believe that gender roles and stereotypes still influence people's thoughts, behaviors, and opportunities in society? Use examples to support your answer if possible.

Psychology Project

What cultural and individual traits do you share with your classmates? Interview your peers to learn about your similarities and differences.

Materials:
- three partners
- a pencil and paper

Instructions:

1. Answer the following questions about your culture and your own personal identity:
   - What are some of your values?
   - How does your family history affect your values?
   - How would you describe yourself?
   - Are you similar to or different from others in your community?
   - How does the area you live in affect your personal identity and your cultures?
   - What culture(s) would you say you belong to?
2. Choose a partner to "interview" and discuss these questions. Write down any responses your partner says.
3. Interview a second and third partner and write down their responses.
4. Review your partners' responses. What are the similarities? Where are there differences? Circle the similarities you share, and underline the differences.
5. Discuss the results. Were all responses similar? How were they different? As a group, talk about what role culture plays in your everyday life, as well as how it affects how you view yourself.

268 CHAPTER 8

Internet Resources

Countries and Their Cultures: www.everyculture.com

This site contains articles about countries and areas of the world, covering topics such as history, economy, marriage and family, sociopolitical organization, and religion.

United Nations Educational, Scientific, and Cultural Organization (UNESCO): www.unesco.org

UNESCO works to create the conditions for dialogue among civilizations, cultures, and peoples, based upon respect for commonly shared values.

World Health Organization—Gender: www.who.int/topics/gender/en/

Includes information, multimedia, and publications about gender issues.

Psychology Today: www.psychologytoday.com/basics/gender

Provides gender blogs and information on gender differences and sexual orientation.

Test Yourself

Pick the best answer.

1. **What is culture?**
   a. a belief system that governs how people act and think
   b. a group of people who live in a particular region or act in a particular way
   c. a shared set of beliefs, behaviors, values, and attitudes held by a group of people or a society
   d. a society composed of a group of individuals who share similar ethnic, racial, and social backgrounds

2. **Gender is defined as**
   a. the psychological aspect of being male or female
   b. a biological distinction between males and females
   c. a cultural role defined by social standards and rules
   d. the identification of a person's physiological aspects

3. **Which of the following questions might a cross-cultural psychologist be interested in investigating?**
   a. How is culture defined by people of different social status?
   b. How do other cultures perceive the American culture?
   c. How do perceptions of love vary in different countries?
   d. How many generations of immigrant families are bilingual?

4. **Research has shown that men tend to talk to each other about**
   a. private concerns   c. relationships
   b. their feelings   d. current events

5. **Cross-cultural psychology is**
   a. the study of cultures from around the world
   b. the study of human thought and behavior across cultures
   c. the study of human thought and behavior in a multicultural country
   d. the study of the spread of culture through communication and technology

6. **A cultural pressure to work together and be part of the group is most common in cultures that have a high degree of**
   a. universalism   c. ethnocentrism
   b. collectivism   d. individualism

7. **What happened to girls who were exposed to masculinizing hormones before birth?**
   a. They were all unaffected by the hormones.
   b. Each girl reacted differently to the hormones.
   c. They acted traditionally feminine as children but became tomboys as adolescents and young adults.
   d. They acted like tomboys as children but became more traditionally feminine as they grew older.

8. **Which of the following is an example of acculturation?**
   a. A young child moves and adapts to a new culture.
   b. An adult learns traditions from a business associate's culture.
   c. A teen travels to experience new cultures and traditions.
   d. An adult speaks multiple languages and eats foreign foods.

9. **Research suggests that differences between males and females in mathematics and verbal skills may be caused by psychological and social issues rather than biology because**
   a. these differences have increased in recent years
   b. these differences have decreased in recent years
   c. these differences have remained constant
   d. females now score higher than males in mathematics

10. **In China, some brides now wear white gowns instead of traditional red gowns. This example demonstrates that**
    a. cultures cannot change over time
    b. one culture can influence another
    c. cultural norms are not powerful
    d. individualism is more popular than collectivism

11. **The term *intersexed* refers to**
    a. a person who does not conform to gender stereotypes
    b. a person who consciously chooses his or her gender
    c. a person who is neither masculine nor feminine
    d. a person who is born with ambiguous sexual organs

12. **Gender roles are created by a(n)**
    a. biological need and response
    b. individual's personal identity
    c. society's strengthening of stereotypes
    d. culture's expectations for male and female behavior

13. **Studies have shown that _____ are more concerned about appropriate gender behavior in their children, particularly their _____ children.**
    a. fathers; male   c. mothers; male
    b. fathers; female   d. mothers; female

14. **Each culture has its own _____ or learned ways of controlling displays of emotion in social settings.**
    a. base feelings
    b. display rules
    c. emotive expressions
    d. social interactions

15. **The development of a person's sense of being male or female is called**
    a. gender role   c. gender typing
    b. gender identity   d. gender stereotyping

16. **Which of the following conclusions does Phoebe Ellsworth's study of emotions suggest?**
    a. Our culture helps us determine how to display our emotions physically.
    b. Our culture gives us a context for interpreting actions and assigning emotions to those actions.
    c. Emotions are not universal, and most emotions are not present in more than one culture.
    d. Cross-cultural studies of emotion do not reveal significant differences between cultures.

CULTURE AND GENDER   269

CHAPTER 8 • Assessment

TEST YOURSELF

1. c	9. b
2. a	10. b
3. c	11. d
4. d	12. d
5. b	13. a
6. b	14. b
7. d	15. b
8. a	16. b

Ready for Testing

STUDENTS KNOW THEY ARE READY FOR TESTING IF THEY ARE ABLE TO . . .

- Define *culture* and discuss how it varies across time and place.
- Explain how culture influences people's conceptions of self and identity.
- Define *gender* and *gender identity*.
- Explain which factors influence the development of gender identity.
- Describe how men and women differ in thinking, social behavior, and personality.

CHAPTER 8 • Concept Summary

MULTIMEDIA CONTENT AVAILABLE AT
www.mypsychlab.com

Map the Concepts on **mypsychlab.com**

Study and Review Flashcards on **mypsychlab.com**

STUDY TIPS

Active Reading Effective readers interact with the material they are reading to help them absorb and comprehend information. Before reading each section in a chapter, students should scan the section by reading the introduction, headings, and conclusion. Tell them to look at photographs, charts, and other visuals. Then they should write a question about the material. As they read, students should look for an answer to their question; this will give them a purpose for reading. Additional strategies include chunking the material into short segments and paraphrasing that section before continuing to read, and drawing diagrams, flowcharts, or other graphic organizers to map ideas visually. Students might also consider reading aloud or photocopying the material so they can highlight or underline key points.

CHAPTER 8 Concept Summary: Culture and Gender

Learning Objectives
21.1 21.2 21.3 21.4   pp. 250–259

Understand Culture's Role in Psychology

- **culture** is a shared set of beliefs, behaviors, values, and attitudes held by a group of people or a society
  - cultures have **norms**, understood rules dictating what behavior is acceptable or unacceptable
  - common characteristics of culture
    - culture is learned
    - culture is shared
    - culture changes over time
- **cultural variation** across place and time
  - cultures can be shaped by
    - **geographic factors**
      - climate
      - natural resources
    - **acculturation** is the process of adapting to a new culture by adopting the new culture's beliefs and behaviors
    - **human factors**
      - population density
      - technological development
- **individualism and collectivism**
  - **individualism** is a cultural style that emphasizes the importance of individuality, independence, and personal needs → **independent self-concept**
  - **collectivism** is a cultural style that emphasizes the importance of interdependence, group goals, and group needs → **interdependent self-concept**

Table 21.1 Independence vs. Interdependence

INDEPENDENT TASKS	INTERDEPENDENT TASKS
Be unique	Belong; try to fit in
Express yourself	Occupy your proper place
Meet your own goals	Help others meet their goals
Say what's on your mind	Be indirect; try to know what others are thinking

Source: Adapted from Markus & Kitayama, 1991.

- **cross-cultural psychology** the study of human thought and behavior across cultures
  - there are many areas of cross-cultural psychology research, including
    - emotion
    - intelligence
    - development across the life span
    - abnormal behavior
  - **culture-bound** thought and behavior is found only in particular cultures
  - **universal** thought and behavior is found across all cultures

---

What Every Student Should Know About . . .

PROCRASTINATION

A perfectionist procrastinator is a person who delays completing his or her project due to constant revisions and changes made to the project that prevent the project itself from being completed. The perfectionist delays his or her work as a means of avoiding failure. Here are some tips for students who are perfectionist procrastinators: (1) Create a schedule or a block of time where you have specifically allocated time for a variety of daily activities. (2) Set realistic goals. Identify the realistic advantages to having high standards of work compared to unrealistic expectations of work. (3) Know when to say, "Enough!" Always set time limits on your work—even if you have to finish your work and you think you could have done a better job if you had more time.

Learn How Gender Identity Develops

Learning Objectives: 22.1, 22.2, 22.3 — pp. 261–265

- **gender** is the psychological aspects of being masculine or feminine
  - **gender roles** are a culture's expectations for masculine or feminine behavior, including attitudes, actions, and personality traits associated with being male or female in that culture
  - **gender typing** is the process of acquiring gender role characteristics
  - **gender identity** is the individual's sense of being male or female
- **biological influences on gender**
  - physical and hormonal differences
- **environmental factors affecting gender**
  - social pressure to conform to gender roles
  - culture personalities that are considered norms
- **gender differences**
  - **cognitive differences** (e.g., listening skills) may be present but are possibly due to psychological and social issues rather than biology
  - **social and personality differences** are often the result of stereotyped thinking about the sexes

CULTURE AND GENDER 271

CHAPTER 8 • Concept Summary

STUDY TIPS

Taking Notes Perhaps the most important point for students to remember when taking notes in class is that they should not attempt to write down everything the teacher says. Rather than writing in sentences, students should use phrases or even a single word when that will suffice. Abbreviations and symbols should be used whenever possible. Caution students, however, that they should copy anything the teacher writes on the board, anything the teacher repeats, and all terms and definitions. It is a good idea to leave space between ideas so that students can go back and add information later. As they write, students should highlight important ideas by underlining, circling, or starring them. If the teacher is talking too fast, suggest that students jot down nouns and verbs only and fill in the rest after class.

Comprehension Check

LIVING IN A DIFFERENT CULTURE

Ask students to think about moving to another part of the country or even another part of the world where the culture is different from the one in which they currently live. What kinds of issues might they come up against? What kinds of difficulties might they confront? What coping mechanisms might they use? Lead a class discussion on this topic.

CHAPTER 9 • Module 23

Launch the Chapter

CHAPTER GOALS AND LEARNING OBJECTIVES

Module 23 Encoding and Storage

Learn how the brain encodes memories.

23.1 What are levels of processing?
23.2 How are memories encoded in the brain?
23.3 How can we make encoding more effective?

Understand how memories are stored in the brain.

23.4 How is information stored in long-term memory?
23.5 How and where are memories stored in the brain?

Module 24 Retrieval and Retrieval Failure

Learn how memories are retrieved from the brain.

24.1 What kinds of cues help people remember?
24.2 What factors influence how memories are retrieved?
24.3 How can we improve our ability to retrieve memories?
24.4 Can memories change? How reliable are they?
24.5 Why do we forget?
24.6 How does amnesia occur?

DIFFERENTIATED INSTRUCTION KEY

Look for these symbols to help you adjust steps in each lesson to meet your students' needs.

- **L1** Special Needs
- **L2** Basic
- **ELL** English Language Learners
- **LPR** Less Proficient Readers
- **L3** All Students
- **L4** Advanced Students

CHAPTER 9 Memory

The Masters of Memory

Most of us, at some point in our busy days, have a little trouble remembering things. That problem doesn't seem to be shared by the people who enter the U.S. Memory Championship, held in New York every year since 1998 (PR Newswire Association, Inc., 2000). The championship has five events: First, contestants have 15 minutes to memorize 99 names and faces and 20 minutes to recite them back. Second, they must memorize an unpublished poem of 50 lines in 15 minutes. The third task is to memorize a list of random numbers, and the fourth is to memorize a list of random words. Finally, contestants must memorize the position of all 52 cards in a shuffled deck of playing cards.

Sound impossible? Scott Hagwood can do it and has done it four times. Scott also holds the world rank of grand master. Grand masters must memorize the following: 1,000 numbers in under an hour, the exact order of 10 shuffled decks of cards (also in less than 1 hour), and the order of 1 shuffled deck of cards in less than 2 minutes. In 2007, David Thomas did it—also a grand master, ranked number 35 in the world in terms of memory masters.

How do they do it? Although they do spend thousands of hours in training, in the end, memory masters like Scott and David simply use a strategy that has been around since the fifth century B.C.E. A Greek poet named Simonides discovered that he could easily remember who was sitting at a large banquet by remembering *where* each person sat—humans apparently have a great memory for location (Schachter, 1996). The memory masters simply take each number or card or person and associate it with a familiar place or even an image. Retrieving such memories becomes fairly simple. In the chapter you are about to read, you will learn why this memory "trick" works so well.

CORRELATION TO APA STANDARDS FOR CHAPTER 9

VA. MEMORY

VA-1. Encoding of memory .... pp. 275–280
VA-2. Storage of memory .... pp. 280–283, 296–297
VA-3. Retrieval of memory....................... pp. 285–295

*W*hy study ?

Memory

Without memory, how would we be able to learn anything? The ability to learn is the key to our very survival, and we cannot learn unless we can remember what happened the last time a particular situation arose. Why study forgetting? If we can learn about the ways in which we forget information, we can apply that learning so that forgetting occurs less frequently.

MEMORY 273

CHAPTER 9 • Module 23

Teacher Prep

Memory is an active system that receives information from the senses, organizes and alters it as it stores it, and retrieves information from storage. Memory involves the three processes of encoding, storage, and retrieval.

The levels-of-processing model of memory proposes that how long a memory will be remembered depends on the depth to which it was processed. The parallel distributed processing model proposes that memories are created and stored across a network of neural circuits in a parallel fashion. The most accepted model of memory is the information-processing model, which proposes three components of memory—sensory, short term, and long term.

The information-processing model proposes that information moves from sensory memory to short-term memory (STM) through the process of selective attention. The duration of STM is 10–30 seconds without rehearsal.

Long-term memory (LTM) is the third stage of memory proposed by the information-processing theory and has an essentially unlimited capacity and duration. Procedural memories are memories for skill and habits—things people can *do*. Declarative memories are memories of facts—things people can *know*.

Retrieval describes the process of pulling memories out of LTM. The retrieval of memories is a constructive process. There are at least four different causes for forgetting: encoding failure, decay, proactive interference, and retroactive interference.

It is still unclear exactly how memories are physically stored in the brain. The concept of the physical change that takes place in the brain when memories are formed is called the engram, and scientists continue their search for the engram.

SCHEDULING

1 Period = 50 min. 1 Block = 90 min.	Semester Course (18 weeks/90 days) Periods/Blocks		Full-Year Course (36 weeks/180 days) Period/Blocks	
Module 23	2.5	1.25	5	2.5
Module 24	2.5	1.25	5	2.5
Total Days for Chapter	5	2.5	10	5

CHAPTER 9 • Module 23

Focus

RESOURCES
For this module, consult the appropriate sections of the Teacher's Manual, Test Bank, and PowerPoint slides, all found on the Teacher's Resource DVD, and the interactive study tools for students on MyPsychLab.

BEFORE CLASS
Students should read the section for homework before coming to class.

BELLRINGER
Ask students to think about their own memories. Poll the class to determine which students think they have good memories and which students find themselves forgetful. Ask students to share the bases of their determinations.

Teach

BRAINSTORM
Have the "good memory" students share some of their tricks or techniques for remembering, and write them on the board. Do the "forgetful" students think these ideas would be helpful? Why or why not?

COVER THE MODULE
- *Memory* can be defined as an active system that receives information from the senses, organizes and alters it as it stores it away, and then retrieves the information from storage.
- Putting It In: *Encoding*
  - Putting information into the memory system

LINK to Chapter Three: Sensation and Perception, pp. 86–88

- Keeping It In: *Storage*
  - Keeping information in the memory system
- Getting it Out: *Retrieval*
  - Pulling up information from memory

Module 23
Encoding and Storage

Module Goals

Learn how the brain encodes memories.

Understand how memories are stored in the brain.

Learning Objectives

23.1 What are levels of processing?
23.2 How are memories encoded in the brain?
23.3 How can we make encoding more effective?
23.4 How is information stored in long-term memory?
23.5 How and where are memories stored in the brain?

Learn How the Brain Encodes Memories

Is memory a place or a process? The answer to that question is not simple. As you read through this module, you'll learn that memory is a process but that it also has a "place" in the brain as well. Perhaps the best definition of **memory** is an active system that receives information from the senses, puts that information into a usable form, organizes it as it stores it away, and then retrieves the information from storage (Baddeley, 1996, 2003).

The first stage in the memory system is to get sensory information (sight, sound, etc.) into a form that the brain can use. This is called **encoding**. Encoding is what the brain does to convert sensory information into a form that is usable in the brain's storage systems. For example, when people hear a sound, their ears turn the vibrations in the air into messages from the auditory neuron cells, which makes it possible for the brain to interpret that sound. LINK to *Chapter Three: Sensation and Perception, pp. 86–88*. After encoding information, the next step in memory is to hold on to the information for some period of time in a process called **storage**. This period of time will be of different lengths, depending on the stage of memory being used. For example, in one stage of memory, people hold on to information just long enough to work with it, about 20 seconds or so. In another stage of memory, people hold on to information more or less permanently.

The biggest problem many people have with memory is **retrieval**—getting the information they know they have out of storage. Have you ever handed in an essay test and *then* remembered several other things you could have said? This is a classic example of a retrieval problem. In this module, we'll discuss encoding and storage, and in the next module, we will learn more about retrieval.

Exactly how does memory work? When the storage process occurs, where does that information go and why? Memory experts have proposed several different ways of looking at memory. The model that many researchers feel is the most complete and perhaps the most influential over the last several decades is the **information processing model**, an approach that focuses on the way infor-

memory an active system that receives information from the senses, puts that information into a usable form, and organizes it as it stores it away, and then retrieves the information from storage.

encoding the set of mental operations that people perform on sensory information to convert that information into a form that is usable in the brain's storage systems.

storage holding onto information for some period of time.

retrieval getting information that is in storage into a form that can be used.

information-processing model model of memory that assumes the processing of information for memory storage is similar to the way a computer processes memory in a series of three stages.

274 CHAPTER 9

Terms

- memory • encoding • storage • retrieval • information-processing model
- levels-of-processing model • sensory memory • short-term memory (STM)
- selective attention • working memory • maintenance rehearsal • long-term memory (LTM) • elaborative rehearsal • procedural (nondeclarative) memory
- implicit memory • declarative memory • semantic memory • episodic memory
- explicit memory

274 Chapter 9 Memory

FIGURE 23.1 Three-Stage Process of Memory
Information enters through the sensory system, briefly registering in sensory memory. Selective attention moves the information into short-term memory, where it is held while attention (rehearsal) continues. If the information receives enough rehearsal, it will enter and be stored in long-term memory.

mation is processed, or handled, through three different stages of memory. The processes of encoding, storage, and retrieval are seen as part of this model, which is illustrated in Figure 23.1. ⊙→ Simulate on **mypsychlab.com**

⊙→ Simulate the information-processing model on **mypsychlab.com**

23.1 What are levels of processing?

The information-processing model assumes that the length of time for which information will be remembered depends on the stage of memory in which it is stored. However, other researchers have proposed that the length of time that a memory will be retained depends on the depth (i.e., the effort made to understand the meaning) to which the information is processed (Cermak & Craik, 1979; Craik & Lockhart, 1972). For example, if the word *BALL* is flashed on a screen and people are asked to report whether the word was in capital letters or lowercase, or if the word "ball" is spoken aloud and people are asked to remember its sound, the word itself does not have to be processed very much at all—only its visual or acoustic characteristics need enter into conscious attention. But if those people were asked to use that word in a sentence, they would have to think about what a ball is and how it can be used. They would have to process its meaning, which requires more mental effort than processing its appearance or sound. Thinking about the meaning of something is a deeper level of processing and results in longer retention of the word, researchers have found in numerous experiments (Cermak & Craik, 1979; Craik & Tulving, 1975; Watson et al., 1999). This model of memory is called the **levels-of-processing model**. (See Figure 23.2 on the next page.)

levels-of-processing model model of memory that assumes information that is more "deeply processed," or processed according to meaning rather than just the sound or physical characteristics of the word or words, will be remembered more efficiently and for a longer period of time.

MEMORY 275

CHAPTER 9 • Module 23

MULTIMEDIA CONTENT AVAILABLE AT
www.mypsychlab.com

⊙→ **Simulate** the information-processing model on **mypsychlab.com**

COVER THE MODULE

23.1 What are the levels of processing?

- *Levels-of-Processing Model*
  - Information that is more deeply processed is more likely to be remembered.

EXTEND THE LESSON

Ask students if they believe that some people (maybe themselves included) are simply born with bad memories that cannot be improved in any substantial way. Explain to students that although some people have naturally better memories than others, this is not as important as one's effort and skills used toward remembering things they deem important. Students should not feel discouraged at their "bad" memories (or, on the other hand, should not use forgetfulness as an excuse).

L3 ELL DIFFERENTIATED INSTRUCTION

English Language Learners Introduce essential words in meaningful contexts, through simple sentences drawing on familiar issues, scenarios, and vocabulary.

Explore

USING INFORMATION FROM THE INTERNET

Ask students to explore memory myths on the Internet. They can search for "memory myths" or use the following sites:

- www.memory-improvement-tips.com/memory-myths.html
- www.supermemo.com/articles/myths.htm
- www.mythbusters.com/busting-the-myths-about-memory-improvement.html

Did students come across any myths that were not addressed in the module? What were they? Were they surprised by any of the information they found? Why or why not?

Module 23 Encoding and Storage 275

CHAPTER 9 • Module 23

COVER THE MODULE

23.2 How are memories encoded in the brain?
- The stages of memory are *sensory memory*, STM, and LTM.
- Iconic memory is the visual sensory memory in which an afterimage or icon will be held in neural form for about one-fourth to one-half of a second.
- Echoic memory is the auditory form of sensory memory and takes the form of an echo that lasts for up to 4 seconds.

EXTEND THE LESSON

Multicultural Focus Ask students if they think that culture has anything to do with memory. Point out that all cultures place certain memory expectations on their members. For example, in Western culture we are expected to remember (through honors, ceremonies, and observances) significant dates, persons, or activities. The Fourth of July, Thanksgiving Day, and, most obviously, Memorial Day are examples of a kind of culturally shared memory system. Although often there are no explicit guidelines for activities on these occasions and no particularly dire sanctions for not observing them, we will certainly be looked at askance if we do not remember when they are or what they signify.

FIGURE 23.2 Levels of Processing

23.2 How are memories encoded in the brain?

Sensory Memory Sensory memory is the first stage of memory, the point at which information enters the nervous system through the sensory systems—eyes, ears, and so on. Think of it as a door that is open for a brief time. Looking through the door, one can see many people and objects, but only some of them will actually make it through the door itself. Sensory memory is a kind of door into the world.

Information is encoded into sensory memory as messages in the nervous system. As long as those messages are traveling through the system, it can be said that people have a "memory" for that information that can be accessed if needed. For example, say Elaina is driving down the street, looking at the people and cars on either side of her vehicle. All of a sudden she thinks, "What? Was that man wearing a cape?" and she looks back to check. How did she know to look back? Her eyes had already moved past the possible cape-wearing person, but some part of her brain must have just processed what she saw. This is called a double-take and can only be explained by the presence, however brief, of a memory for what she saw.

There are two major kinds of sensory memory: iconic (visual) memory and echoic (hearing) sensory memory. When we take in images through the sense of sight, we are using iconic memory. Unless we encode an image and move it into our short-term memory, however, iconic memory does not last very long—research suggests that after only a quarter of a second, old information is replaced by new information (Cowan, 1988).

Echoic memory is a brief memory of something a person has heard. A good example of echoic memory is the "What?" phenomenon. You might be reading or concentrating on the television, and your parent or friend walks

sensory memory the very first stage of memory, the point at which information enters the nervous system through the sensory systems.

276 CHAPTER 9

Class Demonstration

CULTURAL REMINDERS

Cultures and subcultures also have ritualized reminders for memory events. For example, people in Western cultures know that a string around one's finger serves as a reminder to do something, just as a flag at half-mast helps remind a large group to honor someone's memory. The use and form of these reminders can vary from culture to culture, although like the memory tasks themselves they typically are learned implicitly within a cultural context.

Divide the class into groups and ask students to brainstorm other cultural reminders that are used in the United States. Ask students to also gather reminders from other cultures that they may know. Bring the class back together and ask each group to share its thoughts.

276 Chapter 9 Memory

up and says something to you. You sit there for a second or two, and then say "What? Oh—yes, I'm ready to eat now," or whatever comment is appropriate. You didn't really process the statement from the other person as he or she said it. You heard it and paid enough attention to it to remember it briefly, but your brain didn't interpret it immediately.

Echoic memory's capacity is limited to what can be heard at any one moment and is smaller than the capacity of iconic memory, although it lasts longer—about 2 to 4 seconds (Schweickert, 1993).

Short-Term and Working Memory

What is short-term memory, and how does it differ from working memory?
Information typically moves from sensory memory to the next stage of memory, called **short-term memory (STM)**, through the process of **selective attention**, the ability to focus on only one stimulus from among all sensory input (Broadbent, 1958). When a person is thinking actively about some information, that information is said to be conscious. It can also be said to be in STM, the memory system in which information is held for brief periods of time while being used.

Selective attention is responsible for the "cocktail party effect" that has been long established in studies of perception and attention (Cherry, 1953; Handel, 1989). If you've ever been at a party where there's a lot of noise going on in the background but you are able to notice when someone says your name, you have experienced this effect. The areas of the brain that are involved in selective attention were working even though you were not consciously aware of it, and when that important bit of information (your name) appeared, those areas brought the information to your conscious awareness (Hopfinger et al., 2000; Stuss et al., 2002).

The only time this attention filter is not working at its peak is during deep Stage Four sleep, and it is still functioning even then (LaBerge, 1980). For example, a mother might be able to sleep through the noise of a train that passes nearby every night but immediately awakens when hearing the soft sound of her baby crying. The train sound may be louder but is not important, whereas the baby's cry is most certainly important.

When your attention is focused—in other words, when you are paying close attention to only one thing—it is relatively easy to form memories about it. For example, if you were given a list of seven numbers and told to spend a few minutes memorizing them, you most likely wouldn't have much trouble with the task. What would happen, though, if you were asked to memorize those same seven numbers while bouncing a basketball through an obstacle course? Your attention would be divided: You'd be paying attention not only to the list of numbers but also to the basketball and the obstacle course. As a result, you'd most likely have a more difficult time encoding that list of numbers and storing it in your memory. Attention, known also as "attending to" stimuli, is the crucial tool that transforms sensations into memories, and when our attention is divided rather than focused, our memories suffer as a result.

short-term memory (STM) the memory system in which information is held for brief periods of time while being used.

selective attention the ability to focus on only one stimulus from among all sensory input.

◀ What is short-term memory, and how does it differ from working memory?

▲ Each person at this gathering is involved in a conversation with others, with several separate conversations going on at the same time all around. Yet if a person in another conversation says the name of one of the people in the room, that person will be able to selectively attend to his or her name. This is known as the "cocktail party effect."

MEMORY 277

CHAPTER 9 • Module 23

COVER THE MODULE *(continued)*

- STM is where information is held while it is conscious and being used.
  - *Selective attention* occurs when the most important stimulus is extracted from a range of sensory input, as with the "cocktail party effect."

DISCUSS THE STUDENT VOICE QUESTION

Ensure that students understand the difference between STM and working memory. Discuss how working memory operates. When might working memory use the "sketchpad" for storing information? When might it use the "recorder"? In what cases are the two used together?

FAST FACT

Scientists continue to study the cocktail party effect, which is our remarkable ability to filter important information from a sea of background noise. For some animals in the wild, this ability is especially important. Ask students if they can guess which noisy animals are being studied by scientists in an effort to pinpoint the cocktail effect in the human brain. (**Answer:** birds and bats)

Class Demonstration (Kinesthetic)

THE COCKTAIL PARTY EFFECT

Take a "break" during class—tell students that they may get up, move around a bit, and chat with their classmates for a few moments. (You may even invent an errand or an unexpected call and leave the room.) "Plant" one student to talk to another student, or small group of students, on either side of the room, and give them something interesting to say, such as "I heard we're having a pop quiz in psychology tomorrow." Make sure that the student speaks to only a few students or small groups of students and keeps his or her voice at a normal level. When students return to their seats, ask how many of them have heard that there will be a pop quiz tomorrow. Did students recognize their brain's use of selective attention?

Module 23 Encoding and Storage   **277**

CHAPTER 9 • Module 23

COVER THE MODULE (continued)
- *STM* holds about 7 plus or minus 2 chunks of information and lasts about 30 seconds without rehearsal.
- STM can be lost through failure to rehearse, decay, interference by similar information, and the intrusion of new information into the STM system, which pushes out older information.

MULTIMEDIA CONTENT AVAILABLE AT
www.mypsychlab.com

Simulate the digit-span test on mypsychlab.com

UNDERSTANDING VISUALS
Direct students' attention to Figure 23.3 and conduct the digit-span test with the class. (You may want to use different numbers from the ones provided.) After the entire test is completed, write the number spans on the board so that students can check their work. Make a table on the board indicating how many students remembered a maximum of four numbers, five numbers, and so on. What was the longest span remembered? How were the students who remembered the longest span able to do so? What is the mean? What is the mode?

L3 DIFFERENTIATED INSTRUCTION
Visual/Nonverbal Learners Encourage these students to make charts and diagrams and sum up information in tables.

278 Chapter 9 Memory

---

working memory an active system that processes the information in short-term memory.

Simulate the digit-span test on mypsychlab.com

6 8 2 5

5 7 2 1 4

3 5 9 7 2 1

9 2 5 4 6 3 8

2 8 3 7 1 5 6 9

7 3 2 4 9 6 8 5 1

6 5 4 7 8 9 3 2 1 7

FIGURE 23.3 Digit-Span Test
Instructions for the digit-span test: Listen carefully as the instructor reads each string of numbers out loud. As soon as each string is ended (the instructor may say "go"), write down the numbers in the exact order in which they were given. How many digits can you store in short-term memory?

278 CHAPTER 9

STM tends to be encoded in auditory (sound) form. That simply means that people tend to "talk" inside their own heads. Although some images are stored in STM in a kind of visual "sketchpad" (Baddeley, 1986), auditory storage accounts for much of short-term encoding. Even a dancer planning out moves in her head will not only visualize the moves but also be very likely to verbally describe the moves in her head as she plans. Research in which participants were asked to recall numbers and letters showed that errors were nearly always made with numbers or letters that *sounded like* the target but not with those that *looked like* the target word or number (Conrad & Hull, 1964).

Some memory theorists use the term *working memory* as another way of referring to STM. This is not entirely correct: STM has traditionally been thought of as a thing or a space into which information is placed. **Working memory** is more correctly thought of as an active system that processes the information present in STM. Working memory is thought to consist of three interrelated systems led by a central executive (a kind of "big boss") that controls and coordinates the other two systems, a visual "sketchpad" of sorts, and a kind of auditory "recorder" (Baddeley, 1986; Baddeley & Hitch, 1974; Engle & Kane, 2004). The central executive acts as interpreter for both the visual and auditory information, and the visual and auditory information is itself contained in STM. For example, when a person is reading a book, the sketchpad will contain images of the people and events of the particular passage being read, while the recorder "plays" the dialogue in the person's head. The central executive helps interpret the information from both systems and pulls it all together. In a sense, then, STM can be seen as being a part of the working memory system (Bayliss et al., 2005; Colom et al., 2006; Kail & Hall, 2001).

Another way to think about STM is as if it were a kind of desk where you work. You might pull some files out of storage (long-term memory) or someone might hand you some files (sensory input). While the files are on your desk, you can see them, read them, and work with them (working memory). The "files" are now conscious material and will stay that way as long as they are on the desk. If they are not that important or only necessary for a little while, they get "thrown out" (forgotten as you fail to pay attention to them). If they are important, they might get stored away in the permanent filing system (long-term memory), where they are not conscious until they are once again retrieved—brought out onto the desk.

George Miller (1956) wanted to know how much information humans could hold in STM at any one time (or how many "files" would fit on the "desk"). He reviewed several memory studies, including some using a memory test called the *digit-span test*, in which a series of numbers is read to subjects who are then asked to recall the numbers in order. Each series gets longer and longer, until the subjects cannot recall any of the numbers in order (see Figure 23.3). Simulate on mypsychlab.com

What you will probably discover is that everyone you test will get past the first two sequences of numbers, but some people will make errors on the six-digit span, about half of the people you test will slip up on the seven-digit span, and very few will be able to get past the nine-digit span without errors. This led Miller to conclude that the capacity of STM is about seven items or pieces of information, plus or minus two items, or from five to nine bits of information. Miller called this the "magical number seven, plus or minus two." So the "desk" isn't very big and can hold only so many "files."

It also can't hold those files for a significant length of time: Research has shown that STM lasts from about 12 to 30 seconds without rehearsal (Atkinson & Shiffrin, 1968; Brown, 1958; Peterson & Peterson, 1959). After that, the memory seems to rapidly "decay" or disappear: For example, if you review your textbook right before a quiz and then put the book away, you might not be able to remember what you read in the textbook when a question about that material comes up on the quiz 15 minutes later.

What do you mean by rehearsal? How long can STMs last if rehearsal is a factor?

Most people learn that saying something they want to remember over and over again in their heads, such as repeating a phone number they need just long enough to dial it, can help them remember longer. This process is called **maintenance rehearsal**. With this type of rehearsal, information will stay in STM until rehearsal stops. If anything interferes with maintenance rehearsal, memories are also likely to be lost. For example, if someone is trying to count a stack of dollar bills by reciting each number out loud while counting, and someone else asks that person the time and interferes with the counting process, the person who is counting will probably forget what the last number was and have to start all over again.

Long-Term Memory

How is long-term memory different from other types of memory?
The third stage of memory is **long-term memory (LTM)**, the system into which information is placed to be kept more or less permanently. LTM seems to be able to store an unlimited amount of information (Bahrick, 1984; Barnyard & Grayson, 1996), ranging from the names of your friends and family members to the lyrics of your favorite songs—and much, much more. Think about it: Would there ever really come a time when you could not fit one more piece of information into your head? When you could learn nothing more? Perhaps if humans lived much longer lives, there might be a way to "fill up" the brain's memory stores. But in practical terms, there is always room for more information (in spite of what some students may believe).

As for how long it lasts, the name *long term* says it all. There is a physical change in the brain itself when a LTM is formed. This physical change is relatively permanent. That means that many of the memories people have stored away for a long, long time—even since childhood—will probably always exist there. (That does not mean, however, that people can always retrieve those memories. We'll talk about this topic more in the next module.)

23.3 How can we make encoding more effective?

Okay, I think I understand how memories are encoded, but are there any strategies I can use to help myself encode information more easily?

More Effective Encoding in Short-Term Memory Remember "the magical number seven, plus or minus two"? This is the capacity of STM: five to nine bits of information. But there is a way to "fool" STM into holding

maintenance rehearsal practice of saying some information to be remembered over and over in one's head in order to maintain it in short-term memory.

long-term memory (LTM) the system of memory into which all the information is placed to be kept more or less permanently.

◀ What do you mean by rehearsal? How long can STMs last if rehearsal is a factor?

◀ How is long-term memory different from other types of memory?

◀ Okay, I think I understand how memories are encoded, but are there any strategies I can use to help myself encode information more easily?

MEMORY 279

CHAPTER 9 • Module 23

DISCUSS THE STUDENT VOICE QUESTION
Ask students if they used *maintenance rehearsal* during the digit-span test. How effective was it? How many numbers did it get them through? Were there other stimuli that interfered with their rehearsal, such as someone speaking in the hallway, a siren outside, or an announcement over the loudspeaker?

COVER THE MODULE *(continued)*
- *LTM* is the system in which memories that are to be kept more or less permanently are stored, and it is unlimited in capacity and relatively permanent in duration.
- Information that is more deeply processed, or processed according to meaning, will be retained and retrieved more efficiently.

DISCUSS THE STUDENT VOICE QUESTION
Discuss with students the idea that there is always room in the brain for more information. What are their reactions to this information? Are they excited? Surprised? Skeptical? Why?

COVER THE MODULE
23.3 How can we make encoding more effective?
- Chunking can increase the amount of information that can be held in STM.

DISCUSS THE STUDENT VOICE QUESTION
Ask students to share some encoding strategies that they use, for example, when studying for a test. Did they learn them in school? Did they think of any themselves? Can they name any famous ones?

Class Demonstration

THE VALUE OF CHUNKING
In the following two-part demonstration, ask a student to volunteer. Inform the volunteer that he or she will be presented with a set of items to be memorized in exact order. Then read the following list of letters:

X I B M C I A F B I C B S M T V

After a short delay, ask the student to recall as many of the letters as possible.

In the second part of the demonstration, tell the student that you will improve his or her memory with a little help. Then read the letters in the following "chunked format":

X IBM CIA FBI CBS MTV

The student should have nearly perfect recall. Grouping the letters reduced the memory task from 16 items to 6 items.

Module 23 Encoding and Storage **279**

COVER THE MODULE (continued)

- Information can be transferred into LTM through elaborative rehearsal.
  - *Elaborative rehearsal* is a deeper kind of processing than maintenance rehearsal.

COVER THE MODULE

23.4 How is information stored in LTM?

- *Procedural (nondeclarative) memories* are memories for skills, habits, and conditioned responses.

LINK to Chapter Six: Learning and Language Development, pp. 178–185

EXTEND THE LESSON

Give students 5 minutes to write down as many procedural memories as they can think of. When time is up, ask students to share their answers as you write them on the board. How many did they come up with? How long do students think it would take to come up with a full list? Would it be possible?

TEACHING TIP

Celebrate classroom successes and praise students as they work to complete projects.

---

more information than is usual. (Think of it as "stacking" related files on the desk.) If the bits of information are combined into meaningful units, or *chunks*, more information can be held in STM. If someone were to recode the last sequence of numbers as "654-789-3217," for example, instead of 10 bits of information, there would only be three "chunks" that read like a phone number. This process of recoding, or reorganizing, the information is called *chunking*. Chances are that anyone who can easily remember more than eight or nine digits in the digit-span test is probably recoding the numbers into chunks.

More Effective Encoding in Long-Term Memory Most people tend to learn things like poems and the multiplication tables by maintenance rehearsal, otherwise known as rote learning. (You might remember the meaning of the word *rote* by thinking about "rotating" information in your head, saying it over and over again.) But maintenance rehearsal is not the most efficient or effective way of putting information into long-term storage.

Elaborative rehearsal is a way of transferring information from STM into LTM by making that information meaningful in some way (Postman, 1975). The easiest way to do this is to connect new information with something that is already well known (Craik & Lockhart, 1972; Postman, 1975). For example, the French word *maison* means "house." A person could try to memorize that using maintenance rehearsal by saying over and over, "*Maison* means house, *maison* means house." But it would be easier and more efficient if that person simply thought, "*Maison* sounds like masons, and masons build houses." That makes the meaning of the word tie in with something the person already knows (masons, who lay stone or bricks to build houses) and helps in remembering the French term.

As discussed in the beginning of this module, Craik and Lockhart (1972) theorized that information that is more "deeply processed," or processed according to its meaning rather than just the sound or physical characteristics of the word or words, will be remembered more efficiently and for a longer period of time. As the levels-of-processing approach predicts, elaborative rehearsal is a deeper kind of processing than maintenance rehearsal and so leads to better long-term storage (Craik & Tulving, 1975).

Understand How Memories Are Stored in the Brain

23.4 How is information stored in long-term memory?

LTMs include general facts and knowledge, personal facts, and even skills that can be performed. Memories for skills that people know how to do, like tying shoes and riding a bicycle, are a kind of LTM called **procedural (nondeclarative) memory**. Procedural memories also include habits and simple conditioned reflexes, like covering your mouth when you cough, that may or may not be in conscious awareness. LINK *to Chapter Six: Learning and Language Development, pp. 178–185*.

Procedural memory may also be called **implicit memory** because memories for these skills, habits, and learned reflexes are not easily retrieved into conscious awareness (i.e., nondeclarative). The fact that people have the knowledge of how to tie their shoes, for example, is *implied* by the fact that

elaborative rehearsal a method of transferring information from STM into LTM by making that information meaningful in some way.

procedural (nondeclarative) memory type of LTM including memory for skills, procedures, habits, and conditioned responses. These memories are not conscious but are implied to exist because they affect conscious behavior.

implicit memory memory that is not easily brought into conscious awareness, such as procedural memory.

280 CHAPTER 9

Explore

AMNESIA AND IMPLICIT MEMORY

Implicit memory effects occur when there is improvement on a task in which participants are not asked to consciously remember prior information. Implicit memory effects have been found in amnesic individuals who perform poorly on explicit memory tasks of recall and recognition, relative to normal controls. Interestingly, individuals with amnesia perform at the same level as normal controls with implicit memory tests, suggesting that previously learned information is available in memory but not accessible with traditional memory measures of recall and recognition.

H. M. suffered from anterograde amnesia due to the removal of several brain areas associated with memory. While H. M. could not explicitly remember newly experienced events, he showed improved performance on such tasks on later trials, indicating an implicit memory effect.

Have students read the article at http://socrates.berkeley.edu/~kihlstrm/IandMLandM.htm. According to the article, what accounts for the retention of implicit memory in most amnesiacs?

280 Chapter 9 Memory

they can actually tie them. But have you ever tried to tell someone how to tie shoes without using your hands to show them?

Although procedural memories are implicit, not all implicit memories are necessarily procedural. A memory from one's early childhood of being frightened by a dog, for example, may not be a conscious memory in later childhood but may still be the cause of that older child's fear of dogs. Conscious memories for events in childhood, on the other hand, are usually considered to be a different kind of LTM called declarative memory.

Procedural memory is about the things that people can *do*, but **declarative memory** is about all the things that people can *know*—the facts and information that make up knowledge. People know things such as the names of the planets in the solar system, that adding two and two makes four, and that a noun is the name of a person, place, or thing. These are general facts, but people also know about the things that have happened to them personally. For example, I know what I ate for breakfast this morning and what I saw on the way to work, but I don't know what you had for breakfast or what you might have seen. There are two types of declarative LTMs, *semantic* and *episodic* (Nyberg & Tulving, 1996).

One type of declarative memory is general knowledge that anyone has the ability to know. Much of this information is learned in school or by reading. This kind of LTM is called **semantic memory**. The word *semantic* refers to meaning, so this kind of knowledge is the awareness of the meanings of words, concepts, and terms as well as names of objects, math skills, and so on. This is also the type of knowledge that is used on game shows such as *Jeopardy!* and *Who Wants to Be a Millionaire?* Semantic memories, like procedural memories, are relatively permanent. But it is possible to "lose the way to" this kind of memory, as we'll discuss in the next module.

The other kind of factual memory is the personal knowledge that each person has of his or her daily life and personal history, a kind of autobiographical memory, or the story of a person's life, as seen through that person's experience. Memories of what has happened to people each day, certain birthdays, anniversaries that were particularly special, childhood events, and so on are called **episodic memory**, because they represent episodes from their lives. Unlike procedural and semantic LTMs, episodic memories tend to be updated and revised more or less constantly. You can probably remember what you had for breakfast today, but what you had for breakfast 2 years ago on this date is most likely a mystery. Episodic memories that are especially *meaningful*, such as the memory of the first day of school or your first date, are more likely to be kept in LTM (although they may not be as accurate as people sometimes assume they are). The updating process is a kind of survival mechanism, because although semantic and procedural memories are useful and necessary on an ongoing basis, no one really needs to remember every little detail of every day.

Episodic and semantic memories are forms of declarative or **explicit memory**, memories that are easily made conscious and brought from long-term storage into STM. The knowledge of semantic memories such as word meanings, science concepts, and so on can be brought out of the "filing cabinet" and placed on the "desk" where that knowledge becomes *explicit*, or obvious. The same is often true of personal, episodic memories. For a look at the connections among all these types of LTM, see Figure 23.4.

Long-Term Memory Organization As stated before, LTM has to be fairly well organized for retrieval to be so quick. Can you remember the name

declarative memory type of LTM containing information that is conscious and known.

semantic memory type of declarative memory containing general knowledge, such as knowledge of language and information learned in formal education.

episodic memory type of declarative memory containing personal information not readily available to others, such as daily activities and events.

explicit memory memory that is consciously known, such as declarative memory.

MEMORY 281

CHAPTER 9 • Module 23

COVER THE MODULE (continued)

- *Declarative memories* are memories for general facts and personal experiences and include both semantic (facts, information) memories and episodic (autobiographical) memories.
- *Implicit memories* are difficult to bring into conscious awareness, while *explicit memories* are those that a person is aware of possessing.

EXTEND THE LESSON

Tell students that the daily lives of Ling, Carlos, and Kate sound nightmarish. The 14-, 19-, and 22-year-olds cannot remember where they have been shortly after they have been there, cannot recall whom they have seen shortly after they have seen them, and cannot recognize familiar buildings shortly after they have walked out of them. Each of these young people suffered from brain seizures at an early age that produced extensive damage to the hippocampus.

However, Ling, Carlos, and Kate all attended mainstream schools, have good speech and language skills, read and spell as well as their peers, and have acquired lots and lots of factual knowledge. Their abilities in these areas, contrasted with their disabilities in others, highlight the difference between semantic memory and episodic memory. What's more, they suggest that the areas of the brain responsible for these types of memory are different. Researchers have concluded that although the hippocampus regulates recall of personal experiences, it plays only a minor role in the storage and acquisition of factual knowledge. In short, while *episodic memory* has been tragically disrupted for these three, semantic memory has remained largely intact.

Class Demonstration

TIME-GAP EXPERIENCE

"I left school, and then I arrived at home. I'm not sure what happened in between." Most of us have shared the experience of doing a fairly complicated task (such as driving a car) and upon completion realizing that we have no recollection of the task (such as which turns were made and so on). This time-gap experience can be explained using the distinction between automatic and effortful processing. An effortful task, such as one that is new or unfamiliar, demands our cognitive resources for its completion. Even a fairly intricate task, once it has become automatic, can be performed outside conscious awareness.

Ask students to list some tasks during which they may experience, or have experienced, a time gap. Were they complex or simple tasks? Ask students to note when time gaps happen to them while covering this chapter. Consider starting a running list on the board or a large sheet of paper and review it at the end of the chapter.

Module 23 Encoding and Storage **281**

CHAPTER 9 • Module 23

COVER THE MODULE (continued)

- LTM is organized in the form of semantic networks, or nodes of related information spreading out from a central piece of knowledge.
- A good analogy of the LTM is the Internet, with many links and the ability to open several windows at once.

COVER THE MODULE

23.5 How and where are memories stored in the brain?

- Evidence suggests that procedural memories are stored in the cerebellum, while STMs are stored in the prefrontal and temporal lobes of the cortex.
- Semantic and episodic memories may be stored in the frontal and temporal lobes as well but in different locations than LTM, while memory for fear of objects is most likely stored in the amygdala.

LINK to Chapter Two: The Biological Perspective, pp. 57–62.

FIGURE 23.4 Types of Long-Term Memories
LTM can be divided into declarative memories, which are factual and typically conscious (explicit) memories, and nondeclarative memories, which are skills, habits, and conditioned responses that are typically unconscious (implicit). Declarative memories are further divided into episodic memories (personal experiences) and semantic memories (general knowledge).

of your first grade teacher? If you can, how long did it take you to pull that name out of LTM and "put it on the desk" of STM? It probably took hardly any time at all. Think of it this way: If a person who puts documents in a filing cabinet just stuffs them in any drawer with no system of organization, when a particular document is needed, it requires searching through every drawer. But if documents are filed away alphabetically, according to type of document (school records in one drawer, bank statements in another, etc.), and perhaps even cross-referenced (so information is contained in multiple files from which it can be retrieved), it becomes very easy to retrieve a particular document.

Perhaps the best way to think of how information is organized in LTM is to think about the Internet. A person might go to one Web site, and from that site, that person can link to many other related sites. Each related site has its own specific information but is itself also linked to many other related sites, and a person can have more than one site open at the same time. This may be very similar to the way in which the mind organizes the information stored in LTM.

23.5 How and where are memories stored in the brain?

Up to now, we've been talking about the storage of memories in a very abstract way. Comparing memory to a desk can help us understand how memory works, but of course, you don't really have a "memory desk" in your head—you have a brain, and different parts of the brain are responsible for storing different types of memory. For example, procedural memories seem to be stored in the cerebellum (Boyd & Winstein, 2004; Daum & Schugens, 1996), and STMs are most likely stored in the prefrontal cortex (the top layer of the very front of the frontal lobe) and the temporal lobe (Goldman-Rakic, 1998; Rao et al., 1997). LINK *to Chapter Two: The Biological Perspective, pp. 57–62.*

As for semantic and episodic LTMs, evidence suggests that these memories are also stored in the frontal and temporal lobes but not in exactly the

---

Class Demonstration

MEMORY NETWORKS

<u>Purpose</u>: Students learn how information in LTM is organized and stored.

<u>Time</u>: Approximately 15 minutes

<u>Description</u>: Begin with a brief introduction to associative networks and organization in LTM. Divide the class into teams of 3–5 students. Instruct each team member to write down the names of 10 household objects, using one sticky note per item. Have team members stick their notes to a work surface, so that all team members can see and reach them. Students then work silently to construct an affinity diagram by physically manipulating the Post-It notes, grouping them into categories. If students disagree with the placement on an item or want to make a new category, they may rearrange the notes. Continue the activity until the group is satisfied with their arrangement. Have team members discuss their decisions for grouping information the way they did. What rules did they use to group the information? Did they group the information according to the room of the house that you would find this object in? Or, the function of the object?

same locations as STMs (Weis et al., 2004). In general, we know that memories are stored all over the brain.

Neural Activity and Structure in Memory Formation Several studies have offered evidence that a memory is not simply one physical change but many: changes in the number of receptor sites, changes in the sensitivity of a synapse through repeated stimulation (called *long-term potentiation*), and changes in the dendrites and in the proteins within the neurons (Alkon, 1989; Kandel & Schwartz, 1982; Squire & Kandel, 1999). All of these changes serve to increase the neural connections and make connections that already exist more sensitive to stimulation. These changes that take place as a memory is forming are called *consolidation*. Recent research suggests that memory consolidation takes place during sleep (Stickgold, 2005) and that afternoon naps can enhance memory consolidation (Nishida & Walker, 2007)—just one of many reasons why it's important not to skimp on sleep.

The Hippocampus and Memory The *hippocampus* (a part of the limbic system) is the part of the brain that is responsible for the formation of new LTMs. One of the clearest pieces of evidence of this function comes from the study of a man known as H. M. (Milner et al., 1968).

H. M. was about 17 when he began to suffer from severe epileptic seizures. A few years later, the majority of H. M.'s hippocampus was removed (along with the amygdala and portions of the parahippocampal region in each hemisphere) in an attempt to remove what the surgeon believed was the source of the seizures. The last thing H. M. could remember was being rolled on the gurney to the operating room—it was the last memory he was ever able to form.

The hippocampus was not the source of H.M.'s problem, but it was apparently the source of his ability to store any new factual information he encountered, because without it, he was completely unable to remember anything new. He had a magazine that he carried around, reading and rereading the stories, because each time he did so, the stories were completely new to him. As with most amnesiacs of this type (although H. M.'s case was quite severe), his old memories were still intact, but his new memories were lost.

The man that most of the world had only known as H.M., Henry Molaison, died in December 2008. His experience and his brain will continue to educate students and neuroscientists, as he agreed many years ago that his brain would be donated for further scientific study upon his death. It has now been sliced into almost 2,400 slices, each about the width of a human hair, in preparation for further study. You can learn more about the H.M. Project at the Web site of the The Brain Observatory, housed at the University of California, San Diego, **http://thebrainobservatory.ucsd.edu**.

MEMORY 283

Critical Thinking

MEMORY STORAGE

Purpose: Students complete a brief 1-minute assignment that involves critical thinking, personalizing, or deeper processing of information.

Time: 1–5 minutes

Description: Give students a few minutes to answer the following: "Give an example from your own experiences of procedural, declarative, episodic, and semantic knowledge. What are the differences between these types of knowledge?"

CHAPTER 9 • Module 23

COVER THE MODULE *(continued)*

- Consolidation consists of the physical changes in neurons that take place during the formation of a memory.
- The hippocampus appears to be responsible for the storage of new LTMs. If it is removed, the ability to store anything new is completely lost.

EXTEND THE LESSON

Direct students to the H. M. Project at The Brain Observatory website (**http://thebrainobservatory.ucsd.edu**). What is the current status of the project? What kinds of things have researchers learned about the brain and memory from H. M.'s brain? Ask students why he was known so long as simply "H. M." Why do we now know his true name?

L3 DIFFERENTIATED INSTRUCTION

Engaging All Learners Use a variety of strategies to teach and assess understanding. Present ideas orally and visually and, when possible, incorporate tactile and kinesthetic experiences. Think beyond the common modes of reading and writing. Students could present information orally, create a poster or visual representation of a work, record their ideas, or act out their understanding. These activities take into consideration multiple intelligences and can provide access for all learners in the classroom.

CHAPTER 9 • Module 23

Assess

Assign the Module 23 Practice Quiz.

Use the Practice Quiz to identify gaps in student understanding.

REMEDIATE

Have students, individually or in groups, review the module goals, learning objectives, and key terms.

Refer students to the Concept Summary on p. 302 for review.

Close

As a class, discuss the different kinds of memory and the ways in which memory is formed and stored. Ask students to offer theories about why the process of memory is still such an intensive field of study.

Practice Quiz

Pick the best answer.

1. Eldon has just finished his essay test and handed it in. As he walks out of the classroom, he realizes that there were a few more things he should have included in the essay. Eldon's problem is in the memory process of
   a. encoding
   b. storage
   c. retrieval
   d. retention

2. Which type of memory is most likely used to remember names of people whom you have just met at a social gathering?
   a. procedural memory
   b. implicit memory
   c. short-term memory
   d. long-term memory

3. Fethia learned her multiplication tables by repeating them over and over until she had them memorized. Fethia was using which kind of rehearsal?
   a. repetitive
   b. imagery
   c. elaborative
   d. maintenance

4. Of the following, which is the most similar to the concept of long-term memory?
   a. a revolving door
   b. a filing cabinet
   c. a desk top
   d. a computer keyboard

5. Long-term memories are encoded in terms of
   a. sounds
   b. visual images
   c. meanings of words and concepts
   d. all of the above

6. Which type of LTM is seldom, if ever, lost by people with Alzheimer's disease?
   a. procedural
   b. semantic
   c. episodic
   d. both b and c

7. In the game show *Who Wants to Be a Millionaire?* contestants are asked an increasingly difficult series of questions about general information. The type of memory needed to access the answers to these kinds of questions is
   a. procedural
   b. semantic
   c. episodic
   d. working

8. The Internet, with its series of links from one site to many others, is a good analogy for the organization of
   a. short-term memory
   b. episodic memory
   c. long-term memory
   d. procedural memory

9. When Edie studies her psychology terms, she tries to tie each concept into something she already knows. She thinks about the meaning of the concept rather than just saying the words over and over. Which of the following best explains Edie's approach to encoding memories?
   a. information-processing model
   b. levels-of-processing model
   c. selective attention
   d. maintenance rehearsal

10. Which of the following is responsible for the "cocktail party effect," in which you are able to hear someone say your name, even when there is a lot of background noise?
    a. working memory
    b. episodic memory
    c. selective attention
    d. elaborative rehearsal

Practice Quiz Answers

1. c
2. c
3. c
4. b
5. d
6. a
7. b
8. c
9. b
10. c

Module 24: Retrieval and Retrieval Failure

Module Goal
Learn how memories are retrieved from the brain.

Learning Objectives
- 24.1 What kinds of cues help people remember?
- 24.2 What factors influence how memories are retrieved?
- 24.3 How can we improve our ability to retrieve memories?
- 24.4 Can memories change? How reliable are they?
- 24.5 Why do we forget?
- 24.6 How does amnesia occur?

Learn How Memories Are Retrieved From the Brain

When it comes to memory, encoding information from the world around us and storing it in the brain is only half of the challenge. The other half of the challenge is *retrieving* that stored information, bringing it back into working memory when we need it. In this module, we'll examine how we remember information—and how, occasionally, we forget it.

24.1 What kinds of cues help people remember?

One of the main reasons that maintenance rehearsal is not a very good way to get information into LTM is that saying something over and over only gives one kind of **retrieval cue** (a stimulus for remembering)—the sound of the word or phrase. When people try to remember a piece of information by thinking about what it means and how it fits in with what they already know, they are giving themselves cues for meaning in addition to sound. The more cues stored with a piece of information, the easier the retrieval of that information will be (Roediger, 2000; Roediger & Guynn, 1996).

Encoding Specificity and State-Dependent Learning Although most people would assume that cues for retrieval would have to be directly related to the concepts being studied, the fact is that almost anything in one's surroundings is capable of becoming a cue. If you usually watch a particular television show while eating peanuts, for example, the next time you eat peanuts you might find yourself thinking of the show you were watching. This connection between surroundings and remembered information is called *encoding specificity*.

Have you ever had to take a test in a different classroom than the one in which you learned the material being tested? Do you think that your performance on that test was hurt by being in a different physical context? Researchers have found strong evidence for the concept of **encoding specificity**, the tendency for memory of any kind of information to be improved if the physical surroundings available when the memory is first

retrieval cue a stimulus for remembering.

encoding specificity the tendency for memory of information to be improved if related information (such as surroundings or physiological state) available when the memory is first formed is also available when the memory is being retrieved.

MEMORY 285

Terms

- retrieval cue • encoding specificity • recall • recognition • serial position effect
- primacy effect • recency effect • false positive • effortful encoding • automatic encoding • flashbulb memories • mnemonic • constructive processing • hindsight bias • misinformation effect • curve of forgetting • encoding failure • memory trace • decay • disuse • proactive interference • retroactive interference • retrograde amnesia • anterograde amnesia • infantile amnesia • autobiographical memory

---

CHAPTER 9 • Module 24

Focus

RESOURCES
For this module, consult the appropriate sections of the Teacher's Manual, Test Bank, and PowerPoint slides, all found on the Teacher's Resource DVD, and the interactive study tools for students on MyPsychLab.

BEFORE CLASS
Students should read the section for homework before coming to class.

BELLRINGER
Ask students if this module has made them look at remembering—and forgetting—differently. Before reading the material, to what did they attribute their ability to remember things? Did they think that a tendency to forget was a personal failure? Did they give it any thought?

Teach

COVER THE MODULE
24.1 What kinds of cues help people remember?
- *Retrieval cues* are words, meanings, sounds, and other stimuli that are encoded at the same time as a new memory.
- *Encoding specificity* occurs when physical surroundings become encoded as retrieval cues for specific memories.

FAST FACT
The tip-of-the-tongue phenomenon is actually quite common, happening at least once a week to young people and as often as four times per week to older adults. Scientists believe that this phenomenon actually involves two brain functions. Ask students if they know what those functions are. (**Answer:** memory and language)

Module 24 Retrieval and Retrieval Failure **285**

CHAPTER 9 • Module 24

COVER THE MODULE (continued)
- State-dependent learning occurs when physiological or psychological states become encoded as retrieval cues for memories formed while in those states.

UNDERSTANDING VISUALS
Direct students to Figure 24.1, illustrating a study on encoding specificity. Do they find that the graph furthers their understanding of the research and the concept? Do they think that this sort of graph best illustrates the results? Why or why not?

COVER THE MODULE
24.2 What factors influence how memories are retrieved?
- Memories are retrieved through recall and recognition.

DISCUSS THE STUDENT VOICE QUESTION
Ask students what kinds of tests they prefer. Is multiple-choice the unanimous choice? If not, which kind of test "wins"? What other types of tests do students mention? Why?

FIGURE 24.1 Recall of Target Words in Two Contexts
The retrieval of words learned while underwater was higher when the retrieval also took place underwater. Similarly, words learned while out of the water (on land) were retrieved at a higher rate out of the water. Reproduced with permission from the *British Journal of Psychology,* © The British Psychology Society.

formed are also available when the memory is being retrieved (Reder et al., 1974; Tulving & Thomson, 1973). For example, encoding specificity would predict that the best place to take one's chemistry test is in the same room in which you learned the material.

In one study, researchers had students who were learning to scuba dive in a pool memorize lists of words while they were either out of the pool or in the pool under the water (Godden & Baddeley, 1975). Subjects were then asked to remember both lists in each of the two conditions. Words learned out of the pool were remembered significantly better when subjects were out of the pool, and words learned underwater were remembered better when subjects were underwater (see Figure 24.1).

Physical surroundings at the time of encoding a memory are not the only kinds of cues that can help in retrieval. In *state-dependent learning,* memories formed during a particular physiological or psychological state will be easier to remember while in a similar state. For example, when you are fighting with someone and are in a state of anger, it's much easier to remember all of the bad things that person has done than to remember the good times. In one study (Eich & Metcalfe, 1989), researchers had subjects try to remember words that they had read while listening to music. Subjects read one list of words while listening to sad music (influencing their mood to be sad) and another list of words while listening to happy music. When it came time to recall the lists, the researchers again manipulated the mood of the subjects via music. The words that were read while subjects were in a happy mood were remembered better if the manipulated mood was also happy, but remembered far less well if the mood was sad. The reverse was also true.

▶ Why do multiple-choice tests seem so much easier than essay tests?

24.2 What factors influence how memories are retrieved?

Why do multiple-choice tests seem so much easier than essay tests? There are two kinds of retrieval of memories—recall and recognition. It is the difference between these two retrieval methods that makes some kinds

286 CHAPTER 9

Class Demonstration

CONTEXT AND ITS EFFECT ON MEMORY
<u>Objective</u>: To demonstrate the effects of context on memory

<u>Materials</u>: An overhead transparency with the following matrix on it, making sure that the number 13 looks like a cross between a B and 13:

```
        12
    A   13   C
        14
```

<u>Procedure</u>: Divide the room in half by identifying a student in the middle and telling one-half to start from the top of the display and process downward and the other half to process from left to right. Ask for a show of hands and ask, "Who saw 12, 13, and 14?" Most of one side will raise their hands. The other half will look puzzled. Now ask, "Who saw A, B, and C?" The other half will respond. Now show them the matrix again and discuss the effect of psychological set on processing.

of exams seem harder than others. In **recall**, memories are retrieved with few or no external cues, such as filling in the blanks on an application form. **Recognition**, on the other hand, involves looking at or hearing information and matching it to what is already in memory. A word search puzzle, in which the words are already written down in the grid and simply need to be circled, is an example of recognition. The following section takes a closer look at these two important processes.

Recall: Hmm . . . Let Me Think When someone is asked a question such as "Where were you born?" the question acts as the cue for retrieval of the answer. This is an example of recall, as are essay questions, short-answer quizzes, and fill-in-the-blank tests that are used to measure a person's memory for information (Borges et al., 1977; Gillund & Shiffrin, 1984; Raaijmakers & Shiffrin, 1992).

Whenever people find themselves struggling for an answer, recall has failed (at least temporarily). Sometimes the answer seems so very close to the surface of conscious thought that it feels like it's "on the tip of the tongue." This is sometimes called the *tip of the tongue (TOT)* phenomenon (Brown & McNeill, 1966; Burke et al., 1991). Although people may be able to say how long the word is or name letters that start or even end the word, they cannot retrieve the sound or actual spelling of the word to allow it to be pulled into the auditory "recorder" of STM so that it can be fully retrieved.

How can a person overcome TOT? The best solution: Forget about it. When you "forget about it," the brain apparently continues to work on retrieval. Some time later (perhaps when you run across a similar-sounding word in your surroundings), the word or name will just "pop out." This can make for interesting conversations, because when that particular word does "pop out," it usually has little to do with the current conversation.

Another interesting feature of recall is that it is often subject to a kind of "prejudice" of memory retrieval, in which information at the beginning and the end of a list, such as the first and last lines of a poem or song, tends to be remembered more easily and accurately. An item's position in a series affects our ability to recall that item, a phenomenon called the **serial position effect** (Murdock, 1962).

A good demonstration of this phenomenon involves instructing people to listen to and try to remember words that are read to them that are spaced about 4 or 5 seconds apart. People typically use maintenance rehearsal by repeating each word in their heads. They are then asked to write as many of the words down as they can remember. If the frequency of recall for each word in the list is graphed, it will nearly always look like the graph in Figure 24.2 on the next page.

Words at the very beginning of the list tend to be remembered better than those in the middle of the list. This effect is called the **primacy effect** and is due to the fact that the first few words, heard when the listener has nothing already in STM to interfere with rehearsal, will receive far more rehearsal time than the words in the middle, which are constantly being replaced by the next words on the list (Craik, 1970; Murdock, 1962).

At the end of the graph, there is another increase in recall. This is the **recency effect**; it is usually attributed to the fact that the last word or two was *just heard* and is still in STM for easy retrieval, with no new words entering to "push" the most recent word or words out of memory (Bjork & Whitten, 1974; Murdock, 1962).

recall type of memory retrieval in which the information to be retrieved must be "pulled" from memory with very few external cues.

recognition the ability to match a piece of information or a stimulus to a stored image or fact.

serial position effect tendency of information at the beginning and end of a body of information to be remembered more accurately than information in the middle of the body of information.

primacy effect tendency to remember information at the beginning of a body of information better than the information that follows.

recency effect tendency to remember information at the end of a body of information better than the information at the beginning of it.

CHAPTER 9 • Module 24

COVER THE MODULE *(continued)*

- *Recall* is a type of memory retrieval in which the information to be retrieved must be "pulled" out of memory with few or no cues.
- The *serial position effect*, or *primacy-recency effect*, occurs when the first items and the last items in a list of information are recalled more efficiently than items in the middle of the list.

KINESTHETIC ACTIVITY

Place 15 objects, covered, in stations around the room. You may place one object in each station or group the objects (or do the activity two separate times with different objects, once with single items per station, once with items grouped, to see if the results differ). Give students 3–5 minutes to walk around the room looking at the objects. You may want to divide students into smaller groups and have them begin at different stations. Ask students to take note of which station they begin with. After the time is up, have students return to their desks and write down as many objects as they can remember in 2 minutes. On average, how many objects were students able to remember? Did they find it easier to remember groupings or single objects? Did they use any techniques to remember the grouped objects? Did they see the serial position effect at work?

L3 DIFFERENTIATED INSTRUCTION

Auditory/Verbal Learners These students can join or form a study group or find a study partner so they can discuss concepts and ideas.

Explore

SERIAL POSITION EFFECT

Have students complete the following activity to further explore the process of recall, especially as it pertains to the serial position effect. Send them to the Multimedia Library for this chapter at **www.mypsychlab.com** to complete the simulation titled "Experiment: Serial Position Effect." Again, did they find the serial position effect at work in their recall of the grocery list items? What other techniques were they able to use to help them in remembering the list? Were the techniques learned in this chapter or techniques they thought of/regularly use themselves?

CHAPTER 9 • Module 24

COVER THE MODULE (continued)
- Recognition involves matching information with images or facts.

EXTEND THE LESSON

We are all eyewitnesses to our own lives, and we are not completely accurate in what we remember. Ask students which of *their* autobiographical memories they think might be somewhat distorted or inaccurate. Why? (Note: Simply give students a moment to think about this quietly or to write the memories down if it helps them process things better. These memories need not be shared with the entire class.)

Inform students that the purpose of this exercise is to encourage them to understand that memory is reconstructive for them as well as for other people, a notion they often resist. Students typically identify memories of events that occurred early in childhood, unpleasant memories they have tried to forget, memories that threaten their self-image, memories that reflect negatively on someone they care about or positively on someone they dislike, and memories for events that occurred during a stressful period when they were preoccupied with problems. Sometimes students "remember" an event only to discover that it happened to someone else or did not occur at all.

FIGURE 24.2 Serial Position Effect
In the serial position effect, information at the beginning of a list will be recalled at a higher rate than information in the middle of the list (primacy effect), because the beginning information receives more rehearsal and may enter LTM. Information at the end of a list is also retrieved at a higher rate (recency effect), because the end of the list is still in STM, with no information coming after it to interfere with retrieval.

The serial position effect is often used to demonstrate that there are indeed two memory systems, STM and LTM. Memory researchers point to the primacy effect as a result of LTM storage and the recency effect as a result of STM.

Can knowledge of the serial position effect be of help to students trying to remember the information they need for their classes? Yes—students can take advantage of the recency effect by skimming back over their notes just before an exam. Knowing that the middle of a list of information is more likely to be forgotten means that students should pay more attention to that middle, and breaking study sessions up into smaller segments helps reduce the amount of "middle to muddle."

Recognition: Hey, Don't I Know You from Somewhere? The other form of memory retrieval is *recognition*, the ability to match a piece of information or a stimulus to a stored image or fact (Borges et al., 1977; Gillund & Shiffrin, 1984; Raaijmakers & Shiffrin, 1992). Recognition is usually much easier than recall because the cue is the actual object, word, sound, and so on, that the person is trying to detect as familiar and known. Examples of tests that use recognition are multiple-choice, matching, and true-false tests. The answer is right there and simply has to be matched to the information already in memory.

Recognition tends to be very accurate for images, especially human faces. In one study, over 2,500 photographs were shown to participants at the rate of one every 10 seconds. Participants were then shown pairs of photographs in which one member of each pair was one of the previously seen photographs. Accuracy for identifying the previously seen photos was between 85 and 95 percent (Standing et al., 1970). This is most likely why many people are good at recognizing a person's face but not as good at being able to come up with the name to go with it.

Recognition isn't foolproof, however. Sometimes, there is just enough similarity between a stimulus that is not already in memory and one that is in memory so that a **false positive** occurs (Muter, 1978). A false positive occurs

false positive error of recognition in which people think that they recognize some stimulus that is not actually in memory.

288 CHAPTER 9

Explore

RETRIEVAL OF MEMORIES

Direct students to the following websites to learn more about recognition and its fallibility.

- **Creating False Memories:**
  http://faculty.washington.edu/eloftus/Articles/sciam.htm

  A good overview of the literature on the topic by Elizabeth Loftus, originally published in *Scientific American*, September 1997, vol. 277 (3), pp. 70–75.

- **Elizabeth F. Loftus:** http://faculty.washington.edu/eloftus/

  Why not go right to the source? Visit the homepage of Elizabeth Loftus.

- **Elizabeth Loftus Interview for *Frontline's* "What Jennifer Saw"**
  www.pbs.org/wgbh/pages/frontline/shows/dna/interviews/loftus.html

  Elizabeth Loftus has done some of the most important research on eyewitness testimony. This interview touches on the validity of eyewitness testimony as well as on many of the other memory issues. This interview accompanies the *Frontline* documentary "What Jennifer Saw."

when a person thinks that he or she has recognized something or someone but in fact does not have that something or someone in memory. False positives can become disastrous in certain situations. In a series of armed robberies in Delaware, word had leaked out that the suspect sought by police might be a priest. When police put Father Bernard Pagano in a lineup for witnesses to identify, he was the only one in the lineup wearing a priest's collar. Seven eyewitnesses identified him as the man who had robbed them. Fortunately for Father Pagano, the real robber confessed to the crimes halfway through Pagano's trial (Loftus, 1987). Eyewitness recognition can be especially prone to false positives.

Flashbulb Memories Although some LTMs need extensive maintenance rehearsal or **effortful encoding** in the form of elaborative rehearsal to enter from STM into LTM, other kinds of LTMs seem to enter permanent storage with little or no effort at all, in a kind of **automatic encoding** (Mandler, 1967; Schneider et al., 1984). People unconsciously notice and remember a lot of things, such as the passage of time and frequency of events. For example, a person might make no effort to remember how many times cars have passed down the street but when asked can give an answer of "often," "more than usual," or "hardly any."

A special kind of automatic encoding takes place when an unexpected event or episode carries strong emotional associations. Memories of highly emotional events can often seem vivid and detailed, as if the person's mind took a "flash picture" of the moment in time. These kinds of memories are called **flashbulb memories** (Neisser, 1982; Neisser & Harsch, 1992; Winningham et al., 2000).

Many people share certain flashbulb memories. Many people of the "baby boomer" generation remember exactly where they were when the news came that President John F. Kennedy had been shot. Younger generations may similarly remember the horrific events of September 11, 2001. But personal flashbulb memories also exist. These memories tend to involve major emotional events, such as an embarrassing moment, or a particularly memorable birthday party. Although some researchers have found evidence for a high degree of accuracy in flashbulb memories of major events, others have found that flashbulb memories, while often convincingly real, are just as subject to decay and alteration over time as other kinds of memories (Neisser & Harsch, 1992).

effortful encoding conscious process of entering information into LTM, often through elaborative rehearsal.

automatic encoding tendency of certain kinds of information to enter LTM with little or no effortful encoding.

flashbulb memories type of automatic encoding that occurs because an unexpected event has strong emotional associations for the person remembering it.

mnemonic a strategy or trick for aiding memory.

▲ In rush hour on August 7, 2007 in Minneapolis, Minnesota, the Mississippi River bridge collapsed, killing 13 people and injuring at least 100 more. Photographs like this appeared in all newspapers and television news reports for days after the collapse, and the disaster led many cities around the country to check their own bridges for potential problems. Events like this are so emotional for many people that the memories for the event are stored automatically, as if the mind had taken a "flash" picture of that moment in time. Such "flashbulb" memories seem to be very accurate but are actually no more accurate than any other memory.

24.3 How can we improve our ability to retrieve memories?

When we store information in LTM, there's no guarantee that we'll be able to retrieve that information again easily through either recognition or recall. We can, however, use strategies and memory "tricks" to help us remember information more effectively. These strategies are called *mnemonic devices*, or simply **mnemonics**, from the Greek word for memory. Table 24.1

MEMORY 289

CHAPTER 9 • Module 24

COVER THE MODULE (continued)

- *Automatic encoding* of some kinds of information requires very little effort to place information into LTM.
- Memory for particularly emotional or traumatic events can lead to the formation of *flashbulb memories*—memories that seem as vivid and detailed, as if the person were looking at a snapshot of the event but that are no more accurate than any other memories.

UNDERSTANDING VISUALS

Direct students' attention to the photograph on this page. Do they remember this particular event? Do they have a flashbulb memory of it? Bring in photographs of recent and historical events that may have caused flashbulb memories and pass them around or project them on an overhead or your computer. (Consider, for example, a photograph of the Manhattan skyline with the Twin Towers intact.) Why did these events trigger flashbulb memories? Ask students to share some from their own time. Encourage students to ask their parents or other adults about their most vivid flashbulb memories.

COVER THE MODULE

24.3 How can we improve our ability to retrieve memories?

- *Mnemonic* devices such as acrostics, acronyms, linking, and rhythmic organization can help us recall information stored in LTM.

Class Demonstration

CONTROVERSIES IN MEMORY

<u>Purpose</u>: Students have a chance to think about, debate, and discuss controversial topics in memory.

<u>Time</u>: 15 minutes

<u>Description</u>: The teacher poses controversial questions or statements to the class. Students share their answers and contribute to further class discussion. Here are some controversies in the area of memory:

- Our childhood memories are accurate.
- Eyewitness testimony should be used in the courtroom.
- It is possible to improve our memories substantially with training.
- Gender and culture greatly influence our memory.

Module 24 Retrieval and Retrieval Failure

CHAPTER 9 • Module 24

EXTEND THE LESSON
Ask students to take a moment to review Table 24.1. Are these mnemonic devices familiar to them? Can they think of any other mnemonics for the examples used in the table? Go down the list—acronym, acrostic, linking, rhythmic organization—and ask students if they can give examples of each.

COVER THE MODULE
24.4 Can memories change? How reliable are they?
- Memories are revised, edited, and altered on an almost continuous basis.

DISCUSS THE STUDENT VOICE QUESTION
Ask students if they have had similar experiences with relatives, friends, or classmates. What might account for these differences? Students might note age, gender, and ethnic differences, as well as each person's role in the event. (Did they have an active role, or were they a witness?)

Table 24.1	Some Common Mnemonic Devices	
MNEMONIC	**DESCRIPTION**	**EXAMPLE**
Acronym	An easy-to-remember word constructed from the first letters of a list of words to be remembered	The acronym **HOMES** helps people remember the names of the Great Lakes: **H**uron, **O**ntario, **M**ichigan, **E**rie, **S**uperior.
Acrostic	An easy-to-remember sentence in which the first letter of each word corresponds to the first letters of the words to be remembered	The acrostic **M**y **V**ery **E**ducated **M**other **J**ust **S**erved **U**s **N**oodles helps people remember the names of the planets: **M**ercury, **V**enus, **E**arth, **M**ars, **J**upiter, **S**aturn, **U**ranus, **N**eptune.
Linking	A list in which items to be remembered are linked in some way.	**Mercury** was the messenger god, who carried lots of love notes to **Venus**, the beautiful goddess who sprang from the **Earth's** sea. She was married to **Mars**, her brother, which didn't please her father **Jupiter** or his father **Saturn**, and his uncle **Uranus** complained to the sea god, **Neptune**.
Rhythmic Organization	Information to be remembered is organized in a rhyming and rhythmic pattern, sometimes set to a tune.	The alphabet song and the rhyme "Thirty days hath September..." are both examples of rhythmic mnemonic devices.

> I think my memory is pretty good, but my brother and I often have arguments about things that happened when we were kids. Why don't we have the same exact memories? ▶ We were both there!

290 CHAPTER 9

gives descriptions and examples of a few of the more popular mnemonics, but you may have other favorite strategies that work for you.

Many of us use mnemonics to help us study for exams or remember the important bits of information we need in our everyday lives. No matter how many mnemonics we use or how hard we try to remember things, however, we may find over time that inaccuracies slip into our memories. It's not uncommon for people to forget some of the information they used to know—or to change the information they think they remember accurately.

24.4 Can memories change? How reliable are they?

I think my memory is pretty good, but my brother and I often have arguments about things that happened when we were kids. Why don't we have the same exact memories? We were both there!

People tend to assume that their memories are accurate when, in fact, memories are revised, edited, and altered on an almost continuous basis. The reason for the changes that occur in memory has to do with the way in which

Class Demonstration

PATRIOT GAMES
This is a fun demonstration that illustrates retrieval processes in action. Ask the class to join together and sing the "Star-Spangled Banner" from memory. When they are finished, ask, "What is the line after 'through the perilous fight'?" Most students will pause, and inevitably they will probably sing the song to themselves again to find the next line. Use this as an illustration of serial learning and reinstatement of retrieval cues.

The Star-Spangled Banner
Oh, say, can you see,
By the dawn's early light,
What so proudly we hailed
At the twilight's last gleaming,
Whose broad stripes and bright stars,
Through the perilous fight,
O'er the ramparts we watched
Were so gallantly streaming.

And the rockets' red glare,
The bombs bursting in air
Gave proof through the night
That our flag was still there
Oh, say, does that Star-Spangled Banner yet wave
O'er the land of the free
And the home of the brave?

memories are formed as well as how they are retrieved.

Constructive Processing of Memories
Many people have the idea that when they recall a memory, they are recalling it as if it were an "instant replay." In reality, memories are never quite accurate, and the more time that passes, the more inaccuracies creep in. As new memories are created in LTM, old memories can get "lost," but they are more likely to be changed or altered in some way (Baddeley, 1988).

Prominent memory researcher Elizabeth Loftus, along with other researchers (Hyman, 1993; Hyman & Loftus, 1998, 2002), has provided ample evidence for the **constructive processing** view of memory retrieval. In this view, memories are literally "built" from the pieces stored away at encoding. Each time a memory is retrieved, it may be altered or revised in some way to include new information. Details that were there at encoding may be left out of the new retrieval.

An example of how memories are reconstructed occurs when people, upon learning the details of a particular event, revise their memories to reflect their feeling that they "knew it all along." They will discard any incorrect information they actually had and replace it with more accurate information gained after the fact. This tendency of people to falsely believe that they would have accurately predicted an outcome without having been told about it in advance is called **hindsight bias** (Bahrick et al., 1996; Hoffrage et al., 2000). For example, after the results of a close political election are announced, people may say that they felt sure all along that the victorious politician would win, even if they had been far from confident about this fact before the election.

Memory Retrieval Problems Some people may say that they have "total recall." What they usually mean is that they feel that their memories are more accurate than those of other people. As should be obvious by now, true total recall is not a very likely ability for anyone to have.

Police investigators try to keep eyewitnesses to crimes or accidents from talking with each other sometimes. The reason is that if one person tells the other about something she has seen, the other person may later "remember" that same detail, even though he did not actually see it at the time. Such false memories are created by a person being exposed to information after the event. That misleading information can become part of the actual memory, affecting its accuracy. This is called the **misinformation effect**. Elizabeth Loftus has performed several studies that demonstrate the misinformation effect. In one study, subjects viewed a slide presentation of a traffic accident. The actual slide presentation contained a stop sign, but in a written summary of the presentation, the sign was referred to as a yield sign. Subjects who were given this misleading information after viewing the slides were far less accurate in their memories for the kind of sign present than were subjects given no such information (Loftus et al., 1978). One of the interesting points this study makes is that information that comes not only after the original event but also in an entirely different format (i.e., written instead of visual) can cause memories of the event to be incorrectly reconstructed.

▲ *These men may engage in "Monday morning quarterbacking" as they apply hindsight to their memories of this game. Their memories of the game may be altered by information they get afterward from the television, newspapers, or their friends.*

constructive processing referring to the retrieval of memories in which those memories are altered, revised, or influenced by newer information.

hindsight bias the tendency to falsely believe, through revision of older memories to include newer information, that one could have correctly predicted the outcome of an event.

misinformation effect the tendency of misleading information presented after an event to alter the memories of the event itself.

MEMORY 291

CHAPTER 9 • Module 24

COVER THE MODULE (continued)

- Memories are reconstructed from the various bits and pieces of information that have been stored away in different places at the time of encoding in a process called *constructive processing*.
- *Hindsight bias* occurs when people falsely believe that they knew the outcome of some event because they have included knowledge of the event's true outcome into their memories of the event itself.
- The *misinformation effect* refers to the tendency of people who are asked misleading questions or given misleading information to incorporate that information into their memories for a particular event.

CHECK FOR UNDERSTANDING

Do a quick review of the concepts discussed in this module so far. Tell students to close their books and ask them to give examples (not definitions) of encoding specificity, the serial position effect, a flashbulb memory, a mnemonic, the misinformation effect, or any other phenomenon you think bears reviewing. Did students struggle with any particular concepts? If so, prompt them with an example of your own and check their understanding by asking them to then come up with their own examples based upon yours.

L4 DIFFERENTIATED INSTRUCTION

Advanced Learners During class discussion, invite volunteers to contribute additional ideas and point of view, after you call on a reasonable number of students.

Explore

HOW FALSE MEMORIES ARE FORMED

Researchers at Northwestern University have used MRI technology to study how people form false memories. The purpose of the study was to create laboratory conditions that set up a circumstance in which people would remember something that did not happen. Participants were asked to look at pictures of objects and to imagine other objects while their brain activity was being measured. Researchers found that the brain areas associated with generating visual images were highly activated when people imagine images. Many of the images that the participants were asked to imagine were incorrectly identified as actually having been seen. Parts of the brain involved in perceiving an object and those involved in imagining an object appear to overlap. This would allow a vividly imagined event to leave a memory trace in the brain that is similar to a real event. Direct students to learn more about the brain and false memories at:

- www.northwestern.edu/newscenter/stories/2004/10/kenneth.html
- www.eurekalert.org/pub_releases/2004-10/nu-nrp101404.php

Module 24 Retrieval and Retrieval Failure 291

CHAPTER 9 • Module 24

COVER THE MODULE (continued)

- Rather than improving memory retrieval, hypnosis makes the creation of false memories more likely.
  - False memory syndrome is the creation of false or inaccurate memories through suggestion, especially while hypnotized.
  - Kathy Pezdek and colleagues assert that false memories are more likely to be formed for plausible false events than for implausible ones.

LINK to Chapter Four: Consciousness, Sleep, Dreams, Hypnosis, and Drugs, p. 125

- Loftus and others have found that people constantly update and revise their memories of events, adding information to a memory that occurred later even when that information is in error.

MULTIMEDIA CONTENT AVAILABLE AT www.mypsychlab.com

Simulate the creation of false memories on **mypsychlab.com**

DISCUSS THE STUDENT VOICE QUESTION

Discuss the issue of false memory syndrome with students. Have they heard, from people they know or perhaps on the news, of this phenomenon? When does a false memory become dangerous? *(Possible answer: When the false memory of a crime implicates an innocent person.)*

DISCUSS THE STUDENT VOICE QUESTION

How do students feel about the memories of their own lives after reading and discussing the information in this module? What is their reaction to the idea that even memories in which they feel very confident may, in fact, be distorted or outright false?

▶ What is false memory syndrome?

Simulate the creation of false memories on **mypsychlab.com**

▶ So can we trust any of our memories at all?

Reliability of Memory Retrieval

What is false memory syndrome?
If memory is edited and changed when people are in a state of waking consciousness, alert and making an effort to retrieve information, how much more might memory be changed when people are in an altered state of conscious, such as hypnosis? *False memory syndrome* refers to the creation of inaccurate or false memories through the suggestion of others, often while the person is under hypnosis (Hochman, 1994).

In her 1996 paper, Dr. Elizabeth Bowman summarized some of the findings about pseudomemories, or false memories, associated with hypnosis. For example, research has shown that, although hypnosis may make it easier to recall some real memories, it also makes it easier to create false memories. False memories have been accidentally created by therapists' suggestions during hypnotic therapy sessions (especially those that involve age regression). LINK to Chapter Four: Consciousness: Sleep, Dreams, Hypnosis, and Drugs, p. 125. Clearly, memories obtained through hypnosis should not be considered accurate without solid evidence from other sources. Simulate on **mypsychlab.com**

So can we trust any of our memories at all?
There is evidence to suggest that false memories cannot be created for just any kind of event. The memories must at least be plausible, according to the research of cognitive psychologist and memory expert Kathy Pezdek, who, with her colleagues, has done several studies demonstrating the resistance of children to the creation of implausible false memories (Hyman et al., 1998; Pezdek et al., 1997; Pezdek & Hodge, 1999).

In a 1999 study, Pezdek and Hodge asked children to read five different summaries of childhood events. Two of these events were false, but only one of the two false events was plausible (e.g., getting lost). Although the children were all told that all of the events happened to them as small children, the results indicated that the plausible false events were significantly more likely to be remembered as real than were the implausible false events. A second experiment (Pezdek & Hodge, 1999) found similar results: Children were significantly less likely to form a false memory for an implausible false event than for a plausible false event.

Classic Studies In Psychology

Elizabeth Loftus and Eyewitnesses

Elizabeth Loftus is a professor of psychology and adjunct professor of law at the University of California in Irvine. For over 30 years, Dr. Loftus has been one of the world's leading researchers in the area of memory. Her focus has been on the accuracy of recall of memories—or rather, the inaccuracies of memory retrieval. She has been an expert witness at more than 200 trials, including that of Ted Bundy, the serial killer who was ultimately executed in Florida (Neimark, 1996).

Loftus and many others have demonstrated time and again that memory is not an unchanging, stable process but rather is constantly changing. People continually update and revise their memories of events without being aware that they are doing so, and they incorporate information gained after the actual event, whether correct or incorrect.

Explore

HOW RELIABLE ARE MEMORIES?

Direct students to the following websites to learn more about the debate over memory and false memories:

- **Imagination Inflation**: Imagining a Childhood Event Inflates Confidence that It Occurred
  http://faculty.washington.edu/eloftus/Articles/Imagine.htm

  Article by Maryanne Garry, Charles G. Manning, Elizabeth F. Loftus, and Steven J. Sherman summarizing research on the relationship between imagining an event and confidence that the event really occurred.

- **The Recovered Memory Project**:
  www.brown.edu/Departments/Taubman_Center/Recovmem/Archive.html

  Archive of cases of recovered memory with links to related references and resources.

Here is a summary of one of Loftus's classic studies concerning the ways in which eyewitness testimony can be influenced by information given after the event in question (Loftus, 1975).

In this experiment, Loftus showed subjects a 3-minute video clip taken from the movie *Diary of a Student Revolution*. In this clip, eight demonstrators run into a classroom and eventually leave after interrupting the professor's lecture in a noisy confrontation. At the end of the video, two questionnaires were distributed containing one key question and 90 "filler" questions. The key question for half of the subjects was, "Was the leader of the four demonstrators who entered the classroom a male?" The other half was asked, "Was the leader of the 12 demonstrators who entered the classroom a male?" One week later, a new set of questions was given to all subjects in which the key question was, "How many demonstrators did you see entering the classroom?" Subjects who were previously asked the question incorrectly giving the number as "four" stated an average recall of 6.4 people, whereas those who read the question incorrectly giving the number as "twelve" recalled an average of 8.9 people. Loftus concluded that subjects were trying to compromise the memory of what they had actually seen—eight demonstrators—with later information. This study, along with the Father Pagano story and many others, clearly demonstrates the heart of Loftus's research: What people see and hear about an event after the fact can easily affect the accuracy of their memories of that event.

Question for Further Discussion
1. How might police officers taking statements about a crime avoid getting inaccurate information from eyewitnesses?

24.5 Why do we forget?

Think for a minute: What would it be like if people didn't forget anything? At first, the answer seems to be that such a phenomenal memory would be great, right? Anything people learned would always be there. But what if people *couldn't* forget? That is exactly the problem experienced in the case of A. R. Luria's (1968) famous *mnemonist*, Mr. S. (A mnemonist is a memory expert or someone with exceptional memory ability.) Mr. S. was a performing mnemonist, astonishing his audiences with lists of numbers that he memorized in minutes. But Mr. S. found that he *was unable to forget* the lists. He also could not easily separate important memories from trivial ones, and each time he looked at an object or read a word, images stimulated by that object or word would flood his mind. He eventually invented a way to "forget" things—by writing them on a piece of paper and then burning the paper (Luria, 1968).

The ability to forget seems necessary to one's sanity if the experience of Mr. S. is any indicator. But how fast do people forget things? Are there some things that are harder or easier to forget?

The Forgetting Curve Hermann Ebbinghaus (1913) was one of the first researchers to study forgetting. Because he did not want any verbal associations to aid him in remembering, he created several lists of "nonsense

MEMORY   293

CHAPTER 9 • Module 24

EXTEND THE DISCUSSION
Share with the class some of the findings of Dr. Elizabeth Bowman:
- Hypnosis enhances the confidence subjects have in their memories, *regardless* of their accuracy or inaccuracy.
- Subjects *cannot* always distinguish between memories that they have always had and new "memories" recently recovered under hypnosis.
- Hypnotic age regression does not appear to increase the accuracy of childhood recall.
- The impact of hypnosis on the reliability of later memory depends on the type of question asked. Open-ended questions cause less memory "contamination" than closed-ended, leading questions.

COVER THE MODULE
24.5 Why do we forget?
- Hermann Ebbinghaus and the Forgetting Curve
  Information is mostly lost by 1 hour after learning but then gradually fades away. This is known as the curve of forgetting.

CLASSIC STUDIES IN PSYCHOLOGY
1. A person in charge of interrogating witnesses should avoid leading questions and let the witness tell the story in his or her own words. The interrogator might ask the witness to repeat his or her testimony several times to check for consistency. The witness should be questioned as soon after the event as possible, as intervening events could affect the person's memory.

Class Demonstration

MEMORY DISTORTION

Purpose: This exercise is an amusing demonstration of memory distortion.

Time: Approximately 15 minutes

Description: Arrange students in a circle, and whisper the message to the first student:

We were going to talk about memory today, but I'm not feeling very well. I woke up this morning with a strange rash and shooting pain in my lower leg. I have asked a very humorous substitute teacher to give the lecture instead. For your homework assignment, I would like you to comment on how well you liked the guest lecture.

The students must recall the message and pass it on to the person next to them. The last person says the message out loud. The final message is often much different from the original message. This is an excellent example of the idea that memories are constantly undergoing construction. Ask students why they think the final message was so different from the original message.

Module 24 Retrieval and Retrieval Failure   **293**

CHAPTER 9 • Module 24

COVER THE MODULE (continued)

- *Encoding Failure*
  - A failure to encode information will not produce a memory.

EXTEND THE DISCUSSION

Direct students to the Multimedia Library for this chapter at **www.mypsychlab.com**, and ask them to read the biography of Hermann Ebbinghaus. Then ask students to write down as many facts as they can remember about Ebbinghaus. Were they attending to the information they read?

UNDERSTANDING VISUALS

Direct students to the art in Figure 24.4. Were they able to find the real penny? If so, what cues did they use? If not, why did they have trouble identifying it? If they chose the incorrect penny, what made them think it was the actual one?

L2 LPR DIFFERENTIATED INSTRUCTION

Less Proficient Readers For students with difficulties with learning strategies, include explicit use of strategies taught as part of the quiz, report, project, or other formal assessments.

FIGURE 24.3 Curve of Forgetting
Ebbinghaus found that his recall of words was greatest immediately after learning the list but rapidly decreased within the first hour. After the first hour, forgetting leveled off.

syllables," pronounceable but meaningless (such as GEX and WOL). He memorized a list, waited a specific amount of time, and then tried to retrieve the list, graphing his results each time. The result has become a familiar graph: the **curve of forgetting**. This graph clearly shows that forgetting happens quickly within the first hour after learning the lists and then tapers off gradually. (See Figure 24.3.) In other words, forgetting is greatest just after learning.

Encoding Failure There are several reasons why people forget things. One of the simplest is that some things never get encoded in the first place. Your friend, for example, may have said something to you as he walked out the door, and you may have heard him, but if you weren't paying attention to what he said, it would not get past sensory memory. This isn't forgetting so much as it is **encoding failure**, the failure to process information into memory. Figure 24.4 shows an example of a test designed to assess encoding failure.

curve of forgetting a graph showing a distinct pattern in which forgetting is very fast within the first hour after learning a list and then tapers off gradually.

encoding failure failure to process information into memory.

FIGURE 24.4 Which Penny Is Real?
Most people do not really look at the face of a penny. Which of these pennies represents an actual penny? The answer can be found later in the chapter.

Class Demonstration

FORGETTING

Purpose: Students investigate the different causes of forgetting.

Time: 20 minutes

Description: Each team member is assigned to a different cause of forgetting:

- decay and distortion
- consolidation failure
- interference
- motivated forgetting

Students gather information on their assigned topic outside class. Back in class, students meet with others assigned the same topic in expert groups. Then, they return to their home group to teach their topic to their teammates.

Memory Trace Decay Theory One of the oldest theories of forgetting involves the concept of a **memory trace**. A memory trace is a physical change in the brain, perhaps in a neuron or in the activity between neurons, which occurs when a memory is formed (Brown, 1958; Peterson & Peterson, 1959). Over time, if these traces are not used, they may **decay**, fading into nothing. It would be similar to what happens when a number of people walk across a particular patch of grass, causing a path to appear in which the grass is trampled down and perhaps turns brown. If people stop using the path, the grass grows back and the path disappears.

Decay causes us to forget sensory memories: Information that is not brought to attention in sensory memory will fade away. Decay, along with the displacement of old information by new information, can cause us to forget STMs, too. But is decay a good explanation for forgetting LTMs? When referring to LTM, decay theory is usually called **disuse**, and the phrase "use it or lose it" takes on great meaning (Bjork & Bjork, 1992). Although the fading of information from LTM through disuse sounds logical, there are many times when people can recall memories they had assumed were long forgotten. There must be other factors involved in the forgetting of LTMs.

Interference Theory A possible explanation of LTM forgetting is that although LTMs may be stored more or less permanently in the brain, those memories may not always be accessible to attempted retrieval because other information interferes (Anderson & Neely, 1995). (And even memories that are accessible are subject to constructive processing, which can lead to inaccurate recall.) An analogy might be this: The can of paint that Phillip wants may very well be on some shelf in his storeroom, but there's so much other junk in its way that he can't see it and can't get to it. In the case of LTM, interference can come from two different "directions."

Have you ever switched from a sport you had been playing for years, like soccer, to a new sport like field hockey? If the answer is yes, you may have found that you had some trouble picking up the new sport. You may have tried to kick the field hockey ball instead of hitting it with your stick—after all, while kicking the ball isn't allowed in field hockey, it's basically required in soccer. The reason why you accidentally kicked that field hockey ball is called **proactive interference**: the tendency for older, previously learned material to interfere with the retrieval of newer, more recently learned material. (See Figure 24.5.)

Another example of proactive interference can occur when someone gets a new cell phone. People in this situation often find themselves remembering their old cell phone number or some of its digits instead of the new cell phone number when they are trying to give the new number to friends.

When newer information interferes with the retrieval of older information, this is called **retroactive interference**. (See Figure 24.5.) What happens when you decide to quit the field hockey team and start playing soccer again? You might find yourself swinging an imaginary stick to hit the soccer ball because the newer skill retroactively interferes with remembering the old skill. Table 24.2 summarizes all of these reasons for forgetting.

FIGURE 24.5 Proactive and Retroactive Interference
If a student were to study for a French exam and then a Spanish exam, interference could occur in two directions. When taking the Spanish exam, the French information studied first may proactively interfere with retrieval of the Spanish information. But when taking the French exam, the more recently studied Spanish information may retroactively interfere with the retrieval of the French information.

memory trace physical change in the brain that occurs when a memory is formed.

decay loss of memory due to the passage of time, during which the memory trace is not used.

disuse another name for decay, assuming that memories that are not used will eventually decay and disappear.

proactive interference memory retrieval problem that occurs when older information prevents or interferes with the retrieval of newer information.

retroactive interference memory retrieval problem that occurs when newer information prevents or interferes with the retrieval of older information.

MEMORY 295

CHAPTER 9 • Module 24

COVER THE MODULE *(continued)*
- **Memory Trace Decay Theory**
  - This theory assumes the presence of a physical memory trace that decays with disuse over time.
- **Interference Theory**
  - Forgetting in LTM is most likely due to proactive or retroactive interference.
  - *Proactive Interference*: prior learning interferes with new learning.
  - *Retroactive Interference*: new learning interferes with retrieval of previous learning.

CHECK FOR UNDERSTANDING
To reinforce students' understanding of the reasons for forgetting, ask them to name each one. Then ask students if they can name examples of each from their own experience. If students struggle with examples, prompt them with some of your own. If students are still not able to provide their own examples, briefly review the material to ensure understanding.

Class Demonstration

DECAY AND INTERFERENCE IN SHORT-TERM MEMORY

Tell students that you want them to remember a sequence of three consonant letters while counting backward from a number you provide them. When they are ready, say, "W T K" and then "701." They should then say "701, 698, 695, 692, 689, 686," and so on. After 15 to 18 seconds, say "write" as a signal to students to recall the three letters. Students should have a fairly difficult time accomplishing this because the counting task prevents them from rehearsing the letters and thus allows the memory trace to decay.

Researchers have argued that the forgetting in this task was primarily due to the buildup of proactive interference. As evidence, they pointed to the fact that students could often remember the letters during the first trial or two but had much greater difficulty remembering letters on any subsequent trials, when proactive interference would develop. Verify this effect with your students by conducting several trials. Examples of potential letter/number combinations might include PZX 317, BVQ 421, LFC 991, JHG 187, and SRN 275. Students will be astonished at their atrocious performance, which, if typical of experiments of this type, should yield about 1 in 10 correct recalls after only 18 seconds of the distractor task!

Module 24 Retrieval and Retrieval Failure **295**

CHAPTER 9 • Module 24

COVER THE MODULE

24.6 How does amnesia occur?

- In *retrograde amnesia*, memory for the past (prior to the injury) is lost and can be a loss of only minutes or a loss of several years.
- ECT, or electroconvulsive therapy, can disrupt consolidation and cause retrograde amnesia.
- In *anterograde amnesia*, memory for anything new becomes impossible although old memories may still be retrievable.

UNDERSTANDING VISUALS

Direct students to the question in the photograph caption. Moore is most likely to have suffered from retrograde amnesia, which is typically experienced by people who are in accidents in which they received a head injury.

TEACHING TIP

Set aside a few minutes at the middle and end of the lesson to ask: What have we learned? What questions do you have about this topic?

L1 DIFFERENTIATED INSTRUCTION

Special Needs Provide adaptive materials as appropriate (e.g., enlarged print, Braille edition, captioned video programs).

The answer to **Figure 24.4** on page 294 is A.

Table 24.2	Reasons for Forgetting
REASON	**DESCRIPTION**
Encoding Failure	The information is not attended to and fails to be encoded.
Decay or Disuse	Information that is not accessed decays from the storage system over time.
Proactive Interference	Older information already in memory interferes with the retrieval of newer information.
Retroactive Interference	Newer information in memory interferes with the retrieval of older information.

24.6 How does amnesia occur?

There are two forms of severe memory loss disorders caused by problems in the functioning of the memory areas of the brain. These problems can result from concussions, brain injuries brought about by trauma, alcoholism (Korsakoff's syndrome), or disorders of the aging brain.

If the hippocampus is important to the formation of memories, what would happen if it got temporarily "disconnected"? People who are in accidents in which they received a head injury often are unable to recall the accident itself. Sometimes, they cannot remember the last several hours or even days before the accident. This type of amnesia (literally, "without memory") is called **retrograde amnesia**, which is loss of memory from the point of injury backwards (Hodges, 1994). (The prefix *retro-* means "backwards.")

Think about this: You are working on your computer, trying to finish a psychology paper that is due tomorrow. Your computer saves the document every 10 minutes, but you are working so furiously that you've written a lot in the last 10 minutes. Then the power goes out—horrors! When the power comes back on, you find that while all the files you had already saved are still there, your history paper is missing that last 10 minutes' worth of work. This is similar to what happens with retrograde amnesia. All memories that were in the process of being stored but not yet permanent are lost forever.

Another type of amnesia is called **anterograde amnesia**, or the loss of memories from the point of injury or illness forward (Squire & Slater, 1978). (The prefix *antero-* means, in this context, "forward.") People with this kind of amnesia have difficulty remembering anything new. This is also the kind of amnesia most often seen in people with *senile dementia*, a mental disorder in which severe forgetfulness, mental confusion, and mood swings are the primary symptoms. (Dementia patients also may suffer from retrograde amnesia in addition to anterograde amnesia.) If retrograde amnesia is like losing a document in the computer because of a power loss, anterograde amnesia is like discovering that your hard drive has become defective—you can read data that is already on the hard drive, but you can't store any new information. As long as you are looking at the data in your open computer window (i.e., attending to it), you can access it, but as soon as you close that window (stop thinking about it), the information is lost, because it was never transferred to the hard drive (LTM).

▲ *Colorado Avalanche defenseman Steve Moore makes his first public appearance after suffering major injuries in a hockey game in 2004. In addition to a broken neck, Moore suffered a concussion and developed amnesia. From which type of amnesia did he most likely suffer?*

retrograde amnesia loss of memory from the point of some injury or trauma backwards, or loss of memory for the past.

anterograde amnesia loss of memory from the point of injury or trauma forward, or the inability to form new LTMs.

Explore

CAUSES OF AMNESIA

Ask students to visit the "Causes of Amnesia" page of WrongDiagnosis.com at www.wrongdiagnosis.com/a/amnesia/causes.htm. Ask students to choose a cause listed on that page and do some research to bring back to the class. Students should prepare a brief (approximately 5-minute) statement about the cause they chose to share with the class. They should include information such as why that particular event causes amnesia, what type of amnesia it causes, and how long the amnesia typically lasts.

I've tried to remember things from when I was a baby, but I don't seem to be able to recall much. Is this some kind of amnesia, too?

What is the earliest memory you have? Chances are, you cannot remember much that happened to you before age 3. When a person does claim to "remember" some event from infancy, a little investigation usually reveals that the "memory" is really based on what family members have told the person about that event and is not a genuine memory at all. This type of "manufactured" memory often has the quality of watching yourself in the memory as if it was a movie and you were an actor. In a genuine memory, you would remember the event through your own eyes—as if you were the camera.

Why can't people remember events from the first 2 or 3 years of life? One explanation of **infantile amnesia** involves the type of memory that exists in the first few years of life, when a child is still considered an infant. Early memories tend to be implicit and, as stated earlier in this chapter, implicit memories are difficult to bring to consciousness. Explicit memory, which is the more verbal and conscious form of memory, does not really develop until after about age 2, when the hippocampus is more fully developed and language skills blossom (Carver & Bauer, 2001).

Katherine Nelson (1993) also gives credit to the social relationships that small children have with others. As children are able to talk about shared memories with adults, they begin to develop their **autobiographical memory**, or the memory for events and facts related to one's personal life story.

◀ I've tried to remember things from when I was a baby, but I don't seem to be able to recall much. Is this some kind of amnesia, too?

Applying Psychology to Everyday Life

Current Research in Alzheimer's Disease

Nearly 4 million Americans have Alzheimer's disease, including the late former President Ronald Reagan. It is the most common type of dementia found in adults and the elderly. It has also become the third leading cause of death in late adulthood, with only heart disease and cancer responsible for more deaths (Antuono et al., 2001).

Symptoms usually begin with changes in memory, which may be rather mild at first but which become more severe over time, causing the person to become more and more forgetful about everyday tasks, such as remembering to turn off the stove. Eventually, more dangerous forgetting occurs, such as taking extra doses of medication or leaving something cooking on the stove unattended. The person with this disorder repeats things in conversation. Thoughts become disorganized, and messages get garbled. As Alzheimer's progresses, the ability to do simple calculations such as balancing a checkbook is lost, along with remembering how to do simple tasks such as bathing or getting dressed. It is a costly disease to care for, and caregivers often face severe emotional and financial burdens in caring for a loved one who is slowly becoming a stranger.

What can be done? There is at present no cure, but in recent years, several new medications have been developed that seem to slow the progress of the disease, and new research into the cause gives hope that a cure may one day be a reality. ◉ Watch on **mypsychlab.com**

◉ Watch a video about Alzheimer's and dementia on **mypsychlab.com**

infantile amnesia the inability to retrieve memories from much before age 3.

autobiographical memory the memory for events and facts related to one's personal life story.

MEMORY 297

CHAPTER 9 • Module 24

COVER THE MODULE (continued)

- Most people cannot remember events that occurred before the age of 2 or 3. This is called *infantile amnesia* and is most likely due to the implicit nature of infant memory.

- The primary memory difficulty in Alzheimer's disease is anterograde amnesia, although retrograde amnesia can also occur as the disease progresses.

  - There are various drugs that are in use or being researched for use in slowing or stopping the progression of Alzheimer's disease.

DISCUSS THE STUDENT VOICE QUESTION

How far back into their own lives can students remember? Do they claim that they can remember things that happened to them before they were 3 years old? Are they adamant that those memories are real, or have they begun to doubt them based on the information in the module?

MULTIMEDIA CONTENT AVAILABLE AT
www.mypsychlab.com

◉ Watch a video about Alzheimer's and dementia on **mypsychlab.com**

Critical Thinking

AGING, CULTURE, AND MEMORY

Research suggests that cultural beliefs about the elderly and the aging process may play a role in determining the extent to which the elderly "lose" their memories. Researchers compared attitudes about aging in Chinese culture, American deaf culture, and American hearing culture. The researchers tested elderly and young individuals in each culture with several tests of memory and a measure of attitudes toward the elderly. The American hearing sample had the least positive views about the elderly, and the Chinese sample had the most positive. The memory tests indicated that while memory performance did not differ among the younger samples from each culture, the Chinese elderly outperformed the American deaf elderly, who outscored the American hearing elderly. These effects may demonstrate the potential for cultural beliefs about aging to determine memory loss, a cultural "self-fulfilling prophecy."

Ask students to consider other ways in which a society's beliefs, traditions, and practices may influence cognitive development and performance. The data reported here are correlational, and we cannot rule out other explanations. Can students think of any?

Module 24 Retrieval and Retrieval Failure

CHAPTER 9 • Module 24

Assess

Assign the Module 24 Practice Quiz.

Use the Practice Quiz to identify gaps in student understanding.

REMEDIATE

Have students, individually or in groups, review the module goals, learning objectives, and key terms.

Refer students to the Concept Summary on p. 302 for review.

Close

Discuss with students the different ways in which we remember and forget. What information in the module did they find the most useful? Did the module make them look differently at the workings of their own brains, as well as those of their parents or grandparents? How might this knowledge change their behavior or attitudes?

Practice Quiz

Pick the best answer.

1. The best place to take your math exam to ensure good retrieval of math concepts is in
   a. the math classroom
   b. an auditorium, to prevent cheating
   c. your home
   d. a special testing room, used only for exams

2. Sarah can remember the name of the first person she was introduced to at Ted's party, and she can remember the names of the last two people she met, but the names of the dozen or so people in between are gone. This is an example of the
   a. encoding specificity effect
   b. serial position effect
   c. tip-of-the-tongue effect
   d. primacy effect

3. This quiz question, as well as the other quiz questions, makes use of which form of retrieval of memories?
   a. rehearsal
   b. recency
   c. recall
   d. recognition

4. Which of the following statements about Loftus's classic study is TRUE?
   a. All of the subjects were able to correctly recall the number of demonstrators.
   b. Subjects given a question stating that there were four demonstrators remembered only three demonstrators.
   c. Subjects given a question stating that there were twelve demonstrators remembered eight demonstrators.
   d. Subjects either increased or decreased the number of demonstrators in an attempt to compromise their memory with the later false information.

5. Which of the following statements about flashbulb memories is FALSE?
   a. They may be formed by the hormones released during emotional moments.
   b. They are usually vivid and detailed.
   c. They are unusually accurate.
   d. They can be of a personal nature or concern world events.

6. The phenomenon of hindsight bias is an example of the _____ view of long-term memory retrieval.
   a. instant replay
   b. constructive processing
   c. levels-of-processing
   d. curve of forgetting

7. In Loftus's 1978 study, subjects viewed a slide presentation of an accident. Later, some of the subjects were asked a question about a yield sign when the actual slides contained pictures of a stop sign. When these same subjects were later asked about what kind of sign was at the accident, they were very likely to be confused. This is an example of
   a. constructive processing
   b. encoding failure
   c. the serial position effect
   d. the misinformation effect

8. In order for a person to interpret thoughts and fantasies about false events as true memories,
   a. the events must seem plausible
   b. the person must believe in repression
   c. the events must be described in detail
   d. they only need to hear about the events once

9. Brian went from the United States, where he grew up, to England. The first week he was there, he had a terrible time remembering to drive on the left side of the road. His problem was most likely due to
   a. encoding failure
   b. retroactive interference
   c. proactive interference
   d. the curve of forgetting

10. T.J. was in a car accident and suffered a concussion. After he recovered, he found that he could not remember the accident itself or the events of the morning leading up to the accident. T.J. had
    a. retrograde amnesia
    b. anterograde amnesia
    c. Alzheimer's disease
    d. encoding failure

298 CHAPTER 9

Practice Quiz Answers

1. a
2. b
3. d
4. d
5. c
6. b
7. d
8. a
9. c
10. a

298 Chapter 9 Memory

CHAPTER 9 Summary

Listen on mypsychlab.com

Module 23: Encoding and Storage

Learn how the brain encodes memories.

23.1 What are levels of processing?
- The information processing model suggests that there are levels of depth within memory. Information that is stored on a superficial level (such as appearance or sound) is not retained as long as information that requires a deeper level of processing (such as meaning).

23.2 How are memories encoded in the brain?
- The stages of memory are sensory memory, STM, and LTM. Information enters the nervous system through the senses. Once a person becomes conscious of information, it enters STM. STM tends to be encoded in auditory (sound) form. With maintenance rehearsal, information will stay in STM until rehearsal stops.

23.3 How can we make encoding more effective?
- Chunking can increase the amount of information that can be held in STM. Information can be transferred into LTM through elaborative rehearsal.

Understand how memories are stored in the brain.

23.4 How is information stored in LTM?
- Information is stored in LTM as implicit and explicit memories. Implicit memories include skills, habits, and emotional associations. Explicit memories include facts and experiences.

23.5 How and where are memories stored in the brain?
- Procedural memories seem to be stored in the cerebellum. STMs are stored in the prefrontal cortex and the temporal lobe. The hippocampus is responsible for the formation of LTMs.

Listen to an audio file of your chapter on mypsychlab.com

Module 24: Retrieval and Retrieval Failure

Learn how memories are retrieved from the brain.

24.1 What kinds of cues help people remember?
- Almost anything in one's surroundings is capable of becoming a cue for memory retrieval. In state-dependent learning, memories formed during a particular physiological or psychological state will be easier to remember while in a similar state.

24.2 What factors influence how memories are retrieved?
- Information at the beginning or end of a list tends to be remembered more easily and accurately. False positives can occur when there is a similarity between a stimulus that is in memory and a stimulus that is not in memory.

24.3 How can we improve our ability to retrieve memories?
- Mnemonic devices such as acrostics, acronyms, linking, and rhythmic organization can help us recall information stored in LTM.

24.4 Can memories change? How reliable are they?
- Memories are revised, edited, and altered on an almost continuous basis. False memories can be created through the suggestion of others, often while a person is under hypnosis.

24.5 Why do we forget?
- Information that is not brought to attention in sensory memory or continuously rehearsed in STM will fade away. Over time, memory traces that are not used may decay. Other information can interfere with the retrieval of information from LTM. Proactive interference occurs when older or previously learned information interferes with the retrieval of newer information. Retroactive interference occurs when newer information interferes with the retrieval of older information.

24.6 How does amnesia occur?
- Amnesia can result from concussions, brain injuries brought about by trauma, alcoholism, or disorders of the aging brain.

Vocabulary Terms

memory p. 274
encoding p. 274
storage p. 274
retrieval p. 274
information-processing model p. 274
levels-of-processing model p. 275
sensory memory p. 276
short-term memory (STM) p. 277
selective attention p. 277
working memory p. 278
maintenance rehearsal p. 279
long-term memory (LTM) p. 279
elaborative rehearsal p. 280
procedural (nondeclarative) memory p. 280
implicit memory p. 280
declarative memory p. 281
semantic memory p. 281
episodic memory p. 281
explicit memory p. 281
retrieval cue p. 285
encoding specificity p. 285
recall p. 287
recognition p. 287
serial position effect p. 287
primacy effect p. 287
recency effect p. 287
false positive p. 288
effortful encoding p. 289
automatic encoding p. 289
flashbulb memories p. 289
mnemonic p. 289
constructive processing p. 291
hindsight bias p. 291
misinformation effect p. 291
curve of forgetting p. 294
encoding failure p. 294
memory trace p. 295
decay p. 295
disuse p. 295
proactive interference p. 295
retroactive interference p. 295
retrograde amnesia p. 296
anterograde amnesia p. 296
infantile amnesia p. 297
autobiographical memory p. 297

MEMORY 299

CHAPTER 9 • Chapter Summary and Vocabulary

Chapter Summary

Encourage students to carefully review and study the summary. Explain that it provides an overview of key concepts presented in the text.

Have students identify what they find unclear or confusing. Call on volunteers to provide answers, examples, or definitions.

Vocabulary Terms

Remind students that terms are defined within the chapter at point of use. If they are not sure of a term's definition, they should look up the definition on the page.

Encourage students to create study cards of unfamiliar words or to go to www.mypsychlab.com for flash cards. Have them test themselves or a classmate. Advanced students can explain the terms in their own words.

Making Connections

IMPROVING MEMORY

This exercise asks students to put what they have learned to practical use. Students should target some specific aspect of their memory that they would like to improve and then apply one or more memory principles from the text to make the improvement. Students might, for example, strive to enhance their performance on exams, to recall important birthdates and anniversaries, to remember people's names following introductions, or to reduce absentminded actions, such as misplacing keys. After implementing their plan, students should write a short paper about their experiences. Specifically, students should describe (a) the aspect of memory they targeted for improvement (and why); (b) the memory principles or strategies they used (including the rationale behind them); and (c) any results (positive or negative) from applying these techniques. You might want to devote some class time to discussion so that volunteers can share their experiences.

Chapter 9 Summary 299

CHAPTER 9 • Assessment

VOCABULARY REVIEW

1. e
2. a
3. d
4. g
5. b
6. j
7. c
8. h
9. i
10. f

WRITING ABOUT PSYCHOLOGY

1. Students will likely note that they remember the event because it was meaningful to them in some way and that it was encoded through automatic encoding—it was not something they had to rehearse in order to remember. The memory might seem especially vivid because it is attached to a strong emotion, such as happiness or sadness, or even a reaction such as fear.

2. Students should answer no, a witness should not be automatically believed. As Loftus discovered, eyewitness testimony is not infallible, and witnesses' memories may be affected by leading questions, time, and interference from other sources, such as the media.

PSYCHOLOGY PROJECT

If students will be conducting the experiment outside class, remind them that their subjects (and, therefore, the students themselves) should first understand all terminology (such as "proactive interference"). Afterward, conduct a class discussion about everyone's findings. Collect the results of the class as a whole, and graph the results together. What kind of graph would be best to use in this situation? Are the full-class results surprising?

CHAPTER 9 Assessment

Study and Review on mypsychlab.com

Vocabulary Review
Match each vocabulary term to its definition.

1. memory
2. sensory memory
3. declarative memory
4. serial position effect
5. false positive
6. automatic encoding
7. curve of forgetting
8. retroactive interference
9. retrograde amnesia
10. autobiographical memory

a. The very first stage of memory, the point at which information enters the nervous system through the sensory systems.
b. Error of recognition in which people think that they recognize some stimulus that is not actually in memory.
c. A graph showing a distinct pattern in which forgetting is very fast within the first hour after learning a list and then tapers off gradually.
d. Type of long-term memory containing information that is conscious and known.
e. An active system that receives information from the senses, puts that information into a usable form, and organizes it as it stores it away, and then retrieves the information from storage.
f. The memory for events and facts related to one's personal life story.
g. Tendency of information at the beginning and end of a body of information to be remembered more accurately than information in the middle of the body of information.
h. Memory retrieval problem that occurs when newer information prevents or interferes with the retrieval of older information.
i. Loss of memory from the point of some injury or trauma backwards, or loss of memory for the past.
j. Tendency of certain kinds of information to enter long-term memory with little or no effortful encoding.

Writing about Psychology
Respond to each question in complete sentences.

1. Think of an event that you remember vividly. Explain how this event was encoded and stored in your memory, and discuss why you think this memory is so vivid in your mind.

2. Imagine that you are serving on a jury in a criminal trial. During the trial, an eyewitness tells the court what she remembers about the crime. Do you automatically believe the eyewitness's testimony? Why or why not? Refer to findings from memory research to support your answer.

Psychology Project
Is it easier to remember information that is only seen, only heard, or seen and heard? Conduct this experiment in memory to find out.

Materials:
- a group of five or more subjects (can be classmates, family members, etc.)
- a list of 20 random words
- an audio recording of an additional 20 random words (if no audio recording equipment is available, you may read the list aloud)
- an audiovisual presentation (such as a PowerPoint) of an additional 20 random words (if no presentation software is available, you may read the list aloud, and create a flip-book of images to show with each word)
- pencils
- paper

Instructions:
1. Distribute paper and pencils to subjects.
2. Distribute the list of 20 words to subjects. Lists should be typed in a column so that the words are clearly legible. Allow subjects to study the words for 2 minutes. Then, collect the lists, and ask subjects to write down all of the words they remember from the list.
3. After a short break of 5 minutes or so, play the audio recording of 20 words (or read the list aloud). Be sure to read the words clearly and at a medium pace. After subjects have heard the list, ask them to write down all of the words they can remember.
4. Allow subjects another short break. Then, play the audiovisual presentation (or read aloud as you show corresponding images from your flip-book). Again, once you are finished, ask subjects to write down all of the words that they can remember.
5. Collect the lists and count the results. What patterns do you see? Were certain words easier to remember than others? Were subjects able to remember more words in visual (written), audio, or audiovisual format? Did subjects experience proactive interference by the time they were exposed to the third list? Write a summary of your findings, and create a graph of your results if possible.

Internet Resources

Exploratorium: www.exploratorium.edu/memory/magnani/index.html
San Francisco's Exploratorium science museum features work by "a memory artist," who paints his childhood home from memory. A novel application of memory principles that students will enjoy seeing.

H.M. –The Day His World Stood Still:
http://brainconnection.positscience.com/topics/?main=fa/hm-memory
A four-part article that chronicles the life of H. M., the most studied case of anterograde amnesia.

Self-Improvement Online: www.selfgrowth.com/memory.html
This site reviews and recommends memory improvement and memory training websites.

Test Yourself

Pick the best answer.

1. Memory can best be described as
   a. an ongoing visual recording of information
   b. a process of information storage
   c. a system that encodes, stores, and retrieves information
   d. a series of active and passive data files

2. When Greg tried to remember the name of his employer's husband, he had trouble getting the right name. At first, he thought it might be Sandy or Randy, but he finally realized that it was Andy. Greg's confusion is evidence that short-term memories are primarily encoded in _____ form.
   a. visual
   b. auditory
   c. explanatory
   d. sensory

3. Although the capacity of short-term memory is limited, more terms can be held in this kind of storage through the process of
   a. encoding
   b. decoding
   c. chunking
   d. construction

4. The best method for encoding long-term memories is probably to use
   a. maintenance rehearsal
   b. recognition learning
   c. elaborative rehearsal
   d. sleep learning

5. Which type of long-term memory is updated more or less constantly?
   a. procedural
   b. declarative
   c. semantic
   d. episodic

6. Knowledge that is gained in school is called _____ memory.
   a. semantic
   b. nondeclarative
   c. implicit
   d. working

7. State-dependent learning suggests that if you were really happy when you were learning Spanish, for best retrieval, you should be _____ when taking the final exam.
   a. calm
   b. angry
   c. happy
   d. focused

8. The name "ROY G. BIV" helps some people remember the colors of the rainbow: red, orange, yellow, green, blue, indigo, and violet. This is an example of which type of mnemonic device?
   a. acronym
   b. acrostic
   c. linking
   d. rhythmic organization

9. The serial position effect predicts that the information from a list that will be remembered best will come at the _____ of the list.
   a. beginning
   b. middle
   c. end
   d. beginning and end

10. Melanie was having a difficult time describing the man who took her purse in the mall parking lot. The officer showed her some pictures of people who had been involved in similar crimes, and she was quickly able to point out the right man. Melanie's situation is a reminder that in comparing recognition to recall, recognition tends to be
    a. easier
    b. slower
    c. more difficult
    d. less accurate

11. In which part of the brain are procedural memories most likely stored?
    a. prefrontal cortex
    b. cerebellum
    c. temporal lobe
    d. hippocampus

12. When retrieving a long-term memory, bits and pieces of information are gathered from various areas and put back together in a process called
    a. consolidation
    b. reintegration
    c. automatic encoding
    d. constructive processing

13. Ebbinghaus found that information is forgotten
    a. more rapidly as time goes by
    b. gradually at first, then increasing in speed of forgetting
    c. quickly at first, then tapering off gradually
    d. most quickly one day after learning

14. The levels-of-processing model of memory would suggest that which of the following questions would lead to better memory of the word *frog*?
    a. Does it rhyme with *blog*?
    b. Is it written in capital letters?
    c. Is it written in cursive?
    d. Would it be found in a pond?

15. The tendency for previously learned material to interfere with the retrieval of newer material is known as
    a. retroactive interference
    b. proactive interference
    c. decay
    d. disuse

16. Anterograde amnesia is most like
    a. being able to see a can of paint on a shelf, but unable to reach it
    b. being able to reach a can of paint on a shelf, but unable to open it
    c. being able to store new information on a hard drive, but unable to access old information
    d. being able to read data that is already on your hard drive, but unable to store new information

17. How might police officers taking statements about a crime avoid getting inaccurate information from eyewitnesses?
    a. Police officers could keep witnesses from talking with each other.
    b. Police officers could allow witnesses to read each other's accounts of the crime.
    c. Police officers could allow witnesses to gather as a group to discuss the crime.
    d. Police officers could suggest plausible explanations to the witnesses.

MEMORY 301

CHAPTER 9 • Assessment

TEST YOURSELF

1. b	11. b
2. b	12. d
3. b	13. a
4. a	14. d
5. d	15. b
6. a	16. d
7. b	17. a
8. b	
9. a	
10. c	

Ready for Testing

STUDENTS KNOW THEY ARE READY FOR TESTING IF THEY ARE ABLE TO . . .

- Introduce the study of memory, including the basic processes of encoding, storage, and retrieval, as well as current theories of how memory works.
- Discuss the information-processing theory of memory in detail, including the concepts of sensory, STM, and LTM.
- Identify the basic mechanisms and limitations in the retrieval of information, including false memories.
- Describe Ebbinghaus's work on forgetting and proposed explanations for forgetting.
- Explain the biological processes thought to underlie memory and the deterioration of memory.

CHAPTER 9 • Concept Summary

MULTIMEDIA CONTENT AVAILABLE AT
www.mypsychlab.com

Map the Concepts on **mypsychlab.com**

Study and Review Flashcards on **mypsychlab.com**

STUDY TIPS

When to Study Part of effective studying includes choosing the best time to study. Each of us has a time of day when we are at our best, whether it is early in the morning, during the evening, or some other time. Explain to students that once they identify this time of day for themselves, they should try to study during those hours. Additionally, tell students to keep in mind that shorter study sessions of 1 or 2 hours are usually more effective than marathon sessions. Even during short study sessions, students should remember to take a break every hour or so. Whenever possible, encourage students to take time to review class notes as soon after class as possible in order to identify problem areas and questions and to fix the information in their minds. Have students make a study schedule for the week, keeping in mind these pointers.

302 Chapter 9 Memory

CHAPTER 9 Concept Summary: Memory

Learning Objectives

23.1 23.2 23.3 pp. 274–280

Learn How the Brain Encodes Memories

- **memory** is an active system that receives, organizes, stores, and retrieves information
- **three basic steps**
  - encoding
  - storage
  - retrieval
- **the information-processing model** — proposes three stages that vary both in duration and capacity; information must be processed effectively at earlier stages before long-term storage occurs
  - **sensory memory** — capacity limited, duration <1 second to 4 seconds
  - **short-term and working memory** — capacity limited (7 ± 2 items), duration 12–30 seconds without rehearsal — chunking and maintenance rehearsal can be used to increase capacity and duration, respectively
  - **long-term memory** — capacity unlimited, duration relatively permanent
    - associated with physical changes in the brain
    - organized in terms of related meanings and concepts

Learning Objectives

23.4 23.5 pp. 280–283

Understand How Memories Are Stored in the Brain

- **long-term memory organization**
  - procedural memory
  - declarative memory
    - episodic memory
    - semantic memory
- **hippocampus** — the part of the brain that is responsible for the formation of new long-term memories

302 CHAPTER 9

What Every Student Should Know About . . .

CREATING A PORTFOLIO

Typical arrangements for portfolios include chronological order, topic- or theme-based order, skill-based plans (that is, showing works that highlight how you have met particular course goals or that show your strengths in specific skills). Print portfolios generally follow a linear order, moving from section to section, whereas electronic portfolios allow more complex networks of texts whose connections take place through multiple paths. Print portfolios might be delivered within a folder or placed within a binder. Electronic portfolios can be established within content management systems (and your school may have one set up through school-wide systems), or they may be placed on a CD or DVD for limited distribution. Students might also create an electronic portfolio that they post to the Web.

Learning Objectives

24.1 24.2 24.3 24.4 24.5   pp. 285–297

Learn How Memories Are Retrieved from the Brain

- **cues to remember**
  - retrieval cues
  - encoding specificity
  - state-dependent learning

- **how memory is retrieved**
  - **recall vs. recognition**
    - recall: few or no external cues required
    - recognition: match incoming sensory information to what is already in memory
  - **serial position effect** — information at the beginning or end of a list tends to be remembered more easily and accurately
  - **automatic encoding** — strong emotional associations can lead to vivid and detailed "flashbulb" memories

- **mnemonic devices** are strategies for improving memory retrieval
  - acronyms
  - acrostics
  - linking
  - rhythmic organization

- **reliability of memory retrieval**
  - constructive processing: means memories are revised, edited, and altered on an almost continuous basis.
  - hindsight bias
  - misinformation effect

- **Forgetting** originally studied by Ebbinghaus (1913), research produced forgetting curve
  - **encoding failure:** nonattended information is not encoded into memory
  - **memory trace decay:** over time, neural connections can decay if not used
  - **interference**
    - other information interferes with accurate retrieval
    - proactive interference
    - retroactive interference

Proactive Interference
French, learned **beforehand**, interferes proactively
Study French → Study Spanish → Spanish Test

Retroactive Interference
Spanish, learned **afterwards**, interferes retroactively
Study French → Study Spanish → French Test

- **amnesia** can result from concussions, brain injuries brought about by trauma, alcoholism, or disorders of the aging brain
  - retrograde amnesia
  - anterograde amnesia

MEMORY 303

CHAPTER 9 • Concept Summary

STUDY TIPS

Predicting Test Questions Predicting with accuracy what will be on a test can lead to more focused studying and better grades. Suggest the following prediction strategies to students: Above all, pay attention to those things the teacher emphasizes in class. If a particular point is repeated; written on the board, on an overhead, or in a PowerPoint presentation; or appears in a study guide, chances are it will resurface on a test. In addition, suggest that students take note of questions asked by the teacher during class. A review of old tests and quizzes will reveal the types of questions and content the teacher stresses. Advise students to predict both lower-order (factual recall) and higher-order (critical thinking) questions. Students can create their own study guide by writing a few possible questions after every class.

Comprehension Check

MEMORY PROCESSES

To check their understanding, students can visit the Multimedia Library section of the www.mypsychlab.com site and explore the Key Processes in Stages of Memory activity. Advanced students can work alone, while on-level and struggling students can work in pairs or small groups. Students will receive immediate feedback on their answers.

CHAPTER 10 • Module 25

Launch the Chapter

CHAPTER GOALS AND LEARNING OBJECTIVES

Module 25 Thinking

Understand the basic elements of thought.

25.1 How are mental images and concepts involved in the process of thinking?

25.2 What methods do people use to solve problems and make decisions?

25.3 Can a machine be made to think like a person?

Identify obstacles to thought.

25.4 What are some obstacles to problem solving?

25.5 What are some obstacles to making good judgments?

25.6 What are some obstacles to decision making?

Module 26 Intelligence

Compare and contrast perspectives on intelligence.

26.1 How do psychologists define intelligence?

26.2 What are some established theories of intelligence?

26.3 What are intellectual disability and giftedness?

Learn how intelligence is measured.

26.4 What is the history of intelligence testing?

26.5 How is intelligence measured today?

26.6 How can we determine whether intelligence tests are reliable and valid?

Consider key issues in intelligence research.

26.7 How are intelligence tests used in the real world?

26.8 How do heredity and environment influence intelligence?

DIFFERENTIATED INSTRUCTION KEY

Look for these symbols to help you adjust steps in each lesson to meet your students' needs.

- **L1** Special Needs
- **L2** Basic
  - **ELL** English Language Learners
  - **LPR** Less Proficient Readers
- **L3** All Students
- **L4** Advanced Students

CHAPTER 10
Cognition:
Thinking and Intelligence

The Life of Alex

On September 6, 2007, Alex, the African gray parrot, died. No ordinary pet, he was made famous by the groundbreaking work of Dr. Irene Pepperberg and her colleagues in cognition and communication research. Although most people know that parrots can learn to mimic words and sounds made by humans—and even machines—Alex could use language in a very different way. He could identify over 50 different objects, seven colors, and five shapes by naming them out loud. Alex could even count up to six objects. He could verbally identify which of two objects was the bigger or the smaller, sort over 100 objects into categories, and say whether two objects were the same kind of object or different objects—hardly simple imitation.

But does this constitute a real use of language? Is Alex the parrot really thinking much like a human would think about these objects? Many cognitive theorists seem to think so (Pepperberg, 2005, 2007), although some caution against interpreting Alex's behavior in human terms (Premack, 2004). The researchers taught Alex by modeling competitive behavior—for example, one researcher might offer a toy if he could correctly name it, and the second researcher's "reward" would be getting to play with the toy. Through modeling and shaping of Alex's words, the parrot was able to learn concepts similar to those of a very young child. Since Alex's death, Pepperberg and her colleagues have continued to work with their two other African gray parrots, Griffin and Arthur (affectionately known as "Wart"), even teaching the parrots to "surf the Web" by linking simple actions to different recorded sites on a television monitor.

As reported, Alex's last words to Pepperberg were, "You be good, see you tomorrow. I love you."

CORRELATION TO APA STANDARDS FOR CHAPTER 10

VB. THINKING
VB-1. Processes and functions comprising thought . . . . . . pp. 306–313
VB-2. Obstacles related to thought. . . . . pp. 314–319

VC. INTELLIGENCE
VC-1. Perspectives on intelligence . . . . pp. 321–327
VC-2. Assessment of intelligence . . . . pp. 327–330
VC-3. Issues in intelligence . . . . pp. 330–333

MODULE 25 ▶ **THINKING**
MODULE 26 ▶ **INTELLIGENCE**

Why Study?

The Nature of Thought

To fully understand how we do any of the things we do (such as learning, remembering, and behaving), we need to understand how we think. How do we organize our thoughts? How do we communicate those thoughts to others? What do we mean by intelligence? Why are some people able to learn so much faster than others?

COGNITION: THINKING AND INTELLIGENCE 305

SCHEDULING				
1 Period = 50 min. 1 Block = 90 min.	Semester Course (18 weeks/90 days) Periods/Blocks		Full-Year Course (36 weeks/180 days) Period/Blocks	
Module 25	2.5	1.25	5	2.5
Module 26	2.5	1.25	5	2.5
Total Days for Chapter	5	2.5	10	5

CHAPTER 10 • Module 25

Teacher Prep

Mental images represent objects or events; concepts represent a category of events, objects, or activities. Mechanical solutions include trial-and-error learning and rote solutions. A heuristic is a strategy that narrows down the possible solutions for a problem. Insight is the sudden perception of a solution. The true flexibility of human thought processes has yet to be developed in a machine.

Obstacles to problem solving include functional fixedness, mental sets, and confirmation bias. Obstacles to making good judgments include the representative heuristic, the availability heuristic, and the anchoring effect. Obstacles to decision making include a tendency to try to see patterns, the gambler's fallacy, and loss aversion.

Intelligence is the ability to understand the world, think rationally or logically, and use resources effectively when faced with challenges. Spearman proposed general intelligence (g factor) as the ability to reason and solve problems, whereas specific intelligence (s factor) is task-specific. Gardner proposed nine different types of intelligence, while Sternberg proposed three. Intellectual disability or developmental delay is a condition in which adaptive behavior is severely deficient for a person. Gifted persons have IQ scores at the upper end of the normal curve.

Psychologists have recognized the effects of cultural bias in intelligence testing. Measuring IQ using the Stanford-Binet Intelligence Test involves comparing a person's score to a standardized norm. The Wechsler Intelligence Tests are designed for specific age groups. Reliability is the tendency of a test to produce the same scores again and again. Validity is the degree to which a test measures what it is supposed to measure.

Intelligence tests are useful for predicting academic success. Stronger correlations are found between IQ scores as genetic relatedness increases. Environmental factors (such as cultural values) also influence intelligence test scores.

Chapter 10 Cognition: Thinking and Intelligence

CHAPTER 10 • Module 25

Focus

RESOURCES
For this module, consult the appropriate sections of the Teacher's Manual, Test Bank, and PowerPoint slides, all found on the Teacher's Resource DVD, and the interactive study tools for students on MyPsychLab.

BEFORE CLASS
Students should read the section for homework before coming to class.

BELLRINGER
Give students a few minutes to draw a map of the school campus from memory, including as many details as possible. Then ask volunteers to display their maps. Point out that most students will have used mental images to complete this task, visually "walking through" the campus in their mind.

Teach

INTRODUCE THE TOPIC
- *Thinking, or cognition*, is a mental activity in the brain when a person processes information.
- When people think, they are not only aware of the information in the brain but are also making decisions about it, comparing it to other information, and using it to solve problems.

COVER THE MODULE
25.1 How are mental images and concepts involved in the process of thinking?
- **Mental Images**
  - *Mental images* represent objects or events and have a picture-like quality.

306 Chapter 10 Cognition: Thinking and Intelligence

Module 25 Thinking

Module Goals	Learning Objectives
Understand the basic elements of thought.	25.1 How are mental images and concepts involved in the process of thinking?
	25.2 What methods do people use to solve problems and make decisions?
	25.3 Can a machine be made to think like a person?
Identify obstacles to thought.	25.4 What are some obstacles to problem solving?
	25.5 What are some obstacles to making good judgments?
	25.6 What are some obstacles to decision making?

Understand the Basic Elements of Thought

What does it mean to think? People talk about thinking all the time: "What do you think?" "Let me think about that." "I don't think so." **Thinking**, or **cognition** (from a Latin word meaning "to know"), is a mental activity in the brain when a person is processing information—organizing it, understanding it, and communicating it. Thinking includes memory, but it is much more. When people think, they are not only aware of the information in the brain but are also making decisions about it, comparing it to other information, and using it to solve problems. Thinking also includes more than just a kind of verbal "stream of consciousness." When people think, they often have images as well as words in their minds.

In academic contexts, many scientists prefer to use the term *cognition* in place of *thinking*, since *cognition* is a more precise term that refers to information processing. In this chapter, therefore, we'll generally use the word *cognition* to describe the mental activity of processing information.

25.1 How are mental images and concepts involved in the process of thinking?

Mental Images Every day, we encode information from the world around us in the form of sounds and visual images. Thus, **mental images** (picture-like representations that stand in for objects or events) are one of several tools people use in the thought process.

For a demonstration of how we use mental images, gather several people and ask them to tell you *as fast as they can* how many windows are in their home. Usually the first people to shout out an answer have fewer windows than those who take longer to respond. Most people look up, as if looking at some image only they can see. If asked, they'll say that they pictured where they live and simply counted windows as they "walked through" the image.

thinking (cognition) mental activity that goes on in the brain when a person is processing information (organizing and attempting to understand information and communicating information to others).

mental images picture-like representations that stand in for objects or events.

306 CHAPTER 10

Terms

- thinking (cognition) • mental images • concepts • superordinate concept • basic level type • subordinate concept • formal concepts • natural concept • prototype
- problem solving • trial and error (mechanical solution) • algorithm • heuristic
- representativeness heuristic • subgoaling • means-end analysis • artificial intelligence (AI) • functional fixedness • mental set • confirmation bias • creativity
- convergent thinking • divergent thinking • conjunction fallacy • availability heuristic
- anchoring effect • gambler's fallacy • loss aversion

So more windows means more time to count them in your head? I guess mentally "walking" through a bigger house in your head would take longer than "walking" through a smaller one.

It does take longer to view a mental image that is larger or covers more distance than a smaller, more compact one (Kosslyn et al., 2001; Ochsner & Kosslyn, 1994). In one study (Kosslyn et al., 1978), participants studied a map of an imaginary island (see Figure 25.1) that included several landmarks. After viewing and memorizing the map, participants were asked to imagine a specific place on the island, such as the hut, and then to "look" for another place, like the lake. When they mentally "reached" the second place, they pushed a button that recorded reaction time. The greater the physical distance between the two locations on the map, the longer it took participants to scan the image for the second location. The participants were apparently scanning their mental image just as if it were a real, physical map.

People use mental imagery every day. It helps them remember where they park, find furniture that fits their living space, daydream, and find their way around by using their learned "mental maps" of familiar locations. LINK to *Chapter Six: Learning and Language Development, p. 197.* Mental imagery is also a very useful tool for remembering other ideas and concepts; for example, you could remember your grocery list by linking the items on it to a series of standard images (Paivio, 1971, 1986; Thomas, 2001).

People can even rotate mental images (Shepard & Metzler, 1971). Kosslyn (1983) asked subjects questions such as the following: "Do frogs have lips and a stubby tail?" Most people reported visualizing a frog, starting with the face and mentally rotating the image to look for a tail.

In the brain, the process of creating a mental image is almost the opposite of seeing an actual image. With an actual image, the information goes from the eyes to the visual cortex and other areas of the cortex process it by

◀ *So more windows means more time to count them in your head? I guess mentally "walking" through a bigger house in your head would take longer than "walking" through a smaller one.*

FIGURE 25.1 Kosslyn's Fictional Island
In Kosslyn's 1978 study, participants were asked to push a button when they had imagined themselves moving from one place on the island to another. As the graph below the picture shows, participants took longer times to complete the task when the locations on the image were farther apart. *Source:* Kosslyn et al. (1978).

COGNITION: THINKING AND INTELLIGENCE 307

CHAPTER 10 • Module 25

COVER THE MODULE *(continued)*

- It takes longer to view a mental image that is larger or covers more distance than a smaller, more compact one.
- Mental imagery helps people in everyday life and is a useful tool for remembering other ideas and concepts.
- In creating a mental image, areas of the cortex associated with stored knowledge send information to the visual cortex, where the image is perceived in the "mind's eye."

LINK to *Chapter Six: Learning and Language Development, p. 197; Chapter Two: The Biological Perspective, p. 60*

MULTICULTURAL FOCUS

Researchers have found that males and females differ very little in terms of how, and how well, they think. Men and women, on the whole, have equal aptitudes for math and science. Researchers have found no important differences between boys and girls in math performance. Girls were slightly better at calculations in elementary and middle school; in high school, boys showed a slight edge in problem solving, perhaps because they took more science classes, which stress problem solving. Boys and girls understood math concepts equally well. Research suggests that social and cultural factors influence performance differences. The fact that more men than women choose scientific and mathematical careers is due not to differing abilities but rather to cultural factors, such as gender expectations that affect students during high school and college.

Class Demonstration

MENTAL IMAGERY

Read the following questions aloud to the class:

- *Scenario I:* Imagine an elephant standing next to a rabbit. Now, answer this question: Does a rabbit have a beak?
- *Scenario II:* Imagine a fly standing next to a rabbit. Now, answer this question: Does a rabbit have an eyebrow?

Next, ask students to say whether the rabbit was the largest in scenario I or II. Which scenario seemed to have more detail in the area they were examining for the beak or the eyebrow: I or II? Research suggests that the size of an image is an important factor in determining how fast we can make judgments about it. People made faster judgments when relying on a larger mental image (such as the rabbit next to the fly) than when using a smaller mental image (such as the rabbit next to an elephant). Did the students' experiences mirror this result?

Module 25 Thinking 307

CHAPTER 10 • Module 25

COVER THE MODULE (continued)

- **Concepts**
  - *Concepts* are ideas that represent a class or category of events, objects, or activities.
  - People use concepts to think without having to consider all the specific examples of a certain category.
  - A concept not only contains the important features of objects or events, but also allows us to identify new objects or events that may fit into it.

TEACHING TIP
Assign group projects that challenge all students to contribute to the best of their capacities.

L3 DIFFERENTIATED INSTRUCTION
The process of instruction involves differentiating learning activities and strategies. Content can be accessed, or processed, through a combination of methods, such as direct instruction, inquiry-based learning, cooperative learning, and information processing models. It can be done as a class, in groups or pairs, or individually.

---

308 Chapter 10 Cognition: Thinking and Intelligence

Images are not the only way we think, are they? ▶

comparing it to information already in memory. **LINK** to Chapter Two: *The Biological Perspective, p. 60.* In creating a mental image, other areas of the cortex associated with stored knowledge send information to the visual cortex, where the image is perceived in the "mind's eye" (Kosslyn et al., 1993; Sparing et al., 2002). PET scans show areas of the visual cortex being activated during this process, providing evidence for the role of the visual cortex in mental imagery (Kosslyn et al., 1993, 1999, 2001).

Concepts

Images are not the only way we think, are they?

Mental images are only one form of mental representation. Another aspect of thought processes is **concepts**—ideas that represent classes or categories of objects, events, or activities. People use concepts to think without having to consider all the specific examples of a certain category. For example, a person can think about "fruit" without thinking about every kind of existing fruit, which would take far more effort and time. This ability to think in terms of concepts allows us to communicate: If I mention a bird, you know what I am referring to, even if we aren't thinking of the same *type* of bird.

A concept not only contains the important features of objects or events, but also allows us to identify new objects or events that may fit into it. For example, dogs come in all shapes, sizes, colors, and lengths of fur. Yet most people have no trouble recognizing an unfamiliar dog as a dog, even if they have never seen that particular breed. Imagine coming across a photo of a dog called a briard (a kind of sheepdog). Although this dog is easily the size of a small pony, you would probably have no trouble recognizing it as a dog, albeit a huge and extremely shaggy one.

Types of Concepts Concepts can represent many different levels of objects or events. A very general concept, such as "fruit," is a **superordinate concept**

concepts ideas that represent a class or category of objects, events, or activities.

superordinate concept the most general form of a type of concept, such as "animal" or "fruit."

▲ Both of these animals are dogs and share features commonly associated with dogs, such as having four legs, fur, and a tail. In other ways, they are different, but we still recognize that both are dogs.

308 CHAPTER 10

Class Demonstration

LEARNING A CONCEPT

Gather several 3- × 5-inch index cards that you will use to illustrate the concepts of shape, size, color, and position. Draw one square and one triangle on each index card; these will represent the concept of shape. The shapes should vary in size (e.g., large/small); color (e.g., green/red); and position (e.g., up/down). Select *one* of the four concepts, but do not reveal it; ask one student to learn the concept you have chosen but not revealed. For example, select size as the relevant concept. Give the student feedback after each card as to whether the response was correct. If the student selects a card with large blue triangle on the card and guesses that "color" is the concept, tell the student that this choice is wrong. See how many cards it takes the student to discover the relevant concept. You may want to repeat this exercise using a different concept for at least two other students. Discuss how concept formation is an important but, often, difficult task.

(one that is ranked highest). The concept "apple" is more specific but can still be a **basic level type**. "Pear," "orange," and "watermelon" would also be basic level types. A "Granny Smith apple" would be a **subordinate concept** (ranked lowest)—the most specific example (Mandler, 2000, 2003; Rosch et al., 1976). Concepts are thought to form a network of associations based on these levels.

Some concepts have very strict definitions. These **formal concepts**, defined by specific rules or features, are pretty rigid. For example, to be a square, an object must be a two-dimensional figure with four equal sides and four right angles adding up to 360 degrees. An object with those features is not only a square, but also cannot be anything *but* a square. Mathematics and the sciences are full of formal concepts such as *polygon*, *wavelength*, and *double-blind experiment*. Each of these concepts must fit very specific requirements to be considered true examples.

But what about things that don't easily fit the rules or features? What if a thing has some, but not all, features of a concept?

In life, people encounter objects, events, and activities that are not as narrowly defined. What is a vehicle? Cars and trucks leap to mind, but what about a bobsled or a raft? Those last two are harder to classify immediately, but they fit some of the rules for "vehicle." These are examples of **natural concepts**, which people form not by applying strict rules, but rather by experiencing these concepts in the real world (Ahn, 1998; Barton & Komatsu, 1989; Gelman, 1988; Rosch, 1973). Natural concepts are "fuzzy" compared to formal concepts (Hampton, 1998). Is a whale a fish or a mammal? Whales are technically mammals but have some of the characteristics we use to define "fish." Is a platypus a mammal or a bird? Mammals have fur; birds lay eggs and have beaks. The duck-billed platypus, which has all three characteristics, is classified as a mammal.

Natural concepts help people understand their surroundings in a less structured manner than the formal concepts learned in school. They form the basis for interpreting those surroundings and the events of everyday life.

◄ But what about things that don't easily fit the rules or features? What if a thing has some, but not all, features of a concept?

▲ A duck-billed platypus is classified as a mammal yet shares features with birds, such as webbed feet and a bill. It also lays eggs. The platypus is an example of a "fuzzy" natural concept. **Credit:** Courtesy of Dave Watts, Nature Picture Library.

basic level type an example of a type of concept around which other similar concepts are organized, such as "dog," "cat," or "pear."

subordinate concept the most specific category of a concept, such as one's pet dog or a pear in one's hand.

formal concept a concept that is defined by specific rules or features.

natural concept a concept formed as a result of someone's experiences in the real world.

COGNITION: THINKING AND INTELLIGENCE 309

CHAPTER 10 • Module 25

COVER THE MODULE *(continued)*

- **Types of Concepts**
  - A very general concept is called a *superordinate concept* (one that is ranked highest).
  - A *basic level type* is a type of concept around which other similar concepts are organized.
  - The most specific category of a concept is called a *subordinate concept* (ranked lowest).
  - *Formal concepts* are defined by specific rules or features.
  - *Natural concepts* are formed as a result of someone's experience in the real world. They help people understand their surroundings in a less-structured manner than formal concepts.

CHECK FOR UNDERSTANDING

Write the following terms on the board: *superordinate concept, basic level type,* and *subordinate concept.* Divide the class into three groups and ask each group to come up with an example of each kind of concept. After a few minutes, have a volunteer from each group write its examples on the board. Then have the class determine whether the examples are correct.

L1 DIFFERENTIATED INSTRUCTION

Special Needs Require students to demonstrate that they are listening and following along (e.g., taking notes, running a finger along the text).

Explore

TYPES OF CONCEPTS

Remind students that a formal concept is defined by specific rules or features, and that a natural concept is formed as a result of a person's experiences in the real world. Ask students to select an example of a formal concept and an example of a natural concept and then create drawings, cut clippings from magazines, or print visuals from the Internet to illustrate their examples. Have students display their "illustrations" around the classroom.

CHAPTER 10 • Module 25

COVER THE MODULE (continued)

- *Prototypes* are examples of concepts that more closely match the defining characteristics of that concept.
- People tend to automatically compare potential examples of a concept to the prototype to see how well they match.
- People use concepts to deal with the information they encounter each day and organize their perceptions of the world. This organization may take the form of schemas (generalizations about objects, places, events, and people) or scripts (a kind of schema that involves a familiar sequence of activities).
- Concepts are an important tool in problem solving.

FAST FACT

The word *prototype* is from the Greek words meaning "first impression."

CHECK FOR UNDERSTANDING

If students have difficulty grasping the concept of prototypes, refer them to Figure 25.2. Starting with the fruits on the left side of the image, explain why those fruits are the ones that people think of as prototypical examples of fruit. As you move toward the right of the image, indicate why those items are less similar to the common prototypical examples of fruit.

Prototypical — Orange, Apple, Peach, Strawberry, Watermelon, Date, Tomato, Olive — **Atypical**

FIGURE 25.2 Prototypical and Atypical Fruits
The fruits on the left side of the image are the ones that people tend to think of as prototypical examples of fruit. The further to the right a fruit is, the less similar it is to common prototypical examples of fruit. *Source:* Adapted from Rosch & Mervis (1975, p. 576).

When someone says "fruit," what's the first image that comes to mind? Probably, it's something like an apple, pear, or orange. Most people will not say "guava" or "papaya" unless they come from a tropical area. In the United States, apples are a good example of a **prototype** for fruit—an example that closely matches the concept's defining characteristics (Mervis & Rosch, 1981; Rosch, 1977). Fruit is often sweet, often grows on trees, has seeds, and is usually round—all very apple-like qualities.

People whose experiences with fruit are very different will have different prototypes. For instance, coconuts are also sweet and round and grow on trees. People in the Northern Hemisphere are more likely to have seen an apple tree than a coconut tree, but someone who grew up in an area with many coconut trees might think of coconuts as a more prototypical fruit. (Aitchison, 1992). Research suggests that what a person knows about a particular type of object affects the person's prototype for the category (Lynch et al., 2000; Shafto & Coley, 2003). Your personal experiences, cultural background, and level of expertise for a given category can all influence the formation of prototypes.

How do prototypes affect thinking? People tend to automatically compare potential examples of a concept to the prototype to see how well they match. Most people take longer to think of olives and tomatoes as fruit because they aren't sweet, one of the prototype's major characteristics (Rosch & Mervis, 1975). Figure 25.2 presents some prototypical examples of the concept "fruit" as well as less typical examples.

Concepts are one of the ways people deal with all the information they encounter each day and organize their perceptions of the world. This organization may take the form of *schemas*, generalizations about objects, places, events, and people, or *scripts*, a kind of schema that involves a familiar sequence of activities. (For example, one's schema for "library" would no doubt include books and bookshelves; one's script for "going to a movie" would include traveling there, purchasing the ticket and snacks, finding the right theater, etc.) Concepts are also are an important tool in *problem solving*, a type of thinking that people engage in every day and in many different situations.

prototype an example of a concept that closely matches the defining characteristics of a concept.

310   CHAPTER 10

Class Demonstration

PROTOTYPES

<u>Purpose</u>: Students classify colors according to prototypes and atypical examples.

<u>Time</u>: 15 minutes

<u>Description</u>: Divide students into teams and provide each team with a box of 64 crayons. Instruct students to choose eight crayons that represent the most basic or prototypical colors. Students should silently categorize the remaining crayons, ordering them from most typical to least typical examples of each prototype. Teams should then discuss the placement of colors. Students will find that it is more difficult to categorize the crayons that are farther from the prototypes.

310   Chapter 10 Cognition: Thinking and Intelligence

25.2 What methods do people use to solve problems and make decisions?

Problem solving is certainly a big part of any student's life. Is there any one "best" way to go about solving a problem?

Put a coin in a bottle and then cork the opening. How can you get the coin out of the bottle without pulling out the cork or breaking the bottle? (For the solution, see p. 312.)

As stated earlier, people use images and concepts as mental tools to solve problems. For the preceding problem, you are probably trying to create an image of the bottle with a coin in it. **Problem solving** occurs when a person must reach a goal by thinking and behaving in certain ways. Problems range from figuring out how to cut a cookie recipe in half to understanding complex mathematical proofs to deciding on a college major. There are several different ways in which people can think to solve problems.

Trial and Error (Mechanical Solutions) One method is to use a **mechanical solution** such as **trial and error**—trying one solution after another until one works. For example, if Shelana has forgotten the PIN for her online banking Web site, she can try one combination after another. Mechanical solutions can also involve solving by *rote*, or a learned set of rules, such as the rules children use to solve word problems. One type of rote solution is to use an algorithm.

Algorithms **Algorithms** are specific, step-by-step procedures for solving certain types of problems. Algorithms will always result in a correct solution, if there is one and if you have enough time to find it. A mathematical procedure like long division uses an algorithm, a set of steps that will determine the correct answer to the problem. Librarians also use algorithms, such as alphabetizing books within each category, to organize and retrieve books. Many puzzles, such as Rubik's Cubes®, have a set of steps that, if followed exactly, will always result in solving the puzzle. But algorithms aren't always practical. For example, if Shelana had no idea what her PIN was, she *might* be able to figure it out by trying *all possible combinations* of four digits, 0 through 9. She would eventually find the right four-digit combination—but it might take years! Computers can run these systematic searches very quickly, but humans need some other way to narrow down the possible solutions.

Heuristics One possibility is to use a **heuristic**—a simple "rule of thumb" that is intended to apply to many situations. Whereas an algorithm is very specific and will always lead to a solution, a heuristic is an educated guess based on prior experiences. For example, if a student using a word-processing program wants to know how to format a page, reading the entire program manual would take too long. Instead, the student could type "format" into the help feature's search program or click on the word "format" on the tool bar. Either action reduces the amount of information the student will have to look at to get an answer, and both actions will also work for similar problems.

Although using a heuristic is often faster than using an algorithm, heuristics will *not* always lead to the correct solution. What you gain in speed is

Problem solving is certainly a big part of any student's life. Is there any one "best" way to go about solving a problem?

▲ These children try one piece after another until finding the piece that fits. This is an example of trial-and-error learning.

problem solving process of cognition that occurs when a goal must be reached by thinking and behaving in certain ways.

trial and error (mechanical solution) problem-solving method in which one possible solution after another is tried until a successful one is found.

algorithm a very specific, step-by-step procedure for solving a certain type of problem.

heuristic an educated guess based on prior experiences that helps narrow down the possible solutions for a problem. Also known as a "rule of thumb."

COGNITION: THINKING AND INTELLIGENCE

CHAPTER 10 • Module 25

COVER THE MODULE

25.2 What methods do people use to solve problems and make decisions?

- *Problem solving* consists of thinking and behaving in certain ways to reach a goal.
- **Trial and Error (Mechanical Solutions)**
  - *Mechanical solutions* include trial-and-error learning and rote solutions.
    - Trial-and-error learning involves trying one possible solution after another until a successful one is found.
    - Solving a problem by rote involves a learned set of rules.
- **Algorithms**
  - *Algorithms* are a type of rote solution in which one follows step-by-step procedures for solving certain types of problems. Algorithms will always result in a correct solution, if there is one.
- **Heuristics**
  - A *heuristic* or "rule-of-thumb" educated guess is a strategy based on prior experience, which narrows down the possible solutions for a problem. Heuristics will not always lead to the correct solution.

DISCUSS

Remind students that shortcuts used in problem solving are called *heuristics*. Ask: **Can you think of any heuristics you use to solve daily problems such as finding a parking space in a crowded area? How did you develop these heuristics? Are they based on past experience?**

Class Demonstration

PROBLEM SOLVING

Purpose: Students discuss the steps involved in problem solving.

Time: 15 minutes

Description: Provide teams of students with a brainteaser. Brainteasers can be easily found on the Internet. Give students a few minutes to think about the problem and generate possible answers. Have students share both their answer and the process they went through to arrive at their answer. This activity can begin a larger class discussion on the stages of problem solving.

Module 25 Thinking **311**

CHAPTER 10 • Module 25

COVER THE MODULE (continued)

- The *representativeness heuristic* assumes that any object or person that shares characteristics with the members of a particular category is also a member of that category.
- *Subgoaling* is the process of breaking a goal down into smaller goals.
- *Means-end analysis* is a heuristic in which the difference between the starting situation and the goal is determined, and then steps are taken to reduce that difference.

DISCUSS THE STUDENT VOICE QUESTION

Explain to students that other expressions for the word *insight* include "Aha!" or "Eureka! moment," "epiphany," or "breakthrough thinking."

- **Insight**
  - Insight is the sudden perception of a solution to a problem. What usually happens is that the mind simply reorganizes a problem, sometimes, while the person is thinking about something else.

CHECK FOR UNDERSTANDING

Write the following terms on the board: *trial and error, algorithms, heuristics,* and *insight*. Call on volunteers to give an example of each of these ways in which people can solve a problem.

L2 ELL DIFFERENTIATED INSTRUCTION

English Language Learners Ask students to write the definitions of essential terms in their own words and then identify the words when they occur within the reading.

What if my problem is writing a term paper? Can I use a heuristic to solve that problem? ▶

Sometimes I have to find answers to problems one step at a time, but in other cases, the answer seems to just "pop" into my head all of a sudden. Why do some answers come so easily to mind? ▶

representativeness heuristic the tendency to believe that any object (or person) that shares characteristics with the members of a particular category is also a member of that category.

subgoaling process of breaking a goal down into smaller goals.

means-end analysis heuristic in which the difference between the starting situation and the goal is determined and then steps are taken to reduce that difference.

312 CHAPTER 10

---

sometimes lost in accuracy, and using heuristics can sometimes lead to narrow thinking. For example, one kind of heuristic for categorizing objects, the **representativeness heuristic**, simply assumes that any object (or person) that shares characteristics with the members of a particular category is also a member of that category. This is useful for classifying plants (all trees that keep their leaves during the winter are evergreens, for example) but less handy when applied to people. Are all people with dark skin from Africa? Are all blue-eyed blondes from Sweden? The representative heuristic can be used—or misused—to create and sustain stereotypes. (Kahneman & Tversky, 1973; Kahneman et al., 1982).

What if my problem is writing a term paper? Can I use a heuristic to solve that problem?

Sometimes it's better to rely on **subgoaling**—breaking a goal down into smaller goals. Writing a term paper, for example, can seem overwhelming until it is broken down into steps: choose a topic, research it, organize your notes, write one section at a time, and so on.

Another heuristic is **means-end analysis**, in which a person determines the difference between the current situation and the goal and then tries to reduce that difference by various means (methods). You might be familiar with the concept behind means-end analysis if you've ever played the "warmer-colder" game, in which a group of people secretly choose an object in the room and the person who is "it" has to discover which object has been chosen. The person who is "it" has to move around the room; if she gets closer to the object, her friends call out, "Warmer!" and if she gets farther away, they call out "Colder!" By analyzing her friends' calls, the person who is "it" can eventually narrow down the location of the chosen object. In this example, the end (the goal) is finding the object, and the means (the method) is moving around the room under the guidance of friends' instructions.

Insight

Sometimes I have to find answers to problems one step at a time, but in other cases, the answer seems to just "pop" into my head all of a sudden. Why do some answers come so easily to mind?

When the solution to a problem seems to come to mind suddenly, it is called *insight*. Even some animals can solve problems by means of a sudden insight. L(I)N(K) *to Chapter Six: Learning and Language Development, p. 198.* In humans, insight often takes the form of an "aha!" moment. A person may see how this problem is similar to another, previously solved problem or how an object can be used for a new, different purpose (such as using a dime as a screwdriver).

Remember the problem of the bottleneck discussed earlier in this chapter? The task was to get the coin out of the bottle without pulling the cork out or breaking the bottle. The answer is simple: *Push the cork into the bottle and shake out the coin. Aha!*

Insight is not really a magical process, although it can seem like magic. What usually happens is that the mind simply reorganizes a problem, sometimes while the person is thinking about something else (Durso et al., 1994).

In summary, thinking is a form of information processing that involves the use of mental imagery and various types of concepts to organize the events of daily life. Problem solving is a special type of thinking that involves many tools, such as trial-and-error thinking, algorithms, and heuristics, to solve different types of problems.

Critical Thinking

WRITING ABOUT INSIGHT

Remind students that when the solution to a problem seems to come to mind suddenly, it is called *insight*. Ask them to write a short statement about a time when they experienced insight about a person, situation, or event. Tell them to explain the background of the experience and theorize about why they think the solution came to them suddenly. Ask volunteers to read their statements to the class.

312 Chapter 10 Cognition: Thinking and Intelligence

25.3 Can a machine be made to think like a person?

Now that you've seen how complex the process of thinking can be, it probably comes as no surprise that scientists have not yet developed robots or computer programs that can replicate human thought perfectly. There are, however, many researchers working in the field of **artificial intelligence (AI)**, or the creation of machines that can think like humans. For a closer look at this field, see the following special section.

Psychology in the News

Artificial Intelligence (AI)

It was John McCarthy (1959), a computer scientist and professor at Stanford University, who first coined the term *artificial intelligence*. Today, artificial intelligence is represented in computer programs such as Deep Blue, a chess program that beat the world chess champion, Garry Kasparov, in 1997 (Kasparov had beaten Deep Blue in 1996, four games to two). In 2003, Kasparov played Deep Blue's "descendent," Deep Junior, and managed only a draw. Deep Junior, unlike Deep Blue, was programmed to consider only the strongest possible positions in detail (Knight, 2003). Interestingly, Deep Blue was programmed to use heuristics, the same decision-making processes that human chess players use. Deep Junior used algorithms (which are more typical for computer programs) and played Kasparov to a draw using strategies that were less like human thinking than Deep Blue's strategies.

AI researchers debate whether scientists should be trying to create artificial intelligence that mimics human thought processes (Hoffmann, 1998; Weizenbaum, 1976). Scientists will no doubt continue to try to refine robotic machines that can be used to go where humans cannot safely go, such as the depths of the oceans and the farthest reaches of our solar system. Will those machines think like machines, think like humans, or use a blend of mechanical and human cognitive processes? Only the future knows.

▲ One rule of thumb, or heuristic, involves breaking a goal into subgoals. This woman is consulting the map to see which of several possible paths she needs to take to get to her goal destination.

▲ Chess genius Garry Kasparov plays against the artificial intelligence program Deep Junior. The outcome was a draw.

artificial intelligence (AI) the creation of a machine that can think like a human.

COGNITION: THINKING AND INTELLIGENCE 313

CHAPTER 10 • Module 25

COVER THE MODULE

25.3 Can a machine be made to think like a person?

- *Artificial intelligence (AI)* is the creation of a machine that can think like a human.

PSYCHOLOGY IN THE NEWS

- AI researchers debate whether scientists should try to create AI that mimics human thought processes.
- Although some computers have been designed that can play chess and perform in similar ways to a human, the true flexibility of human thought processes has yet to be developed in a machine.

1. Making a robot more "human," with the addition of hands and feet, could make it possible for the robot to perform tasks that require limbs.
2. Designing robots with "human" characteristics might be keeping scientists from creating machines that could go beyond human capabilities. These scientists might be thinking too much "inside the box."
3. AI programs might be more effective than human intelligence in performing complex but boring or repetitive tasks.

L2 LPR DIFFERENTIATED INSTRUCTION

Less Proficient Readers For students with difficulties with learning strategies, explicitly model the use of the strategy, including a significant focus on thinking aloud during the execution of each step in the strategy. Discuss where else in or out of school students could use the strategy.

Class Debate

ARTIFICIAL INTELLIGENCE

Divide the class into two groups for a debate about AI, addressing this issue: "Should machines be made to think like a person? Why or why not?" One group should be ready to argue in favor and the other, against. Have students do some library or Internet research to support their arguments before the debate. Afterward, have the class vote on which side the majority of them support.

Module 25 Thinking 313

CHAPTER 10 • Module 25

COVER THE MODULE

25.4 What are some obstacles to problem solving?

- **Functional Fixedness**
  - *Functional fixedness* is the tendency to perceive objects as having only the use for which they were originally intended, therefore failing to see them as possible tools for solving other problems.
- **Mental Sets**
  - *Mental set* is the tendency for people to persist in using problem-solving patterns that have worked in the past. These people are unwilling to "think outside the box."
- **Confirmation Bias**
  - *Confirmation bias* is the tendency to search for evidence that confirms one's beliefs, ignoring any evidence to the contrary.

MULTIMEDIA CONTENT AVAILABLE AT
www.mypsychlab.com

Explore the two-string problem (icon) and confirmation bias on **mypsychlab.com**

EXTEND THE DISCUSSION

Mention to students the idea of an "incubation period" in problem solving. Ask: **Have you ever been able to solve a problem only after leaving it for a while? What problem were you trying to solve? Explain what happened.**

FIGURE 25.3 The String Problem
The string problem: How do you tie the two strings together if you cannot reach them both at the same time?

FIGURE 25.4 The Dot Problem
The dot problem: Can you draw four straight lines so that they pass through all nine dots *without lifting your pencil from the page or touching any dot more than once*? Hint: The tried-and-true rule that schoolchildren learn—stay within the lines—will not succeed here. The solution involves drawing the lines beyond the actual dots, as seen in Figure 25.6 on page 318.

functional fixedness a block to problem solving that comes from thinking about objects in terms of only their typical functions.

mental set the tendency for people to persist in using problem-solving patterns that have worked for them in the past.

confirmation bias the tendency to search for evidence that fits one's beliefs while ignoring any evidence that does not fit those beliefs.

Questions for Further Thought
1. How might having hands and feet make a robot more useful for certain tasks?
2. How might the tendency to design robots with "human" characteristics be limiting the advance of robotic technology?
3. What types of jobs might AI programs perform better than human intelligence?

Identify Obstacles to Thought

25.4 What are some obstacles to problem solving?

Using the aforementioned strategies to solve a problem is not always foolproof. Sometimes a solution remains just out of reach because the elements of the problem are not arranged properly or because people get stuck in certain ways of thinking that act as barriers. Such ways of thinking occur without any conscious awareness. Here's a classic example:

Two strings are hanging from a ceiling but are too far apart to allow a person to hold one and walk to the other. (See Figure 25.3.) Nearby is a table with a pair of pliers on it. The goal is to tie the two pieces of string together. How? For the solution, see Figure 25.5 on page 317.

In becoming aware of these automatic tendencies, people can abandon them for more appropriate problem-solving methods. Three of the most common barriers to successful problem solving are functional fixedness, mental sets, and confirmation bias.

Functional Fixedness **Functional fixedness** is our tendency to think about objects only in terms of their name or their typical uses. Have you ever searched high and low for a screwdriver to fix something? All the while, you could use several other household objects instead: a butter knife, a key, or even a dime. Because we usually use those objects for different functions—cooking, unlocking, and spending—we may ignore less obvious uses. The string problem is an example of functional fixedness. The pair of pliers seems useless, but it can function as a weight. Similarly, renowned chef Alton Brown overcomes functional fixedness with "multitaskers," kitchen items that can be used for more than one purpose. For example, a cigar cutter can become a tool for cutting carrots and green onions.

Mental Sets Functional fixedness is a kind of **mental set**—that is, the tendency for people to persist in using problem-solving patterns that have worked for them before. People often start with tried-and-true solutions and are hesitant or even unable to think of other possibilities or "think outside the box." Look at Figure 25.4. Can you draw four straight lines so that they pass through all nine dots *without lifting your pencil from the page or touching any dot more than once*?

Confirmation Bias Another barrier to logical thinking, **confirmation bias**, is the tendency to search for evidence that fits one's beliefs while ignoring any contrary evidence. Here, what is "set" is a belief rather than a method. For example, believers in ESP tend to remember psychic predictions that came

---

Class Demonstration

FUNCTIONAL FIXEDNESS

Gather several household items, such as an egg carton, baby food jar, nail, paper clip, baking cup, piece of string, paper napkin, safety pin, Band-Aid, and cotton ball. You may want to have several of each item, depending on your class size. Divide the class into small groups and have each choose several items. Each group must brainstorm as many new uses for their items as possible in 10 to 15 minutes. Have each group report their results to the class. Discuss the nature of creativity and the meaning of functional fixedness. If a person suggests using a baby food jar to store small items, this is still fixating on the function of the jar as a container. A more creative suggestion would be to break the jar and use a piece for cutting or to draw around it to make a circle.

true or studies that seem to support their beliefs, while forgetting predictions that never came to pass or studies that found no proof. They remember only information that confirms their bias toward belief in ESP.

⊕–[Explore on **mypsychlab.com**

Creativity: Divergent and Convergent Thinking

So far, we've only talked about logic and pretty straightforward thinking. How do people come up with totally new ideas, things no one has thought of before?
Not every problem can be answered by using rules of logic to apply known information. Sometimes people need to find entirely new ways of looking at the problem or find unusual, inventive solutions. This kind of thinking is called **creativity**: solving problems by combining ideas or behavior in new ways (Csikszentmihalyi, 1996).

The logical problem-solving methods discussed so far are based on **convergent thinking**. Someone sees a problem as having only one answer and believes all lines of thinking will eventually lead to (converge on) that answer by using previous knowledge and logic (Ciardiello, 1998). For example, the question "In what ways are a pencil and a pen alike?" can be answered by listing their common features: Both can be used to write, have similar shapes, and so on. Convergent thinking works well for routine problem solving but perhaps less well when a creative solution is needed.

Divergent thinking is the reverse of convergent thinking. Here a person comes up with many different, or divergent, ideas (Finke, 1995). For example, if someone asks, "What is a pencil used for?" the convergent answer would be "to write." But if someone asks, "How many different uses can you think of for a pencil?" the answers multiply: "writing, poking holes, weighing down the tail of a kite." The TV character MacGyver, who could find hundreds of life-saving uses for objects like paper clips and rubber bands, is a classic example of a divergent thinker! ⊕–[Explore on **mypsychlab.com**

What are the characteristics of a creative, divergent thinker? Researchers in this field have examined the habits of highly creative people and found their most productive periods of divergent thinking tend to occur during more-or-less automatic activities, such as walking or swimming (Csikszentmihalyi, 1996; Gardner, 1993a; Goleman, 1995). These automatic tasks take up some attention, leaving the remainder to devote to creative thinking. It actually helps when one's attention is not completely focused on the problem, because divergent thinkers often make connections at a level of consciousness just below alert awareness, so that ideas can flow freely without being censored by the higher mental processes (Goleman, 1995). In other words, having part of one's attention elsewhere allows the rest of the mind to "sneak up on" more creative solutions and ideas.

Divergent thinkers are less prone to some common barriers to problem solving, such as functional fixedness. For example, what would most people do if it suddenly started to rain while they were walking home with no umbrella? How many people would think of using a see-through vinyl tote bag as a makeshift umbrella?

Creative, divergent thinking is often a neglected topic in education. Yet the ability to be creative is important—coming up with topics for a research paper, for example, is difficult for many students. Cross-cultural research (Basadur et al., 2002; Colligan, 1983) has found that divergent thinking and problem-solving skills cannot be easily taught in some cultures, such as that of the Japanese and the Omaha Native Americans, where in many cases, people

> *So far, we've only talked about logic and pretty straightforward thinking. How do people come up with totally new ideas, things no one has thought of before?*

⊕–[Explore the two-string problem (icon) and confirmation bias on **mypsychlab.com**

⊕–[Explore problem solving and creativity on **mypsychlab.com**

creativity the process of solving problems by combining ideas or behavior in new ways.

convergent thinking type of thinking in which a problem is seen as having only one answer, and all lines of thinking will eventually lead to that single answer, using previous knowledge and logic.

divergent thinking type of thinking in which a person starts from one point and comes up with many different ideas or possibilities based on that point.

CHAPTER 10 • Module 25

DISCUSS THE STUDENT VOICE QUESTION

To lead off a discussion about creativity, ask students why they think it is important to be able to come up with new ideas.

COVER THE MODULE *(continued)*

- **Creativity: Divergent and Convergent Thinking**
  - *Creativity* is the process of solving problems by combining ideas in new ways.
  - In *convergent thinking*, a problem is seen as having only one answer, and all lines of thinking eventually lead to that single answer. This type of thinking works well for routine problem solving.
  - *Divergent thinking* involves coming up with as many different answers as possible. This is a kind of creativity.
  - Creative people are usually good at mental imagery and have knowledge on a wide range of topics, are unafraid to be different, value their independence, and are often unconventional in their work but not in other areas.
  - Cross-cultural research has found that divergent thinking and problem-solving skills cannot be taught easily in some cultures where people value traditions over creativity.

MULTIMEDIA CONTENT AVAILABLE AT
www.mypsychlab.com

⊕–[Explore problem solving and creativity on mypsychlab.com

Class Demonstration

CREATIVE THINKING

Tell students that you want them to take out a sheet of paper because they will take a quiz. Once the groaning has stopped, have them write down all the uses they can think of for some item (i.e., cat litter or rice). At the end of 5 minutes, have them divide into small groups and see how many uses the groups can come up with for whatever item you have chosen. Have the groups present their lists to the class. Tell them they need not repeat an item that another group has already presented. Find out how many items they originally came up with versus the number of items that the group named. It is interesting how many items are similar between the groups.

CHAPTER 10 • Module 25

UNDERSTANDING VISUALS

Direct students' attention to Table 25.1. Have volunteers read each of the ways in which divergent thinking can be stimulated. Ask students if any of them have used these methods and, if so, whether the techniques were helpful.

COVER THE MODULE

25.5 What are some obstacles to making good judgments?

- Some commonly used heuristics, or mental shortcuts, can interfere with good judgment—what we judge to be true about a situation.
- **The Representativeness Heuristic**
  - This heuristic is often used when people think about whether one event caused, or is caused, by another. It may make people ignore other information that is just as relevant.
  - The conjunction fallacy is the error of believing specific conditions are more probable than a single general one.

L4 DIFFERENTIATED INSTRUCTION

Advanced Learners Ask students to brainstorm what they'd like to learn, and then work with them to create a plan for advanced study based on their interests.

316 Chapter 10 Cognition: Thinking and Intelligence

Table 25.1	Stimulating Divergent Thinking
Brainstorming	Generate as many ideas as possible in a short period of time, without judging each idea's merits until all ideas are recorded.
Keeping a Journal	Carry a journal to write down ideas as they occur or a recorder to capture those same ideas and thoughts.
Freewriting	Write down or record everything that comes to mind about a topic without revising or proofreading until all of the information is recorded. Organize it later.
Mind or Subject Mapping	Start with a central idea and draw lines from the center to related ideas, forming a visual map of the concepts and their connections.

value well-established traditions over creativity. However, it is possible for one to develop creative ability over time; see Table 25.1 for some ways to become a more divergent thinker.

Many people think creative people are also a little "different." Some artists and musicians, for example, encourage others to see them as eccentric. But the fact is that most creative people are pretty normal. Creative people usually have a broad range of knowledge about a lot of subjects and aren't afraid to be different—they are more open to new experiences than many people, and they tend to have more vivid dreams and daydreams. They value their independence, and often are unconventional in their work but not otherwise (Csikszentmihalyi, 1997).

25.5 What are some obstacles to making good judgments?

Problem solving isn't the only mental process that is sometimes hampered by obstacles. Most people can also run into barriers—or can be led astray—when they try to form judgments and make decisions. The next two sections will discuss a few common barriers.

Some commonly used heuristics, or mental shortcuts, often interfere with good judgment—what we judge to be true or likely about a given situation. Most of us are just not very good at judging probability: the likelihood that a certain condition will be true or that a certain event will occur. Instead of "doing the math," we rely on heuristics, particularly the representativeness heuristic and the availability heuristic.

The Representativeness Heuristic As we discussed earlier, the representativeness heuristic is our tendency to believe that any object (or person) that shares characteristics with the members of a particular category is also a member of that category. We also often use this heuristic when we think about whether one event caused, or was caused by, another. Unfortunately, it tends to make us ignore other information that is just as relevant (or more so).

For instance, it is a basic law of probability that, if A and B are unrelated conditions or events, the chance that either A or B alone will be true is greater

316 CHAPTER 10

Class Demonstration

CREATIVITY QUIZ

Draw a circle on the board. Allow students 5 minutes to list all of the things they can think of that your picture could represent. Use a plate and a wedding ring as examples, and urge them to think divergently. Sample responses may include, for example:

> Total eclipse of the sun / Top view of a baldheaded man / Floor plan for an igloo / Porthole at night / The end of a gun as seen by a victim / Belly button / Bucket of tar from the top

than the chance of both A and B being true. That rule is the basis of poker games. Statistically, you are more likely to draw a single ace (A) than to draw a pair of aces (A and B), so a pair is worth more, and three or four of a kind are worth even more. However, we forget about probability when the representativeness heuristic comes into play.

Tversky and Kahneman (1983) asked subjects to read a brief profile of "Linda," described as 31 years old, educated, bright, outspoken, and concerned about social issues. They then had to estimate the probability of each of these statements being true:

(1) *Linda is a bank teller.*
(2) *Linda is a bank teller and active in the feminist movement.*

Over 80 percent of the subjects said that the second statement was more likely to be true. Statistically, Linda is more likely to be a bank teller than to be both a bank teller and a feminist, but subjects were led astray by the representative heuristic, because the profile *represented* their ideas of what a typical feminist was like. This particular error in mathematical logic is known as the **conjunction fallacy**, and the researchers found that even people trained in statistics were prone to it. People ignore other simple laws of probability as well when they use the representative heuristic to make judgments; for example, they might think that a shy, withdrawn man from a sample group consisting of 70 lawyers and 30 engineers is nonetheless more likely to be an engineer than a lawyer (Tversky & Kahneman, 1974).

The Availability Heuristic The **availability heuristic** is our tendency to estimate the likelihood that a certain condition will be true or that a certain event will occur based on how easily we can recall similar instances. This is often useful. For instance, when we see a dark, cloudy sky, we assume there's a good chance of rain and grab an umbrella. We're making a judgment (and in this case, a decision) based on all of our *available* recollections of dark, cloudy skies that were followed by rain.

This heuristic is faulty, however, because human memory is limited. More recent and more dramatic or emotional events stand out for us. For this reason, most people will overestimate the danger of flying, because we can easily recall news stories about disastrous plane crashes. (Statistically, a person is far more likely to be killed in a car accident than a plane crash.) If we have just seen or heard about a car crash, however, our estimate of the frequency of car crashes will go up.

Other times, the problem is that certain events or situations are just difficult to bring to mind. Tversky and Kahneman (1974) asked people to judge whether the English language has more words that begin with the letter *r* or more words that have *r* as their third letter. Most people will incorrectly say that there are more words that begin with *r*, simply because those are much easier for us to think of.

The Anchoring Effect Although it might seem like having more information would always help us make better judgments, this is not always the case, due to the **anchoring effect**—our tendency to make judgments based on a specific initial value or starting point, even when it's not really relevant. For instance, Tversky and Kahneman (1974) examined how subjects' estimates of general knowledge items, such as the average winter temperature in Antarctica, were influenced by the way the question was framed. When the question was "anchored" to a specific number—for instance, "Is the average

FIGURE 25.5 The Solution to the String Problem
The solution to the string problem is to use the pliers as a pendulum to swing the second string closer to you.

conjunction fallacy the error of believing specific conditions are more probable than a single general one.

availability heuristic the tendency to estimate the probability of a certain condition or event based on how many similar instances we can recall.

anchoring effect the tendency to consider all of the information available, even when it is irrelevant.

COGNITION: THINKING AND INTELLIGENCE 317

CHAPTER 10 • Module 25

COVER THE MODULE *(continued)*

- **The Availability Heuristic**
  - This heuristic is the tendency to estimate the probability of a certain condition based on how many similar instances a person can recall.
  - Because human memory is limited, more recent dramatic events stand out for people.

- **The Anchoring Effect**
  - This heuristic is the tendency to make judgments based on considering all available information, even if it is irrelevant.

L3 DIFFERENTIATED INSTRUCTION

Tactile/Kinesthetic Learners Encourage these students to make flash cards, using different colors and diagrams, to lay the cards out on a large surface, and then to practice putting them in order.

L3 DIFFERENTIATED INSTRUCTION

Auditory/Verbal Learners These students can speak out loud while studying or into a recorder that they can play back later.

Explore

THE AVAILABILITY HEURISTIC

Before a discussion of obstacles to making good judgments, ask students to spend time outside class drawing a map of the world. Tell them that they may not "cheat" by looking at maps, globes, or atlases. Reassure students that you will not grade their maps. Have students turn in the maps at least one class prior to your discussion of the topic, so you have time to review and summarize the results of the demonstration. Ask volunteers to display their maps to the class and discuss why they drew the maps as they did. Most students greatly enlarge the size of Europe and reduce the size of Africa; this occurs regardless of the country of origin of the students. This most likely reflects the relative prominence of Europe and the relative obscurity of Africa in the Western view of history. That which we know more about is seen as physically larger, and that which we know little of is diminished in size.

Module 25 Thinking 317

CHAPTER 10 • Module 25

COVER THE MODULE

25.6 What are some obstacles to decision making?

- Decision making is a form of problem solving. Both logic and emotion are involved in the process.
- **The Myth of the "Hot Streak"**
  - The brain misleads people by trying to impose a pattern on events, even when none exist.
- **The Gambler's Fallacy**
  - This is the belief that the chance of something occurring depends on whether it has recently occurred.
- **Loss Aversion**
  - This is the tendency to be more sensitive to actual or potential losses than to gains.

EXTEND THE DISCUSSION

Ask students with athletic experience if they are familiar with the myth of the "hot streak." Did they actually believe they were in the middle of a winning (or losing) streak?

L3 DIFFERENTIATED INSTRUCTION

Engaging All Learners Use visuals throughout the lesson. Outlining key ideas, writing key phrases and vocabulary, and putting notes on the overhead projector or board are critical supports for many students. You may want to provide some students with a copy of your notes ahead of time so they can follow along.

---

318 Chapter 10 Cognition: Thinking and Intelligence

---

temperature higher or lower than 17 °C?"—subjects' answers tended to hover around that number, indicating that they had used it as a starting point and then estimated up or down. Similar studies have found that the anchoring effect occurs even when subjects are asked to consider a completely irrelevant number, such as the last two digits of their Social Security number. The anchoring effect can influence people's decision-making processes in a variety of situations, from buying a new car to determining the appropriate sentence for a crime.

25.6 What are some obstacles to decision making?

Decision making can be viewed as a form of problem solving. Faced with two or more alternatives, a person must choose the best one, based on the information available. Often choosing one alternative means eliminating the others; for example, accepting one job means turning down other offers. Both logic and emotion are involved in the process—and both can lead us astray. In his 2009 book *How We Decide*, Jonah Lehrer describes how "gut feelings" may help or hinder decision making, depending on the situation. He suggests that it's most helpful to listen to your gut feelings when you are making trivial decisions, when you are making a decision about a situation you know a lot about, or when you are performing a skill you've practiced many times before. In other situations, however, it's wisest to rely on logic.

The Myth of the "Hot Streak" One way the brain misleads us is in trying to impose patterns on events, even when none exist. This is especially true when we think we see a pattern of rewards, because we hope to maximize those rewards. For instance, studies of professional basketball teams (Gilovich et al., 1985) have found that, although players often think they're on a winning (or losing) streak, analyzing their actual percentage of successful shots proves them wrong. Players (or gamblers) who feel like they're on a "hot streak" may make riskier decisions, even though the chance of success is no better than usual.

The Gambler's Fallacy A closely related pitfall is the **gambler's fallacy**—the belief that the chance of something occurring depends on whether it has recently occurred. This may be true in some life situations, but it's wrong to think that a flipped coin that's come up heads 10 times in a row is bound to come up tails next time. (The odds for any one coin flip are always 50–50.) We *feel* like it should happen, but that feeling is not based on logic.

These irrational feelings aren't confined to the sports arena and the casino. They also affect people's choices about investments, which can lead to stock market bubbles or panics. We're programmed to see patterns, even when events are random.

Loss Aversion Another obstacle to good decision making is **loss aversion**. Simply put, people prefer to avoid taking a loss, and so losses stand out for us more than gains. Researchers have experimented with asking subjects to make a hypothetical decision. They presented the exact same possible outcomes, framed in slightly different terms, and found that subjects will make different decisions if the situation is presented in a way that emphasizes potential losses (Tversky & Kahneman, 1981). If people perceive themselves as having already suffered a loss, they will often take greater risks to try to recover the loss, instead of knowing when to leave well enough alone.

FIGURE 25.6 The Solution to the Dot Problem When people try to solve this problem, a mental set causes them to think of the dots as representing a box, and they try to draw the line while staying in the box. The only way to connect all nine dots without lifting the pencil from the paper is to think outside the box—drawing the lines so they extend out of the box of dots.

gambler's fallacy the belief that the chance of something occurring depends on whether it has recently occurred.

loss aversion the tendency to be more sensitive to actual or potential losses than to gains.

Class Discussion

"GUT" FEELINGS

According to the textbook, "gut feelings" may help or hinder decision making, depending on the situation. Conduct a class discussion about whether students prefer to go with such feelings when making a decision or if they would rather rely on logic. Are there specific situations in which they might use gut feelings over logic, or vice versa?

This research also partly explains why using cash instead of credit cards typically makes us spend less. Physically handing over a $20 bill forces you to focus on the money you're losing, so you're less likely to decide the purchased item is worth it.

Applying Psychology to Everyday Life

Improving Your Cognitive Health

The brain is not a muscle, but it needs exercise to stay fit, just as muscles do. Research has shown that people who regularly work crossword puzzles, take classes, read, and generally stay mentally active are less likely to develop senile dementia than those who do not (Ball et al., 2002; Cabeza et al., 2002; Wilson et al., 2002). Neuroscientists researching Alzheimer's disease (LINK to Chapter Nine: Memory, p. 297) have found that this kind of "brain exercise" may help to improve the brain's ability to develop new neurons and the axons and dendrites that connect them, an ability called *cognitive reserve* (Scarmeas et al., 2003).

Cognitive reserve may explain why up to two-thirds of the autopsies of elderly women in one study showed signs of advanced Alzheimer's disease at the time of death, in spite of the fact that these women had shown no signs of dementia or cognitive impairment before they died (Katzman et al., 1989). The theory is that having extra neurons and neural connections compensates for the neurons that are being damaged by the Alzheimer's disease progression. Since it is difficult to know whether or not you will develop Alzheimer's disease or one of the many other forms of dementia, building up a cognitive reserve is a good idea.

How can you increase your cognitive reserve? Cognitive reserve is greater in people who finish higher levels of education—the intellectual challenges help form new neural connections, especially early in life (see, aren't you glad you're reading this while you're in high school?). Those who are socially as well as intellectually active are also building up their cognitive reserves (Scarmeas et al., 2001, 2003). And studies have shown that those who follow a "Mediterranean diet"—one high in vegetables, fruits, whole grains, and legumes and low in saturated fats—are less at risk for developing Alzheimer's disease, perhaps because of the increased health of the blood supply to the brain related to this kind of healthy eating (Scarmeas et al., 2006, 2007).

Questions for Further Discussion
1. What other kinds of mental activities might help to keep the brain fit?
2. Should doctors suggest mental fitness exercises to their patients?

COGNITION: THINKING AND INTELLIGENCE

CHAPTER 10 • Module 25

APPLYING PSYCHOLOGY TO EVERYDAY LIFE

- Brain "exercise" may help to improve the brain's ability to develop new neurons and the axons and dendrites that connect them. This ability is called *cognitive reserve*.
- Scientists theorize that having extra neurons and neural connections compensates for neurons damaged by the progression of Alzheimer's disease.
- Cognitive reserve is greater in people who have higher levels of education and are socially and intellectually active.
- Following a "Mediterranean diet" high in fruits, vegetables, and grains and low in fat could also help brain functions.

1. Mental activity that requires creativity and the use of memory abilities, such as learning a foreign language and playing a challenging video game, can help to keep the brain fit.
2. Possible answer: Yes, I think it would be helpful if doctors encourage their patients to eat right and exercise their brains in order to improve cognitive health.

Explore

IMPROVING COGNITIVE HEALTH

Ask students to research ways in which they can increase their cognitive reserve, along with the means by which their cognitive health can be negatively affected (e.g., excessive drinking, smoking). Then have them create audiovisual presentations showing what they have learned. Ask volunteers to present their work to the class.

CHAPTER 10 • Module 25

Assess

Assign the Module 25 Practice Quiz.

Use the Practice Quiz to identify gaps in student understanding.

REMEDIATE

Have students, individually or in groups, review the module goals, learning objectives, and key terms.

Refer students to the Concept Summary on p. 338 for review.

Close

As a class, discuss ways in which people can make better decisions and solve problems more easily.

Practice Quiz

Pick the best answer.

1. Assuming that the correct solution is available, which problem-solving strategy will always result in a correct solution?
   a. means-end analysis
   b. heuristic
   c. algorithm
   d. trial and error

2. A "rule of thumb" is another name for a(n)
   a. anchoring effect
   b. heuristic
   c. formal concept
   d. prototype

3. Laticia has been instructed to write an analysis of the Bolshevik revolution for her 11th grade world history class. The paper is to be between 15 and 20 pages, and is due in 1 month. Laticia is feeling very overwhelmed by such a huge assignment. What shortcut would be most useful as she attempts to conquer this very large task?
   a. the representative heuristic
   b. the availability heuristic
   c. trial and error
   d. the use of subgoals

4. Miguel was struggling with the answer to one of the questions on his psychology midterm. Seeing that the answer was not going to come easily, he went on to answer some of the other easier questions. Then, suddenly, the answer to the problematic question just seemed to "pop" into his head. Miguel's experience is an example of
   a. insight
   b. a mechanical solution
   c. convergent thinking
   d. a natural concept

5. Al goes out one frosty morning to find that his car is covered with a layer of thick frost. He needs to get to work and looks for his ice scraper. Unable to find it, he thinks a moment, goes into the house, and returns with a hard plastic spatula from the kitchen. In using the spatula as a makeshift ice scraper, what has Al overcome?
   a. confirmation bias
   b. functional fixedness
   c. loss aversion
   d. the anchoring effect

6. Randall believes that aliens crashed in the western United States in the 1950s. When looking for information about this on the Internet, he ignores any sites that are skeptical of his belief and only visits and talks with his friends about the sites that support his belief. What is this an example of?
   a. confirmation bias
   b. a mental set
   c. the gambler's fallacy
   d. divergent thinking

7. What type of thinking occurs when a problem is seen as having only one answer, with all lines of thinking leading to that answer?
   a. convergent
   b. divergent
   c. formal
   d. natural

8. Which of the following statements about creative people is true?
   a. They are unconventional in most aspects of their lives.
   b. They tend to focus exclusively on one field of knowledge.
   c. They are more open to new experiences than other people.
   d. They can solve almost any type of problem easily.

9. On her way to school, Jackie must stop and wait at three red lights in a row. She is sure the light at the next intersection will have to be green. Her thinking is an example of which cognitive pitfall?
   a. the representativeness heuristic
   b. the myth of the "hot streak"
   c. the gambler's fallacy
   d. hindsight bias

10. Subjects in an experiment view a photograph of Lee, a teenage boy with long hair who is wearing headphones. The subjects are then asked which statement is more likely to be true: "Lee is a high school student" or "Lee is a high school student who plays guitar in a garage rock band." Most subjects say the second statement is more likely to be true. This is an example of
    a. the conjunction fallacy
    b. the availability heuristic
    c. confirmation bias
    d. functional fixedness

Practice Quiz Answers

1. c
2. b
3. d
4. a
5. b
6. a
7. a
8. c
9. c
10. a

Module 26: Intelligence

Module Goals

Compare and contrast perspectives on intelligence.

Learn how intelligence is measured.

Consider key issues in intelligence research.

Learning Objectives

26.1 How do psychologists define intelligence?
26.2 What are some established theories of intelligence?
26.3 What are intellectual disability and giftedness?
26.4 What is the history of intelligence testing?
26.5 How is intelligence measured today?
26.6 How can we determine whether intelligence tests are reliable and valid?
26.7 How are intelligence tests used in the real world?
26.8 How do heredity and environment influence intelligence?

Compare and Contrast Perspectives on Intelligence

26.1 How do psychologists define intelligence?

Think back to Alex the parrot in the opening story. Whether or not you accept Alex's verbal abilities as true language, one thing is clear: Alex is a smart bird. But what do we mean when we say he is "smart"? Is "smart" in a bird the same thing we mean when we say a human is "smart"? What exactly do we mean by the term *intelligence*?

Is intelligence merely a score on some test, or is it practical knowledge of how to get along in the world? Is it making good grades or being a financial or social success? Ask a dozen people and you will probably get a dozen different answers. Psychologists have come up with a workable definition that combines many of the ideas just listed and applies to people across times and cultures: They define **intelligence** as the ability to learn from one's experiences, acquire knowledge, and use resources effectively in adapting to new situations or solving problems (Sternberg & Kaufman, 1998; Wechsler, 1975). These are the characteristics that people need to be able to survive in their culture.

26.2 What are some established theories of intelligence?

Spearman's g Factor Spearman (1904) saw intelligence as two different abilities. The ability to reason and solve problems was labeled **g factor** for *general intelligence*, whereas task-specific abilities in certain areas, such as music, business, or art, were labeled **s factor** for *specific intelligence*. A traditional IQ test would most likely measure g factor, but Spearman believed that superiority in one type of intelligence predicts superiority overall. Although his early research

intelligence the ability to learn from one's experiences, acquire knowledge, and use resources effectively in adapting to new situations or solving problems.

g factor the ability to reason and solve problems, or general intelligence.

s factor the ability to excel in certain areas, or specific intelligence.

COGNITION: THINKING AND INTELLIGENCE   321

Terms

- intelligence • g factor • s factor • triarchic theory of intelligence • analytical intelligence • creative intelligence • practical intelligence • emotional intelligence • standardization • mean • standard deviation • developmentally delayed • gifted • IQ • deviation IQ scores • cultural bias

---

CHAPTER 10 • Module 26

Focus

RESOURCES

For this module, consult the appropriate sections of the Teacher's Manual, Test Bank, and PowerPoint slides, all found on the Teacher's Resource DVD, and the interactive study tools for students on MyPsychLab.

BEFORE CLASS

Students should read the section for homework before coming to class.

BELLRINGER

Ask students to respond in writing to this topic: **What are the common characteristics of intelligent behavior? In other words, how can you tell if someone is intelligent?**

Teach

INTRODUCE THE TOPIC

Ask several volunteers to read their answers to the Bellringer activity. Point out that there are many different ways to define intelligence.

COVER THE MODULE

26.1 How do psychologists define intelligence?

- *Intelligence* is the ability to understand the world, think rationally or logically, and use resources effectively when faced with challenges or problems.

26.2 What are some established theories of intelligence?

- **Spearman's g Factor**
  - Spearman proposed general intelligence, or "g" factor, as the ability to reason and solve problems, while specific intelligence, or "s" factor, is the ability to excel in certain areas, such as music or business.

Module 26 Intelligence   321

CHAPTER 10 • Module 26

COVER THE MODULE (continued)

- **Sternberg's Triarchic Theory**
  - Sternberg proposed three types of intelligence:
    - *Analytical intelligence* is the ability to break problems down into parts for problem solving. This type of intelligence is measured by intelligence and academic achievement tests.
    - *Creative intelligence* is the ability to deal with new and different concepts and come up with new ways of solving problems.
    - *Practical intelligence* is the ability to use information to get along in life.

MULTIMEDIA CONTENT AVAILABLE AT
www.mypsychlab.com

Watch Robert Sternberg discussing intelligence on **mypsychlab.com**

- **Gardner's Multiple Intelligences**
  - Gardner proposed eight different types of intelligence, ranging from verbal, linguistic, and mathematical to interpersonal and intrapersonal intelligence.

UNDERSTANDING VISUALS

Direct students' attention to Table 26.1. Ask volunteers to read to the class Gardner's multiple intelligences, descriptions, and sample occupations. Ask students if any of them plan on careers that are listed in the table. Would they agree that the type of intelligence for their selected career is important?

- **Emotional Intelligence**
  - *Emotional intelligence* is viewed as a powerful influence on success in life.

This child is displaying only one of the many forms intelligence can take, according to Gardner's theory.

Watch Robert Sternberg discussing intelligence on **mypsychlab.com**

triarchic theory of intelligence Sternberg's theory that there are three kinds of intelligence: analytical, creative, and practical.

analytical intelligence the ability to break problems down into component parts, or analysis, for problem solving.

creative intelligence the ability to deal with new and different concepts and to come up with new ways of solving problems.

practical intelligence the ability to use information to get along in life and become successful.

emotional intelligence the awareness of and ability to manage one's own emotions as well as the ability to be self-motivated, able to feel what others feel, and socially skilled.

322 CHAPTER 10

---

found some support for specific intelligences, later researchers (Guilford, 1967; Thurstone, 1938) felt that Spearman had oversimplified the concept of intelligence. They saw intelligence as being composed of numerous factors. In fact, Guilford (1967) proposed that there were 120 types of intelligence.

Sternberg's Triarchic Theory Sternberg's **triarchic theory of intelligence** (1988, 1997) proposed that there are three kinds of intelligence (*triarchic* means "three"): **analytical, creative,** and **practical intelligence**.

Analytical intelligence is the ability to break problems down into parts, or analysis, for problem solving. This type of intelligence, sometimes called "book smarts," is measured by intelligence tests and academic achievement tests. **Creative intelligence** is the ability to deal with new and different concepts and come up with new ways of solving problems. **Practical intelligence** is best described as "street smarts," or the ability to use information to get along in life. People with a high degree of practical intelligence know how to strategize and use people skills to increase their odds of success.

How might these three types of intelligence be illustrated? All three might come into play when planning and completing an experiment. For example, a person needs analytical intelligence to run a statistical analysis on experimental data, creative intelligence to design the experiment in the first place, and practical intelligence to help get funding for the experiment.

Practical intelligence has become the focus of much interest and research. Sternberg (1996, 1997a, 1997b) has found that practical intelligence predicts success in life but has a surprisingly low relationship to academic (analytical) intelligence. In fact, people with greater practical intelligence may be less likely to succeed in an academic setting. Watch on **mypsychlab.com**

Gardner's Multiple Intelligences One of the later theorists to propose the existence of several kinds of intelligence was Gardner (1993b, 1999a). He originally listed seven different kinds of intelligence, but he later added an eighth intelligence (naturalist intelligence), and thinks there might also be a ninth intelligence (existentialist intelligence) (Gardner, 1998, 1999b). Gardner's multiple intelligences are described in Table 26.1 on the next page.

The idea of multiple intelligences has great appeal, especially for educators. However, while Gardner and others claim that evidence exists for this concept (Gardner & Moran, 2006), some argue that the evidence provided by scientific studies is insufficient (Waterhouse, 2006a, 2006b). Some critics propose that such intelligences are no more than different abilities, which are not necessarily the same thing as intelligence (Hunt, 2001).

Emotional Intelligence What about people who have a lot of "book smarts" but not much common sense? Some people succeed in school but not in life, or vice versa. One possible explanation is that real-world success depends on **emotional intelligence**, the awareness of and ability to manage one's own emotions as well as the ability to be self-motivated, to feel what others feel, and to be socially skilled (Persaud, 2001).

The concept of emotional intelligence is controversial in the world of psychology, and many critics have challenged the concept, citing a lack of supporting evidence. However, those who support the idea of emotional intelligence propose that an emotionally intelligent person can control impulses and intense emotions. Empathy, the ability to understand what others feel, is also a component, as are the awareness of one's own emotions, sensitivity, persistence even in the face of frustrations, and the ability to motivate oneself (Goleman, 1995; Salovey & Mayer, 1990).

Class Demonstration

DEFINING INTELLIGENCE

Purpose: Students work with others to generate a definition of intelligence.

Time: 10 minutes

Description: Each student is given a few minutes to write down his or her definition of intelligence. Team members compare their definitions. Then the team creates a new definition of intelligence that incorporates the elements mentioned in the individual definitions. Teams share their groups' definition with the class. This activity not only gets students thinking about what should be included in the definition of intelligence, but also highlights the difficulty scientists have in agreeing on a definition of intelligence.

Table 26.1 Gardner's Multiple Intelligences

TYPE OF INTELLIGENCE	DESCRIPTION	SAMPLE OCCUPATION
Verbal/linguistic	Ability to use language	Writers, speakers
Musical	Ability to compose and/or perform music	Musicians, even those who do not read musical notes but can perform and compose
Logical/mathematical	Ability to think logically and solve mathematical problems	Scientists, engineers
Visual/spatial	Ability to understand how objects are oriented in space	Pilots, astronauts, artists, navigators
Movement	Ability to control one's body motions	Dancers, athletes
Interpersonal	Sensitivity to others and understanding motivation of others	Psychologists, managers
Intrapersonal	Understanding of one's emotions and how they guide actions	Various people-oriented careers
Naturalist	Ability to recognize the patterns found in nature	Farmers, landscapers, biologists, botanists
Existentialist	Ability to see the "big picture" of the human world by asking questions about life, death, and the ultimate reality of human existence	Various careers, philosophical thinkers

26.3 What are intellectual disability and giftedness?

Defining "Average": Standardization and the Normal Curve To understand the range of human intelligence, it helps to understand what psychologists mean when they discuss "normal" or "average" intelligence as measured by standardized tests. **Standardization** refers to the process of giving the test to a large group of people that represents the population for whom the test is designed. Standardization groups are chosen randomly from the population and, like all samples, can only be representative of the population from which they are drawn. LINK *to Chapter One: The Science of Psychology, p. 19.* If a test is designed for children, for example, then a large sample of randomly selected children would take the test under the same conditions. If a study tests a large enough representative sample, and the frequency of different test scores is plotted out on a curve, the curve will look like something like Figure 26.1 on the next page.

The middle part of the curve represents the frequency of scores that are average, or slightly above or below average. Due to the bell curve's symmetry, the very highest part of the curve represents the **mean**—the number you get if you average all of the test-takers' scores. The middle part of the curve is highest because scores at or near the mean occur most frequently. Very high or low scores, which are farther from the mean, occur less frequently, so the

standardization the process of giving a test to a large group of people that represents the population for whom the test is designed.

mean the average score within a group of scores, calculated by adding all of the scores and then dividing by the number of scores.

COGNITION: THINKING AND INTELLIGENCE 323

CHAPTER 10 • Module 26

COVER THE MODULE

26.3 What are intellectual disability and giftedness?

- **Defining "Average": Standardization and the Normal Curve**
  - *Standardization* refers to the process of giving an intelligence test to a large group of people that represents the population for whom the test is designed.

  LINK *to Chapter One: The Science of Psychology, p. 19*

  - If a study tests a large-enough representative sample and the frequency of different test scores is plotted out on a curve, the curve will look like a normal curve.
    - The middle part of the curve represents the frequency of scores that are average or slightly above or below average.
    - The very highest part of the curve represents the mean—the average score.
    - Researchers use the standard deviation (the average variation from the mean score) to discuss how much difference from the mean is typical.

CHECK FOR UNDERSTANDING

To ensure that students understand standardization and the normal curve, direct their attention to Figure 26.1. Ask volunteers to explain why the figure is a normal curve. If students struggle, refer them to the simulation on the normal curve at **www.mypsychlab.com**.

Class Discussion (Kinesthetic)

GARDNER'S MULTIPLE INTELLIGENCES

Purpose: Students discuss different types of intelligence.

Time: 15 minutes

Description: Distribute "talking chips" to the class. Then tell students to think of a well-known person, who is a good example of one of Gardner's types of intelligence. For example, a student could choose Oprah Winfrey as an example of linguistic intelligence. When a student has shared, he or she places a talking chip on the table. The next student who shares must pick a well-known person, who exemplifies a type of intelligence that has not yet been discussed. Students may not share again until all team members have taken a turn and placed their chips on the table.

CHAPTER 10 • Module 26

COVER THE MODULE (continued)

- **Intellectual Disability**
  - Intellectual disability (formerly "mental retardation") is a condition in which the person's IQ falls below 70, and adaptive behavior is severely deficient for a person of a particular chronological age.
  - These limitations must be present before the age of 18.
  - Intellectual disability occurs in about 3 percent of the population.
  - The term *developmentally delayed* means that a person's behavioral and cognitive skills exist at a later developmental stage than the skills of others, who are of the same chronological age.
  - The diagnosis of intellectual disability/developmental delay is based not only on IQ test scores, but also on adaptive functioning and the onset of impairments.

TEACHING TIP
Provide a range of instructional activities that reinforce concepts and skills, expanding students' opportunities for success.

L3 DIFFERENTIATED INSTRUCTION
Visual/Verbal Learners Encourage students to use "sticky" notes to remind themselves of key terms and information, and put them in their notebook or textbook.

FIGURE 26.1 The Normal Curve
This curve represents the frequency of different scores people get when they take the Wechsler IQ test, a widely used standardized intelligence test. The percentages under each section of the normal curve represent the percentage of scores falling within that section for each *standard deviation (SD)* from the mean. The mean score is 100. To be classified as gifted, a person must score 130 or higher, a score more than two standard deviations above the mean. To be classified as developmentally delayed, a person must score 70 or below—that is, more than two standard deviations below the mean.

ends of the curve taper off. The farther a score is from the mean, the lower the number of people who had that score.

Figure 26.1, with its symmetrical bell shape, is a normal curve. It represents a normal distribution of data, with the greatest number of scores nearest to the mean and the fewest scores at the extremes. Researchers use a statistical measure called the **standard deviation**—basically, the average variation from the mean score—to discuss how much difference from the mean is typical. In a normal distribution, 68 percent of subjects score within one standard deviation, and 95 percent within two standard deviations. Only 5 percent will have scores more than two standard deviations from the mean, and a tiny minority—less than 1 percent—will have scores more than three standard deviations from the mean.

Intellectual Disability *Intellectual disability* (formerly *mental retardation*) is defined in several ways. First, the person's IQ score must fall below 70, or two standard deviations below the mean on the normal curve. (For more information about what IQ scores mean and how they are calculated, see page 327 in this module.) Second, the person's *adaptive behavior* (skills that allow people to live independently, such as being able to work at a job, communicate well with others, and grooming skills such as being able to get dressed, eat, and bathe with little or no help) must be severely below the level appropriate for the person's age. Finally, these limitations must be present before the age of 18 years. Intellectual disability occurs in about 3 percent of the population (American Psychiatric Association, 2000). Although the older term *mental retardation* is still sometimes used to refer to the condition of intellectual disability, individuals with this condition may more commonly be referred to as **developmentally delayed**, meaning that their behavioral and cognitive skills exist at an earlier developmental stage than the skills of others who are the same chronological age (Smith & Mitchell, 2001).

So how would a professional go about deciding whether or not a child is developmentally delayed? Is the IQ test the primary method?

As indicated above, the diagnosis of intellectual disability/developmental delay, according to the *DSM-IV* (American Psychiatric Association, 2000), is based not only on IQ tests scores but also on adaptive functioning and the onset of impairments (American Psychiatric Association, 2000). The American Association on Intellectual and Developmental Disabilities (AAIDD) also defines intellectual disability as significant limitations not only in intellectual functioning but also in adaptive behavior (AAIDD, 2009). Developmental delays, classified by IQ test scores, can vary from mild to extremely severe. (See Table 26.2 on page 326.)

> So how would a professional go about deciding whether or not a child is developmentally delayed? Is the IQ test the primary method? ▶

standard deviation a statistical measure of the average variation from the mean score.

developmentally delayed condition in which a person's behavioral and cognitive skills exist at an earlier developmental stage than the skills of others who are the same chronological age.

324 CHAPTER 10

Class Debate

USING STANDARDIZED TESTS
Point out to students that standardized tests are often used in making educational decisions, such as in placing students in particular classes, or in the case of the SAT and ACT tests, admitting students to colleges. Conduct a class debate on whether it is fair for standardized tests to be used in this way. What are some possible advantages and disadvantages?

▲ *This middle-aged man, named Jack, lives in a small town in Arkansas and serves as a deacon in the local church. He is loved and respected and leads a full and happy life. Jack also has Down syndrome, but he has managed to find his place in the world.*

What causes developmental delay? Unhealthy living conditions can affect brain development. Examples are lead poisoning from eating paint chips (Lanphear et al., 2000), exposure to PCBs (Darvill et al., 2000), prenatal exposure to mercury (Grandjean et al., 1997) as well as other toxicants (Eskenazi et al., 1999; Schroeder, 2000), poor nutrition resulting in inadequate brain development, or a lack of mental stimulation in one's surroundings during infancy and childhood (Shah, 1991). Such environmental conditions can influence brain development, producing what is usually relatively mild intellectual disability (Schroeder, 2000).

The three most common biological causes of developmental delay are Down syndrome (LINK *to Chapter Five: Development Across the Life Span, p. 148*), fetal alcohol syndrome, and fragile X syndrome. *Fetal alcohol syndrome*, caused by exposing a developing embryo to alcohol, results in intelligence levels ranging from below average to developmentally delayed (Olson & Burgess, 1997). In *fragile X syndrome*, a male has a defect in a gene on the X chromosome of the twenty-third pair, leading to a deficiency in a protein needed for brain development. Symptoms can range from mild to severe or profound developmental delay (Dykens et al., 1994; Valverde et al., 2007). Other possible causes of developmental delay (Murphy et al., 1998) include lack of oxygen at birth, damage to the fetus in the womb from diseases, infections, or drug use, and even diseases and accidents during childhood.

One thing should always be remembered: Developmental delay affects a person's *intellectual* capabilities and adaptive behaviors. Developmentally delayed people are just as responsive to love and affection as anyone else and have social needs as all people do. Intelligence is only one characteristic; warmth, friendliness, caring, and compassion also count for a great deal and should not be underrated.

Giftedness At the other end of the spectrum are those who fall on the upper end of the normal curve, with an IQ above 130 (about 2 percent of the population). The term applied to these people is **gifted.** In very rare cases (less than half of 1 percent of the population), a person may have such a high IQ that he or she is referred to as a *genius*.

gifted term used to describe the 2 percent of the population falling on the upper end of the normal curve and typically possessing an IQ of 130 or above.

COGNITION: THINKING AND INTELLIGENCE

CHAPTER 10 • Module 26

COVER THE MODULE *(continued)*

- There are various causes of developmental delay:
  - Unhealthy living conditions, which can affect brain development
  - Poor nutrition, resulting in inadequate brain development
  - A lack of mental stimulation in one's surroundings during infancy and childhood
  - Down syndrome

LINK *to Chapter Five: Development Across the Life Span, p. 148*

  - Fetal alcohol syndrome
  - Fragile X syndrome
  - Lack of oxygen at birth, damage to the fetus in the womb, drug use by the mother, and diseases and accidents during childhood

- Developmentally delayed people have social needs as do all people. Intelligence is just one characteristic.

UNDERSTANDING VISUALS

Refer students to Table 26.2 on page 326, showing classifications of developmental delay. Point out that 90 percent of the developmentally delayed population is classified as "mildly" delayed, meaning that they are capable with training of living independently. Ask students if they are surprised to learn this.

CHECK FOR UNDERSTANDING

If students need remediation in understanding factors affecting intelligence, have them work on the Explore activity on the mypsychlab.com website, titled "Intelligence Testing."

Explore

INTELLECTUAL DISABILITY

Have students select an environmental or biological cause of developmental delay from those discussed in the textbook, and then conduct library or Internet research to learn more on the topic. Ask them to find out how and why the developmental delay occurs, if anything can be done in terms of prevention to avoid the delay, and how persons with the delay can be assisted to function in the world. Students should create a short written report, a poster, or an audiovisual presentation about what they have learned.

Module 26 Intelligence

CHAPTER 10 • Module 26

COVER THE MODULE (continued)

- **Giftedness**
  - Gifted persons are defined as those having IQ scores at the upper end of the normal curve (130 or above).
  - Psychologist Lewis Terman conducted a longitudinal study that demonstrated that gifted children grow up to be successful adults for the most part.
  - Recent studies have found that gifted children who are "pushed" too hard to achieve often grow up to be disappointed, somewhat unhappy adults.
  - Differing life conditions (such as wealth) may be a major factor in gifted adults' success, adjustment, and well-being.

EXTEND THE LESSON
Ask students if they think gifted children should be separated from their peers in our educational system. Why or why not?

CLASS DISCUSSION
Remind students that both developmentally delayed and gifted individuals are often the victims of stereotyping about their abilities. Discuss with students whether the information in this module has dispelled such labels they may have placed on these individuals.

L3 DIFFERENTIATED INSTRUCTION
Technology is one method of information delivery that appeals to a variety of students through a variety of learning styles: visual/spatial, auditory/verbal, kinesthetic/body, and logical/mathematical.

Table 26.2 Classifications of Developmental Delay

CLASSIFICATION	RANGE OF IQ SCORES	ADAPTIVE LIMITATIONS	PERCENTAGE OF DEVELOPMENTALLY DELAYED POPULATION
Mild	55–70	Can reach sixth-grade skill level. Capable with training of living independently and being self-supporting.	90 percent
Moderate	40–55	Can reach second-grade skill level. Can work and live in sheltered environments with supervision.	6 percent
Severe	25–40	Can learn to talk and perform basic self-care but needs constant supervision.	3 percent
Profound	Below 25	Very limited ability to learn, may only be able to learn very simple tasks, poor language skills, and limited self-care.	1 percent

Source: Table based on classifications in *DSM-IV-TR* (American Psychiatric Association, 2000).

> **I've heard that geniuses are sometimes a little "nutty" and odd. Is that true, or is it a myth?**

I've heard that geniuses are sometimes a little "nutty" and odd. Is that true, or is it a myth?

People have long held false beliefs about people who are extremely intelligent. Around the turn of the 20th century, people expected young geniuses to lose their genius early in life (Shurkin, 1992). Others believed that gifted people were weird and socially awkward, physically weak, and prone to mental illness. From these beliefs comes the "mad scientist" of the movies (think "Dr. Evil" of *Austin Powers*) and the "evil genius" of literature—Dr. Frankenstein, Dr. Jekyll, and so on.

These misconceptions were shattered by a groundbreaking study initiated in 1921 by Lewis M. Terman, a psychologist at Stanford University. Terman (1925) selected 1,528 children with IQs ranging from 130 to 200 to participate in a longitudinal study. The early findings (Terman & Oden, 1947) demonstrated that the gifted were socially well adjusted, often skilled leaders, above average in height, weight, and physical attractiveness, and more resistant than average to mental illness. Although some of those with the highest IQs (180 and above) were found to have some social and behavioral adjustment problems *as children* (Janos, 1987), Terman's "Termites" were also typically successful as

---

Explore

INTELLIGENCE AND MENTAL CAPACITY IN FILM
Arrange for students to view the film *Little Man Tate,* which considers the question of how best to nourish genius. Jodie Foster stars in this heart-wrenching tale of an uneducated mother, who knows she cannot provide the stimulating and enriched environment her genius son needs in order to thrive. This extremely well-done film depicts the boy's frustrating struggle to gain both the love and the academic stimulation he needs. Then ask students to write a short statement relating insights in the film to psychological principles covered in the text and classroom discussion.

adults, earning more academic degrees and, for those with access to careers outside the home, higher occupational and financial success.

Studies in recent decades have found that gifted children who are "pushed" too hard to achieve often grow up to be disappointed, somewhat unhappy adults (Freeman, 2001). Differing life conditions (such as wealth) may be a major factor in gifted adults' success, adjustment, and well-being. Yet another longitudinal study (Torrance, 1993) found that enjoyment of one's work, a sense of purpose, a high energy level, and persistence were also very important factors in success.

Learn How Intelligence Is Measured

26.4 What is the history of intelligence testing?

The history of intelligence testing spans the twentieth century and has at times been marked by controversies and misuse. This section will discuss only some of the better-known forms of testing and how they came to be.

It doesn't sound like intelligence would be easy to measure on a test—how do IQ tests work, anyway?

Measuring intelligence through testing is less than a century old. It began when French educators realized that some students needed more help with learning than others and tried to find a way to identify these students.

Binet's Mental Ability Test French psychologist Alfred Binet was asked by the French Ministry of Education to design a formal intelligence test to help identify children who were unable to learn as quickly or as well as others, so that they could be given remedial education. The test that he and colleague Théodore Simon eventually developed distinguished not only between fast and slow learners but also between children of different age groups (Binet & Simon, 1916). They noticed that the fast learners seemed to give answers to questions that older children might give, whereas the slow learners gave answers more typical of a younger child. Binet decided that the key element to test was a child's *mental age*, or the average age at which children could successfully answer a particular level of questions. ◉ Watch on mypsychlab.com

Stanford-Binet and IQ Terman (1916), a researcher at Stanford University, adopted German psychologist William Stern's method for comparing mental age and chronological age for use with the translated and revised Binet test. Stern's (1912) formula was to divide the mental age (MA) by the chronological age (CA) and multiply the result by 100. The resulting score is called an **intelligence quotient**, or **IQ**.

$$IQ = MA/CA \times 100$$

For example, a child who is 10 years old and scores a mental age of 15 (by answering the level of questions typical of a 15-year-old), would have an IQ of 150:

$$IQ = 15/10 \times 100 = 150$$

This formula allowed testers to compare the intelligence levels of people of different age groups.

One problem with Stern's simple IQ formula is that the scores start to become meaningless as the person's chronological age passes 16 years. (After all, what significant differences could there be between questions designed for a 30-

◀ It doesn't sound like intelligence would be easy to measure on a test—how do IQ tests work, anyway?

◉ Watch classic footage on mental age testing with Alfred Binet on mypsychlab.com

IQ a number representing a measure of intelligence, resulting from the division of one's mental age by one's chronological age and then multiplying that quotient by 100.

COGNITION: THINKING AND INTELLIGENCE   327

CHAPTER 10 • Module 26

COVER THE MODULE

26.4 What is the history of intelligence testing?
- The history of intelligence testing is less than a century old. It has been marked, at times, by controversies and misuse.
- **Binet's Mental Ability Test**
  - Alfred Binet's test distinguished not only between fast and slow learners, but also between children of different age groups.
  - The test emphasized a child's mental age (the average age at which children could successfully answer a particular level of questions).

MULTIMEDIA CONTENT AVAILABLE AT www.mypsychlab.com

◉ Watch classic footage on mental age testing with Alfred Binet on **mypsychlab.com**

- **Stanford-Binet and IQ**
  - This test yields an IQ (intelligence quotient) score that is determined by dividing the mental age of the person by the chronological age and multiplying that quotient by 100.
  - Later test designers replaced this formula with deviation IQ scores based on the normal curve distribution. IQ is assumed to be normally distributed with a mean IQ of 100 and a typical standard deviation of about 15.

L I N K to Chapter One: The Science of Psychology, p. 28

Explore

ONLINE IQ TESTS

Send students to the Internet website **www.majon.com/iq.html**, where they can take up to four online IQ tests. Then have them report back to the class on which test(s) they took, what types of questions were asked, whether they thought the test(s) seemed culturally fair, and why or why not. Students should not discuss their specific scores from the test(s).

CHAPTER 10 • Module 26

COVER THE MODULE

26.5 How is intelligence measured today?

- Today, the Stanford-Binet Intelligence Scales uses age-group comparison norms. Most children are given this test at around age 7 or 8.
- The Wechsler Tests yield a verbal and a performance score, as well as an overall score of intelligence.

EXTEND THE LESSON

Ask students if they think skills like art and music should be included in the definition of intelligence. Why or why not?

L3 DIFFERENTIATED INSTRUCTION

Differentiating instruction is an essential tool for adapting technology into classroom activities. Technology, such as online activities, can provide an ideal opportunity for engaging students who struggle with a text-based curriculum. It also can be used to provide additional opportunities to access content.

---

year-old versus a 40-year-old?) Later test designers replaced this formula with **deviation IQ scores** based on the normal curve distribution (Eysenck, 1994). IQ is assumed to be normally distributed with a mean IQ of 100 and a typical standard deviation of about 15, meaning that most scores vary from the mean by an average of 15 points. **LINK** to Chapter One: The Science of Psychology, p. 28. The normal curve allows IQ scores to be more accurately estimated.

26.5 How is intelligence measured today?

Today, the *Stanford-Binet Intelligence Scales,* Fifth Edition (SB5) (Roid, 2003) uses age-group comparison norms like the Wechsler tests described below. Educators often use it when placing students into special educational programs. Most children are given this test in the second grade, around age 7 or 8. See Table 26.3 for descriptions of typical items.

Table 26.3 Paraphrased Items from the Stanford-Binet Intelligence Test

AGE*	TYPE OF ITEM	DESCRIPTION OF ITEM
2	Board with three differently shaped holes	Child can place correct shape into matching hole on board.
4	Building block bridge	Child can build a simple bridge out of blocks after being shown a model.
7	Similarities	Child can answer such questions as "In what way are a ship and a car alike?"
9	Digit reversal	Child can repeat four digits backwards.
Average adult	Vocabulary	Child can define 20 words from a list.

*Age at which item typically is successfully completed.
Source: Roid, G. H. (2003).

The Wechsler Tests The Stanford-Binet test is not the only IQ test that is popular today. David Wechsler (1981, 1990, 1991) devised a series of tests for specific age groups, including an IQ test specifically for adults and tests designed specifically for older school-age children, preschool children, and children in the early grades. The Wechsler Adult Intelligence Scale (WAIS-IV), Wechsler Intelligence Scale for Children (WISC-IV), and the Wechsler Preschool and Primary Scale of Intelligence (WPPSI-III) are the three versions of this test, now used more frequently in the United States than the Stanford-Binet. These tests traditionally have a verbal and a performance scale (see examples of verbal and performance tasks in Table 26.4) as well as providing an overall score of intelligence. While still using both verbal and nonverbal items, the WISC-IV and WAIS-IV currently provide an overall score of intelligence and index scores related to verbal comprehension, perceptual reasoning, working memory, and processing speed.

deviation IQ scores a type of intelligence measure that assumes that IQ is normally distributed around a mean of 100 with a standard deviation of about 15.

Explore

CAN YOU "BECOME SMARTER"?

Tell students that research has shown that thinking about intelligence as flexible and changeable, rather than fixed and constant, can result in greater academic achievement, especially for people who belong to groups that are negatively stereotyped about their intelligence. Have students conduct library or Internet research to learn more about this topic. What kinds of practical applications could such an idea have? Ask students to create a short presentation on what they have found out.

Table 26.4 Paraphrased Sample Items from the Wechsler Adult Intelligence Scale (WAIS–III)

VERBAL SCALE

Information	What is steam made of? What is pepper? Who wrote *Tom Sawyer*?
Comprehension	Why is copper often used in electrical wire? What is the advantage of keeping money in a bank?
Arithmetic	Three women divided 18 golf balls equally among themselves. How many golf balls did each person receive? If two buttons cost $0.15, what will be the cost of a dozen buttons?
Similarities	In what way are a circle and a triangle alike? In what way are a saw and a hammer alike?
Vocabulary	What is a hippopotamus? What does "resemble" mean?

PERFORMANCE SCALE

Picture Arrangement	A story is told in three or more cartoon panels placed in the incorrect order; put them together to tell the story.
Picture Completion	Point out what's missing from each picture.
Block Design	After looking at a pattern or design, try to arrange small cubes in the same pattern.
Object Assembly	Given pieces with part of a picture on each, put them together to form objects such as a hand or a profile.
Digit Symbol	Learn a different symbol for each number and then fill in the blank under the number with the correct symbol. (This test is timed.)

Simulated items similar to those in the *Wechsler Adult Intelligence Scale*, Third Edition (1997).

26.6 How can we determine whether intelligence tests are reliable and valid?

Test Construction: Good Test, Bad Test? All tests are not equally good. Experimenters use two major criteria to evaluate tests: reliability and validity. Reliability refers to the test producing consistent results each time it is given to the same people. Validity is the degree to which a test actually measures what it's supposed to measure. **LINK** to *Chapter One: The Science of Psychology, p. 33*. A truly useful test must satisfy both criteria.

If a test fails to give the same results for the same person on different occasions, even when that person has not changed, it is unreliable and useless. If a test does not actually measure what it is supposed to measure, it is also

COGNITION: THINKING AND INTELLIGENCE 329

CHAPTER 10 • Module 26

COVER THE MODULE

26.6 How can we determine whether intelligence tests are reliable and valid?

- **Test Construction: Good Test, Bad Test?**
  - The two major criteria to evaluate tests are reliability and validity.
    - Reliability refers to the test producing consistent results each time it is given to the same people.
    - Validity is the degree to which a test actually measures what it is supposed to measure.

  LINK to *Chapter One: The Science of Psychology, p. 33*

  - Intelligence tests are useful measuring devices, but they are not necessarily measures of all types of intelligent behavior.

L2 ELL DIFFERENTIATED INSTRUCTION

English Language Learners Get students physically involved with the page, using sticky notes or small pieces of cardboard to focus and guide their reading.

Class Demonstration

LATE BLOOMERS

Explain to students that the term *late bloomer* is commonly used to refer to young children who develop skills such as language, reading, or social interaction later than others of their age. The term also can be used to describe adults who do not discover their talents and abilities until later than normally expected. Ask students to do some research into writers, celebrities, scientists, politicians, musicians, artists, athletes, business people, or others who were considered late bloomers. Have each student create a poster with information he or she learned about one such person, post it in the classroom, and give a brief presentation to fellow students. What has this information taught students about intellectual development?

Module 26 Intelligence 329

CHAPTER 10 • Module 26

COVER THE MODULE

26.7 How are intelligence tests used in the real world?

- **IQ Tests and Cultural Bias**
  - People reared in different cultures, or even a different economic situation, from that of the IQ test designer are not likely to perform well.
  - It is very difficult to design an intelligence test that is completely free of *cultural bias* (the tendency of IQ tests to reflect in language, dialect, and content, the culture of the test designers).

LINK to Chapter Eight: Culture and Gender, pp. 258–259

L4 DIFFERENTIATED INSTRUCTION

Advanced Learners Give students responsibility for part of the assessment of their learning. Allow them to plan, design, and monitor the project or assignment.

---

useless and described as "invalid" (untrue). An invalid test can still be reliable, but a test that is not reliable can never be valid. If the same person gets completely inconsistent results, then clearly the test does not accurately measure what it is supposed to measure.

Take the hypothetical example of Professor Stumpwater, who mistakenly believes that intelligence is related to a person's golf scores and develops a test on that basis. How could we evaluate his test?

First of all, we would want to look at how he tried to standardize his test. In this case, the professor would have his sample members play the same number of rounds of golf on the same course under the same weather conditions, and so on. The scores from the standardization group would be called the *norms*, the standards against which all others who take the test would be compared.

Most intelligence tests follow the normal curve described earlier, in which the scores are the most frequent around the mean, or average, and become less and less frequent the farther from the mean they occur. The professor might find that a certain golf score is the average, which he would interpret as average intelligence. People who scored extremely well or poorly on the golf test would be compared to the average.

The professor's test is not reliable. People who are good, regular golfers might score fairly consistently, but others would have widely varying scores from game to game. For those people, the test would be very unreliable, and if a test is unreliable for some, it's not a good test. More importantly, golf scores do not indicate intelligence, so the test is obviously not a valid, or true, measure of intelligence. Professor Stumpwater's test fails on both counts.

Just because an IQ test gives the same score every time a person takes it doesn't mean that the score is actually measuring real intelligence, right?

Think about the definition of intelligence for a moment: the ability to learn from one's experiences, acquire knowledge, and use resources effectively in adapting to new situations or solving problems. How can anyone define "effective use of resources"? Does everyone have access to the same resources? Is everyone's "world" the same? Intelligence tests are useful measuring devices, but they are not necessarily measures of all types of intelligent behavior, or even good measures for all groups of people.

▶ Just because an IQ test gives the same score every time a person takes it doesn't mean that the score is actually measuring real intelligence, right?

Consider Key Issues in Intelligence Research

26.7 How are intelligence tests used in the real world?

IQ Tests and Cultural Bias The problem with trying to measure intelligence with a test based on understanding the world is that not everyone comes from the same "world." People raised in a different culture, or even a different economic situation, from that of the IQ test designer are not likely to perform well. It is also difficult to take a test written in an unfamiliar language or dialect. Early immigrants to the United States who came from non-English-speaking countries would score very poorly on intelligence tests, in some cases being denied entry on that basis (Allen, 2006).

It is very difficult to design an intelligence test that is completely free of **cultural bias**, the tendency of IQ tests to reflect, in language, dialect, and content, the culture of the test designer(s). LINK to Chapter Eight: Culture

cultural bias the tendency of IQ tests to reflect, in language, dialect, and content, the culture of the test designer(s).

Critical Thinking

CULTURAL BIAS IN INTELLIGENCE TESTS

Have the class go online in order to explore cultural bias in intelligence tests. Tell them to search for and then take the Chitling Intelligence Test (formerly the Dove Counterbalance General Intelligence Test), which was designed as an intelligence test that utilizes distinctively ghetto experiences. Then assemble the class to discuss the kinds of issues or difficulties a test taker might experience when taking a typical "Western" intelligence test. Discuss why a Western intelligence test might not be a fair determination of a person's intelligence.

and Gender, pp. 258–259. Someone from the same culture or socioeconomic background may have an unfair advantage over someone who is not (Helms, 1992). People raised in a non-Western culture who are given a test designed within a Western culture might find that many test items make no sense. For example, one question might be: "Which of these five is least like the other four?"

DOG - CAR - CAT - BIRD - FISH

The answer is supposed to be "car," the only one that is not alive. But a child from Japan, an island nation that relies on the sea for much of its food and culture, might choose "fish," because none of the others are found in the ocean. That child's test score would be lower, but not because the child is not intelligent.

In short, intelligence tests are created by people from a particular culture and background. Test creators might mistakenly think that content based on their own experiences is common knowledge, but that is not necessarily the case for everyone.

People have attempted to create intelligence tests that are as free of cultural influences as possible, but many test designers have concluded that creating a completely bias-free test may be impossible (Carpenter et al., 1990). Instead, they are striving to create tests that are at least *culturally fair*, using questions that do not create a disadvantage for people whose culture differs from that of the majority. Many items on these tests require the use of nonverbal abilities, such as rotating objects, rather than items about verbal knowledge that might be culturally specific.

If intelligence tests are so flawed, why do people still use them?
The one thing that IQ tests do well is predict academic success for those who score at the higher and lower ends of the normal curve. (For those who score in the average range of IQ, the predictive value is less clear.) Because IQ tests are often similar to the kinds of tests students take in school, people who do well on IQ tests typically do well on other kinds of academically oriented tests, such as the Scholastic Assessment Test (SAT), the American College Test (ACT), the Graduate Record Exam (GRE), and actual college examinations.

◀ If intelligence tests are so flawed, why do people still use them?

26.8 How do heredity and environment influence intelligence?

Are people born with all of the "smarts" they will ever have, or does experience and learning count for something in the development of intellect? The influence of nature (heredity or genes) and nurture (environment) on personality traits, including intelligence, has long been debated in the field of human development. **LINK** *to Chapter Five: Development Across the Life Span, pp. 142–146*.

Twin Studies The problem with trying to separate the role of genes from that of environment is that controlled, perfect experiments are neither practical nor ethical. Instead, researchers find out what they can from *natural experiments*, the study of circumstances existing in nature, including *twin studies*.

Because identical twins originally come from one fertilized egg, they share the same genetic inheritance, and so any differences on a certain trait should be caused by environmental factors. Fraternal twins come from two different eggs, each fertilized by a different sperm, and share the same amount of genetic

COGNITION: THINKING AND INTELLIGENCE 331

CHAPTER 10 • Module 26

COVER THE MODULE *(continued)*

- Many test designers have concluded that creating a completely bias-free test may be impossible.
- Instead, they are striving to create tests that are at least culturally fair.
- The one thing that IQ tests do well is predict academic success for those who score at the higher and lower ends of the normal curve. Because IQ tests are similar to the kinds of tests students take in school, people who do well on IQ tests typically do well on other kinds of academically oriented tests.

COVER THE MODULE

26.8 How do heredity and environment influence intelligence?

- The influence of nature (heredity or genes) and nurture (environment) on personality traits, including intelligence, has long been debated.

LINK to Chapter Five: Development Across the Life Span, pp. 142–146

L1 DIFFERENTIATED INSTRUCTION

Special Needs Provide structure and support by clearly explaining responsibilities, assignments, and classroom rules.

Class Demonstration

CREATING A CULTURALLY FAIR INTELLIGENCE TEST

Divide students into small groups. Instruct each group to come to a consensus about the kinds of questions that should be on a culturally fair intelligence test. After the groups have finished, ask each to report on its conclusions. Engage the entire class in discussions of each proposal, carefully examining how culture or specific experiences (e.g., education) might influence the results.

CHAPTER 10 • Module 26

COVER THE MODULE (continued)

- **Twin Studies**
  - By comparing the IQs of identical twins and fraternal twins reared together (similar environment) or apart (different environments), as well as persons of other degrees of relatedness, researchers can get a general idea of how much heredity influences intelligence.
  - The greater the degree of genetic relatedness between two people, the stronger the correlation is between their IQ scores.
  - Researchers have determined that the estimated heritability for intelligence (the proportion of change caused by hereditary factors) is about 0.50 or 50 percent.
  - Estimates of heritability apply only to changes in IQ within a group of people, not to the individual people themselves.
  - Only differences among people in general can be investigated for genetic influences.

CHECK FOR UNDERSTANDING

If students struggle with the information in this section on nature and nurture, direct them to the www.mypsychlab.com website to the Explore activity on correlations between IQ scores of persons of varying relationships.

FIGURE 26.2 Correlations Between IQ Scores of Persons with Various Relationships

In the graph on the left, the degree of genetic relatedness seems to determine the agreement (correlation) between IQ scores of the various comparisons. For example, identical twins, who share 100 percent of their genes, are more similar in IQ than fraternal twins, who share 50 percent of their genes, when raised in the same environment. In the graph on the right, identical twins are still more similar to each other in IQ than are other types of comparisons, but being raised in the same environment increases the similarity considerably.

material as any two siblings. **LINK** to *Chapter Five: Development Across the Life Span, p. 147*. By comparing the IQs of these two types of twins reared together (similar environments) or apart (different environments), as well as persons of other degrees of relatedness, researchers can get a general idea of how much heredity influences intelligence (see Figure 26.2).

The greater the degree of genetic relatedness between two people, the stronger the correlation is between their IQ scores. The correlation of 0.86 for identical twins shows that the environment must play a part in determining intelligence (as measured by IQ tests). If heredity alone were responsible, the correlation should be 1.00. Researchers have determined that the estimated *heritability* for intelligence—the proportion of change caused by hereditary factors—is about 0.50 or 50 percent (Plomin & DeFries, 1998).

Wait a minute—if identical twins have a correlation of 0.86, wouldn't that mean that intelligence is 86 percent inherited?

Although the correlation between identical twins is higher than 0.50, that is not entirely due to genetic similarity, because twins who are raised in the same household also share very similar environments. Even twins who are reared apart are usually placed in homes that are similar in socioeconomic and ethnic background.

Estimates of heritability apply only to changes in IQ within a *group* of people, *not to the individual people themselves*. Each individual is far too different in terms of experience, education, and other nongenetic factors to predict exactly how his or her genes will interact with environmental factors. Only differences among people *in general* can be investigated for genetic influences

▶ Wait a minute—if identical twins have a correlation of 0.86, wouldn't that mean that intelligence is 86 percent inherited?

Critical Thinking

CONTROVERSIES IN INTELLIGENCE

<u>Purpose</u>: Students have a chance to think about, debate, and discuss controversial topics in intelligence.

<u>Time</u>: 15 minutes

<u>Description</u>: Pose the following issue to the class: "Intelligence is primarily genetic." Give students 15 minutes to write down whether they agree or disagree, and why. Then ask students to share their answers and contribute to further class discussion. Or, conduct a class debate on this topic.

(Dickens & Flynn, 2001). Genes always interact with environmental factors, and in some cases, extreme environments can modify even very heritable traits. For instance, height is highly heritable—in a group of people who take in roughly equal nourishment, most differences in height are caused by genetic differences. However, environment can still influence this trait, as would happen if a child were severely malnourished.

The Bell Curve and Misinterpretation of Statistics Researchers have also examined whether differences in test performance could be caused by heritable racial differences. (Keep in mind that the concept of *race* is used to group people with common skin colors or facial features, and one should always question that kind of classification. Cultural background, educational experiences, and socioeconomic factors typically have far more to do with similarities in group performances.) In 1994, Herrnstein and Murray published the controversial book *The Bell Curve*, in which they cite statistical studies (never previously published in scientific journals) that led them to claim that IQ is largely inherited. These authors also imply that people from lower economic levels are poor because they are unintelligent.

Herrnstein and Murray made several statistical errors and ignored the effects of environment and culture. First, they assumed that IQ tests are a completely accurate measure of intelligence, but as discussed earlier, IQ tests are not free of bias. So all they really found was a correlation between race and *IQ score*, not intelligence. Second, they assumed that intelligence itself has a heritability factor of about 0.80. The current estimate of the heritability of intelligence is about 0.50 (Plomin & DeFries, 1998). Finally, Herrnstein and Murray failed to understand that heritability only applies to differences *within* a group of people as opposed to those *between* groups of people or individuals (Gould, 1981). Heritability estimates can only be made from a group that was exposed to a similar environment.

These errors call Herrnstein and Murray's research into question. For instance, they found that Japanese Americans are at the top of the IQ ladder, a finding they attribute to racial and genetic characteristics. They seem to ignore the cultural influence of Japanese American parents' intense focus on education and achievement (Neisser et al., 1996). Scientists (Beardsley, 1995; Kamin, 1995) have concluded that there is no real scientific evidence for genetic differences in intelligence *between* different racial groups. A series of studies, using blood-group testing for racial grouping, found no significant relationship between ethnicity and IQ (Neisser et al., 1996).

CHAPTER 10 • Module 26

COVER THE MODULE *(continued)*

- **The Bell Curve and Misinterpretation of Statistics**
  - Herrnstein and Murray claimed that IQ is largely inherited and implied that people from lower economic levels are poor because they are unintelligent.
  - The researchers made several statistical errors and ignored the effects of environment and culture.
  - They assumed that IQ tests are a completely accurate measure of intelligence; however, IQ tests are not free of bias.
  - They also assumed that intelligence itself has a heritability factor of about 0.80; however, the current estimate of the heritability of intelligence is about 0.50.
  - Finally, they failed to understand that heritability applies only to differences within a group of people, as opposed to those between groups of people or individuals.
  - Scientists have concluded that there is no real scientific evidence for genetic differences in intelligence between different racial groups.

L2 LPR DIFFERENTIATED INSTRUCTION

Less Proficient Readers For students with difficulties with attention and memory, emphasize connections between new and known information. Engage students in collaborative "read/reflect/discuss/note" cycles, filling out a graphic organizer, for example.

Class Discussion

THE BELL CURVE

After you have covered Herrnstein and Murray's research on "the bell curve," conduct a class discussion about what students see, as the controversial issues inherent in the ideas that IQ is largely inherited and that people from lower economic levels are poor because they are unintelligent. What effects might these ideas have on the people involved?

CHAPTER 10 • Module 26

Assess

Assign the Module 26 Practice Quiz.

Use the Practice Quiz to identify gaps in student understanding.

REMEDIATE

Have students, individually or in groups, review the module goals, learning objectives, and key terms.

Refer students to the Concept Summary on p. 339 for review.

Close

As a class, revisit the definitions of intelligence that students provided in the Bellringer activity at the beginning of this module. Have students changed their ideas about what the term *intelligence* means?

Practice Quiz

Pick the best answer.

1. According to Spearman, what would a traditional IQ test most likely measure?
   a. general intelligence
   b. emotional intelligence
   c. specific intelligence
   d. practical intelligence

2. In Gardner's view, astronauts, navigators, and artists would have high levels of which type of intelligence?
   a. naturalist
   b. visual/spatial
   c. interpersonal
   d. kinesthetic

3. What does it mean for an IQ test to be culturally fair?
   a. The test is completely free of cultural bias.
   b. The test does not put people from minority cultures at a disadvantage.
   c. The test assesses how a subject would perform in a different culture.
   d. The test is created by a member of the subjects' own culture.

4. Darla is 4 years old. The intelligence test that would most likely be used to measure her intelligence is the
   a. Binet's Mental Ability Test
   b. Wechsler Intelligence Scale for Children
   c. Wechsler Adult Intelligence Scale
   d. Dove Counterbalance General Intelligence Test

5. Mr. Beckett designed an IQ test. He hopes to use it in high schools throughout the county. Which of the following would be a problem for him if he wanted to standardize the test?
   a. He always administers the test in the same conditions.
   b. He can only give the test to his class of 10 students.
   c. He asks similar questions on the test every time.
   d. He finds that people tend to get similar scores each time they take the test.

6. Jared is 35 years old, but his cognitive abilities have never gone beyond the level of a second-grade child. At what level of developmental delay would Jared be classified?
   a. mild
   b. moderate
   c. severe
   d. profound

7. A male with a defective chromosome leading to severe protein deficiency and poor brain development probably suffers from
   a. Down syndrome
   b. fetal alcohol syndrome
   c. hydrocephaly
   d. fragile X syndrome

8. Elizabeth was tested while in grade school and was found to have an IQ of 134. Elizabeth's intelligence level can be labeled as
   a. average
   b. slightly above average
   c. gifted
   d. genius

9. Current estimates place the heritability of IQ at about
   a. 30 percent
   b. 50 percent
   c. 70 percent
   d. 90 percent

10. According to Sternberg, a person who has "street smarts" and can easily manage situations has what kind of intelligence?
    a. intrapersonal
    b. analytical
    c. creative
    d. practical

334 CHAPTER 10

Practice Quiz Answers

1. a
2. b
3. b
4. b
5. b
6. b
7. d
8. c
9. b
10. d

Chapter 10 Cognition: Thinking and Intelligence

CHAPTER 10 Summary

Listen on mypsychlab.com
Listen to an audio file of your chapter on **mypsychlab.com**

Module 25: Thinking

Understand the basic elements of thought.

25.1 How are mental images and concepts involved in the process of thinking?
- Mental images represent objects or events and have a picture-like quality, while concepts represent a class or category of events, objects, or activities.

25.2 What methods do people use to solve problems and make decisions?
- Mechanical solutions include trial-and-error learning and rote solutions, including algorithms, in which one follows step-by-step procedures.
- A heuristic or "rule of thumb" is a strategy that narrows down the possible solutions for a problem. Insight is the sudden perception of a solution.

25.3 Can a machine be made to think like a person?
- Although some computers can perform in similar ways, the true flexibility of human thought processes has yet to be developed in a machine.

Identify obstacles to thought.

25.4 What are some obstacles to problem solving?
- Obstacles include functional fixedness, mental sets, and confirmation bias.

25.5 What are some obstacles to making good judgments?
- Obstacles include the representative heuristic, the availability heuristic, and the anchoring effect.

25.6 What are some obstacles to decision making?
- Obstacles include our tendency to try to see patterns, the gambler's fallacy, and loss aversion.

Module 26: Intelligence

Compare and contrast perspectives on intelligence.

26.1 How do psychologists define intelligence?
- Intelligence is the ability to understand the world, think rationally or logically, and use resources effectively when faced with challenges or problems.

26.2 Are there other theories of intelligence?
- Spearman proposed general intelligence, or g factor, as the ability to reason and solve problems, whereas specific intelligence, or s factor, is task-specific.
- Gardner proposed nine different types of intelligence.
- Sternberg proposed three types of intelligence: analytical, creative, and practical.

26.3 What are intellectual disability and giftedness?
- Intellectual disability or developmental delay is a condition in which IQ is below 70 and adaptive behavior is severely deficient for a person of a particular age.
- Gifted persons have IQ scores at the upper end of the normal curve (130+).

Learn how intelligence is measured.

26.4 What is the history of intelligence testing?
- Intelligence testing developed in the early twentieth century and initially involved by dividing mental age by chronological age to determine IQ. In recent decades, psychologists have recognized the effects of cultural bias in intelligence testing.

26.5 How is intelligence measured today?
- Measuring IQ using the Stanford-Binet Intelligence Test now involves comparing a person's score to a standardized norm. The Wechsler Intelligence Tests are designed for specific age groups.

26.6 How can we determine whether intelligence tests are reliable and valid?
- Reliability is the tendency of a test to produce the same scores again and again each time it is given to the same people. Validity is the degree to which a test measures what it's supposed to measure.

Consider key issues in intelligence research.

26.7 How are intelligence tests used in the real world?
- Intelligence tests are useful for predicting academic success and success on other types of standardized tests.

26.8 How do heredity and environment influence intelligence?
- Stronger correlations are found between IQ scores as genetic relatedness increases. Heritability of IQ is estimated at 0.50. Environmental factors (such as cultural values) also influence intelligence test scores.

Vocabulary Terms

thinking (cognition) p. 306
mental images p. 306
concepts p. 307
superordinate concept p. 308
basic level type p. 308
subordinate concept p. 308
formal concept p. 308
natural concept p. 309
prototype p. 309
problem solving p. 311
trial and error (mechanical solution) p. 311
algorithm p. 311
heuristic p. 311
representativeness heuristic p. 311
subgoaling p. 312
means-end analysis p. 312
artificial intelligence (AI) p. 313
functional fixedness p. 314
mental set p. 314
confirmation bias p. 314
creativity p. 315
convergent thinking p. 315
divergent thinking p. 315
conjunction fallacy p. 317
availability heuristic p. 317
anchoring effect p. 317
gambler's fallacy p. 318
loss aversion p. 318
intelligence p. 321
g factor p. 321
s factor p. 321
triarchic theory of intelligence p. 322
analytical intelligence p. 322
creative intelligence p. 322
practical intelligence p. 322
emotional intelligence p. 322
standardization p. 323
mean p. 323
standard deviation p. 324
developmentally delayed p. 324
gifted p. 325
IQ p. 327
deviation IQ scores p. 328
cultural bias p. 328

COGNITION: THINKING AND INTELLIGENCE 335

CHAPTER 10 • Summary and Vocabulary

Chapter Summary

Encourage students to carefully review and study the summary. Explain that it provides an overview of key concepts presented in the text.

Have students identify what they find unclear or confusing. Call on volunteers to provide answers, examples, or definitions.

Vocabulary Terms

Remind students that terms are defined within the chapter at point of use. If they are not sure of a term's definition, they should look up the definition on the page.

Encourage students to create study cards of unfamiliar words or to go to www.mypsychlab.com for flashcards. Have them test themselves or a classmate. Advanced students can explain the terms in their own words.

Critical Thinking

MAKING CONNECTIONS

Have students connect the information they have learned in this chapter. Write on the board: "We need to go beyond traditional measures of intelligence and look at how people learn to get along with others. There is value in learning 'people skills' early in life, so that we can use these skills throughout our lives." Ask students to write a personal statement, agreeing or disagreeing with this idea. They should be sure to provide support for their opinion.

CHAPTER 10 • Assessment

VOCABULARY REVIEW

1. d
2. c
3. i
4. j
5. g
6. f
7. h
8. e
9. b
10. a

WRITING ABOUT PSYCHOLOGY

1. Students' answers should include two of the following strategies to solve problems and make decisions: trial and error (obstacle: may take too long); algorithms (obstacle: could be a very lengthy process); heuristics (will not always lead to the correct solution); and insight (obstacle: may not actually come to mind).

2. Sternberg's Triarchic Theory: analytical, creative, and practical intelligence. Gardner's Multiple Intelligences: verbal/linguistic, musical, logical/mathematical, visual/spatial, movement, interpersonal, intrapersonal, naturalist, and existentialist.

PSYCHOLOGY PROJECT

Remind students that cultural biases can exist even when people belong to different subgroups within a larger cultural group. Therefore, even if most of the students in the class have somewhat similar backgrounds, there still may be cultural differences in the way they evaluate the online intelligence tests they review.

CHAPTER 10 Assessment

Study and Review on mypsychlab.com

Vocabulary Review

Match each vocabulary term to its definition.

1. validity
2. mental set
3. anchoring effect
4. analytical intelligence
5. algorithm
6. availability heuristic
7. cultural bias
8. convergent thinking
9. emotional intelligence
10. prototype

a. An example of a concept that closely matches the defining characteristics of a concept.
b. The awareness of and ability to manage one's own emotions as well as the ability to be self-motivated, empathetic, and socially skilled.
c. The tendency for people to persist in using problem-solving patterns that have worked for them in the past.
d. The degree to which a test actually measures what it's supposed to measure.
e. Type of thinking in which a problem is seen as having only one answer, and all lines of thinking will eventually lead to that single answer, using previous knowledge and logic.
f. The tendency to estimate the probability of a certain condition or event based on how many similar instances we can recall.
g. A very specific, step-by-step procedure for solving a certain type of problem.
h. The tendency of IQ tests to reflect, in language, dialect, and content, the culture of the test designer(s).
i. The tendency to consider all of the information available, even when it is irrelevant
j. The ability to break problems down into component parts, or analysis, for problem solving.

Writing about Psychology

Respond to each question in complete sentences.

1. What are two strategies people use to solve problems and make decisions, and what is one obstacle that can interfere with the process? Name and define the strategies and the obstacle, and explain how each one could be involved in a real-life problem or decision.

2. Both Sternberg and Gardner proposed that there is more than one kind of intelligence. Sum up the kinds of intelligence described by EITHER the triarchic intelligence theory OR the multiple intelligences theory. Then briefly explain why "intelligence" is not necessarily limited to academic or "book" smarts.

Psychology Project

How do cultural biases affect the way we assess intelligence? Complete this project to examine how intelligence tests may be culturally biased.

Materials:
- a partner
- a computer with an Internet connection
- a pencil and paper

Instructions:

1. With your partner, use an Internet search engine to locate 1–2 intelligence or IQ tests online. You do not need to use the tests named in this chapter, but do find tests that are substantial enough so that you are looking at least 20 test questions total. You might try the Web site of Mensa International or use other online intelligence tests.

2. Working separately, read through the test(s). Note any test items that could be considered to have a bias that might cause a person from another culture, or from a subculture within the United States, to miss the item even if he or she spoke reasonably fluent English.

   For example, one online test asks people to determine what words the letters stand for in this sentence:

   32 is the T in D F at which W F

   A person raised in the United States, where temperature is commonly measured in degrees Fahrenheit, will probably find the answer fairly easily: 32 is the temperature in degrees Fahrenheit at which water freezes. Someone from a country where temperature is usually measured in degrees Celsius might have a harder time.

3. In evaluating test items, keep in mind that cultural biases can exist even when people are from the same large cultural group but belong to different subgroups. Consider the possible effect of socioeconomic status, geographical location, and so forth.

4. Mark any items that you think are culturally biased and jot down why. Then compare notes with your partner. Did you flag the same items? Why or why not?

Internet Resources

Assessment: http://ericae.net/intbod.htm

Offers definitions, descriptions, resources, and other detailed information about a wide range of assessment measures. Use this site as a starting point for a classroom presentation, demonstrating the different ways to assess mental functioning.

IQ Tests Online: www.2h.com/Tests/iq.phtml

Various online IQ tests. Good for stimulating critical thinking regarding validity of online tests.

Mensa International: www.mensa.org

Organization for high–IQ-scoring individuals. See how the top 2 percent spend their time in this organization.

Multiple Intelligences: http://tip.psychology.org/gardner.html

Overview of Gardner's theory of multiple intelligences.

Test Yourself

Pick the best answer.

1. Algorithms are a type of
   a. heuristic
   b. mental set
   c. rule of thumb
   d. mechanical solution

2. Which heuristic can be used to create and maintain stereotypes?
   a. representative
   b. availability
   c. means-end analysis
   d. convergent thinking

3. Kara needs to jot down a phone number. She searches her purse for a pen, but cannot locate one. However, she does find an eyeliner pencil and uses that instead. What mental limitation has Kara just overcome?
   a. confirmation bias
   b. the anchoring effect
   c. the availability heuristic
   d. functional fixedness

4. Which of the following questions would be most likely to produce divergent thinking?
   a. What is a stapler?
   b. How many different uses can you think of for a stapler?
   c. In what year was the first stapler invented?
   d. What does a typical stapler look like?

5. In Sternberg's view, someone who can easily grasp new concepts and can find unusual solutions for a problem possesses _____ intelligence.
   a. emotional
   b. analytical
   c. creative
   d. naturalist

6. Which of the following makes the Wechsler tests different from the Stanford-Binet?
   a. The Stanford-Binet is designed only for adults.
   b. The Weschler tests have both a verbal and a performance component.
   c. The Stanford-Binet is administered to individuals.
   d. The Wechsler tests are designed only for children.

7. Don's employer requires that all new employees take a popular test that will reveal them to be one of five basic personality types. Don objects, saying that he has taken the same test several times for other jobs and comes up as a different type each time. Don is objecting to the test's lack of
   a. bias
   b. reliability
   c. standard deviation
   d. normal distribution

8. Kim is a 33-year-old with an IQ of 50. Her cognitive abilities are about equal to those of a typical 8-year-old. Kim's developmental delay is
   a. mild
   b. moderate
   c. severe
   d. profound

9. In the following list, which concept is a superordinate concept?
   a. mammal
   b. animal
   c. cocker spaniel
   d. dog

10. Which of the following is an important difference between Deep Blue and Deep Junior?
    a. Deep Blue lost to Garry Kasparov at chess, and Deep Junior beat Garry Kasparov.
    b. Deep Blue was programmed to use heuristics, and Deep Junior was programmed to use algorithms.
    c. Deep Blue was capable of human thought, and Deep Junior was not capable of human thought.
    d. Deep Blue used artificial intelligence, and Deep Junior did not use artificial intelligence.

11. Jane grew up in a traditional religious community in an isolated rural area of the United States, with very little exposure to mass media and popular culture. Because of this, she does not know the common slang meanings of words like "cool" and "awesome." What problem might Jane encounter if she took an intelligence test?
    a. the conjunction fallacy
    b. cultural bias
    c. lack of reliability
    d. lack of standardization

12. Spearman called the ability to reason and solve problems
    a. s factor
    b. g factor
    c. practical intelligence
    d. creative intelligence

13. What do IQ tests predict most effectively?
    a. emotional intelligence
    b. academic success
    c. practical intelligence
    d. success in business.

14. Which of the following was a significant flaw in intelligence testing in the early 20th century?
    a. Early test designers made no attempt to standardize their tests.
    b. The formula for IQ is not meaningful when applied to adults.
    c. Most children did not get consistent scores each time they took the test.
    d. Early IQ tests were so culturally biased that they were invalid for most subjects.

15. Which of the following statements is true?
    a. A test that is reliable is always valid.
    b. A test can be valid but unreliable.
    c. A test that is not valid is always unreliable.
    d. A test that is not reliable is always invalid.

16. Psychologist Timothy Wilson (1993) had college students choose their favorite one of five posters to take home. One group of subjects just had to choose, while the other had to answer questions to explain their preference before making their decision. Later, the subjects who had had to explain their choice were less satisfied. What principle does this study illustrate?
    a. People will make different decisions if a situation is presented in a way that emphasizes potential losses.
    b. The brain often misleads us is in trying to impose a pattern on events, even when none exists.
    c. It is best just to go with your "gut feeling" when you are making a trivial, subjective decision.
    d. If people perceive themselves as having already suffered a loss, they will often take greater risks to try to recover the loss.

CHAPTER 10 • Assessment

TEST YOURSELF

1. d
2. a
3. d
4. b
5. c
6. b
7. b
8. b
9. b
10. b
11. b
12. b
13. b
14. b
15. d
16. a

Ready for Testing

STUDENTS KNOW THEY ARE READY FOR TESTING IF THEY ARE ABLE TO . . .

- Introduce the concept of cognition, as it relates to mental images, concepts, and problem solving.
- Describe artificial intelligence and creative thinking.
- Discuss the measurement of intelligence, including the Stanford-Binet and Wechsler intelligence tests, test construction issues, and the determination of intellectual disability.
- Describe several prominent theories of intelligence, including the concepts of giftedness, developmental delay, heredity, and environment.

CHAPTER 10 • Concept Summary

MULTIMEDIA CONTENT AVAILABLE AT
www.mypsychlab.com

Map the Concepts on **mypsychlab.com**

Study and Review Flashcards on **mypsychlab.com**

STUDY TIPS

Making Audio Study Guides For auditory learners, there is no better way to review and absorb information than an audio study guide. In fact, most types of learners can benefit from listening to information while they are performing other tasks. Even if students are not actively paying attention to the content, they will still retain some of it. Students can make their own audio study guide by using a computer, a CD burner or an MP3 player, and audio software. Students can record their own voices by reading summaries of text information or lectures, asking questions and then providing the answers, reciting terms or key dates followed by their definitions or meanings, and more. The audio files can be listened to while traveling to school, waiting in line, exercising, or during any downtime.

CHAPTER 10 Concept Summary: Cognition

Learning Objectives
25.1 25.2 25.3 pp. 306–313

Understand the Basic Elements of Thought

- **thinking (cognition)** is mental activity that goes on in the brain when a person is organizing and attempting to understand information and communicating information
- **mental images** are picture-like mental representations that stand in for objects or events
- **concepts** are ideas that represent a class or category of objects, events, or activities

Prototypical → Atypical: Orange, Apple, Peach, Strawberry, Watermelon, Date, Tomato, Olive

- **problem solving**
  - a **mechanical solution** relies on trial and error and may involve solving by rote, or a learned set of rules
  - a **heuristic** is a simple "rule of thumb" that is intended to apply to many situations
  - **insight** is an instance when the solution to a problem seems to come to mind suddenly
- **artificial intelligence** although machines can mimic some human thought processes, no machine can think exactly like a human

Learning Objectives
25.4 25.5 25.6 pp. 314–319

Identify Obstacles to Thought

- **obstacles to problem solving**
  - functional fixedness
  - mental set
  - confirmation bias
- **obstacles to making good judgments**
  - the representative heuristic
  - the availability heuristic
  - the anchoring effect
- **obstacles to decision making**
  - the tendency to look for patterns even when none exist
  - the gambler's fallacy
  - loss aversion

338 CHAPTER 10

What Every Student Should Know About . . .

PREPARING EFFECTIVE ORAL PRESENTATIONS

Explain to students that when they write a speech, they should write the words as though they were naturally speaking aloud to other people. An oral presentation should come across as effortless to the speaker. The more conversational the tone and language of the speech, the easier it will be for the audience to follow the speaker. There is little room in a speech for complicated sentence structure. Technical terms and complex ideas must be presented and then explained in such a way that listeners can keep pace. By writing as though they were speaking to a friend, students can create an oral presentation that sounds more natural and can be better understood by its listeners.

Thinking and Intelligence

Map The Concepts on mypsychlab.com

Learning Objectives
26.1 26.2 26.3 pp. 321–327

Compare and Contrast Perspectives on Intelligence

- **intelligence** is the ability to learn from one's experiences, acquire knowledge, and use resources effectively in adapting to new situations or solving problems
- **Spearman (1904): g factor** refers to general intelligence, **s factor** refers to task-specific intelligence in a general area
- **Gardner (1990s)** proposed a theory of **multiple intelligences**
- **Sternberg's triarchic theory (1980s)** analytical intelligence, creative intelligence, and practical intelligence
- **intellectual disability or developmental delay** is a condition in which a person's behavioral and cognitive skills exist at an earlier developmental stage than the skills of others who are the same chronological age
- **gifted** is a term used to describe the 2 percent of the population falling on the upper end of the normal curve and typically possessing an IQ of 130 or above

Learning Objectives
26.4 26.5 26.6 pp. 327–330

Learn How Intelligence Is Measured

- **intelligence testing**
  - **Stanford-Binet Intelligence Scales:** IQ was originally determined by dividing mental age by chronological age and multiplying by 100
  - the **Wechsler Intelligence Tests,** designed for specific age groups, use scores derived from both verbal and nonverbal subtests to determine an overall score
  - a good test must be both **reliable** and **valid**

Learning Objectives
26.7 26.8 pp. 330–333

Consider Key Issues in Intelligence Research

- **cultural bias** is the tendency of IQ tests to reflect, in language, dialect, and content, the culture of the test designer(s)
- **heredity** and **environment** can both affect intelligence

COGNITION: THINKING AND INTELLIGENCE 339

CHAPTER 10 • Concept Summary

STUDY TIPS

Cornell Notes The Cornell note-taking strategy involves several distinct and easy steps. First, students should divide a piece of paper into three sections, with horizontal lines near the top and bottom of the page, and a vertical line running from the top horizontal line to the bottom horizontal line that divides the main body of the papers into a narrow and a wide column. Students should write the topic and the date at the top of the paper. Next, they should use the "5 Rs": record, reduce, recite, reflect, and review. **Record:** Have students use the wide column for taking notes as they read the chapter, using abbreviations and shorthand whenever possible. **Reduce:** Have students identify main ideas, key points, dates, people, and vocabulary in their notes and write them in the narrow column. They will use them to write a summary of the main points in the bottom section of the paper. **Recite:** Direct students to study their notes. Cover up the wide column and respond to the key points listed in the narrow column and the summary. **Reflect:** Are there any parts of their notes that students do not understand? **Review:** Suggest that students spend 10 minutes per week reviewing their notes.

Comprehension Check

KINDS OF INTELLIGENCE

Remind students that in this chapter, they studied several kinds of intelligence, including analytical intelligence, creative intelligence, practical intelligence, and emotional intelligence. Which type of intelligence do students think will be most important to them as they mature and move ahead into careers and their adult lives? What reasons can they provide to support their choice?

CHAPTER 11 • Module 27

Launch the Chapter

CHAPTER GOALS AND LEARNING OBJECTIVES

Module 27 Motivation

Explain the major theories of motivation.

27.1 What are the major cognitive and biological theories of motivation?

27.2 What is the humanist theory of motivation?

Describe motivated behaviors.

27.3 What factors motivate eating?

27.4 What factors motivate sexual behavior and orientation?

27.5 What factors motivate achievement?

27.6 Are there other ways in which humans and animals are motivated?

Module 28 Emotion

Understand theories of emotion and emotional expression.

28.1 What are the biological, behavioral, and cognitive components of emotion?

28.2 What are the major theories of emotion?

28.3 How do cultural and environmental factors influence emotional expression?

Analyze emotional behaviors in depth.

28.4 What biological and environmental factors influence the expression and experience of fear?

28.5 What biological and environmental factors influence the expression and experience of happiness?

DIFFERENTIATED INSTRUCTION KEY

Look for these symbols to help you adjust steps in each lesson to meet your students' needs.

- **L1** Special Needs
- **L2** Basic
  - **ELL** English Language Learners
  - **LPR** Less Proficient Readers
- **L3** All Students
- **L4** Advanced Students

CHAPTER 11
Motivation and Emotion

Walking Tall

Debi R. was a relatively healthy woman in her early 50s whose back began to bother her. Her doctor recommended surgery to relieve two bad disks in her back that had begun to slip out of place, causing the pain.

After the surgery, the pain was still there. The surgeon operated again the next day, saying that another disk had ruptured. When Debi began to recover, she found that she could not move her legs or feel her feet—she was partially paralyzed. Several months later, the truth was revealed. The doctor had operated on the wrong side of her disks the first time and then made matters worse by operating again while her tissues were still swollen. Debi was told that she might never walk again.

That was over a year ago. Today Debi still has pain and numbness in her feet but can walk with only a cane to aid her balance—she is no longer confined to a wheelchair. How did she do it? She refused to accept the doctors' predictions and worked extremely hard to achieve the goal of walking again. She did everything the therapists told her to do, and when the therapy stopped, she continued on her own. She is finally at the point where she can walk for short distances with no help at all.

Debi was able to overcome her disability because she was highly *motivated* to do so. She also overcame her fears about not being able to walk and manages her feelings about the pain and the unfairness of what happened so that her attitude remains sunny and joyful. Each day brings a new hope that more progress will be made. Debi isn't even close to giving up.

CORRELATION TO APA STANDARDS FOR CHAPTER 11

VIA. MOTIVATION
VIA-1. Perspective on motivation . . . . pp. 342–348
VIA-2. Domains of motivated behavior in humans . . . . . . pp. 349–356
     and non-human

VIB. EMOTION
VIB-1. Perspectives on emotion . . . . pp. 358–363
VIB-2. Emotional expression. . . . . pp. 358–359, 363–364
VIB-3. Domains of emotional behavior . . . . pp. 364–367

MODULE 27 ▸ MOTIVATION

MODULE 28 ▸ EMOTION

Why Study?

Motivation and Emotion

The study of motivation not only helps us understand why we eat and drink the way we do, but also why some people are more driven to achieve than others. Emotions are a part of everything we do, affecting our relationships with others and our own health, as well as influencing important decisions. In this chapter, we will explore the motives behind our actions and the origins and influences of emotions.

MOTIVATION AND EMOTION 341

SCHEDULING				
1 Period = 50 min. 1 Block = 90 min.	Semester Course (18 weeks/90 days) Periods/Blocks		Full-Year Course (36 weeks/180 days) Period/Blocks	
Module 27	2.5	1.25	5	2.5
Module 28	2.5	1.25	5	2.5
Total Days for Chapter	5	2.5	10	5

CHAPTER 11 • Module 27

Teacher Prep

Motivation is the process by which activities are started, directed, and continued so that physical or psychological needs or wants are met. When motivation comes from outside the self, it is called extrinsic motivation; if a person does something because it is satisfying in some internal manner, the motivation is called intrinsic motivation. Several theories have been proposed to explain the process of motivation, including the theories of instinct, drive reduction, needs, arousal, incentive, humanistic, and self-determination.

Abraham Maslow was a major proponent of the humanistic approach to motivation and proposed a hierarchy of needs that individuals must fulfill before they can reach the highest need of self-actualization, where a person reaches his or her fullest potential.

One specific area of motivation that has been studied extensively is the motivation to eat, or hunger. The hunger drive can be divided into physiological and social components. Some problems associated with eating behaviors are obesity, anorexia nervosa, and bulimia.

Emotions can be defined as the "feeling" aspect of consciousness, characterized by a certain physical arousal, a certain behavior, and an inner awareness of feelings. Emotions can be divided into three components: physiology, behaviors, and subjective experience.

The positive psychology movement is a new perspective in psychology that recommends shifting the focus of psychology away from the negative and toward the positive.

CHAPTER 11 • Module 27

Focus

RESOURCES
For this module, consult the appropriate sections of the Teacher's Manual, Test Bank, and PowerPoint slides, all found on the Teacher's Resource DVD, and the interactive study tools for students on MyPsychLab.

BEFORE CLASS
Students should read the section for homework before coming to class.

BELLRINGER
Ask students to make a list of what motivates them. It could encompass any aspect of their lives, from grades to eating habits to what they wear. Assure students that even if they think they are above influence or are simply unmotivated, they do in fact have motivators. Encourage them to really think about it. Tell students to keep the list and consult it throughout the module. Is it truly accurate? How well do students understand why they do what they do?

COVER THE MODULE

27.1 What are the major cognitive and biological theories of motivation?

- *Extrinsic motivation* comes from the external world.
- *Intrinsic motivation* is internal.
- **LINK** to Chapter Six: Learning and Language Development, p. 186
- *Instinct approaches* proposed that some human actions may be motivated by instincts, innate patterns of behavior found in both people and animals.

Module 27 Motivation

Module Goals	Learning Objectives
Explain major theories of motivation.	**27.1** What are the major cognitive and biological theories of motivation?
	27.2 What is the humanist theory of motivation?
Describe motivated behaviors.	**27.3** What factors motivate eating?
	27.4 What factors motivate sexual behavior and orientation?
	27.5 What factors motivate achievement?
	27.6 Are there other ways in which humans and animals are motivated?

Explain Major Theories of Motivation

27.1 What are the major cognitive and biological theories of motivation?

Motivation is the process by which activities are started, directed, and continued to meet physical or psychological needs or wants (Petri, 1996). The word itself comes from the Latin *movere*, which means "to move." Motivation "moves" people to do the things they do. For example, when a person is relaxing in front of the television and begins to feel hungry, the physical need for food might cause an action (the person will get up), direct the action (the person will go to the kitchen), and sustain it (the person will search for a snack and perhaps even cook something). Hunger is only one example, of course. Loneliness may lead to calling a friend or going to a place where there are people. The desire to get ahead in life motivates many people to go to college. Just getting out of bed in the morning to go to work is motivated by the need to support oneself. There are two different types of motivation: **extrinsic motivation** and **intrinsic motivation**.

Extrinsic motivation comes from outside the self—the "external" world. A person performs an action because it leads to an outcome that is separate from the person (Ryan & Deci, 2000), such as obtaining an external reward or avoiding an unpleasant consequence. For instance, a person might work to make money and avoid losing possessions such as a house **LINK** *to Chapter Six: Learning and Language Development, p. 186.* People rely on extrinsic motivation when they give a child money for doing chores or offer a bonus to a hardworking employee. Intrinsic motivation is "internal." A person performs an action because it is internally rewarding. For instance, a person might engage in creative pursuits, such as painting, because these activities are satisfying in and of themselves.

Instinct Approaches Early approaches to motivation focused on **instincts**, the innate, biologically determined patterns of behavior in people and animals.

motivation the process by which activities are started, directed, and continued so that physical or psychological needs or wants are met.

extrinsic motivation type of motivation in which a person performs an action because it leads to an outcome that is separate from or external to the person.

intrinsic motivation type of motivation in which a person performs an action because the act itself is rewarding or satisfying in some internal manner.

instincts the biologically determined and innate patterns of behavior that exist in both people and animals.

342 CHAPTER II

Terms

- motivation • extrinsic motivation • intrinsic motivation • instincts • instinct approach • need • drive • drive-reduction theory • primary drives • acquired (secondary) drives • homeostasis • need for achievement (nAch) • need for affiliation (nAff) • need for power (nPow) • stimulus motive • arousal theory • Yerkes-Dodson law • sensation seeker • incentives • incentive approaches • expectancy-value theories • expectancy • deficiency needs • growth needs • self-actualization • peak experiences • self-determination theory (SDT) • insulin • glucagons • weight set point • basal metabolic rate (BMR) • obesity • anorexia nervosa • bulimia nervosa • sexual orientation • internal locus of control • external locus of control • oxytocin

---

342 Chapter 7 Motivation and Emotion

Instincts prompt animals to migrate, build nests, mate, and protect their territory, among other things, and early researchers proposed that human beings might be governed by similar instincts (James, 1890; McDougall, 1908). According to these **instinct approach** theorists, in humans, the instinct to reproduce is responsible for sexual behavior, and the instinct for territorial protection may be related to aggressive behavior.

William McDougall (1908) proposed a total of 18 human instincts, including curiosity, flight (running away), pugnacity (aggressiveness), and acquisition (gathering possessions). Later psychologists proposed many more, but most did little more than name and describe instincts without confirming whether or why they exist (Petri, 1996). Freud's psychoanalytic theory still includes the concept of instincts. LINK *to Chapter Twelve: Theories of Personality, pp. 379–380.* Instinct approaches have otherwise faded away, but they did lead to an enduring realization: Some human behavior is controlled by hereditary factors.

Drive-Reduction Approaches The next major theory of motivation involved needs and drives. A **need** is a requirement of some material (such as food or water) that is essential for survival. Each of an organism's needs leads to psychological tension (called a **drive**) and physical arousal (Hull, 1943). According to **drive-reduction theory,** this physical arousal motivates the organism to reduce the drive and satisfy the need.

Primary drives involve survival needs, such as hunger and thirst. Primary drives are not learned; we are born with them. **Acquired (secondary) drives,** such as the need for money or social approval, are learned through experience or conditioning. The behaviorist concepts of primary and secondary reinforcers are related to these drives. Primary reinforcers satisfy primary drives, and secondary reinforcers satisfy acquired, or secondary, drives. LINK *to Chapter Six: Learning and Language Development, pp. 185–186.*

This theory also includes the concept of **homeostasis**, the body's tendency to maintain a steady state. Homeostasis regulates the body's functions, much as a thermostat maintains a constant temperature. A primary drive need creates a state of imbalance, which stimulates behavior that brings the body back into balance, or homeostasis. For example, if Jarrod needs food, he feels hunger and the associated state of tension, and he will seek to restore homeostasis by eating. (See Figure 27.1.)

FIGURE 27.1 Homeostasis
In homeostasis, the body maintains balance in the body's physical states. For example, this diagram shows how increased hunger (a state of imbalance) prompts a person to eat. Eating increases the level of glucose (blood sugar), causing the feelings of hunger to reduce. After a period without eating, the glucose levels become low enough to stimulate the hunger drive once again, and the entire cycle is repeated.

instinct approach approach to motivation that assumes people are governed by instincts similar to those of animals.

need a requirement of some material (such as food or water) that is essential for survival of the organism.

drive a psychological tension and physical arousal arising when there is a need that motivates the organism to act in order to fulfill the need and reduce the tension.

drive-reduction theory approach to motivation that assumes behavior arises from physiological needs that cause internal drives to push the organism to satisfy the need and reduce tension and arousal.

primary drives those drives that involve needs of the body such as hunger and thirst.

acquired (secondary) drives those drives that are learned through experience or conditioning, such as the need for money or social approval.

homeostasis the tendency of the body to maintain a steady state.

MOTIVATION AND EMOTION 343

CHAPTER 11 • Module 27

COVER THE MODULE (continued)

- McDougall proposed 18 human instincts.

LINK *to Chapter Twelve: Theories of Personality, pp. 379–380*

- *Drive-reduction approaches* state that when an organism has a need (such as hunger), the need leads to psychological tension that motivates the organism to act, fulfilling the need and reducing the tension.
  - *Primary drives* involve needs of the body.
  - *Acquired (secondary) drives* are those learned through experience.

LINK *to Chapter Six: Learning and Language Development, pp. 185–186*

  - *Homeostasis* is the tendency of the body to maintain a steady state.

UNDERSTANDING VISUALS

Direct students to Figure 27.1 on this page. Review the cycle with them to ensure understanding. Then ask students if they can think of other ways in which the body maintains homeostasis. *(Answers may include the regulation of body temperature or respiration.)* Work with the class to construct cycles similar to Figure 27.1 on the board. Your cycles may have more or fewer boxes than the figure in the book.

TEACHING TIP

Help distracted students stay on task by using verbal signals and standing nearby.

Class Demonstration

TYPES OF MOTIVATION

Purpose: Students complete a brief 1-minute assignment that involves critical thinking, personalizing, or deeper processing of information.

Time: 1–5 minutes

Description: Give students several minutes to answer the following questions: (1) What did you do in the hour before you came to school? (2) What was your motive for engaging in that behavior? (3) Would you classify your motive as biological? Social? Achievement-related? Explain.

Module 27 Motivation 343

CHAPTER 11 • Module 27

COVER THE MODULE (continued)

- **Needs**
  - The *need for achievement* is a strong desire to succeed in getting to one's goals, both realistic and challenging.
  - The *need for affiliation* is the desire to have friendly social interactions and relationships with others and a desire to be held in high regard by others.
  - The *need for power* concerns having control over others, influencing them and having an impact on them. Status and prestige are important to people high in this need.
- In *arousal theory*, a person has an optimal level of arousal to maintain.

UNDERSTANDING VISUALS

Direct students' attention to Figure 27.2 on this page. Where do students think they fall on the graph when performing tasks that they find difficult or easy? Do they get too anxious doing difficult tasks? Do they get bored with easy tasks? What can students do to get closer to the optimal middle level of arousal?

---

need for achievement (nAch) a need that involves a strong desire to succeed in attaining goals, not only realistic ones but also challenging ones.

need for affiliation (nAff) the need for friendly social interactions and relationships with others.

need for power (nPow) the need to have control or influence over others.

stimulus motive a motive that appears to be unlearned but causes an increase in stimulation, such as curiosity.

arousal theory theory of motivation in which people are said to have an optimal (best or ideal) level of tension that they seek to maintain by increasing or decreasing stimulation.

Yerkes-Dodson law law stating performance is related to arousal; moderate levels of arousal lead to better performance than do levels of arousal that are too low or too high. This effect varies with the difficulty of the task: Easy tasks require a high-moderate level, whereas more difficult tasks require a low–moderate level.

Drive-reduction theory explains some, but not all, instances of human motivation. The following theories explore additional factors.

Different Strokes for Different Folks: Psychological Needs The instinct and drive-reduction approaches emphasize physical needs, but Harvard University psychologist David C. McClelland (1961, 1987) focused on three *psychological* needs: achievement, affiliation, and power.

The **need for achievement** (abbreviated as **nAch**) is the desire to succeed in attaining goals. People who are high in *nAch* also need others' feedback and evaluation. Although many become wealthy, famous, and publicly successful, others seek personally satisfying achievements in ways that don't necessarily lead to material riches. In other words, they just like challenges. Achievement motivation appears to be strongly related to academic and occupational success and productivity (Collins et al., 2004; Gillespie et al., 2002; Spangler, 1992). Debi R.'s story is a good example of this need. Her goal of walking again had nothing to do with wealth or career success, but she was still strongly motivated to achieve it.

Another psychological need is the **need for affiliation (nAff)**—that is, for friendly social interactions and relationships. People high in *nAff* seek to be liked and held in high regard, which makes them good team players. (A person with high achievement needs but low affiliation needs just might run over a few team members on the way to the top.)

The final psychological need McClelland proposed is the **need for power (nPow)**—influence or even control over others. People high in *nPow* want to make an impact through their ideas. They value status and prestige and are likely to own expensive clothes, houses, and cars and dine in the best restaurants. While high-nAch people may not need a lot of money to validate their achievements, high-nPow people typically see money and possessions as achievements in themselves. In other words, as a popular bumper sticker states, "The one who dies with the most toys wins."

Arousal Approaches Another theory of motivation involves our need for stimulation. **Stimulus motives,** such as curiosity, playing, and exploration, appear to be unlearned but cause an increase in stimulation or tension.

According to **arousal theory**, people are said to have an optimal, or ideal, level of stimulation for successful performance on different tasks. For example, one's performance on a task may suffer if arousal is too high or too low. This relationship between task performance and arousal is called the **Yerkes-Dodson law** (Teigen, 1994; Yerkes & Dodson, 1908).

Maintaining optimal arousal may involve reducing tension or creating it (Hebb, 1955). For example, students who experience test anxiety (high arousal) may try to reduce that anxiety to improve test performance. Students who have no anxiety (low arousal) may also have no motivation to study or try hard—and so they might need to be a little *more* anxious to improve their performance. Many arousal theorists believe the optimal level of arousal is usually somewhere in the middle. However, this effect is modified by the difficulty of the task: Easy tasks demand "high–moderate" arousal for optimal performance, whereas difficult tasks require "low–moderate" arousal. (See Figure 27.2.)

FIGURE 27.2 Arousal and Performance
The optimal level of arousal for task performance depends on the difficulty of the task. We generally perform easy tasks well if we are highly aroused (green) and accomplish difficult tasks well if we are not very aroused (red).

344 CHAPTER 11

Class Demonstration

ACHIEVEMENT AND MOTIVATION

Research shows that girls' pattern of motivation differs from that of boys—very bright females show greater debilitation after failure; they display greater decrease in motivation and performance than do other females or any males. Conversely, the brightest males show facilitation following failure. Females show a lower preference for novel or challenging tasks than do males, and females are more likely to attribute their failure to lack of ability than are males.

In addition, two factors that strongly affect what an individual is likely to achieve are the *value* placed on goal achievement and the *expectation* of achieving the goal.

Before discussing this information with students, poll the class to find out what happens to students' motivation after they fail, what they attribute failures to, what motivates them to set high standards, and whether they actually expect to succeed. Record this information in terms of gender, expectations, and the like, as discussed in the research, and then share the results and this information with the class.

If people are supposed to be seeking a level of arousal somewhere around the middle, why do some people love to do things like bungee jumping?

Some people need less or more arousal than average. People who need more are called **sensation seekers** (Zuckerman, 1979, 1994), and they often seek complex and varied sensory experiences. The need does not always have to involve danger. For example, students who study abroad tend to score higher on scales of sensation seeking than those who stay at home (Schroth & McCormack, 2000). Table 27.1 has sample items from a typical sensation-seeking scale.

Sensation seeking may be related to temperament LINK to Chapter Five: Development Across the Life Span, pp. 140–175. In one study (Putnam & Stifter, 2002), researchers found evidence of "sensation-seeking" behavior in children as young as age 2. Ninety children were studied at the ages of 6, 12, 24, and 25 months. The researchers presented the babies with two sets of toys: a block, a plate, and a cup (low-intensity stimulus); or a flashing light, a toy beeper, and a wind-up dragon (a high-intensity stimulus). The infants who reached out for the toys more quickly, especially the high-intensity toys, were labeled for their "approach-motivation." At age 2, the same children were given an opportunity to explore a black box with a hole in one side. "Low-approach-motivated" children were unwilling to put their hands in the box, whereas "high-approach-motivated" children not only put their hands in the box but sometimes even tried to climb in. These differences could be influenced by factors ranging from innate temperament to past experiences.

Incentive Approaches

Last Thanksgiving, I had eaten about all I could. Then my aunt brought out a piece of her wonderful pumpkin pie and I couldn't resist—I ate it, even though I was not at all hungry. What makes us do things even when we don't have the drive or need to do them?

Incentives are things that attract or lure people into action. A delicious-looking pie may prompt us to eat, even though we don't need to, because we have learned that the experience will be rewarding. **Incentive approaches** explain behavior in terms of external stimuli and their rewarding properties (which exist independently of need or arousal). Thus, these theories are actually partly based on the principles of learning discussed in Chapter Six. LINK to Chapter Six: Learning and Language Development, pp. 176–211.

Table 27.1	Sample Items From the Zuckerman-Kuhlman Personality Questionnaire
SCALE ITEM	**SENSATION SEEKING**
I sometimes do "crazy" things just for fun.	High
I prefer friends who are excitingly unpredictable.	High
I am an impulsive person.	High
Before I begin a complicated job, I make careful plans.	Low
I usually think about what I am going to do before doing it.	Low

Source: Adapted from Zuckerman, M. (2002).

◀ *If people are supposed to be seeking a level of arousal somewhere around the middle, why do some people love to do things like bungee jumping?*

◀ *Last Thanksgiving, I had eaten about all I could. Then my aunt brought out a piece of her wonderful pumpkin pie and I couldn't resist—I ate it, even though I was not at all hungry. What makes us do things even when we don't have the drive or need to do them?*

sensation seeker someone who needs more arousal than the average person and seeks out complex and varied experiences.

incentives things that attract or lure people into action.

incentive approaches theories of motivation in which behavior is explained as a response to the external stimulus and its rewarding properties.

MOTIVATION AND EMOTION 345

CHAPTER 11 • Module 27

COVER THE MODULE (continued)

- People who need more arousal than others are called *sensation seekers*.

LINK to Chapter Five: Development Across the Life Span, pp. 140–175

DISCUSS THE STUDENT VOICE QUESTION

Ask students to answer the items in Table 27.1 for themselves, either "true" or "false." ("True" for the first three items and "false" for the last two indicate high sensation seeking, and vice versa.) You may even pose more questions to them from the questionnaire, which can be found on the web at sites such as www.rta.nsw.gov.au/licensing/tests/driverqualificationtest/sensationseekingscale/ Ask students when high sensation seeking is a good thing. When can it be detrimental?

COVER THE MODULE (continued)

- In the *incentive approach*, an external stimulus may be so rewarding that it motivates a person to act toward that stimulus rather than another stimulus or to satisfy a drive.

LINK to Chapter Six: Learning and Language Development, pp. 176–211

DISCUSS THE STUDENT VOICE QUESTION

Ask students to list some incentives that may motivate them to do something they do not have the drive or need to do. Draw two columns on the board and list the incentives as positive (such as an academic award) or negative (such as the overeating example given here).

Explore

PERSONALITY ASSESSMENT

Ask students to further research the Zuckerman-Kuhlman personality questionnaire on the web at a site such as the following:

- www.dmidi.net/Zuckerman-Kuhlman+Personality+Questionnaire
- http://findarticles.com/p/articles/mi_qa3852/is_200201/ai_n9035331/
- www.samplequestionnaire.com/zuckerman-kuhlman-personality-questionnaire.html

What other types of things might this questionnaire measure? Are there any lines of questioning that students found surprising or seemingly irrelevant? How is this questionnaire useful to the scientific community?

Module 27 Motivation **345**

CHAPTER 11 • Module 27

COVER THE MODULE (continued)

- *Expectancy-value theories* emphasize the importance that people attach to beliefs and values at any given time.

LINK to *Chapter Six: Learning and Language Development, p. 197*

COVER THE MODULE

27.2 What is the humanist theory of motivation?

- Maslow proposed a hierarchy of needs, beginning with basic physiological needs and ending with *self-actualization* needs. The more basic needs must be met before the higher needs can be fulfilled.
- Maslow's hierarchy:
  - physiological needs
  - safety needs
  - belongingness and love
  - self-esteem needs
  - cognitive needs
  - aesthetic needs
  - self-actualization

MULTIMEDIA CONTENT AVAILABLE AT
www.mypsychlab.com

Explore Maslow's Hierarchy of Needs on **mypsychlab.com**

---

expectancy-value theories incentive theories that assume the actions of humans cannot be predicted or fully understood without understanding the beliefs, values, and the importance that a person attaches to those beliefs and values at any given moment in time.

expectancy in expectancy-value theory, a belief about what will happen in the future based on past experiences.

deficiency needs in Maslow's theory, these are physical survival needs, such as the need for food.

growth needs in Maslow's theory, these are psychological needs, such as the need for friendship or accomplishments.

self-actualization according to Maslow, the point that is seldom reached at which people have sufficiently satisfied the lower needs and achieved their full human potential.

Explore Maslow's Hierarchy of Needs on **mypsychlab.com**

Expectancy-value theories, a class of incentive theories based on the work of Edward Tolman and others (Lewin, 1936; Rotter, 1954), clearly demonstrate the relationship to learning. These theories assume that human actions cannot be predicted or understood without understanding people's beliefs, values, and the importance they attach to those beliefs and values at any given time. Organisms can remember past events, anticipate future events, and adjust their own actions according to their cognitive **expectancies**—beliefs about what will happen in the future based on past experiences. LINK to *Chapter Six: Learning and Language Development, p. 197*.

Julian Rotter's (1954) social learning theory included expectancy as one of the three factors that predict people's behavior—if Terry's past experiences with writing papers, for example, have led to an expectancy of failing to get a high grade, Terry is unlikely to take on the task of an extra term paper to earn bonus points. By itself, the incentive approach does not explain all motivation. Many theorists today think motivation results from both the "push" of internal needs or drives (such as hunger) and the "pull" of a rewarding external stimulus (such as a candy bar).

27.2 What is the humanist theory of motivation?

Maslow's Hierarchy of Needs Humanistic approaches to motivation are based on Abraham Maslow's work (1943, 1987). Maslow proposed that a person must strive to meet several levels of needs before achieving the highest level of personal fulfillment. His theory includes both **deficiency needs** (the needs of the body) and **growth needs** (desires like having friends or feeling good about oneself). The rare person who has fulfilled all primary needs and gone on to achieve his or her full human potential has reached the point of **self-actualization**. Explore on **mypsychlab.com**

Figure 27.3 represents Maslow's hierarchy of needs as a pyramid. To understand this hierarchy, consider the movie *Cast Away*, in which Tom Hanks's character is stranded on a deserted island. His first concerns are survival needs: finding food and fresh water and building a crude shelter. Once these needs are met, however, he gets lonely. He finds a volleyball, paints it with a handprint and a crude face, and names it "Wilson." He talks to the volleyball as if it were a person, first to plan what he needs to do and later to keep himself relatively sane. His need for companionship was *that* strong.

Like Hanks's character, we also seek to satisfy the most basic needs first—*physiological needs* such as food, water, and rest, followed by *safety and security needs*. Once those are met, we hunger for a sense of *belonging*: acceptance by others, friendship, and love. Next is the *self-esteem* that results from having worked hard and accomplished something worthwhile. Although Maslow originally included only one more level in his hierarchy, he later inserted two other needs (Maslow, 1971; Maslow & Lowery, 1998). These are *cognitive needs*, which pertain to our natural curiosity and desire to understand the world, and *aesthetic needs*, which pertain to our appreciation of order and beauty. (Most people also seem to like to express themselves artistically.) Once all these needs are met, we can attend to our *self-actualization needs*, which help us reach our full potential as human beings.

346 CHAPTER 11

Class Demonstration

IDENTIFYING HUMAN MOTIVES

Give students about 5 minutes to complete this exercise by matching each statement with the correct need (as listed below), and then ask volunteers to share their responses. You can then use the students' responses to help clarify and elaborate on Maslow's theory.

Self-Actualization Needs (SA); Esteem Needs (ESTEEM); Belonging Needs (BELONG); Safety Needs (SAFE); Biological Needs (BIO)

- "Have I got a terrible headache! It's really splitting." *(BIO)*
- "I get lonely on the weekends. I don't get to see my friends very much." *(BELONG)*
- "I feel really bored by this class. I was hoping it would be more challenging." *(SA)*
- "Uh, listen, do you mind if we don't walk down that street? I hear that someone got beaten up there last week." *(SAFE)*
- "Hey, guess what? I just got an A+ on my paper. Pretty good, huh?" *(ESTEEM)*
- "I've decided to go out of state for college. My parents are upset, but I just want to make it on my own." *(ESTEEM)*

FIGURE 27.3 Maslow's Hierarchy of Needs
Maslow proposed that human beings must fulfill the more basic needs, such as physical and security needs, before being able to fulfill the higher needs of self-actualization and transcendence.

The highest need is transcendence (Maslow, 1971)—the need to help others achieve *their* full potential. This aspect of Maslow's hierarchy is very similar to the stage of generativity, proposed by Erik Erikson, in which mature adults focus on nurturing the next generation. **LINK** *to Chapter Five: Development Across the Life Span, pp. 140–175.*

Throughout life, people move up the pyramid, but a change in circumstances can result in a downward shift. For example, a woman might have a rewarding job that fulfills her esteem needs, but if she loses her job and cannot easily find another, she might take a much less fulfilling job so she can continue to provide food and shelter to her family.

This moving up and down within the lower rungs of the hierarchy can occur frequently—even from one hour to the next. **Peak experiences** are those times when self-actualization is achieved, at least temporarily. For Maslow, the process of growth and self-actualization is the striving to make peak experiences happen again and again.

peak experiences according to Maslow, times in a person's life during which self-actualization is temporarily achieved.

MOTIVATION AND EMOTION 347

Explore

ABRAHAM MASLOW

Ask students to research the life and work of Abraham Maslow at the library or on the Internet, either by doing a web search or using one or more of the sites listed below. Have them submit a one- to two-page report of their findings.

- www.mrdowling.com/602-maslow.html
- http://webspace.ship.edu/cgboer/maslow.html
- www.businessballs.com/maslow.htm

CHAPTER 11 • Module 27

EXTEND THE LESSON

Give students some time to review Maslow's Hierarchy of Needs as illustrated in Figure 27.3. Then divide the class into small groups, and give them 3 to 4 minutes to brainstorm individually. They should write down examples of motivations and record them on individual scraps of paper or sticky notes. Next, students should read their answers aloud and stick their notes to the table. Third, team members should silently order the ideas according to Maslow's Hierarchy of Needs. Finally, teams should discuss the categories and whether any responses need to be moved.

LINK *to Chapter Five: Development Across the Life Span, pp. 140–175*

CLASS DEBATE

Have students read the article regarding Maslow's hierarchy at **http://qedrealestate.wordpress.com/2010/08/24/maslow-updatedself-actualization/** Divide the class into two groups to debate Maslow's findings—one group to defend them and one group to refute them. Students should base their arguments on the textbook, their research on Maslow (see the Explore activity, below), and the Internet article. If time allows, you may want to devote an entire class period to this activity—half of the period for preparation and half for debate.

L3 DIFFERENTIATED INSTRUCTION

Special Needs Openly discuss with students any questions you have about when to offer assistance.

Module 27 Motivation 347

CHAPTER 11 • Module 27

DISCUSS THE STUDENT VOICE QUESTION
Direct students to the Geert Hofstede Cultural Dimensions site at **www.geert-hofstede.com/** Which of Hofstede's dimensions would best predict how closely a country would follow Maslow's hierarchy? *(Answers may include individualism, uncertainty avoidance, and possibly power distance, which may predict whether citizens even strive for values toward the top of the hierarchy.)* In addition to the countries mentioned in the text, for what other countries might Maslow's hierarchy not be applicable?

LINK to Chapter Twelve: Theories of Personality, pp. 399–400

COVER THE MODULE *(continued)*

- *Self-determination theory (SDT)* is a model of motivation in which three basic needs are seen as necessary to an individual's successful development:
  - Autonomy: the need to be in control of one's own behavior
  - Competence: the need to be able to master challenging tasks
  - Relatedness: the need to feel a sense of belonging
- Intrinsic motivation occurs when people act because the act itself is satisfying or rewarding.
- Extrinsic motivation occurs when people receive an external reward (such as money) for the act.

DISCUSS THE STUDENT VOICE QUESTION
Ask students if they can think of anything in their lives that they do for both intrinsic and extrinsic motives. An example may be studying hard for a test, not only for a good grade but also for the satisfaction of doing a good job.

348 Chapter 11 Motivation and Emotion

---

self-determination theory (SDT)
theory of human motivation in which the social context of an action has an effect on the type of motivation existing for the action.

▶ Does this theory apply universally?

However, Maslow's theory is not without its critics. The most serious criticism is that it has little scientific support (Drenth et al., 1984), because it is based on Maslow's personal observations rather than any empirically gathered observations or research. Anecdotal evidence in many people's lives (including those of some well-known people) suggests that we do not always need to satisfy the lower needs first (Drenth et al., 1984). For example, artists and scientists have been known to choose to deny their own physical needs while producing great works, and individuals like Gandhi have chosen to go on hunger strikes in order to achieve goals that they consider more important than their own personal needs.

Does this theory apply universally?
Maslow's work was based on his studies of Americans. Cross-cultural research suggests that the hierarchy does not always hold true for other cultures. For instance, in cultures with a stronger tendency to avoid uncertainty, such as Greece and Japan, job security needs are much more powerful than self-actualization needs (Hofstede, 1980; Hofstede et al., 2002). People may value job security more than they value holding an interesting or challenging job. In countries like Sweden and Norway that stress the quality of life over productivity, social needs may be more important than self-actualization (Hofstede et al., 2002). LINK to Chapter Twelve: Theories of Personality, pp. 399–400.

Self-Determination Theory (SDT) A similar theory of motivation is the **self-determination theory (SDT)** of Ryan and Deci (2000), which proposes three universal needs that help people gain a complete sense of self and healthy relationships:

- **autonomy,** the need to control one's own behavior and goals
- **competence,** the need to master the challenging tasks of one's life
- **relatedness,** the need for belonging, intimacy, and security in relationships

Ryan, Deci, and their colleagues (Deci et al., 1994; Ryan & Deci, 2000) believe that people can satisfy these needs more easily if they have a supportive environment, which will not only foster healthy psychological growth, but will also increase one's intrinsic motivation. Evidence suggests that intrinsic motivation increases when we not only feel competence (through experiencing positive feedback and success at challenging tasks) but also autonomy, the knowledge that our actions are self-determined rather than controlled by others (deCharms, 1968; Deci & Ryan, 1985).

Previous research has found that externally rewarding performance may reduce intrinsic motivation (Deci et al., 1999), but more recent research finds that external rewards produce negative effects only for tasks that are not inherently interesting (Cameron et al., 2001). When we find a task interesting, external rewards may increase our intrinsic motivation, at least in the short term. Further research is needed to understand the long-term effects.

▶ But don't we sometimes do things for both kinds of motives?

But don't we sometimes do things for both kinds of motives?
People often have both intrinsic and extrinsic motives for their actions. Teachers, for example, work for money (an extrinsic motive), but may also feel that they are helping their students to become better adults in the future, which helps teachers feel good about themselves and their work (an intrinsic motive).

348 CHAPTER 11

Class Demonstration

INCENTIVES

<u>Purpose</u>: Students complete a brief 1-minute assignment that involves critical thinking, personalizing, or deeper processing of information.

<u>Time</u>: 1–5 minutes

<u>Description</u>: Ask students to name some incentives (external rewards) that have a powerful effect on them. What incentives do they work for in their daily lives (e.g., grades, paycheck, peer approval)?

Describe Motivated Behaviors

How do basic motivations drive and determine our behaviors every day? Whenever we sit down for a meal, go on a date, or study for an exam, we are performing motivated behaviors. In the following pages, we will explore the physiological and psychological components of a few motivated behaviors in detail.

27.3 What factors motivate eating?

Why do we eat? What causes us to feel hungry in the first place?
Cannon (Cannon & Washburn, 1912) believed that stomach contractions, or "hunger pangs," caused hunger; eating would stop the contractions and appease the hunger drive. When we eat, the stomach's sensory receptors respond to the pressure of its stretching muscles and send signals to the brain indicating that we are full (Geliebter, 1988). However, an empty stomach is not the only source of hunger. Hunger is actually a delicately balanced biochemical dance among hormones, neurotransmitters, and stimuli such as food.

When we haven't eaten for a while, we experience a drop in glucose (sugar in the blood). This triggers us to eat to maintain homeostasis in the body; after we eat, levels of blood glucose rise, and we no longer feel hungry, as shown in Figure 27.1 on page 343. Maintenance of homeostasis involves **insulin** and **glucagons**, hormones secreted by the pancreas to control the body's levels of fats, proteins, and carbohydrates, including glucose. Insulin reduces the level of glucose in the bloodstream, whereas glucagons increase it. (Refined carbohydrates, such as sugary and starchy foods, can cause insulin levels to spike, disrupting the regulation of blood sugar and the way energy from food is stored. Many researchers believe overconsumption of these foods may contribute to appetite disturbances and weight gain.)

The Role of the Hypothalamus The brain is also a significant factor in hunger. The part of the brain called the hypothalamus helps control many kinds of motivational stimuli, including hunger, by influencing the pituitary gland **LINK** *to Chapter Two, The Biological Perspective, pp. 57–59.* But the hypothalamus itself controls eating behavior through at least two additional mechanisms.

First, the ventromedial nucleus (VMN), located toward the bottom and center of the hypothalamus (*ventro* means "underside" and *medial* means "middle"), may be involved in stopping the eating response when glucose levels go up (Neary et al., 2004). In one study, rats whose VMN areas were damaged could not stop eating—they ate and ate until they were obese (Hetherington & Ranson, 1940). (See Figure 27.4.) However, they did not eat everything in sight. They actually got rather picky, overeating only the foods that appealed to them (Ferguson & Keesey, 1975; Parkinson & Weingarten, 1990).

Second, the lateral hypothalamus (LH), an area on the side of the hypothalamus (*lateral* means "side"), seems to influence the onset of eating when insulin levels go up (Neary et al., 2004). Damage to this area caused rats to stop eating to the point of starvation. They would eat only if force-fed (Anand & Brobeck, 1951; Hoebel & Teitelbaum, 1966).

Some researchers (Leibel et al., 1995; Nisbett, 1972) believe the hypothalamus affects the **weight set point**, the particular level of weight that the body tries to maintain. The weight set point is dramatically raised or lowered when the hypothalamus is injured, and it is also influenced by metabolism, the speed at which the body burns available energy, and exercise. Regular,

▶ Why do we eat? What causes us to feel hungry in the first place?

FIGURE 27.4 Obese Laboratory Rat
This rat has reached a high level of obesity because its ventromedial hypothalamus has been deliberately damaged in the laboratory. The result is a rat that no longer receives signals of being satiated, and so the rat continues to eat and eat and eat.

insulin a hormone secreted by the pancreas to control the levels of fats, proteins, and carbohydrates in the body by reducing the level of glucose in the bloodstream.

glucagons hormones that are secreted by the pancreas to control the levels of fats, proteins, and carbohydrates in the body by increasing the level of glucose in the bloodstream.

weight set point the particular level of weight that the body tries to maintain.

MOTIVATION AND EMOTION 349

CHAPTER 11 • Module 27

COVER THE MODULE

27.3 What factors motivate eating?
- The physiological components of hunger include signals from the stomach, the increased secretion of *insulin*, and the hypothalamus.
- When the basal metabolic rate slows down, the *weight set point* increases and makes weight gain more likely.

LINK *to Chapter Two: The Biological Perspective, pp. 57–59*

DISCUSS THE STUDENT VOICE QUESTION

What are students' reactions to the idea that hunger is not just about an empty stomach? Do they find it surprising that one could be full in the physical sense but not feel that way? Or that, maybe more hard to believe, some of the rats studied nearly starved in the presence of food?

L2 ELL DIFFERENTIATED INSTRUCTION

English Language Learners Encourage students to look at textbook visuals for the information they provide.

Class Demonstration

TREATMENT OF OBESITY

The popular press has heralded the discovery of a "magic bullet" for treating obesity. Dr. Jeffrey Friedman, a molecular geneticist, led a research team to successfully isolate the gene (called *ob*) that helps control body weight in mice. From this gene, the researchers synthesized a protein hormone (called *leptin*) that, when injected into obese mice, caused them to lose 40 percent of their body weight within a month. Although the mice had access to ample food, they simply chose to eat less. In addition to curbing the animals' appetites, leptin appeared to speed their metabolism. Also, the weight loss itself was solely due to loss of fat, and no adverse effects were observed. The long-term effects of leptin have yet to be studied, but scientists and pharmaceutical companies are already anticipating applications to human weight loss. It is known that humans produce a hormone similar to leptin. It is possible that leptin could be used to treat obesity and, with sensible diet and exercise, regulate weight in normal-weight individuals. Discuss these findings with students. What do they think about the idea of a "magic" weight-loss drug? Are they skeptical? If it did work, what are the implications? Can they think of any drawbacks to such a successful weight-loss drug?

Module 27 Motivation 349

CHAPTER 11 • Module 27

COVER THE MODULE (continued)

- The social components of hunger include social cues for when meals are to be eaten, cultural customs and food preferences, and the use of food as a comfort device or escape from unpleasantness.
- Some people may be externals, who respond to the anticipation of eating by producing an insulin response, increasing the risk of obesity.

LINK to Chapter Six: Learning and Language Development, pp. 176–211.

- **Maladaptive eating behaviors:**
  - *Obesity* means that the body weight of a person is 20 percent or more over the ideal body weight for that person's height.

LINK to Chapter Thirteen: Psychological Disorders, pp. 418–419.

MULTIMEDIA CONTENT AVAILABLE AT
www.mypsychlab.com

Listen to a Psychology in the News podcast on the biology of obesity on **mypsychlab.com**

CULTURAL CONNECTIONS

Read aloud the paragraph regarding cultural factors and gender influence on eating habits. After having reviewed Hofstede's cultural dimensions, what do students think might account for these differences?

---

moderate exercise helps offset age-related slowing of metabolism and the accompanying increase in the weight set point (Tremblay et al., 1999).

Some people are no doubt genetically wired to have a faster **basal metabolic rate (BMR)**, the rate at which the body burns energy when a person is resting. These people can eat large amounts of food without gaining weight. Others with slower metabolisms may gain weight more easily or have trouble losing weight even when they eat a normal (or less-than-normal) amount of food (Bouchard et al., 1990).

Social Components of Hunger People often eat when they are not really hungry, due to social cues such as the convention of eating breakfast, lunch, and dinner at certain times. Much of that "convention" is actually classical conditioning. **LINK** *to Chapter Six: Learning and Language Development, pp. 176–211.* The body becomes conditioned to respond with hunger at certain times, which have become conditioned stimuli. A person who has eaten a late breakfast may still "feel" hungry at lunchtime. And of course, the sight and smell of food are appealing, and people respond to that. People also may use food as a comforting routine or escape from stress (Dallman et al., 2003).

Rodin (1981, 1985) found that the release of insulin may actually begin *before* eating. This phenomenon may reflect classical conditioning, much as Pavlov's dogs began salivating before receiving their food. Because eating foods with certain visual and sensory characteristics has frequently led to an insulin spike in the past, now just looking at or smelling these foods will produce the spike (Stockhorst, 1999). This may explain why some people, who are called "externals," are so responsive to the external features of food, focusing on these rather than on internal hunger. They produce far more insulin in response to the *anticipation* of eating (Rodin, 1985).

Cultural factors and gender also influence hunger and eating habits. One study of men and women from the United States and Japan found that women in the United States were much more likely to start eating for emotional reasons, such as depression, while Japanese women were more likely to eat because of hunger signals or social demands (Hawks et al., 2003). Americans of both sexes were more likely to eat while watching television or movies than were Japanese people.

Maladaptive Eating Behaviors For complex reasons, people do not always eat just the amount of food that they need, and many people have trouble maintaining a healthy weight. Being over- or underweight is sometimes connected to maladaptive eating behaviors. In extreme cases, maladaptive eating behaviors may lead to one of the clinical eating disorders described in the *Diagnostic and Statistical Manual of Mental Disorders, Fourth Edition, Text Revision* or *DSM-IV-TR* (American Psychiatric Association, 2000). **LINK** *to Chapter Thirteen: Psychological Disorders, pp. 418–419.*

In recent years, increasing rates of **obesity** in developed countries have received much attention. **Obesity** is classified by a high body-mass index (BMI), a measure of the ratio between weight and height. A BMI over 30 (which corresponds to a weight that is about 20 to 30 percent or more above one's ideal weight) is defined as obese. Heredity is a significant factor in obesity. Several sets of genes appear to influence a person's likelihood of becoming obese (Barsh et al., 2000), as does family history (Bouchard, 1997).

Listen on **mypsychlab.com**

Another factor is overeating. As developing countries build stronger economies and more stable food supplies, obesity rates increase dramatically

Listen to a Psychology in the News podcast on the biology of obesity on **mypsychlab.com**

basal metabolic rate (BMR) the rate at which the body burns energy when the organism is resting.

obesity a condition in which people weigh roughly 20 to 30 percent more than the medically defined ideal body weight for their height.

350 CHAPTER 11

Class Demonstration

EVALUATING DIET PLANS

<u>Purpose</u>: Teams discuss the physiology and psychology of popular diet plans.

<u>Time</u>: 30 minutes

<u>Description</u>: Each team of students is assigned to a commercial diet plan (Jenny Craig, Weight Watchers, Atkins, etc.). Either have team members bring in materials from outside class or provide teams with information on their assigned plan. Teams have 15 minutes to examine their information and create a poster outlining the main components of the diet plan. Ideas should be categorized according to the physiology of hunger vs. the psychology of hunger. Students should discuss whether this is a healthy plan. Students may want to consider the following points: (1) Describe the major components of the diet plan; (2) Evaluate the effectiveness of the program from a physiological perspective; (3) Evaluate the effectiveness from a sociocultural perspective; (4) What type of person would find this diet most appealing?; (5) Is this diet healthy? Why or why not?

350 Chapter 11 Motivation and Emotion

and quickly (Barsh et al., 2000). More varied and appealing foods become available, enticing people to eat beyond their physiological needs (Raynor & Epstein, 2001). In industrialized societies, people who work long hours have less time to prepare meals and more incentive to dine out (Chou et al., 2004), often on calorie-rich foods.

Maladaptive eating behaviors also include clinical eating disorders, such as anorexia nervosa and bulimia nervosa, which are also prevalent in industrialized countries. A person with **anorexia nervosa** (typically a teenaged girl) drastically restricts food intake to lose weight. A person with **bulimia nervosa** (typically a woman in her early twenties) binges on enormous amounts of food at one sitting, and then uses unhealthy methods for avoiding weight gain, such as deliberate vomiting or laxative abuse (American Psychiatric Association [APA], 2000).

Both disorders are physically dangerous and psychologically debilitating. Patients have distorted body images, believing they are fat even when they are of normal weight or dangerously underweight. They become obsessed with food, eating, and weight loss and frequently suffer from depression and cognitive impairments as well as potentially life-threatening physical consequences.

Figure 27.5 on the next page summarizes the medical and behavioral characteristics of these eating disorders, as well as possible causes and options for treatment. Unfortunately, only 40 to 60 percent of anorexics who receive treatment will make a recovery, and even if an anorexia patient gains weight, the lasting physical damage (such as heart damage, for example) may result in an early death (Neumarker, 1997). The treatment prognosis for bulimia is somewhat more hopeful.

Culture and Eating Disorders Many researchers once believed that eating disorders, especially anorexia, appeared only in cultures obsessed with being thin. But eating disorders are also found in some other cultures (Miller & Pumariega, 1999). What differs is the rate at which such disorders appear (Pan, 2000). Additionally, examining eating disorders in other cultures is complicated, because the associated behaviors may serve an entirely different purpose—for instance, dieting or fasting not to lose weight but for religious or nutritional reasons (Castillo, 1997). LINK *to Chapter Eight: Culture and Gender, p. 259.*

Anorexia and bulimia were once considered rare in African American women, but researchers are now seeing an increase among young African American women of all socioeconomic levels (Crago et al., 1996; Mintz & Betz, 1998; Pumariega & Gustavson, 1994). Additionally, eating disorders and distorted body images are no longer rare in young men. For instance, young men who must stay within a narrow weight range for sports like wrestling may resort to severe dieting or purging behaviors. Men may also experience another sort of distorted body image. Unlike young women, who often see themselves as heavier than they are, young men may see themselves as too skinny and use steroids or supplements to try to put on muscle. It is important for clinicians and doctors to recognize the signs of eating disorders in patients who do not fit the "typical" profile.

27.4 What factors motivate sexual behavior and orientation?

As we discussed earlier, human beings have innate physiological needs that must be met in order to survive. These needs, such as hunger, motivate behavior, such as eating. The need to reproduce is also physiological, but in this

▲ *Cultural factors play an important part in why people eat. Women in Japan have been found to be motivated to eat by hunger and social demands, as this woman and her family are doing.*

▲ *Women in the United States may eat for emotional reasons. Obviously, this woman does not need the social trappings of a bowl, dining table, and the company of others to motivate her eating habits—unless you count the cat.*

anorexia nervosa a condition in which a person reduces eating to the point that a weight loss of 15 percent below the ideal body weight or more occurs.

bulimia nervosa a condition in which a person develops a cycle of "binging," or overeating enormous amounts of food at one sitting, and then using unhealthy methods to avoid weight gain.

MOTIVATION AND EMOTION 351

CHAPTER 11 • Module 27

COVER THE MODULE (continued)
- **Maladaptive eating problems:**
  - *Anorexia* is a condition in which a person (typically young and female) reduces eating to the point that a weight loss of 15 percent below expected body weight is obtained.
  - *Bulimia* is a condition in which a person develops a cycle of overeating ("binging") large amounts of food and then "purging," or deliberately vomiting after eating.

LINK *to Chapter Eight: Culture and Gender, p. 259*

FAST FACT
Ask students to answer true or false to this statement: "All people with anorexia are emaciated." This statement is false. A better indicator than thinness (as, on the opposite side, not all people who are extremely thin have anorexia) is an extreme obsession with eating—what, how much, how often—and exercising.

L4 DIFFERENTIATED INSTRUCTION
Advanced Learners Assign extension projects that provide students with experience in actual community activities.

Class Demonstration

PHYSIQUE PREFERENCES

Purpose: Students examine gender differences in ideal physiques.

Time: 20 minutes

Description: Students work in same-gender teams. The teacher should provide pictures to the teams of different male and female physiques from magazines, newspapers, or printed from the Internet. Ask students to select the picture that best represents the ideal male and female physiques. Teams then present their choices to the class. There are several different uses for this activity. You will probably find that males prefer a female body type that is heavier than what females select. There may be greater consensus across the genders on what an ideal male physique looks like. You may also want to look at what qualities make for an ideal male or female physique (e.g., muscles vs. thinness). You may want to talk about the problems associated with the pressure to achieve an ideal body type (e.g., steroid use, eating disorders). This exercise can be used to open up a discussion on eating disorders, universal standards of beauty, and gender differences in body image.

CHAPTER 11 • Module 27

EXTEND THE LESSON

Direct students to the information about anorexia nervosa and bulimia nervosa in Figure 27.5. After studying the figure, what do students think are the fundamental differences between the two, beyond the outright facts stated here? What do students think might be the differences in personality or situation between a person with anorexia and a person with bulimia?

COVER THE MODULE

27.4 What factors motivate sexual behavior and orientation?

- Sexual behavior is motivated by the need to reproduce, emotional satisfaction, desire for intimacy, and self-affirmation, among many other factors.

L1 DIFFERENTIATED INSTRUCTION

Special Needs Facilitate students' independence by modifying assignments as needed.

L2 ELL DIFFERENTIATED INSTRUCTION

English Language Learners Where possible, incorporate students' cultural experiences into your classroom instruction.

TEACHING TIP

Some students may be embarrassed by, or laugh at, discussions about sexual behavior and orientation. Try to keep the classroom atmosphere as "professional" as possible.

Anorexia Nervosa	Physical Signs	Behaviors	Possible Causes and Contributing Factors	Treatments
	• dramatic weight loss • weight more than 15% below a healthy weight • amenorrhea • periods of insomnia and hyperactivity alternating with extreme fatigue • frequently feeling cold • hair loss on head; fine hair may grow elsewhere on the body • hormonal and chemical imbalances • loss of muscle tissue • heart arrhythmia and other heart problems • dangerously low blood pressure • dehydration	• drastic reduction of food intake • distorted body image; obsession with losing weight • obsession with calories and fat content of food • preoccupation with food and eating • ritualistic eating behaviors such as hiding food or cutting food into tiny bites • excessive exercise • in some cases, vomiting and laxative abuse • wearing baggy clothes to hide body shape or weight loss • reading books about weight loss and eating disorders	• possible genetic component • chemical disturbance, possibly in the neurotransmitter serotonin and the hormone leptin • rejection of sexual maturity • history of sexual abuse • family dysfunction • family preoccupation with eating, dieting, and weight • cultural influences, such as the prevalence of very slender women in popular media and advertisements	• treatment of immediate physical needs; may involve hospitalization and even force-feeding if patient is severely malnourished • psychological counseling on inpatient or outpatient basis • behavioral therapy • group therapy • family therapy

Bulimia Nervosa	Physical Signs	Behaviors	Possible Causes and Contributing Factors	Treatments
	• frequent weight fluctuations • bruised or callused knuckles • bloodshot eyes with light bruising under the eyes • severe tooth decay • erosion of the lining of the esophagus • enlarged salivary glands • hormonal and chemical imbalances • damage to the intestinal tract • heart problems • seizures • dehydration	• bingeing on large quantities of food, followed by purging through vomiting or laxative abuse • frequent trips to the bathroom following meals • distorted body image; obsession with losing weight • obsession with calories and fat content of food • preoccupation with food and eating • in some cases, use of extreme dieting, fasting, or exercise to control weight • reading books about weight loss and eating disorders	• possible genetic component • chemical disturbance, possibly in the neurotransmitter serotonin and the hormone leptin • rejection of sexual maturity • history of sexual abuse • family dysfunction • family preoccupation with eating, dieting, and weight • cultural influences, such as the prevalence of very slender women in popular media and advertisements	• hospitalization if necessary to address physical needs • drugs that affect serotonin levels • psychological therapy (see therapies listed above) • cognitive therapy

FIGURE 27.5 Anorexia Nervosa and Bulimia Nervosa

---

case, the need is connected with survival of the species. Although sex, unlike food, isn't essential for an individual's survival, the survival of the species depends on people reproducing.

Like hunger and eating, sexual feelings and behavior result in part from physiological causes. Adults sometimes joke about teenagers being moody, unpredictable, and "hormonal," but in fact, teenagers who have experienced puberty

---

Explore

YOUR BRAIN ON FOOD

Send students to the Multimedia Library for this chapter at www.mypsychlab.com to view the video "Your Brain on Food." Explain that the DSM is the *Diagnostic and Statistical Manual of Mental Disorders*, which classifies all known psychological disorders (see Chapter 13). Have the class watch the video and complete the questions at the end of it. Ask students to share their answers to the final question: "Argue both for and against the inclusion of syndromes related to overeating and obesity in a revised version of the DSM." You may even start a list on the board of pros and cons for such a change. Overall, how do students feel about this issue? Did this video and what they have read in the text make them see the issue differently?

are "hormonal"—that is, they experience major hormonal changes related to the onset of reproductive maturity. The chemistry of sexual behavior is too complex to describe at length here, but the hormone testosterone is linked with sexual desire in both sexes. In women, fluctuations in sexual desire may also be linked with fluctuating levels of estrogen during the menstrual cycle. Both sexes are anatomically capable of the same sexual feelings, although men have higher rates of most forms of sexual behavior (Oliver & Hyde, 1993; Peplau, 2003).

Of course, culture influences the expression of human sexuality. Most cultures encourage sex within an official union like marriage because it aids survival and perpetuation of the species; that is, it promotes a way to care for offspring over the long term.

Research on Sexual Behavior Several researchers have conducted large-scale studies of human sexual behavior. Perhaps the best-known is Alfred Kinsey, who relied on interviews in which subjects discussed their sexual behaviors (Kinsey et al., 1948). Kinsey's first published report was highly controversial. Many people found it difficult to believe that so many subjects had strayed from what was considered the only socially acceptable sexual behavior—intercourse between a man and a woman who were married.

Kinsey's research has since been criticized on various grounds: that his subjects were primarily white, middle-class, well-educated Protestants from urban areas; that he focused too much on "abnormal" behaviors; and that, as with any study that relies on subjects' self-reports, the accuracy of the data is questionable. Nevertheless, Kinsey's work paved the way for later researchers, such as Masters and Johnson (1966) and Janus and Janus (1993). *The Janus Report on Sexual Behavior*—a survey begun in 1983 that collected data from 3,000 people, aged 18 to older than 65, in 48 states—relied on both interviews and questionnaires. The survey addressed a variety of sexual behaviors and related topics, including marriage and divorce; the decision to have children; and how religion, political orientation, education, wealth, and geographical region affect sexual behavior.

Sexual Orientation **Sexual orientation** refers to the direction of a person's sexual attraction and affection for others—toward members of either the opposite or the same sex. There are three generally recognized sexual orientations: *heterosexuality, homosexuality,* and *bisexuality.* Heterosexuality (from the Greek *hetero,* meaning "other") is sexual attraction to members of the opposite sex. This is the most common form of sexual behavior and the most widely accepted across different cultures. Homosexuality (from the Greek *homos,* meaning "same"), in contrast, is sexual attraction to members of the same sex. It is estimated that 2 to 10 percent of the population is predominantly homosexual, with a larger percentage having had at least one homosexual experience. Bisexuality (the prefix *bi-* means "two") is sexual attraction to members of both sexes (although the degree of attraction to each sex may vary).

Despite the listing of categories above, research suggests that sexual orientation is a continuum. Some people are exclusively attracted to the opposite sex or to the same sex, but many people fall somewhere in between.

Is sexual orientation a product of the environment, biology, or both?

Researchers have studied whether sexual orientation is strictly biological or is influenced by environmental factors such as learning and experience. Given people's widely varying attitudes about sexuality, this is an emotionally charged question. Although there is no definitive answer about what causes sexual orientation, some research strongly suggests biological influences. One study found that when pregnant women experienced severe stress during the

Is sexual orientation a product of the environment, biology, or both?

sexual orientation the direction of a person's sexual attraction and affection for others.

CHAPTER 11 • Module 27

COVER THE MODULE *(continued)*

- **The Kinsey Study**
  - Alfred Kinsey conducted a series of sexual behavior surveys in the late 1940s and early 1950s, revealing some highly controversial findings about the kinds of sexual behavior common among people in the United States, including homosexuality, premarital sex, and extramarital sex.
  - Kinsey's study, published in 1948, covered a set of data that had been collected since 1938.
  - Kinsey's subjects were mostly white, middle class, and college educated.

- **Janus and Janus**
  - Janus and Janus, in the mid-1990s, published the results of a large-scale survey of sexual behavior in the United States. Their survey results did not differ widely from those of Kinsey but looked at many more types of sexual behavior and factors related to sexual behavior than did Kinsey's surveys.
  - Data was collected through interviews and questionnaires with individuals aged 18 to 65 years.

- Heterosexuals are attracted to people of the opposite sex and represent the largest sexual orientation.

- Homosexuals are primarily attracted to people of the same sex and make up about 9 percent of men and 5 percent of women.

- Bisexuals are people who are attracted to both males and females.

DISCUSS THE STUDENT VOICE QUESTION

Ask students to carefully consider the information presented in the text regarding *sexual orientation*. Make it clear that an attitude of tolerance and understanding is expected and will be maintained in the classroom.

Explore

PRIVILEGES BASED ON SEXUAL ORIENTATION

Many of the most basic privileges denied to homosexuals are taken for granted by heterosexuals: being able to talk openly about one's partner without fear of recrimination or abuse, being able to publicly display affection toward one's partner, obtaining employment benefits from a partner's job, and being able to legally document a relationship commitment or to adopt children. For students who are open to this activity, direct them to Internet sites, such as http://en.wikipedia.org/wiki/LGBT_rights_by_country_or_territory, to see which legal rights are extended to and denied homosexuals in the United States and how the United States compares to the rest of the world.

CHAPTER 11 • Module 27

COVER THE MODULE (continued)
- While research suggests a biological component to heterosexuality, environmental influences may also play a part.

LINK to Chapter Two: The Biological Perspective, p. 68

COVER THE MODULE

27.5 What factors motivate achievement?
- Carol Dweck links achievement to beliefs about the self, specifically locus of control.
  - *Internal locus of control* means that an individual has control over his or her own life.
  - *External locus of control* means that one's life is controlled by outside forces.

LINK to Chapter Six: Learning and Language Development, pp. 198–199

EXTEND THE LESSON

One study in which Dweck participated involved motivation of young children. The children were separated into two groups and asked to do simple puzzle problems. Each group scored well on the problems, but one group was praised for its intelligence, while the other group was praised for its effort. The children were then given progressively harder puzzles to solve. Ask students to predict how each group reacted. What was each group's locus of control? (Answer: The group praised for its intelligence eventually gave up on the puzzles, enjoyed them less, and did not score as well as the other group. These children showed an external locus of control. The group praised for its effort did not feel as defeated by the puzzles. These children showed an internal locus of control.)

---

second trimester, there was a significantly higher chance that any male children would be homosexual (Ellis et al., 1988). Simon LeVay (1991) found that a certain area of the hypothalamus was three times larger in men than in women, and two to three times larger in heterosexual men than in homosexual men.

These results show correlation, not necessarily a cause-and-effect relationship, and it is possible that other factors affected LeVay's findings. Still, the research suggests a biological component to sexual orientation. Studies of twins also suggest a genetic component (Bailey & Pillard, 1991), but environmental influences have not been ruled out. (Of course, genetic and environmental influences continually interact to influence all kinds of behavior.) LINK to Chapter Two: The Biological Perspective, p. 68.

Regardless of how the environment influences sexual orientation, it definitely influences sexual behavior and attitudes toward sexual behavior. In many cultures, homosexuals and bisexuals have faced prejudice, discrimination, harassment, and sometimes violence. Although attitudes are beginning to become more positive (Loftus, 2001; Tucker and Potocky-Tripodi, 2006), full social acceptance is, in many societies, a long way off.

27.5 What factors motivate achievement?

According to psychologist Carol Dweck (1999), one's view of *self* can affect the understanding of how much a person's actions can influence his or her success. (Dweck defines *self* as the beliefs one holds about one's abilities and relationships to others.) This is related to the older notion of *locus of control* (think of *locus* as "location"). People with an **internal locus of control** assume that they have control over their lives, while people with an **external locus of control** feel that their lives are controlled by powerful others, luck, or fate (MacDonald, 1970; Rotter, 1966). This affects people's achievement motivation and their persistence (Dweck, 1986; Dweck & Elliott, 1983; Dweck & Leggett, 1988; Elliott & Dweck, 1988).

Dweck believed people form one of two belief systems about intelligence:
- Intelligence is fixed and unchangeable, *or*
- Intelligence is changeable and can be gradually shaped through our experiences and efforts.

People in the first category often show an external locus of control, leading them to give up easily or avoid situations in which they might fail. They try to "look smart" and outperform others. They are also prone to developing *learned helplessness*, the tendency to stop trying to achieve a goal because past failure has led them to believe they cannot succeed. LINK to Chapter Six: Learning and Language Development, pp. 198–199.

People with this view are not necessarily unsuccessful. In fact, consistently successful students may be most at risk for developing learned helplessness after a failure, precisely because their previous successes have led them to believe in fixed intelligence (Dweck, 1999). A straight-A student who gets a C might become depressed, suddenly convinced he or she isn't so smart after all, and then refuse to do homework, ensuring future failure.

People in the second category believe intelligence is changeable and can be shaped by experiences and effort. They tend to show an internal locus of control. Their belief that they can gradually improve their intelligence motivates them to work at developing new strategies and taking on new tasks. They are motivated to master tasks and don't allow failure to destroy their confidence or prevent them from trying again and again, using new strategies each time.

internal locus of control the assumption that one generally has control over one's life.

external locus of control the assumption that one's life is generally controlled by external forces, such as powerful others, luck, or fate.

Class Demonstration

CONTROVERSIES IN MOTIVATION

<u>Purpose</u>: Students have a chance to think about, debate, and discuss controversial topics in motivation.

<u>Time</u>: 15 minutes

<u>Description</u>: Pose controversial questions to the class. Students share their answers and contribute to further class discussion. Here are some controversies involving motivation and emotion:

- Humans are motivated by their instincts.
- Weight control is all about willpower.
- Being intrinsically motivated by something is better than being extrinsically motivated.

Dweck recommends encouraging children to value the learning process more than always "looking smart." Errors should not be viewed as failures but as a way to improve future performance and eventually master a goal. Dweck also recommends praising students' efforts and strategies, not just successes or ability. Instead of saying, "You're right, how smart you are," the parent or teacher should say something like, "You're really thinking hard," or "That was a very clever way to think about this problem," and should provide not only praise but also constructive criticism.

27.6 Are there other ways in which humans and animals are motivated?

The Motivation to Love *Romantic love* encompasses several different feelings: the initial attraction to another person; *passionate love*, or the intense emotions and physical passion experienced at the beginning of a romantic relationship; and *companionate love*, or the deep intimacy, affection, and trust enjoyed by longtime partners. These feelings are influenced by both biological and environmental factors.

While the idea of romantic love is, in part, a modern Western cultural construction, there is an evolutionary advantage to romantic love: It may lead to sexual reproduction, ensuring the survival of the species. Interestingly, some of the same hormones involved in romantic love are involved in the bonds between infants and their caretakers. This also makes sense from an evolutionary standpoint. A human infant is quite helpless, and humans remain dependent on their caretakers for a relatively long time. Close family bonds are essential for children's survival.

Both infant-caretaker attachments and romantic attraction are experienced as pleasurable. The hormone **oxytocin**—released by women during labor and breastfeeding, and by both sexes during sexual activity—plays a role in these feelings. Administering oxytocin to research subjects can increase feelings of trust (Kosfeld et al., 2005) and expressions of romantic affection (Gonzaga et al., 2006).

Endorphins—the brain's "natural painkillers" that produce feelings of euphoria—also seem to be involved. Animal research suggests that endorphins play a role in responding to the distress we feel when separated from a caregiver or partner, as well as the joy we feel upon reuniting (Diamond, 2004; Panksepp et al., 1980). Researchers using functional MRI have found that the same parts of the brain light up when people look at photographs of their romantic partners and when mothers look at photographs of their children (Bartels and Zeki, 2004).

Of course, environmental factors also influence love. Again, there are parallels between caretaker attachments and romantic attachments. Attachment style in infancy—that is, the nature of the connection between infant and caretaker LINK *to Chapter Five, Development Across the Lifespan, pp. 140–175*—affects our family relationships as children, which in turn is correlated with how we form close relationships as adults. Children who experience close, secure family relationships are more likely to form secure romantic relationships as adults (Mickelson et al., 1997).

Other environmental influences include proximity—who's nearby—and similarity. We tend to become close with people whom we see regularly and

▲ *This young girl seems eager to provide an answer to the teacher's question, and the teacher's positive feedback will help foster the girl's need for achievement. Even if the girl does not answer correctly, the teacher can encourage her efforts, helping her stay motivated to learn.*

oxytocin a hormone released by women during labor and breastfeeding, and by both sexes during sexual activity. Oxytocin is also a neurotransmitter within the brain, where it plays similar roles.

MOTIVATION AND EMOTION   355

CHAPTER 11 • Module 27

UNDERSTANDING VISUALS
Direct students' attention to the photo on this page. Ask students what kinds of things the teacher could say to motivate this kind of reaction in students. If, as the caption suggests, the child does not answer correctly, what specific responses would best keep the student engaged and motivated?

COVER THE MODULE
27.6 Are there other ways in which humans and animals are motivated?

- The motivation to love has an evolutionary basis and is influenced by biological and environmental factors.

LINK *to Chapter Five: Development Across the Life Span, pp. 140–175*

L1 DIFFERENTIATED INSTRUCTION
Special Needs If appropriate, pair students with classmate helpers and provide time for interaction.

Class Demonstration

COMPARISON OF THEORIES OF MOTIVATION

Divide the class into small groups. Draw the chart to the right on the board and ask students to copy it for this exercise. Working together with their notes and textbooks, students should fill in the chart. Ask group volunteers to summarize their answers for the rest of the class.

Theory	Main Ideas
Instinct Theories	
Theorists/researchers:	
Drive-Reduction Theory	
Theorists/researchers:	
Arousal Theory	
Theorists/researchers:	
Hierarchy of Needs	
Theorists/researchers:	

Module 27 Motivation   355

CHAPTER 11 • Module 27

COVER THE MODULE *(continued)*

- The motivation to belong also has a biological basis. It can lead to both positive and destructive behaviors.

CRITICAL THINKING

Ask students to think about the social networking sites they belong to, such as MySpace, Twitter, and Facebook. How do these sites increase their feelings of belonging? Do the sites ever make them feel as if they do not belong? (For example, research has suggested that Facebook can make some people feel bad about themselves because all their "friends" appear so happy and successful—a sense of being out of the happiness loop.) Ask students to consider whether their need to belong encourages them to participate in online bullying, in a sort of bully-or-be-bullied situation. Does social networking fill a void in our country or create one? You may even divide students into two groups and give them time to briefly discuss and/or research, and then debate the last question.

L4 DIFFERENTIATED INSTRUCTION

Advanced Learners For these students, emphasize generalizations, theories, ideas, and concepts within the textbook content.

---

who are like us in terms of looks, interests, attitudes, and so on. Broader social and cultural factors also influence our expression of romantic love and sexual feelings.

The Motivation to Belong Of course, we form many relationships besides family and romantic relationships. Human beings also feel a strong need for friendships and a sense of belonging within a group. Again, this has an evolutionary basis. Early humans were more likely to survive—by finding or producing food and evading dangerous predators—if they traveled in groups, cooperated, and worked toward common goals.

Naturally, then, we want to belong. Feeling connected and accepted makes us happy, while isolation makes us anxious and depressed. Studies of ostracism—being deliberately excluded by a group—have shown that being ostracized causes increased activity in a region of the brain which is also active when we respond to physical pain (Eisenberger et al., 2003). Being left out hurts.

Our need to belong can motivate positive behaviors such as cooperating, helping others, and striving to make a good impression. Unfortunately, it can also motivate us to stay in destructive or even abusive relationships to avoid being alone.

Class Demonstration

HIERARCHY OF BELONGINGNESS

<u>Purpose</u>: Students have a chance to think about where they most belong and what groups are most important to them.

<u>Time</u>: 5 minutes

<u>Description</u>: Ask students to construct their own personal hierarchy of belonging as a pyramid, similar to Maslow's Hierarchy of Needs. Students do not need to share this information with the rest of the class. You may want to help them get started by suggesting that perhaps the base, their basic belonging, would be family. Construct one for yourself on the board that you would be willing to share with the class.

Practice Quiz

Pick the best answer.

1. Liz picked out "her" desk on the first day of class. But in the second class period, someone else was sitting in her chosen seat. Liz's territorial attitude about that desk and her negative feelings toward the "interloper" sitting there is best explained by which of the following?
   a. instinct approach
   b. drive-reduction theory
   c. extrinsic motivation
   d. homeostasis

2. Which of these needs is an example of a primary drive?
   a. the need for love
   b. the need for food
   c. the need for creative expression
   d. the need to belong to a group

3. Ronnie believes that people are just born smart or not smart, and he thinks of himself as "not smart." As a result, Ronnie doesn't try all that hard to succeed in school. Dweck would say that Ronnie's achievement motivation is being affected by his
   a. acquired secondary drives
   b. internal locus of control
   c. primary drives
   d. external locus of control

4. Which approach to motivation claims that people have an optimal level of tension?
   a. arousal
   b. incentive
   c. humanistic
   d. self-determination

5. Which of the following is not one of the physiological factors involved in hunger?
   a. the release of insulin
   b. sensory receptors in the stomach
   c. changes in the corpus collosum
   d. activity in the hypothalamus

6. Which of these is an example of fulfilling an esteem need?
   a. eating a hamburger
   b. graduating from college
   c. purchasing a smoke detector
   d. looking at a work of art

7. Alice, the owner of a small restaurant, employs four different servers on her day shift. All of them try to do a good job, but for different reasons. Which one is motivated by an intrinsic reward?
   a. Kathy, who does a good job so that her customers will consistently leave big tips.
   b. Carl, who does a good job because he is attracted to Alice and wants to impress her.
   c. Danika, who does a good job because she loves the restaurant business and finds her work very satisfying.
   d. Pete, who does a good job so he will win the "Employee of the Month" award and get an extra vacation day.

8. Bulimia, unlike anorexia,
   a. usually involves starvation
   b. is most prevalent in early puberty
   c. involves an obsession with food and weight
   d. usually revolves around a cycle of binging and purging

9. Which of these negative situations can activate the same part of the brain that responds to physical pain?
   a. being excluded from a group
   b. failing at an important task
   c. facing a dangerous threat
   d. being hungry after going too long without eating

10. Which of the following terms describes sexual attraction to members of the opposite sex?
    a. sexuality
    b. bisexuality
    c. homosexuality
    d. heterosexuality

Practice Quiz Answers

1. a
2. b
3. d
4. a
5. c
6. b
7. c
8. d
9. a
10. d

CHAPTER 11 • Module 27

Assess

Assign the Module 27 Practice Quiz.

Use the Practice Quiz to identify gaps in student understanding.

REMEDIATE

Have students, individually or in groups, review the module goals, learning objectives, and key terms.

Refer students to the Concept Summary on pp. 372–373 for review.

Close

The issues of motivation discussed in this module affect us all—hunger, love, belonging. Ask students to write down what they learned about themselves through studying this module. Did it change their outlook about themselves? How can they use this information in their lives?

CHAPTER 11 • Module 28

Focus

RESOURCES

For this module, consult the appropriate sections of the Teacher's Manual, Test Bank, and PowerPoint slides, all found on the Teacher's Resource DVD, and the interactive study tools for students on MyPsychLab.

BEFORE CLASS

Students should read the section for homework before coming to class.

BELLRINGER

Ask students to think about the role emotion plays in their lives. Does emotion affect their grades? Does it affect their health? Their memories? Their sleeping and eating habits? What, if any, aspects of their lives are not touched by emotion?

Teach

COVER THE MODULE

28.1 What are the biological, behavioral, and cognitive components of emotion?

- *Emotion* is the "feeling" aspect of consciousness and includes a:
  - Physical (biological) component
  - Behavioral component
  - Cognitive component (inner awareness and labeling of feelings)

LINK to Chapter Two: The Biological Perspective, pp. 49–50

Module 28 Emotion

Module Goals

Understand theories of emotion and emotional expression.

Analyze emotional behaviors in depth.

Learning Objectives

28.1 What are the biological, behavioral, and cognitive components of emotion?

28.2 What are the major theories of emotion?

28.3 How do cultural and environmental factors influence emotional expression?

28.4 What biological and environmental factors influence the expression and experience of fear?

28.5 What biological and environmental factors influence the expression and experience of happiness?

Understand Theories of Emotion and Emotional Expression

28.1 What are the biological, behavioral, and cognitive components of emotion?

The Latin word *movere*, which means "to move," is the root of the words *motive* and *emotion*. **Emotion** is the "feeling" aspect of consciousness, characterized by three elements:
- physical arousal
- behavior that expresses or reveals the feeling
- an inner awareness of the feeling.

The Physiology of Emotion When a person experiences an emotion, the sympathetic nervous system creates physiological arousal. LINK *to Chapter Two: The Biological Perspective, pp. 49–50*. For instance, the heart rate increases, breathing becomes more rapid, the pupils dilate, and the mouth may become dry. Think about the last time you were angry and then about the last time you were frightened. Weren't the physical symptoms pretty similar?

Although facial expressions differ for various emotions (Ekman, 1980; Ekman et al., 1969; Ekman & Friesen, 1978), emotions are hard to distinguish based on bodily reactions alone. It's easy to mistake fear or anger for arousal if the person's face is not clearly visible. However, researchers have found that some emotions may be associated with different physiological reactions—for example, a decrease in skin temperature when experiencing fear, and an increase in skin temperature and blood pressure when experiencing anger (Levenson, 1992; Levenson et al., 1992).

The amygdala, a small area located at the tip of the hippocampus, toward the front of the temporal lobe on each side of the brain, is associated with fear in both humans and animals (Davis & Whalen, 2001; Fanselow &

emotion the "feeling" aspect of consciousness, characterized by physical arousal, behavior that expresses or reveals the emotion, and an inner awareness of feelings.

Terms

- emotion • James-Lange theory of emotion • Cannon-Bard theory of emotion
- two-factor theory • facial feedback hypothesis • cognitive-mediational theory
- display rules • phobia • desensitization • dopamine • serotonin • adaptation-level phenomenon • relative deprivation • positive psychology movement

358 Chapter 11 Motivation and Emotion

Gale, 2003) and in the facial expressions of human emotions (Morris et al., 1998). Rats with damaged amygdalas cannot be classically conditioned to fear new objects—they apparently cannot remember to be afraid (Davidson et al., 2000; Fanselow & Gale, 2003). Amygdala damage in humans has been associated with similar effects (LaBar et al., 1995) and with problems "reading" others' facial expressions to determine their emotions (Adolphs & Tranel, 2003).

Research also suggests that different emotions are associated with different sides of the brain. Although it's not quite this simple, the general findings are that positive emotions are associated with the left frontal lobe, and negative emotions with the right frontal lobe (Davidson, 2003; Geschwind & Iacoboni, 2007; Heilman, 2002). In studies, where the electrical activity of the brain has been tracked using an electroencephalograph (EEG), **LINK** *to Chapter Two: The Biological Perspective, p. 56*, left frontal lobe activation has been associated with pleasant emotions such as love and happiness, while right frontal lobe activity has been associated with negative emotional states such as anxiety, sadness, and clinical depression (Davidson, 2003). Additionally, the right side of the brain seems to be specialized for interpreting facial expressions. Researchers have found that when people are asked to identify the emotion on another person's face, the right hemisphere is more active than the left, particularly in women (Voyer & Rodgers, 2002).

The Behavioral Expression of Emotion We convey emotion through facial expressions and body movements. Facial expressions can vary across cultures, but some are universal. (See Figure 28.1 for examples.) Charles Darwin (1898)

FIGURE 28.1 Facial Expressions of Emotion
Facial expressions appear to be universal. For example, these faces are interpreted as showing (a) anger, (b) fear, (c) disgust, (d) happiness, (e) surprise, and (f) sadness by people of cultures all over the world. People can also consistently recognize expressions of contempt. Although the situations that cause these emotions may differ from culture to culture, the expression of particular emotions remains strikingly the same.

MOTIVATION AND EMOTION 359

CHAPTER 11 • Module 28

COVER THE MODULE *(continued)*

- Different areas of the brain have been found to be associated with different emotions:
  - Amygdala: fear
  - Left frontal lobe: positive emotions
  - Right frontal lobe: negative emotions
- Additionally, the right hemisphere appears to be specialized for interpreting facial expressions.

LINK *to Chapter Two: The Biological Perspective, p. 56*

UNDERSTANDING VISUALS

To further illustrate the point made in Figure 28.1, write each of the following emotions (along with the given number) on 11 separate index cards: (1) Happiness, (2) Surprise, (3) Jealousy, (4) Disgust, (5) Pride, (6) Sadness, (7) Love, (8) Fear, (9) Disappointment, (10) Anger, (11) Relief.

Explain that you are going to conduct a live demonstration of facial expressions, and that you need 11 students to volunteer to *pose* or *send* emotions while the rest of the class attempts to *receive* or *decode* them. Solicit student volunteers who are not shy about posing facial expressions in front of the class (preferably expressive or outspoken individuals who will "ham it up"). Randomly distribute to each volunteer an index card containing the target emotion that will be posed. Instruct the remainder of the class to number a blank sheet of paper from 1 to 11 and have them try to decode each emotion. Remind student senders that they are restricted to facial expressions only—caution them not to use verbal cues (e.g., sighs or groans) or postural cues (e.g., slumping). How well can students guess the emotion each volunteer is conveying? Do students think it might be harder to interpret facial expressions without real emotion behind them?

Explore

KISMET, THE SOCIABLE ROBOT

Have students read about Kismet, the "sociable humanoid robot," at www.ai.mit.edu/projects/humanoid-robotics-group/kismet/kismet.html Ask them to view Kismet's facial expressions by clicking "The Framework" and "Facial Expression." Do students find Kismet's facial expressions easily readable? Do students think that a robot can accurately convey all facial expressions (e.g., more subtle expressions like disgust, which can easily look like anger)? If not, why not?

Module 28 Emotion 359

CHAPTER 11 • Module 28

COVER THE MODULE (continued)

- Freud suggested that emotions arose through evolution and were, therefore, universal among humans.

LINK to Chapter One: The Science of Psychology, pp. 8–9

- Interpretation and labeling of emotions comprise the third element and can vary greatly among cultures.

MULTIMEDIA CONTENT AVAILABLE AT
www.mypsychlab.com

Simulate recognizing facial expressions of emotions on **mypsychlab.com**

DISCUSS THE STUDENT VOICE QUESTION

Ask students what they think about the theories of emotion presented in the text. Does arousal happen before the consciousness of the emotion? Does it happen simultaneously? Can it vary? (e.g., in an emergency situation, students may say that the physical manifestations of fear may come well after the stimulus is gone.)

COVER THE MODULE

28.2 What are the major theories of emotion?

- The *James-Lange theory* states that a stimulus creates a physiological response, which then leads to the labeling of the emotion.

James-Lange theory of emotion
theory in which a physiological reaction leads to the labeling of an emotion.

Simulate recognizing facial expressions of emotions on **mypsychlab.com**

▶ *So which of the three elements of emotion is the most important?*

proposed that emotions were a product of evolution and, therefore, universal. Humans in all cultures would show the same facial expressions because the facial muscles evolved to communicate specific information. Other researchers have since found evidence for at least seven basic universal emotions: anger, fear, sadness, happiness, disgust, surprise, and contempt (Ekman, 1973; Ekman & Friesen, 1969, 1971). **LINK** to Chapter One: The Science of Psychology, pp. 8–9.

Although our basic emotions and the corresponding facial expressions appear to be universal, environmental factors influence just how we express emotions. These factors, such as cultural differences and gender differences, are discussed in section 28.3. **Simulate** on **mypsychlab.com**

Subjective Experience: The Cognitive Labeling of Emotion The third element is our awareness of emotion—the way we interpret and label our subjective feeling as anger, fear, happiness, and so on. This "cognitive element" involves retrieving memories of similar experiences, perceiving the context of the emotion, and coming up with a label.

Our labels are, to some extent, learned responses influenced by language and culture, and may differ somewhat across cultures. For example, one study (Tsai et al., 2004) found that Chinese Americans who were still firmly rooted in Chinese culture used more labels that referred to bodily sensations (such as "dizzy") or social relationships (such as "friendship") than "Americanized" Chinese Americans and European Americans, who used more directly emotional words (such as "liking" or "love").

Even the subjective feeling of happiness may show cultural differences. For instance, Kitayama & Markus (1994) compared Japanese students with students from the United States, and found that Japanese students were more likely to associate a positive emotional state with friendly or socially engaged feelings, while students from the United States associated this state with socially disengaged feelings, such as pride.

So which of the three elements of emotion is the most important?
Early psychologists assumed that feeling a particular emotion led first to a physical reaction and then to a behavioral one. Seeing a snarling dog in one's path causes the *feeling* of fear, which stimulates the body to *physical arousal*, followed by the *behavior* of running. Later psychologists, however, proposed different theories about the order of these three components.

28.2 What are the major theories of emotion?

James-Lange American psychologist William James (1884, 1890, & 1894) and Danish physiologist and psychologist Carl Lange (1885), independently came up with similar explanations of emotion, which psychologists now refer to as the **James-Lange theory of emotion**. (See Figure 28.2.) In this theory, a stimulus (for example, a snarling dog) produces physiological *arousal*. (In this case, the automatic "fight-or-flight" response of the sympathetic nervous system would

FIGURE 28.2 James-Lange Theory of Emotion
In the James-Lange theory of emotion, a stimulus leads to bodily arousal first, which is then interpreted as an emotion.

	Stimulus	First response	Second response
James-Lange theory			FEAR
"I'm afraid because I'm shaking."	Snarling dog	ANS arousal, changes in body	Conscious fear

360 CHAPTER 11

Class Demonstration (Kinesthetic)

VOCAL CUES AND EMOTION

Ask students to stand at the front of class in pairs and tell them to communicate different emotional states to one another. (You might have one pair demonstrate this for the rest of the class, or use different pairs of people for different sets of emotions, or have partners within a pair trade off.) The students must stand back-to-back, facing away from one another. The person communicating the emotion is allowed to use only one statement: "These pretzels are making me thirsty." Hearing this phrase only, it is the partner's job to guess each of the following emotions:

anger	excitement	dejection	disgust	joy
concern	affection	protection	pleasure	sadness
fear	sympathy	love	frustration	hate

Given the restrictions of the rules, students often are surprised to find that they guess any of the emotions correctly; in fact, they will probably identify a significant number of them. Studies of content-free filtered speech demonstrate that nervousness, anger, sadness, and happiness are the easiest emotions to detect from vocal cues alone, whereas surprise, fear, and love are much more difficult.

360 Chapter 11 Motivation and Emotion

be activated.) Arousal might include sensations such as increased heart rate, dry mouth, and rapid breathing. The physical arousal, in turn, leads us to *label* the emotion (in this case, fear). Think about it. Can you imagine being afraid without feeling any physical symptoms? The James-Lange theory has come to refer to the idea that we process emotion by thinking, "I am afraid because I am aroused," "I am in love because my heart pounds when I look at her," and so on.

The James-Lange theory would predict that people who have spinal cord injuries that prevent the sympathetic nervous system from functioning should show decreased emotion. However, several studies show that these people are capable of experiencing the same emotions after their injuries as before (Bermond et al., 1991; Chwalisz et al., 1988).

Cannon-Bard Physiologists Walter Cannon (1927) and Philip Bard (1934) theorized that the *feeling* and the *arousal* occur more or less simultaneously. Cannon believed that we cannot *label* our emotions based on arousal alone, because the physical responses caused by different emotions are not distinct enough.

For instance, a girl's heart might be pounding because she is looking at a snarling dog (fear) or because she is looking at her boyfriend (love). So how is it that we experience different emotions? That's where Bard expanded on Cannon's idea. Bard believed that when sensory information comes into the brain, the thalamus sends a message to the cortex *and* the organs of the sympathetic nervous system *simultaneously*. The sympathetic nervous system produces the *physical* response, while the cortex *experiences* the subjective feeling ("My heart is pounding; I'm so in love with my guy"). The physical response and the emotion are experienced together. (See Figure 28.3.)

The Cannon-Bard theory of emotion has its critics. Lashley (1938) questioned whether the thalamus was sophisticated enough to make sense of all the possible human emotions and relay them properly. The previously mentioned studies of people with spinal cord injuries seem at first to support the Cannon-Bard theory: People can experience emotion even if they cannot get any feedback from the organs of the sympathetic nervous system. However, an alternate pathway, the vagus nerve (LeDoux, 1994), does provide feedback from these organs to the cortex—which makes the case for Cannon-Bard a little less convincing.

Schachter and Singer and the Two-Factor Theory What about the mental interpretation of the physical reaction? Schachter and Singer's **two-factor theory** (1962) proposed that two things have to happen to produce an emotion: physical *arousal* and our *labeling* of the arousal based on environmental cues. These two things happen more or less at the same time. (See Figure 28.4 on the next page.)

For example, if a person comes across a snarling dog, the *physical arousal* (heart racing, eyes opening wide) is accompanied by thought (cognition) resulting in our *label* of what the arousal means. Only then will the person

Cannon-Bard theory of emotion theory in which the physiological reaction and the emotion are assumed to occur at the same time.

two-factor theory theory of emotion in which both the physical arousal and the labeling of that arousal based on cues from the environment must occur before the emotion is experienced.

FIGURE 28.3 Cannon-Bard Theory of Emotion
In the Cannon-Bard theory of emotion, a stimulus leads to activity in the brain, which then sends signals to arouse the body and interpret the emotion at the same time.

MOTIVATION AND EMOTION 361

CHAPTER 11 • Module 28

COVER THE MODULE *(continued)*

- The *Cannon-Bard theory* asserts that the physiological reaction and the emotion are simultaneous, as the thalamus sends sensory information to both the cortex of the brain and the organs of the sympathetic nervous system.

- In Schachter and Singer's cognitive arousal theory, both the physiological arousal and the actual interpretation of that arousal must occur before the emotion itself is experienced. This interpretation is based on cues from the environment.

EXTEND THE LESSON

Cross-cultural research has found that expressions of happiness are most easily and most accurately detected by members of a variety of cultures. In other cases, different smiles, with different corresponding facial actions, can signal other affective states. For example, researchers studied the smiles shown by nurses who either told the truth or lied about a videotape they were watching. Whereas the smile of enjoyment could be detected (using the Facial Action Coding System) when the nurses truthfully related their positive experiences, "masking" smiles could be measured when the nurses lied. These types of smiles contained facial muscle actions shown when negative emotions, such as disgust, anger, or sadness, are displayed. If considered at a surface level, however ("Is this person smiling?"), the differences in the muscle actions would be difficult to detect by an untrained observer. Can students recognize different kinds of smiles? Can they replicate them?

Class Demonstration (Kinesthetic)

PHYSIOLOGICAL EXPERIENCES OF EMOTION

Allow students a few minutes to stretch their legs and socialize a bit. Once students have begun to move around and are relaxed and talking (and not noticing you), make a loud sound, such as slamming a ruler on the desk. Students should jump, and maybe scream, followed by some laughter. Immediately ask students how they feel, physiologically. They will probably report their hearts are racing, and some will have sweaty palms. Ask them how they feel emotionally. Most will say they felt scared but then relieved.

Module 28 Emotion

CHAPTER 11 • Module 28

COVER THE MODULE (continued)

- In the *facial feedback hypothesis*, facial expressions provide feedback to the brain about the emotion being expressed on the face, intensifying the emotion.
- In the *cognitive-mediational theory* of emotion (Lazarus), the cognitive component of emotion (the interpretation) precedes both the physiological reaction and the emotion itself.

EXTEND THE LESSON

While there are certainly times when we should listen to our negative emotions and act upon them (That big dog is going to chase you! Act on your fear and run!), psychologists warn that negative emotions, though good informants, can be bad advisors. Anger may advise retaliation, depression may advise inactivity, loneliness may advise isolation. Remind students that though it is not necessarily best to outright ignore one's negative emotions—they are often important indicators that a solution needs to be reached—they should approach them thoughtfully, sit with them for a while, feel them, and work toward a constructive way to make things better.

FIGURE 28.4 The Schachter-Singer Two-Factor Theory of Emotion
Schachter and Singer's theory is similar to the James-Lange theory but adds the element of cognitive labeling of the arousal. In this theory, a stimulus leads to both bodily arousal and the labeling of that arousal (based on the surrounding context), which leads to the experience and labeling of the emotional reaction.

experience the emotion. In other words, "My heart is racing, and that's one mean-looking dog—what I'm feeling is fear!" Of course, one person's label of his or her arousal might be completely different from another person's label of that same arousal: During a ride on a roller coaster, for example, you might label your arousal as excitement or happiness, while your friend sitting next to you might label her arousal as fear.

The Facial Feedback Hypothesis: Smile, You'll Feel Better Charles Darwin believed that when an emotion is expressed freely on the face, the emotion itself intensifies. Modern psychologists have proposed a theory that is consistent with much of Darwin's thinking. The **facial feedback hypothesis** assumes that facial expressions provide feedback to the brain about the emotion being expressed. Not only can this phenomenon intensify emotion, it can even cause emotion (Buck, 1980; Ekman, 1980; Ekman & Friesen, 1978; Keillor et al., 2002). (See Figure 28.5.) However, this hypothesis is somewhat questionable. According to the hypothesis, people with facial paralysis should be unable to experience emotions in a normal way, but research shows this is not the case (Keillor et al., 2002).

Lazarus and the Cognitive-Mediational Theory Schachter and Singer's (1962) study stressed the role of cognition in emotion. Lazarus's **cognitive-mediational theory** (1991) builds on this idea. According to this theory, the most important aspect of any emotional experience is how the person interprets, or appraises, the stimulus that causes the emotional reaction. The cognitive appraisal *mediates*, or comes between, the stimulus and the emotional response.

According to Lazarus, we cognitively appraise, or evaluate, a situation *before* we experience either physical arousal or subjective emotion. For example, if we encountered a snarling dog confined behind a sturdy fence, we would judge it as being no threat. We would most likely feel nothing but annoyance, with little or no physical arousal. But if the dog was not confined, we'd make

facial feedback hypothesis theory of emotion that assumes that facial expressions provide feedback to the brain concerning the emotion being expressed, which in turn causes and intensifies the emotion.

cognitive-mediational theory theory of emotion in which a stimulus must be interpreted (appraised) by a person in order to result in a physical response and an emotional reaction.

FIGURE 28.5 Facial Feedback Theory of Emotion
In the facial feedback theory of emotion, a stimulus such as this snarling dog causes arousal and a facial expression. The facial expression then provides feedback to the brain about the emotion. The brain then interprets the emotion and may also intensify it.

362 CHAPTER 11

Class Demonstration

SMILE WHEN YOU SAY THAT

Several researchers have noted the bond between the experience of emotion and the way we describe it to others. When we are *angry*, we feel ready to *blow up*, our *blood is boiling*, and we need to *let off steam*. These metaphors are not accidental; the internal experience of anger is marked by a kind of agitated increase in internal pressure, much like the lid of a boiling pot bouncing up and down on a hot stove.

Have students generate examples such as those just listed. As a start, consider how and when we talk about being *cool, calm, and collected*, or why we're *frozen* with fear, *dumb* with surprise, or *jumping* for joy. To make the activity more involved, have students work in small groups to categorize the metaphors within each emotion. This activity can be a nice lead-in to talking about cultural similarities and differences in emotional experience (i.e., ask your bilingual students for other similar idioms and their meanings) or about the physiological components of emotion.

362 Chapter 11 Motivation and Emotion

FIGURE 28.6 Lazarus's Theory of Emotion
In Lazarus's cognitive-mediational theory of emotion, a stimulus causes an immediate appraisal (e.g., "The dog is snarling and not behind a fence, so this is dangerous"). The cognitive appraisal results in an emotional response, which is then followed by the appropriate bodily response.

an *appraisal* like "Danger! Threatening animal dead ahead!" This would be followed by *physical arousal* and the *subjective experience* of fear. In other words, our cognitive appraisal causes both the physical arousal and the emotion. (See Figure 28.6) This differs from the Schachter-Singer theory, in which we feel arousal first and *then* use cognition to label the feeling.

Not everyone agrees with Lazarus's theory. Some researchers believe our emotional reactions happen almost instantaneously, which would leave little time for a cognitive appraisal to occur first (Zajonc, 1998). Others (Kilhstrom et al., 2000) have found that the human brain can respond to a physical threat before conscious thought enters the picture.

Which theory is right?

Human emotions are so incredibly complex that it might not be out of place to say that all of the theories are correct to at least some degree. In certain situations, the cognitive appraisal might occur in time to mediate the emotion that is experienced (such as falling in love). In other situations, the need to act first, and think and feel later, is more important. ⊕─[Explore on **mypsychlab.com**

28.3 How do cultural and environmental factors influence emotional expression?

Although psychologists have differing theories about exactly how and why we *experience* emotion, most researches agree about the factors that influence our emotional *expression*. These include cultural differences, gender differences, and the influence of particular social groups or circumstances.

Display rules (Ekman, 1973; Ekman & Friesen, 1969) are learned ways of controlling displays of emotion in social settings. These rules vary between cultures. For example, Japanese people have strict social rules about showing emotion in public but express emotions more freely in private. L I N K to *Chapter Eight: Culture and Gender, pp. 257–258*. Display rules tend to be different between individualistic cultures, which value the individual above the social group, and collectivistic cultures, which value the social group above the individual. It is important to avoid stereotyping any particular culture, but of course, cultural customs do govern the types of emotion we express, the circumstances under which we express emotions, and how strongly we express emotions.

Display rules are also different for males and females. Boys are often reluctant to talk about feelings in a social setting, whereas girls are expected and encouraged to do so (Polce-Lynch et al., 1998). Women are generally less willing than men to express negative emotions in the workplace, although factors such as status complicate the findings somewhat (Domagalski & Steelman, 2007). Although both sexes experience romantic love similarly, women are

◀ Which theory is right?

⊕─[Explore Explore the different theories of emotion on **mypsychlab.com**

display rules learned ways of controlling displays of emotion in social settings.

MOTIVATION AND EMOTION 363

CHAPTER 11 • Module 28

DISCUSS THE STUDENT VOICE QUESTION

Ask students why it is so difficult to come up with one universally applicable theory of emotion. Check for understanding by asking how it could be possible that each theory outlined in the text is correct. Can students think of different situations that may apply to different theories?

MULTIMEDIA CONTENT AVAILABLE AT
www.mypsychlab.com

⊕─Explore Explore the different theories of emotion on **mypsychlab.com**

COVER THE MODULE

28.3 How do cultural and environmental factors influence emotional expression?

- *Display rules* of emotional expression are learned through one's society.
- Rules may differ by culture, gender, social group, or circumstances.

L I N K to *Chapter Eight: Culture and Gender, pp. 257–258*

TEACHING TIP

Consider creating "accountability partners" in which students are teamed with a classmate. The pairs meet regularly to monitor the accomplishment of goals by the other person.

Class Demonstration

CULTURAL MEANINGS OF NONVERBAL GESTURES

The study of nonverbal gestures and their meaning has received extensive research attention in psychology, sociology, and communication. We know a great deal about what gestures convey, how they are culturally variable, and how they act as cues to emotional and other internal states of a communicator. An intended message may not always be communicated successfully. Some common miscommunicated meanings include the following: (1) "Hook Ôem horns." Texans know that an outstretched index and pinky finger signal a cheer for the University of Texas Longhorns. This same gesture signals a curse in Africa, good luck in Brazil, and an Italian chide that the recipient is being cheated. (2) Signaling that someone is "crazy" in Germany is done by rotating the forefingers back and forth around one's temples. The gesture of a circular motion around the temple signals "There's a phone call" among Argentineans. (3) "Pointing" is accomplished in North America and Europe by using the index finger. In Malaysia, the thumb is preferred, whereas in Japan and China an open hand is used.

Do students know of other examples?

Module 28 Emotion 363

CHAPTER 11 • Module 28

COVER THE MODULE *(continued)*

- Rules for emotional expression can change, depending on the social situation in which we find ourselves.

LINK *to Chapter Seven: Social Psychology, pp. 214–222*

- Emotional expression is also, to an extent, learned behavior.
- Situational factors also work within the cultural and social context.

COVER THE MODULE

28.4 What biological and environmental factors influence the expression and experience of fear?

- Fear responses can be influenced by several factors, such as:
  - Learned behavior
  - Imitation
  - Genetics

CHECK FOR UNDERSTANDING

A research team studied the relationship between odors and emotional reactions. Women smelled a variety of concoctions while undergoing repeated brain scans. Some of the odors were pleasant, while others ranged from garlic breath to a sulfurous stench crossing rotting vegetables with a sewer. The pleasant smells did not trigger much of a reaction; only the right amygdala responded weakly. The most pungent odors, however, caused both amygdalae to respond swiftly. In fact, the anatomical link between the amygdala and brain centers responsible for processing olfactory sensations suggests a strong link between odor and affect. Pinpointing the amygdala's reaction may help explain why unpleasant odors can produce negative emotional reactions.

---

more likely to express these feelings verbally, while men are often more comfortable expressing love through actions (Baumeister and Bratslavsky, 1999; Cancian, 1987; Swain, 1989).

More specific social and environmental circumstances also affect our emotional expression. As with other behaviors, we may act differently when we are with different social groups. **LINK** *to Chapter Seven: Social Psychology, pp. 214–222.* Just as the larger culture has rules for emotional display, so too do smaller social groups, such as our families and peer groups. A person who has been taught that crying is taboo may be unable to cry in front of a family member but able to do so with a close friend or a therapist. The ways in which we express emotion are also, to some extent, learned behaviors. Bandura, Ross, and Ross (1961) found that young children who were allowed to play with attractive toys and then had these toys taken away were more likely to express their frustration through aggressive behavior if they had also witnessed aggressive behaviors being modeled by an adult.

Situational influences also matter. The same person who yells, cheers, and curses while watching a Monday night football game is unlikely to do so at work on Tuesday morning. Even if the person feels just as thrilled or frustrated, intense emotional displays are frowned upon by most employers. Seemingly minor factors, like the weather, can also influence emotions and their expression. Hot temperatures and crowding have been associated with negative emotion (Bell, Garnand, and Heath, 1984; Griffitt, 1970; Griffitt & Veitch, 1971); hot temperatures in particular have been associated with negative arousal, aggression, and violent crime (Anderson, 1987).

Analyze Emotional Behaviors in Depth

28.4 What biological and environmental factors influence the expression and experience of fear?

Both biological and environmental factors influence our experience and expression of fear. Once again, this emotion has evolutionary roots—it makes us flee dangerous situations, avoid risky behaviors, and bond with others for safety. Some fears are learned early in life. For instance, crawling infants who fall a few times quickly learn to be afraid of heights (Campos et al., 1992). (As you learned earlier, the amygdala is involved in learning to fear a particular situation.) We learn fear not only through our own experiences, but also through imitating others' fearful responses (Mineka 1985, 2002; Olsson et al., 2007).

Of course, some people are inherently more or less fearful than average, and this seems to have a genetic basis. Studies have found similar levels of fearfulness among identical twins (Lykken, 1982). As noted earlier, "sensation-seekers" thrive on risky experiences, like skydiving, that are too scary for the average person. Other people may not seek out dangerous experiences but nevertheless can react to them calmly.

Environmental Influences on Fear Personal experiences, social context, and cognitive interpretations affect our experience and expression of fear. Repeated exposure to a potentially frightening situation can make it less scary (Wolpe, 1958). For instance, giving first aid or CPR to an unconscious accident victim would make most people feel anxious. But for an ambulance crew, that experience is fairly routine. Although the crew still needs to be alert and

▲ *Genetic differences in fearfulness may be one reason that risky activities like rock climbing are enjoyable for some people and too frightening for others.*

364 CHAPTER 11

Class Demonstration (Kinesthetic)

SCENT AND EMOTION

Place unmarked, covered, numbered containers around the room that contain scents (either scented oils or actual objects, as long as the students cannot see them). Examples of scents to use are lavender, peppermint, perfume, coffee, onion, motor oil, cooked broccoli, and so forth. Ask students to bring their notebooks and a pencil, and walk around the room smelling each container. After each smell, students should record their reactions in their notebook. Does the scent provoke an emotional reaction? A memory? Maybe no feeling at all? Observe which scents students react most strongly to. Afterward, discuss students' reactions as a class.

react quickly, they would not necessarily be scared. Even if they were, they would be unlikely to express this feeling, due to the social context. Others expect them to function on the job and not let emotions get in the way.

In treating people who suffer from phobias, psychologists rely on **desensitization**—repeated, gradually more intense exposure to the frightening stimulus—and cognitive behavioral therapies that help the patient use rational thinking to overcome the irrational fear. For instance, a patient who is frightened of spiders may be exposed first to photographs of spiders, then to videotapes, then to the real thing. The patient would also learn to counter their current fearful thoughts ("If a spider bites me, I will die") with rational statements ("Only a few types of spider bites are actually dangerous, and none of those spiders live around here").

Classic Studies In Psychology

The Angry/Happy Man

In 1962, Stanley Schachter and Jerome Singer designed an experiment to test their two-factor theory of emotion. Student volunteers were told they were going to answer a questionnaire about their reactions to a new vitamin. In reality, they were injected with epinephrine, which causes physical arousal in the form of increased heart rate, rapid breathing, and a reddened face.

Each student then participated in one of two conditions. In one condition, the "angry man"—a research colleague posing as a study participant—complained about the experimenter, tore up his questionnaire and stormed out. In the other condition, the "happy man" (also a colleague posing as a participant) acted very happy, almost giddy, and played with objects in the room.

Afterward, participants were asked to describe their own emotions. Those exposed to the "angry" man interpreted their arousal symptoms as anger, whereas those exposed to the "happy" man interpreted their arousal as happiness. In all cases, the actual cause of arousal was the epinephrine and the physical symptoms of arousal were identical. The only difference was the exposure of the two groups to the two different *contexts*. Schachter and Singer's results fit their theory: Physiological arousal must be interpreted cognitively before it is experienced as a specific emotion.

Much of the later research inspired by this experiment has failed to find much support for the two-factor theory (Reisenzein, 1983, 1994). However, this theory did draw attention to the important role that cognition plays in determining emotions.

Questions for Further Discussion

1. In this experiment, what was the independent variable manipulated by the experimenters? What was the dependent variable?
2. This experiment used deception, as the participants were not told the true nature of the injection they received. What kind of ethical problems might have arisen from this deception? What problems would the experimenters have in getting this study approved by an ethics committee today?

phobia an intense fear of a specific object or situation, which may or may not be typically considered frightening.

desensitization in the treatment of phobias, the process of repeated, gradually more intense exposure to a frightening stimulus for the purpose of reducing or eliminating the fear response.

CHAPTER 11 • Module 28

COVER THE MODULE (continued)

- Repeated exposure to a frightening stimulus can make it seem less frightening. This is the process used in *desensitization*, which is commonly employed to treat *phobias*.

CLASSIC STUDIES IN PSYCHOLOGY

- Those participants who were exposed to the "angry" man interpreted their physical arousal as anger, while those who were exposed to the "happy" man interpreted their physical arousal as happiness.

1. The independent variable in the experiment was the man, in one case angry and in one case happy. The dependent variable was the participants' interpretation of their arousal after exposure to the man.

2. The epinephrine injection could cause problems for people with preexisting health conditions. Additionally, the mixture of the epinephrine and the angry man could have caused severe emotional reactions in some participants. Even if researchers asked participants about any health conditions beforehand, ethics committees may be reluctant to allow such a study because people may have physical limitations they do not even know about, which could cause health risks.

Explore

HOW COGNITIONS INFLUENCE EMOTIONS

According to Bernard Weiner's attribution theory of motivation and emotion, success and failure typically evoke the causal attributions of ability, effort, task difficulty, or luck, singly or in combination. Underlying these attributions are the dimensions internal/external; stable/unstable; and controllable/uncontrollable. Students may want to consider the following: (1) Which types of attributions encourage persistence in the face of failure? (2) Why might attributions of success to ability be problematic for subsequent motivation? (3) Which attributions are necessary for the emotional experience of pride? A brief description of Weiner's theory may be found at: http://tip.psychology.org/weiner.html, and a more extensive treatment of attribution in the context of education may be found at: http://education.calumet.purdue.edu/vockell/edpsybook/Edpsy5/Edpsy5_attribution.htm

CHAPTER 11 • Module 28

COVER THE MODULE

28.5 What biological and environmental factors influence the expression and experience of happiness?

- *Dopamine*, long associated with pleasure sensations, is more involved in learning to predict rewards and avoid punishments.
- Endorphins and oxytocin play a role in sources of happiness such as love and friendship.
- *Serotonin* stabilizes mood.
- *Adaption-level phenomenon* describes our tendency to evaluate new experiences relative to previous ones and adjust our expectations up or down in response.
- *Relative deprivation* affects happiness, causing us to feel as though we are worse off than others.

FAST FACT

It is commonly known that serotonin plays a role in regulation of mood, sleep, and memory. Ask students if they know which body parts or systems are affected by serotonin. *(Answer: The cardiovascular system, muscles, and various elements of the endocrine system are among those affected. You might ask students to research further and compile a list of all the functions of serotonin that they can find.)*

L3 DIFFERENTIATED INSTRUCTION

Special Needs Incorporate the same comprehension and learning strategies over time to allow for mastery.

28.5 What biological and environmental factors influence the expression and experience of happiness?

Happiness and the Brain Describing the role of the brain in happiness is complex, because "happiness" encompasses several types of emotional states. We can be happy sitting alone reading a book—or enjoying a noisy social gathering. We feel happy when we're on vacation, carefree and relaxed—but working hard at a challenging task is also fulfilling. So what is known about the biological basis of happiness?

Several hormones and neurotransmitters are associated with happiness. You may have heard that the neurotransmitter **dopamine** has been associated with feelings of pleasure, but newer findings suggest that dopamine is more involved in learning to predict and approach rewards and punishments (Ikemoto & Panksepp, 1999). It may not be the "pleasure chemical" that we previously believed it to be. Perhaps more directly associated with pleasure are endorphins, which are released during intense exercise, creating the sense of well-being sometimes described as "runner's high." Endorphins, and also oxytocin, play a role in romantic love, infant-caretaker bonding, and even close friendships—significant sources of happiness. Yet another neurotransmitter, **serotonin,** is more strongly associated with stability of mood, perhaps helping to buffer overreactions to negative events. Many drugs used widely to treat depression, such as Prozac, act by increasing levels of serotonin in synapses—but this immediate action of the drugs leads to a complex array of other effects. In short, we know far less about how the brain experiences happiness than about how it experiences fear.

Adaptability and Environmental Factors While our environment and day-to-day experiences certainly affect our emotions, for the most part, we tend to stay on a fairly even keel. Our ups and downs balance each other out. Of course, minor stressful experiences get us down, but usually not for very long (Affleck et al., 1994; Bolger et al., 1989; Stone & Neale, 1984). Traumatic experiences, such as losing a loved one, can result in more lasting grief or anxiety. However, many people maintain some level of happiness even in the face of intense negative experiences, such as being diagnosed with a terminal illness. Of course these experiences are very painful, but people adapt to their situation and find ways to feel happiness.

Our adaptability helps us cope with life's difficulties; unfortunately, it also limits our capacity for enjoyment. The **adaptation-level phenomenon** (Helson, 1964; Myers, 1993) is our tendency to evaluate new experiences in terms of previous experiences. Each new experience makes us subtly adjust our expectations up or down. So, for instance, if we buy a house near a noisy highway, we eventually adapt and don't find the noise too annoying. By the same token, the first time we speed down the highway in a new car feels thrilling, but as we repeat the experience, the thrill soon fades. *It's become normal.* To recapture the thrill, we might need to drive faster (not recommended) or buy a newer, better car (an expensive way to stay happy). We continually redefine what "normal" should be, and this affects our sense of happiness.

Another way environmental factors affect happiness is in our tendency to compare ourselves with others. **Relative deprivation** is the feeling that we are worse off than others, and we may experience this feeling even when, objectively speaking, our circumstances are pretty good. This helps explain why,

---

dopamine a neurotransmitter that seems to be involved in learning to predict and approach rewards and avoid punishments.

serotonin a neurotransmitter involved in maintaining stability of mood.

adaptation-level phenomenon the tendency to evaluate new experiences in terms of previous experiences and adjust expectations accordingly.

relative deprivation the feeling that one is worse off than others.

Class Activity

THE PURSUIT OF HAPPINESS

Alex Michalos, at the University of Guelph, Ontario, suggests that maintaining a range of short-term and long-term goals can contribute to well-being. For example, the short-term pleasure of playing the drums can provide ongoing satisfaction, while the long-term goal of becoming a better student propels anticipation and motivation. Michalos also points out that the catalog of pleasures seems to have remained unchanged over the years. Healthy bodies, productive jobs, peace of mind, and family and friends continue to be mainstays in the pursuit of happiness.

Ask students to set two goals for themselves, one short-term (to be accomplished within the next 3 months or so) and one long-term (to be accomplished over the course of year or so). Encourage them to write the goals down and keep them in a place where they will see them often so they will remain motivated.

although happiness is definitely correlated with financial security, accumulating additional wealth doesn't necessarily make people happier. As people enter higher income brackets, they start comparing themselves with people who earn even more. An income that would once have seemed like more than enough now feels like just enough, or perhaps even not good enough. Fortunately, we can work to counteract some of the forces in our lives that tend to interfere with happiness.

positive psychology movement a movement that recommends shifting the focus of psychology away from the negative to a more positive focus on strengths, well-being, and the pursuit of happiness.

Applying Psychology to Everyday Life

A How-To of Happiness?

A number of researchers, including social psychologist David G. Myers, have studied happiness. Myers supports the **positive psychology movement**, which recommends shifting the focus of psychology away from the negative to a more positive focus on strengths, well-being, and the pursuit of happiness (Myers, 1993).

So how can people become happier? In his popular book, *The Pursuit of Happiness*, Myers (1993) lists 10 suggestions based on his many years of research:

1. **Realize that enduring happiness doesn't come from success.** Money, power, and fame do not guarantee happiness.
2. **Take control of your time.** People who feel in control of their lives through good time-management skills and goal-setting are also happier people.
3. **Act happy.** Put on a happy face. When people smile, it releases chemicals that make them feel better, and when they frown, the opposite occurs.
4. **Seek work and leisure activities that engage your skills.** Challenging (but not overwhelming) work and leisure activities can bring happiness, even if they aren't exciting or glamorous.
5. **Join the "movement" movement.** Exercise can help relieve depression and anxiety.
6. **Give your body the sleep it wants.** People who rest adequately are typically happier.
7. **Give priority to close relationships.** A good social support system just can't be beat. Nurture friends, who will offer support and help get you through the bad times.
8. **Focus beyond the self.** Not only do happy people help other people more readily, but also they are happier for doing so. Helping others makes people feel good.
9. **Keep a gratitude journal.** Writing down the positive things that you have boosts a sense of well-being.
10. **Nurture your spiritual self.** People with a strong sense of faith also tend to be happier. Communities based on shared belief systems about faith provide a good support system, a sense of purpose and hope, and opportunities to help others.

▲ *In the pursuit of happiness, many people find that helping others increases their own happiness. These volunteers are experiencing that kind of happiness as they fill sandbags to help control the flooding of a nearby river.*

MOTIVATION AND EMOTION 367

CHAPTER 11 • Module 28

COVER THE MODULE *(continued)*

- The *positive psychology movement* is a viewpoint that recommends shifting the focus of psychology away from negative aspects of psychology, such as abuse, anxiety, depression, and all the things that can go wrong to a more positive focus on strengths, well-being, and the pursuit of happiness.
- David Myers has determined ten things people can do to improve and increase happiness:
  - Realize that enduring happiness does not come from success.
  - Take control of your time.
  - Act happy.
  - Seek work and leisure that engages your skills.
  - Join the "movement" movement.
  - Give your body the sleep it wants.
  - Give priority to close relationships.
  - Focus beyond the self.
  - Keep a gratitude journal.
  - Nurture your spiritual self.

L2 **ELL DIFFERENTIATED INSTRUCTION**

English Language Learners Keep in mind that students' English-speaking ability does not reflect their academic aptitude.

L4 **DIFFERENTIATED INSTRUCTION**

Advanced Learners Create a learning environment in the classroom that encourages risk taking.

Explore

POSITIVE PSYCHOLOGY

Direct students to one of the websites below to explore the psychology of happiness and find tips on how to make their lives and outlooks more positive.

- **Positive Psychology: www.positivepsychology.org/** The Positive Psychology Center promotes research, training, education, dissemination, and the application of positive psychology.
- **The Pursuit of Happiness: www.davidmyers.org/happiness/** Information on *The Pursuit of Happiness*, a book by social psychologist David G. Myers; also includes suggestions for a happier life and links to happiness research websites.

Module 28 Emotion **367**

CHAPTER 11 • Module 28

Assess

Assign the Module 28 Practice Quiz.

Use the Practice Quiz to identify gaps in student understanding.

REMEDIATE

Have students, individually or in groups, review the module goals, learning objectives, and key terms.

Refer students to the Concept Summary on p. 373 for review.

Close

Review with students the many influences on the outward manifestations of our emotions, such as culture, gender, and social setting. Do students believe that one (or a few) of these influences are stronger than the others? Which one(s)? Why?

Practice Quiz

Pick the best answer.

1. What are the three elements of emotion?
   a. attention, behavior, and cognition
   b. attention, behavior, and motivation
   c. physical arousal, behavior, and cognition
   d. physical arousal, cognition, and motivation

2. Which theory of emotion is based on the assumption that the thalamus sends sensory information to the cortex and the organs of the sympathetic nervous system at the same time?
   a. Cannon-Bard
   b. Schachter-Singer
   c. Facial feedback
   d. Cognitive-mediational

3. Giuliana, a generally happy person, is enrolled in a psychology experiment. She is injected with epinephrine and then shown a movie clip of two people fighting. Immediately after watching the clip, Giuliana is most likely to feel
   a. angry
   b. happy
   c. scared
   d. relaxed

4. Ming comes home from school one day in a very bad mood, due to a fight he had with his girlfriend. His mother, hoping to improve his mood, starts telling him jokes. Ming resists laughing, but he can't help but smiling at the jokes his mother is telling him, and soon his mood begins to improve. Which theory of emotion best explains the change?
   a. James-Lange
   b. Cannon-Bard
   c. Schachter-Singer
   d. Facial feedback

5. In which theory of emotion is the most important aspect of an emotional experience, the interpretation or appraisal of the stimulus?
   a. James-Lange
   b. Cannon-Bard
   c. Facial feedback
   d. Cognitive-mediational

6. Suppose a research team conducts an experiment with teenagers from two different countries, Rebelland and Obedia. The two groups sit in different rooms and watch the same video, in which parents argue with their teenage daughter about her grades and eventually tell her she is grounded. From a distance, the experimenters secretly observe both groups reacting to the video with annoyance. When it's just the teenagers in the room, both groups angrily say things like, "Her parents are so unfair! She should sneak out anyway!" However, when the experimenter comes in and asks them about the video, only the teens from Rebelland openly express these feelings. The teens from Obedia politely say things like, "Well, her parents were a little strict, but it's for her own good." What best explains the difference?
   a. display rules
   b. innate temperamental differences
   c. the adaptation-level phenomenon
   d. cognitive-mediational theory

7. Which of the following is most closely linked with maintaining stability of mood?
   a. oxytocin
   b. endorphins
   c. dopamine
   d. serotonin

8. The ability to learn to fear a particular situation is impaired by damage to the
   a. amygdala
   b. lateral hypothalamus
   c. nucleus accumbens
   d. anterior cingulate cortex

9. Which of these situations best illustrates the way that the physical environment can influence the expression of emotion?
   a. Whenever Kyle is frustrated, he is physically aggressive with other children at his preschool. His older sister acts the same way at home.
   b. Even though his boss's jokes are not very funny, Jay enthusiastically laughs at them.
   c. During a trip to a hot, crowded, noisy shopping mall, Denise has a temper tantrum when her mother refuses to buy her a new toy.
   d. Carla sometimes loses patience with her children at home, but she is always cool and calm when responding to stressful situations at work.

10. Our tendency to use each new experience to adjust our expectations about life is known as
    a. adaptation-level phenomenon
    b. relative deprivation
    c. desensitization
    d. positive psychology

Practice Quiz Answers

1. c
2. b
3. a
4. d
5. d
6. a
7. d
8. a
9. c
10. a

CHAPTER 11 Summary

Listen on mypsychlab.com

Listen to an audio file of your chapter on mypsychlab.com

Module 27: Motivation

Explain major theories of motivation.

27.1 What are the major cognitive and biological theories of motivation?
- Early instinct approaches proposed that some human actions may be motivated by instincts. Drive-reduction approaches state that need leads to tension that motivates action, fulfilling the need and reducing the tension to maintain homeostasis. According to arousal theory, people seek to maintain an optimal level of arousal. In the incentive approach, an external stimulus may motivate a person to act even in the absence of a drive. McClelland focused on psychological needs: achievement, affiliation, and power. Expectancy-value theories emphasize the importance that people attach to beliefs and values at any given time.

27.2 What is the humanist theory of motivation?
- Self-determination theory (SDT) focuses on three basic needs: autonomy, competence, and relatedness. Intrinsic motivation occurs when people act because the act itself is satisfying or rewarding. Extrinsic motivation occurs when people receive an external reward.

Describe motivated behaviors.

27.3 What factors motivate eating?
- The physiological components of hunger include signals from the stomach and the hypothalamus as well as increased secretion of insulin. Social components of hunger include social cues, cultural customs and preferences, and the use of food as a comfort or escape.

27.4 What factors motivate sexual behavior and orientation?
- Sexual behavior is motivated by the need to reproduce, emotional satisfaction, desire for intimacy, and self-affirmation, among many other factors. Genetic differences appear to play a role in sexual orientation, but environmental influences have not been ruled out.

27.5 What factors motivate achievement?
- Dweck links achievement to beliefs about the self, specifically locus of control.

27.6 Are there other ways in which humans and animals are motivated?
- The motivation to love has an evolutionary basis and is influenced by biological and environmental factors, as is the motivation to belong.

Module 28: Emotion

Understand theories of emotion and emotional expression.

28.1 What are the biological, behavioral, and cognitive components of emotion?
- Emotion includes a biological component (physical arousal), a behavioral component (behavior that expresses or reveals the emotion), and a cognitive component (our inner awareness and labeling of feelings).

28.2 What are the major theories of emotion?
- The James-Lange theory states that a stimulus creates a physiological response that leads to the labeling of the emotion. The Cannon-Bard theory states that the physiological reaction and the subjective experience of emotion are simultaneous. Schachter and Singer's two-factor theory states that both the physiological arousal and interpretation of that arousal must occur before emotion is experienced. The facial feedback hypothesis proposes that facial expressions provide feedback to the brain about the emotion being expressed, intensifying the emotion. The cognitive-mediational theory states that the cognitive component of emotion precedes both the physiological reaction and the subjective experience of emotion.

28.3 How do cultural and environmental factors influence emotional expression?
- Cultural display rules, gender differences, and the influence of particular social groups or circumstances all influence the expression of emotion.

Analyze emotional behaviors in depth.

28.4 What biological and environmental factors influence the expression and experience of fear?
- Fear has evolutionary roots in the need to avoid danger and seek safety. The amygdala is involved in learning to fear a situation. Personal experiences, social context, and cognitive interpretations affect our experience and expression of fear.

28.5 What biological and environmental factors influence the expression and experience of happiness?
- Hormones and neurotransmitters associated with happiness include dopamine, endorphins, oxytocin, and serotonin. The adaptation-level phenomenon and relative deprivation both affect our sense of happiness.

Vocabulary Terms

motivation p. 342
extrinsic motivation p. 342
intrinsic motivation p. 342
instincts p. 342
instinct approach p. 343
need p. 343
drive p. 343
drive-reduction theory p. 343
primary drives p. 343
acquired (secondary) drives p. 343
homeostasis p. 343
need for achievement (nAch) p. 344
need for affiliation (nAff) p. 344
need for power (nPow) p. 344
stimulus motive p. 344
arousal theory p. 344
Yerkes-Dodson law p. 344
sensation seeker p. 345
incentives p. 345
incentive approaches p. 345
expectancy-value theories p. 346
expectancy p. 346
deficiency needs p. 346
growth needs p. 346
self-actualization p. 346
peak experiences p. 347
self-determination theory (SDT) p. 348
insulin p. 349
glucagons p. 349
weight set point p. 349
basal metabolic rate (BMR) p. 350
obesity p. 350
anorexia nervosa p. 351
bulimia nervosa p. 351
sexual orientation p. 353
internal locus of control p. 354
external locus of control p. 354
oxytocin p. 355
emotion p. 358
James-Lange theory of emotion p. 360
Cannon-Bard theory of emotion p. 361
two-factor theory p. 361
facial feedback hypothesis p. 362
cognitive-mediational theory p. 362
display rules p. 363
phobia p. 365
desensitization p. 365
dopamine p. 366
serotonin p. 366
adaptation-level phenomenon p. 366
relative deprivation p. 366
positive psychology movement p. 367

MOTIVATION AND EMOTION 369

CHAPTER 11 • Chapter Summary and Vocabulary

Chapter Summary

Encourage students to carefully review and study the summary. Explain that it provides an overview of key concepts presented in the text.

Have students identify what they find unclear or confusing. Call on volunteers to provide answers, examples, or definitions.

Vocabulary Terms

Remind students that terms are defined within the chapter at point of use. If they are not sure of a term's definition, they should look up the definition on the page.

Encourage students to create study cards of unfamiliar words or to go to **www.mypsychlab.com** for flashcards. Have them test themselves or a classmate. Advanced students can explain the terms in their own words.

Critical Thinking

MAKING CONNECTIONS

Have students complete the following activity to connect the ideas in this chapter. Send them to the Multimedia Library for this chapter at **www.mypsychlab.com** to view the video titled "College Students and Eating Disorders." Then lead a class discussion based on the following questions: (1) What is the difference between dysfunctional eating and an eating disorder? (2) What do students think of the new classification of binge-eating disorder, which has recently been added to the DSM? (3) What factors, other than the classic "media pressure," may cause eating disorders? (4) Do students agree with the idea that familial dysfunction is a major cause of eating disorders?

CHAPTER 11 • Assessment

VOCABULARY REVIEW

1. d
2. f
3. h
4. e
5. i
6. g
7. j
8. c
9. b
10. a

WRITING ABOUT PSYCHOLOGY

1. Students' answers should show a clear understanding of motivation and the various ways it is sparked and manifested. They should be able to discuss Maslow's Hierarchy of Needs, McClelland's psychological needs, and Dweck's theory of self as motivator.

2. Students should note the stimulus–arousal–labeling order of the James-Lange theory; the Cannon-Bard theory that arousal and feeling happen more or less simultaneously, leading to labeling; the order of the two-factor theory—stimulus, then arousal and labeling together; and the emphasis on interpretation in producing emotion, laid out in the cognitive-mediational theory.

PSYCHOLOGY PROJECT

Encourage students to think about needs across cultures and socioeconomic statuses. Have students mount posters on classroom walls or the bulletin board. Set aside some class time for students to make brief oral presentations explaining their ordering of needs. Afterwards, conduct a class discussion about the major similarities and differences between students' hierarchies. Can the entire class together agree upon one basic hierarchy?

CHAPTER 11 Assessment

Study and Review on mypsychlab.com

Vocabulary Review

Match each vocabulary term to its definition.

1. self-actualization
2. anorexia nervosa
3. sensation seeker
4. display rules
5. two-factor theory
6. relative deprivation
7. emotion
8. extrinsic motivation
9. phobia
10. drive-reduction theory

a. Approach to motivation that assumes behavior arises from physiological needs that cause internal drives to push an organism to satisfy the needs, reducing tension and arousal.
b. Intense fear of specific objects or situations, which may or may not be typically considered frightening.
c. Type of motivation in which a person performs an action because it leads to an outcome that is separate from or external to the person.
d. According to Maslow, the point that is seldom reached at which people have sufficiently satisfied their lower needs and achieved their full human potential.
e. Learned ways of controlling displays of emotion in social settings.
f. A condition in which a person reduces eating to the point that a weight loss of 15 percent below the ideal body weight or more occurs.
g. The feeling that one is worse off than others.
h. Someone who needs more arousal than the average person and seeks out complex and varied experiences.
i. Theory of emotion in which both physical arousal and the labeling of that arousal based on cues from the environment must occur before the emotion is experienced.
j. The "feeling" aspect of consciousness, characterized by physical arousal, behavior that expresses or reveals the emotion, and an inner awareness of feelings.

Writing about Psychology

Respond to each question in complete sentences.

1. Abraham Maslow, David McClelland, and Carol Dweck each address the human need for achievement and accomplishment in their theories. Briefly define this need and provide an example of how a person might fulfill it. Then, in a few short paragraphs, summarize each theorist's major beliefs about the achievement need.

2. You are hiking in the desert when you see a large, poisonous snake poised to attack you, and you feel afraid. In a well-organized essay, describe how each of the following theories would explain your emotional response to this situation:
   a. James-Lange theory
   b. Cannon-Bard theory
   c. Schachter-Singer two-factor theory
   d. Cognitive-mediational theory

Psychology Project

What do Maslow's needs look like in real life? Does his hierarchy make sense—or would you organize these needs differently? Complete this project to examine how people meet their needs and to comment on Maslow's theory.

Materials:
- a large piece of poster board
- colored markers
- magazines and newspapers

Instructions:

1. For this assignment, you will work with a partner to create a poster that visually represents the physical and psychological needs Abraham Maslow identified. With your partner, review the hierarchy of needs described on page 347.

2. Maslow saw these needs as a hierarchy, and they are commonly represented by a pyramid showing the "lower" needs at the bottom and the "higher" needs at the top. However, some theorists have questioned whether this makes sense. (For example, contrary to Maslow's belief, a "starving artist" might still produce great works of art.) With your partner, examine Maslow's hierarchy and discuss how it might be modified. You and your partner may have some differences of opinion. The important thing is to discuss these needs based on your own understanding of the world and find some points you definitely agree on.

3. Now, work with your partner to plan your poster. Based on your discussion, decide on the best way to visually represent Maslow's needs. Find and cut out photographs, illustrations, or brief text clippings that you can use to illustrate the different needs.

4. Create your poster. Make sure each need is clearly labeled. Include additional text as needed to explain why you organized the needs the way you did.

Internet Resources

Motivation: http://mentalhelp.net/psyhelp/chap4/chap4i.htm

Extensive discussion of motivation as it applies to self-help and self-improvement, from Mental Health.net.

National Eating Disorders Association: nationaleatingdisorders.org

National nonprofit eating disorders organization. Information, referrals, support, prevention, conferences, and newsletters.

Emotion Home Page: http://emotion.nsma.arizona.edu/emotion.html

History of emotion theory, information on emotion research, and links to related resources.

Test Yourself
Pick the best answer.

1. Which approach to motivation forced psychologists to consider the hereditary factors in motivation?
   a. instinct
   b. incentive
   c. drive-reduction
   d. self-determination

2. The need for money is an example of a(n)
   a. primary drive
   b. acquired drive
   c. instinctive drive
   d. physiological drive

3. Evidence from a study with 2-year-olds who were given an opportunity to explore a black box with a hole in it suggests that sensation seeking may be
   a. learned from one's peers
   b. learned from one's caregivers
   c. related to attachment style
   d. related to innate temperament

4. Shontia works at a day care center. The pay is low and the hours are long, but she loves being around children and has no desire to look for a higher-paying job. Shontia appears to have a(n)
   a. intrinsic motive
   b. extrinsic motive
   c. affiliation motive
   d. drive-reduction motive

5. Which of these actions is motivated in part by the desire to maintain homeostasis?
   a. caring for one's children
   b. eating when hungry
   c. running away from a threat
   d. fighting to protect one's territory

6. Which theory of emotion would predict that people with spinal cord injuries, which prevent them from experiencing sympathetic arousal, would show decreased emotion?
   a. James-Lange
   b. Cannon-Bard
   c. Schachter-Singer
   d. Cognitive-mediational

7. In Schachter and Singer's classic study, participants were physically aroused by
   a. exercising vigorously
   b. receiving epinephrine
   c. watching an exciting film
   d. arguing with the researchers

8. Which of the following statements is supported by research?
   a. In modern Western cultures, women are more likely than men to express feelings of romantic love through actions.
   b. In modern Western cultures, women are more likely than men to express feelings of romantic love through words.
   c. In modern Western cultures, women and men express feelings of romantic love in nearly identical ways.
   d. In modern Western cultures, women experience more feelings of romantic love than men do.

9. Which of the following is a social cue for hunger?
   a. eating a late breakfast
   b. feeling your stomach rumble
   c. noticing that it is time for dinner
   d. producing higher insulin levels

10. People who want to be liked by others and who are good team players are high in the need for
    a. achievement
    b. affiliation
    c. power
    d. arousal

11. Which of these needs is an example of a primary drive?
    a. the need for love
    b. the need for food
    c. the need for creative expression
    d. the need to belong to a group

12. According to Maslow's hierarchy, our lowest-level needs are
    a. cognitive
    b. social
    c. physiological
    d. aesthetic

13. One of the main differences between anorexia and bulimia is that individuals suffering from anorexia
    a. weigh 15 percent or more below expected body weight
    b. have a negative self-image
    c. are obsessed with body weight
    d. can suffer from heart problems

14. The brain chemistry of romantic love is most similar to which other type of feeling?
    a. friendship
    b. self-actualization
    c. attachment to a caretaker
    d. pleasure in personal achievement

15. Which approach to motivation explains behavior in terms of external stimuli and their rewarding properties?
    a. incentive
    b. drive-reduction
    c. instinct
    d. humanistic

16. Which statement best describes the relationship between the neurotransmitter dopamine and people's experience of pleasure?
    a. Dopamine helps us maintain our emotional stability.
    b. Dopamine helps us know when to anticipate a reward.
    c. Dopamine plays a limited role in some pleasurable experiences.
    d. Dopamine is central to almost every kind of pleasurable experience.

17. Research has shown that some people are inherently more or less fearful than others. Therefore, some people (such as firefighters) may choose to engage in work or other experiences that most people would find terrifying. This finding is most closely related to which of the following motivational theories?
    a. arousal theory
    b. drive-reduction theory
    c. self-determination theory
    d. expectancy-value theories

18. Based on available research, which emotion seems to be the LEAST understood in terms of brain chemistry?
    a. love
    b. fear
    c. happiness
    d. anger

MOTIVATION AND EMOTION 371

Ready for Testing

STUDENTS KNOW THEY ARE READY FOR TESTING IF THEY ARE ABLE TO . . .

- Introduce the concept of motivation and discuss the major theories proposed to explain motivated behavior.
- Discuss the specific motivation of hunger and examine the physiological and social components in addition to common eating disorders.
- Describe the three elements of emotion and present six theories on how emotions are processed.
- Explain what is the positive psychology movement.

CHAPTER 11 • Assessment

TEST YOURSELF

1. b
2. b
3. b
4. a
5. d
6. a
7. b
8. b
9. a
10. c
11. b
12. d
13. a
14. a
15. a
16. a
17. a
18. d
19. c

CHAPTER 11 • Concept Summary

MULTIMEDIA CONTENT AVAILABLE AT
www.mypsychlab.com

Map the Concepts on **mypsychlab.com**

Study and Review Flashcards on **mypsychlab.com**

STUDY TIPS

True/False Tests There are a few concrete strategies students can use when taking true/false tests. First, point out that every part of a statement must be true in order for the answer to be true. If any part of the statement is false, the answer is false. Words that qualify a statement, such as *sometimes, often, generally,* and *most,* often indicate a true answer because they make a statement more accurate. Conversely, qualifiers such as *never, always, all,* and *every* often indicate a false answer because they are too broad. If a sentence uses negatives, try dropping the negative and re-reading it. Decide if that answer is true or false, and then choose the opposite for your real answer. Finally, be sure students realize they should guess at answers they do not know on a true/false test. They have a 50 percent chance of being right.

CHAPTER 11 Concept Summary: Motivation and Emotion

Learning Objectives

27.1 27.2 pp. 342–348

- **motivation** is the process by which activities are started, directed, and continued to meet physical or psychological needs or wants
  - **extrinsic motivation** causes a person to act to obtain an external reward
  - **intrinsic motivation** causes a person to act to feel internal satisfaction
- **early instinct approaches** focused on innate, biologically determined patterns of behavior, such as the need to eat, drink, or reproduce
- **drive-reduction approaches** focus on an organism's need to reduce tension and maintain homeostasis

Explain Major Theories of Motivation

- **arousal theory** emphasizes people's need to maintain an optimal level of tension
- **McClelland** focused on the psychological needs for **achievement, affiliation,** and **power**
- **incentive approaches** explain behavior in terms of the external stimulus and its rewarding properties
- **expectancy-value theories** address people's beliefs, values, and the importance they attach to those beliefs and values at any given time
- **humanist theories** (based on **Maslow's** work) address physical, social, and emotional needs.

372 CHAPTER 11

What Every Student Should Know About...

AVOIDING PLAGIARISM

Tell students that to *paraphrase* information from a source means to restate it in their own words, using their own sentence structure. The chief purpose of paraphrasing is to use one's own writing style. The best way to paraphrase something is to read the original material, put it aside, and then compose a restatement of the information. Specific words and phrases that are included from the original material should be placed in quotation marks. Readers should be able to tell where the paraphrase begins and ends. The paraphrase should be an accurate restatement of the source's specific ideas, and it should be followed by a reference that indicates the source of the information.

Learning Objectives 27.3 27.4 27.5 27.6 pp. 349–356

Describe Motivated Behaviors

- **eating** is motivated by physiological and social factors
  - role of the hormones **insulin** and **glucagons** in regulating blood glucose
  - role of the **hypothalamus** in stopping or starting the eating response
  - social cues
  - appeal of food
  - eating for emotional comfort
- **sexual behavior** is motivated by complex factors
  - drive to reproduce
  - hormonal influences
  - social and emotional influences
- **achievement** is affected by beliefs about the self
  - Dweck: **internal** versus **external locus of control**
- the **motivation to love** and **motivation to belong** are also powerful

Learning Objectives 28.1 28.2 28.3 pp. 358–364

Understand Theories of Emotion and Emotional Expression

- **components of emotion** are biological, behavioral, and cognitive
  - physical arousal
  - behavior that reveals or expresses emotion
  - cognitive awareness, interpretation, and labeling
- **major theories** discuss the order of, and causal relationships between, these components
  - **James-Lange theory**
  - **Cannon-Bard theory**
  - Schachter-Singer's **two-factor theory**
  - **facial feedback hypothesis**
  - Lazarus's **cognitive-mediational theory**
- **cultural factors** and **environmental factors** influence emotional expression
  - cultural **display rules**
  - gender differences
  - social groups and social situations
  - learned behaviors
  - physical environment

Learning Objectives 28.4 28.5 pp. 364–367

Analyze Emotional Behaviors in Depth

- **fear**
  - biological factors: evolutionary roots and genetic differences, role of **amygdala**
  - environmental factors: personal experience, social context
  - cognitive factors: use of cognitive-behavioral therapy in treating phobias
- **happiness**
  - biological factors: role of **dopamine, serotonin, oxytocin, endorphins**
  - adaptability and environmental factors

MOTIVATION AND EMOTION 373

CHAPTER 11 • Concept Summary

STUDY TIPS

Setting Goals for Study Sessions Setting goals can help students achieve both long- and short-term goals. Setting goals for study sessions makes it more likely that students will stay on task and accomplish the necessary work. Ask students to write down a study goal for each subject for the week. Then ask them to write down a study goal for today's study session. Goals should address upcoming tests and assignments that are due. Explain that it is important to prioritize tasks for each study session in order to meet the goal for that session. It can be helpful to assign a length of time to each task, both to organize study time effectively and to help with concentration. Remind students to make goals realistic. For example, a study goal for one session might be to read the chapter or to review the class notes for the day. Have students create a goal chart that lists today's study goals and the priority of each, as well as the length of time to complete the task. Suggest that students reward themselves for meeting each day's goals with something they enjoy doing.

Comprehension Check

EMOTION THEORIES

To check their understanding, students can visit the Multimedia Library section of the www.mypsychlab.com site and explore the Physiological, Evolutionary, and Cognitive Theories of Emotion activity. Advanced students can work alone, while on-level and struggling students can work in pairs or in small groups. Students will receive immediate feedback on their answers.

Chapter 11 Concept Summary **373**

CHAPTER 12 • Module 29

Launch the Chapter

CHAPTER GOALS AND LEARNING OBJECTIVES

Module 29 Perspectives on Personality

Evaluate the major theories of personality.

29.1 What is the psychodynamic theory of personality?

29.2 How do behaviorists and social cognitive theorists explain personality?

29.3 How do humanistic psychologists explain personality?

29.4 What are the history and current views of the trait perspective?

Module 30 Assessment and Issues in Personality

Learn how personality is assessed.

30.1 What techniques do researchers use to measure personality? Are these techniques reliable and valid?

Consider key issues in personality research.

30.2 What part do biology and culture play in personality?

30.3 Is personality stable, or can it change over time?

30.4 How can personality influence our health and our work?

30.5 What is self-esteem, and how does it affect us?

30.6 How do cultural perspectives relate to personality?

DIFFERENTIATED INSTRUCTION KEY

Look for these symbols to help you adjust steps in each lesson to meet your students' needs.

- **L1** Special Needs
- **L2** Basic
  - **ELL** English Language Learners
  - **LPR** Less Proficient Readers
- **L3** All Students
- **L4** Advanced Students

CHAPTER 12
Theories of Personality

Not-So-Identical Twins

Many people have heard the story of the "Jim" twins, James Arthur Springer and James Edward Lewis, identical twins separated at the age of 1 month. At age 39, Springer and Lewis were the first set of twins studied by University of Minnesota psychologist Thomas Bouchard, who examined the differences and similarities between identical and fraternal twins raised apart from each other (Bouchard et al., 1990).

The two "Jims" shared interests in mechanical drawing and carpentry, a love of math and a dread of spelling in high school, and smoked and drank the same amount. It is understandable that many researchers attribute these similarities to the shared genetic material of the "Jim" twins. But Springer and Lewis were both raised in Ohio by parents from relatively similar socioeconomic backgrounds—how much of their similarity to each other might be due to those conditions? And how would genetics explain that they had both divorced women named Linda before marrying women named Betty? Are there genes for "divorce Linda, marry Betty?" Obviously not.

Then there's the case of Oskar and Jack. Like the "Jim" twins, they also exhibited a number of similarities in personality and behavior. No one would accuse Oskar and Jack of being raised in similar environments, however. Born in Trinidad at the time Hitler was rising to power, Jack Yufe was raised by their Jewish father in Trinidad as a Jew, while their mother took Oskar Stohr to occupied Czechoslovakia, where he attended a Nazi-run school and was at one time a Hitler youth. In terms of environment, Oskar and Jack were not-so-identical twins.

If the researchers in the twin study had dug a little deeper, they would also have found countless differences between the twins in the study. To automatically assume that all similarities between identical twins are caused by genetic influences and that all differences are caused by environmental influences is bad science. The fact is that any two randomly selected people will find that they have countless things in common, none of which is likely to be caused by hereditary factors.

CORRELATION TO APA STANDARDS FOR CHAPTER 12

VIC. PERSONALITY

VIC-1. Perspectives on personality . . . . pp. 376–389
VIC-2. Assessment of personality . . . . pp. 391–395
VIC-3. Issues in personality . . . . pp. 396–400

MODULE 29 ▸ **PERSPECTIVES ON PERSONALITY**

MODULE 30 ▸ **ASSESSMENT AND ISSUES IN PERSONALITY**

Why Study? Personality

Personality is the sum total of who you are—your attitudes and reactions, both physical and emotional. It's what makes each person different from every other person in the world. How can any study of human behavior not include the study of who we are and how we got to be that way?

THEORIES OF PERSONALITY 375

SCHEDULING

1 Period = 50 min. 1 Block = 90 min.	Semester Course (18 weeks/90 days) Periods/Blocks		Full-Year Course (36 weeks/180 days) Period/Blocks	
Module 29	2.5	1.25	5	2.5
Module 30	2.5	1.25	5	2.5
Total Days for Chapter	5	2.5	10	5

CHAPTER 12 • Module 29

Teacher Prep

Personality is the unique way in which each individual thinks, acts, and feels throughout life. Two components of personality are character, referring to value judgments made about a person's morals or ethical behavior and temperament, referring to the characteristics with which a person is born, such as irritability or adaptability.

There are four main perspectives in personality theory: (1) the psychodynamic perspective focuses on the role of the unconscious mind and biological causes of personality; (2) the behavioral and social cognitive perspective is based on theories of learning and the effect of environment on behavior; (3) the humanistic perspective focuses on the role of each person's conscious life experiences and choices in personality development; and (4) the trait perspective differs from the other perspectives because it does not seek to explain how personality is formed and, instead, focuses on personality characteristics themselves.

The methods for assessing personality vary due to the theory of personality used to develop the methods and due to the purposes for which they are used. Methods include interviews, projective tests, behavioral assessments, and personality inventories. Each method has strengths and weaknesses and varying degrees of reliability, validity, bias, and objectivity.

Key issues to be considered in personality research are the roles that biology and culture play in personality, how stable personality is over time, and how personality can influence our health, work, and self-esteem.

Chapter 12 Theories of Personality **375**

CHAPTER 12 • Module 29

Focus

RESOURCES
For this module, consult the appropriate sections of the Teacher's Manual, Test Bank, and PowerPoint slides, all found on the Teacher's Resource DVD, and the interactive study tools for students on MyPsychLab.

BEFORE CLASS
Students should read the section for homework before coming to class.

BELLRINGER
Write on the board: **I am (adjective) because _____**. Ask students to think about their personalities and fill out the sentence on the board as many times as they can in 5 minutes. Ask students to then define *personality* and conjecture about how personality is developed.

Teach

INTRODUCE THE TOPIC
- *Personality* is the unique way in which each individual thinks, acts, and feels throughout life. Two elements of personality are *character* and *temperament*.
- There are four main perspectives in personality theory:
  - *Psychodynamic* focuses on the role of the unconscious mind and on biological causes of personality differences.
  - *Behavioral and social cognitive* focuses on how learning and the environment affect personality.
  - *Humanistic* focuses on the role of each person's life experiences in personality development.
  - *Trait perspective* focuses on describing the traits and characteristics of personality in order to predict future behavior.

376 Chapter 12 Theories of Personality

Module 29 Perspectives on Personality

Module Goal
Evaluate the major theories of personality.

Learning Objectives
- 29.1 What is the psychodynamic theory of personality?
- 29.2 How do behaviorists and social cognitive theorists explain personality?
- 29.3 How do humanistic psychologists explain personality?
- 29.4 What are the history and current views of the trait perspective?

Evaluate the Major Theories of Personality

Personality is the unique way in which each individual thinks, acts, and feels throughout life. Personality should not be confused with **character**, which refers to value judgments made about a person's morals or ethical behavior; nor should it be confused with **temperament**, the enduring characteristics with which each person is born, such as irritability or adaptability. Temperament is based in one's biology, either through genetic influences, prenatal influences, or a combination of those influences, and forms the basis upon which one's larger personality is built. Both character and temperament are vital parts of personality.

As an area of psychology, the study of personality deals with various explanations for the characteristic behavior of human beings. Not all psychology experts can agree on one single explanation of personality because characteristics are still difficult to measure precisely and scientifically. At present, there are four main perspectives in personality theory:

- The *psychodynamic perspective*, introduced by Sigmund Freud, focuses on the role of the unconscious mind in the development of personality and on biological causes of personality differences.
- The *behavioral and social cognitive perspective*, based on the theories of learning, focuses on the effect of the environment on behavior.
- The *humanistic perspective* first arose as a reaction against the psychodynamic and behaviorist perspectives and focuses on the role of each person's conscious life experiences and choices in personality development.
- The *trait perspective* differs from the other three in its basic goals: The psychoanalytic, behaviorist, and humanistic perspectives all seek to explain the process that causes personality to form into its unique characteristics, whereas trait theorists are more concerned with the characteristics themselves. Some trait theorists assume that traits are biologically determined and others do not.

personality the unique and relatively stable ways in which people think, feel, and behave.

character value judgments of a person's moral and ethical behavior.

temperament a child's innate personality and emotional characteristics, observable in infancy; the enduring characteristics with which each person is born.

29.1 What is the psychodynamic theory of personality?

Sigmund Freud and his Cultural Background It's hard to understand how Freud developed his ideas about personality without knowledge of the

376 CHAPTER 12

Terms

- personality • character • temperament • unconscious mind • id • pleasure principle
- ego • reality principle • superego • conscience • fixation • psychosexual stages
- oral stage • anal stage • anal expulsive personality • anal retentive personality
- phallic stage • Oedipus complex • identification • latency • psychoanalysis
- neo-Freudians • personal unconscious • collective unconscious • archetypes • basic anxiety • neurotic personalities • habits • social cognitive learning theorists • social cognitive view • reciprocal determinism • self-efficacy • locus of control • expectancy
- humanistic perspective • self-actualizing tendency • self • real self • ideal self
- positive regard • unconditional positive regard • conditional positive regard • fully functioning person • trait theories • trait • surface traits • source traits • introversion
- five-factor model • openness • conscientiousness • extraversion • extraverts
- introverts • agreeableness • neuroticism • trait-situation interaction

world in which he and his patients lived. Born in the Austro-Hungarian Empire in 1856, Freud moved with his family to Vienna when he was only 4 years old. He lived there until 1938, when Germany occupied Austria, and Freud, of Jewish background, moved to England to escape the Nazis. Freud's work in psychology began in the late 19th and early 20th centuries, a period of time commonly known in Europe and America as the Victorian Age. The Victorian Age was a time of sexual repression: Churches instructed that sex should take place only in the context of marriage and then only for the purposes of having children. To enjoy sexual intercourse was considered a sin. Freud's focus on sexual explanations for abnormal behavior seems more understandable in light of this cultural background.

Freud came to believe that there were layers of consciousness in the mind. Freud's first major publication, *The Interpretation of Dreams* (1900), developed his idea of the "unconscious" mind and became one of his most influential works.

The Unconscious Mind Freud believed that the mind was divided into three parts: the conscious, preconscious, and unconscious minds (Freud, 1904). (See Figure 29.1.) The ideas of a conscious mind (in which one's current awareness exists) and a preconscious mind (that contains memories, information, and events that can be pulled into the conscious mind at will) may have been accepted or even familiar to professionals of Freud's day. However, the idea of the **unconscious mind** (also called "the unconscious") was controversial. Freud theorized that there is a hidden part of the mind that surfaces in symbolic form in dreams, as well as in the form of some behaviors people engage in without knowing why they do so. Even when a person makes a determined effort to bring a memory out of the unconscious mind, it will not appear directly, according to Freud. Freud believed that the unconscious mind was the most important determining factor in human behavior and personality.

The Divisions of the Personality Freud believed, based on observations of his patients, that personality could be divided into three parts, each existing

unconscious mind level of the mind in which thoughts, feelings, memories, and other information are kept that are not easily or voluntarily brought into consciousness.

FIGURE 29.1 Freud's Conception of Personality
This iceberg represents the three levels of the mind. The part of the iceberg visible above the surface is the conscious mind. Just below the surface is the preconscious mind, everything that is not yet part of the conscious mind. Hidden deep below the surface is the unconscious mind, feelings, memories, thoughts, and urges that cannot be easily brought into consciousness. While two of the three parts of the personality (ego and superego) exist at all three levels of awareness, the id is completely in the unconscious mind.

THEORIES OF PERSONALITY 377

CHAPTER 12 • Module 29

COVER THE MODULE

29.1 What is the psychodynamic theory of personality?

- Sigmund Freud first introduced the psychodynamic theory of personality.
- Freud worked during the Victorian Age, a time of sexual repression, which likely influenced his focus on sexual explanations for abnormal behavior.
- Freud believed the mind was divided into three layers:
  - Conscious mind: where one's current awareness exists
  - Preconscious mind: contains memories, information, and events that can be pulled into the conscious mind at will
  - *Unconscious mind*: a hidden part of the mind that surfaces in symbolic form in dreams or in behaviors that are unexplained
- Freud believed that the unconscious mind was the most important factor in determining behavior and personality.

UNDERSTANDING VISUALS

Remind students that in Figure 29.1, an iceberg represents Freud's three levels of the mind. Ask the class if they can think of other visual representations of Freud's theory to help them make the visual more personal and, therefore, help students make a more concrete connection with the material.

Explore

A FIRST LOOK AT THE FOUR THEORIES OF PERSONALITY

Purpose: Students explore the four theories of personality in a jigsaw learning format to lay the groundwork for lessons ahead.

Time: 15 minutes

Description: Have students count off by 4's. Assign the 1's Freud's psychodynamic theory; the 2's behavioral and cognitive theory; the 3's humanistic theory; and the 4's trait theories. Allow students to group themselves by their numbers and research online or look through the text to prepare descriptions and explanations of their theories. Descriptions should include the leaders in formulating the theories and the main focuses of the theories, as well as any key terms. Once students have gathered information, create groups of four students (one from each theory study group) and have them share with their groups the information they have found.

CHAPTER 12 • Module 29

COVER THE MODULE (continued)

- Freud believed that personality could be divided into three parts.
- The *id* is the most primitive part of the personality, present in an infant and is the unconscious pleasure-seeking aspect of personality. It contains biological drives such as hunger, thirst, self-preservation, and sex.
  - The *pleasure principle* says that the id functions by seeking immediate satisfaction of needs without regard for consequences.
- The *ego* aspect of personality develops as the infant grows and must deal with the reality of having to wait to get what it desires. The ego is mostly conscious and is more logical than the id.
  - The *reality principle* says that the ego functions by the need to satisfy demands of the id in realistic ways.
- The *superego* is the moral center of personality that develops as preschool-aged children learn right from wrong.
  - *Conscience* is the part of the superego that produces pride or guilt based on behavior and right and wrong

DISCUSS THE STUDENT VOICE QUESTION

Ask students how the world would be different if everyone did, indeed, act only on the pleasure principle. Can they think of examples of adults who do not seem to have learned to control their id? What about fictional characters in movies, cartoons, or television shows? Can they think of times that they caved in to their id?

L3 DIFFERENTIATED INSTRUCTION

Visual/Verbal Learners Encourage students to visualize spellings of words or facts to be remembered and to rewrite things from memory.

---

id part of the personality present at birth and completely unconscious.

pleasure principle principle by which the id functions; the immediate satisfaction of needs without regard for the consequences.

ego part of the personality that develops out of a need to deal with reality; mostly conscious, rational, and logical.

reality principle principle by which the ego functions; the need to satisfy the demands of the id in ways that meet the demands of real life.

superego part of the personality that acts as a moral center.

conscience part of the superego that produces pride or guilt, depending on how acceptable behavior is.

▶ If everyone acted on the pleasure principle, the world would be pretty scary. How does knowing right from wrong come into Freud's theory?

---

at one or more levels of conscious awareness (see Figure 29.1). The way these parts of the personality develop and interact with one another is the heart of his theory (Freud, 1923, 1933, 1940).

The first and most primitive part of the personality, present in the infant, is the **id** (Latin for "it"). The id is a completely unconscious, pleasure-seeking part of the personality that exists at birth and contains basic biological drives: hunger, thirst, self-preservation, and sex, for example.

People do seem to be pleasure-seeking creatures, and even infants seek pleasure from sucking and chewing on whatever they stuff into their mouths. In fact, a newborn infant provides a good picture of the id. Infants are demanding, irrational, illogical, and impulsive. They want their needs satisfied immediately, and they don't care about anyone else's needs or desires. (A word of caution: The fact that infant behavior seems to fit Freud's concept of the id is not proof that the id exists. It simply means that Freud came up with the concept of the id to fit what he already knew about infants, and he supported this concept by referring to infant behavior.)

Freud called this need for immediate gratification with no regard for the consequences the **pleasure principle**. The pleasure principle can be summed up simply as "if it feels good, do it." People normally try to satisfy an infant's needs as quickly as possible. Infants are fed when hungry, changed when wet, and tended to whenever they cry. But as infants begin to grow, adults start restraining some of these "needs." There will be things they cannot touch or hold, and they must learn to wait for certain things. Freud theorized that the id cannot deal with the reality of having to wait or not getting what it wants.

According to Freud, to deal with reality, a second part of the personality develops called the **ego**. The ego (Latin for "I") is mostly conscious and is far more rational and logical than the id. The ego works on the **reality principle**, which is the need to satisfy the demands of the id in ways that meet the demands of real life. Sometimes, for example, the ego decides to deny the id it desires because the real-life consequences of those desires would be painful.

For example, while an infant might reach out and take an object despite a parent's protests, a toddler with a developing ego will avoid taking the object when the parent says, "No!" to avoid punishment—but may go back for the object when the parent is not looking. The ego strives to find a way to meet the id's needs within the confines of the real world's restrictions, social norms, and customs.

If everyone acted on the pleasure principle, the world would be pretty scary. How does knowing right from wrong come into Freud's theory?

Freud called the third part, the moral center of personality, the **superego**. The superego (also Latin, meaning "over the self") develops as a preschool-aged child learns the rules, customs, and expectations of society. The superego contains the **conscience**, the part of personality that makes people feel pride and guilt. It is not until the conscience develops that children have a sense of right and wrong. (Note that the term *conscience* is a different word from *conscious*. They look and sound similar, but they represent totally different concepts.) Like the id, the superego is generally disconnected from reality; it is up to the ego to find realistic ways to meet the demands of both the superego and the id.

Anyone who has ever watched cartoons has probably seen these three parts of the personality shown in animated form—the id is a little devil, the superego is an angel, and the ego is the cartoon character caught in the middle, trying to decide what action to take. The id makes demands, the superego restricts

378 CHAPTER 12

Class Demonstration (Kinesthetic)

ROLE PLAYING THE ID, EGO, AND SUPEREGO

Solicit three student volunteers to role-play the id, ego, and superego. While these students are outside the classroom, deciding which role each will play, have the rest of the class develop a scenario that might cause some ethical/moral difficulty for a high school student. Examples may be cheating on a test, not doing chores, texting too much, watching TV, or playing video games instead of studying, and so forth. Once the volunteers have returned, share the scenario with them and have them act out the three parts of one personality. Repeat the activity, so that all students in the class have a chance to act out the scenarios.

378 Chapter 12 Theories of Personality

how those demands can be met, and the ego must come up with a plan that will quiet the id but satisfy the superego. Sometimes the id or the superego does not get its way, resulting in a great deal of anxiety for the ego. This constant state of conflict is Freud's view of how personality works; according to his theories, all disordered behavior arises from the anxiety created by this conflict.

Explore on **mypsychlab.com**

Psychological defense mechanisms are ways of dealing with stress through unconsciously distorting one's perception of reality. Freud believed these mechanisms are created by the ego to adequately deal with the powerful and often opposing forces of the id, the superego, and reality. Anna Freud (Freud's daughter), who was a psychoanalyst, outlined and studied these defense mechanisms (Benjafield, 1996; Freud, 1946). For the three parts of the personality to function, the constant conflict among them must be managed, and Freud assumed that defense mechanisms were important to help with the anxiety caused by this conflict. One such defense mechanism is *repression*, which involves moving anxiety-causing thoughts out of the conscious mind into the unconscious mind to protect the ego. A list of defense mechanisms, their definitions, and examples of each appears in Table 36.1 in Chapter Fifteen.

LINK *to Chapter Fifteen: Stress and Health, p. 502.*

Stages of Personality Development Freud believed the parts of personality develop in stages, and at each stage, a different *erogenous zone*, or area of the body that produces pleasurable feelings, can become the source of conflicts. Conflicts that are not fully resolved can result in **fixation**, or getting "stuck" to some degree in a stage of development. The child may grow into an adult but will still carry emotional and psychological "baggage" from that earlier fixated stage. The term "hang-ups" comes from this idea of being "stuck" at a previous stage of development, unable to move on in healthy ways.

Because Freud believed that the formation of the personality, or *psyche*, is tied to sexual development, he called these the **psychosexual stages** of personality development. The first stage is called the **oral stage** because the erogenous zone, or pleasure focus, is the mouth. (It makes sense that infants are focused on the mouth, since they must use their mouths to nurse in order to survive, and sucking is a basic instinct that babies are born with.) This stage occurs from the birth of the infant to toddler age and is dominated by the id. The conflict, according to Freud, is about weaning (the transition from the safety and comfort of breastfeeding to the more independent cup feeding). Weaning too soon or too late can result in too little or too much satisfaction of the child's oral needs, resulting in an orally fixated adult personality, typified by overeating, drinking too much, nail biting, gum chewing, and a tendency to be either too dependent and optimistic or too aggressive and pessimistic.

Freud believed that as the child becomes a toddler (1 to 3 years), the erogenous zone moves from the mouth to the bowels, beginning the **anal stage** in which conflict revolves around issues of control and power. These issues are often expressed through toilet training, the demand that the child use the toilet at a particular time and in a particular way. This invasion of reality further stimulates the development of the ego. Fixation resulting from harsh or lenient toilet training can take one of two forms. The child who refuses (or is unable) to make it to the toilet may go to the bathroom where and when he or she feels like doing it. According to Freud, this translates in the adult as a person who sees messiness as a statement of personal control and

Explore the id, ego, and superego on **mypsychlab.com**

fixation disorder in which the person does not fully resolve the conflict in a particular psychosexual stage, resulting in personality traits and behavior associated with that earlier stage.

psychosexual stages five stages of personality development proposed by Freud and tied to the sexual development of the child.

oral stage first stage occurring in the first year of life in which the mouth is the erogenous zone and weaning is the primary conflict.

anal stage second stage occurring from about 1 to 3 years of age, in which the anus is the erogenous zone and toilet training is the source of conflict.

THEORIES OF PERSONALITY 379

CHAPTER 12 • Module 29

COVER THE MODULE (continued)

- Freud believed that the anxiety created by the constant conflict between the id, ego, and superego causes disordered behavior.
- Psychological defense mechanisms are ways of dealing with stress through unconsciously distorting one's perception of reality.
  - The ego creates defense mechanisms to manage the opposing forces of the id, ego, and superego.
  - Repression is one defense mechanism that involves moving anxiety-causing thoughts into the unconscious mind.

LINK *to Chapter Fifteen: Stress and Health p. 502*

- Freud believed personality developed in five psychosexual stages.
- *Fixation* is the failure to resolve the conflict in a psychosexual stage.
- *Oral stage* is the first stage of personality development, occurring from birth to toddler age and is dominated by the id.
  - Conflict in this stage is about weaning.
- *Anal stage* is the second stage, occurring from ages 1 to 3.
  - Conflict is about toilet training and issues of control and power.

MULTIMEDIA CONTENT AVAILABLE AT
www.mypsychlab.com

Explore the id, ego, and superego on **mypsychlab.com**

L4 DIFFERENTIATED INSTRUCTION

Advanced Learners Encourage students to apply standards-based understanding to new situations. Challenge them to take information and use it in novel ways.

Class Demonstration (Kinesthetic)

EXPLORING DEFENSE MECHANISMS

Purpose: Students explore Freud's psychological defense mechanisms and perform skits demonstrating them for the class.

Time: 20 minutes

Description: Direct students to textbook page 502 to examine Table 36.1, which describes Freud's defense mechanisms. Allow students to work in groups and assign each group a defense mechanism. Have students prepare a short skit demonstrating their assigned defense mechanism to perform for the class. After the group performs, have the class guess which defense mechanism was being used.

CHAPTER 12 • Module 29

COVER THE MODULE (continued)

- The *anal expulsive personality* is a person fixated in the anal stage, who views messiness as a statement of personal control and is destructive and hostile.
- The *anal retentive personality* is a person fixated in the anal stage, who dislikes making a mess and is stingy, stubborn, and excessively neat.
- The *phallic stage* is the third stage, occurring at ages 3 to 6.
  - Conflict centers on child's awakening sexual feelings.
  - In the *Oedipus complex*, a boy develops a sexual curiosity about his mother that gets mixed with his feelings of love for her. The boy must repress his feelings for his mother and identify with his father.
  - *Identification* is a defense mechanism in which a person tries to take on the characteristics of someone else to deal with anxiety.
- *Latency* is the fourth stage, occurring from age 6 until puberty.
  - Children grow intellectually, physically, and socially but not sexually, due to the repression of sexual feelings.
- Genital stage is the fifth and final stage of personality development, occurring from puberty until death.
  - Sexual feelings can no longer be repressed and are redirected to appropriate others.
  - This marks the entry into adulthood and sexual behavior.

TEACHING TIP

Some students may laugh at, or be embarrassed by, discussions of Freud's stages of personality development, so try to keep the mood of the class "professional."

---

who can be somewhat destructive and hostile. These **anal expulsive personalities** appear to most people as "messy," but Freud believed that this personality could lead to great creativity. Some children, however, are terrified of making a mess and rebel passively—by refusing to go at all or by "holding it" until they absolutely have to go to the bathroom. As adults, they can be stingy, stubborn, and excessively neat. This type is called the **anal retentive personality**. Freud indicated that orderliness and precision—qualities we value in surgeons and bridge engineers, for example—spring from this type of personality.

As the child grows older (3 to 6 years), the erogenous zone shifts to the genitals. Children have discovered the differences between the sexes by now, and this awakening is the beginning of what Freud termed the **phallic stage**. (*Phallic* comes from the Greek word *phallos* meaning "penis.") Freud believed that when a boy realizes that a girl has no penis, he develops a fear of losing his own penis. This is called *castration anxiety*. He also theorized that girls develop *penis envy* because they are missing a penis. If this seems like an odd focus on male anatomy, remember the era—the Western world at that time was very male oriented and male dominated, and the ideas of castration anxiety and penis envy stem from this cultural background. Fortunately, nearly all psychoanalysts have long since abandoned the concept of penis envy (Horney, 1939, 1973; Slipp, 1993).

The conflict in the phallic stage centers on the child's awakening sexual feelings. Freud essentially believed that boys develop both sexual attraction to their mothers and jealousy of their fathers during this stage, a phenomenon called the **Oedipus complex**. (Oedipus, a king in a Greek tragedy, unknowingly killed his father and married his mother. Freud was classically educated and very familiar with Greek and Roman history and mythology. He believed, as many still do, that Greek myths reflected universal human issues and struggles and expressed universal human suffering.) The sexual attraction is actually a sort of a sexual curiosity that becomes mixed up with the boy's feelings of love and affection for his mother. The resulting jealousy leads to anxiety and fears that his father might get angry and retaliate. To deal with this anxiety, the boy must *repress* his sexual feelings for his mother and *identify* with his father. **Identification** is a defense mechanism used to combat anxiety. The boy tries to take on the father's behavior, mannerisms, values, and moral beliefs as his own, becoming "just like Daddy." Girls go through a similar process, with their father the target of their affections and their mother as the rival. The result of identification is the development of the superego, the internalized moral values of the same-sex parent.

By the end of the phallic stage, children have pushed their sexual feelings into the unconscious through the defense mechanism of repression. From age 6 until the onset of puberty, children remain in this stage of hidden sexual feelings, called **latency** (*latent* means "hidden from view"). In this stage, children grow and develop intellectually, physically, and socially, but not sexually. Boys play with other boys, girls play only with girls, and each thinks the opposite sex is pretty awful. But when puberty does begin, there is a re-emergence of sexual energy which brings about the *genital stage*. The sexual feelings that were once repressed can no longer be ignored, but this time, these feelings are redirected toward appropriate others (rather than toward a parent). Since Freud tied personality development into sexual development, the genital stage

anal expulsive personality a person fixated in the anal stage who is messy, destructive, and hostile.

anal retentive personality a person fixated in the anal stage who is neat, fussy, stingy, and stubborn.

phallic stage third stage occurring from about 3 to 6 years of age in which the child discovers sexual feelings.

Oedipus complex situation occurring in the phallic stage in which a child develops a sexual attraction to the opposite-sex parent and jealousy of the same-sex parent.

identification defense mechanism in which a person tries to become like someone else to deal with anxiety.

latency fourth stage occurring during the school years in which the sexual feelings of the child are repressed while the child develops in other ways.

Class Discussion

FIXATIONS AND PERSONALITY TYPE

Purpose: Students discuss how fixations influence adult personality.

Time: 10 minutes

Description: Begin by putting students in groups. Have the groups brainstorm three characters from television shows or movies that all members of the group are familiar with, who display characteristics of Freud's personality fixations. Each group should outline each character's personality and explain it according to Freud's personality theory. Allow students to share their findings with the class.

Table 29.1 Freud's Psychosexual Stages

STAGE	AGE	FOCUS OF PLEASURE	FOCUS OF CONFLICTS	DIFFICULTIES AT THIS STAGE AFFECT LATER...
Oral	Birth to 1½ years old	Oral activities (such as sucking, feeding, and making noises with the mouth)	Separation from safety and comfort (weaning)	• Ability to form interpersonal attachments • Basic feelings about the world • Tendency to use oral forms of aggression, such as sarcasm • Optimism or pessimism • Tendency to take charge or be passive
Anal	1½ to 3 years old	Bowel and bladder control	Control and power (toilet training)	• Sense of competence and control • Stubbornness or willingness to go along with others • Neatness or messiness • Punctuality or tardiness
Phallic	3 to 6 years old	Genitals	Sexual awareness	• Identification with same-sex parent • Pride or humility
Latency	6 years old to puberty	Social skills (such as the ability to make friends) and intellectual skills; dormant period in terms of psychosexual development	School, play, same-sex friendships	• Ability to get along with others parent
Genital	Puberty to death	Sexual behavior	Sexual relationship with partner	• Immature love or indiscriminate hate • Uncontrollable working or inability to work

represents the final process in Freud's personality theory as well as entry into adult social and sexual behavior. Table 29.1 summarizes the stages of the psychosexual theory of personality development.

The Neo-Freudians At first, Freud's ideas were met with resistance and ridicule by doctors and psychologists. Eventually, a number of early followers, objecting to Freud's emphasis on biology and particularly on sexuality, broke away from a strict interpretation of psychoanalytic theory, instead altering the focus of **psychoanalysis** (the term Freud applied to his explanation of the unconscious mind and development of personality as well as the therapy based on that theory) to emphasize the ego and the impact of the social environment. At the same time, they retained many of Freud's original concepts such as the id, ego, superego, and defense mechanisms. These early psychoanalysts became the **neo-Freudians** (the prefix *neo-* means "new").

Carl Gustav Jung (pronounced "YOONG") believed that the unconscious held much more than personal fears, urges, and memories. He believed that

psychoanalysis Freud's term for both the theory of personality and the therapy based on it.

neo-Freudians followers of Freud who developed their own competing psychodynamic theories.

THEORIES OF PERSONALITY 381

CHAPTER 12 • Module 29

COVER THE MODULE (continued)

- *Psychoanalysis* is Freud's term for the theory of personality and the therapy based on it.
- *Neo-Freudians* altered the focus of psychoanalysis to emphasize the ego and the impact of the social environment on personality.
- Carl Jung was a neo-Freudian, who believed in a personal unconscious, as well as a collective unconscious.

CHECK FOR UNDERSTANDING

If students struggle with the concepts in this section of the module, have them review Table 29.1. Remind students that Freud tied personality development into sexual development.

TEACHING TIP

Avoid assigning too many goals at one time to students, who may become overwhelmed.

Explore

LEARNING MORE ABOUT THE NEO-FREUDIANS

Students can read more about the neo-Freudians at the following websites:

- Carl Jung: www.notablebiographies.com/Jo-Ki/Jung-Carl.html
- Alfred Adler: www.notablebiographies.com/A-An/Adler-Alfred.html
- Karen Horney: www.webster.edu/~woolflm/horney.html
- Erik Erikson: www.nndb.com/people/151/000097857/

Module 29 Perspectives on Personality

CHAPTER 12 • Module 29

COVER THE MODULE (continued)

- *Personal unconscious* is Jung's name for the unconscious mind as described by Freud.
- *Collective unconscious* is Jung's name for the memories shared by all members of the human species.
  - *Archetypes:* Jung's collective universal human memories, such as animal animus and the shadow
- Alfred Adler believed that feelings of inferiority young children experience when comparing themselves to older, more powerful people is the driving force behind all human behavior as we seek superiority.
  - Compensation is a defense mechanism in which people try to overcome inferiority by becoming superior in something else.

LINK to Chapter Fifteen: Stress and Health p. 502

  - Birth order affects personality.
- Karen Horney split with Freud over disagreements concerning gender differences and penis envy.
  - *Basic anxiety* is created when a child is born into the bigger and more powerful world of older children and adults.
  - Children usually overcome this anxiety in a nurturing environment.
  - *Neurotic personality* is the result of maladaptive ways of dealing with relationships, due to trying to cope with anxiety.
- Erik Erikson broke from Freud's emphasis on sex and developed eight psychosocial stages of development.

LINK to Chapter Five: Development Across the Life Span, pp. 158–160

DIFFERENTIATED INSTRUCTION

Tactile/Kinesthetic Learners These students can write out key concepts on a large board or poster or trace letters and words to remember key facts.

Carl Jung (1875–1961) was a Swiss psychoanalyst who eventually broke away from Freud's emphasis on the sexual content of the unconscious mind. He formed his own theory of analysis known as analytical psychology.

personal unconscious Jung's name for the unconscious mind as described by Freud.

collective unconscious Jung's name for the memories shared by all members of the human species.

archetypes Jung's collective, universal human memories.

basic anxiety anxiety created when a child is born into the bigger and more powerful world of older children and adults.

neurotic personalities typified by maladaptive ways of dealing with relationships in Horney's theory.

---

there was not only a **personal unconscious**, as described by Freud, but a **collective unconscious** as well (Jung, 1933).

According to Jung, the collective unconscious contains a kind of collective "species" or "racial" memory, human memories of ancient fears and themes, or **archetypes**, that are often expressed through folktales and cultural customs. Two of the better known archetypes are the *anima/animus* (the feminine side of a man/the masculine side of a woman) and the *shadow* (the dark side of personality). The side of one's personality shown to the world is the *persona*.

Alfred Adler also disagreed with Freud over the importance of sexuality in personality development. Adler (1954) developed the theory that as young, helpless children, people all develop feelings of inferiority when comparing themselves to the more powerful, superior adults. (Adler called this the *inferiority complex*.) The driving force behind all human endeavors, emotions, and thoughts for Adler is the seeking of superiority. (Adler called this the *drive for superiority*.) The defense mechanism of *compensation*, in which people try to overcome feelings of inferiority in one area by striving to be superior in another, figures prominently in Adler's theory. **LINK** to Chapter Fifteen: Stress and Health, p. 502.

Adler (1954) also theorized that birth order affected personality. Firstborn children with younger siblings feel inferior once those younger siblings get attention, and they often compensate by overachieving. Middle children feel superior over the dethroned older child while dominating younger siblings; they tend to be very competitive. Younger children feel inferior because they are not allowed the freedom and responsibility of the older children. Although some researchers have found evidence to support Adler's birth order theory (Stein, 2001; Sulloway, 1996), and some have even linked birth order to career choices (Leong et al., 2001; Watkins & Savickas, 1990), other researchers point to sloppy methodology and the bias of researchers toward the birth order idea (Beer & Horn, 2001; Freese et al., 1999; Ioannidis, 1998).

Karen Horney ("HORN-eye") studied Freud's work and taught psychoanalysis at the Psychoanalytic Institutes of Berlin and New York (1967, 1973). She left the institute because of disagreements with Freud over the concepts of gender differences and penis envy. She countered with her own concept of "womb envy," the idea that men compensate for their inability to bear children by striving for success in other areas (Burger, 1997).

Rather than focusing on sexuality, Horney focused on the child's sense of **basic anxiety** in the face of a world that is much bigger and more powerful than the child. While people whose parents gave them love, affection, and a sense of "belonging" tend to overcome this anxiety, others develop **neurotic personalities** and maladaptive ways of dealing with relationships. Some children, according to Horney, deal with their anxiety by becoming dependent and clingy. Others become aggressive, demanding, and cruel, or simply avoid personal relationships.

Erik Erikson (1950, 1959, 1982), an art teacher who became a psychoanalyst, also broke away from Freud's emphasis on sex. He emphasized eight important psychosocial stages of development, discussed in detail in Chapter Five. **LINK** to Chapter Five: Development Across the Life Span, pp. 158–160.

Explore

BIRTH ORDER

The influence of birth order on personality development is a controversial issue in psychology. The general public tends to believe that personality is strongly influenced by birth order, but many psychologists dispute this. Ask students to conduct an informal survey among family and friends to see if they think birth order influences personality. Do students themselves believe it? Why or why not? Then ask students to do library or Internet research to determine what recent research has shown about this theory. Ask volunteers to report back to the class.

It sounds as if all of these theorists became famous by ditching some of Freud's original ideas. Is Freud even worth studying anymore?

Although Freud's psychoanalytic theory seems less relevant today, these concepts form a basis for many modern personality theories. The idea of the defense mechanisms and the concept of an unconscious mind have research support. And modern researchers have had to admit that there are influences on human behavior that exist beyond normal consciousness, especially in the areas of hypnosis and subliminal perception (Borgeat & Goulet, 1983; Bryant & McConkey, 1989; Kihlstrom, 1987, 1999, 2001).

One major criticism of Freud's theory is that it is solely based on his own observations of his patients. He interpreted their behavior and reminiscences to develop his theory of psychoanalysis. He interpreted whatever his patients told him as fantasy or fact, depending on how well the information fit with his developing theory. For example, many of Freud's patients claimed to be abused by family members. Freud apparently decided that these memories were fantasies, developing the basis of the Oedipal conflict. He later revised his original perceptions of his patients' memories of abuse as real due to public and professional criticism from his German colleagues (Masson, 1984).

Freud based much of his interpretations of a patient's problems on the interpretations of dreams (LINK to *Chapter Four: Consciousness: Sleep, Dreams, Hypnosis, and Drugs, p. 119*) and the results of the patient's free association (talking about anything without fear of negative feedback). These "sources" are often criticized for lack of scientific support. Freud could easily fit the patient's words and recollections to his own interpretation. This increased the possibility that his own suggestions might alter the actual memories of the patient, who would no doubt be in a very suggestible state of mind during therapy (Grünbaum, 1984).

Although many professionals today view Freud's theory with a great deal of skepticism, his influence cannot be ignored. Freudian concepts have impacted literature, movies, and even children's cartoons. People who have never taken a course in psychology are familiar with some of Freud's most basic concepts, such as defense mechanisms. He was also one of the first theorists to emphasize the importance of childhood experiences on personality development—in spite of the fact that he never studied children.

29.2 How do behaviorists and social cognitive theorists explain personality?

At the time that Freud's theory was shocking the Western world, another psychological perspective was making its influence known. *Behaviorists* (researchers who use the principles of conditioning, or learning, to explain the actions and reactions of animals and humans) and *social cognitive theorists* (researchers who emphasize the influence of social and cognitive factors on learning) have a very different view of personality.

For the behaviorist, personality is just a set of learned responses or **habits** (DeGrandpre, 2000; Dollard & Miller, 1950). In the strictest view, everything a person or animal does is shaped by the consequence of his or her response to a stimulus. LINK to *Chapter Six: Learning and Language Development, pp. 178–192.*

habits in behaviorism, sets of well-learned responses that have become automatic.

◀ It sounds as if all of these theorists became famous by ditching some of Freud's original ideas. Is Freud even worth studying anymore?

THEORIES OF PERSONALITY 383

Explore

PHOTOGRAPHS AT THE FREUD MUSEUM IN LONDON

The Freud Museum's website has a link to a photograph library, where students can view portraits of Freud, his family, his colleagues, and his famous couch:
www.freud.org.uk/

CHAPTER 12 • Module 29

COVER THE MODULE (continued)

- Even though Freud's psychoanalytic theory has been criticized, research has supported several of his key ideas, such as defense mechanisms and the idea of the unconscious mind, and his theories are still very influential.
- Criticism includes the following:
  - Freud's theory was based solely on his observations of his patients.
  - His interpretations of his patients were filtered by how well they fit with his developing theories.
  - There is a lack of scientific support for Freud's interpretations of dreams and free associations.

DISCUSS THE STUDENT VOICE QUESTION

Ask students why they think Freud's theories have been so influential and are worth studying.

COVER THE MODULE

29.2 How do behaviorists and social cognitive theorists explain personality?

- Behaviorists turn to conditioning and learning to explain actions of humans.
- Cognitive theorists emphasize the influence of social and cognitive factors on learning.
- Behaviorists believe personality is a set of learned responses called *habits*.
- Behavior is shaped by a response to a stimulus.

LINK to *Chapter Six: Learning and Language Development, pp. 178–192*

L3 DIFFERENTIATED INSTRUCTION

Differentiated instruction provides multiple paths for students to access, use, and transfer understanding of concepts. It integrates instructional strategies to meet the needs of a diverse population of students and thereby enables all students to achieve success.

Module 29 Perspectives on Personality **383**

CHAPTER 12 • Module 29

COVER THE MODULE (continued)

- Behaviorists explain personality development through conditioning and positive and negative reinforcement.
- *Social cognitive learning theorists* believe that learning is affected also through the social environment via observation, modeling, and other techniques.

LINK to *Chapter Six: Learning and Language Development, pp. 195–200.*

- The *social cognitive view* emphasizes learning theory that includes anticipating, judging, memory, and imitation of models as influences on behavior.
- In Albert Bandura's *reciprocal determinism*, three factors interact to determine behavior that develops personality—environment, the behavior itself, and personal factors from earlier experiences.
- *Self-efficacy* is an individual's expectancy of how effective his or her efforts will be to accomplish a goal.

CHECK FOR UNDERSTANDING

Ask students to spend a few moments writing about an aspect of their personality that could be attributed to reciprocal determinism. Ask them to explain how it came about because of environmental factors, the responses the behavior itself received, and how past experiences shaped their desire to perform the behavior in the first place.

▶ *So, how does a pattern of rewarding certain behavior end up becoming part of some kind of personality pattern?*

So, how does a pattern of rewarding certain behavior end up becoming part of some kind of personality pattern?

Think about how a traditional behaviorist might explain a shy personality. A child might be exposed to a parent with a rather harsh discipline style. Avoiding the attention of that parent would result in less punishment and scolding, so that the avoidance response is negatively reinforced—the "bad thing" is avoided by keeping quiet. Later, that child might generalize that avoidance response to other authority figures and adults, such as teachers. In this way, a pattern (habit) of shyness develops, shaped by our experience.

Of course, many learning theorists today do not use only conditioning to explain the development of personality. Expanding on the findings of strict behaviorism, some researchers believe that learning is affected not only through behavior but also through the social environment. **Social cognitive learning theorists**, who emphasize the importance of the influences of other people's behavior and of a person's own expectancies on learning, hold that observational learning, modeling, and other cognitive learning techniques can lead to the formation of patterns of personality. **LINK** to *Chapter Six: Learning and Language Development, pp. 195–200.*

Bandura's Reciprocal Determinism and Self-Efficacy One well-researched learning theory was developed by observational learning expert Albert Bandura. In the **social cognitive view**, behavior is governed not just by the influence of stimuli and response patterns but by cognitive processes such as anticipating, judging, and memory as well as learning through the imitation of models. Bandura (1989) identified three factors in determining the patterns of behavior that make up personality: the environment, the behavior itself, and personal or cognitive factors from earlier experiences. These three factors affect each other in a give-and-take relationship. Bandura calls this relationship **reciprocal determinism**. In the context of reciprocal determinism, the environment includes physical surroundings, other people (who may or may not be present), and the potential for reinforcement in those surroundings. The intensity and frequency of the person's behavior will also impact the environment, as will previous consequences of past responses (personality) and mental processes such as thinking and anticipating.

Here's an example: Richard enters a classroom filled with other students, but no teacher is present. (This is the *environment*.) Richard's *personal* characteristics include the desire to gain attention from other people by talking loudly and telling jokes. His *behavior* will most likely be to talk loudly and tell jokes; it will continue if he gets a rewarding positive reaction from the students. If the teacher walks in (the *environment* changes), or if the other students don't laugh, his behavior will most likely change.

One personal variable that Bandura talks about is **self-efficacy**, a person's expectancy of the effectiveness of his or her efforts to accomplish a goal (Bandura, 1998). A sense of self-efficacy depends on the successes and failures in similar circumstances in the past, other people's opinions of their competence, and their own assessment of their abilities. For example, if Fiona has an opportunity to write an extra-credit paper to improve her grade, she will be more likely to do so if her self-efficacy is high: She has earned good grades on papers before and she feels she is good at writing. According to Bandura, people high in self-efficacy are more persistent and expect to succeed, whereas people low in self-efficacy expect to fail and tend to avoid challenges (Bandura, 1998).

---

social cognitive learning theorists theorists who emphasize the importance of both the influences of other people's behavior and of a person's own expectancies of learning.

social cognitive view learning theory that includes cognitive processes such as anticipating, judging, memory, and imitation of models.

reciprocal determinism Bandura's explanation of how the factors of environment, personal characteristics, and behavior can interact to determine future behavior.

self-efficacy individual's expectancy of how effective his or her efforts to accomplish a goal will be in any particular circumstance.

Critical Thinking

CREATING A CHARACTER WITH PERSONALITY

Place students in groups of five. Write a list of personality descriptors (e.g., shyness) on the board. Tell students that they will write a story entitled "How _____ Came to Be." Students should choose a personality descriptor to insert in the blank. They should imagine a character with that personality trait and write a story. (1) Students write for 2 to 3 minutes, describing the environment where the character develops the trait, beginning with "Once upon a time, in a faraway land... ." (2) Have students pass their papers to their "groupmate" on their right, who must now add to the story by describing the character's motivations that would lead to such a personality trait. (3) Students again pass their papers to the next groupmate and add to the story by describing a situation in which the character would find himself or herself and the behavior the character displays. (4) Students pass their papers and add to the story, describing the reaction or result of the behavior and its consequences. (5) Students pass their papers one more time and describe how the story ends, the lesson the character learned, and how that character embodied that trait.

Rotter's Social Learning Theory: Expectancies Julian Rotter (1966, 1978, 1981, 1990) devised a theory based on a basic principle of motivation: People are motivated to seek reinforcement and avoid punishment. He viewed personality as a relatively stable set of *potential* responses to various situations. If a certain response has led to a reinforcing or pleasurable consequence, that response will become a pattern within the personality. One such pattern led to Rotter's concept of **locus of control**, the tendency for people to determine whether they have control over events and consequences in their own lives (the word *locus* means "location"). LINK to Chapter Eleven: Motivation and Emotion, p. 354. People who assume that their own actions and decisions directly affect the consequences they experience have an *internal* locus of control, while people who assume that their experiences are controlled by powerful others, luck, or fate have an *external* locus of control (MacDonald, 1970; Rotter, 1966). Rotter associated people who have an internal locus of control with high achievement motivation (the power and means to achieve). Those who have an external locus of control can fall into patterns of depression (Abramson et al., 1978, 1980; Gong-Guy & Hammen, 1980).

There are some limits to the behaviorist view of personality formation. In particular, the classic theory does not take mental processes into account at all, nor does it give weight to social influences on learning. The social cognitive view of personality, however, includes social and mental processes and their influence on behavior. Another strength of the social cognitive theory is that its concepts can and have been tested under scientific conditions (Backenstrass et al., 2008; Bandura, 1965; Catanzaro et al., 2000; DeGrandpre, 2000; Domjan et al., 2000).

29.3 How do humanistic psychologists explain personality?

In the middle of the 20th century, psychologists such as Carl Rogers and Abraham Maslow introduced the **humanistic perspective** of psychology, which is focused on things that make people uniquely human, such as subjective emotions and the freedom to choose one's own destiny. LINK to Chapter One: The Science of Psychology, p. 10.

Both Maslow and Rogers (1961) believed that humans have a **self-actualizing tendency**, or a desire to fulfill their innate capacities and capabilities and live up to their potential. Important to self-actualization is the development of an image of oneself, or the *self-concept*, based on how the sense of *self* is reflected in the words and actions of important people in one's life.

Real and Ideal Self Two important components of the self-concept are the **real self** (one's actual perception of characteristics, traits, and abilities) and the **ideal self** (the perception of what one *should be* or *would like to be*). The ideal self primarily comes from important people in a person's life, most often the parents. Rogers believed that when the real self and the ideal self are very similar, people feel competent and capable, but when the real and ideal selves are mismatched, anxiety and disordered behavior can result. (See Figure 29.2 on the next page.)

The two halves of the self are more likely to match if they are similar to begin with. When a person has a clear view of his or her real self, and the ideal self is attainable, there usually isn't a mismatch. When a person's view of self

locus of control the tendency for people to assume that they either have control or do not have control over events and consequences in their lives.

expectancy a person's subjective feeling that a particular behavior will lead to a reinforcing consequence.

humanistic perspective the "third force" in psychology that focuses on those aspects of personality that make people uniquely human, such as subjective feelings and freedom of choice.

self-actualizing tendency the striving to fulfill one's innate capacities and capabilities.

self an individual's awareness of their own personal characteristics and level of functioning.

real self one's perception of actual characteristics, traits, and abilities.

ideal self one's perception of whom one should be or would like to be.

THEORIES OF PERSONALITY 385

CHAPTER 12 • Module 29

COVER THE MODULE (continued)

- Julian Rotter viewed personality as a set of responses to various situations, believing people are motivated to seek reinforcement and avoid punishment.
- *Locus of control* is the belief people have for how much control they have over the events and consequences in their own lives.

LINK: *to Chapter Eleven: Motivation and Emotion, p. 354*

- Internal locus of control means that people believe their own actions and decisions directly affect their consequences.
- External locus of control means that people believe that experiences are controlled by outside forces such as luck or fate.

COVER THE MODULE

29.3 How do humanistic psychologists explain personality?

- Humanistic perspective focuses on what makes us uniquely human, such as emotions and freedom to choose our own destiny, introduced by Carl Rogers and Abraham Maslow.

LINK *to Chapter One: The Science of Psychology, p. 10*

- *Self-actualizing tendency* is striving to live up to one's potential.
  - Development of the self concept: (1) the *real self* is the individual's perception of his or her actual characteristics and (2) *ideal self* is the perception of who that individual wishes to be.

Class Demonstration (Kinesthetic)

ARE YOU IN OR OUT? "MUSICAL CHAIRS"

Purpose: Students identify examples of external or internal locus of control.

Time: 10 minutes

Description: Clear a space in the middle of the room and place a large circle on the floor using cardboard, construction paper, and so forth. Ask students to stand around the circle. Tell them that you will be reading a description of a person and a situation, and they should be thinking about whether you are describing an example of internal or external locus of control. Play music and have the students move in a circle. When you stop the music, students should jump into the circle if they think the example is internal and stay out of the circle for external. Students who make an incorrect choice are "out" and should return to their seats. Pause to explain each example. Repeat the process until one student, "the winner," remains.

Module 29 Perspectives on Personality   385

CHAPTER 12 • Module 29

COVER THE MODULE *(continued)*

- *Positive regard* is warmth, affection, love, and respect that come from significant others.
- *Unconditional positive regard* is positive regard without strings attached or expectations for certain behaviors or outcomes.
- *Conditional positive regard* is positive regard given on the condition that something is given in return or an expectation is met.
- A *fully functioning person* is an individual in touch with his or her own feelings and abilities, with the ability to trust one's own intuitions.
  - A person must receive unconditional positive regard in order to be fully functioning.

CLASS DISCUSSION

Write the following on the board: **"The curious paradox is that when I accept myself just as I am, then I can change."—Carl Rogers**

Lead a discussion about how Rogers's theories of self-actualization and the concept of the fully functioning person explain this quote. Do students agree or disagree? Why would a self-actualized or fully functioning person want to change?

L2 ELL DIFFERENTIATED INSTRUCTION

English Language Learners Lead a quick text prereading, or "text tour," focusing student attention on illustrations, titles and subtopics, and boldfaced words.

FIGURE 29.2 Real and Ideal Selves
According to Rogers, the self-concept includes the real self and the ideal self. The real self is a person's actual perception of traits and abilities, whereas the ideal self is the perception of what a person would like to be or thinks he or she should be. When the ideal self and the real self are very similar (matching), the person is content, but when there is a mismatch between the two selves, the person experiences anxiety.

is distorted or the ideal self is impossible to attain, problems arise. It is mainly the reactions of important people in a person's life (good or bad influences) that influence the match between real and ideal selves.

Conditional and Unconditional Positive Regard Rogers defined **positive regard** as warmth, affection, love, and respect that come from significant others (parents, admired adults, friends, and teachers). Rogers believed that **unconditional positive regard**, or love, affection, and respect with no strings attached, is necessary for people to self-actualize. Unfortunately, some parents, spouses, and friends give **conditional positive regard**, which is love, affection, respect, and warmth that depend, or seem to depend, on doing what those people want.

Take Sasha and Karen, two college freshmen, for example. Sasha is considering becoming a math teacher, a computer programmer, or an elementary school teacher. Karen already knows that she is going to be a doctor. Whereas Sasha's parents had left the choice up to her and told her they'd love her no matter what, Karen's parents, since her childhood, made clear their expectation that she become a doctor. Karen believes, consciously or unconsciously, that if she chooses any other career, she will lose her parents' love and respect. Sasha's parents gave her unconditional positive regard, but Karen's parents (whether they intended to do so or not) gave Karen conditional positive regard. Sasha is freer than Karen to explore her potential and abilities.

According to Rogers, a person who is in the process of self-actualizing, actively exploring potentials and abilities and experiencing a match between his or her real self and ideal self, is a **fully functioning person**. Fully functioning people are in touch with their own feelings and abilities and are able to trust their intuitions (Rogers, 1961). To become fully functioning, a person

positive regard warmth, affection, love, and respect that come from significant others in one's life.

unconditional positive regard warmth, respect, and affection without any conditions attached.

conditional positive regard positive regard that is given only when the person is doing what the providers of positive regard wish.

fully functioning person a person who is in touch with and trusting of the deepest, innermost urges and feelings.

386 CHAPTER 12

Class Demonstration

HARMONY OR ANXIETY?

<u>Purpose</u>: Students create a Venn diagram similar to that pictured in Figure 29.2, describing how well their real and ideal selves match.

<u>Time</u>: 20 minutes

<u>Description</u>: Ask students to draw a Venn diagram on a piece of paper and fill it in with descriptions of their perceptions of their real and ideal selves. Ask them to evaluate how well the two selves line up. Are they on the path to harmony or anxiety? How do they plan to make adjustments to work toward self-actualization?

---

386 Chapter **12** Theories of Personality

needs unconditional positive regard. In Rogers's view, Karen would not be a fully functioning person.

Humanistic views of personality paint a very rosy picture. Some critics believe that the picture is a little too rosy, ignoring the more negative aspects of human nature. Humanistic theory is also very difficult to test scientifically. Its greatest impact has been in the development of therapies to promote self-growth and help people better understand themselves and others.

29.4 What are historical and current views of the trait perspective?

While other perspectives are concerned with explaining how personality develops, **trait theories** attempt to describe personality and predict future behavior based on that description. A **trait** is a consistent, enduring way of thinking, feeling, or behaving, and trait theories attempt to describe personality in terms of a person's traits. Gordon Allport and his colleague H.S. Odbert made one of the earliest attempts to list and describe traits that make up personality (Allport & Odbert, 1936), locating 18,000 words in the dictionary that could be traits and paring that list down to 200 traits by eliminating synonyms. Allport believed (with no scientific evidence) that these traits were literally wired into the nervous system to guide behavior, and that each person's "constellation" of traits was unique. Watch on mypsychlab.com

200 is still a very large number of traits, and a more compact way of describing personality was needed. Raymond Cattell (1990) defined two types of traits: surface traits and source traits. **Surface traits** represent the personality characteristics easily seen by other people. **Source traits** are more basic traits that underlie surface traits. For example, shyness, being quiet, and disliking crowds might all be surface traits that underlie the source trait of **introversion**, a tendency to withdraw from excessive stimulation. Cattell identified 16 source traits (Cattell, 1950, 1966) and developed his assessment questionnaire, *The Sixteen Personality Factor Questionnaire* (16PF) (Cattell, 1995), based on these traits (see Figure 29.3).

The Big Five: OCEAN, or the Five-Factor Model of Personality

Later researchers attempted to reduce the number of trait dimensions, with several groups of researchers arriving at more or less the same five trait dimensions (Botwin & Buss, 1989; Jang et al., 1998; McCrae & Costa, 1996). These five dimensions have become known as the **five-factor model**, or the **Big Five** (see Figure 29.4), and represent the current description of human personality—under trait theory, they are the only dimensions necessary to understand what makes us tick.

These five trait dimensions can be remembered by using the acronym OCEAN:

- **Openness** is a person's willingness to try new things and be open to new experiences. People who don't like change score low on openness.
- **Conscientiousness** refers to a person's organization and motivation. People who score high in this dimension are usually on time and take care of belongings. Someone scoring low is less careful about time or property.
- **Extraversion** is a term first used by Carl Jung (1933), who believed that people could be divided into **extraverts** and **introverts**. Extraverts are outgoing and sociable, and introverts dislike being the center of attention.

Watch classic video footage on personality traits with Allport on **mypsychlab.com**

trait theories theories that endeavor to describe the characteristics that make up human personality in an effort to predict future behavior.

trait a consistent, enduring way of thinking, feeling, or behaving.

surface traits aspects of personality that can easily be seen by other people in the outward actions of a person.

source traits the more basic traits that underlie the surface traits, forming the core of personality.

introversion dimension of personality in which people tend to withdraw from excessive stimulation.

five-factor model (Big Five) model of personality traits that describes five basic trait dimensions.

openness one of the five factors; willingness to try new things and be open to new experiences.

conscientiousness the care a person gives to organization and thoughtfulness of others; dependability.

extraversion dimension of personality referring to one's need to be with other people.

extraverts people who are outgoing and sociable.

introverts people who prefer solitude and dislike being the center of attention.

THEORIES OF PERSONALITY 387

CHAPTER 12 • Module 29

COVER THE MODULE

29.4 What are historical and current views of the trait perspective?

- *Trait theories* describe personality and attempt to predict future behavior based on that description.
- A *trait* is a consistent way of thinking, feeling, and behaving.
- Gordon Allport and H.S. Odbert created a list of 200 traits and believed that traits were wired into the nervous system in a unique constellation.
- Raymond Cattell defined two types of traits:
  - *Surface traits* are personality traits seen by other people.
  - *Source traits* are the traits that define the core personality; Cattell identified 16 source traits.
- The *Five-Factor Model/Big Five*: (1) *openness*, (2) *conscientiousness*, (3) *extraversion*, (4) *agreeableness*, and (5) *neuroticism*

MULTIMEDIA CONTENT AVAILABLE AT www.mypsychlab.com

Watch classic video footage on personality traits with Allport on **mypsychlab.com**

L2 LPR DIFFERENTIATED INSTRUCTION

Less Proficient Readers For students with difficulties with attention and memory, ask them to reorganize, prioritize, and otherwise reflect on the key aspects of the lesson. Monitor and reteach as necessary.

Class Demonstration

EXPLORING CATTELL'S SELF-REPORT INVENTORY

Purpose: Students make connections to the trait theory of personality by assessing themselves according to Cattell's 16 personality traits.

Time: 10 minutes

Description: Prepare a blank version of Cattell's Self-Report Inventory, shown in Figure 29.3. Hand out copies to students and have them assess and graph their personalities. Then ask them to write a short paragraph summarizing their findings.

Module 29 Perspectives on Personality **387**

CHAPTER 12 • Module 29

COVER THE MODULE *(continued)*
- Personality traits may not always be expressed in the same way in all situations.
- In *trait-situation interaction*, the particular circumstances in any given situation will influence how a trait is expressed.

MULTIMEDIA CONTENT AVAILABLE AT
www.mypsychlab.com

Explore the five-factor model on mypsychlab.com

UNDERSTANDING VISUALS

Figure 29.3 points out the personality differences of people working in two considerably different fields. Ask: **In what ways can our personality traits affect our abilities? What are other ways that personality can influence the choices we make in our lives?**

L3 DIFFERENTIATED INSTRUCTION

Engaging All Learners Explicitly teach skills. Model note-taking as you present information to the classroom. Collect and review the students' notes and provide suggestions for improvement. Teach study skills, listening skills, and reading skills along with the content.

FIGURE 29.3 Cattell's Self-Report Inventory
Cattell's 16 source traits are seen as "trait dimensions" in which there are two opposite traits at each end with many possible degrees of traits possible along the dimension. For example, someone scoring near the reserved end of the reserved/outgoing dimension would be more introverted than someone scoring in the middle or at the opposite end. The two groups represented in this example are airline pilots and writers. Notice that airline pilots, when compared to writers, tend to be more controlled, relaxed, self-assured, and far less sensitive. Writers, on the other hand, are more imaginative and better able to think abstractly. *Source:* Cattell (1973).

Explore the five-factor model on mypsychlab.com

agreeableness the emotional style of a person that may range from easygoing, friendly, and likeable to grumpy, crabby, and unpleasant.

neuroticism degree of emotional instability or stability.

trait–situation interaction the assumption that the particular circumstances of any given situation will influence the way in which a trait is expressed.

- **Agreeableness** refers to the basic emotional style of a person. A person at the high end of this scale is easygoing, friendly, and pleasant; at the lower end, a person is grumpy, crabby, and hard to get along with.
- **Neuroticism** refers to the stability of the emotional state. People who are excessive worriers, overanxious, and moody score high on this dimension, and those who are more even-tempered and calm score low.

Costa and McCrae believe that these five traits are not interdependent. Someone's score on one dimension gives no information about scores on the other four dimensions, allowing for a tremendous amount of variety in personality descriptions. Explore on mypsychlab.com

Current Thoughts on the Trait Perspective Some theorists have cautioned that personality traits will not always be expressed in the same way across situations. Walter Mischel, a social cognitive theorist, has emphasized that there is a **trait–situation interaction** in which the circumstances of a given situation influence the expression of a trait (Mischel & Shoda, 1995). An extravert may laugh and talk to strangers at a party where he or she already knows a lot of people, for example, but he or she may be less outgoing at a party at which he or she knows no one.

388 CHAPTER 12

Class Demonstration

WHAT'S MY CAREER PERSONALITY?

Purpose: To continue the discussion of personality and career, students explore how their personalities can influence career choices.

Time: 30 minutes

Description: Ask students to make three columns on a blank piece of paper. Next, have them brainstorm three careers they would like to enter and put these careers at the top of each column. In each career column, students should brainstorm ten personality traits they believe will lead them to that career choice. Students can use traits listed in Figures 29.3 and 29.4 as a guide. Then, ask students to take a career personality test online and compare the online results with their initial ideas.

For a lighthearted, simple test, direct students to:

www.kidzworld.com/quiz/2815-quiz-whats-your-job-personality

For a more in-depth, real-world test, direct students to:

www.funeducation.com/Tests/CareerTest/TakeTest.aspx

High Scorer Characteristics

Openness	Conscientiousness	Extraversion	Agreeableness	Neuroticism
• creative • artistic • curious • imaginative • nonconforming	• organized • reliable • neat • ambitious	• talkative • optimistic • sociable • affectionate	• good-natured • trusting • helpful	• worrying • insecure • anxious • temperamental
• conventional • down-to-earth • uncreative	• unreliable • lazy • careless • negligent • spontaneous	• reserved • comfortable being alone • stays in the background	• rude • uncooperative • irritable • aggressive • competitive	• calm • secure • relaxed • stable

Low Scorer Characteristics

FIGURE 29.4 The Big Five
Source: Adapted from McCrae & Costa (1990).

The five-factor model has been studied and tested by numerous researchers. Cross-cultural studies support the findings in 11 different cultures, including Japan, the Philippines, Germany, China, and Peru (Digman, 1990; John et al., 1988; McCrae et al., 2000; 2005; McCrae & Terracciano, 2007; Paunonen et al., 1996; Piedmont et al., 2002). This cultural commonality raises the question of the origins of the Big Five trait dimensions: Are child-rearing practices across all those cultures similar enough to result in these five aspects of personality, or could these five dimensions have a genetic component that transcends cultural differences? In the next module, we will discuss the evidence for a genetic basis of the Big Five.

THEORIES OF PERSONALITY 389

CHAPTER 12 • Module 29

COVER THE MODULE *(continued)*
- Cross-cultural studies of the five-factor model have raised the question of the origin of the Big Five trait dimensions.
  - Are the cultural commonalities of the Big Five due to child-rearing or genetics?

CLASS DEBATE
Lead the class in a debate discussing whether personality is a result of nature or nurture.

FAST FACT
Tell students that Raymond Cattell vehemently opposed the Big Five model of personality, viewing it as a direct attack on his 16-factor model. Cattell referred to the Five Factor model as "five-factor heresy."

L3 DIFFERENTIATED INSTRUCTION
Special Needs Incorporate active reading strategies (e.g., choral reading, paired reading) to assist in maintaining attention.

Class Demonstration

CELEBRITY ANALYSIS

Purpose: Students review and apply the major theoretical perspectives on personality.

Time: 20 minutes

Description: Divide the class into four groups. Give each group a large sheet of paper or poster board. Ask each group to write the name of a well-known person at the top of the paper and then divide it into four equal sections. In the first section, students should review trait theory by listing the traits the celebrity has. Students then pass their papers to another group and describe how Freud's theory applies. Continue this process for students to review cognitive-behavioral theory and humanistic theory. Allow groups to present the findings for each celebrity for whole-group wrap-up discussion.

Module 29 Perspectives on Personality **389**

CHAPTER 12 • Module 29

Assess

Assign the Module 29 Practice Quiz.

Use the Practice Quiz to identify gaps in student understanding.

REMEDIATE

Have students, individually or in groups, review the module goals, learning objectives, and key terms.

Refer students to the Concept Summary on p. 406 for review.

Close

As a class, discuss which personality theory students think is most accurate or applicable to today's society and why.

Practice Quiz

Pick the best answer.

1. Although Chien knows that he attended his grandmother's funeral at 9 years old, he has no memory of the funeral. Freud would most likely argue that Chien's memory of the funeral is in the
   a. conscious
   b. unconscious
   c. preconscious
   d. superconscious

2. Which of the following operates on the pleasure principle?
   a. id
   b. ego
   c. conscience
   d. superego

3. What are the three factors in Bandura's model of reciprocal determinism?
   a. behavior, self-esteem, and control
   b. environment, behavior, personal/cognitive factors
   c. heredity, self-esteem, personal/cognitive factors
   d. self-esteem, behavior, and neuroticism

4. Which dimension of the Big Five theory refers to a person's basic emotional style?
   a. openness
   b. extraversion
   c. agreeableness
   d. neuroticism

5. Which theorist believed that traits exist as a wired part of the nervous system?
   a. Allport
   b. Cattell
   c. Horney
   d. Bandura

6. Carl Rogers believed that for people to become fully functioning, they must receive
   a. positive reinforcement
   b. reciprocal determinism
   c. an external locus of control
   d. unconditional positive regard

7. In which psychosexual stage would fixation most likely result in a person who is overly neat and fussy?
   a. oral
   b. anal
   c. latency
   d. genital

8. Which of the following is a weakness of humanistic personality theory?
   a. It is biased against women.
   b. It is unnecessarily pessimistic.
   c. It is difficult to test scientifically.
   d. It does not promote healthy relationships.

9. The enduring characteristics with which people are born, such as irritability or adaptability, are known collectively as
   a. morality
   b. character
   c. personality
   d. temperament

10. Eddie does well in his high school art class. His parents have never encouraged him in art because they don't consider art as important as engineering. Therefore, Eddie studies more in his science classes and plans to become a civil engineer after college. If Eddie is working to be who his parents think he should be, he is influenced by his
    a. ego
    b. real self
    c. self-esteem
    d. self-concept

Practice Quiz Answers

1. b
2. a
3. b
4. c
5. a
6. d
7. b
8. c
9. d
10. d

Module 30: Assessment and Issues in Personality

Module Goals

Learn how personality is assessed.

Consider key issues in personality research.

Learning Objectives

30.1 What techniques do researchers use to measure personality? Are these techniques reliable and valid?

30.2 What part do biology and culture play in personality?

30.3 Is personality stable, or can it change over time?

30.4 How can personality influence our health and our work?

30.5 What is self-esteem, and how does it affect us?

30.6 How do cultural perspectives relate to personality?

Learn How Personality Is Assessed

30.1 What techniques do researchers use to measure personality? Are these techniques reliable and valid?

With all the different theories of personality, how do people find out what kind of personality they have?

The methods for measuring or assessing personality vary according to the theory of personality used to develop those methods, as one might expect. However, modern psychological professionals do not necessarily tie themselves down to one theoretical viewpoint of personality. Instead, they choose the parts of different theories that seem best fit a particular situation. In fact, looking at behavior from all four theoretical perspectives can often bring insights that would not easily come from one perspective. Many professionals will also use several of the assessment techniques that follow. Still, certain methods are preferred by certain kinds of theorists, as can be seen in Table 30.1 on the next page.

Personality assessments may also differ in the purposes for which they are conducted. For example, researchers may administer a personality test before or during a research study to compare participants according to certain traits. Clinical and counseling psychologists, psychiatrists, and other psychological professionals use personality assessment in the diagnosis of disorders of personality. **LINK** *to Chapter Thirteen: Psychological Disorders, pp. 433–436.* Personality tests are also available to people who simply want to learn more about their own personalities.

Interviews Some therapists ask questions and note the answers in a survey process called an **interview**. This type of interview may flow naturally, like a discussion, from the beginning comments between the client and the psychologist. When a psychologist interviews a client, the client must report on his or her innermost feelings, urges, and concerns—all things that only he or

◀ With all the different theories of personality, how do people find out what kind of personality they have?

interview method of personality assessment in which the professional asks questions of the client and allows the client to answer, either in a structured or unstructured fashion.

THEORIES OF PERSONALITY 391

Terms

- interview • halo effect • projection • projective tests • Rorschach inkblot test
- subjective • direct observation • rating scale • frequency count • personality inventory • behavioral genetics • heritability • self-esteem

---

CHAPTER 12 • Module 30

Focus

RESOURCES

For this module, consult the appropriate sections of the Teacher's Manual, Test Bank, and PowerPoint slides, all found on the Teacher's Resource DVD, and the interactive study tools for students on MyPsychLab.

BEFORE CLASS

Students should read the section for homework before coming to class.

BELLRINGER

Ask students if they have ever taken a personality assessment. Why did they take it? What did they think of the results? How can personality assessments be useful?

Teach

COVER THE MODULE

30.1 What techniques do researchers use to measure personality? Are these techniques reliable and valid?

- Methods for personality assessment vary, according to the theory used to develop the assessment.
  - Methods of assessment are generally chosen based on the situation they are being used for.
  - Personality assessments are used for different purposes, such as diagnosing personality disorders.

LINK *to Chapter Thirteen: Psychological Disorders, pp. 433–436*

- The *interview* is the method of personality assessment in which a professional asks questions and the client is allowed to answer in either a structured or an unstructured fashion.

Module 30 Assessment and Issues in Personality **391**

CHAPTER 12 • Module 30

COVER THE MODULE (continued)

- Interview assessments have drawbacks including the following:
  - Clients can lie, misremember, or give an answer they believe to be more socially acceptable than their true information.
  - The *halo effect* is the tendency of an interviewer to allow positive characteristics noticed on a first impression to influence assessments.
- Projective tests are based on the defense mechanism of *projection* in which a client projects his or her own unacceptable thoughts onto others as if those thoughts belonged to the others.
  - Professionals show clients ambiguous visual stimuli and hope that the clients project unconscious fears and concerns onto the visual, revealing them to the analyst.

L2 ELL DIFFERENTIATED INSTRUCTION

English Language Learners Praise students' efforts to experiment with new language in class, both in writing and in speaking.

Table 30.1 Who Uses What Method?

TYPE OF ASSESSMENT	MOST LIKELY USED BY . . .
Interviews	Psychoanalysts, Humanistic Therapists

Projective Tests
  Rorschach
  Thematic Apperception Test
	Psychoanalysts

Behavioral Assessments
  Direct Observation
  Rating Scales
  Frequency Counts
	Behavioral and Social Cognitive Therapists

Personality Inventories
  Sixteen Personality Factor Questionnaire (16PF)
  Neuroticism/Extraversion/Openness Personality Inventory (NEO-PI)
  Myers-Briggs Type Indicator (MBTI)
  Eysenck Personality Questionnaire (EPQ)
  Keirsey Temperament Sorter II
  California Psychological Inventory (CPI)
  Minnesota Multiphasic Personality Inventory, Version II (MMPI-2)
	Trait Theorists

she can directly know. However, interviews do have drawbacks: Clients can lie, misremember, or give what they think is a socially acceptable answer instead of true information. Interviewers themselves can interpret what clients say in light of their own belief systems or prejudices.

Another problem with interviews is the **halo effect**, which is a tendency to form a favorable or unfavorable impression of someone at the first meeting, so that all of a person's comments and behavior after that first impression will be interpreted to agree with the impression—positively or negatively. First impressions really do count, and people who make a good first impression because of clothing, personal appearance, or some other unimportant characteristic may seem perfect or angelic (thus the term "halo effect") (Lance et al., 1994; Thorndike, 1920).

Projective Tests Have you ever tried to see shapes in the clouds? You might see a house where another person might see the same cloud as a horse. The cloud isn't really either of those things but can be *interpreted* as one or the other, depending on the interpreter. A cloud is an ambiguous stimulus—something capable of being interpreted in more than one way. Now think about the definition of the defense mechanism of **projection**: placing, or "projecting," one's own unacceptable thoughts onto others, as if the thoughts actually belonged to those others. What if a person could project unacceptable, unconscious thoughts onto some harmless, ambiguous stimulus, like a cloud? In just this way, psychoanalysts (and a few other psychologists) show their

halo effect tendency of an interviewer to allow positive characteristics of a client to influence the assessments of the client's behavior and statements.

projection defense mechanism involving placing, or "projecting," one's own unacceptable thoughts onto others, as if the thoughts actually belonged to those others and not to oneself.

Explore

PERSONALITY ASSESSMENTS

<u>Purpose</u>: Table 30.1 lists personality assessments and the professionals who likely use them. Students will browse the Internet to learn more about the assessments mentioned and hypothesize about why the assessments work for the different theories.

<u>Time</u>: One class period

<u>Description</u>: Assign each student a personality assessment from Table 30.1. Ask students to browse the Internet to learn as much as they can about their assigned assessment, including the test format, how it is administered, its purpose, how it is used by professionals, and its accuracy or validity. Once students have gathered their information, have them hypothesize about why that test would work to gather information for the theory behind it. Allow students to share their findings with the class.

FIGURE 30.1 Thematic Apperception Test Example
A sample from the Thematic Apperception Test (TAT). When you look at this picture, what story does it suggest to you? Who are the people? What is their relationship?

clients ambiguous visual stimuli and ask the clients to tell them what they see. The hope is that the client will project those unconscious concerns and fears onto the visual stimulus, revealing them to the analyst. Tests using this method are called **projective tests**.

One of the more well-known projective tests is the **Rorschach inkblot test** developed in 1921 by Swiss psychiatrist Hermann Rorschach (ROR-shock) and revised in the 1960s by John Exner. Rorschach tested thousands of inkblots until he narrowed down the 10 in use today, 5 in black ink on a white background and 5 in colored ink on a white background. Subjects look at each inkblot and simply say whatever they think it looks like. Using predetermined categories and responses commonly given to each picture (Exner, 1980), psychologists score responses on key factors, such as reference to color, shape, figures seen in the blot, and response to the whole or to details. Inkblots are still frequently used as a factor in describing personality, diagnosing mental disorders, and predicting behavior (Watkins et al., 1995; Weiner, 1997).

First developed in 1935 by psychologist Henry Murray and his colleagues (Morgan & Murray, 1935), the **Thematic Apperception Test (TAT)** consists of 20 pictures, all black and white, of people deliberately drawn in ambiguous situations (see Figure 30.1). The subject is given a picture and asked to tell a story about the person or people in it. The story is interpreted by the psychoanalyst, who looks for revealing statements and projection of the subject's own problems onto the people in the pictures.

Other types of projective tests include the Sentence Completion test, Draw-A-Person, and House-Tree-Person. In the Sentence Completion test, the client is given a series of sentence beginnings, such as "I wish my mother . . ." or "Almost every day I feel . . ." and asked to finish the sentence, whereas in the Draw-A-Person and House-Tree-Person, the client is asked to draw the named items.

Projective tests are by their nature very **subjective** (valid only within the person's own perception), and interpreting the answers of clients is almost an art. It is certainly not a science, and interpretations are not known for their accuracy. The tests, with no standard grading scales, have both low reliability and low validity (Gittelman-Klein, 1978; Lilienfeld, 1999; Wood et al., 1996).

projective tests personality assessments that present ambiguous visual stimuli to the client and ask the client to respond with whatever comes to mind.

Rorschach inkblot test projective test that uses ten inkblots as ambiguous stimuli.

Thematic Apperception Test (TAT) projective test that uses 20 pictures of people in ambiguous situations as the visual stimuli.

subjective referring to concepts and impressions that are only valid within a particular person's perception and may be influenced by biases, prejudice, and personal experiences.

THEORIES OF PERSONALITY   393

CHAPTER 12 • Module 30

COVER THE MODULE *(continued)*
- The *Rorschach inkblot test* is a projective test that uses inkblots as ambiguous stimuli.
  - It is used in diagnosing mental disorders and predicting behavior.
- The *Thematic Apperception Test (TAT)* is a projective test that uses 20 pictures of people in ambiguous situations as the visual stimuli.
- Projective tests are *subjective*, are valid only within a person's own perception and may be influenced by bias, prejudice, and personal experience.
  - *Projective tests* are not a "science" and are low in reliability and validity.

UNDERSTANDING VISUALS
Ask students to write a brief scenario that they believe is suggested by Figure 30.1. Have volunteers share their stories with the class. What do their interpretations say about their personalities?

L3 DIFFERENTIATED INSTRUCTION
Visual/Verbal Learners These students should use flash cards of main points or key terms.

Class Demonstration

PROJECTIVE TEST ASSESSMENT

Purpose: Students think critically about the scoring of projective tests.

Time: 25 minutes

Description: The textbook states that projective tests do not have standard grading scales, leading to low reliability and validity. As a class, after they have completed their answers for the TAT example in Figure 30.1, have students come up with a "grading scale" with specific criteria that would help them bring some consistency to the TAT assessment. Then give students 5 minutes to draw anything they want on a blank sheet of paper. Collect the pictures and randomly pass them back out to students for assessment. Ask students to assess the pictures according to their criteria. Then lead the class in a discussion of how their grading scale worked, what new criteria they should add, what should be removed, and the positives and negatives of using this type of assessment.

CHAPTER 12 • Module 30

COVER THE MODULE *(continued)*

- Reliability is the tendency of a test to give the same score every time it is administered.
- Validity is the ability of a test to measure what it is intended to measure.
- **LINK** to *Chapter One: The Science of Psychology, p. 33*
- Behaviorists believe that personality is a group of learned responses to stimuli, so they prefer to observe behaviors unfold in the real world.
  - *Direct observation* is an assessment in which the professional observes the client's behavior in a natural setting.
  - A *rating scale* is an assessment in which a numerical value is assigned to a behavior that is listed in the scale.
  - *Frequency count* is an assessment in which the frequency of a behavior is counted in a specific time period.
- Behavior assessments are subject to the observer effect and bias of the observer and are limited to what the observer can see during the observation session.
- **LINK** to *Chapter One: The Science of Psychology, pp. 17–18*
- Trait theorists use *personality inventories* that are made up of statements that require standardized responses from the client and are, therefore, more objective and reliable.

TEACHING TIP

Establish measurable objectives and determine how you can help students meet them.

Reliability is the tendency of a test to give the same score every time it is administered to the same person or group of people, and *validity* is the ability of the test to measure what it is intended to measure. **LINK** *to Chapter One: The Science of Psychology, p. 33*. A person's answers to the Rorschach, for example, might be quite different from one day to the next, depending on the person's mood and what scary movie might have been on television the previous night.

Projective tests may sound somewhat outdated in today's world of MRIs and PET scans, but many practicing clinical psychologists and psychiatrists still use this type of testing (Butcher & Rouse, 1996; Camara et al., 2000). Some psychologists believe that the latest versions of these tests still have practical use and some validity (Ganellen, 1996; Weiner, 1997), especially when a client's answers on these tests are used as a starting point for digging deeper into the client's recollections, concerns, and anxieties.

Behavioral Assessments Behaviorists do not typically want to "look into the mind." Because behaviorists assume that personality is merely habitually learned responses to stimuli in the environment, the preferred method for a behaviorist would be to watch behaviors as they unfold in the real world. In **direct observation**, the psychologist observes the client engaging in ordinary, everyday behavior, preferably in the natural setting of home, school, or workplace, for example. Other methods often used by behavioral therapists and other assessors are rating scales and frequency counts. In a **rating scale**, a numerical rating is assigned, either by the assessor or the client, for specific behaviors (Nadeau et al., 2001). For example, an assessor might use a 1–5 scale to rate how strongly a client's behavior matches a description, with a rating of 1 indicating a very weak match and a rating of 5 indicating a very strong match. In a **frequency count**, the assessor literally counts the frequency of certain behaviors within a specified time limit. Educators make use of both rating scales and frequency counts to diagnose behavioral problems such as attention-deficit hyperactivity disorder (ADHD) and aspects of personality such as social skill level through the various grade levels.

Problems with these assessments include the observer effect (when a person's behavior is affected by being watched) and bias on the part of the observer. **LINK** *to Chapter One: The Science of Psychology, pp. 17–18*. As with any kind of observational method, there is no control over the external environment. A person observing a client for a particular behavior may not see that behavior occur within the observation time—just like your little brother never seems to make that face at you whenever your mom is watching.

Personality Inventories Trait theorists, typically more interested in personality descriptions, tend to use an assessment known as a **personality inventory**, a questionnaire that has a standard list of questions and only requires certain specific answers, such as "yes," "no," and "can't decide." The standard nature of the questions (everyone gets the same list) and the lack of open-ended answers make these assessments far more objective and reliable than projective tests (Garb et al., 1998), although they are still a form of self-report. One such personality inventory is Cattell's 16PF Questionnaire, discussed in the last module. Costa and McCrae (2000) have recently revised their original *Neuroticism/Extraversion/Openness Personality Inventory (NEO-PI)*, which is based on the Big Five.

direct observation assessment in which the professional observes the client engaged in ordinary, day-to-day behavior in either a clinical or natural setting.

rating scale assessment in which a numerical value is assigned to specific behavior that is listed in the scale.

frequency count assessment in which the frequency of a particular behavior is counted.

personality inventory paper and pencil or computerized test that consists of statements that require a specific, standardized response from the person taking the test.

Class Demonstration

ASSESSING THE "PERSONALITY" OF PERSONALITY ASSESSMENTS

<u>Purpose</u>: Students collect and examine personality tests from the Internet or media.

<u>Time</u>: 15 minutes

<u>Description</u>: Ask students to come to class with a personality test they've found in a magazine or on the Internet. It may also be a good idea to place limitations on what the students should bring—for example, asking them to find the most ridiculous test, the most scientific test, or a test using a certain technique. Students should bring in a copy of the test, and, where applicable, the answers or methods of scoring. Place students in groups and allow them to exchange tests to take and score. Lead the class in a discussion of the following: (1) How can you tell if a personality test is valid? (2) What elements comprise a good test vs. a bad one? (3) Why do you think personality tests are so popular? (4) How accurate have the results been for tests you've taken?

Another inventory in common use is the *Myers-Briggs Type Indicator (MBTI)*. This inventory, based on the ideas of Carl Jung, looks at four pairs of personality preferences: extraversion (E) vs. introversion (I), sensing (S) vs. intuition (N), thinking (T) vs. feeling (F), and judgment (J) vs. perception (P). Each individual's personality can be described through a combination of four preferences, one from each pair: INTJ, ESTP, ISFP, INFJ, and so on (Briggs & Myers, 1998).

The Myers-Briggs is often used to assess personality for career matches. For example, a person who scored high on the extraversion, sensing, thinking, and judging dimensions would be an ESTJ. A typical description of this personality type would be a person who needs to analyze information and bring order to the outer world. Such people are organizers, energetic in completing tasks, and practical. They also take their responsibilities seriously and expect others to do so as well. School administrators, for example, are often ESTJs.

By far, the most common personality inventory is the *Minnesota Multiphasic Personality Inventory, Version II*, or *MMPI-2*, which specifically tests for normal and abnormal behavior patterns in personality (Butcher & Rouse, 1996; Butcher et al., 2000, 2001). This questionnaire consists of 567 statements such as "I am often very tense" or "I believe I am being plotted against." The responder must answer "true," "false," or "cannot say." The MMPI has 10 clinical scales and eight validity scales in addition to numerous subscales that test for a particular kind of behavior. The behavior patterns include mild personality problems such as excessive worrying and shyness as well as more serious disorders such as schizophrenia and depression. LINK to Chapter Thirteen: Psychological Disorders, p. 421.

How can you tell if a person is telling the truth on a personality inventory?

Validity scales, a component of well-designed psychological inventories, are intended to indicate whether a person is responding honestly. Responses to certain items indicate whether people are trying to make themselves look better or worse, for example, and certain items are repeated throughout the test in slightly different forms, so that anyone trying to "fake" the test will have difficulty responding consistently (Butcher et al., 2001). For example, if one of the statements is "I am always happy" and a person responds "true," this person may be giving a socially acceptable answer. If several of the validity scale questions are answered in this way, the person may not be answering honestly.

The advantage of personality inventories over projective tests and interviews is that inventories are standardized (i.e., everyone gets exactly the same questions and the answers are scored in exactly the same way). In fact, responses to inventories are often scored on a computer. Observer bias and bias of interpretation are simply not possible. The validity and reliability of personality inventories are generally recognized as being greatly superior to those of projective tests (Anastasi & Urbina, 1997).

There are some problems, however. For example, validity scales are not perfect. Some people are still able to fake their answers and respond in what they feel are the socially appropriate ways (Anastasi & Urbina, 1997; Hicklin & Widiger, 2000). Other problems have to do with human nature: Some people may pick a particular answer rather than carefully considering the statement, and others may simply grow tired of responding and start picking answers at random.

◀ How can you tell if a person is telling the truth on a personality inventory?

CHAPTER 12 • Module 30

COVER THE MODULE *(continued)*

- The Myers-Briggs Type Indicator is based on the work of Carl Jung. It evaluates four pairs of personality preferences.
  - It is often used to assess personality for career matches.
- The Minnesota Multiphasic Personality Inventory, Version II tests for normal and abnormal behavior patterns in personality.
  - It consists of a questionnaire of 567 statements to which an answer of "true," "false," or "cannot say" must be given.

LINK to Chapter Thirteen: Psychological Disorders, p. 421

- To assess whether a person is telling the truth on a personality inventory, validity scales are used to indicate whether a person's responses are honest.
- Personality inventories are standardized and are scored by a computer, so observer and interpretation bias are ruled out.

L3 DIFFERENTIATED INSTRUCTION

Engaging All Learners Incorporate active reading strategies. Build vocabulary by teaching the meaning of prefixes and suffixes. Have students use study cards for unfamiliar words. Have students read and summarize the paragraph in their own words. Monitor their work to clarify any misunderstandings.

Critical Thinking

DEBATING EMPLOYERS' USE OF PERSONALITY TESTS

Purpose: Students apply what they have learned about personality tests to form an opinion about the reality that companies are using such tests for the purpose of hiring, training, and motivating a work force.

Time: 30 minutes

Description: Allow students time to read the following two articles, available online at the websites shown. Prepare various scenarios of situations as described in the articles, and assign students a role to play in the scenarios. Ask students to respond to the following statement: "Personality tests should be used by employers in hiring decisions, training, coaching, development, and team building" by role-playing and answering as they believe they would in that situation.

- "The Use and Misuse of Personality Tests for Coaching and Development" www.psychologytoday.com/blog/minds-work/200806/the-use-and-misuse-personality-tests-coaching-and-development
- "Employers Relying on Personality Tests to Screen Applicants" www.washingtonpost.com/ac2/wp-dyn/A4010-2005Mar26?language=printer

CHAPTER 12 • Module 30

COVER THE MODULE

30.2 What part do biology and culture play in personality?

- The field of *behavioral genetics* examines how personality is formed due to inherited traits expressed within a particular environment.
- Twin studies of identical and fraternal twins help researchers find evidence of the effects of genetic versus environmental influences on individual differences.

LINK to *Chapter Two: The Biological Perspective, p. 68; Chapter Five: Development Across the Life Span, p. 147*

- The Minnesota twin study revealed that identical twins are more similar than fraternal twins or unrelated people in terms of factors, such as intelligence, leadership, affection, and assertiveness, even when raised in different environments.
- Studies comparing adopted children to their adoptive parents or siblings and to their biological parents reveal that genetic influences are responsible for a large part of personality development regardless of shared or nonshared environments.
- *Heritability* is the degree to which the changes of a trait in a population are inherited.

MULTIMEDIA CONTENT AVAILABLE AT
www.mypsychlab.com

Watch a video about twin studies on **mypsychlab.com**

396 Chapter 12 Theories of Personality

Consider Key Issues in Personality Research

30.2 What part do biology and culture play in personality?

Are our personalities inherited, or do they develop as a result of environmental factors? The field of **behavioral genetics** is devoted to the study of just how much of an individual's personality is due to inherited traits expressed within a particular environment. Animal breeders know that selective breeding for specific traits can produce not only physical changes but also changes in the temperament of the animals (Isabel, 2003; Trut, 1999). Temperament consists of inborn characteristics and is, therefore, determined by biology to a great degree. If animals' temperaments can be influenced by manipulating patterns of genetic inheritance, then personality characteristics related to temperament in human beings may also be influenced by heredity.

Researchers can attempt to determine biology's role in personality development by performing twin studies. **LINK** to *Chapter Two: The Biological Perspective, p. 68.* There are two types of twins: monozygotic (identical) and dizygotic (fraternal) twins. **LINK** to *Chapter Five: Development Across the Life Span, p. 147.* Identical twins share 100 percent of their genetic material, having shared one fertilized egg, whereas fraternal twins share only about 50 percent of their genetic material, as any other pair of siblings would. By comparing identical twins to fraternal twins, especially twins raised in different environments (like Oskar and Jack or the "Jim" twins in the opening story), researchers can find evidence of the relative effects of genetic versus environmental influences on individual differences. (See Figure 30.2.)

Watch on **mypsychlab.com**

The Minnesota twin study suggests that identical twins are more similar than fraternal twins or unrelated people in terms of intelligence, leadership abilities, the tendency to follow rules, and the tendency to uphold traditional cultural expectations (Bouchard, 1997; Finkel & McGue, 1997); affection and assertiveness (Neale et al., 1986); and aggressiveness (Miles & Carey, 1997). These similarities hold even if the twins are raised in separate environments.

If studying genetically identical twins raised in different environments can help investigators understand genetic influences on personality, then studying *unrelated* people who are raised in the *same* environment should help investigators discover the influence of environment. By comparing adopted children to their adoptive parents and siblings and to their biological parents, researchers can uncover some of the shared and nonshared environmental and genetic influences on personality.

Adoption studies have confirmed what twin studies have shown: Genetic influences account for a great deal of personality development, regardless of shared or nonshared environments (Hershberger et al., 1995; Loehlin et al., 1985, 1998). Through this kind of study, a genetic basis has been suggested for shyness (Plomin et al., 1988) and aggressiveness (Brennan et al., 1997).

Heritability is the degree to which the changes in some trait within a population can be inherited, or passed from one generation to the next. Several studies have found that the personality factors of the five-factor model have nearly a 50 percent rate of heritability across several cultures (Bouchard, 1994; Herbst et al., 2000; Jang et al., 1996; Loehlin, 1992; Loehlin et al., 1998). The Minnesota twin study and other research (Lubinski, 2000; Lykken & Tellegen,

Watch a video about twin studies on **mypsychlab.com**

behavioral genetics field of study examining how personality is formed through inherited traits expressed within a particular environment.

heritability the degree to which the changes in some trait within a population can be considered to be due to genetic influences.

396 CHAPTER 12

Explore

GENETICS AND PERSONALITY

Purpose: Students examine the origin of some of their own personality traits and form opinions on the role of genetics and personality.

Time: 15 minutes

Description: Students can privately revisit lists of their own personality traits they've made for past activities or make a new list. For each trait, students should think about where that trait may have originated and list the source and then whether the source is biological or environmental. For example, for the trait of stubbornness, a student may list that it seems to be a trait also displayed by his or her father and is therefore biological or that it developed out of a need to stand up to an aggressive older sibling and is therefore environmental.

FIGURE 30.2 Personalities of Identical and Fraternal Twins
Identical and fraternal twins differ in the way they express the Big Five personality factors. The scores of identical twins have a correlation of about 50 percent, whereas those of fraternal twins have a correlation of only about 15 to 20 percent. These findings support the idea that some aspects of personality are genetically based. *Source:* Loehlin (1992).

1996; Plomin, 1994) seem to indicate that variations in personality traits are about 25 to 50 percent inherited (Jang et al., 1998). Therefore, about half of the variations in personality traits are due to environmental influences.

Simulate on **mypsychlab.com**

30.3 Is personality stable, or can it change over time?

Researchers have long wondered if the elements of personality change over a person's life. The *plaster hypothesis*, based on a metaphor written by William James, suggests that personality develops until people hit maturity at about age 30. Personality then firms up and sets, similar to plaster, throughout middle age, and begins to crack and crumble as cognitive declines appear with old age. A different take on this theory, the *soft plaster hypothesis*, suggests that there may be some changes after age 30, but the changes between 21 and 30 are much more dramatic than changes between 30 and 60.

Newer research on how some of the Big Five traits change over time shows more complexity than the plaster hypothesis suggests. A large research study on participants younger and older than 30 demonstrates some interesting changes: Both agreeableness and conscientiousness tend to increase in later years: after age 30, subjects' agreeableness changed significantly, almost as much as it had between the ages of 21 and 30. Both extraversion and openness tend to reduce as people age. Openness drops significantly for men after age 30, though the decline is less pronounced for women. Neuroticism drops consistently in women between 21 and 60, but stays relatively stable in men. These findings reject both the plaster hypothesis and the soft plaster hypothesis,

Simulate the biological basis of the "Big Five" personality factors on **mypsychlab.com**

THEORIES OF PERSONALITY 397

CHAPTER 12 • Module 30

COVER THE MODULE

30.3 Is personality stable, or can it change over time?

- The plaster hypothesis suggests that personality develops until maturity, at about age 30; then sets, similar to plaster in middle age; and then begins to crack in old age.

- The soft plaster hypothesis suggests that there may be some changes after age 30, but the changes between ages 21 and 30 are more dramatic than those between ages 31 and 60.

- Recent research suggests that agreeableness and conscientiousness increase in later years, extraversion and openness decrease as people age, and neuroticism drops in women but stays stable in men over time.

MULTIMEDIA CONTENT AVAILABLE AT
www.mypsychlab.com

Simulate the biological basis of the "Big Five" personality factors on **mypsychlab.com**

L1 DIFFERENTIATED INSTRUCTION

Special Needs When having students work in groups or pairs, set up procedures that maintain each student's accountability (e.g., each student having to write, draw, or state a response).

Critical Thinking

INTERVIEW WITH AN ELDER

<u>Purpose</u>: Students examine what they've learned about the theories of personality change over time as they relate to the experiences of a grandparent or other elder.

<u>Time</u>: One class period, divided

<u>Description</u>: Use class time to help students develop a list of questions for an interview with a grandparent or other trusted, older adult to learn how their personalities have changed over time. For homework, students conduct the interview and write a brief interpretation of how their interviewees' personality changes relate to the plaster hypothesis, the soft plaster hypothesis, and the Big Five trait research discussed in the textbook.

Module 30 Assessment and Issues in Personality 397

CHAPTER 12 • Module 30

COVER THE MODULE

30.4 How can personality influence our health and our work?

- Research has linked personality characteristics, such as ambition, pressure, and high stress to coronary disease.
- High levels of hostility and anger can lead to cardiovascular disease and heart attacks.
- **LINK** to *Chapter Fifteen: Stress and Health*, p. 498
- Conscientiousness is a factor in longevity.
- People who are extraverted and are highly conscientious are more successful at work than the less extraverted and more neurotic personalities.

FAST FACT

Although most students are familiar with the idea of bullying at school, ask them if they know where else bullying is an issue. The answer is: at work. The negative behavior includes yelling, name-calling, making threatening statements, micromanaging, or undermining another person's reputation. The abuse may be passed off as "tough" management or a "competitive" work environment, where "wimps" fail to succeed.

L3 DIFFERENTIATED INSTRUCTION

Use peer tutoring. This technique helps teachers accommodate academic diversity. All students can be actively involved in tasks they can perform successfully. Students work in pairs to assist each other in learning, which leads to improved self-esteem, personal interaction, and positive attitudes about school.

---

demonstrating that personalities can change throughout our lives (Srivastava et al., 2003). Other studies have suggested that specific experiences, such as rehabilitation and psychological treatment for recovering addicts, can impact the Big Five, demonstrating a positive effect in changing personality through professional psychological treatment (Piedmont, 2001).

30.4 How can personality influence our health and our work?

Many of us think of personality as internal characteristic that doesn't play a major role in our lives, but psychologists have found that personality can affect our quality of life in a number of significant ways. If you want to live a healthier lifestyle or enjoy a successful career, you'll want to pay attention to the ways in which personality factors contribute to our physical health and our performance in the workplace.

Personality and Health There is some indication that personality can affect the types of diseases people tend to get. Doctors Meyer Friedman and Ray Rosenman worked on a series of studies linking personality characteristics such as ambition, pressure, and high levels of stress to coronary disease (Friedman & Kasanin, 1943; Friedman & Rosenman, 1959). Later studies correlated high levels of hostility and anger to medical problems affecting the heart, such as cardiovascular disease and heart attacks (Chang et al., 2002). Even cancer can be linked to a certain type of personality: People with cancer who experience discomfort expressing emotions and hold in stress and anger tend to have thicker tumors than cancer patients with different personality traits (Eysenck, 1994; Temoshok & Dreher, 1992). **LINK** to *Chapter Fifteen: Stress and Health*, p. 498. Keep in mind, however, that people's personalities should not be blamed for their illnesses—heart disease and cancer are serious medical conditions caused by many factors that have nothing to do with personality.

Conscientiousness also seems to be a factor in longevity (Kern & Friedman, 2008). Researchers broke down conscientiousness into three subcategories, self-control, industriousness, and organization, and compared health and life expectancy of participants. People who scored higher in organization and industriousness lived an average of 2 to 4 years longer, were less likely to smoke, and had more stable marriages and jobs than other participants.

Personality and Work Can personality traits predict a person's success in the professional world? In some cases, the answer seems to be yes. Researchers who studied the Big Five factors in the context of workplace performance found that people who are more extraverted tend to be more successful at work, and people who are more neurotic tend to be less successful at work. These correlations are most likely due to the social nature of many work environments (Judge, Heller, & Mount, 2002), but people who do not thrive in social situations may find professional success working in a less social, more independent profession.

Research has also shown that people who are highly conscientious, whether they are introverts or extraverts, tend to perform well in the workplace (Hurtz & Donovan, 2000). Because they are reliable by definition, conscientious individuals are less likely to be absent from work, which almost guarantees that they will be more productive and helpful in the workplace than their coworkers who are frequently absent. Even if you do not particularly love your job (or your class, or your athletic practice), simply showing up and being a

---

Explore

LEARNING MORE ABOUT HOW PERSONALITY CAN AFFECT HEALTH AND WORK

Students can read more about the effects of personality at the following websites:

- **Personality and health:**
  http://health.usnews.com/health-news/family-health/heart/articles/2010/09/22/how-your-personality-affects-your-health
  www.suite101.com/content/personality-and-health-a14472

- **Personality and work:**
  www.healthyplace.com/anxiety-panic/main/anxiety-at-work-which-traits-predict-job-performance/menu-id-69/
  www.personalityresearch.org/papers/neubert.html

- **Quiz for the "workplace personality":**
  www.lhj.com/lhj/quiz.jsp?quizId=/templatedata/lhj/quiz/data/WhatsYourWorkplacePersonalityQuiz_01022003.xml

conscientious contributor can improve your performance and help you get ahead in your workplace, your class, or your team.

30.5 What is self-esteem, and how does it affect us?

Another element of personality is **self-esteem**, the feeling of worth or value in oneself. Originally, Maslow included self-esteem in his hierarchy of needs. People with high self-esteem sleep better, stand up to peer pressure better, give up less easily, are more outgoing and less anxious, and are generally happier (Greenberg, 2008; Leary, 1999; Murray et al., 2002; Watson et al., 2002). In fact, self-esteem may be able to predict future success. A study from Finland connected positive self-esteem to actual success in career, salary, and job satisfaction 10 years later (Salmela-Aro & Nurmi, 2007).

Self-esteem has been typically measured via self-reporting (answering questions on a survey or questionnaire). Two commonly used self-esteem assessment tools are the Rosenberg Self-Esteem Scale, which asks participants to compare certain statements and their ideas of themselves, and the Coopersmith Self-Esteem Inventory, which asks participants to compare themselves to descriptions of others.

Can having high self-esteem help you do better in school?

Although it might seem that all parents would have to do to ensure future success is to pump up their children's self-esteem, self-esteem can't be given to you by someone else, and having a positive self-image does not necessarily predict school achievement (Marsh & Craven, 2006; Swann et al., 2007; Trautwein et al., 2006). Doing well in school, overcoming obstacles, and achieving personal and professional goals can give someone high self-esteem, but there is no evidence that high self-esteem actually *causes* academic or professional success. While high self-esteem may not boost your performance, however, low self-esteem can hurt you: Research shows a drop in performance when self-esteem is deflated, even temporarily (Ybarra, 1999).

◀ Can having high self-esteem help you do better in school?

30.6 How do cultural perspectives relate to personality?

Although the five personality factors of the five-factor model have been found across several cultures, this does not mean that culture does not have an impact on personality. In the early 1980s, organizational management specialist Geert Hofstede conducted a massive study into the work-related values of employees of IBM, a multinational corporation (Hofstede, 1980; Hofstede et al., 2002). The study surveyed workers in 64 countries across the world. From this survey, Hofstede identified four basic dimensions of personality along which cultures differed.

1. **Individualism/collectivism:** *Individualistic cultures* tend to have loose ties between individuals, with people tending to look after themselves and their immediate families only. Members of such cultures have friends based on shared activities and interests and may belong to many different loosely organized social groups. Self-direction, change, youth, security of the individual, and equality are all highly valued. In a *collectivistic culture*, people are from birth deeply tied into very strong ingroups, typically extended families that include grandparents, aunts and uncles, and cousins. Loyalty to the family is highly stressed, and the care of the family is placed before the care of

self-esteem the feeling of worth or value in oneself.

THEORIES OF PERSONALITY 399

CHAPTER 12 • Module 30

COVER THE MODULE

30.5 What is self-esteem, and how does it affect us?

- *Self-esteem* is the feeling of worth or value in oneself.
  - Self-esteem is typically measured by the Rosenberg Self-Esteem Scale and the Coopersmith Self-Esteem Inventory, both of which use self-reporting.
  - People with high self-esteem usually sleep better, handle peer pressure better, are more outgoing and less anxious, and are happier.
  - There is no evidence that self-esteem causes academic success, but low self-esteem has been linked to drops in performance.

30.6 How do cultural perspectives relate to personality?

- A study by Geert Hofstede of IBM employees identified four dimensions of personality that differed among cultures:
  - Individualism/collectivism: Individualistic cultures tend to have loose ties between people. In collectivist cultures, people are deeply tied into very strong in-groups.

DISCUSS THE STUDENT VOICE QUESTION

Ask students to think back to times of good academic performance. Can they describe their self-esteem during that time period? How did their self-esteem affect other areas of their life at that time? What effects has low self-esteem had on their lives?

L4 DIFFERENTIATED INSTRUCTION

Advanced Learners Let students express themselves in various ways such as through artwork, music, writing, or acting.

Cultural Connection

COLLECTIVISTIC VS. INDIVIDUALISTIC CULTURES

At the following website, students can read more details regarding the differences in personalities of individuals raised in collectivistic and individualistic cultures. After they have read the article, ask students to conjecture how their personalities might be different had they been raised in a different cultural environment.
http://library.thinkquest.org/C004361/develop4.html

Module 30 Assessment and Issues in Personality 399

CHAPTER 12 • Module 30

COVER THE MODULE (continued)

- Hofstede's four dimensions of cultural influence on personality (continued):
  - Power distance: the degree to which the less powerful members of a culture accept and even expect that power within the culture is held in the hands of a select few
  - Masculinity/femininity: how a culture distributes the roles played by men and women within the culture
  - Uncertainty avoidance: Some cultures are more tolerant of uncertainty and unstructured situations.

CLASS DISCUSSION

Divide the classroom chalkboard or white board in half. As a class, decide how the culture of the United States fits into each of Hofstede's dimensions and make a list on one side of the board with space left to fill in during later discussion. On the other half of the board, have the students choose a culture that would be seemingly opposite that of the United States and make a list of the applicable Hofstede dimensions to discuss. Lead the students in a discussion of how cultural dimensions influence personality for both cultures, and the implications of such differences in multicultural situations, such as war, peace negotiations, travel, international business, studying abroad, and foreign exchange students.

L2 ELL DIFFERENTIATED INSTRUCTION

English Language Learners Watch for references in your classroom instruction that could be considered cultural bias or stereotyping.

---

the individual. Group membership is limited to only a few permanent groups that have tremendous influence over the individual. The values of this kind of culture are duty, order, tradition, respect for the elderly, group security, and respect for the group status and authority structure.

2. **Power distance:** This dimension refers to the degree to which the less powerful members of a culture accept and even expect that the power within the culture is held in the hands of a select few rather than being more evenly distributed.

3. **Masculinity/femininity:** Referring to how a culture distributes the roles played by men and women within a culture, this dimension varies more between cultures for men than it does for women. "Masculine" cultures are assertive and competitive, although more so for men than for women, and "feminine" cultures are more modest and caring. Both men and women in "feminine" countries have similar, caring values, but in "masculine" countries, the women are not quite as assertive and competitive as the men, leading to a greater difference between the sexes in masculine countries. Japan, Austria, Venezuela, the United States, and Germany were found to be more masculine countries, whereas Sweden, Costa Rica, Portugal, Thailand, and Denmark were ranked as more feminine.

4. **Uncertainty avoidance:** Some cultures are more tolerant of uncertainty and unstructured situations. Cultures that do not tolerate such uncertainty and lack of structure tend to have strict rules and laws with lots of security and safety measures and tend toward a philosophical/religious belief of One Truth (and "we have it!"). Cultures that are more accepting of uncertainty are more tolerant of different opinions and have fewer rules. They tend to allow many different religious beliefs to exist side by side. People in these cultures are less anxious and emotional than people in uncertainty-avoiding countries.

Note that the Big Five personality dimensions of Costa and McCrae (2000) are not necessarily in competition with Hofstede's dimensions. Hofstede's dimensions are *cultural* personality traits, whereas those of the Big Five refer to individuals.

Applying Psychology to Everyday Life

Personality Testing on the Internet

Most people enjoy finding out something about themselves. In fact, that's part of the attraction of the pseudo-psychological methods of astrology and graphology. People want to know, "What am I really like?"

Numerous online personality tests are available, and more seem to appear each day. Some of these tests are fairly well thought out, and are based on much larger, validated tests. They can give some insight into personality traits. Here are two sample Web sites with fairly serious tests:

- Keirsey Temperament Sorter (based on Jung's theory): http://www.keirsey.com/sorter/register.aspx
- Five-Factor Test (based on the five-factor model): http://users.wmin.ac.uk/~buchant/wwwffi

400 CHAPTER 12

Explore

PERSONALITY TESTS ON THE INTERNET

<u>Purpose</u>: Students try out the online tests listed in the textbook.

<u>Time</u>: 30 minutes

<u>Description</u>: Give students class time to take each of the tests listed in the "Applying Psychology to Everyday Life" section on p. 400. Ask students to reflect on the tests' seeming reliability, validity, and accuracy. Did they learn anything new about themselves? How can students use the results of these tests to affect their self-knowledge and lives in some way?

One of the odder online personality tests is the Color Test in which a person selects certain colored shapes by clicking on them. The Color Test is based on the work of Swiss color psychologist Dr. Max Lüscher, a color consultant for industrial concerns (Lüscher, 1969). Color psychologists study the effects of color on mood, attention, and other human factors, and most often work in the field of consumer or marketing psychology, helping businesses and industries select color schemes that will maximize sales and productivity (Bellizzi & Crowley, 1983; Guerin et al., 1995). There are several Internet sites that allow people to take a free Color Test, such as www.colorquiz.com.

The Color Test as devised by Lüscher consists of eight cards, each a different color, randomly placed color side up in front of the subject. The subject chooses the color card that is most attractive, which is then recorded and removed. Then the subject must choose the most attractive color from those that remain. This is repeated until only one card is left. Various tables in Lüscher's book are used to interpret the color choices.

Although colors have been shown to have an effect on the body's physical reactions, (red creates the highest measurements of blood pressure, respiration, heart rate, and eyeblink frequency and blue the lowest) (Dominy & Lucas, 2001; Kaiser, 1984), there is little scientifically derived research to support the association of certain colors with certain personality traits (Brauen & Bonta, 1979; Holmes et al., 1984; McAloon & Lester, 1979).

The results of color personality tests sound suspiciously like the general readings given by astrologers and graphologists: "Does not wish to be involved in differences of opinion, contention or argument, preferring to be left in peace. Wants to make a favorable impression and be recognized. Needs to feel appreciated and admired. Sensitive and easily hurt if no notice is taken of him or if he is not given adequate acknowledgment." How many of these statements are true of you or someone you know? This is a good example of the *Barnum Effect* in action—keep the statement general with a little something for everyone, and it will please nearly everyone.

Still, it can be fun to participate in tests like these, *so long as people remember that a real personality test should be administered under controlled conditions by an expert*. One danger in taking these "personality tests" too seriously is that there is no one to help put the results in perspective. This can lead people to believe that they have some serious psychological disorder because they don't know how to interpret the results of the test. It can be a little like "medical student disease," in which medical students read up on exotic diseases and become convinced that they have them until the teacher reassures them. Online testing can be good entertainment, but real problems should be handled by real professionals. Listen on **mypsychlab.com**

Listen to the Psychology in the News podcast about online personality testing on **mypsychlab.com**

Questions for Further Discussion

1. What might be some other dangers of taking personality tests online?
2. What should a person look for when trying to judge the quality of an online personality test?

THEORIES OF PERSONALITY 401

CHAPTER 12 • Module 30

APPLYING PSYCHOLOGY TO EVERYDAY LIFE

- Possible points to discuss about this feature:
  - What should online personality tests be used for? What should they not be used for?
  - When discussing the color test, ask students to think of products, restaurants, or businesses that have specific color schemes that have been particularly noticeable. What do students believe the marketing message of the businesses' color choices could be? (e.g., A bread business saturates the restaurant in warm gold, brick red, terracotta, and brown, reminiscent of the colors of bread baking in wood ovens. Colors are possibly chosen to communicate warmth and the feeling of a hearth in a kitchen.)

1. Other possible dangers include the tests using intrusive questions that could be "stolen" for identity theft or are simply violations of privacy, limiting labels applied by faulty tests and flawed theories, and leading people to make uninformed decisions because of less-than-professional results.

2. A person should look for the credibility of the website or the creator of the test, the quality of the questions, the quality of the scoring system, and whether the results are interpreted by a professional.

MULTIMEDIA CONTENT AVAILABLE AT
www.mypsychlab.com

Listen to the Psychology in the News podcast about online personality testing on **mypsychlab.com**

Class Debate

THE VALUE OF PERSONALITY TESTING

Tell students that they will debate the following topic: "Personality testing is valuable and should be done on all students." Divide the class in half; one side will argue in favor and the other side will argue against. Remind students to use information from their work in this chapter to support their viewpoints. After the debate, take a vote to see which side of the issue is supported by the majority of the class.

CHAPTER 12 • Module 30

Assess

Assign the Module 30 Practice Quiz.

Use the Practice Quiz to identify gaps in student understanding.

REMEDIATE

Have students, individually or in groups, review the module goals, learning objectives, and key terms.

Refer students to the Concept Summary on p. 407 for review.

Close

As a class, discuss the following questions:

- How can the assessment of personality improve or adversely affect our lives?
- What are appropriate and inappropriate uses for personality tests?

Practice Quiz

Pick the best answer.

1. **According to the plaster hypothesis, at what age is personality relatively stable?**
   a. before age 21
   b. ages 21–30
   c. ages 30–60
   d. over 60

2. **According to Hofstede, which of the following countries is considered to be more "masculine"?**
   a. Sweden
   b. Japan
   c. Portugal
   d. Thailand

3. **Which of the following is a drawback of behavioral personality assessments?**
   a. The assessments can be affected by observer bias.
   b. The assessments are usually neither reliable nor valid.
   c. The assessments do not examine real-world behaviors.
   d. The assessments seem somewhat outdated to most people.

4. **Which measure of personality assessment offers the most objective measurement?**
   a. interview
   b. direct observation
   c. personality inventory
   d. Rorschach inkblot test

5. **Which of the following is not one of the traits found to have a genetic component in studies of identical twins?**
   a. aggressiveness
   b. antagonism
   c. intelligence
   d. leadership abilities

6. **Which is not associated with high self-esteem?**
   a. self-actualization
   b. future success
   c. improved health
   d. future job satisfaction

7. **Which type of disease is commonly associated with holding in one's emotions?**
   a. cancer
   b. obesity
   c. diabetes
   d. coronary disease

8. **Which of the following Big Five personality traits is positively correlated to longevity?**
   a. low levels of openness
   b. high levels of neuroticism
   c. low levels of extraversion
   d. high levels of conscientiousness

9. **Which of the following personality assessment methods would most likely be used by a psychoanalyst?**
   a. MMPI-2
   b. Myers-Briggs
   c. Frequency counts
   d. Rorschach inkblot test

10. **Which of the following personality traits seems to decline in women and remain stable in men between the ages of 30 and 60?**
    a. neuroticism
    b. openness
    c. agreeableness
    d. conscientiousness

Practice Quiz Answers

1. c
2. b
3. a
4. c
5. b

6. c
7. a
8. d
9. d
10. a

CHAPTER 12 Summary

🎧 **Listen** on **mypsychlab.com**

Module 29: Perspectives on Personality
Evaluate the major theories of personality.

29.1 What is the psychodynamic theory of personality?
- The three parts of the personality are the id, ego, and superego. The id works on the pleasure principle and the ego works on the reality principle. The superego is the moral center of personality, containing the conscience, and is the source of moral anxiety.
- The personality develops in a series of psychosexual stages: oral, anal, phallic, latency, and genital. Fixation occurs when conflicts are not fully resolved during a stage, resulting in adult personality characteristics reflecting childhood inadequacies.

29.2 How do behaviorists and social cognitive theorists explain personality?
- Behaviorists define personality as a set of learned responses or habits. The social cognitive view of personality includes the concept of reciprocal determinism, in which the environment, characteristics of the person, and the behavior itself all interact.

29.3 How do humanistic psychologists explain personality?
- Carl Rogers proposed that self-actualization depends on proper development of the self-concept. The self-concept includes the real self and the ideal self. When these two components do not match or agree, anxiety and disordered behavior result.

29.4 What are historical and current views of the trait perspective?
- Trait theorists describe personality traits in order to predict behavior. Several researchers have arrived at five trait dimensions that have research support across cultures, called the Big Five. The five factors are openness, conscientiousness, extraversion, agreeableness, and neuroticism.

Listen to an audio file of your chapter on **mypsychlab.com**

Module 30: Assessment and Issues in Personality
Learn how personality is assessed.

30.1 What techniques do researchers use to measure personality? Are these techniques reliable and valid?
- Interviews are used primarily by psychoanalysts and humanists. Projective tests are used by psychoanalysts. Behavioral assessments include direct observation of behavior, rating scales of specific behavior, and frequency counts of behavior. Personality inventories provide a detailed description of certain personality traits. Several of these techniques tend not to be reliable or valid.

Consider key issues in personality research.

30.2 What part do biology and culture play in personality?
- Studies of twins and adopted children have found support for a genetic influence on many personality traits.

30.3 Is personality stable, or can it change over time?
- Recent studies show substantial changes in personality can occur between the ages of 30 and 60, weakening the "plaster hypothesis."

30.4 How can personality influence our health and our work?
- People's personalities can affect their risk of developing physical health problems such as cardiovascular disease. People who are extraverted and/or conscientious frequently perform well at work, especially in social work environments. People who have high levels of neuroticism tend not to perform well in certain professions.

30.5 What is self-esteem, and how does it affect us?
- Self-esteem is the feeling of self-worth or value in oneself. People with high self-esteem sleep better, stand up to peer pressure better, give up less easily, are more outgoing and less anxious, and are generally happier.

30.6 How do cultural perspectives relate to personality?
- Hofstede's cross-cultural management study revealed four basic dimensions of personality along which cultures may vary: individualism/collectivism, power distance, masculinity/femininity, and uncertainty avoidance.

Vocabulary Terms

personality p. 376
character p. 376
temperament p. 376
unconscious mind p. 377
id p. 378
pleasure principle p. 378
ego p. 378
reality principle p. 378
superego p. 378
conscience p. 378
fixation p. 379
psychosexual stages p. 379
oral stage p. 379
anal stage p. 379
anal expulsive personality p. 380
anal retentive personality p. 380
phallic stage p. 380
Oedipus complex p. 380
identification p. 380

latency p. 380
psychoanalysis p. 381
neo-Freudians p. 381
personal unconscious p. 382
collective unconscious p. 382
archetypes p. 382
basic anxiety p. 382
neurotic personalities p. 382
habits p. 383
social cognitive learning theorists p. 384
social cognitive view p. 384
reciprocal determinism p. 384
self-efficacy p. 384
locus of control p. 385
expectancy p. 385
humanistic perspective p. 385
self-actualizing tendency p. 385
self p. 385

real self p. 385
ideal self p. 385
positive regard p. 386
unconditional positive regard p. 386
conditional positive regard p. 386
fully functioning person p. 386
trait theories p. 387
trait p. 387
surface traits p. 387
source traits p. 387
introversion p. 387
five-factor model (Big Five) p. 387
openness p. 387
conscientiousness p. 387
extraversion p. 387
extraverts p. 387
introverts p. 387

agreeableness p. 388
neuroticism p. 388
trait–situation interaction p. 388
interview p. 391
halo effect p. 392
projection p. 392
projective tests p. 393
Rorschach inkblot test p. 393
Thematic Apperception Test (TAT) p. 393
subjective p. 393
direct observation p. 394
rating scale p. 394
frequency count p. 394
personality inventory p. 394
behavioral genetics p. 396
heritability p. 396
self-esteem p. 399

Critical Thinking

MAKING CONNECTIONS

Each student should take a piece of poster board and create a collage that illustrates "who they really are," using the information they have collected throughout the study of this chapter of all of the personality assessments and explorations they've done, covering the key components of each theory. Students can draw their collages or use clippings from magazines, newspapers, or online material. Students should then write a short thought-paper, discussing the following: (1) What are some of the major themes about yourself that are depicted in your collage? (2) What key elements from the theories discussed in the text or lecture apply to your collage?

CHAPTER 12 • Summary and Vocabulary

Chapter Summary

Encourage students to carefully review and study the summary. Explain that it provides an overview of key concepts presented in the text.

Have students identify what they find unclear or confusing. Call on volunteers to provide answers, examples, or definitions.

Vocabulary Terms

Remind students that terms are defined within the chapter at point of use. If they are not sure of a term's definition, they should look up the definition on the page.

Encourage students to create study cards of unfamiliar words or go to **www.myspychlab.com** for flashcards. Have them test themselves or a classmate. Advanced students can explain the terms in their own words.

CHAPTER 12 Assessment

✓—Study and Review on mypsychlab.com

Vocabulary Review
Match each vocabulary term to its definition.

1. reciprocal determinism
2. personality
3. self-esteem
4. superego
5. temperament
6. trait
7. real self
8. projection
9. ideal self
10. identification

a. The unique and relatively stable ways in which people think, feel, and behave.
b. The feeling of self-worth or value in oneself.
c. One's perception of whom one should be or would like to be.
d. Defense mechanism in which a person tries to become like someone else to deal with anxiety.
e. Part of the personality that acts as a moral center.
f. Defense mechanism involving placing one's own unacceptable thoughts onto others, as if the thoughts actually belonged to those others and not to oneself.
g. A consistent, enduring way of thinking, feeling, or behaving.
h. A child's innate personality and emotional characteristics, observable in infancy; the enduring characteristics with which each person is born.
i. One's perception of actual characteristics, traits, and abilities.
j. Bandura's explanation of how the factors of environment, personal characteristics, and behavior can interact to determine future behavior.

Writing about Psychology
Respond to each question in complete sentences.

1. Contrast the psychodynamic approach to personality with the behavioral approach to personality. Describe each approach, including advantages and disadvantages, and discuss at least one prominent individual associated with each.
2. Design a set of 10 questions to use in a personality interview. At the end of your list, describe what behavioral approach(es) guided the questions and why you chose to ask those questions.

Psychology Project
How reliable are online personality tests? Perform this experiment to see how your perception of your personality measures up to the results of an online test.

Materials:
- a computer with Internet access
- a pencil and paper

Instructions:
1. First, review the Big Five model of personality. For each trait, think about your own personality and decide whether you are a "high scorer" or a "low scorer" in terms of that trait.
2. Next, take an online personality test based on the five-factor model, such as the one located at **http://users.wmin.ac.uk/~buchant/wwwffi**
3. Review the results of the online personality test. Are the test results similar or different to the conclusions you drew about yourself?
4. After comparing your test results to your own self-assessment, take a few minutes to think about factors that could have affected your results. Is the online test reliable and valid? Is your self-assessment reliable and valid? What are the benefits and drawbacks of each testing method? What methods might give you a more accurate picture of your own personality?

CHAPTER 12 • Assessment

VOCABULARY REVIEW

1. j
2. g
3. b
4. e
5. h
6. g
7. i
8. f
9. c
10. d

WRITING ABOUT PSYCHOLOGY

1. Students' answers should include a detailed definition of each theory, an in-depth address of both advantages and disadvantages, and an explanation of the contributions of the prominent individual associated with the theory.
2. Students' questions should clearly follow a specific personality theory with a defined objective, as well as what information the student hopes the answers would reveal about the interviewee. The end description should explain the student's framework in detail, provide a specific stance on why the student chose that approach, and indicate how the questions demonstrate that approach.

PSYCHOLOGY PROJECT

Students can provide their results in the form of a Venn diagram, outlining their initial assessments, the results of the test, and the similarities and differences of each. On the back of the diagram, students can write a paragraph answering the questions listed in part 4 of the project.

Internet Resources

Great Ideas in Personality: www.personalityresearch.org/
A comprehensive website containing links to every imaginable aspect of personality research, information, and assessment.

Personality and Consciousness: www.wynja.com/personality/theorists.html
A good resource for more information about concepts mentioned in the text.

American Psychoanalytic Association: www.apsa.org/pubinfo/about.htm
Contains information about modern psychoanalysis, information about the field, and quotes by Freud.

The Personality Project: http://personality-project.org/perproj/readings-taxonomies.html
Comprehensive site containing "lists of lists" of everything pertaining to personality.

Test Yourself

Pick the best answer.

1. In which psychosexual stage are sexual feelings repressed?
   a. oral
   b. phallic
   c. genital
   d. latency

2. Which of the following is the feeling of self-worth or value in oneself?
   a. real self
   b. self-esteem
   c. self-concept
   d. self-actualization

3. The concept that personality develops between the ages 21 and 30, but changes very little from 30 to middle age, is called
   a. latency theory
   b. middle age theory
   c. plaster hypothesis
   d. reciprocal determinism

4. Elsie's daughter gave her a cell phone. Elsie has never used a cell phone and is scared to use it. Instead, she leaves it in a drawer and uses her house phone. On the Big Five inventory, Elsie would probably score very low on
   a. openness
   b. extraversion
   c. neuroticism
   d. conscientiousness

5. Which type of disease is commonly associated with aggressiveness?
   a. cancer
   b. obesity
   c. diabetes
   d. coronary disease

6. Which of the following is NOT one of Hofstede's four dimensions of cultural personality?
   a. individualism/collectivism
   b. power distance
   c. masculinity/femininity
   d. locus of control

7. According to behaviorists, personality is
   a. a set of learned responses or habits
   b. driven by unconscious forces
   c. a collection of specific traits
   d. determined by biology and heredity

8. Monik is a generally calm person who stays relaxed even in stressful situations. He does not have a history of mental health problems. On the Big Five inventory, Monik would probably score very low on
   a. openness
   b. neuroticism
   c. extraversion
   d. agreeableness

9. Which of the following personality assessment methods is most likely to be reliable?
   a. projective test
   b. subjective interview
   c. personality inventory
   d. Rorschach inkblot test

10. What component of personality inventories is designed to ensure that responders do not cheat on the test?
    a. validity scales
    b. projective tests
    c. clinical scales
    d. repeated questions

11. According to Rogers, anxiety and neurotic behavior result from
    a. learned habits of behavior
    b. unconscious conflicts and desires
    c. receiving too much unconditional positive regard
    d. a mismatch between the real self and the ideal self

12. According to Cattell, traits that can easily be seen by other people are called
    a. open traits
    b. source traits
    c. surface traits
    d. central traits

13. For Bandura, one of the most important personal variables in determining personality is
    a. self-control
    b. self-concept
    c. self-efficacy
    d. self-actualization

14. According to Freud, which structure of the personality functions on the reality principle?
    a. id
    b. ego
    c. superego
    d. conscience

15. Jake was adopted as an infant and raised by his adoptive family. Jake has always been an extravert, but his adoptive parents are both quite introverted. A researcher discovers that Jake's twin brother, who was adopted by another family as an infant and whom Jake has never met, is also very extraverted. Which of the following concepts seems most related to Jake's extraversion?
    a. extraversion as a heritable trait
    b. extraversion as a learned trait
    c. extraversion as a habitual trait
    d. extraversion as a psychosexual trait

16. The stereotypical concept of the "grumpy old man" is challenged by which of the following findings about how men's personalities change over time?
    a. Openness decreases.
    b. Agreeability increases.
    c. Extraversion decreases.
    d. Neuroticism remains relatively stable.

17. Which of the following is a way in which Jung's beliefs differed from Freud's?
    a. Jung did not believe in archetypes.
    b. Jung did not believe in defense mechanisms.
    c. Jung believed in the collective unconscious.
    d. Jung did not believe in the id, ego, and superego.

18. Which of the following personality traits has the LEAST negative impact on health?
    a. low openness
    b. high neuroticism
    c. low extraversion
    d. high conscientiousness

19. Kavita plans to visit Morocco, so she learns about the culture. She learns that if she plans to travel outside of cities, she, as a woman, must dress modestly and she will have a curfew in certain places. She also learns that there are strict rules throughout Morocco and that the religion of Islam impacts when shops close and when people are publicly called to prayer. From this information, Kavita deduces that Morocco as a culture is
    a. masculine, individualistic
    b. feminine, collectivistic
    c. feminine, uncertainty-tolerant
    d. masculine, uncertainty-avoidant

20. Which is a danger that can occur if an analyst relies too heavily on the biological theories of personality?
    a. The client may learn to cheat on tests.
    b. The client may never self-actualize.
    c. The client's behavior may be considered unchangeable.
    d. The analyst may end up with an incorrect diagnosis.

CHAPTER 12 • Assessment

TEST YOURSELF

1. d	11. d
2. b	12. c
3. c	13. c
4. a	14. b
5. d	15. a
6. d	16. b
7. a	17. c
8. b	18. d
9. c	19. d
10. a	20. c

Ready for Testing

STUDENTS KNOW THEY ARE READY FOR TESTING IF THEY ARE ABLE TO . . .

- Define personality according to the various perspectives in psychology.
- Discuss Freud's psychoanalytical perspective on personality, including the division of the mind, components of personality, stages of development, and modifications of his theory by the neo-Freudians.
- Describe the behaviorists' perspective on personality and the social cognitive theory including Albert Bandura's model.
- Introduce the humanistic perspective of personality including Carl Rogers's view of the self and concept of unconditional positive regard.
- Discuss trait theory with regard to the description of personality.
- Explain what is known about the role of biology and heredity in personality development.
- Describe major methods of personality assessment, including interviews, projective tests, behavioral assessment, and personality inventories.

CHAPTER 12 • Concept Summary

MULTIMEDIA CONTENT AVAILABLE AT
www.mypsychlab.com

Map the Concepts on mypsychlab.com

Study and Review Flashcards on **mypsychlab.com**

STUDY TIPS

Creating Graphic Organizers To review for a test, divide the class into groups of three to five students. Give each group a large piece of paper with a topic written at the top and a set period of time to create a graphic organizer related to the topic, such as a web diagram, a Venn diagram, a table, or a flowchart. Then ask students to pass their paper to the next group, which must expand the organizer. Continue until each group has worked on each topic. If the class is large, two organizers can be prepared for each topic and later compared. Post the completed organizers around the classroom.

CHAPTER 12 Concept Summary: Theories of Personality

Learning Objectives 29.1 29.2 29.3 29.4 pp. 376–389

Theories of Personality

- **psychodynamic perspective**
  - mind made up of different levels of awareness—**conscious, preconscious,** and **unconscious**
  - personality stems from interplay and conflict between demands made by the id, restrictions set by the super-ego, and direction by the ego

  Conscious: Contact with outside world
  Preconscious: Material just beneath the surface of awareness
  Ego
  Super-ego
  Id
  Unconscious: Difficult to retrieve material; well below the surface of awareness

- **behavioral and social cognitive perspective**
  - for behaviorists, personality is set of learned responses and habits, gained through classical and operant conditioning
  - in social cognitive view, both learning (individual and through imitation of models) and cognitive processes (such as anticipation, judgment, and memory) are important

- **humanistic perspective**
  - when there is a match between **real** and **ideal selves,** one is considered to be **fully functioning** and capable of reaching **self-actualization**

- **trait theory**
  - Cattell identified 16 source traits through factor analysis; developed assessment questionnaire to identify original 16 trait dimensions (16PF)
  - several groups' work resulted in the five-factor model (Big Five, OCEAN)

High Scorer Characteristics

Openness	Conscientiousness	Extraversion	Agreeableness	Neuroticism
• creative • artistic • curious • imaginative • nonconforming	• organized • reliable • neat • ambitious	• talkative • optimistic • sociable • affectionate	• good-natured • trusting • helpful	• worrying • insecure • anxious • temperamental
• conventional • down-to-earth • uncreative	• unreliable • lazy • careless • negligent • spontaneous	• reserved • comfortable being alone • stays in the background	• rude • uncooperative • irritable • aggressive • competitive	• calm • secure • relaxed • stable

Low Scorer Characteristics

406 CHAPTER 12

What Every Student Should Know About . . .

DOING ONLINE RESEARCH

In addition to online magazines, most major newspapers, news magazines, and television news networks have searchable websites that allow people to locate a huge array of documents on news events. Articles, photos, and other documents from these sites may not be indexed by the major search engines, so the only way to locate these documents is to go directly to the source. Students should check the website of their local library to see which newspaper and magazine databases it subscribes to. Remind students that forums and blogs can contain worthwhile information; however, they should be aware that blogs and forums may present a particular political point of view.

Learning Objective

30.1 pp. 391–395

Learn How Personality is Assessed

- interviews
- projective tests
- behavioral assessments
- personality inventories

Table 30.1 Who Uses What Method?

TYPE OF ASSESSMENT	MOST LIKELY USED BY...
Interviews	Psychoanalysts, Humanistic Therapists

Projective Tests
  Rorschach
  Thematic Apperception Test
	Psychoanalysts

Behavioral Assessments
  Direct Observation
  Rating Scales
  Frequency Counts
	Behavioral and Social Cognitive Therapists

Personality Inventories
  Sixteen Personality Factor Questionnaire (16PF)
  Neuroticism/Extraversion/Openness Personality Inventory (NEO-PI)
  Myers-Briggs Type Indicator (MBTI)
  Eysenck Personality Questionnaire (EPQ)
  Keirsey Temperament Sorter II
  California Psychological Inventory (CPI)
  Minnesota Multiphasic Personality Inventory, Version II (MMPI-2)
	Trait Theorists

Learning Objectives

30.2 30.3 30.4 30.5 30.6 pp. 396–401

Consider Key Issues in Personality Research

- **biology of personality** — identical twins are more similar than fraternal twins or unrelated people in many facets of personality, and adoption studies of twins confirm that genetic influences account for a great deal of personality development
- **stability of personality** — new research suggests that personality can change throughout the life span
- **connections to health and work** — personality can affect people's susceptibility to diseases, and can also affect job performance
- **self-esteem** — is a person's feeling of his or her own self-worth or value
- **cultural aspects of personality**
  - individualism/collectivism
  - power distance
  - masculinity/femininity
  - uncertainty avoidance/uncertainty tolerance

THEORIES OF PERSONALITY 407

Comprehension Check

WHY STUDY PERSONALITY?

Refer students back to the box on p. 375 titled "Why Study Personality?" Ask them to write a brief statement answering the question. Students should use information from the chapter to support their viewpoints. Ask volunteers to read their statements to the class.

CHAPTER 12 • Concept Summary

STUDY TIPS

Listening in Class Be sure students understand the difference between *hearing* and *listening*. Listening requires effort and concentration. To enhance their listening skills, have students practice the following steps. Before they even arrive at class, students should make sure they have reviewed their notes from the previous class, finished assignments, and kept up with the reading. As they listen, students should watch for main ideas and notice how the details fit into them. To stay focused, suggest that students maintain eye contact with the speaker and try to ignore their physical surroundings. It will also help students stay focused if they are active listeners, which means taking notes, marking content about which they have a question, and asking questions when appropriate. To avoid daydreaming, students can try to anticipate what the speaker will say next, as well as mentally evaluating and summarizing what they hear.

CHAPTER 13 • Module 31

Launch the Chapter

CHAPTER GOALS AND LEARNING OBJECTIVES

Module 31 Defining Abnormal Behavior

Understand the historical, cultural, and current views of abnormality.

- 31.1 How has mental illness been explained in the past and in other cultures?
- 31.2 What is psychologically abnormal behavior?
- 31.3 What are the major models of abnormality?
- 31.4 What is stigma, and how does it relate to mental illness?
- 31.5 How do psychological disorders impact individuals, their families, and society?

Module 32 Types of Psychological Disorders

Learn about psychological disorders, their symptoms, and their causes.

- 32.1 What is the DSM classification system?
- 32.2 What are the challenges of diagnosing a mental illness?
- 32.3 What are the different types of anxiety disorders and their causes?
- 32.4 What are the different types of somatoform disorders and their causes?
- 32.5 What are the different types of dissociative disorders and their causes?
- 32.6 What are the different types of mood disorders and their causes?
- 32.7 What are the main symptoms, types, and causes of schizophrenia?
- 32.8 What are the different types of personality disorders and their causes?
- 32.9 How can family and social influences affect the experience of mental illness?

DIFFERENTIATED INSTRUCTION KEY

Look for these symbols to help you adjust steps in each lesson to meet your students' needs.

- **L1** Special Needs
- **L2** Basic
    - **ELL** English Language Learners
    - **LPR** Less Proficient Readers
- **L3** All Students
- **L4** Advanced Students

---

13 Psychological Disorders

The Harsh Reality of Postpartum Psychosis

What could drive a mother to kill her own children? In Toronto, a 37-year-old woman jumped in front of a subway train with her 6-month-old infant in her arms. Another young mother shut herself and her three children in the garage with the car running. Yet another mother in Texas drowned her five children in the bathtub. Experts believe that these women were suffering from a rare form of depression that is caused by sudden hormonal changes just after a woman gives birth. This condition is called *postpartum psychosis* (Ahokas et al., 2000; Brockington et al., 1982; Hamilton, 1982; Mahe & Dumaine, 2001).

Postpartum psychosis may include actual false beliefs or delusions (such as believing that the baby is possessed by a demon), hallucinations (one woman thought her baby was a rat trying to bite her), frantic energy, and an unwillingness to eat or sleep, in addition to symptoms of depression (Rohde & Marneros, 1993).

Research into this condition has suggested that postpartum psychosis is most likely caused by internal, biological factors rather than any cultural or societal expectations because this disorder is found in many cultures, both Western and non-Western, as well as in both technological and traditional societies (Kumar, 1994). Other research highlights the possible role of lack of estrogen, the female hormone that is lower than usual right after childbirth (Ahokas et al., 2000; Mahe & Dumaine, 2001).

Whatever the cause, how can the delusions and hallucinations seem real enough to these women to cause them to harm their own children? Why does this condition become so severe in some women, whereas many others have only a mild form of it? What factors cause a person to cross over the line from normal to abnormal behavior?

CORRELATION TO APA STANDARDS FOR CHAPTER 13

VID. PSYCHOLOGICAL DISORDERS

VID-1. Perspectives on abnormal behavior . . . . pp. 410–416
VID-2. Categories of psychological disorders . . . . pp. 418–436

MODULE 31 ▸ DEFINING ABNORMAL BEHAVIOR

MODULE 32 ▸ TYPES OF PSYCHOLOGICAL DISORDERS

Why Study?

Abnormal Behavior

Because it is all around us, which raises many questions: How should one react? What should be done to help? What kind of person develops a mental illness? Could this happen to someone close? The key to answering these questions is to develop an understanding of just what is meant by abnormal behavior and the different ways in which behavior can depart from the "normal" path.

PSYCHOLOGICAL DISORDERS 409

SCHEDULING				
1 Period = 50 min. 1 Block = 90 min.	Semester Course (18 weeks/90 days) Periods/Blocks		Full-Year Course (36 weeks/180 days) Period/Blocks	
Module 31	2.5	1.25	5	2.5
Module 32	2.5	1.25	5	2.5
Total Days for Chapter	5	2.5	10	5

CHAPTER 13 • Module 31

Teacher Prep

Psychopathology is the study of abnormal behavior. Throughout history, abnormal behavior and mental illness have been regarded with varying degrees of suspicion, fear, misunderstanding, and shame. Early explanations attributed abnormal behavior to the invasion of evil spirits and subjected victims to trepanning, religious rituals, and death. Today, mental illness is still regarded with a certain stigma, but new understanding about the causes and types of mental illness and growing awareness have brought about greater understanding for victims of mental disorders.

Abnormal behavior today is defined by five criteria: Is the behavior *unusual*? Does it go against *social norms*? Does it cause *subjective discomfort*? Is it *maladaptive*? Does the behavior cause the person to be *dangerous to self or others*?

Three models explain the causes of abnormal behavior. The *biological model* proposes that abnormal behavior is due to biological or medical causes. The *psychological models* include the psychodynamic view, explaining abnormal behavior with theories of repression; the behaviorist view proposing learned behaviors as the cause; and the cognitive view citing maladaptive thinking patterns. Finally, the biopsychosocial view proposes that biological, psychological, social, and cultural causes interact to cause the manifestation of a disorder.

In 1952, the *Diagnostic and Statistical Manual of Mental Disorders* was published to help psychological professionals identify and treat mental disorders. The manual categorizes mental disorders into five axes. The disorders discussed in this chapter are found on Axis I, *Clinical Disorders*. This chapter will discuss various types and possible causes of anxiety, somatoform, dissociative, personality, and mood disorders, as well as schizophrenia.

Chapter 13 Psychological Disorders **409**

CHAPTER 13 • Module 31

Focus

RESOURCES

For this module, consult the appropriate sections of the Teacher's Manual, Test Bank, and PowerPoint slides, all found on the Teacher's Resource DVD, and the interactive study tools for students on MyPsychLab.

BEFORE CLASS

Students should read the section for homework before coming to class.

BELLRINGER

On one side of the room, place a sign that says TRUE and the other, FALSE. Read aloud the following statements, one at a time, and ask students to respond by moving to one side of the room. Allow students to explain their answers and then reveal the actual answer.

1. A clear line can be drawn between what is "normal" and what is "abnormal." *FALSE; abnormality manifests in degrees and is determined by the behavior and the situation.*

2. As a group, former mental patients are unpredictable and dangerous. *FALSE; they are no more so than anyone else, although the media is to blame for sensationalizing the exceptions to this rule.*

3. Most mental disorders are treatable but incurable. *FALSE; 70% to 80% of hospitalized mental patients make a full recovery.*

Teach

COVER THE MODULE

- *Psychopathology* is the study of abnormal behavior.
- 31.1 How has mental illness been explained in the past and in other cultures?
- Skulls with evidence of *trepanning* (the process of cutting holes into the skull to allow demons to escape) date as far back as 10,000 B.C.E.
- It was believed that abnormal behavior was the result of possession of evil spirits.
- In 400 B.C.E., Hippocrates introduced the idea that illnesses of body and mind were the result of imbalances of bodily fluids, which he referred to as *humors*.

410 Chapter 13 Psychological Disorders

Module 31 — Defining Abnormal Behavior

Module Goal
Understand historical, cultural, and current views of abnormality.

Learning Objectives
- 31.1 How has mental illness been explained in the past and in other cultures?
- 31.2 What is psychologically abnormal behavior?
- 31.3 What are the major models of abnormality?
- 31.4 What is stigma, and how does it relate to mental illness?
- 31.5 How do psychological disorders impact individuals, their families, and society?

Understand Historical, Cultural, and Current Views of Abnormality

Exactly what is meant by the term *abnormal behavior*? Abnormal compared to what? Who gets to decide what is normal and what is not? Has the term always meant what it means now? These are just a few questions that come to mind when thinking about the study of abnormal behavior, or **psychopathology** (Wen-Shing & Strelzer, 1997). And the answers to these questions are not always straightforward: Definitions of abnormality have always varied from culture to culture, and from era to era.

31.1 How has mental illness been explained in the past and in other cultures?

A Brief History of Psychological Disorders Archaeologists have found human skulls dating from as early as 10,000 B.C.E. bearing the evidence of an ancient surgical technique. The skulls have holes cut into them, made while the person was still living. In fact, many of the holes show evidence of healing, meaning that the person survived the process. The process of cutting holes into the skull of a living person is called *trepanning* (also spelled *trephining*). Although trepanning is still done today to relieve the pressure of fluids on the brain, in ancient times, the reason may have had more to do with releasing the "demons" possessing the poor victim (Gross, 1999). Ancient cultures might have assumed that people who behaved oddly were possessed by evil spirits. As trepanning had to have been rather unpleasant, the disordered person may very well have tried hard to be "normal" after treatment, too.

Hippocrates was a Greek physician who lived around 400 B.C.E.—a time when the rest of the world and even many Greeks believed in the demon possession explanation of mental illness. Hippocrates, now known by some as the "Father of Medicine," challenged that belief, asserting that illnesses of both the body and the mind were the result of imbalances in the body's vital fluids, or *humors* (phlegm, black bile, blood, and yellow bile). Although Hippocrates was not correct in his assumptions about the humors of the body, his was the first

psychopathology the study of abnormal behavior.

410   CHAPTER 13

Terms

- psychopathology • cultural relativity • culture-bound syndromes • situational context • subjective discomfort • maladaptive • psychological disorders • biological model • biopsychosocial model • stigma recorded attempt to explain abnormal behavior as the result of some kind of biological process.

Many Europeans during the Middle Ages believed in spirit possession (through the teachings of the Roman Catholic Church or the remnants of other religious/cultural systems). The treatment of choice was a religious one: *exorcism*, or the formal casting out of the demon through a religious ritual (Lewis, 1995). During the Renaissance, belief in demon possession (in which the possessed person was at least seen as a victim) gave way to a belief in witchcraft, and mentally ill people were often called witches and put to death. Although there is wide disagreement about exactly how many people were hanged, burned, stoned, or drowned as witches, some estimates place the number at around 100,000 (Barstow, 1995).

Although abnormal behaviors were often attributed to supernatural forces during the prescientific era, psychological professionals today have a much more accurate understanding of the causes and symptoms of abnormal behavior. We'll discuss modern views of abnormality later in this module and in Module 32.

Current Issues in Psychology

A Look at Abnormality in Various Cultures

It's important to realize that what's perceived as normal in one culture may be perceived as abnormal in another culture. In particular, cultural differences in abnormal behavior must be addressed when psychological professionals are attempting to treat members of a culture different from theirs. **Cultural relativity** is a term that refers to the need to consider the unique characteristics of the culture in which a person with a disorder was nurtured in order to be able to correctly diagnose and treat the disorder (Castillo, 1997). For example, in most traditional Asian cultures, mental illness is seen as a shameful thing that brings disgrace to one's family. It may be seen as inheritable and, therefore, something that would hurt the marriage chances of other family members, or it may be seen as stemming from something the family's ancestors did wrong in the past (Ritts, 1999; Ying, 1990). This leads many Asian people suffering from disorders that would be labeled as depression or even schizophrenia to report bodily symptoms rather than emotional or mental ones, as bodily ailments are more socially acceptable (Fedoroff & McFarlane, 1998; Lee, 1995; Ritts, 1999).

Some disorders, called **culture-bound syndromes,** are only found in particular cultures. Here are a few examples, together with the culture in which they are found (Ritts, 1999):

- *Taijin-kyofu-sho (TKS):* TKS is found primarily in Japan and involves the fear that one will do something in public that is socially inappropriate or embarrassing, such as blushing, staring, or having an offensive body odor (Kirmayer, 1991).
- *Susto:* Susto is a kind of magical fright found among the Kechua-speaking Latino Indians of the Andes. It is seen as a "loss of soul" triggered by some frightening experience, after which the person falls to the ground and experiences appetite and weight loss, weakness, problems sleeping, depression, and lack of emotion (Pfeiffer, 1982).

cultural relativity the need to consider the unique characteristics of the culture in which behavior takes place.

culture-bound syndromes disorders found only in particular cultures.

PSYCHOLOGICAL DISORDERS 411

CHAPTER 13 • Module 31

COVER THE MODULE *(continued)*

- During the Middle Ages, abnormal behavior was again attributed to spirit possession.
- Exorcism, the process of expelling the evil spirit through religious ritual, was the treatment of choice.
- During the Renaissance, mental illness was thought to be caused by witchcraft, and the mentally ill often were put to death.

CURRENT ISSUES IN PSYCHOLOGY

- *Cultural relativity* refers to the need to consider the unique characteristics of the culture in which a person with a disorder was raised, so that it is possible to correctly diagnose and treat the disorder.
- *Culture-bound syndromes* are disorders that are found only in a particular culture, including TKS, Susto, and Amok.

1. Possible answers include anorexia nervosa, bulimia nervosa, anxiety, and depression due to high stress levels.

MAKING CONNECTIONS

Ask students to think about a time they experienced as "normal" in one setting and "abnormal" in another (e.g., moving from a northern state to the South, where accents, manners, and social norms can be drastically different). How did they feel about the upheaval in what they thought was "normal?"

Class Discussion

WHAT IS "ABNORMAL" IN OUR CULTURE?

Purpose: Students connect to the idea of cultural relativity by discussing what is "normal" and "abnormal" in their culture.

Time: 20 minutes

Description: Divide the class in half. Give each group a large sheet of paper or poster board. Assign one group to list what is considered normal, mentally healthy behavior in their culture and the other to list behavior considered "abnormal." Allow groups to share with the class. Then divide students into smaller groups, giving each group an item from the lists to discuss in more detail. Groups should decide why the behavior is normal or abnormal and how it could change in a different setting. Allow students to again share findings with the class.

Module 31 Defining Abnormal Behavior 411

CHAPTER 13 • Module 31

COVER THE MODULE

31.2 What is psychologically abnormal behavior?

- *Abnormality* can be defined as the following:
  - A statistical definition on a continuum with "normal" in the middle
  - Social nonconformity, or deviance from the social norms of the society in which the individual lives

  LINK to *Chapter Eight: Culture and Gender,* p. 359

  - In this definition, it is important to consider the *situational context*, defined as the social or environmental setting of a person's behavior because behavior that is unacceptable in one culture or situation may be normal in another.
- *Subjective discomfort* is emotional stress or pain while engaged in a particular behavior.

TEACHING TIP

All people have a need for accomplishment and social acceptance. Within the classroom, these needs can be fulfilled by developing a curriculum that promotes academic success and acceptance by the teacher.

- *Amok:* The term comes from Southeast Asia but similar concepts are found in Latin America, as well as in certain Native American tribes. Amok results from a perceived insult or slight, which is followed by a period of brooding and then a violent or aggressive outburst, during which the person may attack others and may not remember doing so (Pfeiffer, 1982).

Question for Further Discussion

1. Think about your own culture. Is there a disorder or behavior that seems to be unique to your culture?

31.2 What is psychologically abnormal behavior?

As we've seen, defining abnormal behavior or abnormality is not a simple task. The easy way out is to say that abnormal behavior is behavior that is not normal, but what does that mean?

One way to define *normal* and *abnormal* is to use a statistical definition that allows us to consider behaviors along a continuum, with "normal" in the middle. Using such a definition, frequently occurring behavior would be considered normal, and behavior that is rare would be abnormal. That kind of definition works fine with a behavior such as talking to others; the two rarer possibilities would be not talking to anyone at all and talking too much to too many people—both of which would be considered abnormal. What about a behavior such as happiness? Is a medium level of happiness really the "norm" most people strive to reach? We can agree that a total lack of happiness would be abnormal, but should a person who is very happy also be labeled abnormal?

Another way of defining abnormality is to see it as something that goes against the norms or standards of the society in which the individual lives. For example, refusing to wear clothing in a society that does not permit nudity would be seen as abnormal. But deviance, or variation, from social norms is not always labeled as negative, abnormal behavior. For instance, if a person decided to become a monk and live in a monastery in the United States, it would be unusual and society would consider it nonstandard behavior, but it wouldn't be a sign of abnormality.

Using *social nonconformity*, or a failure to follow social norms, as a criterion for abnormality also creates a problem when dealing with different cultures. Behavior that would be labeled disordered in one culture may be quite acceptable in another. LINK to *Chapter Eight: Culture and Gender, p. 359.* Even within one culture, the **situational context** (the social or environmental setting of a person's behavior) can make a difference on how behavior is labeled. For example, if a man comes to a therapist complaining of people listening in on his phone conversations and spying on all his activities, the therapist's first thought might be that the man is suffering from feelings of persecution. But if the man then explains that he is in a witness protection program, the complaints take on an entirely different and quite understandable tone.

One sign of abnormality is when a person experiences a great deal of **subjective discomfort**, or emotional distress while engaging in a particular behavior. A woman who suffers from a fear of going outside her house, for example, would experience a great deal of anxiety when trying to leave home and distress over being unable to leave. However, not all behavior that might

situational context the social or environmental setting of a person's behavior.

subjective discomfort emotional distress or emotional pain as reported by an individual.

412 CHAPTER 13

Class Demonstration

MAKING CONNECTIONS

<u>Purpose</u>: Students apply what they have learned and discussed so far concerning abnormal behavior to fictional characters.

<u>Time</u>: 15 minutes

<u>Description</u>: Ask students to brainstorm a familiar fictional character that would lend itself well to a discussion of abnormal behavior. Tell students to describe, on a blank sheet of paper, the character's behavior and why, according to the concepts in the text, the behavior would be defined as "abnormal." Allow students to pair up and share their papers with other classmates.

412 Chapter 13 Psychological Disorders

be considered abnormal necessarily creates subjective discomfort in the person committing the act—a serial killer, for example, does not experience emotional distress after taking someone's life, and some forms of disordered behavior involve showing no emotions at all.

Behavior that does not allow a person to fit into society or function normally can also be labeled abnormal. This kind of behavior is termed **maladaptive** (the prefix *mal-* comes from the Latin word for "bad"), meaning that the person finds it hard to adapt to the demands of day-to-day living. Maladaptive behavior includes behavior that may initially help a person cope but has harmful or damaging effects in the long run. For example, a woman who cuts herself to relieve anxiety experiences initial relief but is harmed by the action. Maladaptive behavior is a key element in the definition of abnormality.

▶ Simulate on mypsychlab.com

The Final Definition of Abnormality

So, how do psychologists decide what is abnormal?
Perhaps the shortest definition of abnormal behavior, or a **psychological disorder,** is any pattern of behavior that causes people significant distress, causes them to harm themselves or others, or harms their ability to function in daily life. To get a clear picture of abnormality, it is often necessary to take all of the factors discussed thus far into account. Psychologists and other psychological professionals must consider several different criteria in determining whether or not a behavior is abnormal (at least two of these criteria must typically be met to form a diagnosis of abnormality):

1. Is the behavior *unusual*, such as experiencing severe panic when faced with a stranger or being severely depressed in the absence of any stressful life situations?
2. Does the behavior *go against social norms*? (Keep in mind that social norms can change over time.)
3. Does the behavior cause the person *significant subjective discomfort*?
4. Is the behavior *maladaptive*?
5. Does the behavior cause the person to be *dangerous to self or others*, as in the case of someone who tries to commit suicide or attacks other people without reason?

31.3 What are the major models of abnormality?

Now that we have a working definition of abnormality, we can begin to ask what causes psychological disorders. Psychologists use three different types of theoretical models—the biological model, psychological models, and the biopsychosocial model—to explain the causes of abnormal behavior.

The Biological Model: Medical Causes for Psychological Disorders

The **biological model** proposes that psychological disorders have a biological or medical cause (Gamwell & Tomes, 1995). According to this model, disorders such as anxiety, depression, and schizophrenia are caused by chemical imbalances, genetic problems, brain damage and dysfunction, or some combination of those causes. There is a growing body of evidence that basic personality traits are as much influenced by genetic inheritance as they are by experience and upbringing, even across cultures (Bouchard, 1994; Herbst et al., 2000; Jang et al., 1996; Loehlin, 1992; Loehlin et al., 1998). One of the Big Five personality factors LINK to Chapter Twelve: Theories of Personality, pp. 387–388) is

▶ Simulate the definition of psychological disorders on **mypsychlab.com**

◀ So, how do psychologists decide what is abnormal?

maladaptive anything that does not allow a person to function within or adapt to the stresses and everyday demands of life.

psychological disorders any pattern of behavior that causes people significant distress, causes them to harm others, or harms their ability to function in daily life.

biological model model of explaining behavior as caused by biological changes in the chemical, structural, or genetic systems of the body.

PSYCHOLOGICAL DISORDERS 413

CHAPTER 13 • Module 31

COVER THE MODULE (continued)

- *Maladaptive* behavior is anything that would cause a person to find it hard to cope with day-to-day living, including coping mechanisms that help the individual initially but cause long-term harm.
- The most useful modern definition is that of an abnormal behavior that is termed a *psychological disorder*, which is any pattern of behavior that causes distress, harm to oneself or others, or the inability to function in day-to-day life.
- Two of the following criteria must be met for deeming a behavior abnormal: (1) Is the behavior unusual? (2) Does the behavior go against social norms? (3) Does the behavior cause significant subjective discomfort? (4) Is the behavior maladaptive? (5) Does the behavior cause the person to be dangerous to self or others?

COVER THE MODULE

31.3 What are the major models of abnormality?

- In the *biological model*, psychological disorders are caused by biological changes in chemical, structural, or genetic systems of the body.

LINK to Chapter Twelve: *Theories of Personality,* pp. 387–388

MULTIMEDIA CONTENT AVAILABLE AT
www.mypsychlab.com

▶ Simulate the definition of psychological disorders on **mypsychlab.com**

Explore

THE BIOLOGICAL MODEL

Remind students that the biological model proposes that psychological disorders have a biological or medical cause. According to this model, disorders such as anxiety, depression, and schizophrenia are caused by chemical imbalances, genetic problems, brain damage and dysfunction, or some combination of those causes. Have students, individually or in small groups, conduct library or Internet research on one of these proposed causes. They should find out what recent studies suggest and what treatments are being used by proponents of the biological model. Ask students to write a brief report or create an audiovisual presentation on what they learned.

Module 31 Defining Abnormal Behavior 413

CHAPTER 13 • Module 31

COVER THE MODULE (continued)

- The psychological model explains disordered behavior as the result of repressing one's threatening thoughts in the unconscious mind.

  LINK to *Chapter Twelve: Theories of Personality,* pp. 376–383

  - Behaviorists define abnormal behavior as learned responses to stimuli, just like normal behavior.
  - Cognitive psychologists believe abnormal behavior results from maladaptive thinking patterns.

- The *biopsychosocial model* sees abnormal behavior as caused by the interaction of biological, psychological, social, and cultural influences.

L2 LPR DIFFERENTIATED INSTRUCTION

Less Proficient Readers Discuss with students how preparing written questions while the material is fresh in their minds will help them review and remember the important points of the chapter later.

---

neuroticism, for example, and it is easy to see how someone who scores high in neuroticism would be at greater risk for anxiety-based disorders.

The biological or medical model has had a great deal of influence, especially in the language used to describe disorders: phrases like *mental illness* and *symptoms of disorder* and terms such as *diagnosis, mental patient, mental hospital, therapy,* and *remission* all come from medical terminology. The use of such terms, although still widespread, may tend to bias the assumptions of professionals who are not psychiatrists or medical doctors toward a biological cause for disordered behavior.

The Psychological Models Although the biological model of psychological disorders is influential, it is not the only way in which disorders are explained. There are several psychological models that attempt to explain disordered behavior as the result of various forms of emotional, behavioral, or thought-related malfunctioning.

The *psychodynamic model*, based on the work of Freud and his followers, **LINK** to *Chapter Twelve: Theories of Personality, pp. 376–383*, explains disordered behavior as the result of repressing one's threatening thoughts, memories, and concerns in the unconscious mind (Carducci, 1998). These repressed thoughts and urges try to resurface, and disordered behavior develops as a way of keeping the thoughts repressed. For example, a woman who has unacceptable thoughts of harming her family members might feel "dirty" and be compelled to wash her hands every time those thoughts threaten to become conscious, ridding herself symbolically of the "dirty" thoughts.

Behaviorists, who define personality as a set of learned responses, have no trouble explaining disordered behavior as being learned just like normal behavior (Skinner, 1971; Watson, 1913). For example, when Joanne was a small child, a spider dropped onto her leg, causing her to scream and react with fear. Her mother came running and made a big fuss over her, soothing her and giving her lots of attention. The next time Joanne saw a spider, she screamed again because of the prior fear-provoking incident. Again, she was rewarded with the attention of everyone in the room. Eventually, Joanne would experience a fear reaction and scream if someone just said the word *spider*. Behaviorists would say that Joanne's fear of the spider was conditioned to occur to the mere sight of a spider or even the sound of the word, and her screaming reaction was positively reinforced by all the attention and soothing.

Cognitive psychologists, who study the way people think, remember, and mentally organize information, see abnormal behavior as resulting from maladaptive thinking patterns (Mora, 1985). A depressed person, for example, may be taking small problems and blowing them out of proportion, or he may be depressed because he's unhappy with his job or his relationships, but he doesn't believe that he has the power to control and change his situation. A cognitive psychologist might explain Joanne's fear of spiders as distorted thinking: "All spiders are vicious and will bite me, and I will die!" Joanne's particular thinking patterns put her at a higher risk of depression and anxiety than those of a person who thinks more logically.

Biopsychosocial Perspective: All of the Above In recent years, a new perspective has surfaced in which biological, psychological, and sociocultural influences on abnormality are not seen as independent causes of abnormal behavior. Instead, these influences are thought to interact with one another to cause the various forms of disorders. For example, a person may have a genetically inherited tendency for a type of disorder, such as anxiety, but may not

---

Class Demonstration

EXPLAINING PSYCHOPATHOLOGY

<u>Purpose</u>: Students think about and discuss the theoretical models used to explain abnormal behavior.

<u>Time</u>: 15 minutes

<u>Description</u>: Place signs in each corner of the room for "Biological Model," "Psychoanalytic Model," "Behaviorism," and "Cognitive Perspective." Write the following question on the board: "What causes abnormal/mentally disordered behavior?" Allow students to talk with others who share their view by meeting in different corners of the room. Give groups time to discuss and, possibly, conduct outside research online to prepare a defense of their position to present to the rest of the class. Ask students to include specific examples of disorders whose behaviors could be explained by their model.

▲ *Statistically speaking, about one out of every five of the people in this crowd suffers from some form of psychological disorder. If psychological disorders are so common, why do you think they are still stigmatized?*

develop the full-blown disorder unless the family and social environments produce the right stressors at the right time in development. The person's particular culture will also play a part in determining the exact degree of the disorder and the form that it might take. This is known as the **biopsychosocial model** of disorder, which has become a very influential way to view the connection between mind and body.

31.4 What is stigma, and how does it relate to mental illness?

Despite the fact that mental illnesses have existed across all times and cultures, there is still a widespread negative attitude toward people with mental illnesses. This social disapproval is known as **stigma**. People who stigmatize psychological abnormality may incorrectly feel that mental illness is a sign of weakness, possession, or some other negative conditions. These stigmas can be expressed both directly (making a negative statement about a person with mental illness) and more subtly (assuming that a person is violent, or denying a person a service or a job, because he or she has a mental disorder). One illustration of the power of this stigma in everyday life comes from a 1977 study in which an associate of psychologist Stewart Page called 180 people who were advertising rooms for rent in Toronto. Initially, most of the rooms were available. When she mentioned that she was about to be released from a mental hospital, however, 75% of people responded that the rooms were not available. When another associate called the same people, the rooms were again available to rent. Does the fact that a person is being released from a mental health facility indicate that the person will not be a good tenant? Not necessarily. However, the stigma associated with mental illness can create serious obstacles for people in many cultures. This stigma can also discourage people suffering from mental illnesses from seeking the help they need.

Stigmas can come from dramatized media portrayals, negative personal experiences, stereotypes, and cultural misconceptions. However, as mental illness is increasingly recognized as a disease of the brain, rather than a character weakness, the stigma associated with psychological disorders seems to be

biopsychosocial model perspective in which abnormal behavior is seen as the result of the combined and interacting forces of biological, psychological, social, and cultural influences.

stigma social disapproval of conditions or characteristics that are considered abnormal.

PSYCHOLOGICAL DISORDERS 415

CHAPTER 13 • Module 31

COVER THE MODULE

31.4 What is stigma, and how does it relate to mental illness?

- *Stigma* is the social disapproval of conditions or characteristics such as mental illness that are considered abnormal.
  - Stigma can be expressed directly (e.g., making a negative comment).
  - It can be expressed indirectly (e.g., harboring a belief that all mental patients are violent).
- Stigmas create serious problems for people with mental illness, including discouraging them from seeking help.
- Stigmas of mental illness seem to be disappearing in Western culture.

UNDERSTANDING VISUALS

Have one of every five students in your class stand up so that students can see how the statistic applies more directly. Then lead the class in a discussion of why mental disorders are stigmatized if they are so common. Ideas include the following: people with disorders are afraid to talk about them with others, thus allowing misconceptions to spread; the media sensationalizes mental illness; television and movies exaggerate portrayals of mental illness; and people tend to avoid others with mental illness because they do not want to "get involved."

Explore

THE STIGMA OF MENTAL ILLNESS

Purpose: Students read online more details about stigma as it relates to mental illness and what is being done to change it.

Time: 30 minutes

Description: First, lead the class in a quick brainstorming session. Ask students to think of as many examples of stigmas associated with mental illness as they can. Then direct students to the following websites to read more in-depth about the topic. Finally, ask students to answer the following questions in writing: (1) What was something new you learned about stigmas and mental illness? (2) What is one way you can do something about stigmas and mental illness?

- For more information about stigmas: www.mayoclinic.com/health/mental-health/MH00076
- An excellent article by Glenn Close, who represents the Bring Change2Mind organization: www.huffingtonpost.com/glenn-close/mental-illness-the-stigma_b_328591.html
- The Bring Change2Mind website: www.bringchange2mind.org/

Module 31 Defining Abnormal Behavior 415

CHAPTER 13 • Module 31

COVER THE MODULE

31.5 How do psychological disorders impact individuals, their families, and society?

- Individuals with mental illness face judgment from others; loss of friendships, family support, and employment; negative side effects of drugs; and dealing with insurance plans that severely limit coverage of treatment for mental illness.
- Families caring for someone with mental illness undergo a great deal of stress due to the amount of time caring for a loved one takes, the expense of the treatment, and self-blame for the condition of the loved one.
- Societies should devote time and money to the treatment of mental disorders and educational programs.

FAST FACT

The World Health Organization has reported that 4 of the 10 leading causes of disability in the United States and other developed countries are mental disorders. By 2020, major depressive illness will be the leading cause of disability in the world for women and children.

L3 DIFFERENTIATED INSTRUCTION

Auditory/Verbal Learners To reinforce the learning of chapter content, auditory learners should verbally repeat important information to themselves.

---

fading in Western culture (Solomon, 1996). While talking about mental illness in public would have been embarrassing and perhaps even shocking in early 20th century America, public figures have recently begun to speak about their struggles with mental health disorders. Research shows that the more exposure that people have to individuals with mental health disorders, the more informed and understanding they become, and the more accepting their attitudes become (Kolodziej & Johnson, 1996).

31.5 How do psychological disorders impact individuals, their families, and society?

Like other forms of illness, psychological disorders disrupt a person's day-to-day life and come with their own physical and mental challenges. As we've discussed, abnormal behavior is still stigmatized in many societies, and people diagnosed with psychological disorders may feel judged or labeled by others around them, even their friends and family members. The stigmas associated with mental illness, along with the challenging health problems that can occur as a result of certain disorders, may lead to a loss of friendships, family support, and even employment, depending on the severity of the illness. Seeking a diagnosis can be a challenging experience for people who do not want to admit that they need help. Also, individuals who are treated for psychological disorders may have to cope with the side effects of treatment: Some drugs that effectively treat psychological disorders also result in weight loss, weight gain, or other health problems. Additionally, many health insurance plans severely limit coverage of the treatment of mental illnesses, and the lack of comprehensive insurance for mental health services reinforces the idea that mental illnesses are not "real" or common medical issues.

The individual diagnosed with a psychological disorder is not the only person affected by the disorder. It can be extremely stressful for families and friends to care for a loved one with a mental illness. Caring for a person with a mental illness is often time-consuming, and drugs and therapy sessions can be expensive. Some family members may even blame themselves for the person's illness, a pattern of thought which increases stress and causes feelings of guilt. The stress of caretaking can actually put family members at greater risk to develop certain types of mental illnesses if they are genetically predisposed to do so. Children of parents with mental disorders are also at an increased risk of developing mental illnesses—partly as a result of genetic factors, and partly due to environmental factors.

Because psychological disorders can and do affect millions of people's lives, it is increasingly important that societies devote resources and funding to the effective treatment of mental illness. In addition to effective and accessible treatment, educational programs that share the facts of mental illness with all members of society can help people with mental illnesses—along with their friends and families—better understand the challenges they face and learn how to meet those challenges. Taking a psychology class is just one way in which you can educate yourself about the facts of mental illness.

Critical Thinking

WRITING ABOUT PSYCHOLOGY

<u>Purpose</u>: Students write about persons' experiences with mental illness.

<u>Time</u>: 15 minutes

<u>Description</u>: Ask students to research a well-known person, past or present, who suffered with mental illness. Then have them respond, in writing, to the following questions: (1) Who was the person you researched who suffered from a psychological disorder? (2) Describe the person's experience, any treatment received, any experience with stigma, and if the person recovered. (3) What insights can you take away from researching the person's experience?

Practice Quiz

Pick the best answer.

1. Who would be the most likely to assume that psychological disorders are caused by an imbalance in the fluids (humors) of the body?
   a. an ancient Egyptian physician
   b. a modern psychiatrist
   c. an ancient Greek physician
   d. a physician of the Middle Ages

2. In Japan, the disorder called _____ centers around a fear of doing something embarrassing or socially inappropriate.
   a. anxiety
   b. taijin-kyofu-sho
   c. susto
   d. amok

3. Which model of abnormality explains abnormal behavior as caused by illogical thinking?
   a. psychodynamic
   b. cognitive
   c. behavioral
   d. biopsychosocial

4. A biopsychologist might explain the occurrence of a major depressive episode as being the result of
   a. unresolved unconscious conflicts that are left over from a difficult childhood
   b. maladaptive automatic thoughts that lead a person to think negatively about his or her world
   c. chemical imbalances, brain damage or dysfunction, or some combination of the two
   d. a combination of biological, social, and psychological factors

5. Which is NOT one of the criteria that psychological professionals consider when determining whether a behavior is abnormal?
   a. Is the behavior maladaptive?
   b. Does the behavior cause the person to be dangerous to self or others?
   c. Does the behavior cause the person significant subjective discomfort?
   d. Is the behavior a genetically inherited trait?

6. What was the most likely reason that ancient people performed trepanning to others?
   a. to relieve fluid pressure on the brain
   b. to look into the brain to see what was wrong
   c. to release evil spirits that were in the person's head
   d. to restore balance to the body's humors

7. Which model of abnormality talks about reinforcement and imitation as ways of developing abnormal behavior?
   a. psychodynamic
   b. behavioral
   c. cognitive
   d. biological

8. Lisa has started having feelings of fearfulness about going to school. She has begun to suffer from headaches and stomachaches and has missed several days of school already. Lisa's condition is abnormal from the _____ definition.
   a. statistical
   b. situational context
   c. social deviance
   d. subjective discomfort

9. The term _____ can refer to society's disapproval of people with mental illnesses.
   a. stigma
   b. psychopathology
   c. cultural relativity
   d. social nonconformity

10. Which of the following is FALSE about psychological disorders?
    a. Certain disorders may lead to a loss of friendships, family support, and employment.
    b. Some family members may blame themselves for a person's illness.
    c. Children of parents with mental disorders are at decreased risk of developing mental illnesses.
    d. Some drugs that treat psychological disorders can result in weight loss, weight gain, or other health problems.

PSYCHOLOGICAL DISORDERS 417

CHAPTER 13 • Module 31

Assess

Assign the Module 31 Practice Quiz.

Use the Practice Quiz to identify gaps in student understanding.

REMEDIATE

Have students, individually or in groups, review the module goals, learning objectives, and key terms.

Refer students to the Concept Summary on p. 442 for review.

Close

As a class, review how our understanding of psychological disorders has changed over time. Ask students to think about how they or their friends would have been treated in each of the historical eras discussed in the text, if they had had a psychological disorder. Finally, lead a discussion about how our society's view of mental illness might be discussed in a psychology class 100 years from now. What changes and contributions can we make?

Practice Quiz Answers

1. c
2. b
3. b
4. d
5. d
6. c
7. b
8. d
9. a
10. c

Module 31 Defining Abnormal Behavior

CHAPTER 13 • Module 32

Focus

RESOURCES
For this module, consult the appropriate sections of the Teacher's Manual, Test Bank, and PowerPoint slides, all found on the Teacher's Resource DVD, and the interactive study tools for students on MyPsychLab.

BEFORE CLASS
Students should read the section for homework before coming to class.

BELLRINGER
On the board, write the names of some of the disorders discussed in the chapter. Have students work in pairs and assign each a disorder. Have students list any preconceived notions or stereotypes that come to mind about the disorder. On a large piece of paper, record the stereotypes that students list for each disorder. Keep this class "poster" to revisit at the end of the module.

Teach

COVER THE MODULE

32.1 What is the DSM Classification System?

- The first *Diagnostic and Statistical Manual of Disorders* (DSM) was published in 1952. The current edition is entitled *The Diagnostic and Statistical Manual of Mental Disorders, Fourth Edition, Text Revision* (DSM-IV-TR).
  - It contains descriptions of 250 disorders divided into categories along five axes.
- Axis I, Clinical Disorders
  - Addresses the disorders that typically bring individuals to the attention of a psychological professional
  - Does not include personality disorders.
- Axis II, Personality Disorders and Mental Retardation

418 Chapter 13 Psychological Disorders

Module 32: Types of Psychological Disorders

Module Goal
Learn about psychological disorders, their symptoms, and their causes.

Learning Objectives
- 32.1 What is the DSM classification system?
- 32.2 What are the challenges of diagnosing a mental illness?
- 32.3 What are the different types of anxiety disorders and their causes?
- 32.4 What are the different types of somatoform disorders and their causes?
- 32.5 What are the different types of dissociative disorders and their causes?
- 32.6 What are the different types of mood disorders and their causes?
- 32.7 What are the main symptoms, types, and causes of schizophrenia?
- 32.8 What are the different types of personality disorders and their causes?
- 32.9 How can family and social influences affect the experience of mental illness?

Learn About Psychological Disorders, Their Symptoms, and Their Causes

32.1 What is the DSM classification system?

In 1952, the first edition of the *Diagnostic and Statistical Manual of Mental Disorders (DSM)* was published to help psychological professionals diagnose psychological disorders. The current version of the *DSM* is called the *Diagnostic and Statistical Manual of Mental Disorders, Fourth Edition, Text Revision (DSM-IV-TR)* (American Psychiatric Association [APA], 2000).

The *DSM-IV-TR* describes about 250 different psychological disorders. Each disorder is described in terms of its symptoms, the typical path the disorder takes as it progresses, and a checklist of specific criteria that must be met in order for the diagnosis of that disorder to be made. The manual also divides these disorders and relevant diagnostic factors along five different categories, or *axes* (the plural of *axis*). A psychologist or psychiatrist will often assess a client on each of these five axes.

Axis I, *Clinical Disorders*, contains the disorders that bring most people to the attention of a psychological professional. All of the psychological disorders are listed on this axis with the exception of personality disorders, which are found on Axis II, *Personality Disorders and Mental Retardation,* along with intellectual disability (which is a developmental disorder). Unlike most psychological disorders, personality disorders are relatively stable and enduring,

418 CHAPTER 13

Terms

- anxiety disorders • free-floating anxiety • phobia • social phobia • specific phobia • agoraphobia • panic attack • panic disorder • obsessive-compulsive disorder • generalized anxiety disorder • magnification • somatoform disorder • hypochondriasis • somatization disorder • conversion disorder • dissociative disorders • dissociative amnesia • dissociative fugue • dissociative identity disorder • affect • mood disorders • dysthymia • cyclothymia • major depression • manic • bipolar disorder • schizophrenia • psychotic • delusions • delusional disorder • hallucinations • flat affect • disorganized • catatonic • paranoid • positive symptoms • negative symptoms • stress-vulnerability model • personality disorders • antisocial personality disorder • borderline personality disorder • seasonal affective disorder • phototherapy and are therefore most similar to conditions that affect many areas of an individual's life, such as intellectual disability.

Axis III, *General Medical Conditions*, includes physical disorders that affect a person's psychological *adjustment*, such as juvenile diabetes, chromosome disorders such as Klinefelter's syndrome, and high blood pressure. (In psychology, the term *adjustment* refers to a person's ability to function normally in everyday life.) Axis IV, *Psychosocial and Environmental Problems*, contains information about problems in a person's life that might affect adjustment, such as the death of a loved one, the loss of a job, or poverty. Finally, Axis V, *Global Assessment of Functioning*, is a numeric scale (going from 0 to 100) used by psychological professionals to rate a person's mental health and adjustment. Explore on mypsychlab.com

Explore the axes of the *DSM-IV-TR* on mypsychlab.com

For a listing and brief description of the disorders found on Axis I, see Table 32.1.

Table 32.1 Axis I Disorders of the *DSM-IV-TR*

DISORDER	EXAMPLES
Disorders usually first diagnosed in infancy, childhood, or adolescence	Learning disabilities, ADHD, bed-wetting, speech disorders
Delirium, dementia, amnesia, and other cognitive disorders	Alzheimer's, Parkinson's, amnesia due to physical causes
Psychological disorders due to a general medical condition	Personality change because of a brain tumor
Substance-related disorders	Alcoholism, drug addictions
Schizophrenia and other psychotic disorders	Schizophrenia, delusional disorders, paranoid psychosis
Mood disorders	Depression, mania, bipolar disorders
Anxiety disorders	Panic disorder, phobias, stress disorders
Somatoform disorders	Hypochondria, conversion disorder
Factitious disorders	Pathological lying, Munchausen syndrome
Dissociative disorders	Dissociative identity disorder (formerly multiple personality), amnesia not due to physical causes
Sexual and gender identity disorders	Sexual desire disorders, paraphilias
Eating disorders	Anorexia, bulimia
Sleep disorders	Insomnia, sleep terror disorder, sleepwalking, narcolepsy
Impulse-control disorders not classified elsewhere	Kleptomania, pathological gambling, pyromania
Adjustment disorders	Mixed anxiety, conduct disturbances

Adapted from the American Psychiatric Association (APA), *DSM-IV-TR* (2000).

CHAPTER 13 • Module 32

COVER THE MODULE (continued)

- Axis III, General Medical Conditions
  - Lists physical disorders that affect a person's ability to function in everyday life
- Axis IV, Psychosocial and Environmental Problems
  - Contains information about problems in a person's life that may affect adjustment
- Axis V, Global Assessment of Functioning
  - Contains a scale from 0 to 100 for professionals to use to rate a person's mental health and adjustment

MULTIMEDIA CONTENT AVAILABLE AT
www.mypsychlab.com

Explore the axes of the *DSM-IV-TR* on mypsychlab.com

UNDERSTANDING VISUALS

Point out to students all of the disorders listed in Table 32.1 that you will cover in this module.

L3 DIFFERENTIATED INSTRUCTION

Tactile/Kinesthetic Learners Have students collect examples of material related to the chapter content (or print it from the Internet) and prepare a display showing the examples they collected.

Explore

THE AXES OF THE *DSM-IV-TR*

Purpose: Help students familiarize themselves with the *DSM-IV-TR*.

Time: 10 minutes

Description: This activity can be done in groups or as a whole class. Assign each student a brief description of a disorder, and in groups or as a class, decide to which axis of the *DSM-IV-TR* the disorder would belong. Alternatively, give students a handout listing 15 to 20 descriptions to categorize for more practice. Descriptions of disorders listed in each axis of the *DSM-IV-TR* can be found at the following website:

http://allpsych.com/disorders/dsm.html

CHAPTER 13 • Module 32

COVER THE MODULE (continued)

- 44 million people or 22 percent of adults in the United States suffer from a mental disorder.
- Psychological disorders comprise 4 of the 10 leading causes of disability in the United States
- People can suffer from more than one disorder at a time.

FAST FACT

The text discusses statistics for adults suffering from mental disorders. Children and adolescents can also develop severe mental illness. One in 10 children and adolescents develops a severe disorder that impairs his or her ability to function, but only 20 percent of children suffering from a disorder receive the treatment they need.

L3 DIFFERENTIATED INSTRUCTION

Visual/Nonverbal Learners *Provide handouts with important chapter information to be used by these students for taking notes.*

That table has a lot of different kinds of disorders, but most people don't get these problems, right?

How Common are Psychological Disorders?

That table has a lot of different kinds of disorders, but most people don't get these problems, right?

Actually, psychological disorders are more common than you might think. In any given year, about 22 percent of adults over age 18 suffer from a mental disorder (Narrow et al., 2002; National Institute of Mental Health [NIMH] 2001; Regier et al., 1993). That comes to about 44 million people in the United States. (See Figure 32.1.) Four of the 10 leading causes of disability in the United States and other developed countries are psychological disorders of some kind, with major depression leading the list (Murray & Lopez, 1996; NIMH, 2001). In fact, it is quite common for people to suffer from more than one mental disorder at a time, such as a person with depression who also has a substance abuse disorder, or a person with an anxiety disorder who suffers from sleep disorders as well (NIMH, 2001).

Disorder	People	Percentage
Major depressive disorder	9.9 million people	(5%)
Dysthymic disorder	10.9 million people	(5.4%)
Bipolar disorder	2.3 million people	(1.2%)
Schizophrenia	2.2 million people	(1.2%)
Panic disorder	2.4 million people	(1.7%)
Obsessive-compulsive disorder	3.3 million people	(2.3%)
Post-traumatic stress disorder	5.2 million people	(3.6%)
Generalized anxiety disorder	4.0 million people	(2.8%)
Social phobia	5.3 million people	(5.3%)
Agoraphobia	3.2 million people	(3.2%)
Specific Phobia	6.3 million people	(4.4%)

Key: Each icon represents 1 million people. Percentages reflect the percentage of adults over 18 affected annually in the United States. Adapted from NIMH (2001).

FIGURE 32.1 Occurrence of Psychological Disorders in the United States

---

Explore

MOST COMMON MENTAL DISORDERS IN THE UNITED STATES

<u>Purpose</u>: Students explore the information in Figure 32.1 in greater detail.

<u>Time</u>: 30 minutes

<u>Description</u>: Ahead of time and using the information in Figure 32.1, calculate how the statistics listed in the figure would appear, using the number of students in your class. Then assign that number of students the disorder to research on the Internet, and for the remaining students, assign them a topic such as "How to determine what is normal and what is not in mental health." Do not let students know how you have divided up the topics. After students have found information on their disorders, tell students that you have assigned the topics based on the statistics so that they can see how the numbers would affect their class. Have students who have researched similar topics stand up as a group for the class and share their research.

32.2 What are the challenges of diagnosing a mental illness?

Definitions and diagnoses of mental illnesses are subject to change across time and cultures, and the slippery nature of diagnosis can present challenges for psychological professionals attempting to identify and treat abnormal behavior in their patients. For example, the *DSM* once classified homosexuality as a mental illness, but as our society's understanding of sexual orientation has changed, the *DSM* has changed with it, and reputable psychiatrists would no longer consider homosexuality to be a psychological disorder or an illness today.

Another challenge of diagnosing a mental illness is that the diagnosis often relies on patients' self-reports of their feelings and experiences, since there are often no physical or biological symptoms to assess. Patients may not always be forthcoming with this information—more women than men are diagnosed with depression, for example, but this diagnostic gap exists at least in part because women seek diagnoses more often than men do. Patients who do not fully disclose symptoms risk misdiagnosis, which can result in treatments that have no effect or that actually worsen symptoms.

Some critics pose the issue that a mental health diagnosis is as dependent upon the psychiatrist or psychologist as it is upon the symptoms. In other words, the same patient might receive a different diagnosis, or no diagnosis at all, depending on the mental health professional who does the evaluation. Because psychiatrists and psychologists are only human, their personal biases about gender, race, socioeconomic status, or other factors may influence their ability to diagnose their patients effectively.

Mental health professionals may also carry biases or set expectations regarding psychological disorders. In a now-famous experiment performed by psychologist David Rosenhan (1973), healthy associates briefly reported "hearing voices" to falsely gain admission to mental hospitals. All were diagnosed with mental disorders. Following admission, all of the *pseudopatients* (people posing as mental patients) stopped complaining about the voices, and behaved as they normally would. All 12 hospitals in the study continued to treat the pseudopatients as if they were exhibiting ongoing symptoms of psychological disorders, such as schizophrenia and manic-depressive psychosis. Several patients were confined to the facilities for months, and when discharged, all except one were discharged with a diagnosis of schizophrenia "in remission."

In another study, Rosenhan arranged with a well-known hospital that one or more pseudopatients would attempt to gain admittance within a 3-month period. He asked the staff to rate each new patient as to whether or not the patient was an imposter. The hospital rated 41 out of 193 patients as imposters. In reality, Rosenhan did not send any pseudopatients to the hospital. The staff's expectations resulted in inaccurate or problematic diagnoses.

Despite the challenges involved in diagnosing psychological disorders, the major types of disorders do have characteristic symptoms that psychological professionals are trained to recognize and treat, and most people who seek help for mental illness will receive a diagnosis leading to effective treatment.

32.3 What are the different types of anxiety disorders and their causes?

The category of **anxiety disorders** includes all disorders in which the most dominant feature is excessive or unrealistic anxiety, characterized by symptoms

anxiety disorders disorders in which the main symptom is excessive or unrealistic anxiety and fearfulness.

CHAPTER 13 • Module 32

COVER THE MODULE

32.2 What are the challenges of diagnosing a mental illness?

- The challenges of diagnosing mental illness:
  - There are changing definitions of what constitutes abnormal behavior, such as the case of homosexuality.
  - Diagnosis rests on patients' self-reporting, with no physical symptoms to assess; patients may not always include all pertinent information.
  - Diagnosis relies on the skills of the diagnosing professional, who can be influenced by numerous factors including personal bias.

FAST FACT

The next edition of the *DSM-IV-TR* (DSM5) is due to be released in 2013. Students can browse the proposed changes at the following website: www.dsm5.org/Pages/Default.aspx

EXTEND THE LESSON

Allow students to take time to browse the Overview of Clinical Assessment Methods simulation available at www.mypsychlab.com

---

Explore

MISDIAGNOSIS OF MENTAL DISORDERS

Purpose: Students read recent articles discussing the problem of misdiagnosis of mental disorders in children and read about suggested ways to avoid misdiagnosis.

Time: 20 minutes

Description: Ask students to read the articles at the following two websites. As they read, they should note how what they have learned about misdiagnosis applies to the situations in the articles. Finally, have students read the article about how to avoid misdiagnosis and briefly write about or discuss how the suggestions can be applied to the misdiagnosis of children to improve the situation.

- "Half kids labeled bipolar may be misdiagnosed"
  www.msnbc.msn.com/id/20576306/ns/health-mental_health/
- "Can Preschoolers Be Depressed?"
  www.nytimes.com/2010/08/29/magazine/29preschool-t.html?scp510&sq5mental%20disorder%20diagnosis&st5cse
- A comprehensive site on the misdiagnosis of mental illness:
  http://www.wrongdiagnosis.com/m/mental_illness/misdiag.htm
- "Reducing Misdiagnosis of Psychiatric Disorders"
  http://mentalhealth.about.com/library/sci/0101/blbddx0101.htm

CHAPTER 13 • Module 32

COVER THE MODULE

32.3 What are the different types of anxiety disorders and their causes?

- *Anxiety disorders* include all disorders in which the main problem is excessive or unrealistic anxiety or fearfulness.
  - Symptoms include elevated heart rate, trouble breathing, sweaty skin, and a sense of impending doom.
  - To be considered a disorder, the anxiety felt must be excessive for the circumstances or unrealistic.
- *Free-floating anxiety* is anxiety that seems unrelated to any known, realistic factor.
- A *phobia* is a type of anxiety disorder characterized by irrational, disproportionate, and persistent fear of something.
  - *Social phobia* is a fear of interacting with others or being in a social situation in which a negative evaluation may occur.
  - *Specific phobia* is a fear of objects or specific situations or events.
  - *Agoraphobia* is the fear of being in a situation from which escape would be difficult or impossible.

MULTIMEDIA CONTENT AVAILABLE AT
www.mypsychlab.com

👁 **Watch** a video about anxiety disorders on **mypsychlab.com**

422 Chapter 13 Psychological Disorders

---

such as elevated heart rate, breathing issues, clammy or sweaty skin, and fear of impending harm. Anxiety can take very specific forms, such as a fear of a specific object, or it can be a very general feeling, such as that experienced by someone who is worried and doesn't know why.

▶ *But doesn't everybody have anxiety sometimes? What makes it a disorder?*

Everyone does have anxiety, and some people have a great deal of anxiety at times. In the case of anxiety disorders, the anxiety is either excessive—greater than it should be given the circumstances—or unrealistic. If final exams are coming up and a student hasn't studied enough, that student's anxiety is understandable and realistic. But a student who has studied, has done well on all the exams, and is very prepared and still worries *excessively* about passing is showing an unrealistic amount of anxiety. **Free-floating anxiety** is the term given to anxiety that seems to be unrelated to any realistic, known factor, and it is often a symptom of an anxiety disorder (Freud & Gay, 1977). 👁 **Watch** on **mypsychlab.com**

Phobic Disorders One of the more specific anxiety disorders is a **phobia**, an irrational, disproportionate, and persistent fear of something. The "something" might be an object or a situation. For example, many people would feel fear if they suddenly came upon a live snake as they were walking and would take steps to avoid the snake. Although those same people would not necessarily avoid a *picture* of a snake in a book, a person with a phobia of snakes would. Avoiding a live snake is rational; avoiding a picture of a snake is not.

Social phobias (also called *social anxiety disorders*) involve a fear of interacting with others or being in a social situation and are some of the most common phobias people experience (WHO International Consortium in Psychiatric Epidemiology, 2000). People with social phobias are afraid of being evaluated in some negative way by others, so they tend to avoid situations that could lead to something embarrassing or humiliating. Common types of social phobia are stage fright and fear of public speaking. Not surprisingly, people with social phobias often have a history of being shy as children (Sternberger et al., 1995).

A **specific phobia** is an irrational fear of some object or specific situation, such as a fear of dogs, or a fear of being in small, enclosed spaces (**claustrophobia**).

Another common type of phobia is **agoraphobia**, whose Greek name literally means "fear of the marketplace." Although that makes it sound like a social phobia, agoraphobia is actually the fear of being in a place or situation from which escape is difficult or impossible if something should go wrong (APA, 2000). So agoraphobics are often afraid of not only crowds but also crossing bridges, traveling in cars or planes, eating in restaurants, and sometimes even leaving the house. To be in any of these situations or to even think about being in such situations can lead to extreme feelings of anxiety and even *panic attacks* (discussed later in this module).

People with specific phobias can usually avoid the object or situation without too much difficulty, and people with social phobias may simply avoid jobs and situations that involve meeting people face-to-face. But people with agoraphobia cannot avoid their phobia's source because it is simply being outside in the real world. A severe case of agoraphobia can make a person's home a prison, leaving the person trapped inside unable to go to work, shop, or engage in any kind of activity that requires going out of the home.

Panic Disorder Fourteen-year-old Anna was sitting in science class watching a film. All of a sudden, she started feeling really strange. Her ears seemed

👁 **Watch** a video about anxiety disorders on **mypsychlab.com**

free-floating anxiety anxiety that is unrelated to any realistic, known source.

phobia an intense fear of a specific object or situation, which may or may not be typically considered frightening.

social phobia fear of interacting with others or being in social situations that might lead to a negative evaluation.

specific phobia fear of objects or specific situations or events.

agoraphobia fear of being in a place or situation from which escape is difficult or impossible.

422 CHAPTER 13

Class Demonstration (Kinesthetic)

EXPLORING PHOBIAS

Purpose: Students examine phobias in greater depth.

Time: 15 minutes

Description: Ask students to browse the list and descriptions of phobias at the following website: **http://phobialist.com/**. Then have students choose one phobia in which to "specialize." Ask students to stand in two circles, one inside circle and one outside circle, facing each other. Students should interview each other, asking each other questions as if they were interviewing a potential roommate. Students should answer the questions "in character," as if they really had their chosen phobia. Have students try to guess each others' phobias. Every 60 seconds, rotate the circles one position and start again. At the end of the exercise, reassemble the class. Ask students to try to divide the phobias into categories for social phobias and specific phobias.

to be stuffed with cotton and her vision was very dim. She was cold, had broken out in a sweat, and felt extremely afraid for no good reason. Her heart was racing and she immediately became convinced that she was dying. A friend sitting behind her saw how pale she had become and tried to ask her what was wrong, but Anna couldn't speak. The friend got the teacher's attention, who motioned to Anna to come over to him. Although she would have sworn she couldn't move, she stood up to go to him and immediately everything returned to normal.

Anna's symptoms are the classic symptoms of a **panic attack**, a sudden onset of extreme panic with various physical symptoms: racing heart, rapid breathing, a sensation of being "out of one's body," dulled hearing and vision, sweating, and dry mouth (Kumar & Oakley-Browne, 2002). Many people who have a panic attack think that they are having a heart attack and can experience pain as well as panic, but the symptoms are caused by the panic, not by any actual physical disorder. Psychologically, the person having a panic attack is in a state of terror, and many people may feel a need to escape. The attack happens without warning and quite suddenly. Although some panic attacks can last as long as half an hour, some last only a few minutes, with most attacks peaking within 10 to 15 minutes.

Having a panic attack is not that unusual, especially for adolescent girls and young adult women (Eaton et al., 1994; Hayward et al., 1989, 2000). Researchers have also found evidence that cigarette smoking greatly increases the risk of panic attacks in adolescents and young adults (Johnson, 2000; Zvolensky et al., 2003). Regardless of the age of onset, it is only when panic attacks become so frequent that they affect a person's ability to function in day-to-day life that they become a **panic disorder**.

Obsessive-Compulsive Disorder Sometimes people get a thought running through their head that just won't go away. If that particular thought causes a lot of anxiety, it can become the basis for an **obsessive-compulsive disorder** or OCD. OCD is a disorder in which unwanted *thoughts* that occur again and again (obsessions, such as a fear that germs are on one's hands) are followed by some compulsion, a repetitive, ritualistic *behavior* (such as repeated hand washing) or mental act (such as praying or counting). The compulsions are meant to lower the anxiety caused by the thought (Soomro, 2001). While everyone has a little obsessive thinking from time to time, the distress caused by a failure or inability to complete a compulsive behavior is a defining feature of OCD.

Generalized Anxiety Disorder

What about people who are just worriers? Can that become a disorder?
Remember free-floating anxiety? That's the kind of anxiety that has no real source and may be experienced by people with **generalized anxiety disorder** in which excessive anxiety and worries occur more days than not for at least 6 months. People with this disorder may also experience anxiety about a number of events or activities (such as work or school performance). These feelings of anxiety have no real source that can be pinpointed, nor can the person control the feelings even if an effort is made to do so.

People with this disorder worry about money, their children, their friends, and anything else that they think might possibly go wrong. They feel tense and edgy, get tired easily, and may have trouble concentrating. They have muscle aches and tension, they experience sleeping problems, and they are often irritable—all signs of stress. The problem is that the stress comes

panic attack sudden onset of intense panic in which multiple physical symptoms of stress occur, often with feelings that one is dying.

panic disorder disorder in which panic attacks occur frequently enough to cause the person difficulty in adjusting to daily life.

obsessive-compulsive disorder disorder in which intruding, recurring thoughts or obsessions create anxiety that is relieved by performing a repetitive, ritualistic behavior or mental act (compulsion).

generalized anxiety disorder disorder in which a person has feelings of dread and impending doom along with physical symptoms of stress, which last 6 months or more.

◂ What about people who are just worriers? Can that become a disorder?

PSYCHOLOGICAL DISORDERS 423

CHAPTER 13 • Module 32

COVER THE MODULE *(continued)*

- *Panic disorder* is another type of anxiety disorder, characterized by frequent panic attacks that affect an individual's ability to function in everyday life.
  - A *panic attack* is the sudden onset of extreme panic in which physical symptoms of stress occur, and the individual believes he or she is dying.
- *Obsessive-compulsive disorder* is an anxiety disorder in which obsessive thoughts create anxiety that is relieved by a compulsion (ritualistic, repetitive behavior, or mental act).
- *Generalized anxiety disorder* is characterized by free-floating anxiety that is experienced the majority of the time for 6 months or longer, causing people to experience extreme stress as a result of worrying.

L1 DIFFERENTIATED INSTRUCTION

L3 Special Needs Relate new concepts and skills to those already achieved.

Class Demonstration (Kinesthetic)

ANXIETY DISORDER "CATCHPHRASE"

Purpose: Students review what they have learned about anxiety disorders.

Time: 15 minutes

Description: Ahead of time, create a list of words that students cannot use during the game and place it on the board. Also, create a bag or envelope containing all of the anxiety disorders discussed in the text for students to draw from during the game. Divide the class into two teams, which take turns sending a representative up to the front of the class to draw a disorder from the bag. Allow 30 seconds per team for the students to use descriptions to describe the disorder for their team to guess without using the words on the board. As soon as the disorder is guessed by the team, that student should sit down and another student from the team should go up to the front, draw a disorder, and allow the team to guess. This process can be repeated until time runs out. Then the next team gets to do the guessing. Keep score for the students for each correct guess, and after all disorders have been used up, the game is over.

Module 32 Types of Psychological Disorders 423

CHAPTER 13 • Module 32

COVER THE MODULE (continued)

- Causes of anxiety disorders include the following:
  - The psychodynamic model proposes that anxiety is a signal of repressed conflicts.
  - Behaviorists believe that anxiety is learned due to the attention an individual received that reinforced the fearful reaction.
  - Cognitive psychologists believe anxiety is the result of irrational thought processes.
  - The biological model theorizes that some chemical imbalances in the brain are due to genetics and heritability of some disorders.

TEACHING TIP

Be careful about offending or embarrassing students who have a family member or loved one with a disorder. Teachers should encourage sensitivity toward people suffering from psychological disorders. There is a major effort in the field of abnormal psychology to destigmatize people suffering from disorders.

---

magnification the tendency to interpret situations as far more dangerous, harmful, or important than they actually are.

somatoform disorders disorders that take the form of bodily illnesses and symptoms but for which there are no real physical disorders.

▲ Anxiety disorders affect children as well as adults.

from their worrying rather than from any real external source. Generalized anxiety disorder is often found occurring with other anxiety disorders and depression.

Causes of Anxiety Disorders Different perspectives on how personality develops offer different explanations for anxiety disorders. For example, the *psychodynamic model* sees anxiety as a kind of danger signal that repressed urges or conflicts are threatening to surface (Freud & Gay, 1977). According to this model, a phobia is a symbol of whatever the person has buried deep in his or her unconscious mind—the true source of the fear. A fear of knives might mean a fear of one's own aggressive tendencies, for example, or a fear of heights may hide a suicidal desire to jump.

Behaviorists believe that anxious behavioral reactions are learned. They see phobias, as nothing more than conditioned fear responses. Remember Joanne, who was afraid of spiders? She received a lot of attention when she had a phobic reaction. But what if her friends stopped giving her this attention every time she overreacted to seeing a spider or hearing the word? According to behaviorists, by removing the reinforcing attention, the phobic reaction would become almost completely extinguished.

Cognitive psychologists see anxiety disorders as the result of illogical, irrational thought processes. One way in which people with anxiety disorders show irrational thinking (Beck, 1976, 1984) is through **magnification**, or the tendency to "make mountains out of molehills" by interpreting situations as being far more harmful, dangerous, or embarrassing than they actually are. In panic disorder, for example, a person might interpret a racing heartbeat as a sign of a heart attack instead of just a momentary arousal.

Biological factors may also contribute to anxiety disorders. Some evidence suggests that chemical imbalances in the brain may have a genetic component, meaning that anxiety disorders such as OCD, phobias, and panic disorder can be passed from parent to child through more than just observational learning (Karayiorgou et al., 1997; Lesch et al., 1996; Logue et al., 2003). Twin studies have also provided evidence for a genetic basis for anxiety disorders, with some studies finding that the heritability of panic disorder is about 44 percent, agoraphobia about 39 percent, and anxiety disorder about 30 percent (Hettema et al., 2001; Tsuang et al., 2004; Villafuerte & Burmeister, 2003). In addition, anxiety disorders are found around the world, although the disorders might take different forms in various cultures.

32.4 What are the different types of somatoform disorders and their causes?

Another category of abnormal behavior involves the belief that one is physically ill, often accompanied by the experience of physical symptoms despite the lack of any physical illness or problem. Disorders in which people believe they are sick when they are not are called **somatoform disorders**. Somatoform

424 CHAPTER 13

Class Demonstration

HOW DO THE FOUR MAIN PSYCHOLOGICAL MODELS EXPLAIN ANXIETY?

<u>Purpose</u>: Students practice explaining profiles of people suffering from different types of anxiety disorders from the different perspectives.

<u>Time</u>: 20 minutes

<u>Description</u>: Divide the class into four groups, one for each of the main psychological models. Read aloud profiles of people suffering from certain anxiety disorders. Allow the groups to work together to form an explanation of the disorder that follows their assigned psychological model. Allow groups to share their explanations with the class. Reassign the psychological models to different groups and repeat the process with another profile.

Profiles of people suffering from anxiety disorders can be found at the following website: **www.thehealthcenter.info/**

means that these disorders take the form of a bodily (somatic) ailment but are not real physical disorders. Although there is no real physical cause, the symptoms are very real to the person experiencing them.

Hypochondriasis Hypochondriasis (or the older name *hypochondria*) is one of the better-known somatoform disorders. In this disorder, a person worries excessively about getting ill. Although this may sound like an anxiety disorder, the specific worry about illness is the distinguishing feature of this disorder. People with this disorder become very preoccupied with bodily symptoms, which may be imagined, or may be real but unimportant in reality (Phillips, 2001). They go to doctors and health clinics frequently, looking for some medical professionals who will tell them what disease they have (Magarinos et al., 2002).

Somatization Disorder A similar somatoform disorder is **somatization disorder** in which the person complains about a specific physical symptom or symptoms, such as pain, nausea, difficulty swallowing, or trouble catching one's breath (Kellner, 1986). People with this disorder also go to doctors a lot, but they show less worry and more "drama" than people with hypochondriasis do. They tend to get very emotional when describing their symptoms, using phrases like "unbearable" and "beyond description" to describe their pain or other symptom, and they tend to become very dependent on the medical professional, demanding attention and even threatening suicide to get that attention in some cases. The symptoms also seem to multiply and shift frequently, with the main symptom being pain one day and shortness of breath on another, for example (Swartz, 1990).

Conversion Disorder Conversion disorder is limited to those functions controlled by the somatic nervous system. Symptoms are the loss of motor and/or sensory functions (APA, 2000). A person may experience dramatic, sudden, and specific symptoms such as blindness, paralysis, deafness, or numbness of certain body parts, none of which have real physical causes. Typically, the problems occur along with some other psychological disorder, such as depression, at a time when there is a stressful situation either already happening or about to happen (Hurwitz, 1989).

People with conversion disorders tend to exhibit a kind of indifference or lack of concern about the symptom, which is understandable if the person has unconscious knowledge that the symptom is not real (Silver, 1996). These symptoms are often anatomically impossible, as is the case with blindness for which there is no corresponding damage to the eyes, optic nerve, or parts of the brain responsible for vision. (See Figure 32.2.) Finally, conversion disorder symptoms disappear when the person is asleep, hypnotized, under anesthesia, or unconscious (Parobek, 1997; Silver, 1996).

Causes of Somatoform Disorders The psychodynamic view of somatoform disorders proposes that these disorders turn repressed anxiety into physical symptoms. Behaviorists, on the other hand, believe that the behavior of people with somatoform disorders brings them two kinds of reinforcement: positive reinforcement in the form of attention from doctors, family members, and others; and negative reinforcement from eliminating the stressful situation associated with the disorder. Cognitive psychologists would again point to the tendency of people with these disorders to magnify minor physical symptoms and allow false beliefs about their health to dominate their thinking.

hypochondriasis somatoform disorder in which the person is terrified of being sick and worries constantly, going to doctors repeatedly, and becoming preoccupied with every sensation of the body.

somatization disorder somatoform disorder in which the person dramatically complains of a specific symptom such as nausea, difficulty swallowing, or pain for which there is no real physical cause.

conversion disorder somatoform disorder in which the person experiences a specific symptom in the somatic nervous system's functioning, such as paralysis, numbness, or blindness, for which there is no physical cause.

FIGURE 32.2 Glove Anesthesia
Glove anesthesia is a disorder in which the person experiences numbness from the wrist down (see the drawing on the left). However, real nerve damage would produce numbness down one side of the arm and hand, as shown in the drawing on the right. Thus, because glove anesthesia is anatomically impossible, it is actually a sign of a conversion disorder.

PSYCHOLOGICAL DISORDERS   425

CHAPTER 13 • Module 32

COVER THE MODULE

32.4 What are the different types of somatoform disorders?

- In *somatoform disorders*, people believe they are sick when they are not.
- *Hypochondriasis* is a somatoform disorder in which a person is terrified of becoming ill, characterized by a preoccupation with bodily symptoms and frequent visits to doctors to find a diagnosis for the imagined illness.
- *Somatization disorder* is a somatoform disorder in which a person complains of one specific symptom in dramatic language using words such as "unbearable," becomes dependent on a healthcare professional, demands constant attention, and has symptoms that change frequently.
- *Conversion disorder* is a somatoform disorder characterized by symptoms specific to the somatic nervous system, such as numbness, blindness, or paralysis that have no real physical cause, disappearing when the person is in an altered state of consciousness.

FAST FACT

Up to 14 percent of patients examined for health problems in the United States have hypochondriasis. Ask students to estimate how much this costs per year in unnecessary procedures and examinations. *(Answer: over $20 billion)*

Class Demonstration (Kinesthetic)

SOMATOFORM SCENARIOS

<u>Purpose</u>: By writing scenarios displaying somatoform disorders, students become more familiar with the content.

<u>Time</u>: 30 minutes

<u>Description</u>: Divide the class into groups. Assign each group a somatoform disorder about which to write a short scenario. Stipulate that the scenarios should accurately display the symptoms of the disorder. Then have one or more group members read their scenario to the class. The audience can identify the disorders after the groups present their work.

CHAPTER 13 • Module 32

COVER THE MODULE

32.5 What are the different types of dissociative disorders and causes?

- *Dissociative disorders* involve a break or separation in conscious awareness, memory, and/or sense of identity.
- *Dissociative amnesia* symptoms include the inability to remember personal information such as a name or memories of personal events, usually due to a trauma experienced by the individual.

L⦿NK to Chapter Nine: Memory, pp. 281–283

- *Dissociative fugue* occurs when a person suddenly travels away from home and afterward cannot remember the trip or one's own identity.
- *Dissociative identity disorder* is characterized by at least two personalities existing in one body. Signs of this disorder include fugues, blackouts, and loss of memory and time.

MULTIMEDIA CONTENT AVAILABLE AT
www.mypsychlab.com

👁 **Watch** classic footage on *The Three Faces of Eve* on mypsychlab.com

L2 LPR DIFFERENTIATED INSTRUCTION

Less Proficient Readers Encourage these students to create mental pictures of the words as they read.

---

dissociative disorders disorders in which there is a separation in conscious awareness, memory, the sense of identity, or some combination.

dissociative amnesia loss of memory for personal information, either partial or complete.

dissociative fugue traveling away from familiar surroundings with amnesia for the trip and possible amnesia for personal information.

dissociative identity disorder disorder occurring when a person seems to have two or more distinct personalities within one body.

▲ On Christmas Day 1985, James McDonnell came home to his wife in Larchmont, New York, after 14 years of amnesia. After suffering two separate head injuries in auto accidents, he lost his memory. He went to Philadelphia and found a job in a restaurant. On Christmas Eve, according to Mr. McDonnell, he bumped his head and recovered all of his memories. Neurologists remain skeptical that a bump on the head can actually restore a person's memories, but Mr. McDonnell was somehow able to remember who he was and reunite with his wife (shown in this picture). What kinds of emotional and psychological adjustments do you think Mr. McDonnell and his family might have had to make upon his sudden return? Is it possible that his 14-year memory loss may have begun with the head injuries but was maintained for so long because of dissociation from his former life?

426 CHAPTER 13

32.5 What are the different types of dissociative disorders and their causes?

Dissociative disorders involve a break, or dissociation, in consciousness, memory, or a person's sense of identity. This separation is easier to understand if you think about how people sometimes drive somewhere and then wonder how they got there—they don't remember the trip itself at all. This sort of "automatic pilot" driving happens when the route is familiar and frequently traveled. One part of the conscious mind thinks about work, school, or whatever is uppermost in the mind, while lower centers of consciousness focus on driving the car, stopping at signs and lights, and turning when needed. This separation in conscious attention is very similar to what happens in dissociative disorders. The difference is that in the disorders the dissociation is much more pronounced and involuntary.

Dissociative Amnesia You may already know that *amnesia* is a term for memory loss. In **dissociative amnesia**, one cannot remember personal information such as one's own name or specific personal events—the kind of information contained in episodic long-term memory. L⦿NK to Chapter Nine: Memory, pp. 281–283. This memory loss is usually associated with a stressful or emotionally traumatic experience, such as rape or childhood abuse (Chu et al., 1999; Kirby et al., 1993), and cannot be easily explained by simple forgetfulness. It can be a loss of memory for only one small segment of time, or it can involve a total loss of one's past personal memories.

These memories usually resurface, sometimes quickly, and sometimes after a long delay. In one case, a veteran of World War II had amnesia for the time during which he was captured, tortured, and escaped from the Far East. He did not recall these memories, or the fact that he had been an intelligence agent at the time, until 37 years later (Cassiday & Lyons, 1992).

Dissociative Fugue The Latin word *fugere* means "flight" and is the word from which the term *fugue* is taken. A **dissociative fugue** occurs when a person suddenly travels away from home (the flight), and afterward, cannot remember the trip or even personal information such as identity. The person may become confused about identity, sometimes even taking on a whole new identity in the new place (Nijenhuis, 2000). However, the person's skills and abilities learned in his or her previous life will remain intact. Such flights usually take place after an emotional trauma and are more common in times of disasters or war.

Dissociative Identity Disorder Perhaps the most controversial dissociative disorder is **dissociative identity disorder**, formerly known as multiple personality disorder. In this disorder, a person seems to experience at least two or more distinct personalities existing in one body. There may be a "core" personality, who usually knows nothing about the other personalities and is the one who experiences "blackouts" or losses of memory and time. Fugues are common in dissociative identity disorder, with the core personality experiencing unsettling moments of "awakening" in an unfamiliar place or with people who call the person by another name (Kluft, 1984).

With the release of several famous books and movies about dissociative identity disorder during the late 20th century, the disorder became well known

---

Explore

DISSOCIATIVE DISORDERS IN THE NEWS

Purpose: Students read more stories of dissociative disorders online.

Time: 30 minutes

Description: Ask students to read news articles describing the experiences of three people suffering from dissociative disorders.

- Dissociative fugue: "A Life, Interrupted"
  www.nytimes.com/2009/03/01/nyregion/thecity/
  01miss.html?pagewanted=all

- Dissociative amnesia: "Amnesia Patient Doesn't Know Who He Is"
  www.cbsnews.com/stories/2009/09/17/national/main531
  7268.shtml

- Dissociative identity disorder: "Inside Karen's Crowded Mind"
  www.newsweek.com/2007/10/20/inside-karen-s-crowded
  -mind.html
  NOTE: Be sure to preview this article. The description of Karen's childhood trauma may not be appropriate for all students.

426 Chapter 13 Psychological Disorders

to the public. For example, the controversial case of the patient known as "Sybil," who claimed to have 16 alternate personalities, became known worldwide with the publication of *Sybil* in 1973, followed by a film adaptation starring actress Sally Field. More recently, the diagnosis of dissociative identity disorder has come under close examination, with many (but not all) professionals now beginning to doubt the validity of previous diagnoses. Some psychological professionals believe that dissociative identity disorder is actually a misdiagnosis of borderline personality disorder or some other form of anxiety disorder (Lauer et al., 1993). ⊙-Watch on mypsychlab.com

⊙-Watch a classic footage on *The Three Faces of Eve* on mypsychlab.com

Causes of Dissociative Disorders Psychodynamic theory sees disassociation as a defense mechanism, a way for a person to repress threatening or unacceptable thoughts and thus reduce the emotional pain from a stressful or traumatic event (Dorahy, 2001).

Cognitive and behavioral explanations for dissociative disorders are connected: The person may feel guilt, shame, or anxiety when thinking about disturbing experiences or thoughts and start avoiding thoughts about them. This "thought avoidance" is negatively reinforced by the reduction of the anxiety and unpleasant feelings, and eventually, will become a habit of "not thinking about" these things. This is similar to what many people do when faced with something unpleasant or painful: They "think about something else." In doing that, they are deliberately not thinking about what is happening to them at the moment and the experience of pain is decreased. People with dissociative disorders may simply be better at doing this sort of "not thinking" than other people are.

There are some possible biological and cultural sources for dissociations as well. Researchers have found that people with *depersonalization disorder* (a mild dissociative disorder in which people feel detached and disconnected from their bodies and surroundings, sometimes referred to as "out-of-body" experiences) have lower brain activity in the areas responsible for their sense of body awareness than do people without the disorder (Simeon et al., 2000). Dissociative disorders can also be found in other cultures, although researchers believe that disorders such as dissociative amnesia may be more culture bound than universal (Pope et al., 2007).

32.6 What are the different types of mood disorders and their causes?

In psychological terms, the word **affect** is used to mean "emotion" or "mood." **Mood disorders**, also referred to as *affective disorders*, involve disturbances in emotion. Although the range of human emotions runs from deep, intense sadness and despair to extreme happiness and elation, under normal circumstances people stay in between those extremes—neither too sad nor too happy but content. It is when stress or some other factor pushes a person to an extreme state of emotion that mood disorders can result.

There are two relatively mild to moderate mood disorders. **Dysthymia** comes from Greek words meaning "bad spirit" and is a form of mild, persistent depression that lasts for at least 2 years or more (Klein et al., 2000). **Cyclothymia** means "spirit that moves in circles" and involves a cycle of being sad, then feeling quite happy, and then returning to sad, happy, sad, happy, and so on, with the cycle lasting 2 years or more. Like dysthymia, it usually begins in childhood or adolescence and includes times of normal feelings that may last less than 2 months at a time (APA, 2000). Both dysthymia and

affect in psychology, a term indicating "emotion" or "mood."

mood disorders disorders in which mood is severely disturbed.

dysthymia a moderate depression that lasts for 2 years or more and is typically a reaction to some external stressor.

cyclothymia disorder that consists of mood swings from moderate depression to hypomania and lasts 2 years or more.

PSYCHOLOGICAL DISORDERS 427

CHAPTER 13 • Module 32

COVER THE MODULE (continued)

- Causes of dissociative disorders include the following:
  - In the psychodynamic model, disassociation is a defense mechanism for a person to use to reduce repressed threatening thoughts or memories of a traumatic event.
  - In the cognitive and behavioral models, a person feels negative emotions when thinking about disturbing experiences, begins to avoid the memories, and eventually forms a habit of "not thinking about" what is creating anxiety.
  - In the biological model, some studies have shown lower brain activity in the areas responsible for body awareness, and evidence of these disorders has been found in other cultures, suggesting heritability.

COVER THE MODULE

32.6 What are the different types of mood disorders and their causes?

- *Affect* is emotion and mood.
- *Mood disorders*, a.k.a. affective disorders, are characterized by disturbances in emotion.
- *Dysthymia* is a mild depression that persists for at least 2 years.
- *Cyclothymia* involves cycling from happy to sad to happy again, lasting for 2 or more years.
  - Both dysthymia and cyclothymia occur in reaction to external life-changing events.

Module 32 Types of Psychological Disorders **427**

Critical Thinking

WRITING ABOUT PSYCHOLOGY

Purpose: This activity is a precursor to the activity on the next page. Students begin to make connections to the discussion of depression in the text by thinking of a time they felt sad or depressed.

Time: 10 minutes

Description: Play the song "Jumper" by the band Third Eye Blind. Ask students to listen to the song and think about its message and any personal connections they feel as they listen. Replay the song and ask students to write privately about a time of sadness or depression in their lives, in response to the following: (1) Describe when and where you were at the time. (2) What was the situation or cause for these feelings? (3) Was there anyone else involved? Who? Why? (4) Describe your thoughts and feelings. (5) How did this mental state affect your life or your ability to cope with day-to-day living?

CHAPTER 13 • Module 32

COVER THE MODULE (continued)

- *Major depression* includes symptoms such as the following:
  - A depressed mood that lasts for most of every day for 2 or more weeks
  - Taking no pleasure in any experiences
  - Exhaustion
  - Feelings of guilt and worthlessness
  - Disruption in sleep and appetite
  - Thoughts of suicide

UNDERSTANDING VISUALS

Direct students' attention to Figure 32.4. Ask students to hypothesize about why the diagnosis of depression has increased in recent years. *(Possible answers include the following: more people are seeking help; the pace of everyday life has increased and become more stressful and demanding due to longer working hours, less job security, economic hardship, and technological advances that require us to be "plugged in" to work at all times.)*

FAST FACTS

- Approximately 3 to 5 percent of teens experience clinical depression every year.
- Approximately 25 percent of high school students have considered suicide.
- The teen suicide rate has tripled in recent years.

Extreme sadness | Mild sadness | Normal emotions | Mild elation | Extreme elation

FIGURE 32.3 The Range of Emotions
Most people experience a range of emotions over the course of a day or several days, such as mild sadness, calm contentment, or mild elation and happiness. A person with a mood disorder experiences emotions that are extreme and, therefore, abnormal.

cyclothymia usually occur in reaction to external events such as the loss of a job or the death of a loved one.

It is normal to get sad every now and then and even to have mild "mood swings" on occasion. (See Figure 32.3.) But people experiencing normal sadness or moodiness usually return to normal relatively quickly. There's also usually a specific reason for normal sadness. Although both dysthymia and cyclothymia can be triggered by external, stressful events, they go on too long to be considered normal reactions that need no treatment or attention.

Major Depression Major depression is a mood disorder characterized by a depressed mood that lasts for at least 2 weeks, a loss of interest or pleasure in activities, and several other symptoms, such as feelings of worthlessness and exhaustion. People suffering from major depression are depressed for most of every day, take little or no pleasure in any activities, feel tired, have trouble sleeping or sleep too much, experience changes in appetite and significant weight changes, experience excessive guilt or feelings of worthlessness, have trouble concentrating, and may have thoughts of death or suicide, including suicide attempts. Suicide is a real risk faced by people suffering from major depression. Some people with this disorder also suffer from delusional thinking and may experience hallucinations (APA, 2000).

Major depression is the most common of the diagnosed mood disorders (see Figure 32.4) and is about twice as common in women as it is in men (APA,

major depression a mood disorder characterized by a depressed mood that lasts for at least 2 weeks, a loss of interest or pleasure in activities, and several other symptoms, such as feelings of worthlessness and exhaustion.

FIGURE 32.4 Prevalence of Major Depression
Currently the most common mood disorder, major depression has seen an increase in diagnosis with each decade. From 1936 to 1945, the prevalence of major depression in the population was about 3 percent, with the onset of symptoms occurring at around ages 18 to 20. By 1966 to 1975, the prevalence had jumped to about 23 percent of the population, and the age of onset had dropped to the early teens.

428 CHAPTER 13

Class Demonstration

GETTING THE WORD OUT ABOUT DEPRESSION

Purpose: Students make a deeper connection to the content by learning how depression affects their peers and role models.

Time: One class period

Description: Have students view the video "Depression: On the Edge," which is co-hosted by the band Third Eye Blind and funded by PBS. Information about the video's content, how to locate it, and additional lesson connections can be found at this website: **www.pbs.org/inthemix/depression_index.html**

After viewing the video, open the class up for unstructured discussion, allowing students to share their thoughts on viewing the video. Ask them to think about why you are presenting this lesson and what they have learned from it. Finally, discuss methods for students helping themselves or a friend who suffers from depression: *talk, listen, and get help*.

428 Chapter 13 Psychological Disorders

2000). This is true even across various cultures (Blazer et al., 1994; Weissman et al., 1993). Though some believe this gender difference can be explained by differences in hormones and brain structure, research has found little support for hormonal influences and other biological factors in depression. Instead, studies have found that the degree of difference between male and female rates of depression is decreasing and is nonexistent in college students and single adults, leading some to conclude that social factors such as marital status, career type, and number of children may have more importance in this issue than biological differences (McGrath et al., 1992; Nolen-Hoeksema, 1990; Weissman & Klerman, 1977). In addition, research by Susan Nolen-Hoeksema suggests that the way in which men and women cope with stress may explain the gender differences in depression: Women are more likely than men to ruminate, or think about their problems, when they are upset or distressed, and the tendency to ruminate can be a risk factor for depression (Nolen-Hoeksema et al., 1999).

Bipolar Disorders Major depression is sometimes referred to as a *unipolar disorder* because the emotional problem exists at only one end, or "pole," of the emotional range. When a person suffers from severe mood swings that go all the way from severe depression to **manic** episodes (excessive excitement, energy, and elation), that person is said to suffer from **bipolar disorder**, meaning that emotions cycle between the two poles of possible emotions (APA, 2000). Unlike cyclothymia, there is usually no external cause for the extreme ups and downs of the bipolar person. The depressive phases of a bipolar person are identical to major depression but give way to manic episodes that may last from a few weeks to a few months. In these manic episodes, the person is extremely happy or elated without any real cause to be so happy. Restlessness, irritability, an inability to sit still or remain inactive, and seemingly unlimited energy are also common. The person may seem silly to others and can become aggressive when not allowed to carry out the grand (and sometimes delusional) plans that are often the hallmark of the manic phase. Speech may be rapid and jump from one topic to another (Blumer, 2002; McDermott, 2001; Rothenberg, 2001). It's been suggested that a link exists between bipolar disorder and creativity, and several well-known artists and writers, such as the novelist Virginia Woolf and the poet Lord Byron, are believed by some experts to have suffered from bipolar disorder, creating their art during manic periods of intense creativity (Jamison, 1993). Watch on mypsychlab.com

Is there a relationship between bipolar disorder and hyperactivity disorders like ADHD?

There does seem to be a connection between attention-deficit hyperactivity disorder (ADHD) and the onset of bipolar disorder in adolescence (Carlson et al., 1998), but only a small percentage of children with ADHD go on to develop bipolar disorder. The symptoms of bipolar disorder include irrational thinking and other manic symptoms that are not present in ADHD (Geller et al., 1998). Confusion between the two disorders arises because hyperactivity (excessive movement and an inability to concentrate) is a symptom of both disorders.

Causes of Mood Disorders Psychodynamic theorists see depression as anger originally aimed at parents or other authority figures who are too threatening to receive the expressions of anger directly. The child represses the anger and later displaces it in the form of self-blame and self-hate.

manic having the quality of excessive excitement, energy, and elation or irritability.

bipolar disorder severe mood swings between major depressive episodes and manic episodes.

◀ Watch a video on bipolar disorder on mypsychlab.com

◀ Is there a relationship between bipolar disorder and hyperactivity disorders like ADHD?

CHAPTER 13 • Module 32

COVER THE MODULE (continued)

- Major depression is diagnosed in twice as many women as men.
  - Little support has been found for the theory that this is a result of hormones and brain structure.
  - The difference has been attributed to social factors such as marital status, career, and number of children.
  - Another theory explaining the difference pinpoints the idea that women dwell on their troubles much more than do men, which is a risk factor for depression.
- In bipolar disorder, an individual experiences severe mood swings, ranging from one pole (severe depression) to another (manic episodes) on the emotional spectrum.
  - *Mood swings* do not seem to have a specific cause, and time spent during a particular phase can last up to a few months.
  - *Manic* phases are characterized by extreme elation, endless energy, restlessness, grand and sometimes delusional ideas, and creativity.

MULTIMEDIA CONTENT AVAILABLE AT
www.mypsychlab.com

Watch a video on bipolar disorder on **mypsychlab.com**

Explore

BIPOLAR DISORDER

Purpose: Students read descriptions of famous persons' experiences with bipolar disorder to help them realize that not even well-known people are immune to mental illness. They can also conjecture about the link between bipolar disorder and creativity.

Time: 20 minutes

Description: Ask students to browse the Internet to research famous people who are known to have suffered from bipolar disorder. Students should choose a person to research further and read about the individual's life and experiences, recording moments when the person experienced manic (or depressive) episodes. Students should create a visual poster that includes a picture of the person, a description of why the person is or was famous, and a timeline of his or her life, indicating important moments, accomplishments, and bouts with the disorder. Allow students to share their research with the class.

CHAPTER 13 • Module 32

COVER THE MODULE (continued)
- Causes of mood disorders:
  - In the psychodynamic model, depression is anger originally aimed at authority figures the individual is afraid to confront, thereby repressing the anger and displacing it into self-hate.
  - In the social cognitive view, a cycle of self-defeating thoughts leads to depression, leads to more negative thoughts, and spins into a downward spiral.
  - The biological model explains mood disorders as being affected by neurotransmitters and genetics.

COVER THE MODULE
32.7 What are the main symptoms, types, and causes of schizophrenia?
- *Schizophrenia* is a psychotic disorder involving a break from reality, in which the person cannot distinguish between reality and fantasy.
- Symptoms of schizophrenia include the following:
  - *Delusions*, defined as false beliefs held by an individual who cannot accept that they are false, are most common.
  - Types of delusions include delusions of persecution, delusions of reference, delusions of influence, and delusions of grandeur.

In the social cognitive view, depressed people continually have negative, self-defeating thoughts about themselves, which depress them further in a downward spiral of despair. This link between negative thoughts and depression does not necessarily mean that negative thoughts *cause* depression; it may be that depression increases the likelihood of negative thoughts (Gotlib et al., 2001). One study found that when comparing adolescents who were depressed to those who were not, the depressed group faced risk factors specifically associated with the social cognitive environment: being female or a member of an ethnic minority; poverty; regular drug use (including tobacco and alcohol); and engaging in delinquent behavior (Costello et al., 2008). Those in the nondepressed group of adolescents were more likely to come from two-parent households, had higher self-esteem, and felt connected to parents, peers, and school.

Biological explanations of mood disorders focus on the effects of neurotransmitters such as serotonin, norepinephrine, and dopamine; drugs used to treat depression and mania typically affect the levels of these three neurotransmitters, either individually or in combination (Cohen, 1997; Cummings & Coffey, 1994; Ruhe et al., 2007). LINK to Chapter Two: The Biological Perspective, p. 46. Genes also play a part in mood disorders, as mood disorders tend to appear in genetically related individuals at a higher rate (Barondes, 1998; Farmer, 1996).

32.7 What are the main symptoms, types, and causes of schizophrenia?

Schizophrenia was named by Eugen Bleuler (oy-GAIN BLOY-luhr), a Swiss psychiatrist, to illustrate the division (*schizo-*) within the brain (*phren*) among thoughts, feelings, and behavior that seems to take place in people with this disorder (Bleuler, 1911; Möller & Hell, 2002). A more modern definition of schizophrenia describes it as a long-lasting **psychotic** disorder (involving a severe break or split with reality) in which the person cannot distinguish what is real from fantasy and experiences disturbances in thinking, emotions, behavior, and perception.

Schizophrenia includes several different kinds of symptoms, the most common of which are **delusions**. Although delusions are not prominent in all forms of schizophrenia, they are the symptom that most people associate with this disorder. Delusions are false beliefs about the world that the person holds; these beliefs tend to remain fixed and unshakable even in the face of evidence that disproves them. Common schizophrenic delusions include *delusions of persecution* in which people believe that others are trying to hurt them in some way; *delusions of reference* in which people believe that other people, television characters, and even books are specifically talking to them; *delusions of influence* in which people believe that they are being controlled by external forces, such as the devil, aliens, or cosmic forces; and *delusions of grandeur* in which people are convinced that they can save the world or have a special mission (APA, 2000). Contrary to popular belief, schizophrenia is *not* characterized by the development of multiple separate personalities. Dissociative identity disorder, the controversial disorder associated with the phenomenon of multiple personalities, is not the same as schizophrenia.

Dr. John Nash is a famous mathematician who won the Nobel Prize for economics in 1994. Dr. Nash's fame, however, is mostly due to the fact that

schizophrenia severe disorder in which the person suffers from disordered thinking, bizarre behavior, hallucinations, and inability to distinguish between fantasy and reality.

psychotic term applied to a person who is no longer able to perceive what is real and what is fantasy.

delusions false beliefs held by a person who refuses to accept evidence of their falseness.

Class Demonstration

A MONOLOGUE DEMONSTRATING SCHIZOPHRENIA

Put a copy of the monologue below on a transparency or make photocopies and distribute them to the class. Tell students that the monologue demonstrates the language, thought processes, and effect of schizophrenia. Ask students to identify the key characteristics of the disorder.

I'd like to tell you about some personal experiences I've been having lately. You see, I've [pause] been involved in high-abstract [pause] type of contract [pause], which I might try to distract [pause] from your gaze [pause] if it were a new craze [pause]; but the sun god has put me into it. [pause] The planet of the lost star [pause] is before you know [pause] and so you'd better not try to be as if you were one with him [pause] always fails because one and one makes three [pause], and that is the word for three [pause], which must be like the tiger after his prey [pause]; and the zommon is not common [pause]—it is a zommon's zommon. [pause] But really class, [holding your head and pausing] what do you think about what I am thinking about right now? You can hear my thoughts, can't you? I'm thinking I'm crazy, and I know you [point to a student] put that thought in my mind. You put that thought there! Or could it be that the dentist did as I thought? She did! I thought she put that radio transmitter into my brain when I had the Novocain! She's making me think this way and she's stealing my thoughts!

he once suffered from a form of schizophrenia in which he experienced delusions of persecution. He, at one time, believed that aliens were trying to contact him through the newspaper (delusions of reference). His life story and his remarkable management of the symptoms of schizophrenia are portrayed in the 2001 movie *A Beautiful Mind*, which starred Russell Crowe as Nash (Kuhn & Nasar, 2001; Nasar, 1998).

Delusional thinking alone is not enough to merit a diagnosis of schizophrenia. There is a separate category of psychotic disorders called **delusional disorders** in which the primary symptom is some form of delusion. In schizophrenia, other symptoms must be present (APA, 2000; Black & Andreasen, 1999). Speech disturbances are common: People with schizophrenia will make up words, repeat words or sentences persistently, string words together on the basis of sounds (called *clanging*; an example would be something like "come into house, louse, mouse, mouse and cheese, please, sneeze"), and experience sudden interruptions in speech or thought. People suffering from schizophrenia have disturbed thoughts as well; they often have a hard time linking their thoughts together in a logical fashion.

People with schizophrenia may also have **hallucinations** in which they hear voices or see things or people that are not really there. Hearing voices is the more common symptom; it is actually one of the key symptoms in making a diagnosis of schizophrenia. Hallucinations involving touch, smell, and taste are less common but also possible. Although the movie portrayed Nash as having visual hallucinations, he says that in reality he heard voices that he eventually learned to ignore, although he was never cured (Nasar, 1998).

Emotional disturbances are also a key feature of schizophrenia. **Flat affect** is a condition in which the person shows little or no emotion. Emotions can also be excessive and/or inappropriate—a person might laugh when it would be more appropriate to cry or show sorrow, for example.

The person's behavior may also become disorganized and extremely odd. For example, some forms of schizophrenia are accompanied by periods of complete immobility, whereas still others may involve weird facial grimaces and odd gesturing. According to APA (2000), at least two or more of the following symptoms must be present frequently for at least 1 month to diagnose schizophrenia: delusions, hallucinations, disturbed speech, disturbed emotions, and disturbed behavior.

Attention is also a problem for many people with schizophrenia. They seem to have trouble "screening out" information and stimulation that they don't really need, causing them to be unable to focus on information that is relevant (Asarnow et al., 1991).

Categories of Schizophrenia Although all people with schizophrenia share the symptoms already discussed to a certain degree, the way in which these symptoms show up in behavior can be used to distinguish among several different types of schizophrenia (APA, 2000).

People suffering from **disorganized** schizophrenia are very confused in speech, have vivid and frequent hallucinations, and tend to have very inappropriate affect (display of emotion) or flat affect. They are very socially impaired, unable to engage in the normal social rituals of daily life. Giggling, silliness, nonsensical speech, and neglect of cleanliness and hygiene are common.

▲ Actor Russell Crowe portrayed schizophrenic genius John Forbes Nash in the 2001 film *A Beautiful Mind.*

delusional disorder a psychotic disorder in which the primary symptom is one or more delusions.

hallucinations false sensory perceptions, such as hearing voices that do not really exist.

flat affect a lack of emotional responsiveness.

disorganized type of schizophrenia in which behavior is bizarre and childish and thinking, speech, and motor actions are very disordered.

CHAPTER 13 • Module 32

COVER THE MODULE (continued)

- Speech disturbances such as rhyming, repetition, pauses or interruptions in flow of speech, or made-up words
- *Hallucinations*: false sensory perceptions
- *Flat affect*: a condition in which a person shows little or no emotion
- Excessive or inappropriate emotion
- Disturbed or bizarre behavior
- Categories of schizophrenia include the following:
  - *Disorganized*: symptoms include confused speech, vivid and frequent hallucinations, inappropriate or flat affect, and neglect of hygiene.

TEACHING TIP

When creating student work groups, consider a mix of learning styles, ability levels, genders, and cultural or ethnic backgrounds. Group members should be rotated frequently.

Class Discussion

PSYCHOLOGY IN FILM

Show segments from the movie *A Beautiful Mind,* depicting the true story of Dr. John Nash. Ask students to record signs and symptoms of schizophrenia as they appear in the film segments. Allow students to share their remarks with the class. What comments do they have about what they saw in the film?

CHAPTER 13 • Module 32

COVER THE MODULE (continued)

- *Catatonic*: symptoms include disturbed motor behavior in which the individual does not respond to the outside world and either holds a pose for hours or cannot stop moving about wildly.
- *Paranoid*: symptoms include hallucinations and persistent, unshakable delusions.
- *Positive symptoms*: addition of new behaviors or distortion of normal functions.
- *Negative symptoms*: a decrease of normal functions.
- Causes of schizophrenia:
  - Biopsychosocial is the ruling model, with research suggesting genetics, chemical influences, and brain structural defects. Evidence suggests that schizophrenia is consistent among cultures, with 1 percent of the world population suffering from the illness, regardless of culture.

---

catatonic type of schizophrenia in which the person experiences periods of statue-like immobility mixed with occasional bursts of energetic, frantic movement, and talking.

paranoid type of schizophrenia in which the person suffers from delusions of persecution, grandeur, and jealousy, together with hallucinations.

positive symptoms symptoms of schizophrenia that are excesses of behavior or occur in addition to normal behavior; hallucinations, delusions, and distorted thinking.

negative symptoms symptoms of schizophrenia that are less than normal behavior or an absence of normal behavior; poor attention, flat affect, and poor speech production.

> There's something I don't understand. If one identical twin has the gene and the disorder, shouldn't the other one always have it, too? Why is the rate only 50 percent? ▶

Catatonic schizophrenia is an increasingly rare form of the disorder that involves very disturbed motor behavior. The person doesn't respond to the outside world and either doesn't move at all, maintaining often odd-looking postures for hours on end (a condition known as *catatonia*), or moves about wildly in great agitation. It's as if there are only two "speeds" for the catatonic, totally off or totally on.

People diagnosed with **paranoid** schizophrenia suffer from hallucinations and delusions. Auditory hallucinations ("hearing things") are common, and the delusions typically take the form of feelings of persecution, grandeur, or extreme jealousy toward others. Although their thinking is not as scattered as that of someone with disorganized schizophrenia, people with paranoid schizophrenia have delusions that tend to be extremely unusual but very systematic and unshakable.

Another way of categorizing schizophrenia is to look at the kind of symptoms that predominate. **Positive symptoms** appear to reflect the addition of new behavior or distortion of normal functions, such as hallucinations and delusions. **Negative symptoms** appear to reflect a decrease or subtraction of normal functions, such as poor attention or lack of affect (APA, 2000).

Positive symptoms are associated with overactivity in the dopamine-producing areas of the brain. Dopamine-reducing drugs used to treat schizophrenia are usually effective on these symptoms, and the outlook for effective treatment of symptoms is generally good (Davis et al., 1991; Penn, 1998; Rosenzweig et al., 1996).

Negative symptoms include the inability to filter out stimuli to focus attention, flat affect, problems with producing speech, apathy, and withdrawal from others. Negative symptoms, unlike positive symptoms, are associated with *lower* than normal activity in the dopamine systems of the brain and problems in the functioning of the frontal lobe.

Causes of Schizophrenia When trying to explain the cause or causes of schizophrenia, the biopsychological model prevails. Supporters of this model have generated a significant amount of research pointing to genetic origins, chemical influences (dopamine), and brain structural defects as the causes of schizophrenia (Gottesman & Shields, 1982; Harrison, 1999; Kety et al., 1994). Further support for a biological explanation of schizophrenia comes from studies of the disorder across different cultures. If schizophrenia were caused mainly by environmental factors, then rates of schizophrenia would vary widely from culture to culture. In fact, schizophrenia occurs in approximately 1 percent of the population, regardless of the culture (Torrey, 1987), and the disease has most likely existed throughout human history.

The highest risk for developing schizophrenia if one has a blood relative with the disorder is faced by monozygotic (identical) twins, who share 100 percent of their genetic material, with a risk factor of about 50 percent (Gottesman & Shields, 1976, 1982; Gottesman et al., 1987). Dizygotic twins, who share about 50 percent of their genetic material, have about a 17 percent risk, the same as a child with one schizophrenic parent. As genetic relatedness decreases, so does the risk (see Figure 32.5).

There's something I don't understand. If one identical twin has the gene and the disorder, shouldn't the other one always have it, too? Why is the rate only 50 percent?

Critical Thinking

DISPELLING MYTHS ABOUT SCHIZOPHRENIA

Purpose: Students discuss misconceptions about schizophrenia.

Time: 15 minutes

Description: Read the statements below one at a time to the class. Ask students to raise their hand if they believe a statement to be true and to do nothing if they believe it to be false. Before revealing the correct answer, allow students to share their reasons and support for their stance. Then explain the correct answers.

- Schizophrenia leads to split or multiple personalities. *In truth, schizophrenia is a disorder in which the individual experiences a break with reality, not different personalities, as is the case in dissociative identity disorder.*
- Schizophrenia is a rare condition. *The risk of developing schizophrenia is about 1 percent, or 1 in 100.*
- Schizophrenics are dangerous. *Most people with schizophrenia are neither dangerous nor violent.*
- Schizophrenia is untreatable. *When treated properly, many people with schizophrenia can function normally.*

FIGURE 32.5 Genetics and Schizophrenia
This graph shows a definite pattern: the greater the degree of genetic relatedness, the higher the risk of schizophrenia in individuals related to each other. The only individual to carry a risk even close to that of identical twins (who share 100 percent of their genes) is a person who is the child of two schizophrenic parents. **Source:** Gottesman (1991).

Relatedness	Category	Lifetime risk
Third-degree relatives	General population	1%
	Spouses of patients	2%
	First cousins	2%
Second-degree relatives	Uncles/aunts	2%
	Nephews/nieces	4%
	Grandchildren	5%
	Half-siblings	6%
First-degree relatives	Children	12%
	Siblings	9%
	Siblings (with schizophrenic parent)	17%
	Dizygotic twins	17%
	Parents	6%
	Monozygotic twins	48%
	Offspring of two schizophrenic parents	46%

If schizophrenia were entirely controlled by genes, identical twins would indeed both have the disorder at a risk of 100 percent, not merely 50 percent. Obviously, there is some influence of environment on the development of schizophrenia. One model that has been proposed is the **stress-vulnerability model**, which assumes that people with the genetic "markers" for schizophrenia have a physical vulnerability to the disorder but will not develop schizophrenia unless they are exposed to environmental or emotional stress at critical times in development, such as puberty (Harrison, 1999; Weinberger, 1987). That would explain why only one twin out of a pair might develop the disorder when both carry the genetic markers for schizophrenia—the life stresses for the affected twin were different from those of the one who remained healthy. ⊙▶ Simulate on mypsychlab.com

⊙▶ Simulate the diagnosis of schizophrenia on mypsychlab.com

32.8 What are the different types of personality disorders and their causes?

Personality disorders are a little different from other psychological disorders in that they do not affect merely one aspect of the person's life, as would be the case with a higher than normal level of anxiety or a set of distorted beliefs, but instead affect the person's entire life adjustment. The disorder is the personality itself, not one aspect of it. A person with a personality disorder has an excessively rigid, maladaptive pattern of behavior and ways of relating to others (APA, 2000). This rigidity and inability to adapt to social demands and life changes makes it very difficult for the individual with a personality disorder to fit in with others or have relatively normal social relationships.

stress-vulnerability model explanation of disorder that assumes a biological sensitivity, or vulnerability, to a certain disorder will result in the development of that disorder under the right conditions of environmental or emotional stress.

personality disorders disorders in which a person adopts a persistent, rigid, and maladaptive pattern of behavior that interferes with normal social interactions.

PSYCHOLOGICAL DISORDERS 433

CHAPTER 13 • Module 32

COVER THE MODULE (continued)

- Schizophrenia is not entirely controlled by genes; the *stress-vulnerability model* suggests that while a person has the genetic predisposition, environmental factors including exposure to stress at critical times in development, such as puberty, are believed to trigger the onset of the disorder.

COVER THE MODULE

32.8 What are the different types of personality disorders and their causes?

- *Personality disorders* are composed of a persistent, rigid, and maladaptive pattern of behavior that makes it difficult for an individual to fit in with others and have normal relationships.

UNDERSTANDING VISUALS

Discuss with students the following questions: According to Figure 32.5, who has the *least* risk of developing schizophrenia genetically? Who has the most risk? How is risk determined?

MULTIMEDIA CONTENT AVAILABLE AT
www.mypsychlab.com

⊙▶ Simulate the diagnosis of schizophrenia on mypsychlab.com

L2 TEACHING TIP

Requiring students to prepare portfolios gives them a valuable tool for career development. Portfolio materials should appear in several forms, including writing, visual presentations, and notes from oral presentations. When selecting materials, students should decide what benchmarks to use for assessing their work.

Class Demonstration (Kinesthetic)

REVIEWING THE SYMPTOMS OF SCHIZOPHRENIA

Place signs throughout the classroom, one for "Disorganized Schizophrenia," one for "Catatonic Schizophrenia," and one for "Paranoid Schizophrenia." Read symptoms in random order for each of the disorders and have the students move to the appropriate area of the room for the type of schizophrenia the symptoms describe. Some symptoms appear in more than one type of schizophrenia, so be sure to note that with the class during this review session.

Module 32 Types of Psychological Disorders 433

CHAPTER 13 • Module 32

COVER THE MODULE (continued)

- Three categories of personality disorders are listed in the *DSM-IV-TR*: (1) odd or eccentric, (2) dramatic or erratic, and (3) anxious or fearful.
- In the *antisocial personality disorder*, a person is literally "against society" in that he or she has no morals or conscience, is manipulative, and acts without regard for consequences.

L2 TEACHING TIP

Remind students that as their vocabulary skills improve, so do their other communication skills, including speaking and writing. Suggest to students that they keep lists of any new words they add to their vocabulary daily.

Table 32.2   The Personality Disorders

PERSONALITY DISORDER	DESCRIPTION
Odd or Eccentric Types	
Paranoid	Extreme suspicion of others; mistrustful, often jealous
Schizoid	Loners who are cool, distant, and unwilling and unable to form close relationships with others
Schizotypal	Difficulty in forming social relationships, odd and eccentric behavior, tendency to hold magical beliefs
Dramatic or Erratic Types	
Antisocial	Lacking in conscience or morals; users and con artists who experience no regret or strong emotions
Borderline	Moody, unstable, lacking in a clear sense of identity, clinging to others
Histrionic	Tendency to overreact and use excessive emotions to draw attention from and manipulate others. Desire to be the center of attention
Narcissistic	Extremely vain and self-involved
Anxious or Fearful Types	
Avoidant	Fearful of social relationships, tend to avoid social contacts unless absolutely necessary
Dependent	Needy, want others to make decisions for them
Obsessive-Compulsive	Controlling, focused on neatness and order to an extreme degree (not to be confused with obsessive-compulsive disorder, or OCD, which is an anxiety disorder rather than a personality disorder)

Adapted from the American Psychiatric Association (APA), *DSM-IV-TR* (2000).

There are three basic categories of personality disorders listed in the *DSM-IV-TR* (APA, 2000): those in which the people are seen as odd or eccentric by others, those in which the behavior of the person is very dramatic or erratic, and those in which the main emotion is anxiety or fearfulness. There are 10 recognized personality disorders (see Table 32.2 above).

antisocial personality disorder
disorder in which a person has no morals or conscience, manipulates others, and often behaves in an impulsive manner without regard for the consequences of that behavior.

Antisocial Personality Disorder   One of the most well researched of the personality disorders is **antisocial personality disorder**. People with antisocial personality disorder are literally "against society" (its rules, expectations, and norms). The antisocial person, sometimes called a *sociopath* or *psychopath*, habitually breaks the law, disobeys rules, tells lies, and uses other

434   CHAPTER 13

Class Demonstration

PROFILING PERSONALITY DISORDERS

Purpose: Students apply the information in Table 32.2 to synthesize a fictional character with a personality disorder.

Time: 30 minutes

Description: Assign each student a personality disorder described in Table 32.2. Allow students time to imagine a fictional character and situations that character would find himself or herself in while displaying the symptoms and behaviors of the disorder. Students should then create posters to display in the classroom. They should write out the symptoms listed in Table 32.2, followed by paragraphs discussing how their fictional character would display each symptom. Have volunteers review their posters with the rest of the class.

people without worrying about their rights or feelings. In Freudian terms, the antisocial personality has no superego or a very weak superego and, therefore, has no real conscience to create guilty feelings when the person does something morally wrong. As a consequence, people with this disorder typically feel no remorse or guilt at lying, cheating, stealing, or even more serious crimes such as murder.

The first thing that usually comes to most people's minds when they hear the term *sociopath* is the *serial killer*, a person who kills others for the excitement and thrill of killing without feeling any guilt. However, most antisocial personalities are not killers. Typically, they borrow money or belongings and don't bother to repay the debt or return the items; they are impulsive; they don't keep their commitments, either socially or in their jobs; and they tend to be very selfish, self-centered, manipulative, and unable to feel deep emotions.

There is a definite gender difference in antisocial personality disorder with three to six times as many males diagnosed with this disorder as females (APA, 2000; Paris, 2004).

Borderline Personality Disorder People who suffer from **borderline personality disorder** are considered to be "on the border" between being in touch with reality and being in a psychotic state. These individuals have relationships with other people that are intense and relatively unstable. They are often moody, manipulative, and untrusting of others. Periods of depression are not unusual, and some may engage in excessive spending, drug abuse, or suicidal behavior (suicide attempts may be part of the manipulation the borderline personality uses in his or her relationships). Emotions are often inappropriate and excessive, leading to confusion with *histrionic personality disorder*. What makes the borderline different is the confusion over identity issues in which the person may be unable to focus on consistent life goals, career choices, friendships, and sexual behavior (APA, 2000).

The frequency of this disorder in women is two to three times greater than in men (APA, 2000; Swartz et al., 1990). Numerous causes such as genetic or hormonal influences, childhood abuse, and a poor mother–infant relationship during the years in which identity is forming have all been suggested as a cause of the disorder (Torgersen, 2000; Widiger & Weissman, 1991; Zanarini, 2000).

Causes of Personality Disorders There is some evidence of genetic factors in personality disorders. Close biological relatives of people with antisocial, schizotypal, and borderline disorders are more likely to have these disorders than those who are not related, for example (APA, 2000; Battaglia et al., 1995; Faraone et al., 1999; Nigg & Goldsmith, 1994). Adoption studies of children whose biological parents had antisocial personality disorder show an increased risk for that disorder in those children, even though the children were raised in a different environment by different people (APA, 2000).

Other causes of personality disorders have been suggested. Antisocial personalities are emotionally unresponsive to stressful or threatening situations when compared to others, which may be one reason that they are not afraid of getting caught (Arnett et al., 1997; Blair et al., 1995; Lykken, 1995).

borderline personality disorder maladaptive personality pattern in which the person is moody, unstable, lacks a clear sense of identity, and often clings to others.

CHAPTER 13 • Module 32

COVER THE MODULE (continued)

- People with antisocial personality disorder typically feel no remorse for actions such as lying, stealing, or even murder.
- *Borderline personality disorder* describes an individual's state on the borderline of reality and a psychotic state, characterized by unstable or intense relationships, moodiness, and inappropriate and excessive emotions.
  - A person with this disorder has no clear sense of identity, is unable to focus on things like career goals or friendships, and displays erratic sexual behavior.
- Causes of personality disorders have largely been attributed to biological factors.
  - Evidence suggests genetics play a role; close biological relatives of those with personality disorders have a higher chance of developing them.
- People with antisocial personality disorder show lower than normal levels of stress hormones, possibly explaining the lack of fear of consequences for negative behaviors.

FAST FACT

Symptoms of personality disorders tend to manifest differently in teens than in adults. For example, when it comes to unstable relationships, teens differ in that they have a tendency to distort the nature of relationships, such as believing that a teacher is a "girlfriend" or "boyfriend." Other differences manifest in impulsive behaviors; adults will tend to overspend money or drive recklessly, and teens will run away from home, participate in sexual acts beyond their maturity, or abuse drugs.

Critical Thinking

TEEN MOODINESS OR BORDERLINE PERSONALITY DISORDER?

Teens are famous for being irritable and moody, not to mention expressing erratic behavior as they explore who they are and who they want to be. So how is this different from the description of borderline personality disorder? Teens can read the following two articles to find out. After differences they read about and record their responses on the board.

- "An Emotional Hair Trigger, Often Misread"
  www.nytimes.com/2009/06/16/health/16brod.html?_r=2

- Dr. Alec Miller, a professor of psychiatry, has spent 15 years working with adolescents with BDP and responds to questions about the differences in his article "Teen Moodiness, or Borderline Personality Disorder?" http://consults.blogs.nytimes.com/2010/02/25/borderline-personality-disorder-in-teenagers/

CHAPTER 13 • Module 32

COVER THE MODULE

32.9 How can family and social influences affect the experience of mental illness?

- When a person is genetically predisposed to a mental illness, negative environmental factors can contribute to causing the disorder to manifest, and positive environmental factors can lessen the possibility that the disorder will arise.
  - Negative environmental factors include abusive family relationships, personal tragedies, neglect, and low socioeconomic status.
  - Positive environmental factors include healthy parent–child relationships, economic independence, and a general sense of support and security.

APPLYING PSYCHOLOGY TO EVERYDAY LIFE

- *Seasonal affective disorder (SAD)* is a mood disorder caused by the body's reaction to lack of sunlight during winter months, which likely interrupts the body's biological clock.
- Symptoms include daytime sleepiness, lack of energy, overeating, and weight gain.
- Treatment of SAD can include antidepressants, but daily exposure to artificial daylight, known as *phototherapy*, has been most effective.

This unresponsiveness seems to be linked to lower than normal levels of stress hormones in antisocial people (Lykken, 1995).

Disturbances in family relationships and communication have also been linked to personality disorders and, in particular, to antisocial personality disorder (Benjamin, 1996; Livesley, 1995). It is safe to say that many of the same factors (genetics, social relationships, and parenting) that help to create ordinary personalities also create disordered personalities.

32.9 How can family and social influences affect the experience of mental illness?

While environmental influences such as parenting and social relationships do not generally cause mental illness, these factors can cause a person who is genetically predisposed toward an illness to develop the illness. For example, unsupportive or abusive family relationships can aggravate mental illness, as can low socioeconomic status and lack of community support. There is a strong correlation between poverty and mental illness: The stress and negativity experienced as a result of poverty can lead to disorders such as anxiety, depression, and substance abuse (Dohrenwend et al., 1992). Other factors that can negatively influence those with a tendency toward psychological disorders are academic failure, family conflict, personal tragedies, child abuse, and neglect. However, positive family and social influences, such as a healthy parent–child relationship and economic independence, can protect those at risk of mental illnesses by offering stability, support, and security. This isn't to say that if a person comes from a supportive family or community, they *won't* develop a mental illness; it's just less likely.

Applying Psychology to Everyday Life

Seasonal Affective Disorder

Some people find that they only get depressed at certain times of the year. In particular, depression seems to set in during the winter months and goes away during spring and summer. This could be a sign of **seasonal affective disorder (SAD),** a mood disorder caused by the body's reaction to low levels of light present in the winter months (Partonen & Lonnqvist, 1998).

In some people, especially those who live in northern climates where winter is long and the days are very short, the biological clock gets out of "step." This can cause feelings of daytime sleepiness and a lack of energy that the mind interprets as depression. Other symptoms include excessive eating, a craving for sugary and starchy foods, excessive sleeping, and weight gain. The worst months for SAD are January and February, and true SAD disappears in the spring and summer.

Treatment of SAD can include antidepressant drugs, but one of the most effective treatments is **phototherapy,** or daily exposure to bright light (Terman, 2001). Lamps are used to create an "artificial daylight" for a certain number of hours during each day, and the person with SAD sits under that light. Milder symptoms can be controlled with more time spent outdoors when the sun is shining and increasing the amount of sunlight that comes into the workplace or home (see Figure 32.6).

seasonal affective disorder (SAD) a mood disorder caused by the body's reaction to low levels of sunlight in the winter months.

phototherapy the use of lights to treat seasonal affective disorder or other disorders.

Explore

CONTRIBUTING TO THE MENTAL HEALTH OF LOVED ONES

<u>Purpose</u>: Students learn about how to promote mental wellness in their families and communities.

<u>Time</u>: 20 minutes

<u>Description</u>: Allow students to browse the following website. Then ask them to create a one- or two-page brochure reporting what they have learned. Post the brochures around the classroom.

<u>Website</u>: UNC Center for Excellence in Community Mental Health at:
www.unccmh.org/clients-and-families/learn-about-mental-illness/a-family-guide/vi-how-families-can-help/

FIGURE 32.6 Prevalence of SAD in the United States
These data, gathered by Steven G. Potkin and his associates (from Wurtman & Wurtman, 1989), indicate considerably higher rates of seasonal affective disorder (SAD) in the northern latitudes. For example, Washington, Minnesota, and Maine have more than three times the levels of SAD as Florida, Louisiana, and Arizona. Shorter winter days in the more northern areas are thought to trigger a change in the brain's biochemistry resulting in SAD.

Legend:
- MORE THAN .90
- .70 TO .89
- .50 TO .69
- .20 TO .49
- LESS THAN .19
- *SAMPLE SIZE TOO SMALL TO BE STATISTICALLY RELIABLE

CHAPTER 13 • Module 32

UNDERSTANDING VISUALS

Have students look at Figure 32.6 and determine how prevalent SAD is in their area. Ask students to take a moment to write about how they feel during the winter months and whether these emotions are likely symptoms of seasonal affective disorder. Allow students to share with the class.

EXTEND THE LESSON

Experts know that SAD is somehow triggered by the brain's response to low daylight exposure. But how? Researchers believe it has to do with the two hormones, melatonin and serotonin, which help regulate the body's sleep–wake cycles, energy, and mood.

Melatonin is present in the body in greater quantities during periods of darkness or shorter days and is believed to send the body signals to go to sleep. Increased melatonin can create feelings of lethargy, sleepiness, and lower levels of energy. Serotonin is the opposite of melatonin and is present in increasing quantities during periods of daylight. Low levels of serotonin have been linked to depression and can explain why depression increases during the winter months when days are shorter and periods of darkness are longer.

Class Demonstration

WRITING ABOUT PSYCHOLOGICAL DISORDERS

Have students quickly review the list of this module's learning objectives on p. 418, and select one on which to focus. Tell students to write one or two paragraphs in answer to the question posed in the learning objective they chose. Then call on volunteers to read their answers to the class. Ask students from the other groups to say if they think the questions were answered correctly.

CHAPTER 13 • Module 32

Assess

Assign the Module 32 Practice Quiz.

Use the Practice Quiz to identify gaps in student understanding.

REMEDIATE

Have students, individually or in groups, review the module goals, learning objectives, and key terms.

Refer students to the Concept Summary on pp. 442–443 for review.

Close

Revisit the posters made during the Bellringer exercise at the beginning of the module. Ask students to consider their initial ideas about mental illness and discuss how their views have changed or been elaborated upon. Record their comments on the poster in a different-colored marker to show the contrast.

Practice Quiz

Pick the best answer.

1. In the *DSM-IV-TR*, Axis I contains information about
   a. clinical disorders
   b. general medical conditions
   c. global assessment of functioning
   d. psychosocial and environmental problems

2. Alex hates to go over bridges. This is a mild form of
   a. social phobia
   b. specific phobia
   c. agoraphobia
   d. claustrophobia

3. The controversial condition formerly known as multiple personality disorder is now called
   a. panic disorder
   b. depersonalization disorder
   c. generalized anxiety disorder
   d. dissociative identity disorder

4. Which of the following mood disorders is most commonly diagnosed?
   a. dysthymia
   b. cyclothymia
   c. bipolar disorder
   d. major depression

5. Which of the following statements about antisocial personality disorder is TRUE?
   a. Most people with this disorder are serial killers.
   b. Most people with this disorder are men.
   c. People with this disorder suffer terrible guilt but commit crimes anyway.
   d. People with this disorder feel emotions very deeply and intensely.

6. Which of the following is a negative symptom of schizophrenia?
   a. delusions
   b. lack of affect
   c. hallucinations
   d. distorted thinking

7. Which axis of the *DSM-IV-TR* would a therapist use to classify the loss of a person's job?
   a. I
   b. II
   c. III
   d. IV

8. When anxiety is not related to any known, realistic factor, it is called
   a. panic
   b. a phobia
   c. free-floating anxiety
   d. generalized anxiety disorder

9. Drugs used to treat schizophrenia
   a. decrease blood flow to the brain
   b. decrease the activity of dopamine
   c. restructure the brain's frontal lobe
   d. effectively cure negative symptoms

10. Which disorder is characterized by severe mood swings, intense energy, and intense sadness?
    a. dysthymia
    b. bipolar disorder
    c. cyclothymia
    d. major depression

Practice Quiz Answers

1. a
2. b
3. d
4. d
5. b
6. b
7. d
8. c
9. b
10. b

CHAPTER 13 Summary

Listen on mypsychlab.com

Module 31: Defining Abnormal Behavior
Understand historical, cultural, and current views of abnormality.

31.1 How has mental illness been explained in the past and in other cultures?
- In ancient times, holes were cut in an ill person's head to let out evil spirits. Hippocrates believed mental illness came from an imbalance in the body's four humors, whereas in the Middle Ages the mentally ill were labeled as witches.

31.2 What is psychologically abnormal behavior?
- Abnormal behavior is any pattern of behavior that causes people significant distress, causes them to harm themselves or others, or harms their ability to function in daily life.

31.3 What are the major models of abnormality?
- Biological models propose that psychological disorders have a biological cause. Psychological models explain disordered behavior as the result of thought-related malfunctions. The biopsychosocial model proposes that biological, psychological, and sociological factors interact to cause abnormal behavior.

31.4 What is stigma, and how does it relate to mental illness?
- Stigma is social disapproval of conditions or characteristics that are considered abnormal.

31.5 How do psychological disorders impact individuals, their families, and society?
- Individuals must cope with stigma and labels, financial challenges of treatment, and health issues. Friends and family members must cope with the stress of caring for a loved one.

Module 32: Types of Psychological Disorders
Learn about psychological disorders, their symptoms, and their causes.

32.1 What is the DSM classification system?
- *Diagnostic and Statistical Manual of Mental Disorders, Fourth Edition, Text Revision (DSM-IV-TR)* is a manual of psychological disorders and symptoms.

32.2 What are the challenges of diagnosing a mental illness?
- Psychological professionals must rely on self-reports of symptoms and may be swayed by their own biases.

Listen to an audio file of your chapter on **mypsychlab.com**

32.3 What are the different types of anxiety disorders and their causes?
- Anxiety disorders include phobias, obsessive-compulsive disorder, panic disorder, and generalized anxiety disorder. They may be caused by repressed desires, conditioning, illogical thought processes, chemical imbalances in the nervous system, or genetic factors.

32.4 What are the different types of somatoform disorders and their causes?
- Somatoform disorders include hypochondriasis, somatization disorder, and conversion disorder. They may be caused by negative reinforcement or irrational fear.

32.5 What are the different types of dissociative disorders and their causes?
- Dissociative disorders include dissociative amnesia, dissociative fugue, and dissociative identity disorder. They may be caused by repression, avoidance learning, or abnormal brain activity.

32.6 What are the different types of mood disorders and their causes?
- Mood disorders include dysthymia, cyclothymia, major depression, and bipolar disorder. They may be caused by learned helplessness; distorted thinking; or chemical imbalances in the brain.

32.7 What are the main symptoms, types, and causes of schizophrenia?
- Symptoms include delusions, hallucinations, emotional disturbances, attentional difficulties, disturbed speech, and disordered thinking. The three types are disorganized, catatonic, and paranoid. The cause is believed to be primarily biological.

32.8 What are the different types of personality disorders and their causes?
- Personality disorders include antisocial personality disorder and borderline personality disorder. There is some evidence of genetic factors in personality disorders.

32.9 How can family and social influences affect the experience of mental illness?
- Factors that can negatively influence those with a tendency toward psychological disorders are poverty, academic failure, family conflict, personal tragedies, child abuse, and neglect. Positive social influences can protect those at risk.

Vocabulary Terms

psychopathology p. 410
cultural relativity p. 411
culture-bound syndromes p. 411
situational context p. 412
subjective discomfort p. 412
maladaptive p. 413
psychological disorders p. 413
biological model p. 413
biopsychosocial model p. 415
stigma p. 415
anxiety disorders p. 421
free-floating anxiety p. 422
phobia p. 422
social phobia p. 422
specific phobia p. 422
agoraphobia p. 422
panic attack p. 423
panic disorder p. 423
obsessive-compulsive disorder p. 423
generalized anxiety disorder p. 423
magnification p. 424
somatoform disorders p. 424
hypochondriasis p. 425
somatization disorder p. 425
conversion disorder p. 425
dissociative disorders p. 426
dissociative amnesia p. 426
dissociative fugue p. 426
dissociative identity disorder p. 426
affect p. 427
mood disorders p. 427
dysthymia p. 427
cyclothymia p. 427
major depression p. 428
manic p. 429
bipolar disorder p. 429
schizophrenia p. 430
psychotic p. 430
delusions p. 430
delusional disorder p. 431
hallucinations p. 431
disorganized p. 431
catatonic p. 432
paranoid p. 432
positive symptoms p. 432
negative symptoms p. 432
stress-vulnerability model p. 433
personality disorders p. 433
antisocial personality disorder p. 434
borderline personality disorder p. 435
seasonal affective disorder (SAD) p. 436
phototherapy p. 436

PSYCHOLOGICAL DISORDERS 439

CHAPTER 13 • Chapter Summary and Vocabulary

Chapter Summary

Encourage students to carefully review and study the summary. Explain that it provides an overview of key concepts presented in the text.

Have students identify what they find unclear or confusing. Call on volunteers to provide answers, examples, or definitions.

Vocabulary Terms

Remind students that terms are defined within the chapter at point of use. If they are not sure of a term's definition, they should look up the definition on the page.

Encourage students to create study cards of unfamiliar words or go to **www.mypsychlab.com** for flashcards. Have them test themselves or a classmate. Advanced students can explain the terms in their own words.

Critical Thinking

MAKING CONNECTIONS

Have students complete the following activity to connect the ideas in this chapter. Divide the class into pairs or small groups. Tell them to think about a situation in which a person with a mood or anxiety disorder has moved next door to them or has joined their class. How would the students react? Would they keep their distance? Make friends? Ask volunteers to relate their thoughts to the class.

CHAPTER 13 • Assessment

VOCABULARY REVIEW

1. h
2. f
3. c
4. i
5. e
6. j
7. d
8. g
9. a
10. b

WRITING ABOUT PSYCHOLOGY

1. Excellent answers will define and describe each model of abnormality in detail, supply a clear statement of which model best explains the causes of psychological disorders, and support the view with at least three stated reasons or supports with cited evidence from the text for each.
2. Excellent answers will include a clear statement choosing the viewpoint of either Dr. Hashimoto or Dr. Ward. Answers should also include at least three clear, well-explained supports for the side chosen with citations from the text.

CHAPTER 13 Assessment

Study and Review on **mypsychlab.com**

Vocabulary Review
Match each vocabulary term to its definition.

1. borderline personality disorder
2. cyclothymia
3. delusions
4. dissociative disorders
5. phobia
6. disorganized
7. somatoform disorders
8. subjective discomfort
9. catatonic
10. dysthymia

a. A type of schizophrenia in which the person experiences periods of statue-like immobility mixed with occasional bursts of energetic, frantic movement and talking.
b. A moderate depression that lasts for 2 years or more and is typically a reaction to some external stressors.
c. False beliefs held by a person who refuses to accept evidence of his or her falseness.
d. Disorders that take the form of bodily illnesses and symptoms but for which there are no real physical disorders.
e. An intense fear of a specific object or situation, which may or may not be typically considered frightening.
f. A disorder that consists of mood swings from moderate depression to hypomania and lasts 2 years or more.
g. Emotional distress or emotional pain.
h. Maladaptive personality pattern in which the person is moody, unstable, lacks a clear sense of identity, and often clings to others.
i. Disorders in which there is a break in conscious awareness, memory, the sense of identity, or some combination.
j. A type of schizophrenia in which behavior is bizarre and childish and thinking, speech, and motor actions are very disordered.

Writing about Psychology
Respond to each question in complete sentences.

1. Briefly describe the biological, psychological, and biopsychosocial models of abnormality. Which model, if any, do you believe best explains the causes of psychological disorders? Or do you believe that no single model is best? Use evidence from the chapter to support your answer.
2. Two psychologists, Dr. Hashimoto and Dr. Ward, have differing views about the basis of schizophrenia. Dr. Hashimoto believes that schizophrenia has a biological basis, while Dr. Ward believes that schizophrenia is caused primarily by environmental factors. Which psychologist do you think is more correct? Why?

Psychology Project
Although women and members of minority groups were not always fully represented in the early days of psychology, they have always made important contributions to the field. This project will give you a chance to study one psychologist's contributions in depth.

Materials:
- access to print or electronic reference resources
- a pencil and paper, or other note-taking materials
- poster board, markers, and craft supplies (optional)

Instructions:
1. Choose one of the psychological disorders discussed in this chapter to research in more detail.
2. Use print or electronic resources to learn about the history of the disorder you have chosen. Ask yourself, "How long has this disorder been recognized as a mental illness? How were people treated for this disorder in the past? Is the disorder different today than it was in the past? Does this disorder exist in other cultures? Has this disorder become rarer or more common?" Take notes as you gather information.
3. Share what you've learned with your classmates by delivering a short oral presentation or creating a poster filled with the information you've collected.

Internet Resources

Mental Health Net: www.mhnet.org/disorders/
Comprehensive descriptions of the symptoms and treatment of mental disorders are presented here. Brush up on your *DSM-IV* categories and information about a variety of conditions as you prepare your classroom discussions.

Symptoms of Mental Illness: http://psychcentral.com/disorders/
The symptoms and treatments of various mental disorders are summarized.

Teens Health: Your Mind: http://kidshealth.org/teen/your_mind/
A website covering major mental illness affecting teens, written for a teen audience

American Academy of Child and Adolescent Psychiatry:
www.aacap.org/cs/root/resources_for_families/glossary_of_symptoms_and_mental_illnesses_affecting_teenagers
A comprehensive site with information for families as well as teenagers

Test Yourself

Pick the best answer.

1. Which is NOT a reason that stigmas associated with psychological disorders have begun to fade?
   a. Mental illness is increasingly recognized as a disease of the brain.
   b. Public figures have spoken out about their struggles with mental health disorders.
   c. People are becoming less exposed to individuals with mental health disorders.
   d. Mental illness is no longer considered by most people to be a character weakness.

2. Michael decided to give up his job teaching at a small community college in Florida and become a monk. He moved to a nearby town with a monastery, took his vows, and is now living quite happily as a member of that religious order. By what definition might Michael's behavior be considered abnormal?
   a. statistical   c. maladaptive
   b. subjective discomfort   d. harmful to self

3. During the Renaissance, mentally ill people
   a. were considered to have an imbalance in the body's vital fluids, or *humors*
   b. were treated through a religious ceremony known as an exorcism
   c. had holes cut in their skull to allow the demons possessing them to escape
   d. were often called witches and put to death

4. Which is NOT a reason that caring for a loved one with a mental illness is stressful for friends and family?
   a. Family members may blame themselves for the individual's illness, increasing feelings of stress and guilt.
   b. The mental illness sufferer will most likely become violent toward others.
   c. Drugs and therapy sessions are often expensive.
   d. The stress of caretaking can put family members at increased risk of developing mental illness themselves if they are genetically predisposed.

5. Which mood disorder is a consistently sad mood?
   a. bipolar   c. mania
   b. cyclothymia   d. major depression

6. Which of the following is not a typical symptom of schizophrenia?
   a. overly rational thinking   c. delusions
   b. inappropriate emotions   d. hallucinations

7. On which axis of the *DSM-IV-TR* would you find information about juvenile diabetes?
   a. Axis I   c. Axis III
   b. Axis II   d. Axis IV

8. Jennifer worries that someone might come into her house at night while she is sleeping and helpless. She checks the locks on the doors and windows several times before she can relax enough to go to bed. Her constant checking of the locks is most similar to
   a. a compulsion   c. a panic disorder
   b. an obsession   d. a phobia

9. What is the relationship between gender and diagnostic rates of major depression?
   a. Women and men are diagnosed with major depression at the same rate.
   b. Women are diagnosed with major depression twice as often as men are.
   c. Men are diagnosed with major depression twice as often as women are.
   d. Men are diagnosed with major depression three to six times as often as women are.

10. Which is NOT a factor that might negatively influence those with a tendency toward psychological disorders?
    a. economic independence
    b. family conflicts
    c. lack of community support
    d. academic failure

11. What is NOT one of the challenges of diagnosing a mental illness?
    a. Patients do not always fully disclose their symptoms, risking misdiagnosis.
    b. Physicians may have personal biases about gender, race, or socioeconomic status that influence their diagnosis.
    c. The definitions and diagnoses of mental illnesses change across time and cultures.
    d. Most individuals with mental illnesses refuse to believe that anything is wrong with them.

12. Charles believed that a famous song by a popular musical group carried a special, secret message meant only for him. This would be an example of a delusion of
    a. persecution   c. influence
    b. reference   d. grandeur

13. An irrational fear of blood would be
    a. a social phobia   c. agoraphobia
    b. a specific phobia d. claustrophobia

14. Bud's relatives are concerned that Bud worries too much. He worries about little things going wrong, he worries about big things going wrong, and sometimes it seems as though he's worrying because there's nothing to worry about. He worries so much that he has a hard time getting things done. Bud most likely has
    a. panic disorder
    b. a social phobia
    c. generalized anxiety disorder
    d. obsessive-compulsive disorder

15. In an old movie, a madman made weird faces and sounds, jumped about wildly in his cell, and laughed and giggled constantly. This bizarre behavior is typical of the _____ schizophrenic.
    a. disorganized   c. paranoid
    b. catatonic   d. depressed

16. Jane loves to be the center of attention. She tends to manipulate friends and family members into giving her attention, and she is very emotional. Which type of personality disorder is Jane most likely to have?
    a. schizoid   c. histrionic
    b. avoidant   d. borderline

CHAPTER 13 • Assessment

TEST YOURSELF

1. c	9. b
2. a	10. a
3. d	11. d
4. b	12. b
5. d	13. b
6. a	14. c
7. c	15. a
8. a	16. d

Ready for Testing

STUDENTS KNOW THEY ARE READY FOR TESTING IF THEY ARE ABLE TO . . .

- Define abnormality and briefly discuss the historical and cultural impact on defining psychological disorders.
- Present the biological and psychological models of psychopathology.
- Discuss the diagnosis and prevalence rates of psychological disorders in the United States.
- Describe specific categories of psychological disorders, including anxiety, somatoform, dissociative, mood, schizophrenia, and personality disorders.
- Understand the diagnosis of seasonal affective disorder and its treatment.

CHAPTER 13 • Concept Summary

MULTIMEDIA CONTENT AVAILABLE AT
www.mypsychlab.com

- **Map the Concepts** on **mypsychlab.com**
- **Study and Review** Flashcards on **mypsychlab.com**

STUDY TIPS

Preparing a Time Management Schedule If students are unsure how to create a schedule, tell them that for 1 week, they should keep track of everything they do with their time. They should be honest with themselves; no one will be judging them. The process should give them a realistic picture of how they spend their time. When they have completed that step, they should add up the hours and divide them into categories such as family, recreation, class hours, chores, athletics, social activities, and any part-time job. They should create categories that fit their lifestyle. They will want to include all of their activities. Then they should look carefully at their completed information. What can they say about the way they spend their time? What decisions will they make, based on what they have written? After doing this exercise, some people make radical changes in the way they manage their time; others discover that they like things the way they are. Their determination is exactly that—theirs! What works for them might not work for their friends. At this point, they can create an actual schedule of what they will do then.

442 Chapter 13 Psychological Disorders

CHAPTER 13 Concept Summary: Psychological Disorders

Learning Objectives

31.1 31.2 31.3 31.4 31.5   pp. 410–416

Understand Historical, Cultural, and Current Views of Abnormality

- **definition of abnormal behavior** any pattern of behavior that causes significant distress, causes people to harm themselves or others, or harms their ability to function in daily life
- **models of abnormality**
  - biological model
  - psychological models
  - biopsychosocial perspective
- **stigma** refers, in psychology, to social disapproval of conditions or characteristics that are considered abnormal
- **impact of mental illness** may include stigma, labeling, expense, side effects of treatment, stress, and guilt

Learning Objectives

32.1 32.2 32.3 32.4 32.5 32.6 32.7 32.8 32.9   pp. 418–436

Learn About Psychological Disorders, Their Symptoms, and Their Causes

- **DSM-IV-TR** describes approximately 250 different psychological disorders and includes diagnostic criteria along five axes
- **anxiety disorders**
  most dominant symptom is excessive or unrealistic anxiety; can be free-floating or more specific
  - panic disorder
  - obsessive-compulsive disorder (OCD)
  - generalized anxiety disorder
- **somatoform disorders**
  include disorders in which individuals believe they are sick and may experience physical symptoms but there is no physical illness or problem
  - hypochondriasis
  - somatization disorder
  - conversion disorder
- **dissociative disorders**
  involve a dissociation in consciousness, memory, or sense of identity, often associated with extreme stress or trauma
  - dissociative amnesia
  - dissociative fugue
  - dissociative identity disorder

442 CHAPTER 13

What Every Student Should Know About . . .

CREATING A PORTFOLIO

Tell students that there are several essential factors to consider when designing their portfolios: (1) Identify the audience, purpose, and main story or argument of the portfolio. (2) Consider the kind of materials to include and the ways they might be presented. (3) Carefully choose organizational elements (tabs, dividers, links, and the like). (4) Choose a design to match the portfolio's goals. (5) Ensure that the portfolio's readers are given the information they need to find the information they want. (6) Design the portfolio so that users can move through the portfolio easily.

Learning Objectives

32.1 32.2 32.3 32.4 32.5 32.6 32.7 32.8 32.9 pp. 418–436

Learn About Psychological Disorders, Their Symptoms, and Their Causes (continued)

- **mood disorders** involve a disturbance in mood or emotion; can be mild or severe
  - **dysthymia** mild, chronic depression
  - **cyclothymia** cycles of sadness and happiness interspersed with normal mood
  - **major depression** deeply depressed mood
  - **bipolar disorder** extreme mood swings, severe depression and mania

- **schizophrenia** psychotic disorder involving a break with reality and disturbances in thinking, emotions, behavior, and perceptions
  - disorganized
  - catatonic
  - paranoid

- **personality disorders** involve excessively rigid and maladaptive patterns of behavior and ways of relating to others
  - antisocial personality disorder
  - borderline personality disorder

- **family and social influences**
  - negative influences can make predisposed individuals more likely to develop a psychological disorder
  - positive influences can protect against psychological disorders

Table 32.1 Axis I Disorders of the *DSM-IV-TR*

DISORDER	EXAMPLES
Disorders usually first diagnosed in infancy, childhood, or adolescence	Learning disabilities, ADHD, bed-wetting, speech disorders
Delirium, dementia, amnesia, and other cognitive disorders	Alzheimer's, Parkinson's, amnesia due to physical causes
Psychological disorders due to a general medical condition	Personality change because of a brain tumor
Substance-related disorders	Alcoholism, drug addictions
Schizophrenia and other psychotic disorders	Schizophrenia, delusional disorders, paranoid psychosis
Mood disorders	Depression, mania, bipolar disorders
Anxiety disorders	Panic disorder, phobias, stress disorders
Somatoform disorders	Hypochondria, conversion disorder
Factitious disorders	Pathological lying, Munchausen syndrome
Dissociative disorders	Dissociative identity disorder (formerly multiple personality), amnesia not due to physical causes
Sexual and gender	Sexual desire disorders, paraphilias identity disorders
Eating disorders	Anorexia, bulimia
Sleep disorders	Insomnia, sleep terror disorder, sleepwalking, narcolepsy
Impulse-control disorders, not classified elsewhere	Kleptomania, pathological gambling, pyromania
Adjustment disorders	Mixed anxiety, conduct disturbances

Adapted from the American Psychiatric Association (APA), *DSM-IV-TR* (2000).

Comprehension Check

ANSWERING QUESTIONS ABOUT ABNORMAL BEHAVIOR

To check their understanding of the chapter material, students should revisit the paragraph on p. 409 titled "Why Study Abnormal Behavior?" Divide the class into four groups and have each group meet to discuss one of the questions asked in the paragraph. Then reassemble the class and have a representative from each group present the group's answer(s) to the question it discussed.

CHAPTER 13 • Concept Summary

STUDY TIPS

Following a Schedule Remind students that during the early weeks of the year or semester, they are likely to have less homework. They will have to adjust their schedule as the term progresses, because they will be carrying a heavier assignment and study load. Encourage them to schedule in weekend study hours. It is easy to forget about studying on the weekend, with social activities, athletics, and possibly a part-time job. But being a student does not end when classes are over; in fact, the work is just beginning. Another advantage to studying on the weekend is that it keeps information current. Repetition is needed to get information stored in a person's long-term memory. Following a schedule can be challenging, especially if a person has never done it before; its function is to help one manage time well and to minimize stress, not create more of it.

CHAPTER 14 • Module 33

Launch the Chapter

CHAPTER GOALS AND LEARNING OBJECTIVES

Module 33 Psychotherapies

Understand perspectives on treating psychological disorders.

33.1 What are the two modern ways in which psychological disorders can be treated, and how have they been treated in the past?

33.2 Who can treat psychological disorders, and what training is required?

Identify psychological treatments and evaluate their effectiveness.

33.3 What are the different types of psychotherapy?

33.4 How effective is psychotherapy?

33.5 What other factors influence the effectiveness of therapy?

Module 34 Biomedical Therapies and Issues in Therapy

Identify biomedical therapies and evaluate their effectiveness.

34.1 What are biomedical forms of therapy, and how effective are they?

34.2 Should children and adolescents be treated with the same drugs used for adults?

Consider legal, ethical, and professional challenges in therapy.

34.3 What ethical challenges do therapists face when they deliver treatment?

34.4 What resources support people with psychological disorders and their families?

DIFFERENTIATED INSTRUCTION KEY

Look for these symbols to help you adjust steps in each lesson to meet your students' needs.

- **L1** Special Needs
- **L2** Basic
- **ELL** English Language Learners
- **LPR** Less Proficient Readers
- **L3** All Students
- **L4** Advanced Students

CHAPTER 14
Psychological Therapies

Treating Panic Disorder

Marie began having panic attacks at the age of 14. When she started having attacks at school, the school began sending her home. Marie's mother took her to see a child psychiatrist, who diagnosed Marie with mild panic disorder. **LINK** *to Chapter Thirteen: Psychological Disorders, pp. 422–424.*

The psychiatrist recommended two types of treatment: cognitive psychotherapy (performed by a trained psychologist) and a carefully monitored drug treatment. The goal of the first type of therapy, cognitive therapy, is to help clients see how their thinking patterns can be self-defeating and illogical. In cognitive psychotherapy sessions, a trained psychologist let Marie talk about her feelings and fears. Then she showed her where her thinking was going a little off-track. She explained to Marie that panic disorder did not mean that she was "crazy." A small area in her brain that would normally react to fear-provoking situations was "misfiring," making her body think that there was reason to be afraid and causing panic symptoms. She explained that it was like having a smoke detector that went off when there was no smoke and no fire.

The drug treatment consisted of daily doses of an antidepressant medication. The initially small dosage was increased gradually until Marie was on an effective dose. During the course of the drug treatment, the cognitive therapy sessions continued. Marie's panic attacks eventually disappeared completely, and she was able to gradually discontinue taking the drug. Within one year, Marie was able to end her therapy, having successfully conquered her panic.

Marie's story is a successful one, but psychological disorders are not always resolved so simply. Different disorders require different kinds of therapies, and not all disorders can be completely eliminated. Therapies can take many forms, depending on the specific disorder that needs to be treated and on how that particular type of therapy explains psychological disorders to begin with.

CORRELATION TO APA STANDARDS FOR CHAPTER 14

VIIA. TREATMENT OF PSYCHOLOGICAL DISORDERS

VIIA-1. Perspectives on treatment.................. pp. 446–459

VIIA-2. Categories of treatment and types ... pp. 448–462, 465–470 of treatment providers

VIIA-3. Legal, ethical, and professional.............. pp. 470–473 issues in the treatment of psychological disorders

MODULE 33 ▸ **PSYCHOTHERAPIES**

MODULE 34 ▸ **BIOMEDICAL THERAPIES AND ISSUES IN THERAPY**

Why Study?

Therapies for Psychological Disorders

There are almost as many methods of therapy as there are disorders. Correctly matching the type of therapy to the disorder can mean the difference between a cure and a crisis. It is important to know the choices available for treatment and how they relate to the different kinds of disorders, so as to make an informed decision and achieve the best possible outcome.

PSYCHOLOGICAL THERAPIES 445

SCHEDULING

1 Period = 50 min. 1 Block = 90 min.	Semester Course (18 weeks/90 days) Periods/Blocks		Full-Year Course (36 weeks/180 days) Period/Blocks	
Module 33	2.5	1.25	5	2.5
Module 34	2.5	1.25	5	2.5
Total Days for Chapter	5	2.5	10	5

CHAPTER 14 • Module 33

Teacher Prep

Therapy for psychological disorders consists of treatment methods aimed at making people feel better and function more effectively. The two main types of therapy are psychotherapy—talking things out with a professional—and biomedical therapy—using biological methods such as medication to treat a psychological disorder.

Psychoanalysis is an insight therapy developed by Sigmund Freud with the goal of revealing the unconscious conflicts, urges, and desires that Freud assumed were the cause of the psychological disorder.

Humanistic therapy is also an insight therapy, but unlike psychoanalysis, humanistic therapy focuses on conscious experiences of emotion and an individual's sense of self.

Behavior therapies use action-based therapy to change behavior based on principles of classical and operant conditioning. The abnormal behavior is not seen as a symptom, but as the problem itself.

Cognitive therapy is an action therapy that focuses on helping people change the distorted thinking and unrealistic beliefs that lead to maladaptive behaviors.

An alternative to individual therapy is group therapy. A group of clients with similar problems gather and discuss their problems under the guidance of a single therapist.

The effectiveness of the various psychotherapy techniques is difficult to determine due to various time frames required for the different therapies, alternate explanations of "effectiveness," the lack of adequate control groups, experimenter bias, and the inaccuracies of self-report information.

Biomedical therapies directly affect the biological function of the body and include the three categories of drug therapy, shock therapy, and surgical treatments.

CHAPTER 14 • Module 33

Focus

RESOURCES
For this module, consult the appropriate sections of the Teacher's Manual, Test Bank, and PowerPoint slides, all found on the Teacher's Resource DVD, and the interactive study tools for students on MyPsychLab.

BEFORE CLASS
Students should read the section for homework before coming to class.

BELLRINGER
Ask students, after they have read this module, if they were seeking out a therapist for talk therapy, what theoretical perspective would they look for? Cognitive therapy? Behavioral therapies? Humanistic therapies? Why?

Teach

COVER THE MODULE
33.1 What are two modern ways in which psychological disorders can be treated, and how have they been treated in the past?

- *Psychotherapy* involves a person talking to a psychological professional about the person's problems.
- Psychotherapy for the purpose of gaining understanding into one's motives and actions is called *insight therapy*.
- Psychotherapy aimed at changing disordered behavior directly is called *action therapy*.
- *Biomedical therapy* uses a medical procedure to bring about changes in behavior.
- Biomedical therapies include psychosurgery, electroconvulsive therapy, and psychotropic medications.

446 Chapter 14 Psychological Therapies

Module 33 Psychotherapies

Module Goals

Understand perspectives on treating psychological disorders.

Identify psychological treatments and evaluate their effectiveness.

Learning Objectives

33.1 What are the two modern ways in which psychological disorders can be treated, and how have they been treated in the past?

33.2 Who can treat psychological disorders, and what training is required?

33.3 What are the different types of psychotherapy?

33.4 How effective is psychotherapy?

33.5 What other factors influence the effectiveness of therapy?

Understand Perspectives on Treating Psychological Disorders

33.1 What are the two modern ways in which psychological disorders can be treated, and how have they been treated in the past?

Therapy refers to treatment methods aimed at helping people to feel better and function more effectively. Two main types of therapy are used to treat psychological disorders. In **psychotherapy**, people discuss their problems with a therapist, who tries to help them understand those problems or change the underlying behavior. **Biomedical therapy** uses medical interventions to bring the symptoms under control.

Psychotherapy Psychotherapy can be performed in many ways. A person might work with a professional one-on-one, or participate in group therapy in which a professional leads a group of people who have similar psychological problems.

Most psychotherapies aim to help both mentally healthy and psychologically disordered people understand themselves better (Goin, 2005; Wolberg, 1977). This understanding of one's motives and actions is called insight, and so therapies with this as the primary goal are called **insight therapies**. In contrast, **action therapy** (as used by Marie's psychologist) focuses more on changing behavior than providing overarching insights into its causes. Most psychological professionals use a combination of insight and action therapies.

Biomedical Therapy Biomedical therapy relies on medical procedures, such as drugs, electrical shock treatments, and surgical methods, to change disordered thinking or behavior. Alone, it merely alleviates symptoms. This is sometimes enough, but most professionals agree that biomedical therapy should usually be accompanied by some form of psychotherapy (Keller et al., 2000; Rohde et al., 2008). Treating not only the symptoms but also any underlying problems helps ensure that the problem does not recur and no new symptoms develop.

therapy treatment methods aimed at making people feel better and function more effectively.

psychotherapy therapy for mental disorders in which a person with a problem talks with a psychologist, psychiatrist, or counselor.

biomedical therapy therapy for mental disorders in which a person with a problem is treated with biological or medical methods to relieve symptoms.

insight therapies therapies in which the main goal is helping people to gain insight with respect to their behavior, thoughts, and feelings.

action therapy therapy in which the main goal is to change disordered or inappropriate behavior directly.

446 CHAPTER 14

Terms

- therapy • psychotherapy • biomedical therapy • insight therapies • action therapy
- psychiatrist • psychoanalyst • psychoanalysis • psychiatric social worker
- psychologist • free association • manifest content • latent content • resistance
- transference • psychodynamic therapy • unconditional positive regard
- nondirective • person-centered therapy • reflection • empathy • authenticity
- behavior therapies • classical conditioning • operant conditioning • applied behavior analysis (behavior modification) • systematic desensitization • aversion therapy • flooding (exposure and response prevention) • reinforcement • token economy • contingency contracting • modeling • participant modeling • extinction
- time-out • shaping • cognitive therapy • arbitrary inference • selective thinking • overgeneralization • magnification and minimization • personalization
- cognitive-behavioral therapy (CBT) • rational-emotive behavior therapy (REBT)
- family counseling • self-help groups • eclectic therapies • therapeutic alliance

Early Treatment of Mental Illness Throughout much of history, life for the mentally ill was extremely difficult. People with severe mental illnesses were often thought to be possessed by a supernatural force. "Treatments" were severe and sometimes deadly. Even as recently as the 19th and 20th centuries, the mentally ill did not always receive compassionate, humane treatment.

In movies about mental hospitals, they don't look like great places to be in even now. How bad was it back then? What did people do with relatives who were mentally ill?

The first truly organized effort to address mental illness began in England in the mid-1500s. Bethlem Hospital in London (later known as "Bedlam") was converted into an asylum (meaning, "place of safety"). Unfortunately, the first asylums were little more than prisons where the mentally ill were chained to their beds. Supposedly "cleansing" treatments consisted of bloodletting, beatings, induced vomiting, and ice baths in which people were submerged until they passed out or suffered a seizure (Hunt, 1993). ◉ Watch on **mypsychlab.com**

It was not until 1793, during the French Revolution, that efforts were made to develop a "moral treatment" based on kindness and guidance. At this time, Dr. Philippe Pinel personally unchained the inmates at the Bic tre Asylum in Paris, France, beginning the movement toward humane treatment (Brigham, 1844; Curtis, 1993). Others, such as the American activist Dorothea Dix (1802–1887), continued the movement toward reform.

The Origins of Psychotherapy: Freud and Psychoanalysis

So, what exactly happens in psychoanalysis? I've heard lots of stories about it, but what's it really like?

Modern psychotherapy began with the work of Austrian physician Sigmund Freud (1856–1939). Instead of focusing on physical "cleansing," Freud believed effective treatment should resolve the hidden conflicts in the unconscious mind. This very medical viewpoint is reflected in the use of the term "patients" to describe people who sought treatment.

While Freud was a pioneer in the field of psychotherapy, the researchers and theorists who followed in his footsteps developed many different approaches to helping people with mental illness. Professionals today generally prefer the more positive term "clients," which describes people who are not necessarily sick but who need help with a problem and take an active role in treatment.

33.2 Who can treat psychological disorders, and what training is required?

Several types of professionals can treat psychological problems. These professionals have different training with different focuses, and they may have different goals.

Psychiatrists A **psychiatrist** is a medical doctor who specializes in diagnosing and treating psychological disorders, such as schizophrenia or depression. Like other doctors, psychiatrists have a medical doctorate (M.D.) degree and are qualified to write prescriptions and perform medical procedures. Many psychiatrists do not perform therapy, but rather diagnose and prescribe medication with a referral to a psychotherapist on the team. Psychiatrists regularly

◉ Watch a video on the history of mental institutions in the United States on **mypsychlab.com**

▲ *In this famous painting by French artist Robert Fleury, French psychiatrist Dr. Philippe Pinel orders the chains removed from patients at a Paris asylum for insane women. Pinel was one of the first psychiatrists to recommend humane treatment of the mentally ill.*

psychiatrist a medical doctor who specializes in the diagnosis and treatment of psychological disorders.

PSYCHOLOGICAL THERAPIES **447**

Explore

USING INFORMATION FROM THE INTERNET

Send students to the Kirkbride Buildings website at **www.kirkbridebuildings.com/** Ask students to view the photos and read about the Kirkbride buildings and their promoter, Thomas Kirkbride. What feelings do the photographs of the asylums evoke in students? Do students think there could have been a meaning to their architecture? If so, what?

CHAPTER 14 • Module 33

COVER THE MODULE (continued)

- Mentally ill people began to be confined to institutions called asylums in the mid-1500s.
  - Treatments were harsh and often damaging and over the years have included shock treatments and ice water baths.
- Philippe Pinel became famous for demanding that the mentally ill be treated with kindness, personally unlocking the chains at Bicetre Asylum in France.
  - He developed the technique of objective introspection, which involves the process of objectively examining and measuring one's own thoughts and mental activities.
- **The Origins of Psychotherapy: Freud and Psychoanalysis**
  - Sigmund Freud developed a treatment called psychoanalysis that focused on releasing a person's hidden, repressed urges and concerns from the unconscious mind.

DISCUSS THE STUDENT VOICE QUESTION

Ask students why they think people would have sent their loved ones—maybe even their own parents or children—to asylums in the past if they were so inhumane and possibly dangerous. *(Students may, for example, note fear as a primary motivator, either fear of the mentally ill person or fear of societal reprisals.)*

MULTIMEDIA CONTENT AVAILABLE AT
www.mypsychlab.com

◉ Watch a video on the history of mental institutions in the United States on **mypsychlab.com**

COVER THE MODULE

33.2 Who can treat psychological disorders, and what training is required?

- Psychiatrists, as medical doctors, can prescribe medications and perform procedures to treat psychological disorders.

Module 33 Psychotherapies **447**

CHAPTER 14 • Module 33

COVER THE MODULE (continued)

- *Psychoanalysts* are psychiatrists or psychologists with special training in the theory of psychoanalysis.
- *Psychiatric social workers* are social workers with special training in the influences of the environment on mental illness.
- *Psychologists* have academic degrees and can perform counseling, teaching, and research and may specialize in any one of a large number of areas within psychology.

COVER THE MODULE

33.3 Identify psychological treatments and evaluate their effectiveness.

- Freud's insight therapy emphasized the role of the unconscious in disordered emotions and behavior.

TEACHING TIP

A meeting between student and teacher can provide a time to set goals, evaluate performance, and suggest methods for an improved learning environment.

L1 DIFFERENTIATED INSTRUCTION

Special Needs Help students with physical challenges feel comfortable in all activities, including special projects and events.

---

check on the progress of the medication prescribed and its effects on the patient. They have special training in mental health. As medical doctors, they tend to have a biopsychological perspective.

Psychoanalysts A **psychoanalyst** is either a psychiatrist or a psychologist (see below) with special training in Freudian theory and **psychoanalysis**. This training is currently available at nearly three dozen institutes. Compared to Freud and his original followers, modern psychoanalysts may be more direct and take less time to get to the heart of a client's problems, but they still follow many of Freud's principles and methods, working with each client for several hours each week over a period of months or even years.

Psychiatric Social Workers A **psychiatric social worker** is trained in social work, usually possesses a master of social work (M.S.W.) degree, and may be licensed by his or her state of employment as a licensed clinical social worker (L.C.S.W.). These professionals focus more on environmental conditions that can affect mental health, such as poverty, overcrowding, stress, and drug abuse. With special training and licensing, they may administer psychotherapy and often work in a clinical setting with other psychological professionals.

Psychologists A **psychologist** has no medical degree but instead undergoes intense academic and practical training, learning about many areas of psychology before choosing one in which to specialize. According to the American Psychological Association, psychologists must hold either a doctor of philosophy (Ph.D.) or a doctor of psychology (Psy.D.) degree. (In all but a few states, people who hold a master of science (M.S.) or master of arts (M.A.) degree are usually called *therapists* or *counselors*, not psychologists.)

Unlike psychiatrists, clinical psychologists typically cannot prescribe medicines or perform medical procedures. However, some states now allow psychologists to prescribe medication if they have received special training. This relatively recent change helps reduce the cost and delay sometimes experienced by people who need mental health services. If a person sees a psychologist but must then visit a psychiatrist for prescriptions, the cost can be prohibitive. Also, some states have fewer psychiatrists, causing frustrating, sometimes dangerous delays in patients' receiving crucial services.

Although some psychologists are trained as psychoanalysts, most are not. Counselors or therapists today typically use techniques that have little to do with Freud's theories (although Freud's emphasis on creating a safe environment in which clients can talk about their experiences is still very much a part of many kinds of psychotherapy). Additionally, many psychologists work in fields that do not involve counseling. They may teach at colleges or universities, conduct research for academic or other institutions or for industries, or combine these activities. Others design equipment and workplaces, develop educational methods, or work as consultants to businesses and the court system.

Identify Psychological Treatments and Evaluate Their Effectiveness

33.3 What are the different types of psychotherapy?

Freudian Psychoanalysis: Then and Now Freud developed psychoanalysis to help his patients feel more able to explore their innermost feelings without fear of embarrassment or rejection. This insight therapy emphasizes

psychoanalyst either a psychiatrist or a psychologist who has special training in the theories of Sigmund Freud and his method of psychoanalysis.

psychoanalysis an insight therapy based on the theory of Freud, emphasizing the revealing of unconscious conflicts.

psychiatric social worker a social worker with some training in therapy methods who focuses on the environmental conditions that can have an impact on mental disorders, such as poverty, overcrowding, stress, and drug abuse.

psychologist a professional with an academic degree and specialized training in one or more areas of psychology.

448 CHAPTER 14

Class Discussion

ON BEING SANE IN INSANE PLACES

One of the more controversial articles published about mental hospitals is David Rosenhan's "On Being Sane in Insane Places." This account describes how eight sane people gained admission to 12 different mental hospitals by complaining to the admissions office that they had been hearing voices that said, "Empty, hollow, and thud." The pseudopatients behaved normally during the rest of the admission interview and throughout their hospitalization. Although all of them were released from the mental hospitals, all were released with the stigmatizing label "schizophrenia in remission."

Have students read Rosenhan's article at **http://psychrights.org/articles/Rosenham.htm**. (Alternately, you may ask students to read certain sections or break students into groups and assign each a section so they are not overwhelmed with the length.) After students have read the article, conduct a class discussion. How did students feel about the article? What underlying concerns did it address? How could these issues be rectified? Did Rosenhan conduct an effective investigation? Why or why not?

448 Chapter 14 Psychological Therapies

revealing the unconscious conflicts, urges, and desires that are assumed to cause disordered emotions and behavior (Freud, 1904; Mitchell & Black, 1996).

Early psychoanalytic patients lay on a couch so they would feel more relaxed, dependent, and childlike, making it easier for them to recall early childhood memories. The analyst, who took notes about the patient's responses, sat behind the patient to keep patients from being affected by the analyst's reactions. Because Freud believed that without direction from an analyst, the unconscious mind would leak thoughts that could provide insight into urges and inner conflicts, the psychoanalyst would encourage the patient to say whatever came to mind without restraint.

Over the past century, Freudian psychoanalysis has changed somewhat, but it is still based on two core techniques:

- **dream interpretation,** the analysis of the elements within a patient's reported dream
- **free association,** the practice of allowing patients to talk freely about anything that comes to mind

Dream interpretation was central to Freud's method. LINK *to Chapter Four: Consciousness: Sleep, Dreams, Hypnosis, and Drugs, p. 121.* Freud thought repressed material often surfaced in dreams in symbolic form, and he wrote in his classic work *The Interpretation of Dreams* that "dreams are the royal road to the unconscious." He believed in looking beyond the dream's **manifest content** (what literally happened) to the **latent content**—the hidden, symbolic meaning. Latent content, if correctly interpreted, would reveal the patient's unconscious conflicts (Freud, 1900).

Free association was originally devised by Freud's coworker, Josef Breuer (Breuer & Freud, 1895), who encouraged his patients to freely say whatever came into their minds. Breuer believed this uncensored flow of ideas would often reveal unconscious concerns. Freud adopted this method, believing that repressed thoughts were trying to "break free" into consciousness.

Freud thought patients would ultimately reach a point of **resistance** when they became unwilling to talk about certain potentially uncomfortable topics. Patients would also experience **transference**—meaning they would *transfer* feelings about past authority figures onto the therapist. (For example, a patient with unresolved feelings of anger toward a deceased parent might express that anger toward the therapist.) As patients revealed their innermost feelings to an all-accepting therapist, they would come to trust the therapist as they once trusted their parents. Patients would first transfer positive feelings and then, when the therapist remained neutral and seemingly unresponsive, they would transfer negative feelings.

In classical Freudian psychoanalysis, the therapist's first job is to analyze and interpret the information that the patient reveals through dreams, free association, resistance, and transference. Then, the therapist uses this interpretation of the patient's struggles to help the patient achieve a deeper understanding of his or her problems and their causes, perhaps by asking the patient pointed questions about key conflicts and their meanings.

Although some psychoanalysts today still use Freud's original, rather time-consuming methods, most modern psychoanalysts have modified them. The couch is frequently gone, and the client may sit, stand, or walk around. The modern psychoanalyst is also far more directive, asking questions, suggesting helpful behavior, and giving opinions and interpretations early on. This helps speed up the therapeutic process. Today's psychoanalysts also focus less on the id, instead looking more at the ego or sense of self (Prochaska & Norcross, 2003).

free association psychoanalytic technique in which a patient was encouraged to talk about anything that came to mind without fear of negative evaluations.

manifest content the actual content of one's dream.

latent content the hidden, symbolic meaning of a dream.

resistance a patient's reluctance to discuss a certain topic, which typically involves changing the subject or becoming silent.

transference the tendency for a patient or client to project positive or negative feelings for important people from the past onto the therapist.

CHAPTER 14 • Module 33

COVER THE MODULE (continued)

- Dream Interpretation
  - Looking for the underlying *(latent)* content within dream symbols
- *Free Associations*
  - Saying whatever comes to mind in order to reveal the unconscious
- *Resistance*
  - Pointing out client attempts to resist therapeutic breakthroughs
- *Transference*
  - Clients tend to transfer their positive and negative feelings for other people onto the therapist.

LINK *to Chapter Four: Consciousness, Sleep, Dreams, Hypnosis, and Drugs, p. 121*

EXTEND THE LESSON

Have students keep a dream journal for 2 weeks or so. When the time is up, ask students, dream journal in hand, to visit **www.dreammoods.com/dreamdictionary/** and interpret their dreams. Ask if any students would be comfortable sharing some of their findings with the class. (You might also keep a journal and share some of your own findings to get the discussion started and make students more comfortable.) Do students think the interpretations seem feasible?

L4 DIFFERENTIATED INSTRUCTION

Advanced Learners Ask "what if" questions to develop students' thinking skills.

Explore

PSYCHOANALYSIS

Encourage students to learn more about Freud and psychoanalysis at the following websites:

- **About Psychoanalysis: www.apsa.org/pubinfo/about.htm**
  Article on this topic from the American Psychoanalytic Association
- **Freud Links: http://users.rcn.com/brill/freudarc.html**
  A collection of links and other information related to Sigmund Freud
- **Psychoanalysis Techniques and Practices: www.freudfile.org/psychoanalysis/**
  A source of much information on the theory and practice of psychoanalysis

CHAPTER 14 • Module 33

COVER THE MODULE (continued)

- Freud's original therapy technique is criticized for its lack of scientific research and his own personal biases that caused him to misinterpret much of what his patients revealed.
- Modern psychodynamic therapists have modified the technique so that it takes less time and is much more direct, and they do not focus on the id and sexuality as did Freud.
- **Humanistic Therapies**
  - Humanistic therapies focus on the conscious mind and subjective experiences to help clients gain insights.
  - *Person-centered therapy* is very nondirective, allowing the client to talk through problems and concerns, while the therapist provides a supportive background.

LINK to Chapter One: The Science of Psychology, p. 10

DISCUSS THE STUDENT VOICE QUESTION

What are students' opinions about the humanistic therapy techniques? Make two columns on the board, one for advantages and one for disadvantages, and ask students to brainstorm a list of each with regard to nondirective therapy. How does it fare in the end? Do students believe that, barring serious mental illness, such therapy could get one closer to his or her ideal self?

---

psychodynamic therapy a newer and more general term for therapies based on psychoanalysis with an emphasis on transference, shorter treatment times, and a more direct therapeutic approach.

unconditional positive regard warmth, respect, and affection without any conditions attached; this is a crucial part of the accepting atmosphere the therapist creates for the client in person-centered therapy.

nondirective term used to describe a therapy style in which the therapist remains relatively neutral and does not interpret or take direct actions with regard to the client, instead remaining a calm, nonjudgmental listener while the client talks.

person-centered therapy a nondirective insight therapy based on the work of Carl Rogers in which the client does most of the talking and the therapist listens.

reflection therapy technique in which the therapist restates what the client says rather than interpreting those statements.

> So, the key to getting over unhappiness ▶ would be to get the real and ideal selves closer together. How does a therapist do that?

Psychodynamic therapy is a broader term; it includes traditional psychoanalysis as well as more modern approaches that are typically much shorter. These approaches focus more heavily on the process of transference and work best when the client is fairly intelligent and able to verbalize feelings and thoughts effectively. Psychodynamic approaches are most helpful for people with nonpsychotic adjustment disorders, such as affective, anxiety, somatoform, or dissociative disorders. People who are extremely withdrawn or who suffer from the more severe psychotic disorders are not good candidates for this form of psychotherapy.

Although Freud's basic model was very influential, most current methods have moved away from his ideas and modified his practices. Freud's original theory has been criticized because it was based not on scientific research but on his own interpretations of the experiences of a small sample of middle- to upper-class women in Victorian Europe. Critics also argue that Freud was unwilling to believe some of his patients' disturbing revelations and overemphasized the importance of problems with sexuality.

Humanistic Therapies Humanistic theory focuses not on unconscious conflicts but instead on a person's conscious emotional experiences and sense of self. It also emphasizes present-day experiences rather than childhood experiences (Cain & Seeman, 2001; Rowan, 2001; Schneider et al., 2001). LINK to Chapter One: The Science of Psychology, p. 10. Finally, it centers on the individual's choices and the potential to change behavior. Humanistic theory is at the heart of Carl Rogers's person-centered therapy.

Rogers's work emphasizes one's sense of self (Rogers, 1961), which is based on the *real self* (how people see their actual traits and abilities) and the *ideal self* (how people think they should be). The closer the two self-concepts match, the happier and better adjusted the person is.

To create this match, people need to receive **unconditional positive regard**—love, warmth, respect, and affection without any conditions attached. When love seems conditional ("I will love you *if* you are/do X"), people's ideal selves will be determined by those conditions and become more difficult to achieve. This results in mismatched selves and unhappiness.

So, the key to getting over unhappiness would be to get the real and ideal selves closer together. How does a therapist do that?

The therapist provides unconditional positive regard and helps clients recognize the discrepancies between their real and ideal selves. The client does most of the therapeutic "work," talking out problems in an atmosphere of warm acceptance. Rogers's therapy is very **nondirective** because the therapist merely acts as a sounding board. (Over time, Rogers came to replace the word "client" with the more neutral term "person"; his method is now called **person-centered therapy** because the person is the center of the process.)

Rogers identified four crucial elements of the person–therapist relationship: unconditional positive regard, reflection, empathy, and authenticity. Unconditional positive regard is the warm, accepting, completely uncritical atmosphere that the therapist must create. The therapist must always respect clients and their feelings, values, and goals.

Reflection is the technique of restating or *reflecting* the person's stream of ideas in slightly different words, like a mirror—without additional commentary. This allows the person to talk and have insights without any

---

Explore

CARL ROGERS

Share with the class the following quote from Carl Rogers:

"In my early professional years, I was asking the question: How can I treat, or cure, or change this person? Now, I would phrase the question in this way: How can I provide a relationship which this person may use for his own personal growth?

I have gradually come to one negative conclusion about the good life. It seems to me that the good life is not any fixed state. It is not, in my estimation, a state of virtue, or contentment, or nirvana, or happiness. It is not a condition in which the individual is adjusted or fulfilled or actualized. To use psychological terms, it is not a state of drive-reduction, or tension-reduction, or homeostasis.

The good life is a process, not a state of being.

It is a direction, not a destination."—From *On Becoming a Person*, 1961

Ask students to write a short essay about how this quote affects the way they view the role of the therapist in helping people through their issues.

interference due to the therapist's interpretations or biases. Here's an example from one of Rogers's own sessions (Meador & Rogers, 1984, p. 143):

CLIENT: I just ain't no good to nobody, never was, and never will be.

ROGERS: Feeling that now, hm? That you're just no good to yourself, no good to anybody. Never will be any good to anybody. Just that you're completely worthless, huh?

The therapist acknowledges clients' feelings through **empathy**, which involves listening carefully and closely to clients and trying to feel what they feel. Therapists must also avoid getting their own feelings mixed up with clients' feelings. Finally, the therapist must show **authenticity** in genuine, open, and honest responses. Some professionals may find it easier to "hide" behind the therapist's role, but in person-centered therapy, the therapist has to be able to tolerate a client's differences without being judgmental.

Humanistic therapies have been used to treat mental disorders and also in career and marriage counseling. Person-centered therapy can be very ethical because it is so nondirective: The therapist typically says nothing the client hasn't already said, so there is less risk of misinterpretation. Unfortunately, humanistic therapies have several of the same drawbacks as psychoanalysis. The underlying theories are largely based on case studies, with little supporting experimental research. Clients must also be intelligent, verbal, and able to express themselves logically, which makes humanistic therapies a less practical choice for treating more serious mental disorders such as schizophrenia.

Behavior Therapies: Learning New Responses

I've heard behaviorists have a very different way of looking at abnormality—they think abnormal behavior is all learned. So, do behaviorists do any kind of therapy?

Behavior therapies are action-based rather than insight-based. They aim to change behavior through the same kinds of learning techniques people (and animals) use to learn any new responses.

In behaviorism, the abnormal or undesirable behavior isn't a symptom of a problem; it *is* the problem. Learning created it, and new learning can correct it (Onken et al., 1997; Skinner, 1974; Sloan & Mizes, 1999). This method, with its practical focus on controlling behavior rather than analyzing it, usually produces faster results than insight-oriented therapy. (An old joke states that overnight, a behavioral therapist cured a man's fear of things hiding under the bed by simply cutting the legs off the bed.) Behaviorism assumes all behavior is learned through classical and/or operant conditioning, which form the basis of behavioral therapy techniques.

In **classical conditioning**, one learns an involuntary response when a stimulus that normally causes a particular response is paired with a new, neutral stimulus. After enough pairings, the new stimulus will also cause the response to occur LINK *to Chapter Six: Learning and Language Development, pp. 178–182.* (Think of Pavlov's dogs.) Old, undesirable reflex responses can be replaced by new, desirable ones. In **operant conditioning**, one learns a behavioral response because a given behavior produces effects that are rewarding or punishing. (Instead of Pavlov's dogs, think of dogs being trained to do tricks for a TV show or movie.)

▲ A Rogerian person-centered therapist listens with calm acceptance to anything the client says. A sense of empathy with the client's feelings is also important.

◀ *I've heard behaviorists have a very different way of looking at abnormality—they think abnormal behavior is all learned. So, do behaviorists do any kind of therapy?*

empathy the ability of the therapist to understand the feelings of the client.

authenticity the genuine, open, and honest response of the therapist to the client.

behavior therapies action therapies based on the principles of classical and operant conditioning and aimed at changing disordered behavior without concern for the original causes of such behavior.

classical conditioning learning in which one learns an involuntary response when a stimulus that normally causes a particular response is paired with a new, neutral stimulus. After enough pairings, the new stimulus will also cause the response to occur.

operant conditioning learning in which one learns a behavioral response because a given behavior produces certain effects (such as a reward or punishment).

PSYCHOLOGICAL THERAPIES 451

CHAPTER 14 • Module 33

COVER THE MODULE (continued)

- Basic elements
  - Reflection of client's statements by the therapist—restating and repeating client's feelings
  - Unconditional positive regard given to the client by the therapist—acceptance of client
  - The *empathy* of the therapist for the client—ability to put yourself in client's position
  - *Authenticity* of the therapist in the client's perception—being "real"
- Humanistic therapies are also not based in experimental research.
- They work best with intelligent, highly verbal persons.
- **Behavior Therapies**
  - *Behavior therapies* are action therapies that do not look at thought processes, but instead focus on changing the abnormal or disordered behavior itself through classical or operant conditioning.

LINK *to Chapter Six: Learning and Language Development, pp. 178–182*

DISCUSS THE STUDENT VOICE QUESTION

Write some of the behavioral therapy methods, such as systematic desensitization, flooding, and reinforcement on the board. Ask students to brainstorm certain disorders, fears, or psychoses that might be best treated with each. Can they back up their answers? Which specific methods could be used to help people with serious disorders, such as severe depression or schizophrenia, as noted in the text? Again, ask students to explain why they think so.

Critical Thinking

PHOBIAS

<u>Purpose</u>: Students complete a brief assignment that involves critical thinking, personalizing, and deeper processing of information.

<u>Time</u>: 1 to 5 minutes

<u>Description</u>: Give students several minutes to answer the following questions:

(1) Do you have any phobias? (2) How has classical conditioning played a role in these phobias? (3) Can you think of a way to use classical conditioning to reverse your phobia?

Module 33 Psychotherapies **451**

CHAPTER 14 • Module 33

COVER THE MODULE (continued)

- *Systematic desensitization* involves teaching clients to relax in response to a fear-producing stimulus.
- *Aversion therapy* involves pairing negative/aversive images with undesirable behaviors.

UNDERSTANDING VISUALS

Direct students to the process of systematic desensitization depicted in Figure 33.1. Ask them to think about a phobia or serious fear they have, such as a fear of spiders, enclosed places, or heights. Do they believe they could be cured of their fears by this process? Why or why not? Ask if any students have conquered a serious fear. How?

L2 LPR DIFFERENTIATED INSTRUCTION

Less Proficient Readers Pair a less-proficient reader with a more capable reader who can help emphasize the main points of a reading assignment.

FIGURE 33.1 Systematic Desensitization

1. The client is trained in progressive muscle relaxation, learning to relax different sets of muscles until an almost complete state of relaxation is achieved.
2. The client and the therapist construct a list (a "hierarchy of fears"), beginning with the least frightening object or situation and working up to the most frightening.
3. Under the therapist's guidance, the client starts working through the list, confronting each item mentally (by looking at or thinking about it), or more directly (by actually encountering it).

Classical and operant conditioning are the basis of **applied behavior analysis** techniques (formerly called behavior modification), which are used to treat phobias, obsessive-compulsive disorder, and similar anxiety disorders. Specific techniques include systematic desensitization, aversion therapy, and flooding.

In **systematic desensitization**, used to treat phobic disorders, a therapist guides the client through a series of steps meant to reduce fear and anxiety (see Figure 33.1).

The client gradually progresses through the entire list, all while remaining in a relaxed state. The underlying idea here is that each item is a conditioned stimulus the client has learned to fear because it was originally paired with a real frightening stimulus. For instance, a client may fear the sound of a buzzing bee (conditioned stimulus) because he once suffered a painful bee sting (real frightening stimulus). Therapy gradually overcomes the client's phobia by pairing each conditioned stimulus with a new relaxation response that just isn't compatible with fear. (How could someone simultaneously feel physically relaxed and physically anxious?) In this way, fear is reduced as the client works through the list until the phobia is gone. Desensitization can even be done using virtual reality (Rothbaum et al., 1995).

Aversion therapy aims to reduce the frequency of undesirable behaviors by pairing an aversive (unpleasant) stimulus with the stimulus that results in the undesirable behavior. This therapy is often used to help clients stop behaviors such as smoking, excessive alcohol consumption, or overeating unhealthy foods. For example, alcoholism may be treated through use of the drug *disulfiram*, commonly known as Antabuse (Petrakis et al., 2002). When combined with alcohol, this medicine results in several unpleasant reactions—nausea, vomiting, anxiety, and more serious symptoms. Therefore, the person learns to associate a once-desirable stimulus (alcohol) with an aversive stimulus (the symptoms). This makes this drug an effective deterrent for alcohol use.

applied behavior analysis (behavior modification) the use of learning techniques to modify or change undesirable behavior and increase desirable behavior.

systematic desensitization behavior technique used to treat phobias in which a client makes an ordered list of fears and is taught to relax while concentrating on those fears.

aversion therapy the pairing of an undesirable behavior with an aversive stimulus to reduce the frequency of the behavior.

Class Demonstration

SYSTEMATIC DESENSITIZATION

The technique of systematic desensitization is frequently used to treat persons suffering from phobias. In this exercise, divide the class into small groups and have them develop a systematic desensitization treatment for a phobia. Select a phobia that is somewhat concrete and familiar to the students (e.g., a fear of visiting the dentist or a fear of the water). In order to facilitate the discussion after the exercise, all groups should be assigned the same phobic object or situation. After you have briefly explained the phobia, instruct the groups to do the following: (1) Decide upon and justify the type of relaxation techniques to be used by your client, (2) construct a hierarchy of scenes related to the phobia, and (3) based upon their relaxation technique and hierarchy, decide whether to use graduated exposure and be prepared to justify their choice. Give the groups 15 to 20 minutes to complete their tasks and then ask each group to describe its treatment program. Class discussion can focus on the differences and similarities in treatment programs.

▲ Some behavioral therapists now use virtual reality to expose patients to phobic objects and situations—like the cabin of an airplane. As part of systematic desensitization, this patient receives exposure to anxiety-provoking visual displays through a virtual reality headset.

Flooding, another method used to treat phobias, works a bit faster than systematic desensitization. Both techniques involve exposing the client to the phobic object or situation. But in flooding, this exposure is not gradual, but rapid and intense (Gelder, 1976; Olsen, 1975), with the goal of extinguishing the fear response entirely. For example, a person with a dog phobia might be placed in the same room with a small, friendly dog. If the person cannot leave the room or avoid the dog, the fear will eventually extinguish because *nothing bad happens*. (Leaving the room would actually reinforce the fear through the removal of an unpleasant stimulus, otherwise known as negative reinforcement.)

This technique is also called **exposure and response prevention** because it has two steps: *exposure* to the feared stimulus and *prevention* of the old, fearful response. It may require repeated exposure, but it usually brings results within a few brief sessions. Flooding has been successfully used to treat both post-traumatic stress disorder (Foa et al., 2000; Keane et al., 1989) and obsessive-compulsive disorder (Foa & Franklin, 2000). However, therapists must consider whether their clients are physically healthy enough to withstand the initial trauma that might occur as a result of flooding.

Other behavior therapies are based on operant conditioning. Again, the goal is to reduce the frequency of undesirable behavior and increase the frequency of desirable responses. Operant conditioning techniques include **reinforcement** techniques as well as modeling, shaping, and extinction. **LINK** *to Chapter Six: Learning and Language Development, pp. 184–193.*

Reinforcement strengthens a response by following it with some pleasurable consequence (positive reinforcement) or removing an unpleasant stimulus (negative reinforcement). (Note that "negative reinforcement" does not mean "punishment.") One use of reinforcement is to have clients participate in a **token economy** in which they can earn tokens to trade for food, treats, or special privileges. Clients earn tokens for behaving correctly or accomplishing behavioral goals and may lose tokens for inappropriate behavior. **LINK** *to Chapter Six: Learning and Language Development, p. 192.* Token economies have sometimes helped to modify the behavior of relatively disturbed persons in mental institutions (Dickerson et al., 1994; Glynn, 1990; McMonagle & Sultana, 2002).

Another method, **contingency contracting**, relies on a formal agreement between therapist and client (or teacher and student, or parent and child) that clearly states both parties' responsibilities and goals (Salend, 1987). Such con-

flooding (also known as **exposure and response prevention**) technique for treating phobias and other stress disorders in which the person is rapidly and intensely exposed to the fear-provoking situation or object and prevented from avoiding or escaping it.

reinforcement the strengthening of a response by following it with a pleasurable consequence or the removal of an unpleasant stimulus.

token economy the use of objects called tokens to reinforce behavior; tokens can be accumulated and exchanged for desired items or privileges.

contingency contracting the use of a formal, written agreement between the therapist and client (or other parties) that clearly states behavioral goals, reinforcements, and penalties.

PSYCHOLOGICAL THERAPIES 453

CHAPTER 14 • Module 33

COVER THE MODULE (continued)
- *Flooding* involves overwhelming the client with fear-producing stimuli.
- *Reinforcement* is rewarding appropriate behaviors.

LINK to Chapter Six: Learning and Language Development, pp. 184–193.

- The use of *token economies* involves giving secondary rewards (tokens, points, etc.) for specific behaviors.

LINK to Chapter Six: Learning and Language Development, p. 192

EXTEND THE LESSON (KINESTHETIC)
Make sure students understand the concept of an anxiety hierarchy. Ask for a volunteer who has a phobia (or the volunteer could pretend to have a phobia). For example, the volunteer may have a fear of heights. Everyone in the class should write down one situation that would provide anxiety for a person with a fear of heights. They might write "riding in an elevator to the tenth floor" or "looking down from a 20-foot bridge." The volunteer randomly calls on students to come to the front of the room and read their item. As students come up, the volunteer physically orders them according to the level of anxiety. This exercise is a good visual representation of an anxiety hierarchy. Also, a second volunteer with the same phobia may be asked to come up and "reorder" the people according to their personal fears.

Cultural Connections

CULTURAL BELIEFS ABOUT THERAPY
Psychotherapy appears to be much more widely accepted in individualistic cultures, such as that of the United States. In collectivistic cultures, however, psychotherapy is not common, nor does it have a good reputation. Ask students to speculate about the reasons for this difference. One suggestion might be that in collectivist cultures, psychological problems are viewed in the context of shame and humility. People who need psychotherapists bring dishonor to their families. The entire social network is also different in these cultures, and people often find other ways of dealing with problems (such as alcoholism or engaging that social network). Another cultural difference that contributes to beliefs about therapy is varying emphases on religion. Some groups view psychological problems as spiritual in nature. Like collectivist cultures, these groups may provide interventions (e.g., prayer, support groups) that are based in religious institutions for such problems. Engage students in a discussion of their own culturally based ideas about the effectiveness of therapy.

Module 33 Psychotherapies 453

CHAPTER 14 • Module 33

COVER THE MODULE (continued)

- *Modeling* is demonstrating the desired behavior.
- LINK to *Chapter Six: Learning and Language Development, p. 193*
  - *Extinction* is removing reinforcement for the behavior.
- How successful are behavior therapies?
  - They can be effective in treating specific problems such as bedwetting, drug addictions, and phobias and can help improve some of the more troubling behavioral symptoms associated with more severe disorders.

EXTEND THE LESSON

Have students explore virtual reality therapy online and see if they can find some simulations or even photographs of simulations. (For example, in a person with a phobia, simple photographs may evoke fear of heights or a simulation may evoke fear of spiders.) Or, if you have the resources, download several of the free simulations at a site such as **http://vrealities.com/vrtherapy.html** for use in class. What are students' reactions to the virtual reality they encountered? Did they have a real, physical reaction to the simulations or photographs?

L3 DIFFERENTIATED INSTRUCTION

Visual/Nonverbal Learners Allow these students to explain aloud what they see in photographs, figures, or tables in the textbook.

---

tingency contracts help address specific problems such as drug addiction (Talbott & Crosby, 2001), educational problems (Evans & Meyer, 1985; Evans et al., 1989), and eating disorders (Brubaker & Leddy, 2003).

For example, a typical parent–child contract would include the contract's purpose and a specific list of agreed-upon behaviors, such as "completing homework," "making my bed," and "using a respectful tone when speaking to Mom or Dad," along with rewards for fulfilling these tasks and penalties for failing to do so. This method works because the contract spells out expectations clearly. The stated tasks, penalties, and rewards are consistent, making discipline easier; the child *chooses* the behavior and the associated consequences. Both parties sign the contract, and there is no "wiggle room" for either to reinterpret the rules. Consistency is extremely effective when using reinforcement to mold behavior. LINK to *Chapter Six: Learning and Language Development, p. 193*.

Modeling is based on Albert Bandura's work in observational learning, which states that a person can learn to confront fears or develop certain skills by observing and imitating someone else (the model) (Bandura et al., 1969). In **participant modeling**, a model—either physically present or seen on videotape—demonstrates the desired behavior in a step-by-step, gradual process. The therapist encourages the client to imitate the model (Bandura, 1986; Bandura et al., 1974). For example, a person who fears dogs would watch and then imitate a model who might first approach a dog, then touch it, then pet it, and so on.

Modeling has been used to treat dental fears in children (Klorman et al., 1980; Ollendick & King, 1998), social withdrawal (O'Connor, 1972), obsessive-compulsive disorder (Roper et al., 1975), and phobias (Hintze, 2002). Behavioral therapists sometimes teach parents or others how to carry out this fairly simple technique.

Extinction reduces the frequency of a particular behavior by removing a reinforcer. Often, this means not giving a person any attention for inappropriate or undesirable behavior. With children, this may be a form of **time-out**, in which the child is removed from the situation that provides reinforcement (Kazdin, 1980). In adults, simply refusing to acknowledge an undesirable behavior is one way to reduce its frequency.

Shaping behavior works on the opposite principle—it rewards the person for getting closer to demonstrating a desired behavior. For example, if the goal is to teach a child to brush his teeth independently, the child might be rewarded first for holding a toothbrush, then for going through the motions of brushing, and so on. Modeling, shaping, and extinction may be used not only to treat psychological disorders but also to teach daily living skills and appropriate social behavior to children with developmental delays.

Behavior therapies may be more effective than other methods in treating specific behavioral problems, such as bed-wetting, overeating, drug addictions, and phobic reactions (Burgio, 1998; Wetherell, 2002). People with serious psychological disorders, such as severe depression or schizophrenia, do not respond as well to behavior therapies, although specific symptoms may improve, which helps people function more normally in the social world (Glynn, 1990; McMonagle & Sultana, 2002).

Cognitive Therapies: Thinking is Believing Cognitive therapy (Beck, 1979; Freeman et al., 1989), developed by Aaron T. Beck, is another primarily action-based therapy. It focuses on helping people change their ways of thinking. The idea is that maladaptive behavior is caused by distorted thinking and unrealistic beliefs (Hollon & Beck, 1994), especially distortions related

---

modeling learning through the observation and imitation of others.

participant modeling technique in which a model demonstrates the desired behavior in a step-by-step, gradual process while the client is encouraged to imitate the model.

extinction the disappearance or weakening of a learned response following the removal or absence of the unconditioned stimulus (in classical conditioning) or the removal of a reinforcer (in operant conditioning).

time-out an extinction process in which a person is removed from the situation that provides reinforcement for undesirable behavior, usually by being placed in a quiet corner or room away from possible attention and reinforcement opportunities.

shaping technique in which a person is rewarded for gradually coming closer to demonstrating a desirable behavior by reinforcing steps toward the desired behavior and extinguishing behaviors that move away from the desired behavior.

cognitive therapy therapy focused on helping clients recognize distortions in their thinking and replace distorted, unrealistic beliefs with more realistic, helpful thoughts.

Class Demonstration

MODIFY YOUR BEHAVIOR

A way for students to understand the principles of behavioral therapy is for them to design a program to change their own behavior. Have students choose a behavior that they would like to change. You might suggest cutting back on caffeine, eating more healthfully, or studying more effectively. They can then consider ways in which they could alter their own behavior, taking into consideration the need to keep behavioral records in order to recognize the rewards and stimulus conditions that keep the behavior going. Have the students design a program of behavioral change. This could be assigned as a paper topic, or in relatively small classes, you could have students present their programs to the rest of the class.

to depression (Abela & D'Allesandro, 2002; McGinn, 2000). The goal is to help clients objectively evaluate the truth of their beliefs, as well as their attributions concerning their own behavior and others' LINK *to Chapter Seven: Social Psychology, pp. 224–237.* Then they can recognize distorted, negative thoughts and replace them with more positive, helpful thoughts.

What unrealistic beliefs do people have?

Beck's cognitive therapy focuses on common distortions of thinking LINK *to Chapter Twelve: Theories of Personality, pp. 378–389,* listed in the table 33.1 below:

◀ What unrealistic beliefs do people have?

Table 33.1	Common Distortions of Thinking	
TYPE OF DISTORTION	**DESCRIPTION**	**EXAMPLE**
Arbitrary inference (*Arbitrary* means based only on impulse or whim.)	A person makes inferences, or conclusions, that aren't supported by any real evidence.	"Suzy canceled our date—I'll bet she's going out with someone else!"
Selective thinking	A person focuses on only one aspect of a situation, leaving out other relevant facts that might make things seem less negative.	Peter's teacher praised his paper but made a minor comment about a few punctuation errors. Peter ignores the positive feedback and focuses on the one critical comment.
Overgeneralization	A person draws a sweeping conclusion from one incident and then applies it to areas of life that have nothing to do with the original event.	"I insulted my algebra teacher. I'll flunk and I'll never be able to get a decent job—I'll end up on welfare."
Magnification and minimization	A person blows bad things out of proportion while not emphasizing or recognizing good things.	A student who has received good grades on every other exam believes that the C she got on her last quiz means she will do poorly in all of her courses.
Personalization	A person takes responsibility or blame for events that are not really connected to the individual.	When Tara's best friend is in a bad mood because of something that happened at school, Tara immediately assumes that her friend is angry with her.

arbitrary inference distortion in which a person draws a conclusion that is not based on any evidence.

selective thinking distortion in which a person focuses on only one aspect of a situation while ignoring all other relevant aspects.

overgeneralization distortion in which a person draws sweeping conclusions based on only one incident or event and applies those conclusions to events that are unrelated to the original.

magnification and minimization distortions in which a person blows a negative event out of proportion to its importance (magnification) while ignoring relevant positive events (minimization).

personalization distortion in which a person takes responsibility or blame for events that are unconnected to the person.

PSYCHOLOGICAL THERAPIES 455

Explore

YOU ARE WHAT YOU THINK

Have students read more about the topic of cognitive distortions at **http://depression.about.com/health/depression/library/weekly/aa082399.htm**. Ask them to again think about the ones that particularly plague them. Does the article shed any light on why they tend to think that way? What are some methods they can use to break their irrational patterns of thinking?

CHAPTER 14 • Module 33

COVER THE MODULE *(continued)*

- **Cognitive Therapies**
  - Cognitive therapy is oriented toward teaching the client how thinking may be distorted and helping clients to see how inaccurate some of their beliefs may be.

  LINK *to Chapter Seven: Social Psychology, pp. 224–237*

  - Some of the cognitive distortions in thinking include *arbitrary inference, selective thinking, overgeneralization, magnification and minimization,* and *personalization.*

  LINK *to Chapter Twelve: Theories of Personality, pp. 378–389*

DISCUSS THE STUDENT VOICE QUESTION

Ask students to examine the list of unrealistic beliefs in Table 33.1. Have they experienced any (maybe even all) of these feelings or thoughts at one time in their lives? Were they able to reason themselves out of them or at least understand after the fact that their beliefs about that particular circumstance were irrational?

L3 DIFFERENTIATED INSTRUCTION

Auditory/Verbal Learners Write important points from the chapter on the board. Have students read them aloud from the board and summarize each one as it is discussed in class.

Module 33 Psychotherapies 455

CHAPTER 14 • Module 33

COVER THE MODULE (continued)

- *Cognitive-behavioral therapies* are action therapies that work at changing a person's illogical or distorted thinking.
  - The three goals of cognitive-behavior therapies are to relieve the symptoms and solve the problems, to develop strategies for solving future problems, and to help change irrational, distorted thinking.
  - *Rational-emotive behavior therapy* is a very directive therapy in which the therapist challenges the client's irrational beliefs, often arguing with clients and even assigning them homework.

DISCUSS THE STUDENT VOICE QUESTION

This is a good time to discuss the idea that sometimes, dysfunction does not equal abnormality. Just because the cognitive distortions we have examined are common, and are probably experienced a number of times by just about everyone in the class, does not mean that they serve a purpose in our lives. Encourage students to try to step back and look at the situation the next time they let these kinds of distortions take hold. Tell them to think about why they might be feeling that way and what the situation may really mean.

A cognitive therapist encourages clients to examine and test their beliefs. In their initial talks, the client and therapist identify an illogical or unrealistic belief. Then the therapist guides the client to ask questions, such as "When did this belief of mine begin?" or "What is the evidence for this belief?" This is a kind of critical thinking focused specifically on one's own thoughts rather than outside experiences.

While cognitive therapy focuses on thinking rather than behavior, a related technique, **cognitive-behavioral therapy (CBT)**, addresses both. Like behaviorism, CBT focuses on the present, but it also assumes people's interactions with the world are more complicated than simple, automatic or conditioned responses. People observe the world, make assumptions and inferences based on their observations or cognitions, and then decide how to respond (Rachman & Hodgson, 1980).

CBT also assumes that disorders come from illogical, irrational cognitions and that changing the thinking patterns will relieve the symptoms. Cognitive-behavioral therapists may also use behavioral techniques to achieve the following goals:

1. Relieve the symptoms and help clients resolve the problems.
2. Help clients develop strategies to use to cope with future problems.
3. Help clients replace irrational, self-defeating thoughts with more rational, self-helping, positive thoughts.

Albert Ellis proposed a version of CBT called **rational-emotive behavioral therapy (REBT)**, which teaches clients to challenge irrational beliefs with more rational, helpful statements (Ellis, 1997, 1998). Many people hold irrational beliefs like "Everyone should love and approve of me (if they don't, I am awful and unlovable)," or "When things do not go the way I wanted and planned, it is terrible, and I feel very disturbed. I can't stand it!"

But I've felt that way at times. Why are these statements so irrational?

Although common, these all-or-nothing feelings don't make sense. Can anyone expect to receive constant love and affection, or to have everything work out as planned? REBT is about helping people to realize that life can be good without being "perfect."

REBT therapists are very directive and confrontational. They may challenge irrational beliefs, assign homework, use behavioral techniques, and even argue with clients in exchanges like this:

CLIENT: I'm just so shy, I can't bring myself to talk to anyone.

THERAPIST: Really? You're talking to me, aren't you?

CLIENT: But that's different, I know you.

THERAPIST: You didn't know me when you started seeing me, yet you were able to talk to me, right? So obviously, you can talk to other people when you want, right?

CLIENT: Well. . . maybe. But it's hard for me to just start up a conversation with someone I've never met.

THERAPIST: But "hard" isn't the same as "impossible," is it? When you go home tonight, I want you to look at some person you don't know on the bus, the train, the sidewalk, and just say, "Hi." That's all, just "hi." Do that at least twice a day until you see me again, and each time you do it, buy yourself a little treat.

> But I've felt that way at times. Why are these statements so irrational?

cognitive-behavioral therapy (CBT) action therapy in which the goal is to help clients overcome problems by learning to think more rationally and logically.

rational-emotive behavior therapy (REBT) cognitive-behavioral therapy in which clients are directly challenged in their irrational beliefs and helped to restructure their thinking into more rational belief statements.

Class Demonstration

RATIONAL-EMOTIVE THERAPY

Purpose: Students generate examples of irrational beliefs and reword them with more rational, helpful statements.

Time: 5 to 10 minutes

Description: Students work in teams of three to five. Each student chooses an object to use as a "talking chip" (e.g., pen, coin, keys). One student begins by generating an irrational belief. He or she might say, "Nobody likes me." Once they have spoken, they put their talking chip into the center of the table. Other students may respond by trying to replace that irrational statement with a more rational, helpful one. For example, a student might answer with "Is that really true? Let's make a list of all the people who like you." It's now another student's turn to come up with an irrational statement and put his or her chip on the table. Students may not share an irrational statement again until all team members have taken a turn and placed their chips on the table. When everyone has shared, the members retrieve their chips and begin again.

Cognitive and cognitive-behavioral therapies are both action therapies, which are less expensive than most insight therapies because they are comparatively short term. Instead of digging deeply into the problem's source, cognitive therapies tackle the problem itself, helping clients deal with symptoms directly. Both cognitive and behavioral therapies are sometimes criticized for treating the symptom, not the cause (although the cognitive viewpoint does address maladaptive thoughts as a cause). Another criticism is the potential for bias (Westen, 2005). No one is perfectly logical, so can the therapist always decide whether the client's thoughts are rational?

Nevertheless, cognitive and cognitive-behavioral therapies have considerable success in treating many disorders, including depression, stress disorders, eating disorders, anxiety disorders, personality disorders, and even—when combined with other therapies—some types of schizophrenia (Beck, 2007; Clark et al., 1989, in press; DeRubeis et al., 1999; Holcomb, 1986; Jay & Elliot, 1990; Kendall, 1983; Kendall et al., 2008; McGinn, 2000; Meichenbaum, 1996; Mueser et al., 2008). The learning principles on which cognitive therapies are based are considered empirically sound (Masters et al., 1987).

Table 33.2 categorizes the various psychotherapies discussed up to this point.

Table 33.2 Characteristics of Psychotherapies

TYPE OF THERAPY	GOAL	KEY PEOPLE
Psychodynamic therapy	Insight	Freud
Person-centered therapy	Insight	Rogers
Behavior therapy	Action	Watson, Jones, Skinner, Bandura
Cognitive therapy	Action	Beck
CBT	Action	Various professionals
REBT	Action	Ellis

Group Therapies: Not for the Shy An alternative to individual therapy is to gather a group of clients with similar problems to discuss them under a single therapist's guidance (Yalom, 1995). Most of the approaches discussed so far could be done in a group setting, but the ones most suited to groups are person-centered and behavior therapies; the ones least suited to groups are psychoanalysis and cognitive-behavioral therapies (Andrews, 1989). The group structure can also vary, and not all group therapy uses a trained therapist. Common forms of group therapy include family counseling and self-help groups.

In **family counseling**, also called **family therapy**, a family that is experiencing some type of problem—marital or child-discipline problems, for example—visits the therapist as a group. (The group may also include the extended family.) Therapy may also include some one-on-one sessions with individual family members, but the real work in improving family communication happens in the group setting (Frankel & Piercy, 1990; Pinsof & Wynne, 1995). Therapy focuses on the family as a system of interacting parts. No one person is "the problem"; all members of the system are experiencing, rewarding, or contributing to the problem.

family counseling (family therapy) a form of group therapy in which family members meet together with a counselor or therapist to resolve problems that affect the entire family.

PSYCHOLOGICAL THERAPIES 457

Explore

GROUP THERAPY

Encourage students to learn more about the methods and benefits of group and family therapy at the following websites:

- **Family Therapy:** www.abacon.com/famtherapy/history.html
  An historical overview—excellent overview of family therapy
- **Group Therapy:** www.yalom.com
  Irving Yalom—group therapy provides students with a better understanding of group therapy, focusing mainly on Yalom.
- **Divorce Support:** www.divorcesupport.com/
  This website offers suggestions and practical information for coping with divorce.

CHAPTER 14 • Module 33

COVER THE MODULE *(continued)*

- Although cognitive-behavioral therapy has seemed successful in treating depression, stress disorders, and anxiety, it is criticized for focusing on the symptoms and not the causes of disordered behavior.
- **Group Therapy**
  - Group therapy can be accomplished using many styles of psychotherapy and may involve treating people who are all part of the same family, as in family counseling.

CHECK FOR UNDERSTANDING

Make sure students have their books closed and copy Table 33.2 on the board, completing the first column. Either individually on paper, or as a class, have students complete the rest of the table. You may even want to add a fourth column, "Methods," to the end of the table.

L3 DIFFERENTIATED INSTRUCTION

Tactile/Kinesthetic Learners Have these students draw flowcharts to organize chapter information.

CHAPTER 14 • Module 33

COVER THE MODULE (continued)

- Group therapy can also be accomplished without the aid of a trained therapist in the form of *self-help or support groups* composed of other people who have the same or similar problems.
- Group therapy has the advantages of low cost, exposure to other people with similar problems, social interaction with others, and social and emotional support from people with similar disorders or problems.
- Disadvantages of group therapy can include the need to share the therapist's time with others in the group, the lack of a private setting in which to reveal concerns, the possibility that shy people will not be able to speak up within a group setting, and the inability of people with severe disorders to tolerate being in a group.
- Group therapy is less costly than individual therapy and provides a great deal of social and emotional support from other group members.

MULTIMEDIA CONTENT AVAILABLE AT
www.mypsychlab.com

Explore the different schools of therapy on mypsychlab.com

For example, George frequently refused to do chores, treated people rudely, and destroyed his toys for attention. His father had not wanted children and only paid attention to George when he was misbehaving. His mother tolerated his rudeness, wouldn't let his father spank him, and replaced his broken toys with new ones. Clearly, the problems within this family system were not all George's fault. Family therapy aims to discover and change such unhealthy patterns.

Self-help groups or **support groups** constitute another form of group therapy, in which people meet voluntarily with others who have similar problems, with no therapist in charge. Instead of official leaders, self-help groups have members who volunteer to lead individual meetings. The groups usually center on a particular problem; a well-known example is a 12-step group known as Alcoholics Anonymous. Other groups exist for nearly every imaginable psychological disorder or difficult life situation.

People may choose self-help groups for several reasons. Therapists may be costly or in short supply. Self-help groups are free and provide the social and emotional support of a group session (Bussa & Kaufman, 2000). More importantly, people may feel that a therapist who has never experienced a particular problem cannot truly understand it. In contrast, someone who has "been there" can truly empathize and provide practical advice.

With group therapy, people may improve significantly from simply knowing that they are not alone. Studies have shown that breast cancer patients who participated in group therapy had much higher survival and recovery rates than those who received only individual therapy or no psychotherapy (Fawzy et al., 1993; Spiegel et al., 1989). Another study found that adolescent girls in Africa, suffering from depression due to the stresses of the war in Uganda, improved when treated with group therapy (Bolton et al., 2007).

Table 33.3 summarizes the advantages and disadvantages of group therapy.

Table 33.3 Group Therapy: Advantages and Disadvantages

ADVANTAGES	DISADVANTAGES
• Lower cost for therapist-led sessions; no cost for self-help groups	• Possible reluctance to share personal feelings and secrets with a group
• Exposure to the ways in which other people view and handle the same kinds of problems	• Necessity of sharing the therapist's time during sessions
• The opportunity for both the therapist and the person to see how that person interacts with others	• Possible difficulty speaking up due to shyness or discomfort in social situations
• Social and emotional support from people with similar or identical problems	• Inappropriateness for certain types of problems, such as severe psychiatric disorders involving paranoia

self-help groups (support groups)
groups composed of people who have similar problems and who meet together without a therapist or counselor for the purpose of discussion, problem solving, and social and emotional support.

Group therapy can be combined with individual and biomedical therapies. A survey comparing individual and group therapy found that group therapy is only effective if it is long term, and it is more effective when used to promote skilled social interactions rather than treating serious psychotic symptoms (Evans et al., 2000).

Class Demonstration

GROUP THERAPY

Purpose: Students discuss advantages and disadvantages of group therapy.

Time: 10 minutes

Description: Students begin by thinking about their answers to the following questions:

- What are the advantages to group therapy?
- What are the disadvantages to group therapy?
- How many examples of group therapy can you think of?

Students should try to build on advantages and disadvantages already noted or think of some new ones, but they should also feel free to further discuss any that have already been covered in class. Next, students team up in small groups and discuss their answers. Finally, the groups compile their lists of advantages and disadvantages. The lists can be handed in and/or used for a larger class discussion.

Psychotherapeutic methods that work for some people's problems may not work as well with others, and so nearly all psychological professionals use more than one technique. **Eclectic therapy** is a style of therapy that uses several different techniques of psychotherapy to treat a person's problem.

⊕ Explore on **mypsychlab.com**

⊕ Explore the different schools of therapy on **mypsychlab.com**

33.4 How effective is psychotherapy?

There sure are a lot of psychotherapies, but do any of them really work?

The first major analysis of various psychotherapies' effectiveness concluded that therapy really made no difference. Hans Eysenck reviewed 19 studies, dating back to the 1930s, that reported on clients' improvement or lack thereof when treated with psychoanalysis and eclectic therapy (Eysenck, 1957). He compared the results with studies of other people (the control group) who were institutionalized for mental disorders but received only food, shelter, and care for their basic needs. Eysenck concluded that the people receiving psychotherapy did not recover at any higher rate, and the passage of time alone could account for all recovery.

◀ *There sure are a lot of psychotherapies, but do any of them really work?*

Studies of Psychotherapy's Effectiveness Eysenck's classic survey created a major controversy in clinical and counseling psychology. Other researchers searched for evidence that would support Eysenck's controversial findings. One such effort reviewed well-controlled studies and concluded that different psychotherapies did not differ in effectiveness (Luborsky et al., 1975). Of course, that can mean that the psychotherapies were either all equally effective or all equally ineffective.

Studying the effectiveness of psychotherapy is difficult for many reasons:

1. The ethics of treating some people (the experimental group) and not others (the control group)
2. The potential for a "placebo effect" (Shapiro & Shapiro, 1997)
3. Differences in how long different types of therapy take to achieve results
4. Difficulties in defining and measuring "improvement," especially for insight-based therapies (Shadish et al., 2002)
5. Biases and inaccuracies that affect the experimenter's or the client's reporting (Seligman, 1995; Wampold, 1997)

Let's examine the questions each of these problems might raise in real life:

1. In a controlled study of depressed clients, an experimental group receives cognitive therapy and a control group is put on a waiting list. *Is this fair to subjects in the control group? What if they really need help now?*
2. John is receiving psychotherapy to treat his anger-management problems. He feels like he's getting better, but the people around him see no change. *Is he really improving? Or does he just think he is? In what ways is it meaningful and helpful that John* thinks *he is improving?*
3. Researchers want to conduct a short-term study comparing the effectiveness of psychoanalysis and behavioral therapy. But psychoanalysis takes longer. *Isn't the behavioral therapy guaranteed to seem more effective?*
4. Miriam is working with a person-centered therapist. She's gained insights into her life and has a greater sense of control, self-worth, and self-esteem. *How can these subjective changes be measured?*

eclectic therapy therapy style that results from combining elements of several different therapy techniques.

PSYCHOLOGICAL THERAPIES 459

Critical Thinking

CONTROVERSIES IN THE TREATMENT OF MENTAL ILLNESS

Purpose: Students have a chance to think about, debate, and discuss controversial topics in treating mental illness.

Time: 15 minutes

Description: Pose controversial questions to the class. Students share their answers and contribute to further class discussion. Here are some controversies from the area of treatment:

- Psychotherapy is effective.
- Labeling a person with a disorder can hinder effective treatment.
- With a loving family, people can get better without seeking treatment.
- Therapists and their clients can develop a friendship outside the environment of therapy.

CHAPTER 14 • Module 33

COVER THE MODULE

33.4 How effective is psychotherapy?

- Hans Eysenck's early survey of client improvement seemed to suggest that clients would improve as time passed, with or without therapy.
- Surveys of people who have received therapy suggest that psychotherapy is more effective than no treatment at all.
- Surveys reveal that from 75 to 90 percent of people who receive therapy improve; the longer a person stays in therapy, the better the improvement, and psychotherapy works as well alone as with drugs.
- Some types of psychotherapy are more effective for certain types of problems, and no single psychotherapy method is effective for all problems.

L(I)N(K) to *Chapter Seven: Social Psychology, p. 227*

DISCUSS THE STUDENT VOICE QUESTION

Ask students if their views of psychotherapy have changed as the class has discussed this module. Do they think it could be helpful for psychological problems? Is it stigmatized? Or overdone? What kinds of issues do they think merit therapy?

CHAPTER 14 • Module 33

COVER THE MODULE (continued)
- Effective therapy should be matched to the particular client and the particular problem.
- There should be a *therapeutic alliance* between therapist and client.
- There should be a protected setting in which clients can release emotions and reveal private thoughts.

DISCUSS THE STUDENT VOICE QUESTION

Discuss with students what someone in their situation (a student, and most likely a minor, with limited resources) might do if they thought they needed therapy. For example, they might talk to their parents or other relative, family doctor, school counselor, or even a trusted teacher to get them started. They should acknowledge what they need but not be afraid to speak up if they think that their confidante, or therapist, goes in a direction they are not happy or comfortable with.

COVER THE MODULE

33.5 What other factors influence the effectiveness of therapy?
- When the culture, ethnic group, or gender of the therapist and the client differ, misunderstandings and misinterpretations can occur due to differences in cultural/ethnic values, socioeconomic differences, gender roles, and beliefs.

---

5. Researchers attempt to assess a therapist's effectiveness not through a controlled study, but through feedback from the therapist and his clients. *But isn't the therapist biased?* He expects and wants the treatment to work. *Do clients always report their own behavior accurately?*

Despite these research challenges, more recent surveys have shown that, more often than not, people who have received psychotherapy believe that they have been helped (Kotkin et al., 1996). Several surveys (Lambert & Ogles, 2003; Seligman, 1995; Thase, 1999) have found that an estimated 75 to 90 percent of survey participants believe psychotherapy has helped them. The longer the therapy, the greater the improvement. (Remember, this survey information is subject to the same flaws as any other survey information **LINK** to *Chapter Seven: Social Psychology, p. 227.*) Other studies have found that some psychotherapies are more effective for certain types of disorders (Clarkin et al., 2007; Hollon et al., 2002), but no one psychotherapy is the most effective or works for every problem.

Characteristics of Effective Psychotherapy

So, how does a person with a problem know what kind of therapist to go to? How do you pick a good one?

Most psychological professionals today combine methods or switch methods to fit the particular client's needs and goals. No one therapy is best. What matters is finding the right therapy for a specific client.

Several factors matter in any successful therapy (Hubble et al., 1999; Seligman, 1998; Stiles et al., 1998). The most crucial is the **therapeutic alliance** between client and therapist. This relationship should be caring, warm, and accepting, characterized by empathy, mutual respect, and understanding. Therapy should also provide a protected setting in which to release emotions and reveal private thoughts. It should help clients understand why they feel the way they do and provide ways to feel better.

33.5 What other factors influence the effectiveness of therapy?

Cultural, Ethnic, and Gender Concerns in Psychotherapy Cultural, ethnic, and gender concerns also help determine psychotherapy's effectiveness. Consider the following situation (adapted from Wedding, 2004):

> K. is a 24-year-old Korean American living with her parents, who both grew up in Korea before moving to the United States as adults. K. is depressed and unhappy with her lack of independence. K's father is angry about her plans to marry a non-Korean. At K's first session, her therapist began assertiveness training and role-playing to prepare K. to deal with her father. K never came to her second appointment.

This demonstrates one problem that can arise when the client's ethnicity or culture differs from the therapist's. Different cultures and ethnic groups may have different values. K.'s therapist focused on making her more assertive and independent, but these Western values run counter to Korean cultural values, which stress interdependence, connection with family, and obedience to one's elders. K. may have wanted help dealing with the situation and her conflicting feelings, rather than help in becoming independent.

> So, how does a person with a problem know what kind of therapist to go to? How do you pick a good one?

therapeutic alliance the relationship between therapist and client that develops as a warm, caring, accepting relationship characterized by empathy, mutual respect, and understanding.

Class Discussion

HOW CAN I FIND A GOOD THERAPIST?

Although common problems of living are often eliminated simply in time or through the support of friends or family, people with little available social support should consider professional therapy.

To find a therapist, one could contact the American Psychiatric Association or other professional groups, such as the Association of Behavior Therapists. Librarians can help locate the addresses of organizations. Referrals can be obtained from one's family physician or local mental health department.

People considering therapy should know that there is no such thing as the "best" therapist because satisfaction with a particular therapy depends on what is desired. Regardless of the particular therapeutic orientation chosen, people need a therapist with whom they feel comfortable. In fact, this may be the single most important factor in determining the success of therapy. Discuss this information with students for further information on finding psychological help.

For therapy to be effective, the client must continue in treatment until a successful outcome is reached. K., however, never returned after the first session. Clients may drop out of therapy if the therapist projects values onto them and fails to empathize with or even understand their feelings. This is more likely when the client and therapist are from mismatched backgrounds. For example, imagine how difficult it could be for an educated, white, female therapist from an upper-middle-class family to understand the problems of a Hispanic adolescent boy from a poor family living in substandard housing.

Such culture clashes can make it difficult for therapists to understand and help clients (Matsumoto, 1994; Moffic, 2003; Wedding, 2004). Members of minority racial or ethnic groups typically drop out of therapy more frequently than majority group clients, although there seems to be a reduced dropout rate when both the therapist and the client are members of the same ethnic group (Brown et al., 2003; Cooper et al., 2003; Flaskerud, 1991; Sue, 1977, 1992; Sue et al., 1994; Vail, 1976; Vernon & Roberts, 1982). Traditional forms of psychotherapy, developed mainly in Western, individualistic cultures, may need to be modified to fit clients from more collectivistic, interdependent cultures.

Four potential barriers to effective psychotherapy exist when a client and therapist have vastly different backgrounds (Sue & Sue, 2003):

1. **Language.** Having different native languages may create problems in verbal communication and psychological testing (Betancourt & Jacobs, 2000; Lewis, 1996).
2. **Cultural values.** Differing cultural values interfere with forming an empathetic relationship (Sattler, 1977; Wedding, 2004).
3. **Social class.** Clients from impoverished backgrounds may have values and experiences that the therapist cannot understand (Wedding, 2004).
4. **Nonverbal communication.** Body language can also differ between cultures and ethnicities. Different cultures have different "rules" and comfort levels concerning physical distance between people, gestures, eye contact (Galanti, 1997; Like et al., 1996), conversational silences, and even facial expressiveness.

Are gender differences that important? For example, do most people prefer a therapist who is of the same sex?

Research on this question varies. One study found that white, middle-class clients, whether male or female, seemed to prefer a female therapist (Jones et al., 1987). Another found that African American clients were more likely to drop out of therapy if the therapist was of the same sex (Vail, 1976). However, some research (Flaskerud, 1991) has found that the effects of gender differences are insignificant, particularly when compared to the effects of ethnic and cultural differences. It seems that while a therapist's gender may have some effect on a client's willingness to remain in treatment, cultural differences generally play a larger role in therapist–client misunderstandings than gender differences do.

Psychotherapeutic Strategies and Disorder Prevention Psychotherapeutic techniques can treat psychological disorders—but can they *prevent* them? Yes, according to many psychologists. By identifying people or communities at risk and implementing strategies to minimize that risk, it's

◀ Are gender differences that important? For example, do most people prefer a therapist who is of the same sex?

PSYCHOLOGICAL THERAPIES 461

CHAPTER 14 • Module 33

COVER THE MODULE *(continued)*
- The four barriers to effective psychotherapy that exist when the backgrounds of client and therapist differ are language, cultural values, social class, and nonverbal communication.

DISCUSS THE STUDENT VOICE QUESTION
Ask students how they feel about this issue. When does gender matter in dealing with a professional (such as a doctor), and when does it seem irrelevant? When does culture matter, and when does it seem irrelevant? Are there times when both are an issue? Why?

FAST FACT
Ask students who first identified mental illness as a medical condition rather than a sign of demonic possession or other malicious influences. *(The answer is the ancient Greeks, who, though their understanding and treatment of mental illness were not always correct, did see the value of encouraging and consoling words in treatment. The advent of the Middle Ages saw the return of the belief that mental illness was caused by supernatural forces.)*

Cultural Connection

NAVAJO MEDICINE

For the Navajo, sickness is a sign of disharmony with nature. Each person is thought to be part of a universal design that contains all other people and all the elements of nature in a "psychic wholeness" and "cosmic harmony." This orderly universe contains both good and evil held in balance; improper contact with dangerous elements of the universe causes an imbalance, and such an imbalance manifests itself in sickness. Since all people are part of this interrelated pattern of life, medicine must not only restore the health of the sick one but restore universal harmony in the family and in any segments of the tribe that have become disharmonious with nature.

Direct students to the article at **http://www.parkridgecenter.org/Page126.html** to read about Navajo healing today. Conduct a class discussion or ask students to write a short statement about modern Navajos' approach to healing. What is the role of the traditional healer? What is the role of Western medicine? Are the two compatible? Why or why not?

Module 33 Psychotherapies 461

CHAPTER 14 • Module 33

COVER THE MODULE (continued)

- Therapy can be helpful in alleviating unhealthy behaviors even in people who do not have psychological disorders.
- The quality of community resources can affect psychological health and improve communities at large.

L1 DIFFERENTIATED INSTRUCTION

Special Needs Discuss with these students and their parents whether any special procedures or safety precautions are necessary in the classroom.

---

possible to improve people's well-being and avoid the need for expensive drugs and therapy later on.

Many individuals face poverty, racism, and sexism, along with environmental stressors such as a lack of healthy food, child care, or employment. These circumstances can lead to negative thought patterns and emotions, as well as risky or unhealthy behaviors, even in people who do not have psychological disorders. Therapy techniques can help alleviate these problems by helping people change their thought patterns (cognitive therapy), by modeling and reinforcing positive behaviors (behavioral therapy), and even by promoting positive regard and empathy for others (humanistic therapy).

Community members can provide job training, parenting help, and other practical skills to increase people's sense of competence, empowerment, and self-worth. On a larger scale, society can move toward reducing stress and improving people's quality of life by actively combating poverty, unemployment, and inequality.

These actions may help to prevent psychological disorders and improve the quality of life in our communities. How can you use some of the therapeutic strategies discussed here to improve your life and the lives of those around you?

Applying Psychology to Everyday Life

What Is EMDR?

Graduate psychology student Francine Shapiro was walking through a park recalling old, troublesome memories. As she moved her eyes rapidly back and forth, she discovered that her disturbing thoughts seemed to disappear. She quickly found 70 volunteers to try this eye-movement technique, and they, too, found their disturbing thoughts and anxieties decreasing (Butler, 1993).

Shapiro eventually earned her doctorate by developing a controlled study in which 22 survivors of rape, war, or childhood abuse were given 1 hour of what Shapiro called **eye movement desensitization reprocessing**, or **EMDR**. All participants reported that their memories lost much of their tendency to provoke fear and they felt considerably better after undergoing the process (Shapiro, 1989). EMDR has since become a popular therapy for phobias and other anxiety-related disorders, especially post-traumatic stress disorder or PTSD LINK to Chapter Fifteen: Stress and Health, p. 492.

In EMDR, the client is instructed to think of a negative memory and an image that represents it (Shapiro, 1989, 1995). Then, the client focuses on the memory while visually following the therapist's rapidly moving fingers back and forth, until the fear has been eliminated. This is "eye movement desensitization." The client is also asked to focus on some negative self-statement ("I am unlovable") during the EMDR session. When the fear and anxiety are gone, the client focuses on a positive thought ("I am lovable") while looking for signs of stress or tension. If such signs exist, they will be treated with additional EMDR sessions. This is "reprocessing," in which the negative cognitions are reprocessed into positive, helpful ones.

eye movement desensitization reprocessing (EMDR) controversial form of therapy for post-traumatic stress disorder and similar anxiety problems in which the client is directed to move the eyes rapidly back and forth while thinking of a disturbing memory.

462 CHAPTER 14

Explore

MENTAL HEALTH RESOURCES IN THE COMMUNITY

Divide the class into pairs or small groups and ask students to research what mental health resources are available in their community. Do psychologists or psychiatrists practice in the area? Is there a community mental health service? Are there specific mental health issues particular to the community? If students or their families needed mental health services, where could they go? Reassemble the class and ask volunteers to present the information that they found. Conduct a class discussion on what services the community has or needs and whether current resources are threatened by budget cuts or other issues.

462 Chapter 14 Psychological Therapies

Studies supporting Shapiro have shown EMDR to be an effective therapy for stress and various anxiety disorders (Silver et al. 1995; Wilson et al., 1995). Other researchers have found that EMDR is not always effective (Montgomery & Ayllon, 1994; Muris et al., 1998; Oswalt et al., 1993), or that it is no more effective than simple muscle relaxation or exposure therapy (Vaughan et al., 1994). Some researchers and therapists see EMDR as simply another form of exposure therapy (Davidson & Parker, 2001). Still, others point to the lack of objectivity in how clients' "recovery" is measured. Many early studies were done without verifying a diagnosed disorder, and the therapists themselves personally collected all data (much of it potentially inaccurate self-reporting), raising the possibility of experimenter bias or the experimenter effect (Hurst & Milkewicz, 2000).

The Skeptic's Dictionary article on EMDR (Carroll, 2000) states that each time new study results contradict Shapiro's original theories of how EMDR works, she changes the theory so the new research fits. For example, research showed that the eye movements are not necessary; finger tapping or alternating tones in each ear produces the same results (Butler, 1993; Renfrey & Spates, 1994). Shapiro then admitted the eye movements are not essential and shifted the therapy's focus to reprocessing (Carroll, 2000).

This constant revision makes the theory impossible to disprove and sounds suspiciously like what proponents of pseudopsychologies do when confronted with contradictory evidence (Lohr et al., 1995, 1998). Until enough controlled, objective studies are done, EMDR will remain controversial (Lilienfeld et al., 2002).

Questions for Further Discussion

1. Could EMDR be a radically different form of systematic desensitization or exposure therapy, or could it be the simple exposure that brings about the reported relief?
2. If a therapy such as EMDR does produce results, what could be the harm in allowing people to take advantage of it? How might that be similar to a placebo effect?

CHAPTER 14 • Module 33

APPLYING PSYCHOLOGY TO EVERYDAY LIFE

- *Eye-movement desensitization reprocessing (EMDR)* involves moving the eyes back and forth rapidly while concentrating on disturbing thoughts. The disturbing thoughts are supposed to be controlled or eliminated by this process.

  LINK to Chapter Fifteen: Stress and Health, p. 492

- Although studies seem to show that it is effective in treating stress and anxiety disorders, other research has found that it is not always effective and criticizes the way in which recovery is measured in the supportive studies. More controlled studies are needed.

1. Students should show critical thinking skills in evaluating why EMDR is helpful to some people, keeping in mind the arguments for and against it as a feasible procedure as laid out in the text.

2. Because EMDR is not a proven method of therapy, there is potential harm in its use. If it is, as some suggest, pseudopsychology, while it may seem to work for some people, it may not work for them all the time. If it then ceases to work, people may continue to spend time in psychological pain in an ineffective therapy. Or they may blame themselves for its sudden failure to work. Much like the placebo effect, it may work for some people simply because those people want it to work and/or strongly believe that it will work.

PSYCHOLOGICAL THERAPIES

Class Debate

EMDR

Divide the class into two groups: one to defend EMDR as a viable treatment option and one to debunk EMDR as pseudoscience. Give teams several days, both outside class and some in-class meeting time, to formulate their arguments. During the debate, give each side a chance to present its argument and each side a chance to respond. Students may use websites such as the following for research in formulating their arguments.

- **EMDR Treatment: Less Than Meets the Eye?**
  www.quackwatch.org/01QuackeryRelatedTopics/emdr.html
- **Eye Movement Desensitization and Reprocessing (EMDR)**
  www.skepdic.com/emdr.html
- **What Is EMDR?**
  www.psychotherapist.net/emdr-faq.html#anchor702310
- **What Is EMDR?**
  www.emdr.com/

Module 33 Psychotherapies

CHAPTER 14 • Module 33

Assess

Assign the Module 33 Practice Quiz.

Use the Practice Quiz to identify gaps in student understanding.

REMEDIATE

Have students, individually or in groups, review the module goals, learning objectives, and key terms.

Refer students to the Concept Summary on p. 478 for review.

Close

Review with the students the basic forms of therapy and what disorders or problems each best addresses. Discuss why "talk" therapy is so effective for so many people. Why are there so many different methods? Why do students think therapy is so prevalent in our society?

Practice Quiz

Pick the best answer.

1. Psychotherapies that attempt to change inappropriate or disordered behavior directly are known as
   a. action therapies
   b. insight therapies
   c. biomedical therapies
   d. psychoanalytic therapies

2. The process during which a psychoanalyst encourages a patient to talk about whatever comes to mind without fear of negative evaluation is called
   a. resistance
   b. transference
   c. free association
   d. dream interpretation

3. Compared to traditional psychoanalysis, modern psychodynamic therapy is
   a. more directive
   b. more time consuming
   c. more action oriented
   d. more focused on the id

4. Humanistic therapies are different from psychoanalysis because they focus more on
   a. personal insights
   b. childhood events
   c. biomedical approaches
   d. conscious experiences

5. Which of the following is not one of the four basic elements of Roger's person-centered therapy?
   a. empathy
   b. authenticity
   c. reflection
   d. reinforcement

6. Which of the following would most likely be a person-centered therapist's response to the client's claim, "I feel like a failure"?
   a. "I don't think you're a failure."
   b. "Why do you feel like a failure?"
   c. "Have you always felt like a failure?"
   d. "You feel that you're failing in some way."

7. Jeremy is trying to stop biting his fingernails. He wears a rubber band around each of his wrists, and whenever he finds himself biting his nails, he snaps the band. Jeremy is using a form of
   a. flooding
   b. extinction
   c. aversion therapy
   d. systematic desensitization

8. Maya is upset because her tutor teased her about turning in her assignment several hours late. Although her tutor was quite pleased with the report itself and told Maya that her work was excellent, Maya remains unhappy. Which type of distorted thinking is Maya engaging in?
   a. minimization
   b. personalization
   c. arbitrary inference
   d. selective thinking

9. Annelina is frightened of water. Her therapist takes her to the beach and forces her to stand by the ocean for an hour at a time over several sessions. This therapeutic technique is called
   a. flooding
   b. modeling
   c. reinforcement
   d. systematic desensitization

10. According to Sue and Sue (2003), which of the following is not a potential barrier to effective therapy when therapists and clients come from different cultural backgrounds?
    a. age
    b. language
    c. social class
    d. nonverbal communication

Practice Quiz Answers

1. a
2. c
3. a
4. d
5. d
6. d
7. c
8. d
9. a
10. a

Module 34: Biomedical Therapies and Issues in Therapy

Module Goals

Identify biomedical therapies and evaluate their effectiveness.

Consider legal, ethical, and professional challenges in therapy.

Learning Objectives

34.1 What are biomedical forms of therapy, and how effective are they?

34.2 Should children and adolescents be treated with the same drugs used for adults?

34.3 What ethical challenges do therapists face when they deliver treatment?

34.4 What resources support people with psychological disorders and their families?

Identify Biomedical Therapies and Evaluate Their Effectiveness

Biomedical therapies directly affect the biological functioning of the body and brain. Therapists with a biological perspective, such as psychiatrists, will most likely employ medical techniques instead of or in addition to psychotherapy. Even psychotherapists whose orientation is not primarily biological may work with a medical doctor to combine the two forms of therapy. Biomedical therapies fall into three categories: drug therapy, shock therapy, and surgical treatments.

34.1 What are biomedical forms of therapy, and how effective are they?

Psychopharmacology The use of drugs to control or relieve the symptoms of a psychological disorder is called **psychopharmacology**. Although these drugs are sometimes used alone, they are more often combined with some form of psychotherapy and are more effective as a result (Kearney & Silverman, 1998; Keller et al., 2000). The four basic categories of drugs are antipsychotic drugs, antianxiety drugs, antidepressants, and antimanic drugs (also called mood stabilizers). Table 34.1 lists commonly used classes of drugs.

Simulate on **mypsychlab.com**

Antipsychotic drugs are used to treat psychotic symptoms, such as hallucinations, delusions, and bizarre behavior. They fall into three categories: typical neuroleptics, atypical neuroleptics, and partial dopamine agonists. (*Neuroleptic* comes from the French word *neuroleptique*, which means "to have an effect on neurons.")

Typical neuroleptics block certain dopamine receptors in the brain, thereby reducing dopamine's effect in synaptic transmission (Csernansky et al., 2002). However, because they affect dopamine pathways involved in movement as well as pathways involved in psychosis, they may eventually cause side

Simulate different biomedical therapies on **mypsychlab.com**

psychopharmacology the use of drugs to control or relieve the symptoms of psychological disorders.

antipsychotic drugs drugs used to treat psychotic symptoms such as delusions, hallucinations, and other bizarre behavior.

typical neuroleptics antipsychotic drugs that block certain dopamine receptors in the brain, thereby reducing dopamine's effect in synaptic transmission

Terms

- psychopharmacology • antipsychotic drugs • typical neuroleptics • atypical neuroleptics • partial dopamine agonists • antianxiety drugs • benzodiazepines
- antidepressant drugs • monoamine oxidase inhibitors (MAOIs) • tricyclics
- antimanic drugs • lithium • anticonvulsant drugs • electroconvulsive therapy (ECT)
- bilateral ECT • unilateral ECT • psychosurgery • prefrontal lobotomy • bilateral cingulotomy

---

CHAPTER 14 • Module 34

Focus

RESOURCES

For this module, consult the appropriate sections of the Teacher's Manual, Test Bank, and PowerPoint slides, all found on the Teacher's Resource DVD, and the interactive study tools for students on MyPsychLab.

BEFORE CLASS

Students should read the section for homework before coming to class.

BELLRINGER

Encourage students to think critically about the use of medication in psychological treatment as you review and discuss this module. Point out that people may have very different reactions to using medications. While some people may be eager to turn to medication for any issue, some may be hesitant to use it even for serious problems. Ask students to think about where they fall on that continuum now and after further discussion.

Teach

COVER THE MODULE

34.1 What are biomedical forms of therapy, and how effective are they?

- Biomedical therapies include the use of drugs, induced convulsions, and surgery to relieve or control the symptoms of mental disorders.

- **Psychopharmacology**
  - *Antipsychotic drugs* are used to control delusions, hallucination, and bizarre behavior and include the *typical neuroleptics*, atypical neuroleptics, and partial dopamine agonists.

MULTIMEDIA CONTENT AVAILABLE AT
www.mypsychlab.com

Simulate different biomedical therapies on **mypsychlab.com**

CHAPTER 14 • Module 34

COVER THE MODULE (continued)

- *Antianxiety drugs* are used to treat anxiety disorders and include the benzodiazepines and also certain antidepressant drugs.

LINK to *Chapter Two: The Biological Perspective,* p. 46

CHECK FOR UNDERSTANDING (KINESTHETIC)

Copy Table 32.1 on the board, completing the first column and leaving the other two blank except the headings. Place the answers on sticky notes around the board. (For example, you may just want to stick with one or two.) Invite students up to the board in groups—or all the students if your class is small—to complete the table. Then have one student in the group get his or her text for group members to check their answers together.

Table 34.1 Types of Drugs Used in Psychopharmacology

CLASSIFICATION	TREATMENT AREAS	EXAMPLES
Antipsychotic: typical neuroleptic	Positive (excessive) symptoms such as delusions or hallucinations	Chlorpromazine, droperidol, haloperidol
Antipsychotic: atypical neuroleptic	Positive and some negative symptoms of psychoses	Risperidone, clozapine, aripiprazole (a partial dopamine agonist)
Antianxiety: minor tranquilizers	Symptoms of anxiety and phobic reactions	Xanax, Ativan, Valium
Antimanic	Manic behavior	Lithium, anticonvulsant drugs
Antidepressants: MAOIs	Depression	Iproniazid, isocarboxazid, phenelzine sulfite, tranylcypromine sulfate
Antidepressants: tricyclics	Depression	Imipramine, desipramine, amitriptyline, doxepin
Antidepressants: SSRIs	Depression	Fluoxetine, sertraline, paroxetine

effects such as *tardive dyskinesia,* a syndrome involving repetitive, involuntary jerking movements of the face and body that lasts even after a person stops medication (Jones & Pilowsky, 2002).

Atypical neuroleptics also block dopamine receptors but seem to be more selective for those in one particular dopamine pathway related to psychoses. They also block or partially block some subtypes of serotonin receptors. This combination of actions seems to result in fewer side effects and sometimes even improvement in certain schizophrenic symptoms such as withdrawal, apathy, and reduced communication (Jones & Pilowsky, 2002).

Partial dopamine agonists, a newer class of atypical neuroleptics, partly activate certain subtypes of dopamine receptors rather than blocking them (Tamminga, 2002). (An *agonist* is any drug that mimics the action of a neurotransmitter; a partial agonist does the same, but essentially acts like a weaker version of the neurotransmitter. LINK to *Chapter Two: The Biological Perspective, p. 46.*) By 2005, the only partial dopamine agonist approved by the Food and Drug Administration for use in treating schizophrenia was aripiprazole (Abilify).

Some people might need drug treatment for only a few months or a few years. But in most cases, especially when schizophrenia starts in adolescence or young adulthood, the patient must take medication for the rest of his or her life. Long-term use of neuroleptics, particularly the older, typical class, is associated with decreased cognitive functioning (Terry et al., 2002, 2003). A hoped-for advantage of partial dopamine agonists is that they will not only have fewer side effects but will also have less impact on cognitive processes.

Antianxiety drugs are used to treat disorders ranging from mild anxiety to panic disorder, social phobia, and other phobias. Traditional antianxiety drugs are minor tranquilizers or **benzodiazepines** such as Xanax, Ativan, and Valium, which have a sedative effect and, when taken in the right dose, can re-

atypical neuroleptics antipsychotic drugs that suppress dopamine to a much greater degree in one particular dopamine pathway related to psychoses, and which also block or partially block certain serotonin receptors.

partial dopamine agonists a newer class of atypical neuroleptics that affect the release of dopamine rather than blocking its receptors.

antianxiety drugs drugs used to treat and calm anxiety reactions, typically minor tranquilizers.

benzodiazepines drugs that lower anxiety and reduce stress.

Class Discussion

SHOULD PSYCHOLOGISTS PRESCRIBE MEDICATIONS?

Discuss the issue of whether counseling or clinical psychologists should be able to prescribe medication. Some people have argued that it is ludicrous that family physicians and surgical specialists, who may have no psychological training at all, are allowed to prescribe the entire range of psychoactive drugs for treating mental illnesses, while psychologists, who specialize in treating mental illnesses, cannot prescribe any medications. Although historically, most psychologists did not have the training in pharmacology that physicians were given, in recent years many graduate programs in psychology have added coursework in physiology and pharmacology to narrow this gap. While most people would agree that psychologists probably should not be able to prescribe nonpsychoactive medications, the wisdom of prohibiting them from prescribing *any* medications seems doubtful. Because psychologists are pressing for legislative changes in some states that would allow them to prescribe some medications in some circumstances, this debate is likely to become more visible in the near future. How do students feel about this issue? Do they see any potential dangers if psychologists begin prescribing medications?

lieve symptoms within half an hour (Uretsky, 2002). Their main disadvantage is the potential for abuse and physical dependence, the latter being associated with a potentially dangerous withdrawal syndrome (National Institute on Drug Abuse [NIDA], 2002). Benzodiazepines are now used less frequently, and **antidepressant drugs** (discussed below) have often been prescribed for anxiety disorders such as panic disorder, obsessive-compulsive disorder, and post-traumatic stress disorder. These drugs take 3 to 5 weeks to show any effect, but they are less subject to abuse and have fewer side effects.

The first **antidepressant drugs**, now used in the treatment of depression, were originally developed to treat other disorders. Iproniazid, originally used to treat tuberculosis symptoms in the early 1950s, became the first modern antidepressant when it was found to have a positive effect on mood (Trujillo & Chinn, 1996). It was also the first of the **monoamine oxidase inhibitors (MAOIs)**, which block the activity of the enzyme monoamine oxidase.

Monoamine oxidase is one of the brain's "cleanup workers." Its primary function is breaking down norepinephrine, serotonin, and dopamine, three neurotransmitters involved in controlling mood. Normally, these neurotransmitters are reuptaken by the neurons that released them. However, depressed people seem to benefit from having these neurotransmitters remain in the synaptic gap longer. MAOIs enable that to happen by inhibiting the action of the enzyme that breaks them down, which increases the opportunity for the neurotransmitters to bind to receptor sites.

MAOIs prescribed today include Marplan, Nardil, and Parnate. Their associated side effects—including weight gain, constipation, dry mouth, dizziness, headache, drowsiness or insomnia, and sexual arousal disorders—usually lessen with continued treatment. MAOIs also increase the risk of developing severe high blood pressure if combined with certain foods, beverages, and medications (Geddes & Butler, 2002).

The second class of antidepressants, **tricyclic antidepressants**, was discovered in the course of developing treatments for schizophrenia (Trujillo & Chinn, 1996). Tricyclics, so called because of their three-ring molecular structure, increase the activity of serotonin and norepinephrine by inhibiting their reuptake into the neurons' synaptic vesicles. **LINK** *to Chapter Two: The Biological Perspective, pp. 46–47*. Common tricyclics include Tofranil, Norpramin, Pertofrane, Elavil, Sinequan, and Adapin. Side effects, which may lessen over time, are similar to those of MAOIs but may also include skin rashes, blurred vision, lowered blood pressure, and weight loss (APA, 2000b; Geddes & Butler, 2002).

MAOIs and tricyclics affect the action of three critical neurotransmitters: norepinephrine, serotonin, and dopamine. Many of their side effects involve unwanted actions on other neurotransmitter systems. This observation led to the development of the *selective serotonin reuptake inhibitors (SSRIs)*, which inhibit the reuptake process of serotonin only. This causes fewer side effects, making these drugs comparatively safer than older antidepressants. Like other antidepressants, SSRIs may take 2 to 6 weeks to produce effects. Some of the better-known SSRIs are Prozac, Zoloft, and Paxil.

The last major category is **antimanic drugs** (mood stabilizers), used to treat bipolar disorder and episodes of mania. For many years, the treatment of choice has been **lithium**, a metallic chemical element that, when taken as lithium carbonate, evens out the highs and the lows of bipolar disorder. Lithium interferes with some of the chemical events that occur inside neurons when neurotransmitter receptors are activated; this action may underlie its mood-stabilizing effect (Baraban, Worley, & Snyder, 1989).

antidepressant drugs drugs used to treat depression and anxiety.

monoamine oxidase inhibitors (MAOIs) antidepressant drugs that block the activity of the enzyme monoamine oxidase, which breaks down several neurotransmitters involved in regulating mood.

tricyclics antidepressant drugs that increase the activity of serotonin and norepinephrine by inhibiting their reuptake into the neurons' synaptic vesicles.

antimanic drugs drugs used to bipolar disorder and episodes of mania

lithium chemical element that, in the form of lithium carbonate, has traditionally been used as an antimanic drug

---

CHAPTER 14 • Module 34

COVER THE MODULE (continued)

- *Antimanic drugs* are used to treat bipolar disorder and include *lithium* and certain anticonvulsant drugs.
- *Antidepressant drugs* are used in the treatment of depression and include *monoamine oxidase inhibitors (MOAIs)*, *tricyclic* antidepressants, and selective serotonin reuptake inhibitors (SSRIs).

LINK *to Chapter Two: The Biological Perspective, pp. 46–47*

EXTEND THE LESSON

Have students research information regarding antidepressants on the Internet (e.g., go to the following websites: **www.rci.rutgers.edu/~lwh/drugs/psypharm.htm** and **http://skepdic.com/placebo.html**). Did they find any information that they found surprising? What are their thoughts about the argument for the placebo effect in antidepressants? Did they find that argument convincing? Why or why not?

Class Demonstration

INTERVIEWING MENTAL HEALTH PROFESSIONALS

This assignment gives students firsthand knowledge about careers in therapeutic settings. Invite a mental health professional into the classroom to be interviewed by the students. The interviewee could be a member of your school's counseling center, a psychiatric case worker, a clinician, a psychiatrist, a clinical psychologist in private practice, a social worker, a staff member at the local Veteran's Administration hospital, a director of a halfway house, or a doctor at a state or private hospital. The structure of the interview should include: (1) information about the professional's education and training; (2) years of experience on the job; (3) memorable or difficult cases and the solutions used to work with that person; (4) day-to-day responsibilities; (5) pay range; (6) job satisfaction; and (7) information about how and why the professional chose this career path. Discuss as a class beforehand what else, in general, students want to learn from the speaker and specifically what questions will be asked (although follow-up and spontaneous questions during the interview should be encouraged). Remind students to conduct themselves "professionally" during the interview.

CHAPTER 14 • Module 34

COVER THE MODULE (continued)

- **Electroconvulsive Therapy**
  - *Electroconvulsive therapy (ECT)* is used to treat severe depression, bipolar disorder, and schizophrenia.
  - ECT involves the use of a muscle relaxant, a short-term anesthetic, and relatively mild muscular contractions.

LINK to Chapter Nine: Memory, p. 283

DISCUSS THE STUDENT VOICE QUESTION

What are students' thoughts about ECT? Do they have preconceived notions about the procedure? Does it evoke visions of dark, dirty asylums and cruel doctors? Discuss with students how ECT has been portrayed in movies and television shows, and inform them that ECT is, in fact, endorsed by the American Psychiatric Association as safe and effective (see **www.psych.org/Departments/EDU/Library/APAOfficialDocumentsandRelated/PositionStatements/200702.aspx**). Ask students how they feel about the side effects outlined in the text. Under what circumstances, if any, would the side effects be acceptable to them?

TEACHING TIP

Working in small groups offers the chance for students to assess classmates' contributions. By establishing criteria for evaluation, students can assess others' work. Frequently considered factors include creativity, cooperation, and contributions to the completion of tasks.

---

anticonvulsant drugs drugs traditionally used to treat seizure disorders and sometimes used in treating mania

electroconvulsive therapy (ECT) form of biomedical therapy used to treat severe depression, in which electrodes are placed on either one or both sides of a person's head and an electric current is passed through the electrodes that is strong enough to cause a seizure or convulsion.

bilateral ECT electroconvulsive therapy in which the electrodes are placed on both sides of the head.

unilateral ECT electroconvulsive therapy in which the electrodes are placed on only one side of the head and the forehead.

▶ *What are some of the side effects? Can this therapy affect your memory?*

Although the drug has been associated with weight gain, most side effects typically disappear quickly. Patients must monitor diet carefully, because diuretics (substances like caffeine that cause the body to excrete water) or lowered levels of sodium can cause lithium to build up to toxic levels. Doctors generally recommend that people with recurrent bipolar disorder continue lithium treatment at maintenance levels.

Anticonvulsant drugs, normally used to treat seizure disorders, have also been used to treat mania. One example is the drug Depakote. These drugs can be as effective as lithium in regulating mood and may also be combined with lithium treatments (Bowden et al., 2000; Thase & Sachs, 2000). When bouts of mania include psychotic symptoms, patients are often treated with antipsychotic drugs in addition to a combination of anticonvulsants or antidepressants (Tohen et al., 2003).

Electroconvulsive Therapy Many people are surprised to discover that **electroconvulsive therapy (ECT)** may still be used to treat severe depression. ECT involves delivering an electric shock to one or both sides of a person's head, resulting in a seizure or convulsion and the release of a flood of neurotransmitters (APA, 2001). Mood improves almost immediately. ECT is used to treat severe cases of depression, as well as schizophrenia and severe mania, when these disorders don't respond to other treatments (APA, 2001).

ECT originated in the 1930s, when doctors were researching the possible uses of drug-induced seizures in treating schizophrenia. Italian researchers Ugo Cerletti and Lucio Bini first used electricity to induce a seizure in a man with schizophrenia, who fully recovered after just 11 treatments (Endler, 1988; Fink, 1984; Shorter, 1997). Soon, doctors were using ECT on many severe mental disorders—without anesthesia because the severe shock usually resulted in a loss of consciousness. Broken bones, bitten tongues, and fractured teeth were not unusual "side effects."

Understandably, this little-understood treatment developed a bad reputation, especially after its harsh portrayal in the classic 1962 book by Ken Kesey, *One Flew Over the Cuckoo's Nest*. Modern ECT, however, is far more controlled and humane. It is used only to treat severe disorders, and most states require informed, written consent. ECT is most useful for severe, otherwise untreatable depression, especially in cases involving an intent to commit suicide. Because ECT works more quickly than antidepressants, it can help to prevent suicide attempts (APA, 2001). ECT is not a "cure," and no one fully understands how it works or why it is effective, but it does help bring about a state of mind that is more receptive to other treatments.

What are some of the side effects? Can this therapy affect your memory?

ECT has several negative side effects. It may disrupt the memory consolidation process and may prevent the formation of long-term memories. LINK to Chapter Nine: Memory, p. 283. This causes both retrograde amnesia, the loss of memories for events that happen close to the time of the treatment, and anterograde amnesia, the rapid forgetting of new material (APA, 2001; Lisanby et al., 2000; Weiner, 2000).

The anterograde amnesia usually clears up within a few weeks, but the retrograde amnesia can extend to events several months before and a few weeks after treatment. A few patients suffer more severe and long-lasting cognitive difficulties; it is not clear whether these stem from the treatment or the disorder (Smith, 2001).

Modern ECT practices aim to reduce side effects. The patient is given muscle relaxants to reduce the convulsive effects, as well as a short-term

---

Class Discussion

THE ETHICS OF ELECTROCONVULSIVE THERAPY

Ugo Cerletti's (1877 to 1963) contribution to the development of convulsive therapies—the history of which reaches back to the late 1800s—was to advocate the use of electroshock. In 1938, after a series of studies using animals, Cerletti applied electroshock to a 19-year-old man found wandering the streets of Rome in a psychotic state. The patient received 11 electroshock applications and was reported to be "cured" after 1 year and able to return to his former job. Electroshock methods were introduced to the United States in 1939, although the *Journal of the American Medical Association* published editorials warning of the possibility of electrocution. Discuss this history of ECT with students. What are the ethical implications? What would be the problem with proving the effectiveness of ECT (as practiced in the 1930s) on human subjects today? Even if it were able to be proven, would it be put to use?

CHAPTER 14 • Module 34

COVER THE MODULE (continued)

- Research has shown that when both published and unpublished studies are taken into account, all but one antidepressant drug has been associated with an increased risk of suicide when used to treat depression in children and adolescents.
- The one safe antidepressant has been found to be more effective when combined with psychotherapy.

DISCUSS THE STUDENT VOICE QUESTION

Use this question as an illustration of how difficult it is to find a "magic bullet" drug for any disorder or physical problem. Sometimes, it is difficult to know how the medication will affect different people (researchers cannot test every possible scenario) or what the long-term side effects will be.

MULTIMEDIA CONTENT AVAILABLE AT
www.mypsychlab.com

Listen to the Psychology in the News podcast on treating children and adolescents with antidepressant drugs on **mypsychlab.com**

COVER THE MODULE

34.3 What ethical challenges do therapists face when they deliver treatment?

- Therapists confront many ethical issues.

Wait a minute—how can a drug that's meant to help depression increase the risk of suicide?

Listen to the Psychology in the News podcast on treating children and adolescents with antidepressant drugs on **mypsychlab.com**

▲ Depression is not only an adult disorder; children and adolescents, such as this young man, also suffer from depression. Using antidepressant drugs to treat depression in children and adolescents is controversial. What other methods could be used to treat depression in this age group?

children and adolescents, suggests that they be closely monitored, and urges professionals to weigh the drug's possible benefits against the risks.

Wait a minute—how can a drug that's meant to help depression increase the risk of suicide?

Children and adolescents are often affected differently by drugs used to treat adults. Younger people's hormonal and neurological systems are not yet fully functional, and thus, drugs that are safe for adults may have harmful side effects. However, the effects of antidepressants on children and adolescents are not clearly understood. **Listen** on **mypsychlab.com**

A major 2001 study—at that time the largest clinical trial of antidepressant use in cases of adolescent depression—concluded that antidepressants were both safe and effective (Keller et al., 2001). But in April 2004, researchers published a meta-analysis (a comprehensive scientific review) of published and unpublished studies conducted by drug companies that produce antidepressants (Whittington et al., 2004). Although the companies' published research supported the drugs' safety for use with children and adolescents, unpublished research indicated that four out of five SSRIs tested could increase the risk of suicide in children aged 5 to 18. Prozac was the only exception.

Does this mean that these drugs should never be prescribed for children and adolescents? At least one drug in the 2004 study is approved for use in treating obsessive-compulsive disorder in children. When this drug (and possibly others like it) is used to treat anxiety-related disorders rather than depression, there is no apparent increase in risk of suicide.

Obviously, using these drugs to treat depression is risky, especially when the research shows that there are safer drugs and alternative treatments. One study found that treatment of adolescents with major depression was more successful when the approved antidepressant was combined with psychotherapy (March et al., 2004). Doctors and psychiatrists should exercise caution in prescribing powerful psychoactive drugs meant for adult bodies and nervous systems to younger persons.

Consider Legal, Ethical, and Professional Challenges in Therapy

34.3 What ethical challenges do therapists face when they deliver treatment?

Consider the following scenarios:

- Dr. A. is a social worker. One day, a client of hers admits to feeling out of control around his two children and regularly hitting them with a belt. Dr A. knows the importance of maintaining confidentiality but fears for the children's safety.
- Dr. B., a marriage counselor, is treating Mr. and Mrs. Smith. When Dr. B. occasionally sees Mrs. Smith alone, she flirts with him. During one such session, Mrs. Smith announces her plans to leave her husband. She confesses her attraction to Dr. B., who admits the feeling is mutual.

Explore

ANTIDEPRESSANTS AND ADOLESCENTS

Students can learn more about the use of antidepressants for adolescents, and the controversy surrounding it, at the following websites:

- **National Institute of Mental Health**

  www.nimh.nih.gov/health/topics/child-and-adolescent-mental-health/antidepressant-medications-for-children-and-adolescents-information-for-parents-and-caregivers.shtml

- **Healthy Place**

  www.healthyplace.com/depression/children/antidepressants-for-children-and-adolescents/menu-id-68/

- **Antidepressants and Suicide**

  www.alertpubs.com/antidepressants_and_suicide.htm

anesthetic. Electrodes may be placed on both sides of the head (**bilateral ECT**) or only on one side and the forehead (**unilateral ECT**). Unilateral ECT is just as effective as bilateral ECT but causes less severe convulsions and memory and cognitive problems (Sackeim et al., 2000).

Psychosurgery Psychosurgery involves cutting into the brain to remove or destroy brain tissue and thereby relieve psychiatric symptoms. One of the earliest and best-known techniques is the **prefrontal lobotomy**, which severs the connections between the prefrontal lobes and the rest of the brain (Cosgrove & Rauch, 1995; Freeman & Watts, 1937).

But I thought lobotomies left most people worse off than before—didn't it take away their emotions or something?

Some early lobotomy patients did seem less agitated, anxious, and delusional, but their experience was hardly typical. Many patients experienced negative personality changes, including apathy, lack of emotional response, intellectual dullness, and childishness. Others—about 6 percent—did not survive the surgery. As antipsychotic drugs were developed and long-term studies highlighted lobotomies' serious side effects, this technique was eventually discontinued (Cosgrove & Rauch, 1995; Swayze, 1995).

A modern psychosurgical technique is the **bilateral cingulotomy** in which magnetic resonance imaging LINK *to Chapter Two: The Biological Perspective, pp. 55–56* is used to guide an electrode to the cingulate gyrus. This area connects the frontal lobes to the limbic system, which controls emotional reactions. Running a current through the electrode destroys a very small and specific area of brain cells (a process called deep lesioning). LINK *to Chapter Two: The Biological Perspective, p. 54*. Cingulotomies are effective in about one-third to one-half of cases of major depression, bipolar disorder, and certain forms of otherwise unresponsive obsessive-compulsive disorder (Dougherty et al., 2002; Spangler et al., 1996).

Because a bilateral cingulotomy is deliberate and permanent brain damage, doctors will not perform one unless all other possible treatments have been tried, and will do so only with the patient's full and informed consent (Rodgers, 1992; Spangler et al., 1996). Given the ethical, social, and legal implications of psychosurgery in general, today, only very few such surgeries are carried out worldwide (Cosgrove & Rauch, 1995).

Many psychological professionals today believe that combining psychotherapy with medical therapies—particularly drug therapy—is a more effective approach to many disorders. A depressed person may take an antidepressant drug but also participate in therapy. Cognitive-behavioral therapy in combination with drug therapy has been shown to be particularly effective in treating depression (Dew et al., 2007; Frank et al., 2007; Rohde et al., 2008). Another study has found that women with recurrent depression benefit from supplementing antidepressants with monthly maintenance psychotherapy (Frank et al., 2007).

34.2 Should children and adolescents be treated with the same drugs used for adults?

Using antidepressant drugs to treat depression and anxiety-related disorders in adolescents is somewhat controversial (Breggin, 2003, 2004; Breggin & Breggin, 1994). In late 2004, the Food and Drug Administration began requiring all antidepressants to be labeled with a "black box" warning (FDA MedWatch Safety Alert, 2004). The warning describes an increased risk of suicide in

▲ *The woman on the left is Rosemary Kennedy, sister of President John F. Kennedy. The man on the right is her father, U.S. Ambassador to Great Britain Joseph Kennedy. About 6 years after this photograph was taken, Rosemary, who was mildly mentally retarded and whose behavior had become difficult to control, was subjected to a prefrontal lobotomy. The results were disastrous, and she remained institutionalized until her death on January 7, 2005.*

psychosurgery surgery performed on brain tissue to relieve or control severe psychological disorders.

prefrontal lobotomy psychosurgery in which the connections of the prefrontal lobes of the brain to the rear portions are severed.

bilateral cingulotomy psychosurgical technique in which an electrode is inserted into the cingulated gyrus with the guidance of a magnetic resonance imaging machine for the purpose of destroying that area of brain tissue with an electric current.

CHAPTER 14 • Module 34

COVER THE MODULE (continued)

- **Psychosurgery**
  - One of the earliest psychosurgeries was the *prefrontal lobotomy*, in which the front part of the frontal lobe was cut away from the back part of the brain, producing effects ranging from a disappearance of symptoms to a lack of emotional response and mental retardation.
  - Modern psychosurgery includes the *bilateral cingulotomy*, used to treat major depression, bipolar disorders, and certain forms of obsessive-compulsive disorder that have not responded to other forms of treatment.

LINK *to Chapter Two: The Biological Perspective, pp. 54–56*

DISCUSS THE STUDENT VOICE QUESTION

Point out to students that the vast majority of the lobotomies performed in the United States were done in the 1940s and 1950s. Ask students why people might have undergone (or subjected their loved ones to) a dangerous surgery with such frightening side effects. (*Possible answer: The stigma of mental illness at that time might have driven those who could afford it to take drastic measures in hopes of a miracle cure.*)

COVER THE MODULE

34.2 Should children and adolescents be treated with the same drugs used for adults?

- Antidepressant use with adolescents is controversial.

Class Discussion

PREFRONTAL LOBOTOMIES

Most people consider the prefrontal lobotomy to be barbaric and without any redeeming value. Use this assumption to stimulate a class discussion on this topic. Present the following scenario:

Imagine that you are a doctor in a mental hospital in the 1940s. Your hospital, constructed to hold 700 patients, now has over 1300. Many patients are violent and need to be tied to their beds or kept in locked cells. Antipsychotic drugs will not be invented for another decade. Patients regularly attack one another and the attendants; others run through the hallways screaming. You have one patient who has been in the hospital for 25 years, for whom there is no hope of recovery. However, you know that there is a brief procedure that, if successful, will result in a large decrease of episodes of violent behavior. If successful, the patient will appear to be much more content with life. You know that, for most patients receiving this procedure, there will be little difference in measurable IQ. You know of no behavioral test that routinely shows any mental deficit from the procedure. Would you, as this patient's doctor, use this procedure?

- Dr. C., a psychiatrist, has experience providing psychodynamic and humanistic therapy. A new client explains that he would like help in overcoming his social phobia using behavioral therapy. Dr. C has no formal training in this method.
- Dr. D., a psychologist, copies some patient files onto a laptop computer so he can catch up on work over the weekend. He stops at the supermarket on his way home. Upon returning to his car, he discovers that it has been broken into. The briefcase containing his laptop has been stolen.

These scenarios illustrate ethical issues that therapists face. By the nature of their work, they have access to great deal of personal information and may have a powerful influence over their clients' lives and well-being. With such power comes great responsibility.

Good therapists take their ethical responsibilities to clients, other psychological professionals, and the community very seriously. Ethical issues fall into four broad categories:
- commitment to the client's well-being
- confidentiality and privacy
- professional boundaries and conflicts of interest
- competence and professionalism

Commitment to the Client's Well-Being Good therapists commit wholeheartedly to the therapeutic relationship and work to ensure that the client has an active, empowered role. When a client first seeks treatment, the therapist will determine whether he or she can meet the client's needs. A therapist who cannot take on a new client for some reason (such as a too-full schedule or lack of expertise with a certain problem) will attempt to refer the client elsewhere for treatment.

In treatment, the therapist keeps the client informed—about what to expect; the therapist's and client's responsibilities; various treatments' purpose, risks, and benefits; and any other relevant issues. The principle here is "informed consent." Before prescribing a new medication, a psychiatrist must inform the client about potential side effects. If a client is not fluent in English, the therapist must still ensure that treatment decisions are communicated clearly.

Self-determination is also important. The therapist's role is to help the client—not to direct every aspect of his or her life. Therapists must be careful not to exert excessive or unhealthy influence.

Finally, therapists stay committed until the client no longer needs them. Termination of the relationship should occur by mutual consent. If circumstances make it impossible to continue treatment—for instance, if the therapist is moving to another state—the therapist will help the client transition to another qualified provider. Simply not liking a patient isn't grounds for ending the relationship; however, if interpersonal issues are so great that they interfere with treatment, the therapist may refer the patent elsewhere. (Good therapists also won't let therapy drag out for years if the client clearly doesn't need it or isn't improving. In those cases, the ethical thing to do would be to suggest termination or to help the client find someone who could better help them.)

Confidentiality and Its Limits To build trust, therapists must be able to assure the client that personal disclosures will remain confidential and privacy will be protected. Obviously, an ethical therapist would never gossip about clients or reveal information shared in confidence to the client's spouse, employer, or other connections. Although therapists treating minors may

---

CHAPTER 14 • Module 34

COVER THE MODULE (continued)
- There are four categories of ethical issues:
  - Commitment to clients' well-being
  - Confidentiality and privacy
  - Professional boundaries and conflicts of interest
  - Competence and professionalism
- Therapists should work with clients for a good outcome rather than telling the client what to do.

EXTEND THE LESSON
Discuss with students the ethical scenarios posed in the text. Where does the ethical lapse, or potential lapse, lie? What can the therapist in each scenario do to stop or prevent the issue? In the first scenario, where is the line between confidentiality and the children's safety? What should the therapist do if he or she is not sure?

L2 LPR DIFFERENTIATED INSTRUCTION

Less Proficient Readers Emphasize the organization of a chapter before the student begins reading. Point out relationships among objectives and major headings. A simple chart of the chapter's organization may be useful.

Explore

ETHICAL ISSUES

Ask students to do some research on ethical issues in psychotherapy. They may use the library or the Internet in their research. Some websites they may consult include:

- **The American Psychological Association**
  www.apa.org/topics/ethics/index.aspx
- **The American Psychiatric Association**
  www.psych.org/MainMenu/PsychiatricPractice/Ethics.aspx
- **The American Psychotherapy Association**
  www.groupsinc.org/group/ethicalguide.html

- **Psychotherapy Networker**
  www.psychotherapynetworker.org/magazine/populartopics/ethics

Ask students to write a short report on their findings. What are some common ethical dilemmas? Were some of the issues that fell under the heading of "ethics" surprising to them? Why is it sometimes difficult to recognize an ethical problem? How can therapists avoid getting into risky ethical territory? Is it always avoidable?

CHAPTER 14 • Module 34

COVER THE MODULE *(continued)*
- Therapists are bound to break their promise of confidentiality if they believe a client is a danger to himself or herself or others.
- Therapists should be careful to keep their relationships with their clients professional.
- Therapists should be forthcoming about their expertise and only treat clients they are qualified to treat.

EXTEND THE LESSON

Discuss with students the problems that the issue of confidentiality might pose for a therapist. Not everyone says, "I'm going to kill myself" or "I'm going to hurt someone." What if clients claim that they do not plan to kill themselves, but it has occurred to them before? What if clients confide that they once committed a crime and got away with it? What rights of confidentiality should children have? What about confidentiality in family and group therapy? (You can find more on these issues at **www.guidetopsychology.com/confid.htm**. The laws on this site apply to the state of California. You might encourage students to check out the laws in your own state.)

---

update parents or guardians about the client's progress, they should not disclose information shared in therapy sessions.

Additionally, therapists must exercise discretion and omit potentially identifying details when discussing cases with colleagues and publishing articles or books. If the therapist wishes to record a session on audio or video, or have colleagues observe a session, it must be done with the client's consent. Finally, therapists follow strict guidelines for ensuring confidentiality of records, including destroying those records when appropriate. In the hypothetical scenario described above, Dr. D's carelessness grossly endangered clients' right to privacy.

What about Dr. A's dilemma? In situations where clients are clearly a danger to themselves or others, a therapist must break confidentiality and alert appropriate medical or legal professionals. (Behaviors that are illegal but do not endanger anyone, such as shoplifting, do not meet this criterion.) For instance, if a client revealed detailed plans to commit suicide, the therapist would be professionally obligated to seek emergency inpatient care. In many states, psychological professionals are among the people legally required to report suspected child abuse or neglect, so Dr. A should contact her local child protective services agency.

▲ *Clients may share their innermost feelings with a therapist, along with very personal details about their lives. For this reason, therapists must scrupulously honor their clients' right to confidentiality and privacy.*

Professional Boundaries and Conflicts of Interest Ethical therapists must maintain appropriate professional boundaries and avoid conflicts of interest—that is, situations where the therapist's personal interests or motives might interfere with his or her professional obligations. To fulfill this responsibility, therapists avoid forming other types of relationships with the client—personal friendships, romantic relationships, business partnerships, and so on. Therapist also do not treat clients with whom they have a preexisting relationship, including family relationships.

In Dr. B's case, acting on or even revealing his attraction to Mrs. Smith would violate professional boundaries. It would also place his own interests above his obligations to both Mr. and Mrs. Smith. Therapists are prohibited from having romantic or sexual relationships with clients, and professional organizations also stipulate that, even if therapy is terminated, the therapist cannot enter into such a relationship for a period of years afterward. (It is also unacceptable to terminate therapy for the sake of pursuing a romantic or other personal relationship.)

Less dramatic, but still important, conflicts of interest include accepting gifts from a client, socializing together, and the like. While it is important for therapists and clients to relate to each other as people, their relationship must have clearly defined limits.

Competence and Professionalism Finally, good therapists fulfill a high standard of competence and behave professionally not only with clients, but also with colleagues and with the psychology community as a whole. This responsibility encompasses a wide range of day-to-day actions.

Good therapists are continually learning. They keep informed about new research, new therapeutic practices, and medical, social, or legal developments that affect the treatment they provide. They also represent themselves honestly—in person, in publications, and in any form of advertising or business promotion. They do not claim expertise they don't possess. In Dr. C's case, if she knows behavioral therapy would be the best treatment for her potential new client but she herself isn't qualified to provide it, the ethical choice would be to help the client find someone who is.

Class Discussion

THERAPISTS' VISIT TO THE CLASSROOM

Ask one or more therapists from your area to meet with your class to discuss issues covered in the text, such as professional ethics, confidentiality, and dealing with clients. Therapists could include a social worker, psychologist, or marriage counselor. Ask students to submit questions to you ahead of time, which you can pass along to the visitors. Remind students to treat their guests with courtesy and respect.

Many treatment professionals also have other responsibilities such as research, writing, or teaching. Just as they are expected to be thoughtful, ethical, and honest when treating clients, they must also bring these qualities to other aspects of their work, including their interactions with students, colleagues, employees they supervise, and others. This doesn't mean therapists never have a bad day or make a mistake—just that they hold themselves to a high standard.

34.4 What resources support people with psychological disorders and their families?

Given the many different forms of therapy and the importance of choosing the best treatment, seeking help might seem like an overwhelming task. A person who needs a mental health specialist but isn't sure where to begin finding one might start by talking with another healthcare provider (such as a family doctor), a social services agency, or a student or employee assistance program. Additionally, numerous national and local resources are dedicated to helping people locate the services they need.

Several national organizations provide information about mental health services. One of the best known is the National Alliance on Mental Illness (NAMI; see more at www.nami.org). This grassroots organization advocates for patients and clients in several ways: through educating people about mental illness (and combating stigma), working to improve national policies, sponsoring initiatives such as walk-a-thons to raise money and awareness, and maintaining connections to more specialized support groups. NAMI has branches in all 50 states, and affiliated organizations also exist in many communities. Some affiliates provide support to specific groups, such as veterans, children, and adolescents.

Additionally, several other national organizations can help put people in touch with local treatment resources and support groups. These groups include Mental Health America (www.nmha.org), the American Self-Help Clearinghouse (www.mentalhelp.net/selfhelp/), the National Mental Health Consumers' Self-Help Clearinghouse (www.mhselfhelp.org/), and Network of Care (networkofcare.org/).

Other national resources provide information and support for people coping with a specific problem or disorder. These include groups like the Depression and Bipolar Support Alliance (www.dbsalliance.org/) the National Eating Disorders Association (www.nationaleatingdisorders.org), and the Anxiety Disorders Association of America (www.adaa.org/), to name just a few.

Local support groups exist to help people cope with many challenging situations—not only clinical psychological disorders but also specific life situations that can cause psychological symptoms. (For example, many adults experience profound grief and show signs of clinical depression after the death of a parent; support groups can help them cope.) Information about local support groups can be found in the phone book or online. Many support groups help people struggling with substance-abuse problems or addictive behaviors. These include 12-step groups with numerous local chapters, such as Alcoholics Anonymous and Gamblers Anonymous.

What mental health resources are available to students? Primary care doctors and school counselors can provide some basic services, and they can give students information about additional services and resources available in the community. A teacher or adult you trust can help you get in touch with your doctor or school counselor if you are looking for help, advice, or information.

PSYCHOLOGICAL THERAPIES 473

Explore

TREATMENT OPTIONS

Divide the class into three or four groups, and give each group a cluster of the websites listed in the text to explore. What primary problems or disorders do these organizations help with? What kinds of therapies are used? How long do they typically take? What kinds of professionals are involved? Ask students to research other organizations along the same vein as the group from the text with which they're working. Are there many? How similar are they?

CHAPTER 14 • Module 34

COVER THE MODULE

34.4 What resources support people with psychological disorders and their families?

- Resources include national advocacy organizations that provide support for people with a specific disorder, local support groups, and community health centers.

EXTEND THE LESSON

Remind students that for many people, therapy is a good way to get through a passing difficult phase of their lives. It need not be exhaustive, expensive, or even conducted by a trained professional, as in organizations such as Alcoholics Anonymous. Whether students think they need help coping with divorce or the death of a loved one, or they are struggling with something more severe, such as extreme depression or anxiety, they have a wide range of options in the psychotherapeutic community and should not feel weak or ashamed for getting help. The websites listed here in the text are a good starting point to finding it.

L3 DIFFERENTIATED INSTRUCTION

Visual/Nonverbal Learners Have these students research well-known psychologists (e.g., Freud, Jung) to find quotes from them about topics the students are studying. Ask students to prepare posters containing the quotes, with credit assigned to each quote.

Module 34 Biomedical Therapies 473

CHAPTER 14 • Module 34

Assess

Assign the Module 34 Practice Quiz.

Use the Practice Quiz to identify gaps in student understanding.

REMEDIATE

Have students, individually or in groups, review the module goals, learning objectives, and key terms.

Refer students to the Concept Summary on p. 479 for review.

Close

How do students feel about medical interventions for psychological problems? How do they think they are best used? With all that is still unknown about them, do students think they're still worthwhile? If so, in which kinds of cases?

Practice Quiz

Pick the best answer.

1. The newest class of drugs used to treat psychotic symptoms is called
   a. anticonvulsants
   b. partial dopamine agonists
   c. atypical neuroleptics
   d. selective serotonin reuptake inhibitors

2. Which of the following treatments involves running a current through an electrode to destroy a small, specific area of brain cells?
   a. bilateral cingulotomy
   b. prefrontal lobotomy
   c. electroconvulsive therapy
   d. psychopharmacology

3. The main disadvantage of the benzodiazepines traditionally used to treat anxiety disorders is that benzodiazepines
   a. can be addictive
   b. are slow to take effect
   c. have many unpleasant side effects
   d. cannot be combined with certain foods and beverages

4. Tricyclic antidepressants treat depression by
   a. producing a sedative effect
   b. suppressing dopamine receptors in the brain
   c. affecting the transportation of sodium ions in cells
   d. inhibiting the reuptake of serotonin and norepinephrine

5. Drugs in the newest class of antidepressants, which includes Prozac and Paxil, have fewer side effects because
   a. these drugs inhibit serotonin reuptake, but not reuptake of norepinephrine and dopamine.
   b. these drugs inhibit the reuptake of norepinephrine, dopamine, and serotonin.
   c. these drugs inhibit norepinephrine and serotonin reuptake, but not reuptake of dopamine.
   d. these drugs inhibit dopamine and serotonin reuptake but have a limited effect on norepinephrine.

6. Which of the following is most commonly used to treat manic episodes and bipolar disorder?
   a. ECT
   b. MAOIs
   c. lithium
   d. psychosurgery

7. ECT, or electroconvulsive therapy, is most strongly associated with which of the following?
   a. temporary loss of memory
   b. apathy and lack of emotional response
   c. increased risk of suicidal behavior
   d. potentially dangerous increases in blood pressure

8. Which of the following statements about psychosurgery is true?
   a. Psychosurgery is a popular treatment for mental illness today.
   b. Psychosurgery is no longer performed in the United States.
   c. Psychosurgery is still performed today, but only as a last resort.
   d. Psychosurgery is never an ethical course of treatment.

9. Which of the following situations would most clearly create a conflict of interest for a therapist?
   a. discussing a client's problems with the therapist's colleagues
   b. forming a business partnership with a current client
   c. working with a client to set a mutually agreed-upon target end-date for therapy
   d. providing a teenage client's parents with a general update on the client's progress

10. Which of the following is a 12-step group designed to help people suffering from substance abuse?
    a. Alcoholics Anonymous
    b. Mental Health America
    c. Network of Care
    d. the National Alliance on Mental Illness (NAMI)

Practice Quiz Answers

1. b
2. c
3. a
4. d
5. a
6. a
7. a
8. c
9. b
10. a

---

474 Chapter 14 Psychological Therapies

CHAPTER 14 Summary

Listen on **mypsychlab.com**

Module 33: Psychotherapies

Understand perspectives on treating psychological disorders.

33.1 What are the two modern ways in which psychological disorders can be treated?
- The two modern forms of therapy are psychotherapy and biomedical therapy.

33.2 Who can treat psychological disorders?
- Psychiatrists, psychoanalysts, psychiatric social workers, and psychologists all treat psychological disorders.

Identify psychological treatments and evaluate their effectiveness.

33.3 What are the different types of psychotherapy?
- Psychoanalysis helps patients reveal their unconscious concerns. Modern psychodynamic therapists have modified the technique so that it takes less time and is more directive.
- Person-centered therapy allows the client to talk through problems and concerns, while the therapist provides support. Essential elements of therapy are unconditional positive regard, reflection, empathy, and authenticity.
- Behavior therapies focus on changing the abnormal or disordered behavior itself through classical or operant conditioning.
- Cognitive therapy teaches clients to recognize distorted thinking and inaccurate beliefs. The goals are to relieve symptoms and solve problems, develop strategies for solving future problems, and help change irrational, distorted thinking.
- Rational-emotive behavior therapy is a directive therapy in which the therapist directly challenges clients' irrational beliefs.
- Group therapy involves treating people in a group setting.

33.4 How effective is psychotherapy?
- Current surveys of people who have received therapy suggest that psychotherapy is more effective than no treatment at all. Surveys reveal that 75 to 90 percent of clients improve, longer times in therapy is linked with greater improvement, and psychotherapy sometimes works as well alone as with drugs.

Listen to an audio file of your chapter on **mypsychlab.com**

33.5 What other factors influence the effectiveness of therapy?
- Good therapy depends on the therapeutic alliance and the existence of a protected setting in which to reveal and release thoughts and emotions. Cultural, ethnic, and gender differences between therapist and client can result in misunderstandings.

Module 34: Biomedical Therapies and Issues in Therapy

Identify biomedical therapies and evaluate their effectiveness.

34.1 What are biomedical forms of therapy?
- Four major categories of drugs used for treatment are antipsychotic drugs, antianxiety drugs, antidepressants, and antimanic drugs.
- Electroconvulsive therapy (ECT) is used to treat severe depression, bipolar disorder, and schizophrenia.
- Modern psychosurgery relies on the bilateral cingulotomy, used to treat major depression, bipolar disorders, and certain forms of obsessive-compulsive disorder.

34.2 Should children and adolescents be treated with the same drugs used for adults?
- Research has shown that all but one antidepressant has been associated with an increased risk of suicide in children and adolescents.

Consider legal, ethical, and professional challenges in therapy.

34.3 What ethical challenges do therapists face?
- Therapists' ethical challenges include the responsibility of maintaining a relationship with the client; the need to maintain confidentiality; the need to maintain professional boundaries; and the need to be professional in dealing with clients.

34.4 What resources support people with psychological disorders and their families?
- Resources include national advocacy organizations, organizations that provide support for people with a specific disorder, local support groups, and community health centers.

Vocabulary Terms

therapy p. 446
psychotherapy p. 446
biomedical therapy p. 446
insight therapies p. 446
action therapy p. 446
psychiatrist p. 447
psychoanalyst p. 448
psychoanalysis p. 448
psychiatric social worker p. 448
psychologist p. 448
free association p. 449
manifest content p. 449
latent content p. 449
resistance p. 449
transference p. 449
psychodynamic therapy p. 450
unconditional positive regard p. 450
nondirective p. 450
person-centered therapy p. 450
reflection p. 450
empathy p. 451
authenticity p. 451
behavior therapies p. 451
classical conditioning p. 451
operant conditioning p. 451
applied behavior analysis (behavior modification) p. 452
systematic desensitization p. 452
aversion therapy p. 452
flooding (exposure and response prevention) p. 453
reinforcement p. 453
token economy p. 453
contingency contracting p. 453
modeling p. 454
participant modeling p. 454
extinction p. 454
time-out p. 454
shaping p. 454
cognitive therapy p. 454
arbitrary inference p. 455
selective thinking p. 455
overgeneralization p. 455
magnification and minimization p. 455
personalization p. 455
cognitive-behavioral therapy (CBT) p. 456
rational-emotive behavior therapy (REBT) p. 456
family counseling p. 457
self-help groups p. 458
eclectic therapies p. 459
therapeutic alliance p. 460
eye movement desensitization reprocessing (EMDR) p. 462
psychopharmacology p. 465
antipsychotic drugs p. 465
typical neuroleptics p. 465
atypical neuroleptics p. 466
partial dopamine agonists p. 466
antianxiety drugs p. 466
benzodiazepines p. 466
antidepressant drugs p. 467
monoamine oxidase inhibitors (MAOIs) p. 467
tricyclics p. 467
antimanic drugs p. 467
lithium p. 467
anticonvulsant drugs p. 468
electroconvulsive therapy (ECT) p. 468
bilateral ECT p. 468
unilateral ECT p. 468
psychosurgery p. 469
prefrontal lobotomy p. 469
bilateral cingulotomy p. 469

PSYCHOLOGICAL THERAPIES 475

CHAPTER 14 • Chapter Summary and Vocabulary

Chapter Summary

Encourage students to carefully review and study the summary. Explain that it provides an overview of key concepts presented in the text.

Have students identify what they find unclear or confusing. Call on volunteers to provide answers, examples, or definitions.

Vocabulary Terms

Remind students that terms are defined within the chapter at point of use. If they are not sure of a term's definition, they should look up the definition on the page.

Encourage students to create study cards of unfamiliar words or to go to **www.mypsychlab.com** for flashcards. Have them test themselves or a classmate. Advanced students can explain the terms in their own words.

Critical Thinking

MAKING CONNECTIONS

Have students complete the following activity to connect the ideas in this chapter. Send them to the Multimedia Library for this chapter at **www.mypsychlab.com** to view the video titled "Asylum: A History of the Mental Institution in America," which illustrates some of the strains that asylums were under in the 1950s. Then lead a class discussion based on the following questions: (1) What do you think might have been some of the underlying issues causing the asylums to be so crowded in the first place? (2) Does the video shed light on some of the hype surrounding now-unused radical therapies, such as lobotomy? (3) Does it seem as though the doctors and nurses in the asylums were looking to do real good by helping people get better?

Chapter 34 Summary 475

CHAPTER 14 • Assessment

VOCABULARY REVIEW

1. f
2. b
3. a
4. h
5. c
6. j
7. i
8. d
9. g
10. e

WRITING ABOUT PSYCHOLOGY

1. Students should show in their answers that they understand the basic characteristics of each therapy method, as well as the specific methods used within each type of therapy for treating specific problems or disorders.

2. Students should note two of the four ethical issues in therapy: commitment to the client's well-being, confidentiality and privacy, professional boundaries and conflicts of interest, or competence and professionalism. They should be able to identify how these issues affect both "talk therapy" and biomedical therapies using medicine, ECT, or psychosurgery.

PSYCHOLOGY PROJECT

After students have turned in materials for review, have each group give a short presentation outlining the disorder they treated and the treatment methods they chose. If any groups used the same disorder, compare the treatment methods of each group. Are they similar? If not, could they all be effective nonetheless?

CHAPTER 14 Assessment

Study and Review on mypsychlab.com

Vocabulary Review
Match each vocabulary term to its definition.

1. therapeutic alliance
2. cognitive-behavioral therapy (CBT)
3. nondirective
4. eclectic therapies
5. benzodiazepines
6. contingency contracting
7. eye movement desensitization reprocessing (EMDR)
8. action therapy
9. bilateral cingulotomy
10. psychopharmacology

a. Term used to describe a therapy style in which the therapist remains relatively neutral and does not interpret or take direct actions with regard to the client, instead remaining a calm, nonjudgmental listener while the client talks.
b. Action therapy in which the goal is to help clients overcome problems by learning to think more rationally and logically.
c. Drugs that lower anxiety and reduce stress.
d. Therapy in which the main goal is to change disordered or inappropriate behavior directly.
e. The use of drugs to control or relieve the symptoms of psychological disorders.
f. The relationship between therapist and client that develops as a warm, caring, accepting relationship characterized by empathy, mutual respect, and understanding.
g. Psychosurgical technique in which an electrode is inserted into the cingulated gyrus with the guidance of a magnetic resonance imaging machine for the purpose of destroying that area of brain tissue with an electric current.
h. Therapy style that results from combining elements of several different therapy techniques.
i. Controversial form of therapy for post-traumatic stress disorder and similar anxiety problems in which the client is directed to move the eyes rapidly back and forth while thinking of a disturbing memory.
j. The use of a formal, written agreement between the therapist and client (or other parties) that clearly states behavioral goals, reinforcements, and penalties.

Writing about Psychology
Respond to each question in complete sentences.

1. Matilda becomes anxious whenever she has to speak in public, and she has developed a phobia of public speaking. In a well-organized essay, describe how Matilda's anxiety phobia would be treated in the context of each of the following therapies:
   a. Behavior therapy
   b. Cognitive therapy
   c. Biomedical therapy

2. Identify and briefly describe two types of ethical issues therapists commonly face. Then provide examples of how each type of issue might come up
   a. when using a psychotherapy for treatment
   b. when using a biomedical therapy for treatment

Psychology Project
How do psychological professionals collaborate on treatment approaches? Complete this project to improve your understanding of different therapeutic approaches.

Materials:
- three partners (to form a group of four)
- access to print or electronic reference resources
- a pencil and paper, or other note-taking materials

Instructions:

1. Assign the following roles to the four members of your group: Case Manager, Action-oriented Therapist, Insight-oriented Therapist, Biomedically Oriented Therapist.
2. Have the Case Manager complete a one to two paragraph description of a client suffering from a common psychological disorder. You may wish to consult *Chapter Thirteen: Psychological Disorders*, or other references. Include specific details.
3. Have each of the Therapists review the available methods in his or her assigned treatment category and choose the most appropriate method to treat the client's particular problem.
4. Have each of the Therapists complete a one to two paragraph description of how and why you would use your chosen method to treat the client's problem. Include advantages and possible disadvantages of using this method.
5. As a group, come to an agreement about the best treatment plan for this client. Is there any one method that clearly stands out as the best for this particular problem, or would it make sense to combine methods? If so, why? Based on the group discussion, have the Case Manager write a paragraph summarizing which treatment method(s) will be used and why.

Internet Resources

About Psychotherapy: www.aboutpsychotherapy.com
Educational site for individuals seeking therapy; written by a practicing clinical psychologist in New York City

4Therapy: www.4therapy.com/
A megasite devoted to therapy of all kinds

Internet Mental Health: www.mentalhealth.com
Comprehensive educational site

Mental Help Net: www.mentalhelp.net
Very informative up-to-date site that includes featured topics and current news in psychological treatments

Test Yourself

Pick the best answer.

1. Larisa is going to a therapist to gain a better understanding of what makes her do the things she does. This type of therapy is known as
   a. action therapy
   b. insight therapy
   c. behavioral therapy
   d. biomedical therapy

2. Ioana is seeing a psychoanalyst. She begins to feel safe and protected by the psychoanalyst, the same way she feels about her parents. Freud would most likely argue that Ioana is experiencing
   a. latency
   b. resistance
   c. transference
   d. free association

3. Lashonna was afraid of dogs. She wanted to get over this fear, so she began by thinking about seeing a dog but staying calm. Then she walked past her neighbor's dog in its fenced yard until she no longer felt afraid. Next, she visited a pet store and petted a dog while the sales clerk held it. Finally, she bought herself a puppy and was no longer afraid. Lashonna's method of getting over her fear is most similar to
   a. flooding
   b. extinction
   c. aversion therapy
   d. systematic desensitization

4. Cara sat down with her daughter, Morgan, and together they wrote out a list of things that Morgan was expected to do each day and the rewards she would get if she accomplished them, as well as the penalties she would face if she did not do them. This system is most similar to
   a. shaping behavior
   b. a token economy
   c. participant modeling
   d. a contingency contract

5. When 5-year-old Cathy began acting out, her parents took her to a therapist who suggested that her parents may have caused the problem by using the wrong kind of discipline. The kind of therapy that would best help Cathy would most likely be
   a. family therapy
   b. behavioral therapy
   c. cognitive therapy
   d. psychodynamic therapy

6. The use of benzodiazepines to treat anxiety disorders is gradually being phased out in favor of treatment with
   a. psychosurgery
   b. antidepressant drugs
   c. antimanic drugs
   d. antipsychotic drugs

7. Jessica sends a poem she wrote to a magazine for publication, but the magazine rejects her poem. Jessica feels awful about the rejection and tells herself that she'll never be a published writer, she'll never find a good job, and she'll die unhappy and alone. Jessica is engaging in
   a. overgeneralization
   b. personalization
   c. arbitrary inference
   d. selective thinking

8. Albert Bandura's research was most influential in the area of
   a. psychoanalysis
   b. behavioral therapy
   c. person-centered therapy
   d. cognitive-behavioral therapy

9. Which of the following is NOT an ethical principle of mental health treatment?
   a. The therapist must permit the client to give informed consent before starting treatment.
   b. The therapist must direct as many aspects of the client's life as possible in order to help the client fully recover.
   c. The therapist and the client should end their relationship through mutual consent.
   d. The therapist should not gossip about clients or reveal confidential information about the client to others.

10. Which of the following people is least likely to find psychodynamic therapy effective?
    a. a person suffering from anxiety
    b. a person suffering from schizophrenia
    c. a person suffering from mild depression
    d. a person suffering from a dissociative disorder

11. The organization NAMI
    a. ensures that psychological therapies are effective, ethical, and available to everyone
    b. grants undergraduate and graduate degrees to students training to be psychological professionals
    c. oversees the testing and regulation of new drugs designed to treat mental illness
    d. advocates for those struggling with mental illness through education, politics, sponsorship, and practical support

12. A psychologist and a psychiatrist are working together to treat a severely depressed patient who is frequently suicidal. Which combination of therapies would they most likely use?
    a. group therapy, followed by psychosurgery if the group therapy is not effective
    b. psychotherapy and antidepressant medication, followed by electroconvulsive therapy if the psychotherapy and medication are not effective
    c. psychodynamic therapy, followed by antidepressant medication if the psychodynamic therapy is not effective
    d. eye movement desensitization reprocessing (EMDR), followed by antidepressant medication and electroconvulsive therapy if the EMDR is not effective

13. Which statement best summarizes available research on how cultural and gender differences influence the effectiveness of psychotherapy?
    a. Cultural differences clearly help determine the effectiveness of psychotherapy, but the effect of gender differences is less clear.
    b. Gender differences matter more than cultural differences in predicting the effectiveness of psychotherapy.
    c. Cultural and gender differences are about equally important in determining the effectiveness of psychotherapy.
    d. Gender differences are not at all related to the effectiveness of psychotherapy, but cultural differences are.

CHAPTER 14 • Assessment

TEST YOURSELF

1. b
2. b
3. b
4. a
5. d
6. a
7. b
8. b
9. a
10. c
11. b
12. d
13. a
14. a
15. a
16. a
17. a
18. d
19. c

Ready for Testing

STUDENTS KNOW THEY ARE READY FOR TESTING IF THEY ARE ABLE TO . . .

- Define two modern ways in which psychological disorders can be treated, and briefly discuss the history of treatment of the mentally ill.
- Introduce the major types of psychotherapy, including psychoanalysis, humanistic, behavior, cognitive, and group therapy.
- Discuss the assessment and effectiveness of the psychotherapy treatments.
- Describe the biomedical approaches of treating psychological disorders, including the use of drugs, electroconvulsive therapy, and psychosurgery.
- Understand the controversy surrounding the treatment of youth with antidepressant drugs.

CHAPTER 14 • Assessment

MULTIMEDIA CONTENT AVAILABLE AT
www.mypsychlab.com

Map the Concepts on **mypsychlab.com**

Study and Review Flashcards on **mypsychlab.com**

STUDY TIPS

Becoming an Active Listener Help students become better listeners in class by giving them these suggestions:

- Keep your eyes on the teacher. It will help keep distractions to a minimum.
- Listen for main ideas and think about how the supporting details fit for each one.
- Be alert. Recognize when a new idea is being introduced.
- Aim for excellent concentration. Engage in self-talk. Tell yourself that you are understanding all the information.
- Test your active listening skills by practicing with a friend. When you are engaged in conversation, listen actively and do not talk for a while. You may be surprised at the outcome.
- Get enough sleep the night before school. It is hard to listen and take good notes when you are tired.
- Do not come to school hungry. Low blood sugar can affect your ability to concentrate.
- Think about the material you are learning.

478 Chapter 14 Psychological Therapies

CHAPTER 14 Concept Summary: Psychological Therapies

Learning Objectives 33.1 33.2 pp. 446–448

Understand Perspectives on Treating Psychological Disorders

- **psychotherapy** involves having the person with a psychological problem talk with a psychological professional
- **biomedical therapy** involves treating the person with a psychological problem using biological or medical methods

Table 33.2 Characteristics of Psychotherapies

TYPE OF THERAPY	GOAL	KEY PEOPLE
Psychodynamic therapy	Insight	Freud
Person-centered therapy	Insight	Rogers
Behavior therapy	Action	Watson, Jones, Skinner, Bandura
Cognitive therapy	Action	Beck
CBT	Action	Various professionals
REBT	Action	Ellis

Learning Objectives 33.3 33.4 33.5 pp. 448–463

Identify Psychological Treatments and Evaluate Their Effectiveness

- **Freudian psychoanalysis** (Sigmund Freud)
  - uses **dream interpretation** and **free association** to uncover unconscious conflicts
  - modern **psychodynamic therapy** is shorter, more direct, and more focused on transference
- **humanistic therapies**
  - **person-centered therapy** (Carl Rogers) emphasizes sense of self and reconciling one's real self and ideal self
- **cognitive therapies**
  - **common thinking distortions**
  - **cognitive-behavioral therapies (CBT)** address distorted thinking and the resulting behavioral responses; may involve behavioral techniques
- **effectiveness of therapy**
  - Eysenck (1957) found psychotherapy made no difference in improvement
  - recent surveys find that many people feel psychotherapy has helped them

- **behavior therapies**
  - **classical conditioning** techniques:
    - systematic desensitization
    - aversion therapy
    - flooding
  - **operant conditioning** techniques:
    - **reinforcement** techniques
    - modeling
    - shaping
    - extinction
- **group therapies** involve gathering a group of people with similar problems; may or may not involve a trained therapist
- **factors influencing effectiveness of therapy**
  - length of therapy
  - **therapeutic alliance** between patient and therapist
  - differences in cultural or ethnic background
  - gender differences

478 CHAPTER 14

What Every Student Should Know About . . .

PREPARING EFFECTIVE ORAL PRESENTATIONS

Remind students that delivering an oral presentation effectively is critical in getting their message across to an audience. Provide the following tips: (1) Speak in a conversational style. (2) Vary your tone, volume, and pacing. (3) Maintain eye contact with the audience. (4) Project your voice to the size of the room. (5) Speak at a pleasing rate. (6) Be aware of your gestures. (7) Maintain good posture. (8) Have fun!

Map The Concepts on mypsychlab.com

Learning Objectives
34.1 34.2 pp. 465–470

Identify Biomedical Therapies and Evaluate Their Effectiveness

- **psychopharmacology** is the use of drugs to control or relieve the symptoms of a psychological disorder
  - antipsychotic drugs
  - antidepressant drugs
  - antianxiety drugs
  - antimanic drugs
- **electroconvulsive therapy** involves delivering an electric shock to one side (**unilateral ECT**) or both sides (**bilateral ECT**) of a person's head
- **psychosurgery** involves cutting into the brain to remove or destroy brain tissue and thereby relieve psychiatric symptoms

Learning Objectives
34.3 34.4 pp. 470–473

Consider Legal, Ethical, and Professional Challenges in Therapy

- **ethical issues** in therapy
  - requires intense commitment to clients' well-being
  - confidentiality and privacy issues
  - boundaries and conflicts of interest
  - competence and professionalism
- **resources and support**
  - national organizations (e.g., NAMI) that provide information about mental health services
  - national organizations that address specific disorders
  - local support groups
  - community mental health centers

PSYCHOLOGICAL THERAPIES 479

CHAPTER 14 • Concept Summary

STUDY TIPS

Just Do It! Many students have problems beginning homework assignments. Explain that the best method to use is to stop thinking about the assignment and just begin to do it. For example, if they have a 30-page reading assignment and they find themselves sitting and staring at the textbook, they should take action. Open the book and start skimming. Turn the pages and let their eyes skim over the material. Now they should tell themselves that they will read five pages. After they have read five pages, they should tell themselves that they will read five more and then do it. The trick is to break down large tasks into manageable smaller ones. Ask them to imagine a large sandwich they are about to eat. They could not possibly put the whole thing in their mouth and consume it at one time; however, they can manage it by eating one bite at a time. An assignment that feels overwhelming can surely trigger procrastination. It is important to just begin.

Comprehension Check

TYPES OF THERAPY

To check their understanding, students can visit the Multimedia Library section of the www.mypsychlab.com site and explore the Key Components of Psychoanalytic, Humanistic, Behavior, and Cognitive Therapies activity. Advanced students can work alone, while on-level and struggling students can work in pairs or small groups. Students will receive immediate feedback on their answers.

Chapter 34 Concept Summary

CHAPTER 15 • Module 35

Launch the Chapter

CHAPTER GOALS AND LEARNING OBJECTIVES

Module 35 Stress and Stressors

Understand the causes and consequences of stress.

35.1 How do psychologists define stress?

35.2 What kinds of events and situations can cause stress?

35.3 How can stress affect physiological and psychological health?

Module 36 Coping with Stress and Promoting Wellness

Learn strategies for promoting mental and physical health.

36.1 How do people think about stress?

36.2 What are effective and ineffective ways to deal with stressors?

36.3 What are some strategies for coping with stress?

36.4 What is optimism, and how can people become more optimistic?

36.5 What are some ways to promote wellness?

DIFFERENTIATED INSTRUCTION KEY

Look for these symbols to help you adjust steps in each lesson to meet your students' needs.

- **L1** Special Needs
- **L2** Basic
  - **ELL** English Language Learners
  - **LPR** Less Proficient Readers
- **L3** All Students
- **L4** Advanced Students

CHAPTER 15 Stress and Health

The Chilean Mine Miracle

In October 13, 2010, a news story captivated people around the world: One by one, 33 men emerged from a collapsed mine in Chile. The miners, who had been trapped during an accident in early August, spent 69 days a half-mile under the earth before they were rescued. In the underground shelter in which they survived, there was no sunlight, no fresh air, and barely any food. When the miners were rescued at last, however, Chile's health minister announced that all 33 men were in surprisingly good physical and emotional health (Reinberg, 2010). How were these miners able to cope with the stress of living underground for more than 2 months, unsure if they'd ever be rescued from the mine or see their families and friends again? How did they remain relatively physically and mentally healthy under such extraordinary circumstances?

The miners, along with several experts who evaluated them, attributed their resilience to a number of factors. The camaraderie and friendship that the miners shared most likely helped to sustain them, as did the schedule they followed in order to keep themselves busy (Hansen, 2010). Deep in the mine, the men joked with each other, talked about sports, and attended makeshift religious services led by the oldest member of their group, whom they appointed their spiritual advisor (Hansen, 2010; Sibley, 2010). Some of them even exercised in the mine: To keep his mind and body healthy, Edison Peña ran through the mine's corridors, sometimes running up to 6 miles a day (Robbins, 2010).

The support systems that the miners relied on to survive their long entrapment—including friendship, humor, spirituality, and exercise—are effective for relieving stress and promoting wellness above ground, too. The field of health psychology focuses on how our physical activities, psychological traits, and social relationships affect our overall health, and psychologists in this field seek to understand how humans can effectively cope with stress and become their healthiest selves—physically, mentally, and emotionally.

CORRELATION TO APA STANDARDS FOR CHAPTER 15

VIIB. HEALTH

VIIB-1. Stress and coping . . . . pp. 482–492, 495–498, 500–503

VIIB-2. Behaviors and attitudes . . . . pp. 499, 503–505 that promote health

MODULE 35 ▸ STRESS AND STRESSORS

MODULE 36 ▸ COPING WITH STRESS AND PROMOTING WELLNESS

Why Study?

Health and Stress

How are they related? Stress is not a rare experience but something that all people experience in varying degrees every day. This chapter will explore the sources of stress in daily life, the factors that can make the experience of stress easier or more difficult, and how stress influences our physical and mental health, as well as ways to cope with the stresses of everyday life and extraordinary experiences.

Teacher Prep

Stress is the physical, emotional, cognitive, and behavioral response to events that are perceived as threatening or challenging. The events that cause stress are called stressors and can be either internal or external events.

Conflict is a source of stress and occurs when a person feels pulled toward two or more goals but can only achieve one of them. Kurt Lewin defined three types of conflict: approach-approach conflict, avoidance-avoidance conflict, and approach-avoidance conflict.

Hans Selye was a pioneer in the study of the physical consequences of stressors. He proposed that the body goes through three stages called the general adaptation syndrome (GAS). The stages are alarm, resistance, and exhaustion.

The cognitive-mediational theory of emotions proposed by Richard Lazarus states that the way people think about and appraise a stressor is a major factor in their stress response. Primary appraisal involves estimating the severity of the stressor and classifying it. In secondary appraisal, an individual determines what resources he or she has available for dealing with the threat or loss.

Social factors also play a key role in the amount of stress an individual experiences. Living in poverty and job stress are two major sources of stress.

Coping strategies are actions that people take to master, tolerate, or reduce the effects of stressors. Individuals can promote wellness in their own lives by exercising, getting involved with others, getting enough sleep, eating healthy foods, and reserving time for fun.

SCHEDULING

1 Period = 50 min. 1 Block = 90 min.	Semester Course (18 weeks/90 days) Periods/Blocks		Full-Year Course (36 weeks/180 days) Period/Blocks	
Module 35	3	1.5	6	3
Module 36	3	1.5	6	3
Total Days for Chapter	6	3	12	6

CHAPTER 15 • Module 35

Focus

RESOURCES
For this module, consult the appropriate sections of the Teacher's Manual, Test Bank, and PowerPoint slides, all found on the Teacher's Resource DVD, and the interactive study tools for students on MyPsychLab.

BEFORE CLASS
Students should read the section for homework before coming to class.

BELLRINGER
Ask students to think about what makes them feel stress and write down their five biggest stressors. How do they react to these stressors? Does their reaction depend on the kind of stressor they're facing? Ask them to consult their list throughout the chapter and note what they have learned about the stressors and how they can best cope with them.

Teach

COVER THE MODULE
35.1 How do psychologists define stress?
- *Stress* occurs when events are identified as threatening or challenging.
- *Stressors*, or stress-causing events, can be internal or external.

DISCUSS THE STUDENT VOICE QUESTION
Ask students how stressed they feel on a daily basis. Do they think they are stressed all the time? Ask them to stop and think the next time they are consciously feeling stressed (maybe at one of the, likely many, times during the day when they say, "I am SO stressed."). Is the stress internal or external?

482 Chapter 15 Stress and Health

Module 35: Stress and Stressors

Module Goal
Understand the causes and consequences of stress.

Learning Objectives
- 35.1 How do psychologists define stress?
- 35.2 What kinds of events and situations can cause stress?
- 35.3 How can stress affect physiological and psychological health?

Understand the Causes and Consequences of Stress

Life is really about change. Every day, each person faces some kind of challenge, big or small. Just deciding what to wear to school can be a challenge for some people, whereas others find the morning commute the most challenging part of the day. There are decisions to be made and changes that will require adapting plans already made. Sometimes there are actual threats to well-being—an accident, a fight with friends, a failed exam, or a parent's job loss, to name a few. All of these challenges, threats, and changes require people to respond in some way.

35.1 How do psychologists define stress?

Stress is the term used to describe the physical, emotional, cognitive, and behavioral responses to events that are judged to be threatening or challenging.

Stress can show itself in many ways. Physical problems can include unusual fatigue, sleeping problems, frequent colds, and even chest pains and nausea. People under stress may behave differently, too: pacing, eating too much, crying a lot, or physically striking out at others. Emotionally, people under stress experience anxiety, depression, fear, and irritability, as well as anger and frustration. Mental symptoms of stress include problems in concentration, memory, and decision making, and people under stress often lose their sense of humor.

I feel like that most of the time!

Most people experience some degree of stress on a daily basis, and students are even more likely to face situations and events that require them to make changes and adapt their behavior: Assigned readings, papers, studying for tests, juggling part-time jobs, relationships, and dealing with deadlines are all examples of things that can cause a person to experience stress. Some people feel the effects of stress more than others because what is appraised as a threat by one person might be appraised as an opportunity by another. (For example, think of how you and your friends might respond differently to the opportunity to write a 10-page paper for extra credit in the last 3 weeks of the semester.) Stress-causing events are called **stressors**; they can come from within a person or from an external source and range from relatively mild to severe.

Stressors can range from the deadly serious (hurricanes, fires, crashes, combat) to the merely irritating and annoying (delays, rude people, losing your house keys). Stressors can even be imaginary, as when a student puts off

> I feel like that most of the time!

stress the term used to describe the physical, emotional, cognitive, and behavioral responses to events that are appraised as threatening or challenging.

stressors events that cause a stress reaction.

482 CHAPTER 15

Terms

- stress • stressors • distress • eustress • catastrophe • hassles • burnout
- acculturative stress • pressure • frustration • general adaptation syndrome (GAS)
- immune system • natural killer cell • acute stress disorder (ASD) • post-traumatic stress disorder (PTSD)

opening a report card, imagining that it will be full of failing grades, or when a parent imagines the worst happening to a teenage child who hasn't come home from an evening out.

Actually, there are two kinds of stressors: those that cause **distress**, which occurs when people experience unpleasant stressors, and those that cause *eustress*, which occurs when people experience stress from positive events. Hans Selye (ZEL-yeh) coined the term *eustress* to describe the stress experienced when positive events require the body to adapt or change (1936). Starting college, getting married, and earning a job promotion may all be positive events for most people, but they all require a great deal of adaptation or change in people's habits, duties, and even lifestyle, thereby creating stress.

In an update of Selye's original definition, researchers now define **eustress** as the optimal amount of stress that people need to promote health and well-being. The arousal theory is based on the idea that a certain level of stress, or arousal, is actually necessary for people to feel content (Zuckerman, 1994). L**I**N**K to Chapter Eleven: Motivation and Emotion, p. 334. That arousal can be viewed in terms of eustress. For example, many students are aware that experiencing a little anxiety or stress is helpful to them because it motivates them to study. Without the eustress created by the impending exam, many students might not study very much or at all.

What about the student who is so stressed out that everything he's studied just flies right out of his head? Obviously, a high level of anxiety concerning an impending exam that actually interferes with the ability to study or to retrieve the information at exam time is not eustress but is, in fact, distress. The difference is not only in the degree of anxiety but also in how the person *interprets* the exam situation. A number of events, great and small, good and bad, can cause us to feel "stressed out." Simulate on mypsychlab.com

35.2 What kinds of events and situations can cause stress?

Environmental Factors: Life's Ups and Downs Losing one's home in a tornado is an example of a stressor called a **catastrophe**, an unpredictable event that happens on a large scale and creates tremendous amounts of stress and feelings of threat. Wars, hurricanes, floods, fires, airplane crashes, and other disasters are catastrophes. The terrorist-driven destruction of the World Trade Center in New York City on September 11, 2001, is a prime example of a catastrophe. In one study, nearly 8 percent of the people living in the area near the attacks developed a severe stress disorder, and nearly 10 percent reported symptoms of depression even as late as 2 months after the attack (Galea et al., 2002). Another example of a catastrophe was the devastation caused by Hurricane Katrina on August 29, 2005. A Category 3 hurricane when it made landfall in Louisiana, Katrina laid waste to the north-central coastal area of the Gulf of Mexico. In New Orleans, the damage from Katrina was increased by the failure of the levees to hold back flood waters. Eighty percent of the city and many neighboring areas were flooded for weeks (Swenson & Marshall, 2005).

Thankfully, most people do not have to face the extreme stress of a catastrophe. But stress is present even in relatively ordinary life experiences and does not have to come from only negative events, such as job loss. Sometimes there are big events, such as going to college, getting married, or having a baby,

Simulate stress and stressors on mypsychlab.com

distress the effect of unpleasant and undesirable stressors.

eustress the effect of positive events, or the optimal amount of stress that people need to promote health and well-being.

catastrophe an unpredictable, large-scale event that creates a tremendous need to adapt and adjust as well as overwhelming feelings of threat.

STRESS AND HEALTH 483

CHAPTER 15 • Module 35

COVER THE MODULE *(continued)*

- Stress that has a negative impact is called *distress*.
- *Eustress* is the optimal amount of stress that people need to function well.

L**I**N**K to Chapter Eleven: Motivation and Emotion, p. 334

MULTIMEDIA CONTENT AVAILABLE AT
www.mypsychlab.com

Simulate stress and stressors on mypsychlab.com

COVER THE MODULE

35.2 What kinds of events and situations can cause stress?

- *Catastrophes* are events such as floods or crashes that can result in high levels of stress, including acute stress disorder (ASD) and post-traumatic stress disorder (PTSD).

TEACHING TIP

Explain to students that when they work in teams, each team member is usually responsible for a specific task. If one team member does not complete the responsibility for a task, the other team members cannot finish their tasks and the entire team suffers.

Explore

CATASTROPHES AND STRESS

Discuss with students the effects of catastrophes on mental health. Have they ever been profoundly affected by a catastrophe that they or a loved one did not directly experience? What kind of event might cause such a reaction? For example, you might point out that, while large-scale disasters such as the March 2011 earthquake and tsunami in Japan caused many Americans sadness and sympathy for the people affected, the events of September 11, 2001, caused a serious, nationwide stress reaction. Why is there a difference? *(Possible answers might include the loss of American life, the attack on American soil, and the threat of terrorism.)* Direct students to the American Psychological Association's" Natural Disasters" page at **www.apa.org/topics/disasters/index.aspx** for further information, coping tips, and links to current events on the topic.

Module 35 Stress and Stressors **483**

CHAPTER 15 • Module 35

COVER THE MODULE (continued)

- Major life changes create stress by requiring adjustments. Major life changes have an impact on chronic health problems and risk of accidents.

UNDERSTANDING VISUALS

Direct students' attention to Table 35.1. Ask them to think about whether any of these issues have affected them or a member of their immediate family. How did they react? Does the information on the table put their reactions into perspective? (For example, if they reacted severely to a divorce or death of a loved one, do they now understand that these are top stressors in anyone's life?) Which of these might they consider "positive" stressors? Are they surprised with where the positive stressors fall? (For example, most people would consider marriage a positive event, but it ranks toward the top of the list as a stressor.)

EXTEND THE LESSON

Encourage students to visit the website referenced in the text, **www.stresstips.com/lifeevents.htm**, and take the quiz to calculate their SRRS scores. Ask them to note the information that is given along with their scores. Was the information applicable? Do they think they perceive more or less stress than the assessment indicates, or did they find it accurate to their stress levels?

Table 35.1 Sample Items from the Social Readjustment Rating Scale (SRRS)

MAJOR LIFE EVENT	LIFE CHANGE UNITS
Death of spouse	100
Divorce	75
Marital separation	65
Death of a close family member	63
Personal injury or illness	53
Marriage	50
Dismissal from work	47
Pregnancy	40
Change to different line of work	36
Major mortgage	31
Begin or end school	26
Change in living conditions	25
Change in work hours or conditions	20
Change in residence/schools/recreation	19
Vacation	13
Christmas	12

Source: Adapted and abridged from Holmes & Rahe (1967).

that also require a person to make adjustments and changes—and adjustments and changes are really the core of stress, according to early researchers in the field (Holmes & Rahe, 1967).

Holmes and Rahe (1967) believed that any life event that required people to change, adapt, or adjust their lifestyles would result in stress. Like Selye, they assume that both negative events (such as getting fired) and positive events (such as getting a promotion) demand that a person adjust in some way, and so both kinds of events are associated with stress. Holmes and Rahe devised a way to measure the amount of stress in a person's life by having that person add up the total "life change units" associated with each major event in their Social Readjustment Rating Scale (SRRS) (see Table 35.1).

When an individual adds up the points for each event that has happened to him or her within the past 12 months (and counting points for repeat events as well), the resulting score can provide a good estimate of the degree of stress being experienced by that person. The researchers found that certain ranges of scores on the SRRS could be associated with increased risk of illness or accidents. (Warning: Table 35.1 is *not* a complete listing of the original 43 events and associated life change units and should not be used to calculate a stress "score"! If you would like to calculate your SRRS score, try this free site: **http://www.stresstips.com/lifeevents.htm**.)

Scores of 150 or below were not associated with any significant problems, but scores between 150 and 199 were considered a "mild life crisis" and associated with a 33 percent increase in the risk of that person experiencing an illness or accident in the near future (when compared to persons not experiencing any crisis). Scores between 200 and 299 were labeled "moderate life crisis"

Class Discussion

WHAT IS THE PURPOSE OF STRESS?

By asking your students this question, you cannot only explore their thoughts on the topic but also explain to them why stress exists. The stress response exists for the purpose of survival. When we experience stress, our sympathetic nervous systems activate, blood pressure and heart rate increase, and, often, we begin to sweat. These reactions prepare us for "fight or flight," and we are optimized for survival in a physically challenging situation. Most of us are not faced with challenging, potentially life-threatening situations on a daily basis.

However, we are capable of generating large amounts of psychological stress, and the physiological response is the same. So the problem with psychological stress is that we create it with our minds, and our bodies produce the necessary fuel to react physically, but we do not (or cannot) react physically. The health consequences of this cycle are potentially hazardous, as the stress response can lead to many cardiovascular maladies. Chronic stress can lead to insomnia, weight gain, and suppression of immune function. Students should discuss the somewhat paradoxical existence of stress in modern life.

and associated with a 50 percent increase in risk, whereas scores over 300 were considered a "major life crisis" and represented an 80 percent increase in risk (Holmes & Masuda, 1973). Simply put, if a person's score is 300 or above, that person has a very high chance of becoming physically or mentally ill or having an accident (caused by stress-related distractions) in the near future.

The SRRS as it was originally designed seems more appropriate for adults who are already established in their careers. There are variations of the SRRS that use as life events some of those things more likely to be experienced by teenagers and young adults. One of these variations is the College Undergraduate Stress Scale (CUSS) that is represented in part in Table 35.2 (Renner & Mackin, 1998). This scale looks quite different from Holmes and Rahe's original scale because the stressful events listed and rated include those that would be more common or more likely to happen to a student.

Wait, how can falling asleep in class be stressful? It's what happens when the teacher catches you that's stressful, isn't it?

Ah, but if you fall asleep in class, even if the teacher doesn't catch on, you'll miss everything that happened in class that day. You might then have to borrow a friend's notes, copy out the notes yourself, try to read your friend's handwriting, and so on—all of which can be stressful situations. Actually, all the events listed on both the SRRS and the CUSS are stressful not just because some of them are emotionally intense but also because there are so many little details, changes, adjustments, adaptations, frustrations, and delays that are caused by the events themselves. The death of a spouse, for example, rates 100 life change units because it requires the greatest amount of adjustment in a person's life. A lot of those adjustments are the little details: planning the funeral, getting the notice in the obituaries, and eventually deciding what to do with the spouse's belongings.

Although it's easy to think about big disasters and major changes in life as sources of stress, the bulk of the stress we experience daily actually comes from little frustrations, delays, irritations, minor disagreements, and similar annoyances. These daily annoyances are called **hassles** (Lazarus, 1993; Lazarus & Folkman, 1984).

◀ Wait, how can falling asleep in class be stressful? It's what happens when the teacher catches you that's stressful, isn't it?

Table 35.2	Sample Items from the College Undergraduate Stress Scale (CUSS)
EVENT	RATING
Death of a close friend	97
Finals week	90
Flunking a class	89
Financial difficulties	84
Writing a major term paper	83
Difficulties with parents	73
Difficulties with a roommate	66
A class you hate	62
Maintaining a steady dating relationship	55
Peer pressures	53
Being away from home for the first time	53
Falling asleep in class	40

Source: Adapted and abridged from Renner & Mackin (1998).

hassles the daily annoyances of everyday life.

STRESS AND HEALTH 485

CHAPTER 15 • Module 35

COVER THE MODULE *(continued)*
- The daily frustrations and irritations experienced by people are called *hassles* and have an impact on day-to-day health.

DISCUSS THE STUDENT VOICE QUESTION
Discuss with students how hassles in their daily lives make small adjustments necessary. Give the example of oversleeping and missing their ride to school. Is it simply a free day off? What are the implications?

UNDERSTANDING VISUALS
Now, direct students' attention to Table 35.2. Do they find it more applicable to their lives than Table 35.1? Have they experienced more of these stressors? What is their opinion of the rankings of the stressors?

L1 DIFFERENTIATED INSTRUCTION
Special Needs Seat students where they can more easily see and hear speakers.

Class Demonstration

STUDENTS' DAILY HASSLES

After discussing Table 35.2, give students the opportunity to create their own lists. Have students work in groups to generate a list of 20 to 30 hassles that are present in their lives using the information below. Students should be as specific as possible in identifying the hassle. Next, ask students to rank-order the hassles in terms of their importance. A volunteer from each group should read to the class the top five from the list.

Instructions to students: List the hassles you must cope with in your daily life. Group them in the following categories:

- household/living arrangement hassles
- financial responsibility hassles
- time-pressure hassles
- inner concern hassles
- health hassles
- environmental hassles
- family hassles
- work hassles
- school hassles
- future/security hassles
- social hassles
- other hassles

Rank each hassle on a scale of 1 to 10 (1 = least important; 10 = most important).

Module 35 Stress and Stressors **485**

CHAPTER 15 • Module 35

COVER THE MODULE *(continued)*
- The nature of one's hassles may vary, depending on one's life stage.

MULTIMEDIA CONTENT AVAILABLE AT
www.mypsychlab.com

◉ Simulate how stressed you are on **mypsychlab.com**

COVER THE MODULE
- Several social factors can increase the effects of stress: poverty, stresses on the job or in the workplace, and entering a majority culture that is different from one's culture of origin.
- *Burnout* is a condition that occurs when job stress is so great that the person develops negative thoughts, emotions, and behavior, as well as an extreme dissatisfaction with the job and a desire to quit.

MULTIMEDIA CONTENT AVAILABLE AT
www.mypsychlab.com

◉ Watch a video on rude atmospheres in the workplace on **mypsychlab.com**

L3 DIFFERENTIATED INSTRUCTION

Auditory/Verbal Learners To reinforce learning, ask these students to recite information to another student or group of students.

Lazarus and Folkman (1984) developed a "hassles" scale that has items such as "misplacing or losing things" and "troublesome neighbors." A person taking the test for hassles would rate each item in the scale in terms of how much of a hassle that particular item was for the person. The ratings range from 0 (no hassle or didn't occur) to 3 (extremely severe hassle). Whereas the major life events of Holmes and Rahe's scale (1967) may have a long-term effect on a person's chronic physical and mental health, the day-to-day minor annoyances, delays, and irritations that affect immediate health and well-being are far better predictors of short-term illnesses such as headaches, colds, backaches, and similar symptoms (Burks & Martin, 1985; DeLongis et al., 1988; Dunn et al., 2006). ◉ Simulate on **mypsychlab.com**

A recent study has indicated that hassles may also come from quite different sources depending on a person's developmental stage (Ellis et al., 2001). In this study, researchers surveyed 270 randomly selected people from ages 3–75. The participants were asked to check off a list of daily hassles and pleasures associated with having "bad days" and "good days," respectively, as well as ranking the hassles in terms of frequency and severity of impact. For children ages 3–5, getting teased was the biggest daily hassle. For children in the 6–10 age group, the biggest hassle was getting bad grades. Children 11–15 years old reported feeling pressured to use drugs, whereas older adolescents (ages 16–22) cited trouble at school or work. Adults found fighting among family members the greatest source of stress, whereas the elderly people in the study cited a lack of money. No matter how old you are, however, chances are extremely good that you will have to put up with day-to-day annoyances and frustrations that can increase your levels of stress.

Social Factors: Poverty, Job Stress, and Culture Sometimes, a source of stress is social: Much of the stress in everyday life comes from our interactions with other people and our own place in society. Two of the more prominent social factors that contribute to stress are poverty and job stress.

Living in poverty is stressful for many reasons. Lack of sufficient money to provide the basic necessities of life can lead to many stressors for both adults and children: overcrowding, lack of medical care, increased rates of disabilities due to poor prenatal care, noisy environments, increased rates of illness (such as asthma in childhood) and violence, and substance abuse (Aligne et al., 2000; Bracey, 1997; Leroy & Symes, 2001; Park et al., 2002; Renchler, 1993; Rouse, 1998; Schmitz et al., 2001).

Even if a person has a job and is making an adequate salary, there are stresses associated with the workplace that add to daily stressors. Some of the typical sources of stress in the workplace include the workload, a lack of variety or meaningfulness in work, lack of control over decisions, long hours, poor physical work conditions, and lack of job security (Murphy, 1995).
◉ Watch on **mypsychlab.com**

One of the more serious effects of workplace stress is a condition called burnout. **Burnout** can be defined as negative changes in thoughts, emotions, and behavior as a result of prolonged stress or frustration (Miller & Smith, 1993). Symptoms of burnout are extreme dissatisfaction, pessimism, lowered job satisfaction, and a desire to quit. Although burnout is most commonly associated with job stress, students can also suffer from burnout when the stresses of school life—term papers, exams, assignments, and the like—become overwhelming. The emotional exhaustion associated with burnout can be lessened when a person at risk of burnout is a member of a social group within the work environment that provides support and the motivation to continue to perform despite being exhausted (Halbesleben & Bowler, 2007).

◉ Watch a video on rude atmospheres in the workplace on **mypsychlab.com**

burnout negative changes in thoughts, emotions, and behavior as a result of prolonged stress or frustration.

486 CHAPTER 15

Class Demonstration

STRESS AT WORK

<u>Purpose</u>: Students complete a brief assignment that involves critical thinking, personalizing, or deeper processing of information.

<u>Time</u>: Approximately 5 minutes

<u>Description</u>: Give students several minutes to answer the following questions: (1) Have you ever had a job or done work (such as babysitting, community work, or even chores at home) that was stressful? (2) What was it about the work or job that made it stressful? (3) What occupation do you think would be the most stressful and why? Ask volunteers to read their responses to the class.

When a person from one culture must live in another culture, that person may experience a great deal of stress. *Acculturation* means the process of adapting to a new or different culture, often the dominant culture (Sodowsky et al., 1991). LINK *to Chapter Eight: Culture and Gender, p. 254.* The stress resulting from the need to change and adapt to the dominant or majority culture is called **acculturative stress** (Berry & Kim, 1998; Berry & Sam, 1997).

The method that a minority person chooses to enter into the majority culture can also have an impact on the degree of stress that person will experience (Berry & Kim, 1988). One method is *integration*, in which the individual tries to maintain a sense of the original cultural identity while also trying to form a positive relationship with members of the dominant culture. For example, an integrated person will maintain a lot of original cultural traditions within the home and with immediate family members but will dress like the majority culture and adopt some of those characteristics as well. Some research has suggested that acculturative stress due to integration is usually low (Ward & Rana-Deuba, 1999). However, other researchers have suggested that this interpretation has been affected by confounding factors, and we may not truly understand the effect—if any—that integration has on mental health (Rudmin, 2010).

In *assimilation*, the minority person gives up the old cultural identity and completely adopts the majority culture's ways. In the early days of the United States, many immigrants were assimilated into the mainstream American culture, even changing their names to sound more "American." Assimilation leads to moderate levels of stress, most likely due to the loss of cultural patterns and rejection by other members of the minority culture who have not chosen assimilation (LaFromboise et al., 1993; Lay & Nguyen, 1998).

Separation is a pattern in which the minority person rejects the majority culture's ways and tries to maintain the original cultural identity. Members of the minority culture refuse to learn the language of the dominant culture, and they live where others from their culture live, socializing only with others from their original culture. Separation can result in a fairly high degree of stress.

The greatest acculturative stress will most likely be experienced by people who have chosen to be *marginalized*, neither maintaining contact with the original culture nor joining the majority culture. They essentially live on the "margins" of both cultures without feeling or becoming part of either culture. Marginalized individuals do not have the security of the familiar culture of origin or the acceptance of the majority culture and may suffer a loss of identity and feel alienated from others (Roysircai-Sodowsky & Maestas, 2000). Obviously, marginalized people have little in the way of a social support system to help them deal with both everyday stresses and major life changes.

Psychological Factors: Pressure, Lack of Control, and Frustration

While many factors that contribute to stress come from the world around us, some stressful situations are caused or intensified by our thoughts and perceptions. **Pressure,** which occurs when people feel that they must work harder, work faster, or do more, is one of these psychological factors. Although some people claim to "work well under pressure," the truth is that pressure can have a negative impact on a person's ability to be creative. Psychologist Teresa Amabile has gathered research within actual work settings strongly indicating that when time pressure is applied to workers who are trying to come up with creative, innovative ideas, creativity levels decrease dramatically—even though the workers may think they have been quite productive because of the effort they have made (Amabile et al., 2002).

▲ This Buddhist group is celebrating Songkran, the New Year, by performing their cultural ritual of pouring water over their elders' palms. Although they are wearing clothing typical of people living in Los Angeles, California, where the ceremony is taking place, they still maintain some of their cultural traditions.

acculturative stress stress resulting from the need to change and adapt a person's ways to the majority culture.

pressure the psychological experience produced by urgent demands or expectations for a person's behavior that come from an outside source.

STRESS AND HEALTH 487

CHAPTER 15 • Module 35

COVER THE MODULE *(continued)*

- The four methods of acculturation are:
  - *Integration*: The individual tries to maintain a sense of the original cultural identity while also trying to form a positive relationship with members of the dominant culture.
  - *Assimilation*: The minority person gives up the old cultural identity and completely adopts the majority culture's ways.
  - *Separation*: A pattern in which the minority person rejects the majority culture's ways and tries to maintain the original cultural identity.
  - *Marginalization*: The person neither maintains contact with the original culture nor joins the majority culture.
- Social support systems are important in helping people cope with stress.
- *Pressure* is the psychological experience produced by urgent demands or expectations.

Cultural Connections

ADAPTING TO A NEW CULTURE

Purpose: Students explore and discuss different patterns for adapting to a new culture.

Time: 15 minutes

Description: Begin the assignment by asking students to think about a fictional person who has just moved out of his or her country to a new culture. The job of the students is to provide advice on how to make this transition as least stressful as possible. Students should have a few minutes to look over the different patterns of adapting to a new culture—integration, assimilation, separation, and marginalization. Students should then share answers with a team of their classmates. Team members should try to reach consensus on which advice is best, and then teams should share their answers with the class.

Module 35 Stress and Stressors **487**

CHAPTER 15 • Module 35

COVER THE MODULE (continued)

- Uncontrollability involves being unable to handle a situation as you believe it should be handled.
- *Frustration* is the psychological experience produced by the blocking of a desired goal or the fulfillment of a perceived need.
  - Frustrations can be internal or external. Frustration may result in persistence, aggression, displaced aggression, or withdrawal.

COVER THE MODULE

35.3 How can stress affect physiological and psychological health?

- The autonomic nervous system consists of the sympathetic system, which responds to stressful events, and the parasympathetic system, which restores the body to normal functioning after the stress has ceased.

LINK *to Chapter Two: The Biological Perspective, pp. 48–50*

Another factor that increases a person's experience of stress is the degree of control that the person has over a particular event or situation. The less control a person has, the greater the degree of stress. In two studies carried out in a nursing home with the elderly residents as the participants, researchers Rodin and Langer (Langer & Rodin, 1976; Rodin & Langer, 1977) gave each of the residents a houseplant. Decisions about watering and how much sun each plant should have were up to each resident. These residents, who comprised the experimental group, were also given choices such as whether they wanted to see a weekly movie, on which of the two evenings that the movie was shown did they want to attend, and in what area or room they would like to see their visitors.

Participants in the control group, although also given plants, were told that the nurses would take care of the plants and were not encouraged to make decisions for themselves. The follow-up study took place a year and a half later. Using participation in activities, measures of happiness, and other assessments, the researchers found that those who had more control over their lives and who had been given more responsibility were more vigorous, active, and sociable than those in the control group.

Frustration occurs when people are blocked or prevented from achieving a desired goal or fulfilling a perceived need. As a stressor, frustration can be *external*, as when you're stuck in traffic on the way to an important event, you're cut from a sports team or a musical group, or your wallet is stolen. Losses, rejections, failures, and delays are all sources of external frustration. *Internal frustrations*, also known as *personal frustrations*, occur when a person's goal or need can not be attained because of his or her internal or personal characteristics. A person who wants to be an engineer but has no math skills would find it difficult to attain that goal.

Obviously, some frustrations are minor and others are more serious. The seriousness of a frustration is affected by how important the goal or need actually is. A person who is delayed in traffic while driving to the mall to do some shopping just for fun will be less frustrated than a person who is trying to get to the mall before it closes to get that last-minute forgotten and important birthday gift.

35.3 How can stress affect physiological and psychological health?

Effects on Physical Health No matter where stress comes from—whether from major life events or daily hassles, from social conditions, or from a person's own pressures and frustrations—it can take a serious toll on our health. Even though stress is not a physical illness, it can actually damage the body, weaken the immune system, and make people more likely to develop a variety of health problems.

How does stress affect the body? We'll start our investigation by considering the *autonomic nervous system* (ANS), the part of the human nervous system that is responsible for all automatic, involuntary, and life-sustaining activities. **LINK** *to Chapter Two: The Biological Perspective, pp. 48–50.* The ANS consists of two divisions: the *parasympathetic* and the *sympathetic*. It is the sympathetic nervous system (the "fight-or-flight" system) that reacts when the human body is subjected to stress: Heart rate increases, digestion slows or shuts down, and energy is sent to the muscles to help deal with whatever action the stressful situation requires. The parasympathetic system returns

frustration the psychological experience produced by the blocking of a desired goal or fulfillment of a perceived need.

Explore

STRESS AND HEALTH

For further information about the effects of stress on health, direct students to the following websites:

American Heart Association: www.americanheart.org/
Offers news, risk-assessment tests, addresses for local offices, a heart and stroke guide, and other information

HealthFinder: www.healthfinder.gov
Contains resources for questions about health and health maintenance

National Center for Health Statistics: www.cdc.gov/nchs/
Provides news, health statistics, answers to frequently asked questions, and links to other health sites

World Health Organization: www.who.int/home-page/
Provides updated health and disease statistics, links to other sites, and advice for international travelers

Alarm Stage
Sympathetic nervous system is activated by adrenal glands
- Forehead, neck, shoulder, arm, and leg muscles contract
- Pupils enlarge
- Sugar is released into the bloodstream for energy
- Accelerated heart rate increases blood flow to muscles; blood pressure increases

Resistance Stage
- Breathing is frequent and shallow
- Blood pressure remains high
- Hormones from adrenal glands are released into bloodstream

Exhaustion Stage
- Liver runs out of sugar
- Prolonged muscle tension causes fatigue

FIGURE 35.1 General Adaptation Syndrome
The diagram at the top shows some of the physical reactions to stress in each of the three stages of the general adaptation syndrome. The diagram at the bottom shows the relationship of each of the three stages to the individual's ability to resist a stressor. In the alarm stage, resistance drops at first as the sympathetic system quickly activates. But resistance then rapidly increases as the body mobilizes its defense systems. In the resistance stage, the body is working at a much increased level of resistance, using resources until the stress ends or the resources run out. In the exhaustion stage, the body is no longer able to resist as resources have been depleted, and at this point disease and even death are possible.

Graph: Resistance to stress across Stage 1 Alarm (Shock), Stage 2 Resistance (Normal level of resistance to stress), Stage 3 Exhaustion

the body to normal, day-to-day functioning after the stress is ended. If the stress is great enough and lasts long enough, the parasympathetic system may shut the body down, causing a collapse into what some people might call "nervous exhaustion." Both systems figure prominently in a classic theory of the body's physiological reactions to stress, the general adaptation syndrome.

Psychologist Hans Selye was the founder of the field of research concerning stress and its effects on the human body. He studied the sequence of physiological reactions that the body goes through when adapting to a stressor. This sequence (see Figure 35.1) is called the **general adaptation syndrome (GAS)** and consists of three stages (Selye, 1956):

- **Alarm:** When the body first reacts to a stressor, the sympathetic nervous system is activated. The adrenal glands release hormones that increase heart rate, blood pressure, and the supply of blood sugar, resulting in a burst of energy. Reactions such as fever, nausea, and headache are common.
- **Resistance:** As the stress continues, the body settles into sympathetic division activity, continuing to release the stress hormones that help the body fight off, or resist, the stressor. The early symptoms of alarm lessen and the person or animal may actually feel better. Researchers have found that one of the hormones released under stress, noradrenaline, actually

general adaptation syndrome (GAS) the three stages of the body's physiological reaction to stress, including alarm, resistance, and exhaustion.

STRESS AND HEALTH   489

CHAPTER 15 • Module 35

COVER THE MODULE *(continued)*

- The *GAS* is the body's reaction to stress and includes three stages of reaction:
  - *Alarm*: When the body first reacts to a stressor, the sympathetic nervous system is activated.
  - *Resistance*: The body settles into sympathetic division activity, continuing to release the stress hormones that help the body fight off, or resist, the stressor.
  - *Exhaustion*: When the body's resources are gone, resistance ends, the parasympathetic division activates, and exhaustion occurs.

UNDERSTANDING VISUALS

Direct students' attention to the illustration in Figure 35.1. The stress experienced by a firefighter is a prime example of the GAS. Ask students if they can think of any other examples of people or professions that might experience this phenomenon. Do any students think that they have been through this process? Did it involve a serious or even life-threatening situation? Have students ever experienced GAS in a situation that was not dangerous? Do they think it served a purpose for them in that situation?

Class Demonstration

THINKING CRITICALLY ABOUT STRESS

Students should apply their understanding of the causes of stress to these questions:

1. Our perceptions and interpretations of events help determine how stressful these events are for us. Describe two daily hassles that often annoy, frustrate, or irritate you, and include how altering your perceptions or interpretations might reduce their stressfulness. (**Possible answer:** *Driving behind a slow driver is a common daily hassle. It might help to ask yourself why you are in such a hurry or remind yourself that slow drivers, too, need to be able to shop for groceries or go to the doctor.*)

2. Stress is not all bad. What do you think is good about stress? List at least two things. (**Possible answers:** *Some worthwhile goals in life cannot be achieved without experiencing stress. As Selye suggested, this kind of stress is probably not as harmful as the stress of a boring, meaningless, aimless existence. Stress may protect us from fatigue or exhaustion by warning us that we are doing more than we can handle and need to rearrange our priorities.*)

CHAPTER 15 • Module 35

MULTIMEDIA CONTENT AVAILABLE AT
www.mypsychlab.com

⊕ **Explore** Selye's General Adaptation Syndrome on **mypsychlab.com**

COVER THE MODULE (continued)

- Stress causes the *immune system* to react as though an illness or invading organism had been detected, increasing the functioning of the immune system.
- As the stress continues or increases, the immune system can begin to fail.

🔗 **LINK** to *Chapter Two: The Biological Perspective, p. 52*

DISCUSS THE STUDENT VOICE QUESTION

Discuss with students the timing issues related to stress and immunity, when stress ceases to boost immunity and instead reduces it (refer to Figure 35.2 as needed). Students may primarily associate immunity with viruses and infections. Ensure that students understand how immunity affects things such as heart disease and cancer progression.

⊕ **Explore** Selye's General Adaptation Syndrome on **mypsychlab.com**

▶ So stress actually increases the activity of the immune system? But then, how do people under stress end up having medical problems like high blood pressure? ▶

immune system the system of cells, organs, and chemicals of the body that responds to attacks from diseases, infections, and injuries.

---

seems to affect the brain's processing of pain, so that when under stress a person may experience insensitivity to pain (Delaney et al., 2007).

- **Exhaustion:** When the body's resources are gone, exhaustion occurs. Exhaustion can lead to the formation of stress-related diseases (i.e., high blood pressure or a weakened immune system) or the death of the organism if outside help is unavailable (Stein-Behrens et al., 1994). When the stressor ends, the parasympathetic division activates and the body attempts to replenish its resources.

Alarm and resistance are stages that people experience many times throughout life, allowing people to adapt to life's demands (Selye, 1976), but the prolonged secretion of the stress hormones during the exhaustion stage can lead to the most harmful effects of stress. This aspect of Selye's work convinced other researchers of the connection between stress and certain "diseases of adaptation," as Selye termed them. The most common of these diseases are ulcers and high blood pressure. ⊕ **Explore** on **mypsychlab.com**

As Selye first discovered, the **immune system** (the system of cells, organs, and chemicals in the body that responds to attacks on the body from diseases and injuries) is affected by stress. Researchers have found that stress triggers the same response in the immune system that infection triggers (Maier & Watkins, 1998): When the body's immune cells, or white blood cells, encounter an infection, they create certain enzymes and other chemicals to fight the infection. The white blood cells surround the bacteria or other infectious material and release the chemicals and enzymes into the bloodstream. From there, these chemicals activate receptor sites on the *vagus nerve*, the longest nerve that connects the body's organs to the brain. The activation of these receptor sites signals to the brain that the body is sick, causing the brain to respond by further activation of the immune system.

Stress activates this same system but starts in the brain rather than in the bloodstream. The same chemical changes that occur in the brain when it has been alerted by the vagus nerve to infection in the body occurred in laboratory animals when they were kept isolated from other animals or given electric shocks (Maier & Watkins, 1998). This has the effect of "priming" the immune system, allowing it to more successfully resist the effects of the stress, as in Selye's resistance stage of the GAS.

So stress actually increases the activity of the immune system? But then, how do people under stress end up having medical problems like high blood pressure?

The positive effects of stress on the immune system only seem to work when the stress is not a chronic condition. (See Figure 35.2 on page 491.) As stress continues, the body's resources begin to fail in the exhaustion phase of the general adaptation to stress (Kiecolt-Glaser et al., 1987, 1995, 1996; Prigerson et al., 1997). In one study, students who were undergoing a stressful series of exams were compared to a group of similar students relaxing during a time of no classes and no exams (Deinzer et al., 2000). The exam group tested significantly lower for immune system chemicals that help fight off disease than did the relaxing control group, even as long as 14 days after the exams were over. The hormone *cortisol*, released by the adrenal glands when the body experiences stress, can suppress the immune system, and this suppression of immune system functioning can continue even after the stress itself is over. 🔗 **LINK** to *Chapter Two: The Biological Perspective, p. 52.*

Of course, anything that can weaken the immune system can have a negative effect on other bodily systems. The sympathetic system (active during stress) cannot work at the same time as the parasympathetic system, and the

---

Class Demonstration

HEALTH BELIEFS AND COPING

Pose the following questions to students and ask them to write down how they would answer them on a scale of 1 (almost always) to 5 (never).

- I eat at least one healthy, balanced meal a day.
- I get 7 to 8 hours of sleep at least 4 nights a week.
- I exercise to the point of perspiration at least twice a week.
- I regularly attend a club or social activities.
- I have a network of friends and acquaintances.
- I have one or more friends in whom to confide about personal matters.
- I do something for fun at least once a week.
- I am able to organize my time effectively.
- I take quiet time for myself during the day.

Ask students to evaluate their answers. Are they, on average, high or low? Discuss with students how taking care of themselves can be cyclical. If they live as healthfully as they can, they are likely to be better able to cope with stress and, therefore, are better able to avoid the negative health consequences that chronic stress can cause.

FIGURE 35.2 Stress Duration and Illness
In this graph, the risk of getting a cold virus increases greatly as the months of exposure to a stressor increase. Although a stress reaction can be useful in its early phase, prolonged stress has a negative impact on the immune system, leaving the body vulnerable to illnesses such as a cold. *Source:* Cohen et al. (1998).

parasympathetic system is responsible for normal, day-to-day functioning of the body, including repairs and "system maintenance." For example, stress has been shown to put people at a higher risk for heart attacks and strokes at least in part because the liver, which is activated during parasympathetic functioning, does not have a chance to clear the fat and cholesterol from the bloodstream, leading to clogged arteries and eventually, the possibility of heart attacks. One study looked at the heart health of people who suffered acute stress reactions after the 9/11 terrorist attacks and found a 53 percent increase in heart ailments over the 3 years following the attacks (Holman et al., 2008). Another large-scale study found that work stress is highly associated with an increased risk of coronary heart disease due to negative effects of stress on the ANS and glandular activity (Chandola et al., 2008). Simply put, prolonged stress is not good for the heart.

Stress can also play a role in the progression of cancer. Cancer is not one disease but rather a collection of diseases that can affect any part of the body. Unlike normal cells, which divide and reproduce according to genetic instructions and stop dividing according to those same instructions, cancer cells divide without stopping. The resulting tumors affect the normal functioning of the organs and systems they invade, causing organs to fail and eventually killing the organism.

Although stress itself cannot give a person cancer, stress can have a suppressing effect on the immune system, making the unchecked growth of cancer more likely. In particular, an immune system cell called a **natural killer cell** has as its main functions the suppression of viruses and the destruction of tumor cells (Herberman & Ortaldo, 1981). Stress has been shown to depress the release of natural killer cells, making it more difficult for the body's systems to fight cancerous growths (Zorilla et al., 2001). The hormone adrenaline is released under stress and has been found to interfere with a protein that normally would suppress the growth of cancer cells (Sastry et al., 2007). In other research, stress has been linked to the accumulation of genetic errors that can lead to the formation of cancer cells and tumors: Stress causes the release of hormones such as adrenaline and noradrenaline that, over time, can cause mistakes in the instructions given by the genes to the cells of the body. As these mistakes "pile up" over the years, cells can begin to grow out of control, causing the growth of tumors and possibly cancer (Kiecolt-Glaser et al., 2002).

Heart disease and cancer are not the only diseases affected by stress. Studies have shown that children in families experiencing ongoing stress are more

natural killer cell immune system cell responsible for suppressing viruses and destroying tumor cells.

STRESS AND HEALTH 491

CHAPTER 15 • Module 35

COVER THE MODULE *(continued)*

- Some health associated with stress are:
  - Higher risk for heart attacks and strokes
  - Increased growth of cancer due to depression of *natural killer cells*

FAST FACT

According to the American Psychological Association, stress is linked to the six leading causes of death: heart disease, cancer, lung ailments, accidents, liver cirrhosis, and suicide. Direct students to **http://facts.randomhistory.com/stress-facts.html** for some interesting facts about stress. Discuss some of these facts in class. Which ones did students find surprising? Interesting? Disturbing? Did the list dispel any myths students previously held?

UNDERSTANDING VISUALS

Discuss with students Figure 35.2. Ask them if they have ever experienced a time when they felt under severe, prolonged stress, and then, on top of it all, they got sick. Did they consider at the time that maybe not Murphy's Law but instead the stress itself contributed to their illness? Ensure that students understand how stress can make a person more susceptible to the common cold and even play a role in the progression of cancer.

Class Demonstration

CONTROVERSIES ABOUT STRESS

Purpose: Students have a chance to think about, debate, and discuss controversial topics about stress.

Time: 15 minutes

Description: Pose any of the following controversial questions to the class. Students should share their answers and contribute to further class discussion.

- The government should encourage employers to implement policies that help their employees deal with stress, such as quiet places for meditation and more opportunities for physical exertion.
- Daily hassles are worse for your health than major life events.
- Females can handle more stress than males can.

CHAPTER 15 • Module 35

COVER THE MODULE *(continued)*

- High levels of stress can also affect mental health.
- *ASD* may result from traumatic experiences.
- When ASD lasts longer than 1 month, it is then classified as *PTSD*.

L I N K to Chapter Fourteen: Psychological Therapy, pp. 456–475; Chapter Nine: Memory, p. 283

L3 DIFFERENTIATED INSTRUCTION

Tactile/Kinesthetic Learners Encourage students to create collages covering important chapter information, which can be posted around the classroom.

TEACHING TIP

Rather than asking students whether they understand what you have said, have them restate what you have said in their own words.

---

acute stress disorder (ASD)
a disorder resulting from exposure to a major stressor, with symptoms of anxiety, dissociation, recurring nightmares, sleep disturbances, problems in concentration, and moments in which people seem to "relive" the event in dreams and flashbacks for as long as 1 month following the event.

post-traumatic stress disorder (PTSD)
a disorder resulting from exposure to a major stressor, with symptoms of anxiety, nightmares, poor sleep, reliving the event, and concentration problems, lasting for more than 1 month.

---

likely to develop fevers with illness than are other children (Wyman et al., 2007). A review of research and scientific literature (Cohen et al., 2007) found stress to be a contributing factor in many human diseases, including not only heart disease but also depression and HIV/AIDS.

Effects on Psychological Health People who experience high levels of stress are at risk not only for physical illnesses but also for mental illnesses, particularly a type of anxiety disorder called **acute stress disorder (ASD)**. ASD is a severe stress disorder suffered by people who experience a traumatic event, particularly a traumatic event that most humans don't experience in their lifetimes (like a natural disaster, a combat experience, or the death of a child). Symptoms of ASD occur within 4 weeks of the traumatic event and include anxiety, dissociative symptoms (such as emotional numbness/lack of responsiveness, not being aware of surroundings, and dissociative amnesia), recurring nightmares, sleep disturbances, problems in concentration, and moments in which people seem to "relive" the event in dreams and flashbacks for as long as 1 month following the event. One recently published study gathered survey information from Hurricane Katrina evacuees at a major emergency shelter and found that 62 percent of those sampled met the criteria for having ASD (Mills et al., 2007). When the symptoms associated with ASD last for more than 1 month, the disorder is then called **post-traumatic stress disorder (PTSD)**. In that same study, researchers concluded that it was likely that anywhere from 38 to 49 percent of all the evacuees sampled were at risk of developing PTSD that would still be present 2 years after the disaster. Furthermore, whereas the onset of ASD occurs within 4 weeks of the traumatic event, the symptoms of PTSD may not occur until 6 months or later after the event (American Psychiatric Association, 2000). Treatment of these stress disorders may involve psychotherapy and the use of drugs to control anxiety. L I N K *to Chapter Fourteen: Psychological Therapies, pp. 456–475.*

Women seem to be more vulnerable to PTSD than men. Researchers have found that women have almost twice the risk of developing PTSD than do men and that the likelihood increases if the traumatic experience took place before the woman was 15 years old (Breslau et al., 1997, 1999). Children may also suffer different effects from stress than do adults. Severe PTSD has been linked to a decrease in the size of the hippocampus in children with the disorder (Carrion et al., 2007). The hippocampus is important in the formation of new long-term declarative memories (L I N K *to Chapter Nine: Memory, p. 283*), and this may have a detrimental effect on learning and the effectiveness of treatments for these children. The rate of PTSD (self-reported) among combat-exposed military personnel has tripled since 2001 (Smith et al., 2008), so the problems associated with this long-term stress disorder are not going away any time soon.

Applying Psychology to Everyday Life

Suicide in America

Some people experience so much stress that they feel they have no choice but to escape, and tragically, some of these people choose to escape by ending their own lives. Here are the facts about suicide in the United States:

- More people in the United States die from suicide than from homicide. In 1996, among teenagers and young adults, suicide

---

Explore

POST-TRAUMATIC STRESS DISORDER

Ask students to watch the video "PTSD 911" on this chapter's resources at **www.mypsychlab.com**. Does the virtual reality therapy used in this case look familiar to them? How is PTSD similar to phobias, discussed earlier in the text? **(Possible answers:** *PTSD is an anxiety disorder, as are phobias. PTSD is triggered by an external event, as phobias can be.)* Does the use of virtual reality (VR) in treating PTSD make as much sense to students as using VR to treat phobias? Why or why not? Encourage students to visit the National Institute of Mental Health's page on phobias at **www.nimh.nih.gov/publicat/reliving.cfm** for more information.

took more lives than cancer, heart disease, AIDS, birth defects, strokes, pneumonia, the flu, and chronic lung diseases *combined* (Satcher, 1999).

- From 1980 to 1996, the rate of suicides among children 10 to 14 years of age increased by 100 percent. Suicide is the third leading cause of death among adolescents (Centers for Disease Control and Prevention [CDC], 2006), and the eleventh leading cause of death for all ages (CDC, 2005).
- Women are about three times more likely than men to attempt suicide, but men are nearly four times more likely to complete the attempt (CDC, 2005).
- Suicide rates in both completed and attempted suicides among adolescents vary according to ethnicity as well as gender, with suicide *deaths* highest among male American Indian/Alaska natives, and suicide *attempts* highest among female American Indian/Alaska natives (Goldston et al., 2008). The lowest rates of deaths were African American females, and the lowest rates of attempts were among African American and White males.

What are the signs of impending suicide? Sometimes there are none, but depression is one of the most common mental disorders associated with suicide, and depression does have signs, including feelings of hopelessness, lack of energy, sleeping problems, and persistent physical symptoms such as headaches or stomachaches. People who are depressed and intend to commit suicide usually *do* talk about it, and this communication should always be taken seriously.

What can be done to help prevent suicides? The most important thing a person can do for a suicidal individual is to seek professional help. Most of us are not trained to provide this help, but medical and psychological professionals *do* have this training, and they should be made aware of the suicidal person's case. The American Foundation for Suicide Prevention (http://www.afsp.org) advises those in a position to help a suicidal individual to listen with a sincere attitude of concern and avoid giving unasked-for advice. Other recommendations include assuring the person that things can and will change, staying with the person, and calling the police if an emergency intervention is necessary. Suicidal individuals should also be encouraged to call the National Suicide Prevention Lifeline: it is toll-free, confidential, and available 24 hours a day, 7 days a week: 1-800-273-TALK (8255).

Above all, a person who tries to prevent a suicide and fails should not feel responsible. In the end, if a person committed to the act of suicide succeeds, there may have been nothing that any bystander really could have done to prevent it. **Listen** on **mypsychlab.com**

▲ *Suicide-prevention hotline centers are designed to provide help and support to people who are on the verge of committing suicide. Volunteers, such as the one pictured here, act as concerned listeners for the depressed people who call in to the hotline centers.*

Listen to a Psychology in the News podcast about suicide on **mypsychlab.com**

Questions for Further Thought
1. How might a parent's suicide affect the children left behind?
2. How might a teenager's suicide affect parents, siblings, and friends?

STRESS AND HEALTH 493

CHAPTER 15 • Module 35

APPLYING PSYCHOLOGY TO EVERYDAY LIFE

- More people in the United States die from suicide than from homicide.
- Suicidal behavior is strongly linked to depression. People who talk about suicide should be taken seriously and need help.

1. Possible answer: Children left behind by a parent's suicide may feel abandoned and unloved. They may feel that the parent's suicide is somehow their fault, much like children of divorce are likely to internalize the divorce as their fault.

2. Possible answer: Parents, siblings, and friends may feel guilty about a teenager's suicide—that they did not recognize or take the signs seriously, that they were not as supportive as they think they should have been, or that the suicide is their fault. People left behind may even feel anger that their loved one chose to take his or her own life rather than seek help.

MULTIMEDIA CONTENT AVAILABLE AT
www.mypsychlab.com

Listen to a Psychology in the News podcast about suicide on **mypsychlab.com**

EXTEND THE LESSON

Encourage students to explore the American Foundation for Suicide Prevention's website at **www.afsp.org** for information about suicide prevention and where to go for help if a person contemplates suicide. Suggest that students bookmark this site for future reference.

Class Demonstration

THE MANY FACES OF STRESS

As a class or in small groups, have students give examples that illustrate the following sources and experiences of stress:

- Fear or apprehension (**Possible answers:** *A soldier going into battle; teenagers concerned that their parents will discover they have an eating disorder*)
- Anxiety (*An "A" student who worries about failing courses; a person who was in an airplane crash in which many people died*)
- Depression (*A person who has experienced the death of a loved one; an adolescent who suffers physical disfigurement*)
- Frustration (*A person stuck in traffic; a hungry person who doesn't have a can opener for his soup*)
- Guilt (*Soldiers who have survived a battle in which their best friend died; a student who is praised for a good grade she acquired by cheating*)

Module 35 Stress and Stressors

CHAPTER 15 • Module 35

Assess

Assign the Module 35 Practice Quiz.

Use the Practice Quiz to identify gaps in student understanding.

REMEDIATE

Have students, individually or in groups, review the module goals, learning objectives, and key terms.

Refer students to the Concept Summary on p. 510 for review.

Close

Discuss with students the purpose that stress serves in their lives. Do they think there are times in their lives when it serves a positive purpose? If so, when? Has this module motivated them to evaluate their stress levels?

Practice Quiz

Pick the best answer.

1. The optimal amount of stress that people need to promote their health and sense of well-being is called
   a. intensity
   b. distress
   c. eustress
   d. acute stress

2. Research has shown that _____ have a long-term effect on physical and mental health, but _____ have a greater impact on short-term health.
   a. hassles; major life events
   b. major life events; hassles
   c. major life events; catastrophes
   d. hassles; catastrophes

3. Eduardo is on his way to an important job interview when his car breaks down on the highway. Eduardo is likely to experience what kind of frustration?
   a. external
   b. internal
   c. personal
   d. uncontrollable

4. In the _____ stage of the GAS, the person may actually start to feel better.
   a. alarm
   b. resistance
   c. exhaustion
   d. termination

5. The activation of the immune system response by stress differs from the activation of that system by illness in that
   a. illness activates areas in the brain first
   b. stress increases the release of natural killer cells
   c. illness increases the release of natural killer cells
   d. stress activates areas in the brain first

6. Which of the following is NOT a typical source of stress in the workplace?
   a. heavy workload
   b. lack of variety
   c. lack of shift work
   d. lack of job security

7. Larysa moved from Ukraine to the United States. She learned to speak and write English, changed her last name so that it would sound more "American," and no longer maintains any of her old culture's styles of dress or customs. Larysa has used which method of entering the majority culture?
   a. assimilation
   b. integration
   c. separation
   d. acute stress

8. Which of the following experiences is a better predictor of stress-related headaches?
   a. having a parent die
   b. becoming pregnant
   c. living through an earthquake
   d. misplacing important documents

9. Anxiety, recurring nightmares, sleep disturbances, and concentration problems that occur for more than 1 month after a major stressor are symptoms of
   a. acute stress disorder
   b. post-traumatic stress disorder
   c. general adaptation syndrome
   d. general stress disorder

10. Which of the following events is considered the most stressful, according to the Social Readjustment Rating Scale (SRRS)?
    a. death of a spouse
    b. divorce
    c. pregnancy
    d. dismissal from work

494 CHAPTER 15

Practice Quiz Answers

1. c
2. b
3. a
4. b
5. d
6. c
7. a
8. c
9. b
10. a

494 Chapter 15 Stress and Health

Module 36: Coping with Stress and Promoting Wellness

Module Goal
Learn strategies for promoting mental and physical health.

Learning Objectives
- 36.1 How do people think about stress?
- 36.2 What are effective and ineffective ways to deal with stressors?
- 36.3 What are some strategies for coping with stress?
- 36.4 What is optimism, and how can people become more optimistic?
- 36.5 What are some ways to promote wellness?

Learn Strategies for Promoting Mental and Physical Health

We may not be able to control the stressors in our lives, but we can have some control over how we deal with those stressors. In this module, we will explore the factors that affect how different people react to stress on a cognitive level, and we'll discuss some of the most effective strategies for coping with stress and keeping the mind and body healthy.

36.1 How do people think about stress?

The Cognitive Appraisal Approach Not all people react to the same stressors in the same ways. In fact, there are multiple ways of thinking about stress, and our cognitive assessment of a stressor plays a large role in determining how exactly that stressor will affect us. Cognitive psychologist Richard Lazarus developed a cognitive view of stress called the *cognitive appraisal theory* of emotions, in which the way people think about and appraise a stressor is a major factor in how stressful that particular stressor becomes (Lazarus, 1991, 1999; Lazarus & Folkman, 1984). According to Lazarus, there is a two-step process in assessing the degree of threat or harm of a stressor and how one should react to that stressor. (See Figure 36.1 on page 496.)

The first step in appraising a stressor is called **primary appraisal**, which involves estimating the severity of the stressor and classifying it as a threat (something that could be harmful in the future), a challenge (something to be met and defeated), or a harm or loss that has already occurred. If the stressor is appraised as a threat, negative emotions may arise that inhibit the person's ability to cope with the threat. For example, a student who has not read the text or taken good notes will certainly appraise a pop quiz as a threat. If the stressor is seen as a challenge, however, it is possible to plan to meet that challenge, which is a more positive and less stressful approach. For example, the student who has studied, read, and feels prepared is much more likely to appraise the upcoming exam as an opportunity to do well.

Perceiving a stressor as a challenge instead of a threat makes coping with the stressor or the harm it may already have caused more likely to be successful,

primary appraisal the first step in assessing stress, which involves estimating the severity of a stressor and classifying it as either a threat or a challenge.

Terms

- primary appraisal • secondary appraisal • Type A personality • Type B personality • Type C personality • hardy personality • aggression • displaced aggression • escape or withdrawal • coping strategies • problem-focused coping • emotion-focused coping • psychological defense mechanisms • social support system • denial • repression • rationalization • projection • reaction formation • displacement • regression • identification • compensation (substitution) • sublimation • optimists • pessimists

---

CHAPTER 15 • Module 36

Focus

RESOURCES
For this module, consult the appropriate sections of the Teacher's Manual, Test Bank, and PowerPoint slides, all found on the Teacher's Resource DVD, and the interactive study tools for students on MyPsychLab.

BEFORE CLASS
Students should read the section for homework before coming to class.

BELLRINGER
Ask students what kinds of things they do to relieve stress. Do they exercise? Spend time with friends? Spend quiet time alone? Do they do these things specifically to relieve stress, or is that just a secondary benefit? Encourage students who do not engage in stress-relieving activities to think of some that may work for them as you discuss the module.

Teach

COVER THE MODULE
36.1 How do people think about stress?

- The cognitive appraisal approach holds that how people think about a stressor determines, at least in part, how stressful that stressor will become.
  - The first step is *primary appraisal,* in which the person determines whether an event is threatening, challenging, or of no consequence. Threatening events are more stressful than those seen as challenging.

CHAPTER 15 • Module 36

COVER THE MODULE (continued)

- The second step is *secondary appraisal*, in which the person assesses the resources available to deal with the stressor, such as time, money, and social support.

UNDERSTANDING VISUALS

Discuss with students the sequence shown in Figure 36.1. Have students considered the idea that they can think themselves into or out of stress and that stress can be as much a construction of their own minds as a consequence of outside influences? Have students ever been conscious of this thought process? How quickly do they think it happens? Could it be possible to consciously think through this process, or do students think it is mainly influenced by their personality and is out of their control?

TEACHING TIP

Field trips are a good way to expose students to the business world. In lieu of such trips, ask adults to visit your classroom to discuss pertinent topics with the students.

496 Chapter 15 Stress and Health

FIGURE 36.1 Responses to a Stressor

Lazarus's Cognitive Appraisal Approach. According to this approach, there are two steps in cognitively determining the degree of stress created by a potential stressor. Primary appraisal involves determining if the potential stressor is a threat. If it is perceived as a threat, secondary appraisal occurs. Secondary appraisal involves determining the resources one has available to deal with the stress, such as time, money, physical ability, and so on. Inadequate resources lead to increased feelings of stress and the possibility of developing new resources to deal with the stress.

```
Potential stressor occurs
         │
         ▼
   Primary appraisal
(How threatening is this event to my well-being?)
    │              │
    ▼              ▼
Perceived as    Perceived as
harmless or     potentially harmful
a challenge       │        │
    │             ▼        ▼
    ▼        Biological   Emotional
 No stress   reaction     reaction
                 │
                 ▼
            Secondary
            appraisal
        (Do I have the
        resources to deal
        with the stressor?)
                 │
                 ▼
        Weighing coping strategies
           │              │
           ▼              ▼
    Adequate resources   Inadequate resources
       perceived            perceived
           │                   │
           ▼                   ▼
      Use of existing         Stress
      coping resources          │
                        ┌───────┴────────┐
                        ▼                ▼
                Discovering new      Remaining
                ways of responding    stressed
                or new resources
```

whereas perceiving it as an embarrassment or imagining failure or rejection is more likely to lead to increased stress reactions, negative emotions, and an inability to cope well (Folkman, 1997; Lazarus, 1993). In other words, how we *think* about something affects how well we deal with it, so think positively!

In **secondary appraisal**, people who have identified a threat or harmful effect must estimate the resources that they have available for coping with the stressor. Potential resources include social support, money, time, energy, and ability, depending on the threat. If resources are perceived as adequate or abundant, the degree of stress will be considerably less than if resources are missing or lacking. For example, a student who feels that she has the time to study for an exam and the ability to understand the material in that time will feel much less distress than the student who has little time to study and doesn't feel that she understood much of the material.

The Effects of Personality How one cognitively assesses a stressor has a lot to do with one's personality. People with certain kinds of personality traits—such as aggressiveness or a naturally high level of anxiety, for example—seem to create more stress for themselves than may exist in the actual stressor. In fact,

secondary appraisal the second step in assessing a threat, which involves estimating the resources available to the person for coping with the stressor.

496 CHAPTER 15

Class Demonstration

PERCEPTION AND STRESS

What is a petty annoyance for one person can be a crisis for another. You have used a computer to type your term paper. Another user of the computer inadvertently erases it. One person will take the attitude that "crying over spilled milk" will not help and rewrites the paper with a minimum of stress. Another person's first reaction is anger: find out who did it and get even. This person will have to redo the paper, too, but as he sits at the computer, his lingering anger causes him to make mistakes, and making mistakes adds to his frustration. Discuss with students some of the petty annoyances they face in the course of a day. How easy is it for them to decide whether to turn them into larger stressors? Have students come up with a list of daily hassles that increase in severity. Where on the continuum do students hit the point at which they are unable to take the annoyance in stride?

personality characteristics seem to be a major factor in predicting overall health. Researchers have found that people who live to be very old—into their 90s and even over 100 years—tend to be relaxed, easygoing, cheerful, and active. People who have opposite personality traits such as aggressiveness, stubbornness, inflexibility, and tenseness typically do not live as long as the average life expectancy (Levy et al., 2002). Those personality traits are some of the factors associated with two personality types that have been related to how people deal with stress and the influence of certain personality characteristics on coronary heart disease.

In 1974, medical doctors Meyer Friedman and Ray Rosenman published a book titled *Type A Behavior and Your Heart*. The book was the result of studies spanning three decades of research into the influence of certain personality characteristics and coronary heart disease (Friedman & Kasanin, 1943; Friedman & Rosenman, 1959; Rosenman et al., 1975). Since then, numerous researchers have explored the link between what Friedman called Type A and Type B personalities.

Type A people are workaholics—they are very competitive, ambitious, hate to waste time, and are easily annoyed. There is a constant sense of pressure and a strong tendency to try to do several things at once. Often successful but frequently unsatisfied, they always seem to want to go faster and do more, and they get easily upset over small things. A typical Type A finds it difficult to relax and do nothing—Type A people take work with them on vacation, bring a laptop to the beach, and do business on their cell phones while they travel. **Type B** people, on the other hand, are not that competitive or driven, tend to be easygoing and slow to anger, and seem relaxed and at peace. Type B people are more likely to take a book to the beach than schoolwork or office work. (See Figure 36.2.)

In 1961, the *Western Collaborative Group Study* (Rosenman et al., 1975) followed 3,500 men over an 8-year period and found that Type A men were three times more likely to develop heart disease than Type B men. The *Framingham Heart Study* found that the risk of coronary heart disease for Type A working women is four times that of Type B working women (Eaker & Castelli, 1988). Other research has narrowed the key factors in Type A personality and heart disease to one characteristic: hostility, or long-lasting feelings of conflict and anger (Matthews et al., 2004; Williams, 1999; Williams et al., 1980).

Many studies support the link between hostility and increased risk of coronary heart disease. A study of hostility levels and risk factors for heart disease in young adults found that increases in hostility over a 5-year follow-up study were associated with a rise in high blood pressure, one of the major risk factors of heart disease (Markovitz et al., 1997). Another study found that over a period of slightly more than three decades, men who had exhibited high

FIGURE 36.2 Personality and Coronary Heart Disease
The two bars on the left represent men with Type A personalities. Notice that within the Type A men, there are more than twice as many who suffer from coronary heart disease as those who are healthy. The two bars on the right represent men with Type B personalities. Far more Type B personalities are healthy than Type A personalities, and there are far fewer Type B personalities with coronary heart disease when compared to Type A personalities. *Source:* Miller et al., (1991, 1996).

Type A personality person who is ambitious, time conscious, extremely hardworking, and tends to have high levels of hostility and anger as well as being easily annoyed.

Type B personality person who is relaxed and laid-back, less driven and competitive than Type A, and slow to anger.

STRESS AND HEALTH 497

CHAPTER 15 • Module 36

COVER THE MODULE *(continued)*

- **The Effects of Personality**
  - *Type A personalities* are ambitious, time-conscious, hostile, and angry workaholics who are at increased risk of coronary heart disease, primarily due to the anger and hostility.
  - *Type B personalities* are relaxed and easy-going and have one third the risk of coronary heart disease as do Type A personalities if male, and one-fourth the risk if female and working outside the home.

EXTEND THE DISCUSSION

Discuss with students the idea of being a personality "type." Do they think they are locked into a certain personality? Do they think personalities exist on a continuum, or are they mostly identified with their defining characteristics? What evidence do they see in themselves that they have certain set personality traits?

TEACHING TIP

Collaborative learning can increase student behavior, incentive, and accomplishment. It is more successful with heterogeneous than with homogeneous groups.

Class Demonstration

PERSONALITY AND STRESS

Purpose: Students discuss personality factors that are related to stress.

Time: 10 minutes

Description: Students begin by taking 5 minutes to review their textbook on personality variables that are related to stress. These variables may include Types A, B, or C personality, the hardy personality, or optimistic/pessimistic explanatory style. Divide students into four-member teams, and ask each student to come up with some possible questions to use when interviewing a partner. Then the four-member teams are divided into two A's and two B's. First, A's interview B's, and then B's interview A's, in an attempt to uncover how their partner's personality may influence their reaction to stressors. Finally, the whole team reunites for sharing and discussion.

Module 36 Coping with Stress 497

CHAPTER 15 • Module 36

COVER THE MODULE (continued)

- *Type C personalities* are pleasant but repressed, internalizing their negative emotions.
- *Hardy people* are hard workers who lack the anger and hostility of the Type A, instead seeming to thrive on stress.

DISCUSS THE STUDENT VOICE QUESTION

Talk to students about the obvious importance of being able to handle stress and negative emotions in a positive way. Studies have shown that when it comes to emotions such as anger or frustration, "getting it out" with yelling or aggression is not healthy. Nor, as we now see here, is holding it all inside. Without asking them at which end they fall, poll the class to see if, when angry, they tend to react at these extremes. Discuss healthy ways in which anger can be released. Possibly students may need some release from the physical tension, such as exercise. Other suggestions might be identifying the true, underlying problem (if there really is one) and going about fixing it, or talking about it with a trusted friend or relative (who is not the target of the anger).

What about people who don't blow their top but try to keep everything in instead? Wouldn't that be bad for a person's health?

levels of hostility in their youth were far more likely to develop premature cardiovascular disease, particularly heart attacks, than were those men who had lower levels of anger and hostility (Chang et al., 2002). Similar studies found that hostility in college-aged male and females was significantly related to increased risk of heart disease, particularly if levels of hostility rose in middle age (Brondolo et al., 2003; Siegler et al., 2003).

What about people who don't blow their top but try to keep everything in instead? Wouldn't that be bad for a person's health?

Researchers Temoshok and Dreher (1992) identified a third personality type associated with a higher incidence of cancer. **Type C** people tend to be pleasant and try to keep the peace but find it difficult to express emotions, especially negative ones. They internalize their anger and often experience loneliness and despair over the loss of a loved one or a loss of hope. Type C people who have cancer often have thicker cancerous tumors (Eysenck, 1994; Temoshok & Dreher, 1992). Just as the stress of hostility puts the cardiovascular systems of Type A people at greater risk, the internalized negative emotions of the Type C personality may increase the levels of the stress hormone cortisol, which can weaken the immune system and slow recovery.

Not all Type A people are prone to heart disease—some people actually seem to thrive on stress. These people have a **hardy personality**, a term first coined by psychologist Suzanne Kobasa (1979). Hardy people (call them "Type H") differ from ordinary, hostile Type A people—and from others who suffer ill effects due to stress—in three ways:

- Hardy people have a deep sense of *commitment* to their values, beliefs, sense of identity, work, and family life.
- Hardy people also feel that they are in *control* of their lives and what happens to them.
- Hardy people tend to appraise stressful events and situations differently than people who are not hardy. When things go wrong, they do not see a frightening problem to be avoided but instead a *challenge* to be met and answered.

Why would those three characteristics (often known as the three "Cs" of hardiness [Kobasa, 1979]) lessen the negative impact of stress? Commitment makes a person more willing to make sacrifices and deal with hardships than if commitment were lacking. Think about it: Have you ever been forced to participate in an activity that you hated? Every little frustration and snag was very stressful, right? Now think about doing something you love to do. The frustrations and snags that inevitably come with any endeavor just don't seem quite as bad when you are doing something you have a commitment to do.

As for control, uncontrollability is one of the major factors cited as increasing stress. Appraising events as challenges rather than problems also changes the level of stress experienced, a difference similar to that felt when riding a roller coaster: If riding the roller coaster is your own idea, it's fun; if someone makes you ride it, it's not fun.

The four personality types discussed so far could be summed up this way: If life gives you lemons,

- Type A people get enraged and throw the lemons back, possibly increasing risk of a minor heart attack while doing so.
- Type B people gather all the lemons and make lemonade.
- Type C people don't say anything but fume inside where no one can see.
- Those with a hardy personality gather the lemons, make lemonade, sell it, turn it into a franchise business, and make millions.

Type C personality pleasant but repressed person, who tends to internalize his or her anger and anxiety and who finds expressing emotions difficult.

hardy personality a person who seems to thrive on stress but lacks the anger and hostility of the Type A personality.

Cultural Connections

BREAKDOWN OR SMASHUP?

A recent survey revealed that 6 in 10 Japanese workers feel significant stress on the job. Many business people cope by heavy drinking bouts after work or lying in the house in a vegetable-like state all weekend. Yoshie Ogasawara's funhouse, however, stocks a large supply of antique reproductions that patrons gleefully smash into walls. Groups of at least five workers pay $80 each for the privilege of destroying large porcelain vases, small statues, and figurines. The psychological benefits of this quick release remain to be seen. But in a country where a visit to a mental health professional still carries a strong social stigma, this may provide a socially sanctioned means of letting off steam.

Ask students, in light of their study in this module, if this seems like a healthy way to vent one's aggression and frustration. On the one hand, this may look like the extreme hostility that can cause heart disease. On the other hand, the Japanese would otherwise be likely to keep their negative emotions inside, causing other health concerns. Do students think that one might be better than the other—that maybe in this case, letting it out in a safe environment is best?

498 Chapter 15 Stress and Health

36.2 What are effective and ineffective ways to deal with stressors?

I understand that people with different personality types react to stressors differently, but are some reactions more helpful than others?

You know by now that people deal with stress in a variety of different ways: Some of us go out and take action to fix the problem; others stay at home and punch a pillow. Unfortunately, some of the most typical responses to stressors are not the most practical, helpful, or healthy responses.

A typical first response to a frustrating situation is *persistence*, or the continuation of efforts to get around whatever is causing the frustration. Persistence may involve making more intense efforts or changing the style of response. For example, anyone who has ever put coins into a drink machine only to find that the drink does not come out has probably (1) pushed the button again, more forcefully, and (2) pushed several other buttons in an effort to get some kind of response from the machine. If neither of these strategies works, many people may hit or kick the machine itself in an act of aggression.

Aggression, or actions meant to harm or destroy, is unfortunately another typical reaction to frustration. Although aggression is a frequent and persistent response to frustration, it is seldom the *first* response. Berkowitz (1993) stated that frustration creates an internal "readiness to aggress," but that aggression will not follow unless certain external cues are also present. For example, if the human source of a person's frustration is far larger and stronger in appearance than the frustrated person, aggression is an unlikely outcome!

Instead of using aggression, one could try to reason with the person who is the source of frustration. Reasoning with someone is a form of persistence. Trying to "get around" the problem is another way in which people can deal with frustration. Another possibility is to take out one's frustrations on less threatening, more available targets, in a process called **displaced aggression**. Anyone who has ever been frustrated by things that occurred at work or school and then later yelled at another person (such as a spouse, parent, child, or friend) has experienced displaced aggression. The person one really wants to strike out at is one's boss or teacher, or whoever or whatever caused the frustration in the first place. That could be dangerous, so the aggression is reserved for another less threatening or weaker target. For example, unemployment and financial difficulties are extremely frustrating, as they block a person's ability to achieve or maintain a certain standard of living. In one study, male unemployment and single parenthood were the two factors most highly correlated to rates of child abuse (Gillham et al., 1998). Unemployment is also one of the factors correlated most highly with the murder of abused women, creating four times the risk of murder for women in abusive relationships (Campbell & Wolf, 2003). Both studies are examples of displaced aggression toward the weaker and more available targets of children and women. Such targets often become *scapegoats*, or habitual targets of displaced aggression. Scapegoats are often pets, children, spouses, and even minority groups (who are seen as having less power).

Another possible reaction to frustration is **escape** or **withdrawal**. Escape or withdrawal can take the form of leaving, dropping out of school, quitting a job, or ending a relationship. Some people manage a psychological escape or withdrawal into apathy (ceasing to care about or act upon the situation), fantasy (which is only a temporary escape), or the use of drugs. Obviously, the latter reaction can lead to even more problems.

◀ I understand that people with different personality types react to stressors differently, but are some reactions more helpful than others?

aggression actions meant to harm or destroy.

displaced aggression taking out one's frustrations on some less threatening or more available target, a form of displacement.

escape or withdrawal leaving the presence of a stressor, either literally or by a psychological withdrawal into fantasy, drug abuse, or apathy.

STRESS AND HEALTH 499

CHAPTER 15 • Module 36

COVER THE MODULE

36.2 What are effective and ineffective ways to deal with stressors?

- Persistence, or trying harder to work one's way out of a situation, is a typical first response to frustration.
- A common subsequent response is *aggression*, actions meant to harm or destroy.
- If aggression toward the target of one's frustration is inadvisable, one may resort to *displaced aggression* toward a safer target that is not the source of the frustration.
- *Escape or withdrawal*, leaving the situation physically or psychologically, is another common reaction to frustration.

DISCUSS THE STUDENT VOICE QUESTION

This discussion follows from earlier discussions on personality types and healthy reactions to stress. Discuss with students why aggression and, probably more likely, displaced aggression are such typical reactions to frustration. Often, they happen without the perpetrator perceiving much thought behind it. Displaced aggression may not even be linked to the original frustration in the mind of the aggressor. What are students' suggestions for stopping these unhealthy reactions?

Class Demonstration

TYPE A BEHAVIOR PATTERNS

You can use an activity described by Eagleston (1987) to help increase your students' understanding of Type A behavior. You should note to your students that people exhibiting Type A behavior "engage in a set of observable behaviors that can be grouped into three areas: (1) excessive competitiveness and achievement orientation, (3) time urgency and impatience, and (3) easily aroused anger and hostility" (Eagleston, 1987). After writing these three areas on the board, divide students into small groups and tell each group to develop a list of specific and observable behaviors representing each of the areas. After 10 minutes, ask the groups to share their behaviors and have the class develop a consensus list of behaviors. The ensuing class discussion will help facilitate an understanding of the characteristics associated with Type A behavior.

Module 36 Coping with Stress 499

CHAPTER 15 • Module 36

COVER THE MODULE

36.3 What are some strategies for coping with stress?

- *Problem-focused coping* is used when the problem can be eliminated or changed so that it is no longer stressful or so that the impact of the stressor is reduced.
- *Emotion-focused coping* is often used with problem-focused coping and involves changing one's emotional reactions to a stressor.

DISCUSS THE STUDENT VOICE QUESTION

Talk to students about the differences between problem-focused coping and emotion-focused coping. Ensure they understand that, though they should try to "fix" any stressors they can, emotion-focused coping will come into play when a fix is not available. Ask students to give examples of when they've used problem-focused coping and emotion-focused coping to ensure they get the distinction.

EXTEND THE LESSON (KINESTHETIC)

In the middle of your class period, announce that you are giving a pop quiz and that it will part of students' final grade for the class. (If this is especially unusual, you may need to come up with a ruse, such as administrative pressure to get more grades on the books, etc.) Tell students that first they may have a break to stretch their legs, talk to their classmates, and so on, as long as they do not discuss the current module. Reconvene the class in about 5 minutes for the "quiz." Ask students how they feel now. How did they feel when you announced the quiz? Students will likely indicate that the announcement caused them stress, but they felt better after talking with their classmates. Use this to illustrate the effect of social support, either through commiseration or simple interaction, on stress reduction.

500 Chapter 15 Stress and Health

It doesn't sound like aggression, escape, or withdrawal are very good ways to deal with stressful situations. How do people deal with all the stress they face every day? ▶

coping strategies actions that people can take to master, tolerate, reduce, or minimize the effects of stressors.

problem-focused coping coping strategies that try to eliminate the source of a stress or reduce its impact through direct actions.

emotion-focused coping coping strategies that change the impact of a stressor by changing the emotional reaction to the stressor.

500 CHAPTER 15

36.3 What are some strategies for coping with stress?

It doesn't sound like aggression, escape, or withdrawal are very good ways to deal with stressful situations. How do people deal with all the stress they face every day? People who can deal effectively with stress and minimize the effect of stressful situations in their lives have learned to *cope* with stress. These people often use specific **coping strategies**, which are actions that people can take to master, tolerate, reduce, or minimize the effects of stressors.

Problem-Focused Coping One type of coping strategy is to work on eliminating or changing the stressor itself. When people try to eliminate the source of a stress or reduce its impact through their own actions, it is called **problem-focused coping** (Folkman & Lazarus, 1980; Lazarus, 1993). For example, a student might have a problem understanding a particular teacher. The teacher is knowledgeable but has trouble explaining the concepts of the course in a way that this student can understand. Problem-focused coping might include talking to the teacher after class, asking fellow students to clarify the concepts, getting a tutor, or forming a study group with other students who are also having difficulty and pooling the group's resources.

Emotion-Focused Coping Problem-focused coping is not the only effective way to deal with stress. Most people use both problem-focused coping and **emotion-focused coping** to successfully deal with stressful events (Eschenbeck et al., 2008; Folkman & Lazarus, 1980; Lazarus, 1993; Stowell et al., 2001). Emotion-focused coping is a strategy that involves changing the way a person feels or emotionally reacts to a stressor. You may have heard the saying that we may not be able to change a situation, but we can change how we *think* or *feel* about a situation. This strategy reduces the emotional impact of the stressor and makes it possible to deal with the problem more effectively. For example, the student who is faced with a teacher who isn't easy to understand might share his concerns with a friend, talking it through until he is calm enough to tackle the problem in a more direct manner. Emotion-focused coping also works for stressors that are uncontrollable and for which problem-focused coping is not possible. Someone using emotion-focused coping may decide to view the stressor as a challenge rather than a threat, decide that the problem is a minor one, write down concerns in a journal, or even ignore the problem altogether. True, ignoring a problem is not a good strategy when there is something a person can actively do to solve the problem. But when it is not possible to change or eliminate the stressor, or when worrying about the stressor can be a problem itself, ignoring the problem can help a person cope with the stress.

Using humor can also be a form of emotion-focused coping, as the old saying "laughter is the best medicine" suggests. A recent study on the effects of laughter found that laughter actually boosted the action of the immune system by increasing the work of natural killer cells (cells that attack viruses in the body). In this study, participants were shown a humorous video for 1 hour. Blood samples were taken 10 minutes before the viewing, 30 minutes into the viewing, 30 minutes after viewing, and 12 hours after viewing the video. There were significant increases in natural killer cell activity and nearly half a dozen other immune system cells and systems, with some effects lasting the full 12 hours after the video ended (Berk et al., 2001).

Emotion-focused coping is highly related to several forms of psychological defenses first proposed by Sigmund Freud, as the next section discusses.

Explore

LAUGHING OUT LOUD TO GOOD HEALTH

Direct students to http://library.thinkquest.org/25500/index2.htm, a site dedicated to the philosophy that laughter is the best medicine. This site contains a wealth of information, both serious and silly: material about emotions and stress, information about why we laugh and why it is good for us, how to tell a joke, as well as specific jokes and other laugh-worthy fun. Ask students to write a short report on what they learned from the site.

Psychological Defense Mechanisms In Freud's writings on psychoanalysis, he stated that when people experience anxiety (stress) from conflicts between the demands of the body's needs and desires and society's rules for proper behavior, there are certain unconscious distortions of thought that can protect their sense of self from that anxiety (Freud, 1915). *LINK* to *Chapter Twelve: Theories of Personality, p. 379.* These unconscious distortions of the perception of reality are called **psychological defense mechanisms** and were further explained by Freud's daughter, Anna Freud (1946). Although Freudian theory has fallen in and out of favor over the last century, the concept of these defense mechanisms has remained quite useful in clinical psychology as a way of describing people's defensive behavior and irrational thinking.

Table 36.1 on page 502 lists, defines, and gives examples of some of the more common defense mechanisms. Nearly all of these resemble emotion-focused coping strategies, although their use as substitutes for healthy coping techniques can easily lead to more problems. *Simulate* on **mypsychlab.com**

How Social Support Affects Coping

I hear the term "social support system" all the time now. Exactly what is it?

A **social support system** is the network of friends, family members, neighbors, coworkers, and others who can offer help to a person in need. That help can take the form of advice, physical or monetary support, information, emotional support, love and affection, or companionship. Research has consistently shown that having a good social support system is of critical importance in a person's ability to cope with stressors: People with good social support systems are less likely to die from illnesses or injuries than those without such support (Kulik & Mahler, 1989, 1993). Marriage, itself a form of social support, is a good predictor of healthy aging and longevity (Gardner & Oswald, 2004; Vaillant, 2002).

Social support can make a stressor seem less threatening because people with such support know that there is help available. Having people to talk to about one's problems reduces the physical symptoms of stress—talking about frightening or frustrating events with others can help people think more realistically about the threat, for example, and talking with people who have had similar experiences can help put the event into perspective. The negative emotions of loneliness and depression, which are less likely to occur with someone who has social support, can adversely affect one's ability to cope (Beehr et al., 2000; Weisse, 1992). Positive emotions are more likely to occur in the presence of friends and family and have a decidedly beneficial effect on health, helping people recover from stressful experiences more quickly and effectively (Tugade & Fredrickson, 2004).

How Culture Affects Coping Imagine this scene: You are driving out in the country when you come upon an elderly man working on a large wooden box, polishing it with great care. You stop to talk to the man and find out that the box is his own coffin, and he spends his days getting it ready, tending to it with great care. He isn't frightened of dying and doesn't feel strange about polishing his own coffin. How would you react?

If you were from the same rural area of Vietnam as the elderly man, you would probably think nothing strange is going on. For elderly people in the Vietnamese culture, thoughts of death and the things that go along with dying, such as a coffin, are not as stressful as they are to people from Western cultures. In fact, *stress* isn't all that common a term in Vietnamese society compared to Western societies (Phan & Silove, 1999).

psychological defense mechanisms unconscious distortions of a person's perception of reality that reduce stress and anxiety.

social support system the network of family, friends, neighbors, coworkers, and others who can offer support, comfort, or aid to a person in need.

Simulate factors in stress reduction on **mypsychlab.com**

◀ I hear the term "social support system" all the time now. Exactly what is it?

▲ These life-size models of Marge and Homer Simpson were created for the 350th episode of The Simpsons in April 2005. A large part of the success of such comedies can be attributed to the human need to laugh—laughter helps us cope with many of life's stresses.

STRESS AND HEALTH 501

CHAPTER 15 • Module 36

COVER THE MODULE *(continued)*

- *Psychological defense mechanisms* are unconscious distortions of perceived reality and can be a form of emotion-focused coping.
- *Social support*, or people who are available for help and comfort, is a valuable tool in managing stress.
- Different cultures perceive stressors differently. Coping strategies will also vary from culture to culture.

MULTIMEDIA CONTENT AVAILABLE AT www.mypsychlab.com

Simulate factors in stress reduction on **mypsychlab.com**

DISCUSS THE STUDENT VOICE QUESTION

Talk to students about the different forms social support can take—family, friends, even clubs of which they are members. Ask students what social support means to them. Is it mostly friends? Mostly relatives? An extended group of people? A more intimate group? Point out that their modes of social support will reflect their different situations and personalities and will certainly differ, probably in several ways, from one person to the next.

Class Demonstration

COPING WITH FINAL EXAM STRESS

Purpose: Students generate examples of how to cope with stress.

Time: 5–10 minutes

Description: Read the following scenario to the class:

It is three weeks before finals, and Kara is starting to worry. She has two papers, four exams, and on top of that she is graduating and hasn't committed to a college yet. What are some strategies Kara could use to cope with her stress?

Students should begin by writing their answer to the question. Next, students should share their answer with a partner. They may want to combine their answers or come up with the best three coping strategies. In the final step, students can pair with a larger team, or you can call on a few pairs to share their responses with the entire class.

Module 36 Coping with Stress **501**

CHAPTER 15 • Module 36

COVER THE MODULE (continued)

- Common defense mechanisms:
  - *Denial*
  - *Repression*
  - *Rationalization*
  - *Projection*
  - *Reaction formation*
  - *Displacement*
  - *Regression*
  - *Identification*
  - *Compensation (substitution)*
  - *Sublimation*

UNDERSTANDING VISUALS

Discuss with students the various defense mechanisms as illustrated in Table 36.1. Then ask students to close their books, and read to them the examples from the table. Can they identify each corresponding defense mechanism?

FAST FACT

Share with students some other defense mechanisms that have been identified, such as acting out, dissociation, compartmentalization, intellectualization, undoing, and assertiveness (see http://psychcentral.com/lib/2007/15-common-defense-mechanisms/).

---

denial psychological defense mechanism in which the person refuses to acknowledge or recognize a threatening situation.

repression psychological defense mechanism in which the person refuses to consciously remember a threatening or unacceptable event, instead pushing those events into the unconscious mind.

rationalization psychological defense mechanism in which a person invents acceptable excuses for unacceptable behavior.

projection psychological defense mechanism in which unacceptable or threatening impulses or feelings are seen as originating with someone else, usually the target of the impulses or feelings.

reaction formation psychological defense mechanism in which a person forms an opposite emotional or behavioral reaction to the way he or she really feels to keep those true feelings hidden from self and others.

displacement redirecting feelings from a threatening target to a less threatening one.

regression psychological defense mechanism in which a person falls back on childlike patterns of responding in reaction to stressful situations.

identification defense mechanism in which a person tries to become like someone else to deal with anxiety.

compensation (substitution) defense mechanism in which a person makes up for inferiorities in one area by becoming superior in another area.

sublimation channeling socially unacceptable impulses and urges into socially acceptable behavior.

Table 36.1 Psychological Defense Mechanisms

DEFENSE MECHANISM AND DEFINITION	EXAMPLE
Denial: refusal to recognize or acknowledge a threatening situation.	Ben is failing his classes but denies struggling academically. He is surprised when he receives low grades on his report card.
Repression: "pushing" threatening or conflicting events or situations out of conscious awareness.	Elise, who was badly injured in a fire as a child, cannot remember the fire at all.
Rationalization: making up acceptable excuses for unacceptable behavior.	"If I don't have breakfast, I can have that piece of cake later on without hurting my diet."
Projection: placing one's own unacceptable thoughts onto others, as if the thoughts belonged to them and not to oneself.	Keisha is attracted to her friend's boyfriend but denies this and believes the boyfriend is attracted to her.
Reaction formation: forming an emotional reaction or attitude that is the opposite of one's threatening or unacceptable actual thoughts.	Seven-year-old Darnell likes his female classmate, Annie, but he makes fun of her and acts rudely in her presence.
Displacement: expressing feelings that would be threatening if directed at the real target onto a less threatening substitute target.	Sandra gets reprimanded by her teacher and goes home to angrily pick a fight with her brother.
Regression: falling back on childlike patterns as a way of coping with stressful situations.	Four-year-old Jeff starts wetting his bed after his parents bring home a new baby.
Identification: trying to become like someone else to deal with one's anxiety.	Marie really admires Suzy, the most popular girl in school, and tries to copy her behavior and dress.
Compensation (substitution): trying to make up for areas in which a lack is perceived by becoming superior in some other area.	Reggie is not good at athletics, so he puts all of his energies into becoming an academic scholar.
Sublimation: turning socially unacceptable urges into socially acceptable behavior.	Alain, who is very aggressive, becomes a professional hockey player.

In the case of many people living in Vietnam and even Vietnamese immigrants to other countries, mental illness is explained by an imbalance between the male and female elements of a person, or by a loss of soul, evil spirits, or a weakening of the nerves. Coping with stress in Vietnamese culture may include rituals, consulting a fortune-teller, or eating certain foods (Phan & Silove, 1999).

Class Demonstration

DEFENSE MECHANISMS

<u>Purpose</u>: Students learn about defense mechanisms.

<u>Time</u>: 10 minutes or more

<u>Description</u>: In this role-play exercise, students work in pairs. Assign each student pair to a defense mechanism (e.g., denial, repression). Students should generate a role-play in which a person illustrates the defense mechanism during a conversation with a fictional friend or family member. Pairs may practice their role plays a few times and then perform them for the rest of the class. The audience can try to guess which defense mechanism is being illustrated by each role-play.

Obviously, culture is an important factor in the kinds of coping strategies an individual may adopt and even in determining the degree of stress that is experienced. Mental health professionals should make an effort to include an assessment of a person's cultural background as well as immediate circumstances when dealing with adjustment problems due to stress.

How Religion Affects Coping A belief in a higher power can also be a source of great comfort in times of stress. There are several ways that religious beliefs can affect the degree of stress people experience and the ability to cope with that stress (Hill & Butter, 1995; Pargament, 1997).

First, most people who hold strong religious beliefs belong to a religious organization and attend regular religious functions, such as services at a church, synagogue, mosque, or temple. This membership can be a vital part of a person's social support system. People do not feel alone in their struggle, both literally because of the people who surround them in their religious community and spiritually because of the intangible presence of their deity (Koenig et al., 1999).

Another way that religion helps people cope involves the rituals and rites that help people feel better about personal weaknesses, failures, or feelings of inadequacy (Koenig et al., 2001). These include rituals such as confession of sins or prayer services during times of stress. Finally, religious beliefs can give meaning to things that otherwise seem to have no meaning or purpose, such as viewing death as a pathway to a paradise, or the destruction of one's home in a natural disaster as a reminder to place less attachment on material things. ◆ Explore on mypsychlab.com

◆ Explore coping strategies on mypsychlab.com

36.4 What is optimism, and how can people become more optimistic?

Can the way in which you see the world affect your stress levels and your overall health? As it turns out, the answer is yes: Having a positive outlook can actually improve your physical and mental health.

Optimists are people who always tend to look for positive outcomes. (In contrast, **pessimists** seem to expect the worst to happen.) For an optimist, a glass is half full, whereas for a pessimist, the glass is half empty. Researchers have found that optimism is associated with longer life and increased immune system functioning. Mayo Clinic researchers conducted a longitudinal study of optimists and pessimists (as assessed by a scale) over a period of 30 years (Maruta et al., 2002). The results for pessimists were not good: They had a much higher death rate than did the optimists, and those that were still living in 1994 had more problems with physical and emotional health, more pain, less ability to take part in social activities, and less energy than optimists. The optimists had a 50 percent lower risk of premature death and were more calm, peaceful, and happy than the pessimists (Maruta et al., 2002).

Psychologist Martin Seligman (2002) has outlined four ways in which optimism may affect how long a person lives:

1. Optimists are less likely to develop learned helplessness, the tendency to stop trying to achieve a goal that has been blocked in the past. ⓁⒾⓃⓀ to *Chapter Six: Learning and Language Development, p. 199.*
2. Optimists are more likely than pessimists to take care of their health by preventive measures (such as going to the doctor for checkups

optimists people who expect positive outcomes.

pessimists people who expect negative outcomes.

STRESS AND HEALTH 503

CHAPTER 15 • Module 36

COVER THE MODULE (continued)
- People with religious beliefs also have been found to cope better with stressful events.

MULTIMEDIA CONTENT AVAILABLE AT
www.mypsychlab.com

◆ Explore coping strategies on mypsychlab.com

COVER THE MODULE

36.4 What is optimism, and how can people become more optimistic?

- *Optimists* look for positive outcomes and experience far less stress than *pessimists*, who take a more negative view.

ⓁⒾⓃⓀ to *Chapter Six: Learning and Language Development, p. 199*

L1 DIFFERENTIATED INSTRUCTION

Special Needs Give these students extra time to finish assignments.

Class Demonstration

LIFESTYLE AWARENESS TRIANGLE

Have students draw a "lifestyle triangle" to help them visualize the stress in their lives. The three sides of the triangle should represent (1) school and/or work, (2) leisure/recreational activities, and (3) relationships with others. The length of each side should accurately reflect the amount of time and energy spent on this aspect, so that longer sides represent more time and energy expended. Ask students to draw two lifestyle triangles, one representing their *ideal* triangle (i.e., how they wished their triangle looked) and one representing their *actual* triangle (i.e., the way it really looks). In general, bigger discrepancies between the two triangles reflect greater perceived stress experienced by students. Sometimes, the school/work side of a triangle is so long that the other sides cannot possibly connect with each other! Discuss with students the implications of the triangles they have drawn (perhaps volunteers would be willing to share their depictions) and brainstorm ways that they can change their behavior so that their actual triangle can become more like their ideal triangle—which should ultimately reduce some of the stress in their lives.

Module 36 Coping with Stress **503**

CHAPTER 15 • Module 36

DISCUSS THE STUDENT VOICE QUESTION

Ask students if it makes sense to them that optimists should get better grades in school. Tell them to read to themselves the paragraph beginning, "Optimism is associated with a person's belief that he or she can control moods. . . ." Then ask them if this sounds like any other concepts they have covered in the class so far. Students should be able to identify that optimists have an internal locus of control. The example of an optimist's attribution of poor exam grades should illustrate this to students.

UNDERSTANDING VISUALS

Direct students' attention to the steps in Figure 36.3. Ask students if there is a situation in their lives right now, or if there are situations that they commonly experience, that could be approached this way. Give them some time during class to think about this and then write out how they would fill in the thought bubbles in this figure using their own stressful situations. You may want to do this for yourself ahead of time and share your thought bubbles with the class after they have completed theirs.

Whoa—optimistic students get better grades? How do I become an optimist? ▶ Sign me up!

and eating right) because they believe that their actions make a difference in what happens to them. (Remember, a feeling of control over one's situation is a characteristic of hardy people as well.)

3. Optimists are far less likely than pessimists to become depressed, and depression is associated with mortality because of the effect of depression on the immune system.
4. Optimists generally have a more effectively functioning immune system than pessimists, perhaps because they experience less psychological stress.

Seligman (1998) has also found that optimists are more successful in their life endeavors than pessimists. Optimistic politicians win more elections, optimistic students get better grades, and optimistic athletes win more contests.

Whoa—optimistic students get better grades? How do I become an optimist? Sign me up!

Optimism is associated with a person's belief that he or she can control moods or emotional reactions to situations. According to psychiatrist Dr. Susan Vaughan (2000), optimists tend to engage in *alternative thinking*, coming up with alternative explanations for why the bad thing happened. For example, optimists tend to attribute poor exam grades to the difficulty of that particular material or to not having enough time to study. They appraise it as a challenge and assume that they will perform more successfully in the future. See Figure 36.3 for more ways to become an optimistic thinker. Optimists also use *downward social comparison* frequently, comparing their performance to that of less competent others, which makes them feel better and protects their self-esteem. Finally, some optimists improve their mood through relaxation techniques such as exercising, meditating, or reading a good book.

Step 1: When a bad mood strikes, stop and think about what just went through your head. *(I'll never get this term paper finished. It's too hard!)*

Step 2: Recognize the negative statements. Think about the damage each statement is doing to you. *(That statement isn't going to help me; it just makes me feel worse.)*

Step 3: Argue with your negative thoughts. Replace each negative statement with a more positive statement. *(I can finish the term paper. I'm just going to have to devote more time to working on it. I can manage this situation.)*

FIGURE 36.3 Steps to Optimistic Thinking

Class Demonstration

THE CONTROL PROCESS

A broader approach to understanding people's reactions to stress involves understanding their sense of control. Below are some specific control strategies and their effects on adjustment to stressful events.

- *Behavior control.* This strategy involves taking concrete steps to reduce the unpleasantness of a negative event. This kind of direct control will often alleviate the stress associated with the aversive event. Actual (or perceived) behavior control can also help reduce stress prior to the anxiety-provoking event, or at least increase tolerance of the event when it occurs.

- *Cognitive control.* Cognitive control means thinking about the unpleasant event differently or reevaluating the nonaversive aspects of the event. This strategy seems to help adjustment at all levels of the event—prior, during, and after.

- *Decision control.* Being able to make decisions about the onset, timing, or type of aversive event can be helpful if the outcomes of the decision are favorable.

36.5 What are some ways to promote wellness?

Wellness can be defined as the practice of behaviors and lifestyle choices that promote both physical and mental health. Here are some helpful hints on how to promote wellness in your own life:

- **Exercise.** No one likes to admit it, but exercise is the best way to become healthier. Exercise makes the heart healthier, raises the body's metabolic rate to help maintain a healthy weight, raises good cholesterol and lowers bad cholesterol, strengthens bones, improves sleep quality, reduces tiredness, increases natural killer cell activity to help ward off viruses and cancer, and is a great way to reduce the effects of stress (Fiatarone et al., 1993; Manson et al., 2002). In fact, aerobic exercise has been found to reduce feelings of tiredness and increase energy in young adults who, because of a sedentary lifestyle, have been diagnosed with persistent fatigue (Puetz et al., 2008).
- **Get involved with others.** Make some new friends, join a club, or perform community service. Make it a point to do things with other people. Ask friends over to watch a movie, or work on a service project with a group of classmates or other people in your community.
- **Get some sleep.** Sleep serves to restore the body physically and provides a way to manage stress during dreaming. LINK to Chapter Four: Consciousness: Sleep, Dreams, Hypnosis, and Drugs, p. 118. Try to get at least 7 to 8 hours of sleep each night, including weekends. Try to go to bed and get up at the same time every day to maintain your sleep–wake cycle. Sleep deprivation can lead to a lower production of natural killer cells, which are a necessary and vital part of the immune system (Irwin et al., 1994, 1996).
- **Eat healthy foods.** Eat breakfast every day, making sure to include a good amount of protein in that meal. Protein in the morning helps improve concentration and alertness, and eating breakfast helps you to avoid overeating at lunch or dinner. Eating breakfast has even been shown to decrease the risk of stroke, obesity, and diabetes (Pereira et al., 2003). Be sure to include some healthy snacks at least twice a day.
- **Have some fun.** Playing is important! Schedule some time to just relax, play a game with a friend, read a book, or do something fun. Playing helps prevent burnout.
- **Manage your time.** One of the things that can create a lot of stress is feeling overwhelmed when there are lots of tasks to do. Make a list of the tasks you need to accomplish, and check each item off the list as you finish it. This gives you a sense of control over your day's activities and rewards you with a sense of accomplishment each time you can check off an item.
- **Take a deep breath.** When you feel stressed, take a moment to cope. Take some deep breaths to help calm yourself and relax tension. If you're so stressed that you feel like crying, find a quiet, private place and cry—crying can relieve stress.

▲ *Regular exercise increases the functioning of the immune system and helps give people a sense of control over their health. Having a sense of control decreases feelings of stress, which also helps the immune system to function well.*

CHAPTER 15 • Module 36

COVER THE MODULE

36.5 What are some ways to promote wellness?

- Factors that promote wellness include exercise, social activities, getting enough sleep, eating healthily, having fun, managing one's time, and practicing good coping skills.

LINK to *Chapter Four: Consciousness, Sleep, Dreams, Hypnosis, and Drugs*, p. 118

EXTEND THE LESSON

Meditation can produce a state of relaxation and reduce the physical reactions common to stressful situations. Concentrative meditation involves focusing inward on some repetitive stimulus, such as one's breathing. Receptive meditation involves focusing outward to expand conscious awareness. There are many resources on the Internet, such as www.meditationcenter.com/index.html, that provide information about meditation, as well as guided meditations to get a person started.

Class Demonstration (Kinesthetic)

RELAX BEFORE THE BIG GAME

Have your class compare performances of students who do and do not use relaxation and imagery. Bring a bucket and several tennis balls to class. Depending on the size of the bucket, place it 10 to 15 feet away. Randomly divide the class in half. Ask half of the students to come up individually and shoot one ball into the bucket. Count how many are made by those students.

Lead the other half of the class in a progressive relaxation exercise. Once they are relaxed, ask them to picture standing in front of the class with a tennis ball in their hand, aiming the ball into the bucket, smoothly shooting the ball at the bucket, and watching the ball go in the bucket as their arm completes the follow-through. Have them imagine shooting and making 10 shots in a row. Now have those students come up in front of the class and shoot one bucket. Ask them to maintain their visual image of making the bucket while they are shooting. Again, count the number of shots made.

Lead the class in a discussion of the differences in number of shots made by both groups. What effect, if any, did relaxation and imagery have on the second group's score?

CHAPTER 15 • Module 36

Assess

Assign the Module 36 Practice Quiz.

Use the Practice Quiz to identify gaps in student understanding.

REMEDIATE

Have students, individually or in groups, review the module goals, learning objectives, and key terms.

Refer students to the Concept Summary on p. 511 for review.

Close

As a class, discuss with students the many unhealthy and healthy ways in which people deal with stress. Encourage to them to think about their own coping mechanisms and how they can be improved. Ask students to consult the list of stressors they made in the Bellringer in Module 35. How can they use this module to deal with those stressors?

Practice Quiz

Pick the best answer.

1. According to Lazarus, secondary appraisal involves
   a. estimating the severity of the stressor
   b. classifying the stressor as a threat or challenge
   c. deciding whether the stressor is a problem
   d. estimating the resources a person has available for coping

2. Which of the following people is most at risk for coronary heart disease?
   a. a workaholic who has a hostile personality
   b. an easygoing person who can relax without guilt
   c. a diligent worker who views life as a challenge to be overcome
   d. an outwardly pleasant person who stores negative emotions inside

3. Which of the following statements about optimists is true?
   a. Optimists are more likely than pessimists to develop coronary heart disease.
   b. Optimists are less likely than pessimists to go to the doctor regularly.
   c. Optimists are more likely than pessimists to develop learned helplessness.
   d. Optimists are less likely than pessimists to experience premature death.

4. Mima is knitting a scarf, but she keeps making mistakes, and she becomes frustrated. Which of the following is most likely Mima's first response to frustration?
   a. deciding to make a hat instead
   b. yelling and tearing the scarf apart
   c. taking out the frustration on a friend
   d. continuing to attempt to fix the scarf

5. Which of the following is an example of problem-focused coping?
   a. ignoring an argument with a friend and focusing on other things
   b. venting to mutual acquaintances about an argument with a friend
   c. making excuses for behavior that led to an argument with a friend
   d. attempting to settle an argument with a friend by apologizing

6. Clarissa feels anxious because she is having trouble making new friends. She knows that another girl in her class, Patrice, is very social and has lots of friends. Clarissa begins copying Patrice's mannerisms and interests. Clarissa is engaging in
   a. repression
   b. projection
   c. displacement
   d. identification

7. Ellie sucks her thumb when she is under stress. Ellie is engaging in
   a. reaction formation
   b. displacement
   c. regression
   d. projection

8. When a person tries to cope by eliminating or changing the stressor directly, it is known as
   a. a defense mechanism
   b. problem-focused coping
   c. self-focused coping
   d. emotion-focused coping

9. Which of the following is NOT an effective way to promote wellness?
   a. exercising
   b. getting enough sleep
   c. holding back tears
   d. playing with friends

10. Which of the following statements about aggression is true?
    a. Aggression is rarely the first response to frustration.
    b. Aggression will always follow frustration.
    c. Aggression is not a typical response to frustration.
    d. Aggression is not affected by external cues.

Practice Quiz Answers

1. d
2. a
3. d
4. d
5. d
6. d
7. c
8. b
9. c
10. a

CHAPTER 15 Summary

Listen on **mypsychlab.com**

Module 35: Stress and Stressors
Understand the causes and consequences of stress.

35.1 How do psychologists define stress?
- Stress is the term used to describe the physical, emotional, cognitive, and behavioral responses to events that are judged to be threatening or challenging. Stressors, or stress-causing events, can be internal or external. Unpleasant stressors can cause distress and pleasant stressors can cause eustress.

35.2 What kinds of events and situations can cause stress?
- Environmental causes of stress include catastrophes, major life events or changes, and everyday hassles. Social causes of stress include poverty, workplace conditions, and adapting to a new culture. Psychological factors that cause or intensify stressful situations include pressure, uncontrollability, and frustration.

35.3 How can stress affect physiological and psychological health?
- The general adaptation syndrome (GAS) is a sequence of physiological responses to a stressor: alarm (activation of the sympathetic nervous system), resistance (the release of stress hormones), and exhaustion (when the body has used up its resources in response to stress). Chronic stress can suppress the immune system, put heart health at risk, and harm the body's ability to fight cancer.
- People who experience high levels of stress are at risk for anxiety disorders such as acute stress disorder (ASD) and post-traumatic stress disorder (PTSD).

Module 36: Coping with Stress and Promoting Wellness
Learn strategies for promoting mental and physical health.

36.1 How do people think about stress?
- Lazarus's cognitive-mediational theory of emotion consists of two steps: primary appraisal, which involves estimating the severity of a stressor and classifying it as a threat, a challenge, or a harm or loss; and secondary appraisal, which involves estimating the resources available for coping with the stressor.

Listen to an audio file of your chapter on **mypsychlab.com**
- How one cognitively assesses a stressor has a lot to do with one's personality. Type A people are under constant pressure and tend to create more stress for themselves than Type B people, who are more relaxed. Type C people internalize anger and other emotions, which may increase stress. People with hardy personalities thrive on stress and appraise stressors as challenges to be overcome.

36.2 What are effective and ineffective ways to deal with stressors?
- Typical responses to frustration include persistence, aggression, displaced aggression, and escape or withdrawal. Most of these responses are not effective ways to minimize stressors, and aggression and withdrawal can be dangerous strategies.

36.3 What are some strategies for coping with stress?
- Problem-focused coping involves eliminating the stressor or reducing its impact through practical actions. Emotion-focused coping involves changing the way a person reacts emotionally to a stressor.
- Some people cope with stress by protecting themselves with psychological defense mechanisms.
- A strong social support network, cultural support, and religious support can increase people's ability to cope with stress.

36.4 What is optimism, and how can people become more optimistic?
- Optimists are people who tend to look for positive outcomes. People can become more optimistic by engaging in alternative thinking, making downward social comparisons, and improving mood through relaxation techniques.

36.5 What are some ways to promote wellness?
- Behaviors and lifestyle choices that promote physical and mental health include exercising, socializing, sleeping enough, eating healthy foods, having fun, managing time effectively, and taking deep breaths to release tension.

Vocabulary Terms

stress p. 482
stressors p. 482
distress p. 483
eustress p. 483
catastrophe p. 483
hassles p. 485
burnout p. 486
acculturative stress p. 487
pressure p. 487
frustration p. 488
general adaptation syndrome (GAS) p. 489
immune system p. 490
natural killer cell p. 491
acute stress disorder (ASD) p. 492
post-traumatic stress disorder (PTSD) p. 492
primary appraisal p. 495
secondary appraisal p. 496
Type A personality p. 497
Type B personality p. 497
Type C personality p. 498
hardy personality p. 498
aggression p. 499
displaced aggression p. 499
escape or withdrawal p. 499
coping strategies p. 500
problem-focused coping p. 500
emotion-focused coping p. 500
psychological defense mechanisms p. 501
social support system p. 501
denial p. 502
repression p. 502
rationalization p. 502
projection p. 502
reaction formation p. 502
displacement p. 502
regression p. 502
identification p. 502
compensation (substitution) p. 502
sublimation p. 502
optimists p. 503
pessimists p. 503

STRESS AND HEALTH 507

CHAPTER 15 • Chapter Summary and Vocabulary

Chapter Summary

Encourage students to carefully review and study the summary. Explain that it provides an overview of key concepts presented in the text.

Have students identify what they find unclear or confusing. Call on volunteers to provide answers, examples, or definitions.

Vocabulary Terms

Remind students that terms are defined within the chapter at point of use. If they are not sure of a term's definition, they should look up the definition on the page.

Encourage students to create study cards of unfamiliar words or to go to **www.mypsychlab.com** for flashcards. Have them test themselves or a classmate. Advanced students can explain the terms in their own words.

Critical Thinking

MAKING CONNECTIONS

Have students complete the following activity to connect the ideas in this chapter. Send them to the Multimedia Library for this chapter at **www.mypsychlab.com** to view the video titled "Socializing and Stress," which discusses how our genetics may affect our need to socialize, or not, in stressful situations. Then lead a class discussion based on the following questions: (1) How does studying animals such as worms help scientists to understand human behavior? (2) What are students' own instincts when it comes to stressful situations—to seek out social interaction or to shy away from it? (3) What are the implications of developing drugs to help people curb stress and overeating?

CHAPTER 15 • Assessment

Vocabulary Review

Match each vocabulary term to its definition.

1. eustress
2. catastrophe
3. primary appraisal
4. withdrawal
5. aggression
6. sublimation
7. hassles
8. repression
9. coping strategies
10. pressure

a. The effect of positive events, or the optimal amount of stress that people need to promote health and well-being.
b. The daily annoyances of everyday life.
c. Actions meant to harm or destroy.
d. The psychological experience produced by urgent demands or expectations for a person's behavior that come from an outside source.
e. An unpredictable, large-scale event that creates a tremendous need to adapt and adjust as well as overwhelming feelings of threat.
f. Psychological defense mechanism in which the person refuses to consciously remember a threatening or unacceptable event, instead pushing those events into the unconscious mind.
g. Leaving the presence of a stressor.
h. Actions that people can take to master, tolerate, reduce, or minimize the effects of stressors.
i. The first step in assessing stress, which involves estimating the severity of a stressor and classifying it as either a threat or a challenge.
j. Channeling socially unacceptable impulses and urges into socially acceptable behavior.

Writing about Psychology

Respond to each question in complete sentences.

1. Describe three common stressors that affect you, people you know, or your community. Identify each stressor as an environmental factor, a social factor, a psychological factor, or a combination of factors. Then, explain at least one effective way to cope with each stressor. Consider problem-focused coping, emotion-focused coping, and other coping techniques discussed in this chapter as you develop your response.

2. Imagine a stressful situation that might occur on a typical day at school, at work, or at home. Describe this situation. Then, write about how each of the following people would react to the situation: a Type A person, a Type B person, a Type C person, and a person with a hardy personality. Finally, explain which reaction is most similar to the reaction you think you would have. What does your answer tell you about your personality type?

Psychology Project

Can simple lifestyle changes really affect your physical and psychological health? Perform this activity to find out.

Materials:
- a notebook and pencil

Instructions:

1. You've learned that some ways to promote physical and mental health include exercising more, joining a club or organization, getting more sleep, eating healthier foods, spending some time relaxing or playing each day, making to-do lists, and taking deep breaths to calm yourself and relax tension. Now, choose one of these activities that you think you can realistically incorporate into your daily life for at least 2 weeks.

2. On the first page of your notebook, write down the lifestyle change that you plan to make for the next 2 weeks. For example, you might plan to eat more vegetables, make a to-do list of your homework assignments every day, or get at least 8 hours of sleep each night. Then, write down how you plan to meet this goal.

3. Put your plan into action. Over the next 2 weeks, spend some time every day participating in the activity that you have chosen. Record a brief summary of your daily experiences in your notebook at the end of every day. If you notice changes in your physical health or the amount of stress in your life, record those changes in your notebook, too.

4. At the end of the 2-week period, evaluate your notes. Has your life changed at all since you put your plan into action? Do you feel more physically healthy or less stressed out? Remember that 2 weeks is not a very long time, and consider continuing the changes you have made for a longer period of time if you feel that they are helping you become healthier.

CHAPTER 15 • Assessment

VOCABULARY REVIEW

1. a
2. e
3. i
4. g
5. c
6. j
7. b
8. f
9. h
10. d

WRITING ABOUT PSYCHOLOGY

1. Students' answers may range from school worries to local poverty to a catastrophe that has affected the area in which they live. They should show an understanding of when problem solving is possible and when acceptance is the best course and understand healthy ways of dealing with stress and pressure.

2. Students should display a clear understanding of each personality type and that type's typical reactions to stressful situations. They should show a thoughtful evaluation of their own personalities and likely reactions.

PSYCHOLOGY PROJECT

Consider asking students to share the changes they made and their effectiveness with the class. Make a class list of the changes that seem to be the most beneficial and somewhat easily accomplished, and encourage other students to consider trying them.

Internet Resources

Psychometric Properties of QueenDom's Tests:
www.queendom.com/tests/psychometrics/index.html/sts_lc.html
Contains links to various online tests that assess health, locus of control, and coping, including a Burnout Inventory, Coping Skills Inventory, and Locus of Control and Attributional Style Inventory

Stress Reduction Techniques: www.mindtools.com/stresstq.html
Contains tips on stress reduction from MindTools.com and links to additional information on this topic

Stress Management and Emotional Wellness:
www.optimalhealthconcepts.com/Stress
Includes links, a discussion forum, and information about maximizing health and performance, managing stress, and enhancing one's emotional well-being

Test Yourself

Pick the best answer.

1. Which of the following is a cognitive symptom of stress?
   a. frequent colds
   b. anxiety
   c. overeating
   d. memory problems

2. How do today's researchers differ from Selye in their definition of eustress?
   a. They feel that eustress is more harmful than distress.
   b. They have not found evidence for eustress.
   c. They believe that a certain level of eustress is necessary to promote health.
   d. They believe that eustress is basically the same as distress.

3. Unpredictable, large-scale events that create a great deal of stress and feelings of threat are called
   a. major life events
   b. catastrophes
   c. hassles
   d. frustrations

4. After the car accident, Yoshiko suffered from nightmares and other sleeping problems, and she could not concentrate on her work. After about 2 weeks, these symptoms disappeared and she was able to work and sleep normally again. Yoshiko was suffering from
   a. acute stress disorder
   b. post-traumatic stress disorder
   c. mild stress reaction
   d. shell shock

5. For which of the following groups of people would a lack of money be more stressful than for the other groups, according to Ellis et al. (2001)?
   a. children
   b. adolescents
   c. young adults
   d. elderly people

6. Rachel's employer gives her a bad review, making Rachel feel lousy. When she arrives at home, she yells at her husband and children. Rachel is displaying
   a. aggression
   b. withdrawal
   c. persistence
   d. displaced aggression

7. In which stage of the general adaptation syndrome is death a possible outcome?
   a. alarm
   b. resistance
   c. reaction
   d. exhaustion

8. Appraising a stressor as a challenge results in _____ than if the stressor is appraised as a threat.
   a. more stress
   b. less stress
   c. less successful coping
   d. more negative emotions

9. Which of the following is a psychological factor in stress?
   a. poverty
   b. prejudice
   c. uncontrollability
   d. hassles

10. Which of the following is NOT one of the three methods suggested by Vaughan to promote a positive, optimistic mood?
    a. alternative thinking
    b. relaxation
    c. using a scapegoat
    d. downward social comparison

11. Shawna is having trouble in algebra. She goes to the school's academic help center for tutoring and spends extra time working algebra problems at home. Shawna's method of coping is
    a. problem-focused
    b. emotion-focused
    c. a defense mechanism
    d. meditative

12. Displacement is a psychological defense mechanism that involves
    a. expressing feelings that would be threatening if directed at the real target onto a less threatening substitute target
    b. falling back on childlike patterns as a way of coping with stressful situations
    c. refusal to acknowledge or recognize a threatening situation
    d. making up acceptable excuses for unacceptable behavior

13. Which of the following is one of the ways to promote wellness in one's life?
    a. Get enough sleep.
    b. Eat whatever you want, as long as it tastes good.
    c. Don't worry about managing your time.
    d. Avoid getting too involved with other people.

14. Who among the following probably has the least ability to cope effectively with stress?
    a. Marian, who is a very religious person
    b. Mei Ling, who comes from a culture that emphasizes the family
    c. Jackie, who has few friends and whose family lives far away from her
    d. Lenora, who has recently gotten married

15. Which of the following people is most likely to experience job stress?
    a. a worker who must handle a variety of tasks each day
    b. a worker who controls his or her own daily schedule
    c. a worker who is well compensated for any overtime
    d. a worker who has no contract and may be fired at any time

16. Negative changes in thoughts, emotions, and behavior as a result of prolonged stress and frustration are known as
    a. burnout
    b. job stress
    c. exhaustion
    d. marginalization

17. An increased rate of PTSD in a population would most likely be a result of which of the following factors?
    a. an ongoing, large-scale military conflict
    b. an increase in technological hassles
    c. a sustained economic recession
    d. a lack of highly trained psychology professionals

18. Which of the following is the most valid criticism of the Social Readjustment Rating Scale (SRRS)?
    a. Most people do not experience most of the events on the SRRS, so it is irrelevant to real life.
    b. Positive life events, no matter how major, are not stressful, so the SSRS contains incorrect information.
    c. Different events may be more or less stressful in different cultures, so the SRRS may not be effective across cultures.
    d. The SRRS was revised in 1997, so it is only relevant for people who were working adults in 1997.

19. Joe rarely takes any work home, preferring to leave his work worries at the office. He is not ambitious and likes to have a lot of leisure time when it is possible. He is also easygoing and doesn't lose his temper often, preferring to avoid conflict. Joe most likely has a
    a. Type A personality
    b. Type B personality
    c. Type C personality
    d. Type H personality

STRESS AND HEALTH 509

CHAPTER 15 • Assessment

TEST YOURSELF

1. b
2. b
3. b
4. a
5. d
6. a
7. b
8. b
9. a
10. c
11. b
12. d
13. a
14. a
15. a
16. a
17. a
18. d
19. c

Ready for Testing

STUDENTS KNOW THEY ARE READY FOR TESTING IF THEY ARE ABLE TO . . .

- Define stress and identify the external and psychological factors that influence an individual's experience of stress.
- Discuss the causes of stress.
- Describe the physical reaction to stress and the relation of this reaction to cognitive, personality, and social factors.
- Explain the methods used to cope with stress including those influenced by culture and religion.

CHAPTER 15 • Concept Summary

MULTIMEDIA CONTENT AVAILABLE AT
www.mypsychlab.com

Map the Concepts on **mypsychlab.com**

Study and Review Flashcards on **mypsychlab.com**

STUDY TIPS

Setting Goals Tell students that a goal represents something you wish to achieve in life. It is what you make happen. Along with good time management skills, "successful" people have goals. Success means different things to different people; whether having a 4.0 GPA, getting a dream job after college, having a spouse and family, or traveling around the world, success and goals go hand in hand. Explain to students that people tend to believe what they read more than what they hear. Reading what you have written is powerful; therefore, it makes sense to put your goals down on paper. It is easy for people to fantasize about all of the wonderful things that they want to have or to be, but those thoughts will just linger as thoughts. Writing a goal down makes it more real and will help them focus on the daily and weekly tasks needed to make it a reality. It can help keep them stay focused when they feel overwhelmed.

CHAPTER 15 Concept Summary: Stress and Health

Learning Objectives

35.1 35.2 35.3   pp. 482–493

Understand the Causes and Consequences of Stress

- **stress** is the physical, emotional, cognitive, and behavioral responses to events that are judged to be threatening or challenging
  - **stressors** are stress-causing events
    - unpleasant stressors cause **distress**
    - pleasant stressors cause **eustress**

- **factors that cause stress**
  - environmental factors
    - **catastrophes**
    - **major life changes** — measured on the Social Readjustment Rating Scale (SRRS)
    - **hassles**
  - social factors
    - **poverty**
    - **job stress** — can lead to **burnout**
    - **acculturative stress** — methods of entering a majority culture include integration, assimilation, separation, and marginalization
  - psychological factors
    - **pressure**
    - **uncontrollability**
    - **frustration**

- **effects on health**
  - physical health
    - the **general adaptation syndrome (GAS)** is a sequence of physiological reactions in response to a stressor
      - **alarm**
      - **resistance**
      - **exhaustion**
    - prolonged stress suppresses the immune system
    - stress can impair heart health and weaken the body's ability to fight cancer
  - psychological health
    - stress-related disorders with symptoms including anxiety, recurring nightmares, sleep problems, problems concentrating, and "reliving" experiences through flashbacks or dreams
      - **acute stress disorder (ASD)**
      - **post-traumatic stress disorder (PTSD)**

What Every Student Should Know About . . .

RESEARCHING ONLINE

Remind students that when they do online research, they need to save pertinent information about the sources they use. Unfortunately, it is very easy to download or copy-and-paste material without keeping track of where it came from. Encourage students to document their sources by taking down the following: (1) author name; (2) title (of web page, etc.); (3) title of larger work containing the source (website, etc.); (4) publication date; (5) URL; (6) access date; and (7) a brief summary of the site's contents and relevance to the topic.

Map The Concepts on mypsychlab.com

Learning Objectives
36.1 36.2 36.3 36.4 36.5 pp. 495–505

Learn Strategies for Promoting Mental and Physical Health

- **cognitive factors**
  - **Lazarus's cognitive-mediational theory of emotions** suggests an individual's appraisal of a stressor is a major factor in determining how stressful that stressor becomes
    - primary appraisal
    - secondary appraisal
  - **personality differences** affect how one assesses a stressor, the coping strategies used, and possible health outcomes
    - Type A
    - Type B
    - Type C
    - "Type H"

- **typical reactions to stressors**
  - persistence
  - aggression — displaced aggression
  - withdrawal or escape

- **coping strategies** are behavioral and psychological actions taken to master, tolerate, reduce, or minimize the effects of stressors
  - **problem-focused coping** involves working to change or eliminate the stressor itself
  - **emotion-focused coping** involves changing the way a person feels or emotionally reacts to a stressor
    - psychological defense mechanisms
  - religious beliefs, culture, and social support systems can influence coping strategies

- **optimism** is associated with controlling mood or emotional reactions; can be a learned skill through alternative thinking, downward social comparison, relaxation, and correcting faulty thinking

- **strategies for promoting wellness**
  - exercise
  - social involvement
  - adequate sleep
  - healthy diet
  - having fun
  - time management
  - relaxation

STRESS AND HEALTH 511

CHAPTER 14 • Concept Summary

STUDY TIPS

Rewarding Yourself Students should understand that rewarding themselves for reaching a goal is a positive behavior. They should choose an activity that they enjoy doing but that they do not always have time to do, such as seeing a film or reading a favorite magazine. However, even though they may feel great after accomplishing a goal, they should not reward themselves with something expensive, compliments of a credit card. Getting into debt will create stress, and that is not relaxing. Students are always busy; taking the time for a relaxing walk or drive is a reward in itself. Often it is the small things in life that are the best rewards. Students can be creative. They could catch up on e-mails and phone calls, or play their favorite sport. Only they know what is the best reward system for them.

Comprehension Check

INEFFECTIVE THERAPIES

To check their understanding, students can visit the Multimedia Library section of the www.mypsychlab.com site and explore the Coping Strategies and Their Effects activity. Advanced students can work alone, while on-level and struggling students can work in pairs or small groups. Students will receive immediate feedback on their answers.

Chapter 15 Concept Summary **511**

CHAPTER 16 • Module 37

Launch the Chapter

CHAPTER GOALS AND LEARNING OBJECTIVES

Module 37 Careers in Psychology

Identify educational requirements for careers in psychology.

- 37.1 What are the degree requirements for psychological professionals?
- 37.2 What resources are available for people who want to study psychology in the future?

Explore career options in psychology.

- 37.3 What types of careers are available to someone with a bachelor's degree in psychology?
- 37.4 How does psychology interact with other career fields?

DIFFERENTIATED INSTRUCTION KEY

Look for these symbols to help you adjust steps in each lesson to meet your students' needs.

- **L1** Special Needs
- **L2** Basic
- **ELL** English Language Learners
- **LPR** Less Proficient Readers
- **L3** All Students
- **L4** Advanced Students

---

16 Applied Psychology and Psychology Careers

Psychology in the Real World

Mrs. Patel was a little startled when she received a phone call from her daughter Katy's grade school counselor. The counselor asked Mrs. Patel to come to the school the following afternoon for a conference with Katy's teachers. At the conference, Mrs. Patel was relieved to learn that Katy had been tested and found to be a gifted child. Gifted children are those who score on the upper end of intelligence tests, and Katy had scored very well indeed. She had also been evaluated by a school psychologist, who confirmed that Katy was gifted and identified areas in which Katy could benefit from further help from her teachers.

The counselor and teachers explained that Katy, as a gifted child, needed to have a special educational plan drawn up to ensure that she received the education best suited to her abilities. This plan is called an *individualized educational program,* or *IEP* (Sellin & Birch, 1981; U.S. Department of Education, 2000). An IEP is required for children with special needs, such as learning problems or intellectual delay, but IEPs can also be used for gifted children.

Mrs. Patel was asked to look at the plan that Katy's teachers and counselor had developed, which included a summary of Katy's current performance levels and both short-term and long-term goals for her educational future. For example, the counselor and teachers wanted to work on helping Katy develop better organizational skills and improve her handwriting. Mrs. Patel was asked for her input, and then she and the teachers and counselor signed the IEP for Katy. They told Mrs. Patel that a new IEP would be developed for Katy each year.

Mrs. Patel's experience with the IEP is one small example of how psychology can be used in the real world, in this case, by those in the field of *educational psychology* who examine the process of learning and look for ways to improve learning in children and adults. Educational psychology is one of many areas in which psychological principles can be applied to issues and concerns of everyday life. This chapter will look at just some of the areas of applied psychology, as well as the types of careers open to someone who studies psychology today.

CORRELATION TO APA STANDARDS FOR CHAPTER 16

VIIC. CAREERS

VIIC-1. Educational requirements .... pp. 515–520
VIIC-2. Career options .... pp. 520–527

MODULE 37 • CAREERS IN PSYCHOLOGY

Why Study?

Applied Psychology and Psychology Careers

Many different kinds of psychologists study or work in many different fields. While early psychologists were still discovering the processes that govern the human mind, today's psychologists are more often applying information and principles gained from research to people in the real world. Why study careers in psychology? With so many different areas of focus, a career in psychology can be varied and exciting. There is much more to psychology than helping people who have mental health problems.

APPLIED PSYCHOLOGY 513

SCHEDULING

1 Period = 50 min.
1 Block = 90 min.

	Semester Course (18 weeks/90 days) Periods/Blocks	Full-Year Course (36 weeks/180 days) Period/Blocks
Module 37	2 1	4 2
Total Days for Chapter	2 1	4 2

CHAPTER 16 • Module 37

Teacher Prep

The field of psychology is not limited to diagnosing and treating individuals with mental disorders. The term *applied psychology* refers to using findings from psychological research to solve real-world problems. Clinical and counseling psychology is just one well-known area of applied psychology, but there are numerous other ways that psychological research can be applied to improve lives, health, education, environment, sports, architecture, urban planning, the workplace, the justice system, and marketing techniques, to name a few. There are many careers available within the field of psychology that interact with other career fields to accomplish the aforementioned improvements, such as health psychology, forensic psychology, sports psychology, and industrial/organizational psychology.

There are four levels of educational degrees and training that psychology students can complete, each leading to a unique set of career paths. The 4-year bachelor's degree is the first-level students can complete. In earning a bachelor's of arts or science (B.A. or B.S.), students will gain an introductory knowledge of the general concepts in psychology, as well as research skills and some practical experience in the field. With a B.S. or B.A. in psychology, students are qualified to find entry-level jobs in a variety of fields. The next level is the master's degree, and psychology students can earn a master's of arts or science (M.A. or M.S.) or a master's in social work (M.S.W.) and go on to work in a research lab or clinical setting under the supervision of another, more advanced psychologist or psychiatrist. Students who earn a doctorate degree such as a Ph.D. or a Psy.D. are officially considered to be qualified psychologists, working in academic research settings or providing treatment as clinical or counseling psychologists. The doctorate degree is more advanced than a master's, takes longer to complete, and is far more specialized. If students go on to earn a medical degree, they are qualified to diagnose and treat mental disorders with prescription medication, conduct medical procedures, and work as psychoanalysts.

Chapter 16 Applied Psychology and Careers   **513**

CHAPTER 16 • Module 37

Focus

RESOURCES

For this module, consult the appropriate sections of the Teacher's Manual, Test Bank, and PowerPoint slides, all found on the Teacher's Resource DVD, and the interactive study tools for students on MyPsychLab.

BELLRINGER

Ask students to make three columns on a blank sheet of paper, with the following headings: **What I Know, What I Want to Know,** and **What I Learned**. Ask students to fill in the first two columns about their thoughts for careers in psychology. Instruct students to think about careers of which they are aware, what a typical day for that job would be like, and what degrees and requirements are necessary to work in the field. Allow students to share their responses. Ask students to keep their papers until the end of the module, where they will be revisiting their responses and filling in the third column.

Teach

COVER THE MODULE

- *Applied psychology* is the use of psychological concepts to solve real-world problems by assessing the problem and then devising a plan of action.
- Psychology is not just about diagnosing mental disorders for patients, as is the case in clinical and counseling psychology; areas in applied psychology include clinical and counseling psychology, health psychology, educational psychology, industrial/organizational psychology, and many more.

514 Chapter 16 Applied Psychology and Careers

Module 37 Careers in Psychology

Module Goals

Identify educational requirements for careers in psychology.

Explore career options in psychology.

Learning Objectives

37.1 What are the degree requirements for psychological professionals?

37.2 What resources are available for people who want to study psychology in the future?

37.3 What types of careers are available to someone with a bachelor's degree in psychology?

37.4 How does psychology interact with other career fields?

Identify Educational Requirements for Careers in Psychology

The term **applied psychology** refers to using findings from psychological research to solve real-world problems. The psychological professional, who might be a psychiatrist, psychologist, or even a psychiatric social worker, may do testing or use some other type of assessment and then describe a plan of action intended to solve whatever problem is of concern. In the opening story, the problem revolved around delivering the best possible education to a gifted child. The teacher may have noticed signs of Katy's giftedness and referred Katy to the school counselor for an evaluation. The counselor then contacted Katy's parents and a school psychologist. The school psychologist tested Katy in several different ways to determine not only her gifted status but also areas in which she needed help, such as her organizational skills. Then the counselor and teachers used that information to devise Katy's IEP. This is a practical application of psychological tools to a real problem—the teacher, school psychologist, and counselor literally "apply" psychology.

▶ *It seems to me that psychology could be useful in a lot of different areas, not just education.*

The field of applied psychology isn't just one field but rather many different areas that all share the common goal of using psychology in a practical way. Numerous areas can be considered applied psychology, including one of the broadest areas of psychology: clinical and counseling psychology. There are health psychologists, who examine the effects of stress on physical as well as mental health; educational and school psychologists, who look for ways to improve learning in children and adults; sports psychologists, who help athletes prepare themselves mentally for competition; human factors psychologists, who deal with the way people and machines interact; forensic psychologists, who deal with psychological issues within the legal system; and industrial/organizational (I/O) psychologists, who deal with the work environment. There are also environmental psychologists, who look at the interaction of people with their surroundings at work, in social

◀ It seems to me that psychology could be useful in a lot of different areas, not just education.

applied psychology the use of psychological concepts in solving real-world problems.

514 CHAPTER 16

Terms

- applied psychology • master's degree • doctorate • doctor of philosophy (Ph.D.)
- doctor of psychology (Psy.D.) • health psychology • educational psychology • school psychology • sports psychology • forensic psychology • environmental psychology
- industrial/organizational psychology • human factors psychology

settings, and in schools, homes, and other buildings. Those surroundings include not just the physical structures but also the particular population of people who live, work, and play in those surroundings. Consumer psychologists look at the factors that influence people to buy certain products or the best ways to market a product and examine the buying habits of the typical consumer.

This module includes information on the different types of psychological professionals and the type of education required for each profession, with a brief overview of many of the specialized areas in psychology. It also explores how psychology can be used in a practical way in several different areas of life: the environment, law, education, sports, and the world of work.

37.1 What are the degree requirements for psychological professionals?

Majoring in psychology to earn a 4-year bachelor's degree at college is a valuable and important achievement because a general understanding of psychology can be useful in many career fields. However, keep in mind that most professional positions in psychology require higher education beyond the undergraduate level—a master's degree, a doctorate, or in some cases, even a medical degree.

In psychology, as in many other fields, education tends to become more and more specialized as students progress to a higher level. Undergraduate programs usually aim to provide students with a good foundation in psychology—an understanding of major concepts and of the many different branches of this field. Once students complete their undergraduate education, they may choose to apply their learning in a career that requires only a broad foundation. Section 37.3 describes some of the careers open to people who have earned a bachelor's degree in psychology, such as teaching, research, health services, marketing, and social work.

Other careers in psychology require more specialized knowledge and training at the graduate level. This is the case for careers that involve teaching at the college level, conducting experimental research, or working directly with people who need treatment for psychological problems. Specific careers are described later in this chapter. The sections below provide an overview of what paths are open to students who pursue a bachelor's degree, master's degree, a doctorate, or a medical degree.

The Bachelor's Degree in Psychology Students who attend college may choose to take courses in psychology, often beginning with an introductory-level survey course that covers a broad range of topics in psychology. Most schools offer required courses for psychology majors and minors (such as experimental psychology, which teaches students how to design and conduct experiments). Students may also choose electives that focus in more depth on specific areas of interest, such as developmental psychology, abnormal psychology, social psychology, or cognitive psychology. Many institutions give psychology students the opportunity to perform research, and students who choose to major in psychology may be required to do independent, original research. Students who successfully complete a 4-year psychology major will earn a bachelor of arts degree (B.A.) or a bachelor of science degree (B.S.) in psychology. With a B.A. or a B.S. in psychology,

▲ *Constance Newman (left) is a Peace Corps volunteer. Using skills she developed while obtaining a bachelor's degree in psychology, Constance is trying to help this Mbankono woman understand the importance of having her child immunized against diseases such as measles.*

APPLIED PSYCHOLOGY AND PSYCHOLOGY CAREERS 515

CHAPTER 16 • Module 37

COVER THE MODULE

37.1 What are the degree requirements for psychological professionals?

- Psychology careers require at least a 4-year bachelor's degree, and most professional positions require a master's degree, a doctorate, and sometimes a medical degree.
- Most colleges offer majors and minors in psychology.
  - Course study typically begins with a survey class covering a broad range of topics in psychology.
  - Students may also take electives focusing on a more specific area of interest such as social or cognitive psychology.
  - Students are often given the opportunity to conduct research and may even be required to perform individual, original research to earn a psychology degree.
  - After 4 years at the undergraduate level, students can earn a B.A. or B.S. in psychology.

EXTEND THE LESSON

Many students may be unfamiliar with terms used in collegiate-level course descriptions. It may be helpful to define the following:

- *Elective:* a course taken to enhance your degree, but that is not a required part of your program
- *Major:* a student's main field of specialization in pursuit of a degree in college
- *Minor:* a declared secondary field of study
- *Bachelor of arts:* an undergraduate degree granted upon completion of a program in a branch of liberal arts or humanities
- *Bachelor of science:* an undergraduate degree granted upon completion of a program in the sciences

---

Research Project

INTRODUCTION TO THE "PASSPORT TO PSYCHOLOGY" PORTFOLIO PROJECT

Purpose: Students create a compilation of what they learn as they explore careers in the field of psychology. During their study of the topics in this chapter, they complete various activities to contribute to a "Passport to Psychology" portfolio. At the end of the chapter, the portfolio they create will be a snapshot of how they envision themselves in a possible career in psychology.

Time: 10 minutes

Description: Ask students to make a list of their interests and strengths that they plan to pursue in a future career. Then ask them to imagine and write about how their aptitudes could be applied to a career in psychology; for example, an artistic student may be able to translate his or her talent into the field of art therapy and may want to work with children.

CHAPTER 16 • Module 37

COVER THE MODULE *(continued)*

- After completing a bachelor's degree, students can choose to work toward a master's degree in psychology.
  - A *master's degree* takes approximately 2 to 3 years to complete, and coursework is focused on a specialized field.
  - Students are also usually required to complete a thesis in the final year.
  - A *master's degree* provides students with a deeper understanding of the field of study and more research and hands-on experience in the field.
- In addition to an M.A. or M.S in psychology, students can earn an M.S.W., which focuses more on the relationship of environmental conditions and mental health.

FAST FACT

Read the names of the following celebrities (along with a serial killer) to the class and ask students what the individuals all have in common. The answer is: a B.A. in psychology!

- Jerry Bruckheimer, producer of several hit TV shows and movies such as *CSI, Lost,* and *Pirates of the Caribbean*
- Natalie Portman, actress in movies such as *Star Wars* and *The Black Swan*
- Ted Bundy, serial killer
- Wes Craven, horror film writer and director of movies including *Scream* and *Nightmare on Elm Street*

---

graduates can find entry-level jobs in a wide variety of fields, from law and business management to health services, education, and the arts, or they can choose to continue their academic study of psychology in graduate school (American Psychological Association [APA], 2010).

The Master's Degree: Psychology and Social Work Students who are interested in psychology but don't necessarily want to become psychologists or psychiatrists may pursue a **master's degree**. Generally a master's degree takes 2 to 3 years to complete. However, some programs may be shorter or longer, and the length of time needed to complete the degree will vary, depending on whether one is a part-time or full-time student. Some students earn the master's degree as an end in itself and choose a career that doesn't require further education. Many students, however, complete the master's as one stepping stone on the path toward earning a higher degree.

A master of arts (M.A.) or master of science (M.S.) psychology degree requires students to complete specific coursework, as undergraduates do. In contrast to most undergraduate programs, coursework is concentrated in a specialized field, such as counseling or sports psychology. Many programs also require students to complete a thesis in their final year. A thesis is an extensive paper—perhaps 60 to 100 pages—on a particular area of focus that the student chooses; this paper represents the culmination of the student's learning. Graduating students may also be required to pass an oral examination, participate in an internship, and take comprehensive exams, often called "comps," that assess what they have learned throughout the program.

Students pursuing a master's may specialize in any branch of psychology—industrial/organizational psychology, substance abuse, and so on. The master's degree provides students with a deep understanding of a specific branch of psychology, more advanced research skills than what undergraduate students typically learn, and, depending on the type of program, hands-on experience working directly with people.

Upon completing the degree, students may go on to work in a research lab or in a clinical setting, often under the supervision of a psychologist or psychiatrist who has completed more advanced training. A student who has specialized in counseling and taken board exams to earn a counseling license may work independently as a counselor or therapist—for instance, in vocational counseling or marriage and family therapy. However, in most states, only people who have completed a doctorate are considered psychologists, and according to the APA, only those who have completed a Ph.D. or Psy.D. may be considered a "psychologist."

Students with a master's degree may also work in other settings, such as schools, corporate training departments, and the like, and if they have also completed teacher training, they may teach psychology at the high school level or part-time at a community college. (A full-time position teaching at the college level usually requires a doctorate.)

Additionally, working in psychology doesn't necessarily require students to have earned a master's degree *in psychology*. Many students choose instead to pursue a master's in the related field of social work—the M.S.W. degree. A social worker's job may be extremely similar to a counselor's or therapist's. Psychiatric social workers, for example, may provide psychotherapy, work with other mental health professionals, and even be licensed by the state as clinical social workers (L.C.S.W.). However, compared to many other branches of psychology, social work focuses more on the relationship between environmental conditions and psychological health.

master's degree a graduate degree students may pursue after completing a 4-year college degree. Generally a master's degree takes 2 to 3 years to complete. It provides more specialized knowledge, training, and experience than students typically receive as undergraduates.

Explore

"PASSPORT TO PSYCHOLOGY" PORTFOLIO PROJECT

Purpose: Students learn more about how an undergraduate degree in psychology is structured at a college of interest to them.

Time: 30 minutes

Description: Have students think of a college they are interested in possibly attending; for students who may not be college-bound, perhaps they can choose a college that is the home of a sports team they enjoy following. Allow students to research the course requirements to earn an undergraduate psychology degree from that college. Students should imagine that they are planning to earn this degree and create a written plan of courses they will be taking as well as course descriptions. A helpful model can be found at Ohio State University's website: http://undergrad.psy.ohio-state.edu/html/degree-requirements.php. Students should prepare a final copy of their course list to place in their portfolio.

Not all social workers directly provide therapy or counseling. For instance, many work with government or nonprofit social service agencies. Social workers are involved in areas where psychology and the social world intersect—foster care programs, drug addiction, health care, and so on.

Finally, people who plan to become school psychologists often pursue an educational specialist degree (Ed.S.), which is more intensive than most master's degree programs but less intensive than a doctorate. The Ed.S. typically takes about 3 years to complete and requires coursework in education and psychology, as well as a year-long internship. Not all school psychologists hold Ed.S. degrees, but most hold a graduate degree of some sort.

Becoming a Psychologist: The Doctoral Degree To work as a psychologist—whether in a research, clinical, or other setting—a person must earn a **doctorate**. This degree is more advanced than the master's, takes more time to complete, and involves an even greater degree of specialization. A doctoral program typically takes from 5 to 7 years to complete. Like a master's program, a doctoral program involves in-depth research and writing and hands-on experience in experimental research or in clinical practice. However, a doctoral program is far more demanding; students must be highly motivated, self-disciplined, and able to work more and more independently as they progress through the program.

Psychologists are addressed by the title "Doctor"—they've earned it with years of hard work!—but this degree is academic, not medical. Psychologists may have either a **doctor of philosophy (Ph.D.)** or **doctor of psychology (Psy.D.)** degree.

What's the difference between a Ph.D. and a Psy.D.?

In almost all academic subject areas—psychology, languages, education, philosophy, the sciences, and many others—the Ph.D. indicates the highest degree of learning available. This degree is very research oriented. Earning it usually requires a previous master's degree, course work for the doctorate, and finally, a dissertation—typically a book-length scholarly work based on original research. In psychology, this often includes designing and carrying out an experimental study.

The Psy.D. degree, developed in the late 1970s, involves an equally advanced level of expertise, but the expertise is of a different kind. The Psy.D. is focused less on research and more on the practical application of psychological principles (Peterson, 1976, 1982). Instead of a dissertation, Psy.D. candidates are likely to complete a major paper that does not involve original experimental research. Each year of a Psy.D. program will also require the student to participate in a *practicum,* which provides hands-on experience observing and eventually conducting therapy and treatments under supervision.

Psychologists who have earned a Ph.D. typically go on to work in fields where they continue to do original research, usually in collaboration with others. Many hold academic positions at colleges or universities. Their job responsibilities include teaching psychology courses, conducting research and publishing scholarly articles or books, and in many cases, advising graduate students who are pursuing their own master's or doctorate. Other psychologists hold what are called "quasi-academic" positions in government or industry. They may not be university professors, but they often have some teaching responsibilities, such as presenting lectures and supervising research staff. They may be expected to publish their research findings regularly in professional journals or other publications.

◀ What's the difference between a Ph.D. and a Psy.D.?

doctorate a graduate degree students may pursue after completing a 4-year college degree or a master's degree. Generally, a doctorate takes 5 to 7 years to complete. It provides highly advanced academic training and requires extensive research and/or clinical practice.

doctor of philosophy (Ph.D.) a doctorate that is research oriented and culminates in a dissertation based on original research.

doctor of psychology (Psy.D.) a doctorate that focuses on applying psychological principles and provides extensive hands-on experience working in a clinical or counseling setting.

APPLIED PSYCHOLOGY AND PSYCHOLOGY CAREERS   517

CHAPTER 16 • Module 37

COVER THE MODULE *(continued)*

- Social workers may provide counseling and therapy, but other career options with an M.S.W. include working in government or nonprofit social services, foster care, drug addiction, and health care.
- A *doctorate* degree is required to work as a psychologist.
  - A doctorate program takes 5 to 7 years to complete.
  - The degree has highly specialized requirements involving more in-depth research, experience, and writing.
  - Students can earn a doctor of philosophy, a doctor of psychology, or a doctor of education.
- A *Ph.D.* is research oriented and requires the completion of a dissertation about an original research study.
  - People with a Ph.D. usually go on to academic careers, teaching, research, and publish regularly.
- A *Psy.D.* focuses less on research and more on practical application of psychology principles and requires a lengthy paper, as well as completion of practicums.

TEACHING TIP

Be sensitive to students' possible career choices. Remind students that getting a degree in psychology would not "limit" them to working as a psychologist; rather, such a degree could be applicable to other fields as well.

Critical Thinking

"PASSPORT TO PSYCHOLOGY" PORTFOLIO PROJECT

Purpose: Students can compare and contrast what they like and dislike about careers available with a Ph.D., a Psy.D., and an Ed.D.

Time: 30 minutes

Description: On a sheet of paper, students should create a table with three horizontal columns labeled **Ph.D., Psy.D.,** and **Ed.D.** Two vertical columns should be labeled **Like** and **Dislike**. Students can use the resources mentioned in the text on page 519 and also browse the Internet (the following website is a good one: http://psychology.about.com/od/education/a/phd-in-psychology.htm). Students can research a career for each degree that attracts their interest, filling out their charts as they read. Once they have completed their charts, students can write a brief paragraph comparing and contrasting the degrees and careers they read about. Students should include a discussion of which degree/career they think would suit them best.

Students should prepare a final copy of their written material to include in their portfolios.

Module 37 Careers in Psychology   517

CHAPTER 16 • Module 37

COVER THE MODULE (continued)

- People with a Psy.D. degree go on to careers in clinical or counseling psychology.

LINK to *Chapter One: The Science of Psychology, p. 12*

- The Ed.D. is for people interested in pursuing a career in education, such as an educational psychologist.
- To become a psychiatrist, a medical degree is required.
  - Psychiatrists attend medical school and specialize in diagnosing and treating mental disorders, usually through prescription medication.
  - Psychiatrists are authorized to perform medical procedures.
- Psychoanalysts complete several years of training in addition to the Ph.D., the Psy.D., or the M.D., specializing in psychoanalysis.

LINK to *Chapter Fourteen: Psychological Therapies, pp. 455–458.*

FAST FACT

Beginning salaries for people with a Ph.D. in psychology average in range from $44,000 to $88,000 a year. The salary for a full professor with a Ph.D. can range from $63,000 to $150,000 a year. Send interested students to **www.payscale.com** for additional information.

▲ Psychologists specialize in many different areas and work in many different settings. This child psychologist is evaluating the young boy by using puppets and dolls to encourage the boy to talk about his feelings.

Psychologists who have earned a Psy.D. go on to work in fields that involve providing treatment—clinical or counseling psychology. (See Chapter 1 for an explanation of the difference between clinical and counseling psychology. **LINK** to *Chapter One: The Science of Psychology, p. 12.*) They may have their own clinical practice or be affiliated with a larger organization, such as a community mental health program. These professionals may also hold academic positions that involve teaching courses and supervising students as they gain their clinical experience. They may not be expected to publish academic work as often as their counterparts with Ph.D.s; however, many clinical psychologists do publish books or articles for an academic or a general audience.

Another type of doctoral degree is the Ed.D., or doctorate of education. This degree is similar to a Ph.D., but it is specifically intended to prepare students for a position in the field of education. Educational psychologists—those psychologists who research the process of human learning and help design improvements in the field of education—may pursue an Ed.D. instead of a Ph.D.

Becoming a Psychiatrist: The Medical Degree Most careers in psychology are open to people who have obtained one of the doctoral degrees described above. However, someone who wants to be a psychiatrist and provide medical treatment (instead of or in addition to psychotherapy) must obtain a medical degree, or M.D.

Psychiatrists attend medical school and go through the same types of training that other doctors do. Just as other doctors might specialize in pediatric medicine or heart surgery, a psychiatrist specializes in diagnosing and treating psychological disorders, mainly through prescriptions of drugs. Psychiatrists, as medical doctors, are authorized to write prescriptions and perform medical procedures. Compared to other psychological professionals, they usually place a greater emphasis on the biological roots of psychological disorders and on medical means of treatment. (For many years, psychiatrists were the only psychological professionals who could write prescriptions; however, this is changing: In an effort to reduce costs and avoid treatment delays for patients, some states now allow psychologists with special training to prescribe medication.)

Finally, a small subset of psychological professionals is trained as psychoanalysts. Psychoanalysts have usually obtained a Psy.D., Ph.D., or M.D. and have several additional years of specialized training in the theory and methods of psychoanalysis developed by Sigmund Freud **LINK** to *Chapter Fourteen, Psychological Therapies, pp. 455–458.*

37.2 *What resources are available for people who want to study psychology in the future?*

If you're interested in studying psychology in the future, your head might be spinning by now. There are so many different branches of psychology, and so many possible careers in the field, that you might not be sure where to begin. Your school guidance counselor (and perhaps your psychology teacher

---

Explore

"PASSPORT TO PSYCHOLOGY" PORTFOLIO PROJECT

At the following websites, students can take quizzes that will assess their individual preferences and abilities and report a list of careers in the field of psychology that would best fit their propensities. Once students have taken the quizzes, they should record the career suggestions offered by the website and take some time to read about them by following the provided links. For this page in their portfolios, students should provide a list of the suggested careers along with brief descriptions and a discussion of what they thought about each suggestion in terms of how well they believe they would be suited for that career.

- "Should You Become a Psychologist?"
  http://careerplanning.about.com/library/quiz/career_quizzes/blpsychologist_quiz.htm
- "Which Psychology Career is Right for You?"
  http://careerplanning.about.com/library/quiz/career_quizzes/blpsychologist_quiz.htm
- A website listing many careers in psychology with brief descriptions:
  http://maxweber.hunter.cuny.edu/~bseegmil/hdbk/fields.htm

as well) can help you get started; a number of print and online resources can also help you.

For an extensive collection of resources specific to psychology, visit the Web site of the APA at http://www.apa.org. Its Education section (http://www.apa.org/education/index.aspx) can help you determine whether to major in psychology in college and, later, how to get into a graduate program and get the most out of it. It also provides information about psychology careers, including brief articles written by people who use psychology in various nonacademic careers (see http://www.apa.org/careers/resources/profiles/index.aspx). Much of the information on this site is geared toward people who are already working as psychology professionals, but it is still a valuable resource, and students can obtain affiliate membership status from the APA.

In addition to online information, the APA site also provides links for various print publications. Specific books you might find helpful as a high school or college student include:

- *The Insider's Guide to the Psychology Major: Everything You Need to Know About the Degree and Profession* (Wegenek & Buskist, 2010)
- *Career Paths in Psychology: Where Your Degree Can Take You,* 2nd edition (Sternberg, 2006)
- *What Psychology Majors Could (and Should) Be Doing: An Informal Guide to Research Experience and Professional Skills* (Silvia, Delaney, & Marcovitch, 2009)

Another resource to consult is the *Occupational Outlook Handbook* (OOH), which is published and regularly updated by the Bureau of Labor Statistics. This publication provides detailed information about hundred of different occupations, including the education and training required, typical job responsibilities and working conditions, average salaries, and the prospects for growth in that field.

Many psychology careers require education beyond the 4-year college degree. Useful resources about choosing and applying to a graduate program (and figuring out how to pay for it) include:

- *Graduate Study in Psychology,* 2011 edition (APA, 2011)
- *Getting In: A Step-by-Step Plan for Gaining Admission to Graduate School in Psychology,* 2nd edition (APA, 2007)

It sounds like many psych careers require a ton of education! How do people pay for all those years of schooling?

Pursuing higher education does require a significant investment of time and money—which can be a bit intimidating. Fortunately, undergraduate and graduate students have several options to help them finance their educations.

Undergraduates and grad students may pay for their education through college financial aid programs or government student loans. They may also be awarded academic or other scholarships that pay tuition and other costs, in part or in full. Numerous reference books, such as the *Ferguson Career Resource Guide to Grants, Scholarships, and Other Financial Resources* (2007), provide information about sources of financial aid for students pursuing an undergraduate or graduate education. (This resource is organized according to several broad fields of study; if you're interested in studying psychology, look through the "social sciences" section.) College financial aid offices can also help students plan for paying for their education.

◀ It sounds like many psych careers require a ton of education! How do people pay for all those years of schooling?

APPLIED PSYCHOLOGY AND PSYCHOLOGY CAREERS 519

CHAPTER 16 • Module 37

COVER THE MODULE

37.2 What resources are available for people who want to study psychology in the future?

- To begin, students can speak with the school psychologist or guidance counselor.
- For online resources, the education section of the American Psychology Association website is helpful.
- Various print resources are also available covering topics such as: what to expect in psychology majors, what to look for in a good program, discussions of the various careers available in the field of psychology, and lists of careers, responsibilities, and average salaries.
- Financial resources are available from a variety of resources such as college financial aid programs, government loans, and scholarships.
  - College financial aid officers are available to help students create a plan to fund their education.

L1 DIFFERENTIATED INSTRUCTION

Visual Learners Encourage these students to create flowcharts, and diagrams using bright colors and put them where they can be viewed frequently.

Explore

"PASSPORT TO PSYCHOLOGY" PORTFOLIO PROJECT

Now that students have had the opportunity to learn more about careers in psychology, obtain the resources mentioned on this page in the text. Ask them to choose one or two careers that interest them from the research they've done so far. Devise a list of questions for students to answer as they read through the resources from page 519, asking them to focus specifically on their chosen careers. Sample questions:
(1) What degree do you need to earn to qualify for your career choice? (2) Of the colleges/universities that offer the degree you need, which ones interest you? (3) What research experience and professional skills will you need? (4) What is the average salary you could earn in your career? (5) What is the working environment for this career? (6) What internships and resources are available to help you, as a student, get ahead?

Students should create a final copy of this assignment to be included in their portfolio.

Module 37 Careers in Psychology **519**

CHAPTER 16 • Module 37

COVER THE MODULE *(continued)*

- Merit-based awards are available in scholarships, grants, and fellowships and are available at the colleges and universities offering the programs and by many outside organizations.
- Students interested in applying for merit-based funds would be wise to familiarize themselves with the requirements and begin working toward them as soon as possible, to gain an advantage in the intense competition for the awards.
- The option of becoming a teaching assistant (TA) is available to graduate students.
  - In return for a small salary and help with tuition and fees, a TA may perform such duties as assisting a professor's research, teaching undergraduate classes, and grading papers and exams.

COVER THE MODULE

37.3 What types of careers are available to someone with a bachelor's degree in psychology?

- The content and skills learned in the completion of a bachelor's degree in psychology are useful in many careers students may not expect, including sales, statistical analysis, education, and health services.

Some merit-based scholarships, grants, and fellowships are awarded by the college or university itself. Others are given out by external organizations. For example, the APA and affiliated organizations finance a number of scholarships, grants, and other awards each year. A detailed, searchable list is available at the APA Web site (http://www.apa.org/about/awards/index.aspx). Psi Chi, the college-level International Honor Society in Psychology, also gives out a number of grants and awards (see http://www.psichi.org/Awards/), as do numerous other organizations.

Competition for these awards can be intense, but sometimes just knowing what programs are out there can give students an advantage. Awards based on academic merit usually require the student to maintain a certain grade-point average. Depending on the nature of the award, they may also have other built-in requirements, such as completing a research project in a specific area of psychology.

For graduate students, most universities also have a limited number of graduate assistantships. A student who qualifies for a graduate assistantship may work part-time as a professor's research assistant or teaching assistant (TA). For instance, he or she may help run lab experiments, grade papers and exams, or even lead discussion sections for undergraduate courses. (In your classes in college, you may work with a TA in addition to—or instead of—a professor.) In return, tuition and fees are partially or completely waived, and the student usually also receives a small salary in exchange for the work. Nobody gets rich working as a graduate assistant, but these positions do help students finance their education and pay basic living expenses. Additionally, students who are further along in their education—for instance, a student who is just a couple of years away from completing a Ph.D.—may be qualified to teach classes part-time at their university. These part-time instructors earn much less than full-time faculty, but nevertheless, the extra income can help graduate students make ends meet, while also providing valuable teaching experience.

Finally, students may choose to attend school part-time while working a full-time job. This is usually more manageable at the undergraduate or master's level than the doctoral level, and of course, it takes longer to earn the degree that way. However, for many students, this is the best path, and many employers will partially finance the degree if it is relevant to the student's job.

Explore Career Options in Psychology

37.3 What types of careers are available to someone with a bachelor's degree in psychology?

Although people earning the bachelor's degree in psychology cannot be called psychologists or provide therapy in a private practice, there are many career fields open to people with undergraduate degrees in psychology. A bachelor's degree in psychology can be highly flexible and adaptable to many different kinds of careers (Landrum & Davis, 2007; Schwartz, 2000). In the 1994–1995 *Psychology Baccalaureate Survey* conducted by the APA (Grocer & Kohout, 1997), people with bachelor's degrees in psychology found careers in the following areas: education and teaching, sales, consulting and statistical analysis, administration or clerical services, health and health-related services, professional services, and research and development. (See Figure 37.1.)

Research

"PASSPORT TO PSYCHOLOGY" PORTFOLIO PROJECT

Divide students into four groups. Assign each group a type of financial aid to research: fellowship, grant, scholarship, and teaching assistantship. Direct students to each choose one financial aid option within their category to research in more detail, answering the following questions: (1) Is the money awarded expected to be paid back? If so, what are the requirements? (2) What are the requirements for applying for the aid? (3) How are applications assessed and how much money is available? (4) What are the requirements to maintain the reward over time? Students should share their information with their category groups. Then they should break into groups of four (one student from each category) and share what they have learned.

For their portfolio, students should create a concept map displaying what they have learned about the various financial aid options and include a written paragraph about what options they think would be right for them.

Helpful websites to begin research: APA Scholarships, Grants and Awards: **www.apa.org/about/awards/index.aspx**; Psychologymajors.com, "Psychology Degree Financial Aid Advice": **www.psychologymajors.com/student-financial-aid-paying-for-your-psychology-degree**

FIGURE 37.1 Some Potential Careers for College Graduates with Psychology Degrees

Other possible careers include marketing researcher, social worker, and communications specialist (Landrum & Davis, 2007; Schwartz, 2000). With its emphasis on critical thinking and empirical observation, psychology trains people for a variety of potential workplace environments and requirements. Psychology is an excellent undergraduate major even if you intend to do graduate work in another career. Business, law, child care, teaching, and management are only a few of the areas that relate to psychology.

If you major in psychology in college, you will develop excellent interpretive and analytical skills, and you will become experienced in areas such as statistical analysis and experimental design. Many employers from all sorts

APPLIED PSYCHOLOGY AND PSYCHOLOGY CAREERS 521

CHAPTER 16 • Module 37

COVER THE MODULE (continued)
- Many people with undergraduate degrees in psychology do not go on to pursue a career in psychology itself. However, skills and knowledge amassed during the completion of a bachelor's degree in psychology are transferrable and useful in many other careers.
  - Critical thinking, empirical observation, interpretive and analytical skills, statistical analysis, experimental design, and interpersonal skills are all attractive to employers in various career fields.

FAST FACT
According to Shelly K. Schwartz's article "Working Your Degree," the top 10 jobs employing people with a bachelor's degree in psychology are top or mid-level managers/executives, sales, social work, management-related occupations, personnel training/human resources, administrative jobs, insurance/real estate/business services, marketing, registered nurse/pharmacist/physical therapist/physician's assistant, and accountant/auditor/financial specialist.

Critical Thinking

HOW CAN A DEGREE IN PSYCHOLOGY TRANSFER TO OTHER CAREERS?
Place signs around the room for the careers listed in Figure 37.1 or from those listed in the above "Fast Fact." Give students a moment to think about careers they are considering for their future and have them move to the area of the room that best fits the category their career would fit into. This will be their "career group" for this activity.

Ask students to read the articles at the following websites:

- "What Can You Do with a Psychology Degree?"
  www.allpsychologyschools.com/psychology-careers/article/careers-psych-bachelor-degree

- "Working Your Degree" by Shelly K. Schwartz
  http://money.cnn.com/2000/12/08/career/q_degreepsychology/

Students should return to their groups and share their findings. Have each group present a summary to the rest of the class.

"Passport to Psychology" Portfolio Project For their portfolios, students can create a resume and cover letter to apply for an imaginary job in the career field they just researched to include in their portfolio.

Module 37 Careers in Psychology

CHAPTER 16 • Module 37

COVER THE MODULE

37.4 How does psychology interact with other career fields?

- *Health psychology* focuses on the relationship of human behavior patterns and stress reaction to physical health.
  - The goal is to improve and maintain good health while preventing and treating illness.
  - Health psychologists may work in hospitals, clinics, medical schools, health agencies, academic settings, or private practice.

LINK to *Chapter Fifteen: Stress and Health, pp. 503–505*

- *Educational psychology* focuses on human learning and developing new learning techniques.
  - Educational psychologists may have an Ed.D. rather than a Ph.D.

L1 DIFFERENTIATED INSTRUCTION

Auditory Learners Suggest that these students discuss with friends or a study group the material that they have been learning.

---

of different companies actively look for people with these skills and experiences, and psychology majors can be particularly attractive to employers as a result. In fact, most psychology majors do not go on to pursue careers in psychology. However, they frequently cite their training in psychology as one of the factors that makes them a successful employee, manager, or parent (APA, 2010).

37.4 How does psychology interact with other career fields?

Psychology and Health **Health psychology** focuses on the relationship of human behavior patterns and stress reactions to physical health with the goal of improving and helping to maintain good health while preventing and treating illness. A health psychologist might design a program to help people lose weight or stop smoking, for example. Stress management techniques are also a major focus of this area. Health psychologists may work in hospitals, clinics, medical schools, health agencies, academic settings, or private practice.

In one study, health psychologists examined the effects of social support and social burden (strain in social activities, negative experiences, and the need for taking care of others) on the number of times women went for breast cancer screening in a special study of breast cancer (Messina et al., 2004). The researchers found that women who had more social support and less of a social burden tended to go for screenings more often than women who had less social support and more social demands. Those with higher social demands and less support tended to rely more on self-examination at home rather than clinical tests. Relying only on self-examination without the support of clinical tests such as mammography puts these women at greater health risk.

This is just one example of the kinds of research that health psychologists conduct. Other areas studied by health psychologists include the influence of optimistic attitudes on the progress of disease, the link between mental distress and health, and the promotion of wellness and hope in an effort to prevent illness. LINK to *Chapter Fifteen: Stress and Health, pp. 503–505.*

Psychology and Education **Educational psychology** is concerned with the study of human learning. As educational psychologists come to understand some of the basic aspects of learning, they develop methods and materials for aiding the process of learning. For example, educational psychologists helped to design the phonics method of teaching children to read. This type of psychologist may have a doctorate of education (Ed.D.) rather than a Ph.D. and typically works in academic settings.

What types of research might an educational psychologist conduct? The November 2009 issue of *Journal of Educational Psychology* included articles on the role that students' oral language and decoding skills play in reading comprehension, a method of teaching anatomy with interactional three-dimensional graphics, and the impact of teacher–student interactions and various presentation strategies in kindergarten and first grade on learning outcomes—just to name a few.

▲ *This woman is a health psychologist. She is helping the girl to control her fear of receiving an injection by letting her act out giving an injection to a special doll.*

health psychology area of psychology in which the psychologists focus on the relationship of human behavior patterns and stress reaction to physical health.

educational psychology area of psychology in which the psychologists are concerned with the study of human learning and development of new learning techniques.

Explore

LET THE EXPERTS DO THE TALKING

Invite some psychology professionals to speak to your class about the nature of their job, their experiences in the field, and the training they received to go into their career. Ask them to touch on what motivated them to choose psychology and their particular specialty. If possible, try to get professionals with varying degree types and career fields discussed in Section 37.4.

"Passport to Psychology" Portfolio Project Ahead of time, ask students to prepare a list of questions about things they would like to learn about from the speakers. Students can either choose to ask the questions directly or listen and take notes as the speaker talks to the class. A list of questions and answers, plus a brief description about what the students learned from the speakers should be placed in the portfolio.

School psychology is related to, but not at all the same as, educational psychology. Whereas educational psychologists may do research and develop new learning techniques, school psychologists may take the results of that research or those methods and apply them in the actual school system. School psychologists work directly with children in the school setting. They do testing and other forms of assessment to place children in special programs such as gifted and talented or reading programs, or to diagnose educational problems such as dyslexia or attention deficit disorder. They may act as consultants to teachers, parents, and educational administrators.

Counseling students is actually a relatively small part of the job of a school psychologist, although counseling takes a much bigger role when tragedies strike a school. When traumatic events, such as the unexpected death of a classmate or the tragic Columbine High School shootings in 1999, take place, school psychologists are often called on to offer help and counseling to students.

Psychology and Sports *Sports psychology* is a relatively new and fast-growing field in which the main focus is on helping athletes and others involved in sports activities prepare mentally, rather than just physically, for participation in sports. The idea behind this field is that a superior physical performance is not enough to guarantee success; rather, the mind must be prepared for the activity by setting clear, short-term goals; holding positive thoughts, using visualization of the goal; stopping negative thoughts; and employing other techniques based primarily in the cognitive perspective.

For example, a sports psychologist might have a golfer who has been having trouble hitting the ball where he wants it to go do visualization exercises, mentally seeing himself hit the ball down the fairway again and again. The most successful athletes—in golf or any other sport—succeed in part because of their ability to remain focused under the most intense pressure. Sports psychologists work in athletic organizations and may have a private practice or do consulting work.

▲ *One technique used by sports psychologists is relaxation training, which teaches athletes to use specific physical techniques to reduce performance anxiety. Here the Wisconsin Badgers college football team participates in a relaxation exercise before the big game.*

Psychology and the Law Psychologists have often been involved in the world of legal matters in various ways. Social psychologists often do research in the areas of criminal behavior and may consult with attorneys or other agents of the court system on such topics as witness credibility, jury selection, and the kind of influences that exist for decision-making processes. Developmental psychologists may become involved in determining the accuracy of and influences on the testimony of children and adolescents, as well as the needs of children caught up in a custody battle between divorced or divorcing parents. Cognitive psychologists may become expert witnesses on the accuracy of memory and eyewitness testimony or on ways to determine the truth or falsehood of statements made by witnesses or defendants. Clinical psychologists may deliver their services directly to prisoners in prisons and jails or may conduct assessments of intelligence and/or mental status to determine whether or not a person charged with a crime should stand trial.

All of the forms of psychological involvement in legal matters mentioned here can be considered as part of the growing field of **forensic psychology**.

school psychology area of psychology in which the psychologists work directly in the schools, doing assessments, educational placement, and diagnosing educational problems.

sports psychology area of psychology in which the psychologists help athletes and others to prepare themselves mentally for participation in sports activities.

forensic psychology area of psychology concerned with people in the legal system, including profiling of criminals, jury selection, and expert witnessing.

APPLIED PSYCHOLOGY AND PSYCHOLOGY CAREERS 523

CHAPTER 16 • Module 37

COVER THE MODULE *(continued)*

- *School psychology* is a field in which school psychologists take the information gleaned from educational psychology research and apply it in the school setting.
  - School psychologists work directly with children, assessing children for special programs, diagnosing educational problems such as dyslexia, or counseling students in the aftermath of a tragedy.
- *Sports psychology* focuses on helping athletes mentally prepare for participation in sports.
  - Sports psychologists work with athletes by helping them set goals, visualizing the goals, maintaining a positive mentality, and focusing under extreme pressure.
- *Forensic psychology* is concerned with people in the legal system with numerous applications, including witness credibility, jury selection, criminal behavior, and being expert witnesses in testifying in the court.

L1 DIFFERENTIATED INSTRUCTION

Kinesthetic Learners Suggest that these students "walk and talk" the information they learn, by reciting as they move.

Class Discussion

THINK LIKE A FORENSIC PSYCHOLOGIST

Explain to students why and how forensic psychologists are consulted on criminal cases and asked to give expert testimony. Then ask students to debate the guilt of the following individuals:

- An adolescent with an IQ of 55 sees a violent video game in which a character is hit on the head with a hammer but springs up again, unharmed. The adolescent then hits his sister with a hammer and kills her but states that he just wanted to play with her, like the video-game characters did with each other.

- A college student drinks something laced with LSD, hallucinates, and kills a person who, in the hallucination, was trying to attack her, supposedly in self-defense. She has no memory of the event.

"Passport to Psychology" Portfolio Project Following the class discussion, students should write about what they learned about a forensic psychologist's role in the justice system.

Module 37 Careers in Psychology **523**

CHAPTER 16 • Module 37

COVER THE MODULE (continued)

- *Environmental psychology* focuses on the relationship of human behavior and the environment in which it takes place, such as an office, store, or school.
  - Environmental psychologists may work with urban or city planners, engineers, and architects to plan the most efficient buildings, parks, housing, and plants.

EXTEND THE LESSON

Environmental psychology has recently become a "hot field" to work in, due to a surge of interest and growing concern for learning more about sustainable living and the green movement. Environmental psychologists work closely with a team of professionals, including architects, interior designers, and urban planners to improve the overall human environment, working to motivate people to change their behavior and live greener. One method of doing so is to change the way zoos are designed. Many zoos are now creating exhibits that place people inside the animals' environments, rather than outside a cage. At the Dallas, Texas, zoo visitors are placed in glass bubbles inside the gorilla habitat, thus enclosing the visitors instead of the gorillas. Signs describing endangered species and habitat loss surrounding exhibits are also meant to encourage people to think more carefully about their behaviors and the environment.

▲ *Some forensic psychologists serve as expert witnesses in criminal cases and may be asked to perform psychological assessments of defendants.*

(*Forensic* comes from the Latin word *forens*, meaning "public.") Forensic psychology is the practice of psychology related to the legal system and involves examining criminal evidence and aiding law enforcement investigations into criminal activities. If you have watched TV shows like *CSI*, you may have seen dramatized examples of forensic psychology in action.

As discussed earlier, some forensic psychologists provide information and advice to legal officials such as lawyers or judges, some act as expert witnesses, some diagnose and treat criminals within the prison system, and others administer psychological tests to criminal defendants. Forensic psychologists may aid either the prosecution or the defense in a trial by helping to determine which potential jurors would be the best or worst choices. This type of professional may do consulting work in addition to a regular private practice in clinical or counseling psychology or may work entirely within the justice system as a police psychologist, a profiler of serial criminals for federal agencies, or a full-time jury expert, for example.

Psychology and the Environment Another broad area in which psychological principles can be applied to solve practical problems is the area of managing the environment. **Environmental psychology** is an area that focuses on the relationship between human behavior and the environment in which the behavior takes place, such as an office, store, school, dormitory, or hospital. Because the concern of researchers in this field deals directly with behavior in a particular setting, research is always conducted in that setting rather than in a laboratory. Environmental psychologists may work with other professionals such as urban or city planners, economists, engineers, and architects, helping those professionals to plan the most efficient buildings, parks, housing developments, or plants, for example.

Psychology and Work Work is a tremendous part of many people's lives. People often spend more time at work than they do with their families or in social activities. One of the largest branches of applied psychology focuses on

environmental psychology area of psychology in which the focus is on how people interact with and are affected by their physical environments.

Application (Kinesthetic)

THINK LIKE AN ENVIRONMENTAL PSYCHOLOGIST

Ask students to look at two different environments outside their homes; they can choose restaurants, malls, stores, their own school, or a healthcare facility. To do this assignment, they should be in the environment they are studying. Ask them to note in writing the following: (1) Using their five senses, describe their surroundings, noting dominant colors, patterns, sounds, and aesthetics. (2) Describe the behaviors they observe in people around them; are they happy, grumpy, loud, soft, patient, efficient, stressed, and so forth? (3) Describe the efficiency of the environment. How well is it organized for its purpose? Do people seem to have an easy time accomplishing whatever it is they are there to do? (4) How well does the design of the environment accomplish the goals of the facility?

"Passport to Psychology" Portfolio Project Students should create a final copy of their observations to be placed in their portfolio, along with a description of their interest in environmental psychology and whether it appeals to them.

524 Chapter 16 Applied Psychology and Careers

Current Issues in Psychology

Workplace Violence

Violent incidents in the workplace are quite rare, but they do happen. Over the past few decades, psychologists have devoted time and energy to studying the reasons for this violence and ways to recognize and prevent future incidents. Professor John Gambon of Ozarks Technical Community College in Springfield, Missouri, is an industrial/organizational psychologist who has been studying this issue and gathering data for presentation to his classes. Here are some highlights from his research into this issue:

1. People in some types of jobs face a higher probability of becoming a victim of a crime because of the characteristics of the job. For example, two of the occupations most at risk for workplace violence are nighttime convenience store clerk and cab driver. The availability of cash and the solitary nature of these jobs entice many criminals to attempt robbery.
2. Some forms of workplace violence are domestic issues that spill over into the world of work, such as the angry spouse who goes to the employee's place of business and attacks the employee, either on the premises or in the parking lot.
3. In some cases, it is not an outside criminal who commits workplace violence but a current or former employee. What are the characteristics of persons who commit violence in the workplace? Typically, they have at least a high school diploma or some college. Their self-esteem, or sense of worth as a person, is intimately tied to their job. They tend to like watching violent television or movies. There is a small correlation between these individuals and those with delusional disorders: People who become violent in the workplace are somewhat likely to suffer from a delusional disorder such as paranoia. LINK to Chapter Thirteen: Psychological Disorders, pp. 430–434.

Prevention of violence in the workplace includes some simple, common-sense items as well as some less simple methods (Arbury, 2005; Harvey & Keashly, 2003; Security Director's Report, 2008; Vandenbos & Bulatao, 1996):

1. Entrances and exits that are well lighted
2. Presence of video cameras or security guards, especially at night
3. Criminal background checks performed on all potential new employees
4. Training for managers and supervisors to learn how to identify signs of potential workplace violence, such as verbal threats by an employee; an employee's fascination with/access to firearms; desensitization of an employee to television and movie violence, with a preference for watching such media; and employee's low-grade acts of violence, such as pushing or shoving.

APPLIED PSYCHOLOGY AND PSYCHOLOGY CAREERS 525

CHAPTER 16 • Module 37

CURRENT ISSUES IN PSYCHOLOGY

- In his research, Professor John Gambon has isolated the following information on workplace violence: (1) certain jobs such as those with solitary working conditions or high cash availability are more susceptible to violence; (2) violence is sometimes caused by domestic issues spilling into the workplace; and (3) sometimes, violent acts are committed by employees who have certain characteristics that predispose them to aggression.

- Research into how to prevent workplace violence is ongoing, but providing better lighting, security cameras and guards, background checks on employees, and monitoring even mildly violent behavior or interest in violent media and firearms have been cited as important preventative measures.

FAST FACT

According to the Bureau of Labor Statistics, at least 2 million Americans are affected by workplace violence every year.

L1 DIFFERENTIATED INSTRUCTION

Special Needs Distribute written instructions or display them on the board or an overhead.

Critical Thinking

PREVENTING VIOLENCE IN THE WORKPLACE

Purpose: Students research information about how to prevent violence in the workplace and create a public service announcement poster to educate employees.

Time: 40 minutes

Description: Direct students to the following websites to read about preventing violence in the workplace. Students should then create posters displaying what they have learned. Consider requirements for the poster, including a catchy tagline, an eye-catching visual, and an engaging message.

- Prevention of workplace violence websites:
  http://crimeprevention.rutgers.edu/crime/violence/workplace/prevention.htm
  www.usda.gov/news/pubs/violence/wpv.htm
  http://workplaceviolencenews.com/2011/03/28/warning-signs-of-workplace-violence-2/

- Sample public service announcement posters:
  http://tomstirr.com/posters/html/bullying_violence.php

"Passport to Psychology" Portfolio Project Students should place a final copy of their poster in their portfolio.

CHAPTER 16 • Module 37

COVER THE MODULE (continued)

- *Industrial/organizational psychologists* focus on the relationship between people and their work environment. They are often hired by businesses to hire and assess employees, design new work schedules, or create ways to boost employee morale.
- *Human factors psychology* is a branch of I/O that studies how humans interact with machines to help engineers create the most efficient, practical, and comfortable equipment possible.
- **Psychologists who influenced this field**
  - Walter D. Scott first applied psychological principles to hiring, management, and advertising techniques in the early 1900s.
  - During World War I, Robert Yerkes devised the Army Alpha and Army Beta tests to help test the intelligence of recruits.
  - In the 1920s, Elton Mayo was the first to view the workplace as a social system rather than an assembly line and suggest that allowing workers to give their input would improve attitudes and reduce resistance.

MULTIMEDIA CONTENT AVAILABLE AT
www.mypsychlab.com

Explore psychologists at work on mypsychlab.com

TEACHING TIP
Incorporate material from magazines, newspapers, or the Internet to identify current topics of interest to students.

---

industrial/organizational (I/O) psychology area of psychology concerned with the relationships between people and their work environment.

human factors psychology area of industrial/organizational psychology concerned with the study of the way humans and machines interact with each other.

▲ *These women were participants in one of the early industrial/organizational psychology experiments conducted by Elton Mayo for the Western Electric Company.*

how psychology can help people in management, productivity, morale, and many other areas of the world of work.

Industrial/organizational (I/O) psychology is concerned with the relationships between people and their work environments. I/O psychologists may help in personnel selection, administer job performance assessments, design work schedules that help workers adjust to new time periods of work hours with less difficulty, or design new work areas to increase morale and productivity. Psychologists in this field may study the behavior of entire organizations. They are often hired by corporations and businesses to deal with the hiring and assessment of employees. They may research and develop ways for workers to be more efficient and productive. They may work in business, government and nonprofit agencies, and academic settings.

A certain kind of I/O specialist, called a *human factors engineer*, focuses on designing machines, furniture, and other devices that people have to use so that those devices are the most practical, comfortable, and logical for human use. **Human factors psychology** consists of these researchers and designers who study the way humans and machines interact with each other. They may work in the design of appliances, airplane controls, and computers or other mechanical devices. For example, they may design interfaces that help people use computer programs (like self-checkout machines at the grocery store or ATMs) in more intuitive, less error-prone ways. Human factors psychologists tend to work directly in the businesses that design and manufacture the machines they study.

Industrial/organizational psychology got its start near the beginning of the 20th century with the work of Walter D. Scott. Scott applied psychological principles to hiring, management, and advertising techniques (Schultz & Schultz, 2004). Another early figure in the newly developing field of industrial/organizational psychology was Hugo Munsterberg, a psychologist also trained by Wundt who conducted research on such varied topics as the power of prayer and eyewitness testimony (Hothersall, 1995).

The field became important during World War I when the army needed a way to test the intelligence of potential recruits. Psychologist Robert Yerkes, who would later become known for his groundbreaking research in comparative psychology while working with the great apes, developed the Army Alpha and Army Beta tests. The Army Alpha test was used with applicants who were able to read, whereas the Army Beta test was administered to applicants who were illiterate (McGuire, 1994; Yerkes, 1921). In the mid-1920s, a series of studies conducted by Elton Mayo for the Western Electric Company (Franke & Kaul, 1978; Parsons, 1992; Roethlisberger & Dickson, 1939) broadened the field. These were the first studies to view the workplace as a social system rather than simply a production line. Rather than treating workers as simply other pieces of equipment, these studies suggested that allowing workers some input into the decision-making process not only improved workers' attitudes but also reduced workers' resistance to changes in the workplace. These studies led the way for others to examine how management of employees and production could be im-

526 CHAPTER 16

Explore

INTERVIEW AN EXPERT

For the final portfolio piece, work with students to select a professional to interview to learn more about a branch of psychology that students are interested in. Students may want to consult the results of earlier explorations and career quizzes while making their selection. Consider conferring individually with students to help them select a professional to interview and write interview questions, as well as reviewing questions and procuring parent approval before the student conducts the interview. (For the sake of efficiency, consider grouping all students who are interested in a specific branch and having the group interview the professional.) Students can report their findings in a format of your choosing, but interesting methods would be in the form of a visual chart containing the following columns: (1) What I Know About This Field, (2) What I Want to Learn About This Field, and (3) What I Learned as a Result of This Interview, or as a magazine article entitled "A Day in the Life of . . ." or "Diary of a _____ Psychologist."

526 Chapter 16 Applied Psychology and Careers

proved. Management theories and strategies may also be applied to other kinds of settings such as schools, colleges, and universities.

+[Explore on mypsychlab.com

+[Explore psychologists at work on mypsychlab.com

Applying Psychology to *Your* Life Our journey through the fascinating science of psychology has given you a glimpse of how this science of human behavior and mental processes can relate to almost every aspect of life: how we think, how we feel, and how we behave when we are alone and when we are with others. You've learned about how we grow and change, but also about how we stay the same throughout our lives. You've seen what makes us healthy and what makes us sick, what helps us learn and what makes us forget. Ultimately, this knowledge of human behavior will help you gain a deeper understanding of yourself and of the world around you.

For years, psychologists have been helping to make the world a better place, and they'll continue this work in the future, developing new innovations in fields like sports, forensics, education, and industry. They will work in health fields and legal fields, research labs and social services. They'll work as psychiatrists, human factors engineers, and clinical psychologists and they'll make fascinating, valuable discoveries. Will you be one of them?

Applying Psychology to Everyday Life

Techniques Used by Sports Psychologists

Many athletes become frustrated when their performance seems to be less than it could be or when they reach a roadblock on their way to achieving new goals. Here are a few techniques designed to help athletes get around the roadblocks and get the most out of their performance.

1. *Visualization.* In this technique, athletes try to "see" their performance in their minds as if watching from the sidelines before actually doing it.
2. *Thought stopping.* People often have negative thoughts about things that might happen: "I'm going to miss it, I just know it!" is a good example of a negative, self-defeating thought. Sports psychologists train athletes to stop such thoughts in the making, replacing them with more positive thoughts: "I can do this. I've done it before and it was easy."
3. *Confidence training.* Another thing that sports psychologists do is try to build confidence and self-esteem in the athletes who come to them for help. Lack of confidence in one's own abilities is a major roadblock.
4. *Fostering realistic goals and expectations.* Sports psychologists try to teach athletes that although setting goals is important, setting unrealistic goals can lead to burnout, frustration, and feelings of failure. Sports psychologists try to help athletes modify their expectations and goals to be more realistic.
5. *Fostering team unity.* Sports psychologists may also work with entire teams of athletes, helping them to become a unit that works as one single "organism" while still providing support for each individual athlete.

APPLIED PSYCHOLOGY AND PSYCHOLOGY CAREERS 527

Final Project

PSYCHOLOGY CAREER FAIR

<u>Purpose</u>: Students showcase what they have learned about themselves and careers in psychology.

<u>Time</u>: One class period

<u>Description</u>: Ask students to imagine that they have decided to pursue a career in psychology. Based on what they have learned in the creation of their portfolio, ask them to create a visual aid mapping their career path in their chosen field, including the college they plan to attend, the degree(s) they plan to complete, and how they will finance their education. They should then describe a typical day at work once they are working in the field. Invite parents to attend the career fair and set up students' visual displays in a gallery format so attendees can browse the displays and query students.

CHAPTER 16 • Module 37

APPLYING PSYCHOLOGY TO YOUR LIFE

As a class, brainstorm ways that the branches of psychology studied in this chapter have influenced students' lives by improving them or the world around them in some way. Record student responses on the board. Ask for a show of hands of students who are considering pursuing a career in psychology. Allow them to share which careers they are interested in and what piqued their interest.

APPLYING PSYCHOLOGY TO EVERYDAY LIFE

After discussing the techniques in this section with the class, ask students to volunteer how sports psychology may have been present in their own experiences with sports or extracurricular activities. What advice or techniques have their coaches given to them during practices and games?

Divide students into five groups. Assign each group a technique discussed in this section. Ask the students in each group to work together to brainstorm how the technique can be used in situations outside sports.

CHECK FOR UNDERSTANDING (KINESTHETIC)

Place signs around the room, perhaps on the floor, that contain terms and careers studied in this chapter. Break students into teams and for each question, the teams should select a representative. Read a definition or description of an occupation, and team representatives should find the sign for the answer and move to it. The student who arrives first wins the point for the team. Continue until all terms have been reviewed.

Module 37 Careers in Psychology 527

CHAPTER 16 • Module 37

Assess

Assign the Module 37 Practice Quiz.

Use the Practice Quiz to identify gaps in student understanding.

REMEDIATE

Have students, individually or in groups, review the module goals, learning objectives, and key terms.

Refer students to the Concept Summary on pp. 532–533 for review.

Close

Ask students to take out the papers containing the charts from the Bellringer activity at the beginning of the module. Have them fill in the final "What I Learned" column. Allow students to share with the class and track responses on the board.

Practice Quiz

Pick the best answer.

1. Which of the following professionals in psychology focuses most on the environmental conditions that affect mental disorders?
   a. psychiatrist
   b. psychology professor
   c. psychologist
   d. psychiatric social worker

2. Which type of psychologist would be most likely to administer an IQ test to a child to determine the child's eligibility for a gifted program?
   a. health
   b. educational
   c. school
   d. environmental

3. Which of the following degrees always has a clinical or counseling focus?
   a. an M.S.
   b. an Ed.D.
   c. a Ph.D.
   d. a Psy.D.

4. One of the early figures in I/O psychology who developed the Army Alpha and the Army Beta tests was
   a. Elton Mayo
   b. Hugo Munsterberg
   c. Walter D. Scott
   d. Robert Yerkes

5. Yolanda would like to spend her career studying cognitive science. She hopes to work at a university where she can conduct research and also teach undergraduate students. What type of degree should Yolanda pursue to meet her goals?
   a. a master's degree in psychology
   b. a master's degree in social work
   c. a Psy.D.
   d. a Ph.D. in psychology

6. What type of psychologist would be most likely to put together a personality profile of a criminal for the FBI?
   a. clinical
   b. forensic
   c. industrial/organizational
   d. sports

7. Suzanne is about to compete in a gymnastics tournament, and she begins to have second thoughts about her ability. She realizes that such negative thoughts will not help and tells herself that she has done these exercises perfectly in practice, and she can do them perfectly now. Suzanne's ability to replace her negative thinking with more helpful, positive thinking is a form of
   a. relaxation training
   b. thought stopping
   c. distraction desensitization
   d. autogenic training

8. Which of the following publications is published by the Bureau of Labor Statistics and includes detailed information about psychology careers?
   a. *Career Paths in Psychology: Where Your Degree Can Take You*
   b. *Occupational Outlook Handbook*
   c. *Graduate Study in Psychology*
   d. *The Insider's Guide to the Psychology Major: Everything You Need to Know About the Degree and Profession*

9. Which of the following psychological professionals would be LEAST likely to study factors that can lead to workplace violence?
   a. an industrial/organizational psychologist
   b. a social psychologist
   c. a comparative psychologist
   d. an environmental psychologist

10. The professional most likely to use Freudian concepts in therapy is a
    a. psychiatrist
    b. psychologist
    c. psychiatric social worker
    d. psychoanalyst

Practice Quiz Answers

1. d
2. c
3. d
4. d
5. d
6. b
7. b
8. b
9. c
10. d

CHAPTER 16 Summary

Listen on **mypsychlab.com**

Module 37: Applied Psychology and Psychology Careers

Identify educational requirements for careers in psychology.

37.1 What are the degree requirements for psychological professionals?
- The different types of psychological professionals are psychiatrists, psychoanalysts, psychiatric social workers, and psychologists.
- Areas of specialization include clinical and counseling psychology, developmental, experimental, social, personality, physiological, and comparative psychology.
- Counselors and therapists must hold at least a master's (M.A. or M.S.) degree.
- Social workers hold a master of social work (M.S.W.) degree.
- School psychologists often hold an educational specialist (Ed.S.) degree.
- Psychologists hold either a Ph.D. or a Psy.D. degree. Educational psychologists may hold an Ed.D. degree.
- Psychiatrists must hold a medical degree (M.D.).

37.2 What resources are available for people who want to study psychology in the future?
- The *Occupational Outlook Handbook* provides detailed information about educational requirements, working conditions, job prospects, and job responsibilities for careers in psychology and other fields.
- The Web site of the American Psychological Association provides general information about topics in psychology as well as resources on pursuing psychology degrees and careers and reference links for many valuable print resources.
- Students may finance their education through financial aid programs, scholarships and awards, and graduate assistantships. Numerous references provide general information about these options for a wide variety of career fields.

Listen to an audio file of your chapter on **mypsychlab.com**
- The Web sites of the American Psychological Association and Psi Chi, the International Honor Society in Psychology, provide information about scholarships and awards for students in psychology.

Explore career options in psychology.

37.3 What types of careers are available to someone with a bachelor's degree in psychology?
- Education, statistical consulting, administration and other business careers, as well as health services, are examples of careers that a person with a bachelor's degree in psychology might enter.

37.4 How does psychology interact with other career fields?
- Psychology interacts with various other career fields including health, education, sports, law, and business.
- In health psychology, the goal is to discover relationships between human behavior, including stress factors, and physical health with the intention of preventing and treating ill health.
- Educational psychologists study the processes of human learning to develop new educational techniques and methods. School psychologists apply those methods in the school, administer assessments, recommend placement, and provide counseling and diagnosis of educational problems.
- Sports psychologists help athletes prepare themselves mentally for participation in sports.
- Forensic psychologists may act as expert witnesses for legal matters, help in jury selection, provide clinical services to defendants or prisoners, or produce personality profiles of various types of criminals.
- Environmental psychology looks at the relationship between human behavior and the physical environment in which that behavior takes place.
- Industrial/organizational psychology is concerned with how people function in and are affected by their work environments.
- Human factors psychology is a type of I/O psychology that focuses on the way humans and machines interact with each other.

Vocabulary Terms

applied psychology p. 514
master's degree p. 516
doctorate p. 517
doctor of philosophy (Ph.D.) p. 517
doctor of psychology (Psy.D.) p. 517
health psychology p. 522
educational psychology p. 522
school psychology p. 523
sports psychology p. 523
forensic psychology p. 524
environmental psychology p. 524
industrial/organizational (I/O) psychology p. 526
human factors psychology p. 526

APPLIED PSYCHOLOGY AND PSYCHOLOGY CAREERS 529

CHAPTER 16 • Summary and Vocabulary

Chapter Summary

Encourage students to carefully review and study the summary. Explain that it provides an overview of key concepts presented in the text.

Have students identify what they find unclear or confusing. Call on volunteers to provide answers, examples, or definitions.

Vocabulary Terms

Remind students that terms are defined within the chapter at point of use. If they are not sure of a term's definition, they should look up the definition on the page.

Encourage students to create study cards of unfamiliar words or go to **www.mypsychlab.com** for flashcards. Have them test themselves or a classmate. Advanced students can explain the terms in their own words.

Critical Thinking

THE FINAL STEP IN BEGINNING A CAREER IN PSYCHOLOGY

Most states require not only a bachelor's degree, master's degree, doctoral degree, or medical degree to practice psychology; they also require state licensure. Direct students to the following websites, allow them to browse, and have them answer the following questions: (1) Why do states require an additional license to practice? (2) What are the prerequisites that states require to apply for each type of license? (3) What are the specific requirements for your state?

- www.allpsychologyschools.com/psychology-careers/article/licensing
- www.asppb.org/
- www.allpsychologycareers.com/psychology-license.html

Chapter 16 Summary 529

CHAPTER 16 • Assessment

VOCABULARY REVIEW

1. i
2. a
3. h
4. c
5. e
6. b
7. d
8. f
9. g
10. j

WRITING ABOUT PSYCHOLOGY

1. Students' answers should describe, in detail, the scope and focus of two of the listed choices, as well as providing at least one detailed discussion of a way that the two fields are alike, and one detailed discussion of a way that the two fields differ. Excellent answers will include more than one of each.

2. Students' answers should describe at least two clear differences between the Ph.D. and the Psy.D. and include discussion of the differences in training to earn the degrees and the career paths available upon completion of each degree. Excellent answers will include brief descriptions of what those careers entail.

PSYCHOLOGY PROJECT

It may be helpful to group students according to interests in careers to research. Additionally, confer with each pair to devise questions for them to answer during their research using the resources available. Because the answers to the questions will be the key information on the poster, consider requiring a certain number of questions that would need some thought to answer. Provide students with guidelines to follow in creating the final product, giving instructions about format, number and creativity of visuals, and detail in written responses. Allow students to present their findings to the class and allow students in the audience to ask their peers questions about the careers they researched.

CHAPTER 16 Assessment

Study and Review on mypsychlab.com

Vocabulary Review
Match each vocabulary term to its definition.

1. applied psychology
2. master's degree
3. school psychology
4. forensic psychology
5. doctor of philosophy (Ph.D.)
6. educational psychology
7. industrial/organizational (I/O) psychology
8. doctor of psychology (Psy.D.)
9. human factors psychology
10. sports psychology

a. A graduate degree students may pursue after completing a 4-year college degree, generally taking 2 to 3 years to complete and providing more specialized knowledge, training, and experience than students typically receive as undergraduates.
b. Area of psychology in which the psychologists are concerned with the study of human learning and development of new learning techniques.
c. Area of psychology concerned with people in the legal system, including profiling of criminals, jury selection, and expert witnessing.
d. Area of psychology concerned with the relationships between people and their work environment.
e. A doctorate that is research oriented and culminates in a dissertation based on original research.
f. A doctorate that focuses on applying psychological principles and provides extensive hands-on experience working in a clinical or counseling setting.
g. Area of industrial/organizational psychology concerned with the study of the way humans and machines interact with each other.
h. Area of psychology in which the psychologists work directly in the schools, doing assessments, educational placement, and diagnosing educational problems.
i. The use of psychological concepts in solving real-world problems.
j. Area of psychology in which the psychologists help athletes and others to prepare themselves mentally for participation in sports activities.

Writing about Psychology
Respond to each question in complete sentences.

1. Choose any two of the following areas of psychology. In a paragraph, compare and contrast the two areas, describing what each area focuses on and what type of work professionals in this branch of psychology typically do.
   a. health psychology
   b. sports psychology
   c. educational psychology
   d. industrial/organizational psychology
   e. environmental psychology
2. Briefly explain the difference between a Ph.D. and a Psy.D. Give examples of the type of work students would do while pursuing this degree and what careers they might enter after receiving the degree.

Psychology Project
What do different types of psychological professionals do in their day-to-day work? Complete this project to improve your understanding of careers in psychology.

Materials:
- access to print or electronic reference resources
- a pencil and paper, or other note-taking materials
- poster board
- markers or other drawing materials

Instructions:

1. With your partner, choose one career in psychology to research. (You may also choose a career in a related field, such as social work, but it must be a field that requires an understanding of psychology.) You will work with your partner to create an informational poster about this career.
2. Review the information in this chapter about the career you selected.
3. Conduct additional research about this career using print or online references. Take notes on important details. To guide your research, you may want to start with a few key questions, such as: What are the educational training and licensing requirements for this career? Why do people choose this career? What kinds of day-to-day responsibilities are associated with this career? What is the typical working environment for people who pursue this career? (For example, do they work independently or within an organization? With laboratory rats or with people?) Where could someone learn more about how to pursue this career?
4. Prepare a poster that provides information about the career you chose. Include text that answers questions like the ones listed above. Use Internet sources and/or magazines to find images related to this career and include them in your poster.

Internet Resources

AllPsychologyCareers.com, "The Psychology Career Center":
www.allpsychologycareers.com/

About.com Psychology, "Top 10 Psychology Career Trends":
http://psychology.about.com/od/careersinpsychology/tp/psychology-career-trends.htm

AllPsychologySchools.com "Your Guide to Psychology Education and Careers":
www.allpsychologyschools.com/psychology-careers/article/article-archive

American Psychology Association, Careers Page
www.apa.org/careers/resources/guides/careers.aspx

Test Yourself

Pick the best answer.

1. Max is interested in becoming a psychologist. He is most interested in how people become attracted to other people. He would most likely specialize in
   a. social psychology
   b. comparative psychology
   c. environmental psychology
   d. personality psychology

2. What type of degree does a person usually need to complete to be called a psychologist?
   a. a bachelor's degree
   b. a master's degree
   c. a doctorate degree
   d. a medical degree

3. Which type of psychologist would most likely study the effects of psychological stress on the growth rate of cancer cells?
   a. sports
   b. health
   c. environmental
   d. forensic

4. The Web site of the American Psychological Association provides information about
   a. choosing psychology as a college major
   b. scholarships, grants, and other funding sources
   c. possible career paths in psychology
   d. all of the above

5. Bernard works in a factory and is responsible for making sure that the office equipment made in the factory is practical and easy to use. He sometimes suggests changes in the design of certain equipment to accomplish this goal. Bernard is most likely what type of psychologist?
   a. conflict management
   b. human factors
   c. industrial/organizational
   d. management/design

6. Some psychologists believe that panic attacks occur because of a malfunction in a small area of the brain normally responsible for alerting the person to real danger. This view is most compatible with which area of specialization in psychology?
   a. health
   b. human factors
   c. counseling
   d. physiological

7. John would like to become a mental health professional who treats schizophrenic patients. Although a number of different factors contribute to the development of schizophrenia, John is most interested in studying the associated brain dysfunctions and prescribing medication to help patients manage their symptoms. What type of degree should John pursue?
   a. a master's degree in psychology
   b. a Psy.D.
   c. a Ph.D. in psychology
   d. an M.D. with a specialization in psychiatry

8. A sports psychologist tells Michaela, a tennis player, to try to see herself actually hitting the ball over the net. The psychologist is using
   a. focus training
   b. autogenic training
   c. thought stopping
   d. visualization

9. Hector is interested in working with families who have been affected by drug abuse and addiction. He does not want a career doing research, but instead would like to work for a local government agency or community outreach center and interact directly with families who have been affected by this problem. What degree should Hector pursue?
   a. a bachelor's degree
   b. a master's in social work
   c. a Ph.D. in psychology
   d. a medical degree

10. Individuals who want to pursue a career as a(n) _____ are most likely to obtain an Ed.S. degree.
    a. social worker
    b. psychiatrist
    c. school psychologist
    d. developmental psychologist

CHAPTER 16 • Assessment

TEST YOURSELF

1. a
2. c
3. b
4. d
5. b
6. d
7. d
8. d
9. b
10. c

Ready for Testing

STUDENTS KNOW THEY ARE READY FOR TESTING IF THEY ARE ABLE TO . . .

- Explain the degree requirements for psychology professionals.
- Discuss the resources that are available for people who want to study psychology in the future.
- Describe the types of careers that are available to someone with a bachelor's degree in psychology.
- Explain how psychology interacts with other career fields.

CHAPTER 16 • Concept Summary

MULTIMEDIA CONTENT AVAILABLE AT
www.mypsychlab.com

Map the Concepts on **mypsychlab.com**

Study and Review Flashcards on **mypsychlab.com**

STUDY TIPS

Positive Self-Affirmations Encourage students to put their thoughts into positive language. Tell them that *affirmations* are statements using positive language. If they have heard someone answer a question with "Affirmative!" instead of a simple "Yes," they know the power of that word. It seems charged with energy. There isn't any doubt in that response. *Self-affirmations* are positive statements that you say to yourself. Most people don't think that they talk to themselves, but they do it all the time. What might students say to themselves? Is it, "I'll never have enough time to complete this assignment," or "This is so hard," or "I'm going to be late for class—I'm always late." How can a person change negative statements like these to positive ones? "I'll never have enough time to complete this assignment" could be changed to, "I have enough time to complete this assignment." "This is so hard" could be changed to, "This is getting easier every day." Changing how they think might be a challenge, but it's one that will put them on a direct path to success.

CHAPTER 16 Concept Summary: Applied Psychology and

Learning Objectives

37.1 **37.2** pp. 514–520

Identify Educational Requirements for Careers in Psychology

- **graduate degrees** are often required for professional positions
  - a **master's degree** is required to work as a counselor, therapist, or social worker
  - a **medical degree (M.D.)** is required to work as a psychiatrist
  - a **doctorate** is required to work as a psychologist
    - **Ph.D. (doctor of philosophy)** has a research focus
    - **Psy.D. (doctor of psychology)** has a clinical focus

- **print, electronic, and in-person resources** provide detailed information about studying psychology and pursuing psychology careers

- **financial aid resources** exist to help students finance the advanced education required for many psychology careers

---

What Every Student Should Know About . . .

PROCRASTINATION

Give students the following suggestions for stopping procrastination and getting on with their lives: (1) *Plan*. Stay focused and stay organized. Break down your project into individual steps, with realistic timeframes for the completion of each step. (2) *Prioritize*. Identify which step should come first, second, and so on. (3) *Perform*. Provide yourself with an incentive or a reason to finish that job or task you have been delaying. Then just do it!

532 Chapter 16 Applied Psychology and Careers

Psychology Careers

Map The Concepts on mypsychlab.com

Learning Objectives
37.3 **37.4** pp. 520–527

Explore Career Options in Psychology

- **a bachelor's degree** in psychology can be used in many career fields.
  - education and teaching
  - consulting and statistical analysis
  - administration or clerical services
  - professional services
  - sales and marketing
  - health and health-related services
  - research and development
  - market research
  - social work
  - communications

- **areas that interact with other career fields**
  - **health psychologists** study the relationship between behavior patterns, stress reactions, and physical health
  - **educational psychology** focuses on the nature of human learning
  - **sports psychologists** help athletes prepare mentally for sports using a variety of specialized techniques such as relaxation training
  - **forensic psychology** helps people in the legal system by examining criminal evidence and aiding law enforcement investigations
  - **environmental psychologists** study the relationship between human behavior and the environment where the behavior takes place
  - **industrial/organizational (I/O) psychologists** study the relationship between people and their work environments.
  - **human factors psychologists** study the way humans and machines interact with each other.
  - **educational psychologists** conduct research to help people understand and improve learning processes
  - **school psychologists** apply research through working directly with students and school personnel

APPLIED PSYCHOLOGY AND PSYCHOLOGY CAREERS 533

Comprehension Check

ONLINE QUIZ: SPECIALTY AREAS IN PSYCHOLOGY

Direct students to the website listed below, where they can take a quiz to see how much they remember about what they just studied about specialties in psychology. They will receive immediate feedback for their answers. Challenge them to try the most difficult level!

http://psychology.about.com/library/quiz/bl_specialty_quiz.htm

---

CHAPTER 16 • Concept Summary

STUDY TIPS

Strategies for Reading Texts Help students get more out of reading their textbook by giving them the following tips:

- Look for main ideas that are often the first sentence of a paragraph. Pay attention to when a new idea begins.

- Review often. Reviewing is an essential skill for learning and remembering. Studying textbook material is similar to studying class notes; they both require ongoing review. Spend time with your textbooks and notes. The payoff is worth the energy and time.

- If you think you need additional information in order to understand something, try doing an Internet search to find related materials.

- Pretend that you are having a discussion with the author. Do you agree or disagree with his or her ideas? This process helps you become an active reader.

- Without looking, recite the information that you have in your summaries.

- If the material is difficult to understand, read it out loud. Hearing the material can help you understand it (auditory learning).

Glossary/Glosario

A

absolute threshold: the lowest level of stimulation that a person can consciously perceive 50 percent of the time the stimulation is present by 50 percent of the people tested. 79
umbral absoluto: nivel más bajo de estimulación que puede percibir la persona de manera consciente el 50 por ciento de las veces que la estimulación está presente por parte del 50 por ciento de las personas sometidas a prueba.

accommodation: the process of altering or adjusting old schemes to fit new information and experience, or, as a monocular clue, the brain's use of information about the changing thickness of the lens of the eye in response to looking at objects that are close or far away. 98, 153
adaptación: proceso de alterar o adecuar viejos procesos para ajustar información y experiencia nueva o, como pista monocular, uso de información por parte del cerebro concerniente al espesor cambiante del cristalino en respuesta a la visión de objetos cercanos o lejanos.

acculturation: the process of adapting to a new culture by adopting the new culture's beliefs and behaviors. 254
aculturación: proceso de adaptarse a una nueva cultura mediante la adopción de las creencias y conductas de esta.

acculturative stress: stress resulting from the need to change and adapt a person's ways to the majority culture. 487
estrés cultural: estrés que se produce como resultado de la necesidad de cambiar y adaptar la manera de ser de una persona a la cultura mayoritaria.

acquired (secondary) drives: those drives that are learned through experience or conditioning, such as the need for money or social approval. 343
impulsos adquiridos (secundarios): impulsos que se aprenden mediante la experiencia o el condicionamiento, como la necesidad de dinero o aprobación social.

action potential: the release of the neural impulse consisting of a reversal of the electrical charge within the axon. 45
potencial de acción: liberación del impulso neural consistente en la inversión de la carga eléctrica dentro del axón.

action therapy: therapy in which the main goal is to change disordered or inappropriate behavior directly. 446
terapia activa: tipo de terapia en la cual el objetivo principal es cambiar de manera directa una conducta inapropiada o alterada.

activation-information-mode model (AIM): revised version of the activation-synthesis explanation of dreams in which information that is accessed during waking hours can have an influence on the synthesis of dreams. 120
modelo activación-información-modulación: versión revisada de la explicación de los sueños "activación-síntesis", según la cual la información que se recibe durante las horas de vigilia puede tener influencia en la síntesis de los sueños.

activation-synthesis hypothesis: explanation that states that dreams are created by the higher centers of the cortex to explain the activation by the brain stem of cortical cells during REM sleep periods. 120
hipótesis activación-síntesis: teoría que sostiene que los sueños son creados por los centros superiores de la corteza cerebral para explicar la activación de las células corticales del tronco cerebral durante los períodos de sueño REM.

activity theory: theory of adjustment to aging that assumes older people are happier if they remain active in some way, such as volunteering or developing a hobby. 168
teoría de la actividad: teoría de adaptación al envejecimiento que supone que las personas mayores son más felices si permanecen activas de alguna manera, como al hacer servicios de voluntariado o al desarrollar algún pasatiempo.

acute stress disorder (ASD): a disorder resulting from exposure to a major stressor, with symptoms of anxiety, dissociation, recurring nightmares, sleep disturbances, problems in concentration, and moments in which people seem to "relive" the event in dreams and flashbacks for as long as one month following the event. 492
trastorno de estrés agudo: trastorno que se produce como resultado de la exposición a un factor estresante mayor, con síntomas de ansiedad, disociación, pesadillas recurrentes, perturbaciones del sueño, problemas de concentración y momentos en los que la persona parece "revivir" el suceso en sueños y reviviscencias durante períodos de hasta un mes después de ocurrido el evento.

adaptation-level phenomenon: the tendency to evaluate new experiences in terms of previous experiences and adjust expectations accordingly. 366
fenómeno adaptación-nivel: tendencia a evaluar las experiencias nuevas en términos de experiencias anteriores y ajustar las expectativas en consecuencia.

adaptive theory: theory of sleep proposing that animals and humans evolved sleep patterns to avoid predators by sleeping when predators are most active. 113
teoría de adaptación: teoría del sueño que propone que los animales y los seres humanos desarrollaron patrones de sueño para evitar a los depredadores, al dormir cuando los depredadores están más activos.

adrenal glands: endocrine glands located on top of each kidney that secrete over 30 different hormones to deal with stress, regulate salt intake, and provide a secondary source of sex hormones affecting the sexual changes that occur during adolescence. 51
glándulas suprarrenales: glándulas endocrinas ubicadas en la parte superior de cada riñón que secretan más de 30 hormonas distintas para afrontar el estrés, regular la ingesta de sal y brindar una fuente extra de hormonas sexuales que afectan los cambios sexuales durante la adolescencia.

aerial perspective: the haziness that surrounds objects that are farther away from the viewer, causing the distance to be perceived as greater. 98
perspectiva aérea: nebulosidad que rodea a los objetos más alejados del observador, que causa que la distancia se perciba como mayor.

affect: in psychology, a term indicating "emotion" or "mood." 427
afecto: en psicología, término que indica "emoción" o "estado de ánimo".

afterimages: images that occur when a visual sensation persists for a brief time even after the original stimulus is removed. 85
imágenes residuales: imágenes que ocurren cuando la sensación visual persiste por un instante incluso después de que el estímulo original desaparece.

aggression: actions meant to harm or destroy. 238, 499
agresión: acciones destinadas a dañar o destruir.

agoraphobia: fear of being in a place or situation from which escape is difficult or impossible. 422
agorafobia: temor a estar en un lugar o en una situación de la cual es imposible o muy difícil escapar.

agreeableness: the emotional style of a person that may range from easygoing, friendly, and likeable to grumpy, crabby, and unpleasant. 389
amabilidad: estilo emocional de una persona que puede ir de relajado, amistoso y simpático a gruñón, malhumorado y desagradable.

alcohol: the chemical resulting from fermentation or distillation of various kinds of vegetable matter. 128
  alcohol: químico que se produce como resultado de la fermentación o destilación de distintos tipos de materia vegetal.

algorithm: a very specific, step-by-step procedure for solving a certain type of problem. 311
  algoritmo: procedimiento muy específico, paso a paso, para resolver un determinado tipo de problema.

alpha waves: brain waves that indicate a state of relaxation or light sleep. 113
  ondas alfa: ondas cerebrales que indican un estado de relajación o sueño ligero.

altered state of consciousness: state in which there is a shift in the quality or pattern of mental activity as compared to waking consciousness. 110
  estado alterado de conciencia: estado en el cual hay un cambio en la calidad o el patrón de la actividad mental, en comparación con la conciencia activa.

altruism: prosocial behavior that is done with no expectation of reward and may involve the risk of harm to oneself. 240
  altruismo: conducta prosocial que se realiza sin esperar gratificación y que puede implicar el riesgo de dañarse a sí mismo.

amphetamines: stimulants that are synthesized (made) in laboratories rather than being found in nature. 126
  anfetaminas: estimulantes que se sintetizan (se fabrican) en laboratorio y no se encuentran en la naturaleza.

amygdala: brain structure located near the hippocampus, responsible for fear responses and memory of fear. 60
  núcleo amigdalino o cuerpo amigdaloide cerebral: estructura cerebral ubicada cerca del hipocampo, responsable de las respuestas al miedo y la memoria del miedo.

anal expulsive personality: a person fixated in the anal stage who is messy, destructive, and hostile. 380
  personalidad anal expulsiva: persona obsesionada en la etapa anal que es desordenada, destructiva y hostil.

anal retentive personality: a person fixated in the anal stage who is neat, fussy, stingy, and stubborn. 380
  personalidad anal retentiva: persona obsesionada en la etapa anal que es pulcra, meticulosa, mezquina y terca.

anal stage: second stage occurring from about one to three years of age, in which the anus is the erogenous zone, and toilet training is the source of conflict. 379
  etapa anal: segunda etapa que tiene lugar desde aproximadamente el año a los tres años de edad, en la cual el ano es la zona erógena y el entrenamiento para controlar los esfínteres es una fuente de conflicto.

analytical intelligence: the ability to break problems down into component parts, or analysis, for problem solving. 322
  inteligencia analítica: habilidad para descomponer los problemas en partes, o analizarlos, para resolverlos.

anchoring effect: the tendency to consider all of the information available, even when it is irrelevant. 317
  efecto anclaje: tendencia a considerar toda la información disponible, aunque sea irrelevante.

andropause: gradual changes in the sexual hormones and reproductive system of middle-aged males. 167
  andropausia: cambios graduales en las hormonas sexuales y en el sistema reproductor masculino en hombres de mediana edad.

anorexia nervosa: a condition in which a person reduces eating to the point that a weight loss of 15 percent below the ideal body weight or more occurs. 351
  anorexia nerviosa: afección en la cual la persona reduce la ingesta al punto que se produce una pérdida de peso de por lo menos el 15 por ciento por debajo del peso ideal o más.

anterograde amnesia: loss of memory from the point of injury or trauma forward, or the inability to form new long-term memories. 296
  amnesia anterógrada: pérdida de la memoria desde el punto de lesión o trauma hacia adelante, o incapacidad de formar recuerdos a largo plazo.

antianxiety drugs: drugs used to treat and calm anxiety reactions, typically minor tranquilizers. 466
  fármacos ansiolíticos: fármacos que se u san para tratar y calmar reacciones de ansiedad; generalmente son tranquilizantes suaves.

anticonvulsant drugs: drugs traditionally used to treat seizure disorders and sometimes used in treating mania. 468
  fármacos anticonvulsivos: fármacos que tradicionalmente se usan para tratar trastornos convulsivos y, algunas veces, las manías.

antidepressant drugs: drugs used to treat depression and anxiety. 467
  fármacos antidepresivos: fármacos que se usan para tratar la depresión y la ansiedad.

antimanic drugs: drugs used to bipolar disorder and episodes of mania. 467
  fármacos antimaníacos: fármacos que se usan para el tratamiento de trastornos bipolares y episodios de manías.

antipsychotic drugs: drugs used to treat psychotic symptoms such as delusions, hallucinations, and other bizarre behavior. 465
  fármacos antipsicóticos: fármacos que se usan para tratar síntomas psicóticos como delirios, alucinaciones y otras conductas extravagantes.

antisocial personality disorder: disorder in which a person has no morals or conscience, manipulates others, and often behaves in an impulsive manner without regard for the consequences of that behavior. 434
  trastorno de personalidad antisocial: trastorno en el cual la persona no tiene moral ni conciencia, manipula a otros y, con frecuencia, se comporta de manera impulsiva sin tener en cuenta las consecuencias de ese comportamiento.

anxiety disorders: disorders in which the main symptom is excessive or unrealistic anxiety and fearfulness. 421
  trastornos de ansiedad: trastornos en los cuales el síntoma principal es la ansiedad y el temor excesivo o irreal.

applied behavior analysis (ABA): modern term for a form of behavior modification that uses shaping techniques to mold a desired behavior or response. 192
  análisis conductual aplicado: término moderno que describe una forma de modificación de la conducta que usa técnicas de modelado para obtener una conducta o respuesta deseada.

applied behavior analysis (behavior modification): the use of learning techniques to modify or change undesirable behavior and increase desirable behavior. 452
  análisis conductual aplicado (modificación de conducta): uso de técnicas de aprendizaje para modificar o cambiar conductas no deseadas e incrementar las conductas deseadas.

applied psychology: the use of psychological concepts in solving real-world problems. 514
  psicología aplicada: uso de conceptos de psicología para resolver problemas de la vida real.

arbitrary inference: distortion in which a person draws a conclusion that is not based on any evidence. 455
  inferencia arbitraria: distorsión en la cual la persona saca una conclusión que no se basa en ninguna evidencia.

archetypes: Jung's collective, universal human memories. 382
  arquetipos: recuerdos humanos universales y colectivos de Jung.

arousal theory: theory of motivation in which people are said to have an optimal (best or ideal) level of tension that they seek to maintain by increasing or decreasing stimulation. 344
  teoría de la excitación: teoría de la motivación que sostiene que las personas tienen un nivel de tensión óptimo (mejor o ideal) que buscan mantener, aumentando o disminuyendo la estimulación.

artificial intelligence (AI): the creation of a machine that can think like a human. 312
  inteligencia artificial: creación de una máquina que puede pensar como un ser humano.

assimilation: the process of trying to understand new things in terms of schemes one already possesses. 153
  asimilación: proceso de tratar de comprender cosas nuevas en términos de patrones que uno ya posee.

association areas: areas within each lobe of the cortex responsible for the coordination and interpretation of information, as well as higher mental processing. 61
  áreas de asociación: áreas dentro de cada lóbulo de la corteza cerebral responsables de la coordinación e interpretación de la información, así como del procesamiento mental superior.

attachment: the first emotional bond a child forms with its primary caretaker. 143
  apego: primer vínculo emocional que forma un niño con su cuidador primario.

attitude: a tendency to respond positively or negatively toward a certain person, object, idea, or situation. 224
  actitud: tendencia a responder de manera positiva o negativa a cierta persona, objeto, idea o situación.

attribution: the process of explaining one's own behavior and the behavior of others. 229
  atribución: proceso de explicar el propio comportamiento y el de los otros.

attribution theory: the theory of how people make attributions. 229
  teoría de la atribución: teoría de cómo las personas hacen atribuciones.

atypical neuroleptics: antipsychotic drugs that suppress dopamine to a much greater degree in one particular dopamine pathway related to psychoses, and which also block or partially block certain serotonin receptors. 466
  antipsicóticos atípicos: fármacos antipsicóticos que suprimen la dopamina en un grado mucho mayor en una vía de dopamina particular relacionada con las psicosis y que también bloquean total o parcialmente algunos receptores de la serotonina.

auditory canal: short tunnel that runs from the pinna to the eardrum. 87
  canal auditivo: pequeño túnel que se extiende desde el pabellón de la oreja hasta el tímpano.

auditory nerve: bundle of axons from the hair cells in the inner ear. 87
  nervio auditivo: grupo de axones en las células pilosas del oído interno.

authenticity: the genuine, open, and honest response of the therapist to the client. 451
  autenticidad: respuesta genuina, abierta y honesta del terapeuta a su cliente.

autobiographical memory: the memory for events and facts related to one's personal life story. 297
  memoria autobiográfica: recuerdo de eventos y hechos relacionados con la historia personal.

automatic encoding: tendency of certain kinds of information to enter long-term memory with little or no effortful encoding. 289
  procesamiento automático: tendencia de ciertos tipos de información a ingresar en la memoria a largo plazo con poco o ningún esfuerzo de codificación.

autonomic nervous system (ANS): division of the PNS consisting of nerves that control all of the involuntary muscles, organs, and glands. 49
  sistema nervioso autónomo: división del sistema nervioso periférico que consiste en los nervios que controlan todos los músculos, los órganos y las glándulas involuntarias.

availability heuristic: the tendency to estimate the probability of a certain condition or event based on how many similar instances we can recall. 317
  disponibilidad heurística: tendencia a estimar la probabilidad de cierta condición o evento sobre la base de la cantidad de instancias similares que podemos recordar.

aversion therapy: the pairing of an undesirable behavior with an aversive stimulus to reduce the frequency of the behavior. 452
  terapia de aversión: unión de una conducta indeseable con un estímulo desagradable para reducir la frecuencia de la conducta.

axon: tubelike structure that carries the neural message to other cells. 42
  axón: estructura tubular que transporta el mensaje neural a otras células.

axon terminals: branches at the end of the axon. 46
  terminales del axón: ramales en el extremo del axón.

B

barbiturates: depressant drugs that have a sedative effect. 128
  barbitúricos: fármacos depresivos que tienen un efecto sedante.

basal metabolic rate (BMR): the rate at which the body burns energy when the organism is resting. 350
  metabolismo basal: velocidad a la cual el cuerpo quema energía cuando el organismo está en reposo.

basic anxiety: anxiety created when a child is born into the bigger and more powerful world of older children and adults. 382
  ansiedad básica: ansiedad que aparece cuando el niño nace en el grande y poderoso mundo de adultos y niños mayores.

basic level type: an example of a type of concept around which other similar concepts are organized, such as "dog," "cat," or "pear." 308
  tipo de nivel básico: ejemplo de un tipo de concepto alrededor del cual se organizan otros conceptos similares, como "perro", "gato" o "pera".

behavior modification: the use of operant conditioning techniques to bring about desired changes in behavior. 192
  modificación de conducta: uso de técnicas de condicionamiento operante para producir cambios de conducta deseados.

behavior therapies: action therapies based on the principles of classical and operant conditioning and aimed at changing disordered behavior without concern for the original causes of such behavior. 451
  terapias de conducta: terapias de acción que se basan en principios de condicionamiento clásico u operante y que apuntan a cambiar conductas alteradas sin preocuparse por las causas originales de tal conducta.

behavioral genetics: field of study examining how personality is formed through inherited traits expressed within a particular environment. 396
  genética conductual: ciencia que estudia cómo se forma la personalidad mediante los rasgos heredados que se expresan en un ambiente particular.

behaviorism: the science of behavior that focuses on observable behavior only. 8
  conductismo: ciencia de la conducta que se focaliza solo en la conducta observable.

bell curve: alternate name for the normal curve, which is said to be shaped like a bell. 30
  curva de campana: nombre alternativo de la curva normal, que se dice que tiene la forma de una campana.

benzodiazepines: drugs that lower anxiety and reduce stress. 128, 466
  benzodiazepinas: fármacos que reducen la ansiedad y el estrés.

bilateral cingulotomy: psychosurgical technique in which an electrode wire is inserted into the cingulated gyrus with the guidance of a magnetic resonance imaging machine for the purpose of destroying that area of brain tissue with an electric current. 469
  cingulotomía bilateral: técnica psicoquirúrgica en la cual se inserta un electrodo en la circunvolución cingular con la guía de una máquina de imagen por resonancia magnética con el propósito de destruir esa área de tejido cerebral con una corriente eléctrica.

bilateral ECT: electroconvulsive therapy in which the electrodes are placed on both sides of the head. 468
  terapia electroconvulsiva bilateral: terapia electroconvulsiva en la cual se colocan electrodos en ambos lados de la cabeza.

binocular cues: cues for perceiving depth based on both eyes. 97
  pistas binoculares: pistas para percibir la profundidad con base en ambos ojos.

binocular disparity: the difference in images between the two eyes, which is greater for objects that are close and smaller for distant objects. 98
disparidad binocular: diferencia en imágenes entre ambos ojos, que es mayor para los objetos cercanos y menor para los objetos lejanos.

biofeedback: using feedback about biological conditions to bring involuntary responses, such as blood pressure and relaxation, under voluntary control. 192
biorretroalimentación: uso de la retroalimentación de las condiciones biológicas para lograr que ciertas respuestas involuntarias, como tensión arterial y relajación, estén bajo control voluntario.

biological model: model of explaining behavior as caused by biological changes in the chemical, structural, or genetic systems of the body. 413
modelo biológico: modelo que sostiene que la conducta es causada por cambios biológicos en el sistema químico, estructural o genético del cuerpo.

biological preparedness: referring to the tendency of animals to learn certain associations, such as taste and nausea, with only one or few pairings due to the survival value of the learning. 182
predisposición biológica: tendencia de los animales a aprender ciertas asociaciones, como gusto y náusea, con solo una o algunas uniones debido al valor de supervivencia de la enseñanza.

biomedical therapy: therapy for mental disorders in which a person with a problem is treated with biological or medical methods to relieve symptoms. 446
terapia biomédica: terapia para trastornos mentales en la cual se trata a la persona que tiene un problema con métodos biológicos o médicos para aliviar los síntomas.

biopsychological perspective: perspective that attributes human and animal behavior to biological events occurring in the body, such as genetic influences, hormones, and the activity of the nervous system. 11
perspectiva biopsicológica: perspectiva que atribuye la conducta humana y animal a los eventos biológicos que ocurren en el cuerpo, como influencias genéticas, hormonas y la actividad del sistema nervioso.

biopsychosocial model: perspective in which abnormal behavior is seen as the result of the combined and interacting forces of biological, psychological, social, and cultural influences. 413
modelo biopsicosocial: perspectiva según la cual la conducta anormal es vista como el resultado de las fuerzas interrelacionadas y combinadas de influencias biológicas, psicológicas, sociales y culturales.

bipolar disorder: severe mood swings between major depressive episodes and manic episodes. 429
trastorno bipolar: cambios drásticos del estado de ánimo entre grandes episodios depresivos y episodios maníacos.

blind spot: the area in the retina where the axons of the three layers of retinal cells exit the eye to form the optic nerve, insensitive to light. 82
punto ciego: área de la retina donde los axones de las tres capas de células retinales salen del ojo para formar el nervio óptico, insensible a la luz.

borderline personality disorder: maladaptive personality pattern in which the person is moody, unstable, lacks a clear sense of identity, and often clings to others. 435
trastorno límite de la personalidad: esquema de personalidad inadaptiva en el cual la persona es temperamental, inestable, carece de un sentido de la identidad claro y con frecuencia se aferra a otros.

bottom-up processing: the analysis of the smaller features to build up to a complete perception. 101
procesamiento del fondo hacia arriba: análisis de las características más pequeñas hasta llegar a una percepción completa.

brightness constancy: the tendency to perceive the apparent brightness of an object as the same even when the light conditions change. 95
constancia de brillantez: tendencia a percibir la brillantez aparente de un objeto como constante incluso cuando las condiciones de luz varían.

Broca's aphasia: condition resulting from damage to Broca's area, causing the affected person to be unable to speak fluently, to mispronounce words, and to speak haltingly. 205
afasia de Broca: afección que se produce como resultado de una lesión en el área de Broca, que causa que la persona afectada sea incapaz de hablar de manera fluida, pronuncie palabras incorrectamente y hable de manera entrecortada.

bulimia nervosa: a condition in which a person develops a cycle of "binging," or overeating enormous amounts of food at one sitting, and then using unhealthy methods to avoid weight gain. 351
bulimia nerviosa: afección en la cual la persona desarrolla un ciclo en el cual ingiere grandes cantidades de alimentos de una vez (atracones) y luego usa métodos no saludables para evitar ganar peso.

burnout: negative changes in thoughts, emotions, and behavior as a result of prolonged stress or frustration. 486
agotamiento: cambios negativos en los pensamientos, las emociones y la conducta como resultado de estrés o frustración prolongada.

bystander effect: referring to the effect that the presence of other people has on the decision to help or not help, with help becoming less likely as the number of bystanders increases. 240
efecto espectador: efecto que tiene la presencia de otras personas sobre la decisión de ayudar o no ayudar, donde la probabilidad de ayudar disminuye a medida que la cantidad de espectadores aumenta.

C

caffeine: a mild stimulant found in coffee, tea, and several other plant-based substances. 128
cafeína: estimulante suave que se encuentra en el café, el té y otras sustancias de origen vegetal.

Cannon-Bard theory of emotion: theory in which the physiological reaction and the emotion are assumed to occur at the same time. 361
teoría de la emoción de Cannon-Bard: teoría que sostiene que la reacción fisiológica y la emoción ocurren al mismo tiempo.

case study: study of one individual in great detail. 18
estudio de caso: estudio de una persona con gran detalle.

catastrophe: an unpredictable, large-scale event that creates a tremendous need to adapt and adjust, as well as overwhelming feelings of threat. 483
catástrofe: evento impredecible de gran escala que crea una necesidad tremenda de adaptación, así como un sobrecogedor sentimiento de amenaza.

catatonic: type of schizophrenia in which the person experiences periods of statue-like immobility mixed with occasional bursts of energetic, frantic movement, and talking. 432
catatónica: tipo de esquizofrenia en la cual la persona experimenta períodos de inmovilidad similar a la de una estatua mezclados con ocasionales despliegues de movimientos energéticos y frenéticos y habla.

central nervous system (CNS): part of the nervous system consisting of the brain and spinal cord. 47
sistema nervioso central: parte del sistema nervioso que consiste en el cerebro y la médula espinal.

central-route processing: type of information processing that involves attending to the content of the message itself. 229
procesamiento a través de ruta central: tipo de procesamiento de la información que implica prestar atención al contenido mismo del mensaje.

centration: in Piaget's theory, the tendency of a young child to focus only on one feature of an object while ignoring other relevant features. 154
centración: en la teoría de Piaget, tendencia de los niños pequeños a focalizarse solo en una característica de un objeto, mientras ignoran otras características relevantes.

cerebellum: part of the lower brain located behind the pons that controls and coordinates involuntary, rapid, fine motor movement. 58
   cerebelo: parte del cerebro inferior ubicada detrás del puente de Varolio que controla y coordina el movimiento involuntario, rápido y motor fino.

cerebral hemispheres: the two sections of the cortex on the left and right sides of the brain. 60
   hemisferios cerebrales: las dos secciones de la corteza cerebral a los lados derecho e izquierdo del cerebro.

character: value judgments of a person's moral and ethical behavior. 376
   carácter: juicio de valor de la conducta moral y ética de una persona.

chromosome: tightly wound strand of genetic material or DNA. 66, 142
   cromosoma: segmento de material genético o ADN.

circadian rhythm: a cycle of bodily rhythm that occurs over a 24-hour period. 112
   ritmo circadiano: ciclo de ritmo corporal que ocurre en un período de 24 horas.

classical conditioning: learning in which one learns an involuntary response when a stimulus that normally causes a particular response is paired with a new neutral stimulus. After enough pairings, the new stimulus will also cause the response to occur. 178, 451
   condicionamiento clásico: aprendizaje en el cual uno aprende una respuesta involuntaria cuando un estímulo que normalmente causa una respuesta particular se une con un estímulo nuevo y neutral. Después de las suficientes uniones, el nuevo estímulo también motiva la respuesta.

clinical psychology: area of psychology in which the psychologists diagnose and treat people with psychological disorders that may range from mild to severe. 12
   psicología clínica: área de la psicología que diagnostica y trata a las personas con trastornos psicológicos que van de moderados a severos.

closure: the tendency to complete figures that are incomplete. 95
   cierre: tendencia a completar figuras que están incompletas.

cocaine: a natural drug derived from the leaves of the coca plant. 127
   cocaína: droga natural derivada de las hojas de la planta de coca.

cochlea: snail-shaped structure of the inner ear that is filled with fluid. 87
   cóclea: estructura con forma de caracol ubicada en el oído interno que está llena de líquido.

cognitive development: development of thinking and reasoning skills, such as problem-solving and memory. 142
   desarrollo cognitivo: desarrollo de habilidades de pensamiento y razonamiento, como resolución de problemas y memoria.

cognitive dissonance: sense of discomfort or distress that occurs when a person's behavior does not correspond to that person's attitudes. 227
   disonancia cognitiva: sensación de incomodidad o angustia que ocurre cuando la conducta de una persona no corresponde a su actitud.

cognitive neuroscience: study of the physical changes in the brain and nervous system during thinking. 10
   neurociencia cognitiva: estudio de los cambios físicos en el cerebro y el sistema nervioso durante el razonamiento.

cognitive perspective: modern perspective that focuses on memory, intelligence, perception, problem solving, and learning. 10
   perspectiva cognitiva: perspectiva moderna que se focaliza en la memoria, la inteligencia, la percepción, la resolución de problemas y el aprendizaje.

cognitive therapy: therapy focused on helping clients recognize distortions in their thinking and replace distorted, unrealistic beliefs with more realistic, helpful thoughts. 454
   terapia cognitiva: terapia que se focaliza en ayudar a los clientes a reconocer las distorsiones en su razonamiento y a reemplazar creencias distorsionadas y poco realistas con pensamientos más realistas y útiles.

cognitive universalism: theory that concepts are universal and influence the development of language. 203
   universalismo cognitivo: teoría que sostiene que los conceptos son universales y que influyen en el desarrollo del lenguaje.

cognitive-behavioral therapy (CBT): action therapy in which the goal is to help clients overcome problems by learning to think more rationally and logically. 456
   terapia cognitivo-conductual: terapia activa en la cual el objetivo es ayudar a los clientes a superar los problemas enseñándoles a pensar de manera más racional y lógica.

cognitive-mediational theory: theory of emotion in which a stimulus must be interpreted (appraised) by a person in order to result in a physical response and an emotional reaction. 362
   teoría de mediación cognitiva: teoría de la emoción en la cual el estímulo debe ser interpretado (evaluado) por la persona para dar como resultado una respuesta física y una reacción emocional.

collective unconscious: Jung's name for the memories shared by all members of the human species. 382
   inconsciente colectivo: nombre dado por Jung a los recuerdos compartidos por todos los miembros de la especie humana.

collectivism: a cultural style that emphasizes the importance of interdependence, group goals, and group needs. 255
   colectivismo: estilo cultural que hace hincapié en la importancia de la interdependencia, los objetivos grupales y las necesidades del grupo.

companionate love: type of love consisting of intimacy and commitment. 237
   amor de compañía o sociable: tipo de amor consistente en intimidad y compromiso.

comparative psychology: area of psychology in which the psychologists study animals and their behavior for the purpose of comparing and contrasting it to human behavior. 14
   psicología comparada: área de la psicología que estudia a los animales y su conducta con el propósito de compararla y contrastarla con la conducta humana.

compensation (substitution): defense mechanism in which a person makes up for inferiorities in one area by becoming superior in another area. 502
   compensación (sustitución): mecanismo de defensa en el cual la persona compensa su inferioridad en un área al convertirse en superior en otra.

compliance: changing one's behavior as a result of other people directing or asking for the change. 216
   sumisión: cambio en la conducta personal a solicitud de otras personas.

computed tomography (CT): brain-imaging method using computer-controlled X-rays of the brain. 55
   tomografía computarizada: método de diagnóstico por imágenes del cerebro que usa rayos X controlados por computadora.

concentrative meditation: form of meditation in which a person focuses the mind on some repetitive or unchanging stimulus so that the mind can be cleared of disturbing thoughts, and the body can experience relaxation. 123
   meditación focalizada: forma de meditación en la cual la persona focaliza el pensamiento en un estímulo repetitivo o constante, para que la mente se limpie de pensamientos perturbadores y el cuerpo pueda relajarse.

conception: the moment at which a sperm and egg unite to form a single cell. 147
   concepción: momento en el que se unen el espermatozoide y el óvulo para formar una sola célula.

concepts: ideas that represent a class or category of objects, events, or activities. 307
   conceptos: ideas que representan una clase o categoría de objetos, eventos o actividades.

concrete operations stage: third stage of cognitive development in which the school-age child becomes capable of logical thought processes but is not yet capable of abstract thinking. 154
etapa de las operaciones concretas: tercera etapa del desarrollo cognitivo en el cual el niño en edad escolar se vuelve capaz de tener procesos de razonamiento lógico si bien todavía no es capaz de tener un razonamiento abstracto.

conditional positive regard: positive regard that is given only when the person is doing what the providers of positive regard wish. 386
aprecio positivo condicional: aprecio positivo que se brinda solamente cuando la persona lleva a cabo lo que el proveedor de aprecio positivo desea.

conditioned emotional response (CER): emotional response that has become classically conditioned to occur to learned stimuli, such as a fear of dogs or the emotional reaction that occurs when seeing an attractive person. 181
respuesta emocional condicionada: respuesta emocional condicionada de manera clásica frente a un estímulo aprendido, como el temor a los perros o la reacción emocional que tiene lugar al ver a una persona atractiva.

conditioned response (CR): learned reflex response to a conditioned stimulus. 179
respuesta condicionada: respuesta refleja aprendida a un estímulo condicionado.

conditioned stimulus (CS): stimulus that becomes able to produce a learned reflex response by being paired with the original unconditioned stimulus. 179
estímulo condicionado: estímulo capaz de producir una respuesta refleja aprendida al unirse con el estímulo original no condicionado.

conditioned taste aversion: development of a nauseated or aversive response to a particular taste because that taste was followed by a nausea reaction, occurring after only one association. 182
aversión del gusto condicionada: desarrollo de una respuesta repugnante o desagradable a un sabor particular debido a que ese sabor fue seguido de una reacción repugnante, después de una sola asociación.

cones: visual sensory receptors found at the back of the retina, responsible for color vision and sharpness of vision. 82
conos: receptores sensoriales visuales que se encuentran en la parte posterior de la retina y son responsables de la visión de los colores y de la agudeza visual.

confirmation bias: the tendency to search for evidence that fits one's beliefs while ignoring any evidence that does not fit those beliefs. 314
sesgo de confirmación: tendencia a buscar evidencia que satisface las propias creencias, ignorando toda otra evidencia en contrario.

conformity: changing one's own behavior to match that of other people. 215
conformidad: cambiar la conducta personal para adecuarse a la de otras personas.

confounding variable: variable in an experiment that may unintentionally affect the dependent variable. 21
variable de confusión: variable de un experimento que puede afectar de manera no intencional la variable dependiente.

conjunction fallacy: the error of believing specific conditions are more probable than a single general one. 317
falacia de la conjunción: error de creer que ciertas condiciones específicas son más probables que una condición general simple.

conscience: part of the superego that produces pride or guilt, depending on how acceptable behavior is. 378
conciencia: parte del superyó que produce orgullo o culpa, según qué tan aceptable es la conducta.

conscientiousness: the care a person gives to organization and thoughtfulness of others; dependability. 388
escrupulosidad: atención que una persona presta a la organización y a la consideración hacia los otros; confiabilidad.

consciousness: a person's awareness of everything that is going on around him or her at any given moment, which is used to organize behavior. 110
conciencia: conocimiento de la persona de todo lo que ocurre a su alrededor en todo momento, que se usa para organizar la conducta.

conservation: in Piaget's theory, the ability to understand that simply changing the appearance of an object does not change the object's nature. 154
conservación: en la teoría de Piaget, habilidad de comprender que solo cambiar la apariencia de un objeto no hace que cambie su naturaleza.

constructive processing: referring to the retrieval of memories in which those memories are altered, revised, or influenced by newer information. 291
procesamiento constructivo: recuperación de recuerdos en la cual tales recuerdos se ven alterados, revisados o influenciados por información nueva.

consumer psychology: branch of psychology that studies the habits of consumers in the marketplace. 216
psicología del consumidor: rama de la psicología que estudia los hábitos de los consumidores en el mercado.

contiguity: the tendency to perceive two things that happen close together in time as being related. 96
contigüidad: tendencia a percibir que dos cosas que suceden casi al mismo tiempo están relacionadas.

contingency contracting: the use of a formal, written agreement between the therapist and client (or other parties) that clearly states behavioral goals, reinforcements, and penalties. 453
contrato de contingencias: uso de un acuerdo formal, por escrito, entre el terapeuta y el cliente (o terceros) que establece claramente los objetivos, los refuerzos y las penalidades conductuales.

continuity: the tendency to perceive things as simply as possible with a continuous pattern rather than with a complex, broken-up pattern. 95
continuidad: tendencia a percibir las cosas de la manera más simple posible con un patrón continuo en lugar de hacerlo con un patrón complejo y discontinuo.

continuous reinforcement: the reinforcement of each and every correct response. 189
refuerzo continuo: refuerzo de todas y cada una de las respuestas correctas.

control group: subjects in an experiment who are not subjected to the independent variable and who may receive a placebo treatment. 21
grupo de control: en un experimento, sujetos que no están sometidos a la variable independiente y que pueden recibir un tratamiento placebo.

conventional morality: second level of Kohlberg's stages of moral development in which the child's behavior is governed by conforming to the society's norms of behavior. 164
moral convencional: segundo nivel de desarrollo moral de las etapas de Kohlberg en el cual la conducta del niño es gobernada por el cumplimiento de las normas de conducta de la sociedad.

convergence: the rotation of the two eyes in their sockets to focus on a single object, resulting in greater convergence for closer objects and lesser convergence if objects are distant. 98
convergencia: rotación de ambos ojos en sus órbitas para focalizarse en un solo objeto, que da como resultado mayor convergencia para los objetos cercanos y menor convergencia para los objetos lejanos.

convergent thinking: type of thinking in which a problem is seen as having only one answer, and all lines of thinking will eventually lead to that single answer, using previous knowledge and logic. 315
pensamiento convergente: tipo de pensamiento en el cual se considera que el problema tiene una sola solución y todas las líneas de pensamiento eventualmente llevan a esa única respuesta, usando los conocimientos previos y la lógica.

conversion disorder: somatoform disorder in which the person experiences a specific symptom in the somatic nervous system's functioning, such as paralysis, numbness, or blindness, for which there is no physical cause. 425
trastorno de conversión: trastorno somatoforme en el cual la persona experimenta un síntoma específico en el funcionamiento del sistema nervioso somático, como parálisis, entumecimiento o ceguera, para el cual no hay causa física.

coping strategies: actions that people can take to master, tolerate, reduce, or minimize the effects of stressors. 500
estrategias de afrontamiento: acciones que inician las personas para controlar, tolerar, reducir o minimizar los efectos de un factor estresante.

corpus callosum: thick band of neurons that connects the right and left cerebral hemispheres. 60
cuerpo calloso: banda gruesa de neuronas que conecta los hemisferios cerebrales izquierdo y derecho.

correlation: a measure of the relationship between two variables. 19
correlación: medida de la relación entre dos variables.

correlation coefficient: a number derived from the formula for measuring a correlation and indicating the strength and direction of a correlation. 19
coeficiente de correlación: número derivado de la fórmula para medir una correlación y que indica la fuerza y dirección de la correlación.

cortex: outermost covering of the brain consisting of densely packed neurons, responsible for higher thought processes and interpretation of sensory input. 60
corteza cerebral: cubierta exterior del cerebro que consiste en un denso conjunto de neuronas, responsables de los procesos de pensamiento superiores y de la interpretación de los datos sensoriales.

counseling psychology: area of psychology in which the psychologists help people with problems of adjustment. 12
orientación: área de la psicología que ayuda a las personas con problemas de adaptación.

creative intelligence: the ability to deal with new and different concepts and to come up with new ways of solving problems. 322
inteligencia creativa: habilidad para afrontar conceptos nuevos y diferentes y encontrar nuevas maneras de resolver problemas.

creativity: the process of solving problems by combining ideas or behavior in new ways. 315
creatividad: proceso de resolver problemas mediante la combinación de ideas o conductas de maneras nuevas.

critical period: a time when a child is developmentally most susceptible to the presence or absence of particular stimuli in the environment and must progress to the next stage of development if development is to continue normally. 144
período crítico: período en el cual el niño está madurativamente más susceptible a la presencia o ausencia de estímulos particulares en el entorno y debe progresar a la siguiente etapa de desarrollo si su crecimiento continúa normalmente.

cross-cultural psychology: the study of human thought and behavior across cultures. 257
psicología transcultural: estudio del pensamiento y la conducta humana en distintas culturas.

cross-sectional design: research design in which several different age groups are studied at one time. 144
diseño transversal: diseño de investigación en el cual se estudian distintos grupos de edad al mismo tiempo.

cross-sequential design: a combination of the longitudinal and cross-sectional designs in which different participants of various ages are compared at several points in time. 144
diseño secuencial: combinación de los diseños longitudinal y transversal, en la cual los distintos participantes de distintas edades se comparan en varios puntos en el tiempo.

cultural bias: the tendency of IQ tests to reflect, in language, dialect, and content, the culture of the test designer(s). 328
sesgo cultural: tendencia de las pruebas de coeficiente intelectual que refleja, en lenguaje, dialecto y contenido, la cultura de sus diseñadores.

cultural relativity: the need to consider the unique characteristics of the culture in which behavior takes place. 411
relatividad cultural: necesidad de considerar las características únicas de la cultura en la cual ocurre determinada conducta.

culture: a shared set of beliefs, behaviors, values, and attitudes held by a group of people or a society. 250
cultura: conjunto de creencias, conductas, valores y actitudes compartidas por un grupo de personas o una sociedad.

culture-bound: found only in particular cultures. 257
ligado a la cultura: que solo se encuentra en determinadas culturas.

culture-bound syndromes: disorders found only in particular cultures. 411
síndromes ligados a la cultura: trastornos que solo se encuentran en determinadas culturas.

curve of forgetting: a graph showing a distinct pattern in which forgetting is very fast within the first hour after learning a list and then tapers off gradually. 294
curva del olvido: gráfica que muestra un patrón distintivo en el cual el olvido es muy rápido durante la primera hora después de aprender una lista y luego disminuye gradualmente.

cyclothymia: disorder that consists of mood swings from moderate depression to hypomania and lasts two years or more. 427
ciclotimia: trastorno que consiste en cambios del estado de ánimo de depresión moderada a hipomanía y que dura dos años o más.

D

dark adaptation: the recovery of the eye's sensitivity to visual stimuli in darkness after exposure to bright lights. 83
adaptación a la oscuridad: recuperación de la sensibilidad del ojo al estímulo visual en la oscuridad después de haber estado expuesto a la luz brillante.

decay: loss of memory due to the passage of time, during which the memory trace is not used. 295
deterioro: pérdida de la memoria debido al paso del tiempo, durante el cual no se usa el rastro de memoria.

declarative memory: type of long-term memory containing information that is conscious and known. 281
memoria declarativa: tipo de memoria a largo plazo que contiene información consciente y conocida.

deep lesioning: insertion of a thin, insulated wire into the brain through which an electrical current is sent that destroys the brain cells at the tip of the wire. 54
lesión cerebral por radiofrecuencia: inserción de un cable delgado y aislado en el cerebro mediante el cual se envía una corriente eléctrica que destruye las células que se encuentran en el extremo del cable.

deficiency needs: in Maslow's theory, these are physical survival needs, such as the need for food. 346
necesidades de deficiencia: en la teoría de Maslow, necesidades de supervivencia física, como la necesidad de alimentos.

delta waves: long, slow waves that indicate the deepest stage of sleep. 113
ondas delta: ondas largas y lentas que indican un estado profundo de sueño.

delusional disorder: a psychotic disorder in which the primary symptom is one or more delusions. 431
trastorno delusorio: trastorno psicótico en el cual el síntoma principal es uno o varios delirios.

delusions: false beliefs held by a person who refuses to accept evidence of their falseness. 430
delirios: creencias falsas que sostiene la persona que rehúsa aceptar evidencia de su falsedad.

dendrites: branchlike structures that receive messages from other neurons. 42
   dendritas: estructuras similares a ramas que reciben los mensajes de otras neuronas.

denial: psychological defense mechanism in which the person refuses to acknowledge or recognize a threatening situation. 502
   negación: mecanismo psicológico de defensa en el cual la persona se niega a aceptar o reconocer una situación de amenaza.

dependent variable: variable in an experiment that represents the measurable response or behavior of the subjects in the experiment. 21
   variable dependiente: en un experimento, variable que representa la respuesta o conducta mensurable de un sujeto dentro del experimento.

depressants: drugs that decrease the functioning of the nervous system. 126
   depresor: fármacos que disminuyen el funcionamiento del sistema nervioso.

depth perception: the ability to perceive the world in three dimensions. 96
   percepción de profundidad: capacidad de percibir el mundo en tres dimensiones.

descriptive statistics: a way of organizing numbers and summarizing them so that patterns can be determined. 26
   estadística descriptiva: manera de organizar números y sintetizarlos para hallar patrones.

desensitization: in the treatment of phobias, the process of repeated, gradually more intense exposure to a frightening stimulus for the purpose of reducing or eliminating the fear response. 365
   desensibilización: en el tratamiento de fobias, proceso de exponer de manera gradual y repetida a la persona a un estímulo atemorizante con el propósito de reducir o eliminar la respuesta de miedo.

developmental psychology: area of psychology in which the psychologists study the changes in the way people think, relate to others, and feel as they age. 13
   psicología evolutiva: área de la psicología que estudia los cambios en la manera de pensar de las personas, de relacionarse con otros y de sentir a medida que envejecen.

developmentally delayed: condition in which a person's behavioral and cognitive skills exist at an earlier developmental stage than the skills of others who are the same chronological age. 324
   evolutivamente retrasado: afección en la cual las habilidades cognitivas y conductuales de la persona están en una etapa evolutiva anterior a las de otros que tienen la misma edad cronológica.

deviation IQ scores: a type of intelligence measure that assumes that IQ is normally distributed around a mean of 100 with a standard deviation of about 15. 328
   coeficiente intelectual de desviación: tipo de medida de la inteligencia que supone que el coeficiente intelectual normalmente se distribuye alrededor de una media de 100 con una desviación estándar de alrededor de 15.

diffusion of responsibility: occurring when a person fails to take responsibility for actions or for inaction because of the presence of other people who are seen to share the responsibility. 240
   difusión de la responsabilidad: ocurre cuando una persona no asume la responsabilidad de sus acciones o inacciones debido a la presencia de otras personas que se considera que comparten la responsabilidad.

direct observation: assessment in which the professional observes the client engaged in ordinary, day-to-day behavior in either a clinical or natural setting. 394
   observación directa: evaluación en la cual el profesional observa al cliente mientras está ocupado en actividades habituales tanto en un entorno clínico como en un entorno natural.

discrimination: treating people differently because of prejudice toward the social group to which they belong. 232
   discriminación: tratamiento diferencial que se da a otras personas debido a prejuicios hacia el grupo social al cual pertenecen.

discriminative stimulus: any stimulus, such as a stop sign or a doorknob, that provides the organism with a cue for making a certain response in order to obtain reinforcement. 188
   estímulo discriminativo: todo estímulo, como una señal de alto o la perilla de una puerta, que brinda al organismo una pista para realizar cierta respuesta para obtener un refuerzo.

disorganized: type of schizophrenia in which behavior is bizarre and childish and thinking, speech, and motor actions are very disordered. 431
   desorganizada: tipo de esquizofrenia en la cual la conducta es extravagante e infantil y el razonamiento, el discurso y las acciones motoras son muy desorganizadas.

displaced aggression: taking out one's frustrations on some less threatening or more available target, a form of displacement. 499
   agresión desplazada: descargar las frustraciones personales en un objetivo menos amenazante o más accesible; forma de desplazamiento.

displacement: redirecting feelings from a threatening target to a less threatening one. 502
   desplazamiento: redireccionamiento de los sentimientos de un objetivo amenazante a uno menos amenazante.

display rules: learned ways of controlling displays of emotion in social settings. 258, 363
   reglas de exhibición: maneras aprendidas de controlar la exhibición de las emociones en entornos sociales.

dispositional cause: cause of behavior attributed to internal factors such as personality or character. 229
   causa disposicional: causa de conducta atribuida a factores internos como la personalidad o el carácter.

dissociative amnesia: loss of memory for personal information, either partial or complete. 426
   amnesia disociativa: pérdida de la memoria de la información personal, ya sea de manera parcial o completa.

dissociative disorders: disorders in which there is a separation in conscious awareness, memory, the sense of identity, or some combination. 426
   trastornos disociativos: trastornos en los cuales hay una separación de la percepción consciente, la memoria, el sentido de la identidad, o una combinación de ellos.

dissociative fugue: traveling away from familiar surroundings with amnesia for the trip and possible amnesia for personal information. 426
   fuga disociativa: viaje lejos del entorno familiar con pérdida de la memoria con respecto al viaje y posiblemente también con respecto a la información personal.

dissociative identity disorder: disorder occurring when a person seems to have two or more distinct personalities within one body. 426
   trastorno de identidad disociativo: trastorno que ocurre cuando una persona parece tener dos o más personalidades distintas dentro de su cuerpo.

distress: the effect of unpleasant and undesirable stressors. 483
   angustia: efecto producido por factores estresantes desagradables y no deseados.

disuse: another name for decay, assuming that memories that are not used will eventually decay and disappear. 295
   desuso: otro término para deterioro, que supone que los recuerdos que no se usan eventualmente se deterioran y desaparecen.

divergent thinking: type of thinking in which a person starts from one point and comes up with many different ideas or possibilities based on that point. 315
   pensamiento divergente: tipo de pensamiento en el cual la persona comienza desde un punto y surgen muchas ideas distintas o posibilidades sobre la base de ese punto.

DNA (deoxyribonucleic acid): special molecule that contains the genetic material of the organism. 66, 142
   ADN (ácido desoxirribonucleico): molécula especial que contiene el material genético del organismo.

doctor of philosophy (Ph.D.): a doctorate that is research oriented and culminates in a dissertation based on original research. 517
  doctor en filosofía: doctorado orientado a la investigación que culmina con una disertación que se basa en una investigación original.

doctor of psychology (Psy.D.): a doctorate that focuses on applying psychological principles and provides extensive hands-on experience working in a clinical or counseling setting. 517
  doctor en psicología: doctorado orientado a la aplicación de principios psicológicos y que brinda amplia experiencia práctica para el trabajo en un entorno clínico o de orientación.

doctorate: a graduate degree students may pursue after completing a four-year college degree or a master's degree. Generally, a doctorate takes 5–7 years to complete. It provides highly advanced academic training and requires extensive research and/or clinical practice. 517
  doctorado: título de grado al que los estudiantes pueden aspirar después de finalizar cuatro años de estudios universitarios o de maestría. Generalmente, un doctorado tarda de 5 a 7 años en finalizarse. Brinda entrenamiento académico muy avanzado y requiere amplia investigación y/o práctica clínica.

dominant: referring to a gene that actively controls the expression of a trait. 66, 142
  dominante: gen que controla activamente la expresión de un rasgo.

door-in-the-face technique: asking for a large commitment and being refused and then asking for a smaller commitment. 216
  técnica del portazo en la cara: procedimiento que consiste en solicitar un compromiso importante y, una vez rechazado, solicitar un compromiso menor.

dopamine: a neurotransmitter that seems to be involved in learning to predict and approach rewards and avoid punishments. 366
  dopamina: neurotransmisor que parece estar implicado en aprender a predecir y acercarse a las recompensas y aprender a evitar los castigos.

double-blind experiment: study in which neither the experimenter nor the subjects know if the subjects are in the experimental or control group. 22
  experimento doble ciego: estudio en el cual ni el experimentador ni los sujetos saben si los sujetos están en el grupo experimental o de control.

drive: a psychological tension and physical arousal arising when there is a need that motivates the organism to act in order to fulfill the need and reduce the tension. 343
  impulso: tensión psicológica y excitación física que aparece donde hay una necesidad que motiva al organismo a actuar para satisfacer la necesidad y reducir la tensión.

drive-reduction theory: approach to motivation that assumes behavior arises from physiological needs that cause internal drives to push the organism to satisfy the need and reduce tension and arousal. 343
  teoría de reducción del impulso: enfoque de la motivación que supone que el comportamiento surge de las necesidades fisiológicas que causan que los impulsos internos muevan al organismo para satisfacer la necesidad y reducir la tensión.

dysthymia: a moderate depression that lasts for two years or more and is typically a reaction to some external stressor. 427
  distimia: depresión moderada que dura dos años o más y que comúnmente es la reacción a un factor estresante externo.

E

eclectic therapies: therapy style that results from combining elements of several different therapy techniques. 459
  terapias eclécticas: estilo de terapia que es el resultado de la combinación de elementos de distintas técnicas de terapia.

educational psychology: area of psychology in which the psychologists are concerned with the study of human learning and development of new learning techniques. 522
  psicología educacional: área de la psicología que estudia el aprendizaje humano y el desarrollo de nuevas técnicas de aprendizaje.

effortful encoding: conscious process of entering information into long-term memory, often through elaborative rehearsal. 289
  codificación consciente: proceso consciente de ingresar información en la memoria a largo plazo, con frecuencia mediante repeticiones elaboradas.

ego: part of the personality that develops out of a need to deal with reality, mostly conscious, rational, and logical. 378
  yo: parte de la personalidad que se desarrolla a partir de la necesidad de manejar la realidad, mayormente consciente, racional y lógica.

ego integrity: sense of wholeness that comes from having lived a full life and the ability to let go of regrets; the final completion of the ego. 166
  integridad del yo: sentido de la integridad que deriva de haber vivido una vida plena y sin arrepentimientos; realización del yo.

egocentrism: the inability to see the world through anyone else's eyes. 154
  egocentrismo: incapacidad de ver el mundo a través de los ojos de otra persona.

elaboration likelihood model: model of persuasion stating that people will either elaborate on the persuasive message or fail to elaborate on it and, that the future actions of those who do elaborate are more predictable than those who do not. 228
  modelo de la probabilidad de la elaboración: modelo de persuasión que sostiene que las personas procesan o no el mensaje persuasivo y que las acciones de aquellos que lo procesan son más predecibles que las de aquellos que no.

elaborative rehearsal: a method of transferring information from STM into LTM by making that information meaningful in some way. 280
  ensayo elaborativo: método por el que se transfiere la información de la memoria a corto plazo a la memoria a largo plazo al volverla importante de alguna manera.

electroconvulsive therapy (ECT): form of biomedical therapy used to treat severe depression, in which electrodes are placed on either one or both sides of a person's head, and an electric current is passed through the electrodes that is strong enough to cause a seizure or convulsion. 468
  terapia electroconvulsiva: forma de terapia biomédica que se usa para tratar depresiones severas, en la cual se colocan electrodos en uno o ambos lados de la cabeza de la persona y se pasa una corriente eléctrica lo suficientemente fuerte través de los electrodos para causar un ataque o una convulsión.

electroencephalograph (EEG): Equipment designed to record the brain-wave patterns produced by electrical activity of the surface of the brain. 56
  electroencefalógrafo: equipo diseñado para grabar los patrones de ondas cerebrales producidos por la actividad eléctrica de la superficie del cerebro.

embryo: name for the developing organism from two weeks to eight weeks after fertilization. 148
  embrión: nombre del organismo en desarrollo desde las dos hasta las ocho semanas después de la fertilización.

embryonic period: the period from two to eight weeks after fertilization during which the major organs and structures of the organism develop. 148
  período embrionario: período desde las dos hasta las ocho semanas después de la fertilización durante el cual se desarrollan los órganos y las estructuras principales del organismo.

emotion: the "feeling" aspect of consciousness, characterized by physical arousal, behavior that expresses or reveals the emotion, and an inner awareness of feelings. 358
  emoción: aspecto "sensible" de la conciencia, caracterizado por excitación física, conducta que expresa o revela la emoción y conciencia interna de los sentimientos.

emotional intelligence: the awareness of and ability to manage one's own emotions, as well as the ability to be self-motivated, able to feel what others feel, and socially skilled. 322
  inteligencia emocional: percepción y capacidad para manejar las propias emociones así como la capacidad de automotivarse, sentir lo que otros sienten y estar socialmente calificado.

emotion-focused coping: coping strategies that change the impact of a stressor by changing the emotional reaction to the stressor. 500
estrategia de afrontamiento focalizada en la emoción: estrategias de afrontamiento que cambian el impacto del factor estresante al cambiar la reacción emocional a este.

empathy: the ability of the therapist to understand the feelings of the client. 451
empatía: capacidad del terapeuta de comprender los sentimientos del cliente.

encoding: the set of mental operations that people perform on sensory information to convert that information into a form that is usable in the brain's storage systems. 274
codificación: conjunto de operaciones mentales que realizan las personas sobre la base de la información sensorial para convertir esa información en una forma utilizable en los sistemas de almacenamiento del cerebro.

encoding failure: failure to process information into memory. 294
falla de codificación: incapacidad de procesar la información para convertirla en memoria.

encoding specificity: the tendency for memory of information to be improved if related information (such as surroundings or physiological state) available when the memory is first formed is also available when the memory is being retrieved. 285
especificidad de codificación: tendencia a mejorar la memoria de la información si la información relacionada (como el entorno o el estado fisiológico) disponible en el momento de formación del recuerdo también está disponible en el momento en que se recupera ese recuerdo.

endocrine glands: glands that secrete chemicals called hormones directly into the bloodstream. 50
glándulas endocrinas: glándulas que secretan químicos llamados hormonas directamente en el torrente sanguíneo.

environmental psychology: area of psychology in which the focus is on how people interact with and are affected by their physical environments. 524
psicología ambiental: área de la psicología en la cual el foco se encuentra en cómo las personas interactúan con sus entornos físicos y se ven afectadas por estos.

episodic memory: type of declarative memory containing personal information not readily available to others, such as daily activities and events. 281
memoria episódica: tipo de memoria declarativa que contiene información personal que no está disponible para otros, como actividades y eventos diarios.

equal status contact: contact between groups in which the groups have equal status, with neither group having power over the other. 235
contacto en estado igualitario: contacto entre grupos de igual estado, cuando ninguno de ellos tiene poder sobre el otro.

escape or withdrawal: leaving the presence of a stressor, either literally or by a psychological withdrawal into fantasy, drug abuse, or apathy. 499
escape o repliegue: abandonar el lugar en presencia de un factor estresante, ya sea de manera literal o mediante un repliegue psicológico en la fantasía, el abuso de drogas o la apatía.

eustress: the effect of positive events, or the optimal amount of stress that people need to promote health and well-being. 483
eustrés: efecto de los eventos positivos o cantidad de estrés óptima que las personas necesitan para promover la salud y el bienestar.

evolution: a process of gradual change over time. 69
evolución: proceso de cambio gradual en el tiempo.

evolutionary psychology: perspective that focuses on the biological bases of universal mental characteristics that all humans share. 11
psicología evolutiva: perspectiva que se focaliza en las bases biológicas de las características mentales universales que comparten todos los seres humanos.

expectancy: (1) a person's subjective feeling that a particular behavior will lead to a reinforcing consequence. 385 (2) in expectancy-value theory, a belief about what will happen in the future based on past experiences. 346
expectativa: (1) sentimiento subjetivo de la persona de que una conducta particular dará como resultado una consecuencia de refuerzo. (2) en la teoría de las expectativas, creencia en lo que sucederá en el futuro basándose en experiencias pasadas.

expectancy-value theories: incentive theories that assume the actions of humans cannot be predicted or fully understood without understanding the beliefs, values, and the importance that a person attaches to those beliefs and values at any given moment in time. 346
teoría de las expectativas: teorías de la motivación que suponen que las acciones de los seres humanos no pueden ser totalmente predecibles o completamente entendibles sin la comprensión de las creencias, los valores y la importancia que la persona le confiere a esas creencias y valores en determinado momento.

experiment: a deliberate manipulation of a variable to see if corresponding changes in behavior result, allowing the determination of cause-and-effect relationships. 20
experimento: manipulación deliberada de una variable para ver si los cambios correspondientes en la conducta resultan, permitiendo la determinación de relaciones de causa y efecto.

experimental group: subjects in an experiment who are subjected to the independent variable. 21
grupo experimental: sujetos de un experimento que están sujetos a la variable independiente.

experimental psychology: area of psychology in which the psychologists primarily do research and experiments in the areas of learning, memory, thinking, perception, motivation, and language. 13
psicología experimental: área de la psicología que principalmente realiza experimentos e investiga en las áreas de aprendizaje, memoria, razonamiento, percepción, motivación y lenguaje.

experimenter effect: tendency of the experimenter's expectations for a study to unintentionally influence the results of the study. 22
efecto del experimentador: tendencia a que las expectativas de la persona que lleva a cabo el estudio influyan involuntariamente en los resultados.

explicit memory: memory that is consciously known, such as declarative memory. 281
memoria explícita: memoria que se conoce de manera consciente, como la memoria declarativa.

expressive language delay: the apparent ability of infants to understand far more language than they can produce. 156
retardo de lenguaje expresivo: capacidad aparente de los niños pequeños de comprender más lenguaje del que pueden producir.

extinction: the disappearance or weakening of a learned response following the removal or absence of the unconditioned stimulus (in classical conditioning) or the removal of a reinforcer (in operant conditioning). 180, 454
extinción: desaparición o debilitamiento de una respuesta aprendida después de quitar el estímulo no condicionado o ante la ausencia de este (en el condicionamiento clásico), o después de quitar el refuerzo (en el condicionamiento operante).

extraversion: dimension of personality referring to one's need to be with other people. 388
extraversión: dimensión de la personalidad que hace referencia a la necesidad de estar con otras personas.

extraverts: people who are outgoing and sociable. 388
extravertidas: personas extrovertidas y sociables.

extrinsic motivation: type of motivation in which a person performs an action because it leads to an outcome that is separate from or external to the person. 342
motivación extrínseca: tipo de motivación en la cual la persona realiza una acción porque llega a un resultado separado o externo a la persona.

GL-10 GLOSSARY/GLOSARIO

eye-movement desensitization reprocessing (EMDR): controversial form of therapy for post-traumatic stress disorder and similar anxiety problems in which the client is directed to move the eyes rapidly back and forth while thinking of a disturbing memory. 462
   desensibilización y reprocesamiento por movimientos oculares: controvertida forma de terapia para el trastorno de estrés postraumático y problemas de ansiedad similares en la cual se instruye al cliente para que mueva los ojos de un lado a otro rápidamente mientras piensa en un recuerdo perturbador.

F

facial feedback hypothesis: theory of emotion that assumes that facial expressions provide feedback to the brain concerning the emotion being expressed, which, in turn, causes and intensifies the emotion. 362
   hipótesis de la retroalimentación facial: teoría de la emoción que supone que las expresiones faciales brindan retroalimentación al cerebro con respecto a la emoción que expresan, que a su vez causa e intensifica la emoción.

false positive: error of recognition in which people think that they recognize some stimulus that is not actually in memory. 288
   falso positivo: error de reconocimiento en el cual las personas piensan que reconocieron algún estímulo que en realidad no está en la memoria.

family counseling (family therapy): a form of group therapy in which family members meet together with a counselor or therapist to resolve problems that affect the entire family. 457
   orientación familiar (terapia familiar): forma de terapia grupal en la cual los miembros de la familia se encuentran con un consejero o terapeuta para resolver problemas que afectan a toda la familia.

fertilization: the union of the ovum and sperm in the fallopian tube. 147
   fertilización: unión del óvulo y el espermatozoide en la trompa de Falopio.

fetal period: the time from about eight weeks after conception to the birth of the child. 148
   período fetal: tiempo que se extiende desde aproximadamente ocho semanas después de la concepción hasta el nacimiento de la criatura.

fetus: name for the developing organism from eight weeks after fertilization to the birth of the baby. 148
   feto: nombre que recibe el organismo en desarrollo desde las ocho semanas después de la fertilización hasta el nacimiento del bebé.

figure–ground: the tendency to perceive objects, or figures, as existing on a background. 95
   figura-fondo: tendencia a percibir objetos, o figuras, como partes del entorno.

five-factor model (Big Five): model of personality traits that describes five basic trait dimensions. 388
   modelo de los cinco factores: modelo de atributos de personalidad que describe cinco dimensiones de atributos básicos.

fixation: disorder in which the person does not fully resolve the conflict in a particular psychosexual stage, resulting in personality traits and behavior associated with that earlier stage. 379
   fijación: trastorno en el cual la persona no resuelve totalmente el conflicto en una etapa psicosexual particular, que causa atributos de personalidad y conducta asociados con esa etapa anterior.

fixed interval schedule of reinforcement: schedule of reinforcement in which the interval of time that must pass before reinforcement becomes possible is always the same. 189
   programa de refuerzo de intervalo fijo: programa de refuerzo en el cual el intervalo de tiempo que debe transcurrir antes de que pueda ocurrir el refuerzo es siempre el mismo.

fixed ratio schedule of reinforcement: schedule of reinforcement in which the number of responses required for reinforcement is always the same. 190
   programa de refuerzo de razón fija: programa de refuerzo en el cual el número de respuestas necesarias para el refuerzo es siempre el mismo.

flashbulb memories: type of automatic encoding that occurs because an unexpected event has strong emotional associations for the person remembering it. 289
   destellos de memoria: tipo de codificación automática que ocurre porque un evento inesperado tiene fuertes asociaciones emocionales para la persona que lo recuerda.

flat affect: a lack of emotional responsiveness. 431
   afecto plano: falta de respuesta emocional.

flooding (also known as **exposure and response prevention**): technique for treating phobias and other stress disorders in which the person is rapidly and intensely exposed to the fear-provoking situation or object and prevented from avoiding or escaping it. 453
   inundación (también se conoce como **exposición y prevención de la respuesta**): técnica para el tratamiento de fobias y otros trastornos de estrés en la cual se expone a la persona de manera rápida e intensa a la situación u objeto que provoca temor y se impide que pueda eludirlo o escapar.

foot-in-the-door technique: asking for a small commitment and, after gaining compliance, asking for a bigger commitment. 216
   técnica del pie en la puerta: procedimiento que consiste en solicitar un compromiso pequeño y, una vez obtenido, solicitar un compromiso mayor.

forensic psychology: area of psychology concerned with people in the legal system, including profiling of criminals, jury selection, and expert witnessing. 524
   psicología forense: área de la psicología que se ocupa de las personas en el sistema legal, que incluye perfiles de criminales, selección de jurados y testigos expertos.

formal concept: a concept that is defined by specific rules or features. 308
   concepto formal: concepto que se define por reglas o características específicas.

formal operations stage: Piaget's last stage of cognitive development, in which the adolescent becomes capable of abstract thinking. 155
   etapa de las operaciones formales: última etapa del desarrollo cognitivo de Piaget, en la cual el adolescente se vuelve capaz de tener un razonamiento abstracto.

free association: psychoanalytic technique in which a patient was encouraged to talk about anything that came to mind without fear of negative evaluations. 449
   asociación libre: técnica psicoanalítica en la cual se anima al paciente a que hable de cualquier cosa sin miedo a ser juzgado negativamente.

free-floating anxiety: anxiety that is unrelated to any realistic, known source. 421
   ansiedad flotante: ansiedad que no está relacionada con una fuente conocida o realista.

frequency count: assessment in which the frequency of a particular behavior is counted. 394
   medida de frecuencia: evaluación en la cual se mide la frecuencia de una conducta particular.

frequency distribution: table or graph that shows how often different numbers or scores appear in a particular set of scores. 28
   distribución de frecuencia: tabla o gráfica que muestra con qué frecuencia ocurre un número o resultado en un grupo particular de resultados.

frequency theory: theory of pitch that states that pitch is related to the speed of vibrations in the basilar membrane. 88
   teoría de la frecuencia: teoría de que el tono está relacionado con la velocidad de las vibraciones en la membrana basilar.

frontal lobes: areas of the cortex located in the front and top of the brain, responsible for higher mental processes and decision making, as well as the production of fluent speech. 61
   lóbulos frontales: áreas de la corteza cerebral ubicadas en la zona frontal y superior del cerebro, responsables de los procesos mentales superiores, de la toma de decisiones y de la fluidez del habla.

frustration: the psychological experience produced by the blocking of a desired goal or fulfillment of a perceived need. 488
  frustración: experiencia psicológica que se produce por el bloqueo de un objetivo deseado o por no satisfacer una necesidad percibida.

fully functioning person: a person who is in touch with and trusting of the deepest, innermost urges and feelings. 386
  persona completamente funcional: persona que está en contacto con sus necesidades y sentimientos más profundos.

functional fixedness: a block to problem solving that comes from thinking about objects in terms of only their typical functions. 314
  fijación funcional: incapacidad de resolver problemas que proviene de pensar en los objetos solo en términos de su función típica.

functional MRI (fMRI): A specialized MRI scan that tracks changes in oxygen levels of the blood to show which areas of the brain are active. 56
  resonancia magnética functional: tipo especializado de resonancia magnética que rastrea los cambios en los niveles de oxígeno de la sangre para mostrar qué áreas del cerebro están activas.

functionalism: early perspective in psychology associated with William James, in which the focus of study is how the mind allows people to adapt, live, work, and play. 6
  funcionalismo: perspectiva temprana de la psicología asociada con William James en la cual el foco de estudio es de qué manera la mente permite a las personas adaptarse, vivir, trabajar y jugar.

fundamental attribution error: the tendency to overestimate the influence of internal factors in determining the behavior of others while underestimating situational factors. 229
  error fundamental de atribución: tendencia a sobrestimar la influencia de factores internos en la determinación de la conducta de otros y subestimar los factores situacionales.

G

g factor: the ability to reason and solve problems or general intelligence. 321
  factor g: capacidad de una persona para razonar y resolver problemas, o inteligencia general.

gambler's fallacy: the belief that the chance of something occurring depends on whether it has recently occurred. 318
  falacia del jugador: creencia de que la probabilidad de que algo ocurra depende de si ha ocurrido recientemente o no.

gender: the psychological aspects of being male or female. 261
  género: aspectos psicológicos de ser hombre o mujer.

gender identity: the individual's sense of being male or female. 261
  identidad de género: percepción individual de ser hombre o mujer.

gender roles: a culture's expectations for masculine or feminine behavior, including attitudes, actions, and personality traits associated with being male or female in that culture. 261
  roles de género: expectativas de la cultura con respecto a las conductas masculinas y femeninas, que incluyen actitudes, acciones y atributos de personalidad asociados con ser hombre o mujer en esa cultura.

gender typing: the process of acquiring gender role characteristics. 261
  clasificación de género: proceso de adquirir características de roles de género.

gene: section of DNA having the same arrangement of chemical elements. 66, 142
  gen: sección de ADN que tiene la misma disposición de elementos químicos.

general adaptation syndrome (GAS): the three stages of the body's physiological reaction to stress, including alarm, resistance, and exhaustion. 489
  síndrome general de adaptación: las tres etapas de la reacción fisiológica del cuerpo al estrés, que incluyen alarma, resistencia y agotamiento.

generalized anxiety disorder: disorder in which a person has feelings of dread and impending doom along with physical symptoms of stress, which last six months or more. 423
  trastorno de ansiedad generalizada: trastorno en el cual la persona tiene sentimientos de temor y desastre inminente, junto con síntomas físicos de estrés, y que dura seis meses o más.

generativity: providing guidance to one's children or the next generation, or contributing to the well-being of the next generation through career or volunteer work. 165
  generatividad: brindar guía a los hijos o a la siguiente generación, o contribuir al bienestar de la siguiente generación mediante trabajo voluntario o profesional.

germinal period: first two weeks after fertilization, during which the zygote moves down to the uterus and begins to implant in the lining. 148
  período germinal: primeras dos semanas después de la fertilización, durante las cuales el cigoto se traslada al útero y comienza a implantarse en el revestimiento de este.

Gestalt psychology: early perspective in psychology focusing on perception and sensation, particularly the perception of patterns and whole figures. 95
  psicología gestáltica: perspectiva temprana de la psicología que se focaliza en la percepción y la sensación, particularmente en la percepción de patrones y figuras completas.

gifted: term used to describe the two percent of the population falling on the upper end of the normal curve and typically possessing an IQ of 130 or above. 325
  dotado: término que se usa para describir al dos por ciento de la población que se encuentra dentro del extremo superior de la curva normal y que típicamente posee un coeficiente intelectual de 130 o mayor.

glucagons: hormones that are secreted by the pancreas to control the levels of fats, proteins, and carbohydrates in the body by increasing the level of glucose in the bloodstream. 349
  glucagones: hormonas que secreta el páncreas para controlar los niveles de grasas, proteínas y carbohidratos del cuerpo mediante un aumento del nivel de glucosa en el torrente sanguíneo.

gonads: sex glands; secrete hormones that regulate sexual development and behavior as well as reproduction. 51
  gónadas: glándulas sexuales; secretan hormonas que regulan el desarrollo y el comportamiento sexual, así como la reproducción.

grammar: the system of rules governing the structure and use of a language. 201
  gramática: sistema de reglas que gobiernan la estructura y el uso del lenguaje.

groupthink: kind of thinking that occurs when people place more importance on maintaining group cohesiveness than on assessing the facts of the problem with which the group is concerned. 219
  pensamiento de grupo: tipo de pensamiento que ocurre cuando las personas le dan mayor importancia a resguardar la unión del grupo que a evaluar los hechos del problema con el cual el grupo se enfrenta.

growth needs: in Maslow's theory, these are psychological needs, such as the need for friendship or accomplishments. 346
  necesidades de crecimiento: en la teoría de Maslow, estas son necesidades psicológicas, como la necesidad de amistad y logros.

gustation: the sensation of a taste. 88
  gustación: percepción de un sabor.

H

habits: in behaviorism, sets of well-learned responses that have become automatic. 383
  hábitos: en el conductismo, conjuntos de respuestas bien aprendidas que se han vuelto automáticas.

habituation: tendency of the brain to stop attending to constant, unchanging information. 79
  habituación: tendencia del cerebro a dejar de prestar atención a la información constante y monótona.

hallucinations: false sensory perceptions, such as hearing voices that do not really exist. 431
  alucinaciones: falsas percepciones sensoriales, como oír voces que realmente no existen.

hallucinogenics (hallucinogens): drugs that cause false sensory messages, altering the perception of reality. 126, 130
  alucinógenos: drogas que causan mensajes sensoriales falsos y alteran la percepción de la realidad.

halo effect: tendency of an interviewer to allow positive characteristics of a client to influence the assessments of the client's behavior and statements. 392
  efecto de halo: tendencia del entrevistador a permitir que las características positivas del cliente influyan en la evaluación de su conducta y sus declaraciones.

hardy personality: a person who seems to thrive on stress but lacks the anger and hostility of the Type A personality. 498
  personalidad fuerte: persona que parece estar mejor bajo estrés pero que carece de la ira y la hostilidad de la personalidad tipo A.

hassles: the daily annoyances of everyday life. 485
  complicaciones: molestias de la vida cotidiana.

health psychology: area of psychology in which the psychologists focus on the relationship of human behavior patterns and stress reaction to physical health. 522
  psicología de la salud: área de la psicología que se focaliza en la relación de los patrones de la conducta humana y la reacción al estrés con la salud física.

heritability: the degree to which the changes in some trait within a population can be considered to be due to genetic influences. 396
  heredabilidad: grado en el cual los cambios en algún rasgo dentro de una población pueden atribuirse a las influencias genéticas.

heroin: narcotic drug derived from opium that is extremely addictive. 130
  heroína: droga narcótica derivada del opio que es extremadamente adictiva.

hertz (Hz): cycles or waves per second, a measurement of frequency. 86
  hercio: ciclos u ondas por segundo; una medida de la frecuencia.

heuristic: an educated guess based on prior experiences that helps narrow down the possible solutions for a problem. Also known as a "rule of thumb." 311
  heurística: conjetura educada que se basa en experiencias previas y que ayuda a limitar las posibles soluciones a un problema. También se conoce como "regla general".

hindsight bias: the tendency to falsely believe, through revision of older memories to include newer information, that one could have correctly predicted the outcome of an event. 291
  sesgo retrospectivo: tendencia falsa a creer que, mediante la revisión de recuerdos más antiguos que incluyen nueva información, uno podría haber predicho correctamente el resultado de un evento.

hippocampus: curved structure located within each temporal lobe, responsible for the formation of long-term memories and the storage of memory for location of objects. 59
  hipocampo: estructura curva ubicada dentro de cada lóbulo temporal, responsable de la formación de recuerdos a largo plazo y del almacenamiento de la memoria para la ubicación de los objetos.

histogram: graph showing a frequency distribution. 29
  histograma: gráfica que muestra una distribución de frecuencia.

homeostasis: the tendency of the body to maintain a steady state. 59, 343
  homeostasis: tendencia del cuerpo a mantener un estado estable.

hormones: chemicals released into the bloodstream by endocrine glands. 50
  hormonas: químicos que las glándulas endocrinas liberan en el torrente sanguíneo.

human development: the scientific study of the changes that occur in people as they age, from conception until death. 142
  desarrollo humano: estudio científico de los cambios que ocurren a medida que las personas envejecen, desde la concepción hasta la muerte.

human factors psychology: area of industrial/organizational psychology concerned with the study of the way humans and machines interact with each other. 526
  psicología de los factores humanos: área de la psicología industrial/organizacional que se ocupa de la manera en que los seres humanos y las máquinas interactúan.

humanistic perspective: the "third force" in psychology that focuses on those aspects of personality that make people uniquely human, such as subjective feelings and freedom of choice. 385
  perspectiva humanística: "tercera fuerza" en psicología que se centra en aquellos aspectos de la personalidad que hacen a las personas esencialmente humanas, como los sentimientos subjetivos y la libertad de elección.

hypnosis: state of consciousness in which a person is especially susceptible to suggestion. 124
  hipnosis: estado de conciencia en el cual la persona es especialmente susceptible a la sugestión.

hypochondriasis: somatoform disorder in which the person is terrified of being sick and worries constantly, going to doctors repeatedly, and becoming preoccupied with every sensation of the body. 425
  hipocondriasis: trastorno somatoforme en el que la persona está aterrada de estar enferma y se preocupa constantemente, acude a los médicos repetidas veces y se inquieta con cada sensación corporal.

hypothalamus: small structure in the brain located below the thalamus and directly above the pituitary gland, responsible for motivational behavior such as sleep, hunger, thirst, and sex. 59
  hipotálamo: pequeña estructura del cerebro ubicada debajo del tálamo y directamente encima de la glándula pituitaria, responsable de las conductas motivacionales como el sueño, el hambre, la sed y el sexo.

hypothesis: tentative explanation of a phenomenon based on observations. 16
  hipótesis: explicación tentativa de un fenómeno sobre la base de la observación.

I

id: part of the personality present at birth and completely unconscious. 378
  ello: parte de la personalidad que está presente en el nacimiento y es completamente inconsciente.

ideal self: one's perception of whom one should be or would like to be. 385
  yo ideal: percepción propia de quien uno debería ser o le gustaría ser.

identification: defense mechanism in which a person tries to become like someone else to deal with anxiety. 380, 502
  identificación: mecanismo de defensa en el cual la persona trata de volverse como alguien más para manejar la ansiedad.

imaginary audience: type of thought common to adolescents in which young people believe that other people are just as concerned about the adolescent's thoughts and characteristics as they themselves are. 163
  audiencia imaginaria: tipo de pensamiento común en los adolescentes que piensan que otras personas están tan preocupadas por los pensamientos y las características adolescentes como ellos mismos.

immune system: the system of cells, organs, and chemicals of the body that responds to attacks from diseases, infections, and injuries. 490
  sistema inmunológico: sistema de células, órganos y químicos del cuerpo que responde a los ataques de las enfermedades, las infecciones y las lesiones.

implicit memory: memory that is not easily brought into conscious awareness, such as procedural memory. 280
  memoria implícita: memoria que no es fácil de traer al conocimiento consciente, como la memoria de procedimiento.

incentive approaches: theories of motivation in which behavior is explained as a response to the external stimulus and its rewarding properties. 345
  método de los incentivos: teorías de la motivación en las cuales se explica la conducta como una respuesta al estímulo externo y a sus propiedades gratificantes.

incentives: things that attract or lure people into action. 345
  incentivos: cosas que atraen o tientan a las personas para ponerse en acción.

independent self-concept: an individual's perception of self as entirely independent from others. 255
  autoconcepto independiente: percepción de un individuo de su propio ser como totalmente independiente de otros.

independent variable: variable in an experiment that is manipulated by the experimenter. 20
  variable independiente: variable de un experimento que es manipulada por el experimentador.

individualism: a cultural style that emphasizes the importance of individuality, independence, and personal needs. 255
  individualismo: estilo cultural que enfatiza la importancia de la individualidad, la independencia y las necesidades personales.

industrial/organizational (I/O) psychology: area of psychology concerned with the relationships between people and their work environment. 14, 526
  psicología industrial/organizacional: área de la psicología que se ocupa de la relación entre las personas y su entorno de trabajo. 14, 526

infantile amnesia: the inability to retrieve memories from much before age three. 297
  amnesia infantil: incapacidad de recuperar recuerdos desde mucho antes que los tres años.

inferential statistics: statistical analysis of two or more sets of numerical data to reduce the possibility of error in measurement and to determine if the differences between the data sets are greater than chance variation would predict. 26
  estadística inferencial: análisis estadístico de dos o más grupos de datos numéricos para reducir la probabilidad de un error de medida y determinar si las diferencias entre los conjuntos de datos son mayores que lo que predice la variación accidental.

information-processing model: model of memory that assumes the processing of information for memory storage is similar to the way a computer processes memory in a series of three stages. 274
  modelo de procesamiento de la información: modelo de memoria que sostiene que el procesamiento de recuerdos para almacenamiento en la memoria es similar a la manera en que una computadora procesa la memoria en tres etapas.

informed consent: permission from a person (or a parent or guardian, in the case of minors) to participate in an experiment after the risks and purpose of the experiment have been explained. 20
  consentimiento informado: permiso de una persona (o de los padres o tutores, en el caso de menores) para participar en un experimento, después de conocidos los riesgos y el objetivo del experimento.

in-groups: social groups with whom a person identifies; "us." 232
  grupos exclusivos: grupos sociales con los que se identifica la persona; "nosotros".

insight: the seemingly sudden perception of relationships among various parts of a problem, allowing the solution to the problem to come quickly. 198
  perspectiva: aparentemente súbita percepción de las relaciones entre las distintas partes de un problema, que permite que la resolución del problema sea rápida.

insight therapies: therapies in which the main goal is helping people to gain insight with respect to their behavior, thoughts, and feelings. 466
  terapias de introspección: terapias en las cuales el objetivo principal es ayudar a las personas a conocer en profundidad su conducta, pensamientos y sentimientos.

insomnia: the inability to get to sleep, stay asleep, or get a good quality of sleep. 118
  insomnio: incapacidad de conciliar el sueño, mantenerlo o lograr un sueño de buena calidad.

instinct approach: approach to motivation that assumes people are governed by instincts similar to those of animals. 342
  enfoque instintivista: enfoque de la motivación que supone que las personas son gobernadas por los instintos, al igual que los animales.

instinctive drift: tendency for an animal's behavior to revert to genetically controlled patterns. 191
  tendencia instintiva: tendencia de la conducta de los animales a volver a patrones genéticamente controlados.

instincts: the biologically determined and innate patterns of behavior that exist in both people and animals. 342
  instintos: patrones de conducta biológicamente determinados e innatos que existen tanto en las personas como en los animales.

insulin: a hormone secreted by the pancreas to control the levels of fats, proteins, and carbohydrates in the body by reducing the level of glucose in the bloodstream. 349
  insulina: hormona secretada por el páncreas para controlar los niveles de grasas, proteínas y carbohidratos del cuerpo mediante la reducción de los niveles de glucosa en el torrente sanguíneo.

intelligence: the ability to learn from one's experiences, acquire knowledge, and use resources effectively in adapting to new situations or solving problems. 321
  inteligencia: capacidad de aprender de las propias experiencias, adquirir conocimientos y usar los recursos de manera efectiva para adaptarse a nuevas situaciones o para resolver problemas.

interdependent self-concept: an individual's perception of self as fundamentally connected to others. 255
  autoconcepto interdependiente: percepción de un individuo de sí mismo como fundamentalmente conectado a otros.

internal locus of control: the assumption that one generally has control over one's life. 354
  locus de control interno: suposición de que generalmente uno tiene control sobre la propia vida.

external locus of control: the assumption that one's life is generally controlled by external forces, such as powerful others, luck, or fate. 354
  locus de control externo: suposición de que la vida de uno generalmente está controlada por fuerzas externas, como personas poderosas, la suerte o el destino.

interneuron: a neuron found in the center of the spinal cord that receives information from the sensory neurons and sends commands to the muscles through the motor neurons. Interneurons also make up the bulk of the neurons in the brain. 49
  interneurona: neurona que se encuentra en el centro de la médula espinal que recibe información de las neuronas sensoriales y envía órdenes a los músculos mediante las neuronas motoras. Las interneuronas también conforman la gran mayoría de las neuronas cerebrales.

interpersonal attraction: liking or having the desire for a relationship with another person. 235
  atracción interpersonal: deseo de tener una relación con otra persona.

interview: method of personality assessment in which the professional asks questions of the client and allows the client to answer, either in a structured or unstructured fashion. 391
  entrevista: método de evaluación de la personalidad en el cual el profesional formula preguntas al cliente y le permite responder, ya sea de manera estructurada o no.

intrinsic motivation: type of motivation in which a person performs an action because the act itself is rewarding or satisfying in some internal manner. 342
  motivación intrínseca: tipo de motivación en el cual la persona realiza una acción porque el acto en sí es gratificante o satisfactorio de alguna manera interior.

introversion: dimension of personality in which people tend to withdraw from excessive stimulation. 387
  introversión: dimensión de la personalidad en la cual las personas tienden a distanciarse de la estimulación excesiva.

introverts: people who prefer solitude and dislike being the center of attention. 388
  introvertidas: personas que prefieren la soledad y a las que no les gusta ser el centro de atención.

IQ: a number representing a measure of intelligence, resulting from the division of one's mental age by one's chronological age and then multiplying that quotient by 100. 327
  coeficiente intelectual: número que representa una medida de la inteligencia, que es el resultado de dividir la edad mental entre la edad cronológica y luego multiplicar ese cociente por 100.

J

James-Lange theory of emotion: theory in which a physiological reaction leads to the labeling of an emotion. 360
  teoría de la emoción de James-Lange: teoría en la cual una reacción fisiológica lleva a rotular una emoción.

just noticeable difference (jnd or the difference threshold): the smallest difference between two stimuli that is detectable 50 percent of the time by 50 percent of the people tested. 78
  umbral diferencial: diferencia más pequeña entre dos estímulos que es detectable el 50 por ciento de las veces por parte del 50 por ciento de las personas sometidas a prueba.

K

kinesthetic sense: sense of the location of body parts in relation to the ground and each other. 91
  sentido cinestésico: sentido de la ubicación de las partes del cuerpo en relación con el suelo y entre ellas.

L

laboratory method: method of conducting research in a controlled environment. 18
  método de laboratorio: método de llevar a cabo una investigación en un entorno controlado.

language: a system for combining symbols (such as words) so that an unlimited number of meaningful statements can be made for the purpose of communicating with others. 201
  lenguaje: sistema para combinar símbolos (como las palabras) para formar un número ilimitado de enunciados importantes con el propósito de comunicarse con otros.

latency: fourth stage occurring during the school years, in which the sexual feelings of the child are repressed while the child develops in other ways. 380
  latencia: cuarta etapa que ocurre durante los años escolares, en la cual los sentimientos sexuales del niño son reprimidos mientras se desarrolla en otros aspectos.

latent content: the hidden, symbolic meaning of a dream. 449
  contenido latente: significado oculto y simbólico de un sueño.

latent learning: learning that remains hidden until its application becomes useful. 197
  enseñanza latente: enseñanza que permanece oculta hasta que su aplicación resulta útil.

Law of Effect: law stating that if an action is followed by a pleasurable consequence, it will tend to be repeated, and if followed by an unpleasant consequence, it will tend not to be repeated. 185
  Ley del efecto: ley que sostiene que si a una acción le sigue una consecuencia agradable, tenderá a repetirse, mientras que si es seguida por una consecuencia desagradable, tenderá a no repetirse.

learned helplessness: the tendency to fail to act to escape from a situation because of a history of repeated failures in the past. 199
  incapacidad aprendida: tendencia a dejar de actuar para escapar de una situación debido a una historia de fracasos repetidos en el pasado.

learning: any relatively permanent change in behavior brought about by experience or practice. 178
  aprendizaje: todo cambio relativamente permanente en la conducta causado por la experiencia o la práctica.

levels-of-processing model: model of memory that assumes information that is more "deeply processed," or processed according to meaning rather than just the sound or physical characteristics of the word or words, will be remembered more efficiently and for a longer period of time. 275
  modelo de niveles de procesamiento: modelo de memoria que supone que aquella información que se "procesa profundamente", o que se procesa de acuerdo con el significado en lugar de solo el sonido o las características físicas de las palabras, será recordada de manera más eficiente y durante un período de tiempo mayor.

light adaptation: the recovery of the eye's sensitivity to visual stimuli in light after exposure to darkness. 84
  adaptación a la luz: recuperación de la sensibilidad del ojo a los estímulos visuales a la luz después de una exposición a la oscuridad.

limbic system: a group of several brain structures located under the cortex and involved in learning, emotion, memory, and motivation. 58
  sistema límbico: grupo de varias estructuras cerebrales ubicadas debajo de la corteza cerebral y que están implicadas en el aprendizaje, la emoción, la memoria y la motivación.

linear perspective: the tendency for parallel lines to appear to converge on each other. 98
  perspectiva lineal: tendencia a que las líneas paralelas parezcan converger entre sí.

lithium: chemical element that, in the form of lithium carbonate, has traditionally been used as an antimanic drug. 467
  litio: elemento químico que, bajo la forma de carbonato de litio, se ha usado tradicionalmente como fármaco antimaníaco.

locus of control: the tendency for people to assume that they either have control or do not have control over events and consequences in their lives. 385
  locus de control: tendencia de las personas a suponer que ellas tienen o no tienen control sobre los eventos y consecuencias de su vida.

longitudinal design: research design in which one group of people is followed and assessed at different times as the group ages. 144
  diseño longitudinal: diseño de investigación en el cual un grupo de personas es seguido y evaluado en diferentes momentos a medida que el grupo envejece.

long-term memory (LTM): the system of memory into which all the information is placed to be kept more or less permanently. 279
  memoria a largo plazo: sistema de memoria en el que toda la información se guarda para su mantenimiento de manera más o menos permanente.

loss aversion: the tendency to be more sensitive to actual or potential losses than to gains. 318
  aversión a la pérdida: tendencia a ser más o menos sensible a las pérdidas reales o potenciales que a las ganancias.

lowball technique: getting a commitment from a person and then raising the cost of that commitment. 216
  técnica del engaño: obtener un compromiso de una persona y luego subir el costo de tal compromiso.

LSD (lysergic acid diethylamide): powerful synthetic hallucinogen. 130
  LSD (dietilamida de ácido lisérgico): poderoso alucinógeno sintético.

M

magnetic resonance imaging (MRI): brain-imaging method using radio waves and magnetic fields of the body to produce detailed images of the brain. 55
  imagen por resonancia magnética: método de resonancia del cerebro que usa ondas de radio y campos magnéticos del cuerpo para producir imágenes detalladas del cerebro.

magnification: the tendency to interpret situations as far more dangerous, harmful, or important than they actually are. 424
magnificación: tendencia a interpretar las situaciones como más peligrosas, perjudiciales e importantes de lo que realmente son.

magnification and minimization: distortions in which a person blows a negative event out of proportion to its importance (magnification) while ignoring relevant positive events (minimization). 455
magnificación y minimización: distorsiones en las cuales la persona exagera un evento negativo (magnificación) mientras ignora eventos positivos relevantes (minimización).

maintenance rehearsal: practice of saying some information to be remembered over and over in one's head in order to maintain it in short-term memory. 279
ensayo de mantenimiento: práctica que implica la repetición de la información una y otra vez, para mantenerla en la memoria a corto plazo.

major depression: a mood disorder characterized by a depressed mood that lasts for at least two weeks, a loss of interest or pleasure in activities, and several other symptoms, such as feelings of worthlessness and exhaustion. 428
depresión severa: trastorno del estado de ánimo caracterizado por un estado deprimido que dura al menos dos semanas, pérdida de interés o placer en las actividades y otros síntomas, como sentimientos de desvalorización y cansancio.

maladaptive: anything that does not allow a person to function within or adapt to the stresses and everyday demands of life. 413
inadaptivo: todo lo que no le permite a la persona funcionar dentro de las presiones o demandas de la vida cotidiana o adaptarse a ellas.

manic: having the quality of excessive excitement, energy, and elation or irritability. 429
maníaco: que tiene excitación, energía y euforia o irritabilidad excesivas.

manifest content: the actual content of one's dream. 449
contenido manifiesto: contenido real del sueño.

marijuana: mild hallucinogen (also known as *pot* or *weed*) derived from the leaves and flowers of a particular type of hemp plant. 131
marihuana: alucinógeno suave derivado de las hojas y las flores un un tipo particular de planta de cáñamo.

master's degree: a graduate degree students may pursue after completing a four-year college degree. Generally a master's degree takes 2–3 years to complete. It provides more specialized knowledge, training, and experience than students typically receive as undergraduates. 516
maestría: título de grado al que los estudiantes pueden aspirar después de finalizar cuatro años de estudios universitarios. Generalmente, una maestría tarda de 2 a 3 años en finalizarse. Brinda más conocimientos especializados, entrenamiento y experiencia que la que reciben los estudiantes universitarios.

MDMA (Ecstasy or X): designer drug that can have both stimulant and hallucinatory effects. 130
MDMA (éxtasis): droga de diseño que puede tener tanto un efecto estimulante como un efecto alucinatorio.

mean: the average score within a group of scores, calculated by adding all of the scores and then dividing by the number of scores. 27, 323
media: resultado promedio dentro de un grupo de resultados, que se calcula al sumar todos los resultados y luego al dividir entre el número de resultados.

means-end analysis: heuristic, in which the difference between the starting situation and the goal is determined and then steps are taken to reduce that difference. 312
análisis medio-fin: método heurístico en el cual se determina la diferencia entre la situación inicial y el objetivo, y luego se dan pasos para reducir esa diferencia.

measures of central tendency: numbers that best represent the most typical score of a frequency distribution. 27
medidas de tendencia central: números que representan mejor el resultado más típico de una distribución de frecuencia.

measures of variability: measurement of the degree of differences within a distribution or how the scores are spread out. 27
medidas de variabilidad: medida del grado de diferencia dentro de una distribución o cómo se distribuyen los resultados.

median: the middle score in an ordered distribution of scores, or the mean of the two middle numbers; the 50th percentile. 27
mediana: resultado del medio en una distribución ordenada de resultados o la media de los los números del medio; percentil 50.

meditation: mental series of exercises meant to refocus attention and achieve a trancelike state of consciousness. 123
meditación: serie de ejercicios mentales diseñados para reubicar la atención y lograr un estado de conciencia similar al trance.

medulla: the first large swelling at the top of the spinal cord, forming the lowest part of the brain, which is responsible for life-sustaining functions such as breathing, swallowing, and heart rate. 57
bulbo raquídeo: primera gran protuberancia que se encuentra en la parte superior de la médula espinal y forma la parte inferior del cerebro, responsable de funciones vitales como la respiración, la deglución y la frecuencia cardíaca.

memory: an active system that receives information from the senses, puts that information into a usable form, and organizes it as it stores it away, and then retrieves the information from storage. 274
memoria: sistema activo que recibe información de los sentidos, la transforma en utilizable, la organiza, la almacena y finalmente la recupera.

memory trace: physical change in the brain that occurs when a memory is formed. 295
rastro de memoria: cambio físico en el cerebro que ocurre cuando se forma un recuerdo.

menopause: the cessation of ovulation and menstrual cycles, and the end of a woman's reproductive capability. 167
menopausia: cese de la ovulación y los ciclos menstruales y finalización de la capacidad reproductiva de la mujer.

mental images: picture-like representations that stand in for objects or events. 306
imágenes mentales: representaciones similares a dibujos que representan objetos o eventos.

mental set: the tendency for people to persist in using problem solving patterns that have worked for them in the past. 314
predisposición mental: tendencia de las personas a persistir en el uso de patrones de resolución de problemas que ya han usado en el pasado.

mescaline: natural hallucinogen derived from the peyote cactus buttons. 130
mescalina: alucinógeno natural derivado de los botones del peyote, un tipo de cactus.

microsleeps: brief sidesteps into sleep lasting only a few seconds. 112
microsueños: breves períodos de sueño que duran apenas unos pocos segundos.

misinformation effect: the tendency of misleading information presented after an event to alter the memories of the event itself. 291
efecto equívoco: tendencia a presentar información engañosa después de un evento para alterar los recuerdos del evento en sí mismo.

mnemonic: a strategy or trick for aiding memory. 289
nemotécnico: estrategia o truco para ayudar a la memoria.

mode: the most frequent score in a distribution of scores. 27
modo: resultado más frecuente en una distribución de resultados.

modeling: learning through the observation and imitation of others. 454
modelado: aprendizaje que se da a través de la observación e imitación de otros.

monoamine oxidase inhibitors (MAOIs): antidepressant drugs that block the activity of the enzyme monoamine oxidase, which breaks down several neurotransmitters involved in regulating mood. 467
inhibidores de la monoaminooxidasa: fármacos antidepresivos que bloquean la actividad de la enzima monoaminooxidasa, que rompe varios neurotransmisores implicados en la regulación del estado de ánimo.

GLOSSARY/GLOSARIO

monocular cues (pictorial depth cues): cues for perceiving depth based on one eye only. 97
   pistas monoculares: pistas para percibir la profundidad con base en un solo ojo.

mood disorders: disorders in which mood is severely disturbed. 427
   trastornos del estado de ánimo: trastornos en los que se perturba severamente el estado de ánimo.

morphemes: the smallest units of meaning within a language. 202
   morfemas: unidades más pequeñas de significado dentro de un lenguaje.

morphine: narcotic drug derived from opium, used to treat severe pain. 129
   morfina: droga narcótica derivada del opio, que se usa para el tratamiento del dolor agudo.

motion parallax: the perception of motion of objects in which close objects appear to move more quickly than objects that are farther away. 98
   paralaje de movimiento: percepción del movimiento de los objetos en la cual los objetos cercanos parecen moverse más rápido que los objetos lejanos.

motivation: the process by which activities are started, directed, and continued so that physical or psychological needs or wants are met. 342
   motivación: proceso por el cual se comienza, controla y continúa una actividad para satisfacer una necesidad o deseo físico o psicológico.

motor cortex: section of the frontal lobe located at the back, responsible for sending motor commands to the muscles of the somatic nervous system. 61
   corteza motora: sección del lóbulo frontal ubicada en la parte posterior, responsable de enviar órdenes motoras a los músculos del sistema nervioso somático.

motor neuron: a neuron that carries messages from the central nervous system to the muscles of the body. 48
   neurona motora: neurona que transmite información desde el sistema nervioso central hasta los músculos del cuerpo.

Müller-Lyer illusion: illusion of line length that is distorted by inward-turning or outward-turning corners on the ends of the lines, causing lines of equal length to appear to be different. 99
   ilusión de Müller-Lyer: ilusión óptica en la cual las líneas rectas parecen más largas o más cortas según si las puntas de flecha añadidas en sus extremos apuntan hacia adentro o hacia afuera; esto causa que líneas rectas de la misma longitud parezcan diferentes.

myelin: fatty substances that coat the axons of neurons to insulate, protect, and speed up the neural impulse. 43
   mielina: sustancia grasa que recubre los axones de las neuronas para aislar, proteger y acelerar el impulso neural.

N

narcolepsy: sleep disorder in which a person falls immediately into REM sleep during the day without warning. 118
   narcolepsia: trastorno del sueño en el cual la persona cae inmediatamente en sueño REM durante el día, sin previo aviso.

narcotics: a class of opium-related drugs that suppress the sensation of pain by binding to and stimulating the nervous system's natural receptor sites for endorphins. 126
   narcóticos: clase de drogas relacionadas con el opio que eliminan la sensación de dolor al unirse y estimular los receptores naturales de endorfinas del sistema nervioso.

natural concept: a concept formed as a result of someone's experiences in the real world. 309
   concepto natural concepto que se forma como resultado de las experiencias en el mundo real.

natural killer cell: immune system cell responsible for suppressing viruses and destroying tumor cells. 491
   célula asesina natural: célula del sistema inmunológico responsable de la eliminación de virus y de la destrucción de células cancerosas.

natural selection: principle stating that inherited characteristics that give a survival advantage are more likely to be passed on to future generations. 69
   selección natural: principio que sostiene que las características heredadas que brindan una ventaja de supervivencia son más propensas a pasar a las futuras generaciones.

naturalistic observation: the study of people or animals in their natural environment. 17
   observación naturalista: estudio de las personas o los animales en su entorno natural.

nature: the influence of our inherited characteristics on our personality, physical growth, intellectual growth, and social interactions. 66, 142
   naturaleza: influencia de nuestras características heredadas en nuestra personalidad, crecimiento físico, crecimiento intelectual e interacciones sociales.

need: a requirement of some material (such as food or water) that is essential for survival of the organism. 343
   necesidad: requerimiento de algún material (como alimentos o agua) que es esencial para la supervivencia del organismo.

need for achievement (nAch): a need that involves a strong desire to succeed in attaining goals, not only realistic ones but also challenging ones. 344
   necesidad de logro: necesidad que implica un fuerte deseo de triunfar en la obtención de logros, no solo realistas sino también los que implican un desafío.

need for affiliation (nAff): the need for friendly social interactions and relationships with others. 344
   necesidad de afiliación: necesidad de interacciones sociales amistosas y relaciones con otros.

need for power (nPow): the need to have control or influence over others. 344
   necesidad de poder: necesidad de tener control o influencia sobre otros.

negative reinforcement: the reinforcement of a response that removes or allows escape from something unpleasant. 186
   refuerzo negativo: refuerzo de una respuesta que elimina o permite escapar de algo desagradable.

negative symptoms: symptoms of schizophrenia that are less than normal behavior or an absence of normal behavior; poor attention, flat affect, and poor speech production. 432
   síntomas negativos: síntomas de esquizofrenia que representan una conducta poco normal o una ausencia de conducta normal; poca atención, afecto plano y pobre producción de habla.

neo-Freudians: followers of Freud who developed their own competing psychodynamic theories. 381
   neofreudianos: seguidores de Freud que desarrollaron sus propias teorías psicodinámicas contrapuestas.

neurofeedback: form of biofeedback using brain-scanning devices to provide feedback about brain activity in an effort to modify behavior. 192
   neurorretroalimentación: forma de biorretroalimentación que usa dispositivos de escaneo cerebral para brindar retroalimentación sobre la actividad cerebral con el fin de modificar la conducta.

neuron: the basic cell that makes up the nervous system and that receives and sends messages within that system. 42
   neurona: célula básica que conforma el sistema nervioso y que recibe y envía mensajes dentro de ese sistema.

neuroplasticity: the ability within the brain to constantly change both the structure and function of many cells in response to experience or trauma. 56
   neuroplasticidad: capacidad del cerebro de cambiar constantemente tanto la estructura como la función de muchas células como respuesta a experiencias o traumas.

neurotic personalities: typified by maladaptive ways of dealing with relationships in Horney's theory. 382
   personalidades neuróticas: personalidades caracterizadas por maneras inadaptivas de tratar con las relaciones en la teoría de Horney.

neuroticism: degree of emotional instability or stability. 389
  neurosis: grado de inestabilidad o estabilidad emocional.

neurotransmitter: chemical found in the synaptic vesicles that, when released, has an effect on the next cell. 46
  neurotransmisor: químico que se encuentra en las vesículas sinápticas y que, cuando se libera, tiene efecto en la célula siguiente.

neutral stimulus (NS): stimulus that has no effect on the desired response. 179
  estímulo neutral: estímulo que no tiene efecto en la respuesta deseada.

nicotine: the active ingredient in tobacco. 127
  nicotina: ingrediente activo del tabaco.

night terrors: relatively rare disorder in which the person experiences extreme fear and screams or runs around during deep sleep without waking fully. 117
  terrores nocturnos: trastorno relativamente raro en el cual la persona experimenta temor excesivo y grita o corre durante el sueño profundo sin despertarse del todo.

nightmares: bad dreams occurring during REM sleep. 117
  pesadillas: sueños que causan angustia y que ocurren durante el sueño REM.

nondirective: term used to describe a therapy style in which the therapist remains relatively neutral and does not interpret or take direct actions with regard to the client, instead remaining a calm, nonjudgmental listener while the client talks. 450
  no directiva: término que se usa para describir un estilo de terapia en el cual el terapeuta permanece relativamente neutral y no interpreta o inicia acciones directas con respecto al cliente, sino que permanece calmo y escucha sin juzgar mientras el cliente habla.

non-REM (NREM) sleep: any of the stages of sleep that do not include REM. 113
  sueño no REM: cualquiera de las etapas del sueño que no incluyen el sueño REM.

norm of reciprocity: assumption that if someone does something for a person, that person should do something for the other in return. 216
  norma de reciprocidad: suposición de que si alguien hace algo por una persona, esa persona debe hacer algo a cambio.

normal curve: special frequency polygon in which the scores are symmetrically distributed around the mean, and the mean, median, and mode are all located on the same point on the curve with scores decreasing as the curve extends from the mean. 30
  curva normal: polígono de frecuencia especial en el que los valores están simétricamente distribuidos alrededor de la media, y la media, la mediana y la moda están ubicadas en el mismo punto de la curva con valores decrecientes a medida que la curva se separa de la media.

norms: a culture's understood rules for expected behavior, values, beliefs, and attitudes. 250
  normas: reglas implícitas de una cultura sobre conducta esperada, valores, creencias y actitudes.

nurture: the influence of the environment on personality, physical growth, intellectual growth, and social interactions. 66, 142
  crianza: influencia del medio ambiente en la personalidad, el crecimiento físico, el crecimiento intelectual y las interacciones sociales.

O

obedience: changing one's behavior at the command of an authority figure. 217
  obediencia: cambiar la propia conducta bajo las órdenes de una figura de autoridad.

obesity: a condition in which people weigh roughly 20 to 30 percent more than the medically defined ideal body weight for their height. 350
  obesidad: afección en la cual las personas pesan alrededor del 20 al 30 por ciento más del peso ideal médicamente definido para su estatura.

object permanence: the knowledge that an object exists even when it is not in sight. 154
  permanencia del objeto: conocimiento de que el objeto existe incluso cuando no está a la vista.

observational learning: learning new behavior by watching a model perform that behavior. 195
  aprendizaje observacional: aprender nuevas conductas mirando al modelo realizar esa conducta.

observer bias: tendency of observers to see what they expect to see. 17
  sesgo del observador: tendencia del observador a ver lo que desea ver.

observer effect: tendency of people or animals to behave differently from normal when they know they are being observed. 17
  efecto del observador: tendencia de personas o animales a comportarse de manera diferente de lo normal cuando saben que están siendo observados.

obsessive-compulsive disorder: disorder in which intruding, recurring thoughts or obsessions create anxiety that is relieved by performing a repetitive, ritualistic behavior or mental act (compulsion). 423
  trastorno obsesivo-compulsivo: trastorno en el cual pensamientos y obsesiones recurrentes e invasivas provocan ansiedad que se alivia mediante la realización de una conducta o de un acto mental (compulsión) repetitivo y ritual.

occipital lobe: section of the brain located at the rear and bottom of each cerebral hemisphere containing the visual centers of the brain. 60
  lóbulo occipital: sección del cerebro ubicada en la parte posterior inferior de cada hemisferio cerebral y que contiene los centros visuales del cerebro.

Oedipus complex: situation occurring in the phallic stage in which a child develops a sexual attraction to the opposite-sex parent and jealousy of the same-sex parent. 380
  complejo de Edipo: situación que ocurre durante la etapa fálica en la cual el niño desarrolla atracción sexual hacia el progenitor del sexo opuesto y celos del progenitor del mismo sexo.

olfaction (olfactory sense): the sensation of smell. 90
  olfato: percibir aromas y olores; sentido del olfato.

openness: one of the five factors; willingness to try new things and be open to new experiences. 388
  apertura: uno de los cinco factores; predisposición a probar cosas nuevas y estar abierto a nuevas experiencias.

operant: any behavior that is voluntary. 185
  operante: toda conducta que sea voluntaria.

operant conditioning: the learning of voluntary behavior through the effects of pleasant and unpleasant consequences to responses. 184, 451
  condicionamiento operante: aprendizaje de conductas voluntarias a través de los efectos de las consecuencias agradables y desagradables de las respuestas.

operational definition: definition of a variable of interest that allows it to be measured. 20
  definición operacional: definición de una variable de interés que permite que esta sea medida.

opium: substance derived from the opium poppy from which all narcotic drugs are derived. 129
  opio: sustancia derivada de la amapola del opio de la cual se derivan todas las drogas narcóticas.

opponent-process theory: theory of color vision that proposes four primary colors with cones arranged in pairs: red and green, blue and yellow. 85
  teoría oponente-proceso: teoría de la visión de los colores que propone cuatro colores primarios agrupados en pares: rojo y verde, azul y amarillo.

optimists: people who expect positive outcomes. 503
  optimistas: personas que esperan resultados positivos.

oral stage: first stage occurring in the first year of life in which the mouth is the erogenous zone and weaning is the primary conflict. 379
etapa oral: primera etapa que ocurre durante el primer año de vida, en la cual la boca es la zona erógena y el conflicto primario es el destete.

out-groups: social groups with whom a person does not identify; "them." 232
grupos externos: grupos sociales con los que la persona no se identifica; "ellos".

overgeneralization: distortion in which a person draws sweeping conclusions based on only one incident or event and applies those conclusions to events that are unrelated to the original. 455
sobregeneralización: distorsión en la cual la persona saca conclusiones rápidas basadas en un solo accidente o evento y aplica esas conclusiones a eventos no relacionados con el original.

overlap (interposition): the assumption that an object that appears to be blocking part of another object is in front of the second object and closer to the viewer. 98
superposición (interposición): suposición de que un objeto que parece bloquear parte de otro objeto está delante de ese objeto y más cercano al observador.

ovum: the female sex cell, or egg. 147
óvulo: célula sexual femenina.

oxytocin: a hormone released by women during labor and breastfeeding, and by both sexes during sexual activity. Oxytocin is also a neurotransmitter within the brain, where it plays similar roles. 355
oxitocina: hormona liberada por las mujeres durante el parto y la lactancia, y por ambos sexos durante la actividad sexual. La oxitocina también es un neurotransmisor dentro del cerebro, donde tiene un papel similar.

P

pancreas: endocrine gland; controls the levels of sugar in the blood. 51
páncreas: glándula endocrina que controla los niveles de azúcar en la sangre.

panic attack: sudden onset of intense panic in which multiple physical symptoms of stress occur, often with feelings that one is dying. 423
ataque de pánico: comienzo repentino de pánico intenso en el cual ocurren múltiples síntomas físicos de estrés, con frecuencia con sentimientos de muerte.

panic disorder: disorder in which panic attacks occur frequently enough to cause the person difficulty in adjusting to daily life. 423
trastorno de pánico: trastorno en el cual los ataques de pánico ocurren con la frecuencia suficiente para causar dificultades para ajustarse a la vida diaria de la persona.

paranoid: type of schizophrenia in which the person suffers from delusions of persecution, grandeur, and jealousy, together with hallucinations. 432
paranoia: tipo de esquizofrenia en la cual la persona sufre de delirios de persecución, grandeza y celos, junto con alucinaciones.

parasympathetic division: part of the ANS that restores the body to normal functioning after arousal and is responsible for the day-to-day functioning of the organs and glands. 49
división parasimpática: parte del sistema nervioso autónomo que restablece la función normal del cuerpo al despertar y es responsable del funcionamiento diario de órganos y glándulas.

parietal lobes: sections of the brain located at the top and back of each cerebral hemisphere containing the centers for touch, taste, and temperature sensations. 60
lóbulos parietales: secciones del cerebro ubicadas en la parte superior posterior de cada hemisferio cerebral y que contienen los centros del tacto, el gusto y las sensaciones de temperatura.

partial dopamine agonists: a newer class of atypical neuroleptics that affect the release of dopamine rather than blocking its receptors. 466
agonistas parciales de la dopamina: nueva clase de antipsicóticos atípicos que afectan la liberación de dopamina en lugar de bloquear sus receptores.

partial reinforcement effect: the tendency for a response that is reinforced after some, but not all, correct responses to be very resistant to extinction. 189
efecto de refuerzo parcial: tendencia de una respuesta resistente a la extinción que se refuerza después de algunas, pero no todas, respuestas correctas.

participant modeling: technique in which a model demonstrates the desired behavior in a step-by-step, gradual process while the client is encouraged to imitate the model. 454
modelado participante: técnica en la cual el modelo demuestra la conducta deseada en un proceso gradual y paso a paso mientras se anima al cliente a imitar el modelo.

PCP: synthesized drug now used as an animal tranquilizer that can cause stimulant, depressant, narcotic, or hallucinogenic effects. 130
PCP: droga sintética que en la actualidad se usa como tranquilizante animal y que puede causar efectos estimulantes, depresivos, narcóticos o alucinógenos.

peak experiences: according to Maslow, times in a person's life during which self-actualization is temporarily achieved. 347
experiencias pico: según Maslow, momentos en la vida de una persona durante los cuales se consigue temporalmente la autorrealización.

perception: the method by which the sensations experienced at any given moment are interpreted and organized in some meaningful fashion. 78
percepción: método mediante el cual las sensaciones que se experimentan en un momento dado se interpretan y organizan de manera importante.

perceptual set (perceptual expectancy): the tendency to perceive things a certain way because previous experiences or expectations influence those perceptions. 100
expectativa perceptiva: tendencia a percibir las cosas de determinada manera debido a que las experiencias o expectativas previas influyen en esas percepciones.

peripheral nervous system (PNS): all nerves and neurons that are not contained in the brain and spinal cord but that run through the body itself. 49
sistema nervioso periférico: todos los nervios y las neuronas que no están contenidas en el cerebro y la médula espinal sino en el cuerpo en sí.

peripheral-route processing: type of information processing that involves attending to factors not involved in the message, such as the appearance of the source of the message, the length of the message, and other noncontent factors. 229
procesamiento a través de ruta periférica: tipo de procesamiento de la información que implica prestar atención a factores que no participan en el mensaje, como la apariencia de la fuente del mensaje, la longitud del mensaje y otros factores que no tienen que ver con el contenido.

personal fable: type of thought common to adolescents in which young people believe themselves to be unique and protected from harm. 163
fábula personal: tipo de pensamiento común en los adolescentes en el cual creen ser únicos y estar protegidos de todo mal.

personal unconscious: Jung's name for the unconscious mind as described by Freud. 382
inconsciente personal: nombre dado por Jung a la mente inconsciente que describe Freud.

personality: the unique and relatively stable ways in which people think, feel, and behave. 376
personalidad: modo único y relativamente estable en el cual las personas piensan, sienten y se comportan.

personality disorders: disorders in which a person adopts a persistent, rigid, and maladaptive pattern of behavior that interferes with normal social interactions. 433
trastornos de la personalidad: trastornos en los que la persona adopta patrones de conducta persistentes, rígidos e inadaptivos que interfieren con las interacciones sociales normales.

personality inventory: paper and pencil or computerized test that consists of statements that require a specific, standardized response from the person taking the test. 394
  inventario de personalidad: prueba en papel y lápiz o computarizada que consiste en enunciados que requieren una respuesta específica y estandarizada.

personality psychology: area of psychology in which the psychologists study the differences in personality among people. 13
  psicología de la personalidad: área de la psicología que estudia las diferencias de personalidad entre las personas.

personalization: distortion in which a person takes responsibility or blame for events that are unconnected to the person. 455
  personalización: distorsión en la cual la persona siente responsabilidad o culpa por eventos que no están conectados con ella.

person-centered therapy: a nondirective insight therapy based on the work of Carl Rogers in which the client does all the talking and the therapist listens. 450
  terapia centrada en la persona: terapia interna no directiva basada en el trabajo de Carl Rogers en la cual el cliente es el que habla y el terapeuta solo escucha.

persuasion: the process by which one person tries to change the belief, opinion, position, or course of action of another person through argument, pleading, or explanation. 228
  persuasión: proceso por el cual la persona trata de cambiar las creencias, la opinión, la posicion o el curso de acción de otra mediante el argumento, la súplica o la explicación.

pessimists: people who expect negative outcomes. 503
  pesimistas: personas que esperan resultados negativos.

phallic stage: third stage occurring from about three to six years of age, in which the child discovers sexual feelings. 380
  etapa fálica: tercera etapa que ocurre desde alrededor de los tres hasta los seis años de edad en la cual el niño descubre los sentimientos sexuales.

phobia: an intense fear of a specific object or situation, which may or may not be typically considered frightening. 365, 422
  fobia: miedo intenso a un objeto o una situación específica, que puede o no ser considerada típicamente aterradora.

phonemes: the basic units of sound in language. 202
  fonemas: unidades básicas de sonido del lenguaje.

phototherapy: the use of lights to treat seasonal affective disorder or other disorders. 436
  fototerapia: uso de luces para tratar el trastorno afectivo estacional y otros trastornos.

physical dependence: condition occurring when a person's body becomes unable to function normally without a particular drug. 132
  dependencia física: afección que ocurre cuando el cuerpo de una persona se vuelve incapaz de funcionar normalmente sin una droga específica.

physical development: development of the body. 142
  desarrollo físico: desarrollo del cuerpo.

physiological psychology: area of psychology in which the psychologists study the biological bases of behavior. 13
  psicología fisiológica: área de la psicología que estudia las bases biológicas de la conducta.

pineal gland: endocrine gland located near the base of the cerebrum; secretes melatonin. 51
  glándula pineal: glándula endocrina ubicada cerca de la base del cerebro; secreta melatonina.

pinna: the visible part of the ear. 87
  pabellón auricular: parte visible del oído.

pitch: psychological experience of sound that corresponds to the frequency of the sound waves; higher frequencies are perceived as higher pitches. 88
  tono: experiencia psicológica del sonido que corresponde a la frecuencia de las ondas sonoras; las frecuencias más altas se perciben como tonos más agudos.

pituitary gland: gland located in the brain that secretes human growth hormone and influences all other hormone-secreting glands (also known as the master gland). 51
  glándula pituitaria: glándula ubicada en el cerebro que secreta la hormona del crecimiento humano e influye en todas las otras glándulas secretoras de hormonas (también se conoce como hipófisis).

place theory: theory of pitch that states that different pitches are experienced by the stimulation of hair cells in different locations on the organ of Corti. 88
  teoría del lugar: teoría del tono que sostiene que los distintos tonos se experimentan debido a la estimulación de las células pilosas en distintos lugares del órgano de Corti.

placebo effect: phenomenon in which the expectations of the participants in a study can influence their behavior. 22
  efecto placebo: fenómeno por el cual las expectativas de los participantes en un estudio pueden tener influencia sobre su conducta.

placenta: a specialized organ that develops out of fetal tissue, providing nourishment and filtering away waste products. 148
  placenta: órgano especializado que se desarrolla a partir del tejido fetal, brinda nutrición y filtra los productos de desecho.

pleasure principle: principle by which the id functions; the immediate satisfaction of needs without regard for the consequences. 378
  principio del placer: principio mediante el cual funciona el ello; satisfacción inmediata de las necesidades sin tener en cuenta las consecuencias.

polygon: line graph showing a frequency distribution. 30
  polígono: gráfica lineal que muestra una distribución de frecuencia.

pons: the larger swelling above the medulla that connects the top of the brain to the bottom and that plays a part in sleep, dreaming, left–right body coordination, and arousal. 58
  puente de Varolio: gran protuberancia que se ubica encima del bulbo raquídeo que conecta las partes superior e inferior del cerebro y que tiene un papel importante en el dormir, los sueños, la coordinación izquierda-derecha del cuerpo y el despertar.

population: the entire group of people or animals in which the researcher is interested. 19
  población: todo el grupo de personas o animales en el cual está interesado el investigador.

positive psychology or **positive psychology movement:** a viewpoint that recommends shifting the focus of psychology away from the negative aspects to a more positive focus on strengths, well-being, and the pursuit of happiness. 11, 367
  psicología positiva o **movimiento de psicología positiva:** punto de vista que recomienda quitar el foco de la psicología de los aspectos negativos y llevarlo hacia otros más positivos como las fortalezas, el bienestar y la búsqueda de la felicidad.

positive regard: warmth, affection, love, and respect that come from significant others in one's life. 386
  aprecio positivo: calidez, ternura, amor y respeto que surgen de las personas importantes en la propia vida.

positive reinforcement: the reinforcement of a response by the addition or experiencing of a pleasurable stimulus (a reward following a response). 186
  refuerzo positivo: refuerzo de una respuesta por el agregado o la experiencia de un estímulo placentero (una recompensa que sigue a la respuesta).

positive symptoms: symptoms of schizophrenia that are excesses of behavior or occur in addition to normal behavior; hallucinations, delusions, and distorted thinking. 432
  síntomas positivos: síntomas de esquizofrenia que son excesos de conducta o que ocurren además de la conducta normal; alucinaciones, delirios y pensamiento distorsionado.

positron emission tomography (PET): Brain-imaging method in which a radioactive sugar is injected into the subject, and a computer compiles a color-coded image of the activity of the brain, with lighter colors indicating more activity. 55

tomografía por emisión de positrones: método de diagnóstico por imágenes cerebrales en el cual se inyecta un azúcar radiactivo en el sujeto y la computadora compila una imagen codificada por colores de la actividad del cerebro, que muestra colores más claros donde hay mayor actividad.

postconventional morality: third level of Kohlberg's stages of moral development in which the person's behavior is governed by moral principles that have been decided on by the individual and that may be in disagreement with accepted social norms. 164
moral posconvencional: tercer nivel de desarrollo moral de las etapas de Kohlberg en el cual la conducta de la persona está gobernada por principios morales que fueron decididos por el individuo y que pueden estar en desacuerdo con las normas sociales aceptadas.

post-traumatic stress disorder (PTSD): a disorder resulting from exposure to a major stressor, with symptoms of anxiety, nightmares, poor sleep, reliving the event, and concentration problems, lasting for more than one month. 492
trastorno de estrés postraumático: trastorno que se produce como resultado de la exposición a un factor estresante importante, con síntomas de ansiedad, pesadillas, poco sueño, sensación de revivir el evento y problemas de concentración, que dura más de un mes.

practical intelligence: the ability to use information to get along in life and become successful. 322
inteligencia práctica: capacidad de usar información para avanzar en la vida y ser exitoso.

pragmatics: aspects of language involving the practical ways of communicating with others, or the social "niceties" of language. 202
pragmática: aspectos del lenguaje que implican las maneras prácticas de comunicarse con otros, o las "sutilezas" sociales del lenguaje.

preconventional morality: first level of Kohlberg's stages of moral development in which the child's behavior is governed by the consequences of the behavior. 164
moral preconvencional: primer nivel de desarrollo moral de las etapas de Kohlberg en el cual la conducta del niño es gobernada por las consecuencias de la conducta.

predisposition: tendency or possibility. 67
predisposición: tendencia o probabilidad.

prefrontal lobotomy: psychosurgery in which the connections of the prefrontal lobes of the brain to the rear portions are severed. 469
lobotomía prefrontal: psicocirugía en la cual se cortan las conexiones de los lóbulos prefrontales del cerebro a las partes posteriores.

prejudice: negative attitude held by a person about the members of a particular social group. 232
prejuicio: actitud negativa que tiene una persona hacia los miembros de un grupo social particular.

preoperational stage: Piaget's second stage of cognitive development in which the preschool child learns to use language as a means of exploring the world. 154
etapa preoperacional: segunda etapa del desarrollo cognitivo de Piaget, en la cual el niño en edad preescolar aprende a usar el lenguaje como un medio de explorar el mundo.

pressure: the psychological experience produced by urgent demands or expectations for a person's behavior that come from an outside source. 487
presión: experiencia psicológica producida por exigencias o expectativas urgentes de la conducta de la persona que provienen de una fuente externa.

primacy effect: tendency to remember information at the beginning of a body of information better than the information that follows. 287
efecto de primacía: tendencia a recordar mejor la información al comienzo de un conjunto de información que la información que sigue.

primary appraisal: the first step in assessing stress, which involves estimating the severity of a stressor and classifying it as either a threat or a challenge. 495
apreciación primaria: primer paso en la valoración del estrés, que implica estimar la gravedad del factor estresante y clasificarlo como una amenaza o un desafío.

primary drives: those drives that involve needs of the body, such as hunger and thirst. 343
instintos primarios: aquellos instintos que implican las necesidades del cuerpo, como el hambre y la sed.

primary reinforcer: any reinforcer that is naturally reinforcing by meeting a basic biological need, such as hunger, thirst, or touch. 186
reforzador primario: todo reforzador que refuerza de manera natural, cubriendo una necesidad biológica básica como el hambre, la sed o el contacto.

proactive interference: memory retrieval problem that occurs when older information prevents or interferes with the retrieval of newer information. 295
interferencia proactiva: problema que ocurre en la recuperación de la memoria cuando la información más vieja evita o interfiere en la recuperación de la información más nueva.

problem solving: process of cognition that occurs when a goal must be reached by thinking and behaving in certain ways. 311
resolución de problemas: proceso de cognición que ocurre cuando se debe alcanzar un objetivo mediante el razonamiento y cierta conducta.

problem-focused coping: coping strategies that try to eliminate the source of a stress or reduce its impact through direct actions. 500
estrategia de afrontamiento focalizada en el problema: estrategias de afrontamiento que tratan de eliminar la fuente de estrés o reducir su impacto mediante acciones directas.

procedural (nondeclarative) memory: type of long-term memory including memory for skills, procedures, habits, and conditioned responses. These memories are not conscious but are implied to exist because they affect conscious behavior. 280
memoria de procedimiento (no declarativa): tipo de memoria a largo plazo que incluye la memoria de las habilidades, los procedimientos, los hábitos y las respuestas condicionadas. Esta memoria no es consciente, pero es implícita y afecta la conducta consciente.

projection: defense mechanism involving placing or "projecting" one's own unacceptable thoughts onto others, as if the thoughts actually belonged to those others and not to oneself. 392, 502
proyección: mecanismo de defensa que implica colocar o "proyectar" nuestros propios pensamientos inaceptables en otros, como si los pensamientos realmente pertenecieran a esas personas y no a nosotros.

projective tests: personality assessments that present ambiguous visual stimuli to the client and ask the client to respond with whatever comes to mind. 393
pruebas proyectivas: evaluaciones de la personalidad que presentan estímulos visuales ambiguos al cliente y se le solicita responder lo que le viene a la mente.

prosocial behavior: socially desirable behavior that benefits others. 240
conducta prosocial: conducta socialmente deseable que beneficia a otros.

prototype: an example of a concept that closely matches the defining characteristics of a concept. 309
prototipo: ejemplo de un concepto que concuerda fuertemente con las características definitorias del concepto.

proximity: physical or geographical nearness, or the tendency to perceive objects that are close to each other as part of the same grouping. 95, 236
proximidad: cercanía física o geográfica o tendencia a percibir objetos que están cerca como parte del mismo grupo.

psilocybin: natural hallucinogen found in certain mushrooms. 131
psilocibina: alucinógeno natural que se encuentra en ciertos hongos.

psychiatric social worker: a social worker with some training in therapy methods who focuses on the environmental conditions that can have an impact on mental disorders, such as poverty, overcrowding, stress, and drug abuse. 448
trabajador social psiquiátrico: trabajador social con algún entrenamiento en métodos de terapia que se focaliza en las condiciones ambientales que pueden tener un impacto en los trastornos mentales, como la pobreza, el hacinamiento, el estrés y el abuso de drogas.

psychiatrist: a medical doctor who specializes in the diagnosis and treatment of psychological disorders. 447
  psiquiatra: doctor en medicina que se especializa en el diagnóstico y tratamiento de trastornos psicológicos.

psychoactive drugs: drugs that alter thinking, perception, and memory. 126
  drogas psicoactivas: drogas que alteran el pensamiento, la percepción y la memoria.

psychoanalysis: the theory and therapy based on the work of Sigmund Freud, emphasizing the revealing of unconscious conflicts. 8, 381, 448
  psicoanálisis: teoría y terapia que se basa en el trabajo de Sigmund Freud, que hace hincapié en la revelación de conflictos inconscientes.

psychoanalyst: either a psychiatrist or a psychologist who has special training in the theories of Sigmund Freud and his method of psychoanalysis. 448
  psicoanalista: psiquiatra o psicólogo con entrenamiento especial en las teorías de Sigmund Freud y su método de psicoanálisis.

psychodynamic perspective: a modern version of psychoanalysis that is more focused on the development of a sense of self and the discovery of other motivations behind a person's behavior than repressed desires. 10
  perspectiva psicodinámica: visión moderna del psicoanálisis que está más focalizada en el desarrollo de un sentido del yo y en el descubrimiento de otras motivaciones detrás de la conducta de la persona que en los deseos reprimidos.

psychodynamic therapy: a newer and more general term for therapies based on psychoanalysis with an emphasis on transference, shorter treatment times, and a more direct therapeutic approach. 450
  terapia psicodinámica: término nuevo y más general para las terapias que están basadas en el psicoanálisis con énfasis en la transferencia, períodos de tratamiento más cortos y un enfoque terapéutico más directo.

psychological defense mechanisms: unconscious distortions of a person's perception of reality that reduce stress and anxiety. 501
  mecanismos psicológicos de defensa: distorsiones inconscientes de la percepción de la realidad de la persona, que reducen el estrés y la ansiedad.

psychological dependence: the feeling that a drug is needed to continue a feeling of emotional or psychological well-being. 132
  dependencia psicológica: sensación de que una droga es necesaria para continuar con el bienestar emocional o psicológico.

psychological disorders: any pattern of behavior that causes people significant distress, causes them to harm others, or harms their ability to function in daily life. 413
  trastornos psicológicos: todo patrón de conducta que causa en las personas una angustia importante, les lleva a lesionar a otros o les incapacita para funcionar en la vida cotidiana.

psychologist: a professional with an academic degree and specialized training in one or more areas of psychology. 448
  psicólogo: profesional con un título académico que tiene entrenamiento especializado en una o más áreas de la psicología.

psychology: the scientific study of behavior and mental processes. 4
  psicología: estudio científico de la conducta y los procesos mentales.

psychopathology: the study of abnormal behavior. 410
  psicopatología estudio de las conductas anormales.

psychopharmacology: the use of drugs to control or relieve the symptoms of psychological disorders. 465
  psicofarmacología: uso de fármacos para controlar o aliviar los síntomas de los trastornos psicológicos.

psychosexual stages: five stages of personality development proposed by Freud and tied to the sexual development of the child. 379
  etapas psicosexuales: cinco etapas del desarrollo de la personalidad propuestas por Freud y ligadas al desarrollo sexual del niño.

psychosocial development: development affecting our emotional and social lives. 143
  desarrollo psicosocial: desarrollo que afecta nuestra vida emocional y social.

psychosurgery: surgery performed on brain tissue to relieve or control severe psychological disorders. 469
  psicocirugía: cirugía que se lleva a cabo en el tejido cerebral para aliviar o controlar trastornos psicológicos severos.

psychotherapy: therapy for mental disorders in which a person with a problem talks with a psychologist, psychiatrist, or counselor. 446
  psicoterapia: terapia para los trastornos mentales en la cual la persona con problemas conversa con un psicólogo, un psiquiatra o un consejero.

psychotic: term applied to a person who is no longer able to perceive what is real and what is fantasy. 430
  psicótica: término que se aplica a la persona que ya no es capaz de percibir qué es real y qué es fantasía.

puberty: the physical changes in both primary and secondary sex characteristics that occur as part of sexual development. 162
  pubertad: cambios físicos de las características sexuales primarias y secundarias que ocurren como parte del desarrollo sexual.

punishment: any event or object that, when following a response, makes that response less likely to happen again. 186
  castigo: evento u objeto que, cuando sigue a una respuesta, hace que esa respuesta tenga menos probabilidades ocurrir nuevamente.

punishment by application: the punishment of a response by the addition or experiencing of an unpleasant stimulus. 186
  castigo por aplicación: castigo de una respuesta mediante el agregado o la experiencia de un estímulo desagradable.

punishment by removal: the punishment of a response by the removal of a pleasurable stimulus. 186
  castigo por supresión: castigo de una respuesta mediante la eliminación de un estímulo agradable.

R

random assignment: process of assigning subjects to the experimental or control groups randomly so that each subject has an equal chance of being in either group. 21
  asignación aleatoria: proceso de asignar sujetos a los grupos experimentales o de control de manera aleatoria, para que cada sujeto tenga la misma probabilidad de estar en cualquiera de los grupos.

range: the difference between the highest and lowest scores in a distribution. 28
  rango: diferencia entre el resultado mayor y el menor en una distribución.

rapid eye movement (REM): stage of sleep in which the eyes move rapidly under the eyelids and the person is typically experiencing a dream. 113
  movimientos oculares rápidos: etapa del sueño en la que los ojos se mueven rápidamente debajo de los párpados y la persona por lo general sueña.

rating scale: assessment in which a numerical value is assigned to specific behavior that is listed in the scale. 394
  escala de valoración: evaluación en la cual al valor numérico le es asignado una conducta específica enumerada en la lista.

rational-emotive behavior therapy (REBT): cognitive-behavioral therapy in which clients are directly challenged in their irrational beliefs and helped to restructure their thinking into more rational belief statements. 456
  terapia conductual racional-emotiva: terapia cognitivo-conductual en la cual el cliente es directamente confrontado con sus creencias irracionales y se le ayuda a reestructurar su pensamiento en enunciados más racionales.

rationalization: psychological defense mechanism in which a person invents acceptable excuses for unacceptable behavior. 502
  racionalización: mecanismo psicológico de defensa en el cual la persona inventa excusas aceptables para conductas inaceptables.

reaction formation: psychological defense mechanism in which a person forms an opposite emotional or behavioral reaction to the way he or she really feels to keep those true feelings hidden from self and others. 502
  formación reactiva: mecanismo psicológico de defensa en el cual la persona forma una reacción emocional o conductual opuesta a la manera que realmente desea para mantener esos sentimientos ocultos de sí misma y de otros.

real self: one's perception of actual characteristics, traits, and abilities. 385
  yo real: percepción de las características, los atributos y las capacidades reales propios.

realistic conflict theory: theory stating that prejudice and discrimination will be increased between groups that are in conflict over a limited resource. 233
  teoría realista del conflicto: teoría que sostiene que el prejuicio y la discriminación se incrementan entre grupos que están en conflicto por un recurso limitado.

reality principle: principle by which the ego functions; the need to satisfy the demands of the id in ways that meet the demands of real life. 378
  principio de realidad: principio por el que funciona el yo; necesidad de satisfacer las demandas del ello para satisfacer las exigencias de la vida real.

recall: type of memory retrieval in which the information to be retrieved must be "pulled" from memory with very few external cues. 287
  recuerdo: tipo de recupero de memoria en el cual la información debe ser "extraída" de la memoria con muy pocas pistas externas.

recency effect: tendency to remember information at the end of a body of information better than the information at the beginning of it. 287
  efecto de lo más reciente: tendencia a recordar mejor la información al final de un conjunto de información que al principio.

receptive meditation: form of meditation in which a person attempts to become aware of everything in immediate conscious experience, or an expansion of consciousness. 123
  meditación receptiva: forma de meditación en la cual la persona intenta estar consciente de todo en la experiencia consciente inmediata o expansión de la conciencia.

receptor sites: holes in the surface of the dendrites or certain cells of the muscles and glands, which are shaped to fit only certain neurotransmitters. 46
  sitios receptores: orificios en la superficie de las dendritas o ciertas células de los músculos y las glándulas que están preparados para recibir solo ciertos neurotransmisores.

recessive: referring to a gene that only influences the expression of a trait when paired with an identical gene. 67, 142
  recesivo: gen que solo influye en la expresión de un rasgo cuando se une con un gen idéntico.

reciprocal determinism: Bandura's explanation of how the factors of environment, personal characteristics, and behavior can interact to determine future behavior. 384
  determinismo recíproco: explicación de Bandura de cómo los factores del entorno, las características personales y la conducta pueden interactuar para determinar conductas futuras.

reciprocity of liking: tendency of people to like other people who like them in return. 236
  reciprocidad de la atracción: tendencia de las personas a sentirse atraídas por otras personas a las que a su vez atraen.

recognition: the ability to match a piece of information or a stimulus to a stored image or fact. 287
  reconocimiento: capacidad de unir una información o un estímulo a una imagen o un hecho almacenado.

reflection: therapy technique in which the therapist restates what the client says rather than interpreting those statements. 450
  reflexión: técnica de terapia en la cual el terapeuta reformula lo que el cliente dice en lugar de interpretar tales dichos.

regression: psychological defense mechanism in which a person falls back on childlike patterns of responding in reaction to stressful situations. 502
  regresión: mecanismo psicológico de defensa en el cual la persona comienza a tener patrones infantiles de respuesta en reacción a situaciones estresantes.

reinforcement: the strengthening of a response by following it with a pleasurable consequence or the removal of an unpleasant stimulus. 185, 453
  refuerzo: fortalecimiento de una respuesta mediante la aplicación de una consecuencia agradable o la eliminación de un estímulo desagradable.

reinforcer: any event or object that, when following a response, increases the likelihood of that response occurring again. 185
  reforzador: todo evento u objeto que, cuando sigue a una respuesta, incrementa la probabilidad de que esa respuesta vuelva a ocurrir.

relative deprivation: the feeling that one is worse off than others. 366
  privación relativa: sentimiento de que uno está peor que el resto.

relative size: perception that occurs when objects that a person expects to be of a certain size appear to be small and are, therefore, assumed to be much farther away. 98
  tamaño relativo: percepción que ocurre cuando un objeto que se espera sea de determinado tamaño es más pequeño y, por lo tanto, se supone que está más lejos.

reliability: the tendency of a test to produce the same scores again and again each time it is given to the same people. 33
  confiabilidad: tendencia de una prueba a producir los mismos resultados una y otra vez cuando se le administra a las mismas personas.

REM behavior disorder: a rare disorder in which the mechanism that blocks the movement of the voluntary muscles fails, allowing the person to thrash around and even get up and act out nightmares. 117
  trastorno de conducta del sueño REM: trastorno raro en el cual el mecanismo que bloquea el movimiento de los músculos voluntarios falla y permite que la persona se agite e incluso se levante y actúe las pesadillas.

REM paralysis: the inability of the voluntary muscles to move during REM sleep. 115
  parálisis del sueño REM: incapacidad de mover los músculos voluntarios durante el sueño REM.

REM rebound: increased amounts of REM sleep after being deprived of REM sleep on earlier nights. 116
  rebote del sueño REM: mayor cantidad de sueño REM después de haber sido privado de este tipo de sueño en noches anteriores.

representative sample: randomly selected sample of subjects from a larger population of subjects. 19
  muestra representativa: muestra de los sujetos de una población más grande seleccionada aleatoriamente.

representativeness heuristic: the tendency to believe that any object (or person) that shares characteristics with the members of a particular category is also a member of that category. 312
  representatividad heurística: tendencia a creer que un objeto (o una persona) que comparte características con los miembros de una categoría especial también es un miembro de esa categoría.

repression: psychological defense mechanism in which the person refuses to consciously remember a threatening or unacceptable event, instead pushing those events into the unconscious mind. 502
  represión: mecanismo psicológico de defensa en el cual la persona se niega a recordar de manera consciente un evento amenazante o no aceptable y en cambio empuja esos eventos más profundamente en la mente inconsciente.

resistance: a patient's reluctance to discuss a certain topic, which typically involves changing the subject or becoming silent. 449
  resistencia: negativa del paciente a discutir ciertos temas, que normalmente implica cambiar de tema o permanecer en silencio.

GLOSSARY/GLOSARIO GL-23

restorative theory: theory of sleep proposing that sleep is necessary to the physical health of the body and serves to replenish chemicals and repair cellular damage. 113
teoría del sueño reparador: teoría del sueño que propone que este es necesario para la salud física del cuerpo y sirve para reponer químicos y reparar el daño celular.

reticular formation (RF): an area of neurons running through the middle of the medulla and the pons and slightly beyond that play a role in general arousal, alertness, and sleep. 58
formación reticular: área de neuronas que se extiende a través del centro del bulbo raquídeo y el puente de Varolio y un poco más allá, que tiene un papel en el despertar general, la vigilia y el sueño.

retrieval: getting information that is in storage into a form that can be used. 274
recuperación: obtener información que está almacenada y darle una forma que se pueda usar.

retrieval cue: a stimulus for remembering. 285
pista de recuperación: estímulo para recordar.

retroactive interference: memory retrieval problem that occurs when newer information prevents or interferes with the retrieval of older information. 295
interferencia retroactiva: problema que ocurre en la recuperación de la memoria cuando la información más nueva evita o interfiere en la recuperación de la información más vieja.

retrograde amnesia: loss of memory from the point of some injury or trauma backwards, or loss of memory for the past. 296
amnesia retrógrada: pérdida de la memoria desde el punto de una lesión o trauma hacia atrás o pérdida de la memoria del pasado.

reversible figures: visual illusions in which the figure and ground can be reversed. 95
figuras reversibles: ilusiones visuales en las cuales la figura y el fondo pueden invertirse.

rods: visual sensory receptors found at the back of the retina, responsible for noncolor sensitivity to low levels of light. 82
bastoncillos: receptores sensoriales visuales que se encuentran en la parte posterior de la retina y son responsables de la no sensibilidad al color en bajos niveles de luz.

romantic love: type of love consisting of intimacy and passion. 237
amor romántico: tipo de amor que consiste en intimidad y pasión.

Rorschach inkblot test: projective test that uses ten inkblots as ambiguous stimuli. 393
test de Rorschach: prueba proyectiva que usa diez manchas de tinta como estímulos ambiguos.

S

s factor: the ability to excel in certain areas, or specific intelligence. 321
factor s: capacidad de sobresalir en determinadas áreas, o inteligencia específica.

schizophrenia: severe disorder in which the person suffers from disordered thinking, bizarre behavior, hallucinations, and inability to distinguish between fantasy and reality. 430
esquizofrenia: trastorno severo en el cual la persona sufre de pensamiento desordenado, conducta extravagante, alucinaciones e incapacidad de distinguir entre fantasía y realidad.

school psychology: area of psychology in which the psychologists work directly in the schools, doing assessments, educational placement, and diagnosing educational problems. 523
psicología escolar: área de la psicología cuyo trabajo transcurre en las escuelas, haciendo evaluaciones, colocación y diagnóstico de problemas educacionales.

scientific method: system of gathering data so that bias and error in measurement are reduced. 16
método científico: sistema de recolección de datos que reduce el sesgo y los errores de medida.

seasonal affective disorder (SAD): a mood disorder caused by the body's reaction to low levels of sunlight in the winter months. 436
trastorno afectivo estacional: trastorno del estado de ánimo causado por la reacción del cuerpo a los bajos niveles de luz solar durante los meses de invierno.

secondary appraisal: the second step in assessing a threat, which involves estimating the resources available to the person for coping with the stressor. 496
apreciación secundaria: segundo paso en la evaluación de una amenaza, que implica estimar los recursos disponibles para afrontar el factor estresante.

secondary reinforcer: any reinforcer, such as praise, tokens, or gold stars, that becomes reinforcing after being paired with a primary reinforcer. 186
reforzador secundario: todo reforzador, como elogios, fichas o estrellas doradas, que se vuelven reforzadores al unirse con un reforzador primario.

selective attention: the ability to focus on only one stimulus from among all sensory input. 277
atención selectiva: capacidad de focalizarse en un solo estímulo entre todas las entradas sensoriales.

selective thinking: distortion in which a person focuses on only one aspect of a situation while ignoring all other relevant aspects. 455
pensamiento selectivo: distorsión en la cual la persona se focaliza solo en un aspecto de la situación e ignora todos los otros aspectos relevantes.

self: an individual's awareness of their own personal characteristics and level of functioning. 385
yo: conciencia del individuo de sus propias características personales y nivel de funcionamiento.

self-actualization: according to Maslow, the point that is seldom reached at which people have sufficiently satisfied the lower needs and achieved their full human potential. 346
autorrealización: según Maslow, punto que casi nunca se alcanza en el cual las personas tienen suficientemente cubiertas las necesidades menores y han alcanzado su potencial humano completo.

self-actualizing tendency: the striving to fulfill one's innate capacities and capabilities. 385
tendencia a la autorrealización: esfuerzo por desarrollar las propias capacidades innatas.

self-determination theory (SDT): theory of human motivation in which the social context of an action has an effect on the type of motivation existing for the action. 348
teoría de la autodeterminación: teoría de la motivación humana en la cual el contexto social de una acción tiene efecto en el tipo de motivación que existe para la acción.

self-efficacy: individual's expectancy of how effective his or her efforts to accomplish a goal will be in any particular circumstance. 384
autoeficacia: expectativa del individuo de qué tan efectivos son sus esfuerzos para alcanzar una meta en una circunstancia particular.

self-esteem: the feeling of worth or value in oneself. 399
autoestima: sensación de valor o aprecio de uno mismo.

self-fulfilling prophecy: the tendency of one's expectations to affect one's behavior in such a way as to make the expectations more likely to occur. 235
profesía autocumplida: tendencia de que las propias expectativas afecten la propia conducta de manera tal que esas expectativas tienen mayores probabilidades de ocurrir.

self-help groups (support groups): groups composed of people who have similar problems and who meet together without a therapist or counselor for the purpose of discussion, problem solving, and social and emotional support. 458
grupos de autoayuda (grupos de apoyo): grupos compuestos de personas que tienen problemas similares y se encuentran, sin la presencia de un terapeuta o un consejero, para debatir, resolver problemas y para apoyarse unos a otros social y emocionalmente.

semantic memory: type of declarative memory containing general knowledge, such as knowledge of language and information learned in formal education. 281
  memoria semántica: tipo de memoria declarativa que contiene conocimientos generales, como conocimiento del lenguaje e información aprendida durante la educación formal.

semantics: the rules for determining the meaning of words and sentences. 202
  semántica: reglas que determinan el significado de palabras y oraciones.

sensation: the process that occurs when special receptors in the sense organs are activated, allowing various forms of outside stimuli to become neural signals in the brain. 78
  sensación: proceso que ocurre cuando se activan receptores especiales en los órganos sensoriales, que permiten que varios estímulos externos se transformen en señales neurales en el cerebro.

sensation seeker: someone who needs more arousal than the average person and seeks out complex and varied experiences. 345
  buscador de emociones: alguien que necesita más excitación que las personas promedio y busca experiencias variadas y complejas.

sensitive period: a time when a child is susceptible to stimuli and receptive to learning from particular types of experiences. 145
  período sensitivo: período cuando el niño es susceptible a los estímulos y receptivo a las enseñanzas de algunas experiencias particulares.

sensorimotor stage: Piaget's first stage of cognitive development in which the infant uses its senses and motor abilities to interact with objects in the environment. 153
  etapa sensoriomotriz: primera etapa del desarrollo cognitivo de Piaget, en la cual el niño pequeño usa sus sentidos y capacidades motrices para interactuar con los objetos del entorno.

sensory adaptation: tendency of sensory receptor cells to become less responsive to a stimulus that is unchanging. 79
  adaptación sensorial: tendencia de las células receptoras de los sentidos a reccionar menos ante un estímulo permanente.

sensory memory: the very first stage of memory; the point at which information enters the nervous system through the sensory systems. 276
  memoria sensorial: primera etapa de la memoria, punto en el que la información entra en el sistema nervioso a través de los sistemas sensoriales.

sensory neuron: a neuron that carries information from the senses to the central nervous system. 48
  neurona sensorial: neurona que lleva información desde los sentidos hacia el sistema nervioso central.

serial position effect: tendency of information at the beginning and end of a body of information to be remembered more accurately than information in the middle of the body of information. 287
  efecto de posición serial: tendencia a recordar la información ubicada al principio y al final de un conjunto de información con mayor precisión que aquella que se encuentra en el medio.

serotonin: a neurotransmitter involved in maintaining stability of mood. 366
  serotonina: neurotransmisor que mantiene la estabilidad del estado de ánimo.

sexual orientation: the direction of a person's sexual attraction and affection for others. 353
  orientación sexual: dirección de la atracción sexual y del afecto de una persona.

shape constancy: the tendency to interpret the shape of an object as being constant, even when its shape changes on the retina. 95
  constancia de la forma: tendencia a interpretar la forma de un objeto como constante, incluso cuando su forma en la retina cambia.

shaping: technique in which a person is rewarded for gradually coming closer to demonstrating a desirable behavior by reinforcing steps toward the desired behavior and extinguishing behaviors that move away from the desired behavior. 188, 454
  modelado: técnica en la cual se recompensa a la persona por acercarse gradualmente a la conducta deseada reforzando los pasos hacia dicha conducta y eliminando aquellas que se alejan de la conducta deseada.

short-term memory (STM): the memory system in which information is held for brief periods of time while being used. 277
  memoria a corto plazo: sistema de memoria en el cual la información se mantiene por períodos cortos de tiempo mientras se usa.

similarity: the tendency to perceive things that look similar to each other as being part of the same group. 95
  similaridad: tendencia a percibir cosas que parecen similares como parte del mismo grupo.

situational cause: cause of behavior attributed to external factors, such as delays, the action of others, or some other aspect of the situation. 229
  causa situacional: causa de conducta que se atribuye a factores externos, como retrasos, acciones de otros o algún otro aspecto de la situación.

situational context: the social or environmental setting of a person's behavior. 412
  contexto situacional: entorno social o ambiental de la conducta de una persona.

size constancy: the tendency to interpret an object as always being the same actual size, regardless of its distance. 94
  constancia del tamaño: tendencia a interpretar un objeto como del mismo tamaño, sin importar la distancia, siempre.

skin senses: the sensations of touch, pressure, temperature, and pain. 91
  sentido cutáneo: sensación de tacto, presión, temperatura y dolor.

sleep apnea: disorder in which the person stops breathing for nearly half a minute or more. 118
  apnea del sueño: trastorno en el cual la persona deja de respirar durante casi medio minuto o más.

sleep deprivation: any significant loss of sleep, resulting in problems in concentration and irritability. 112
  privación del sueño: toda pérdida importante de sueño, que da como resultado problemas de concentración e irritabilidad.

sleepwalking (somnambulism): an episode, occurring during Stages Three and Four sleep, of moving around or walking around in one's sleep. 117
  sonambulismo: episodio, que ocurre durante las etapas tres y cuatro del sueño, en el que la persona se mueve o camina mientras está dormida.

social cognitive learning theorists: theorists who emphasize the importance of both the influences of other people's behavior and of a person's own expectancies of learning. 384
  teorizadores del aprendizaje sociocognitivo: teorizadores que hacen hincapié en la importancia tanto de las influencias de la conducta de otras personas como de las propias expectativas de aprendizaje de la persona.

social cognitive theory: referring to the use of cognitive processes in relation to understanding the social world. 234
  teoría sociocognitiva: teoría que hace referencia al uso de procesos cognitivos en relación con la comprensión del mundo social.

social cognitive view: learning theory that includes cognitive processes such as anticipating, judging, memory, and imitation of models. 384
  visión sociocognitiva: teoría del aprendizaje que incluye procesos cognitivos como anticipación, juicio, memoria e imitación de modelos.

social comparison: the comparison of oneself to others in ways that raise one's self-esteem. 234
  comparación social: comparse con otros para levantar la propia autoestima.

social facilitation: the tendency for the presence of other people to have a positive impact on the performance of an easy task. 219
  facilitación social: tendencia a que la presencia de otras personas tenga un impacto positivo en la realización de tareas sencillas.

social identity: the part of the self-concept including one's view of self as a member of a particular social category. 234
  identidad social: parte del autoconcepto que incluye la propia visión como miembro de una categoría social particular.

social identity theory: theory in which the formation of a person's identity within a particular social group is explained by social categorization, social identification, and social comparison. 234
  teoría de la identidad social: teoría en la cual la formación de la identidad de una persona dentro de un grupo social particular se explica mediante la categorización social, la identificación social y la comparación social.

social impairment: the tendency for the presence of other people to have a negative impact on the performance of a difficult task. 219
  deterioro social: tendencia a que la presencia de otras personas tenga un impacto negativo en la realización de una tarea compleja.

social influence: the process through which the real or implied presence of others can directly or indirectly influence the thoughts, feelings, and behavior of an individual. 214
  influencia social: proceso por el cual la presencia real o implícita de otros puede tener influencia directa o indirecta sobre los pensamientos, los sentimientos y la conducta de un individuo.

social loafing: the tendency for people to put less effort into a simple task when working with others on that task. 219
  pereza social: tendencia de las personas a poner menos esfuerzo en una tarea simple cuando se trabaja con otras personas.

social phobia: fear of interacting with others or being in social situations that might lead to a negative evaluation. 422
  fobia social: temor a interactuar con otros o a estar en situaciones sociales que puedan llevar a una evaluación negativa.

social psychology: the scientific study of how a person's thoughts, feelings, and behavior are influenced by the real, imagined, or implied presence of others. 13, 214
  psicología social: estudio científico de cómo la presencia real, imaginaria o implícita de otros afecta los pensamientos, los sentimientos y la conducta de una persona.

social role: the pattern of behavior that is expected of a person who is in a particular social position. 239
  rol social: patrón de conducta que se espera de una persona que está en determinada posición social.

social support system: the network of family, friends, neighbors, coworkers, and others who can offer support, comfort, or aid to a person in need. 501
  sistema de apoyo social: red comprendida por familia, amigos, vecinos, compañeros de trabajo y otros que pueden ofrecer apoyo, consuelo y ayuda a un persona necesitada.

social-cognitive theory of hypnosis: theory that assumes that people who are hypnotized are not in an altered state but are merely playing the role expected of them in the situation. 126
  teoría sociocognitiva de la hipnosis: teoría que supone que las personas hipnotizadas no están en un estado alterado sino solamente actuando el papel que se espera de ellos en esa situación.

sociocultural perspective: perspective that focuses on the relationship between social behavior and culture. 11
  perspectiva sociocultural: perspectiva que se focaliza en la relación entre la conducta social y la cultura.

soma: the cell body of the neuron responsible for maintaining the life of the cell. 42
  soma: cuerpo celular de la neurona responsable de mantener la vida de la célula.

somatization disorder: somatoform disorder in which the person dramatically complains of a specific symptom, such as nausea, difficulty swallowing, or pain, for which there is no real physical cause. 425
  trastorno de somatización: trastorno somatoforme en el que la persona se queja de un síntoma específico como náuseas, dificultad para tragar o dolor, para el cual no hay una causa física real.

somatoform disorders: disorders that take the form of bodily illnesses and symptoms but for which there are no real physical disorders. 424
  trastornos somatoformes: trastornos que toman la forma de enfermedades y síntomas corporales pero para los cuales no hay un trastorno físico real.

somatosensory cortex: area of neurons running down the front of the parietal lobes responsible for processing information from the skin and internal body receptors for touch, temperature, body position, and possibly taste. 60
  corteza somatosensorial: área de neuronas que se extiende en la parte frontal de los lóbulos parietales y es responsable del procesamiento de la información de los receptores internos del cuerpo y de la piel para el tacto, la temperatura, la posición del cuerpo y posiblemente el gusto.

somesthetic senses: the body senses consisting of the skin senses, the kinesthetic sense, and the vestibular senses. 91
  sentidos somestésicos: sentidos corporales que consisten en el sentido cutáneo, el sentido cinestésico y el sentido vestibular.

source traits: the more basic traits that underlie the surface traits, forming the core of personality. 387
  atributos fuente: atributos más básicos que yacen por debajo de los atributos superficiales y forman el núcleo de la personalidad.

specific phobia: fear of objects or specific situations or events. 422
  fobia específica: temor a objetos, situaciones o eventos específicos.

spontaneous recovery: the reappearance of a learned response after extinction has occurred. 180
  recuperación espontánea: reaparición de una respuesta aprendida después de haberla eliminado.

sports psychology: area of psychology in which the psychologists help athletes and others to prepare themselves mentally for participation in sports activities. 523
  psicología del deporte: área de la psicología que ayuda a los atletas y otros deportistas a prepararse mentalmente para participar en actividades deportivas.

standard deviation: a statistical measure of the average variation from the mean score. 28, 324
  desviación estándar: medida estadística de la variación promedio de la media.. 324

standardization: the process of giving a test to a large group of people that represents the population for whom the test is designed. 19, 323
  estandarización: proceso de dar una prueba a un grupo grande de personas que representa la población para la cual la prueba fue diseñad.

statistically significant: referring to differences in data sets that are larger than chance variation would predict. 33
  estadísticamente importante: diferencias entre grupos de datos que son mayores de lo que puede predecir la variación accidental.

statistics: branch of mathematics concerned with the collection and interpretation of numerical data. 26
  estadística: rama de las matemáticas que se ocupa de la recolección e interpretación de datos numéricos.

stem cells: special cells found in all the tissues of the body that are capable of becoming other cell types when those cells need to be replaced due to damage or wear and tear. 56
  células madre: células especiales que se hallan en todos los tejidos del cuerpo y son capaces de transformarse en otros tipos de células cuando esas células deben ser reemplazadas debido a lesiones o deterioro.

stereotype: a set of characteristics that people believe is shared by all members of a particular social category. 232
  estereotipo: conjunto de características que se cree que comparten todos los miembros de una categoría social particular.

stereotype vulnerability: the effect that people's awareness of the stereotypes associated with their social group has on their behavior. 234
  vulnerabilidad de los estereotipos: efecto que la conciencia de los estereotipos asociados con el grupo social tiene en la conducta de cada uno.

stigma: social disapproval of conditions or characteristics that are considered abnormal. 415
  estigma: desaprobación social de las condiciones o características que son consideradas anormales.

stimulants: drugs that increase the functioning of the nervous system. 126
  estimulantes: drogas que incrementan el funcionamiento del sistema nervioso.

stimulatory hallucinogenics: drugs that produce a mixture of psychomotor stimulant and hallucinogenic effects. 130
  alucinógenos estimulantes: drogas que producen una mezcla de estimulación psicomotriz y efectos alucinógenos.

stimulus discrimination: the tendency to stop making a generalized response to a stimulus that is similar to the original conditioned stimulus because the similar stimulus is never paired with the unconditioned stimulus. 180
  discriminación de estímulo: tendencia a dejar de dar una respuesta generalizada a un estímulo que es similar al estímulo original condicionado porque el estímulo similar nunca se une con el estímulo no condicionado.

stimulus generalization: the tendency to respond to a stimulus that is only similar to the original conditioned stimulus with the conditioned response. 180
  generalización de estímulo: tendencia a responder a un estímulo que solo es similar al estímulo original condicionado con la respuesta condicionada.

stimulus motive: a motive that appears to be unlearned but causes an increase in stimulation, such as curiosity. 344
  motivo del estímulo: motivo que parece ser no aprendido pero causa un incremento en la estimulación, como la curiosidad.

storage: holding onto information for some period of time. 274
  almacenar: mantener información durante algún tiempo.

stress: the term used to describe the physical, emotional, cognitive, and behavioral responses to events that are appraised as threatening or challenging. 482
  estrés: término que se usa para describir las respuestas físicas, emocionales, cognitivas y conductuales a los eventos que se perciben como amenazantes o desafiantes.

stressors: events that cause a stress reaction. 482
  factores estresantes: eventos que causan una reacción de estrés.

stress-vulnerability model: explanation of disorder that assumes a biological sensitivity or vulnerability to a certain disorder will result in the development of that disorder under the right conditions of environmental or emotional stress. 433
  modelo estrés-vulnerabilidad: explicación de un trastorno que supone que una sensibilidad biológica, o vulnerabilidad, a cierto trastorno dará como resultado el desarrollo de ese trastorno en condiciones correctas de estrés emocional y ambiental.

structuralism: early perspective in psychology associated with Wilhelm Wundt and Edward Titchener, in which the focus of study is the structure or basic elements of the mind. 6
  estructuralismo: perspectiva temprana de la psicología asociada con Wilhelm Wundt y Edward Titchener, en la cual el foco de estudio es la estructura o los elementos básicos de la mente.

subgoaling: process of breaking a goal down into smaller goals. 312
  subobjetivación: proceso de dividir un objetivo en objetivos más pequeños.

subjective: referring to concepts and impressions that are only valid within a particular person's perception and may be influenced by biases, prejudice, and personal experiences. 393
  subjetivos: conceptos e impresiones que son válidas solo en la percepción particular de una persona y pueden verse influenciados por sesgos, prejuicios y experiencias personales.

subjective discomfort: emotional distress or emotional pain as reported by an individual. 412
  incomodidad subjetiva: distrés emocional o dolor emocional según lo que describe el individuo.

sublimation: channeling socially unacceptable impulses and urges into socially acceptable behavior. 502
  sublimación: canalizar impulsos y deseos socialmente inaceptables mediante conductas aceptables.

subordinate concept: the most specific category of a concept, such as one's pet dog or a pear in one's hand. 308
  concepto subordinado: categoría más específica de un concepto, como la propia mascota o una pera en la propia mano.

successive approximations: small steps in behavior, one after the other, that lead to a particular goal behavior. 188
  aproximaciones sucesivas: pequeños pasos de conducta, uno detrás del otro, que llevan a una conducta-objetivo particular.

superego: part of the personality that acts as a moral center. 378
  superyó: parte de la personalidad que actúa como centro moral.

superordinate concept: the most general form of a type of concept, such as "animal" or "fruit." 308
  hiperónimo: tipo más general de concepto, como "animal" o "fruta".

surface traits: aspects of personality that can easily be seen by other people in the outward actions of a person. 387
  atributos superficiales: aspectos de la personalidad que los otros pueden ver fácilmente en las acciones externas de la persona.

survey method: method of conducting research in the form of interviews. 18
  método de encuesta: método para llevar a cabo investigaciones en forma de entrevistas.

sympathetic division (fight-or-flight system): part of the ANS that is responsible for reacting to stressful events and bodily arousal. 49
  división simpática (sistema de lucha o huida): parte del sistema nervioso autónomo responsable de reaccionar ante eventos estresantes y de la excitación corporal.

synaptic vesicles: saclike structures found inside the synaptic knob containing chemicals. 46
  vesículas sinápticas: estructuras similares a sacos que se encuentran dentro de la protuberancia sináptica y que contienen químicos.

syntax: the system of rules for combining words and phrases to form grammatically correct sentences. 202
  sintaxis: sistema de reglas para combinar palabras y frases para formar una oración gramaticalmente correcta.

systematic desensitization: behavior technique used to treat phobias in which a client makes an ordered list of fears and is taught to relax while concentrating on those fears. 452
  desensibilización sistemática: técnica de conducta que se usa para tratar fobias en la que el cliente hace una lista ordenada de los miedos y se le enseña a relajarse mientras se concentra en esos miedos.

T

temperament: a child's innate personality and emotional characteristics, observable in infancy; the enduring characteristics with which each person is born. 143, 376
  temperamento: personalidad innata y características emocionales de un niño, observables durante la infancia; características perdurables con las que nace cada persona.

temporal lobes: areas of the cortex located just behind the temples containing the neurons responsible for the sense of hearing and meaningful speech. 60
  lóbulos temporales: áreas de la corteza cerebral ubicadas justo detrás de las sienes y que contienen las neuronas responsables del sentido del oído y del lenguaje.

teratogen: any factor that can cause a birth defect. 148
  teratógeno: todo factor que puede causar un defecto de nacimiento.

texture gradient: the tendency for textured surfaces to appear to become smaller and finer as distance from the viewer increases. 98
  gradiente de textura: tendencia a que las superficies texturadas parezcan más pequeñas y mejores a medida que se incrementa la distancia del observador.

thalamus: part of the limbic system located in the center of the brain, this structure relays sensory information from the lower part of the brain to the proper areas of the cortex and processes some sensory information before sending it to its proper area. 59
  tálamo: parte del sistema límbico ubicado en el centro del cerebro. Esta estructura transmite información sensorial desde la parte inferior del cerebro a las áreas correspondientes de la corteza cerebral y procesa parte de la información sensorial antes de enviarla al área correspondiente.

that's-not-all technique: a sales technique in which the persuader makes an offer and then adds something extra to make the offer look better before the target person can make a decision. 217
  técnica "eso no es todo": técnica de ventas en la cual el vendedor hace una oferta y luego agrega algo extra para que la oferta se vea mejor antes de que el comprador tome una decisión.

Thematic Apperception Test (TAT): projective test that uses 20 pictures of people in ambiguous situations as the visual stimuli. 393
  test de apercepción temática: prueba proyectiva que usa 20 dibujos de personas en situaciones ambiguas como estímulo visual.

therapeutic alliance: the relationship between therapist and client that develops as a warm, caring, accepting relationship characterized by empathy, mutual respect, and understanding. 460
  alianza terapéutica: relación entre terapeuta y cliente que se desarrolla como una relación cálida, afectuosa y acogedora, caracterizada por empatía, respeto mutuo y comprensión.

therapy: treatment methods aimed at making people feel better and function more effectively. 446
  terapia: métodos de tratamiento que apuntan a que las personas se sientan mejor y funcionen de manera más efectiva.

theta waves: brain waves indicating the early stages of sleep. 113
  ondas theta: ondas cerebrales que indican las primeras etapas del sueño.

thinking (cognition): mental activity that goes on in the brain when a person is processing information (organizing and attempting to understand information and communicating information to others). 306
  razonamiento (cognición): actividad mental que ocurre en el cerebro cuando una persona está procesando información (organizando y tratando de comprender la información y comunicándola a otros).

thyroid gland: endocrine gland found in the neck; regulates metabolism. 51
  glándula tiroides: glándula endocrina que se encuentra en el cuello y regula el metabolismo.

time-out: an extinction process in which a person is removed from the situation that provides reinforcement for undesirable behavior, usually by being placed in a quiet corner or room away from possible attention and reinforcement opportunities. 454
  tiempo muerto: proceso de extinción en el cual se quita a la persona de la situación que brinda refuerzo de la conducta no deseada, usualmente poniéndola en un rincón tranquilo o alejándola de posibles oportunidades de atención y refuerzo.

token economy: the use of objects called tokens to reinforce behavior; tokens can be accumulated and exchanged for desired items or privileges. 192, 453
  economía de fichas: uso de objetos que se denominan "fichas" para reforzar la conducta; las fichas pueden acumularse y cambiarse por artículos o privilegios deseados.

top-down processing: the use of preexisting knowledge to organize individual features into a unified whole. 100
  procesamiento de arriba hacia abajo: uso de conocimientos preexistentes para organizar características individuales en un todo unificado.

trait: a consistent, enduring way of thinking, feeling, or behaving. 387
  atributo: forma consistente y perdurable de pensar, sentir y comportarse.

trait theories: theories that endeavor to describe the characteristics that make up human personality in an effort to predict future behavior. 387
  teorías de los atributos: teorías que tratan de describir las características que conforman la personalidad humana en un esfuerzo por predecir conductas futuras.

trait–situation interaction: the assumption that the particular circumstances of any given situation will influence the way in which a trait is expressed. 389
  interacción atributo-situación: suposición de que las circunstancias particulares de una situación dada influirán en el modo en que se expresa un atributo.

transduction: the transformation of energy from one form to another. 82
  transducción: transformación de la energía de una forma en otra.

transference: the tendency for a patient or client to project positive or negative feelings for important people from the past onto the therapist. 449
  transferencia: tendencia del paciente o cliente a proyectar sentimientos positivos o negativos hacia personas importantes del pasado en el terapeuta.

trial-and-error (mechanical solution): problem-solving method in which one possible solution after another is tried until a successful one is found. 311
  prueba y error (solución mecánica): método de resolución de problemas en el cual se trata una solución posible detrás de la otra hasta que se halla una solución exitosa.

triarchic theory of intelligence: Sternberg's theory that there are three kinds of intelligence: analytical, creative, and practical. 322
  teoría triárquica de la inteligencia: teoría de Sternberg que sostiene que hay tres tipos de inteligencia: analítica, creativa y práctica.

trichromatic theory: theory of color vision that proposes three types of cones: red, blue, and green. 84
  teoría tricromática: teoría de la visión de los colores que propone tres tipos de conos: rojos, azules y verdes.

tricyclics: antidepressant drugs that increase the activity of serotonin and norepinephrine by inhibiting their reuptake into the neurons' synaptic vesicles. 467
  antidepresivos tricíclicos: fármacos antidepresivos que incrementan la actividad de la serotonina y la norepinefrina mediante la inhibición de su reabsorción en las vesículas sinápticas de las neuronas.

two-factor theory: theory of emotion in which both the physical arousal and the labeling of that arousal based on cues from the environment must occur before the emotion is experienced. 361
  teoría de los dos factores: teoría de la emoción en la cual tanto la excitación física como la identificación de esa excitación basándose en pistas del entorno deben ocurrir antes de que se experimente la emoción.

Type A personality: person who is ambitious, time conscious, extremely hardworking, and tends to have high levels of hostility and anger as well as being easily annoyed. 497
  personalidad tipo A: persona ambiciosa, consciente del tiempo, extremadamente trabajadora y que tiende a tener altos niveles de hostilidad y agresividad y se enoja fácilmente.

Type B personality: person who is relaxed and laid-back, less driven and competitive than Type A, and slow to anger. 497
  personalidad tipo B: persona relajada y flexible, menos impulsiva y competitiva que el tipo A y que no se enoja fácilmente.

Type C personality: pleasant but repressed person, who tends to internalize his or her anger and anxiety and who finds expressing emotions difficult. 498
  personalidad tipo C: persona agradable pero reprimida, que tiende a internalizar su enojo y ansiedad y a la que no le resulta fácil expresar sus emociones.

typical neuroleptics: antipsychotic drugs that block certain dopamine receptors in the brain, thereby reducing dopamine's effect in synaptic transmission. 465
  antipsicóticos típicos: fármacos antipsicóticos que bloquean algunos receptores de la dopamina en el cerebro, por lo que reducen el efecto de la dopamina en la transmisión sináptica.

U

umbilical cord: cord that connects the baby to the placenta and implants itself in the uterine wall. 148
  cordón umbilical: cordón que conecta al bebé con la placenta y que se implanta en la pared uterina.

unconditional positive regard: warmth, respect, and affection without any conditions attached; this is a crucial part of the accepting atmosphere the therapist creates for the client in person-centered therapy. 386, 450
  aprecio positivo incondicional: calidez, respeto y afecto sin condiciones; parte esencial de la atmósfera de aceptación que crea el terapeuta en la terapia focalizada en la persona.

unconditioned response (UCR): an involuntary (reflex) response to a naturally occurring or unconditioned stimulus. 179
  respuesta no condicionada: respuesta involuntaria (refleja) a un estímulo natural o no condicionado.

unconditioned stimulus (UCS): a naturally occurring stimulus that leads to an involuntary (reflex) response. 179
  estímulo no condicionado: estímulo que ocurre naturalmente y lleva a una respuesta involuntaria (refleja).

unconscious mind: level of the mind in which thoughts, feelings, memories, and other information are kept that are not easily or voluntarily brought into consciousness. 377
  mente inconsciente: nivel de la mente en el que los pensamientos, los sentimientos, los recuerdos y otra información que se mantiene no se puede traer fácilmente o voluntariamente a la conciencia.

unilateral ECT: electroconvulsive therapy in which the electrodes are placed on only one side of the head and the forehead. 468
  terapia electroconvulsiva unilateral: terapia electroconvulsiva en la cual se colocan los electrodos solo en una parte de la cabeza y la frente.

universal: found across all cultures. 257
  universal: que se encuentra en todas las culturas.

uterus: the muscular organ that will contain and protect the developing infant. 148
  útero: órgano muscular que contiene y protege al niño en desarrollo.

V

validity: the degree to which a test actually measures what it is supposed to measure. 33
  validez: grado en el cual una prueba mide en realidad lo que se supone que mide.

variable interval schedule of reinforcement: schedule of reinforcement in which the interval of time that must pass before reinforcement becomes possible is different for each trial or event. 189
  programa de refuerzo de intervalo variable: patrón de refuerzo en el cual el intervalo de tiempo que debe pasar antes de que sea posible el refuerzo es diferente en cada prueba o evento.

variable ratio schedule of reinforcement: schedule of reinforcement in which the number of responses required for reinforcement is different for each trial or event. 190
  programa de refuerzo de razón variable: patrón de refuerzo en el cual el número de respuestas que se requieren para el refuerzo es diferente en cada prueba o evento.

vestibular senses: the sensations of movement, balance, and body position. 91
  sentidos vestibulares: sensaciones de movimiento, equilibrio y posición corporal.

vicarious conditioning: classical conditioning of a reflex response or emotion by watching the reaction of another person. 182
  condicionamiento vicario: condicionamiento clásico de un reflejo de respuesta o emoción que se produce al observar la reacción de otra persona.

visual accommodation: the change in the thickness of the lens as the eye focuses on objects that are far away or close. 82
  adaptación visual: cambio en el espesor del cristalino a medida que el ojo se enfoca en objetos cercanos o lejanos.

volley principle: theory of pitch that states that frequencies from about 400 Hz to 4000 Hz cause the hair cells (auditory neurons) to fire in a volley pattern, or take turns in firing. 88
  principio de la volea: teoría del tono que sostiene que las frecuencias de 400 Hz a 4000 Hz causan que las células pilosas (neuronas auditivas) descarguen en un patrón de volea, es decir, lo hagan por turno.

W

waking consciousness: state in which thoughts, feelings, and sensations are clear, organized, and the person feels alert. 110
  vigilia: estado en el cual los pensamientos, los sentimientos y las sensaciones son claras, organizadas y la persona se siente alerta.

weight set point: the particular level of weight that the body tries to maintain. 349
  punto fijo de peso: nivel particular de peso que el cuerpo trata de mantener.

Wernicke's aphasia: condition resulting from damage to Wernicke's area, causing the affected person to be unable to understand or produce meaningful language. 206
  afasia de Wernicke: afección que se produce como resultado de una lesión en el área de Wernicke y causa que la persona afectada sea incapaz de comprender o producir el lenguaje.

withdrawal: physical symptoms that can include nausea, pain, tremors, crankiness, and high blood pressure, resulting from a lack of an addictive drug in the body systems. 132
  abstinencia: síntomas físicos que incluyen náuseas, dolor, temblores, irritabilidad y tensión arterial alta y son el resultado de la falta de una droga adictiva en los sistemas del cuerpo.

working memory: an active system that processes the information in short-term memory. 278
  memoria de trabajo: sistema activo que procesa la información en la memoria a corto plazo.

Y

Yerkes-Dodson law: law stating performance is related to arousal; moderate levels of arousal lead to better performance than do levels of arousal that are too low or too high. This effect varies with the difficulty of the task: Easy tasks require a high-moderate level whereas more difficult tasks require a low-moderate level. 344

Ley de Yerkes-Dodson: ley que sostiene que el rendimiento está relacionado con la activación; niveles moderados de activación llevan a un mejor rendimiento que niveles demasiado bajos o demasiado altos. Este efecto varía según la dificultad de la tarea: las tareas fáciles requieren un nivel alto-moderado, mientras que las más difíciles requieren un nivel bajo-moderado.

Z

zygote: a single cell that contains all the information needed to form a complete human being, resulting from the union of ovum and sperm. 147

cigoto: célula única que contiene toda la información necesaria para formar un ser humano completo, que se produce como resultado de la unión del óvulo y el espermatozoide.

References

Abadinsky, H. (1989). *Drug abuse: An introduction.* Chicago: Nelson-Hall Series in Law, Crime, and Justice.

Abbott, L., Nadler, J., & Rude, R. K. (1994). Magnesium deficiency in alcoholism: Possible contribution to osteoporosis and cardiovascular disease in alcoholics. *Alcoholism, Clinical & Experimental Research, 18*(5), 1076–1082.

Abe, K., Amatomi, M., & Oda, N. (1984). Sleepwalking and recurrent sleep talking in children of childhood sleepwalkers. *American Journal of Psychiatry, 141,* 800–801.

Abela, J. R. Z., & D'Allesandro, D. U. (2002). Beck's cognitive theory of depression: The diathesis-stress and causal mediation components. *British Journal of Clinical Psychology, 41,* 111–128.

Abraham, W. C., & Williams, J. M. (2003). Properties and mechanisms of LTP maintenance. *The Neuroscientist, 9*(6), 463–474.

Abramson, L. Y., Garber, J., & Seligman, M. E. P. (1980). Learned helplessness in humans: An attributional analysis. In J. Garber & M. E. P. Seligman (Eds.), *Human Helplessness* (pp. 3–34). New York: Academic Press.

Abramson, L. Y., Seligman, M. E. P., & Teasdale, J. D. (1978). Learned helplessness in humans: Critique and reformulation. *Journal of Abnormal Psychology, 87,* 49–74.

Adam, K. (1980). Sleep as a restorative process and a theory to explain why. *Progressive Brain Research, 53,* 289–305.

Adams, D. B. (1968). The activity of single cells in the midbrain and hypothalamus of the cat during affective defense behavior. *Archives Italiennes de Biologie, 106,* 243–269.

Adams, R. J. (1987). An evaluation of colour preferences in early infancy. *Infant Behaviour and Development, 10,* 143–150.

Adler, A. (1954). *Understanding human nature.* New York: Greenburg Publisher.

Adolphs, R., Gosselin, F., Buchanan, T. W., Tranel, D., Schyns, P., & Damasio, A. R. (2005). A mechanism for impaired fear recognition after amygdala damage. *Nature, 433,* 68–72.

Adolphs, R., & Tranel, D. (2003). Amygdala damage impairs emotion recognition from scenes only when they contain facial expressions. *Neuropsychologia, 41,* 1281–1289.

Affleck, G., Tennen, H., Urrows, S., & Higgins, P. (1994). Person and contextual features of daily stress reactivity: Individual differences in relations of undesirable daily events with mood disturbance and chronic pain intensity. *Journal of Personality and Social Psychology, 66,* 329–340.

Aghajanian, G. K., & Marek, G. J. (1999). Serotonin and hallucinogens. *Neuropsychopharmacology, 21,* 16S–23S.

Agresti, A., & Finlay, B. (1997). *Statistical methods for the social sciences,* (3rd ed.). Upper Saddle River, NJ: Prentice Hall.

Aguiar, A., & Baillargeon, R. (2003). Perseverative responding in a violation-of-expectation task in 6.5-month-old infants. *Cognition, 88*(3), 277–316.

Ahn, W. (1998). Why are different features central for natural kinds and artifacts?: The role of causal status in determining feature centrality. *Cognition, 69,* 135–178.

Ahokas, A., Aito, M., & Rimon, R. (2000). Positive treatment effect of estradiol in post-partum psychosis: A pilot study. *Journal of Clinical Psychiatry, 61*(3), 166–169.

Aiello, J. R., & Douthitt, E. A. (2001). Social facilitation from Triplett to electronic performance monitoring. *Group Dynamics: Theory, Research, and Practice, 5*(3), 163–180.

Ainsworth, M. D. S. (1985). Attachments across the life span. *Bulletin of the New York Academy of Medicine, 61,* 792–812.

Ainsworth, M. D. S., Blehar, M. C., Waters, E., & Wall, S. (1978). *Patterns of attachment: A study of the strange situation.* Hillsdale, NJ: Erlbaum.

Aitchison, J. (1992). Good birds, better birds, & amazing birds: The development of prototypes. In P. J. Arnaud & H. Béjoint (Eds.), *Vocabulary and applied linguistics* (pp. 71–84). London: Macmillan.

Ajzen, I. (2001). Nature and operation of attitudes. *Annual Review of Psychology, 52,* 27–58.

Ajzen, I., & Fishbein, M. (2000). Attitudes and the attitude–behavior relation: Reasoned and automatic processes. In W. Stroebe & M. Hewstone (Eds.), *European review of social psychology* (pp. 1–33). New York: John Wiley & Sons.

Albert, D. J., & Richmond, S. E. (1977). Reactivity and aggression in the rat: Induction by alpha–adrenergic blocking agents injected ventral to anterior septum but not into lateral septum. *Journal of Comparative and Physiological Psychology, 91,* 886–896 [DBA] *Physiology and Behavior, 20,* 755–761.

Aligne, C. A., Auinger, P., Byrd, R. S., & Weitzman, M. (2000). Risk factors for pediatric asthma contributions of poverty, race, and urban residence. *American Journal of Respiratory Critical Care Medicine, 162*(5), 873–877.

Alkon, D. (1989). Memory storage and neural systems. *Scientific American, 261*(1), 42–50.

Allen, G. E. (2006). *Intelligence tests and immigration to the United States, 1900–1940.* Hoboken, NJ: John Wiley and Sons.

Allen, L. S., & Gorski, R. A. (1991). Sexual dimorphism of the anterior commissure and massa intermedia of the human brain. *Journal of Comparative Neurology, 312,* 97–104.

Allen, L. S., Hines, M., Shryne, J. E., & Gorski, R. A. (1989). Two sexually dimorphic cell groups in the human brain. *Journal of Neuroscience, 9*(9), 496–506.

Alloy, L. B., & Clements, C. M. (1998). Hopelessness theory of depression: Tests of the symptom component. *Cognitive Therapy and Research, 22,* 303–335.

Allport, G. W., & Odbert, H. S. (1936). Trait names: A psycho-lexical study. *Psychological Monographs, 47*(211).

Alm, H., & Nilsson, L. (1995). The effects of a mobile telephone conversation on driver behaviour in a car following situation. *Accident Analysis and Prevention, 27*(5), 707–715.

Amabile, T., Hadley, C. N., & Kramer, S. J. (2002). Creativity under the gun. *Harvard Business Review, 80*(8), 52–60.

American Association of University Women. (1992). *How schools shortchange girls.* Washington, DC: Author.

American Association of University Women. (1998). *Separated by sex: A critical look at single-sex education for girls.* Washington, DC: Author.

American Association on Intellectual and Developmental Disabilities (2009). FAQ on intellectual disability. Retrieved from **http://www.aamr.org/content_104.cfm**

American Psychiatric Association. (2000). *DSM-IV-TR: Diagnostic and statistical manual of mental disorders* (4th ed., text rev.). Washington, DC: Author. [Appendix I: Outline for Cultural Formulation and Glossary of Culture-Bound Syndromes].

American Psychiatric Association. (2000a). *Diagnostic and statistical manual of mental disorders: DSM-IV-TR.* Washington, DC: Author.

American Psychiatric Association. (2000b). Practice guidelines for the treatment of patients with major depressive disorder (Rev. ed.). *American Journal of Psychiatry, 157*(4, Suppl.): 1–45.

American Psychiatric Association Committee on Electroconvulsive Therapy. (2001). *The practice of electroconvulsive therapy: Recommendations for treatment, training, and privileging* (2nd ed). Washington, DC: American Psychiatric Association.

American Psychological Association. (2002). *Ethical Principles of Psychologists and Code of Conduct.* Retrieved from http://www.apa.org/ethics/code/index.aspx

American Psychiatric Association, DSM-V Neurodevelopmental Disorders Work Group. (2009). *Report of the DSM-V Neurodevelopmental Disorders Work Group.* Retrieved from **http://www.psych.org/MainMenu/Research/DSMIV/DSMV/DSMRevisionActivities/DSM-V-Work-Group-Reports/Neurodevelopmental-Disorders-Work-Group-Report.aspx**

American Psychological Association. (2010). *Careers in psychology.* Retrieved from **http://www.apa.org/careers/resources/guides/careers.aspx**

Anand, B. K., & Brobeck, J. R. (1951.) Hypothalamic control of food intake in rats and cats. *Yale Journal of Biological Medicine, 24,* 123–146.

Anastasi, A., & Urbina, S. (1997). *Psychological testing* (7th ed.). Upper Saddle River, NJ: Prentice-Hall.

Anderson, C. A. (1987). Temperature and aggression: Effects on quarterly, yearly, and city rates of violent and nonviolent crime. *Journal of Personality and Social Psychology, 52*(6), 1161–1173.

Anderson, C. A. (2003). Video games and aggressive behavior. In D. Ravitch & J. P. Viteritti (Eds.), *Kid stuff: Marketing sex and violence to America's children* (p. 157). Baltimore and London: The Johns Hopkins University Press.

Anderson, C. A., Berkowitz, L., Donnerstein, E., Huesmann, R. L., Johnson, J., Linz, D., et al. (2003). The influence of media violence on youth. *Psychological Science in the Public Interest, 4,* 81–110.

Anderson, M. C., & Neely, J. H. (1995). Interference and inhibition in memory retrieval. In E. L. Bjork & R. A. Bjork (Eds.), *Handbook of perception and cognition, Volume 10, Memory.* San Diego, CA: Academic Press.

Andrews, J. D. W. (1989). Integrating visions of reality: Interpersonal diagnosis and the existential vision. *American Psychologist, 44,* 803–817.

Antuono, P. G., Jones, J. L., Wang, Y., & Li, S. (2001). Decreased glutamate [plus] glutamine in Alzheimer's disease detected in vivo with (1)H-MRS at 0.5 T. *Neurology, 56*(6), 737–742.

Arbury, S. (2005). Workplace violence: Training young workers in preventative strategies. NFIB Business Toolbox, March 4.

Archer, J. (1991). The influence of testosterone on human aggression. *British Journal of Psychology, 82,* 1–28.

Argamon, S., Koppel, M., Fine, J., & Shimoni, A. (2003). Gender, genre, and writing style in formal written texts. *Text, 23*(3).

Argyle, M. (1986). Rules for social relationships in four cultures. *Australian Journal of Psychology, 38,* 309–318.

Arnett, P. A., Smith, S. S., & Newman, J. P. (1997). Approach and avoidance motivation in psychopathic criminal offenders during passive avoidance. *Journal of Personality and Social Psychology, 72*(6), 1413–1428.

Aron, A., Aron, E. N., & Coups, E. (2005). *Statistics for psychology*. Upper Saddle River, NJ: Pearson/Prentice-Hall.

Aronson, E. (1997). Back to the future. Retrospective review of Leon Festinger's—a theory of cognitive dissonance. *American Journal of Psychology, 110*, 127–137.

Asarnow, R. F., Granholm, E., & Sherman, T. (1991). Span of apprehension in schizophrenia. In H. A. Nasrallah (Ed.), *Handbook of Schizophrenia, Vol. 5*, S. R. Steinhauer, J. H. Gruzelie, & J. Zubin, (Eds.), *Neuropsychology, psychophysiology and information processing* (pp. 335–370). Amsterdam: Elsevier.

Asch, S. E. (1951). Effects of group pressure upon the modification and distortion of judgement. In H. Guetzkow (Ed.), *Groups, leadership and men*. Pittsburgh, PA: Carnegie Press.

Asch, S. E. (1956). Studies of independence and conformity: A minority of one against a unanimous majority. *Psychological Monographs, 70* (Whole No. 416).

Aserinsky, E., & Kleitman, N. (1953). Regularly occurring periods of eye motility, and concomitant phenomena, during sleep. *Science, 118*, 273–274.

Atkinson, R. C., & Shiffrin, R. M. (1968). Human memory: A proposed system and its control processes. In K. W. Spence & J. T. Spence (Eds.), *The psychology of learning and motivation* (Vol. 2, pp. 89–105). New York: Academic Press.

Bachman, J., Wadsworth, K., O'Malley, P., Johnston, L., & Schulenberg, J. (1997). *Smoking, drinking, and drug use in young adulthood: The impact of new freedoms and new responsibilities*. Mahwah, NJ: Erlbaum.

Backenstraß, M., Pfeiffer, N., Schwarz, T., Catanzaro, S. J., & Mearns, J. (2008). Reliability and validity of the German version of the Generalized Expectancies for Negative Mood Regulation (NMR) Scale. *Diagnostica, 54*, 43–51.

Backer, B., Hannon, R., & Russell, N. (1994). *Death and dying: Understanding and care*, 2nd ed. Albany, NY: Delmar Publishers.

Baddeley, A. (1988). Cognitive psychology and human memory. *Trends in Neurosciences, 11*, 176–181.

Baddeley, A. D. (1986). *Working memory*. London/New York: Oxford University Press.

Baddeley, A. D. (1996). Exploring the central executive. *Quarterly Journal of Experimental Psychology, 49A*, 5–28.

Baddeley, A. D. (2003). Working Memory: Looking back and looking visual forward. *Nature Reviews Neuroscience, 4*(10), 829–839.

Baddeley, A. D., & Hitch, G. (1974). Working memory. In G. A. Bower (Ed.), *The psychology of learning and motivation*, (Vol. 8, pp. 47–89). New York: Academic Press.

Baehr, E. K., Revelle, W., & Eastman, C. I. (2000). Individual difference in the phase amplitude of the human circadian temperature rhythm: With an emphasis on morningness-eveningness. *Journal of Sleep Research, 9*, 117–127.

Baer, D. M., Wolf, M. M., & Risley, T. R. (1968). Some current dimensions of applied behavior analysis. *Journal of Applied Behavior Analysis, 1*, 91–97.

Bahrick, H. (1984). Fifty years of second language attrition: Implications for programmatic research. *Modern Language Journal, 68*, 105–118.

Bahrick, H. P., Hall, L. K., & Berger, S. A. (1996). Accuracy and distortion in memory for high school grades. *Psychological Science, 7*, 265–271.

Bailey, J. M., & Pillard, R. C. (1991). A genetic study of male sexual orientation. *Archives of General Psychiatry, 48*, 1089–1096.

Baillargeon, R. (1986). Representing the existence and the location of hidden objects: Object permanence in 6- and 8-month-old infants. *Cognition, 23*, 21–41.

Ball, K., Berch, D. B., Helmers, K. F., Jobe, J. B., Leveck, M. D., Marsiske, M., et al. (2002). Advanced cognitive training for Independent and Vital Elderly Study Group. Effects of cognitive training interventions with older adults: A randomized controlled trial. *Journal of the American Medical Association, 288*, 2271–2281.

Bandura, A. (1965). Influence of models' reinforcement contingencies on the acquisition of imitative responses. *Journal of Social Psychology, 1*, 589–595.

Bandura, A. (1980). The social learning theory of aggression. In R. A. Falk & S. S. Kim (Eds.), *The war system: An interdisciplinary approach* (p. 146). Boulder, CO: Westview Press.

Bandura, A. (1986). *Social foundations of thought and action: A social cognitive theory*. Englewood Cliffs, NJ: Prentice Hall.

Bandura, A. (1989). Human agency in social cognitive theory. *American Psychologist, 44*, 1175–1184.

Bandura, A. (1998). Exploration of fortuitous determinants of life paths. *Psychological Inquiry, 9*, 95–99.

Bandura, A., Blanchard, E. B., & Ritter, B. (1969). Relative efficacy of desensitization and modeling approaches for inducing behavioral, affective, and attitudinal changes. *Journal of Personality and Social Psychology, 13*, 173–199.

Bandura, A., Jeffrey, R. W., & Wright, C. L. (1974). Efficacy of participant modeling as a function of response induction aids. *Journal of Abnormal Psychology, 83*, 56–64.

Bandura, A., & Rosenthal, T. L. (1966). Vicarious classical conditioning as a functioning of arousal level. *Journal of Personality and Social Psychology, 3*, 54–62.

Bandura, A., Ross, D., & Ross, S. A. (1961). Transmission of aggression through imitation of aggressive models. *Journal of Abnormal and Social Psychology, 63*, 575–582.

Baraban, J. M., Worley, P. F., & Snyder, S. H. (1989). Second messenger systems and psychoactive drug action: Focus on the phosphoinositide system and lithium. *American Journal of Psychiatry, 146*(10), 1251–1260.

Bard, P. (1934). On emotional expression after decortication with some remark on certain theoretical views. *Psychological Review, 41*, 309–329, 424–449.

Bargh, J. A., Chen, M., & Burrows, C. (1996). Automaticity of social behavior: Direct effects of trait construct and stereotype activation on action. *Journal of Personality & Social Psychology, 71*(2), 230–244.

Barkley, R. A. (1998). *Attention deficit hyperactivity disorder: A handbook for diagnosis and treatment*. New York: Guilford Press.

Barkley, R. A., Fischer, M., Fletcher, K., & Smallish, L. (2001). *Young adult outcome of hyperactive children as a function of severity of childhood conduct problems, I: Psychiatric status and mental health treatment*. Submitted for publication.

Barnes, V., Schneider, R., Alexander, C., & Staggers, F. (1997). Stress, stress reduction, and hypertension in African Americans: An updated review. *Journal of the National Medical Association, 89*(7), 464–476.

Barnyard, P., & Grayson, A. (1996). *Introducing psychological research*. London: Macmillan Press.

Baron, J. N., & Reiss, P. C. (1985). Same time, next year: Aggregate analyses of the mass media and violent behavior. *American Sociological Review, 50*, 347–363.

Barondes, S. H. (1998). *Mood genes: Hunting for origins of mania and depression*. New York: W. H. Freeman.

Barsalou, L. W. (1992). *Cognitive psychology: An overview for cognitive scientists*. Hillsdale, NJ: Lawrence Erlbaum Associates.

Barsh, G. S., Farooqi, I. S., & O'Rahilly, S. (2000). Genetics of body-weight regulation. *Nature, 404*, 644–651.

Barstow, A. L. (1995). *Witchcraze: A new history of the European witch hunts*. London: Pandora.

Bartels, A., & Zeki, S. (2000). The neural basis of romantic love. *NeuroReport, 11*, 3829–3834.

Bartels, A., & Zeki, S. (2004). The neural correlates of material and romantic love. *NeuroImage, 21*, 1155–1166.

Bartlett, N. R. (1965). Dark and light adaptation. Chapter 8. In C. H. Graham, (Ed.), *Vision and visual perception*. New York: John Wiley and Sons.

Barton, M. E., & Komatsu, L. K. (1989). Defining features of natural kinds and artifacts. *Journal of Psycholinguistic Research, 18*, 433–447.

Bartoshuk, L. M. (1993). The biological basis for food perception and acceptance. *Food Quality and Preference, 4*(1/2), 21–32.

Basadur, M., Pringle, P., & Kirkland, D. (2002). Crossing cultures: Training effects on the divergent thinking attitudes of Spanish-speaking South American managers. *Creativity Research Journal, 14*(3, 4), 395–408.

Battaglia, M., Bernardeschi, L., Franchini, L., Bellodi, L., & Smeraldi, E. (1995). A family study of schizotypal disorder. *Schizophrenia Bulletin, 21*(1), 33–45.

Baumeister, R. F., & Bratslavsky, E. (1999). Passion, intimacy, and time: Passionate love as a function of change in intimacy. *Personality and Social Psychology Review, 3*, 49–69.

Bayliss, D. M., Baddeley, J. C., & Gunn, D. M. (2005). The relationship between short-term memory and working memory: Complex span made simple? *Memory, 13*(3–4), 414–421.

Beardsley, T. (1995, January). For whom the bell curve really tolls. *Scientific American*, 14–17.

Beck, A. T. (1976). *Cognitive therapy and the emotional disorders*. New York: International Universities Press.

Beck, A. T. (1979). *Cognitive therapy and the emotional disorders*. New York: Penguin Books.

Beck, A. T. (1984). Cognitive approaches to stress. In C. Lehrer & R. L. Woolfolk (Eds.), *Clinical guide to stress management*. New York: Guilford Press.

Beck, A. T., Freeman, A., Davis, D. D., & Associates (2007). *Cognitive therapy of personality disorders*. (2nd ed.). New York: Guilford Press.

Beehr, T. A., Jex, S. M., Stacy, B. A., & Murray, M. A. (2000). Work stressors and coworker support as predictors of individual strain and job performance. *Journal of Organizational Behavior, 21*(4), 391–405.

Beer, J. M., & Horn, J. M. (2000). The influence of rearing order on personality development within two adoption cohorts. *Journal of Personality, 68*, 789–819.

Bell, P. A., Garnand, D. B., & Heath, D. (1984). Effects of ambient temperature and setaing arrangement on personal and environmental evaluations. *Journal of General Psychology, 110*, 197–200.

Bellizzi, J. A., & Crowley, A. E. (1983). The effects of color in store design. *Journal of Retailing, 59*, 21–45.

Belsky, J. (2005). Differential susceptibility to rearing influence: An evolutionary hypothesis and some evidence. In B. Ellis & D. Bjorklund (Eds.), *Origins of the social mind: Evolutionary psychology and child development* (pp. 139–163). New York: Guilford (#) Press.

Belsky, J., & Johnson, C. D. (2005). Developmental outcome of children in day care. In J. Murph, S. D. Palmer, & D. Glassy (Eds.), *Health in child care: A manual for health professionals* (4th ed., pp. 81–95). Elks Grove Village, IL: American Academy of Pediatrics.

Belsky, J., Vandell, D., Burchinal, M., Clarke-Stewart, K. A., McCartney, K., Owen, M., et al. (2007). Are there long-term effects of early child care? *Child Development, 78*, 681–701.

Bemporad, J. R. (1997). Cultural and historical aspects of eating disorders. *Theoretical Medicine, 18*(4), 401–420.

Benjafield, J. J. G. (1996). *A history of psychology*. Boston: Allyn and Bacon.

Benjamin, S. L. (1996). An interpersonal theory of personality disorders. In J. F. Clarkin & M. F. Lenzenweger (Eds.), *Major theories of personality disorder*. New York: Guilford Press.

Bennis, W. G., & Nanus, B. (1985). *Leaders: The strategies for taking charge*. New York: Harper & Row.

Benowitz, N. L. (1996). Pharmacology of nicotine: Addiction and therapeutics. *Annual Review of Pharmacology and Toxicology, 36*, 597–613.

Benson, H. (1975). *The relaxation response*. New York: Morrow.

Benson, H., Beary, J., & Carol, M. (1974a). The relaxation response. *Psychiatry, 37*, 37–46.

Benson, H., Rosner, B. A., Marzetta, B. R., & Klemchuk, H. M. (1974b). Decreased blood pressure in pharmacologically treated hypertensive patients who regularly elicited the relaxation response. *Lancet, 1*(7852), 289–291.

Berenbaum, S. A., & Snyder, E. (1995). Early hormonal influences on childhood sex-typed activity and playmate preferences: Implications for the development of sexual orientation. *Developmental Psychology, 31*, 31–42.

Berk, L. E. (1992). Children's private speech: An overview of theory and the status of research. In R. M. Diaz & L. E. Berk (Eds.), *Private speech: From social interaction to self-regulation* (pp. 17–53). Hillsdale, NJ: Erlbaum.

Berk, L. E., & Spuhl, S. T. (1995). Maternal interaction, private speech, and task performance in preschool children. *Early Childhood Research Quarterly, 10*, 145–169.

Berk, L. S., Felten, D. L., Tan, S. A., Bittman, B. B., & Westengard, J. (2001, March). Modulation of neuroimmune parameters during the eustress of humor-associated mirthful laughter. *Alternative Therapy Health Medicines, 7*(2), 62–72, 74–76.

Berkowitz, L. (1993). *Aggression: Its causes, consequences and control*. New York: McGraw-Hill.

Bermond, B., Nieuwenhuyse, B., Fasotti, L., & Schuerman, J. (1991). Spinal cord lesions, peripheral feedback, and intensities of emotional feelings. *Cognition and Emotion, 5*, 201–220.

Berry, J. W., & Kim, U. (1998). Acculturation and mental health. In P. R. Dasen, J. W. Berry, & N. Sartorius (Eds.), *Health and cross-cultural psychology: Toward applications* (pp. 207–236). Newbury Park, CA: Sage.

Berry, J. W., & Sam, D. L. (1997). Acculturation and adaptation. In J. W. Berry, M. H. Segall, & C. Kagitcibasi (Eds.), *Handbook of cross-cultural psychology, Vol. 3: Social behaviour and applications* (2nd ed., pp. 291–326). Boston: Allyn & Bacon.

Berscheid, E., & Reis, H. T. (1998). Attraction and close relationships. In D. T. Gilbert & S. T. Fiske et al. (Eds.), *The handbook of social psychology, Vol. 2* (4th ed., pp. 193–281), New York: McGraw-Hill.

Berteretche, M. V., Dalix, A. M., Cesar d'Ornano, A. M., Bellisle, F., Khayat, D., & Faurion, A. (2004). Decreased taste sensitivity in cancer patients under chemotherapy. *Supportive Care in Cancer, 12*(8), 571–576.

Best, D. L., & Williams, J. E. (2001). Gender and culture. In D. Matsumoto (Ed.), *The handbook of culture and psychology* (pp. 195–212). New York: Oxford University Press.

Betancourt, J. R., & Jacobs, E. A. (2000). Language barriers to informed consent and confidentiality: The impact on women's health. *Journal of American Medical Women's Association, 55*, 294–295.

Binet, A., & Simon, T. (1916). *The development of intelligence in children*. Baltimore: Williams & Wilkins.

Binkofski, F., & Buccino G. (2006). The role of ventral premotor cortex in action execution and action understanding. *Journal of Physiology, 99*, 396–405.

Birman, D., & Trickett, E. J. (2001). Cultural transitions in first-generation immigrants: Acculturation of Soviet Jewish refugee adolescents and parents. *Journal of Cross-Cultural Psychology, 32*(4), 456–477.

Bivens, J. A., & Berk, L. E. (1990). A longitudinal study of the development of elementary school children's private speech. *Merrill-Palmer Quarterly, 36*, 443–463.

Bjork, R. A., & Bjork, E. L. (1992). A new theory of disuse and an old theory of stimulus fluctuation. In A. Healy, S. Kosslyn, & R. Shiffrin (Eds.), *From learning processes to cognitive processes: Essays in honor of William K. Estes* (Vol. 2, pp. 35–67). Hillsdale, NJ: Erlbaum.

Bjork, R. A., & Whitten, W. B. (1974). Recency-sensitive retrieval processes in long-term free recall. *Cognitive Psychology, 6*, 173–189.

Black, D. W., & Andreasen, N. C. (1999). Schizophrenia, schizophreniform disorder, and delusional (paranoid) disorders. In R. E. Hales et al. (Eds.), *Textbook of psychiatry* (3rd ed., pp. 425–477). Washington, DC: American Psychiatric Press.

Blair, R. J. R., Sellars, C., Strickland, I., Clark, F., Williams, A. O., Smith, M., et al. (1995). Emotion attributions in the psychopath. *Personality and Individual Differences, 19*(4), 431–437.

Blanchard, M., & Main, M. (1979). Avoidance of the attachment figure and social-emotional adjustment in day-care infants. *Developmental Psychology, 15*, 445–446.

Blanchard-Fields, F., Chen, Y., Horhota, M., & Wang, M. (2007). Cultural differences in the relationship between aging and the correspondence bias. *Journals of Gerontology Series B: Psychological Sciences and Social Sciences, 62*(6), 362–365.

Blanchard-Fields, F., & Horhota, M. (2005). Age differences in the correspondence bias: When a plausible explanation matters. *Journals of Gerontology: Psychological Sciences, 60B*, P259–P267.

Blass, T. (1991). Understanding behavior in the Milgram obedience experiment: The role of personality, situations, and their interactions. *Journal of Personality and Social Psychology, 60*, 398–413.

Blass, T. (1999). The Milgram paradigm after 35 years: Some things we now know about obedience to authority. *Journal of Applied Social Psychology, 25*, 955–978.

Blatt, S. D., Meguid, V., & Church, C. C. (2000). Prenatal cocaine: What's known about outcomes? *Contemporary Ob/Gyn, 9*, 67–83.

Blazer, D. G., Kessler, R. C., McGonagle, K. A., & Swartz, M. S. (1994). The prevalence and distribution of major depression in a national community sample: The National Comorbidity Survey. *American Journal of Psychiatry, 151*, 979–986.

Bleuler, E. (1911, reissued 1950). *Dementia praecox or the group of schizophrenias*. New York: International Universities Press.

Blits, B., & Bunge, M. B. (2006). Direct gene therapy for repair of the spinal cord. *Journal of Neurotrauma, 23*(3–4), 508–520.

Block, R. I., & Ghoneim, M. M. (1993). Effects of chronic marijuana use on human cognition. *Psychopharmacology, 100*(1–2), 219–228.

Bloom, L. (1974). Talking, understanding and thinking. In R. Schiefelbusch & L. L. Lloyd (Eds.), *Language perspectives: Acquisition, retardation and intervention*. New York: Macmillan.

Bloom, P. (2000). *How children learn the meaning of words*. Cambridge, MA: MIT Press.

Blumer, D. (2002). The illness of Vincent van Gogh. *American Journal of Psychiatry, 159*(4), 519–526.

Bogle, K. D. (2000). Effect of perspective, type of student, and gender on the attribution of cheating. *Proceedings of the Oklahoma Academy of Science, 80*, 91–97.

Bolger, N., DeLongis, A., Kessler, R. C., & Schilling, E. A. (1989). Effects of daily stress on negative mood. *Journal of Personality and Social Psychology, 57*, 808–818.

Bolton, P., Bass, J., Betancourt, T., Speelman, L., Onyango, G., Clougherty, K. F., et al. (2007). Interventions for depression symptoms among adolescent survivors of war and displacement in northern Uganda. *Journal of Medical Association, 298*, 519–527.

Bonnet, M., & Arand, D. (1995). We are chronically sleep deprived. *Sleep, 18*(10), 908–911.

Booth-Butterfield, S. (1996). Message characteristics. *Steve's primer of practical persuasion and influence*. Retrieved August 2, 2004, from www.as.wvu.edu/~sbb/comm221/chapters/message.htm.

Borgeat, F., & Goulet, J. (1983, June). Psychophysiological changes following auditory subliminal suggestions for activation and deactivation. *Perceptual & Motor Skills, 56*(3), 759–766.

Borges, M. A., Stepnowsky, M. A., & Holt, L. H. (1977). Recall and recognition of words and pictures by adults and children. *Bulletin of the Psychonomic Society, 9*, 113–114.

Bosworth, H. B., & Schaie, K. W. (1997). The relationship of social environment, social networks, and health outcomes in the Seattle Longitudinal Study: Two analytical approaches. *Journals of Gerontology Series B: Psychological Sciences and Social Sciences, 52*(5), 197–205.

Botwin, M. D., & Buss, D. M. (1989). The structure of act data: Is the five-factor model of personality recaptured? *Journal of Personality and Social Psychology, 56*, 988–1001.

Bouchard, C., Tremblay, A., Nadeau, A., Dussault, J., Despres, J. P., Theriault, G., et al. (1990). Long-term exercise training with constant energy intake. 1: Effect on body composition and selected metabolic variables. *International Journal on Obesity, 14*(1), 57–73.

Bouchard, T. (1994). Genes, environment, and personality. *Science, 264*, 1700–1701.

Bouchard, T. J., Jr. (1997). Whenever the twain shall meet. *The Science, 37*(5), 52–57.

Bowden, C. L., Calabrese, J. R., McElroy, S. L., Gyulai, L., Wassef, A., Petty, F., et al. (2000). For the Divalproex Maintenance Study Group. A randomized, placebo-controlled 12-month trial of divalproex and lithium in treatment of outpatients with bipolar I disorder. *Archives of General Psychiatry, 57*(5), 481–489.

Bowers, K. S., & Woody, E. Z. (1996). Hypnotic amnesia and the paradox of intentional forgetting. *Journal of Abnormal Psychology, 105*, 381–390.

Bowman, E. S. (1996). Delayed memories of child abuse: Part II. An overview of research findings relevant to understanding their reliability and suggestibility. *Dissociation: Progress in the Dissociative Disorders, 9*, 232–243.

Boyd, L. A., & Winstein, C. J. (2004). Cerebellar stroke impairs temporal but not spatial accuracy during implicit motor learning. *Neurorehabilitation and Neural Repair, 18*(3), 134–143.

Boyson-Bardies, B., deHalle, P., Sagart, L., & Durand, C. (1989). A cross-linguistic investigation of vowel formats in babbling. *Journal of Child Language, 16*, 1–17.

Bracey, G. (1997). A few facts about poverty. *Phi Delta Kappan, 79*, 163–164.

Brauen, C. M., & Bonta, J. L. (1979). Cross-cultural validity, reliability, and stimulus characteristics of the Luscher Color Test. *Journal of Personality Assessment, 43*, 459–460.

Braun, S. (1996). *Buzz: The science and lore of alcohol and caffeine.* New York: Oxford University Press, 107–192.

Brecher, M., Wang, B. W., Wong, H., & Morgan, J. P. (1988). Phencyclidine and violence: Clinical and legal issues. *Journal of Clinical Psychopharmacology, 8*, 397–401.

Breedlove, S. M., Rosenzweig, M. R., & Watson, N. V. (2007). *Biological psychology: An introduction to behavioral and cognitive neurosciences* (5th ed., pp. 23–34). Sunderland, MA: Sinauer Associates.

Breggin, P. R. (2003/2004). Suicidality, violence and mania caused by selective serotonin reuptake inhibitors (SSRIs): A review and analysis. *International Journal of Risk & Safety in Medicine, 16*, 31–49.

Breggin, P. R., & Breggin, G. R. (1994). *Talking back to Prozac.* New York: St. Martin's Press.

Breland, K., & Breland, M. (1961). The misbehavior of organisms. *American Psychologist, 16*, 681–684.

Brennan, J. F. (2002). *History and systems of psychology* (6th ed.). Upper Saddle River, NJ: Prentice Hall.

Brennan, P. A., Raine, A., Schulsinger, F., Kirkegaard-Sorensen, L., Knop, J., Hutchings, B., et al. (1997). Psychophysiological protective factors for male subjects at high risk for criminal behavior. *American Journal of Psychiatry, 154*, 853–855.

Breslau, N., Chilcoat, H. D., Kessler, R. C., Peterson, E. L., & Lucia, V. C. (1999). Vulnerability to assaultive violence: Further specification of the sex difference in posttraumatic stress disorder. *Psychological Medicine, 29*, 813–821.

Breslau, N., Davis, G. C., Andreski, P., & Peterson, E. L. (1997). Sex differences in posttraumatic stress disorder. *Archives of General Psychiatry, 54*(11), 1044–1048.

Breuer, J., & Freud, S. (1895). *Studies on hysteria (cathartic method). Special Edition, 2*, 1–309.

Brewer, M. B. (2001). Ingroup identification and intergroup conflict: When does ingroup love become outgroup hate? In R. D. Ashmore, L. Jussim, & D. Wilder (Eds.), *Social identity, intergroup conflict, and conflict reduction.* New York: Oxford University Press.

Brick, J. (2003). The characteristics of alcohol: Chemistry, use and abuse. In J. Brick (Ed.), *Handbook of the medical consequences of alcohol and drug abuse* (pp. 1–11). New York: Haworth Medical Press.

Briem, V., & Hedman, L. R. (1995). Behavioural effects of mobile telephone use during simulated driving. *Ergonomics, 38*, 2536–2562.

Briggs, K. C., & Myers, I. B. (1998). *The Myers-Briggs Type Indicator-Form M.* Palo Alto, CA: Consulting Psychologists Press.

Brigham, A. (1844). Asylums exclusively for the incurably insane. Classic article in *American Journal of Psychiatry, 151*, 50–70.

Broadbent, D. (1958). *Perception and communication.* Elmsford, NY: Pergamon.

Brockington, I. F., Winokur, G., & Dean, C. (1982). Puerperal psychosis. In I. F. Brockington & R. Kumar (Eds.), *Motherhood and mental illness* (pp. 37–69). London: Academic Press.

Brondolo, E., Rieppi, R., Erickson, S. A., Bagiella, E., Shapiro, P. A., McKinley, P., et al. (2003). Hostility, interpersonal interactions, and ambulatory blood pressure. *Psychosomatic Medicine, 65*, 1003–1011.

Brown, C., Taylor, J., Green, A., Lee, B. E., Thomas, S. B., & Ford, A. (2003). *Managing depression in African Americans: Consumer and provider perspectives.* (Final Report to Funders). Pittsburgh: Mental Health Association of Allegheny County.

Brown, J. (1958). Some tests of the decay theory of immediate memory. *Quarterly Journal of Experimental Psychology, 10*, 12–21.

Brown, R. (1973). *A first language: The early stages.* Cambridge, MA: Harvard University Press.

Brown, R., & McNeill, D. (1966). The "tip of the tongue" phenomenon. *Journal of Verbal Learning & Verbal Behavior, 5*(4), 325–337.

Brubaker, D. A., & Leddy, J. J. (2003). Behavioral contracting in the treatment of eating disorders. *The Physician and Sportsmedicine, 31*(9).

Bryant, R. A., & McConkey, K. M. (1989). Hypnotic blindness: A behavioral and experimental analysis. *Journal of Abnormal Psychology, 98*, 71–77.

Buccino, G., Binkofski, F., Fink, G. R., Fadiga, L., Fogassi, L., Gallese, V., et al. (2001). Action observation activates premotor and parietal areas in a somatotopic manner: An fMRI study. *European Journal of Neuroscience, 13*(2), 400–404.

Buccino, G., Binkofski, F., & Riggio, L. (2004). The mirror neuron system and action recognition. *Brain and Language, 89*(2), 370–376.

Buck, R. (1980). Nonverbal behavior and the theory of emotion: The facial feedback hypothesis. *Journal of Personality and Social Psychology, 38*, 811–824.

Budney, A. J., Hughes, J. R., Moore, B. A., & Novy, P. L. (2001). Marijuana abstinence effects in marijuana smokers maintained in their environment. *Archives of General Psychiatry, 58*, 917–924.

Bunge, M. B., & Pearse, D. D. (2003). Transplantation strategies to promote repair of the injured spinal cord. *Journal of Rehabilitative Research & Development, 40*(4), 55–62.

Bureau of Labor Statistics, U.S. Department of Labor. (2008). *Occupational Outlook Handbook, 2008–09 Edition.* Retrieved May 28, 2008, from **http://www.bls.gov/oco/ocos056.htm**

Burger, J. M. (1986). Increasing compliance by improving the deal: The that's not all technique. *Journal of Personality and Social Psychology, 51*, 277–283.

Burger, J. M. (1997). The psychoanalytic approach: Neo-Freudian theory, application, and assessment. *Personality* (4th ed.). Pacific Grove, CA: Brooks/Cole.

Burger, J. M., & Petty, R. E. (1981). The low-ball compliance technique: Task or person commitment? *Journal of Personality and Social Psychology, 40*, 492–500.

Burgio, K. L. (1998). Behavioral vs. drug treatment for urge urinary incontinence in older women: A randomized controlled trail. *Journal of the American Medical Association, 280*, 1995–2000.

Burke, D. M., MacKay, D. G., Worthley, J. S., & Wade, E. (1991). On the tip of the tongue: What causes word finding failures in young and older adults. *Journal of Memory and Language, 30*, 542–579.

Burks, N., & Martin, B. (1985). Everyday problems and life change events: Ongoing versus acute sources of stress. *Journal of Human Stress, 11*, 27–35.

Burrows, P., & Elstrom, P. (1999, August 2). HP's Carly Fiorina: The boss. *Bloomberg Businessweek.* Retrieved from **http://www.businessweek.com/1999/99_31/b3640001.htm**

Bushman, B. J. (1997). Effects of alcohol on human aggression: Validity of proposed explanations. In M. Galanter (Ed.), *Recent developments in alcoholism* (Vol. 13, pp. 227–243). New York: Plenum Press.

Bushman, B. J., & Huesmann, L. R. (2001). Effects of televised violence on aggression. In D. G. Singer & J. L. Singer (Eds.), *Handbook of children and the media* (Ch. 11, pp. 223–254). Thousand Oaks, CA: Sage.

Bussa, B., & Kaufman, C. (2000). What can self-help do? *The Journal of the California Alliance of the Mentally Ill, 2*(2).

Butcher, J. N., Graham, J. R., Ben-Poarth, Y. S., Tellegen, A., Dahlstrom, W. G., & Kaemmer, B. (2001). *Minnesota Multiphasic Personality Inventory-2. Manual for administration, scoring, and interpretation* (Rev. ed.). Minneapolis, MN: University of Minnesota Press.

Butcher, J. N., & Rouse, S. V. (1996). Personality: Individual differences and clinical assessment. *Annual Review of Psychology, 47*, 87–111.

Butcher, J. N., Rouse, S. V., & Perry, J. N. (2000). Empirical description of psychopathology in therapy clients: Correlates of MMPI-2 scales. In J. N. Butcher (Ed.), *Basic sources on the MMPI-2* (pp. 487–500). Minneapolis, MN: University of Minnesota Press.

Butler, K. (1993). Too good to be true? *Networker, 6*, 19–31.

Cabeza, R., Anderson, N. D., Locantore, J. K. & McIntosh, A. R. (2002). Aging gracefully: Compensatory brain activity in high-performing older adults. *NeuroImage, 17*(3), 1394–1402.

Cain, D., & Seeman, J. (Eds.). (2001). *Humanistic psychotherapies: Handbook of research and practice.* Washington, DC: APA Publications.

Califia, P. (1997). *Sex changes: The politics of transgenderism.* San Francisco: Cleis Press.

Camara, W. J., Nathan, J. S., & Puente, A. E. (2000). Psychological test usage: Implications in professional psychology. *Professional Psychology: Research and Practice, 31*(2), 141–154.

Cameron, J. A., Alvarez, J. M., Ruble, D. N., & Fuligni, A. J. (2001). Children's lay theories about ingroups and outgroups: Reconceptualizing research on prejudice. *Personality and Social Psychology Review, 5*, 118–128.

Cameron, J., Banko, K. M., & Pierce, W. D. (2001). Pervasive negative effects of rewards on intrinsic motivation: The myth continues. *The Behavior Analyst, 24*, 1–44.

Cami, J., Farre, M., Mas, M., Roset, P. N., Poudevida, S., Mas, A., et al. (2000). Human pharmacology of 3,4-methylenedioxymethamphetamine ("ecstasy"): Psychomotor performance and subjective effects. *Journal of Clinical Psychopharmacology, 20*, 455–466.

Campbell, J. C., & Wolf, A. D. (2003). Risk factors for femicide in abusive relationships: Results from a multisite case control study. *American Journal of Public Health, 93*(7).

Campos, J. J., Bertenthal, B. I., & Kermoian, R. (1992). Early experience and emotional development: The emergence of wariness and heights. *Psychological Science, 3*, 61–64.

Cancian, F. M. (1987). *Love in America: Gender and self-development.* Cambridge, England: Cambridge University Press.

Cannon, W. B. (1927). The James-Lange theory of emotion: A critical examination and an alternative theory. *American Journal of Psychology, 39*, 10–124.

Cannon, W. B., & Washburn, A. L. (1912). An explanation of hunger. *American Journal of Physiology, 29*, 444–454.

Carducci, B. (1998). *The psychology of personality.* Pacific Grove, CA: Brooks/Cole.

Carlson, G. A., Jensen, P. S., & Nottelmann, E. D. (Eds.). (1998). Special issue: Current issues in childhood bipolarity. *Journal of Affective Disorders, 51*.

Carpenter, P. A., Just, M. A., & Shell, P. (1990). What one intelligence test measures: A theoretical account of the processing in the Raven Progressive Matrices test. *Psychological Review, 97*(3), 404–431.

Carrion, V. G., Weems, C. F., & Reiss, A. L. (2007). Stress predicts brain changes in children: A pilot longitudinal study on youth stress, posttraumatic stress disorder, and the hippocampus. *Pediatrics, 119*(3), 509–516.

Carroll, R. T. (2000). Eye movement desensitization and reprocessing (EMDR). The Skeptic's Dictionary. Retrieved July 14, 2004, from **www.skepdic.com/pseudosc.html**

Carruthers, M. (2001). A multifactorial approach to understanding andropause. *Journal of Sexual and Reproductive Medicine, 1*, 69–74.

Carson, R. C. (1969). *Interaction concepts of personality*. Chicago: Aldine.

Carver, L. J., & Bauer, P. J. (2001). The dawning of a past: The emergence of long-term explicit memory in infancy. *Journal of Experimental Psychology: General, 130*, 726–745.

Cassiday, K. L., & Lyons, J. A. (1992). Recall of traumatic memories following cerebral vascular accident. *Journal of Traumatic Stress, 5*, 627–631.

Castillo, R. J. (1997). Eating disorders. In R. J. Castillo (Ed.), *Culture and mental illness: A client-centered approach* (p. 152). Pacific Grove, CA: Brooks/Cole Publishing Co.

Catanzaro, S. J., Wasch, H. H., Kirsch, I., & Mearns, J. (2000). Coping-related expectancies and dispositions as prospective predictors of coping responses and symptoms: Distinguishing mood regulation expectancies, dispositional coping, and optimism. *Journal of Personality, 68*, 757–788.

Cattell, R. B. (1950). *Personality: A systematic, theoretical, and factual study*. New York: McGraw-Hill.

Cattell, R. B. (1973). *Personality and mood by questionnaire*. San Francisco: Jossey-Bass.

Cattell, R. B. (1990). Advances in Cattellian personality theory. In L. A. Pervin (Ed.), *Handbook of personality: Theory and research* (pp. 101–110). New York: Guilford (#) Press.

Cattell, R. B. (1994). *Sixteen Personality Factor Questionnaire* (5th ed.). Champaign, IL: Institute for Personality and Ability Testing.

Cattell, R. B. (1995). Personality structure and the new fifth edition of the 16PF. *Educational & Psychological Measurement, 55*(6), 926–937.

Cattell, R. B. (Ed.). (1966). *Handbook of multivariate experimental psychology*. Chicago: Rand McNally.

Cave, K. R., & Kim, M. (1999). Top-down and bottom-up attentional control: On the nature of interference from a salient distractor. *Perception & Psychophysics, 61*, 1009–1023.

Centers for Disease Control and Prevention. (1992). *Smoking and health in the Americas: The Surgeon General's report*. National Center for Chronic Disease Prevention and Health Promotion.

Centers for Disease Control and Prevention. (2005). Web-based Injury Statistics Query and Reporting System (WISQARS) [Online]. National Center for Injury Prevention and Control, CDC (producer). Available at **http://www.cdc.gov/ncipc/wisqars/default.htm**

Centers for Disease Control and Prevention. (2006). Welcome to WISQARS (Web-based Injury Statistics Query and Reporting System). Retrieved February 27, 2008, from Centers for Disease Control and Prevention, National Center for Injury and Prevention Control Web site: **http://www.cdc.gov/ncipc/wisqars/**

Centerwall, B. S. (1989). Exposure to television as a risk factor for violence. *American Journal of Epidemiology, 129*, 643–652.

Cermak, L., & Craik, F. (1979). *Levels of processing in human memory*. Hillsdale, NJ: Erlbaum.

Chandola, T., Britton, A., Brunner, E., Hemingway, H., Malik, M., Kumari, M., et al. (2008). Work stress and coronary heart disease: What are the mechanisms? *European Heart Journal*. doi:10.1093/eurheartj/ehm584

Chang, P. P., Ford, D. E., Meoni, L. A., Wang, N., & Klag, M. J. (2002). Anger in young men and subsequent premature cardiovascular disease: The precursors study. *Archives of Internal Medicine, 162*, 901–906.

Chee, M. W. L., & Choo, W. C. (2004). Functional imaging of working memory following 24 hours of total sleep deprivation. Program and abstracts of the 56th Annual Meeting of the American Academy of Neurology; April 24–May 1, 2004, San Francisco, CA.

Chen, C., & Farruggia, S. (2002). Culture and adolescent development. In W. J. Lonner, D. L. Dinnel, S. A. Hayes, & D. N. Sattler (Eds.), *Online Readings in Psychology and Culture* (Unit 11, Chapter 2), (**http://www.wwu.edu/~culture**), Center for Cross-Cultural Research, Western Washington University, Bellingham, Washington.

Cheng, H., Cao, Y., & Olson, L. (1996). Spinal cord repair in adult paraplegic rats: Partial restoration of hind limb function. *Science, 273*, 510–513.

Cherry, E. C. (1953). Some experiments on the recognition of speech, with one and with two ears. *Journal of the Acoustical Society of America, 25*(5), 975–979.

Chomsky, N. (2006). *Language and mind* (3rd ed.). New York: Cambridge University Press.

Chomsky, N., Belletti, A., & Rizzi, L. (2002). *On nature and language*. New York: Cambridge University Press.

Chou, S. Y., Grossman, M., & Saffer, H. (2004). An economic analysis of adult obesity: Results from the behavioral risk factor surveillance system. *Journal of Health Economics, 23*, 565–587.

Chu, J. A., Frey, L. M., Ganzel, B. L., & Matthews, J. A. (1999). Memories of childhood abuse: Dissociation, amnesia, and corroboration. *American Journal of Psychiatry, 156*, 749–755.

Chwalisz, K., Diener, E., & Gallagher, D. (1988). Autonomic arousal feedback and emotional experience: Evidence from the spinal cord injured. *Journal of Personality and Social Psychology, 54*, 820–828.

Cialdini, R. B., Trost, M. R., & Newsom, J. T. (1995). Preference for consistency: The development of a valid measure and the discovery of surprising behavioral implications. *Journal of Personality and Social Psychology, 69*, 318–328.

Cialdini, R. B., Vincent, J., Lewis, S., Catalan, J., Wheeler, D., & Darby, B. (1975). Reciprocal concessions procedure for inducing compliance: The door-in-the-face technique. *Journal of Personality and Social Psychology, 31*, 206–215.

Cialdini, R. B., Wosinska, W., Barrett, D., Butner, J., & Gornik-Durose, M. (1999). Compliance with a request in two cultures: The differential influence of social proof and commitment/consistency on collectivists and individualists. *Personality and Social Psychology Bulletin, 25*, 1242–1253.

Ciardiello, A. (1998). Did you ask a good question today? Alternative cognitive and metacognitive strategies. *Journal of Adolescent & Adult Literacy, 42*, 210–219.

Clark, D. A., Beck, A. T., & Brown, G. (1989). Cognitive mediation in general psychiatric outpatients: A test of the content-specificity hypothesis. *Journal of Personality and Social Psychology, 56*, 958–964.

Clark, D. A., Hollifield, M., Leahy, R. L., & Beck, J. S. (in press). The cognitive theory for psychiatric disorders. In G. Gabbard, J. S. Beck, & J. Wright (Eds.), *Textbook of psychotherapeutic treatments in psychiatry*. Washington, DC: American Psychiatric Press.

Clarkin, J. F., Levy, K. N., Lenzenweger, M. F., & Kernberg, O. F. (2007). Evaluating three treatments for borderline personality disorder: A multiwave study. *American Journal of Psychiatry, 164*(6), 922–928.

Coates, J. (1986). *Women, men, and language*. New York: Longman.

Cohen, L. J. (1997). Rational drug use in the treatment of depression. *Pharmacotherapy, 17*, 45–61.

Cohen, S., Frank, E., Doyle, B. J., Skoner, D. P., Rabin, B. S., & Gwaltney, J. M. (1998). Types of stressors that increase susceptibility to the common cold. *Health Psychology, 17*, 214–223.

Cohen, S., Janicki-Deverts, D., & Miller, G. E. (2007). Psychological stress and disease. *Journal of the American Medical Association, 298*(14), 1685–1687.

Colcombe, S. J., Erickson, K. I., Raz, N., Webb, A. G., Cohen, N. J., McAuley, E., et al. (2003). Aerobic fitness reduces brain tissue loss in aging humans. *Journal of Gerontology Series A: Biological Sciences and Medical Sciences, 58*, 176–180.

Colligan, J. (1983). Musical creativity and social rules in four cultures. *Creative Child and Adult Quarterly, 8*, 39–44.

Collins, C. J., Hanges, P. J., & Locke, E. A. (2004). The relationship of achievement motivation to entrepreneurial behavior: A meta-analysis. *Human Performance, 17*(1), 95–117.

Colom, R., Shih, P. C., Flores-Mendoza, C., & Quiroga, M. A. (2006). The real relationship between short-term memory and working memory. *Memory, 14*(7), 804–813.

Committee on Animal Research and Ethics. (2004). *Research with animals in psychology*. APAOnline. Retrieved October 12, 2004, from **www.apa.org/science/animal2.html**

Conrad, R., & Hull, A. J. (1964). Information, acoustic confusion, and memory span. *British Journal of Psychology, 55*, 429–432.

Cooper, L. A., Gonzales, J. J., Gallo, J. J., Rost, K. M., Meredith, L. S., Rubenstein, L. V., et al. (2003). The acceptability of treatment for depression among African-American, Hispanic, and white primary care patients. *Medical Care, 41*(4), 479–489.

Cosgrove, G. R., & Rauch, S. L. (1995). Psychosurgery. *Neurosurgery Clinics of North America, 6*, 167–176.

Costa, P. T., Jr., & McCrae, R. R. (2000). The revised NEO Personality Inventory (NEO PI-R). In J. Cheek & E. M. Donahue (Eds.), *Handbook of personality inventories*. New York: Plenum (#) Press.

Costello, D. M., Swendsen, J., Rose, J. S., & Dierker, L. C. (2008). Risk and protective factors associated with trajectories of depressed mood from adolescence to early adulthood. *Journal of Consulting and Clinical Psychology, 76*(2), 173–183.

Courage, M. L., & Howe, M. L. (2002). From infant to child: The dynamics of cognitive change in the second year of life. *Psychological Bulletin, 128*, 250–277.

Cowan, N. (1988). Evolving conceptions of memory storage, selective attention, and their mutual constraints within the human information processing system. *Psychological Bulletin, 104*, 163–191.

Crago, M. B., Shisslak, C. M., & Estes, L. S. (1996). Eating disturbances among American minority groups: A review. *International Journal of Eating Disorders, 19*, 239–248.

Craik, F. I. M. (1970). The fate of primary memory items in free recall. *Journal of Verbal Learning and Verbal Behavior, 9,* 143–148.

Craik, F. I. M. (1994). Memory changes in normal aging. *Current Directions in Psychological Science, 3*(5), 155–158.

Craik, F. I. M., & Lockhart, R. S. (1972). Levels of processing. A framework for memory research. *Journal of Verbal Learning and Verbal Behaviour, 11,* 671–684.

Craik, F. I. M., & Tulving, E. (1975). Depth of processing and the retention of words in episodic memory. *Journal of Experimental Psychology: General, 104,* 268–294.

Crawford, M., & Unger, R. (2004). *Women and gender: A feminist psychology* (4th ed.). Boston: McGraw-Hill.

Crowley, A. E., & Hoyer, W. D. (1994). An integrative framework for understanding two-sided persuasion. *Journal of Consumer Research, 20,* 561–574.

Csernansky, J. G., Mahmoud, R., & Brenner, R. (2002). A comparison of reperidone and haloperidol for the prevention of relapse in patients with schizophrenia. *New England Journal of Medicine, 346,* 16–22.

Csikszentmihalyi, M. (1996). *Creativity: Flow and the psychology of discovery and Invention.* New York: Harper Perennial.

Csikszentmihalyi, M. (1997). *Finding flow: The psychology of engagement with everyday life.* New York: Basic Books.

Cua, A. B., Wilhelm, K. P., & Maibach, H. I. (1990). Elastic properties of human skin: Relation to age, sex and anatomical region. *Archives of Dermatology Research, 282,* 283–288.

Cummings, J. L., & Coffey C. E. (1994). Neurobiological basis of behavior. In C. E. Coffey & J. L. Cummings (Eds.), *Textbook of geriatric neuropsychiatry* (pp. 72–96). Washington, DC: American Psychiatric Press.

Cummings, S. R., & Melton, L. J., III. (2002). Epidemiology and outcomes of osteoporotic fractures. *Lancet, 359*(9319), 1761–1767.

Curtis, R. C., & Miller, K. (1986). Believing another likes or dislikes you: Behaviors making the beliefs come true. *Journal of Personality and Social Psychology, 51,* 284–290.

Curtis, R. H. (1993). *Great lives: Medicine.* New York: Charles Scribner's Sons Books for Young Readers.

Curtiss, S., Fromkin, V., Krashen, S., Rigler, D., & Rigler, M. (1974). The linguistic development of Genie. *Language: Journal of the Linguistic Society of America, 50*(3), 528–554.

Cytowic, R. E. (1989). Synesthesia and mapping of subjective sensory dimensions. *Neurology, 39,* 849–850.

Dallman, M., Pecoraro, N., Akana, S., la Fleur, S. E., Gomez, F., Houshyar, H., et al. (2003). Chronic stress and obesity: A new view of "comfort food." *Proceedings of the National Academy of Sciences, 100*(20), 11696–11701.

Damasio, H., Grabowski, T., Frank, R., Galaburda, A. M., & Damasion, A. R. (1994). The return of Phineas Gage: Clues about the brain from the skull of a famous patient. *Science, 264,* 1102–1105.

Darley, J. M., & Latané, B. (1968). Bystander intervention in emergencies: Diffusion of responsibility. *Journal of Personality and Social Psychology, 8,* 377–383.

Darvill, T., Lonky, E., Reihman, J., Stewart, P., & Pagano, J. (2000). Prenatal exposure to PCBs and infant performance on the Fagan test of infant intelligence. *Neurotoxicology, 21*(6), 1029–1038.

Darwin, C. (1859). *The origin of species by means of natural selection.* London: John Murray.

Darwin, C. (1898). *The expression of the emotions in man and animals.* New York: D. Appleton.

Daum, I., & Schugens, M. M. (1996). On the cerebellum and classical conditioning. *Current Directions in Psychological Science, 5,* 58–61.

Davidson, P. R., & Parker, K. C. H. (2001). Eye movement desensitization and reprocessing (EMDR): A meta-analysis. *Journal of Counseling and Clinical Psychology, 69*(2), 305–316.

Davidson, R. J. (2003). Affective neuroscience and psychophysiology: Toward a synthesis. *Psychophysiology, 40*(5), 655–665.

Davidson, R. J., Putman, K. M., & Larson, C. L. (2000). Dysfunction in the neural circuitry of emotion regulation—a possible prelude to violence. *Science, 289,* 591–594.

Davies, I. R. L., Laws, G., Corbett, G. G., & Jerrett, D. J. (1998a). Crosscultural differences in colour vision: Acquired "colour blindness" in Africa. *Personality and Individual Differences, 25,* 1153–1162.

Davies, I. R. L., Sowden, P., Jerrett, D. T., Jerrett, T., & Corbett, G. G. (1998b). A cross-cultural study of English and Setswana speakers on a colour triads task: A test of the Sapir-Whorf hypothesis. *British Journal of Psychology, 89,* 1–15.

Davis, K. L., Kahn, R. S., Ko, G., & Davidson, M. (1991). Dopamine in schizophrenia: A review and reconceptualization. *American Journal of Psychiatry, 148,* 1474–1486.

Davis, M., & Whalen, P. J. (2001). The amygdala: Vigilance and emotion. *Molecular Psychiatry, 6,* 13–34.

De Valois, R. L., & Jacobs, G. H. (1968). Primate color vision. *Science, 162,* 553–540.

deCharms, R. (1968). *Personal causation.* New York: Academic Press.

Deci, E. L., Eghrari, H., Patrick, B. C., & Leone, D. R. (1994). Facilitating internalization: The self-determination theory perspective. *Journal of Personality, 62,* 119–142.

Deci, E. L., Koestner, R., & Ryan, R. M. (1999). A meta-analytic review of experiments examining the effects of extrinsic rewards on intrinsic motivation. *Psychological Bulletin, 125,* 627–668.

Deci, E. L., & Ryan, R. M. (1985). *Intrinsic motivation and self–determination in human behavior.* New York: Plenum Press.

DeGrandpre, R. J. (2000). A science of meaning: Can behaviorism bring meaning to psychological science? *American Psychologist, 55,* 721–739.

Deinzer, R., Kleineidam, C. H., Winkler, R., Idel, H., & Bachg, D. (2000). Prolonged reduction of salivary immunoglobulin A (sIgA) after a major academic exam. *International Journal of Psychophysiology, 37,* 219–232.

Delaney, A. J., Crane, J. W., & Sah, P. (2007). Noradrenaline modulates transmission at a central synapse by a presynaptic mechanism. *Neuron, 56*(6), 880–892.

Delfiner, R. (2001, November 16). "Kitty Left at Death's Door." *The New York Post.*

DeLongis, A., Lazarus, R. S., & Folkman, S. (1988). The impact of daily stress on health and mood: Psychological and social resources as mediators. *Journal of Personality and Social Psychology, 54*(3), 486–495.

Demers, R. A. (1988). Linguistics and animal communication. In F. J. Newmeyer (Ed.), *Language form and language function* (pp. 314–335). Cambridge, MA: MIT Press.

Denno, D. W. (2002). Crime and consciousness: Science and involuntary acts. *Minnesota Law Review, 87,* 269–399.

Deregowski, J. B. (1969). Perception of the two-pronged trident by two- and three-dimensional perceivers. *Journal of Experimental Psychology, 82,* 9–13.

DeRubeis, R. J., Gelfand, L. A., Tang, T. Z., & Simons, A. D. (1999). Medications versus cognitive behavior therapy for severely depressed outpatients: Mega-analysis of four randomized comparisons. *American Journal of Psychiatry, 156*(7), 1007–1013.

Dew, M. A., Whyte, E. M., Lenze, E. J., Houck, P. R., Mulsant, B. H., Pollock, B. G., et al. (2007). Recovery from major depression in older adults receiving augmentation of antidepressant pharmacotherapy. *American Journal of Psychiatry, 164*(6), 892–899.

Diamond, L. M. (2003). What does sexual orientation orient? A biobehavioral model distinguishing romantic love and sexual desire. *Psychological Review, 110,* 173–192.

Diamond, L. M. (2004). Emerging perspectives on distinctions between romantic love and sexual desire. *Current Directions in Psychological Science, 13,* 116–119.

Diamond, M. C. (1991). Hormonal effects on the development of cerebral lateralization. *Psychoneuroendocrinology, 16,* 121–129.

Diamond, M., & Sigmundson, H. K. (1997). Sex reassignment at birth. Long-term review and clinical implications. *Archives of Pediatric Adolescent Medicine, 151*(3), 298–304.

Dickens, W. T., & Flynn, J. R. (2001 April). Heritability estimates vs. large environmental effects: The IQ paradox resolved. *Psychological Review, 108*(2), 346–369.

Dickerson, F., Ringel, N., Parente, F., & Boronow, J. (1994). Seclusion and restraint, assaultiveness, and patient performance in a token economy. *Hospital and Community Psychiatry, 45,* 168–170.

Digman, J. M. (1990). Personality structure: Emergence of the five-factor model. *Annual Review of Psychology, 41,* 417–440.

Dillard, J. (1990). Self-inference and the foot-in-the-door technique: Quantity of behavior and attitudinal mediation. *Human Communication Research, 16,* 422–447.

Dillard, J. (1991). The current status of research on sequential–request compliance techniques. *Personality and Social Psychology Bulletin, 17,* 282–288.

Dinges, D. F. (1995). An overview of sleepiness and accidents. *Journal of Sleep Research, 4*(2), 4–14.

Dohrenwend, B. P., Levav, I. Shrout, P. E., Schwartz, S., Naveh, G., Link, B. G., et al. (1992). Socioeconomic status and psychiatric disorders: The causation-selection issue. *Science, 313,* 979–982.

Doidge, N. (2007). *The brain that changes itself.* New York: Viking.

Dollard, J., & Miller, N. F. (1950). *Personality and psychotherapy.* New York: McGraw-Hill.

Domagalski, T. A., & Steelman, L. A. (2007). The impact of gender and organizational status on workplace anger expression. *Management Communication Quarterly, 20*(3), 297–315.

Domhoff, G. W. (1996). *Finding meaning in dreams: A quantitative approach.* New York: Plenum Press.

Dominey, P. F., & Dodane, C. (2004). Indeterminacy in language acquisition: The role of child-directed speech and joint attention. *Journal of Neurolinguistics, 17*(2–3), 121–145.

Dominy, N. J., & Lucas, P. W. (2001). Ecological importance of trichromatic vision to primates. *Nature, 410,* 363–366.

Domjan, M., Cusato, B., & Villarreal, R. (2000). Pavlovian feed-forward mechanisms in the control of social behavior. *Behavioral and Brain Sciences, 23,* 235–282.

Dorahy, M. J. (2001). Dissociative identity disorder and memory dysfunction: The current state of experimental research and its future directions. *Clinical Psychology Review, 21*(5), 771–795.

Dougherty, D. D., Baer, L., Cosgrove, G. R., Cassem, E. H., Price, B. H., Nierenberg, A. A., et al. (2002). Prospective long-term follow-up of 44 patients who received cingulotomy for treatment-refractory obsessive-compulsive disorder. *The American Journal of Psychiatry, 159*(2), 269–275.

Drenth, P. J., Thierry, H., Willems, P. J., & de Wolff, C. J. (1984). *Handbook of work and organizational psychology.* Chichester: John Wiley and Sons.

Druckman, D., & Bjork, R. A. (Eds.). (1994). *Learning, remembering, believing: Enhancing human performance.* (Study conducted by the National Research Council). Washington, DC: National Academy Press.

Duben, A., & Behar, C. (1991). *Istanbul households: Marriage, family and fertility 1880–1940.* Cambridge: Cambridge University Press.

Dubowitz, H., & Bennett, S. (2007). Physical abuse and neglect of children. *Lancet, 369*(9576), 1891–1899.

Duncan, R. M. (1995). Piaget and Vygotsky revisited: Dialogue or assimilation? *Developmental Review, 15*, 458–472.

Dunn, J. C., Whelton, W. J., & Sharpe, D. (2006). Maladaptive perfectionism, hassles, coping, and psychological distress in university professors. *Journal of Counseling Psychology, 53*(4), 511–523.

Durso, F., Rea, C., & Dayton, T. (1994). Graph-theoretic confirmation of restructuring during insight. *Psychological Science, 5*, 94–98.

Dweck, C. S. (1986). Motivational processes affecting learning. *American Psychologist, 41*(10), 1040–1048.

Dweck, C. S. (1999). *Self-theories: Their role in motivation, personality and development.* Philadelphia: Psychology Press.

Dweck, C. S., & Leggett, E. L. (1988). A social-cognitive approach to motivation and personality. *Psychological Review, 95*, 256–273.

Dweck, C. S., & Elliott, E. (1983). Achievement motivation. In P. Mussen (Ed.), *Handbook of child psychology. Vol. 4. Socialization, personality, and social development* (pp. 643–691). New York: Wiley.

Dykens, E. M., Hodapp, R. M., & Leckman, J. F. (1994). *Behavior and development in Fragile X syndrome.* Thousand Oaks, CA: Sage.

Eagly, A. H. (1987). *Sex difference in social behavior: A social-role interpretation.* Hillsdale, NJ: Lawrence Erlbaum Associates.

Eagly, A. H., Ashmore, R. D., Makhijani, M. G., & Longo, L. C. (1991). What is beautiful is good, but...: A meta-analytic review of the physical attractiveness stereotype. *Psychological Bulletin, 110*, 109–128.

Eagly, A. H., & Chaiken, S. (1975). An attribution analysis of the effect of communicator characteristics on opinion change: The case of communicator attractiveness. *Journal of Personality and Social Psychology, 37*, 136–144.

Eagly, A. H., & Chaiken, S. (1993). *The psychology of attitudes.* Fort Worth, TX: Harcourt Brace.

Eagly, A. H., & Chaiken, S. (1998). Attitude structure and function. In D. T. Gilbert, S. T. Fiske, & G. Lindzey (Eds.), *The handbook of social psychology* (4th ed., pp. 269–322). New York: McGraw–Hill.

Eagly, A. H., & Crowley, M. (1986). Gender and helping behavior: A meta-analytic review of the social psychological literature. *Psychological Bulletin, 100*, 283–308.

Eagly, A. H., Wood, W., & Diekman, A. B. (2000). Social role theory of sex differences and similarities: A current appraisal. In T. Eckes & H. M. Trautner (Eds.), *The developmental social psychology of gender* (pp. 123–174). Mahwah, NJ: Lawrence Erlbaum Associates.

Eaker, E. D., & Castelli, W. P. (1988). Type A behavior and mortality from coronary disease in the Framingham Study. *New England Journal of Medicine, 319*, 1480–1481.

Eaton, W. W., Kessler, R. C., Wittchen, H. U., & Magee, W. J. (1994). Panic and panic disorder in the United States. *American Journal of Psychiatry, 151*(3), 413–420.

Ebbinghaus, H. (1885). *Memory: A contribution to experimental psychology.* New York: Dover.

Ebbinghaus, H. (1913). *Memory: A contribution to experimental psychology.* New York: Teachers College Press. (Translated from the 1885 German original.)

Egan, L. C., Santos, L. R., & Bloom, P. (2007). The origins of cognitive dissonance. Evidence from children and monkeys. *Psychological Science, 18*(11), 978–983.

Eich, E., & Metcalfe, J. (1989). Mood dependent memory for internal vs. external events. *Journal of Experimental Psychology: Learning, Memory and Cognition, 15*, 443–455.

Eisenberger, N. I., Lieberman, M. D., & Williams, K. D. (2003). Does rejection hurt? An fMRI study of social exclusion. *Science, 302*, 290–292.

Eisenegger, C., Naef, M., Snozzi, R., Heinrichs, M., & Fehr, E. (2010). Prejudice and truth about the effect of testosterone on human bargaining behavior. *Nature, 463*, 356–359.

Ekman, P. (1972). Universal and cultural differences in facial expressions of emotion. In J. Cole (Ed.), *Nebraska Symposium of Motivation, 1871* (Vol. 19). Lincoln: University of Nebraska Press.

Ekman, P. (1973). Darwin and cross-cultural studies of facial expression. In P. Ekman (Ed.), *Darwin and facial expression: A century of research in review.* New York: Academic Press.

Ekman, P. (1980). Asymmetry in facial expression. *Science, 209*, 833–834.

Ekman, P., & Friesen, W. V. (1969). The repertoire of nonverbal behavior: Categories, origins, usage, and coding. *Semiotica, 1*, 49–98.

Ekman, P., & Friesen, W. V. (1971). Constants across cultures in the face and emotion. *Journal of Personality and Social Psychology, 17*(2), 124–129.

Ekman, P., & Friesen, W. V. (1978). *The facial action coding system.* Palo Alto, CA: Consulting Psychologists Press.

Ekman, P., Sorensen, E. R., & Friesen, W. V. (1969). Pan-cultural elements in facial displays of emotion. *Science, 164*, 86–88.

Elkind, D. (1985). Egocentrism redux. *Developmental Review, 5*, 218–226.

Elliott, E., & Dweck, C. (1988). Goals: An approach to motivation and achievement. *Journal of Personality and Social Psychology, 54*, 5–12.

Ellis, A. (1997). *The practice of rational emotive behavior therapy.* New York: Springer Publishing.

Ellis, A. (1998). *The Albert Ellis reader: A guide to well-being using rational emotive behavior therapy.* Secaucus, NJ: Carol Publishing Group.

Ellis, L., Ames, M. A., Peckham, W., & Burke, D. (1988). Sexual orientation of human offspring may be altered by severe maternal stress during pregnancy. *The Journal of Sex Research, 25*, 152–157.

Ellis, L. K., Gay, P. E., & Paige, E. (2001). Daily pleasures and hassles across the lifespan. Poster presented at the annual meeting of the American Psychological Association, San Francisco, CA.

Endler, N. S. (1988). The origins of electroconvulsive therapy (ECT). *Convulsive Therapy, 4*, 5–23.

Engle, R. W., & Kane, M. J. (2004). Executive attention, working memory capacity, and a two-factor theory of cognitive control. *The Psychology of Learning and Motivation, 44*, 145–199.

Enns, J. T., & Coren, S. (1995). The box alignment illusion: An orientation illusion induced by pictorial depth. *Perception & Psychophysics, 57*, 1163–1174.

Epping-Jordan, M., Waltkins, S. S., Koob, G. F., & Markou, A. (1998). Dramatic decreases in brain reward function during nicotine withdrawal. *Nature (Lond), 393*, 76–79.

Erikson, E. (1980). Elements of a psychoanalytic theory of psychosocial development. In S. Greenspan & G. Pollock (Eds.), *The course of life* (Vol. 1, pp. 11–61). Washington, DC: U.S. Dept. of Health and Human Services.

Erikson, E. H. (1950). *Childhood and society.* New York: Norton.

Erikson, E. H. (1959). Growth and crises of the healthy personality. *Psychological Issues, 1*, 50–100.

Erikson, E. H. (1982). *The life cycle completed.* New York: Norton.

Erikson, E. H., & Erikson, J. M. (1997). *The life cycle completed.* New York: Norton.

Ertelt, D., Small, S., Solodkin, A., Dettmers, C., McNamara, A., Binkofski, F., et al. (2007). Action observation has a positive impact on rehabilitation of motor deficits after stroke. *NeuroImage, 36*, (Suppl.2), T164–T173.

Eschenbeck, H., Kohlmann, C. W., & Lohaus, A. (2007). Gender differences in coping strategies in children and adolescents. *Journal of Individual Differences, 28*(1), 18–26.

Eskenazi, B., Bradman, A., & Castorina, R. (1999). Exposures of children to organophosphate pesticides and their potential adverse health effects. *Environmental Health Perspectives, 107*(Suppl. 3), 409–419.

Evans, D., Hodgkinson, B., O'Donnell, A., Nicholson, J., & Walsh, K. (2000). The effectiveness of individual therapy and group therapy in the treatment of schizophrenia. In *Best Practice, 5*(3), 1–54. Published by the Joanna Briggs Institute for Evidence Based Nursing and Midwifery.

Evans, I. M., & Meyer, L. H. (1985). *An educative approach to behavior problems: A practical decision model for interventions with severely handicapped learners.* Baltimore: Paul H. Brookes.

Evans, W. H., Evans, S. S., & Schmid, R. E. (1989). *Behavior and instructional management: An ecological approach.* Boston: Allyn and Bacon.

Exner, J. E. (1980). But it's only an inkblot. *Journal of Personality Assessment, 44*, 562–577.

Eysenck, H. (1994). *Test your IQ.* Toronto: Penguin Books.

Eysenck, H. J. (1957). The effects of psychotherapy: An evaluation. *Journal of Consulting Psychology, 16*, 319–324.

Eysenck, H. J. (1994). Synergistic interaction between psychosocial and physical factors in the causation of lung cancer. In C. Lewis, C. O'Sullivan, & J. Barraclough (Eds.), *The psychoimmunology of human cancer* (pp. 163–178). London: Oxford University Press.

Fahey, V. (1993). How sleep deprived are you? *Health, 7*(5), 3–4.

Fanselow, M. S., & Gale, G. D. (2003). The amygdala, fear, and memory. *Annals of the New York Academy of Sciences, 985*, 125–134.

Faraone, S. V., Biederman, J., & Friedman, D. (2000). Validity of DSM-IV subtypes of attention-deficit/hyperactivity disorder: A family study perspective. *Journal of the American Academy of Child and Adolescent Psychiatry, 39*, 300–307.

Faraone, S. V., Biederman, J., Lehman, B. K., Keenan, K., Norman, D., Seidman, L. J., et al. (1993). Evidence for independent familial transmission of attention deficit hyperactivity disorder and learning disabilities: Result from a family genetic study. *American Journal of Psychiatry, 150,* 891–895.

Faraone, S. V., Tsuang, M. T., & Tsuang, D. W. (1999). *Genetics of mental disorders: A guide for students, clinicians, and researchers.* New York: Guilford Press.

Farmer, A. E. (1996). The genetics of depressive disorders. *International Review of Psychiatry, 8*(4).

Farthing, W. (1992). *The psychology of consciousness.* Upper Saddle River, NJ: Prentice-Hall.

Fawzy, F. I., Fawzy, N. W., Hyun, C. S., Elashoff, R., Guthrie, D., Fahey, J. L., & et al. (1993). Malignant melanoma effects of an early structured psychiatric intervention, coping, and affective state on recurrence and survival 6 years later. *Archives of General Psychiatry, 50*(9), 681–689.

FDA MedWatch Safety Alert. (October 15, 2004). Public health advisory: Suicidality in children and adolescents being treated with antidepressant medications. Retrieved December 15, 2004, from **www.fda.gov/medwatch/SAFETY/2004/safety04.htm#ssri**

Fechner, G. T. (1860). *Elemente der Psykophysik.* Leipzig: Breitkopf und Härtel.

Fedoroff, I. C., & McFarlane, T. (1998). Cultural aspects of eating disorders. In S. S. Kazarian & D. R. Evans (Eds.), *Cultural clinical psychology: Theory, research and practice* (pp. 152–176). New York: Oxford University Press.

Feingold, A. (1992). Good-looking people are not what we think. *Psychological Bulletin, 111,* 304–341.

Feldman, D. H. (2003). Cognitive development in childhood. In R. M. Lerner, M. A. Easterbrooks, et al. (Eds.), *Handbook of psychology: Developmental psychology,* (Vol. 6, pp. 195–201). New York: Wiley.

Fenn, K. M., Nusbaum, H. C., & Margoliash, D. (2003). Consolidation during sleep of perceptual learning of spoken language. *Nature, 425,* 614–616.

Ferguson, N. B., & Keesey, R. E. (1975). Effect of a quinine-adulterated diet upon body weight maintenance in male rats with ventromedial hypothalamic lesions. *Journal of Comparative Physiological Psychology, 89*(5), 478–488.

Fernald, A. (1984). The perceptual and affective salience of mothers' speech to infants. In L. Feagans, C. Garvey, & R. Golinkoff (Eds.), *The origins and growth of communication.* Norwood, NJ: Ablex.

Fernald, A. (1992). Human maternal vocalizations to infants as biologically relevant signals: An evolutionary perspective. In J. H. Barkow, L. Cosmides, & J. Tooby (Eds.), *The adapted mind: Evolutionary psychology and the generation of culture.* New York: Oxford University Press.

Feroah, T. R., Sleeper, T., Brozoski, D., Forder, J., Rice, T. B., & Forster, H. V. (2004). *Circadian slow wave sleep and movement behavior are under genetic control in inbred strains of rat.* Paper presented at the American Physiological Society Annual Conference, April 17–21, 2004, at the Washington, DC, Convention Center.

Festinger, L. (1954). A theory of social comparison processes. *Human Relations, 7,* 117–140.

Festinger, L. (1957). *A theory of cognitive dissonance.* Stanford, CA: Stanford University Press.

Festinger, L., & Carlsmith, J. (1959). $1/$20 Experiment: Cognitive consequences of forced compliance. *Journal of Abnormal and Social Psychology, 58*(2), 203–210.

Fiatarone, M. (1996). Physical activity and functional independence in aging. *Research Quarterly for Exercise & Sport, 67,* 70–75.

Fiatarone, M. A., O'Neill, E. F., Doyle, N., Clements, K. M., Roberts, S. B., Kehayias, J. et al. (1993). The Boston FICSIT study: The effects of resistance training and nutritional supplementation on physical frailty in the oldest old. *Journal of American Geriatrics, 41,* 333–337.

Fiedler, F. E. (1967). *A theory of leadership effectiveness.* New York: McGraw-Hill.

Fincham, F. D., Harold, G. T., & Gano-Phillips, S. (2000). The longitudinal association between attributions and marital satisfaction: Direction of effects and role of efficacy expectations. *Journal of Family Psychology, 14,* 267–285.

Fink, M. (1984). Meduna and the origins of convulsive therapy. *American Journal of Psychiatry, 141,* 1034–1041.

Finke, R. (1995). Creative realism. In S. Smith, T. Ward, & R. Finke (Eds.), *The creative cognition approach* (pp. 301–326). Cambridge: Cambridge University Press.

Finkel, D., & McGue, M. (1997). Sex differences and nonadditivity in heritability of the Multidimensional Personality Questionnaire scales. *Journal of Personality and Social Psychology, 72,* 929–938.

Fischer, A. (1993). Sex differences in emotionality: Fact or Stereotype? *Feminism & Psychology, 3,* 303–318.

Fischl, B., Liu, A., & Dale, A. M. (2001). Automated manifold surgery: Constructing geometrically accurate and topologically correct models of the human cerebral cortex. *IEEE Transactions on Medical Imaging, 20,* 70–80.

Fiske, S. T. (1998). Stereotyping, prejudice, and discrimination. In D. T. Gilbert & S. T. Fiske (Eds.), *The handbook of social psychology* (4th ed., Vol. 2, pp. 357–411). New York: McGraw-Hill.

Flaskerud, J. H. (1991). Effects of an Asian client–therapist language, ethnicity and gender match on utilization and outcome of therapy. *Community Mental Health Journal, 27,* 31–42.

Flavell, J. H. (1999). Cognitive development: Children's knowledge about the mind. *Annual Review of Psychology, 50,* 21–45.

Fleming, M. F., & Barry, K. L. (1992). Clinical overview of alcohol and drug disorders. In M. F. Fleming & K. L. Barry (Eds.), *Addictive disorders.* St. Louis, MO: Mosby Year Book.

Flemons, W. W. (2002). Obstructive sleep apnea. *New England Journal of Medicine, 347,* 498–504.

Foa, E. B., & Franklin, M. E. (2000). Psychotherapies for obsessive-compulsive disorder: A review. In M. Maj, N. Sartorius, A. Okasha, & J. Zohar, (Eds.), *Obsessive-compulsive disorder* (pp. 93–115). New York: John Wiley & Sons.

Foa, E. B., Keane, T. M., & Friedman, M. J. (Eds). (2000). *Effective treatments for PTSD.* New York: Guilford Press.

Folkman, S. (1997). Positive psychological states and coping with severe stress. *Social Science & Medicine, 45,* 1207–1221.

Folkman, S., & Lazarus, R. S. (1980). An analysis of coping in a middle-aged community sample. *Journal of Health and Social Behavior, 21*(3), 219–239.

Follett, K. J., & Hess, T. M. (2002). Aging, cognitive complexity, and the fundamental attribution error. *Journals of Gerontology Series B: Psychological Sciences and Social Sciences, 57,* 312–323.

Foulkes, D., & Schmidt, M. (1983). Temporal sequence and unit comparison composition in dream reports from different stages of sleep. *Sleep, 6,* 265–280.

Frank, D. A., Augustyn, M., Knight, W. G., Pell, T., & Zuckerman, B. (2001). Growth, development, and behavior in early childhood following prenatal cocaine exposure. *Journal of the American Medical Association, 285*(12), 1613–1625.

Frank, E., Kupfer, D. J., Buysse, D. J., Swartz, H. A., Pilkonis, P. A., Houck, P. R., et al. (2007). Randomized trial of weekly, twice-monthly, and monthly interpersonal psychotherapy as maintenance treatment for women with recurrent depression. *American Journal of Psychiatry, 164*(5), 761–767.

Franke, R. H., & Kaul, J. D. (1978). The Hawthorne Experiments: First statistical interpretation. *American Sociological Review, 43,* 623–643.

Frankel, B. R., & Piercy, F. P. (1990). The relationship among selected supervisor, therapist, and client behaviors. *Journal of Marital and Family Therapy, 16,* 407–421.

Freedman, J., & Fraser, S. (1966). Compliance without pressure: The foot-in-the-door technique. *Journal of Personality and Social Psychology, 4,* 195–202.

Freeman, A., Simon, K. M., Beutler, L. E., & Arkowitz, H. (Eds.). (1989). *Comprehensive handbook of cognitive therapy.* New York: Plenum Press.

Freeman, J. (2001). *Gifted children grown up.* London: David Fulton Publishers Ltd.

Freeman, W., & Watts, J. W. (1937). Prefrontal lobotomy in the treatment of mental disorders. *Southern Medical Journal, 30,* 23–31.

Freese, J., Powell, B., & Steelman, L. C. (1999). Rebel without a cause or effect: Birth order and social attitudes. *American Sociological Review, 64,* 207–231.

Fresquet, N., Angst, M., & Sandner, G. (2004). Insular cortex lesions alter conditioned taste avoidance in rats differentially when using two methods of sucrose delivery. *Behavioral Brain Research, 153*(2), 357–365.

Freud, A. (1946). *The ego and the mechanisms of defense. American Edition.* New York: I.U.P.

Freud, S. (1900). *The interpretation of dreams. S.E., 4–5.* (cf. Joyce Crick, Trans., 1999). London: Oxford University Press.

Freud, S. (1900). *The interpretation of dreams.* Translated by A. A. Brill, 1913. New York: Macmillan.

Freud, S. (1904). *Freud's psycho-analytic procedure, S.E., 7,* 249–254.

Freud, S. (1904). *Psychopathology of everyday life.* New York: Macmillan; London: Fisher Unwin.

Freud, S. (1915). *Repression, the standard edition of the complete psychological works of Sigmund Freud,* (Vol. 14). Edited by James Strachey. London: The Hogart Press and the Institute of Psychoanalysis, 1974.

Freud, S. (1923). *The ego and the id, S.E., 19,* 12–66.

Freud, S. (1930). *Civilization and its discontents.* New York: Jonathon Cape.

Freud, S. (1933). *New introductory lectures on psycho-analysis.* London: Hogarth.

Freud, S. (1940). Splitting of the ego in the process of defence. *International Journal of Psychoanalysis, 22,* 65 [1938], S.E., 23:275–278.

Freud, S., & Gay, P. (1977). *Inhibitions, symptoms and anxiety. Standard edition of the complete works of Sigmund Freud.* New York: W. W. Norton.

Freud, S., Strachey, J., & Riviere, J. (1990). *The ego and the id (The Standard Edition of the Complete Psychological Works of Sigmund Freud).* New York: W. W. Norton.

Friedman, M., & Kasanin, J. D. (1943). Hypertension in only one of identical twins. *Archives of Internal Medicine, 72,* 767–774.

Friedman, M., & Rosenman, R. H. (1959). Association of specific behavior pattern with blood and cardiovascular findings. *Journal of the American Medical Association, 169,* 1286–1296.

Friesen, W. V. (1972). *Cultural differences in facial expressions in a social situation: An experimental test of the concept of display rules.* Unpublished doctoral dissertation, University of California—San Francisco.

Frontera, W. R., Hughes, V. A., Lutz, K. J., & Evans, W. J. (1991). A cross-sectional study of muscle strength and mass in 45- to 78-year-old men and women. *Journal of Applied Physiology, 71*, 644–650.

Furumoto, L. (1979). Mary Whiton Calkins (1863–1930): Fourteenth president of the American Psychological Association. *Journal of the History of Behavioral Sciences, 15*, 346–356.

Gado, M. (2004). A cry in the night: The Kitty Genovese murder. *Court TV's Crime Library: Criminal Minds and Methods.* Retrieved August 2, 2004, from www.crimelibrary.com/serial_killers/predators/kitty_genovese/1.html?sect=2

Galanti, G. A. (1997). *Caring for patients from different cultures* (2nd ed.). Philadelphia: University of Pennsylvania Press.

Galea, S., Resnick, H., Kilpatrick, D., Bucuvalas, M., Gold, J., & Vlahov, D. (2002). Psychological sequelae of the September 11 terrorist attacks in New York City. *New England Journal of Medicine, 346*(13), 982–987.

Gamwell, L., & Tomes, N. (1995). *Madness in America: Cultural and medical perspectives of mental illness before 1914.* Ithaca, NY: Cornell University Press.

Ganchrow, J. R., Steiner, J. E., & Munif, D. (1983). Neonatal facial expressions in response to different qualities and intensities of gustatory stimuli. *Infant Behavior Development, 6*, 473–478.

Ganellen, R. J. (1996). *Integrating the Rorschach and the MMPI-2 in personality assessment.* Mahwah, NJ: Erlbaum.

Garb, H. N., Florio, C. M., & Grove, W. M. (1998). The validity of the Rorschach and the Minnesota Multiphasic Personality Inventory: Results from meta-analyses. *Psychological Science, 9*, 402–404.

Garcia, J., Brett, L. P., & Rusiniak, K. W. (1989). Limits of Darwinian conditioning. In S. B. Klein & R. R. Mowrer (Eds.), *Contemporary learning theories: Instrumental conditioning theory and the impact of biological constraints on learning* (pp. 237–275). Hillsdale, NJ: Erlbaum.

Garcia, J., & Koelling, R. A. (1966). Relation of cue to consequence in avoidance learning. *Psychonomic Science, 4*, 123.

Gardner, H. (1993a). *Creating minds: An anatomy of creativity seen through the lives of Freud, Einstein, Picasso, Stravinsky, Eliot, Graham, and Ghandi.* New York: Basic Books.

Gardner, H. (1993b). *Multiple intelligences: The theory in practice.* New York: Basic Books.

Gardner, H. (1998). Are there additional intelligences? The case for naturalist, spiritual, and existential intelligences. In J. Kane (Ed.), *Education, information, and transformation* (pp. 111–131). Upper Saddle River, NJ: Merrill-Prentice Hall.

Gardner, H. (1999a). *Intelligence reframed: Multiple intelligences for the 21st century.* New York: Basic Books.

Gardner, H. (1999b, February). Who owns intelligence? *Atlantic Monthly*, 67–76.

Gardner, H., & Moran, S. (2006). The science in multiple intelligences: A response to Lynn Waterhouse. *Educational Psychologist, 41*, 227–232.

Gardner, J., & Oswald, A. J. (2004). How is mortality affected by money, marriage, and stress? *Journal of Health Economics, 23*(6), 1181–1207.

Garland, E. J., & Smith, D. H. (1991). Simultaneous prepubertal onset of panic disorder, night terrors, and somnambulism. *Journal of American Academic Child and Adolescent Psychiatry, 30*(4), 553–555.

Garner, D. M., & Garfinkel, P. E. (1980). Socio-cultural factors in the development of anorexia nervosa. *Psychological Medicine, 10*, 647–656.

Geddes, J., & Butler, R. (2002). Depressive disorders. *Clinical Evidence, 7*, 867–882.

Geen, R. G., & Thomas, S. L. (1986). The immediate effects of media violence on behavior. *Journal of Social Issues, 42*, 7–27.

Gelder, M. (1976). Flooding. In T. Thompson & W. Dockens (Eds.), *Applications of behavior modification* (pp. 250–298). New York: Academic Press.

Geliebter, A. (1988). Gastric distension and gastric capacity in relation to food intake in humans. *Physiological Behavior, 44*, 665–668.

Geller, B., Williams, M., Zimerman, B., Frazier, J., Beringer, L., & Warner, K. L. (1998). Prepubertal and early adolescent bipolarity differentiate from ADHD by manic symptoms, grandiose delusions, ultra-rapid or ultradian cycling. *Journal of Affective Disorders, 51*(2), 81–91.

Gelman, S. A. (1988). The development of induction within natural kind and artifact categories. *Cognitive Psychology, 20*, 65–95.

Geschwind, D. H., & Iacoboni, M. (2007). Structural and functional asymmetries of the frontal lobes. In B. L. Miller & J. K. Cummings (Eds.), *The human frontal lobes* (2nd ed., pp. 68–91). New York: Guilford Press.

Gibbons, J. L., Stiles, D. A., & Shkodriani, G. M. (1991). Adolescents' attitudes toward family and gender roles: An international comparison. *Sex Roles, 25*, 625–643.

Gibson, E. J., & Walk, R. D. (1960). The "visual cliff." *Scientific American, 202*, 67–71.

Giedd, J. N., Blumenthal, J., Jeffries, N. O., Castellanos, F. X., Liui, H., Zijdenbos, A., et al. (1999). Brain development during childhood and adolescence: A longitudinal MRI study. *Nature Neuroscience, 2*(10), 861–863.

Gillespie, M. A., Kim, B. H., Manheim, L. J., Yoo, T., Oswald, F. L., & Schmitt, N. (2002). The development and validation of biographical data and situational judgment tests in the prediction of college student success. Presented in A. M. Ryan (Chair), *Beyond g: Expanding thinking on predictors of college success.* Symposium conducted at the 14th Annual Convention of the American Psychological Society, New Orleans, LA.

Gillham, B., Tanner, G., Cheyne, B., Freeman, I., Rooney, M., & Lambie, A. (1998). Unemployment rates, single parent density, and indices of child poverty: Their relationship to different categories of child abuse and neglect. *Child Abuse and Neglect, 22*(2), 79–90.

Gilligan, C. (1982). *In a different voice: Psychological theory and women's development.* Cambridge, MA: Harvard University Press.

Gillund, G., & Shiffrin, R. M. (1984). A retrieval model for both recognition and recall. *Psychological Review, 91*, 1–67.

Gilovich, T., Vallone, R., & Tversky, A. (1985). The hot hand in basketball: On the misperception of random sequences. *Cognitive Psychology, 17*, 295–314.

Gittelman-Klein, R. (1978). Validity in projective tests for psychodiagnosis in children. In R. L. Spitzer & D. F. Klein (Eds.), *Critical issues in psychiatric diagnosis* (pp. 141–166). New York: Raven Press.

Glynn, S. M. (1990). Token economy approaches for psychiatric patients: Progress and pitfalls over 25 years. *Behavior Modification, 14*, 383–407.

Godden, D. R., & Baddeley, A. D. (1975). Context-dependent memory in two natural environments: On land and underwater. *British Journal of Psychology, 66*, 325–331.

Goin, M. K. (2005). Practical psychotherapy: A current perspective on the psychotherapies. *Psychiatric Services, 56*(3), 255–257.

Goldman-Rakic, P. S. (1998). The prefrontal landscape: Implications of functional architecture for understanding human mentation and the central executive. In A. C. Roberts, T. W. Robbins, & L. Weiskrantz (Eds.), *The prefrontal cortex: Executive and cognitive functions* (pp. 87–102). Oxford, UK: Oxford University Press.

Goldsmith, H. H., & Campos, J. (1982). Toward a theory of infant temperament. In R. Emde & R. Harmon (Eds.), *The development of attachment and affiliative systems: Psychobiological aspects* (pp. 161–193). New York: Plenum Press.

Goldstein, S. (1997). *Managing attention and learning disorders in late adolescence and adulthood: A guide for practitioners.* New York: John Wiley.

Goldston, D. B., Molock, S. D., Whitbeck, L. B., Murakami, J. L., Zayas, L. H., & Hall, G. C. (2008). Cultural considerations in adolescent suicide prevention and psychosocial treatment. *American Psychologist, 63*(1), 14–31.

Goleman, D. (1982). Staying up: The rebellion against sleep's gentle tyranny. *Psychology Today, 3*, 24–35.

Goleman, D. (1995). *Emotional intelligence: Why it can matter more than IQ.* New York: Bantam Books.

Gong-Guy, E., & Hammen, C. (1980). Causal perceptions of stressful events in depressed and nondepressed outpatients. *Journal of Abnormal Psychology, 89*, 662–669.

Gonzaga, G. C., Turner, R. A., Keltner, D., Campos, B. C., & Altemus, M. (2006). Romantic love and sexual desire in close relationships. *Emotion 6*, 163–179.

Goodglass, H., Kaplan, E., & Barresi, B., (2001). *The assessment of aphasia and related disorders* (3rd ed.). Baltimore: Lippincott, Williams & Wilkins.

Gotlib, I. H., Sivers, H., Canli, T., Kasch, K. L., & Gabrieli, J. D. E. (2001). Neural activation in depression in response to emotional stimuli. In I. H. Gotlib (Chair), *New directions in the neurobiology of affective disorders.* Symposium presented at the Annual Meeting of the Society for Research in Psychopathology, Madison, WI.

Gottesman, I. I. (1991). *Schizophrenia genesis: The origins of madness.* New York: Freeman.

Gottesman, I. I., McGuffin, P., & Farmer, A. E. (1987). Clinical genetics as clues to the "real" genetics of schizophrenia (a decade of modest gains while playing for time). *Schizophrenia Bulletin, 13*(1), 23–48.

Gottesman, I. I., & Shields, J. (1976). A critical review of recent adoption, twin and family studies of schizophrenia: Behavioural genetics perspectives. *Schizophrenia Bulletin, 2*, 360–401.

Gottesman, I., & Shields, J. (1982). *Schizophrenia: The epigenetic puzzle.* New York: Cambridge University Press.

Gottman, J. M., & Krokoff, L. J. (1989). Marital interaction and satisfaction: A longitudinal view. *Journal of Consulting and Clinical Psychology, 57*, 47–52.

Gould, S. J. (1981). *The mismeasure of man.* New York: Norton.

Gouldner, A. W. (1960). The norm of reciprocity: A preliminary statement. *American Sociological Review, 25*, 161–178.

Grandjean, P., Weihe, P., White, R. F., Debes, F., Araki, S., Yokoyama, et al. (1997). Cognitive deficit in 7-year-old children with prenatal exposure to methylmercury. *Neurotoxicology and Teratology, 19*(6), 417–428.

Greenberg, J. (2008). Understanding the vital human quest for self-esteem. *Perspectives on Psychological Science, 3*, 48–55.

Gregory, R. L. (1990). *Eye and brain, the psychology of seeing.* Princeton, NJ: Princeton University Press.

Gresham, L. G., & Shimp, T. A. (1985). Attitude toward the advertisement and brand attitudes: A classical conditioning prospective. *Journal of Advertising, 14*(1), 10–17, 49.

Griffit, W. (1970). Environmental effects on interpersonal affective behavior: Ambient effective temperature and attraction. *Journal of Personality and Social Psychology, 15*, 240–244.

Griffit, W., & Veitch, R. (1971). Hot and crowded: Influences of population density and temperature on interpersonal affective behavior. *Journal of Personality and Social Psychology, 17*, 92–98.

Grocer, S., & Kohout, J. (1997). *The 1995 APA survey of 1992 baccalaureate recipients*. Washington, DC: American Psychological Association.

Gross, C. G. (1999). A hole in the head. *The Neuroscientist, 5*, 263–269.

Grünbaum, A. (1984). *The foundations of psychoanalysis: A philosophical critique*. Berkeley, CA: University of California Press.

Guerin, D. A., Park, Y., & Yang, S. (1995). Development of an instrument to study the meaning of color in interior environments. *Journal of Interior Design, 20*(2), 31–41.

Guilford, J. P. (1967). *The nature of human intelligence*. New York: McGraw-Hill.

Guthrie, R. V. (2004). *Even the rat was white: A historical view of psychology*. Boston: Allyn and Bacon.

Halbesleben, J. R. B., & Bowler, W. M. (2007). Emotional exhaustion and job performance: The mediating role of motivation. *Journal of Applied Psychology, 91*, 93–106.

Hall, C. (1966). Studies of dreams collected in the laboratory and at home. *Institute of Dream Research Monograph Series* (No. 1). Santa Cruz, CA: Privately printed.

Hamilton, D. L., & Gifford, R. K. (1976). Illusory correlation in interpersonal perception: A cognitive basis of stereotypic judgments. *Journal of Experimental Social Psychology, 12*, 392–407.

Hamilton, J. A. (1982). The identity of postpartum psychosis. In I. F. Brockington, & R. Kumar (Eds.), *Motherhood and mental illness* (pp. 1–17). London: Academic Press.

Hampton, J. A. (1998). Similarity-based categorization and fuzziness of natural categories. *Cognition, 65*, 137–165.

Handel, S. (1989). *Listening: An introduction to the perception of auditory events*. Cambridge, MA: MIT Press.

Hansen, D. (2010, October 10). Chilean mining rescue offers lessons on handling office stress. *Vancouver Sun*. Retrieved from http://www.vancouversun.com/business/Chilean+mining+rescue+offers+lessons+handling+office+stress/3687996/story.html

Harlow, H. F. (1958). The nature of love. *American Psychologist, 13*, 573–685.

Harman, G. (1999). Moral philosophy meets social psychology: Virtue ethics and the fundamental attribution error. *Proceedings of the Aristotelian Society, 1998–99, 99*, 315–331.

Harmon-Jones, E. (2000). Cognitive dissonance and experienced negative affect: Evidence that dissonance increases experienced negative affect even in the absence of aversive consequences. *Personality and Social Psychology Bulletin, 26*, 1490–1501.

Harmon-Jones, E. (2004). Insights on asymmetrical frontal brain activity gleaned from research on anger and cognitive dissonance. *Biological Psychology, 67*, 51–76.

Harmon-Jones, E. (2006). Integrating cognitive dissonance theory with neurocognitive models of control. *Psychophysiology, 43*, S16.

Harmon-Jones, E., Harmon-Jones, C., Fearn, M., Sigelman, J. D., & Johnson, P. (2008). Action orientation, relative left frontal cortical activation, and spreading of alternatives: A test of the action-based model of dissonance. *Journal of Personality and Social Psychology, 94*(1), 1–15.

Harrison, P. J. (1999). The neuropathology of schizophrenia: A critical review of the data and their interpretation. *Brain, 122*, 593–624.

Hart, P. (1998). Preventing groupthink revisited: Evaluating and reforming groups in government. *Organizational Behavior & Human Decision Processes, 73*(2–3), 306–326.

Hartfield, E. (1987). Passionate and companionate love. In R. J. Sternberg & M. L. Barnes (Eds.), *The psychology of love* (pp. 191–217). New Haven, CT: Yale University Press.

Hartfield, E., & Rapson, R. L. (1992). Similarity and attraction in intimate relationships. *Communication Monographs, 59*, 209–212.

Harvey, S. & Keashly, L. (2003). Predicting the risk for aggression in the workplace: Risk factors, self-esteem and time at work. *Social Behaviour & Personality: An International Journal, 31*(8), 807–814.

Hauck, S. J., & Bartke, A. (2001). Free radical defenses in the liver and kidney of human growth hormone transgenic mice. *Journal of Gerontology and Biological Science, 56*, 153–162.

Havighurst R. J., Neugarten B. L., & Tobin S. N. S. (1968). Disengagement and patterns of aging. In B. L. Neugarten (Ed.), *Middle age and aging: A reader in social psychology* (pp. 161–172). Chicago: University of Chicago Press.

Hawks, S. R., Madanat, H. N., Merrill, R. M., Goudy, M. B., & Miyagawa, T. (2003). A cross-cultural analysis of "motivation for eating" as a potential factor in the emergence of global obesity: Japan and the United States. *Health Promotion International, 18*(2), 153–162.

Hayflick, L. (1977). The cellular basis for biological aging. In C. E. Finch & L. Hayflick (Eds.), *Handbook of biology of aging* (p. 159). New York: Van Nostrand Reinhold

Hayward, C., Killen, J. D., Kraemer, H. C., & Taylor, C. B. (2000). Predictors of panic attacks in adolescents. *Journal of the American Academy of Child and Adolescent Psychiatry, 39*(2), 207–214.

Hayward, C., Killen, J. D., & Taylor, C. B. (1989). Panic attacks in young adolescents. *American Journal of Psychiatry, 146*(8), 1061–1062.

Hebb, D. O. (1955). Drives and the C.N.S. (Conceptual Nervous System). *Psychological Review, 62*, 243–254.

Hegeman, R. (2007). Police: Shoppers stepped over victim. *The Associated Press*. Retrieved February 21, 2008, from http://abcnews.go.com/US/wireStory?id=3342724

Heider, F. (1958). *The psychology of interpersonal relations*. New York: John Wiley & Sons.

Heilman, K. M. (2002). *Matter of mind: A neurologist's view of brain-behavior relationships*. New York: Oxford University Press.

Heinrich, B. (2000). Testing insight in ravens. In C. Heyes & L. Huber (Eds.), *The evolution of cognition*. Cambridge, MA: MIT Press.

Helms, J. E. (1992). Why is there no study of cultural equivalence in standardized cognitive ability testing? *American Psychologist, 47*(9), 1083–1101.

Helson, H. (1964). *Adaptation level theory*. New York: Harper & Row.

Henning, H. (1916). Die qualitätenreihe des geschmacks. *Zsch. f. Psychol., 74*, 203–219.

Henningfield, J. E. (1995). Nicotine medications for smoking cessation. *New England Journal of Medicine, 333*(18), 1196–1203.

Henningfield, J. E., Clayton, R., & Pollin, W. (1990). Involvement of tobacco in alcoholism and illicit drug use. *British Journal of Addition, 85*, 279–292.

Herberman, R. B., & Ortaldo, J. R. (1981). Natural killer cells: Their role in defenses against disease. *Science, 214*, 24–30.

Herbst, J. H., Zonderman, A. B., McCrae, R. R., & Costa, P. T., Jr. (2000). Do the dimensions of the Temperament and Character Inventory map a simple genetic architecture? Evidence from molecular genetics and factor analysis. *American Journal of Psychiatry, 157*, 1285–1290.

Hermann, A., Maisel, M., Wegner, F., Liebau, S., Kim, D. W., Gerlach, M., et al. (2006). Multipotent neural stem cells from the adult tegmentum with dopaminergic potential develop essential properties of functional neurons. *Stem Cells, 24*(4), 949–964.

Hersh, S. M. (2004, May 10). Annals of national security: Torture at Abu Ghraib. *The New Yorker*.

Hershberger, S. L., Plomin, R., & Pedersen, N. L. (1995, October). Traits and metatraits: Their reliability, stability, and shared genetic influence. *Journal of Personality and Social Psychology, 69*(4), 673–685.

Hetherington, A. W., & Ranson, S. W. (1940). Hypothalamic lesions and adiposity in rats. *Anatomical Records, 78*, 149–172.

Hettema, J. M., Neale, M. C., & Kendler, K. S. (2001). A review and meta-analysis of the genetic epidemiology of anxiety disorders. *Amercian Journal of Psychiatry, 158*, 1568–1578.

Hewstone, M., Rubin, M., & Willis, H. (2002). Intergroup bias. *Annual Review of Psychology, 53*, 575–604.

Heyes, C. M. (1998). Theory of mind in nonhuman primates. *Behavior and Brain Science, 21*, 101–148.

Hicklin, J., & Widiger, T. A. (2000). Convergent validity of alternative MMPI-2 personality disorder scales. *Journal of Personality Assessment, 75*(3), 502–518.

Hilgard, E. R. (1991). A neodissociation interpretation of hypnosis. In S. J. Lynn & J. W. Rhue (Eds.), *Theories of hypnosis* (pp. 83–104). New York: Guilford Press.

Hilgard, E. R., & Hilgard, J. R. (1994). *Hypnosis in the relief of pain* (Rev. ed.). New York: Brunner/Mazel.

Hill, P. C., & Butter E. M. (1995). The role of religion in promoting physical health. *Journal of Psychology and Christianity, 14*(2), 141–155.

Hintze, J. M. (2002). Interventions for fears and anxiety problems. In M. R. Shinn, H. R. Walker, & G. Stoner (Eds.), *Interventions for academic and behavior problems II: Preventive and remedial approaches* (pp. 939–954). Bethesda, MD: National Association of School Psychologists.

Hobson, J. A. (1988). *The dreaming brain*. New York: Basic Books.

Hobson, J. A., & McCarley, R. (1977). The brain as a dream state generator: An activation-synthesis hypothesis of the dream process. *American Journal of Psychiatry, 134*, 1335–1348.

Hobson, J., Pace-Schott, E., & Stickgold, R. (2000). Dreaming and the brain: Towards a cognitive neuroscience of conscious states. *Behavioral and Brain Sciences, 23*(6), 793–1121.

Hochman, J. (1994). Buried memories challenge the law. *National Law Journal, 1*, 17–18.

Hodges, J. R. (1994). Retrograde amnesia. In A. Baddeley, B. A. Wilson, & F. Watts (Eds.), *Handbook of memory disorders* (pp. 81–107). New York: Wiley.

Hodson, D. S., & Skeen, P. (1994). Sexuality and aging: The hammerlock of myths. *The Journal of Applied Gerontology, 13*, 219–235.

Hoebel, B. G., & Teitelbaum, P. (1966). Weight regulation in normal and hypothalamic hyperphagic rats. *Journal of Comparative Physiological Psychology, 61*, 189–193.

Hoffmann, A. (1998). *Paradigms of artificial intelligence: A methodological and computational analysis.* London: Springer-Verlag.

Hoffrage, U., Hertwig, R., & Gigerenzer, G. (2000). Hindsight bias: A by-product of knowledge updating? *Journal of Experimental Psychology: Learning, Memory, and Cognition, 26,* 566–581.

Hofstede, G. H. (1980). *Culture's consequences, international differences in work-related values.* Beverly Hills, CA: Sage.

Hofstede, G. J., Pedersen, P. B., & Hofstede, G. H. (2002). *Exploring culture: Exercises, stories, and synthetic cultures.* Yarmouth, ME: Intercultural Press.

Hogg, M. A., & Hains, S. C. (1998). Friendship and group identification: A new look at the role of cohesiveness in groupthink. *European Journal of Social Psychology, 28*(1), 323–341.

Holcomb, W. R. (1986). Stress inoculation therapy with anxiety and stress disorders of acute psychiatric patients. *Journal of Clinical Psychology, 42,* 864–872.

Hollon, S. D., & Beck, A. T. (1994). Cognitive and cognitive-behavioral therapies. In A. E. Bergin & and S. L. Garfield (Eds.), *Handbook of psychotherapy and behavior change* (4th ed., p. 428). Chichester, UK: John Wiley & Sons.

Hollon, S. D., These, M., & Markowitz, J. (2002). Treatment and prevention of depression. *Psychological Science in the Public Interest, 3,* 39–77.

Holman, E. A., Silver, R. C., Poulin, M., Andersen, J., Gil-Rivas, V., & McIntosh, D. N. (2008). Terrorism, acute stress, and cardiovascular health: A 3-year national study following the September 11th attacks. *Archives of General Psychiatry, 65,* 73–80.

Holmes, C. B., Wurtz, P. J., Waln, R. F., Dungan, D. S., & Joseph, C. A. (1984). Relationship between the Luscher Color Test and the MMPI. *Journal of Clinical Psychology, 40,* 126–128.

Holmes, T. H., & Masuda, M. (1973). Psychosomatic syndrome: When mothers-in-law or other disasters visit, a person can develop a bad, bad cold. *Psychology Today, 5*(11), 71–72, 106.

Holmes, T. H., & Rahe, R. H. (1967). The Social Readjustment Rating Scale. *Journal of Psychosomatic Research II,* 213–218.

Holroyd, J. (1996). Hypnosis treatment of clinical pain: Understanding why hypnosis is useful. *International Journal of Clinical and Experimental Hypnosis, 44,* 33–51.

Hood, D. C. (1998). Lower-level visual processing and models of light adaptation. *Annual Review of Psychology, 49,* 503–535.

Hopfinger, J. B., Buonocore, M. H., & Mangun, G. R. (2000). The neural mechanisms of top-down attentional control. *Nature Neuroscience, 3,* 284–291.

Horne, J. A., & Staff, C. H. (1983). Exercise and sleep: Body heating effects. *Sleep, 6,* 36–46.

Horney, K. (1939). *New ways in psychoanalysis.* New York: W. W. Norton.

Horney, K. (1967/1973). *Feminine psychology.* New York: W. W. Norton.

Horowitz, D. L. (1985). *Ethnic groups in conflict.* Berkeley, CA: University of California Press.

Hortaçsu, N. (1999). The first year of family and couple initiated marriages of a Turkish sample: A longitudinal investigation. *International Journal of Psychology, 34*(1), 29–41.

Hothersall, D. (1995). *History of psychology.* Boston: McGraw Hill.

Hu, P., & Meng, Z. (1996). *An examination of infant–mother attachment in China.* Poster presented at the meeting of the International Society for the Study of Behavioral Development, Quebec City, Quebec, Canada.

Hubble, M. A., Duncan, B. L., & Miller, S. D. (1999). Directing attention to what works. In M. A. Hubble, B. L. Duncan, & S. D. Miller (Eds.), *The heart and soul of change: What works in therapy* (pp. 407–447). Washington, DC: American Psychological Association.

Huesmann, L. R., & Eron, L. (1986). *Television and the aggressive child: A cross-national comparison.* Hillsdale, NJ: Erlbaum.

Huesmann, L. R., & Miller, L. S. (1994). Long-term effects of repeated exposure to media violence in childhood. In L. R. Huesmann (Ed.), *Aggressive behavior: Current perspectives* (pp. 153–183). New York: Plenum Press.

Huesmann, L. R., Moise, J. F., & Podolski, C. L. (1997). The effects of media violence on the development of antisocial behavior. In D. M. Stoff, J. Breiling, & J. D. Maser (Eds.), *Handbook of antisocial behavior* (pp. 181–193). New York: John Wiley.

Huesmann, L. R., Moise-Titus, J., Podolski, C. L., & Eron, L. D. (2003). Longitudinal relations between children's exposure to TV violence and their aggressive and violent behavior in young adulthood: 1977–1992. *Developmental Psychology, 39*(2), 201–221.

Hull, C. L. (1943). *Principles of behavior.* New York: Appleton-Century.

Hunt, E. (2001). Multiple views of multiple intelligence. [Review of Intelligence reframed: Multiple intelligence in the 21st century.] *Contemporary Psychology, 46,* 5–7.

Hunt, M. (1993). *The story of psychology.* New York: Doubleday.

Hurst, S., & Milkewicz, N. (2000). Eye movement desensitization and reprocessing: A controversial treatment technique. Retrieved July 14, 2004, from www.netpsych.com/health/emd.htm

Hurtz, G. M., & Donovan, J. J. (2000). Personality and job performance: The Big Five revisited. *Journal of Applied Psychology, 85,* 869–879.

Hurvich, L. M. (1969). Hering and the scientific establishment. *American Psychologist, 24,* 497–514.

Hurwitz, T. A. (1989). Approach to the patient with psychogenic neurological disturbance. In W. N. Kelley (Ed.), *Textbook of internal medicine.* (Vol. 2, pp. 2518–2521). Philadelphia: J. B. Lippincott.

Hyde, J. S., & Kling, K. C. (2001). Women, motivation, and achievement. *Psychology of Women Quarterly, 25,* 264–378.

Hyde, J. S., & Plant, E. A. (1995). Magnitude of psychological gender differences. *American Psychologist, 50,* 159–161.

Hyman, I. E., Jr. (1993). Imagery, reconstructive memory, and discovery. In B. Roskos-Ewoldsen, M. J. Intons-Peterson, & R. E. Anderson (Eds.), *Imagery, creativity, and discovery: A cognitive perspective* (pp. 99–121). The Netherlands: Elsevier Science.

Hyman, I. E., Jr., Gilstrap, L. L., Decker, K., & Wilkinson, C. (1998). Manipulating remember and know judgements of autobiographical memories. *Applied Cognitive Psychology, 12,* 371–386

Hyman, I. E., Jr., & Loftus, E. F. (1998). Errors in autobiographical memories. *Clinical Psychology Review, 18,* 933–947.

Hyman, I. E., Jr., & Loftus, E. F. (2002). False childhood memories and eyewitness memory errors. In M. L. Eisen, J. A. Quas, & G. S. Goodman (Eds.), *Memory and suggestibility in the forensic interview* (pp. 63–84). Mahwah, NJ: Erlbaum.

Iacoboni, M., Woods, R. P., Brass, M., Bekkering, H., Mazziotta, J. C., & Rizzolatti, G. (1999). Cortical mechanisms of human imitation. *Science, 286,* 2526–2528.

Ikemoto, S., & Panksepp, J. (1999). The role of nucleus accumbens dopamine in motivated behavior: A unifying interpretation with special reference to reward-seeking. *Brain Research Reviews, 31,* 6–41.

Ioannidis, J. P. A. (1998, January 28). Effect of the statistical significance of results on the time to completion and publication of randomized efficacy trials. *Journal of the American Medical Association, 279,* 281–286.

Irwin, A. R., & Gross, A. M. (1995). Cognitive tempo, violent video games, and aggressive behavior in young boys. *Journal of Family Violence, 10*(3), 337–350.

Irwin, M., Mascovich A., Gillin, J. C., Willoughby, R., Pike, J., & Smith, T. L. (1994). Partial sleep deprivation reduces natural killer cell activity in humans. *Psychosomatic Medicine, 56,* 493–498.

Irwin, M., McClintick, J., Costlow, C., Fortner, M., White, J., & Gillin, J. C. (1996). Partial night sleep deprivation reduces natural killer and cellular immune responses in humans. *The Federation of American Societies for Experimental Biology Journal, 10,* 643–653.

Isabel, J. (2003). *Genetics: An introduction for dog breeders.* Loveland, CO: Alpine Publications.

Jacobson, S. G., Cideciyan A. V., Regunath, G., et al. (1995). Night blindness in Sorsby's fundus dystrophy reversed by vitamin A. *Nature Genetics, 11,* 27–32.

Jaeger, J. J., Lockwood, A. H., Van Valin, R. D., Kemmerer, D. L., Murphy, B. W., & Wack, D. S. (1998). Sex differences in brain regions activated by grammatical and reading tasks. *Neuroreport, 9,* 2803–2807.

James, W. (1884). What is an emotion? *Mind, 9,* 188–205.

James, W. (1890). *Principles of psychology.* New York: Henry Holt.

James, W. (1890, 2002). *The principles of psychology (Vols. 1 and 2).* Cambridge, MA: Harvard University Press.

James, W. (1894). The physical basis of emotion. *Psychological Review, 1,* 516–529.

Jameson, M., Diehl, R., & Danso, H. (2007). Stereotype threat impacts college athletes' academic performance. *Current Research in Social Psychology, 12*(5), 68–79.

Jamison, K. R. (1993.) *Touched with fire: Manic-depressive illness and the artistic temperament.* New York: Free Press (Macmillan).

Jang, K. L., Livesley, W. J., & Vernon, P. A. (1996). Heritability of the Big Five personality dimensions and their facets: A twin study. *Journal of Personality, 64,* 577–591.

Jang, K. L., McCrae, R. R., Angleitner, A., Riemann, R., & Livesley, W. J. (1998). Heritability of facet-level traits in a cross-cultural twin sample: Support for a hierarchical model of personality. *Journal of Personality and Social Psychology, 74,* 1556–1565.

Janis, I. (1972). *Victims of groupthink.* Boston: Houghton-Mifflin.

Janis, I. (1982). *Groupthink* (2nd ed.) Boston: Houghton-Mifflin.

Janos, P. M. (1987). A fifty-year follow-up of Terman's youngest college students and IQ-matched agemates. *Gifted Child Quarterly, 31,* 55–58.

Janus, S. S., & Janus, C. L. (1993). *The Janus report on sexual behavior.* New York: John Wiley & Sons

Jay, S. M., & Elliot, C. H. (1990). A stress inoculation program for parents whose children are undergoing medical procedures. *Journal of Consulting and Clinical Psychology, 58,* 799–804.

Jilek, W. G. (2001, July). Cultural factors in psychiatric disorders. Paper presented at the 26th Congress of the World Federation for Mental Health.

John, O. P., Angleitner, A., & Ostendorf, F. (1988). The lexical approach to personality: A historical review of trait taxonomic research. *European Journal of Personality, 2,* 171–203.

Johnson, G. (1995, June 6). Chimp talk debate: Is it really language? *The New York Times.*

Johnson, J., Cohen, P., Pine, D. S., Klein, D. F., Kasen, S., & Brook, J. S. (2000). Association between cigarette smoking and anxiety disorders during adolescence and early adulthood. *Journal of the American Medical Association, 284*(18), 2348–2351.

Jones, E. E., & Harris, V. A. (1967). The attribution of attitudes. *Journal of Experimental Social Psychology, 3,* 1–24.

Jones, E. J., Krupnick, J. L., & Kerig, P. K. (1987). Some gender effects in a brief psychotherapy. *Psychotherapy, 24,* 336–352.

Jones, G. W. (1997). Modernization and divorce: Contrasting trends in Islamic Southeast Asia and the West. *Population and Development Review, 23*(1), 95–113.

Jones, H. M., & Pilowsky, L. S. (2002). Dopamine and antipsychotic drug action revisited. *British Journal of Psychiatry, 181,* 271–275.

Jones, M. C. (1924). A laboratory study of fear: The case of Peter. *Pedagogical Seminary, 31,* 308–315.

Judge, T. A., Heller, D., & Mount, M. K. (2002). Five-factor model of personality and job satisfaction: A meta-analysis. *Journal of Applied Psychology, 87,* 530–541.

Juffer, F., & Rosenboom, L. G. (1997). Infant–mother attachment of internationally adopted children in the Netherlands. *International Journal of Behavioral Development, 20*(1), 93–107.

Jung, C. (1933). *Modern man in search of a soul.* New York: Harcourt Brace.

Kabat-Zinn, J., Lipworth, L., & Burney, R. (1985). The clinical use of mindfulness meditation for the self-regulation of chronic pain. *Journal of Behavioral Medicine, 8,* 163–190.

Kabat-Zinn, J., Lipworth, L., Burney, R., & Sellers, W. (1986). Four year follow-up of a meditation-based program for the self regulation of chronic pain: Treatment outcomes and compliance. *Clinical Journal of Pain, 2,* 159–173.

Kahneman, D., Slovic, P., & Tversky, A. (1982). *Judgment under uncertainty: Heuristics and biases.* New York: Cambridge University Press.

Kahneman, D., & Tversky, A. (1973). On the psychology of prediction. *Psychological Review, 80,* 237–251.

Kail, R. & Hall, L. K. (2001). Distinguishing short-term memory from working memory. *Memory & Cognition, 29*(1), 1–9.

Kaiser, P. K. (1984). Physiological response to color: Critical review. *Color Research and Application, 9,* 29–36.

Kales, A., Soldatos, C., Bixler, E., Ladda, R. L., Charney, D. S., Weber, G., et al. (1980). Hereditary factors in sleepwalking and night terrors. *British Journal of Psychiatry, 137,* 111–118.

Kamin, L. J. (1995, February). Behind the curve. *Scientific American,* 99–103.

Kandel, E. R., & Schwartz, J. H. (1982). Molecular biology of learning: Modulation of transmitter release. *Science, 218,* 433–443.

Karau, S. J., & Williams, K. D. (1993). Social loafing: A meta-analytic review and theoretical integration. *Journal of Personality and Social Psychology, 65,* 681–706.

Karau, S. J., & Williams, K. D. (1997). The effects of group cohesiveness on social loafing and social compensation. *Group Dynamics: Theory, Research and Practice, 1,* 156–168.

Karayiorgou, M., Altemus, M., Galke, B., Goldman, D., Murphy, D., Ott, J., et al. (1997). Genotype determining low catechol-O-methyltransferase activity as a risk factor for obsessive-compulsive disorder. *Proceeds of the National Academy of Science, 94,* 4572–4575.

Karney, B. R., & Bradbury, T. N. (2000). Attributions in marriage: State or trait? A growth curve analysis. *Journal of Personality and Social Psychology, 78,* 295–309.

Kastenbaum, R. (1985). Dying and death: A life-span approach. In J. E. Birren & K. W. Schaie (Eds.), *Handbook of the psychology of aging* (2nd ed., pp. 619–643). New York: Van Nostrand Reinhold.

Kastenbaum, R., & Costa, P. T., Jr. (1977). Psychological perspective on death. *Annual Review of Psychology, 28,* 225–249.

Katzman, R., Aronson, M., Fuld, P., Kawas, C. K., Brown, T., Morgenstern, H., et al. (1989). Development of dementing illnesses in an 80-year-old volunteer cohort. *Annals of Neurology, 25*(4), 317–324.

Kazdin, A. E. (1980). Acceptability of time out from reinforcement procedures for disruptive behavior. *Behavior Therapy, 11*(3), 329–344.

Keane, T. M., Fairbank, J. A., Caddell, J. M., & Zimering, R. T. (1989). Implosive (flooding) therapy reduced symptoms of PTSD in Vietnam combat veterans. *Behavior Therapy, 20,* 245–260.

Kearney, C. A., & Silverman, W. K. (1998). A critical review of pharmacotherapy for youth with anxiety disorders: Things are not as they seem. *Journal of Anxiety Disorders, 12,* 83–102.

Keillor, J., Barrett, A., Crucian, G., Kortenkamp, S., & Heilman, K. (2002). Emotional experience and perception in the absence of facial feedback. *Journal of the International Neuropsychological Society, 8*(1), 130–135.

Keller, M. B., McCullough, J. P., Klein, D. N., Arnow, B., Dunner, D., Gelenberg, A., et al. (2000). A comparison of nefazodone, the cognitive behavioral-analysis system of psychotherapy, and their combination for the treatment of chronic depression. *New England Journal of Medicine, 342*(20), 1462–1470.

Keller, M. B., Ryan, N. D., Strober, M., Klein, R. G., Kutcher, S. P., Birmaher, B., et al. (2001). Efficacy of paroxetine in the treatment of adolescent major depression: A randomized, controlled trial. *Journal of the Academy of Child and Adolescent Psychiatry, 40*(7), 762–772.

Kellner, R. (1986). *Somatization and hypochondriasis.* New York: Praeger-Greenwood.

Kelly, J. A., McAuliffe, T. L., Sikkema, K. J., Murphy, D. A., Somlai, A. M., Mulry, G., et al. (1997). Reduction in risk behavior among adults with severe mental illness who learned to advocate for HIV prevention. *Psychiatric Services, 48*(10), 1283–1288.

Kempe, R. S., & Kempe, C. C. (1978). *Child abuse.* Cambridge, MA: Harvard University Press.

Kendall, P. (1983). Stressful medical procedures: Cognitive-behavioral strategies for stress management and prevention. In D. Meichenbaum & M. Jaremko (Eds.), *Stress reduction and prevention* (pp. 159–190). New York: Plenum Press.

Kendall, P. C., Hudson, J. L., Gosch, E., Flannery-Schroeder, E., & Suveg, C. (2008). Cognitive-behavioral therapy for anxiety disordered youth: A randomized clinical trial evaluating child and family modalities. *Journal of Consulting and Clinical Psychology, 76*(2), 282–297.

Kendler, K. S. (1985). Diagnostic approaches to schizotypal personality disorders: A historical perspective. *Schizophrenia Bulletin, 11,* 538–553.

Kern, M. L., & Friedman, H. S. (2008). Do conscientious individuals live longer? A quantitative review. *Health Psychology, 27*(5), 505–512.

Keromoian, R., & Leiderman, P. H. (1986). Infant attachment to mother and child caretaker in an East African community. *International Journal of Behavioral Development, 9,* 455–469.

Kety, S. S., Wender, P. H., Jacobsen, B., Ingaham, L. J., Jansson, L., Faber, B., et al. (1994). Mental illness in the biological and adoptive relatives of schizophrenic adoptees. *Archives of General Psychiatry, 51,* 442–455.

Kiecolt-Glaser, J. K., Fisher, L. D., Ogrocki, P., Stout, J. C., Speicher, C. E., & Glaser, R. (1987). Marital quality, marital disruption, and immune function. *Psychosomatic Medicine, 49,* 13–34.

Kiecolt-Glaser, J. K., Glaser, R., Gravenstein, S., Malarkey, W. B., & Sheridan, J. (1996). Chronic stress alters the immune response to influenza virus vaccine in older adults. *Processes of the National Academy of Science, 93*(7), 3043–3047.

Kiecolt-Glaser, J. K., Marucha, P. T., Malarkey, W. B., & Marcado, A. M. (1995). Slowing of wound healing by psychological stress. *Lancet, 346,* 1194–1196.

Kiecolt-Glaser, J. K., McGuire, L., Robles, T., & Glaser, R. (2002). Psychoneuroimmunology: Psychological influences on immune function and health. *Journal of Consulting and Clinical Psychology, 70,* 537–547.

Kihlstrom, J. F. (1987). The cognitive unconscious. *Science, 237,* 1445–1452.

Kihlstrom, J. F. (1999). Conscious and unconscious cognition. In R. J. Sternberg (Ed.), *The nature of cognition* (pp. 173–203). Cambridge, MA: MIT Press.

Kihlstrom, J. F. (2001). Hypnosis and the psychological unconscious. In H. S. Friedman (Ed.), *Assessment and therapy: Specialty articles from the Encyclopedia of Mental Health* (pp. 215–226). Adelman (Ed.), San Diego, CA: Academic Press.

Kihlstrom, J., Mulvaney, S., Tobias, B., & Tobis, I. (2000). The emotional unconscious. In E. Eich, J. Kihlstrom, G. Bower, J. Forgas, & P. Niedenthal (Eds.), *Cognition and emotion* (pp. 30–86). New York: Oxford University Press.

Kimura, D. (1999). *Sex and cognition.* Cambridge, MA: MIT Press.

Kimura, D. (2002, May 13). Sex differences in the brain. *Scientific American.* Special issue "The hidden mind," *12,* 32–37.

Kinsey, A. C., Pomeroy, W. B., & Martin, C. E. (1948). *Sexual behavior in the human male.* Philadelphia: W. B. Saunders.

Kirby, J. S., Chu, J. A., & Dill, D. L. (1993). Correlates of dissociative symptomatology in patients with physical and sexual abuse histories. *Comprehensive Psychiatry, 34,* 250–263.

Kirmayer, L. J. (1991). The place of culture in psychiatric nosology: Taijinkyofusho and the DSM-III-R. *Journal of Nervous and Mental Disease, 179,* 19–28.

Kirsch, I. (2000). The response set theory of hypnosis. *American Journal of Clinical Hypnosis, 42,* 3/42, 4, 274–292.

Kirsch, I., & Lynn, S. J. (1995). The altered state of hypnosis: Changes in the theoretical landscape. *American Psychologist, 50,* 846–858.

Kitayama, S., & Markus, H. R. (1994). Introduction to cultural psychology and emotion research. In S. Kitayama & H. R. Markus (Eds.), *Emotion and culture: Empirical studies of mutual influence* (pp. 1–22). Washington, DC: American Psychological Association.

Klaver, C. C., Wolfs, R. C., Vingerling, J. R., Hofman, A., & de Jong, P. T. (1998). Age-specific prevalence and causes of blindness and visual impairment in an older population: The Rotterdam Study. *Archives of Ophthalmology, 116,* 653–658.

Klein, D., Schwartz, J., Rose, S., & Leader, J. (2000). Five-year course and outcome of dysthymic disorder: A prospective, naturalistic follow-up study. *American Journal of Psychiatry, 157*(6), 931–939.

Klein, S. B., & Mowrer, R. R. (1989). *Contemporary learning theories: Pavlovian conditioning and the status of traditional learning theory.* Hillsdale, NJ: Lawrence Erlbaum Associates.

Klein, S. B., & Thorne, B. M. (2007). *Biological psychology*. New York: Worth Publishers.

Kleinot, M. C., & Rogers, R. W. (1982). Identifying effective components of alcohol misuse prevention programs. *Journal of Studies on Alcohol, 43*, 802–811.

Kligman, A. M., & Balin, A. K. (1989). Aging of human skin. In A. K. Balin & A. M. Kligman (Eds.), *Aging and the skin* (pp. 1–42). New York: Raven Press.

Klorman, R., Hilpert, P. L., Michael, R., LaGana, C., & Sveen, O. B. (1980). Effects of coping and mastery modeling on experienced and inexperienced pedodontic patients' disruptiveness. *Behavior Therapy, 11*, 156–168.

Kluft, R. P. (1984). Introduction to multiple personality disorder. *Psychiatric Annals, 14*, 19–24.

Klüver, H., & Bucy, P. C. (1939). Preliminary analysis of functions of the temporal lobes in monkeys. *Archives of Neurological Psychiatry, 42*, 979–1000.

Knight, A. H. (1996). *The life of the law: The people and cases that have shaped our society, from King Alfred to Rodney King*. New York: Crown Publishing Group.

Knight, J. A. (1998). Free radicals: Their history and current status in aging and disease. *Annals of Clinical and Laboratory Science, 28*, 331–346.

Knight, W. (2003). Man vs. machine chess match ends in stalemate. *NewScientist.com News Service*, February. Retrieved November 4, 2004, from http://www.newscientist.com/news/news.jsp?id=ns99993370.

Knox, R. (2010). The teen brain: It's just not grown up yet. *Morning Edition*. National Public Radio.

Kobasa, S. (1979). Stressful life events, personality, and health: An inquiry into hardiness. *Journal of Personality and Social Psychology, 37*(1), 1–11.

Koenig, H. G., Hays, J. C., Larson, D. B., George, L. K., Cohen, H. J., McCullough, M. E., et al. (1999). Does religious attendance prolong survival? A six-year follow-up study of 3,968 older adults. *Journal of Gerontology, 54A*, M370–M377.

Koenig, H. G., McCullough, M. E., & Larson, D. B. (2001). *Handbook of religion and health*. Oxford, UK: Oxford University Press.

Koh, J. K. (1996). A guide to common Singapore spiders. *BP Guide to Nature* series. Singapore: Singapore Science Center.

Kohlberg, L. (1973). Continuities in childhood and adult moral development revisited. In P. Baltes & K. W. Schaie (Eds.), *Life-span development psychology: Personality and socialization*. San Diego, CA: Academic Press.

Köhler, W. (1925, 1992). *Gestalt psychology: An introduction to new concepts in modern psychology (reissue)*. New York: Liveright.

Kolodziej, M., & Johnson, B. T. (1996.) Interpersonal contact and acceptance of persons with psychiatric disorders: A research synthesis. *Journal of Consulting and Clinical Psychology, 64*, 1387–1396.

Konowal, N. M., Van Dongen, H. P. A., Powell, J. W., Mallis, M. M., & Dinges, D. F. (1999). Determinants of microsleeps during experimental sleep deprivation. *Sleep, 22* (1 Suppl.), 328.

Kosfeld, M., Heinrichs, M., Zak, P. J., Fischbacher, U., & Fehr, E. (2005). Oxytocin increase trust in humans. *Nature, 435*, 673–676.

Kosslyn, S. M. (1983). Mental imagery. In Z. Rubin (Ed.), *The psychology of being human*. New York: Harper & Row.

Kosslyn, S. M., Alpert, N. M., Thompson, W. L., Maljkovic, V., Weise, S. B., Chabris, C. F., et al. (1993). Visual mental imagery activates topographically organized visual cortex: PET investigations. *Journal of Cognitive Neuroscience, 5*, 263–287.

Kosslyn, S. M., Ball, T. M., & Reiser, B. J. (1978). Visual images preserve metric spatial information: Evidence from studies of image scanning. *Journal of Experimental Psychology: Human Perception and Performance, 4*, 47–60.

Kosslyn, S. M., Ganis, G., & Thompson, W. L. (2001). Neural foundations of imagery. *Nature Reviews Neuroscience, 2*, 635–642.

Kosslyn, S. M., Pascual-Leone, A., Felician, O., Camposano, S., Keenan, J. P., Thompson, W. L., et al. (1999). The role of area 17 in visual imagery: Convergent evidence from PET and rTMS. *Science, 284*, 167–170.

Kosslyn, S. M., Thompson, W. L., Wraga, M. J., & Alpert, N. M. (2001). Imagining rotation by endogenous and exogenous forces: Distinct neural mechanisms for different strategies. *Neuroreport, 12*, 2519–2525.

Kotkin, M., Daviet, C., & Gurin, J. (1996). The *Consumer Reports* mental health survey. *American Psychologist, 51*(10), 1080–1082.

Kouri, E. M., Pope, H. G., & Lukas, S. E. (1999). Changes in aggressive behavior during withdrawal from long-term marijuana use. *Psychopharmacology, 143*, 302–308.

Kratofil, P. H., Baberg, H. T., & Dimsdale, J. E. (1996). Self-mutilation and severe self-injurious behavior associated with amphetamine psychosis. *General Hospital Psychiatry, 18*, 117–120.

Kryger, M., Lavie, P., & Rosen, R. (1999). Recognition and diagnosis of insomnia. *Sleep, 22*, S421–S426.

Kübler-Ross, E. (1997). *The wheel of life: A memoir of living and dying*. New York: Touchstone.

Kuhn, H. W., & Nasar, S. (Eds.). (2001). *The essential John Nash*. Princeton, NJ: Princeton University Press.

Kulik, J. A., & Mahler, H. I. M. (1989). Social support and recovery from surgery. *Health Psychology, 8*, 221–238.

Kulik, J. A., & Mahler, H. I. M. (1993). Emotional support as a moderator of adjustment and compliance after coronary bypass surgery: A longitudinal study. *Journal of Behavioral Medicine, 16*, 45–63.

Kumar, R. (1994). Postnatal mental illness: A transcultural perspective. *Social Psychiatry and Psychiatric Epidemiology, 29*(6), 250–264.

Kumar, S., & Oakley-Browne, M. (2002). Panic disorder. *Clinical Evidence, 7*, 906–912.

Küntay, A., & Slobin, D. I. (2002). Putting interaction back into child language: Examples from Turkish. *Psychology of Language and Communication, 6*, 5–14.

Kupfer, D. J., & Reynolds, C. F., III. (1997). Management of insomnia. *New England Journal of Medicine, 336*(5), 341–346.

LaBar, K. S., LeDoux, J. E., Spencer, D. D., & Phelps, E. A. (1995). Impaired fear conditioning following unilateral temporal lobectomy to humans. *Journal of Neuroscience, 15*, 6846–6855.

LaBerge, D. (1980). Unitization and automaticity in perception. In J. H. Flowers (Ed.), *Nebraska symposium on motivation* (pp. 53–71). Lincoln, NE: University of Nebraska Press.

Lacayo, A. (1995). Neurologic and psychiatric complications of cocaine abuse. *Neuropsychiatry, Neuropsychology, and Behavioral Neurology, 8*(1), 53–60.

LaFromboise, T., Coleman, H. L. K., & Gerton J. (1993). Psychological impact of biculturalism: Evidence and theory. *Psychological Bulletin, 114*, 395–412.

Lambert, M. J., & Ogles, B. M. (2003). The efficacy and effectiveness of psychotherapy. In M. J. Lambert (Ed.), *Handbook of psychotherapy and behavior change* (5th ed.) (5th ed., pp. 139–193). New York: Wiley.

Lance, C. J., LaPointe, J. A., & Fisicaro, S. A. (1994). Tests of three causal models of halo rater error. *Organizational Behavior and Human Decision Performance, 57*, 83–96.

Landrum, R. E., & Davis, S. F. (2007). *The psychology major: Career options and strategies for success* (3rd ed.) Upper Saddle River, NJ: Prentice Hall.

Lange, C. (1885/1967). The emotions. Reprinted in Lange, C. G. & James, W., (Eds.), *The emotions*. New York: Harner Publishing Co.

Langer, E. J., & Rodin, J. (1976). The effects of enhanced personal responsibility for the aged: A field experiment in an institutional setting. *Journal of Personality and Social Psychology, 34*, 191–198.

Lanphear, B. P., Dietrich, K., Auinger, P., & Cox, C. (2000). Cognitive deficits associated with blood lead concentrations <10 micrograms/dL in U.S. children and adolescents. *Public Health Reports, 115*(6), 521–529.

Lapsley, D. K., Milstead, M., Quintana, S. M., Flannery, D., & Buss, R. R. (1986). Adolescent egocentricism and formal operations: Tests of a theoretical assumption. *Developmental Psychology, 22*, 800–807.

Lashley, K. S. (1938). The thalamus and emotion. *The Psychological Review, 45*, 21–61.

Lasnik, H. (1990). Metrics and morphophonemics in early English verse. *University of Connecticut Working Papers in Linguistics, 3*, 29–40. Storrs, CT: University of Connecticut

Latané, B., & Darley, J. M. (1969). Bystander "apathy." *American Scientist, 57*(2), 244–268.

Latané, B., Williams, K., & Harkins, S. (1979). Many hands make light the work: The causes and consequences of social loafing. *Journal of Personality & Social Psychology, 37*(6), 822–832.

Lauer, J., Black, D. W., & Keen, P. (1993). Multiple personality disorder and borderline personality disorder: Distinct entities or variations on a common theme? *Annals of Clinical Psychiatry, 5*, 129–134.

Launer, L., Masaki, K., Petrovitch, H., Foley, D., & Havlik, R. (1995). The association between midlife blood pressure levels and late-life cognitive function. *Journal of the American Medical Association, 272*(23), 1846–1851.

Laws, G., Davies, I., & Andrews, C. (1995). Linguistic structure and nonlinguistic cognition: English and Russian blues compared. *Language and Cognitive Processes, 10*, 59–94.

Lay, C., & Nguyen, T. T. I. (1998). The role of acculturation-related and acculturation non-specific daily hassles: Vietnamese-Canadian students and psychological distress. *Canadian Journal of Behavioural Science, 30*(3), 172–181.

Lazarus, R. S. (1991). *Emotion and adaptation*. New York: Oxford University Press.

Lazarus, R. S. (1993). From psychological stress to the emotions: A history of changing outlooks. *Annual Review of Psychology, 44*, 1–22.

Lazarus, R. S. (1999). *Stress and emotion: A new synthesis*. New York: Springer Publishing.

Lazarus, R. S., & Folkman, S. (1984). *Stress, appraisal and coping*. New York: Springer Publishing.

Leary, M. R. (1999). The social and psychological importance of self-esteem. In R. M. Kowalski & M. R. Leary (Eds.), *The social psychology of emotional and behavioral problems*. Washington, DC: APA Books.

Leary, M. R., & Forsyth, D. R. (1987). Attributions of responsibility for collective endeavors. *Review of Personality and Social Psychology, 8*, 167–188.

Leclerc, C. M., & Hess, T. M. (2007). Age differences in the bases for social judgments: Tests of a social expertise perspective. *Experimental Aging Research, 33*(1), 95–120.

LeDoux, J. (1994). Emotion, memory and the brain. *Scientific American, 270*, 32–39.

Lee, M., & Shlain, B. (1986). *Acid dreams: The complete social history of LSD: The CIA, the sixties, and beyond.* New York: Grove Press.

Lee, P. A. (1995). Physiology of puberty. In K. L. Becker (Ed.), *Principles and practice of endocrinology and metabolism* (pp. 822–830). Philadelphia: J.B. Lippincott.

Lehnert, B. (2007). Joint wave-particle properties of the individual photon. *Progress in Physics, 4*(10), 104–108.

Lehrer, J. (2009). *How we decide.* New York: Houghton Mifflin Harcourt.

Leibel, R. L., Rosenbaum, M., & Hirsch, J. (1995). Changes in energy expenditure resulting from altered body weight. *The New England Journal of Medicine, 332*, 621–628.

Leonard, L. (1997). *Children with specific language impairment.* Cambridge, MA: MIT Press.

Leong, F. T. L., Hartung, P. J., Goh, D., & Gaylor, M. (2001). Appraising birth order in career assessment: Linkages to Holland's and Super's models. *Journal of Career Assessment, 9*, 25–39.

Leroy, C., & Symes, B. (2001). Teachers' perspectives on the family backgrounds of children at risk. *McGill Journal of Education, 36*(1), 45–60.

Lesch, K. P., Bengel, D., Heils, A., Sabol, S. Z., Greenberg, B. D., Petri, S., et al (1996). Association of anxiety-related traits with a polymorphism in the serotonin transporter gene regulatory region. *Science, 274*(5292), 1527–1531.

LeVay, S. (1991). A difference in hypothalamic structure between heterosexual and homosexual men. *Science, 253*, 1034–1037.

Levenson, R. W. (1992). Autonomic nervous system differences among emotions. *Psychological Sciences, 3*, 23–27.

Levenson, R. W., Ekman, P., Heider, K., & Friesen, W. V. (1992). Emotion and autonomic nervous system activity in the Minangkabau of West Sumatra. *Journal of Personality and Social Psychology, 62*, 972–988.

Levy, B. R., Slade, M. D., Kunkel, S. R., & Kasl, S. V. (2002). Longevity increased by positive self-perceptions of aging. *Journal of Personality and Social Psychology, 83*, 261–269.

Lewin, K. (1936). *Principles of topological psychology.* New York: McGraw-Hill.

Lewin, K., Lippit, R., & White, R. K. (1939). Patterns of aggressive behavior in experimentally created social climates. *Journal of Social Psychology, 10*, 271–301

Lewis, D. K. (1996, June). A cross-cultural model for psychotherapy: Working with the African-American client. *Perspectives on Multiculturalism and Cultural Diversity*, VI(2).

Lewis, J. R. (1995). *Encyclopedia of afterlife beliefs and phenomenon.* Detroit, MI: Visible Ink Press.

Like, R., Steiner, P., & Rubel, A. (1996). Recommended core curriculum guidelines on culturally sensitive and competent care. *Family Medicine, 27*, 291–297.

Lilienfeld, S. O. (1999). Projective measures of personality and psychopathology: How well do they work? *Skeptical Inquirer, 23*(5), 32–39.

Lilienfeld, S. O., Lynn, S. J., & Lohr, J. M. (2002). *Science and pseudoscience in clinical psychology.* New York: Guilford Press.

Lilienfeld, S. O., Lynn, S. J., & Lohr, J. M. (2004). Science and pseudoscience in clinical psychology: Initial thoughts, reflections, and considerations. In S. O. Lilienfeld, S. J Lynn, & J. M. Lohr (Eds.), *Science and pseudoscience in clinical psychology* (p. 2). New York: Guilford Press.

Lim, J., Choo, W. C., & Chee, M. W. L. (2007). Reproducibility of changes in behavior and fMRI activation associated with sleep deprivation in a working memory task. *Sleep, 30*, 61–70.

Lin, C. S., Lyons, J. L., & Berkowitz, F. (2007). Somatotopic identification of language-SMA in language processing via fMRI. *Journal of Scientific and Practical Computing 1*(2), 3–8.

Lindemann, B. (1996). Taste reception. *Physiological Review, 76*, 719–766.

Lisanby, S. H., Maddox, J. H., Prudic, J., Devanand, D. P., & Sackeim, H. A. (2000). The effects of electroconvulsive therapy on memory of autobiographical and public events. *Archives of General Psychiatry, 57*, 581–590.

Livesley, J. W. (Ed.). (1995). *The DSM-IV personality disorders.* New York: Guilford Press.

Loehlin, J. C. (1992). *Genes and environment in personality development.* Newbury Park, CA: Sage.

Loehlin, J. C., McCrae, R. R., Costa, P. T., Jr., & John, O. P. (1998). Heritabilities of common and measure-specific components of the Big Five personality factors. *Journal of Research in Personality, 32*, 431–453.

Loehlin, J. C., Willerman, L., & Horn, J. M. (1985). Personality resemblances in adoptive families when the children are late-adolescent or adult. *Journal of Personality and Social Psychology, 48*, 376–392.

Loftus, E. (1975). Leading questions and the eyewitness report. *Cognitive Psychology, 7*, 560–572.

Loftus, E. (1987, June 29). Trials of an expert witness. *Newsweek.*

Loftus, E. F., Miller, D. G., & Burns H. J. (1978). Semantic integration of verbal information into a visual memory. *Journal of Experimental Psychology: Human Learning, 4*, 19–31.

Loftus, J. (2001). America's liberalization in attitudes toward homosexuality, 1973 to 1998. *American Sociological Review, 66*(5), 762–782.

Logue, M. W., Vieland, V. J., Goedken, R. J., & Crowe, R. R. (2003). Bayesian analysis of a previously published genome screen for panic disorder reveals new and compelling evidence for linkage to chromosome 7. *American Journal of Medical Genetics, 121B*, 95–99.

Lohr, J. M., Kleinknecht, R. A., Tolin, D. F., & Barrett, R. H. (1995). The empirical status of the clinical application of eye movement desensitization and reprocessing. *Journal of Behavior Therapy and Experimental Psychiatry, 26*, 285–302.

Lohr, J. M., Tolin, D. F., & Lilienfield, S. O. (1998). Efficacy of eye movement desensitization and reprocessing: Implications for behavior therapy. *Behavior Therapy, 29*, 123–156.

Lovaas, O. I. (1964). Cue properties of words: The control of operant responding by rate and content of verbal operants. *Child Development, 35*, 245–256.

Lubinski, D. (2000). Scientific and social significance of assessing individual differences: "Sinking shafts at a few critical points." *Annual Review of Psychology, 51*, 405–444.

Luborsky, L., Singer, B., & Luborsky, L. (1975). Comparative studies of psychotherapies: Is it true that "everyone has won and all must have prizes"? *Archives of General Psychiatry, 32*, 995–1008.

Lucy, J. A., & Shweder, R. A. (1979). Whorf and his critics: Linguistic and nonlinguistic influences on color memory. *American Anthropologist, 81*, 581–615.

Luria, A. R. (1968). *The mind of a mnemonist.* New York: Basic Books.

Lurito, J. T., Dzemidzic, M., Mathews, V. P., Lowe, M. J., Kareken, D. A., Phillips, M. D., et al. (2000). Comparison of hemispheric lateralization using four language tasks. *NeuroImage, 11*, S358.

Lüscher, M. (1969). *The Lüscher Color Test.* New York: Random House.

Lutkenhaus, P., Grossmann, K. E., & Grossman, K. (1985). Infant–mother attachment at twelve months and style of interaction with a stranger at the age of three years. *Child Development, 56*, 1538–1542.

Lykken, D. T. (1982, September). Fearlessness: Its carefree charm and deadly risks. *Psychology Today*, 20–28.

Lykken, D. T. (1995). *The antisocial personalities.* Hillsdale, NJ: Lawrence Erlbaum Associates.

Lykken, D. T., & Tellegen, A. (1996). Happiness is a stochastic phenomenon. *Psychological Science, 7*, 186–189.

Lynch, E. B., Coley, J. D., & Medin, D. L. (2000). Tall is typical: Central tendency, ideal dimensions, and graded category structure among tree experts and novices. *Memory & Cognition, 28*(1), 41–50.

Lytton, H., & Romney, D. M. (1991). Parents' sex-differentiated socialization of boys and girls: A meta-analysis. *Psychological Bulletin, 109*, 267–296.

Lyvers, M. (2003). The neurochemistry of psychedelic experiences. *Science & Consciousness Review, 1*, 1–5.

Lyznicki, J. M., Doege, T. C., Davis, R. M., & Williams, M. A. (1998). Sleepiness, driving, and motor-vehicle crashes. Council on Scientific Affairs, American Medical Association. *Journal of the American Medical Association, 279*(23), 1908–1913.

Maccoby, E. E. (1998). *The two sexes: Growing up apart: Coming together.* Cambridge, MA: Belknap Press of Harvard University Press.

MacDonald, A. P. (1970). Internal-external locus of control and the practice of birth control. *Psychological Reports, 27*, 206.

MacDonald, D., Kabani, N., Avis, D., & Evens, A. C. (2000). Automated 3D extraction of inner and outer surfaces of cerebral cortex from MRI. *NeuroImage, 12*, 340–356.

MacKenzie, S. B., Lutz, R. J., & Belch, G. E. (1986, May). The role of attitude toward the ad as a mediator of advertising effectiveness: A test of competing explanations. *Journal of Marketing Research, 23*, 130–143.

Macquet, P., & Franck, G. (1996). Functional neuroanatomy of human rapid eye movement sleep and dreaming. *Nature, 383*, 163–166.

Magarinos, M., Zafar, U., Nissenson, K., & Blanco, C. (2002). Epidemiology and treatment of hypochondriasis. *CNS Drugs, 16*(1), 9–22.

Magid, L. (2005, February 10). The rise & fall of Carly Fiorina. *CBS News.* Retrieved from **http://www.cbsnews.com/stories/2005/02/09/scitech/pcanswer/main672809.shtml**

Mahe, V., & Dumaine, A. (2001). Oestrogen withdrawal associated psychoses. *Acta Psychiatrica Scandinavica, 104*(5), 323–331.

Maier, S. F., & Watkins, L. R. (1998). Cytokines for psychologists: Implications of bidirectional immune-to-brain communication for understanding behavior, mood, and cognition. *Psychological Review, 105*, 83–107.

Main, M., & Cassidy, J. (1988). Categories of response to reunion with the parent at age 6: Predictable from infant attachment classifications and stable over a 1-month period. *Developmental Psychology, 24*, 415–426.

Main, M., & Hesse, E. (1990). Parents' unresolved traumatic experiences are related to infant disorganized attachment status: Is frightened and/or frightening parental behaviour the linking mechanism? In M. T. Greenberg, D. Cicchetti, & E. M. Cummings (Eds.), *Attachment in the preschool years: Theory, research and intervention* (pp. 161–182). Chicago: University of Chicago Press.

Main, M., & Solomon, J. (1990). Procedures for identifying infants as disorganized/disoriented during the Ainsworth Strange Situation. In M. T. Greenberg,

Miller, G. A. (1956). The magical number seven, plus or minus two: Some limits on our capacity for processing information. *Psychological Review, 63*, 81–97.

Miller, J. G. (1984). Culture and the development of everyday social explanation. *Journal of Personality and Social Psychology, 46*, 961–978.

Miller, L. H., & Smith, A. D. (1993). *The stress solution.* New York: Pocket Books.

Miller, M. E., & Bowers, K. S. (1993). Hypnotic analgesia: Dissociated experience or dissociated control? *Journal of Abnormal Psychology, 102*, 29–38.

Miller, M. N., & Pumariega, A. (1999). Culture and eating disorders. *Psychiatric Times, 16*(2), 1–4.

Miller, N. E., Sears, R. R., Mowrer, O. H., Doob, L. W., & Dollard, J. (1941). The frustration-aggression hypothesis. *Psychological Review, 48*, 337–342.

Miller, T. Q., Smith, T. W., Turner, C. W., Guijarro, M. L., & Hallet, A. J. (1996). A meta-analytic review of research on hostility and physical health. *Psychological Bulletin, 119*, 322–348.

Miller, T. Q., Turner, C. W., Tindale, R. S., Posavac, E. J., & Dugoni, B. L. (1991). Reasons for the trend toward null findings in research on Type A behavior. *Psychological Bulletin, 110*, 469–485.

Mills, M. A., Edmondson, D., & Park, C. L. (2007). Trauma and stress response among Hurricane Katrina evacuees. *American Journal of Public Health, 97*(1), 116–123.

Milner, B., Corkin, S., & Teuber, H. L. (1968). Further analysis of the hippocampal syndrome: 14-year follow-up study of H. M. *Neuropsychologia, 6*, 215–234.

Mineka, S. (1985). The frightful complexity of the origins of fears. In F. R. Brush & J. B. Overmier (Eds.), *Affect, conditioning, and cognition: Essays on the determinants of behavior.* Hillsdale, NJ: Erlbaum.

Mineka, S. (2002). Animal models of clinical psychology. In N. Smelser & P. Baltes (Eds.), *International encyclopedia of the social and behavioral sciences.* Oxford, England: Elsevier Science.

Mintz, L. B., & Betz, N. E. (1988). Prevalence and correlates of eating disordered behaviors among undergraduate women. *Journal of Counseling Psychology, 35*, 463–471.

Mischel, W., & Shoda, Y. (1995). A cognitive-affective system theory of personality: Reconceptualizing situations, dispositions, dynamics, and invariances in personality structure. *Psychological Review, 102*, 246–268.

Mishell, D. R. (2001). Menopause. In M. A. Stenchever, et al. (Eds.), *Comprehensive gynecology* (4th ed., pp. 1217–1258). St. Louis, MO: Mosby.

Mitchell, S. A., & Black, M. J. (1996). *Freud and beyond: A history of modern psychoanalytic thought* (reprint). New York: HarperCollins Publishers.

Moffic, H. S. (2003). Seven ways to improve "cultural competence." *Current Psychiatry, 2*(5), 78.

Mok, A., Morris, M. W., Benet-Martínez, V., & Karakitapoglu-Aygun, Z. (2007). Embracing American culture: Structures of social identity and social networks among first-generation biculturals. *Journal of Cross-Cultural Psychology, 38*(5), 629–635.

Moldofsky, H. (1995). Sleep and the immune system. *International Journal of Immunopharmacology, 17*(8), 649–654.

Möller, A., & Hell, D. (2002). Eugen Bleuler and forensic psychiatry. *International Journal of Law and Psychiatry, 25*, 351–360.

Money, J. (1994). *Sex errors of the body and related syndromes.* Baltimore: Paul H. Brookes.

Money, J., & Mathews, D. (1982). Prenatal exposure to virilizing progestins: An adult follow-up study of 12 women. *Archives of Sexual Behavior, 11*(1), 73–83.

Money, J., & Norman, B. F. (1987). Gender identity and gender transposition: Longitudinal outcome study of 24 male hermaphrodites assigned as boys. *Journal of Sex and Marriage Therapy, 13*, 75–79.

Montgomery, R. W., & Ayllon, T. (1994). Eye movement desensitization across subjects: Subjective and physiological measures of treatment efficacy. *Journal of Behavior Therapy and Experimental Psychiatry, 25*, 217–230.

Moody, R., & Perry, P. (1993). *Reunions: Visionary encounters with departed loved ones.* London: Little, Brown and Company.

Moore, T. E. (1988). The case against subliminal manipulation. *Psychology and Marketing, 5*, 297–316.

Moore-Ede, M. C., Sulzman, F. M., & Fuller, C. A. (1982). *The clocks that time us.* Cambridge, MA: Harvard University Press.

Moorhead, G., Neck, C. P., & West, M. S. (1998). The tendency toward defective decision making within self-managing teams: The relevance of groupthink for the 21st century. *Organizational Behavior & Human Decision Processes, 73*(2–3), 327–351.

Mora, G. (1985). History of psychiatry. In H. I. Kaplan & B. J. Sadock (Eds.), *Comprehensive textbook of psychiatry* (pp. 2034–2054). Baltimore: Williams & Wilkins.

Moreland, R. L., & Zajonc, R. B. (1982). Exposure effects in person perceptions: Familiarity, similarity, and attraction. *Journal of Experimental Social Psychology, 18*(5), 395–415.

Morgan, C. D., & Murray, H. A. (1935). A method for investigating fantasies: The Thematic Appercetion Test. *Archives of Neurology and Psychiatry, 34*, 298–306.

Morris, J. S., Friston, K. J., Buche, L. C., Frith, C. D., Young, A. W., Calder, A. J., et al. (1998). A neuromodulatory role for the human amygdala in processing emotional facial expressions. *Brain, 121*, 47–57.

Moscovici, S., and Zavalloni, M. (1969). The group as a polarizer of attitudes. *Journal of Personality and Social Psychology, 12*, 125–135.

Mueser, K. T., Rosenberg, S. D., Xie, H., Jankowski, M. K., Bolton, E. E., Lu, W., et al. (2008). A randomized controlled trial of cognitive-behavioral treatment for posttraumatic stress disorder in severe mental illness. *Journal of Consulting and Clinical Psychology, 76*(2), 259–271.

Muhlberger, A., Herrmann, M. J., Wiedemann, G. C., Ellgring., H., & Pauli, P. (2001). Repeated exposure of flight phobics to flights in virtual reality. *Behaviour Research and Therapy, 39*(9), 1033–1050.

Murdock, B. B., Jr. (1962). The serial position effect in free recall. *Journal of Experimental Psychology, 64*, 482–488.

Muris, P., Harald, M., Irit, H., & Sijsenaar, M. (1998). Treating phobic children: Effects of EMDR versus exposure. *Journal of Consulting and Clinical Psychology, 66*, 193–198.

Murphy, C. C., Boyle, C., Schendel, D., Decouflé, P., & Yeargin-Allsopp, M. (1998). Epidemiology of mental retardation in children. *Mental Retardation and Developmental Disabilities Research Reviews, 4*, 6–13.

Murphy, K. R., & LeVert, S. (1995). *Out of the fog: Treatment options and coping strategies for adult attention deficit disorder.* New York: Hyperion.

Murphy, L. R. (1995). Managing job stress: An employee assistance/human resource management partnership. *Personnel Review, 24*(1), 41–50.

Murphy, M., & Donavan, S. (1997). *The physical and psychological effects of meditation: A review of contemporary research with a comprehensive bibliography.* Petaluma, CA: Institute of Noetic Sciences.

Murray, C. J. L., & Lopez, A. D. (Eds.). (1996). *Summary: The global burden of disease: A comprehensive assessment of mortality and disability from diseases, injuries, and risk factors in 1990 and projected to 2020.* Cambridge, MA: Published by the Harvard School of Public Health on behalf of the World Health Organization and the World Bank, Harvard University Press.

Murray, S. L., Holmes, J. G., MacDonald, G., & Ellsworth, P. C. (1998). Through the looking glass darkly? When self-doubts turn into relationship insecurities. *Journal of Personality and Social Psychology, 75*, 1459–1480.

Murray, S. L., Rose, P., Bellavia, G. M., Holmes, J. G., & Kusche, A. G. (2002). When rejection stings: How self-esteem constrains relationship-enhancement processes. *Journal of Personality and Social Psychology, 54B*, 173–180.

Muter, P. (1978). Recognition failure of recallable words in semantic memory. *Memory & Cognition, 6*(1), 9–12.

Myers, D. (1993). *The pursuit of happiness: Who is happy, and why?* New York: Avon.

Nadeau, K. G. (1995). *A comprehensive guide to attention deficit disorder in adults: Research, diagnosis, and treatment.* New York: Brunner/Mazel.

Nadeau, K. G., Quinn, P., & Littman, E. (2001). *AD/HD Self-Rating Scale for Girls.* Springfield, MD: Advantage Books.

Naitoh, P., Kelly, T. L., & Englund, C. E. (1989). *Health effects of sleep deprivation.* Naval Health Research Centre, Report No. 89–46.

Narrow, W. E., Rae, D. S., Robbins, L. N., & Regier, D. A. (2002). Revised prevalence estimates of mental disorders in the United States. *Archives of General Psychiatry, 59*, 115–123.

Nasar, S. (1998). *A beautiful mind: A biography of John Forbes Nash, Jr., winner of the Nobel Prize in economics 1994.* New York: Simon & Schuster.

National Center for Health Statistics. (2007). Alcohol use. Retrieved July 25, 2007, from **http://www.cdc.gov/nchs/fastats/alcohol.htm**

National Institute of Mental Health. (2001). The numbers count: Mental disorders in America. *NIH Publication No. 01-4584.* Bethesda, MD: Author.

National Institute on Alcoholism and Alcohol Abuse. (2007). *Data/statistical tables.* Retrieved July 25, 2007, from **http://www.niaaa.nih.gov/Resources/DatabaseResources/QuickFacts/default.htm**

National Institute on Drug Abuse. (2002). Research report series—Prescription drugs: Abuse and addiction. National Institutes of Health (NIH). Retrieved July 19, 2008, from **www.drugabuse.gov/ResearchReports/Prescription/prescription5.html**

National Institutes of Health. (2007). *Stem cell basics.* Retrieved February 6, 2008, **http://stemcells.nih.gov/info/basics/**

Neale, M. C., Rushton, J. P., & Fulker, D. W. (1986). The heritability of items from the Eysenck Personality Questionnaire. *Personality and Individual Differences, 7*, 771–779.

Neary, N. M., Goldstone, A. P., & Bloom, S. R. (2004). Appetite regulations: From the gut to the hypothalamus. *Clinical Endocrinology, 60*(2), 153–160.

Neimark, J. (1996). The diva of disclosure, memory researcher Elizabeth Loftus. *Psychology Today, 29*(1), 48–80.

Neimeyer, R. A., & Mitchell, K. A. (1998). Similarity and attraction: A longitudinal study. *Journal of Social and Personality Relationships, 5*, 131–148.

Neisser, U. (1982). Snapshots or benchmarks? In U. Neisser (Ed.), *Memory observed: Remembering in natural contexts* (pp. 43–48). San Francisco: W. H. Freeman.

Neisser, U., Boodoo, G., Bouchard, T. J., Boykin, A. W., Brody, N., Ceci, S. J., et al. (1996). Intelligence: Knowns and unknowns. *American Psychologist, 51*, 77–101.

Cicchetti, D., & Cummings, E. M. (Eds.), *Attachment in the preschool years: Theory, research and intervention* (pp. 121–160). Chicago: University of Chicago Press.

Mandler, G. (1967). Organization and memory. In K. W. Spence & J. T. Spence (Eds.), *The psychology of learning and motivation* (Vol. 1, pp. 327–372). New York: Academic Press.

Mandler, J. M. (2000). Perceptual and conceptual processes. *Journal of Cognition and Development, 1,* 3–36.

Mandler, J. M. (2003). Conceptual categorization. In D. H. Rakison & L. M. Oakes (Eds.), *Early category and concept development: Making sense of the blooming, buzzing confusion* (pp. 103–131). Oxford, England: Oxford University Press.

Manson, J., Greenland, P., LaCroix, A. Z., Stefanick, M. L., Mouton, C. P., Oberman, A., et al. (2002). Walking compared with vigorous exercise for the prevention of cardiovascular events in women. *The New England Journal of Medicine, 347*(10), 716–725.

Manusov, V., & Patterson, M. L. (Eds.). (2006). *The Sage handbook of nonverbal communication* (p. 289). Thousand Oaks, CA: Sage.

March, J., Silva, S., Petrycki, S., Curry, J., Wells, K., Fairbank, J., et al. (Treatment for Adolescents with Depression Study [TADS] Team). (2004). Fluoxetine, cognitive-behavioral therapy, and their combination for adolescents with depression: Treatment for Adolescents with Depression Study (TADS) randomized controlled trial. *Journal of the American Medical Association, 292*(7), 807–820.

Margolin, S., & Kubic, L. S. (1944). An apparatus for the use of breath sounds as a hypnogogic stimulus. *American Journal of Psychiatry, 100,* 610.

Markovitz, J. H., Lewis, C. E., Sanders, P. W., Tucker, D., & Warnock, D. G. (1997). Relationship of diastolic blood pressure with cyclic GMP excretion among young adults (the CARDIA study): Influence of a family history of hypertension. *Journal of Hypertension, 15*(9), 955–962.

Markus, H. R., & Kitayama, S. (1991). Culture and the self: Implications for cognition, emotion, and motivation. *Psychological Review, 98*(2), 224–253.

Marsh, H. W., & Craven, R. G. (2006). Reciprocal effects of self-concept and performance from a multidimensional perspective: Beyond seductive pleasure and unidimensional perspectives. *Perspectives on Psychological Science, 1,* 133–163.

Martin, J. A., & Buckwalter, J. J. (2001). Telomere erosion and senescence in human articular cartilage chondrocytes. *Journal of Gerontology and Biological Science, 56*(4), 172–179.

Martin, L. (2004). *Can sleepwalking be a murder defense?* Retrieved October 19, 2004, from www.mtsinai.org/pulmonary/Sleep/sleep-murder.htm

Maruta, T., Colligan, R. C., Malinchoc, M., & Offord, K. P. (2002, August). Optimism-pessimism assessed in the 1960s and self-reported health status 30 years later. *Mayo Clinic Proceedings, 77,* 748–753.

Maslow, A. H. (1943). A theory of human motivation. *Psychological Review, 50,* 370–396.

Maslow, A. H. (1968). *Toward a psychology of being.* Princeton, NJ: Van Nostrand Reinhold.

Maslow, A. H. (1971). *The farther reaches of human nature.* New York: The Viking Press.

Maslow, A. H. (1987). *Motivation and personality* (3rd ed.). New York: Harper & Row.

Maslow, A. H., & Lowery, R. (Ed.). (1998). *Toward a psychology of being* (3rd ed.). New York: Wiley & Sons.

Masson, J. M. (1984). *The assault on truth: Freud's suppression of the seduction theory.* New York: Farrar, Straus and Giroux.

Masters, J. C., Burish, T. G., Holton, S. D., & Rimm, D. C. (1987). *Behavior therapy: Techniques and empirical finding.* San Diego, CA: Harcourt Brace Jovanovich.

Masters, W., & Johnson, V. (1966). *Human sexual response.* Boston: Little, Brown and Company.

Masuda, T., & Kitayama, S. (2004). Perceiver-induced constraint and attitude attribution in Japan and the US: A case for the cultural dependence of the correspondence bias. *Journal of Experimental Social Psychology, 40,* 409–416.

Matsumoto, D. (1993). Ethnic differences in affect intensity, emotion judgments, display rule attitudes, and self-reported emotional expression in an American sample. *Motivation and Emotion, 17*(2), 107–123.

Matsumoto, D. (1994). *People: Psychology from a cultural perspective.* Pacific Grove, CA: Brooks-Cole.

Matsumoto, D. (1999). *People: Psychology from a cultural perspective* (2nd ed.). Pacific Grove, CA: Brooks/Cole.

Matsumoto, D., Takeuchi, S., Andayani, S., Kouznetsova, N., & Krupp, D. (1998). The contribution of individualism vs. collectivism to cross-national differences in display rules. *Asian Journal of Social Psychology,* 147–165.

Matthews, K. A., Gump, B. B., Harris, K. F., Haney, T. L., & Barefoot, J. C. (2004). Hostile behaviors predict cardiovascular mortality among men enrolled in the Multiple Risk Factor Intervention Trial. *Circulation, 109,* 66–70.

Mavromatis, A. (1987). *Hypnagogia: The unique state of consciousness between wakefulness and sleep.* London: Routledge & Kegan Paul.

Mavromatis, A., & Richardson, J. T. E. (1984). Hypnagogic imagery. *International Review of Mental Imagery, 1,* 159–189.

McAloon, M., & Lester, D. (1979). The Luscher Color Test as a measure of anxiety in juvenile delinquents. *Psychological Reports, 45,* 228.

McCann, S. J. H., & Stewin, L. L. (1988). Worry, anxiety, and preferred length of sleep. *Journal of Genetic Psychology, 149,* 413–418.

McCarthy, J. (1959). Programs with common sense. In *Mechanisation of thought processes, proceedings of the Symposium of the National Physics Laboratory* (pp. 77–84). London: Her Majesty's Stationery Office.

McCauley, C. (1998). Group dynamics in Janis's theory of groupthink: Backward and forward. *Organizational Behavior & Human Decision Processes, 73*(2–3), 142–162.

McClelland, D. C. (1961). *The achieving society.* Princeton, NJ: Van Nostrand.

McClelland, D. C. (1987). *Human motivation.* Cambridge, MA: Cambridge University Press.

McCrae, R. R., & Costa, P. T., Jr. (1990). *Personality in adulthood.* New York: Guilford Press.

McCrae, R. R., & Costa, P. T., Jr. (1996). Toward a new generation of personality theories: Theoretical contexts for the five-factor model. In J. S. Wiggins (Ed.), *The five-factor model of personality: Theoretical perspectives* (pp. 51–87). New York: Guilford Press.

McCrae, R. R., Costa, P. T., Jr., Ostendorf, F., Angleitner, A., Hrebickova, M., Avia, M. D., et al. (2000). Nature over nurture: Temperament, personality, and life span development. *Journal of Personality and Social Psychology, 78,* 173–186.

McCrae, R. R., & Terracciano, A. (2007). The five-factor model and its correlates in individuals and cultures. In F. J. R. van de Vijver, D. A. van Hemert, & Y. Poortinga (Eds.), *Individuals and cultures in multi-level analysis* (pp. 247–281). Mahwah, NJ: Erlbaum.

McCrae, R. R., Terracciano A., & 78 Members of the Personality Profiles of Cultures Project. (2005). Universal features of personality traits from the observer's perspective: Data from 50 cultures. *Journal of Personality and Social Psychology, 88,* 547–561.

McDermott, J. F. (2001). Emily Dickinson revisited: A study of periodicity in her work. *American Journal of Psychiatry, 158*(5), 686–690.

McDougall, W. (1908). *An introduction to social psychology.* London: Methuen & Co.

McGinn, L. K. (2000). Cognitive behavioral therapy of depression: Theory, treatment, and empirical status. *American Journal of Psychotherapy, 54,* 254–260.

McGinnis, J. M., & Foege, W. H. (1993). Actual causes of death in the United States. *Journal of the American Medical Association, 270*(18), 2207–2212.

McGrath, E., Keita, G. P., Strickland, B. R., & Russo, N. F. (1992). *Women and depression: Risk factors and treatment issues.* Washington, DC: American Psychological Association.

McGuire, F. (1994). Army alpha and beta tests of intelligence. In R. J. Sternberg (Ed.), *Encyclopedia of intelligence* (Vol. 1, pp. 125–129.) New York: Macmillan.

McMonagle, T., & Sultana, A. (2002). Token economy for schizophrenia (Cochrane Review). In *The Cochrane Library, Issue 2.* Oxford, UK: Update Software.

McPherson, M., Smith-Lovin, L., & Cook, J. M. (2001). Birds of a feather: Homophily in social networks. *Annual Review of Sociology, 27,* 415–444.

Meador, B. D., & Rogers, C. R. (1984). Person-centered therapy. In R. J. Corsini (Ed.), *Current psychotherapies* (3rd ed., pp. 142–195). Itasca, IL: Peacock Publishers.

Medicine, B. (2002). Directions in gender research in American Indian societies: Two spirits and other categories. In W. J. Lonner, D. L. Dinnel, S. A. Hayes, & D. N. Sattler (Eds.), *Online readings in psychology and culture* (Unit 3, Chapter 2), (www.wwu.edu/~culture), Center for Cross-Cultural Research, Western Washington University, Bellingham, WA.

Meichenbaum, D. (1996). Stress inoculation training for coping with stressors. *The Clinical Psychologist, 49,* 4–7.

Melzack, R., & Wall, P. D. (1965). Pain mechanisms: A new theory. *Science, 150,* 971–979.

Melzack, R., & Wall, P. D. (1996). *The challenge of pain.* London: Penguin Books.

Menon, T., Morris, M., Chiu, C. Y., & Hong, Y. I. (1999). Culture and the construal of agency: Attribution to individual versus group dispositions. *Journal of Personality and Social Psychology, 76,* 701–727.

Merikle, M. P. (2000). Subliminal perception. In A. E. Kazdin (Ed.), *Encyclopedia of psychology* (Vol. 7, pp. 497–499). New York: Oxford University Press.

Mervis, C. B., & Rosch, E. (1981). Categorization of natural objects. *Annual Review of Psychology, 32,* 89–115.

Messina, C. R., Lane, D. S., Glanz, K., West, D. S., Taylor, V., Frishman, W., & et al. (2004). Relationship of social support and social burden to repeated breast cancer screening in the Women's Health Initiative. *Health Psychology, 23,* 582–594.

Meyrick, J. (2001). Forget the blood and gore: An alternative message strategy to help adolescents avoid cigarette smoking. *Health Education, 101*(3), 99–107.

Michaels, J. W., Blommel, J. M., Brocato, R. M., Linkous, R. A., & Rowe, J. S. (1982). Social facilitation and inhibition in a natural setting. *Replications in Social Psychology, 2,* 21–24.

Mickelson, K. D., Kessler, R. C., & Shaver, P. R. (1997). Adult attachment in a nationally representative sample. *Journal of Personality and Social Psychology, 73,* 1092–1106.

Miles, D. R., & Carey, G. (1997). Genetic and environmental architecture of human aggression. *Journal of Personality and Social Psychology, 72,* 207–217.

Milgram, S. (1964). Behavioral study of obedience. *Journal of Abnormal and Social Psychology, 67,* 371–378.

Milgram, S. (1974). *Obedience to authority: An experimental view.* New York: Harper & Row.

Neisser, U., & Harsch, N. (1992). Phantom flashbulbs: False recollections of hearing the news about *Challenger*. In E. Winograd & U. Neisser (Eds.), *Affect and accuracy in recall: Studies of "flashbulb memories"* (pp. 9–31). New York: Cambridge University Press.

Nelson, K. (1993). The psychological and social origins of autobiographical memory. *Psychological Science, 4*, 7–14.

Neumarker, K. (1997). Mortality and sudden death in anorexia nervosa. *International Journal of Eating Disorders, 21*, 205–212.

Neville, H. J., & Bavelier, D. (2000). Specificity and plasticity in neurocognitive development in humans. In M. S. Gazzaniga (Ed.), *The new cognitive neurosciences* (2nd ed., pp. 83–99). Cambridge, MA: MIT Press.

Newcomb, M. D., & Harlow, L. L. (1986). Life events and substance use among adolescents: Mediating effects of perceived loss of control and meaninglessness in life. *Journal of Personality and Social Psychology, 51*, 564–577.

Nigg, J. T., & Goldsmith, H. H. (1994). Genetics of personality disorders: Perspectives from personality and psychopathology research. *Psychological Bulletin, 115*, 346–380.

Nijenhuis, E. R. (2000). Somatoform dissociation: Major symptoms of dissociative disorders. *Journal of Trauma and Dissociation, 1*(4), 7–29.

Nisbett, R. E. (1972). Hunger, obesity, and the ventromedial hypothalamus. *Psychological Review, 79*, 433–453.

Nishida, M., & Walker, M. P. (2007). Daytime naps, motor memory consolidation and regionally specific sleep spindles. *PLoS One, 2*, e341.

Nolen-Hoeksema, S. (1990). *Sex differences in depression*. Palo Alto, CA: Stanford University Press.

Nolen-Hoeksema, S., Larson, J., & Grayson, C. (1999.) Explaining the gender differences in depressive symptoms. *Journal of Personality and Social Psychology, 77*, 1061–1072.

Nunes, A., & Kramer, A. F. (2009). Experience-based mitigation of age-related performance declines: Evidence from air traffic control. *Journal of Experimental Psychology: Applied, 15*(1), 12–24.

Nyberg, L., & Tulving, E. (1996). Classifying human long-term memory: Evidence from converging dissociations. *European Journal of Cognitive Psychology, 8*(2), 163–183.

O'Brien, J. (2009). *Encyclopedia of gender and society*. Thousand Oaks, CA: Sage.

Ochsner, K., & Kosslyn, S. M. (1994). Mental imagery. In V. S. Ramaschandran (Ed.), *Encyclopedia of human behavior*. New York: Academic Press.

O'Connor, R. D. (1972). Relative efficacy of modeling, shaping, and the combined procedures for modification of social withdrawal. *Journal of Abnormal Psychology, 79*, 327–334.

Olin, B. R. (Ed.). (1993). Central nervous system drugs, sedatives and hypnotics, barbiturates. In *Facts and comparisons drug information* (pp. 1398–1413). St. Louis, MO: Facts and Comparisons.

Oliver, J. E. (1993). Intergenerational transmission of child abuse: Rates, research, and clinical interpretations. *American Journal of Psychiatry, 150*, 1315–1324.

Ollendick, T. H., & King, N. J. (1998). Empirically supported treatments for children with phobic and anxiety disorders: Current status. *Journal of Clinical Child Psychology, 27*(2), 156–167.

Olsen, P. (1975). *Emotional flooding*. Baltimore: Penguin Books.

Olson, H. C., & Burgess, D. M. (1997). Early intervention for children prenatally exposed to alcohol and other drugs. In M. J. Guralnick (Ed.), *The effectiveness of early intervention* (pp. 109–146). Baltimore: Brookes.

Olsson, A., Nearing, K. I., & Phelps, E. A. (2007). Learning fears by observing others: The neural systems of social fear transmission. *Social Cognitive and Affective Neuroscience, 2*, 3–11.

Onken, L. S., Blaine, J. D., & Battjes, R. J. (1997). Behavioral therapy research: A conceptualization of a process. In S. W. Henggeler & A. B. Santos (Eds.), *Innovative approaches for difficult-to-treat populations* (pp. 477–485). Washington, DC: American Psychiatric Press.

Oswalt, R., Anderson, M., Hagstrom, K., & Berkowitz, B. (1993). Evaluation of the one-session eye-movement desensitization reprocessing procedure for eliminating traumatic memories. *Psychological Reports, 73*, 99–104.

Overeem, S., Mignot, E., Gert van Dijk, J., & Lammers, G. J. (2001). Narcolepsy: Clinical features, new pathophysiological insights, and future perspectives. *Journal of Clinical Neurophysiology, 18*(2), 78–105.

Overmier, J. B., & Seligman, M. E. P. (1967). Effects of inescapable shock on subsequent escape and avoidance behavior. *Journal of Comparative Physiology and Psychology, 63*, 23–33.

Owen, M. T., Easterbrooks, M. A., Chase-Lansdale, L., & Goldberg, W. A. (1984). The relation between maternal employment status and the stability of attachments to mother and to father. *Child Development, 55*, 1894–1901.

Page, S. (1977). Effects of the mental illness label in attempts to obtain accommodation. *Canadian Journal of Behavioral Science, 9*, 84–90.

Paivio, A. (1971). *Imagery and verbal processes*. New York: Holt, Rinehart & Winston.

Paivio, A. (1986). *Mental representations: A dual coding approach*. New York: Oxford University Press.

Palmer, S. E. (1992). Common region: A new principle of perceptual grouping. *Cognitive Psychology, 24*(3), 436–447.

Pan, A. S. (2000). Body image, eating attitudes, and eating behaviors among Chinese, Chinese-American and non-Hispanic White women. *Dissertation Abstracts International, Section B: The Sciences and Engineering, 61*(1-B), 544.

Panksepp, J., Herman, B. H., Vilberg, T., Bishop, P., & Deeskinazi, F. G. (1980). Endogenous opioids and social behavior. *Neuroscience and Biobehavioral Reviews, 4*, 473–487.

Pargament, K. I. (1997). *The psychology of religion and coping: Theory, research, and practice*. New York: Guilford Press.

Paris, J. (2004). Gender differences in personality traits and disorders. *Current Psychiatry Reports, 6*, 71–74.

Park, J., Turnbull, A. P., & Turnbull, H. R. (2002). Impacts of poverty on quality of life in families of children with disabilities. *Exceptional Children, 68*, 151–170.

Parkinson, W. L., & Weingarten, H. P. (1990). Dissociative analysis of ventromedial hypothalamic obesity syndrome. *American Journal of Physiology: Regulatory, Integrative, and Comparative Physiology, 259*, R829–R835.

Parobek, V. M. (1997). Distinguishing conversion disorder from neurologic impairment. *Journal of Neuroscience Nursing, 29*(2), 128.

Parsons, H. M. (1992). Hawthorne: An early OBM experiment. *Journal of Organizational Behavior Management, 12*(1), 2743.

Partonen, T., & Lonnqvist, J. (1998). Seasonal affective disorder. *Lancet, 352*(9137), 1369–1374.

Paunonen, S. V., Keinonen, M., Trzbinski, J., Forsterling, F., Grishenko-Roze, N., Kouznetsova, L., et al. (1996). The structure of personality in six cultures. *Journal of Cross Cultural Psychology, 27*, 339–353.

Pavlov, I. P. (1906). The scientific investigation of the psychical faculties or processes in the higher animals. *Science, 24*, 613–619.

Pavlov, I. P. (1926). *Conditioned reflexes*. London: Oxford University Press.

Peng, K., Ames, D. R., & Knowles, E. D. (2000). Culture and human inference: Perspectives from three traditions. In D. Matsumoto (Ed.), *The handbook of culture and psychology* (pp. 245–264). New York: Oxford University Press.

Penn, D. L. (1998). Assessment and treatment of social dysfunction in schizophrenia. *Clinicians Research Digest, Supplemental Bulletin, 18*, 1–2.

Peplau, L. A., & Taylor, S. E. (1997). *Sociocultural perspectives in social psychology: Current readings*. Upper Saddle River, NJ: Prentice-Hall.

Pepperberg, I. M. (2005). An avian perspective on language evolution: Implications of simultaneous development of vocal and physical object combinations by a grey parrot (*Psittacus erithacus*). In M. Tallerman (Ed.), *Language origins: Perspectives on evolution* (pp. 239–261). New York: Oxford University Press.

Pepperberg, I. M. (2007). Grey parrots do not always "parrot": The roles of imitation and phonological awareness in the creation of new labels from existing vocalizations. *Language Sciences, 29*(1), 1–13.

Pereira, M. A., Kartashov, A. I., Van Horn, L., Slattery, M., Jacobs, D. R., Jr., & Ludwig, D. S. (2003). Eating breakfast may reduce risk of obesity, diabetes, heart disease. Paper presented March 6 at the American Heart Association's 2003 Annual Conference on Cardiovascular Disease Epidemiology and Prevention in Miami, FL.

Persaud, R. (2001). *Staying sane: How to make your mind work for you*. New York: Bantam.

Peters, W. A. (1971). *A class divided*. Garden City, NY: Doubleday.

Peterson, D. (2009). Myra Bluebond-Langer: Bearing witness. *LASNews*. Retrieved from **http://www.las.illinois.edu/alumni/magazine/articles/2009/bluebond/**

Peterson, D. R. (1976). Need for the doctor of psychology degree in professional psychology. *American Psychologist, 31*, 792–798.

Peterson, D. R. (1982). Origins and development of the Doctor of Psychology concept. In G. R. Caddy, D. C. Rimm, N. Watson, & J. H. Johnson (Eds.), *Educating professional psychologists* (pp. 19–38). New Brunswick, NJ: Transaction Books.

Peterson, L. R., & Peterson, M. J. (1959). Short-term retention of individual items. *Journal of Experimental Psychology, 58*, 193–198.

Petitto, L. A., Holowka, S., Sergio, L. E., & Ostry, D. (2001). Language rhythms in baby hand movements. *Nature, 413*, 35.

Petitto, L. A., & Marentette, P. F. (1991). Babbling in the manual mode: Evidence for the ontogeny of language. *Science, 251*, 1493–1496.

Petrakis, I. L., Gonzalez, G., Rosenheck, R., & Krystal, J. H. (2002). Comorbidity of alcoholism and psychiatric disorders. *Alcohol Research and Health, 26*(2), 81–89.

Petri, H. (1996). *Motivation: Theory, research and application* (4th ed.). Belmont, CA: Wadsworth.

Petrova, P. K., Cialdini, R. B., & Sills, S. J. (2003). Compliance, consistency, and culture: Personal consistency and compliance across cultures. *Journal of Experimental Social Psychology* [submitted]. Retrieved August 6, 2004, from **www.public.asu.edu/~liulang/Compliance.pdf**

Pettigrew, T. F., & Tropp, L. R. (2000). Does intergroup contact reduce prejudice? Recent meta-analytic findings. In S. Oskamp (Ed.), *Reducing prejudice and discrimination: Social psychological perspectives* (pp. 93–114). Mahwah, NJ: Erlbaum.

Petty, R. E. (1995). Attitude change. In A. Tesser (Ed.), *Advances in social psychology* (pp. 194–255). New York: McGraw-Hill.

Petty, R. E., & Cacioppo, J. T. (1986). *Communication and persuasion: Central and peripheral routes to attitude change*. New York: Springer-Verlag.

Petty, R. E., & Cacioppo, J. T. (1996). *Attitudes and persuasion: Classic and contemporary approaches* (reprint). Boulder, CO: Westview Press.

Petty, R. E., Wheeler, S. C., & Tormala, Z. L. (2003). Persuasion and attitude change. In T. Millon & M. J. Lerner (Eds.), *Handbook of psychology: Volume 5: Personality and social psychology* (pp. 353–382). Hoboken, NJ: John Wiley & Sons.

Pezdek, K., Finger, K., & Hodge, D. (1997). Planting false childhood memories: The role of event plausibility. *Psychological Science, 8*, 437–441.

Pezdek, K., & Hodge, D. (1999). Planting false childhood memories in children: The role of event plausibility. *Child Development, 70*, 887–895.

Pfeiffer, W. M. (1982). Culture-bound syndromes. In I. Al-Issa (Ed.), *Culture and psychopathology* (pp. 201–218). Baltimore: University Park Press.

Phan, T., & Silove, D. (1999). An overview of indigenous descriptions of mental phenomena and the range of traditional healing practices amongst the Vietnamese. *Transcultural Psychiatry, 36*, 79–94.

Phillips, K. A. (2001). Somatoform and factitious disorders. *Review of Psychiatry, 20*(3), 27–65.

Piaget, J. (1926). *The language and thought of the child*. New York: Harcourt Brace.

Piaget, J. (1952). *The origins of intelligence in children*. New York: W. W. Norton.

Piaget, J. (1962). *Play, dreams and imitation in childhood*. New York: W. W. Norton.

Piaget, J. (1983). Piaget's theory. In W. Kessen (Ed.), *Handbook of child psychology*, (Vol. 1, pp. 103–128). New York: Wiley.

Piedmont, R. L. (2001). Cracking the plaster cast: Big Five personality change during intensive outpatient counseling. *Journal of Research in Personality, 35*(4), 500–520.

Piedmont, R. L., Bain, E., McCrae, R. R., & Costa, P. T., Jr. (2002). The applicability of the Five-Factor Model in a sub-Saharan culture: The NEO-PI-R in Shona. In R. R. McCrae & J. Allik (Eds.), *The Five-Factor Model across cultures* (pp. 105–126). New York: Kluwer Academic/Plenum Press.

Pilkington, J. (1998). "Don't try and make out that I'm nice": The different strategies women and men use when gossiping. In J. Coates (Ed.), *Language and gender: A reader* (pp. 254–269). Oxford, UK: Blackwell.

Pinker, S. (1995). Language acquisition. In L. R. Gleitman et al. (Eds.), *An invitation to cognitive science* (2nd ed., pp. 135–182). Cambridge, MA: MIT Press.

Pinker, S., & Bloom, P. (1990). Natural language and natural selection. *Behavioral and Brain Sciences, 13*(4), 707–784.

Pinsof, W. M., & Wynne, L. C. (1995). The efficacy of marital and family therapy: An empirical overview, conclusions, and recommendations. *Journal of Marital and Family Therapy, 21*, 585–613.

Pittam, J., Gallois, C., Iwawaki, S., & Kroonenberg, P. (1995). Australian and Japanese concepts of expressive behavior. *Journal of Cross-Cultural Psychology, 26*(5), 451–473.

Pizarro, D. A., & Salovey, P. (2002). On being and becoming a good person: The role of emotional intelligence in moral development and behavior. In J. Aronson (Ed.), *Improving academic achievement: Impact of psychological factors on education* (pp. 247–266). San Diego, CA: Academic Press.

Plomin, R. (1994). The nature of nurture: The environment beyond the family. In R. Plomin (Ed.), *Genetics and experience: The interplay between nature and nurture* (pp. 82–107). Thousand Oaks, CA: Sage.

Plomin, R., & DeFries, J. C. (1998). Genetics of cognitive abilities and disabilities. *Scientific American*, 62–69.

Plomin, R. N. L., Pederson, G. E., McClearn, J. R., Nesselroade, C. S., & Bergman, H. F. (1988). EAS temperaments during the last half year of the life span: Twins reared apart and twins raised together. *Psychology of Aging, 4*, 43–50.

Plug, C., & Ross, H. E. (1994). The natural moon illusion: A multi-factor angular account. *Perception, 23*, 321–333.

Polce-Lynch, M., Myers, B. J., Kilmartin, C. T., Forssmann-Falck, R., & Kliewer, W. (1998). Gender and age patterns in emotional expression, body image, and self-esteem. A qualitative analysis. *Sex Roles, 38*, 1025–1050.

Polgreen, L. (2010, July 31). India digs under top of the world to match rival. *New York Times*. Retrieved from **http://www.nytimes.com/2010/08/01/world/asia/01pass.html**

Pope, H. G., Gruber, A. J., Hudson, J. I., Huestis, M. A., & Yurgelun-Todd, D. (2001). Neuropsychological performance in long-term cannabis users. *Archives of General Psychiatry, 58*(10), 909–915.

Pope, H. G., Poliakoff, M. B., Parker, M. P., Boynes, M., & Hudson, J. I. (2007). Is dissociative amnesia a culture-bound syndrome? Findings from a survey of historical literature. *Psychological Medicine, 37*(2), 225–233.

Pormerleau, C. S., & Pormerleau, O. F. (1994). Euphoriant effects of nicotine. *Tobacco Control, 3*, 374.

Postman, L. (1975). Tests of the generality of the principle of encoding specificity. *Memory & Cognition, 3*, 663–672.

Pratkanis, A. R. (1992). The cargo-cult science of subliminal persuasion. *Skeptical Inquirer, 16*, 260–272.

Pratkanis, A. R., & Greenwald, A. G. (1988). Recent perspectives on unconscious processing: Still no marketing applications. *Psychology and Marketing, 5*, 337–353.

Pratt, J. A. (1991). Psychotropic drug tolerance and dependence: Common underlying mechanisms? In E. Pratt (Ed.), *The biological bases of drug tolerance and dependence* (pp. 2–28). London: Academic Press, Harcourt Brace Jovanovich.

Premack, D. (2004). Is language the key to human intelligence? *Science, 303*(5656), 318–320.

Priester, J. M., & Petty, R. E. (1995). Source attributions and persuasion: Perceived honesty as a determinant of message scrutiny. *Personality and Social Psychology Bulletin, 21*, 637–654.

Prigerson, H. G., Bierhals, A. J., Kasi, S. V., Reynolds, C. F., Shear, M. K., Day, N., et al. (1997). Traumatic grief as a risk factor for mental and physical morbidity. *American Journal of Psychiatry, 154I*, 616–623.

Prochaska, J. O., & Norcross, J. C. (2003). *Systems of psychotherapy* (5th ed.). Belmont, CA: Wadsworth.

PR Newswire Association, Inc. (2000). Con Edison Hosts the U.S. Memory Championship at Corporate Headquarters in New York. *Gale Group: Farmington Hills, MI*. Retrieved August 15, 2007, from **http://www.highbeam.com/doc1G1-f9201135.html**

Puetz, T. W., Flowers, S. S., & O'Connor, P. J. (2008). A randomized controlled trial of the effect of aerobic exercise training on feelings of energy and fatigue in sedentary young adults with persistent fatigue. *Psychotherapy and Psychosomatics, 77*(3), 167–174.

Pumariega, A. J., & Gustavson, C. R. (1994). Eating attitudes in African-American women: The essence. *Eating Disorders: Journal of Treatment and Prevention, 2*, 5–16.

Putnam, S. P., & Stifter, C. A. (2002). Development of approach and inhibition in the first year: Parallel findings for motor behavior, temperament ratings and directional cardiac response. *Developmental Science, 5*, 441–451.

Raaijmakers, J. G. W., & Shiffrin, R. M. (1992). Models for recall and recognition. *Annual Review of Psychology, 43*, 205–234.

Rachman, S. J., & Hodgson, R. J. (1980). *Obsessions and compulsions*. Englewood Cliffs, NJ: Prentice Hall.

Radford, B. (2004). *New technique used in treating A.D.D.* Retrieved August 28, 2004, from **www.kansascity.com/mld/kansascity**

Rainforth, M. V., Schneider, R. H., Nidich, S. I., Gaylord-King, C., Salerno, J. W., & Anderson, J. W. (2007). Stress reduction programs in patients with elevated blood pressure: A systematic review and meta-analysis. *Current Hypertension Reports, 9*, 520–528.

Ramachandran, V. S., & Hubbard, E. M. (2003). Hearing colors, tasting shapes. *Scientific American, 5*, 52–59.

Ramón y Cajal, S. (1995.) *Histology of the nervous system of man and vertebrates* (N. Swanson & L. M. Swanson, Trans.). New York: Oxford University Press.

Rao, S. C., Rainer, G., & Miller, E. K. (1997). Integration of what and where in the primate prefrontal cortex. *Science, 276*, 821–824.

Raynor, H. A., & Epstein, L. H. (2001). Dietary variety, energy regulation and obesity. *Psychological Bulletin, 127*(3), 325–341.

Reder, L. M., Anderson, J. R., & Bjork, R. A. (1974). A semantic interpretation of encoding specificity. *Journal of Experimental Psychology, 102*, 648–656.

Regier, D. A., Narrow, W. E., Rae, D. S., Manderscheid, R. W., Locke, B. Z., & Goodwin, F. K. (1993). The de facto mental and addictive disorders service system. Epidemiologic Catchment Area prospective 1-year prevalence rates of disorders and services. *Archives of General Psychiatry, 50*(2), 85–94.

Reinberg, S. (2010, October 14). Rescued Chilean miners in good heath. *Bloomberg Businessweek*. Retrieved from **http://www.businessweek.com/lifestyle/content/healthday/644394.html**

Reiner, W. G. (1999). Assignment of sex in neonates with ambiguous genitalia. *Current Opinions in Pediatrics, 11*(4), 363–365.

Reiner, W. G. (2000). The genesis of gender identity in the male: Prenatal androgen effects on gender identity and gender role. Talk given at New York University Child Study Center, Grand Rounds Summary.

Reisenzein, R. (1983). The Schachter theory of emotion: Two decades later. *Psychological Bulletin, 94*, 239–264.

Reisenzein, R. (1994). Pleasure-arousal theory and the intensity of emotions. *Journal of Personality and Social Psychology, 7*(6), 1313–1329.

Renchler, R. (1993). Poverty and learning. *ERIC Digests*, ERIC Clearinghouse on Educational Management, Eugene, OR. Retrieved June 1, 2004, from **www.ed.gov/databases/ERIC_Digests/ed357433.html**

Renfrey, G., & Spates, R. C. (1994). Eye movement desensitization: A partial dismantling study. *Journal of Behavior Therapy and Experimental Psychiatry, 25*, 231–239.

Renner, M. J., & Mackin, R. S. (1998). A life stress instrument for classroom use. *Teaching of Psychology, 25*, 47.

Rezvani, A. H., & Levin, E. D. (2001). Cognitive effects of nicotine. *Biological Psychiatry, 49*, 258–267.

Richards, C. F., & Lowe, R. A. (2003). Researching racial and ethnic disparities in emergency medicine. *Academic Emergency Medicine, 10*(11), 1169–1175.

Ridley, M. (1999). *Genome: The autobiography of a species in 23 chapters*. London: Fourth Estate.

Ritts, V. (1999). Infusing culture into psychopathology: A supplement for psychology instructors. Retrieved June 19, 2004, from www.stlcc.cc.mo.us/mc/users/vritts/psypath.htm

Rizzolatti, G., Fadiga, L., Gallese, V., & Fogassi, L. (1996). Premotor cortex and the recognition of motor actions. *Cognitive Brain Research, 3*, 131–141.

Robbins, L. (2010, October 14). Chilean miner to be invited to New York marathon. *New York Times*. Retrieved from http://thelede.blogs.nytimes.com/2010/10/14/chilean-miner-invited-to-new-york-marathon/

Robinson, J. W., & Preston, J. D. (1976). Equal status contact and modification of racial prejudice: A reexamination of the contact hypothesis. *Social Forces, 54*, 911–924.

Rodgers, J. E. (1992). *Psychosurgery: Damaging the brain to save the mind*. New York: HarperCollins.

Rodin, J. (1981). Current status of the internal-external hypothesis for obesity. *American Psychologist, 36*, 361–372.

Rodin, J. (1985). Insulin levels, hunger, and food intake: An example of feedback loops in body weight regulation. *Health Psychology, 4*, 1–24.

Rodin, J., & Langer, E. J. (1977). Long-term effects of a control-relevant intervention among the institutionalized aged. *Journal of Personality and Social Psychology, 35*, 275–282.

Roediger, H. L., III. (2000). Why retrieval is the key process to understanding human memory. In E. Tulving (Ed.), *Memory, consciousness and the brain: The Tallinn Conference* (pp. 52–75). Philadelphia: Psychology Press.

Roediger, H. L., III, & Guynn, M. J. (1996). Retrieval processes. In E. L. Bjork & R. A. Bjork (Eds.), *Memory* (pp. 197–236). New York: Academic Press.

Roethlisberger, F. J., & Dickson, W. J. (1939). *Management and the worker*. Cambridge, MA: Harvard University Press.

Roffman, R. A., Stephens, R. S., Simpson, E. E., & Whitaker, D. L. (1988). Treatment of marijuana dependence: Preliminary results. *Journal of Psychoactive Drugs, 20*(1), 129–137.

Roffwarg, H. P., Muzio, J. N., & Dement, W. C. (1966). Ontogenetic development of the human sleep-dream cycle. *Science, 152*(3722), 604–619.

Rogers, C. (1961). *On becoming a person: A therapist's view of psychotherapy*. Boston: Houghton/Mifflin.

Rogers, R. W., & Mewborn, C. R. (1976). Fear appeals and attitude change: Effects of a threat's noxiousness, probability of occurrence, and the efficacy of the coping responses. *Journal of Personality and Social Psychology, 34*, 54–61.

Rohde, A., & Marneros, A. (1993). Postpartum psychoses: Onset and long-term course. *Psychopathology, 26*, 203–209.

Rohde, P., Silva, S. G., Tonev, S. T., Kennard, B. D., Vitiello, B., Kratochvil, C. J., et al. (2008). Achievement and maintenance of sustained improvement during TADS continuation and maintenance therapy. *Archives of General Psychiatry, 65*(4), 447–455.

Roid, G. H. (2003). *Stanford-Binet intelligence scales* (5th ed.). Itasca, IL: Riverside Publishing.

Roper, G., Rachman, S., & Marks, I. (1975). Passive and participant modeling in exposure treatment of obsessive-compulsive neurotics. *Behaviour Research and Therapy, 13*, 271–279.

Rosch, E. (1973). On the internal structure of perceptual and semantic categories. In T. E. Moore (Ed.), *Cognitive development and the acquisition of language* (pp. 111–144). New York: Academic Press.

Rosch, E. (1977). Human categorization. In N. Warren (Ed.), *Advances in cross-cultural psychology* (Vol. 1, pp. 1–72). London: Academic Press.

Rosch, E., & Mervis, C. (1975). Family resemblances: Studies in the internal structures of categories. *Cognitive Psychology, 7*, 573–605.

Rosch, E., Mervis, C. B., Gray, W. D., Johnson, D. M., & Boyes-Braem, P. (1976). Basic objects in natural categories. *Cognitive Psychology, 8*, 382–439.

Rosch-Heider, E. (1972). Universals in color naming and memory. *Journal of Experimental Psychology, 93*, 10–20.

Rosch-Heider, E., & Olivier, D. C. (1972). The structure of the color space in naming and memory for two languages. *Cognitive Psychology, 3*, 337–354.

Rosenhan, D. L. (1973). On being sane in insane places. *Science, 179*, 250–258.

Rosenman, R. H., Brand, R. I., Jenkins, C. D., Friedman, M., Straus, R., & Wurm, M. (1975). Coronary heart disease in the Western Collaborative Group Study, final follow-up experience of 1/2 years. *Journal of the American Medical Association, 233*, 812–817.

Rosenthal, A. M. (1964). *Thirty-eight witnesses: The Kitty Genovese case*. New York: McGraw-Hill.

Rosenzweig, M. R., Leiman, A. L., & Breedlove, A. M. (1996). *Biological psychology*. Sunderland, MA: Sinaur Associates.

Ross, H. E., & Ross, G. M. (1976). Did Ptolemy understand the moon illusion? *Perception, 5*, 377–385.

Rossini, P. M., Altamura, C., Ferreri, F., Melgari, J. M., Tecchio, F., Tombini, M., et al. (2007). Neuroimaging experimental studies on brain plasticity in recovery from stroke. *Eura Medicophys, 43*(2), 241–254.

Rothbaum, B. O., Hodges, L. F., Kooper, R., Opdyke, D., Williford, J. S., & North, M. (1995). Effectiveness of computer-generated (virtual reality) graded exposure in the treatment of acrophobia. *American Journal of Psychiatry, 152*, 626–628.

Rothenberg, A. (2001). Bipolar illness, creativity, and treatment. *Psychiatric Quarterly, 72*(2), 131–147.

Rotter, J. B. (1954). *Social learning and clinical psychology*. New York: Prentice Hall.

Rotter, J. B. (1966). Generalized expectancies for internal versus external control of reinforcements. *Psychological Monographs, 80*, Whole No. 609.

Rotter, J. B. (1978). Generalized expectancies for problem solving and psychotherapy. *Cognitive Therapy and Research, 2*, 1–10.

Rotter, J. B. (1981). The psychological situation in social learning theory. In D. Magnusson (Ed.), *Toward a psychology of situations: An interactional perspective*. Hillsdale, NJ: Lawrence Erlbaum Associates.

Rotter, J. B. (1990). Internal versus external control of reinforcement: A case history of a variable. *American Psychologist, 45*, 489–493.

Rotton, J., & Frey, J. (1985). Air pollution, weather, and violent crime: Concomitant time-series analysis of archival data. *Journal of Personality and Social Psychology, 49*, 1207–1220.

Rotton, J., Frey, J., Barry, T., Milligan, M., & Fitzpatrick, M. (1979). The air pollution experience and physical aggression. *Journal of Applied Social Psychology, 9*, 397–412.

Rouse, B. A. (1998). *Substance and mental health statistics source book*. Rockville, MD: Department of Health and Human Services, Substance Abuse and Mental Health Services Administration (SAMHSA).

Rouw, R., & Scholte, H. S. (2007). Increased structural connectivity in grapheme-color synesthesia. *Nature Neuroscience*. Published online: May 21, 2007.

Rowan, J. (2001). *Ordinary ecstasy*. Hove, UK: Brunner-Routledge.

Rowe, D. C., Almeida, D. A., & Jacobson, K. C. (1999). School context and genetic influences on aggression in adolescence. *Psychological Science, 10*, 277–280.

Roysircai-Sodowsky, G. R., & Maestas, M. V. (2000). Acculturation, ethnic identity, and acculturative stress: Evidence and measurement. In R. H. Dana (Ed.), *Handbook of cross-cultural and multicultural assessment* (pp. 131–172). Mahwah, NJ: Lawrence Erlbaum Associates.

Ruble, D., Alvarez, J., Bachman, M., Cameron, J., Fuligni, A., Garcia Coll, C., et al. (2004). The development of a sense of "we": The emergence and implications of children's collective identity. In M. Bennett & F. Sani (Eds.), *The development of the social self*. New York: Psychology Press.

Ruhe, H. G., Mason, N. S., & Schene, A. H. (2007). Mood is indirectly related to serotonin, norepinephrine and dopamine levels in humans: A meta-analysis of monoamine depletion studies. *Molecular Psychiatry, 12*(4), 331–359.

Ryan, R. M., & Deci, E. L. (2000). Intrinsic and extrinsic motivations: Classic definitions and new directions. *Contemporary Educational Psychology, 25*, 54–67.

Sackeim, H. A., Prudic, J., Devanand, D. P., Nobler, M. S., Lisanby, S. H., Peyser, S., et al. (2000). A prospective, randomized, double-blind comparison of bilateral and right unilateral electroconvulsive therapy at different stimulus intensities. *Archives of General Psychiatry, 57*, 425–434.

Sadker, M., & Sadker, D. (1994). *Failing at fairness: How America's schools cheat girls*. New York: Scribner.

Salend, S. J. (1987). Contingency management systems. *Academic Therapy, 22*, 245–253.

Salmela-Aro, K., & Nurmi, J-E. (2007). Self-esteem during university studies predicts career characteristics 10 years later. *Journal of Vocational Behavior, 70*, 463–477.

Salovey, P., & Mayer, J. D. (1990). Emotional intelligence. *Imagination, Cognition, and Personality, 9*, 185–211.

Salovey, P., Rothman, A. J., Detweiler, J. B., & Steward, W. (2000). Emotional states and physical health. *American Psychologist, 55*, 110–121.

Sam, D. L., & Moreira, V. (2002). The mutual embeddedness of culture and mental illness. In W. J. Lonner, D. L. Dinnel, S. A. Hayes, & D. N. Sattler (Eds.), *Online Readings in Psychology and Culture* (Unit 9, Chapter 1), (http://www.wwu.edu/~culture), Center for Cross-Cultural Research, Western Washington University, Bellingham, Washington.

Sanders, L. D., Weber-Fox, C. M., & Neville, H. J. (2008). Varying degrees of plasticity in different subsystems within language. In J. R. Pomerantz & M. Crair (Eds.), *Topics in integrative neuroscience: From cells to cognition*. New York: Cambridge University Press.

Sands, L. P., & Meredith, W. (1992). Intellectual functioning in late midlife. *Journal of Gerontological and Psychological Science, 47*, 81–84.

Sarbin, T. R., & Coe, W. C. (1972). *Hypnosis: A social psychological analysis of influence communication*. New York: Holt, Rinehart & Winston.

Sastry, K. S., Karpova, Y., Prokopovich, S., Smith, A. J., Essau, B., Gersappe, A., et al. (2007). Epinephrine protects cancer cells from apoptosis via activation of cAMP-dependent protein kinase and BAD phosphorylation. *Journal of Biological Chemistry, 282*(19), 14094–14100.

Satcher, D. (2001). *The surgeon general's national strategy to prevent suicide*. Washington, DC: Office of the Surgeon General of the United States.

Sattler, J. M. (1977). The effects of therapist–client racial similarity. In A. S. Gurman & A. M. Razin (Eds.), *Effective psychotherapy: A handbook of research* (pp. 252–290). Elmsford, NY: Pergamon.

Saunders, B., & Goddard, C. R. (1998). Why do we condone the "physical punishment" of children? *Children Australia, 23*, 23–28.

Savage-Rumbaugh, S., & Lewin, R. (1994). *Kanzi*. New York: Wiley.

Savage-Rumbaugh, S., Shanker, S., & Taylor, T. J. (1998). *Apes, language and the human mind*. Oxford, UK: Oxford University Press.

Scarmeas, N., Levy, G., Tang, M.-X., Manly, J., & Stern, Y. (2001). Influence of leisure activity on the incidence of Alzheimer's disease. *Neurology, 57*, 2236–2242.

Scarmeas, N., Luchsinger, J. A., Mayeux, R., & Stern, Y. (2007). Mediterranean diet and Alzheimer disease mortality. *Neurology, 69*, 1084–1093.

Scarmeas, N., Stern, Y., Mayeux, R., & Luchsinger, J. A. (2006). Mediterranean diet, Alzheimer disease, and vascular mediation. *Archives of Neurology, 63*, 1709–1717.

Scarmeas, N., Zarahn, E., Anderson, K. E., Habeck, C. G., Hilton, J., Flynn, J., et al. (2003). Association of life activities with cerebral blood flow in Alzheimer disease: Implications for the cognitive reserve hypothesis. *Archives of Neurology, 60*(3), 317–318.

Schachter, S., & Singer, J. E. (1962). Cognitive, social and physiological determinants of emotional states. *Psychological Review, 69*, 379–399.

Schacter, D. L. (1996). *Searching for memory. The brain, the mind, and the past*. New York: Basic Books.

Schafer, M., & Crichlow S. (1996). Antecedents of groupthink: A quantitative study. *Journal of Conflict Resolution, 40*, 415–435.

Schaffhauser, D. (2010, March 25). STEM review suggests small measures to close gender gap. *Campus Technology*. Retrieved from **http://campustechnology.com/articles/2010/03/25/stem-review-suggests-small-measures-to-close-gender-gap.aspx#**

Schmitt, D. P. (2002). Personality, attachment and sexuality related to dating relationship outcomes: Contrasting three perspectives on personal attribute interaction. *British Journal of Social Psychology, 41*(4), 589–610.

Schmitz, C., Wagner, J., & Menke, E. (2001). The interconnection of childhood poverty and homelessness: Negative impact/points of access. *Families in Society, 82*(1), 69–77.

Schneider, K. J., Bugental, J. F. T., & Fraser, J. F. (Eds.). (2001). *Handbook of humanistic psychology*. Thousand Oaks, CA: Sage.

Schneider, R. H., Staggers, F., Alexander, C. N., Sheppard, W., Rainforth, M., Kondwani, K., et al. (1995). A randomized controlled trial of stress reduction for hypertension in older African Americans. *Hypertension, 26*(5), 820–827.

Schneider, W., Dumais, S., & Shriffrin, R. (1984). *Automatic and control processing and attention*. London: Academic Press.

Schneidman, E. (1983). *Death of man*. New York: Jason Aronson.

Schneidman, E. (1994). *Death: Current perspectives*. New York: McGraw-Hill.

Schreiber, F. R. (1973, reissued 1995). *Sybil*. New York: Warner.

Schroeder, S. R. (2000). Mental retardation and developmental disabilities influenced by environmental neurotoxic insults. *Environmental Health Perspectives, 108*(Suppl. 3), 395–399.

Schroth, M. L., & McCormack, W. A. (2000). Sensation seeking and need for achievement among study-abroad students. *The Journal of Social Psychology, 140*, 533–535.

Schultz, D., & Schultz, S. E. (2004). *Psychology and work today*. Upper Saddle River, NJ: Pearson.

Schwartz, S. K. (2000). *Working your degree*. Retrieved from **http://cnnfn.cnn.com/2000/12/08/career/q_degreepsychology/**

Schweickert, R. (1993). A multinomial processing tree model for degradation and redintegration in immediate recall. *Memory and Cognition, 21*, 168–175.

Schwitzgebel, E. (1999). Representation and desire: A philosophical error with consequences for theory-of-mind research. *Philosophical Psychology, 12*, 157–180.

ScienceDaily. (2008, September 8). Tracking the reasons many girls avoid science and math. *Science Daily*. Retrieved from **http://www.sciencedaily.com/releases/2008/09/080905153807.htm**

Scott, S. K., Young, A. W., Calder, A. J., Hellawell, D. J., Aggleton, J. P., & Johnson, M. (1997). Impaired auditory recognition of fear and anger following bilateral amygdala lesions. *Nature, 385*(6613), 254–257.

Searight, H. R., Burke, J. M., & Rottnek, F. (2000). Adult ADHD: Evaluation and treatment in family medicine. *American Family Physician, 62*(9), 2077–2086, 2091–2092.

Security Director's Report. (2008). Experts identify four trends in workplace violence. *Institute of Management and Administration, 8*(6), 1–15.

Segall, M. H., Campbell, D. T., & Herskovits, M. J. (1966). *The influence of culture on perception*. Indianapolis, IN: Bobbs-Merrill.

Seligman, L. (1998). *Selecting effective treatments: A comprehensive guide to treating mental disorders*. San Francisco: Jossey-Bass.

Seligman, M. E. P. (1970). On the generality of the laws of learning. *Psychological Review, 77*, 406–418.

Seligman, M. E. P. (1975). *Helplessness—On depression, development, and death*. San Francisco: Freeman.

Seligman, M. E. P. (1995). The effectiveness of psychotherapy: The *Consumer Reports* study. *American Psychologist, 50*, 965–975.

Seligman, M. E. P. (1998). *Learned optimism: How to change your mind and your life* (2nd ed.). New York: Pocket Books.

Seligman, M. E. P. (2002). *Authentic happiness*. New York: Free Press.

Seligman, M. E. P., & Maier, S. F. (1967). Failure to escape traumatic shock. *Journal of Experimental Psychology, 74*, 1–9.

Sellin, D. F., & Birch, J. W. (1981). *Psychoeducational development of gifted and talented Learners*. Rockville, MD: Aspen Publications

Selye, H. (1936). Syndrome produced by diverse nocuous agents. *Nature, 138*, 32.

Selye, H. (1956). *The stress of life*. New York: McGraw-Hill.

Selye, H. (1976). *The stress of life* (Rev. ed.). New York: McGraw-Hill.

Shadish, R., Cook, T. D., & Campbell, D. T. (2002). *Experimental and quasi-experimental designs for generalized causal inferences*. New York: Houghton Mifflin.

Shafto, P., & Coley, J. D. (2003). Development of categorization and reasoning in the natural world: Novices to experts, naïve similarity to ecological knowledge. *Journal of Experimental Psychology: Learning, Memory & Cognition, 29*, 641–649.

Shafton, A. (1995). *Dream reader: Contemporary approaches to the understanding of dreams (SUNY series in dream studies)* New York: State University of New York Press.

Shah, P. M. (1991). Prevention of mental handicaps in children in primary health care. *Bulletin of the World Health Organization, 69*, 779–789.

Shapiro, A. K., & Shapiro, E. (1997). *The powerful placebo*. Baltimore: Johns Hopkins University Press.

Shapiro, F. (1989). Eye movement desensitization: A new treatment for post-traumatic stress disorder. *Journal of Behavior Therapy and Experimental Psychiatry, 20*, 211–217.

Shapiro, F. (1995). *Eye movement desensitization and reprocessing: Basic principles, protocols, and procedure*. New York: Guilford Press.

Shaver, K. (2007, June 17). Stay-at-home dads forge new identities, roles. *Washington Post*. Retrieved from **http://www.washingtonpost.com/wp-dyn/content/article/2007/06/16/AR2007061601289.html**

Shepard, R. N., & Metzler, J. (1971). Mental rotation of three-dimensional objects. *Science, 171*, 701–703.

Shepard, T. H. (2001). *Catalog of teratogenic agents* (10th ed.). Baltimore: Johns Hopkins University Press.

Sherif, M. (1936). *The psychology of social norms*. New York: Harper & Row.

Sherif, M., Harvey, O. J., White, B. J., Hood, W. R., & Sherif, C. W. (1961). *Intergroup conflict and cooperation: The Robber's Cave experiment*. Norman, OK: University of Oklahoma Book Exchange.

Shorter E. (1997). *A history of psychiatry: From the era of the asylum to the age of Prozac*. New York: John Wiley & Sons.

Shuglin, A. (1986). The background chemistry of MDMA. *Journal of Psychoactive Drugs, 18*(4), 291–304.

Shurkin, J. N. (1992). *Terman's kids: The groundbreaking study of how the gifted grow up*. Boston: Little, Brown and Company.

Shweder, R. A. (1998). *Welcome to middle age!: (And other cultural fictions)*. New York: Oxford University Press.

Shweder, R. A. (2003). *Why do men barbecue?: Recipes for cultural psychology*. Cambridge, MA: Harvard University Press.

Sibley, R. (2010, October 14). Reborn from the belly of the Earth. *Ottawa Citizen*. Retrieved from **http://www.ottawacitizen.com/opinion/Reborn+from+belly+Earth/3669061/story.html**

Siegler, I. C., Costa, P. T., Brummett, B. H., Helms, M. J., Barefoot, J. C., Williams, R. B., et al. (2003). Patterns of change in hostility from college to midlife in the UNC alumni heart study predict high-risk status. *Psychosomatic Medicine, 65*, 738–745.

Siegler, R. S. (1996). *Emerging minds: The process of change in children's thinking*. New York: Oxford University Press.

Silva, C. E., & Kirsch, I. (1992). Interpretive sets, expectancy, fantasy proneness, and dissociation as predictors of hypnotic response. *Journal of Personality & Social Psychology, 63*, 847–856.

Silver, F. W. (1996). Management of conversion disorder. *American Journal of Physical Medicine and Rehabilitation, 75*, 134–140.

Silver, L. (2000). Attention deficit/hyperactivity in adult lives. *Child & Adolescent Psychiatric Clinics of North America, 9*, 511–523.

Silver, S. M., Brooks, A., & Obenchain, J. (1995). Eye movement desensitization and reprocessing treatment of Vietnam war veterans with PTSD: Comparative effects with biofeedback and relaxation training. *Journal of Traumatic Stress, 8*(2), 337–342.

Simeon, D., Guralnik, O., Hazlett, E. A., Spiegel-Cohen, J., Hollander, E., & Buchsbaum, M. S. (2000). Feeling unreal: A PET study of depersonalization disorder. *American Journal of Psychiatry, 157*, 1782–1788.

Singh-Manoux, A., Richards, M., & Marmot, M. (2003). Leisure activities and cognitive function in middle age: Evidence from the Whitehall II study. *Journal of Epidemiology and Community Health, 57*, 907–913.

Skarin, B., Skorinko, J., Saeed, K., & Pavlov, O. (2009, July 26–30). Modeling the cycles of gangs and criminal behavior. Paper presented at the 27th International Conference of the System Dynamics Society, Albuquerque, NM.

Skinner, B. F. (1938). *The behavior of organisms: An experimental analysis.* New York: Appleton-Century-Crofts.

Skinner, B. F. (1956). A case history in scientific method. *American Psychologist, 11*, 221–233.

Skinner, B. F. (1961). *Cumulative record: Definitive edition.* New York: Appelton-Century-Crofts.

Skinner, B. F. (1971). *Beyond freedom and dignity.* New York: Alfred A. Knopf.

Skinner, B. F. (1974). *About behaviorism.* New York: Alfred A. Knopf.

Skolnick, A. (1986). Early attachment and personal relationships across the life course. In P. B. Baltes, D. L. Featherman, & R. M. Lerner (Eds.), *Life-span development and behavior* (Vol. 7). Hillsdale, NJ: Erlbaum.

Skrandies, W., Reik, P., & Kunze, C. (1999). Topography of evoked brain activity during mental arithmetic and language tasks: Sex differences. *Neuropsychologia, 37*, 421–430.

Slater, A. (2000). Visual perception in the young infant: Early organisation and rapid learning. In D. Muir & A. Slater (Eds.), *Infant development: The essential readings.* Oxford, UK: Blackwell.

Slipp, S. (1993). *The Freudian mystique: Freud, women and feminism.* New York: New York University Press.

Sloan, D. M., & Mizes, J. S. (1999). Foundations of behavior therapy in the contemporary healthcare context. *Clinical Psychology Review, 19*, 255–274.

Smith, D. (2001). Shock and disbelief. *Atlantic Monthly, 2*, 79–90.

Smith, J. D., & Mitchell, A. (2001). "Me? I'm not a drooler. I'm the assistant": Is it time to abandon mental retardation as a classification? *Mental Retardation, 39*(2), 144–146.

Smith, T. C., Ryan, M. A. K., Wingard, D. L., Sallis, J. F., & Kritz-Silverstein, D. (2008). New onset and persistent symptoms of post-traumatic stress disorder self-reported after deployment and combat exposures: Prospective population based U.S. military cohort study. *British Medical Journal, 336*(7640), 366–371.

Smith-Spark, L. (2005, March 18). How sleepwalking can lead to killing. *BBC News.* Retrieved February 14, 2008, from **http://news.bbc.co.uk/1/hi/uk/4362081.stm**

Snyder, M., Tanke, E. D., & Berscheid, E. (1977). Social perception and interpersonal behavior: On the self-fulfilling nature of social stereotypes. *Journal of Personality and Social Psychology, 35*, 656–666.

Solomon, J. (1996, May 20). Breaking the silence. *Newsweek,* 20–22.

Soomro, G. M. (2001). Obsessive-compulsive disorder. *Clinical Evidence, 6*, 754–762.

Sowell, E. R., Thompson, P. M., Holmes, C. J., Jernigan, T. L., & Toga, A. W. (1999). In vivo evidence for post-adolescent brain maturation in frontal and striatal regions. *Nature Neuroscience, 2*(10), 859–861.

Spangler, W. D. (1992). Validity of questionnaire and TAT measures of need for achievement: Two meta-analyses. *Psychological Bulletin, 112*, 140–154.

Spangler, W. J., Cosgrove, G. R., Ballantine, H. T., Jr., Cassem, E. H., Rauch, S. L., Nierenberg, A., et al. (1996). Magnetic resonance image-guided stereotactic cingulotomy for intractable psychiatric disease. *Neurosurgery, 38*, 1071–1076.

Sparing, R., Mottaghy, F., Ganis, G., Thompson, W. L., Toepper, R., Kosslyn, S. M., & et al. (2002). Visual cortex excitability increases during visual mental imagery—A TMS study in healthy human subjects. *Brain Research, 938*, 92–97.

Spearman, C. (1904). "General intelligence" objectively determined and measured. *American Journal of Psychology, 15*, 201–293.

Sperry, R. W. (1968). Mental unity following surgical disconnection of the cerebral hemispheres. *The Harvey Lectures.* Series 62, 293–323. New York: Academic Press.

Spiegel, D., Bloom, J. R., & Gottheil, E. (1989). Effects of psychosocial treatment on survival of patients with metastatic breast cancer. *Lancet, 2*, 888–891.

Squire, L. R., & Kandel, E. R. (1999). *Memory: From mind to molecule.* New York: Scientific American Library.

Squire, L. R., & Slater, P. C. (1978). Anterograde and retrograde memory impairment in chronic amnesia. *Neuropsychologia, 16*, 313–322.

Srivastava, S., John, O. P., Gosling, S. D, & Potter, J. (2003). Development of personality in early and middle adulthood: Set like plaster or persistent change? *Journal of Personality and Social Psychology, 84*(5), 1041–1053.

Standing, L., Conezio, J., & Haber, R. N. (1970). Perception and memory for pictures: Single-trial learning of 2500 visual stimuli. *Psychonomic Science, 19*, 73–74.

Steele, C. M. (1992). Race and the schooling of black Americans. *The Atlantic Monthly, 269*(4), 68–78.

Steele, C. M. (1997). A threat in the air: How stereotypes shape intellectual identity and performance. *American Psychologist, 52*, 613–629.

Steele, C. M. (1999, August). Thin ice: "Stereotype threat" and Black college students. *The Atlantic Monthly, 284*, 44–54.

Steele, C. M., & Aronson J. (1995). Stereotype threat and the intellectual test performance of African Americans. *Journal of Personality and Social Psychology, 69*, 797–811.

Steen, C. (1996). Synesthesia. *Health Report with Robin Hughes.* ABC Radio National Transcripts.

Stein, H. T. (2001). Adlerian overview of birth order characteristics. Alfred Adler Institute of San Francisco. Retrieved June 16, 2004, from **http://ourworld.compuserve.com/homepages/hstein/birthord.htm**

Stein, S. (1984). *Girls and boys: The limits of non-sexist rearing.* London: Chatto and Windus.

Stein-Behrens, B., Mattson, M. P., Chang, I., Yeh, M., & Sapolsky, R. (1994). Stress exacerbates neuron loss and cytoskeletal pathology in the hippocampus. *Journal of Neuroscience, 14*, 5373–5380.

Steinberg, L., & Silverberg, S. B. (1987). Influences on marital satisfaction during the middle stages of the family life cycle. *Journal of Marriage and the Family, 49*, 751–760.

Stern, W. (1912). The psychological methods of testing intelligence (G. M. Whipple, Trans.). *Educational Psychology Monographs,* 13.

Sternberg, R. J. (1986). A triangular theory of love. *Psychological Review, 93*, 119–135.

Sternberg, R. J. (1988a). *The triarchic mind: A new theory of human intelligence.* New York: Viking-Penguin.

Sternberg, R. J. (1988b). Triangulating love. In R. Sternberg & M. Barnes (Eds.), *The psychology of love* (pp. 119–138). New Haven, CT: Yale University Press.

Sternberg, R. J. (1996). *Successful intelligence: How practical and creative intelligence determine success in life.* New York: Simon & Schuster.

Sternberg, R. J. (1997a). Construct validation of a triangular love scale. *European Journal of Social Psychology, 27*, 313–335.

Sternberg, R. J. (1997b). The triarchic theory of intelligence. In P. Flannagan, J. L. Genshaft, & P. L. Harrison (Eds.), *Contemporary intellectual assessment: Theories, tests, and issues* (pp. 92–104). New York: Guilford Press.

Sternberg, R. J. (2002). Cultural explorations of human intelligence around the world. In W. J. Lonner, D. L. Dinnel, S. A. Hayes, & D. N. Sattler (Eds.), *Online Readings in Psychology and Culture* (Unit 5, Chapter 1), (**http://www.wwu.edu/~culture**), Center for Cross-Cultural Research, Western Washington University, Bellingham, Washington.

Sternberg, R. J., & Kaufman, J. C. (1998). Human abilities. *Annual Review of Psychology, 49*, 479–502.

Sternberger, R. R., et al. (1995). Social phobia: An analysis of possible developmental factors. *Journal of Abnormal Psychology, 194*, 526–531.

Stevenson, M. B., Roach, M. A., Leavitt, L. A., Miller, J. F., & Chapman, R. S. (1988). Early receptive and productive language skills in preterm and full-term 8-month-old infants. *Journal of Psycholinguistic Research, 17*(2), 169–183.

Stickgold, R. (2005). Sleep-dependent memory consolidation. *Nature, 437*: 1272–1278.

Stickgold, R., Hobson, J. A., Fosse, R., & Fosse, M. (2001). Sleep, learning, and dreams: Off-line memory reprocessing. *Science, 294*, 1052–1057.

Stickgold R., Malia, A., Maquire, D., Roddenberry, D., & O'Connor, M. (2000). Replaying the game: Hypnagogic images in normals and amnesiacs. *Science, 290*, 350–353.

Stiff, J. B., & Mongeau, P. A. (2002). *Persuasive communication* (2nd ed.). New York: Guilford Press.

Stiles, W. B., Agnew-Davies, R., Hardy, G. E., Barkham, M., & Shapiro, D. A. (1998). Relations of the alliance with psychotherapy outcome: Findings in the second Sheffield Psychotherapy Project. *Journal of Consulting and Clinical Psychology, 66*, 791–802.

Stitzer, M. L., & De Wit, H. (1998). Abuse liability of nicotine. In N. L. Benowitz (Ed.), *Nicotine safety and toxicity* (pp. 119–131). New York: Oxford University Press.

Stockhorst, U., Gritzmann, E., Klopp, K., Schottenfeld-Naor, Y., Hübinger, A., Berresheim, H., Steingrüber, H., & Gries, F. A. (1999). Classical conditioning of insulin effects in healthy humans. *Psychosomatic Medicine, 61*, 424–435.

Stone, A. A., & Neale, J. M. (1984). Effects of severe daily events on mood. *Journal of Personality and Social Psychology, 46*, 137–144.

Stowell, J. R., Kiecolt-Glaser, J. K., & Glaser, R. (2001). Perceived stress and cellular immunity: When coping counts. *Journal of Behavioral Medicine, 24*(4), 323–339.

Straus, M. A. (2000). Corporal punishment of children and adult depression and suicidal ideation. In *Beating the devil out of them: Corporal punishment in American families and its effects on children* (pp. 60–77). New York: Lexington Books.

Straus, M. A., & Stewart, J. H. (1999). Corporal punishment by American parents: National data on prevalence, chronicity, severity, and duration, in relation to child, and family characteristics. *Clinical Child and Family Psychology Review, 2*, 55–70.

Straus, M. A., & Yodanis, C. L. (1994). Physical abuse. In M. A. Straus (Ed.), *Beating the devil out of them: Corporal punishment in American families* (pp. 81–98). San Francisco: New Lexington Press.

Strauss, V. (2005, February 1). Decoding why few girls choose science, math. *Washington Post.* Retrieved from **http://www.washingtonpost.com/ac2/wp-dyn/A52344-2005Jan31**

Strayer, D. L., & Drews, F. A. (2007). Cell-phone-induced driver distraction. *Current Directions in Psychological Science, 16*, 128–131.

Strayer, D. L., Drews, F. A., & Crouch, D. J. (2006). A comparison of the cell phone driver and the drunk driver. *Human Factors, 48,* 381–391.

Strayer, D. L., & Johnston, W. A. (2001). Driven to distraction: Dual-task studies of simulated driving and conversing on a cellular phone. *Psychological Science, 12,* 462–466.

Stuss, D. T., Binns, M. A., Murphy, K. J., & Alexander, M. P. (2002). Dissociations within the anterior attentional system: Effects of task complexity and irrelevant information on reaction time speed and accuracy. *Neuropsychology, 16,* 500–513.

Sue, D. W., & Sue, D. (2003). *Counseling the culturally different: Theory and practice* (4th ed.). New York: John Wiley & Sons.

Sue, S. (1977). Community mental health services to minority groups: Some optimism, some pessimism. *American Psychologist, 32,* 616–624.

Sue, S. (1992). Ethnicity and mental health: Research and policy issues. *Journal of Social Issues, 48*(2), 187–205.

Sue, S., Zane, N., & Young, K. (1994). Research on psychotherapy in culturally diverse populations. In A. Bergin & S. Garfield (Eds.), *Handbook of psychotherapy and behavior change* (pp. 783–817). New York: Wiley.

Sulloway, F. J. (1996). *Born to rebel: Birth order, family dynamics, and creative lives.* New York: Pantheon.

Sutherland, P. (1992). *Cognitive development today: Piaget and his critics.* London: Paul Chapman.

Swain, S. (1989). Covert intimacy: Closeness in men's friendships. In B. J. Risman & P. Schwartz (Eds.), *Plasticity of development.* Cambridge, MA: MIT Press.

Swanbrow, D. (1998, March 25). Red fish, blue fish help clarify cultural aspects of emotion. *The University Record.* Retrieved from **http://ur.umich.edu/9798/Mar25_98/fish.htm**

Swann, J. (1998). Talk control: An illustration from the classroom of problems in analyzing male dominance of conversation. In J. Coates (Ed.), *Language and gender: A reader* (pp. 185–196). Oxford, UK: Blackwell.

Swann, W. B., Jr., Chang-Schneider, C., & McClarty, K. L. (2007). Do people's self-views matter? Self-concept and self-esteem in everyday life. *American Psychologist, 62,* 84–94.

Swartz, M. (1990). Somatization disorder. In L. N. Robins (Ed.), *Psychiatric disorder in America* (pp. 220–257). New York: Free Press.

Swartz, M., Blazer, D., George, L., & Winfield, I. (1990). Estimating the prevalence of borderline personality disorder in the community. *Journal of Personality Disorders, 4*(3), 257–272.

Swayze, V. W., II. (1995). Frontal leukotomy and related psychosurgical procedures in the era before antipsychotics (1935–1954): A historical overview. *American Journal of Psychiatry, 152*(4), 505–515.

Swenson, D. D., & Marshall, B. (2005, May 14). Flash flood: Hurricane Katrina's inundation of New Orleans, August 29, 2005 (SWF). *Times-Picayune.*

Taglialatela, J. P., Savage-Rumbaugh, E. S., & Baker, L. A. (2003). Vocal production by a language-competent bonobo (Pan Paniscus). *International Journal of Comparative Psychology, 24,* 1–17.

Tajfel, H., & Turner, J. C. (1986). The social identity theory of intergroup behaviour. In S. Worchel & W. G. Austin (Eds.), *The psychology of intergroup relations* (Vol. 2, pp. 7–24) New York: Nelson Hall.

Takeuchi, T., Ogilvie, R. D., Murphy, T. I., & Ferrelli, A. V. (2003). EEG activities during elicited sleep onset. REM and NREM periods reflect difference mechanisms of dream generation. *Clinical Neurophysiology, 114*(2), 210–220.

Talbot, M. (2010, January 20). Marriage rates and the defense. *The New Yorker.* Retrieved from **http://www.newyorker.com/online/blogs/newsdesk/2010/01/marriage-rates-and-the-defense.html**

Talbott, G. D., & Crosby, L. R. (2001). Recovery contracts: Seven key elements. In R. H. Coombs (Ed.), *Addiction recovery tools* (pp. 127–144). Thousand Oaks, CA: Sage.

Tamminga, C. A. (2002). Partial dopamine agonists in the treatment of psychosis. *Journal of Neural Transmission, 109,* 411–420.

Tart, C. T. (1970). Marijuana intoxication: Common experiences. *Nature, 226,* 701.

Tart, C. T. (1986). *Waking up: Overcoming the obstacles to human potential.* Boston: New Science Library.

Taylor, D. M., & Moghaddam, F. M. (1994). *Theories of intergroup relations: International social psychological perspectives* (2nd ed.). Westport, CT: Praeger.

Teigen, K. (1994). Yerkes–Dodson: A law for all seasons. *Theory & Psychology, 4,* 525–547.

Temoshok, L., & Dreher, H. (1992). *The Type C connection: The behavioral links to cancer and your health.* New York: Random House.

Terman, J. S. (2001). Circadian time of morning light administration and therapeutic response in winter depression. *Archives of General Psychiatry, 58,* 69–75.

Terman, L. M. (1916). *The measurement of intelligence.* Boston: Houghton Mifflin.

Terman, L. M. (1925). *Mental and physical traits of a thousand gifted children* (Vol. 1) Stanford, CA: Stanford University Press.

Terman, L. M., & Oden, M. H. (1947). *The gifted child grows up: 25 years' follow-up of a superior group: Genetic studies of genius* (Vol. 4). Stanford, CA: Stanford University Press.

Terry, A. V., Jr., Hill, W. D., Parikh, V., Evans, D. R., Waller, J. L., & Mahadik, S. P. (2002). Differential effects of chronic haloperidol and olanzapine exposure on brain cholinergic markers and spatial learning in rats. *Psychopharmacology, 164*(4), 360–368.

Terry, A. V., Jr., Hill, W. D., Parikh, V., Waller, J. L., Evans, D. R., & Mahadik, S. P. (2003). Differential effects of haloperidol, risperidone, and clozapine exposure on cholinergic markers and spatial learning performance in rats. *Neuropsychopharmacology, 28*(2), 300–309.

Thase, M. E. (1999). When are psychotherapy and pharmacotherapy combinations the treatment of choice for major depressive disorders? *Psychiatric Quarterly, 70*(4), 333–346.

Thase, M. E., & Sachs, G. S. (2000). Bipolar depression: Pharmacotherapy and related therapeutic strategies. *Biological Psychiatry, 48*(6), 558–572.

Thomas, M., Thorne, D., Sing, H., Redmond, D., Balkin, T., Wesensten, N., et al. (1998). The relationship between driving accidents and microsleep during cumulative partial sleep deprivation. *Journal of Sleep Research, 7*(2), 275.

Thomas, N. J. T. (2001). Mental imagery. In E. N. Zalta (Ed.), *The Stanford encyclopedia of philosophy* (Winter 2001 edition). Retrieved January 20, 2008, from **http://plato.stanford.edu/entries/ mental-imagery/**

Thorndike, E. L. (1911). *Animal intelligence: Experimental studies.* New York: Macmillan.

Thorndike, E. L. (1920). A constant error on psychological rating. *Journal of Applied Psychology, 4,* 25–29.

Thornton, A., & Hui-Sheng, L. (1994). Continuity and change. In A. Thornton & L. Hui-Sheng (Eds.), *Social change and the family in Taiwan* (pp. 396–410). Chicago: University of Chicago Press.

Thurstone, L. L. (1938). *Primary mental abilities.* Chicago: University of Chicago Press.

Tobach, E. (2001). Development of sex and gender. In J. Worell (Ed.), *Encyclopedia of women and gender* (pp. 315–332). San Diego, CA: Academic Press.

Toga, A. W., & Thompson, P. M. (2003). Mapping brain asymmetry. *Natural Neuroscience, 4,* 37–48.

Tohen, M., Vieta, E., Calabrese, J., Ketter, T. A., Sachs, G., Bowden, C., et al. (2003). Efficacy of olanzapine and olanzapine-fluoxetine combination in the treatment of bipolar I depression. *Archives of General Psychiatry, 60*(11), 1079–1088.

Tolman, E. C. (1932). *Purposive behavior in animals and man.* New York: Century.

Tolman, E. C., & Honzik, C. H. (1930). Introduction and removal of reward and maze learning in rats. *University of California Publications in Psychology, 4,* 257–275.

Torgersen, S. (2000). Genetics of patients with borderline personality disorder. *Psychiatric Clinics of North America, 23,* 1–9.

Torrance, E. P. (1993). The Beyonders in a thirty-year longitudinal study of creative achievement. *Roeper Review, 15*(3), 131–135.

Torrey, E. F. (1987). Prevalence studies in schizophrenia. *British Journal of Psychiatry, 150,* 598–608.

Trappey, C. (1996). A meta-analysis of consumer choice and subliminal advertising. *Psychology and Marketing, 13,* 517–530.

Trautwein, U., Lüdtke, O., Köller, O., & Baumert, J. (2006). Self-esteem, academic self-concept, and achievement: How the learning environment moderates the dynamics of self-concept. *Journal of Personality and Social Psychology, 90,* 334–349.

Tremblay, A., Doucet, E., & Imbeault, P. (1999). Physical activity and weight maintenance. *International Journal of Obesity, 23*(3), S50–S54.

Tresniowski, A. (1999, July 12). Troubled sleep. *People Weekly,* 56–59.

Triandis, H. (1971). *Attitude and attitude change.* New York: Wiley.

Trocmé, N., MacLaurin, B., Fallon, B., Daciuk, J., Billingsley, D., Tourigny, M., et al. (2001). *Canadian incidence study of reported child abuse and neglect: Final report, pp. 30–31.* Ottawa, ON: Minister of Public Works and Government Services Canada.

Trujillo, K. A., & Chinn, A. B. (1996). Antidepressants. *Drugs and the Brain*: California State University. Retrieved July 20, 2004, from **www.csusm.edu/DandB/AD.html#history**.

Trut, L. M. (1999). Early canid domestication: The Farm-Fox Experiment. *Science,* 283.

Tsai, J. L., Simeonova, D. I., & Watanabe, J. T. (2004). Somatic and social: Chinese Americans talk about emotion. *Personality and Social Psychology Bulletin, 30*(9), 1226–1238.

Tsuang, M., Domschke, K., Jerskey, B. A., & Lyons, M. J. (2004). Agoraphobic behavior and panic attack: A study of male twins. *Journal of Anxiety Disorders, 18*(6), 799–807.

Tucker, E. W., & Potocky-Tripodi, M. (2006). Changing heterosexuals' attitudes toward homosexuals: A systematic review of the empirical literature. *Research on Social Work Practice, 16*(2), 176–190.

Tugade, M. M., & Fredrickson, B. L. (2004). Resilient individuals use positive emotions to bounce back from negative emotional experiences. *Journal of Personality and Social Psychology, 86*(2), 320–333.

Tukuitonga, C. F., & Bindman, A. B. (2002). Ethnic and gender differences in the use of coronary artery revascularisation procedures in New Zealand. *New Zealand Medical Journal*, 115, 179–182.

Tulving, E., & Thomson, D. M. (1973). Encoding specificity and retrieval processes in episodic memory. *Psychological Review*, 80, 352–373.

Tversky, A., & Kahneman, D. (1974). Judgment under uncertainty: Heuristics and biases. *Science*, 185, 1124–1130.

Tversky, A., & Kahneman, D. (1981). The framing of decisions and the psychology of choice. *Science*, 211(4481), 453–458.

Udry, J. R. (1971). *The social context of marriage*, (2nd ed.) Philadelphia: J.B. Lippincott.

Unger, R. (1979). Toward a redefinition of sex and gender. *American Psychologist*, 34, 1085–1094.

Uretsky, S. D. (2002). Antianxiety drugs. *Gale Encyclopedia of Medicine*. The Gale Group. Retrieved July 19, from **www.healthatoz.com/healthatoz/Atoz/ency/antianxiety_drugs.html#**.

U.S. Department of Education. (2007). *Encouraging girls in math and science: IES practice guide*. Retrieved from **http://ies.ed.gov/ncee/wwc/pdf/practiceguides/20072003.pdf**

Vail, A. (1976). Factors influencing lower class, black patients' remaining in treatment. *Clinical Psychology*, 29, 12–14.

Vaillant, G. E. (2002). Adaptive mental mechanisms: Their role in a positive psychology. *American Psychologist*, 55, 89–98.

Valverde, R., Pozdnyakova, I., Kajander, T., Venkatraman, J., & Regan, L. (2007). Fragile X mental retardation syndrome: Structure of the KH1-KH2 domains of fragile X mental retardation protein. *Structure*, 9, 1090–1098.

van der Merwe, A., & Garuccio, A. (Eds.). (1994). *Waves and particles in light and matter*. New York: Plenum Press.

Vartanian, L. R. (2000). Revisiting the imaginary audience and personal fable constructs of adolescent egocentricism: A conceptual review. *Adolescence*, 35(140), 639–661.

Vaughan, K., Armstrong, M. S., Gold, R., O'Connor N., Jenneke, W., & Tarrier, N. (1994). A trial of eye movement desensitization compared to image habituation training and applied muscle relaxation in post-traumatic stress disorder. *Journal of Behavior Therapy and Experimental Psychology*, 25, 283–291.

Vaughan, S. (2000). *Half empty, half full: The psychological roots of optimism*. New York: Harcourt.

Vernon, S. W., & Roberts, R. E. (1982). Use of RDC in a tri-ethnic community survey. *Archives of General Psychiatry*, 39, 47.

Vigil, J. D. (1988). Group processes and street identity: Adolescent Chicano gang members. *Ethos*, 16(4), 421–445.

Villafuerte, S., & Burmeister, M. (2003). Untangling genetic networks of panic, phobia, fear and anxiety. *Genome Biology*, 4(8), 224.

Villani, S. (2001). Impact of media on children and adolescents: A 10-year review of the research. *Journal of the American Academy on Child and Adolescent Psychiatry*, 40(4), 392–401.

Visser, P. S., & Krosnick, J. A. (1998). Development of attitude strength over the life cycle: Surge and decline. *Journal of Personality and Social Psychology*, 75(6), 1389–1410.

Vogel, G. W. (1975). A review of REM sleep deprivation. *Archives of General Psychiatry*, 32, 749–761.

Vogel, G. W. (1993). Selective deprivation, REM sleep. In M. A. Carskadon (Ed.), *The encyclopedia of sleep and dreaming*. New York: Macmillan Publishing Company.

Vokey, J. R., & Read J. D. (1985). Subliminal messages: Between the devil and the media. *American Psychologist*, 40, 1231–1239.

von Helmholtz, H. (1852). On the theory of compound colours. *Philosophical Magazine*, 4, 519–535.

Voyer, D., & Rodgers, M. (2002). Reliability of laterality effects in a dichotic listening task with nonverbal material. *Brain & Cognition*, 48, 602–606.

Voyer, D., Voyer, S., & Bryden, M. (1995). Magnitude of sex differences in spatial abilities: A meta-analysis and consideration of critical variables. *Psychological Bulletin*, 117(2), 250–270.

Vygotsky, L. S. (1934/1962). *Thought and language*. Cambridge, MA: MIT Press.

Vygotsky, L. S. (1978). *Mind in society: The development of higher psychological processes*. Cambridge, MA: Harvard University Press.

Vygotsky, L. S. (1987). Thought and word. In R. W. Riebe & A. S. Carton (Eds.), *The collected works of L. S. Vygotsky: Vol. 1. Problems of general psychology* (pp. 243–288). New York: Plenum Press.

Walker, L. J. (1991). Sex differences in moral reasoning. In W. M. Kurtines & J. L. Gewirtz (Eds.), *Handbook of moral behavior and development: Vol. 2. Research* (pp. 333–364). Hillsdale, NJ: Lawrence Erlbaum Associates.

Wampold, B. E. (1997). Methodological problems in identifying efficacious psychotherapies. *Psychotherapy Research*, 7, 21–43.

Ward, C., & Rana-Deuba, A. (1999). Acculturation and adaptation revisited. *Journal of Cross-Cultural Psychology*, 30, 422–442.

Ward, I. L. (1992). Sexual behavior: The product of parinatal hormonal and prepubertal social factors. In A. A. Gerall, H. Moltz, & I. L. Ward. (Eds.), *Handbook of behavioral neurobiology: Vol. 11. Sexual differentiation* (pp. 157–178). New York: Plenum Press.

Wartner, U. G., Grossmann, K., Fremmer-Bombik, E., & Suess, G. (1994). Attachment patterns at age six in south Germany: Predictability from infancy and implications for preschool behavior. *Child Development*, 65, 1014–1027.

Waterhouse, L. (2006a). Inadequate evidence for multiple intelligences, Mozart effect, and emotional intelligence theories. *Educational Psychologist*, 41(4), 247–255.

Waterhouse, L. (2006b). Multiple intelligences, the Mozart effect, and emotional intelligence: A critical review. *Educational Psychologist*, 41, 207–225.

Watkins, C. E., Campbell, V. L., Nieberding, R., & Hallmark, R. (1995). Contemporary practice of psychological assessment by clinical psychologists. *Professional Psychology: Research and Practice*, 26, 54–60.

Watkins, C. E., Jr., & Savickas, M. L. (1990). Psychodynamic career counseling. In W. B. Walsh & S. H. Osipow (Eds.), *Career counseling: Contemporary topics in vocational psychology* (pp. 79–116). Hillsdale, NJ: Lawrence Erlbaum Associates.

Watson, D., Suis, J., & Haig, J. (2002). Global self-esteem in relation to structural models of personality and affectivity. *Journal of Personality and Social Psychology*, 83, 185–197.

Watson, D. L., Hagihara, D. K., & Tenney, A. L. (1999). Skill-building exercises and generalizing psychological concepts to daily life. *Teaching of Psychology*, 26, 193–195.

Watson, J. B. (1913). Psychology as the behaviorist views it. *Psychological Review*, 20, 158–177.

Watson, J. B. (1924). *Behaviorism*. New York: W. W. Norton.

Watson, J. B., & Rayner, R. (1920). Conditioned emotional responses. *Journal of Experimental Psychology*, 3, 1–14.

Watt, H. M. G. (2000). Measuring attitudinal change in mathematics and English over the 1st year of junior high school: A multi-dimensional analysis. *Journal of Experimental Education*, 68, 331–361.

Webb, W. B. (1992). *Sleep: The gentle tyrant* (2nd ed.). Bolton, MA: Ander.

Wechsler, D. (1975). *The collected papers of David Wechsler*. New York: Academic Press.

Wechsler, D. (1981). *Wechsler Adult Intelligence Scale* (Rev.). San Antonio, TX: The Psychological Corporation.

Wechsler, D. (1990). *Wechsler Preschool and Primary Scale of Intelligence* (Rev.). Sidcup, Kent: The Psychological Corporation.

Wechsler, D. (1991). *Wechsler Intelligence Scale for Children* (3rd ed.). New York: The Psychological Corporation.

Wedding, D. (2004). Cross-cultural counseling and psychotherapy. In R. J. Corsini & D. Wedding (Eds.), *Current psychotherapies* (7th ed., p. 485). Itasca, IL: Peacock.

Weinberger, D. R. (1987). Implications of normal brain development for the pathogenesis of schizophrenia. *Archives of General Psychiatry*, 44, 660–668.

Weiner, B. (1985). An attributional theory of achievement motivation. *Psychological Review*, 92, 548–573.

Weiner, I. B. (1997). Current status of the Rorschach Inkblot Method. *Journal of Personality Assessment*, 68, 5–19.

Weiner, R. D. (2000). Retrograde amnesia with electroconvulsive therapy: Characteristics and implications. *Archives of General Psychiatry*, 57, 591–592.

Weis, S., Klaver, P., Reul, J., Elger, C. E., & Fernandez, G. (2004). Temporal and cerebellar brain regions that support both declarative memory formation and retrieval. *Cerebral Cortex*, 14, 256–267.

Weisman, A. (1972). *On dying and denying*. New York: Behavioral Publications.

Weisse, C. S. (1992). Depression and immunocompetence: A review of the literature. *Psychological Bulletin*, 111, 475–489.

Weissman, M. M., & Klerman, G. L. (1977). Sex differences and the epidemiology of depression. *Archives of General Psychiatry*, 34, 98–111.

Weissman, M. M., Bland, R., Joyce, P. R., Newman, S., Wells, J. E., & Wittchen, H. U. (1993). Sex differences in rates of depression: Cross-national perspectives. *Journal of Affective Disorders*, 29, 77–84.

Weizenbaum, J. (1976). *Computer power and human reason*. San Francisco: W. H. Freeman and Company.

Wender, P. H., Wolf, L. E., & Wasserstein, J. (2001). Adults with ADHD. An overview. *Annals of the New York Academy of Sciences*, 931, 1–16.

Wenneberg, S. R., Schneider, R. H., Walton, K. G., Maclean, C. R., Levitsky, D. K., Mandarino, J. V., et al. (1997). Anger expression correlates with platelet aggregation. *Behavioral Medicine*, 22(4), 174–177.

Wen-Shing, T., & Strelzer, J. (Eds.). (1997). *Culture and psychopathology: A guide to clinical assessment*. Bristol, PA: Brunner/Mazel.

Werker, J. F., & Lalonde, C. E. (1988). Cross-language speech perceptions: Initial capabilities and developmental change. *Developmental Psychology*, 24, 672–683.

Wertheimer, M. (1982). *Productive thinking*. Chicago: University of Chicago Press.

Westen, D. (2005). Cognitive neuroscience and psychotherapy: Implications for psychotherapy's second century. In G. Gabbard, J. Beck, & J. Holmes (Eds.), *Oxford textbook of psychotherapy*. Oxford, UK: Oxford University Press.

Wetherell, J. L. (2002). Behavior therapy for anxious older adults. *Behavior Therapist, 25*, 16–17.

White, G. L. (1980). Physical attractiveness and courtship progress. *Journal of Personality and Social Psychology, 39*, 660–668.

White, S. (2000). *The transgender debate (the crisis surrounding gender identity)*. Reading, UK Garnet Publishing.

Whittington, C. J., Kendall, T., Fonagy, P., Cottrell, D., Cotgrove, A., & Boddington, E. (2004). Selective serotonin reuptake inhibitors in childhood depression: Systematic review of published versus unpublished data. *Lancet, 363*(9418), 1341–1345.

WHO International Consortium in Psychiatric Epidemiology. (2000). Cross-national comparisons of the prevalences and correlates of mental disorders. *Bulletin of the World Health Organization, 78*(4), 413–426.

Widiger, T. A., & Weissman, M. M. (1991). Epidemiology of borderline personality disorder. *Hospital and Community Psychiatry, 42*, 1015–1021.

Williams, M. E. (1995). *The American Geriatrics Society's complete guide to aging and mental health*. New York: Random House, Inc.

Williams, R. B. (1999). A 69-year-old man with anger and angina. *Journal of the American Medical Association, 282*, 763–770.

Williams, R. B., Haney, T. L., Lee, K. L., Kong, Y. H., Blumenthal, J. A., & Whalen, R. E. (1980). Type A behavior, hostility, and coronary atherosclerosis. *Psychosomatic Medicine, 42*(6), 539–549.

Williamson, A. M., & Feyer, A. M. (2000). Moderate sleep deprivation produces impairments in cognitive and motor performance equivalent to legally prescribed levels of alcohol intoxication. *Journal of Occupational and Environmental Medicine, 57*(10), 649–655.

Wilson, R. S., Mendes de Leon, C. F., Barnes, L. L., Schneider, J. A., Bienias, J. L., Evans, D. A., et al. (2002). Participation in cognitively stimulating activities and risk of incident Alzheimer disease. *Journal of the American Medical Association, 287*, 742–748.

Wilson, S., Becker, L., & Tinker, R. (1995). Eye movement desensitization and reprocessing (EMDR) treatment for psychologically traumatized individuals. *Journal of Consulting and Clinical Psychology, 63*, 928–937.

Winningham, R. G., Hyman, I. E., Jr., & Dinnel, D. L. (2000). Flashbulb memories? The effects of when the initial memory report was obtained. *Memory, 8*, 209–216.

Witelson, S. F. (1991). Neural sexual mosaicism: Sexual differentiation of the human temporo-pariatal region for functional asymmetry. *Psychoneuroendocrinology, 16*, 131–153.

Wolberg, L. R. (1977). *The technique of psychotherapy*. New York: Grune & Stratton.

Wolpe, J. (1958). *Psychotherapy by reciprocal inhibition*. Stanford, CA: Stanford University Press.

Wood, J. M., Nezworski, M. T., & Stejskal, W. J. (1996). The comprehensive system for the Rorschach: A critical examination. *Psychological Science, 7*(1), 3–10, 14–17.

Wurtman, R., & Wurtman, J. (1989, January). Carbohydrates and depression. *Scientific American*.

Wyman, P. A., Moynihan, J., Eberly, S., Cox, C., Cross, W., Jin, X., et al. (2007). Association of family stress with natural killer cell activity and the frequency of illnesses in children. *Archives of Pediatric and Adolescent Medicine, 161*, 228–234.

Wynne, C. (1999). Do animals think? The case against the animal mind. *Psychology Today, 32*(6), 50–53.

Yalom, I. (1995). *The theory and practice of group psychotherapy* (4th ed.). New York: Basic Books.

Ybarra, O. (1999). Misanthropic person memory when the need to self-enhance is absent. *Personality and Social Psychology Bulletin, 25*, 261–269.

Yerkes, R. M. (1921). Psychological examining in the United States Army. *Memoirs of the National Academy of Sciences, 15*, 1–890.

Yerkes, R. M., & Dodson, J. D. (1908). The relation of strength of stimulus to rapidity of habit formation. *Journal of Comparative Neurology and Psychology, 18*, 459–482.

Ying, Y. W. (1990). Explanatory models of major depression and implications for help-seeking among immigrant Chinese-American women. *Culture, Medicine, and Psychiatry, 14*, 393–408.

Young, T. (1802). On the theory of light and colors. *Philosophical Transactions of the Royal Society, 91*, 12–49.

Yule, G. (1996). *Pragmatics*. Oxford, UK: Oxford University Press.

Zajonc, R. B. (1965). Social facilitation. *Science, 149*, 269–274.

Zajonc, R. B. (1968). Attitudinal effects of mere exposure. *Journal of Personality and Social Psychology Monographs, 9*(2), 1–27.

Zajonc, R. B. (1998). Emotions. In D. T. Gilbert & S. T. Fiske (Eds.), *Handbook of social psychology* (4th ed., vol. 1, pp. 591–632). New York: McGraw-Hill.

Zajonc, R. B., Heingartner, A., & Herman, E. M. (1970). Social enhancement and impairment of performance in the cockroach. *Journal of Social Psychology, 13*(2), 83–92.

Zanarini, M. C. (2000). Childhood experiences associated with the development of borderline personality disorder. *Psychiatric Clinics of North America, 23*(1), 89–101.

Zeki, S. (2001). Localization and globalization in conscious vision. *Annual Review of Neuroscience, 24*, 57–86.

Zentall, T. R. (2000). Animal intelligence. In R. J. Sternberg (Ed.), *Handbook of intelligence*. Cambridge: Cambridge University Press.

Zhou, J. N., Hofman, M. A., Gooren, L. J. G., & Swaab, D. F. (1995). A sex difference in the human brain and its relation to transsexuality. *Nature, 378*, 68–70.

Zilles, K. (1990). Cortex. In G. Paxinos (Ed.), *The human nervous system* (pp. 757–802). San Diego, CA: Academic.

Zillmann, D., Baron, R., & Tamborini, R. (1981). Social costs of smoking: Effects of tobacco smoke on hostile behavior. *Psychology Journal of Applied Social, 11*, 548–561.

Zimbardo, P. (1971). The pathology of imprisonment. *Society, 9*(4–8), 4.

Zorilla, E. P., Luborsky, L., McKay, J. R., Rosenthal, R., Houldin, A., Tax, A., et al. (2001). The relationship of depression and stressors to immunological assays: A meta-analytic review. *Brain, Behavior, and Immunity, 15*, 199–226.

Zuckerman, M. (1979). *Sensation seeking: Beyond the optimal level of arousal*. Hillsdale, NJ: Lawrence Erlbaum Associates.

Zuckerman, M. (1994). *Behavioral expression and biosocial bases of sensation seeking*. New York: Cambridge University Press.

Zuckerman, M. (2002). Zuckerman-Kuhlman Personality Questionnaire (ZKPQ): An alternative five-factorial model. In B. De Raad & M. Perugini (Eds.), *Big five assessment* (pp. 377–396). Seattle, WA: Hogrefe & Huber Publishers.

Zvolensky, M. J., Schmidt, M. B., & Stewart, S. H. (2003). Panic disorder and smoking. *Clinical Psychology: Science and Practice, 10*, 29–51.

Credits

PHOTO CREDITS

Chapter 1
Page 2 Thomas Northcut/Photodisc/Getty Images; 3D4Medical.com/Getty Images, Inc–3DClinic; **Page 3** Digital Zoo/Getty Images, Inc.; Dave King © Dorling Kindersley; Andy Crawford © Dorling Kindersley; Photodisc/Getty Images; Dex Image\Jupiter Images Royalty Free; Alperium\Shutterstock; **Page 5** Jeff Greenberg\The Image Works; Courtesy of Matthew Paul Gendler; **Page 6** German Information Center; **Page 7** Archives of the History of American Psychology–The University of Akron; **Page 8** Courtesy of Gina Chedid; Getty Images, Inc.–Hulton Archive Photos; **Page 9** G. Paul Bishop; **Page 10** "Courtesy of Dr. Arthur W. Toga, Laboratory of Neuro Imaging"; **Page 11** © Peter Barrett/CORBIS All Rights Reserved; **Page 17** Michael K. Nichols/National Geographic Image Collection; **Page 18** The Warren Anatomical Museum, Francis A. Countway Library of Medicine, Harvard Medical School; **Page 19** Courtesy of Adel Ephraheey; **Page 20** © The New Yorker Collection 1994 Leo Cullum from cartoonbank.com. All Rights Reserved; **Page 21** Courtesy of Chris Meola; **Page 22** © John Henley/CORBIS All Rights Reserved; Courtesy of Glenn Brown; **Page 23** ©The New Yorker Collection 1999 Tom Chalkley from cartoonbank.com. All Rights Reserved; **Page 24** © Peter M. Fisher/CORBIS All Rights Reserved; **Page 27** Courtesy of Joanna DePierro; **Page 38** Michael K. Nichols/National Geographic Image Collection; **Page 39** © The New Yorker Collection 1999 Tom Chalkley from cartoonbank.com. All Rights Reserved.

Chapter 2
Page 40 3D4Medicalcom\Getty Images, Inc–3DClinic; **Page 41** 3D4Medicalcom\Getty Images, Inc–3DClinic; Ryan McVay/Image Bank/Getty Images; **Page 51** Courtesy of Sara Watson; **Page 55** SPL\Photo Researchers, Inc.; Alfred Pasieka\Photo Researchers, Inc.; Pete Saloutos\CORBIS–NY; Tim Beddow\Photo Researchers, Inc.; Philippe Psaila\Photo Researchers, Inc.; **Page 62** Courtesy of Christina Petruzzelli; **Page 63** Medicalpicture\Alamy Images; **Page 64** © George Simian/CORBIS All Rights Reserved; **Page 67** Courtesy of Matthew Paul Taylor; Courtesy of Santi Aragon; **Page 68** Courtesy of Myesha Oowtin; Peter Hvizdak\The Image Works; **Page 69** Julia Margaret Cameron/bilwissedition.com/Photolibrary; **Page 70** ClassicStock\Alamy Images.

Chapter 3
Page 76 Dave King © Dorling Kindersley; **Page 77** Dave King © Dorling Kindersley; PM Images/Taxi/Getty Images; **Page 79** Courtesy of Zenaida Oyola; **Page 80** Design Pics Inc\Alamy Images Royalty Free; Science Photo Library\Alamy Images Royalty Free; D. Hurst\Alamy Images Royalty Free; CreativeAct-Emotions Series\Alamy Images Royalty Free; Cris Cordeiro\Photolibrary.com; Corbis\Superstock Royalty Free; **Page 83** Photo Researchers, Inc.; **Page 84** Fritz Goro\Getty Images/Time Life Pictures; **Page 85** Courtesy of Francine Y. Kelly; **Page 89** Omikron/Photo Researchers, Inc.; **Page 90** Courtesy of Savannah Boyd; **Page 91** Robin Sachs\PhotoEdit, Inc.; Courtesy of Samantha Vitello; **Page 92** © Vince Streano/CORBIS All Rights Reserved; **Page 97** Mark Richards/PhotoEdit; **Page 100** Larry Landolfi\Photo Researchers, Inc.; **Page 107** © Vince Streano/CORBIS All Rights Reserved.

Chapter 4
Page 108 Corbis RF; Photodisc/Getty Images; Photodisc/Getty Images; **Page 109** Corbis RF; Photodisc/Getty Images; Jean Luc Morales/Image Bank/Getty Images; **Page 110** Courtesy of Bryan Scott; **Page 113** Courtesy of Molly Jansen; **Page 116** © Mark Seelen/Zefa/CORBIS All Rights Reserved; **Page 117** Pool/Getty Images, Inc.; **Page 118** Courtesy of Brenda Smith; **Page 119** © Sven Hagolani/Zefa/CORBIS All Rights Reserved; **Page 120** Courtesy of Daniel Wilson; **Page 121** Doug Menuez\Getty Images, Inc.–Photodisc; **Page 123** © Solus-Veer/CORBIS All Rights Reserved; **Page 124** Courtesy of Amanda Ramirez; **Page 128** © Thinkstock/CORBIS All Rights Reserved; **Page 131** © Ed Kashi/CORBIS All Rights Reserved; Courtesy of John Martin; **Page 132** Courtesy of Santi Aragon; **Page 139** © Solus-Veer/CORBIS All Rights Reserved.

Chapter 5
Page 140–141 DAJ/Getty Images, Inc.; **Page 140** © Mark Seelen/CORBIS All Rights Reserved; Joos Mind/Taxi/Getty Images; **Page 141** Soren Hald/Stone/Getty Images; Joos Mind/Taxi/Getty Images; C-Squared Studios\Getty Images, Inc.–Photodisc/Royalty Free; **Page 143** Digital Art\CORBIS–NY; Courtesy of Christina Petruzzelli; **Page 149** Photo Lennart Nilsson/Bonnier Alba AB, A CHILD IS BORN, Dell Publishing Company; Lennart Nilsson\Scanpix Sweden AB; **Page 150** Bloomimage\Corbis RF; Mimi Forsyth; Laura Elliott\Jupiter Images Royalty Free; E. Crews\The Image Works; Laura Dwight\Laura Dwight Photography; Courtesy of Matthew Paul Gendler; **Page 152** Elizabeth Crews\Elizabeth Crews Photography; Geri Engberg\Geri Engberg Photography; Kathleen Sleys; Jo Foord © Dorling Kindersley; Dave King © Dorling Kindersley; **Page 154** Courtesy of Molly Jansen; **Page 156** Mike Good © Dorling Kindersley; **Page 158** Harry F. Harlow\Harlow Primate Laboratory/University of Wisconsin; **Page 164** Courtesy of Joni Saladino; **Page 165** Michael Gibson/Paramount Pictures\CORBIS–NY; **Page 168** Mike Greenlar\The Image Works; **Page 174** Digital Art\CORBIS–NY; E. Crews\The Image Works; **Page 189** Courtesy of Ryan Ryan; **Page 199** Courtesy of Jennifer Crisp.

Chapter 6
Page 176 Stockbyte/Getty Images, Inc.; **Page 177** Stockbyte/Getty Images, Inc.; Dave King © Dorling Kindersley; Tim Ridley © Dorling Kindersley; **Page 180** Courtesy of Tracy Klopfer; **Page 191** Bonnie Kamin\PhotoEdit Inc.; **Page 196** Albert Bandura, Stanford University; **Page 202** © Carson Ganci/Design Pics/Corbis; **Page 203** © (Photographer)/CORBIS All Rights Reserved; **Page 210** Albert Bandura, Stanford University; **Page 211** © Carson Ganci/Design Pics/Corbis; © (Photographer)/CORBIS All Rights Reserved.

Chapter 7
Page 212 Alperium\Shutterstock; Bryan Mullennix/Iconica/Getty Images, Inc.; **Page 213** Ryan McVay/Photodisc/Getty Images; Dex Image\Jupiter Images; Bill Reitzel/Photographer's Choice/Getty Images; Bryan Mullennix/Iconica/Getty Images, Inc.; Iconica\Getty Images–Iconica; **Page 216** Courtesy of Danielle N. Ring; **Page 218** Courtesy of Anthony Yetto; **Page 224** Courtesy of Zenaida Oyola; **Page 226** Courtesy of Laura Duffy; **Page 230** Courtesy of Mike Burns; **Page 233** CORBIS–NY; **Page 236** Courtesy of Myesha Oowtin; Courtesy of Alondra Santos; **Page 238** Courtesy of Adel Ebraheey; **Page 239** Philip G. Zimbardo, Inc.; **Page 240** Courtesy of Bryan Scott.

Chapter 8
Page 248 Geoff Brightling/Peter Minister–modelmaker © Dorling Kindersley; Clive Boursnell © Dorling Kindersley; **Page 249** Shutterstock; Clive Boursnell © Dorling Kindersley; Shutterstock; Image Source\Jupiter Images; **Page 251** Jim West\Alamy Images; Courtesy of Gina Chedid; **Page 253** Peter Titmuss\Alamy Images; **Page 254** Courtesy of Adel Ephraheey; **Page 255** Courtesy of Matthew Paul Gendler; **Page 258** Fotosearch\Superstock Royalty Free; **Page 262** David Young-Wolff/Stone/Getty Images; Courtesy of Morgan Soltes; **Page 263** Ellen Senisi; **Page 264** © (Photographer)/CORBIS All Rights Reserved; **Page 270** Peter Titmuss\Alamy Images; **Page 271** David Young-Wolff/Stone/Getty Images; © (Photographer)/CORBIS All Rights Reserved.

Chapter 9
Page 272 Digital Zoo/Getty Images, Inc.; **Page 273** PunchStock–Royalty Free; Digital Zoo/Getty Images, Inc.; **Page 277** Courtesy of Meredith Werbler; Juliet Brauner\Alamy Images; **Page 279** Courtesy of Anthony Yetto; **Page 286** Courtesy of Julie Asher; **Page 289** © Craig Lassig/EPA/CORBIS All Rights Reserved; **Page 290** Courtesy of Catherine Murphy; **Page 291** Jim Cummins\Getty Images, Inc.–Taxi; **Page 292** Courtesy of Alondra Santos; **Page 296** © Gary Caskey/EPA/CORBIS All Rights Reserved; **Page 297** Courtesy of John Martin.

Chapter 10
Page 305 Jupiter Images; Rosemary Calvert\Getty Images–Digital Vision; **Page 307** Courtesy of Christina Falcon; **Page 308** © Phil Banko/CORBIS All Rights Reserved; **Page 309** Dave Watts\Nature Picture Library; **Page 310** Creative Studios\Alamy Images Royalty Free; D. Hurst\Alamy Images Royalty Free; Anatoly Vartanov\Alamy Images Royalty Free; Ocean\Corbis RF; Aleksandr Ugorenkov\Alamy Images Royalty Free; Shawn Hempel\Shutterstock; Valentyn Volkov\Alamy Images Royalty Free; Photosindia.com LLC\Alamy Images Royalty Free; Courtesy of Jessica Decker; **Page 311** Laura Dwight Photography; **Page 312** Courtesy of Ryan Ryan; **Page 313** © Simon Marcus/CORBIS All Rights Reserved; AP Wide World Photos; **Page 322** David Grossman\Photo Researchers, Inc.; **Page 325** Randy Olson\Aurora Photos, Inc.; **Page 331** Courtesy of Everton Allen; **Page 332** Courtesy of Andria Randazzo; **Page 338** Photosindia.com LLC\Alamy Images Royalty Free; Creative Studios\Alamy Images Royalty Free; D. Hurst\Alamy Images Royalty Free; Anatoly Vartanov\Alamy Images Royalty Free; Ocean\Corbis RF; Aleksandr Ugorenkov\Alamy Images Royalty Free; Shawn Hempel\Shutterstock; Valentyn Volkov\Alamy Images Royalty Free.

Chapter 11
Page 340–341 Steve Gorton © Dorling Kindersley; **Page 340** Andy Crawford © Dorling Kindersley; **Page 341** PunchStock–Royalty Free; **Page 345** Courtesy of Christopher Baker; **Page 348** Courtesy of Glen Brown; **Page 349** Dr. Neal E. Miller, Yale University; **Page 351** Ryan McVay/Getty Images, Inc.; Trinette Reed\CORBIS–NY; **Page 353** Courtesy of Joanna DePierro; **Page 355** David Roth/Stone/Getty Images; **Page 359** Barbara Penoya\Getty Images, Inc.–Photodisc/Royalty Free; © Morgan David de Lossy/CORBIS All Rights Reserved; © Pixland/CORBIS All Rights Reserved; © Guido Alberto Rossi/TIPS Images; Chris Carroll\CORBIS–NY; Costa Manos\Magnum Photos, Inc.; **Page 360** Courtesy of Francine Y. Kelly; **Page 364** Vixit\Shutterstock; **Page 367** Skjold Photographs.

CR-1

Chapter 12
Page 374 ColorBlind Images/Iconica/Getty Images, Inc.; VALUELINE/PUNCHSTOCK/GETTY IMAGES, Inc.; **Page 375** Emilio Simion/Photodisc/Getty Images; Riko Pictures/Digital Vision/Getty Images, Inc.; (Photographer)/Image Bank/Getty Images; © Image Source/Corbis; Ron Krisel\Jupiter Images; Comstock Images\Thinkstock; **Page 378** Courtesy of Britany Hayes; **Page 382** © Bettmann/CORBIS All Rights Reserved; **Page 383** Courtesy of John Martin; **Page 384** Courtesy of Matthew V. Store; **Page 391** Courtesy of Everton Allen; **Page 393** Don Martinetti; **Page 395** Courtesy of Luke Thema; **Page 399** Courtesy of Myesha Oowtin.

Chapter 13
Page 408 Andy Crawford © Dorling Kindersley; **Page 409** Kevin Mackintosh/Stone/Getty Images; Andy Crawford © Dorling Kindersley; **Page 413** Courtesy of Jessica Decker; **Page 415** © Alan Schein Photography/CORBIS All Rights Reserved; **Page 420** Courtesy of Matthew Paul Gendler; **Page 423** Courtesy of Bryan Scott; **Page 424** © B. Bird/Zefa/CORBIS All Rights Reserved; **Page 426** New York Daily News; **Page 429** Courtesy of Santi Aragon; **Page 431** Eli Reed\Everett Collection.

Chapter 14
Page 444 Stockbyte\Getty Images–Stockbyte, Royalty Free; **Page 445** Stockbyte\Getty Images–Stockbyte, Royalty Free; **Page 447** Charles Ciccione\Photo Researchers, Inc.; **Page 450** Courtesy of Vincent Apellaniz; **Page 451** Zigy Kaluzny\Getty Images, Inc.–Stone Allstock; **Page 453** Charles Vandermast, Delft University of Technology; **Page 456** Courtesy of Jennifer Crisp; **Page 461** Courtesy of Meredith Werbler; **Page 469** © Bettmann/CORBIS All Rights Reserved; **Page 470** © M. Deutsch/Zefa/CORBIS All Rights Reserved; **Page 472** © Tom Stewart/CORBIS All Rights Reserved; **Page 479** © Tom Stewart/CORBIS All Rights Reserved.

Chapter 15
Page 480–481 Jupiter Images PictureArts Corporation/Brand X Royalty Free; **Page 480** Ian Sanderson/Photographer's Choice/Getty Images; Giantstep Inc./Image Bank/Getty Images; **Page 481** Giantstep Inc./Image Bank/Getty Images; Ron Chappie\Jupiter Images–Thinkstock Images Royalty Free; Ian Sanderson/Photographer's Choice/Getty Images; **Page 482** Courtesy of Catherine Murphy; **Page 485** Courtesy of John Martin; **Page 487** Gary Conner\PhotoEdit, Inc.; **Page 493** © Mary Kate Denny/PhotoEdit, Inc.; **Page 498** Courtesy of Akeem James; **Page 499** Courtesy of Luke Thema; **Page 501** Fred Prouser/Reuters\CORBIS–NY; **Page 504** Lev Olkha\Shutterstock; Lev Olkha\Shutterstock; Lev Olkha\Shutterstock; Courtesy of Victoria A. King; **Page 505** Getty Images–Stockbyte, Royalty Free.

Chapter 16
Page 512–513 Marc Romanelli/Photodisc/Getty Images; **Page 513** Ryan McVay/Photodisc/Getty Images; Getty Images, Inc–Stockbyte, Royalty Free; **Page 515** Peace Corps; **Page 517** Courtesy of Mike Burns; **Page 518** Michal Heron\Michal Heron Photography; **Page 519** Courtesy of Andria Randazzo; **Page 522** Will & Deni McIntyre/Science Source\Photo Researchers, Inc.; **Page 523** Dan McCoy\Rainbow Image Library; **Page 524** John Neubauer\PhotoEdit, Inc.; **Page 526** Courtesy of AT&T Archives and History Center, Warren, NJ; **Page 532** Michal Heron\Michal Heron Photography; **Page 533** Peace Corps; Courtesy of AT&T Archives and History Center, Warren, NJ.

TEXT CREDITS

Chapter 1
Page 11, F1.01a Characteristics of Doctoral Scientists and Engineers in the United States, 2003. NSF 06320; 1.01b "Subfields of Psychology" by M. Hess, T. B. Hoffer, V. Welch, Jr., K. Williams, Doctorate Recipients from United States Universities: Summary Report 2006. Copyright © 2007. Reprinted by permission of Tom W. Smith, GSS Director, NORC.

Chapter 4
Page 4–11, Figure 9.1 Figure, "Sleep Patterns of Infants and Adults" from "Ontogenetic Development of the Human Sleep Dream Cycle" by Howard P. Roffwarg, Joseph N. Muzio, William C. Dement, Science (1966), 152, pp. 604–619. Copyright © 2966 by American Association for the Advancement of Science. Reprinted by permission of AAAS; **Page 4–15,** Module 9.02 Figure, "EEG Results of brain activity during both waking and sleeping." Courtesy of Dr. Leslie Sherlin.

Chapter 7
Page 7–31, Figure 20.1 Figure from "Triangulating Love" (pp. 119–138) by Robert Sternberg in THE PSYCHOLOGY OF LOVE, ed. by Robert J. Sternberg. Copyright © 1986. Reprinted by permission of Yale University Press.

Chapter 8
Page 8:16–17, Table 8.2 Excerpt from Shepard, Thomas H., MD CATALOG OF TERATOGENIC AGENTS 10th edition. Copyright © 2001 by The Johns Hopkins University Press. Reprinted with permission of The Johns Hopkins University Press; Figure 21.1 Adapted from Markus & Kitayama, 1991; **Page 240,** Table 21.1 Adapted from Markus & Kitayama, 1991.

Chapter 9
Page 9–26, Module 24.01 Derived from data in Godden & Baddeley, 1975; **Page 9–41,** Module 24.04 From "Long-Term Memory for a Common Object" by R. S. Nickerson & J. J. Adams, Cognitive Psychology (1979), 11, 287–307. Copyright © 1979. Reprinted by permission from Elsevier.

Chapter 10
Page 7, Figure 25.1 From "Visual Images Preserve Metric Spatial Information: Evidence from Studies of Image Scanning" by Kosslyn et al., Journal of Experimental Psychology: Human Perception and Performance (1978), 4, 47–60. American Psychological Association; **Page 14,** Figure 25.2 Adapted from p. 576 in "Family Resemblances: Studies in the Internal Structures of Categories" by E. Rosch and C. Mervis, Cognitive Psychology, (1975), 7, 573–605. Elsevier Publishing Company; **Page 56–57,** Table 26.2 DSM-IV-TR Classification for Mental Retardation from THE DIAGNOSTIC AND STATISTICAL MANUAL OF MENTAL DISORDERS, Fourth Edition, Text Revision. Copyright © 2000 by American Psychiatric Association. Reprinted by permission of American Psychiatric Publishing, Inc.; Table 32.1 "The Axis I Disorders" from DIAGNOSTIC AND STATISTICAL MANUAL FOR MENTAL DISORDERS, Fourth Edition. Copyright © 2000 by American Psychiatric Association. Reprinted by permission of American Psychiatric Publishing, Inc.; **Page 63,** Table 26.3 STANFORD-BINET INTELLIGENCE SCALES, Fifth Edition by G. H. Roid. Riverside Publishing Company, 2003; **Page 64,** Table 26.4 Simulated items similar to those in the WECHSLER ADULT INTELLIGENCE SCALE, Third Edition (1997);

Chapter 11
Page 16, Figure 27.3 From MOTIVATION AND PERSONALITY, 3rd edition by Abraham H. Maslow, ed. by Robert D. Frager & James Fadiman. Copyright © 1987. Printed and electronically reproduced by Pearson Education, Inc., Upper Saddle River, New Jersey; Table 27.1 Five sample items from the Zuckerman-Kuhlman Personality Questionnaire (ZKPQ): An alternative five-factorial model by Marvin Zuckerman, published on pp. 377–396 in BIG FIVE ASSESSMENT by Boele de Raad & Marco Perugini, ISBN-0-88937-242-X. Copyright © 2002 by Hogrefe & Huber Publishers. Seattle-Toronto-Bern-Gottingen. Reprinted by permission of the publisher; Table 27.1 "Sample items from the Zuckerman-Kuhlman Personality Questionnaire" by Marvin Zuckerman in BIG FIVE ASSESSMENT, ed. by B. De Raad and M. Perugini. Copyright © 2002. Reprinted by permission of Dr. Marvin Zuckerman.

Chapter 12
Page 25, Figure 30.2 Data derived from Cattell, Eber, and Tatsuoka: HANDBOOK FOR THE SIXTEEN PERSONALITY FACTOR QUESTIONNAIRE (16PF [R]), Copyright © 1970, 1988, 1992 by the Institute for Personality and Ability Testing, Inc. (IPAT), Champaign, Illinois, USA. All rights reserved. 16PF is a registered trademark of IPAT, Inc.; Figure 29.4 Figure, "The Big Five" from PERSONALITY IN ADULTHOOD, 2nd edition by Paul T. Costa and Robert R. MacCrae. Copyright © 1990. Reprinted by permission of Guilford Publications, Inc.; Figure 30.2 Figure, "Personalities of Identical and Fraternal Twins" from GENES AND ENVIRONMENT IN PERSONALITY DEVELOPMENT, 2nd edition by J. C. Loehlin. Copyright © 1992. Reprinted by permission of Sage Publications, Inc.

Chapter 13
Page 13–28, Figure 32.4 From DSM-IV-TR, 2000; **Page 13–36,** Figure 32.5 "Genetics and Schizophrenia-Incidence of Schizophrenia Among Related and Unrelated Individuals" graph from SCHIZOPHRENIA GENESIS: The Origins of Madness by Irving I. Gottesman. Copyright © 1990 by Irving I. Gottesman. Reprinted by arrangement with Henry Holt and Company, LLC; **Page 13–39,** Figure 32.6 Courtesy of Steven Potkin, MD, Professor of Psychiatry, University of California Irvine Medical Center.

Chapter 14
Page 14: 61–62, Table 14.5 "Summary of Personality Disorders Types" from DIAGNOSTIC AND STATISTICAL MANUAL FOR MENTAL DISORDERS, Fourth Edition. Copyright © 2000 by American Psychiatric Association. Reprinted by permission of American Psychiatric Publishing, Inc.

Chapter 15
Page 23, Figure 36.2 Miller et al., 1991, 1996; Table 35.1 "The Social Readjustment Rating Scale" by T. H. Holmes & R. H. Rahe, Journal of Psychosomatic Research (1967), 11, 213–218. Elsevier Science Ltd; Table 35.2 "A Life Stress Instrument for Classroom Use" by M. J. Renner & R. S. Mackin, Teaching of Psychology (1998), 25, 47. Reprinted by permission of Taylor & Francis, Inc.

CR-2 CREDITS

Name Index

A

Abadinsky, H., 132
Abbott, L., 128
Abe, K., 116
Abela, J. R. Z., 454
Abramson, L. Y., 385
Adam, K., 113
Adams, D. B., 238
Adams, R. J., 151
Adler, A., T381–382, 382
Adolphs, R., 60, 359
Affleck, G., 366
Aggleton, J. P., 238
Aghajanian, G. K., 131
Agnew-Davies, R., 460
Agresti, A., 26
Aguiar, A., 155
Ahn, W., 309
Ahokas, A., 408
Aiello, J. R., 219
Ainsworth, M. D. S., 156, T157
Aitchison, J., 309
Aito, M., 408
Ajzen, I., 225
Akana, S., 350
Aladdin, R., 112
Albert, D. J., 238
Alexander, C., 123
Alexander, C. N., 123
Al-Hazan, 100
Aligne, C. A., 486
Alkon, D., 283
Allen, G. E., 330
Allen, L. S., 264
Alloy, L. B., 199
Allport, G. W., T387, 387
Alm, H., 111
Almeida, D. A., 238
Alpert, N. M., 307
Altamura, C., 56
Altemus, M., 355, 424
Alvarez, J., 232, 233
Alvarez, J. M., 348
Amabile, T., 487
Amatomi, M., 116
American Association of University Women, 264
American Association on Intellectual and Developmental Disabilities, 324
American Foundation for Suicide Prevention, 493
American Psychiatric Association, 261, 324, 326, 350, 351, 418, 419, 422, 425, 427, 428, 429, 430, 431, 432, 433, 434, 435, 467, 468, 492
American Psychological Association, 6–7, 23, 516, 519, 520, 522
American Self-Help Clearinghouse, 473
Ames, D. R., 230
Ames, M. A., 354
Anand, B. K., 349
Anastasi, A., 395
Andayani, S., 258
Andersen, J., 491
Anderson, C. A., 238, 240, 364
Anderson, J. R., 286
Anderson, J. W., 123
Anderson, K. E., 319
Anderson, M., 463
Anderson, M. C., 295
Anderson, N. D., 168, 319
Andreasen, N. C., 431
Andreski, P., 492
Andrews, C., 203
Andrews, J. D. W., 457
Angleitner, A., 387, 389
Angst, M., 61
Antuono, P. G., 297
Anxiety Disorders Association of America, 473
Araki, S., 325
Arand, D., 121
Archer, J., 238
Argamon, S., 265
Argyle, M., 263
Arkowitz, H., 454
Armstrong, M. S., 463
Arnett, P. A., 435
Arnow, B., 446, 465, 470
Aron, A., 26
Aron, E. N., 26
Aronson, E., 226
Aronson J., 235
Aronson, M., 319
Asarnow, R. F., 431
Asch, S. E., T215, 215–216
Aserinsky, E., 113
Ashmore, R. D., 236
Atkinson, R. C., 279
Augustyn, M., 127
Auinger, P., 325, 486
Avia, M. D., 389
Avis, D., 60
Ayllon, T., 463

B

Baberg, H. T., 127
Bachg, D., 490
Bachman, J., 133
Bachman, M., 232
Backenstraβ, M., 385
Backer, B., 168
Baddeley, A. D., 274, 278, 286, 291
Baddeley, J. C., 278
Badrick, E., 491
Baehr, E. K., 111
Baer, D. M., 192
Baer, L., 469
Bagiella, E., 498
Bahrick, H., 279
Bahrick, H. P., 291
Bailey, J. M., 354
Baillargeon, R., 155
Bain, E., 389
Baker, L. A., 204
Baker, R. W., 468
Balin, A. K., 167
Balkin, T., 112
Ball, K., 168, 319
Ball, T. M., 307
Ballantine, H. T., Jr., 469
Bandura, A., T384, 182, 195, 196, 239, 364, 384, 385, 454
Baraban, J. M., 467
Bard, P., T361, 361
Barefoot, J. C., 497, 498
Bargh, J. A., 101
Barkham, M., 460
Barkley, R. A., 169
Barnes, L. L., 319
Barnes, V., 123
Barnyard, P., 279
Baron, J. N., 240
Baron, R., 238
Barondes, S. H., 430
Barresi, B., 205
Barrett, A., 362
Barrett, D., 217
Barrett, R. H., 463
Barry, K. L., 132
Barry, T., 238
Barsalou, L. W., 178
Barsh, G. S., 350, 351
Barstow, A. L., 411
Bartels, A., 237, 355
Barter, K., 186
Bartlett, N. R., 83
Barton, M. E., 309
Bartoshuk, L. M., 89
Basadur, M., 315
Bass, J., 458
Battaglia, M., 435
Battjes, R. J., 451
Bauer, P. J., 297
Baumeister, R. F., 364
Baumert, J., 399
Bavelier, D., 56
Bayliss, D. M., 278
Beardsley, T., 333
Beary, J., 123
Beck, A. T., 424, 454, 457
Beck, J. S., 457
Becker, L., 463
Beehr, T. A., 501
Beer, J. M., 382
Beery, L. C., 490
Behar, C., 238
Bekkering, H., 64
Belch, G. E., 226
Belenky, G., 112
Bell, K. L., 319
Bell, M. E., 350
Bell, P. A., 364
Bellavia, G. M., 399
Belletti, A., 201
Bellisle, F., 182
Bellizzi, J. A., 401
Bellodi, L., 435
Belsky, J., 157
Bemporad, J. R., 259
Benet-Martínez, V., 254
Bengel, D., 424
Benjafield, J. J. G., 379
Benjamin, J., 424
Benjamin, S. L., 436
Bennet, D. A., 319
Bennett, S., 186
Bennis, W.G., 221
Benowitz, N. L., 128
Ben-Poarth, Y. S., 395
Bensasi, S., 469
Benson, H., 123
Berch, D. B., 168, 319
Berenbaum, S. A., 262
Berger, S. A., 291
Bergman, H. F., 396
Beringer, L., 429
Berk, L. E., 203
Berk, L. S., 500
Berkowitz, B., 463
Berkowitz, F., 56
Berkowitz, L., 238, 240, 499
Bermond, B., 361
Bernardeschi, L., 435
Berry, J. W., 487
Berscheid, E., 234, 236
Bertenthal, B. I., 364
Berteretche, M. V., 182
Best, D. L., 263
Betancourt, J. R., 461
Betancourt, T., 458
Betz, N. E., 351
Beutler, L. E., 454
Beymer, K., 468
Bhatnagar, S., 350
Biederman, J., 169
Bienias, J. L., 319
Bierhals, A. J., 490
Billingsley, D., 186
Bindman, A. B., 241
Binet, A., T327, 327
Binkofski, F., 64
Birch, J. W., 512
Birman, D., 254
Bishop, P., 355
Bittman, B. B., 500
Bivens, J. A., 203
Bixler, E., 116
Bjork, E. L., 295
Bjork, R. A., 124, 286, 287, 295
Black, D. W., 427, 431
Black, M. J., 449
Blaine, J. D., 451
Blair, R. J. R., 435
Blanchard, E. B., 454
Blanchard, M., 157
Blanchard-Fields, F., 230
Blanco, C., 425
Bland, R., 429
Blass, T., 218
Blatt, S. D., 127
Blazer, D., 435
Blazer, D. G., 429, 503
Blehar, M. C., 156
Bleuler, E., 430
Blits, B., 56
Block, R. I., 131
Blommel, J. M., 219
Bloom, J. R., 458
Bloom, L., 156
Bloom, P., 156, 203, 227
Bloom, S. R., 349
Blumenthal, J., 163

NI-1

Name Index

Blumenthal, J. A., 497
Blumer, D., 429
Boddington, E., 470
Bogle, K. D., 230
Bolger, N., 366
Bolton, E. E., 457
Bolton, P., 458
Bonnet, M., 121
Bonta, J. L., 401
Boodoo, G., 333
Booth-Butterfield, S., 228
Borgeat, F., 383
Borges, M. A., 287, 288
Boronow, J., 453
Bosworth, H. B., 168
Botwin, M. D., 387
Bouchard, C., 350, 374
Bouchard, T., 396, 413
Bouchard, T. J., 333
Bouchard, T. J., Jr., 350, 396
Boulay, M. R., 350, 374
Bowden, C., 468
Bowden, C. L., 468
Bowers, K. S., 125
Bowler, W. M., 486
Bowman, E. S., T293, 292
Boyd, L. A., 282
Boyes-Braem, P., 308
Boykin, A. W., 333
Boyle, C., 325
Boynes, M., 427
Boyson-Bardies, B., 202
Bracey, G., 486
Bradbury, T. N., 229
Bradman, A., 325
Brand, R. I., 497
Brass, M., 64
Bratslavsky, E., 364
Brauen, C. M., 401
Braun, S., 128
Brecher, M., 130
Breedlove, A. M., 432
Breedlove, S. M., 88
Breggin, G.R., 469
Breggin, P. R., 469
Breier, A., 468
Breland, K., 191
Breland, M., 191
Brennan, J. F., 6
Brennan, P. A., 396
Brenner, R., 465
Breslau, N., 492
Breuer, J., 449
Brewer, M. B., 232
Briem, V., 111
Briggs, K. C., 395
Brigham, A., 447
Britton, A., 491
Broadbent, D., 277
Brobeck, J. R., 349
Brocato, R. M., 219
Brockington, I. F., 408
Brody, N., 333
Brondolo, E., 498
Brooks, A., 463
Brown, C., 461
Brown, G., 457

Brown, J., 279, 295
Brown, R., 287
Brown, T., 319
Brozoski, D., 113
Brubaker, D. A., 453
Brummett, B. H., 498
Brunner, E., 491
Bryant, R. A., 383
Bryden, M., 264
Buccino, G., 64
Buchanan, T. W., 60
Buche, L. C., 359
Buchsbaum, M. S., 427
Buck, R., 362
Buckwalter, J. J., 167
Bucuvalas, M., 483
Bucy, P. C., 60
Budney, A. J., 131
Bugental, J. F. T., 450
Bunge, M. B., 56
Buonano, F. S., 307
Buonocore, M. H., 277
Burchinal, M., 157
Bureau of Labor Statistics, 519
Burger, J. M., 216, 217, 382
Burgess, D. M., 325
Burgio, K. L., 454
Burish, T. G., 457
Burke, D., 354
Burke, D. M., 287
Burke, J. M., 169
Burks, N., 486
Burmeister, M., 424
Burney, R., 123
Burns, B., 470
Burns H. J., 291
Burrows, C., 101
Burrows, P., 221
Bushman, B. J., 196, 238, 240
Buss, D. M., 387
Buss, R. R., 163
Bussa, B., 458
Butcher, J. N., 394, 395
Butler, K., 462, 463
Butler, R., 467
Butner, J., 217
Butter E. M., 503
Buysse, D. J., 469
Byrd, R. S., 486

C

Cabeza, R., 168, 319
Cacioppo, J., 228, 229
Caddell, J. M., 453
Cain, D., 450
Calabrese, J., 468
Calder, A. J., 238, 359
Califia, P., 261
Calkins, M. W., T7
Camara, W. J., 394
Cameron, J., 232
Cameron, J. A., 233, 348
Cami, J., 130
Campbell, D. T., 99, 459
Campbell, J. C., 499
Campbell, V. L., 393

Campos, B. C., 355
Campos, J., 157
Campos, J. J., 364
Camposano, S., 307
Cancian, F. M., 364
Canli, T., 430
Cannon, W. B., T361, 349, 361
Cao, Y., 56
Carducci, B., 414
Carey, G., 238, 396
Carlsmith, J., 227
Carlson, G. A., 429
Carlyle, T., 220
Carol, M., 123
Carpenter, P. A., 258, 331
Carrion, V. G., 492
Carroll, R. T., 463
Carruthers, M., 167
Carson, J. P., 491
Carson, R. C., 236
Carver, L. J., 297
Caserta, M. T., 492
Cassem, E. H., 469
Cassiday, K. L., 426
Cassidy, J., 157
Castellanos, F. X., 163
Castelli, W. P., 497
Castillo, R. J., 351, 411
Castorina, R., 325
Catalan, J., 216
Catanzaro, S. J., 385
Cattell, R. B., T387, T389, 387, 388
Cave, K. R., 101
Ceci, S. J., 333
Centers for Disease Control and Prevention, 127, 493
Centerwall, B. S., 240
Centorrino, F., 468
Cephus, R., 112
Cerletti, U., T468, 468
Cermak, L., 275
Cesar d'Ornano, A. M., 182
Chabris, C. F., 307
Chaiken, S., 224, 225, 228
Chan, D. W., 389
Chandola, T., 491
Chang, I., 490
Chang, P. P., 398, 498
Chang-Schneider, C., 399
Chapman, R. S., 156, 205
Charney, D. S., 116
Chase-Lansdale, L., 157
Chee, M. W. L., 112
Chen, C., 259
Chen, M., 101
Chen, W. J., 169
Chen, Y., 230
Chen, Y. Q., 491
Cheng, H., 56
Cherry, E. C., 277
Cheyne, B., 499
Chilcoat, H. D., 492
Chinn, A. B., 467
Chiu, C. Y., 219
Chomsky, N., T204, 201, 204
Choo, W. C., 112
Chou, J. C., 468

Chou, S. Y., 351
Chu, J. A., 426
Church, C. C., 127
Chwalisz, K., 361
Cialdini, R., 217
Cialdini, R. B., 216
Ciardiello, A., 315
Cideciyan A. V., 83
Clark, D. A., 457
Clark, F., 435
Clark, J., 469
Clarke-Stewart, K. A., 157
Clarkin, J. F., 460
Clayton, R., 127
Clements, C. M., 199
Clements, K. M., 505
Clougherty, K. F., 458
Coates, J., 265
Coe, W. C., 125
Coffey C. E., 430
Cohen, H. J., 503
Cohen, L. J., 430
Cohen, N. J., 168
Cohen, S., 492
Colcombe, S. J., 168
Coleman, H. L. K., 487
Coley, J. D., 309–310
Colligan, J., 315
Colligan, R. C., 503
Collins, C. J., 344
Colom, R., 278
Committee on Animal Research and Ethics, 24
Conezio, J., 288
Conrad, R., 278
Cook, J. M., 236
Cook, T. D., 459
Cooper, L. A., 461
Corbett, G. G., 203
Coren, S., 99
Corkin, S., 283
Cosgrove, G. R., 469
Costa, P. T., Jr., 168, 387, 389, 394, 396, 400, 413, 498
Costello, D. M., 430
Costlow, C., 505
Cotgrove, A., 470
Cottrell, D., 470
Coups, E., 26
Courage, M. L., 155
Cowan, N., 276
Cox, C., 325, 492
Crago, M. B., 351
Craik, F., 275
Craik, F. I. M., 166, 280, 287
Craven, R. G., 399
Crawford, M., 261
Crichlow S., 219
Crosby, L. R., 453
Cross, W., 492
Crouch, D. J., 111
Crowe, R. R., 424
Crowley, A. E., 228, 401
Crowley, M., 241
Crucian, G., 362
Csernansky, J. G., 465
Csikszentmihalyi, M., 315, 316

NI-2

Cua, A. B., 167
Cummings, J. L., 430
Cummings, S. R., 166
Curry, J., 470
Curry, J. F., 446, 469
Curtis, R. C., 236
Curtis, R. H., 447
Curtiss, S., 145
Cusato, B., 385
Cytowic, R. E., 76

D

Daciuk, J., 186
Dahl, R., 325
Dahlstrom, G., 498
Dahlstrom, W. G., 395
Dale, A. M., 60
Dalix, A. M., 182
D'Allesandro, D. U., 454
Dallman, M., 350
Damasio, A. R., 60
Damasio, H., 18
Damasion, A. R., 18
Danso, H., 24
Darby, B., 216
Darley, J. M., 241
Darvill, T., 325
Darwin, C., T69, 7, 11, 69, 359, 362
Daum, I., 282
Davidson, M., 432
Davidson, P. R., 463
Davidson, R. J., 359
Davies, I. R. L., 203
Daviet, C., 460
Davis, G. C., 492
Davis, K. L., 432
Davis, M., 358
Davis, R. M., 112
Davis, S. F., 520, 521
Day, N., 490
Day, S., 498
Dayton, T., 312
de Jong, P. T., 83
de la Torre, R., 130
De Valois, R. L., 85
De Wit, H., 128
de Wolff, C. J., 348
Dean, C., 408
Debes, F., 325
deCharms, R., 348
Deci, E. L., 342, 348
Decker, K., 292
Decouflé, P., 325
Deeskinazi, F. G., 355
DeFries, J. C., 332, 333
DeGrandpre, R. J., 383, 385
deHalle, P., 202
Deinzer, R., 490
Delaney, A. J., 490
Delfiner, R., 212
DeLongis, A., 366, 486
Demers, R. A., 204
Denno, D. W., 117
Depression and Bipolar Support Alliance, 473

Deregowski, J. B., 101
DeRubeis, R. J., 457
Despres, J. P., 350, 374
Dettmers, C., 64
Detweiler, J. B., 12
Devanand, D. P., 468, 469
Dew, M. A., 469
Diamond, L. M., 237, 355
Diamond, M., 261
Diamond, M. C., 264
Dickens, W. T., 333
Dickerson, F., 453
Dickson, W. J., 526
Diehl, R., 24
Diekman, A. B., 216
Diener, E., 361
Dierker, L. C., 430
Dietrich, K., 325
Digman, J. M., 389
Dill, D. L., 426
Dillard, J., 216
Dimsdale, J. E., 127
Dinges, D. F., 112
Dinnel, D. L., 289
Dodane, C., 156, 205
Dodson, J. D., 344
Doege, T. C., 112
Dohrenwend, B. P., 436
Doidge, N., 40
Dolan, R. J., 359
Dollard, J., 238, 383
Domagalski, T. A., 363
Domhoff, W., 120
Dominey, P. F., 156, 205
Domino, M., 470
Dominy, N. J., 401
Domjan, M., 385
Domschke, K., 424
Donavan, S., 124
Donnerstein, E., 240
Donovan, J. J., 398
Doob, L. W., 238
Dorahy, M. J., 427
Doucet, E., 350
Dougherty, D. D., 469
Douthitt, E. A., 219
Doyle, N., 505
Dreher, H., 398, 498
Drenth, P. J., 348
Drews, F. A., 111
Druckman, D., 124
Dube, S., 468
Duben, A., 238
Dubowitz, H., 186
Dumaine, A., 408
Dumais, S., 289
Duncan, B. L., 460
Duncan, R. M., 202
Dungan, D. S., 401
Dunn, J. C., 486
Dunner, D., 446, 465, 470
Durand, C., 202
Durso, F., 312
Dussault, J., 350, 374
Dweck, C. S., T354, 354, 355
Dykens, E. M., 325
Dzemidzic, M., 264

E

Eagly, A., 241
Eagly, A. H., 216, 224, 225, 228, 236
Eaker, E. D., 497
Easterbrooks, M. A., 157
Eastman, C. I., 111
Eaton, W. W., 423
Ebbinghaus, H., T293, 293
Eberly, S., 492
Eder, H., 319
Edmondson, D., 492
Egan, L. C., 227
Eghrari, H., 348
Eich, E., 286
Eisenberger, N. I., 356
Eisenegger, C., 238
Ekman, P., 257, 258, 358, 360, 362, 363
Elashoff, R., 458
Elger, C. E., 283
Elkind, D., 163
Ellgring, H., 125
Elliot, C. H., 457
Elliot, J., T233, 233
Elliott, E., 354
Ellis, A., 456
Ellis, L., 354
Ellis, L. K., 486
Ellsworth, P. C., 236, 257
Endler, N. S., 468
Engle, R. W., 278
Englund, C. E., 112
Enns, J. T., 99
Epping-Jordan, M., 127
Epstein, L. H., 351
Erickson, K. I., 168
Erickson, S. A., 498
Erikson, E. H., 158, T158–160, 164–166, T381–382, 382
Erikson, J. M., 158
Eron, L., 196
Eron, L. D., 240
Ertelt, D., 64
Eschenbeck, H., 500
Eskenazi, B., 325
Essau, B., 491
Estes, L. S., 351
Evans, A. C., 163
Evans, A. R., 468
Evans, D., 458
Evans, D. A., 319
Evans, D. R., 466
Evans, I. M., 453
Evans, S. S., 453
Evans, W. H., 453
Evans, W. J., 166, 505
Evens, A. C., 60
Exner, J. E., 393
Eysenck, H. J., 328, 398, T459, 459, 498

F

Faber, B., 432
Fadiga, L., 64
Fahey, J. L., 458
Fahey, V., 121

Fairbank, J., 470
Fairbank, J. A., 453
Falater, S., 117
Fallon, B., 186
Fanselow, M. S, 358, 359
Faraone, S. V., 169, 435
Farmer, A. E., 430, 432
Farooqi, I. S., 350, 351
Farre, M., 130
Farruggia, S., 259
Farthing, W., 110
Fasotti, L., 361
Faurion, A., 182
Fawzy, F. I., 458
Fawzy, N. W., 458
FDA MedWatch Safety Alert, 469
Fearn, M., 227
Fedoroff, I. C., 411
Fehr, E., 238, 355
Feingold, A., 236
Feldman, D. H., 155, 164
Felician, O., 307
Felten, D. L., 500
Fenn, K.M., 112
Ferguson, N. B., 349
Fernald, A., 156, 205
Fernandez, G., 283
Fernandez, M. I., 226
Feroah, T. R., 113
Ferrelli, A. V., 115
Ferreri, F., 56
Festinger, L., 226, 227, 234
Feyer, A. M., 120
Fiatarone, M. A., 168, 505
Fiedler, F.E., 221
Fincham, F. D., 229
Fine, J., 265
Finger, K., 292
Fink, G. R., 64
Fink, M., 468
Finke, R., 315
Finkel, D., 396
Finlay, B., 26
Fischbacher, U., 355
Fischer, A., 263
Fischer, M., 169
Fischl, B., 60
Fishbein, M., 225
Fisher, L. D., 490
Fiske, S. T., 232
Fitzpatrick, M., 238
Fitzsimons, L., 469
Flannery, D., 163
Flannery-Schroeder, E., 457
Flaskerud, J. H., 461
Flavell, J. H., 155
Fleming, M. F., 132
Flemons, W. W., 118
Fletcher, K., 169
Flores-Mendoza, C., 278
Florio, C. M., 394
Flowers, S. S., 505
Flynn, J. R., 319, 333
Foa, E. B., 453
Foege, W. H., 167
Fogassi, L., 64
Foley, D., 166

Name Index

Folkman, S., 485, 486, 495, 496, 500
Follett, K. J., 230
Fonagy, P., 470
Ford, A., 461
Ford, D. E., 398, 461, 498
Forder, J., 113
Forssmann-Falck, R., 363
Forster, H. V., 113
Forsterling, F., 389
Forsyth, D. R., 241
Fortner, M., 505
Fosse, M., 112
Fosse, R., 112
Foulkes, D., 115
Fournier, G., 350, 374
Franchini, L., 435
Franck, G., 120
Frank, D. A., 127
Frank, E., 469
Frank, R., 18
Franke, R. H., 526
Frankel, B. R., 457
Franklin, M. E., 453
Fraser, J. F., 450
Fraser, S., 216
Frazier, J., 429
Fredrickson, B. L., 501
Freedman, J., 216
Freeman, A., 454
Freeman, I., 499
Freeman, J., 327
Freeman, W., 469
Freese, J., 382
Fremmer-Bombik, E., 157
Fresquet, N., 61
Freud, A., 379, 501
Freud, S., T8, 8–9, T109, T119, 119, 127, 238, T360, 376–381, T377–383, 422, 424, T445, T447, 447, 449, 501
Frey, J., 238
Frey, L. M., 426
Friedman, D., 169
Friedman, H. S., 398
Friedman, M., 398, 497
Friedman, M. J., 453
Friesen, W., 257, 258, 360, 362, 363
Friesen, W. V., 358
Frishman, W., 319, 522
Friston, K. J., 359
Frith, C. D., 359
Fromkin, V., 145
Frontera, W. R., 166
Fuld, P., 319
Fuligni, A., 232, 233
Fuligni, A. J., 348
Fulker, D. W., 396
Fuller, C. A., 111
Furford, G., 186
Furumoto, L., 7

G

Gabrieli, J. D. E., 430
Gado, M., 212
Galaburda, A. M., 18
Galanti, G. A., 461
Gale, G. D., 358, 359
Galea, S., 483
Galke, B., 424
Gallagher, D., 361
Gallese, V., 64
Gallo, J. J., 461
Gallois, C., 263
Gambon, J., T525
Gamwell, L., 413
Ganchrow, J. R., 151
Ganellen, R. J., 394
Ganis, G., 307
Gano–Phillips, S., 229
Ganzel, B. L., 426
Garb, H. N., 394
Garber, J., 385
Garcia Coll, C., 232
Garcia, J., 182
Garcia, J., 7
Gardner, H., T305, 315, 322, T322–323
Gardner, J., 501
Garfinkel, P. E., 259
Garland, E. J., 116
Garnand, D. B., 364
Garner, D. M., 259
Garry, M., T292
Garuccio, A., 81
Gay, P., 422, 424
Gay, P. E., 486
Gaylor, M., 382
Gaylord-King, C., 123
Geddes, J., 467
Geen, R. G., 240
Gelder, M., 453
Gelenberg, A., 446, 465, 470
Gelfand, L. A., 457
Geliebter, A., 349
Geller, B., 429
Gelman, S. A., 309
George, L., 435
George, L. K., 503
Gerlach, M., 57
Gersappe, A., 491
Gerton J., 487
Geschwind, D. H., 359
Ghoneim, M. M., 131
Gibbons, J. L., 263
Gibson, E. J., 97
Gidez, L., 319
Giedd, J. N., 163
Gillespie, M. A., 344
Gillham, B., 499
Gilligan, C., 164
Gillin, J. C., 505
Gillund, G., 287, 288
Gil-Rivas, V., 491
Gilstrap, L. L., 292
Gittelman-Klein, R., 393
Glanz, K., 522
Glaser, R., 490, 491, 500
Glynn, S. M., 453, 454
Goddard, C. R., 186
Godden, D. R., 286
Goedken, R. J., 424

Gogos, J., 424
Goh, D., 382
Goin, M. K., 446
Gold, J., 483
Gold, R., 463
Goldberg, W. A., 157
Goldman, D., 424
Goldman-Rakic, P. S., 282
Goldsmith, H. H., 157, 435
Goldstein, S., 86, 169
Goldston, D. B., 493
Goldstone, A. P., 349
Goleman, D., 112, 315, 322
Gomez, F., 350
Gong-Guy, E., 385
Gonzaga, G. C., 355
Gonzales, J. J., 461
Gonzalez, A., 453
Goodall, J., T17
Goodglass, H., 205
Goodwin, F. K., 420
Gooren, L. J. G., 262, 264
Gornik–Durose, M., 217
Gorski, R. A., 264
Gosch, E., 457
Gosling, S.D., 398
Gosselin, F., 60
Gotlib, I. H., 430
Gottesman, I. I., 432
Gottheil, E., 458
Gottman, J. M., 238
Goudy, M. B., 350
Gouldner, A. W., 216
Goulet, J., 383
Grabowski, T., 18
Graham, J. R., 395
Grandjean, P, 325
Granholm, E., 431
Gravenstein, S., 490
Gray, W. D., 308
Grayson, A., 279
Grayson, C., 429
Green, A., 461
Greenberg, B. D., 424
Greenberg, J., 399
Greenland, P., 505
Greenwald, A. G., 101
Gregory, R. L., 99
Gresham, L. G., 226
Griffit, W., 364
Grishenko-Roze, N., 389
Grocer, S., 520
Grochocinski, V. J., 469
Gross, A. M., 240
Gross, C. G., 410
Grossman, K., 157
Grossman, M., 351
Grossmann, K. E., 157
Grove, W. M., 394
Gruber, A. J., 131
Grünbaum, A., 383
Guerin, D. A., 401
Guilford, J. P., 322
Gump, B. B., 497
Guralnik, O., 427
Gurin, J., 460

Gustavson, C. R., 351
Guthrie, D., 458
Guthrie, R. V., 7
Guynn, M. J., 285
Gyulai, L., 468

H

Habeck, C. G., 319
Haber, R. N., 288
Hadley, C. N., 487
Hagihara, D. K., 275
Hagstrom, K., 463
Haig, J., 399
Hains, S. C., 219
Halbesleben, J. R. B., 486
Hall, C., 120
Hall, G. C., 493
Hall, G. S., 6
Hall, L. K., 278, 291
Hall, S., 112
Hallmark, R., 393
Halpern, D. F., 333
Hamblen, J.L., 457
Hamer, D. H., 424
Hamilton, D. L., 233
Hamilton, J. A., 408
Hamilton, S. E., 307
Hammen, C., 385
Handel, S., 277
Haney, T. L., 497
Hanges, P. J., 344
Hannon, R., 168
Hansen, D., 480
Harald, M., 463
Hardy, G. E., 460
Harkins, S., 219
Harlow, H. F., T158, 158
Harlow, L.L., 133
Harman, G., 230
Harmon-Jones, C., 227
Harmon-Jones, E., 227
Harold, G. T., 229
Harris, K. F., 497
Harrison, P. J., 432, 433
Harsch, N., 289
Hart, P., 219
Hartfield, E., 236, 237
Hartung, P. J., 382
Harvey, O. J., 235
Harvey, S., 525
Hauck, S. J., 167
Havighurst R. J., 168
Havlik, R., 166
Hawks, S. R., 350
Hayflick, L., 167
Hays, J. C., 503
Hayward, C., 423
Hazlett, E. A., 427
Heath, D., 364
Hebb, D. O., 344
Hedman, L. R., 111
Hegeman, R., 212
Heider, F., 229
Heider, K., 358
Heilman, K., 362

NI-4

Heilman, K. M., 359
Heils, A., 424
Heingartner, A., 219
Heinrich, B., 198
Heinrichs, M., 238, 355
Hell, D., 430
Hellawell, D. J., 238
Heller, D., 398
Helmers, K. F., 168, 319
Helms, J. E., 331
Helms, M. J., 498
Helson, H., 366
Hemingway, H., 491
Henning, H., 89
Henningfield, J. E., 127, 128
Herberman, R. B., 491
Herbst, J. H., 396, 413
Herman, B. H., 355
Herman, E. M., 219
Hermann, A., 57
Herrmann, M. J., 125
Herrnstein, R. J., T333, 333
Hersh, S. M., 240
Hershberger, S. L., 396
Herskovits, M. J., 99
Hess, T. M., 230
Hesse, E., 157
Hetherington, A. W., 349
Hettema, J. M., 424
Hewstone, M., 232
Heyes, C. M., 198
Hicklin, J., 395
Higgins, P., 366
Hilgard, E. R., 125
Hilgard, J. R., 125
Hill, P. C., 503
Hill, W. D., 466
Hilpert, P. L., 454
Hilton, J., 319
Hines, M., 264
Hintze, J. M., 454
Hippocrates, T410
Hirsch, J., 349
Hirschfeld, R. M., 468
Hitch, G., 278
Hobson, J., T120, 120
Hobson, J.A., 112
Hochman, J., 292
Hodapp, R. M., 325
Hodge, D., 292
Hodges, J. R., 296
Hodges, L. F., 452
Hodgkinson, B., 458
Hodgson, R. J., 456
Hodson, D. S., 166
Hoebel, B. G., 349
Hoffmann, A., 313
Hofman, A., 83
Hofman, M. A., 262, 264
Hofstede, G. H., T348, 348, 399, T399–400
Hogg, M. A., 219
Holcomb, W. R., 457
Hollander, E., 427
Hollifield, M., 457
Hollon, S., 460

Hollon, S. D., 454
Holman, E. A., 491
Holmes, C. B., 401
Holmes, C. J., 163
Holmes, J. G., 236, 399
Holmes, T. H., 484, 485, 486
Holowka, S., 156
Holroyd, J., 125
Holt, L. H., 287
Holton, S. D., 457
Hong, Y. I., 219
Honzik, C. H., 197
Hood, D. C., 84
Hood, W. R., 235
Hopfinger, J. B., 277
Horhota, M., 230
Horn, J. M., 382, 396
Horne, J. A., 116
Horney, K., 380, T381–382, 382
Hornick, J., 186
Horowitz, D. L., 233
Hortaçsu, N., 238
Hothersall, D., 526
Houck, P. R., 469
Houldin, A., 491
Houshyar, H., 350
Howe, M. L., 155
Hoyer, W. D., 228
Hrebickova, M., 389
Hu, P., 156
Hubbard, E. M., 76
Hubble, M. A., 460
Hudson, J. I., 131, 427
Hudson, J. L., 457
Huesmann, L. R., 196, 240
Huesmann, R. L, 240
Huestis, M. A., 131
Hughes, J. R., 131
Hughes, V. A., 166
Hui-Sheng, L., 238
Hull, A. J., 278
Hull, C. L., 343
Hunt, E., 322
Hunt, M., 447
Hurst, S., 463
Hurtz, G. M., 398
Hurvich, L. M., 85
Hurwitz, T. A., 425
Hutchings, B., 396
Hyde, J. S., 235, 264
Hyman, I. E., 292
Hyman, I. E., Jr., 289, 291
Hyun, C. S., 458

I

Iacoboni, M., 64, 359
Idel, H., 490
Ikemoto, S., 366
Imbeault, P., 350
Ingaham, L. J., 432
International Honor Society in Psychology, 520
Ioannidis, J. P. A., 382
Irit, H., 463
Irwin, A. R., 240

Irwin, M., 505
Isabel, J., 396
Iwawaki, S., 263

J

Jacobs, D. R., Jr., 505
Jacobs, E. A., 461
Jacobs, G. H., 85
Jacobs, S., 490
Jacobsen, B., 432
Jacobson, K. C., 238
Jacobson, S. G., 83
Jaeger, J. J., 263
James, W., T6, 6–7, 343, T360, 360
Jameson, M., 24
Jamison, K.R., 429
Jang, K. L., 387, 396, 397, 413
Janicki-Deverts, D., 492
Janis, I., 219
Jankowski, M. K., 457
Janos, P. M., 326
Jansson, L., 432
Janus, C. L., T353, 353
Janus, S. S., T353, 353
Jay, S. M., 457
Jeffrey, R. W., 454
Jeffries, N. O., 163
Jenike, M. A., 469
Jenkins, C. D., 497
Jenneke, W., 463
Jensen, P. S., 429
Jernigan, T. L., 163
Jerrett, D. T., 203
Jerrett, T., 203
Jerskey, B. A., 424
Jex, S. M., 501
Jilek, W.G., 259
Jin, X., 492
Jobe, J. B., 168, 319
John, O. P., 389, 396, 398, 413
Johnson, B. T., 416
Johnson, C. D., 157
Johnson, D., 112
Johnson, D. M., 308
Johnson, G., 204
Johnson, J., 240, 423
Johnson, M., 238
Johnson, P., 227
Johnson, V., 353
Johnston, L., 133
Johnston, W. A., 111
Jones, E. E., 230
Jones, E. J., 461
Jones, G. W., 238
Jones, H. M., 466
Jones, J. L., 297
Jones, L., 435
Jones, M. C., T8–9, 9
Jorgensen, P. J., 325
Joseph, C. A., 401
Joyce, P. R., 429
Judge, T. A., 398
Juffer, F., 156
Jung, C., T381–382, 381–382, 387
Just, M. A., 258, 331

K

Kabani, N., 60
Kabat-Zinn, J., 123
Kaemmer, B., 395
Kahn, R. S., 432
Kahneman, D., 311, 317, 318
Kail, R., 278
Kaiser, P. K., 401
Kajander, T., 325
Kales, A., 116
Kamin, L. J., 333
Kandel, E. R., 283
Kane, M. J., 278
Kaplan, B. H., 498
Kaplan, E., 205
Karakitapoglu-Aygun, Z., 254
Karau, S. J., 219
Karayiorgou, M., 424
Kareken, D. A., 264
Karney, B. R., 229
Karpova, Y., 491
Kartashov, A. I., 505
Kasanin, J. D., 398, 497
Kasch, K. L., 430
Kasi, S. V., 490
Kasl, S. V., 497
Kasparov, G., 313
Kastenbaum, R., 168, 169
Katzman, R., 319
Kaufman, C., 458
Kaufman, J. C., 321
Kaul, J. D., 526
Kawas, C. K., 319
Kazdin, A. E., 454
Keane, T. M., 453
Kearney, C. A., 465
Keashly, L., 525
Keck, P. E. Jr., 468
Keen, P., 427
Keenan, J. P., 307
Keenan, K., 169
Keesey, R. E., 349
Kehayias, J. J., 505
Keillor, J., 362
Keinonen, M., 389
Keita, G. P., 429
Keller, M. B., 446, 465, 470
Kellner, R., 425
Kelly, J. A., 226
Kelly, T. L., 112
Keltner, D., 355
Kemmerer, D. L., 263
Kempe, C.C., 67
Kempe, R.S., 67
Kendall, P. C., 457
Kendall, T., 470
Kendler, K. S., 197, 424
Kennard, B. D., 446, 469
Kerig, P. K., 461
Kermoian, R., 364
Kern, M.L., 398
Kernberg, O. F., 460
Keromoian, R., 156
Kesey, K., 468
Kessler, R. C., 355, 366, 423, 429, 492
Ketter, T. A., 468

Name Index

Kety, S. S., 432
Khayat, D., 182
Kiecolt-Glaser, J. K., 490, 491, 500
Kihlstrom, J., 363
Kihlstrom, J. F., 383
Killen, J. D., 423
Kilmartin, C. T., 363
Kilpatrick, D., 483
Kim, B. H., 344
Kim, D-W., 57
Kim, K-S., 57
Kim, M., 101
Kim, U., 487
Kimura, D., 263, 264
King, C. G., 123
King, N. J., 454
Kinney, D. K., 432
Kinsey, A. C., T353, 353
Kirby, J. S., 426
Kirkegaard-Sorensen, L., 396
Kirkland, D., 315
Kirmayer, L. J., 411
Kirsch, I., 124, 126, 385
Kitayama, S., 230, 255, 256, 360
Kivimaki, M., 491
Klag, M. J., 398, 498
Klaver, C. C., 83
Klaver, P., 283
Klein, D., 427
Klein, D. N., 446, 465, 470
Klein, S. B., 8, 88
Kleineidam, C. H., 490
Kleinknecht, R. A., 463
Kleinot, M. C., 228
Kleitman, N., 113
Klemchuk, H. M., 123
Klerman, G. L., 429
Kliewer, W., 363
Kligman, A. M., 167
Kling, K. C., 235
Klorman, R., 454
Kluft, R. P., 426
Klüver, H., 60
Knight, A., 234
Knight, J. A., 167
Knight, W., 313
Knight, W. G., 127
Knop, J., 396
Knowles, E. D., 230
Knox, R., 163
Ko, G., 432
Kobasa, S., 498
Koelling, R. A., 182
Koenig, H. G., 503
Koestner, R., 348
Koh, J. K., 241
Kohlberg, L., 163–164, T164
Köhler, W., 197–198, T198
Kohlmann, C-W., 500
Kohout, J., 520
Köller, O., 399
Kolodny, R., 169
Kolodziej, M., 416
Komatsu, L. K., 309
Kondwani, K., 123
Kong, Y. H., 497
Konowal, N. M., 112

Koob, G. F., 127
Kooper, R., 452
Koppel, M., 265
Kortenkamp, S., 362
Kosfeld, M., 355
Kosslyn, S. M., 307
Kotkin, M., 460
Kouri, E. M., 131
Kouznetsova, L., 389
Kouznetsova, N., 258
Kraemer, H. C., 423
Kramer, A. F., 168
Kramer, A.F., 166
Kramer, S. J., 487
Krashen, S., 145
Kratochvil, C. J., 446, 469
Kratofil, P. H., 127
Kraus, I., 169
Kritz-Silverstein, D., 492
Krokoff, L. J., 238
Kroonenberg, P., 263
Krosnick, J. A., 228
Krupnick, J. L., 461
Krupp, D., 258
Kryger, M., 118
Krystal, J. H., 453
Kubic, L. S., 192
Kübler-Ross, E., 168
Kuhl, P., T156
Kuhn, H. W., 431
Kulik, G., 491
Kulik, J. A., 501
Kumar, R., 408
Kumar, S., 423
Kumari, M., 491
Kunkel, S. R., 497
Küntay, A., 156, 205
Kunze, C., 263
Kupfer, D. J., 118, 469
Kusche, A. G., 399
Kusdil, M. E., 389

L

la Fleur, S. E., 350
LaBar, K. S., 238, 359
LaBerge, D., 277
LaCroix, A. Z., 505
Ladda, R. L., 116
LaFromboise, T., 487
LaGana, C., 454
Lalonde, C. E., 202
Lambert, M. J., 460
Lambie, A., 499
Lance, C. J., 392
Landrum, R. E., 520, 521
Lane, D. S., 522
Lange, C., T360, 360
Langer, E. J., 488
Lanphear, B. P., 325
Lapsley, D. K., 163
Larson, C. L., 359
Larson, D. B., 503
Larson, J., 429
Lashley, K. S., 361
Lasnik, H., 202
Latané, B., 219, 241

Lauer, J., 427
Laugero, K. D., 350
Launer, L., 166
Lavie, P., 118
Laws, G., 203
Lay, C., 487
Lazarus, R. S., T362, 362, T481, 485, 486, 495, 496, 500
Leader, J., 427
Leahy, R. L., 457
Leary, M. R., 241, 399
Leavitt, L. A., 156, 205
Leckman, J. F., 325
Leclerc, C. M., 230
Leddy, J. J., 453
LeDoux, I., 361
LeDoux, J. E., 238, 359
Lee, B. E., 461
Lee, K. L., 497
Lee, M., 130
Lee, P. A., 411
Leggett, E. L., 354
Lehman, B. K., 169
Lehnert, B., 81
Lehrer, J., 318
Leibel, R. L., 349
Leiderman, P. H., 156
Leiman, A. L., 432
Lenze, E. J., 469
Lenzenweger, M. F., 460
Leonard, L., 205
Leone, D. R., 348
Leong, F. T. L., 382
Leroy, C., 486
Lesch, K. P., 424
Lester, D., 401
Levav, I., 436
LeVay, S., 354
Leveck, M. D., 168, 319
Levenson, R. W., 358
LeVert, S., 169
Levin, E. D., 127
Levitsky, D. K., 123
Levy, B. R., 497
Levy, G., 319
Levy, K. N., 460
Lewin, K., 214, 346
Lewin, R., 204
Lewis, C. E., 497
Lewis, D. K., 411, 461
Lewis, S., 216
Li, S., 297
Liebau, S., 57
Lieberman, M. D., 356
Like, R., 461
Lilienfeld, S. O., 393, 463
Lim, J., 112
Lin, C. S., 56
Lindemann, B., 89
Link, B. G., 436
Linkous, R. A., 219
Linz, D., 240
Lippit, R., 214
Lipsitz, L. A., 505
Lipworth, L., 123
Lisanby, S. H, 468–469

Littman, E., 394
Liu, A., 60
Liui, H., 163
Livesley, J. W., 436
Livesley, W. J., 387, 396, 397, 413
Locantore, J. K., 168, 319
Locke, B. Z., 420
Locke, E. A., 344
Lockhart, R. S., 275, 280
Lockwood, A. H., 263
Loehlin, J. C., 333, 396, 413
Loftus, E. F., T292, 289, 291, 292, 293
Loftus, J., 354
Logue, M. W., 424
Lohaus, A., 500
Lohr, J. M., 463
Longo, L. C., 236
Lonky, E., 325
Lonnqvist, J., 436
Lopez, A. D., 420
Lovaas, O. I., 192
Lowe, M. J., 264
Lowe, R. A., 241
Lowery, R., 346
Lu, E., 457
Lubinski, D., 396
Luborsky, L., 459, 491
Lucas, P. W., 401
Luchsinger, J. A., 319
Lucia, V. C., 492
Lucy, J. A., 203
Lüdtke, O., 399
Ludwig, D. S., 505
Lukas, S. E., 131
Lupien, P. J., 350, 374
Luria, A. R., 293
Lurito, J. T., 264
Lüscher, M., 401
Lutkenhaus, P., 157
Lutz, K. J., 166
Lutz, R. J., 226
Lykken, D. T., 364, 396, 435, 436
Lynch, E. B., 309–310
Lynn, S., 463
Lynn, S. J., 124
Lyons, J. A., 426
Lyons, J. L., 56
Lyons, M. J., 424
Lytton, H., 263
Lyvers, M., 130
Lyznicki, J. M., 112

M

Maccoby, E. E., 263
MacDonald, A. P., 385
MacDonald, D., 60
MacDonald, G., 236
MacKay, D. G., 287
MacKenzie, S. B., 226
Mackin, R. S., 485
MacLaurin, B., 186
Maclean, C. R., 123
Macquet, P., 120
Madanat, H. N., 350
Maddox, J. H., 468

NI-6

Maestas, M. V., 487
Magarinos, M., 425
Magee, W. J., 423
Magid, L., 221
Mahadik, S. P., 466
Mahe, V., 408
Mahler, H. I. M., 501
Mahmoud, R., 465
Maibach, H. I., 167
Maier, S. F., 198, 490
Main, M., 157
Maisel, M., 57
Makhijani, M. G., 236
Malamuth, N., 240
Malarkey, W. B., 490
Malia, A., 112
Malik, M., 491
Malinchoc, M., 503
Maljkovic, V., 307
Mallis, M. M., 112
Manalo, S., 350
Mandarino, J. V., 123
Manderscheid, R. W., 420
Mandler, G., 289
Mandler, J. M., 308
Mangun, G. R., 277
Manheim, L. J., 344
Manly, J., 319
Manning, C. G., T292
Manson, J., 505
Manusov, V., 7
Maquire, D., 112
Marcado, A. M., 490
March, J., 470
March, J. S., 446, 469
Marder, K. S., 319
Marek, G. J., 131
Marentette, P. F., 156
Margoliash, D., 112
Margolin, S., 192
Markou, A., 127
Markovitz, J. H., 497
Markowitz, J., 460
Markowitz, J. C., 446, 465, 470
Marks, I., 454
Markus, H. R., 255–256, 360
Marmot, M., 168, 491
Marneros, A., 408
Marsh, H. W., 399
Marshall, B., 483
Marsiske, M., 168, 319
Martin, B., 486
Martin, C. E., 353
Martin, J. A., 167
Martin, L., 117
Marucha, P. T., 490
Maruta, T., 503
Marzetta, B. R., 123
Mas, A., 130
Mas, M., 130
Masaki, K., 166
Mascovich A., 505
Maslow, A., 10, T341, T346–347, 346, 347, 348, 385
Mason, N. S., 430
Masson, J. M., 383
Masters, J. C., 457

Masters, W., 353
Masuda, M., 485
Masuda, T., 230
Mathews, D., 262
Mathews, V. P., 264
Matsumoto, D., 7–8, 250, 251, 258, 461
Matthews, J. A., 426
Matthews, K. A., 497
Mattson, M. P., 490
Mavromatis, A., 114
Mayer, J. D., 322
Mayer, M., 186
Mayeux, R., 319
Mayo, E., T526
Mazziotta, J. C., 64
McAloon, M., 401
McAuley, E., 168
McAuliffe, T. L., 226
McCann, S. J. H., 113
McCarley, R., T120, 120
McCarthy, J., 313
McCartney, K., 157
McCauley, C., 219
McClarty, K. L., 399
McClearn, J. R., 396
McClelland, D. C., 344
McClintick, J., 505
McConkey, K. M., 383
McCorkle, R., 491
McCormack, W. A., 345
McCrae, R. R., 387, 389, 394, 396, 400, 413
McCullough, J. P., 446, 465, 470
McCullough, M. E., 503
McDermott, J. F., 429
McDougall, W., T343, 343
McElroy, S. L., 468
McFarlane, T., 411
McGinn, L. K., 454, 457
McGinnis, J. M., 167
McGonagle, K. A., 429
McGrath, E., 429
McGue, M., 396
McGuffin, P., 432
McGuire, F., 526
McGuire, L., 491
McHugo, G. J., 457
McIntosh, A. R., 168, 319
McIntosh, D. N., 491
McKay, J. R., 491
McKenzie, B., 186
McKinley, P., 498
McMonagle, T., 453, 454
McNamara, A., 64
McNeill, D., 287
McNulty, S., 470
McPherson, M., 236
Meador, B. D., 451
Meador, K. G., 503
Mearns, J., 385
Medicine, B., 262
Medin, D. L., 309–310
Mednick, S. A., 396
Meguid, V., 127
Meichenbaum, D., 457
Melgari, J. M., 56

Melton, L. J., III., 166
Melzack, R., 91
Mendes de Leon, C. F., 319
Meng, Z., 156
Menke, E., 486
Menon, T., 219
Mental Health America, 473
Meoni, L. A., 398, 498
Meredith, L. S., 461
Meredith, W., 166
Merrill, R. M., 350
Mervis, C. B., 308, 310
Messina, C. R., 522
Metcalfe, J., 286
Metzler, J., 307
Mewborn, C. R., 228
Meyer, L. H., 453
Meyrick, J., 228
Michael, R., 454
Michaels, J. W., 219
Michalos, A., T366
Mickelson, K. D., 355
Miles, D. R., 238, 396
Milgram, S., T217–218, 217–218
Milkewicz, N., 463
Miller, A., T435
Miller, D. G., 291
Miller, E. K., 282
Miller, G. A., 278–279
Miller, G. E., 492
Miller, J. F., 156, 205
Miller, J. G., 226, 255
Miller, K., 236
Miller, L. H., 486
Miller, L. S., 240
Miller, M. E., 125
Miller, M. N., 351
Miller, N. E., 238
Miller, N. F., 383
Miller, S. D., 460
Milligan, M., 238
Mills, M. A., 492
Milner, B., 283
Milstead, M., 163
Mineka, S., 364
Mintz, L. B., 351
Mischel, W., 388
Mishell, D. R., 167
Mitchell, A., 324
Mitchell, K. A., 236
Mitchell, P. B., 468
Mitchell, S. A., 449
Miyagawa, T., 350
Mizes, J. S., 451
Moeller, J. R., 319
Moffic, H. S., 461
Moghaddam, F. M., 233
Moise, J. F., 240
Moise-Titus, J., 240
Mok, A., 254
Moldofsky, H., 113
Möller, A., 430
Molock, S. D., 493
Money, J., 261, 262
Mongeau, P. A., 229
Montgomery, R. W., 463
Moody, B. J., 469

Moody, R., 114
Moore, B. A., 131
Moore, T. E., 101
Moore-Ede, M. C., 111
Moorhead, G., 219
Mora, G., 414
Moran, S., 322
Moreira, V., 259
Moreland, R. L., 236
Morgan, C. D., 393
Morgan, J. P., 130
Morgenstern, H., 319
Morris, J. N., 168, 319
Morris, J. S., 359
Morris, M., 219
Morris, M.W., 254
Morton, D. L., 458
Moscovici, S., 220
Mott, F., T145
Mottaghy, F., 307
Mount, M. K., 398
Mouton, C. P., 505
Mowrer, O. H., 238
Mowrer, R. R., 8
Moynihan, J., 492
Mueser, K. T., 457
Muhlberger, A., 125
Muller, C. R., 424
Mulry, G., 226
Mulsant, B. H., 469
Mulvaney, S., 363
Munif, D., 151
Munsterberg, H., 526
Murakami, J. L., 493
Murata, K., 325
Murdock, B. B., Jr., 287
Muris, P., 463
Murphy, B. W., 263
Murphy, C. C., 325
Murphy, D., 424
Murphy, D. A., 226
Murphy, D. L., 424
Murphy, K. R., 169
Murphy, L. R., 486
Murphy, M., 124
Murphy, T. I., 115
Murray, C., T333, 333
Murray, C. J. L., 420
Murray, H. A., 393
Murray, M. A., 501
Murray, S. L., 236, 399
Muter, P., 288
Myers, B. J., 363
Myers, D. G., 12, 366, T367, 367
Myers, I. B., 395

N

Nadeau, A., 350, 374
Nadeau, K. G., 169, 394
Nadler, J., 128
Naef, M., 238
Naitoh, P., 112
Nanus, B., 221
Narrow, W. E., 420
Nasar, S., 431
Nash, J., T430, 430–431

NI-7

Name Index

Nathan, J. S., 394
National Alliance on Mental Illness, 473
National Center for Health Statistics, 128
National Eating Disorders Association, 473
National Institute of Mental Health, 420, T470
National Institute on Drug Abuse, 467
National Institutes of Health, 56
National Mental Health Consumers' Self-Help Clearinghouse, 473
Naveh, G., 436
Neale, J. M., 366
Neale, M. C., 396, 424
Nearing, K. I., 364
Neary, N. M., 349
Neck, C. P., 219
Neely, J. H., 295
Neimark, J., 292
Neimeyer, R. A., 236
Neisser, U., 289, 333
Nelson, K., 297
Nemeroff, C. B., 446, 465, 470
Nesselroade, C. S., 396
Network of Care, 473
Neugarten B. L., 168
Neumarker, K., 351
Neville, H. J., 56
Newcomb, M.D., 133
Newman, J. P., 435
Newman, S., 429
Newsom, J. T., 216
Newsome, J. T., 490
Nezworski, M. T., 393
Nguyen, T. T. I., 487
Nichaman, M. Z., 498
NICHD Early Child Care Research Network, 157
Nicholson, J., 458
Nidich, S. I., 123
Nieberding, R., 393
Nierenberg, A. A., 469
Nieuwenhuyse, B., 361
Nigg, J. T., 435
Nijenhuis, E. R., 426
Nilsson, L., 111
Nisbett, R. E., 349
Nishida, M., 283
Nissenson, K., 425
Nobler, M. S., 469
Nolen-Hoeksema, S., 429
Norcross, J. C., 449
Norman, B. F., 262
Norman, D., 169
North, M., 452
Nottelmann, E. D., 429
Novick, D. M., 469
Novy, P. L., 131
Nunes, A., 166
Nurmi, J-E., 399
Nusbaum, H.C., 112
Nyberg, L., 281

O

Oakley-Browne, M., 423
Obenchain, J., 463
Oberman, A., 505
O'Brien, J., 254
Ochsner, K., 307
O'Connor, M., 112
O'Connor, N., 463
O'Connor, P. J., 505
O'Connor, R. D., 454
Odbert, H. S., T387, 387
Oden, M. H., 326
O'Donnell, A., 458
Offord, K. P., 503
Ogilvie, R. D., 115
Ogles, B. M., 460
Ogrocki, P., 490
Olin, B. R., 129, 130, 131
Oliver, J. E., 353
Olivier, D. C., 203
Ollendick, T. H., 454
Olsen, P., 453
Olson, H. C., 325
Olson, L., 56
Olsson, A., 364
O'Malley, P., 133
O'Neill, E. F., 505
Onken, L. S., 451
Onyango, G., 458
Ooi, W. L., 319
Opdyke, D., 452
O'Rahilly, S., 350, 351
Ortaldo, J. R., 491
Ostendorf, F., 389
Ostry, D., 156
Oswald, A. J., 501
Oswald, F. L., 344
Oswalt, R., 463
Ott, J., 424
Overmier, J. B., 197–199
Owen, M. T., 157

P

Pace-Schott, E., 120
Pagano, J., 325
Page, S., 415
Paige, E., 486
Paivio, A., 307
Palmer, S., 96
Pan, A. S., 351
Panksepp, J., 355, 366
Parente, F., 453
Pargament, K. I., 503
Parikh, V., 466
Paris, J., 435
Park, C. L., 492
Park, J., 486
Park, Y., 401
Parker, K. C. H., 463
Parker, M. P., 427
Parkinson, W. L., 349
Parks, K., 117
Parobek, V. M., 425
Parsons, H. M., 526
Partonen, T., 436
Pascual-Leone, A., 307
Pasqualetti, P., 56
Patrick, B. C., 348
Patterson, M. L., 7
Pauli, P., 125
Paunonen, S. V., 389
Paus, T., 163
Pavlov, I., T8, 8, T179, 178–181
Pavlov, O., 222
Pearse, D. D., 56
Peckham, W., 354
Pecoraro, N., 350
Pedersen, N. L., 396
Pedersen, P. B., 348, 399
Pederson, G. E., 396
Pell, T., 127
Peng, K., 230
Penn, D. L., 432
Penn, R. B., 491
Peplau, L. A., 11, 353
Pepperberg, I. M., 304
Pereira, M. A., 505
Perloff, R., 333
Perri, M. G., 505
Perrin, J., 169
Perry, J. N., 395
Perry, P., 114
Persaud, R., 322
Peters, W. A., 233
Peterson, D., 169
Peterson, D. R., 517
Peterson, E. L., 492
Peterson, L. R., 279, 295
Peterson, M. J., 279, 295
Petitto, L. A., 156
Petrakis, I. L., 453
Petri, H., 342
Petri, S., 424
Petrova, P. K., 217
Petrovitch, H., 166
Petrycki, S., 470
Pettigrew, T. F., 235
Pettinger, M. B., 505
Petty, F., 468
Petty, R., 228, 229
Petty, R. E., 216, 224, 228
Peyser, S., 469
Pezdek, K., T292, 292
Pfeiffer, N., 385
Pfeiffer, W. M., 411, 412
Phan, T., 501, 502
Phelps, E. A., 238, 359
Phelps, E.A., 364
Phillips, K. A., 425
Phillips, M. D., 264
Piaget, J., T141, 153, T153–155, 155, 163, T202, 202
Piedmont, R. L., 389, 398
Piercy, F. P., 457
Pike, J., 505
Pilkington, J., 265
Pilkonis, P. A., 469
Pillard, R. C., 354
Pilowsky, L. S., 466
Pinel, P., T447

Pinker, S., 203, 204
Pinsof, W. M., 457
Pittam, J., 263
Pizarro, D. A., 12
Plant, E. A., 264
Plomin, R., 332, 333, 396
Plomin, R. N. L., 396
Plug, C., 99
Podolski, C. L., 240
Polce-Lynch, M., 363
Polgreen, L., 252
Poliakoff, M. B., 427
Pollin, W., 127
Pollock, B. G., 469
Pomeroy, W. B., 353
Pope, H. G., 131, 427
Pope, H. G. Jr., 468
Pormerleau, C. S., 127
Pormerleau, O. F., 127
Postman, L., 280
Potocky-Tripodi, M., 354
Potter, J., 398
Poudevida, S., 130
Poulin, M., 491
Powell, B., 382
Powell, J. W., 112
Powell, L., 522
Pozdnyakova, I., 325
PR Newswire Association, Inc., 272
Pratkanis, A. R., 101
Pratt, J. A, 132
Premack, D., 304
Preston, J. D., 235
Price, B. H., 469
Priester, J. M., 228
Prigerson, H. G., 490
Pringle, P., 315
Prochaska, J. O., 449
Prokopovich, S., 491
Prudic, J., 468, 469
Pringle, P., 315
Ptolemy, 100
Puente, A. E., 394
Puetz, T. W., 505
Pumariega, A., 351
Putman, K. M., 359
Putnam, S. P., 345

Q

Quinn, P., 394
Quintana, S. M., 163
Quiroga, M. A., 278

R

Raaijmakers, J. G. W., 287, 288
Rachman, S., 454
Rachman, S. J., 456
Radford, B., 192
Rae, D. S., 420
Rahe, R. H., 484, 486
Raine, A., 396
Rainer, G., 282
Rainforth, M., 123
Rainforth, M. V., 123
Ramachandran, V. S., 76
Rana-Deuba, A., 487

NI-8

Ranson, S. W., 349
Rao, S. C., 282
Rapson, R. L., 236
Rauch, S. L., 469
Rayner, R., 181
Raynor, H. A., 351
Raz, N., 168
Rea, C., 312
Read J. D., 101
Rebok, G. W., 168, 319
Reder, L. M., 286
Redmond, D., 112
Regan, L., 325
Regier, D. A., 420
Register, T. C., 491
Regunath, G., 83
Reihman, J., 325
Reik, P., 263
Reinberg, S., 480
Reinecke, M. A., 446, 469
Reiner, W. G., 261
Reis, H. T., 236
Reisenzein, R., 365
Reiser, B. J., 307
Reiss, P. C., 240
Renchler, R., 486
Renfrey, G., 463
Renner, M. J., 485
Resnick, H., 483
Reul, J., 283
Revelle, W., 111
Reynolds, C. F., 469, 490
Reynolds, C. F., III., 118
Rezvani, A. H., 127
Rhee, E., 232
Rhodes, L. J., 468
Rice, T. B., 113
Richards, C. F., 241
Richards, M., 168
Richardson, J. T. E., 114
Richmond, S. E., 238
Ridley, M., 67
Riemann, R., 387
Rieppi, R., 498
Riggio, L., 64
Rigler, D., 145
Rigler, M., 145
Rimer, B. K., 498
Rimm, D. C., 457
Rimon, R., 408
Ringel, N., 453
Risley, T. R., 192
Risser, R., 468
Ritter, B., 454
Ritts, V., 411
Riviere, J., 8
Rizzi, L., 201
Rizzolatti, G., 64
Roach, M. A., 156, 205
Robbins, L., 480
Robbins, L. N., 420
Roberts, R. E., 461
Roberts, S. B., 505
Robinson, J. W., 235
Robles, T., 491
Roddenberry, D., 112

Rodgers, J. E., 469
Rodgers, M., 359
Rodin, J., 350, 488
Roediger, H. L., III, 285
Roethlisberger, F. J., 526
Roffman, R. A., 133
Rogers, C., 10, 385, 386, T450, 450, 451
Rogers, R. W., 228
Rohde, A., 408
Rohde, P., 446, 469
Roid, G. H., 328
Romney, D. M., 263
Rooney, M., 499
Roper, G., 454
Rorschach, H., 393
Rosch, E., 308, 309, 310
Rosch-Heider, E., 203
Rose, J. S., 430
Rose, P., 399
Rose, S., 427
Rosen, R., 118
Rosenbaum, M., 349
Rosenberg, H. J., 457
Rosenberg, R., 396
Rosenberg, St. D., 457
Rosenboom, L. G., 156
Rosenhan, D. L., 421, T448
Rosenheck, R., 453
Rosenman, R. H., 398
Rosenthal, A. M., 212
Rosenthal, R., 491
Rosenthal, T. L., 182
Rosenzweig, M. R., 88, 432
Roset, P. N., 130
Rosner, B. A., 123
Ross, D., 195, 239, 364
Ross, G. M., 100
Ross, H. E., 99, 100
Ross, S. A., 195, 239, 364
Rossini, P. M., 56
Rost, K. M., 461
Rothbaum, B. O., 452
Rothenberg, A., 429
Rothman, A. J., 12
Rotter, J. B., 346, T385, 385
Rottnek, F., 169
Rotton, J., 238
Rouse, B. A., 486
Rouse, S. V., 394, 395
Rouw, R., 76
Rowan, J., 450
Rowe, D. C., 238
Rowe, J. S., 219
Rowland, L., 112
Roysircai-Sodowsky, G. R., 487
Rubel, A., 461
Rubenstein, L. V., 461
Rubin, M., 232
Ruble, D., 232
Ruble, D. N., 233, 348
Rucci, P., 469
Rude, R. K., 128
Rudmin, F., 487
Ruhe, H. G., 430
Rushton, J. P., 396

Russell, J. M., 446, 465, 470
Russell, N., 168
Russo, M., 112
Russo, N. F., 429
Ryan, M. A. K., 492
Ryan, R. M., 342, 348

S

Sabol, S. Z., 424
Sachs, G. S., 468
Sackeim, H. A., 319, 468, 469
Sadker, D., 264
Sadker, M., 264
Saeed, K., 222
Saffer, H., 351
Sagart, L., 202
Sah, P., 490
Salend, S. J., 453
Salerno, J. W., 123
Sallis, J. F., 492
Salmela-Aro, K., 399
Salovey, P, 322
Salovey, P., 12
Sam, D. L., 259, 487
San, L., 130
Sánchez, G. I., 7
Sanchez-Bernardos, M. L., 389
Sanders, L. D., 56
Sanders, P. W., 497
Sandner, G., 61
Sands, L. P., 166
Santos, L. R., 227
Sanz, J., 389
Sapolsky, R., 490
Sarbin, T. R., 125
Sastry, K. S., 491
Satcher, D., 493
Sattler, J. M., 461
Saunders, B., 186
Saunders, P. R., 389
Savage-Rumbaugh, S., 204
Savickas, M. L., 382
Scarmeas, N., 319
Schachter, D. L., 272
Schachter, S., T361, 361, 362, 365
Schafer, M., 219
Schaffhauser, D., 265
Schaie, K. W., 144, 168
Schendel, D., 325
Schene, A. H., 430
Schilling, E. A., 366
Schmid, R. E., 453
Schmidt, K., 491
Schmidt, M., 115
Schmidt, M. B., 423
Schmitt, D. P., 236
Schmitt, N., 344
Schmitz, C., 486
Schneider, J. A., 319
Schneider, K. J., 450
Schneider, R. H., 123
Schneider, W., 289
Schneidman, E., 168
Scholte, H. S., 76
Schroeder, S. R., 325

Schroth, M. L., 345
Schuerman, J., 361
Schugens, M. M., 282
Schulenberg, J., 133
Schulsinger, F., 396
Schultz, D., 526
Schultz, S. E., 526
Schwartz, J., 427
Schwartz, J. H., 283
Schwartz, S., 436
Schwartz, S. K., 520, T521, 521
Schwarz, J., 57
Schwarz, T., 385
Schweickert, R., 277
Schweitzer, P. K., 116
Schyns, P., 60
ScienceDaily, 265
Scott, S. K., 238
Scott, W. D., T526, 526
Searight, H. R., 169
Sears, R. R., 238
Security Director's Report, 525
Seeman, J., 450
Segall, M. H., 99
Seidman, L. J., 169
Seligman, D. A., 491
Seligman, M. E. P., 11–12, 182, T198, 197–199, 385, 459, 460, 503, 504
Sellars, C., 435
Sellers, W., 123
Sellin, D.F., 512
Selye, H., T481, 483, 489, 490
Sergio, L. E., 156
Serresse, O., 350, 374
Severe, J., 470
Shadish, R., 459
Shafto, P., 310
Shafton, A., 115, 116
Shanker, S., 204
Shapiro, A. K., 459
Shapiro, D. A., 460
Shapiro, E., 459
Shapiro, F., 462
Shapiro, P. A., 498
Sharpe, D., 486
Shaver, K., 251
Shaver, P. R., 355
Shear, M. K., 490
Shell, P., 258, 331
Shepard, R. N., 307
Shepard, T. H., 148
Sheppard, W., 123
Sheps, D. S., 505
Sheridan, J., 490
Sherif, C. W., 235
Sherif, M., T215, 215, 235
Sherman, S J., T292
Sherman, T., 431
Shields, J., 432
Shiffrin, R. M., 279, 287, 288
Shih, P. C., 278
Shimoni, A., 265
Shimp, T. A., 226
Shisslak, C. M., 351
Shkodriani, G. M., 263

Name Index

Shlain, B., 130
Shoda, Y., 388
Shorter E., 468
Shriffrin, R., 289
Shrout, P. E., 436
Shryne, J. E., 264
Shuglin, A., 130
Shurkin, J. N., 326
Shweder, R. A., 165, 203
Sibley, R., 480
Siegler, I. C., 498
Siegler, R. S., 155
Sigelman, J. D., 227
Sigmundson, H. K., 261
Sijsenaar, M., 463
Sikkema, K. J., 226
Sills, S. J., 217
Silove, D., 501, 502
Silva, C. E., 124
Silva, S., 470
Silva, S. G., 446, 469
Silver, F. W., 425
Silver, L., 169
Silver, R. C., 491
Silver, S. M., 463
Silverberg, S. B., 238
Silverman, W. K., 465
Simeon, D., 427
Simeonova, D. I., 360
Simon, K. M., 454
Simon, T., 327
Simons, A. D., 446, 457, 469
Simpson, E. E., 133
Sing, H., 112
Singer, B., 459
Singer, J. E., T361, 361, 362, 365
Singh-Manoux, A., 168
Siscovick, D. S., 505
Sivers, H., 430
Skarin, B., 222
Skeen, P., 166
Skinner, B. F., T10, 10, 185, 188, 189, 197, 414, 451
Skodol, A. E., 436
Skolnick, A., 157
Skorinko, J., 222
Skrandies, W., 263
Slade, M. D., 497
Slater, A., 151
Slater, P. C., 296
Slattery, M., 505
Sleeper, T., 113
Slipp, S., 380
Sloan, D. M., 451
Sloan, R. P., 498
Slobin, D. I., 156, 205
Slovic, P., 311
Small, S., 64
Smallish, L., 169
Smeraldi, E., 435
Smith, A. D., 486
Smith, A. J., 491
Smith, D., 468
Smith, D. H., 116
Smith, D. M., 168, 319
Smith, J. D., 324
Smith, M., 435
Smith, P. B., 389

Smith, S., 123
Smith, S. S., 435
Smith, T. C., 492
Smith, T. L., 505
Smith-Lovin, L., 236
Smith-Spark, L., 117
Snozzi, R., 238
Snyder, E., 262
Snyder, M., 234
Snyder, S. H., 467
Soldatos, C., 116
Solodkin, A., 64
Solomon, J., 157, 416
Somlai, A. M., 226
Soomro, G. M., 423
Sorensen, E. R., 358
Sorensen, N., 325
Sowden, P., 203
Sowell, E. R., 163
Spangler, W. D., 344
Spangler, W. J., 469
Sparing, R., 307
Spates, R. C., 463
Spearman, C., T305, T321, 321
Speelman, L., 458
Speicher, C. E., 490
Spencer, D. D., 238, 359
Sperry, R. W., 62, 63
Spiegel, D., 458
Spiegel-Cohen, J., 427
Spuhl, S. T., 203
Squire, L., 283
Squire, L. R., 296
Srivastava, S., 398
Stack, J. A., 469
Stacy, B. A., 501
Staff, C. H., 116
Staggers, F., 123
Standing, L., 288
Stapf, D. M., 469
Steele, C. M., 234, 235
Steelman, L. A., 363
Steelman, L. C., 382
Steen, C., 76
Stefanick, M. L., 505
Stein, H. T., 382
Stein, S., 262
Stein-Behrens, B., 490
Steinberg, L, 238
Steiner, J. E., 151
Steiner, P., 461
Stejskal, W. J., 393
Stephens, R. S., 133
Stepnowsky, M. A., 287, 288
Stern, W., 327
Stern, Y., 319
Sternberg, R. J., 236–237, T237, 258, T305, 321, T322, 322, 333
Sternberger, R. R, 422
Stevenson, L. Y., 226
Stevenson, M. B., 156, 205
Steward, W., 12
Stewart, J. H., 186
Stewart, P., 325
Stewart, S. H., 423
Stewin, L. L., 113
Stickgold, R., 112, 120, 283

Stiff, J. B., 229
Stifter, C. A., 345
Stiles, D. A., 263
Stiles, W. B., 460
Stitzer, M. L., 128
Stockhorst, U., 350
Stone, A. A., 366
Storch, A., 57
Stout, J. C., 490
Stowell, J. R., 500
Strachey, J., 8
Straus, M. A., 186
Straus, R., 497
Strauss, V., 265
Strayer, D. L., 111
Strelzer, J., 410
Strickland, B. R., 429
Strickland, I., 435
Stueve, A., 436
Sue, D., 461
Sue, D. W., 461
Sue, S., 461
Suess, G., 157
Sukel, K. E., 307
Sullivan, R., 186
Sulloway, F. J., 382
Sultana, A., 453, 454
Sulzman, F. M., 111
Sumner, F. C., 7
Sutherland, P., 155
Suveg, C., 457
Sveen, O. B., 454
Swaab, D. F., 262, 264
Swain, S., 364
Swanbrow, D., 257
Swann, A. C., 468
Swann, J., 265
Swann, W. B., Jr., 399
Swartz, H. A., 469
Swartz, M., 425, 435
Swartz, M. S., 429
Swayze, V. W., II, 469
Swendsen, J., 430
Swenson, D. D., 483
Symes, B., 486

T

Taglialatela, J. P., 204
Tajfel, H., 232, 234
Takeuchi, S., 258
Takeuchi, T., 115
Talbot, M., 259
Talbott, G. D., 453
Tamborini, R., 238
Tamminga, C. A., 466
Tan, S. A., 500
Tang, M.-X., 319
Tang, T. Z., 457
Tanke, E. D., 234
Tanner, G., 499
Tart, C., 110
Tart, C. T., 131
Tax, A., 491
Taylor, C. B., 423
Taylor, D. M., 233
Taylor, J., 461

Taylor, S. E., 11
Taylor, T. J., 204
Taylor, V., 522
Teasdale, J. D., 385
Tecchio, F., 56
Teitelbaum, P., 349
Tellegen, A., 395, 396
Temoshok, L., 398, 498
Tennen, H., 366
Tenney, A. L., 275
Tennstedt, S. L., 168, 319
Terman, J. S., 436
Terman, L. M., T326, 326, 327
Terracciano A., 389
Terry, A. V., Jr., 466
Teuber, H. L., 283
Thase, M. E., 446, 460, 465, 468, 470
Theriault, G., 350, 374
These, M., 460
Thierry, H., 348
Thomas, M., 112
Thomas, N. J. T., 307
Thomas, S. B., 461
Thomas, S. L., 240
Thompson, P. M., 62, 163
Thompson, W. L., 307
Thomson, D. M., 286
Thorndike, E. L., T177, 184–185, 392
Thorne, B.M., 88
Thorne, D., 112
Thornton, A., 238
Thurstone, L. L., 322
Tinker, R., 463
Titchener, E., T6, 6
Tobach, E., 261
Tobias, B., 363
Tobin S. N. S., 168
Tobis, I., 363
Toepper, R., 307
Toga, A. W., 62, 163
Tohen, M., 468
Tolin, D. F., 463
Tollefson, G. D., 468
Tolman, E. C., T197, 197
Tombini, M., 56
Tomes, N., 413
Tonev, S. T., 446, 469
Torgersen, S., 435
Tormala, Z. L., 224, 228
Torrance, E. P., 327
Torrey, E. F., 432
Tourigny, M., 186
Tranel, D., 60
Trappey, C., 101
Trautwein, U., 399
Tremblay, A., 350, 374
Tresniowski, A., 117
Triandis, H., 224
Trickett, E.J., 254
Trivedi, M. H., 446, 465, 470
Trocmé, N., 186
Tropp, L. R., 235
Trost, M. R., 216
Trujillo, K. A., 467
Trut, L. M., 396
Trzbinski, J., 389
Tsai, J. L., 360
Tsuang, D. W., 435

NI-10

Tsuang, M., 424
Tsuang, M. T., 435
Tucker, D., 497
Tucker, E. W., 354
Tugade, M. M., 501
Tukuitonga, C. F., 241
Tulving, E., 275, 280, 281, 286
Turnbull, H. R., 486
Turner, J. C., 232, 234
Turner, R. A., 355
Tversky, A., 311, 317, 318

U

Udry, J. R., 236
Unger, R., 261
United Nations Population Fund, 259
Unverzagt, F. W., 168, 319
Urbina, S., 333, 395
Uretsky, S. D., 467
Urrows, S., 366
U.S. Department of Education, 265, 512

V

Vail, A., 461
Vaillant, G. E., 501
Valverde, R., 325
van der Merwe, A., 81
Van Dongen, H. P. A., 112
Van Heertum, R. L., 319
Van Horn, L., 505
Van Valin, R. D., 263
Vandell, D., 157
Vartanian, L. R., 163
Vaughan, K., 463
Vaughan, S., 504
Veitch, R., 364
Venkatraman, J., 325
Vernieri, F., 56
Vernon, P. A., 396, 397, 413
Vernon, S. W., 461
Vicary, J., 101
Vieland, V. J., 424
Vieta, E., 468
Vigil, J.D., 221, 222
Vilberg, T., 355
Villafuerte, S., 424
Villani, S., 240
Villarreal, R., 385
Vincent, J., 216
Vingerling, J. R., 83
Visser, P. S., 228
Vitaliano, P. P., 498
Vitiello, B., 446, 469, 470
Vlahov, D., 483
Vogel, G. W., 116
Vokey, J. R., 101
von Helmholtz, H., 84
Voyer, D., 264, 359
Voyer, S., 264
Vygotsky, L. S., T202, 202–203

W

Wack, D. S., 263
Wade, E., 287
Wadsworth, K., 133
Wagner, J., 486
Walker, L. J., 164
Walker, M. P., 283
Wall, P. D., 91
Wall, S., 156
Wallace, R. K., 123
Waller, J. L., 466
Waln, R. F., 401
Walsh, K., 458
Waltkins, S. S., 127
Walton, K. G., 123
Wang, B. W., 130
Wang, M., 230
Wang, N., 398, 498
Wang, N. Y., 461
Wang, Y., 264, 297
Ward, C., 487
Ward, I. L., 262
Warner, K. L., 429
Warnock, D. G., 497
Wartella, E., 240
Wartner, U. G., 157
Wasch, H. H., 385
Washburn, A. L., 349
Washburn, M.F., T6
Wassef, A., 468
Wasserstein, J., 169
Watanabe, J. T., 360
Waterhouse, L., 322
Waters, E., 156
Watkins, C. E., 393
Watkins, C. E., Jr., 382
Watkins, L. R., 490
Watson, D., 399
Watson, D. L., 275
Watson, J. B., T8, 8–9, T181, 181, 197, 414
Watson, N. V., 88
Watt, H. M. G., 264
Waziri, R., 123
Webb, A. G., 168
Webb, W. B., 111, 113
Weber, E., 78–79
Weber, G., 116
Weber, M. J., 491
Weber-Fox, C. M., 56
Wechsler, D., 321, 328
Wedding, D., 460, 461
Weems, C. F., 492
Wegner, F., 57
Weihe, P., 325
Weinberger, D. R., 433
Weiner, B., T365
Weiner, I. B., 393, 394
Weiner, R. D., 468
Weingarten, H. P., 349
Weis, S., 283
Weise, S. B., 307
Weisman, A., 168
Weisse, C. S., 501
Weissman, M. M., 429
Weitzman, M., 486
Weizenbaum, J., 313
Wells, J. E., 429
Wells, K., 470
Welsh, A., 112
Wender, P. H., 169, 432
Wenneberg, S. R., 123
Wen-Shing, T., 410
Werker, J. F., 202
Wertheimer, M., 95
Wesensten, N., 112
West, D. S., 522
West, M. S., 219
Westen, D., 457
Westengard, J., 500
Wetherell, J. L., 454
Whalen, P. J., 358
Whalen, R. E., 497
Wheeler, D., 216
Wheeler, S. C., 224, 228
Whelton, W. J., 486
Whitaker, D. L., 133
Whitbeck, L. B., 493
White, B. J., 235
White, G. L., 236
White, J., 505
White, R. F., 325
White, R. K., 214
White, S., 261
Whiton, M., 7
Whitten, W. B., 287
Whittington, C. J., 470
WHO International Consortium in Psychiatric Epidemiology, 422
Whyte, E. M., 469
Widiger, T. A., 395, 435
Wiedemann, G. C., 125
Wilhelm, K. P., 167
Wilkinson, C., 292
Willems, P. J., 348
Willerman, L., 396
Williams, A. O., 435
Williams, J. E., 263
Williams, J. M., 56
Williams, K., 219
Williams, K. D., 219, 356
Williams, M., 429
Williams, M. A., 112
Williams, M. E., 166
Williams, R. B., 497, 498
Williamson, A. M., 120
Williford, J. S., 452
Willis, H., 232
Willis, S. L., 168, 319
Willoughby, R., 505
Wilson, R. S., 319
Wilson, S., 463
Winfield, I., 435
Wingard, D. L., 492
Winkler, R., 490
Winningham, R. G., 289
Winokur, G., 408
Winstein, C. J., 282
Witelson, S. F., 264
Wittchen, H. U., 423, 429
Wolberg, L. R., 446
Wolf, A. D., 499
Wolf, L. E., 169
Wolf, M. M., 192
Wolfe, R., 457
Wolfs, R. C., 83
Wolpe, J., 364
Wong, H., 130
Wood, J. M., 393
Wood, W., 216
Woodfield, R., 389
Woods, R. P., 64
Woody, E. Z., 125
Worley, P. F., 467
Worthley, J. S., 287
Wosinska, W., 217
Wozniak, P. J., 468
Wright, C. L., 454
Wright, J., 186
Wundt, W., T5, 5–6
Wurm, M., 497
Wurtman, J., 437
Wurtman, R., 437
Wurtz, P. J., 401
Wyman, P. A., 492
Wynne, C., 198
Wynne, L. C., 457

X

Xie, H., 457

Y

Yalom, I., 457
Yang, S., 401
Ybarra, O., 399
Yeargin-Allsopp, M., 325
Yeh, M., 490
Yerkes, R. M., 344, T526, 526
Ying, Y. W., 411
Yodanis, C. L., 186
Yokoyama, K., 325
Yoo, T., 344
Young, A. W., 238, 359
Young, K., 461
Young, T., 84
Yule, G., 202
Yurgelun-Todd, D., 131

Z

Zafar, U., 425
Zajecka, J., 446, 465, 470
Zajonc, R. B., 219, 236, 363
Zak, P. J., 355
Zanarini, M. C., 435
Zane, N., 461
Zarahn, E., 319
Zavalloni, M., 220
Zayas, L. H., 493
Zeki, S., 95, 237, 355
Zentall, T. R., 198
Zhou, J. N., 262, 264
Zijdenbos, A., 163
Zilles, K., 60
Zillmann, D., 238
Zimbardo, P., T239, 239–240
Zimerman, B., 429
Zonderman, A. B., 396, 413
Zorilla, E. P., 491
Zuckerman, B., 127
Zuckerman, M., 345, 483
Zvolensky, M. J., 423

Subject Index

A

ABC model of attitudes, T224–225, 224–225, 225f
Abnormal behavior. *See also* psychological disorders
   class demonstration, T412, T414
   class discussion, T411
   comprehension check, T443
   critical thinking, T416
   current issues, T411
   defining, T259, T409, T411, T412–413, 259, 412–413
   history of, T409, T410–411, 410–411
   impacts, T416, 416
   models of, T409, T413–414, 413–415
   stigma, T415, 415–416
   terms, T410
   understanding visuals, T415
Abnormality, T412
Absolute threshold, T77–79, 79, 79t
Abu Ghraib prison, 240
Accelerated learning, T198
Accommodation, T98, T104, 98, 153
Acculturation, T254, 254
Acculturative stress, 487
Achievement, T344, T354, 354–355
Acquired (secondary) drives, T343, 343
Action potential, T45, 45, 45f
Action therapy, T446, 446
Activation-information-mode model (AIM), T109, T120, 120
Activation-synthesis hypothesis, T120, 120
Activity theory, T168, 168
Acute stress disorder (ASD), T483, T492, 492
Adaptation, T40, T66–73, 66–70
Adaptation-level phenomenon, T366, 366
Adaptive behavior, 324
Adaptive theory, T109, 113
ADHD. *See* attention deficit hyperactivity disorder
Adler, Alfred, T381–382, 382
Adolescents
   antidepressant use, T469–470
   depression, T428
   mental illness, T420
   personality disorder, T435
Adolescents, development
   antidepressants, T469–470
   authority, resentment of, T165
   critical thinking, T163
   family members, peers, T164–165, 164–165
   identity formation, T164, 164
   mental changes, T141
   personal fables, writing about, T163
   physical changes, T141, T162, 162–163
   reasoning, morals, T163–164, 163–164
   student voice question, T163
   terms, T162
Adoption studies, T68, 68–69
Adrenal glands, T51, 50–51

Adults
   ADHD, T169, 169
   psychopharmacology treatment, 469–470
   sleep patterns, 112f
Adults, development, T141
   aging, T167–168, 167–168
   cognitive changes, T165–166, 166
   death, dying, T166, T168–169, 168–169
   physical changes, T166–167, 166–167
   social changes, T165–166, 165–166
   terms, T162
Aerial (atmospheric) perspective, T98, T104, 98
Aesthetic needs, 346
Affect, T427, 427
Affective disorders. *See* mood disorders
African-Americans, obstacles, T7
Afterimages, T85, 85, 85f
Aggression
   alcohol and, T238
   defined, T238, 238
   and the media, T240, 240
   social roles, T239, 239–240
   stress, T499, 499
Aging, T167–168, T297, 167–168
Agonists, drugs, T132
Agoraphobia, T422, 422
Agreeableness, 388
Ainsworth, Mary, T157, 156–157
Alarm, T489, 489
Alcohol, T128–129
   aggression, T238, 238
   aversion therapy, 452–453
   effects of, T48, T132, 128–129, 129f
Algorithm, T311, 311
Al-Hazan, 100
Alpha waves, T113, 113
Altered state of consciousness, T110, 110–111
Alternative thinking, 504
Altruism, T240, 240–241
Alzheimer's disease, 21, 22f
American Association on Intellectual and Developmental Disabilities (AAIDD), 324
American Psychological Association (APA)
   first female president, 7
   founding of, 6
   psychological education, 519–520
   Psychology Baccalaureate Survey, 520
Amnesia, T280, T296–297, 296–297, 426
Amok, 412
Amphetamines, 126
Amygdala, T58, T60, 59, 358
Anal explosive personality, T380, 380
Anal retentive personality, T380, 380
Anal stage, T379, 379
Analytical intelligence, T322, 322
Anchoring effect, T305, T317, 317–318
Andropause, T167, 167
The Animal Mind (Washburn), T6
Animals
   language, T203, 203–204
   research, T22, T24, 22–24

Anorexia nervosa, T351–352, 351, 352f
Antagonists, drugs, T132
Anterograde amnesia, T296, 296
Antianxiety drugs, T466, 466–467
Anticonvulsant drugs, T467, 468
Antidepressant drugs, T467, 467, 469–470
Antimanic drugs, T467, 467
Antipsychotic drugs, T465, 465
Antisocial personality disorder, T434, 434–435
Anxiety disorders, T422–424, 421–424
Anxiety hierarchy, T453
Apparent distance hypothesis, 100
Applied behavior analysis (ABA), T192, T208, T454, 192, 452
Applied psychology, T513, T514, 514–515. *See also* careers in psychology
Approach-approach conflict, T481
Approach-avoidance conflict, T481
Aqueous humor, T77, 81
Arbitrary interference, 455t
Archetypes, T382, 382
Arousal theory, T344–345, T361, 344f, 344–345
Artificial intelligence (AI), T313, 312–313
Asch, Solomon, 215–216
Assimilation, T487, 153, 487
Association areas, T61, 61–62
Asylums, T447, T475
Athletes, test performance, T24, 24
Atmospheric perspective, 98
Attachment, 143
Attachment styles, T157–158, 156–157
Attention, 94
Attention deficit hyperactivity disorder (ADHD), T169, 169, 429
Attitude
   ABC model, T224–225, 224–225, 225f
   changing, T228, 228–229
   cognitive dissonance, T226–227, 226–228
   defined, T213, T224, 224
   formation, T226, 225–226, 226f
Attraction, love, T236–237, 235–238
Attribution, T213, T229, 229
Attribution theory, T229–230, T365, 229–230
Atypical neuroleptics, T465, 466
Auditory canal, T87, 87
Auditory nerve, T87, 87
Authenticity, 451
Autism, T151
Autobiographical amnesia, 297
Autokinetic effect, 100
Automatic encoding, T289, 289
Automatic processing, 111
Autonomic arousal, 50
Autonomic nervous system (ANS), T41, T49, T488, 48–50, 488–489
Autonomy, T348
Availability heuristic, T305, T317, 317
Aversion therapy, T452, 452–453
Avoidance-avoidance conflict, T481
Axon, T41, T43, 42
Axon terminals, 46

B

Babbling, T204, 204
Babies. *See* infants
Bachelor of arts, T515
Bachelor of science, T515
Bachelor's degree, T515, T520–521, 515–516
Bandura, Albert, T195–196, T384, 195, 384
Barbiturates, T128, 128
Bard, Philip, 361
Basal metabolic rate (BMR), 350
Basic anxiety, T382, 382
Basic level type, T309, 308
Basilar membrane, 87
***A Beautiful Mind*,** T431, 431
Beck, Aaron T., 454
Behavior. *See also* abnormal behavior; behaviorism; social psychology
   defined, 4
   emotional expression, 359–360
   evolutionary influences, T40, 69–70
   hormone effects, 51
   operant, 185
   physiological basis of, T75
   sexual, T352–353, 351–353
   species-specific, T191
   study methods, 17–19
Behavior control, T504
Behavior modification. *See* applied behavior analysis (ABA)
Behavior therapies, T192, T445, T451–454, 451–454
Behavioral genetics, T396, 396
Behaviorism
   abnormal behavior, T414, 414
   anxiety disorders, T424, 424
   assessments, 394
   classical conditioning, 181
   dissociative disorders, T427, 427
   history of, T8, T10, 8–9, 10
   personality, T383, 383–385
   therapy, 451–454
Bell curve, T30, T333, 30f, 30–31
The Bell Curve (Herrnstein, Murray), 333
Belonging needs (BELONG), T346, T356, 346
Benzodiazepines, T128, T466, 128, 466–467
Beta waves, T113
Big Five model, T387–388, 387–389, 389f
Bilateral cingulotomy, T469, 469
Bilateral ECT, 469
Bilingualism, T202
Binet, Alfred, T327, 327
Binet's mental ability test, T327, 327
Binge drinking, T129
Bini, Lucio, 468
Binocular cues, T96, T98, T104, 97–99
Binocular disparity, T98, T104, 98–99
BIO. *See* biological needs
Biofeedback, T192, 192
Biological influences. *See also* genetics; heredity
   anxiety disorders, T424, 424
   gender identity, 262
   mood disorders, T430, 429
   motivation, 342–346
   personality, 396–397
   personality disorders, 435

SI-1

schizophrenia, 432–433, 433f
sexual orientation, 353–354
Biological model, psychological disorders, T413–414, T424, 413–414
Biological needs (BIO), T346
Biological preparedness, 182
Biological rhythms, 111
Biomedical therapy. *See also* psychotherapy
   APA standards correlation, T444
   chapter goals, learning objectives, T444
   children, adults, 469–470
   class demonstration, T467
   class discussion, T466, T468, T469, T472
   comprehension check, T479
   defined, T446, 446
   electroconvulsive therapy, 468–469
   internet resources, T476
   psychopharmacology, T465–467, 465–468, 466t
   psychosurgery, T469, 469
   scheduling, T445
   student voice question, T468, T469, T470
   teacher prep, T445
   terms, T465
   testing readiness, T477
   understanding, check for, T466
Biopsychological perspective, T11, 11
   APA standards correlation, T40
   chapter goals, learning objectives, T40
   critical thinking, T71
   scheduling, T41
   teacher prep, T41
Biopsychosocial model, psychological disorders, T414, T432, 414–415
Bipolar disorders, T429, 429
Birth order, T382
Bisexual, T353
Bleuler, Eugen, 430
Blind spot, T82, 82
Bluebond-Langner, Myra, 169
Bobo doll, observational learning, T195, 195
Body, in balance, T59
Borderline personality disorder, T435, 435
Bottom-up processing, 101
Bouchard, Thomas, 68, 374
Brain
   aging and, T168
   class demonstration, T56, T58, T59, T60, T61, T62, T63
   critical thinking, T64
   culture and, T55
   diagram of, T57
   diet and, T319, T352
   drug use and, T131
   emotions and, T359
   functions, T61, 47
   impairment from birth, 40
   internet resources, T72
   language and, T205
   largest, of mammals, T198
   right, left hemispheres, T62–63, 62–63, 63f
   structure, function, T40, T40–41, T47, T58, T60–61, 57f, 57–62
   student voice question, T60, T61, T62
   study of, T40, T54–56, 54–56
   terms, T54
   understanding, check for, T61
   understanding visuals, T62, T63
   waves, T114–115
The Brain Observatory, 283
Brain surgery, T57
Brain-imaging techniques, T41, T55–56
Breland, Keller, 191
Breland, Marian, 191
Brightness, T81, 81
Brightness constancy, T77, T95, 95
Broca, Paul, 54
Broca's aphasia, 205
Broca's area, T61, T205, 61, 205
Bulimia nervosa, T351–352, 351, 352f
Bullying
   social influence and, T219
   work and, T398
Bureau of Labor Statistics, 519
Burnout, T486, 486
Bystander effect, T241, 212, 241

C

Caffeine, T128, 128
Calkins, Mary Whiton, 7, 7f
Calloway, LaShanda, 212, 241
Cancer, 491
Cannon, Walter, T361, 361
Cannon-Bard theory of emotion, T361, 361, 361f
Careers in psychology, T13
   bachelor's degree, T515, T520–521, 515–516
   career options, T520, 520–522, 521f
   comprehension check, T533
   critical thinking, T529
   degree requirements, T515–518, 515–518
   doctoral degree, T517, 517–518
   internet resources, T530
   master's degree, T516, 516–517
   medical degree, T517, 518
   other career field interaction, T521–526, T522–526, 522–527
   portfolio project, T515, T516, T517, T518, T519, T520, T521, T522, T523, T524, T525, T526
   psychology career fair, T527
   reasons to study, 513
   resources available, T518–520, 518–520
   salaries, T518
   scheduling, T513
   teacher prep, T513
   terms, T514–515
   testing readiness, T531
   understanding, check for, T527
Carlyle, thomas, 220
Carroll, R. T., 463
Case study, defined, T18, 18
Cast Away, 346
Castelli, W. P., 497
Catastrophe, T483, 483
Catatonic schizophrenia, T432, 432
Cattell, Raymond, T387, 387
Cell body, T41
Cellular clock theory, T167, 167
Central nervous system (CNS), T41, T47–49, 47–48
Central-route processing, 229
Centration, T154, 154, 155f
Cerebellum, T58, 58
Cerebral hemispheres, T60, 60
Cerebrum, 58
Cerletti, Ugo, T468, 468
***Challenger* disaster,** 219
Character, 376
Children
   ADHD, T169, 169
   antidepressants, T469–470, 469–470
   giftedness, T326, 326–327
   mental illness, T420
Children, development. *See* adolescents, development; infants/children, development
Chilean mine miracle, 480
China, 252–253
Chomsky, Noam, T204, 202, 204
Chromosome, 66, 142
Chunking, T279, 280
Cigarettes, sense of taste and, T89
Cilia, 90
Circadian rhythm, T109, T112, T121, 112
A Class Divided (Peters), 233
Classical conditioning
   affecting emotions, 181–182
   chapter goals, learning objectives, T176
   class demonstration, T179, T180
   defined, 178, 179f
   in everyday life, 182
   example case, 176
   internet resources, T208
   principles of, T179, 178–181
   psychotherapy, 451–452
   television advertisements and, T181
   understanding, check for, T180, T182
   understanding visuals, T179
Clicker training, operant conditioning and, T189
Clinical psychology, T12–13, 12
Cloning, humans, ethics of, T23
Closure, T95, 95
Cocaine, T127, T132, 127
Cochlea, T87, 87
Cognition, T306, 306. *See also* intelligence; thinking
Cognition, emotions and, T365
Cognitive appraisal approach, T495–496, 495–496, 496f
Cognitive control, T504
Cognitive development
   adulthood, T165–166, 166
   defined, 143
   infants, children, T152–155, 152–155, 153t
   men *vs.* women, T264, 264
Cognitive dissonance, T226–227, 226–228
Cognitive health, T319
Cognitive learning theory, T197, 197–199
Cognitive maps, T197
Cognitive needs, 346
Cognitive neuroscience, T10, 10–11
Cognitive perspective, T10, 10–11
Cognitive psychology
   abnormal behavior, T414, 414
   anxiety disorders, T424, 424
   dissociative disorders, T427, 427
Cognitive reserve, T319, 319
Cognitive therapy, T445, T455–457, 454–457
Cognitive universalism, T203, 203
Cognitive-behavioral therapy (CBT), T456–457, 456–457
Cognitive-mediational theory, T362, T481, 362–363, 363f
Collagen, 167
Collective monologue, 202
Collective unconscious, T382, 382
Collectivism, T255, 255–256
Collectivistic cultures, T399, 399–400
College Undergraduate Stress Scale (CUSS), 485, 485t
Color, 81, 84–85
Color blindness, T85
Color test, 401
Commitment, T237, 237
Common region, T96
Companionate love, T237, 237–238, 355
Comparative psychology, T14, 14
Compensation (substitution), T382, 502t
Competence, T348
Compliance, T216, 216–217
Computed Tomography (CT) scan, T55–56, 55, 55f
Concentrative meditation, T123, T505, 123
Conception, T147, 147
Concepts, T308–310, 307–310
Concrete operations stage, 154
Concussion, T54
Conditional positive regard, T386, 386–387
Conditioned emotional response (CER), T181, 181
Conditioned response (CR), T179, 179–180
Conditioned stimulus (CS), T177, T179, 179–180
Conditioned taste aversion, T182, 182
Conditioning, T8, 8. *See also* classical conditioning; operant conditioning
Conductive impairment, T88, 88
Cones, T84, 82
Confederate, 22, 215
Confidentiality, T472, 23, 471–472
Confirmation bias, T305, T314, 314–315
Conflict, T481
Conformity, T213, T215, 215, 215f
Confounding variable, T21, 21
Conjunction fallacy, T316, 317
Conscience, T378, 378
Conscientiousness, T387, 387
Conscious mind, T377
Consciousness
   APA standards correlation, T108
   chapter goals, learning objectives, T108
   class debate, T111, T121
   class demonstration, T112, T115, T117, T119
   critical thinking, T118, T135
   defined, T109, 110

Subject Index

Consciousness. (continued)
   hypnosis, meditation, T108–109, T123–125, 123–126
   internet resources, T136
   levels of, T110, 110–111
   nature and purpose of, T111
   psychoactive drugs, T109, T126–133, 126–133
   reasons to study, 109
   scheduling, T109
   sleep, dreams, T109, T111–121, 110–121
   states of, brain waves, 114f
   student voice question, T120
   teacher prep, T109
   terms, T110
   testing readiness, T137
   vs. unconsciousness, T108, 110–111
Conservation, cognitive development, T155, 154
Consolidation, T283, 283
Constructive processing, T291, 291
Consumer psychology, T216, 216–217
Contiguity, T96, 96
Contingency contracting, 453–454
Continuity, T95, 95–96
Continuous reinforcement, T189, 189
Control group, T21, 21
Conventional morality, T164, 164
Convergence, T98, T104, 98
Convergent thinking, T315, 315
Conversion disorder, T425, 425
Cooing, T204, 204
Coopersmith Self-Esteem Inventory, T399
Coping strategies, T500–505, 500–503
Cornea, T77, 81
Coronary heart disease, stress, 497f, 497–498
Corporal punishment, T157
Corpus callosotomy, T62
Corpus callosum, T60, 60
Correlation, T19–20, T31–32, 19–20, 31, 32f
Correlation coefficient, T19, T31–32, 19, 31–32
Correlation method, T19–21, 19–20
Cortex, T41, T58, T60, 58–62
Corticoids, 51
Cortisol, 51
Costa, P. T., 387, 394
Counseling psychology, T12, 12–13
Counterconditioning, 9
Creative enhancement, T198
Creative intelligence, T322, 322
Creativity, T315–316, 315–316
Critical period, T144, 144–146
Cross-cultural psychology, T257, 257–259
Cross-sectional design, T144, 144, 145t
Cross-sequential design, T144, 144, 145t
Crowe, Russell, 431, 431f
Cultural bias, T305, T330–331, 330–331
Cultural neuroscience, T55
Cultural psychology, 11
Cultural relativism, T256
Cultural relativity, T411, 411
Culture, cultural influences
   abnormal behavior, T259, T411, 259, 411–412
   advertisements, legal drug use and, T133
   aging, attitudes and, T168
   aging, memory and, T297
   APA standards correlation, T248
   beliefs, behavior and, T68
   brain and, T55
   chapter goals, learning objectives, T248
   comprehension check, T271
   conceptions of self, identity, 255–256
   consumer psychology, T216, 217
   creativity, T315–316, 315–316
   cross-cultural psychology, T257, 257–259
   culture-based support, 248
   death, dying, T169
   defined, T250, 250–251
   development, 68, 258–259
   eating habits, disorders, T350, 351
   emotion, T257, T361, T363, 257–258, 363–364
   five-factor model, T389
   gender, T263, 262–265
   happiness, T361
   immigration, acculturation, T254, 254
   independence, interdependence, T256
   intelligence, T258, 258
   internet resources, T268
   language, T204
   meditation, T124
   memory and, T276
   nonverbal gestures, T363
   perception, T77, T101, 101
   personality, T399–400, 399–400
   in psychology, T11, 250–251
   psychotherapy, T453, 460–461
   reasons to study, 249
   scheduling, T249
   social loafing, 219
   stress factors, T501, 486–487, 501–503
   student voice question, T251
   teacher prep, T249
   terms, T250
   testing readiness, T269
   understanding visuals, T251, T256, T258
   variations across time, place, T252–253, 251–254
Culture-bound, T257, 257
Culture-bound syndromes, T411, 411–412
Curve of forgetting, T293, 293–294, 294f
Cyclothymia, T427, 427–428

D
Da Vinci, Leonardo, 54
Dark adaptation, T83, 83
Darwin, Charles, 7, 11, 69–70, 362
Data analysis, 26–33
Day care
   designing of, T158
   social development and, T145
Death, dying, T168–169, 168–169
Debriefing, 23

Decay of memory, T295, 295
Decibels, 86f
Decision control, T504
Decision making, T318, 310–312, 318–319
Declarative memory, T281, 281
Deep Blue, 313
Deep lesioning, T54, 54
Defense mechanisms, T379, T502, 501, 502t
Deficiency needs, 346
Degrees in psychology, T515–518, 515–518
Deindividuation, T219, 219
Delta waves, T113, T115, 113–115
Delusional disorder, 431
Delusions, T430, 430
Dendrites, T41, T42, 42
Denial, 502t
Deoxyribonucleic acid. See DNA
Department of Education, 265
Dependent variable, T20, 21
Depersonalization disorder, 427
Depolarization, T45, 45
Depressants, T109, T126, T128, 126, 128–129
Depression, T198–199. See also major depression
   adolescents, T428
   class demonstration, T428
   treatment of, 467, 469–470
Depth perception, T96, T98, T104, 96
Descriptive statistics, T26–27, 26–28
Desensitization, T365, 365
Development. See human development
Developmental delay, T324–325, 324–325, 326t
Developmental psychology, T13, T143, T145, 13, 143. See also human development
Deviation IQ scores, 328
Devil's trident, 101, 101f
Diabetes, 51
Diagnostic and Statistical Manual of Mental Disorders (DSM), T409, T418–419, 418–420, 419t
Diet
   brain and, T319
   plans, physiology and psychology of, T350
Difference threshold, 78–79
Diffusion of responsibility, T241, 241
Digit-span test, 278, 278f
Direct observation, T394, 394
Discrimination, T232–233, 232–233
Discriminative stimulus, 188
Disorganized schizophrenia, T431, 431
Displaced aggression, T499, 499
Displacement, 502t
Display rules, T363, 258, 363–364
Dispositional cause, T229, 229
Dissociation, 124–125
Dissociative amnesia, T426, 426
Dissociative disorders, T426–427, 426–427
Dissociative fugue, T426, 426
Dissociative identity disorder, T426, 426–427
Distress, T43, 483
Disuse, 295
Divergent thinking, T315, 315–316, 316t
Dizygotic twins, T147
DNA (deoxyribonucleic acid), T41, T66–67, 66, 142, 143f

Doctor of philosophy (Ph.D.), T517, 517–518
Doctor of psychology (Psy.D.), T517, 517–518
Doctorate, T517, 517–518
Domhoff, William, 120
Dominant genes, T67, 66–67, T142, 142–143
Door-in-the-face technique, T216, 216
Dopamine, T47, T366, 366
Dot problem, 314, 314f, 318f
Double-blind experiment, T22, 22
Down syndrome, 325
Downward social comparison, 504
Draw-A-Person, 393
Dreams
   class demonstration, T119
   critical thinking, T120
   functions of, T109, 119–120
   interpretation, T119, T449, 449
   nightmares, T116, 116–118, T118
   REM sleep, T113, T115–116, 115–116, T118
   student voice question, T118
   understanding visuals, T119
Drive, 343
Drive-reduction theory, T343, 343–344
Drug abuse, body, brain and, T48
Drug tolerance, T127, 127
Drugs. See psychoactive drugs; psychopharmacology
Dweck, Carol, T354, 354–355
Dysthymia, T427, 427–428

E
Eaker, E. D., 497
Ear
   sound and, T77
   structure of, 87f, 87–88
Eating, T341, T349–352, T369, 349–351
Ebbinghaus, Hermann, T293, 293–294
Ebrahim, Irshaad, 117
Echoic memory, T276
Eclectic therapy, 459
Ecstasy (MDMA), T130, 130
Educational psychology, 512, T522, 522–523
EEG. See electroencephalograph
Effortful encoding, 289
Effortful processing, 111
Ego, T378, 378
Ego integrity, 166
Egocentrism, T154, 154
Einstein, Albert, 81
Elaboration likelihood model, 228–229, T229
Elaborative rehearsal, T280, 280
Elective, T515
Electrochemical messages, T44–45, 43–45
Electroconvulsive therapy (ECT), T296, T468, 468–469
Electroencephalograph (EEG), T56, 55f, 56, T114
Elliot, Jane, T233, 233
Embryo, T149, 149
Embryonic period, T148, 148
Emotion
   angry/happy man experiment, T365, 365
   behavioral expression, T358–360, 359–360

SI-3

chapter goals, learning objectives, T340
class activity, T366
class demonstration, T360, T361, T362, T363, T364
classical conditioning, 181–182
cognitions and, T365
cognitive labeling, 360
cultural, environmental factors, T257, 257–258, T361, T363, 363–364
defined, T358–360, 358
description of, T362
development in children, 158, 159–160t
fear, T364–365, 364–365
happiness, T366, 366–367
internet resources, T370
Kismet, sociable robot, T359
mood disorders, T427, 427–430
negative, T362
nonverbal gestures, T363
odors and, T364
physiology of, T361, 358–359
range of, 428f
reasons to study, 341
scheduling, T341
student voice question, T360, T363
teacher prep, T341
terms, T358
testing readiness, T371
theories of, T360–363, 360–363, T373
understanding, check for, T364
understanding visuals, T359
vocal cues and, T360
Emotional intelligence, T322, 322
Emotion-focused coping, T500, 500
Empathy, T451, 451
Encoding
class demonstration, T276, T277, T278, T279, T281, T282
critical thinking, T283
defined, 274, 275f
failure, T294, 294, 294f
internet resources, T275
more effectively, 279–280
multicultural focus, T276
specificity, T285, 285–286, 286f
student voice question, T277, T279
terms, T274
understanding visuals, T278
Endocrine glands, T41, T50–51, 50
Endorphins, T47, T366
Environment, environmental influence
emotion, T363, 363–364
fear, T364–365, 364–365
gender identity, 263
happiness, T366, 366–367
heredity, adaptation, T40, 66–70, T66–73
human development, T143, 67–69, 143
intelligence, T331, 331–333, 332f
mental illness, T436
personality, 396–397
sexual orientation, 353–354

stress factors, 483–486
terms, T66
Environmental psychology, T524, 524
Episodic memory, T281, 281
Equal status contact, T235, 235
Ergot, T130
Erikson, Erik, 158, 165–166, T381–382, 382
Erikson's psychological stages of development, T158–160, T166, 158, 159–160t
Erikson's theories of adulthood, 165–166
Erogenous zone, 379
Escape, stress, T499
Esteem needs (ESTEEM), T346
Ethical issues
humans vs. animals, 24
psychological research, 23
psychotherapy, T471–472, 470–473
Ethnicity, psychotherapy, 460–461
Eustress, T49, 483
Evolution, T69, 69–70
Evolutionary psychology, T11, 11
Exercise, T52, 505
Exhaustion, T489, 490
Exner, John, 393
Exorcism, T411
Expectancy, T100, 346, 385
Expectancy-value theories, T346, 346
Experiment, defined, T20, 20
Experimental group, T21, 21
Experimental hazards, T21–22
Experimental method, T20–21, 20–21
Experimental psychology, T13, 13
Experimenter effect, 21–22, T22
Explicit memory, 281
Explicit processing, T111, 111, T136
Exposure and response prevention, 453
Expressive language delay, 156
External locus of control, T354, 354, T385
Extinction, T180, T188
classical conditioning, 180, 181f
operant conditioning, T188, 188
therapy, T454, 454
Extraversion, extraverts, 387, T398
Extrinsic motivation, T342, 342, T348
Eye, T81–83, 81–84, 82f
Eye-movement desensitization reprocessing (EMDR), 462–463, T463
Eysenck, Hans, T459, 459

F

Facial expressions, T359, 359f, 359–360
Facial feedback hypothesis, T362, 362, 362f
Falater, Scott, 117
False memory syndrome, T291–292, 292
False positive, 288–289
Family counseling, 457
Family influence, psychological disorders, T436, 436
Family therapy, 457
Fear, T364–365, 364–365
Fechner, Gustav, 79
Femininity, T400, 400
Fertilization, T147, 147
Fetal alcohol syndrome, 325
Fetal period, T148, 148
Fetus, 149
Field, Sally, 427

Fight-or-flight system, T49, 49–50
Figure-ground, T95, 95, 95f
Finding Meaning in Dreams (Domhoff), 120
Fiorina, Carly, 221
Five-factor model, T387–388, 387–389, 389f
Five-Factor test, 400
Fixation, T379, T380, 379
Fixed interval schedule of reinforcement, T189, 189
Fixed ratio schedule of reinforcement, T190, 190
Flashbulb memories, T289, 289
Flat affect, T431, 431
Flavor, T90
Flooding, T453, 453
FMRI. *See* functional MRI
Food and Drug Administration, 469
Foot-in-the-door technique, T216, 216
Forensic psychology, T523, 523–524
Forgetting
amnesia, T280, 296–297
curve of, 293–294, 294f
reasons for, T294, 296t
theories of, T295, 295
Formal concept, T309, 308
Formal operations stage, T155, 155
Fragile X syndrome, T325, 325
Framingham Heart Study (Eaker, Castelli), 497
Free association, T449, 449
Free radical theory, T167, 167
Free-floating anxiety, T422, 422
Frequency count, T394, 394
Frequency distribution, T28–29, 28–29, 29t
Frequency polygon, T30, 31, 31f
Frequency theory, T88, 88
Freud, Anna, 8f
Freud, Sigmund
aggression, 238
background, 8f, 8–9, 376–377
cocaine use, 127
dreams, T109, T119, 119
emotions, T360
instincts, 343
psychoanalysis, T445, T447, 447–450, T450
psychodynamic theory of personality, 376–383, T377–383
Friedman, Meyer, 497
Frontal lobes, T61, 61, 61f
Frustration, T488, 488
Frustration-aggression hypothesis, T238, 238
Fully functioning person, T386, 386–387
Functional fixedness, T305, T314, 314
Functional MRI (fMRI), T56, 55f, 56
Functionalism, T6, 7
Fundamental attribution error, T229–230, 229–230

G

G factor, T321, 321–322
GABA (gamma-Aminobutyric acid), alcohol and, T132
Gage, Phineas, 18, 18f
Gambler's fallacy, T305, T318, 318
Gambon, John, 525
Ganglia, T77
Gangs, T221–222, 221–222

Garcia, John, 7
Gardner's multiple intelligences, T305, T322–323, 322, 323t
Gate-control theory, T91, 91–92
Gates, T44, 44
Geert Hofstede Cultural Dimensions, T348
Gender
APA standards correlation, T248
career stereotypes, T265
chapter goals, learning objectives, T248
children's toys, analyzing, T262
controversies in, T264
culture and, T263
defined, 261
depression, men and, T264
internet resources, T268
math, science gap, T265, 265
men/women, differences, T264, 264–265
physique preferences, T351
psychotherapy, T460–461
reasons to study, 249
scheduling, T249
student voice question, T262
teacher prep, T249
terms, T261
testing readiness, T269
Gender identity
biological influence, T262, 262
cultural influence, T263, 263–264
defined, T261, 261–262
environmental influence, T263, 263
Gender identity disorder, 261–262
Gender roles, T261, T263, 261
Gender typing, T261, 261
General adaptation syndrome (GAS), T481, T489, 489f, 489–490
Generalization, operant conditioning, T188, 188
Generalized anxiety disorder, T423, 423–424
Generativity, 165–166
Genes, T66–67, 66–67, T142, 142
Genetics, T66–67. *See also* biological influences; heredity
defined, T40, 66–67
human development, T142, 142–143
personality, T396, 396–397
Genital stage, T380, 380–381
Genovese, Catherine, 212, 241
Germinal period, T148, 148
Gestalt, T95
Gestalt psychology, T77, T95–96, 95–96, 96f
Gibson, Eleanor, 97
Gifted, T326, 325–327
Giftedness, T326, 323–327
Gilligan, Carol, 164
Glands, 41, T51 50–52
Glove anesthesia, 425f
Glucagons, 51, 349
Gonads, T51, 51
Goodall, Jane, 17f
Grammar, T201, 201
Graphs, tables, T28–29, 28–31
Great person theory, T220, 220
Group polarization, T219, T220, 220
Group therapy, T457–458, 457–458, 458t

SI-4

Subject Index

Groupthink, T213, T219, 219–220, 220t
Growth hormone (GH), 51
Growth needs, 346
Gustation, T89, 88–89
Gut feelings, T318

H

H. M., 283
Habits, 383
Habituation, T79, 79–80, T104
Hagwood, Scott, 272
Hair cells, 87
Haiti, 248
Hall, G. Stanley, 6
Hallucinations, T431, 431
Hallucinogenics, hallucinogens, T109, T126, 126, T130–131, 130–131
Halo effect, T392, 392
Hanks, Tom, 346
Happiness, T366, 366–367
Hardy personality, T498, 498
Harlow, Harry, T158, 158
Harman, Denham, 167
Hassles, 485–486
Hayflick Limit, 167
Health, aging, T166, 167
Health, personality, T398, 398
Health psychology, T522, 522
Health, stress. See stress, stressors
Hearing, T86–88, 86–88
Hearing impairment, T88
Heider, Fritz, 229
Helping, factors in, T241
Henning, Hans, 89
Heredity. See also biological influences; genetics
    class demonstration, T68, T69
    development, 67–69
    environment, adaptation, T40, 66–70, T66–73
    genetics, T67, 66–67
    intelligence, T331, 331–333, 332f
    terms, T66
    writing about, T67
Heritability, 386–397
Heroin, T130, 130
Herrnstein, R. J., 333
Hertz (Hz), T86, 86
Heterosexual, T353
Heuristic, T311, 311–312
Hierarchy of needs, 346–348, 347f
Hindbrain, T41, T57, 57–58
Hindsight bias, T291, 291
Hippocampus, T58–59, 59, T283, 283
Hippocrates, 410
Histogram, T29, 29, 29f
Hofstede, Geert, T348, T399–400, 399–400
Holophrases, 156, 204
Homeostasis, T59, 59, T343, 343, 343f
Homosexual, T353
Hormones, T41, T50–52, 50–52
Horney, Karen, T381–382, 382
Hot streak, T318
House-Tree-Person, 393
How We Decide (Lehrer), 318
Human development
    adolescence, T141, 162–165
    adulthood, T141, 165–169
    APA standards correlation, T140
    chapter goals, learning objectives, T140

    class discussion, T144
    controversies, T144
    critical, sensitive periods, T144, 144–146
    critical thinking, T171
    cultural differences, T259, 258–259
    defined, T141, 142
    environmental influences, T142–143, 143
    genetic influences, T142, 142–143
    infancy, childhood development, T141, 151–160
    internet resources, T143, T145, T172, T175
    newborn development, 150–151
    prenatal development, T147–149, 147–149
    reasons to study, 141
    research issues, 143
    scheduling, T141
    student voice question, T143
    teacher prep, T141
    terms, T142
    testing readiness, T173
    ways to study, T144, 144
Human factors psychology, T526, 526
The Human Zoo **(television),** T239
Humanistic perspective, T10, 10, 376, T376–377, 385–387
Humanistic theory, psychotherapy, T445, T450–451, 450–451
Humanitarian guidelines, 23
Humors, T410
Hunger. See eating
Hypnagogic images, T114, 114
Hypnos, T124
Hypnosis, T108–109, T124–125, 124–126, 125t, T136, T292, T293
Hypochondriasis, T425, 425
Hypoglycemia, 51
Hypothalamus
    circadian rhythm, T109, T112, 112
    eating motivation, 349–350
    functions of, T58–59, 59
Hypothesis, T16, 16

I

Iconic memory, T276
Id, T378–379, 378
Ideal self, T385, 385–386, 386f
Identification, T380, 380, 502t
Identity crisis, T160
Ikeda, Kikunae, 89
Illusions, T77, T99, 99–100
Imaginary audience, T163, 163
Immigration, T254, 254
Immune system, T52, 51–52, T490, 490–491, 491f
Impermeable, 44
Implicit memory, T280–281, 280–281
Implicit processing, T111, 111, T136
Impulse buying, consumer psychologists and, T182
Incentive approaches, T345, 345–346
Incentives, 345, T348
Independent self-concept, T255, 255–256, 256f
Independent variable, T20, 20–21
Individualism, T255, 255–256
Individualistic cultures, T399, 399

Individualized educational program (IEP), 512
Industrial/organizational (I/O) psychology, 14, T526, 526–527
Ineffective therapies, T39
Infantile amnesia, T297, 297
Infants, 112f, 156–157
Infants/children, development
    children's books, as illustration, T160
    class demonstration, T156, T158, T160
    cognitive skills, T141, T152–155, 152–155, 153t
    innate reflexes, T141
    intelligence, measuring, T150
    internet resources, T152
    language, 155–156, T156
    newborns, T150–151, 150–151
    physical changes, T151, 151, 152f
    relationships, T156–157, 156–157
    social, emotional, 158, 159–160t
    student voice question, T154
    terms, T147
    understanding visuals, T158
    videos, to teach, T157
Inferential statistics, 26, T33, 33
Inferiority complex, 382
Information-processing model, 274–275, T275
Informed consent, T20, 20, 23
In-groups, T232, 232
Insight, T198, 198, T312, 312
Insight therapy, T446, 446, T448
Insomnia, T118, 118
Instinct approach, T342–343, 343
Instinctive drift, T191, 191
Instincts, 342–343
Institutional review boards (IRBs), 23
Insulin, 51, 349
Integration, T487, 487
Intellectual disability, T324–325, 324–325
Intelligence
    APA standards correlation, T304
    chapter goals, learning objectives, T304
    class debate, T324
    class demonstration, T322, T329, T331
    class discussion, T323, T333
    comprehension check, T339
    controversies in, T332
    critical thinking, T330, T332, T335
    culture, T258, 258
    defined, T305, 321, T321
    disability, 323–325, T324–325, 326t
    in film, T326
    flexibility of, T328
    giftedness, T323, T326, 323–327
    heredity, environment, T331, 331–333, 332f
    in infants, T150
    internet resources, T336
    late bloomers, T329
    scheduling, T305
    teacher prep, T305
    terms, T321
    testing readiness, T337

    theories of, T321–322, 321–323
    understanding, check for, T323, T325
    understanding visuals, T322, T325
Intelligence quotient (IQ), T327, T330–333, 327–328
Intelligence testing
    cultural bias in, T330–331
    history of, T327, 327–328
    modern, T328, 328–329
    reliability, validity, T329, 329–330
    use of, T330–331, 330–331
Interdependent self-concept, T255, 255–256, 256f
Interference theory, T295, 295
Intergroup contact, 235
Internal locus of control, T354, 354, T385
Internet resources
    autism, T151
    brain, T72
    brain waves, T114
    careers in psychology, T530
    classical conditioning, T208
    consciousness, T136
    culture, cultural influences, T268
    developmental psychology, T145
    dissociative disorders, T426
    emotion, T370
    encoding, T275
    gender, T268
    human development, T143, T145, T172, T175
    hypnosis, T124
    infants/children, development, T152
    information from, T406
    intelligence, T336
    language, T208
    learning, T198, T208
    Maslow, T347
    memory, T300
    memory myths, T275
    memory retrieval, T288, T292
    motivation, T370
    neo-Freudians, T381
    nervous system, T43
    neuropsychology, T72
    neuroscience, T43, T72
    operant conditioning, T208
    perception, T104
    personality, T404
    personality tests, T400, 400–401
    positive psychology, T367
    psychological disorders, T421, T440
    psychologists, finding on, T14
    psychology, T5, T7, T30, T36
    psychology-related, evaluation of, T30
    research results, T33
    sensation and perception, T104
    sleep studies, T113
    social psychology, T244
    statistics, T33
    storage, T275
    teen alcohol abuse, T128
    wikis, T74
    Zuckerman-Kuhlman personality questionnaire, T345

Interneurons, T48, 48
Interpersonal attraction, T236, 235–238
Interposition, 98
The Interpretation of Dreams **(Freud),** T119, 119, 377
Interviews, T391–392, 391–392
Intimacy, T237, 237
Intonation, 202
Intrinsic motivation, T342, 342, T348
Introversion, introverts, 387
Ions, 43, T44
IQ (intelligence quotient), T327, 327–328, T330–333

J
James, William, 6–7, 360–361, 397
James-Lange theory of emotion, T360, 360f, 360–361
The Janus Report on Sexual Behavior, 352, T353
Jim twins, 68, 374
Job stress, T486, 486–487
Jones, Mary Cover, 9
Journal of Educational Psychology, 522
Judgements, T305, T316–317, 316–318
Jung, Carl Gustav, T381–382, 381–382, 382f
Just noticeable difference (jnd, difference threshold), T78–79, 78–79
Justification, T23, 23

K
Kasparov, Garry, 313
Keirsey Temperament Sorter, 400
Kennedy, John F., 469f
Kennedy, Joseph, 469f
Kennedy, Rosemary, 469f
Kesey, Ken, 468
Kinesthetic senses, T91–92, 91–92
King, Rodney, 234
Kinsey, Alfred, T353, 353
Kinsey Study, T353
Kohlberg, Lawrence, 163–164
Kohlberg's levels of morality, T164, 164, 164t
Köhler, Wolfgang, 197–198, T198
Kübler-Ross, Elisabeth, 168

L
Laboratory method, T18, 18
Lahaul Valley, 252
Lange, Carl, 360–361
Language
  acquisition of, T204
  animal studies, T203, 203–204, T208
  APA standards correlation, T176
  brain areas associated with, 205
  chapter goals, learning objectives, T176
  culture and, T204
  defined, T201, 201
  development stages, 155–156, T156, 204–205
  internet resources, T208
  nonhandicapping, T205
  scheduling, T177
  structure of, 201–202
  teacher prep, T177
  terms, T201
  testing readiness, T209
  thought and, T202–203, 202–204
Language acquisition device (LAD), 201, 204
Late bloomers, T329
Latency, T380, 380
Latent content, T119, 449
Latent learning, 197, 198f
Lateral thinking, T198
Law of Effect, 184–185
Law, psychology, 523–524
Lazarus, Richard, T362, 362–363, T481, 495–496
Leadership, 220–221, T221
Learned helplessness, T198, 198–199
Learning. See also classical conditioning; operant conditioning
  APA standards correlation, T176
  chapter goals, learning objectives, T176
  cognitive, T197, 197–199
  controversies in, T187
  defined, 178
  forms of, T207
  insight, T198
  internet resources, T198, T208
  observational, T195–196, 195–196
  reasons to study, 177
  scheduling, T177
  teacher prep, T177
  techniques, methods of, T198
  testing readiness, T209
  theory, in everyday life, T193
Learning environment, T46
Left-handed people, workplace problems, T64
Lehrer, Jonah, 318
Lens, T77, T82, 82
Levels-of-processing model, T273, T275, 275, 276f
Lewis, James, 68, 374
Lifespan development. See human development
Lifestyle awareness triangle, T503
Lifestyle, healthy, T52
Light, T77, T81, 81
Light adaptation, T84, 84
Limbic system, T58, 58–60, 59f
Lindemann, Bernd, 89
Linear perspective, T98, 98, T104
Lithium, T467, 467–468
Little Albert experiment, T8–9, 9, T181, 181
Little Man Tate **(movie),** T326
Little Peter experiment, T9, 9, T23
Lobes, T60–61, 60–61, 61f
Locus of control, T385, 385
Loftus, Elizabeth, T292, 292–293
Longitudinal design, T144, 144, 145t
Long-term memory (LTM)
  defined, T273, T279, 279
  more effective encoding, 280
  organization, T282, 282
  storage, 280–281, T280–283
  types of, 281, 282f
Loss aversion, T305, T318, 318–319
Loudness, T86
Love, T236–237, 235–238, 355–356
Lowball technique, T216, 216–217
Lowe, Jules, 117
LSD (lysergic acid diethylamide), T130, 130
Lucent Technologies, 221

M
Magnetic resonance imaging (MRI), T55–56, 55, 55f
Magnification, 424
Magnification and minimization, 455t
Maintenance rehearsal, T279, 279
Major, college, T515
Major depression, 428f, 428–429, T428–430
Maladaptive, T413, 413
Manic, T429, 429
Manifest content, T119, 449
Marginalization, T487, 487
Marijuana, T48, T130–131, 131
Martin, Lawrence, 117
Masculinity, T400, 400
Maslow, Abraham, T341, 10, T346–347, 346–348, 385–387
Maslow's hierarchy of needs, T346–347, 346–348, 347f
Master's degree, T516, 516–517
Matsumoto, David, 7–8
Maturation, 178
Mayo, Elton, T526, 526
McCarthy, John, 313
McCrae, R. R., 387, 394
McDonnell, James, 426
McDougall, William, T343, 343
MDMA (ecstasy, X), T130, 130
Mean, T27, 27, 323–324
Means-end analysis, T312, 312
Measure of central tendency, T26–27, 26–27
Measure of variability, T26, 26–28, T28
Mechanical solution, T311, 311
Media, violence, T240, 240
Median, T27, 27
Meditation, T109, T123–124, 123–124, T136, T505
Mediterranean diet, brain and, T319
Medulla, T57, 57–58
Melatonin, T51, 51
Memory
  amnesia, T280, T296–297, 296–297
  APA standards correlation, T272
  chapter goals, learning objectives, T272
  cocktail party effect, T277
  defined, T274, 274
  encoding process, T274–279, 274–279
  forgetting process, T293–295, 293–296
  improving, T299
  internet resources, T300
  levels of processing, T273, T275, 275, 276f
  masters of, 272
  more effective encoding, T279–280
  myths, internet resources, T275
  reasons to study, 273
  reliability, T290–293, 290–293
  scheduling, T273
  storage location, T282–283, 282–283
  storage process, T282–283, 280–283
  teacher prep, T273
  testing readiness, T301
  time-gap experience, T281
Memory distortion, T293
Memory retrieval
  class demonstration, T286, T289, T290, T293, T294, T295
  comprehension check, T303
  controversies, T289
  cues, T285–286, 285–286, 286f
  factors, T286–289, 286–289
  improvement, T289–290, 289–290
  internet resources, T288, T292
  problems, 291
  reliability, T290–292, 292–293
  serial position effect, T287
  student voice question, T286, T290, T292, T296
  terms, T285
  understanding, check for, T291, T295
  understanding visuals, T286, T289, T294, T296
Memory trace, T295, 295
Men
  depression, T264
  eating disorders, 351
  emotional display rules, 363–364
  in math, science, 265
  physique preferences, T351
  women, differences, T264, 264–265, T307
Menopause, T166, 167
Mental illness. See abnormal behavior; psychological disorders
Mental images, T306–307, 306–307, 307f
Mental retardation. See intellectual disability
Mental set, T305, T314, 314, 314f
Mere exposure effect, T236, 236
Mescaline, T130, 130
Microsleeps, T112, 112
Milgram, Stanley, T217–218, 217–218
Milgram's Study of Obedience to Authority, T217–218, 217–218, 218t
Miller, George, 278
Minnesota Multiphasic Personality Inventory, Version II (MMPI-2), T395, 395
Minnesota Twin Family Study, 68
Minnesota/Texas Adoption Project, T68, 68
Minor, college, T515
Minorities
  mental health care and, T17
  in psychology, T7, 7–8
Mirror neurons, T41, T64, 64
Misinformation effect, T291, 291
Mnemonics, T289–290, 289–290, 290f
Mode, T27, 27
Modeling, T454, 454
Molaison, Henry, 283
Monoamine oxidase inhibitors (MAOIs), T467, 467
Monocular cues (pictorial depth cues), T96, T98, 97–98, T104
Monozygotic twins, T147
Mood disorders, T427–430, 427–430
Mood swings, T429
Moon illusion, 99–100, 100f
Moore, Steve, 296
Moral development, 163–164, T164
Morphemes, T202, 202
Morphine, T129, 129
Motion parallax, T98, 98, T104

Subject Index

Motion sickness, T92
Motivation
  achievement, T344, T354, 354–355
  APA standards correlation, T340
  to belong, T356, 356
  chapter goals, learning objectives, T340
  class debate, T347
  class demonstration, T343, T344, T346, T348, T349, T354, T355, T356
  cognitive, biological theories, T342–344, 342–346, T355
  controversies in, T354
  critical thinking, T356
  defined, 342
  eating, T341, T349–352, 349–351, T369
  humanist theory of, T346–348, 346–348
  internet resources, T370
  to love, 355–356
  needs and, T344–345
  reasons to study, 341
  sexual behavior, T352–353, 351–353
  sexual orientation, T352–354, 351–354
  student voice question, T345, T348, T349, T353
  teacher prep, T341
  terms, T342
  testing readiness, T371
  types of, T343
  understanding visuals, T343, T344, T355
  will to recover, 340
Motor cortex, 61, T62, 62*f*
Motor neurons, T48, 48
Müller-Lyer illusion, T99, 99, 99*f*
Murder while sleepwalking, T117, 117
Murray, C., 333
Murray, Henry, 393
Myelin, T43, 43
Myers, David G., 12, 367, T367
Myers-Briggs Type Indicator (MBTI), T395, 395

N

Narcolepsy, T118, 118–119
Narcotics, T109, T126, 126, T129–130, 129–130
Nash, John, T430, 430–431
National Alliance on Mental Illness (NAMI), 473
Natural concept, T309, 309
Natural killer cell, T491, 491
Natural selection, 7, T69, 69
Naturalistic observation, T17, 17
Nature, T66, 66, T142, 142, T172
Nature *vs.* nurture, T66–67, T69, T141
Navajo medicine, T461
Need, T344, 343
Need for achievement (nAch), T344, 344
Need for affiliation (nAff), T344, 344
Need for power (nPow), T344, 344
Negative correlation, T19, T32
Negative reinforcement, T186, 186, 187*f*, 188*t*

Negative symptoms, T432, 432
Negatively skewed, T31, 31
Neo-Freudians, T381, 381–383
Nervous system
  class debate, T52
  class demonstration, T45, T46, T47, T49, T51
  divisions of, T42, 42, 43*f*
  functions of, T40–53, 47–50
  internet resources, T43
  neuroendocrine system, 50–52
  neurons, T42–47, 42–47
  reasons to study, 41
  student voice question, T43, T45, T46, T48
  terms, T42
  understanding visuals, T44
Neuroendocrine system, 50–52
Neurofeedback, T192, 192
Neuroleptics, 465–466
Neurons
  defined, T41, 42
  electrochemical messages, 43–45, T44–45
  memory, T283, 283
  mirror, T64, 64
  psychoactive drugs, T132, 131–132
  speed of, T45
  spinal cord, T48, 48
  structure, function, 42–43, 44*f*, T42–45
  synapses, T46–47, 46–47
Neuroplasticity, 56
Neuropsychology, T72
Neuroscience, T40, 56–57
  controversies in, T59
  internet resources, T43, T72
  recent innovations, T56
Neurotic personalities, T382, 382
Neuroticism, 388
Neuroticism/Extraversion/Openness Personality Inventory (NEO-PI), 394
Neurotransmitters, T46–47, 46–47, 47*t*, T132
Neutral stimulus (NS), T177, T179, 179–180
Newborn development, T150–151, 150–151
Newman, Constance, 515*f*
Nicotine, T127, 127–128
Night blindness, 83
Night Terrors, 108, T116, 116–118, T118
Nightmares, T116, 116–118, T118
Nondeclarative memory, 280
Nondirective therapy, 450
Nonexperimental methods, T17–18, 17–19
Nonhandicapping language, T205
Non-REM (NREM) sleep, 113–115, 115*f*, T113–116, T118
Nonverbal gestures, T363
Norm of reciprocity, T216, 216
Normal curve, 30*f*, T30–31, 30–31, T323, 323–324, 324*f*
Norms, 250, T250–251
Nurture, T66, 66, T142, 142, T172

O

Obedience, T217–218, 217–218
Obesity, 349*f*, T349–350, 350–351
Object permanence, T154, 154

Observable behavior, 8
Observational learning, 195–196, T196
Observational research, T18
Observer bias, T17, 17–18
Observer effect, T17, 17
Obsessive-compulsive disorder (OCD), T423, 423
Occipital lobe, T60, 60, 61*f*
Occupational Outlook Handbook (OOH) **(Bureau of Labor Statistics),** 519
OCEAN, 387–388
Oedipus complex, T380, 380
Olfaction, T90, 90
Olfactory receptors, 90, 90*f*
"On Being Sane in Insane Places" (Rosenhan), T448
One Flew Over the Cuckoo's Nest **(Kesey),** 468
Openness, 387
Operant behavior, 185
Operant conditioning
  animal training and, T189, T191
  biological constraints on, 190–191
  chapter goals, learning objectives, T176
  class demonstration, T185
  clicker Training and, T189
  defined, 10, T177, 184
  in everyday life, T192, 192
  internet resources, T208
  Law of Effect, 184–185
  principles of, T185, 185–187
  psychotherapy, 451–452
  punishment, 186–187, 193
  specializations of, 187–190
  superstition and, T190
  terms, T184
  understanding, check for, T185
Operational definition, T20, 20
Opium, T129–130, 129
Opponent-process theory, T85, 85
Optic nerve, 82, 84*f*
Optical illusions, T99
Optimists, T503, 503–504, 504*f*
Oral presentations, T106, T338, T478
Oral stage, T379, 379
Organ of Corti, T87, 87
Otolith organs, 92
Out-groups, T232, 232
Ovaries, 51
Overgeneralization, 455*t*
Overlap (interposition), T98, 98, T104
Ovum, 147
Oxytocin, 355

P

Pagano, Bernard, 289
Page, Steward, 415
Pain, 91–92
Painkillers, T129
Pancreas, T51, 51
Panic attack, 422–423, T423
Panic disorder, 422–423, T423, 444
Papillae, 89
Paranoid schizophrenia, T432, 432
Parasympathetic division, T41, T49, 49–50, 488–489
Parenting styles, T166
Parents, T67, 67–68, 164–165
Parietal lobes, T60, 60, 61*f*
Parks, Kenneth, 117
Parrots, language, 304

Partial dopamine agonists, 466, T465
Partial reinforcement effect, T189, 189
Participant modeling, 454
Participants, 19
Passion, T237, 237
Passionate love, 355
Pavlov, Ivan, 8, T179, 178–180
Pavlov's dogs, 178–180, 179*f*
PCP (phenyl cyclohexyl piperidine), T130, 130
Peak experiences, 347
Peer pressure, 165
Peers, T67, 67–68
Pepperberg, Irene, 304
Perception
  APA standards correlation, T76
  attention, 94
  chapter goals, learning objectives, T76
  class demonstration, T95, T98, T99, T100
  constancies, T94–95, 94–95
  controversies, T101
  critical thinking, T101, T103
  defined, T77–78, 78, T94
  experiences, expectation, 100–101
  Gestalt principles, T95–96, 95–96, 96*f*
  internet resources, T104
  monocular, binocular depth cues, T96, T98, 96–99, T104
  multicultural focus, T101
  reasons to study, 77
  scheduling, T77
  stress and, T496
  student voice question, T99
  teacher prep, T77
  terms, T94
  testing readiness, T105
  understanding, check for, T96
  visual illusions, 99–100
  vs. sensation, 78
Perceptual illusions, T96
Perceptual set (perceptual expectancy), T100, 100, 100*f*
Perfect pitch, T88
Peripheral nervous system (PNS), T41, T48, 48, 49*f*
Peripheral-route processing, 229
Peripheria, T48
Personal fable, T163, 163
Personal unconscious, T382, 382
Personality
  behavioral theories, T375, 376, T376–377, T383–385, 383–385
  biological, cultural influences, T396, 396–397, 399–400
  career and, T388
  celebrity analysis, T389
  chapter goals, learning objectives, T374
  class debate, T389
  class demonstration, T378, T379, T384, T385, T386, T387, T388, T389
  class discussion, T380, T386
  comprehension check, T407
  critical thinking, T384, T403
  defense mechanisms, T379, T502
  defined, T376, 376

SI-7

health, T398, 398
humanistic perspective, T375, 376, T376–377, T385–386, 385–387
internet resources, T404
internet tests, T345, 400–401
measuring, T391–395, 391–395, 392t, T401
men vs. women, T264, 264–265
psychodynamic theory, T375–383, 376–383
reasons to study, 375, T407
scheduling, T375
self-esteem, T399, 399
social cognitive theories, T375, 376, T376–377, T383–385, 383–385
stability of, T397, 397–398
stress, T497, 496–498
student voice question, T378, T383
teacher prep, T375
terms, T376
testing readiness, T405
trait perspective, T375, 376, T376–377, T387–389, 387–389
Types A, B, C, 497–498, T497–499
understanding, check for, T381, T384
understanding visuals, T377, T388
work, T398, 398–399

Personality assessment
class debate, T395, T401
class demonstration, T393, T394
class discussion, T400
critical thinking, T397
cultural connection, T399
methods for, T391–395, T401
terms, T391
understanding visuals, T393
value of, T401

Personality disorders, T433–435, 433–436, 434t
Personality inventory, T394, 394–395
Personality psychology, T13, 13
Personalization, 455t
Person-centered therapy, T450, 450
Persuasion, 228, 228t, T228–229
Pessimists, 503
PET scan. See positron emission tomography scan
Peters, W. A., 233
Phallic stage, T380, 380
Phi phenomenon, 100
Phobia
classical conditioning, T181, 181
critical thinking, T451
defined, 9, T422, 422
desensitization, T365, 365
disorders, 422
writing about, T182
Phonemes, T202, 202
Photoreceptors, 82, 83f
Phototherapy, 436
Physical dependence, T132, 132
Physical development
adolescence, T141, T162, 162–163
adulthood, T166–167, 166–167
defined, 143
infancy, childhood, 151, 152f
Physiological arousal. See emotion
Physiological needs, 346
Physiological psychology, T13, 13–14
Physiologist, 178
Physique preferences, T351
Piaget, Jean, T153–155, 153–155, T202, 202
Piaget's stages of cognitive development, 53t, T153–155, 153–155
Pictorial depth cues, 98
Pineal gland, T51, 51
Pinna, T87, 87
Pitch, T86, 86, T88, 88
Pituitary gland, T51, 51
Place theory, T88, 88
Placebo effect, 21–22, T22
Placenta, 149
Plagiarism, T174, T372
Plaster hypothesis, T397, 397–398
Pleasure principle, T378, 378
Polygon, T29–30, 30, 30f
Pons, T58, 58
Population, 19
Portfolio, T138, T302, T442
Positive correlation, T19, T32
Positive psychology, T11, 11–12
Positive psychology movement, T341, T367, 367
Positive regard, T386, 386–387
Positive reinforcement, T186, 186, 187f
Positive symptoms, T432, 432
Positively skewed, T31, 31
Positron emission tomography (PET) scan, 55f, T55–56, 55–56
Postconventional morality, T164, 164
Postpartum psychosis, 408
Post-traumatic stress disorder (PTSD), 248, T483, 492, T493
Poverty, T486, 486–487
Power distance, T400, 400
Practical intelligence, T322, 322
Pragmatics, T202, 202
Preconscious mind, T377
Preconventional morality, T164, 164
Predictive validity, 33
Predisposition, T67, 67
Prefrontal lobotomy, T469, 469
Prejudice, T232–235, 232–235
Prenatal development
class demonstration, T148
critical periods, T148, 148
stages of, T147–149, 147–149, 149f
student voice question, T148
teratogens, T148, 148, 148t
terms, T147
Preoperational stage, T154, 154
Prescription drugs, teen abuse of, T129
Pressure perception, 91
Pressure, stress, T487, 487–488
Primacy effect, T287
Primary appraisal, T495
Primary drives, T343, 343
Primary reinforcer, T186, 186
Primary sex characteristics, 162
Prioritizing, T211
Proactive interference, 295, 295f
Problem solving, 310–312, T311–312, T314–315, 314–316
Problem-focused coping, T500, 500

Procedural (nondeclarative) memory, T280, 280
Procrastination, T38, T270, T532
Projection, 392, 502t
Projective tests, T392–393, 392–394
Prosocial behavior, T240–241, 240–241
Prototype, 309–310, T310, 310f
Proximity, 95, T236, 236
Psi Chi, 520
Psilocybin, T130, 131
Psyche, 379
Psychiatric social worker, T448, 448
Psychiatrist, T447, 447–448, T518, 518
Psychoactive drugs, T109, T126–133
categories of, 126–131
class debate, T131
class demonstration, T126, T127, T129, T132, T133
cultural pressures, expectations, 133
effects of, 132–133
functioning of, 131–132
student voice question, T131, T132
understanding, check for, T127
Psychoanalysis, T8, 8, T381, 381, T445, T447, T449, 447–450
Psychoanalyst, T448, 448, T518
Psychodynamic perspective
abnormal behavior, T414, 414
anxiety disorders, T424, 424
defined, T10, 10
dissociative disorders, T427, 427
mood disorders, 429, T430
Psychodynamic theory of personality
background, T376–377, 376–377
personality development stages, T379–381, 379–381, 381f
personality divisions, 377f, T377–379, 377–379
unconscious mind, 377
Psychodynamic therapy, 450
Psychological defense mechanisms, T379, T501, 501, 502t
Psychological dependence, T132, 132–133
Psychological development, 158, 159–160t
Psychological disorders. See also abnormal behavior
anxiety disorders, 421–424, T422–424
APA standards correlation, T408
chapter goals, learning objectives, T408
class demonstration, T422, T423, T424, T425, T428, T430, T433, T434, T437
class discussion, T431
critical thinking, T416, T427, T432, T435, T439
defined, T413, 413
diagnosing, T421, 421
dissociative disorders, T426–427, 426–427
DSM classification system, T418–419, 418–420
early Treatment of, 447

family, social influences, T436, 436
history, T410–411, 410–411
impacts of, T416, 416
internet resources, T421, T440
mood disorders, T427–430, 427–430
occurrence of, T420, 420, 420f
personality disorders, T433–435, 433–436, 434t
resources, T473, 473
SAD, 436–437, 437f
scheduling, T409
schizophrenia, T430–433, 430–433
somatoform disorders, 424–425, T425
teacher prep, T409
terms, T418
testing readiness, T441
treatment professionals, T447–448, 447–448
understanding visuals, T419, T428, T433, T437
Psychological disorders, treatment. See psychotherapy
Psychological education. See careers in psychology
Psychological needs, 344
Psychological professionals. See careers in psychology; treatment professionals
Psychological research. See research
Psychological therapies. See biomedical therapy; psychotherapy
Psychologist(s)
contributions of, T6, T8
defined, T448, 448
finding, on internet, T14
medication prescribing, T466
as scientists, T12
Psychology
APA standards, correlation to, T2
chapter goals, learning objectives, T2
class debate, T9
class demonstration, T6, T8, T10, T12
classic studies in, T9
critical thinking, T9, T35
culture and, T11, 250–251
defined, T3, 4
development of, T2, T5
differentiated instruction, T6, T13
in everyday life, 527
field growth, change, 11–12
goals of, T4, 4–5
history of, T5, 5–9, 6f
internet resources, T5, T7, T30, T36
minorities in, T7, 7–8
modern perspectives, T3, T10–11, 10–11
multicultural focus, T7
other field interaction, 522–527
project, T36
reasons to study, 2–3
research, T2, T12, T16–25
scheduling, T3
societal benefits of, T14–15
statistics, T2, T26–34

SI-8

Subject Index

Psychology. (*continued*)
subfields, T2, 13f, T12–14, 12–14
teacher prep, T3
terms, T4
testing, readiness of, T37
Psychology Baccalaureate Survey (APA), 520
Psychology, careers. *See* careers in psychology
Psychopathology, T409, T410, 410
Psychopharmacology, T465–467, 465–470, 466t
Psychosexual stages, T379, 379–381, 381t
Psychosocial development, 143
Psychosurgery, T469
Psychotherapy. *See also* biomedical therapy
APA standards correlation, T444
behavior therapies, 451–454
chapter goals, learning objectives, T444
class debate, T463
class demonstration, T452, T454, T456, T458
class discussion, T448, T460
cognitive therapies, 454–457
comprehension check, T479
concerns, 460–461
controversies in, T459
cultural connection, T453, T461
defined, 8, T446, 446
effectiveness, T459–462, 459–462
EMDR, T463, 462–463
ethical challenges, T471, 470–473
group therapy, T457–458, 457–458, 458t
humanistic therapies, T450–451, 450–451
internet resources, T447, T476
origins of, T447, 447
psychoanalysis, 448–450
reasons to study, 445
resources, T462, 473
scheduling, T445
strategies, disorder prevention, 461–462
student voice question, T450, T451, T455, T456, T460, T461
teacher prep, T445
terms, T446
testing readiness, T477
treating panic disorder, 444
treatment professionals, T447–448, 447–448
types of, T448–458, 448–459, 457t
understanding, check for, T457
understanding visuals, T452
Psychotic, 430
Ptolemy, 100
Puberty, 162
Punishment, T186–187, 186–187, T193, 193
Punishment by application, T186, 186

Punishment by removal, T186, 186–187, 188t
Pupil, T77, 82
The Pursuit of Happiness (Myers), 367

R

Raccoons, behavior, 190–191
Random assignment, T21, 21
Range, T28, 28
Rapid eye movement (REM) sleep. *See* REM (rapid eye movement) sleep
Rating scale, T394, 394
Rational-emotive behavioral therapy (REBT), T456, 456
Rationalization, 502t
Reaction formation, 502t
Real self, 385–386, 386f
Realistic conflict theory, T233, 233
Reality principle, T378, 378
Reasoning development, 163–164
Recall, T287, 287–288
Recency effect, 287
Receptive meditation, T123, 123–124, T505
Receptor sites, 46
Recessive genes, T67, 67, T142, 143
Reciprocal determinism, 384
Reciprocity of liking, T236, 236
Recognition, T288, 287–289
Reflection, 450–451
Reflex, classical conditioning, 178
Reflexes, in infants, T141, 150, 150f, T150–151
Regression, 502t
Reinforcement, reinforcer, 10, 185–186, T189, T453, 453
Relatedness, T348
Relationship development, T156–157, 156–158
Relative deprivation, T366, 366–367
Relative size, T98, 98, T104
Relaxation, stress and, T505
Reliability, 33, T394, 394
Religion, 503
REM behavior disorder, T116, 116
REM paralysis, T115, 115
REM rebound, T116, 116
REM (rapid eye movement) sleep, T113, 113, T115–116, 115f, 115–116, T118
Representative sample, 19
Representativeness heuristic, T305, 311, T312, T316, 316–317
Repression, T379, 502t
Research
on animals vs. humans, T22, T24, 22–24
claims, in tabloids, T20
class debate, T22
class demonstration, T19, T20, T24
controversies in, T24
critical thinking, T20, T23
data analysis, 26–33
developmental psychology, 143
ensuring validity, 21–22
ethical issues, 23–24
importance of, T12, 12, 14
methods, T16–25, 16–23
observational, T18
personality, 396–400

psychotherapy effectiveness, 459–462
student voice question, T19, T21, T22
terms, T16
understanding visuals, T20, T23, T24
Resistance, T449, T489, 449, 489–490
Response, 178
Resting potential, 44
Restorative theory, T109, 113
Reticular formation (RF), T58, 58
Retina, T77, 82, T82–83, 83f
Retrieval, T273, 274, 275f
Retrieval cue, T285, 285
Retroactive interference, 295, 295f
Retrograde amnesia, T296, 296
Reversible figures, 95, 95f
Right to withdraw, 23
Risks/benefits, 23
Rizzolatti, Giacomo, 64
Rods, 82, T83–84
Rogers, Carl, 10, 385–387, T450, 450–451
Role models, T211
Romantic love, T237, 237, 355
Rorschach, Herman, 393
Rorschach inkblot test, T393, 393
Rosenberg Self-Esteem Scale, T399
Rosenhan, David, 421, T448
Rosenman, Ray, 497
Rote, 311
Rotter, Julian, T385, 385

S

S factor, T321, 321–322
SA. *See* self-actualization needs
Safety needs (SAFE), T346, 346
Sánchez, George I., 7
Saturation, T81, 81
Scapegoat, T234, 234
Scent, emotion and, T364
Schachter, Stanley, T361, 361, 365
Schaie, K. Warner, 144
Schizophrenia, 10f, T430–433, 430–433, 433f
School psychology, T523, 523
Scientific method, T3, T16–17, 16–17
Scott, Walter D., T526, 526
Seasonal affective disorder (SAD), T436–437, 436–437, 437f
Seattle Longitudinal Study, 144
Secondary appraisal, T496, 496
Secondary reinforcer, T186, 186
Secondary sex characteristics, 162–163
Selective attention, T81, T277, 277
Selective serotonin reuptake inhibitors (SSRIs), T467
Selective thinking, 455t
Self, 385
Self-actualization needs (SA), T346, 346
Self-actualizing tendency, T385, 385
Self-concept, 255–256
Self-determination theory (SDT), T348, 348
Self-efficacy, T384, 384
Self-esteem, T399, 399
Self-fulfilling prophecy, T235, 235
Self-help groups, T458, 458
Seligman, Martin, 11, T198, 197–199
Selye, Hans, T481, 483, 489–490
Semantic memory, 281

Semantics, T202, 202
Semicircular canals, 92
Semipermeable, 44
Senile dementia, 296
Sensation
APA standards correlation, T76
chapter goals, learning objectives, T76
class demonstration, T79, T80, T83, T84, T85, T89, T90, T91
critical thinking, T92, T103
defined, T77–78, 78
development, newborns, 150–151
energy sensing, 80f, 80–81
gustation, 88–89
hearing, 86–88
internet resources, T104
olfaction, 90
reasons to study, 77
scheduling, T77
sensory adaptation, T79, 79–80
sensory thresholds, 78–79
student voice question, T79, T81, T84, T90, T91
teacher prep, T77
terms, T78
testing readiness, T105
touch, 91–92
understanding, check for, T85, T90
understanding visuals, T83, T86
vision, 81–85
vs. perception, 78
Sensation seeker, T345, 345, 345t
Senses
in careers, T107
critical thinking, T92
Sensitive period, T144, 145–146
Sensorimotor stage, 153–154
Sensorineural impairment, T88, 88
Sensory adaptation, T77, 79–80, T80, T104
Sensory memory, T276–277, 276–277
Sensory neurons, 48
Sensory receptors, T77, T80, 80
Sensory thresholds, T78–79, 78–79
Sentence Completion test, 393
Separation, T487, 487
Serial position effect, T287, 287–288, 288f
Serotonin, T47, T366, 366
Sexual behavior, T352–353, 351–353
Sexual orientation, T352–354, 351–354
Shape constancy, T77, 94f, T95, 95
Shaping, T188, 188, 454
Shapiro, Francine, 462–463
Shock box, T217
Short-term memory (STM), T273, T276–278, 277–280, T295
Similarity, T95, 95
Simon, Théodore, 327
Simonides, 272
Simulated Shock Generator and Event Recorder, T217
Singer, Jerome, T361, 361, 365
Situational cause, 229, T229–230
Situational context, T412, 412
The Sixteen Personality Factor Questionnaire, 387, 388f
Size constancy, T77, T94, 94

SI-9

The Skeptic's Dictionary (Carroll), 463
Skewed distributions, T31, 31
Skin senses, T77, T91, 91–92
Skinner, B. F., 10, T185, 185, 189
Sleep
    biological rhythms, 111
    circadian rhythm, T109, 112
    class demonstration, T115, T117
    dreams, T109, T111, T115–116, T118–120, 119–120, T122, T449
    functions of, 113
    internet resources, T113
    patterns, 112f
    REM cycle, T113, 113–116, T115–116, T118, 114f, 115f
    stages, T109, 113–115
    understanding visuals, T112, T114
Sleep apnea, T118, 118
Sleep deprivation, T112, 112, 120–121, T121
Sleep disorders, T116–118, 116–119, 119t
Sleep spindles, 114–115
Sleepwalking, 116–117, T116–118
Sleepwalking defense, T116–117
Smell, sense of, T90, 90
Social cognition, T213
    attitude changing, T228, 228–229
    attitudes, behavior, T224–228, 224–228
    attribution theory, T229–230, 229–230, T365
    class demonstration, T226–227, T229, T230
    mood disorders, 429, T430
    terms, T224
Social cognitive learning theorists, 384
Social cognitive theory, T234, 234, T383–385, 383–385
Social cognitive view, T384, 384
Social comparison, T234, 234
Social development
    adults, T165–166, 165–166
    children, 158, 159–160t
    day care and, T145
    men *vs.* women, T264, 264–265
Social facilitation, T218, 218–219
Social identity, social identity theory, T234, 234
Social impairment, T219, 219
Social influence
    on behavior, 215–219
    chapter goals, learning objectives, T212
    class demonstration, T215, T216, T217, T220
    compliance, T216, 216–217
    conformity, T213, T215, 215, 215f
    critical thinking, T219, T222
    defined, T213, T214, 214
    gangs, T221–222, 221–222
    group dynamics, T220, 219–220
    leadership, 220–221, T221
    obedience, T217–218, 217–218
    psychological disorders, 436
    task performance, 218–219, T219

Social interaction, T213
    aggression, 238–240, T239–240
    attraction, love, T236–237, 235–238
    cartoons, analyzing, T240
    chapter goals, learning objectives, T212
    class demonstration, T233, T234, T238, T240, T241
    class discussion, T236
    critical thinking, T235, T237
    prejudice, discrimination, T232–235, 232–235
    prosocial behavior, 240–241
    terms, T232
Social loafing, 218–219, T219
Social nonconformity, 412
Social phobia, T422, 422
Social psychology
    APA standards correlation, T212
    chapter goals, learning objectives, T212
    critical thinking, T243
    defined, 11, T13, 13, T214, 214
    internet resources, T244
    reasons to study, 213
    scheduling, T213
    social cognition, T213, 224–230
    social influence, T213, 214–222
    social interaction, T213, 232–241
    teacher prep, T213
    terms, T214
    testing readiness, T245
Social Readjustment Rating Scale (SRRS), 484t, 484–485
Social role, T239, 239–240
Social support system, T501, 501
Social-cognitive theory of hypnosis, T125, 126
Sociocultural perspective, T11, 11
Soma, T41, 42
Somatic nervous system, T49, 48–50
Somatic pain, 91
Somatization disorder, T425, 425
Somatoform disorders, 424–425, T425
Somatosensory cortex, 60, 62f
Somesthetic senses, T77, T91, 91
Somnambulism, T116–118, 116–117
Sound
    ear, entrance in, T77
    perception of, T86
Sound perception, 86–88
Sound waves, T86, 86f
Source traits, T387, 387
Spanking, T157
Spearman's factors, T305, T321, 321–322
Species-specific behaviors, 191
Specific phobia, T422, 422
Speech disturbances, T431
Sperry, Roger, 62
Spinal cord, T41, 47–48, 48f, T48
Split brain, T62
Spontaneous recovery, T180, 180, 181f, T188, 188–189
Sports psychology, T523, 523, T527, 527
Springer, James, 68, 374
Squid, studying, T44
SSRIs. *See* selective serotonin reuptake inhibitors
Standard deviation, T28, 28, 28t, 324
Standardization, T323, 323, T323–324

Stanford Prison Experiment, T239
Stanford-Binet Intelligence Scales, T305, T327, T328, 327–328, 328t
State-dependent learning, T286, 286
Statistically significant, 33
Statistics, 26
    class demonstration, T27, T28, T29
    critical thinking, T32, T35
    differentiated instruction, T30
    importance of, T29
    internet resources, T33
    terms, T26
    understanding visuals, T29
Steen, Carol, 76
Stem cells, T41, 56–57
Stereotype vulnerability, T234, 234–235
Stereotypes
    class demonstration, T233
    defined, T232, 232–233
    math/science gender gap, 265
    representativeness heuristic, 311
    test performance, 24
Stern, William, 327
Sternberg, Robert, T237, 236–237, T305
Sternberg's triarchic theory, T322, 322
Stigma, T415, 415–416
Stimulants, T109, T126–128, 126–128
Stimulatory hallucinogenics, 130
Stimulus, T177, 178
Stimulus discrimination, T180, 180
Stimulus generalization, T180, 180
Stimulus motive, 344
Stirrup, ear, T87
Stohr, Oskar, 374
Storage
    class demonstration, T276, T277, T278, T279, T281, T282
    critical thinking, T283
    defined, 274, 275f
    internet resources, T275
    multicultural focus, T276
    student voice question, T277, T279
    terms, T274
Storch, Alexander, 57
Stress, coping with, T49
    APA standards correlation, T480
    chapter goals, learning objectives, T480
    class demonstrations, T499, T501, T502, T503, T504, T505
    cognitive appraisal approach, T495–496, 495–496, 496f
    critical thinking, T507
    cultural connections, T498
    effective, ineffective ways, T499, 499, T511
    internet resources, T508
    optimism, 503–504, 504f
    personality effects, 496–498
    promoting wellness, T505, 505
    scheduling, T481
    strategies for, T481, T500–505, 500–503

    student voice question, T498, T499, T500, T501
    teacher prep, T481
    terms, T495
    testing readiness, T509
    understanding visuals, T502, T504
Stress, stressors
    APA standards correlation, T480
    chapter goals, learning objectives, T480
    class demonstration, T485, T489, T491, T493
    class discussion, T484
    controversies, T491
    defined, T481, T482, 482–483
    environmental factors, T483–486, 483–486
    internet resources, T508
    physical health effects, T488–492, 488–492
    psychological factors, 487–488
    psychological health effects, 482
    purpose of, T484
    reasons to study, 481
    scheduling, T481
    social factors, T486–488, 486–487
    student voice question, T482, T485, T490
    suicide, T493, 492–493
    teacher prep, T481
    terms, T482
    testing readiness, T509
    understanding visuals, T484, T485, T489, T491
Stress-vulnerability model, T433, 433
Stroboscopic motion, 100
Structuralism, T6, 6
Study skills, T246
Study tips, T479
    active reading, T270
    audio study guides, T338
    Cornell notes, T339
    essay tests, T138
    goals, T510
    graphic organizers, T406
    learning styles, T39
    listening in class, T407, T478
    multiple choice Tests, T246
    notebook organization, T211
    notes taking, T271
    organization, T74
    outlines, T75
    place to study, T38
    positive self-affirmations, T532
    rewards, T511
    rewriting and color-coding notes, T210
    schedule, T106, T442–443
    setting priorities, T174
    SQ3R, T247
    study groups, T107
    study session goals, T373
    summarizing, T175
    test question prediction, T303
    test reading strategies, T533
    test-taking skills, T139
    true/false Tests, T372
    when to study, T302
Subgoaling, T312, 312

Subject Index

Subjective, 393
Subjective discomfort, T412, 412–413
Sublimation, 502t
Subliminal advertising, T101, 101
Subordinate concept, 308, T309
Substitution (compensation), 502t
Successive approximation, 188
Sudden infant death syndrome (SIDS), 168
Suicide, T428, 492–493, T493
Sumner, Francis Cecil, 7
Superego, 378, T378–379
Superordinate concept, 308, T309
Superstition, operant conditioning and, T190
Support groups, T458, 458, 473
Surface traits, T387, 387
Survey method, T18, 18–19
Survival instincts, 140
Susto, 411
Sybil, 427
Sympathetic division, T41, T49–50, 49–50, 488–489
Synapses, T46, 46f, 46–47
Synaptic vesicles, T46, 46
Synesthesia, 76
Syntax, T202, 202
Systematic desensitization, T452, 452, 452f

T

Tables, graphs, T28–29, 28–31
Taijin-kyofu-sho (TKS), 411
Task performance, 218–219, T219
Taste, 88–89, T89
Taste buds, 89, 89f
Teenagers. *See* adolescents; adolescents, development
Television
  advertisements, classical conditioning and, T181
  children and, T159
Telomeres, 167
Temperament, 143, T157, 376
Temperature, 91
Temporal lobes, T60, 60–61, 61f
Teratogens, T148, 148, 148t
Terman, Lewis M., T326, 326–327
Test performance, 24
Testes, 51
Texture gradient, T98, 98, T104
Thalamus, T58–59, 59
That's-not-all technique, T216, 217
Thematic, T393
Thematic Apperception Test (TAT), 393, 393f
Theory, 4–5
Therapeutic alliance, T460, 460
Therapy, 446. *See also* biomedical therapy; psychotherapy
Theta waves, T113–114, 113–115
Thinking
  AI, 312–313, T313
  APA standards correlation, T304
  chapter goals, learning objectives, T304
  class debate, T313
  class demonstration, T307, T308, T310, T311, T314, T315, T316
  class discussion, T318
  common distortions, 455t
  concepts, 307–308, T308, T309–310
  concepts, Types of, 308–310
  creative, T315
  critical Thinking, T312
  decision making, 310–312, T318, 318–319
  defined, T306, 306
  insight, T312
  language relationship, 202–204
  making judgements, T305, T316–317, 316–318
  mental images, T305, T306–307, 306–307, 307f
  multicultural focus, T307
  optimism, 503–504, 504f
  problem solving, T305, 310–312, T311–312, T314–315, 314–316
  reasons to study, 305
  scheduling, T305
  student voice question, T312
  teacher prep, T305
  terms, T306
  testing readiness, T337
  understanding, check for, T312
  understanding visuals, T316
Thomas, David, 272
Thorndike, Edward L., T177, 184–185
Thought. *See* thinking
Thymus gland, T52, 52
Thyroid gland, T51, 51
Thyroxin, 51
Timbre, T86, 86
Time-out, 454
Tinnitus, T88, 88
Tip-of-the-tongue phenomenon, T285
Titchener, Edward, 6
Token economy, T192, 192, 453
Tolman, Edward, T197, 197
Tongue, 89, 89f
Top-down processing, T100, 100
Touch, T91, 91
Trait, T387, 387
Trait theories, 376, T387, 387–389
Trait-situation interaction, T388, 388
Tranquilizers, 128
Transactional view, 221
Transduction, 82
Transference, T449, 449
Transformational view, 221
Transgendered, 261
Transsexual, 262
Treatment professionals, 447–448
Trepanning (trephining), T410, 410
Trial and error, T311, 311
Triangular theory of love, 236–237, T237, 237f
Triarchic theory of intelligence, 322

Trichromatic theory, 84, T84–85
Tricyclics, T467, 467
Twins
  aggression, T238, 238
  identical *vs.* fraternal, T147, 147f
  intelligence studies, T332, 331–333
  personality, T396, 396–397, 397f
  studies of, T68, 68, 374
Two-factor theory of emotion, 361–362, 362f, 365
Tympanic membrane, 87
Type A Behavior and Your Heart (Friedman, Rosenman), 497
Types A, B, C personalities, T497–499, 497–498
Typical neuroleptics, T465, 465–466

U

Umami, 89
Umbilical cord, 149
Uncertainty avoidance, T400, 400
Unconditional positive regard, T386, 386–387, 450
Unconditioned response (UCR), T179, 179–180
Unconditioned stimulus (UCS), T177, T179, 179–180
Unconscious, 8
Unconscious mind, T377, 377
Unconscious processes, 110–111
Unilateral ECT, 469
Unipolar disorder. *See* major depression
United States (U.S.)
  cultural traditions, 252–253
  occurrence of psychological disorders, T416, 420, 420f
  suicide, 492–493, T493
Universal, 257
The Up Series, 144
U.S. Memory Championship, 272
Uterus, 149

V

Vagus nerve, 490
Validity, T33, 33, 394
Validity scales, 395
Variable, 19
Variable interval schedule of reinforcement, T189, 189–190
Variable ratio schedule of reinforcement, T190, 190
Vestibular senses, T77, T91, 91–92, T92
Vicarious conditioning, T182, 182
Vicary, James, 101
Vietnam, 501–502
Violence, 240, 525
Visceral pain, 91
Visible spectrum, 81, 81f
Vision, 81–85
Visual accommodation, T82, 82
Visual cliff, T97, 97

Visual illusions, T99, 99–100
Vitreous humor, 82
Volley principle, T88, 88
Volume, 86
Vygotsky, Lev, T202, 202–203

W

Waking consciousness, T110, 110
Walk, Richard, 97
Washburn, Margaret, T6
Watson, John B., 8–10, T181, 181
Wear-and-tear theory of aging, T167, 167
Weber, Ernst, 78–79
Weber's law, T78, 78–79
Wechsler tests, T305, T328, 328, 329t
Weight set point, 349–350
Wellness, T505, 505
Wernicke's aphasia, T205, 205
Wernicke's area, T61, 61, T205, 205
Wertheimer, Max, 95
Western Collaborative Group Study (Rosenman), 497
Western Electric Company, 526
Wikipedia, T74
Wikis, T74
Winkte, 262
Witchcraft, T411
Withdrawal, 132, 499
Withdrawal, stress, T499
Women
  eating disorders, 351
  emotional display rules, 363–364
  major depression, T429
  in math, science, 265
  men, differences, T264, T307, 264–265
  obstacles, psychology participation and, T7
  physique preferences, T351
Word webs, T31
Working memory, 278–279
Workplace
  bullying, T398
  personality, T398, 398–399
  psychology and, 524–527
  violence prevention, T525
Wundt, Wilhelm, 5, 6f

X

X (MDMA), 130

Y

Yerkes, Robert, T526, 526
Yerkes-Dodson law, 344
Yufe, Jack, 374

Z

Zimbardo, Philip, T239, 239–240
Zuckerman-Kuhlman personality questionnaire, T345, 345t
Zygote, T147, 147